W9-BFE-693

United States GOVERNMENT

Democracy In Action

Authors

Richard C. Remy, Ph.D.

Congressional Quarterly

Glencoe
McGraw-Hill

New York, New York   Columbus, Ohio   Woodland Hills, California   Peoria, Illinois

Authors

Richard C. Remy, Ph.D., is Professor Emeritus in the College of Education, The Ohio State University, and Senior Consultant on Civic Education with the Mershon Center for International Security and Public Policy at Ohio State. He received his Ph.D. in political science from Northwestern University, taught in the Chicago public schools, and has served as a consultant to numerous school systems, state departments of education, federal government agencies, and East European ministries of education. His books include: *Building Civic Education for Democracy in Poland, Teaching About International Conflict and Peace, Approaches to World Studies, Teaching About National Security, American Government and National Security, Civics for Americans, Lessons on the Constitution,* and *Citizenship Decision Making.* He is General Editor for *American Government at Work,* a nine-volume encyclopedia for middle schools and high schools.

During the 1990s Dr. Remy created and then co-directed a long-term project with the Polish Ministry of National Education and the Center for Citizenship Education, Warsaw, to develop new civic education programs for Polish students, teachers, and teacher educators. He has also served as a consultant on civic education to educators, government officials, and non-governmental organizations from Armenia, Bulgaria, Estonia, Latvia, Lithuania, Romania, Moldova and Ukraine, as well as to the United States Information Agency and the National Endowment for Democracy. Dr. Remy has served on national advisory boards for such organizations as the American Bar Association, the ERIC Clearinghouse for Social Studies/Social Science Education, and the James Madison Memorial Fellowship Foundation.

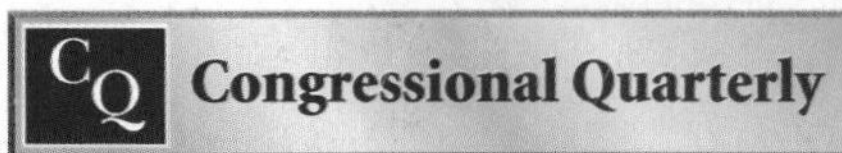

For more than 50 years, Congressional Quarterly has been a recognized leader in political and congressional journalism and publishing. Congressional Quarterly Books, its award-winning book publishing division, publishes more than fifty titles annually on all levels and aspects of American politics and world affairs. Its authoritative and accessible works include directories, encyclopedias, databooks, specialized references, and college political science texts.

Congressional Quarterly's subscription publications and online services have long been an essential source of comprehensive and nonpartisan information on Congress. Flagship publications include the "CQ Weekly Report," considered by many to be the ultimate source on Congress, and "The CQ Researcher," a weekly issue-oriented publication. "Governing," a sister publication, covers state and local government. CQ also publishes a variety of Web-based products on government, politics, and policy.

Glencoe/McGraw-Hill

A Division of The ***McGraw-Hill*** *Companies*

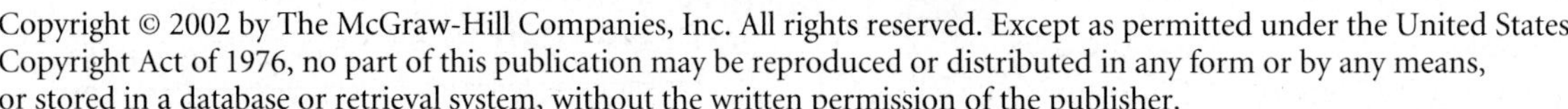
Copyright © 2002 by The McGraw-Hill Companies, Inc. All rights reserved. Except as permitted under the United States Copyright Act of 1976, no part of this publication may be reproduced or distributed in any form or by any means, or stored in a database or retrieval system, without the written permission of the publisher.

Design and Production: DECODE, Inc.

Send all inquiries to
Glencoe/McGraw-Hill, 8787 Orion Place, Columbus, OH 43240

ISBN 0-07-823907-9 (Student Edition) ISBN 0-07-823908-7 (Teacher's Wraparound Edition)

Printed in the United States of America

2 3 4 5 6 7 8 9 10 071/043 06 05 04 03 02 01

Academic Consultants

Glen Blankenship, Ph.D.
Program Director, Georgia Council on Economic Education
Georgia State University
Atlanta, Georgia

Gary E. Clayton, Ph.D.
Professor of Economics
Northern Kentucky University
Highland Heights, Kentucky

Robert L. Lineberry, Ph.D.
Professor of Political Science
University of Houston
Houston, Texas

William E. Nelson, Ph.D.
Research Professor of Black Studies and Professor of Political Science
The Ohio State University
Columbus, Ohio

Jack N. Rakove, Ph.D.
Coe Professor of History and American Studies
Stanford University
Stanford, California

Anita Richardson, J.D., Ph.D.
Senior Law Analyst
American Bar Association
Chicago, Illinois

Donald A. Ritchie, Ph.D.
Associate Historian of the United States Senate Historical Office
Washington, D.C.

Charles E. Walcott, Ph.D.
Associate Professor of Political Science
Virginia Polytechnic Institute and State University
Blacksburg, Virginia

Presidential seal

Educational Reviewers

Barbara Adams
Coronado High School
Lubbock, Texas

Robert Addonizio
Lake Howell High School
Winterpark, Florida

Jerry Chabola
Culver City High School
Culver City, California

Linda Davis
Dadeville High School
Dadeville, Alabama

Richard A. Fagerstrom
College Park High School
Concord, California

Rita Fitzgibbons Fox
McAuley Catholic High School
Chicago, Illinois

Rose Harp
J.J. Pearce High School
Richardson, Texas

Dodie Kasper
Plano High School
Plano, Texas

Maria Martin
Berkner High School
Richardson, Texas

Andy Meyer
Malibu High School
Culver City, California

Willie Mitchell, Jr.
Bullock County High School
Union Spring, Alabama

Manya E. Ogle
Robert E. Lee High School
Montgomery, Alabama

Marcella Osterhaus
Fresno High School
Fresno, California

Steven M. Pricer
Lely High School
Naples, Florida

Edward Schaadt
Gull Lake High School
Richland, Michigan

Mary Stack
Canyon High School
Canyon Country, California

Felicia L. Watts
Camp Verde High School
Camp Verde, Arizona

TABLE OF CONTENTS

Senate flag

Members of the House of Representatives take the oath of office.

TABLE OF CONTENTS

The Supreme Court

TABLE OF CONTENTS

The Democratic National Convention

TABLE OF CONTENTS

Europa hot-air balloon

TABLE OF CONTENTS

Congressional Quarterly's

Speaking of WASHINGTON...

DEMOCRACY WORKSHOP IN ACTION

Multimedia Activities

Democracy in Action: Electronic Field Trips

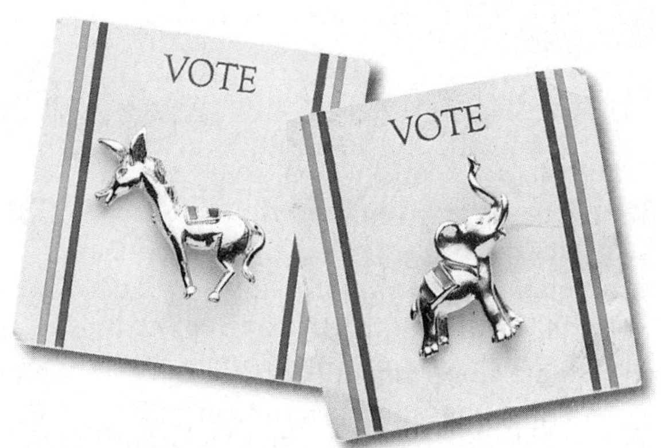

Democratic and Republican Party pins

TABLE OF CONTENTS

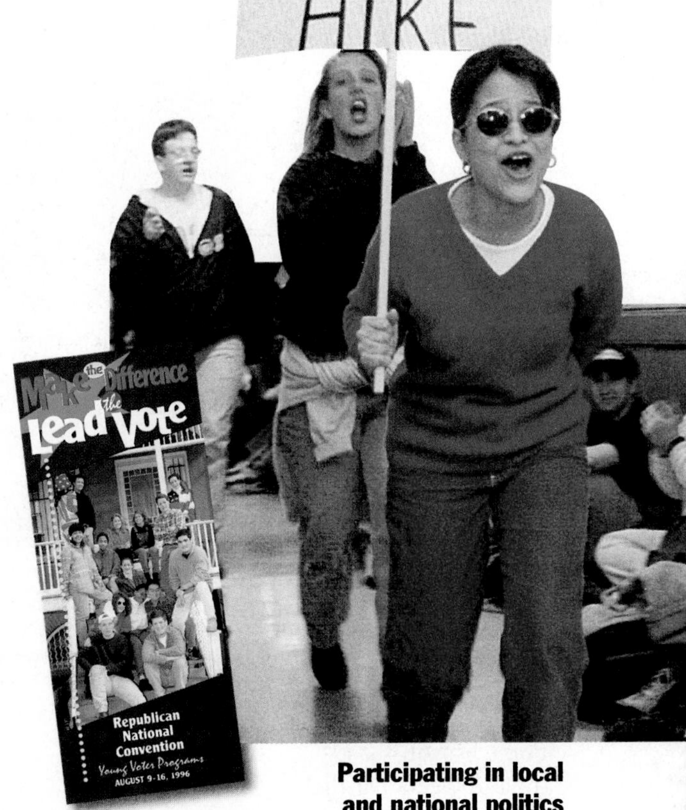

Participating in local and national politics

Participating IN GOVERNMENT

TABLE OF CONTENTS

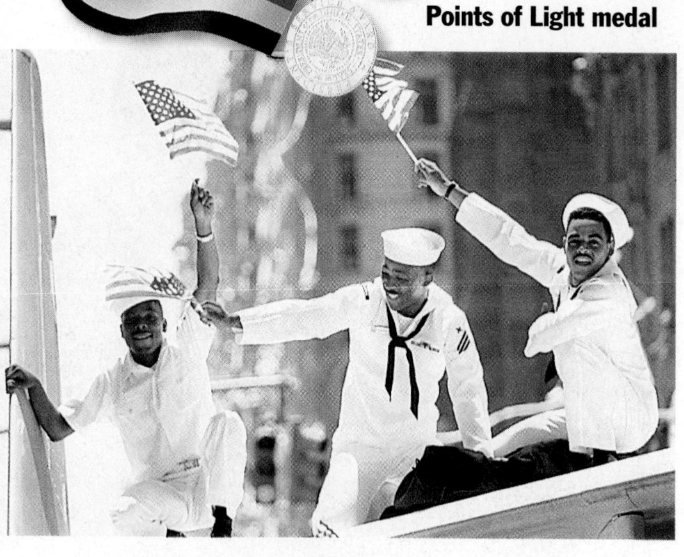
Points of Light medal

United States sailors wave the flag.

We the People
Making a Difference

GOVERNMENT *and You*

THE LAW *and You*

POLITICS *and You*

TABLE OF CONTENTS

Critical Thinking Skills

Social Studies Skills

Study and Writing Skills

Technology Skills

Students use a personal computer to build and program robots.

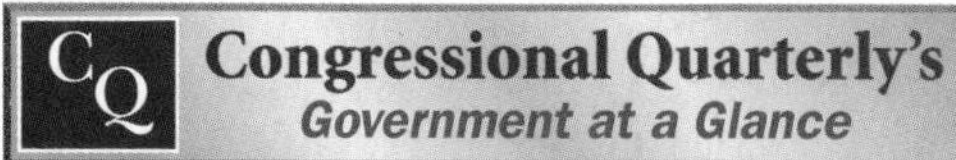

Charts, Graphs, and Maps

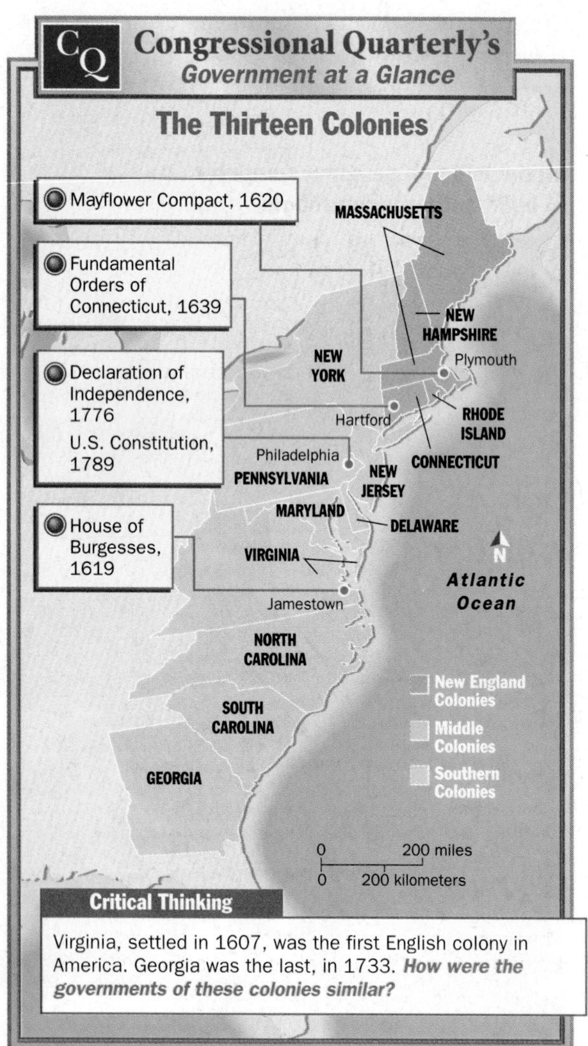

TABLE OF CONTENTS

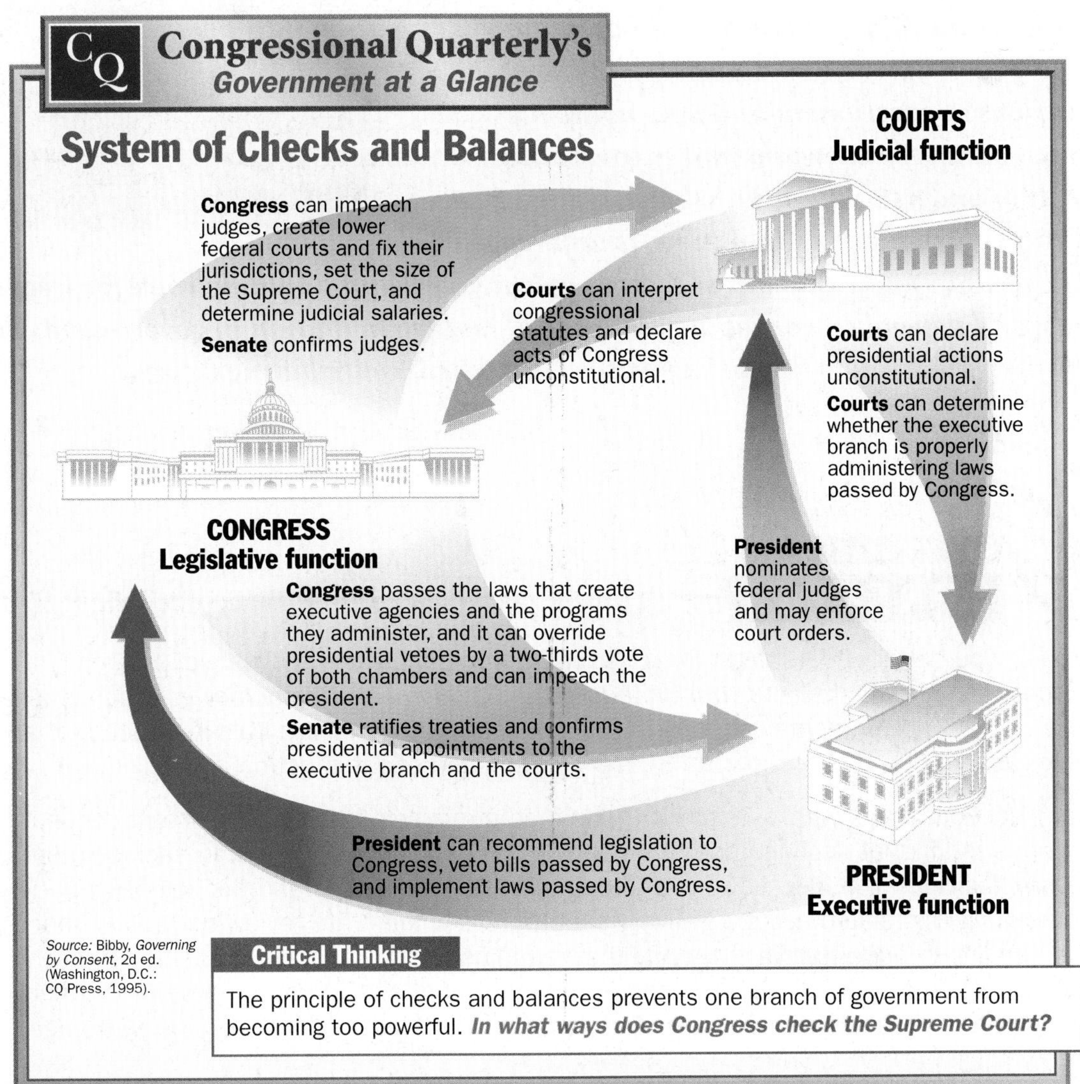

Why Do I Have to Study Government?

When asked about government, many high school students respond that it is uninteresting. Yet, politics is an exciting subject. People fight and die for political beliefs. Governments address some of the most basic issues in your life—the purity of the food you eat, your personal safety, your education, and your right to voice an opinion.

A textbook that deals primarily with the institutions of government and does not relate them to your everyday world makes government difficult to understand. This textbook,* United States Government: Democracy in Action, *is different.

The authors know that our success as a democracy and a leading voice for freedom in the world depend on your understanding of and participation in government. That is why they want you to become a positive, interested, contributing citizen.

★ ★ ★ ★ ★ ★ ★ ★ ★ ★ ★ ★

To help you better understand how government works, how it is a dynamic, exciting process, and how it impacts you, *United States Government: Democracy in Action* emphasizes 14 key government concepts. In this textbook, you will find a built-in structure that helps you identify the key concept in every lesson and see it in action.

Each section begins with a *Reader's Guide* that introduces the key government concept emphasized in that section under the heading, **Understanding Concepts**. In each section review, **Concepts in Action** allows you to demonstrate you understand the key concept by completing the related activity. In every chapter review there are review questions under the heading of **Understanding Concepts** that reinforce the key concept presented in each section of the chapter. These concepts will help you better understand government and see why it is important to you today. ***Read more about these concepts on the next page.***

Growth of Democracy We take democracy for granted, but it has taken generations to develop. This concept will help you understand how democracy grows and why.

Federalism The Founders established a system of shared powers known as federalism. This system is dynamic. The constantly changing relationship between the states and the federal government is a central issue in the study of United States government.

Separation of Powers To prevent a concentration of power the Constitution divided power among three branches of government—legislative, executive, and judicial. This is a source of our government's strength and also, at times, a source of conflict.

Checks and Balances Closely related to the concept of separation of powers, checks and balances outlines specific ways in which each branch affects the powers of the other branches.

Civil Liberties The United States has a long history of personal freedoms. An appreciation for the struggle to preserve and extend these freedoms is vital to the understanding of democracy.

Civil Rights Like personal freedoms, civil rights have developed throughout our history. Citizens should understand the important concept of civil rights—your guarantee of equality under the law.

Civic Participation For a democratic system to survive, its citizens must take an active role in government. Not only do you have important responsibilities such as voting and understanding the laws, you also have opportunities to contribute through your unique abilities. Look for features and activities called Participating in Government throughout this book.

Comparative Government A better understanding of United States government is gained by comparing it to other governments in the world. The text includes an entire unit devoted to these comparisons, as well as special features called Comparing Governments.

Global Perspectives We live in an interdependent world in which every nation's actions contribute to the world's political, social, and economic environment. The text examines this interdependence in the concept of global perspectives.

Constitutional Interpretations The Constitution outlines the framework of our government. The Founders, however, realized that the government would have to deal with unforeseen changes. Therefore, they wrote the Constitution in language that provides the necessary flexibility.

***Three Flags* by Jasper Johns, 1958**

Political Processes The procedures for governing the nation on a daily basis are known as political processes. *United States Government: Democracy in Action* details the dynamic processes of government as they affect both the officeholders and you—the citizen.

Public Policy The course of action a government takes in response to issues is called public policy. This text examines the concept in relation to specific government decisions at every level.

Free Enterprise The free enterprise economy of the United States is consistent with the nation's history of rights and freedoms. Freedom of choice in economic decisions supports other freedoms. Understanding the concept of free enterprise is basic to studying American political institutions.

Cultural Pluralism The United States is not only a nation of immigrants, it is a nation that has benefited from the cultural contributions of all the various groups that now make up its population. Cultural pluralism also serves as a constraint on government, requiring political solutions within a consensus of a variety of views.

UNIT 1

Foundations of American Government

Participating IN GOVERNMENT

Public Opinion *Create a short questionnaire to find out how people in your community feel about government. Ask questions such as, "Do public officials care about what people like you think? Yes or no?" After tabulating the survey results, draw a circle graph that portrays public attitudes and display the graphs in class.*

Electronic Field Trip

Independence Hall

Take a virtual tour of Independence Hall in Philadelphia, where the Continental Congress met and founded the United States of America.

Glencoe's Democracy in Action Video Program

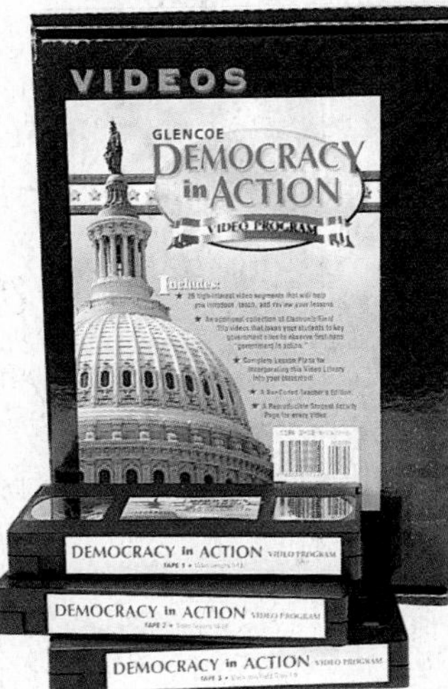

Independence Hall, or the Old State House, was the birthplace of both the Declaration of Independence and the U.S. Constitution. The **Democracy in Action** video program "Independence Hall," referenced below, shows the unique role of Independence Hall in American history.

As you view the video program, try to identify some of the people involved in framing the United States government.

◀ The first die for the Great Seal of the United States and the larger die of the Old Treaty Seal, used to make pendant seals for American treaties

Also available in videodisc format.

View the videodisc by scanning the barcode or by entering the chapter number on your keypad and pressing Search.

Disc 2, Side 1, Chapter 1

Hands-On Activity

Use your school's computerized card catalog or the Internet to research additional information about the historical significance of Independence Hall. How did its location contribute to the events that unfolded there? Using multimedia tools or software, create a multimedia presentation about the role of Independence Hall during the early years of our nation. Incorporate images from the Internet.

★ ★ ★ ★ ★ ★ ★ ★

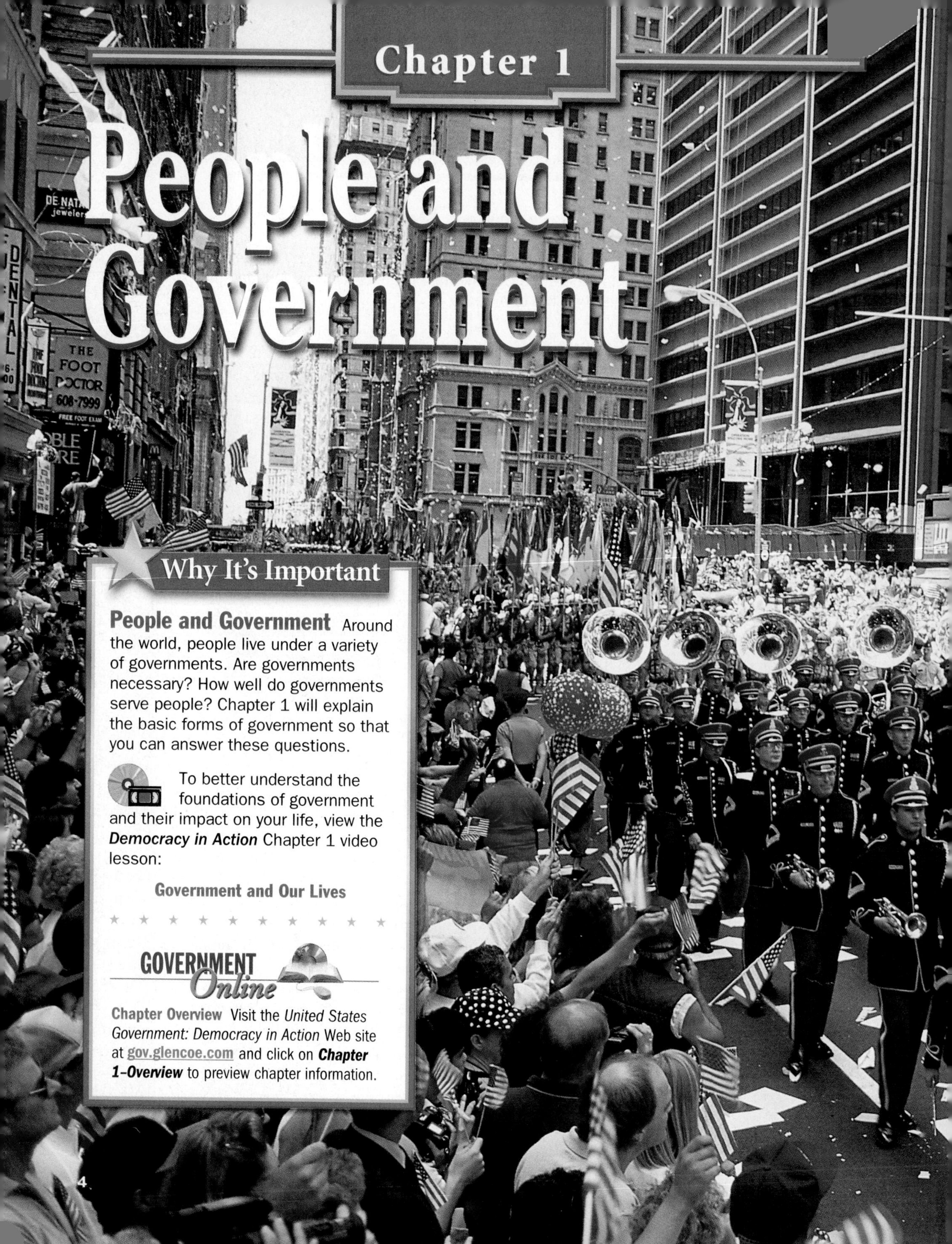

Chapter 1

People and Government

Why It's Important

People and Government Around the world, people live under a variety of governments. Are governments necessary? How well do governments serve people? Chapter 1 will explain the basic forms of government so that you can answer these questions.

To better understand the foundations of government and their impact on your life, view the *Democracy in Action* Chapter 1 video lesson:

Government and Our Lives

GOVERNMENT Online

Chapter Overview Visit the *United States Government: Democracy in Action* Web site at gov.glencoe.com and click on ***Chapter 1–Overview*** to preview chapter information.

Section 1

Principles of Government

Reader's Guide

Key Terms

state, nation, nation-state, consensus, sovereignty, government, social contract

Find Out

- What are the four main purposes of government?
- How do various theories explain the origin of government?

Understanding Concepts

Public Policy Which policies of the government make your life better? Which do you think make life worse?

COVER STORY

Teens Get the Vote

WASHINGTON, D.C., JULY 1, 1971

Several states jockeyed today to become the 38th state to ratify the Twenty-sixth Amendment to the Constitution, which lowers the voting age to 18. Ohio seems to have won the contest; its legislature voted approval in a rare evening meeting. This surprise move deprived Oklahoma of the honor; its legislature was not in session. Also thwarted was North Carolina, which approved the amendment earlier today but delayed official ratification until tomorrow morning. Proposed by Congress on March 23, no other amendment has won such rapid approval. The old record was just over six months in 1804 for the Twelfth Amendment.

A teen's first vote

In 1972, for the first time, many 18-year-olds were allowed to vote. Perhaps waiting in line to vote allowed time for reflection. Why am I doing this? Will it make a difference? Is government really necessary? What does government have to do with my life?

While most of us realize that government is necessary, people have asked basic questions about the institution of government for centuries. What is the proper function of government? What form of government serves best? Where or why did government originate? Many scholars have written much about these issues. This text will help answer some of these basic questions.

The State

Aristotle, a scholar in ancient Greece, was one of the first students of government. He studied the polis, the ancient Greek city-state. Many terms and concepts of government, such as *politics, democracy,* and *republic,* originated in ancient Greece and Rome.

The familiar terms *country* and *state* have basically the same meaning. The word *state* comes from a form of the Latin word *stare,* meaning "to stand." Today the word **state** precisely identifies a political community that occupies a definite territory and has an organized government with the power to make and enforce laws without approval from any higher authority. The United States is one of more than 160 states in the world today.

To citizens of the United States, the term *state* sometimes has a different meaning. The name *United States* was first used in 1776 when the thirteen British colonies became states by declaring their independence. At that time, each state thought of itself as a country. Even though the states later joined together as one nation under the Constitution, the term *state* continued to be used to describe the main political units within the United States.

◀ **Fourth of July parade**

Changing Population and State Power

◀ **Past** Between 1941 and 1945 more than 700,000 African Americans moved from one part of the United States to another seeking opportunity.

Present As people seek a better life, the population of the United States changes, sometimes straining existing facilities, as illustrated in this overcrowded classroom in San Antonio, Texas. ▼

Political Processes
How does a shifting population affect the power of each of the states?

The term *nation* is often used to describe an independent state or country. Strictly speaking, however, a **nation** is any sizable group of people who are united by common bonds of race, language, custom, tradition, and, sometimes, religion. Usually the territorial boundaries of modern states and those of nations are the same. For example, although not all citizens of France are of French descent, the territories of both the nation of France and the state of France coincide. The term **nation-state** is often used to describe such a country.

Not all groups that consider themselves to be nations have their own states. Eastern Canada, for example, includes many French-speaking Catholics who prefer to follow French culture and traditions rather than those of the English-speaking non-Catholic majority of Canada. Some of these people want to break away from Canada and establish their own state. On the other hand, in Africa the populations of some national groups are divided among several African states, the result of artificial borders established during European colonialism. The popular use of the term *nation*, however, fits the standard definition of state. For this reason this text will use the terms *state* and *nation* interchangeably.

Essential Features of a State

The states that make up today's political world share four essential features: population, territory, sovereignty, and government.

Population The most obvious essential for a state is people. The nature of a state's population affects its stability. States where the population shares a general political and social **consensus**, or agreement about basic beliefs, have the most stable governments. For example, most Americans share basic beliefs about the value of democratic government.

Another way that population affects the political organization of a state is through its mobility. Millions of Americans change residences each year. As a result, political power is slowly changing and being modified. A major shift in population from the North and East to the South and West caused Southern and Western states to gain representatives in Congress based on the census, while some states in the North and East lost representation. The movement of some of the population from inner cities to suburban areas resulted in a similar shift in political power.

Territory A state has established boundaries. The United States's continental boundaries are the Atlantic and Pacific Oceans and recognized borders with Canada and Mexico.

The exact location or shape of political boundaries is often a source of conflict among states. Territorial boundaries may change as a result of war, negotiations, or purchase. The territory of the United States, like that of some other states, has grown considerably since the original thirteen states declared their independence. By purchase, negotiation, and war the United States extended its territory to the shores of the Pacific Ocean.

Sovereignty The key characteristic of a state is its sovereignty. Political **sovereignty** means that the state has supreme and absolute authority within its territorial boundaries. It has complete independence, and complete power to make laws, shape foreign policy, and determine its own course of action. In theory, at least, no state has the right to interfere with the internal affairs of another state.

Because every state is considered sovereign, every state is equal with respect to legal rights and duties—at least in theory. In practice, of course, states with great economic strength and military capabilities have more power than other states.

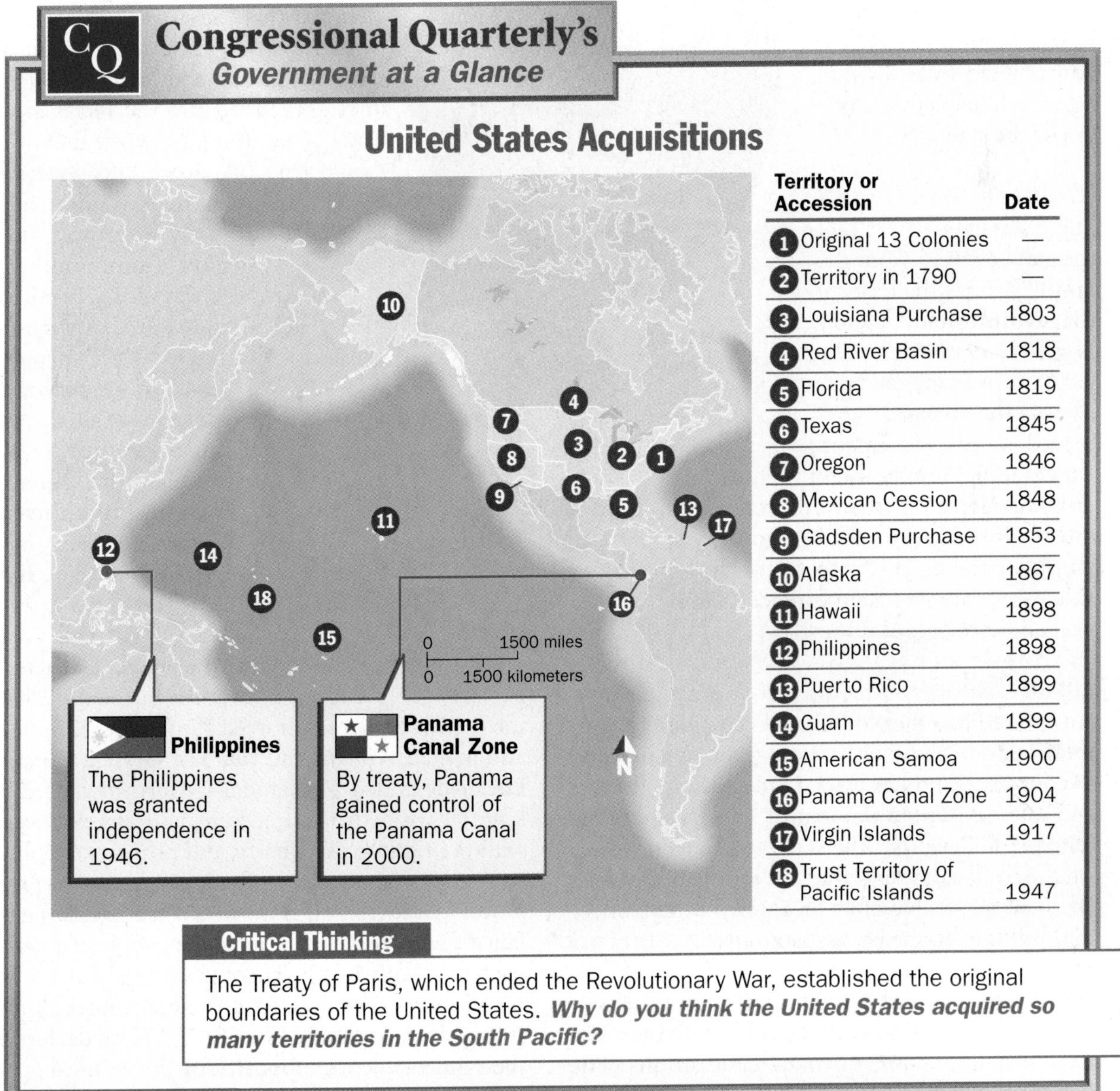

Territory or Accession	Date
1 Original 13 Colonies	—
2 Territory in 1790	—
3 Louisiana Purchase	1803
4 Red River Basin	1818
5 Florida	1819
6 Texas	1845
7 Oregon	1846
8 Mexican Cession	1848
9 Gadsden Purchase	1853
10 Alaska	1867
11 Hawaii	1898
12 Philippines	1898
13 Puerto Rico	1899
14 Guam	1899
15 American Samoa	1900
16 Panama Canal Zone	1904
17 Virgin Islands	1917
18 Trust Territory of Pacific Islands	1947

Critical Thinking

The Treaty of Paris, which ended the Revolutionary War, established the original boundaries of the United States. ***Why do you think the United States acquired so many territories in the South Pacific?***

Government Every state has some form of government. **Government** is the institution through which the state maintains social order, provides public services, and enforces decisions that are binding on all people living within the state.

Theories of the Origin of the State

How did the state or government come to be? No one knows precisely how or why people created the earliest governments. Many scholars have constructed theories that attempt to explain the origin of the state.

Evolutionary Theory Some scholars believe that the state evolved from the family. This is the basis of the **evolutionary theory** of government origin. The head of the primitive family was the authority that served as a government. An extended family might include hundreds of people. Abraham's descendents in the Old Testament of the Bible are an example of the emergence of this kind of rule. Gradually the large extended family needed more organization.

Force Theory In the earliest civilizations people worked together to build walled cities, to control floods, to construct buildings for worship, and to cooperate in other ways. Leaders issued decrees and soldiers went to war to protect their city. Some scholars believe that the state was born of force. The **force theory** says that government emerged when all the people of an area were brought under the authority of one person or group.

Divine Right Theory The notion that the gods have chosen certain people to rule by **divine right** has been important in many civilizations. The Egyptians, Chinese, and Aztec were among those who believed that their rulers were either descendents of gods or at least chosen by gods. In Europe beginning in the 1400s, monarchs often referred to their right to rule as coming from God. People believed that the state was created by God, and those who were born to royalty were chosen by God to govern. To oppose the monarch was to oppose God and was both treason and sin.

Thomas Hobbes (above) and John Locke (right)

Social Contract Theory Beginning in the 1600s, Europeans challenged the rule of sovereigns who ruled by divine right. They were often supported by the writings of philosophers who believed that the origin of the state was in a social contract. **Thomas Hobbes** in England was one of the first to theorize how the **social contract** came about. He wrote that in a "state of nature," no government existed. Without an authority to protect one person from another, life was "cruel, brutish, and short." By contract, people surrendered to the state the power needed to maintain order. The state, in turn, agreed to protect its citizens. Hobbes believed that people did not have the right to break this agreement.

John Locke took the social contract a step further. In 1688 the British Parliament forced King James II to flee and invited William and Mary of Orange to rule. Locke defended Parliament's overthrow of the king. He wrote that people were naturally endowed with the right to life, liberty, and property. To preserve their rights, they willingly contracted to give power to a governing authority. When government failed to preserve the rights of the people, the people could justly break the contract.

Nearly a century later, the American colonies revolted against King George III. They declared their independence supported by the political philosophy of natural rights that Locke had written.

The Purposes of Government

Today governments serve several major purposes for the state: (1) to maintain social order; (2) to provide public services; (3) to provide for national security and a common defense; and (4) to provide for and control the economic system. In carrying out these tasks, governments must make decisions that are binding on all citizens of the state. Government has the authority to require all individuals to obey these decisions and the power to punish those who do not obey them.

The decisions of government are authoritative—that is, they can be enforced upon all of society. Governments derive their authority from two sources—their legitimacy and their ability to use coercive force. Legitimacy means the willingness of citizens to obey the government. In democratic countries legitimacy is based on the consent of the people. Americans understand that if their elected officials fail to respond to the interests of the people, they can be voted out of office. Therefore, the people entrust their government with power.

Coercive force, the second source of government authority, derives from the police, judicial, and military institutions of government. Government can force people to pay taxes and can punish offenders by fines or imprisonment.

Maintaining Social Order John Locke, writing in *Two Treatises of Government* **1** in 1690, explained:

> " *Men being, as has been said, by Nature, all free, equal and independent, no one can be put out of this Estate, and subjected to the Political Power of another, without his own Consent. The only way whereby any one divests himself of his Natural Liberty, and puts on the bonds of Civil Society is by agreeing with other Men to joyn [join] and unite into a Community. . . .* "
>
> —John Locke, 1690

According to the social contract theory, people need government to maintain social order because they have not yet discovered a way to live in groups

See the following footnoted materials in the **Reference Handbook:**
1. *Two Treatises of Government,* page 806.

GOVERNMENT *and You*

Government in Daily Life

Government is much closer than the officials working in Washington, your state capital, or even city hall. Many things that Americans take for granted result from services and protections offered by government.

The roads on which you drive are constructed and maintained by the government. Traffic laws dictate how you drive on those roads. When you go to the store, government regulations make it likely that the groceries you buy will not poison you. Your hair stylist and dentist are expected to be skilled professionals because government licenses these and other businesses and sets minimum standards. Turn on your radio or TV. The program you receive will be clear because government prevents stations from interfering with each other's signals. All in all, the presence of government in daily life is greater than you may think.

Ensuring traffic safety

Participating IN GOVERNMENT ACTIVITY

Solving Problems Assume you serve on your city council. A group of citizens has petitioned the city to change the speed limit on all nonresidential streets from 35 mph to 50 mph. Brainstorm the advantages and disadvantages of each alternative and how it would impact citizens. Recommend what speed limit should be in effect and why.

Naming the Nation **The term *United States of America* was first used officially in the Declaration of Independence, adopted July 4, 1776. Later, on September 9, 1776, the Continental Congress formally resolved to replace the name "United Colonies" with "United States." For a time, the country was officially called "United States of North America," but in 1778, the Continental Congress shortened it to "United States of America."**

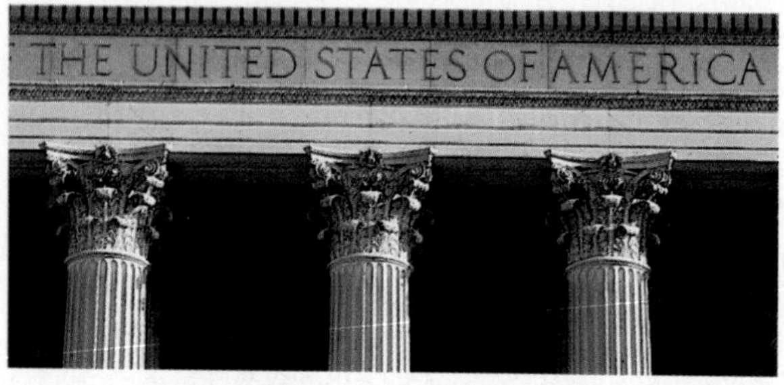

without conflict. There are many sources of conflict in any group. Two people may argue over the boundary line between their properties. Members of a community may disagree about what is best for the group. In any group, some members may try to take unfair advantage of others. Conflict seems to be an inescapable part of group life.

Governments provide ways of resolving conflicts among group members, helping to maintain social order. Governments have the power to make and enforce laws. Governments can require people to do things they might not do voluntarily, such as pay taxes or serve in the army. Governments also provide structures such as courts to help people resolve disagreements in an orderly manner.

Without government, civilized life would not be possible. Government controls and contains conflict between people by placing limits on what individuals are permitted to do. Government provides a group with law and order. An effective government allows citizens to plan for the future, get an education, raise a family, and live orderly lives.

Providing Public Services Abraham Lincoln identified one purpose of government:

> "*The legitimate object of government is to do for a community of people whatever they need to have done but cannot do at all, or cannot so well do for themselves in their separate and individual capacities. But in all that people can individually do for themselves, government ought not to interfere.*"
>
> —Abraham Lincoln, 1854

One of the important purposes of government is to provide essential services that make community life possible and promote the general welfare. Governments undertake projects, such as building sewer systems, that individuals could not or would not do on their own.

Governments also provide an essential service by making and enforcing laws that promote public health and safety. Government inspectors check meat and produce to prevent the sale of spoiled food. State legislators pass laws that require people to pass a driving test.

Providing National Security A third task of government is to protect the people against attack by other states or from threats such as terrorism. Protecting its national security is a major concern of each sovereign state. In today's world of nuclear weapons, spy satellites, international terrorists, and huge armies, the job of providing for the defense and security of the state is complex.

In addition to protecting the nation from attack, government handles normal relations with other nations. The United States Constitution gives our national government a monopoly over our nation's dealings with foreign countries. Thus, our national government has the exclusive power to make treaties with other nations. Government helps to provide economic security by enacting

GOVERNMENT *Online*

Student Web Activity Visit the *United States Government: Democracy in Action* Web site at gov.glencoe.com and click on ***Chapter 1–Student Web Activities*** for an activity about principles of government.

trade agreements with other countries. Some state governments maintain informal relations with foreign governments for trade and cultural purposes. The national government, however, has the power to limit these arrangements.

The government enforces laws that protect the public safety and health.

Making Economic Decisions Nations vary greatly in their ability to provide their citizens with economic opportunities or resources. No country provides its citizens with everything they need or desire. Even in a wealthy country like the United States, many people are poorly clothed, housed, and fed. The problem of scarcity is far greater in many other nations around the world.

Material scarcity is often the cause of conflict in society. Countries in which the gap between rich and poor is great may experience civil unrest. Historically this has been the primary cause of several full-blown revolutions. For this reason governments often use their power to reduce the cause of such conflict by intervening in the economic system.

Governments do not limit their intervention to only domestic necessities. They may intervene in the economic affairs of another nation. For example, after World War II, the United States provided economic aid to nations in which it believed economic conditions might foster Communist revolutions.

Governments pass the laws that determine and control the economic environment of the nation. Such a function could be as limited as simply providing a national currency, or it could be as extensive as controlling every individual's economic decisions.

Governments also may make choices that distribute benefits and public services among citizens. For example, the government can make payments to farmers who raise certain crops or allow tax advantages to certain industries. The government's decision to build a veterans' hospital in a certain town benefits some of the people and not others. Governments usually try to stimulate economic growth and stability through controlling inflation, encouraging trade, and regulating the development of natural resources.

Section 1 Assessment

Checking for Understanding

1. **Main Idea** In a graphic organizer similar to the one below, identify four major purposes of government and give an example of each.

Purpose	Example

2. **Define** state, nation, nation-state, consensus, sovereignty, government, social contract.
3. **Identify** Aristotle, Thomas Hobbes, John Locke.
4. What are the four essential features of a state?

Critical Thinking

5. **Making Comparisons** Thomas Hobbes and John Locke both subscribed to the social contract theory of government. Compare and contrast their views of that theory.

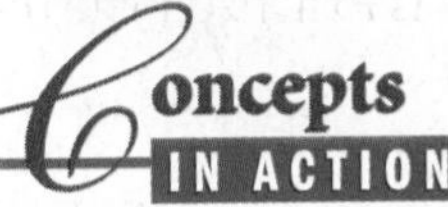

Public Policy Read news articles concerning decisions made by foreign governments. Classify those decisions that you believe are making life better for their citizens and those you believe are making life worse.

Section 2

The Formation of Governments

Reader's Guide

Key Terms

unitary system, federal system, confederacy, constitution, constitutional government, preamble, constitutional law, politics, industrialized nation, developing nation

Find Out

- What are the similarities and differences between a unitary government and a federal government system?
- What are the main purposes of a constitution?

Understanding Concepts

Global Perspectives The United States Constitution is the oldest written constitution still in use. What does this imply about the stability of governments in the world?

COVER STORY

Debates Rage On

RICHMOND, VIRGINIA, 1788

The proposed national constitution, written last summer in Philadelphia, is stirring controversy throughout the state. Although it is based on a design developed by Virginians, many state leaders believe the planned government is too strong. "It squints toward monarchy," says former governor Patrick Henry. James Madison, a leading Virginia delegate at Philadelphia, defends the convention's work. He asks, "What is government itself but the greatest of all reflections on human nature? If men were gods," he observes, "no government would be necessary."

Patrick Henry

The government of each nation has unique characteristics that relate to that nation's historic development. To carry out their functions, governments have been organized in a variety of ways. Most large countries have several different levels of government. These usually include a central or national government, as well as the governments of smaller divisions within the country, such as provinces, states, counties, cities, towns, and villages.

Government Systems

The relationship among the national government and the smaller divisions can be described as either unitary or federal.

Unitary System A unitary system of government gives all key powers to the national or central government. This does not mean that only one level of government exists. Rather, it means that the central government creates state, provincial, or other local governments and gives them limited sovereignty. Great Britain, Italy, and France developed unitary governments as these nations gradually emerged from smaller kingdoms.

Federal System A federal system of government divides the powers of government between the national government and state or provincial governments. Each level of government has sovereignty in some areas. The United States developed a federal system after the thirteen colonies became states.

To begin with, the United States formed a confederacy, a loose union of independent states. When the confederacy failed to provide an effective national government, the Constitution made the national government supreme, while preserving some state government powers. Today, other countries with federal systems include Canada, Switzerland, Mexico, Australia, and India.

Constitutions and Government

A **constitution** is a plan that provides the rules for government. A constitution serves several major purposes. (1) It sets out ideals that the people bound by the constitution believe in and share. (2) It establishes the basic structure of government and defines the government's powers and duties. (3) It provides the supreme law for the country. Constitutions provide rules that shape the actions of government and politics, much as the rules of basketball define the action in a basketball game.

Constitutions may be written or unwritten; however, in most modern states, constitutions are written. The United States Constitution, drawn up in 1787, is the oldest written constitution still serving a nation today. Other nations with written constitutions include France, Kenya, India, Italy, and Switzerland. Great Britain, on the other hand, has an unwritten constitution based on hundreds of years of legislative acts, court decisions, and customs.

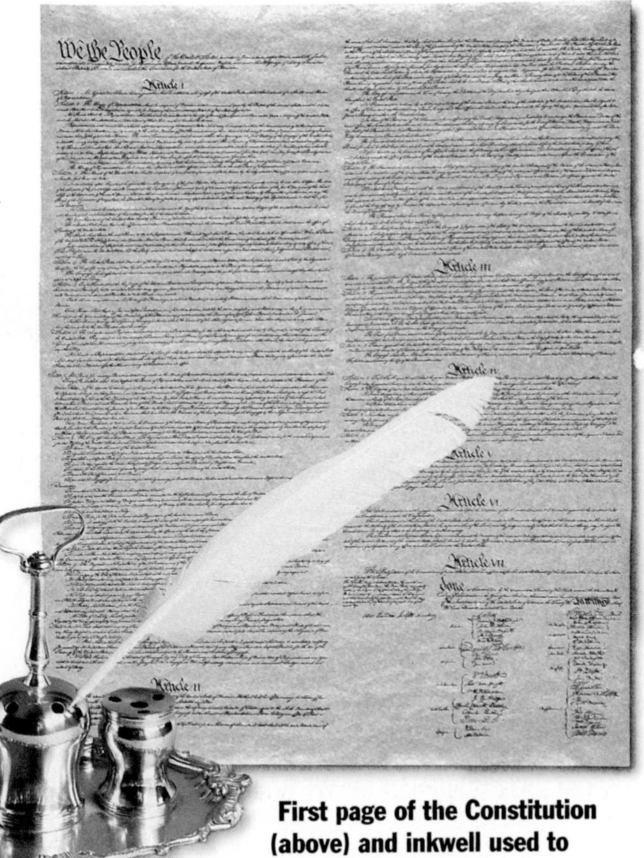

First page of the Constitution (above) and inkwell used to sign the Constitution

All governments have a constitution in the sense that they have some plan for organizing and operating the government. In this sense the People's Republic of China has a constitution. The term **constitutional government,** however, has a special meaning. It refers to a government in which a constitution has authority to place clearly recognized limits on the powers of those who govern. Thus, constitutional government is *limited* government. Despite the existence of a written constitution, the People's Republic of China does not have constitutional government. In that country, there are few limits on the power of the government.

Incomplete Guides

Constitutions themselves are important but incomplete guides to how a country is actually governed. They are incomplete for two reasons. First, no written constitution by itself can possibly spell out all the laws, customs, and ideas that grow up around the document itself. In the United States, for example, until Franklin D. Roosevelt was elected president four times, it was custom, rather than law, that no person should be elected president more than twice. Only when the Twenty-second Amendment went into effect was a president limited by law to two elected terms.

Second, a constitution does not always reflect the actual practice of government in a country. The People's Republic of China, for example, has a written constitution filled with statements about the basic rights, freedoms, and duties of citizens. Yet, for years the Chinese government has maintained an extensive police force to spy on Chinese citizens and punish those whose ideas are not acceptable to the state. Although the government relaxed some restrictions in the late 1980s, authorities crushed a pro-democracy movement in 1989.

A Statement of Goals

Most constitutions contain a statement that sets forth the goals and purposes to be served by the government. This statement is usually called the **preamble.** The Preamble to the United States Constitution states the major goals of American government:

Breaking Precedent

Constitutional Interpretations Wendell Lewis Willkie became the Republican nominee for president in 1940 when Franklin D. Roosevelt ran for an unprecedented third term. Roosevelt violated George Washington's precedent that limited presidents to two terms. ***How did George Washington's precedent reflect the idea of limited government?***

> *We, the people of the United States, in Order to form a more perfect Union, establish Justice, insure domestic Tranquility, provide for the common defence [defense], promote the general Welfare, and secure the Blessings of Liberty to ourselves and our Posterity, do ordain and establish this Constitution for the United States of America.*
>
> —Preamble to the Constitution, 1787

A Framework for Government The main body of a constitution sets out the plan for government. In federal states, such as the United States, the constitution also describes the relationship between the national government and state governments. Most written constitutions also describe the procedure for amending, or changing, the constitution.

The main body of a constitution is usually divided into parts called articles and sections. The United States Constitution has 7 articles containing a total of 21 sections. The French constitution has 92 articles grouped under 15 titles. The Indian constitution, the longest in the world, consists of hundreds of articles.

The Highest Law Constitutions provide the supreme law for states. A constitution is usually accepted as a superior, morally binding force. It draws its authority from the people or from a special assembly chosen by the people to create the constitution. **Constitutional law** involves the interpretation and application of the constitution. Thus, constitutional law primarily concerns defining the extent and limits of government power and the rights of citizens.

Politics and Government

The effort to control or influence the conduct and policies of government is called **politics.** The Constitution did not prevent the development of politics because politics and government are closely related. In fact, a major political struggle developed over the ratification of the Constitution itself. Within a few years major political parties played key roles in elections.

People are taking part in politics when they join a citizens' group protesting higher taxes or when they meet with the mayor to ask the city to repave the streets in their neighborhood. Legislators are acting politically when they vote to have government buildings constructed in the districts they represent.

Seeking Government Benefits Participation in politics arises because people realize that government has the potential to influence their lives in many ways. Different people make different demands on government. Construction workers may want government to support the building of new highways to create jobs. Conservationists may want the government to spend its money on mass transit and public parks instead. Still other people, who favor lower taxes, may want neither the new highways nor more public parks.

In a large, diverse nation like the United States, there is a continual struggle over what benefits and services government should provide, how much they should cost, and who should pay for them. Through politics, individuals and groups seek to maximize the benefits they get from government while they try to reduce the costs of these benefits. Through politics, people also seek to use government to turn their values and beliefs into public policy. One group, for example, tries to influence government to ban smoking in public places. Other people pressure government not to restrict smoking in any way.

Importance of Politics Through politics, conflicts in society are managed. As people seek rewards and benefits, politics provides a peaceful way for them to compete with one another. The outcomes of politics—the struggle to control government—affect such key matters as the quality of air and water, economic conditions, peace and war, and the extent of citizens' rights and freedoms.

Special Interests The Constitution says that government should promote the *general* welfare. The Framers believed government should operate in the interests of *all* the people, not favoring any special group or person. One of the issues that concerned the Framers of the United States Constitution was the possibility that groups of people, united by special political interests, would hinder the launching of the new government. James Madison explained his concerns in a series of articles called ***The Federalist:***

> "*Among the numerous advantages promised by a well-constructed Union... [is] its tendency to break and control the violence of faction.... By a faction, I understand a number of citizens... who are united and actuated [moved] by some common impulse of passion, or of interest, adverse to the rights of other citizens, or to the permanent and aggregate interests of the community....*"
>
> —James Madison, 1787

Some people equate politics with bribery or corruption. They believe the general welfare may be sacrificed to the desires of a special-interest group. The misuse of politics, however, should not obscure the value of a political system.

We the People

Making a Difference

Laura Epstein

Laura Epstein did not plan to stir her community to action when she spent the summer of 1996 with a paint brush. She and eight other young people only wanted to paint over graffiti-covered walls to help beautify downtown Seattle.

Working with Seattle's waste department, Laura and her team painted murals on many of the city's graffiti-covered walls. Volunteers helped decorate one of the park walls, once a graffiti eyesore, with giant bugs.

Laura was surprised when the graffiti-erasing campaign turned into a creative project for the community and the children in the neighborhood. "That was the best part—having the neighbor kids help us paint and get involved," she said. Laura feels she has contributed to the neighborhood by leaving behind something that neighborhood kids can point to and say, "Hey, I helped make that!"

The antigraffiti project is just one of hundreds of projects being carried out by youth teams across the nation who are members of the Youth Volunteer Corps of America (YVCA). The YVCA is a project funded by the federal government that gives young people a way to get involved in their communities. According to Bill Barrett, who works for the national program, "People who serve others are providing the solutions to our country's problems."

Destruction and Development

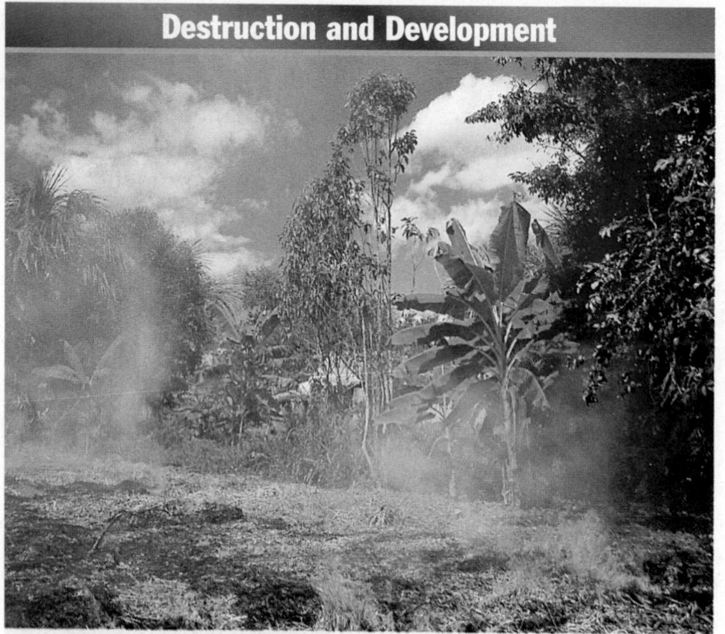

Inequalities Among Countries Nations must cooperate to solve worldwide concerns. Today the increasing demands for natural resources threaten many tropical rain forests, like this one in South America. ***What tensions do you think occur between developing nations and industrialized nations over the destruction of the rain forests?***

Governing in the Twentieth Century

The United States government conducts policy in a complex world. Changing relationships challenge the policies of every nation. It is not easy to define the boundaries of government.

Major Inequalities Among States Because of great inequalities among countries, the world today is full of contrasts. The United States and about 20 other states, such as Japan, Canada, Australia, and France, are **industrialized nations.** Industrialized nations have generally large industries and advanced technology that provide a more comfortable way of life than developing nations do. **Developing nations** are only beginning to develop industrially. More than 100 developing nations have average per capita, or per person, incomes that are a fraction of those of industrialized nations. In the poorest countries, starvation, disease, and political turmoil are a way of life. Many states of Africa south of the Sahara and of Southeast Asia are developing nations. Between these two levels of nations are many newly industrialized states like Mexico, South Korea, and Argentina, as well as other states in South America, Eastern Europe, and the Middle East.

Growing Interdependence Although each state is sovereign, it must exist in a world of many nations. Nations today are in constant contact with one another, and they are becoming more and more interdependent.

Interdependence means that nations must interact or depend on one another, especially economically and politically. The larger countries of North America—Canada, Mexico, and the United States—are developing greater economic, social, and political ties. In 1993 the United States signed the North American Free Trade Agreement (NAFTA) that linked North America in a far-reaching trade partnership that affected goods produced and sold between the United States, Canada, and Mexico.

Interdependence affects the developing states. Many of the developing states have become very dependent on the industrialized ones for economic aid, medical supplies and services, financial investment, assistance to cope with natural disasters, and military aid.

Growing interdependence means that events in one nation affect events throughout the world. In 1990, for example, President Bush sent troops to Saudi Arabia after Iraq invaded neighboring Kuwait. The United States relied on the Middle Eastern states for an important part of its oil supply. As war threatened to break out in the region, people feared that there would be an oil shortage in the United States. The United States and its allies defeated Iraq in the Persian Gulf War in 1991; however, tensions in the Gulf have continued. In 1996 the United States launched 27 missile attacks against Iraq because the policies of its president, Saddam Hussein, had threatened oil-producing countries again. In 1997 new tensions arose when Iraq refused to comply with the terms of the United Nations cease-fire agreement.

Travel, trade, and communications among states are increasing. In 1970 United States exports of goods and services were more than $62 billion, while imports were nearly $60 billion. By 2000 United States yearly exports climbed to more than $950 billion, and imports passed the one trillion mark. An increase in international communications more than matched this huge increase in trade. Fiber optic telephone cable enabled Americans to exceed a tenfold increase in overseas telephone contacts between 1977 and the early 1990s. Satellite television has connected people of every continent.

Nonstate International Groups Today's world also contains some groups that are not states but that play an important role in international politics. These nonstate groups fall into three categories: (1) political movements such as national liberation organizations; (2) multinational corporations; and (3) international organizations. Nonstate groups play major roles in international affairs because they impact policies and decisions of the diverse states of the world.

Some national liberation organizations, such as the Palestine Liberation Organization (PLO), maintain diplomatic relations with many states. States may refuse to recognize those that conduct terrorist activities, however.

Multinational corporations are huge companies with offices and factories in many countries. While they do not have political sovereignty, they do carry out their activities on a global scale, selling their products worldwide and entering into agreements with foreign governments. Thus, multinational corporations influence international politics and the internal decisions of their host countries. Richard Holder, president of Reynolds Metals Company, explained that a global company is one that

> "*. . . operates as a worldwide, integrated system in which all operations, wherever they may be, are interdependent in terms of operations and strategies. Every decision . . . is considered in the light of a worldwide system.*"
>
> —Richard Holder, October 1989

General Motors, American Telephone and Telegraph, Unilever, Nabisco, British Petroleum, Royal Dutch Shell, Mitsubishi, and Sony are examples of global corporations that have attained worldwide economic importance.

Finally, the modern world includes many international organizations. These groups range from the United Nations (UN) to more specialized organizations such as the International Sugar Council and the Universal Postal Union. These organizations undertake a wide variety of tasks, often to serve the needs of member states. The World Meteorological Organization, for example, facilitates the exchange of weather information among states.

Section 2 Assessment

Checking for Understanding

1. **Main Idea** In a Venn diagram similar to the one at the right, show the similarities and differences between a constitutional government and a government that merely has a constitution.

2. **Define** unitary system, federal system, confederacy, constitution, constitutional government, preamble, constitutional law, politics, industrialized nation, developing nation.
3. **Identify** *The Federalist.*
4. Compare sovereignty in a unitary system of government with sovereignty in a federal system.

Critical Thinking

5. **Drawing Conclusions** The Framers of the Constitution wanted to prevent "factions," or special interest groups. Would it be possible to have government without interest groups? Explain.

Concepts IN ACTION

Global Perspectives Choose five foreign nations and find out about each nation's basic structure of government. When was its constitution adopted? Is the government democratic? Obtain information from a local library or on the Internet.

Section 3

Types of Government

Reader's Guide

Key Terms

autocracy, monarchy, oligarchy, democracy, republic, political party, free enterprise

Find Out

- What are the main characteristics of a democracy?
- Why is free enterprise conducive to the growth and preservation of democracy?

Understanding Concepts

Cultural Pluralism How does a representative democracy provide a good government for diverse peoples?

COVER STORY

Democracy Assaulted

BEIJING, CHINA, MAY 1989

Some 10,000 Chinese troops surprised sleeping protesters in Tiananmen Square early this morning. The brutal assault, one of the worst days of bloodshed in China's history, ended seven weeks of demonstrations by students calling for democracy in China. The protesters scattered in terror as soldiers sprayed them with automatic weapons fire. Once government forces gained control of the 100-acre square, they used a tank to crush the Goddess of Democracy, a 30-foot polystyrene statue that students had recently erected. The Chinese Red Cross put the death toll at almost 2,600.

The "Goddess of Democracy"

The United States has established a representative democracy that serves as a model for government and inspires people around the world. Students in China in 1989 marched for "government of the people, by the people, and for the people." Yet other forms of government outnumber true democracies.

Over the centuries, people have organized their governments in many different ways. In Saudi Arabia, for example, the ruling royal family controls the government and its resources. Family members choose the king from among themselves. Thousands of miles away, in Burkina Faso in Africa, a small group of wealthy landowners and military officers governs that country. In Sweden the people elect the Riksdag, the national legislature, which in turn selects the prime minister to carry out the laws.

Major Types of Government

Governments can be classified in many ways. The most time-honored system comes from the ideas of the ancient Greek philosopher Aristotle. It is based on a key question: Who governs the state? Under this system of classification, all governments belong to one of three major groups: (1) autocracy—rule by one person; (2) oligarchy—rule by a few persons; or (3) democracy—rule by many persons.

Autocracy Any system of government in which the power and authority to rule are in the hands of a single individual is an **autocracy**. This is the oldest and one of the most common forms of government. Historically, most autocrats have maintained their positions of authority by inheritance or the ruthless use of military or police power. Several forms of autocracy exist. One is an absolute or **totalitarian dictatorship.** In a totalitarian dictatorship, the ideas of a single leader or group of leaders are glorified. The government seeks to control all aspects of social and economic life. Examples of totalitarian dictatorship include Adolf Hitler's government in Nazi Germany (from 1933 to 1945), Benito Mussolini's rule in Italy (from 1922 to 1943), and Joseph Stalin's regime in the Soviet Union (from 1924 to 1953). In such dictatorships, government is not responsible to the people, and the people lack the power to limit their rulers.

Monarchy is another form of autocratic government. In a monarchy a king, queen, or emperor exercises the supreme powers of government. Monarchs usually inherit their positions. **Absolute monarchs** have complete and unlimited power to rule their people. The king of Saudi Arabia, for example, is such an absolute monarch. Absolute monarchs are rare today, but from the 1400s to the 1700s, kings or queens with absolute powers ruled most of Western Europe.

Today some countries, such as Great Britain, Sweden, Japan, and the Netherlands, have **constitutional monarchs.** These monarchs share governmental powers with elected legislatures or serve mainly as the ceremonial leaders of their governments.

French Dictator

Comparative Government Artist Jacques-Louis David depicts absolute ruler and military leader Napoleon Bonaparte in *Napoleon Crossing the Great St. Bernard* in the late 1790s. ***Why do you think dictatorships require large armies?***

Oligarchy

An oligarchy is any system of government in which a small group holds power. The group derives its power from wealth, military power, social position, or a combination of these elements. Sometimes religion is the source of power. Today the governments of Communist countries, such as China, are mostly oligarchies. In such countries, leaders in the Communist Party and the armed forces control the government.

Both dictatorships and oligarchies sometimes claim they rule for the people. Such governments may try to give the appearance of control by the people. For example, they might hold elections, but offer only one candidate, or control the election results in other ways. Such governments may also have some type of legislature or national assembly elected by or representing the people. These legislatures, however, approve only policies and decisions already made by the leaders. As in a dictatorship, oligarchies usually suppress all political opposition—sometimes ruthlessly.

Democracy

A democracy is any system of government in which rule is by the people. The term *democracy* comes from the Greek *demos* (meaning "the people") and *kratia* (meaning "rule"). The ancient Greeks used the word *democracy* to mean government by the many in contrast to government by the few. Pericles, a great leader of ancient Athens, declared, "Our constitution is named a democracy because it is in the hands not of the few, but of the many."

The key idea of democracy is that the people hold sovereign power. Abraham Lincoln captured this spirit best when he described democracy as "government of the people, by the people, and for the people."

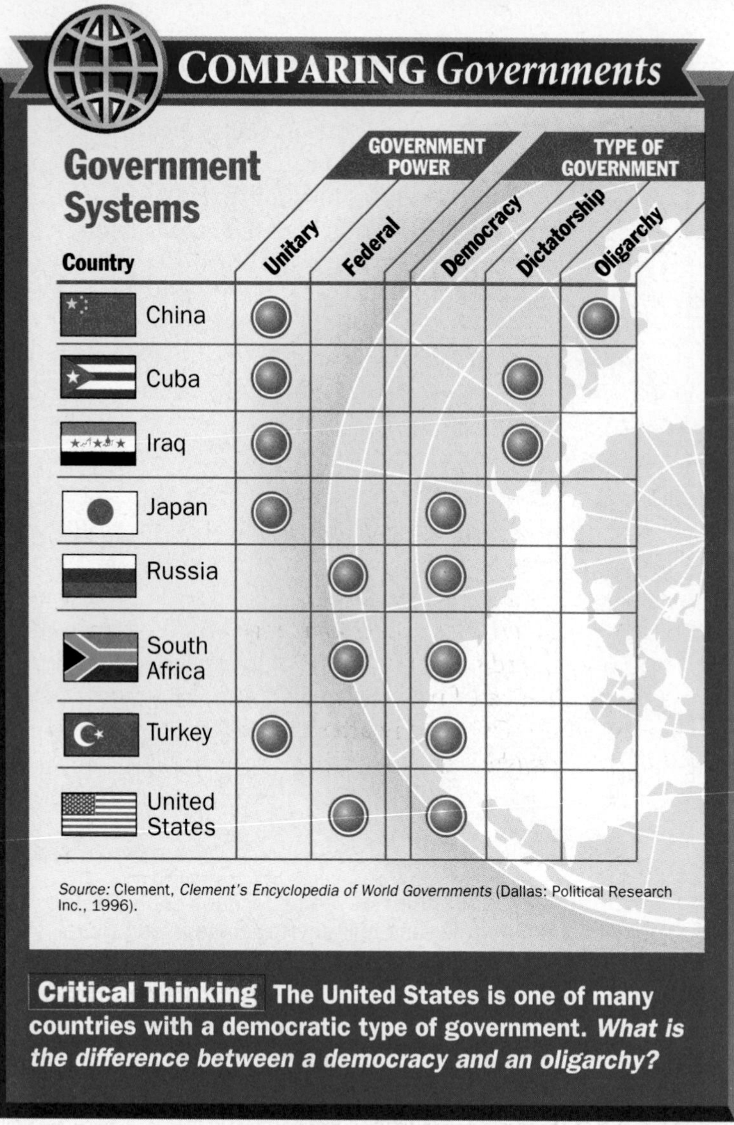

COMPARING *Governments*

Government Systems

Country	Government Power: Unitary	Government Power: Federal	Type of Government: Democracy	Type of Government: Dictatorship	Type of Government: Oligarchy
China	●				●
Cuba	●			●	
Iraq	●			●	
Japan	●		●		
Russia		●	●		
South Africa		●	●		
Turkey	●		●		
United States		●	●		

Source: Clement, *Clement's Encyclopedia of World Governments* (Dallas: Political Research Inc., 1996).

Critical Thinking **The United States is one of many countries with a democratic type of government.** ***What is the difference between a democracy and an oligarchy?***

Democracy may take one of two forms. In a **direct democracy,** the people govern themselves by voting on issues individually as citizens. Direct democracy exists only in very small societies where citizens can actually meet regularly to discuss and decide key issues and problems. Direct democracy is still found in some New England town meetings and in some of the smaller states, called cantons, of Switzerland. No country today, however, has a government based on direct democracy.

In an indirect or **representative democracy,** the people elect representatives and give them the responsibility and power to make laws and conduct government. An assembly of the people's representatives may be called a council, a legislature, a congress, or a parliament. Representative democracy is practiced in cities, states, provinces, and countries where the population is too large to meet regularly in one place. It is the most efficient way to ensure that the rights of individual citizens, who are part of a large group, are represented.

In a **republic,** voters hold sovereign power. Elected representatives who are responsible to the people exercise that power. As Benjamin Franklin was leaving the last session of the Constitutional Convention in Philadelphia in 1787, a woman approached him and asked, "What kind of government have you given us, Dr. Franklin? A republic or a monarchy?" Franklin answered, "A republic, Madam, if you can keep it." Franklin's response indicated that the Founders preferred a republic over a monarchy but that a republic requires citizen participation.

For most Americans today, the terms *representative democracy, republic,* and *constitutional republic* mean the same thing: a system of limited government where the people are the ultimate source of governmental power. It should be understood, however, that throughout the world not every democracy is a republic. Great Britain, for example, is a democracy but not a republic because it has a constitutional monarch as the head of state.

Characteristics of Democracy

Today some nations of the world misuse the word *democracy.* Many countries call their governments "democratic" or "republic" whether they really are or not. The government of North Korea, for example, is an oligarchy, because a small number of Communist Party leaders run the government. Yet their country is called the Democratic People's Republic of Korea. A true democratic government, as opposed to one that only uses the term *democracy* in its name, has characteristics that distinguish it from other forms of government.

Individual Liberty No individual, of course, can be completely free to do absolutely anything he or she wants. That would result in chaos. Rather, democracy requires that all people be as free as possible to develop their own capacities. Government in a democracy works to promote the kind of equality in which all people have an equal opportunity to develop their talents to the fullest extent possible.

Majority Rule with Minority Rights Democracy also requires that government decisions be based on majority rule. In a democracy people usually accept decisions made by the majority of voters in a free election. Representative democracy means that laws enacted in the legislatures represent the will of the majority of lawmakers. Because these lawmakers are elected by the people, the laws are accepted by the people.

At the same time, the American concept of democracy includes a concern about the possible tyranny of the majority. The Constitution helps ensure that the rights of the minority will be protected.

Respect for minority rights can be difficult to maintain, especially when society is under great stress. For example, during World War II, the government imprisoned more than 100,000 Japanese Americans in relocation camps because it feared they would be disloyal. The relocation program caused severe hardships for many Japanese Americans and deprived them of their basic liberties. Even so, the program was upheld by the Supreme Court in 1944 in *Korematsu* v. *United States* [1] and in two similar cases.

 **Landmark Cases**

Endo* v. *United States The Supreme Court, however, upheld the rights of Mitsuye Endo in 1944. A native-born citizen, Endo was fired from a California state job in 1942 and sent to a relocation center. Her lawyer challenged the War Relocation board's right to detain a loyal American citizen. The case finally reached the Supreme Court in 1944.

On the day after the exclusionary order was revoked by the military commander, the Court

See the following footnoted materials in the **Reference Handbook:**
1. *Korematsu* v. *United States* case summary, page 760.

Relocation and Discrimination

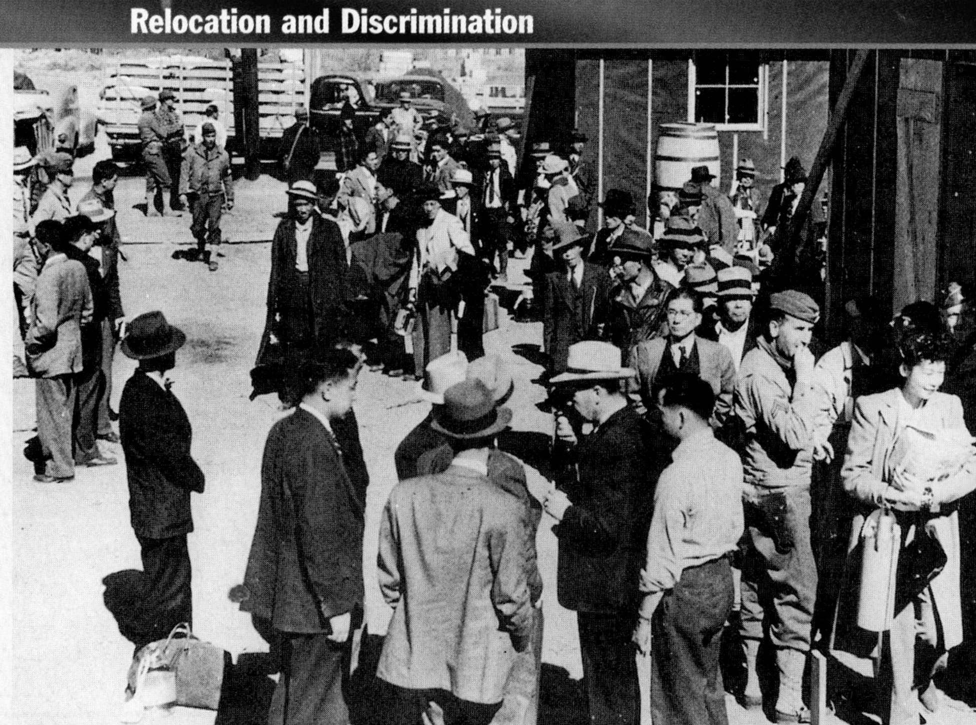

Civil Liberties More than 70,000 of the people of Japanese descent interned during World War II were *Nisei,* or American-born. ***What kind of recompense did internment victims receive in the 1980s?***

ruled that Mitsuye Endo could no longer be held in custody. Justice Frank Murphy wrote:

> *Detention in Relocation Centers of people of Japanese ancestry regardless of loyalty is not only unauthorized by Congress or the Executive, but is another example of the unconstitutional resort to racism inherent in the entire evacuation program. . . . Racial discrimination of this nature bears no reasonable relation to military necessity and is utterly foreign to the ideals and traditions of American people.*
>
> —Justice Frank Murphy, 1944

In recent years the wartime relocation program has been criticized as a denial of individual rights and as proof that tyranny can occur in even the most democratic societies. In 1988 Congress acknowledged the "grave injustice" of the relocation experience and offered payments of $20,000 to those Japanese Americans still living who had been relocated.

Free Elections As we have seen, democratic governments receive their legitimacy by the consent of the governed. The authority to create and run the government rests with the people. All genuine democracies have free and open elections. Free elections give people the chance to choose their leaders and to voice their opinions on various issues. Free elections also help ensure that public officials pay attention to the wishes of the people.

In a democracy several characteristics mark free elections. First, everyone's vote carries the same weight—a principle often expressed in the phrase **"one person, one vote."** Second, all candidates have the right to express their views freely, giving voters access to competing ideas. Third, citizens are free to help candidates or support issues. Fourth, the legal requirements for voting, such as age, residence, and citizenship, are kept to a minimum. Thus, racial, ethnic, religious, or other discriminatory tests cannot be used to restrict voting. Fifth, citizens may vote freely by secret ballot, without coercion or fear of punishment for their voting decisions.

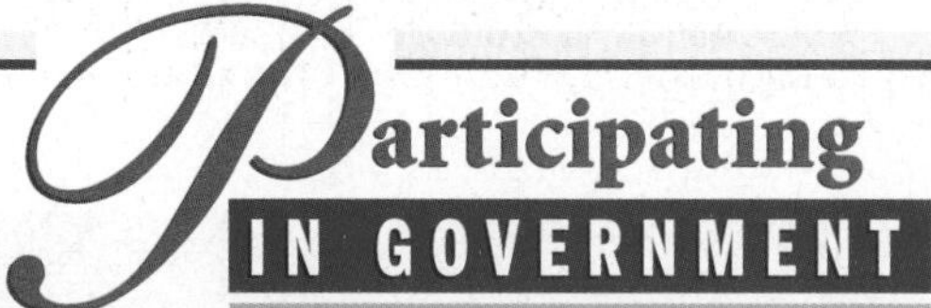

Determining the Social Consensus

Democracy depends, in part, on a social consensus. Certain ideas, values, and beliefs that are shared by a great majority of people help to support and stabilize democratic governments. What are the key elements in the social consensus of your community?

Survey a variety of people asking whether they agree or disagree with the following:

1. Everyone should be given an opportunity for a free public education.
2. Burning the American flag as a symbol of protest should be made unconstitutional.
3. Freedom of speech includes the right to lie on your income tax form.
4. Wealthy people should pay a higher percentage of taxes than low-income people.
5. People or companies should be fined for dumping trash on public property.
6. Scientists should not be permitted to use animals for experiments.

Analyzing survey results

Activity

Compile the results of your survey. Analyze the data and create a poster that illustrates the social consensus of your survey group. Be sure your poster includes charts and graphs that display the survey results.

Prerequisites of Democracy: An Educated Public

Past As the nation grew, ▶ standards and methods of education also expanded. A teacher at a school in Nebraska teaches a multiplication lesson in 1895.

Present Today students use computer technology to develop skills needed in modern society. ▼

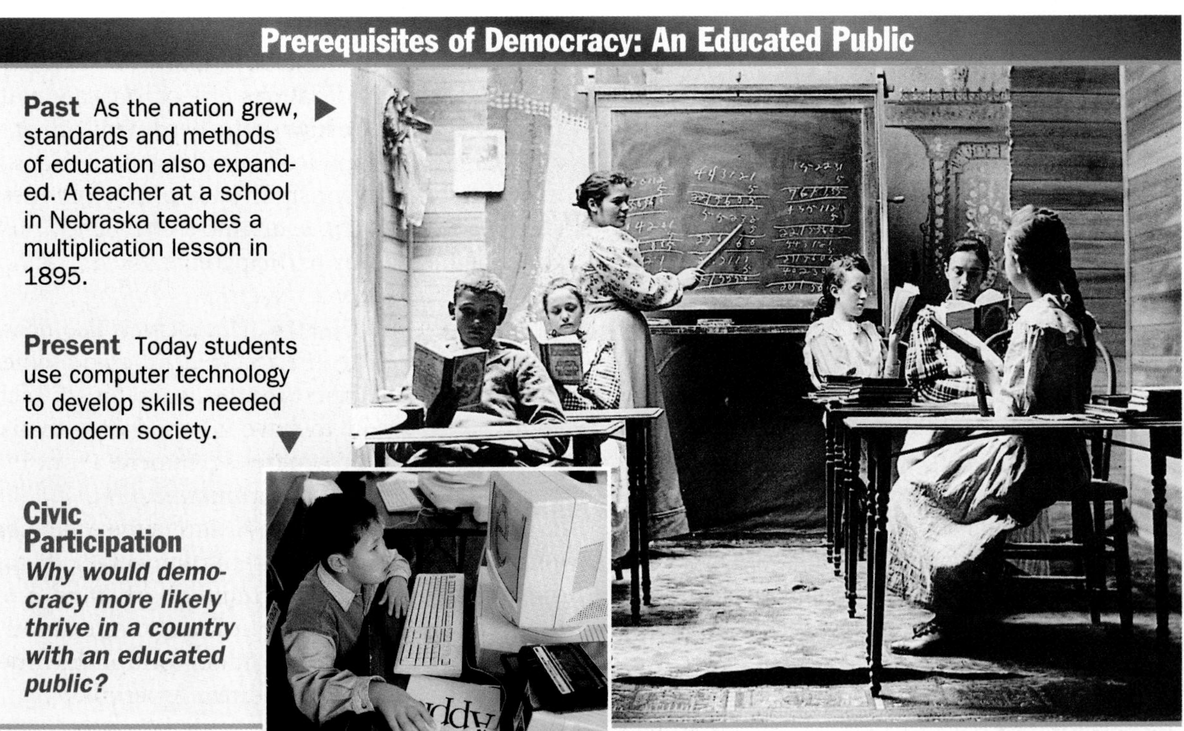

Civic Participation
Why would democracy more likely thrive in a country with an educated public?

Competing Political Parties Political parties are an important element of democratic government. A political party is a group of individuals with broad common interests who organize to nominate candidates for office, win elections, conduct government, and determine public policy. In the United States, while any number of political parties may compete, a two-party system in which the Republicans and the Democrats have become the major political parties has developed.

Rival parties help make elections meaningful. They give voters a choice among candidates. They also help simplify and focus attention on key issues for voters. Finally, in democratic countries, the political party or parties that are out of power serve as a "loyal opposition." That is, by criticizing the policies and actions of the party in power, they can help make those in power more responsible to the people.

The Soil of Democracy

Historically, few nations have practiced democracy. One reason may be that real democracy seems to require a special environment. Democratic government is more likely to succeed in countries which to some degree meet five general criteria that reflect the quality of life of citizens.

Active Citizen Participation Democracy requires citizens who are willing to participate in civic life. Countries in which citizens are able to inform themselves about issues, to vote in elections, to serve on juries, to work for candidates, and to run for government office are more likely to maintain a strong democracy than countries where citizens do not participate fully in their government.

A Favorable Economy Democracy succeeds more in countries that do not have extremes of wealth and poverty and that have a large middle class. The opportunity to control one's economic decisions provides a base for making independent political decisions. In the United States this concept is called free enterprise. If people do not have control of their economic lives, they will not likely be free to make political decisions.

Countries with stable, growing economies seem better able to support democratic government. In the past, autocrats who promised citizens jobs and food have toppled many democratic governments during times of severe economic depression. People who are out of work or unable to feed their families often become more concerned about security than about voting or exercising other political rights.

Widespread Education Democracy is more likely to succeed in countries with an educated public. The debate over public education in America was settled in the 1830s. For example, in 1835 Pennsylvania voted to fund public schools. Thaddeus Stevens, speaking to the Pennsylvania state legislature in favor of the funding legislation, said:

> "*If an elective republic is to endure for any great length of time, every elector must have sufficient information . . . to direct wisely the legislature, the ambassadors, and the executive of the nation. . . . [I]t is the duty of government to see that the means of information be diffused to every citizen.*"
>
> —Thaddeus Stevens, April 1835

Strong Civil Society Democracy is not possible without a **civil society,** a complex network of voluntary associations, economic groups, religious organizations, and many other kinds of groups that exist independently of government. The United States has thousands of such organizations—the Red Cross, the Humane Society, the Sierra Club, the National Rifle Association, your local church and newspaper, labor unions, and business groups. These organizations give citizens a way to make their views known to government officials and the general public. They also give citizens a means to take responsibility for protecting their rights, and they give everyone a chance to learn about democracy by participating in it.

A Social Consensus Democracy also prospers where most people accept democratic values such as individual liberty and equality for all. Such countries are said to have a **social consensus.** There also must be general agreement about the purpose and limits of government.

History shows that conditions in the American colonies favored the growth of democracy. Many individuals had an opportunity to get ahead economically. The American colonists were among the most educated people of the world at the time. Thomas Jefferson remarked that Americans

> "*. . . seem to have deposited the monarchial and taken up the republican government with as much ease as . . . [they] would throwing off an old and putting on a new suit of clothes.*"
>
> —Thomas Jefferson, 1776

The English heritage provided a consensus of political and social values. In time, the benefits of democracy would extend to all Americans.

Section 3 Assessment

Checking for Understanding

1. **Main Idea** In a graphic organizer similar to the one at the right, show who rules the state in each of Aristotle's three classifications of government.

Classification	Ruler(s)

2. **Define** autocracy, monarchy, oligarchy, democracy, republic, political party, free enterprise.
3. **Identify** "one person, one vote."
4. What characteristics of democracy distinguish it from other forms of government?

Critical Thinking

5. **Distinguishing Fact from Opinion** Suppose you are assigned to interview the president of the Republic of Mauritania. What questions would help you determine if democracy exists there?

Concepts IN ACTION

Cultural Pluralism How well are the will of the majority and the rights of minorities being preserved in the United States? Ask several people their opinions. Come to class prepared to share your findings.

Ward v. Rock Against Racism, 1989

The Constitution limits the power of government to restrict free speech. At the same time, a legitimate purpose of government is to maintain public order, including protecting citizens from unwelcome and excessive noise. Does the First Amendment allow a city to regulate the sound level at rock concerts held in a public park? The case of Ward v. Rock Against Racism *addressed this question.*

Students enjoying a Central Park concert

Background of the Case

Rock concerts are regularly held in New York City's Central Park. Area residents had complained of too much noise at some events. At other events audiences said the sound was not loud enough. In 1986 the city passed a regulation requiring groups performing in the park to use a sound system provided and operated by the city.

Rock Against Racism, an anti-racist rock group, had sponsored annual concerts in Central Park and had always provided their own sound equipment and sound technician. Rock Against Racism charged that the city regulation violated their rights to free speech under the First Amendment. The group won a lower federal court case. The Supreme Court agreed to hear the case in 1989.

The Constitutional Issue

Music has long been considered a form of protected speech under the First Amendment. However, the courts do allow governments to make regulations that may incidentally limit speech in an effort to accomplish a legitimate purpose of government. Thus, in several cases the Supreme Court had said that the governments can limit the time, place, and manner of speech if the aim is not to censor the content of the speech but to help further such interests as health and safety. To be constitutional, however, such regulations must not be directed at the content of the speech.

Rock Against Racism argued that the regulation violated the First Amendment by giving city officials artistic control over performers in the park. The group claimed the regulation was not narrowly focused and gave city officials the chance to select poor equipment or to modify the sound if they did not like the message. The city responded that it had a legitimate purpose in protecting citizens from excessive noise and that its guidelines were focused on controlling noise levels in a way that was fair to the audience, the performers, and citizens living nearby.

Debating the Case

Questions to Consider

1. Was the regulation a proper exercise of the government's power to maintain order, or was it a violation of the First Amendment?
2. If officials did not like the message in the music, could they use the regulation to control the content?

You Be the Judge

The courts have established that governments may enforce regulations that incidentally limit speech if the regulation serves a legitimate government interest. What was the city's goal in drawing up the regulation? Was there another, less intrusive way the city could have handled this issue?

Section 4

Economic Theories

Reader's Guide

Key Terms

economics, capitalism, free market, laissez-faire, socialism, bourgeoisie, proletariat, communism, command economy

Find Out

- In what three ways has the United States modified its free enterprise system?
- According to Karl Marx, what was the ultimate goal of true communism?

Understanding Concepts

Free Enterprise What features of the American economy provide incentive for people to achieve economic goals?

COVER STORY

Teen Entrepreneurs

RICHLAND, WASHINGTON, AUGUST 17, 2000

Instead of yard work this summer, Mark Michael, Ryan Robinson, and Charlie Cannon decided to make big money. They started their own dot-com travel company and plan to earn $3 million in the next year.

The bopLOP.com logo

Michael has been clipping *Wall Street Journal* stories about young entrepreneurs since the ninth grade. "I've read them a million times," he says. Cannon searched the Web for travel-related sites. Robinson designed the Web pages, and Michael called companies to sell on-site ads. On July 1 they launched bopLOP.com with over 2,100 links to travel-related Web sites. "We are the only (search engine) that has actually 100 percent travel," Cannon says.

Employment and wages, taxes and spending, production and distribution of products—these are economic concepts. **Economics** can be defined as the study of human efforts to satisfy seemingly unlimited wants through the use of limited resources. Resources include natural materials such as land, water, minerals, and trees. Resources also include such human factors as skills, knowledge, and physical capabilities. There are never enough resources to produce all the goods and services people could possibly want. Therefore, people in every nation must decide how these resources are to be used. Governments generally regulate this economic activity.

The Role of Economic Systems

Governments around the world provide for many kinds of economic systems. All economic systems, however, must make three major economic decisions: (1) what and how much should be produced; (2) how goods and services should be produced; and (3) who gets the goods and services that are produced. Each major type of economic system in the world—capitalism, socialism, and communism—answers these questions differently.

Capitalism

At one end of the spectrum is an economic system in which freedom of choice and individual incentive for workers, investors, consumers, and business enterprises is emphasized. The government assumes that society will be best served by any productive economic activity that free individuals choose. This system is usually referred to as free enterprise, or **capitalism.** Pure capitalism has five main characteristics: (1) private ownership and control of property and economic resources; (2) free enterprise; (3) competition among businesses; (4) freedom of choice; and (5) the possibility of profits.

Tools of Capitalism

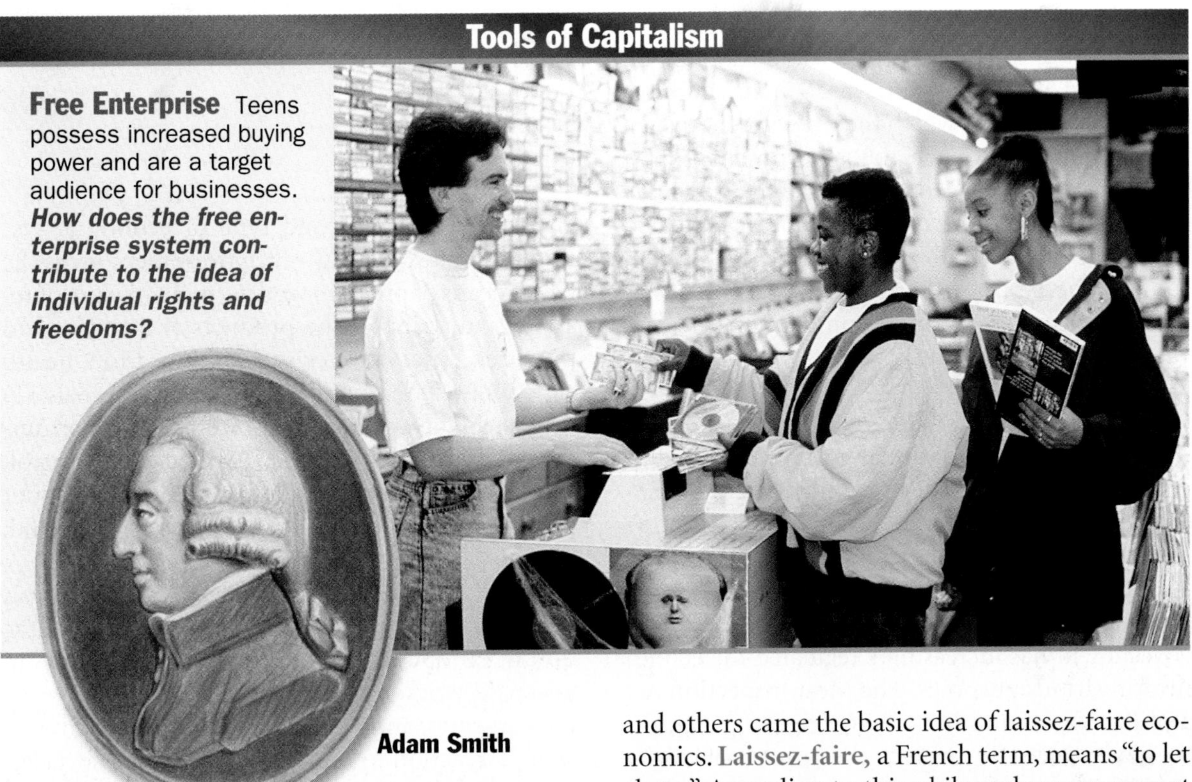

Free Enterprise Teens possess increased buying power and are a target audience for businesses. ***How does the free enterprise system contribute to the idea of individual rights and freedoms?***

Adam Smith

Origins of Capitalism No one person invented the idea of capitalism. It developed gradually from the economic and political changes in medieval and early modern Europe over hundreds of years. Two important concepts laid the foundation for the market system that is at the heart of capitalism. First is the idea that people could work for economic gain. Second is the idea that wealth should be used aggressively.

Major changes in the economic organization of Europe began with the opening of trade routes to the East in the thirteenth century. As trade increased, people began to invest money to make profits. By the eighteenth century, Europe had national states, a wealthy middle class familiar with money and markets, and a new attitude toward work and wealth. Included in this new attitude were the ideas of progress, invention, and the free market. The free market meant that buyers and sellers were free to make unlimited economic decisions in the marketplace.

In 1776 **Adam Smith,** a Scottish philosopher and economist, provided a philosophy for this new system. Smith described capitalism in his book *The Wealth of Nations.*[1] From the writings of Smith and others came the basic idea of laissez-faire economics. Laissez-faire, a French term, means "to let alone." According to this philosophy, government should keep its hands off the economy. In laissez-faire economics, the government's role is strictly limited to those few actions needed to ensure free competition in the marketplace.

In theory, what does a free-enterprise economy mean? In a free-enterprise or pure market economy, economic decisions are made by buyers (consumers) and sellers (producers). Sellers own businesses that produce goods or services. Buyers pay for those goods and services that they believe best fit their needs. Thus, the answer to the question of what to produce is determined in the marketplace by the actions of buyers and sellers, rather than by the government.

Competition plays a key role in a free-enterprise economy. Sellers compete with one another to produce goods and services at reasonable prices. Sellers also compete for resources. At the same time, consumers compete with one another to buy what they want and need. These same consumers in their roles as workers try to sell their skills and labor for the best wages or salaries they can get.

See the following footnoted materials in the **Reference Handbook:**
1. *The Wealth of Nations,* page 807.

Free Enterprise in the United States No nation in the world has a pure capitalist system. The United States, however, is a leading example of a capitalist system in which the government plays a role. For the most part, the government's main economic task has been to preserve the free market. The national government has always regulated American foreign trade, and it has always owned some property. Nevertheless, the government has tried to encourage business competition and private property ownership.

Governmental Influence Since the early 1900s, however, the national government's influence on the economy of the United States has increased in several ways. First, as the nation's government has grown, it has become the single largest buyer of goods and services in the country. Second, since the early 1900s, the United States government has increasingly regulated the economy for various purposes. The Meat Inspection Act and Pure Food and Drug Act were early attempts by government to protect the consumer. Since then, many laws have been passed giving the government a role in such areas as labor-management relations, the regulation of environmental pollution, and control over many banking and investment practices.

Third, the Great Depression of the 1930s left millions of Americans without jobs. The national government set up the Social Security system, programs to aid the unemployed, and a variety of social programs. In addition, the government began to set up public corporations like the Tennessee Valley Authority that competed directly with private companies to provide services such as electricity.

Mixed-Market Economy Today the American economy and others like it are described by economists as **mixed-market economies.** A mixed-market economy is an economy in which free enterprise is combined with and supported by government decisions in the marketplace. Government keeps competition free and fair and protects the public interest.

Even though it is a mixed-market economy, the American economic system is rooted deeply in the idea of individual initiative—that each person knows what is best for himself or herself. Further, it respects the right of all persons to own private property. Finally, it recognizes that freedom to make economic choices is a part of the freedom of political choice.

Socialism

Under the second type of economic system—socialism—the government owns the basic means of production, determines the use of resources, distributes the products and wages, and provides social services such as education, health care, and welfare. Socialism has three main goals: (1) the distribution of wealth and economic opportunity equally among people; (2) society's control, through its government, of all major decisions about production; and (3) public ownership of most land, of factories, and of other means of production.

The basic ideas behind modern socialism began to develop in the nineteenth century. Industrialization in Europe caused several problems. A class of low-paid workers lived in terrible poverty, slums grew in cities, and working conditions were miserable. In reaction to these problems, some socialists rejected capitalism and favored violent revolution. Others planned and built socialist communities where laborers were supposed to share equally in the benefits of industrial production.

Democratic Socialism The socialists who believed in peaceful changes wanted to work within the democratic political system to improve economic conditions, under a system called **democratic socialism.** Under this system the people have basic human rights and have some control over government officials through free elections and multiparty systems. However, the government owns the basic means of production and makes most economic decisions.

Great Britain, Tanzania, Denmark, Norway, and Sweden today operate under a form of democratic socialism. The government controls steel mills, shipyards, railroads, and airlines. It also provides services such as health and medical care.

Opponents of socialism say that it stifles individual initiative. They also claim that socialist nations' high tax rates hinder economic growth. Further, some people argue that, because socialism requires increased governmental regulation, it helps create big government and thus may lead to dictatorship.

Communism

Karl Marx (1818–1883), a German thinker and writer, was a socialist who advocated violent revolution. After studying the conditions of his time, he concluded that the capitalist system would collapse. He first published his ideas in 1848 in a pamphlet called *The Communist Manifesto.* He later expanded his ideas in his book called *Das Kapital* (1867). Marx believed that in industrialized nations the population is divided into capitalists, or the **bourgeoisie** who own the means of production, and workers, or the **proletariat,** who work to produce the goods. Capitalists are a ruling class because they use their economic power to force their will on the workers. The workers, Marx argued, do not receive full compensation for their labor because the owners keep the profits from the goods the workers make. Marx believed that wages in a capitalist system would never rise above a subsistence level—just enough for workers to survive.

Class Struggles Marx interpreted all human history as a class struggle between the workers and the owners of the means of production. Friedrich Engels, a close associate of Marx, wrote:

> "*Former society, moving in class antagonisms, had need of a state, that is, an organization of the exploiting class at each period for the maintenance of external conditions of production: . . . for the forcible holding down of the exploited class in the conditions of oppression.*"
>
> —Friedrich Engels

Marx predicted that, as time passed, a smaller and smaller group of capitalists would control all means of production and, hence, all wealth. Eventually the workers would rise in violent revolution and overthrow the capitalists. The goal of this revolution was government ownership of the means of production and distribution.

Glorification of the Proletariat

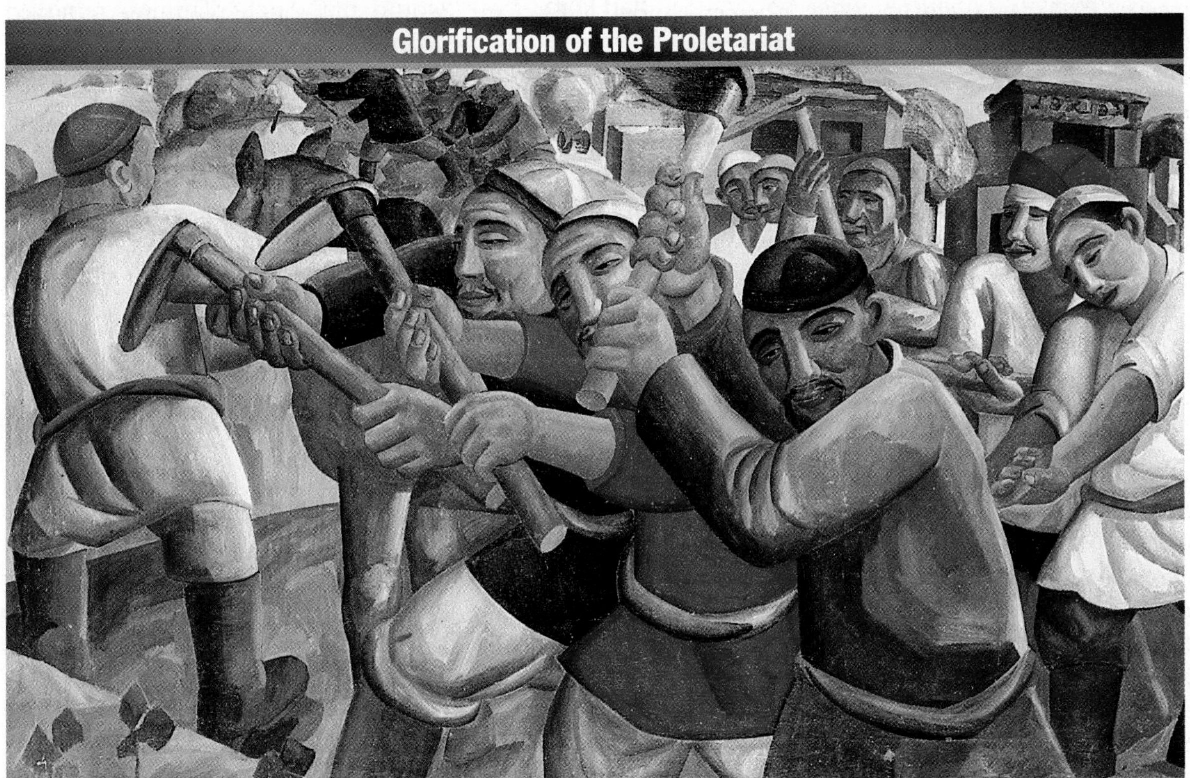

Comparative Government This painting, *The Cultivation of Cotton* by Aleksandr Volkov, is a piece of propaganda exalting the virtues of hard work and workers. ***What message is this painting supposed to send to citizens laboring under a Communist government?***

Karl Marx first called his own ideas "scientific socialism." He believed that in time, socialism would develop into full communism. Under **communism** one class would evolve, property would all be held in common, and there would be no need for government.

In *The Communist Manifesto,* Karl Marx not only wrote that economic events would finally lead to communism by means of revolution, but in fact encouraged it:

> *In short, Communists everywhere support every revolutionary movement against the existing social and political order of things. . . . Let the ruling class tremble at the Communist revolution. The proletarians have nothing to lose but their chains. Working men of all countries, unite!*
>
> —Karl Marx, 1848

Karl Marx

Communism as a Command Economy

In Communist nations, government planners decide how much to produce, what to produce, and how to distribute the goods and services produced. This system is called a **command economy** because decisions are made at the upper levels of government and handed down to managers. In Communist countries this means that the state owns the land, natural resources, industry, banks, and transportation facilities. The state also controls mass communication including newspapers, magazines, television, radio, and motion picture production.

Many nations have developed their own styles of communism. The economy is a full-time responsibility of the People's Republic of China, for example. Government planners adopted a five-year plan that agreed with the goals of the Communist Party. The plan specified, for example, how many new housing units would be produced over the next five years. It also dictated where this housing would be built, what kinds of materials would be used, who would be eligible to live in the new housing, and how much rent they would pay. Such planning removed economic freedom from individual builders, but also political freedom from consumers who were told where to live.

Because Communist countries sometimes fail to provide adequate standards of living, these governments have had to choose between change and revolt by the people. China has begun to loosen its controls and decentralize some business decisions.

Section 4 Assessment

Checking for Understanding

1. **Main Idea** In a graphic organizer similar to the one at the right, identify three functions of economic systems.

2. **Define** economics, capitalism, free market, laissez-faire, socialism, bourgeoisie, proletariat, communism, command economy.
3. **Identify** Adam Smith, Karl Marx.
4. What did Marx believe would happen in a true communist economy?

Critical Thinking

5. **Making Inferences** What ideas presented by Karl Marx appealed to people in nations where wealth was unevenly distributed?

Concepts IN ACTION

Free Enterprise Competition is an important factor in the United States economy. Find advertisements in newspapers that illustrate various kinds of competition. Display these ads on a bulletin board. Should the government regulate prices? Why or why not?

Skills

Critical Thinking

Identifying Central Issues

Identifying central issues is finding the key themes, or major ideas, in a body of information. Central issues are the framework that holds a body of information together.

Learning the Skill

To identify a central issue:

1. Find out the setting and purpose of the selection.
2. Skim the material to identify its general subject.
3. Read the information to pinpoint the ideas that the details support.
4. Identify the central issue. Ask: What part of the material conveys the main idea?

Read the following excerpt from a speech by Pericles honoring the soldiers of Athens.

> *"Our constitution is called a democracy because power is in the hands not of a minority but of the whole people. When it is a question of settling private disputes, everyone is equal before the law, when it is a question of putting one person before another in positions of public responsibility, what counts is not membership of a particular class, but the actual ability which the man possesses. . . . And, just as our political life is free and open, so is our day-to-day life in our relations with each other."*
>
> —Thucydides, from *The History of the Peloponnesian Wars,* 400s B.C.

Pericles emphasizes equality before the law, ability as the basis of public service, and freedom. The central issue: Athens is a democracy.

Aristotle (384–322 B.C.)

Practicing the Skill

Aristotle, a philosopher from Athens, wrote about government in *Politics.* Read the excerpt from *Politics* below and answer the questions that follow.

> *"The basis of a democratic state is liberty; which, according to the common opinion of men, can only be enjoyed in such a state:—this they affirm to be the great end of every democracy. One principle of liberty is for all to rule and be ruled in turn . . . whence it follows that the majority must be supreme, and that whatever the majority approve must be the end and the just. Every citizen, it is said, must have equality, and therefore in a democracy the poor have more power than the rich, because there are more of them."*
>
> —Aristotle

1. According to Aristotle, which group holds the most power in a democracy?
2. Summarize the central issue in one sentence.

Application Activity

Bring to class a news article that deals with some governmental issue. Identify the central issue and explain why it is important.

The Glencoe Skillbuilder Interactive Workbook, Level 2 provides instruction and practice in key social studies skills.

Assessment and Activities

GOVERNMENT Online

Self-Check Quiz Visit the *United States Government: Democracy in Action* Web site at gov.glencoe.com and click on ***Chapter 1–Self-Check Quizzes*** to prepare for the chapter test.

Reviewing Key Terms

Insert the terms below into the following paragraph to describe the nature of government and differing political and economic systems. Each term should be used only once.

constitution, sovereignty, democracy, communism, autocracy, capitalism, state, free market, republic, command economy

Every (1) has a form of government that has (2) within its territorial boundaries. A (3) is a government of and by the people that may have a (4) that protects the rights of the people—unlike an (5) that concentrates power in the hands of one person. The United States is a (6) with elected representation. It has a mixed economy based on (7). The (8) allows buyers and sellers to make economic decisions about what to produce, how much to produce, and who gets the goods and services produced. In contrast, under (9), the People's Republic of China and other states have operated a (10) with government planning.

Current Events JOURNAL

Purposes of Government Use the electronic newspaper index and microfilm in your local library to find current news articles that provide examples of ways the federal government serves one of the four purposes of government. Summarize the articles. Include the summaries on a poster under headings such as "Providing National Security."

Recalling Facts

1. Why did the thirteen British colonies in America become known as "states"?
2. What system of government divides power among different levels rather than giving all power to a central government?
3. Describe three kinds of nonstate groups that influence national politics.
4. Identify two types of monarchs ruling today.
5. How is a direct democracy different from a representative democracy?
6. What is the role of government in a laissez-faire economic system?
7. List the two classes into which Karl Marx divided all people in industrialized nations.
8. Identify two countries that operate under a form of democratic socialism.
9. Who makes most economic decisions in a command economy?

Understanding Concepts

1. **Public Policy** List the major disadvantages and advantages, if any, of living under a totalitarian dictatorship. Explain.
2. **Global Perspectives** Which of the following ideas do you perceive to be the most powerful force in the world today: communism, socialism, or capitalism? Explain.
3. **Cultural Pluralism** How does a federal system provide for the expression of a variety of opinions?
4. **Free Enterprise** Why do totalitarian states often limit economic choices for their citizens?

Chapter 1

Critical Thinking

1. **Understanding Cause and Effect** Why is widespread educational opportunity necessary for a nation to develop a democratic system?
2. **Drawing Conclusions** Political parties usually disagree over issues. Write a brief statement favoring or opposing the concept of giving more power to the states rather than the national government
3. **Identifying Central Issues** What do you think would be the most difficult problem faced by government officials in a command economy?
4. **Making Comparisons** In a Venn Diagram like the one below, show how capitalism, democratic socialism, and communism are alike and different.

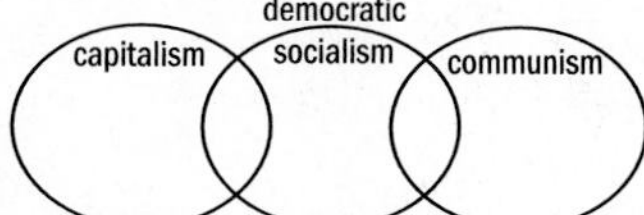

Interpreting Political Cartoons Activity

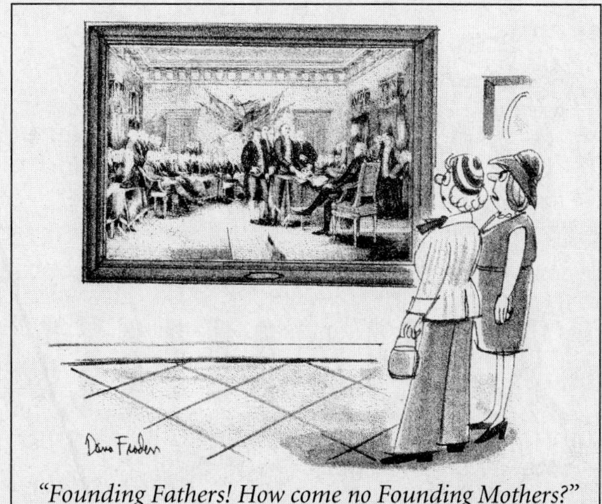

"Founding Fathers! How come no Founding Mothers?"

1. What is the subject of the painting in the cartoon?
2. According to the painting, who were the Founders of the United States?
3. What message is the cartoonist trying to communicate?
4. Do you think women influenced the creation of the United States government? Why or why not?

Cooperative Learning Activity

Tracking Imports Organize into groups of five students. Have each group member locate the following items: a radio, a watch, a shirt, a pair of shoes, and a pair of sunglasses. Compile a list noting the item and the country that manufactured it. Compare the lists to determine which nations are mentioned most frequently. Then have each group make a chart showing the various products and the number of products from each of the countries represented.

Technology Activity

Using the Internet The United Nations (UN) is a major nonstate international organization. Use the Internet to find out the current activities of a UN organization. Summarize this UN organization's involvement around the world.

Skill Practice Activity

Identifying Central Issues Reread the subsection titled "Sovereignty" on page 7. What is the central issue of those paragraphs? Summarize that issue in one sentence.

Participating in Local Government

Constitutions provide a plan for organizing and operating governments. What plan provides the rules for your local government? Does your local government operate under a constitution? Contact a local government official to find out about the basic plan of your city or town. Where did it originate? Present your findings in a diagram to share with the class.

Chapter 2

Origins of American Government

Why It's Important

Your Heritage When you go to sleep tonight, you may take for granted that government officials will not break in to perform an unreasonable search of your house. The security provided by government and the protection from government are a heritage of the period you will study in Chapter 2.

To learn more about the federal government and its origins, view the ***Democracy in Action*** Chapter 2 video lesson:

The Creation of the Federal Government

GOVERNMENT Online

Chapter Overview Visit the *United States Government: Democracy in Action* Web site at gov.glencoe.com and click on ***Chapter 2–Overview*** to preview chapter information.

The Colonial Period

Reader's Guide

Key Terms

limited government, representative government, separation of powers

Find Out

- What events of the early American colonial experience led colonists to believe they would have representative government?
- In what ways were the American colonies democratic? In what ways were they not democratic?

Understanding Concepts

Growth of Democracy What elements of the English political heritage helped develop representative governments in the American colonies?

COVER STORY

Law and Order

JAMESTOWN, VIRGINIA, 1611

New governor Sir Thomas Dale, recently arrived from England, has announced a sweeping set of laws for the colony. Called the "Laws Divine, Morall, and Martial," the new rules are likely to change life here. Each resident will be assigned specific duties. Refusal to cooperate will be dealt with severely. First offenders will be forced to lie down with neck and heels together for one night. Repeat violators will be whipped. A third offense will result in enslavement aboard a convict ship for a period of one year. Authorities expect the new laws to bring order and prosperity to the colony.

Sir Thomas Dale

Every year thousands of foreign and American tourists flock to Virginia to visit the remains of Jamestown, the first permanent English settlement in North America. Crumbling foundations and the ruins of the old church tower mark the site of the original Jamestown, founded in 1607. The decaying brick and mortar offer a striking contrast to the enduring principles of self-government inherited from the English colonists. This legacy of self-government enables Americans today to voice their opinions without fear of reprisal, to choose their leaders, and to take an active role in shaping the nation and communities in which they live.

An English Political Heritage

During the 1600s people from many regions, such as Spain, the Netherlands, France, Germany, Sweden, and West Africa, came to North America. Most colonists, however, came from England. It was the English who established and governed the original thirteen colonies along the Atlantic coast.

The English colonists brought with them ideas about government that had been developing in England for centuries. By the 1600s the English people had won political liberties, such as trial by jury, that were largely unknown elsewhere. At the heart of the English system were two principles of government. These principles—limited government and representative government—greatly influenced the development of the United States.

Limited Government By the time the first colonists reached North America, the idea that government was not all-powerful had become an accepted part of the English system. The idea first appeared in the **Magna Carta,[1]** or Great

See the following footnoted materials in the **Reference Handbook:**
1. *Magna Carta,* page 802.

◀ ***The Signing of the Declaration of Independence* (detail) by John Trumbull, 1824**

Charter, that King John was forced to sign in 1215. The Magna Carta established the principle of **limited government,** in which the power of the monarch, or government, was limited, not absolute. This document provided for protection against unjust punishment and the loss of life, liberty, and property except according to law. Under the Magna Carta, the king agreed that certain taxes could not be levied without popular consent.

The rights in the Magna Carta originally applied only to the nobility. During the next few centuries, however, other groups won political liberties, primarily through agreements between English monarchs and the nobility and merchants.

Petition of Right While Parliament maintained some influence, strong monarchs dominated England for centuries. In 1625 Charles I took the throne. He dissolved Parliament, lodged troops in private homes, and placed some areas under martial law. When he called Parliament back into session in 1628, the representatives forced the king to sign the **Petition of Right,** severely limiting the king's power. No longer could the English monarch collect taxes without Parliament's consent, imprison people without just cause, house troops in private homes without the permission of the owner, or declare martial law unless the country was at war.

English Bill of Rights In 1688 Parliament removed James II from the throne and crowned William III and Mary II. This peaceful transfer of power was called the Glorious Revolution. William and Mary swore an oath to govern England according to the "statutes in Parliament agreed upon, and the laws and customs of the same." Parliament also passed the **English Bill of Rights,** a document that would later be very important to the American colonies.

The English Bill of Rights set clear limits on what a ruler could and could not do. It applied to the American colonists—who were English subjects—as well as to the people in England. Incorporating elements from the Magna Carta, the key ideas of the English Bill of Rights included: (1) Monarchs do not have a divine right to rule. They rule with the consent of the people's representatives in Parliament. (2) The monarch must have Parliament's consent to suspend laws, levy taxes, or

Participating IN GOVERNMENT

Being Represented

Participating in their community

One reason for the War for Independence was that Britain was depriving the colonists, who were British citizens, of representation. By being represented in some of the various organizations in your community, you can provide input to these organizations from a student's perspective. Organizations such as crime patrols, community development groups, youth associations, environmental groups, and volunteer organizations hold regular committee meetings that make decisions that affect you. What can you do to be represented in these organizations?

Activity

1. Call your chamber of commerce or local government offices and ask for a listing of such organizations mentioned.
2. After you have decided on an issue and a committee that interests you, ask to become a part of the committee. You are more likely to serve as a student adviser than as a voting member. As an adviser, though, you will still have the ability to influence decisions and to provide ideas for the future plans of the committee.
3. Attend meetings and ask questions when there are issues that you do not understand. Provide suggestions for getting things done.

maintain an army. (3) The monarch cannot interfere with parliamentary elections and debates. (4) The people have a right to petition the government and to have a fair and speedy trial by a jury of their peers. (5) The people should not be subject to cruel and unusual punishments or to excessive fines and bail.

The English colonists in North America shared a belief in these rights with the people of England. In fact, a major cause of the American Revolution was that the colonists felt they were being deprived of these basic rights.

Beginnings of Representative Government in America

▲ The House of Burgesses was the first elected lawmaking body in the English colonies. The royal governor of Jamestown, Sir George Yeardley, allowed the men of the colony to elect representatives to the assembly.

This report of the Virginia General Assembly contains a partial list of the 22 men who hoped to be elected to serve as burgesses. The burgesses made local laws for the colony. ▶

Growth of Democracy ***What aspects of the English government influenced the creation of the House of Burgesses?***

Representative Government

The colonists had a firm belief in **representative government,** a government in which people elect delegates to make laws and conduct government. The English Parliament was a representative assembly with the power to enact laws. It consisted of an upper chamber, or legislative body, and a lower chamber. The upper chamber, called the House of Lords, included members of the aristocracy. The lower chamber, called the House of Commons, included commoners—mostly merchants or property owners elected by other property owners. American legislatures grew out of the English practice of representation.

The Ideas of John Locke The ideas and writings of seventeenth-century English philosopher John Locke deeply influenced the American colonists. Locke spelled out his political ideas in *Two Treatises on Government,*[1] first published in 1690. His writings were widely read and discussed in both Europe and America. Colonial leaders such as Benjamin Franklin, Thomas Jefferson, and James Madison regarded these ideas as political truth. Locke's ideas have been called the "textbook of the American Revolution."

Locke reasoned that all people were born free, equal, and independent. Locke believed that people possessed natural rights to life, liberty, and property at the time they lived in a state of nature, before governments were formed. People contracted among themselves to form governments to protect their natural rights. Locke argued that if a government failed to protect these natural rights, the people could change that government.

Locke's ideas were revolutionary in an age when monarchs still claimed they had God-given absolute powers. Locke denied that people were born with an obligation to obey their rulers. Rather, in his "Second Treatise of Government," Locke insisted that:

See the following footnoted materials in the **Reference Handbook:**
1. *Two Treatises on Government,* page 806.

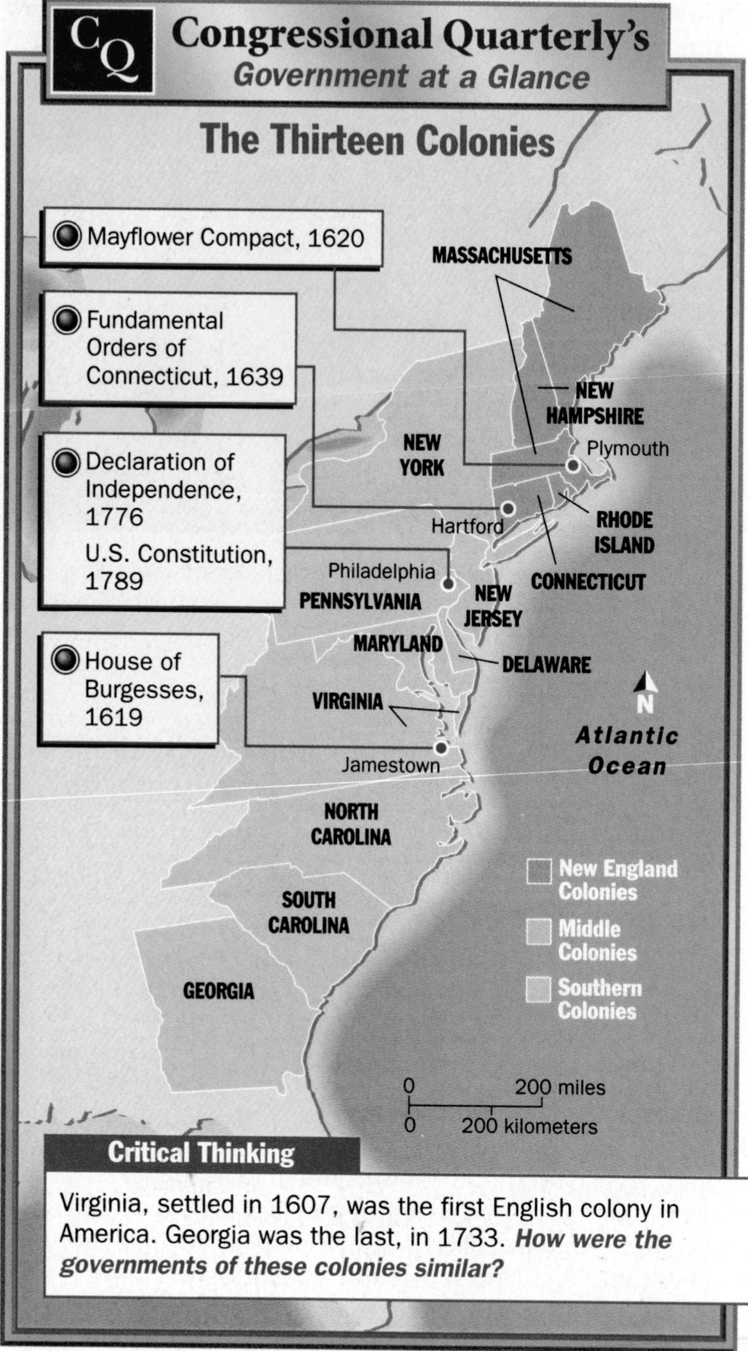

Government, then, was legitimate only as long as people continued to consent to it. Both the Declaration of Independence and the Constitution, written nearly a century after Locke lived, reflected Locke's revolutionary ideas.

Government in the Colonies

The English founded thirteen colonies along the eastern coast of North America between 1607 and 1733. From these colonies the present system of American government evolved. Each English colony had its own government consisting of a governor, a legislature, and a court system. Nevertheless, the British believed that all colonists owed allegiance to the monarch. For many years the colonists agreed.

Democracy grew rapidly in all the colonies, but it did not yet exist in its current form. Women and enslaved persons could not vote, and every colony had some type of property qualification for voting. Nine of the thirteen colonies had an official or established church, and many colonists remained intolerant of religious dissent. In Virginia, for example, the penalty for breaking the Sabbath for the third time was death.

Despite such shortcomings, the colonial governments did in fact establish practices that became a key part of the nation's system of government. Chief among these practices were (1) a written constitution that guaranteed basic liberties and limited the power of government; (2) a legislature of elected representatives; and (3) the separation of powers between the governor (the chief executive) and the legislature. Today the United States government embodies each of these practices.

> *"Freedom of [people] under government is to have a standing rule to live by . . . made by the legislative power vested in it; a liberty to follow [one's] own will in all things, when the rule prescribes not, and not to be subject to the inconstant, uncertain, unknown, arbitrary will of another. . . ."*
>
> —John Locke, 1690

Written Constitutions A key feature of the colonial period was government according to a written plan. The **Mayflower Compact**[1] that the Pilgrims signed in 1620 stands as the first example of many colonial plans for self-government.

Forty-one men, representing all the Pilgrim families, drew up the Mayflower Compact in the tiny cabin of their ship, the *Mayflower,* anchored off the New England coast. The Pilgrim leaders realized they needed rules to govern themselves if they were to survive in the new land. Through the Mayflower Compact, they agreed to:

> *Solemnly and mutually in the Presence of God and one of another, covenant [pledge] and combine ourselves together into a Body Politick, for our better Ordering and Preservation and Furtherance of the Ends aforesaid. . . .*
>
> —The Mayflower Compact, 1620

The Pilgrims also agreed to choose their own leaders and to make their own laws, which they would design for their own benefit.

Beginning in 1629, new Puritan immigrants settled nearby. Massachusetts Bay added many towns to the original Plymouth settlement. In 1636 the colony realized a need for more comprehensive laws. It adopted the **Great Fundamentals,** the first basic system of laws in the English colonies.

In 1639 Puritans who had left the Massachusetts Bay Colony to colonize Connecticut drew up America's first formal constitution, or charter, called the **Fundamental Orders of Connecticut.**[2] This document laid out a plan for government that gave the people the right to elect the governor, judges, and representatives to make laws. While it was based on the Massachusetts model, it did not restrict voting rights to church members.

Soon after, other English colonies began drawing up their own charters. These documents established a system of limited government and rule by law in each of the colonies. Several of these colonial constitutions were very democratic for their time. The Rhode Island and Connecticut charters were so democratic that they continued to serve as state constitutions even after the adoption of the United States Constitution.

Colonial Legislatures Representative assemblies also became firmly established in the colonies. The Virginia House of Burgesses, the first legislature in America, was established in 1619, only 12 years after the settlement of Jamestown. The newly elected lawmakers passed laws aiding farmers and curbing idleness, improper dress, and drunkenness. It was not long before other colonies set up their own legislatures. By the mid-1700s most colonial legislatures had been operating for more than 100

Forming a Government

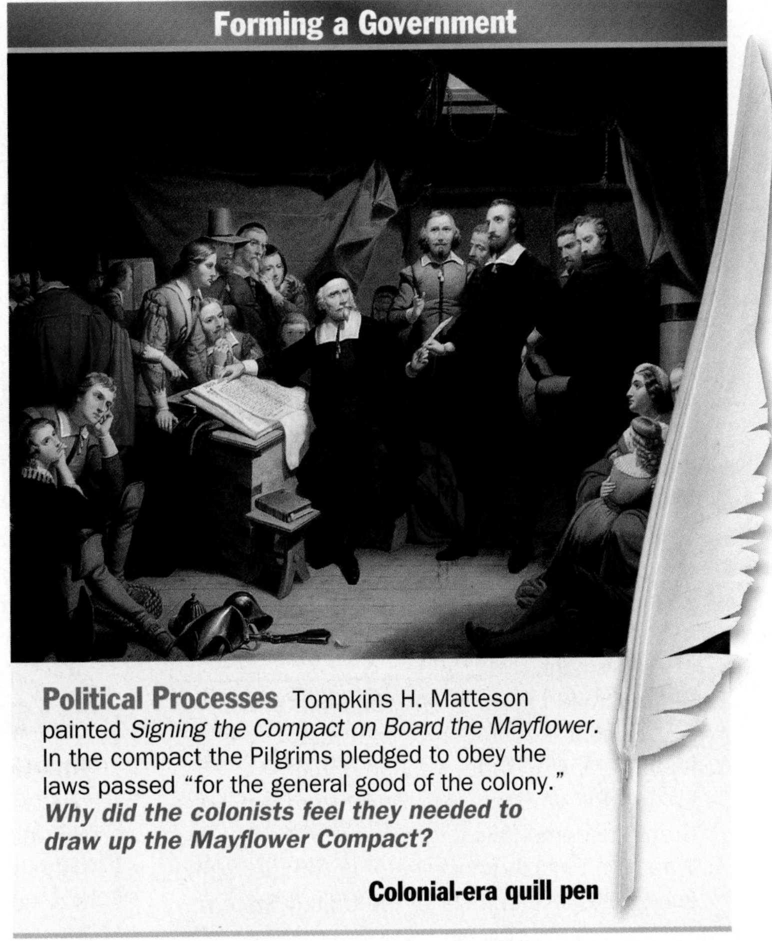

Political Processes Tompkins H. Matteson painted *Signing the Compact on Board the Mayflower.* In the compact the Pilgrims pledged to obey the laws passed "for the general good of the colony." ***Why did the colonists feel they needed to draw up the Mayflower Compact?***

Colonial-era quill pen

See the following footnoted materials in the ***Reference Handbook:***

1. *Mayflower Compact,* page 804.
2. *Fundamental Orders of Connecticut,* page 805.

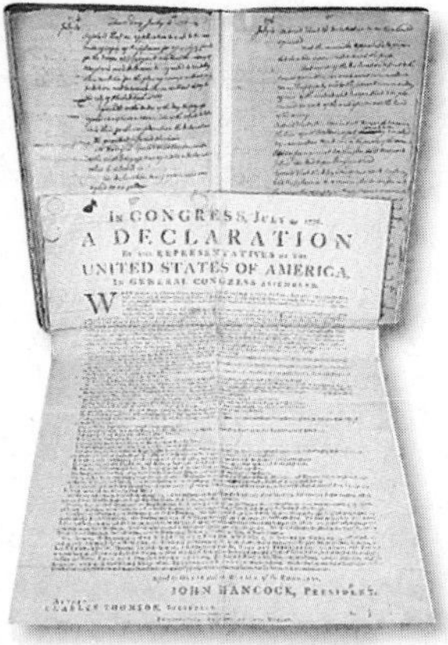

In CONGRESS, July 4, 1776.
A DECLARATION
By the REPRESENTATIVES of the
UNITED STATES OF AMERICA,
In GENERAL CONGRESS assembled.

JOHN HANCOCK, President.

Broadsides **On the night of July 4, 1776, John Dunlap, Congress's official printer, turned out numerous large poster copies (called broadsides) of the Declaration of Independence, which had just been approved. Today, Dunlap's broadsides are valuable. Only 24 are known to exist. Most are held by such institutions as the National Archives and the Library of Congress, with a few owned by private collectors.**

years. As a result, representative government was an established tradition in America well before the colonists declared their independence from Great Britain in 1776.

These legislatures dominated colonial government. The rapidly growing colonies constantly needed new laws to cope with new circumstances. For example, they had to control the distribution of land and construct public buildings and facilities such as roads, ferries, and wharves. The colonies also had to establish new towns, schools, and civil and criminal courts.

Colonial legislatures were examples of the consent of the governed because a large number of qualified men voted. Although there were property qualifications for voting, land was abundant and most colonists could afford property.

Separation of Powers Colonial charters divided the power of government. The governor, the king's agent in the colonies, had executive power. Colonial legislatures had the power to pass laws, and colonial courts heard cases. This principle of **separation of powers** was later incorporated into the United States Constitution. Of course, colonial legislatures and courts were not autonomous—both could be reviewed by a special committee of the king's Privy Council. In practice, however, the colonies had considerable self-government.

Colonial legislatures became the political training grounds for the leaders who later would write the Constitution. Many of these leaders were active in politics and had served in colonial legislatures. Thus, the combination of their English heritage and colonial experience in representative self-government made them leaders in what one historian called "the seedtime of the republic."

Section 1 Assessment

Checking for Understanding

1. **Main Idea** In a graphic organizer similar to the one below, list three practices that were established by colonial governments and became a key part of the nation's system of government.

Key practices of American government

2. **Define** limited government, representative government, separation of powers.
3. **Identify** Magna Carta, Petition of Right, English Bill of Rights, Mayflower Compact, Great Fundamentals.
4. What two English principles of government influenced the development of the United States?

Critical Thinking

5. **Identifying Central Issues** The idea of limited government, first established by the Magna Carta, is an important principle of American government. Why must government be limited?

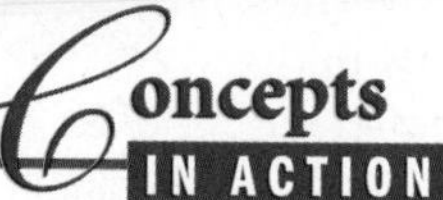

Growth of Democracy Review the key ideas of the English Bill of Rights outlined on pages 36 and 37. Write an essay explaining which rights granted in the English Bill of Rights are the most important today. Include reasons for your opinion.

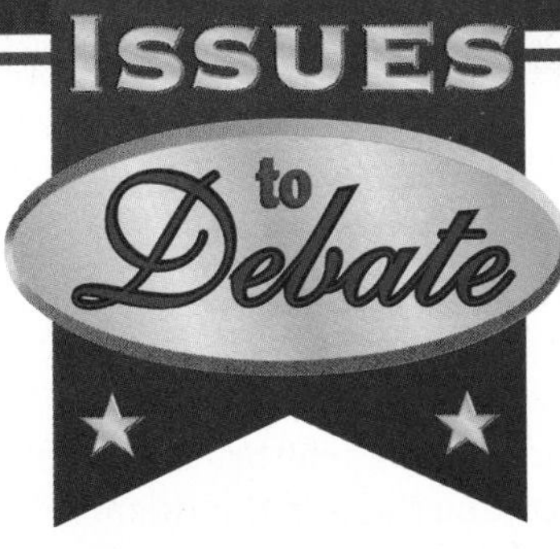

Should Song Lyrics Be Protected by the First Amendment?

Some people claim that rock music glamorizes destructive behavior. Critics of rock music say that it encourages violence. Some people want to protect minors from being exposed to the messages these types of songs convey.

Protected and Unprotected Speech

The Supreme Court has generally agreed that the right of free speech should be balanced against the needs of society. Therefore, some forms of speech are not given constitutional protection. Defamatory speech, obscene speech, as well as seditious speech, or speech that provokes acts of violence fall outside First Amendment protection.

Social Concerns vs. Artistic Expression

Parent groups, community leaders, and police organizations are voicing their disapproval of some kinds of music. They argue that lyrics condoning murder and degrading women give listeners the impression that this behavior is acceptable in our society. Critics point to examples of violence and drug use associated with the performers as evidence that this type of music affects behavior.

Some radio stations have voluntarily stopped playing the most controversial music. Congressional hearings have been held to listen to recommendations that range from putting parent advisory labels on music to establishing a rating system like the one used for movies. Some record companies are now producing two versions of songs with offensive lyrics—a "radio" version and a "street" version.

Many people, however, are reluctant to ask for government involvement for fear of treading on First Amendment rights. Although the music may be unacceptable to them, they do not think it should be subject to censorship.

Debating the Issue

Do You Think Song Lyrics Should Be Protected by the First Amendment Despite Their Content?

Take on the role of a concerned parent of a teenager. You could influence your congressional representative to vote for more controls over musical content, or for more freedom of expression in the music industry.

Key Issues

✔Does society's need to maintain order outweigh the right for artistic expression, if the art promotes violence or defames a portion of our population?

✔Are there dangers in limiting artistic expression?

Debate Allow time for students on both sides of the issue to prepare speeches to be presented to the class. Debate the issue in class.

Vote Make your own personal decision. As a class, vote on the issue and record the results.

Section 2

Uniting for Independence

Reader's Guide

Key Terms

revenue, embargo

Find Out

- What factors caused the British to allow the colonists to operate with little interference between 1607 and 1763?
- Why were the colonists and the British unable to compromise and settle their differences?

Understanding Concepts

Growth of Democracy How did the colonial experience during the dispute with Britain help shape American ideals of constitutional democracy?

COVER STORY

British Battle Militias

BOSTON, MASSACHUSETTS, APRIL 1776

A force ordered to destroy the supplies of self-styled patriot militias and to arrest two of their leaders met armed resistance outside the city early today. About 700 British troops scattered some 70 militia members, called Minute Men, who had gathered in the town of Lexington. The troops then marched on to Concord. Later, fighting broke out with another militia u nit at North Concord Bridge. As the troops returned to Boston, they came under attack from more militia groups before reaching the safety of the city. Losses totaled 73 dead and 174 wounded. Rebel casualties were set at 93.

Drum used at Lexington

Until the mid-1700s Great Britain had allowed its colonies across the Atlantic to develop politically on their own. By the 1760s, however, things had begun to change dramatically as the British government felt a need to tighten its control over the colonies.

The Colonies on Their Own

As British subjects, the colonists in North America owed allegiance to the monarch and the British government. As with other parts of the British empire, the colonies were supposed to serve as a source of raw materials and a market for British goods. Thus, in the eyes of the British crown, the American colonies existed for the economic benefit of Great Britain.

In practice, during the 150 years following the settling of Jamestown in 1607, the colonies in America did pretty much as they pleased. The colonies were more than 3,000 miles (5,556 km) from Great Britain. Orders from the monarch took two months or more to cross the Atlantic. In addition, only the colonial legislatures were actually in a position to deal with the everyday problems facing the colonies. As a result, the colonists grew accustomed to governing themselves through their representatives.

Until the mid-1700s the British government was generally satisfied with this arrangement. The British needed the colonists' loyalty to counter the threat of the French in Canada. The colonists remained loyal in return for a large measure of self-rule and protection from the French.

Britain Tightens Control Two events drastically changed the easy relationship between the colonies and Britain. First, the French and Indian War, fought between 1754 and 1763, threatened Britain's hold on the continent. Second, George III, who became king in 1760, had different ideas about how the colonies should be governed.

The French and Indian War started as a struggle between the French and British over lands in western Pennsylvania and Ohio. By 1756 several other European countries became involved as well. Great Britain eventually won the war in 1763 and gained complete control of what later became the eastern United States. The French were driven out.

The defeat of France in America meant the American colonists no longer needed the British to protect them from the French. The war, however, left the British government with a large war debt that the British expected the colonies to help repay.

Taxing the Colonies When he took the throne, George III was determined to deal more firmly with the American colonies. To help pay for the war, the king and his ministers levied taxes on tea, sugar, glass, paper, and other products. The **Stamp Act** of 1765 imposed the first direct tax on the colonists. It required them to pay a tax on legal documents, pamphlets, newspapers, and even dice and playing cards. Parliament also passed laws to control colonial trade in ways that benefited Great Britain but not the colonies.

Britain's **revenue**—the money a government collects from taxes or other sources—from the colonies increased. Colonial resentment, however, grew along with the revenues. Political protests began to spread throughout the colonies. Colonists refused to buy British goods. This move led to the repeal of the Stamp Act, but the British passed other tax laws to replace it. In 1773 a group of colonists, dressed as Mohawk, dumped 342 chests of British tea into Boston Harbor. This protest against further taxes on tea became known as the Boston Tea Party.

In retaliation Parliament passed the Coercive Acts, which the colonists called the **Intolerable Acts.** One of these acts closed Boston Harbor. Another withdrew the right of the Massachusetts colony to govern itself. By the early 1770s, events clearly showed that revolution was not far off.

We the People

Making a Difference

George Mason

American students have all heard of George Washington, Thomas Jefferson, and James Madison. A key, but less known, figure in the founding of our nation was George Mason. A Virginian, Mason was a neighbor of George Washington. Mason and Washington often visited for friendly discussions about politics.

In 1774, when the British closed the port of Boston, Washington and Mason drew up the Fairfax Resolves. These stated the colonists' objections to the closing and were the first of Mason's writings on constitutional issues.

In 1776 Virginians met at Williamsburg to draw up a constitution and a "Declaration of Rights." Mason headed the drafting committee. His fellow committee member was James Madison, a 25 year old just beginning his political career. Meanwhile, the Continental Congress was meeting in Philadelphia where Madison's close friend Jefferson was chosen to write a declaration of the colonies' independence.

On June 12, the delegates at Williamsburg adopted Mason's Virginia Declaration of Rights. It began:

"That all men are by nature equally free and independent, and have certain inherent rights... namely, the enjoyment of life and liberty, with the means of acquiring and possessing property, and pursuing and obtaining happiness and safety."

Madison kept Jefferson apprised of the work in Virginia. As a result, Mason's ideas were embodied in Jefferson's most famous work — the Declaration of Independence.

Growing Distrust

Civic Rights New British laws caused discontent among colonists who believed their civic rights were being denied. ***Which civic rights do you think Britain denied the colonists?***

Teapot—a symbol of resistance

George III's crown—a symbol of authority

Colonial Unity

Before the mid-1770s most colonists thought of themselves as British subjects. At the same time, each of the colonies developed largely on its own. Thus, most colonists also thought of themselves as Virginians or New Yorkers or Georgians. Indeed, early attempts to bring the colonies together had failed.

Responding to French attacks on the frontier, in 1754 Benjamin Franklin had proposed an innovative plan for uniting the colonies—the **Albany Plan of Union.** The colonies rejected the plan, however, because it gave too much power to an assembly made up of representatives from all thirteen colonies.

By the 1760s the harsh new British policies spurred an American sense of community. A growing number of colonists began to think of themselves as Americans united by their hostility to British authority. At the same time, colonial leaders began to take political action against what they felt was British oppression.

Taking Action In 1765 nine colonies sent delegates to a meeting in New York called the Stamp Act Congress. This was the first meeting organized by the colonies to protest King George's actions. Delegates to the Congress sent a petition to the king, arguing that only colonial legislatures could impose direct taxes such as the Stamp Tax.

By 1773 organizations called **committees of correspondence** were urging resistance to the British. These committees consisted of colonists who wanted to keep in touch with one another as events unfolded. Samuel Adams established the first committee in Boston. The idea spread quickly, and within a few months, Massachusetts alone had more than 80 such committees. Virginia and other colonies soon joined in this communication network.

The First Continental Congress The Intolerable Acts prompted Virginia and Massachusetts to call a general meeting of the colonies. Delegates from all the colonies except Georgia met in Philadelphia on September 5, 1774, for the First Continental Congress. Key colonial leaders such as Patrick Henry, Samuel Adams, Richard Henry Lee, and George Washington attended.

The delegates debated what to do about the relationship with Great Britain. They finally imposed an **embargo,** an agreement prohibiting trade, on Britain, and agreed not to use British goods. They also proposed a meeting the following year if Britain did not change its policies.

Events then moved quickly. The British adopted stronger measures. "The New England governments are in a state of rebellion," George III firmly announced. "Blows must decide whether they are to be subject to this country or independent."

The first blow fell early on the morning of April 19, 1775. British Redcoats clashed with colonial minutemen at Lexington and Concord in Massachusetts. This clash, later called the "shot heard 'round the world," was the first battle of the Revolutionary War.

The Second Continental Congress Within three weeks, delegates from all thirteen colonies gathered in Philadelphia for the Second Continental Congress. This Congress assumed the powers of a central government. It chose John Hancock as president, voted to organize an army and navy and to issue money, and made George Washington commander of a newly organizing Continental Army.

Although it had no constitutional authority, the Second Continental Congress served as the acting government of the colonies throughout the war. It purchased supplies, negotiated treaties, and rallied support for the colonists' cause.

Independence

As the Congress set to work, the independence movement was growing rapidly. A brilliant pamphlet titled *Common Sense*, written by Thomas Paine, influenced many colonists. Paine, a onetime British corset-maker, argued that monarchy was a corrupt form of government and that George III was an enemy to liberty:

> "*First, the powers of governing still remaining in the hands of the king, he will have a negative over the whole legislation on this continent. And as he has shown himself such an inveterate enemy to liberty and discovered such a thirst for arbitrary power, is he, or is he not, a proper person to say to these colonies, 'You shall make no laws but what I please!'*"
>
> —Thomas Paine

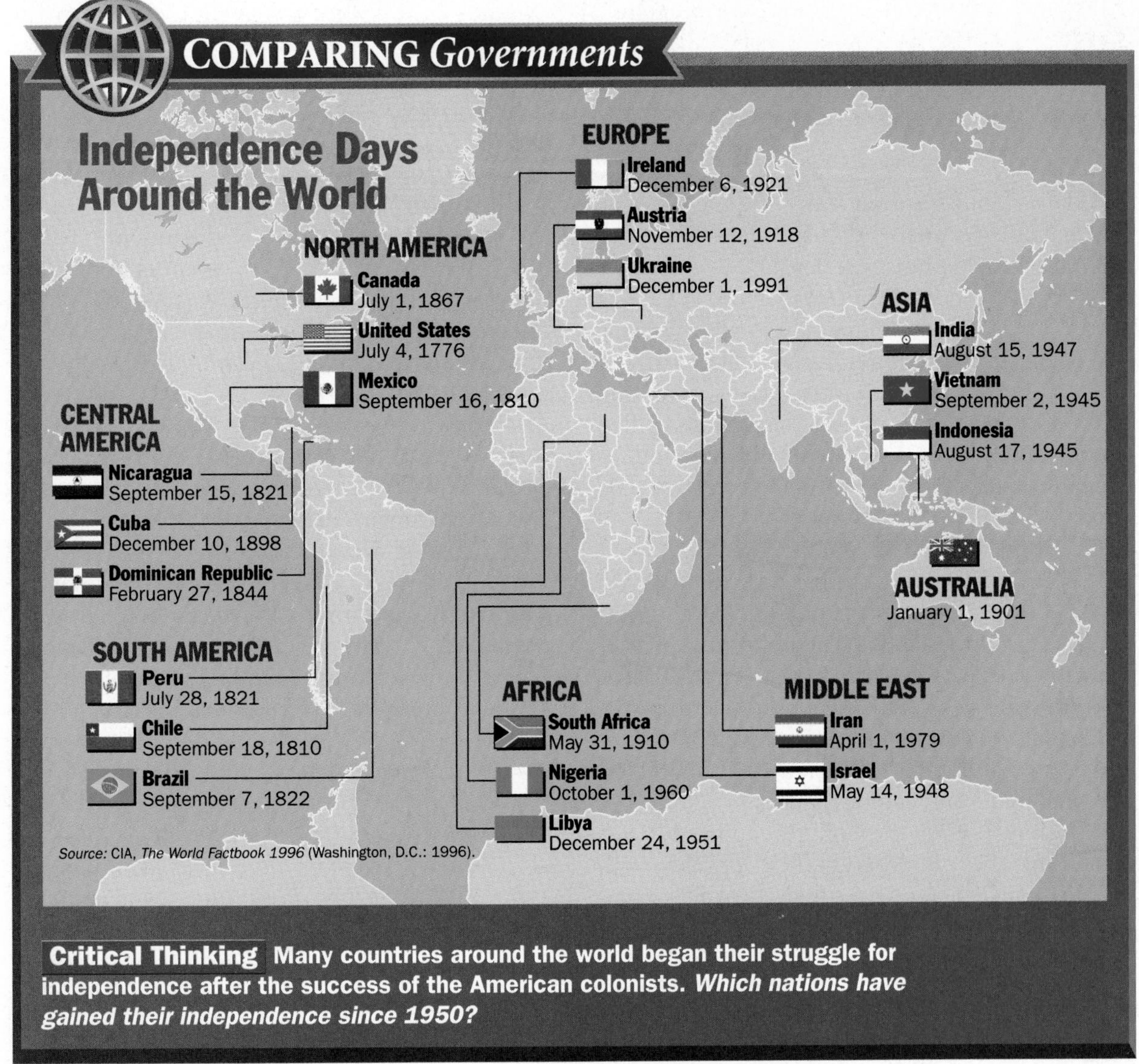

Critical Thinking Many countries around the world began their struggle for independence after the success of the American colonists. ***Which nations have gained their independence since 1950?***

Ready for Independence

Growth of Democracy In *Pulling Down the Statue of George III*, William Walcutt depicted Americans celebrating their independence by tearing down the statue of King George III in New York on July 9, 1776. The statue was later melted down into bullets to be used against the king's troops. ***Why was the Declaration of Independence revolutionary?***

Lap desk Jefferson used to draft the Declaration of Independence

Many colonists agreed with the patriot Samuel Adams. Adams asked, "Is not America already independent? Why not then declare it?"

In June 1776, more than a year after fighting had begun in the colonies, Richard Henry Lee of Virginia did just that. Lee introduced a resolution in the Continental Congress "That these United Colonies are, and of right ought to be, free and independent states."

The Declaration of Independence Congress promptly named a committee to prepare a written declaration of independence. The committee asked Thomas Jefferson, a Virginia planter known for his writing skills, to write the draft. For the next two weeks, Jefferson worked alone on the document. On June 28 Jefferson asked John Adams and Benjamin Franklin to look over his draft. The two men made only minor changes.

On July 2, 1776, the Congress approved Lee's resolution. The colonies had officially broken with Great Britain. The Congress then turned its attention to Jefferson's draft. After considerable debate a few passages were removed and some editorial changes made. On July 4 Congress approved the final draft of the Declaration of Independence. John Hancock, the president of the Congress, was the first to sign the document which eventually held the signatures of all 56 delegates. A statement of the reasons for independence, the document's actual title was *The unanimous Declaration of the thirteen united States of America.*

Key Parts of the Declaration The American Declaration of Independence[1] is one of the most famous documents in history. In writing the document Jefferson drew together the ideas of thinkers such as Locke and others to set out the colonies' reasons for proclaiming their freedom. The purpose of the Declaration was to justify the Revolution and put forth the founding principles of the new nation. Jefferson later wrote:

> "*I did not consider it any part of my charge to invent new ideas, but to place before mankind the common sense of the subject in terms so plain and firm as to command their assent. . . . It was intended to be an expression of the American mind.*"
>
> —Thomas Jefferson

See the following footnoted materials in the **Reference Handbook:**
1. *The Declaration of Independence*, pages 774–799.

The revolutionary document stirred the hearts of the American people. No government at the time had been founded on the principles of human liberty and consent of the governed. The Declaration won praise the world over and influenced the French Revolution of 1789. Over the years many nations, particularly in Latin America, have used it as a model in their own efforts to gain freedom.

The Declaration has three parts. It begins with a statement of purpose and basic human rights:

> "*We hold these truths to be self-evident, that all men are created equal, that they are endowed by their Creator with certain unalienable Rights, that among these are Life, Liberty and the Pursuit of Happiness. That to secure these rights, Governments are instituted among Men, deriving their just powers from the consent of the governed. . . .*"

The middle section of the Declaration lists specific complaints against George III. Each item describes a violation of the colonists' political, civil, and economic liberties. These paragraphs were designed to justify the break with Great Britain.

The conclusion states the colonists' determination to separate from Great Britain. Their efforts to reach a peaceful solution to their problems had failed, leaving them no choice but to declare their freedom.

The First State Constitutions The Declaration of Independence recognized the changes taking place in the colonies. One of the most important of these was the transformation of the colonies into states subject to no higher authority. Thus, the states saw themselves as "states" in the sense in which this term is used in Chapter 1.

Almost two months before the Declaration of Independence, the Second Continental Congress had instructed each of the colonies to form "such governments as shall . . . best conduce [lead] to the happiness and safety of their constituents." By 1776 eight states had adopted written constitutions. Within a few years every former colony had a new constitution or had converted the old colonial charters into state constitutions.

Seven of the new constitutions contained a bill of rights defining the personal liberties of citizens. All recognized the people as the sole source of authority in a limited government with only those powers given by the people.

GOVERNMENT Online

Student Web Activity Visit the *United States Government: Democracy in Action* Web site at gov.glencoe.com and click on ***Chapter 2–Student Web Activities*** for an activity about uniting for independence.

Section 2 Assessment

Checking for Understanding

1. **Main Idea** In a graphic organizer similar to the one below, identify the series of events that led the colonies to declare their independence.

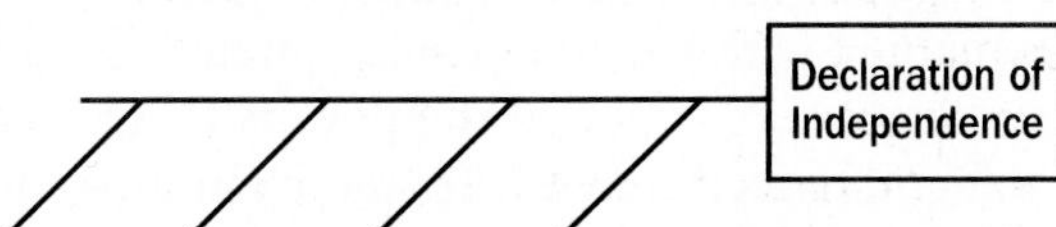

2. **Define** revenue, embargo.
3. **Identify** Stamp Act, Intolerable Acts, Albany Plan of Union.
4. What actions did George III take to make the Americans pay for the French and Indian War?

Critical Thinking

5. **Understanding Cause and Effect** At what point was it too late for Great Britain and the colonies to work out a peaceful settlement? Explain.

Concepts IN ACTION

Growth of Democracy The right of people to complain to the government is one of the fundamental American rights. Identify a recent government action or policy with which you disagree. Decide on a protest method that would be an effective way for you to express your feelings about the issue. Support your method in the form of a letter to the editor.

Section 3

The Articles of Confederation

Reader's Guide

Key Terms

ratify, unicameral, cede, ordinance

Find Out

- What weakness of the Articles of Confederation made enforcing the laws of Congress impossible?
- What evidence shows that financial problems were the main cause of the call to amend the Articles of Confederation?

Understanding Concepts

Federalism What deficiencies in the Articles of Confederation made them too weak to ensure the peace and tranquility of the United States?

COVER STORY

Congress Flees Capital

PHILADELPHIA, JUNE 1783

Nearly 300 unpaid and unhappy soldiers from the recently disbanded Continental Army demonstrated outside the statehouse this week. The protesters shouted curses and threats at the Confederation Congress, which was meeting inside. Some poked their bayonets through the windows of the meeting chambers. The legislators are said to be extremely frightened. Congress has asked the state for protection, but Pennsylvania officials have provided no assistance. At last report the congressmen have left the city and will reconvene the government at Princeton, New Jersey.

Continental soldier

When Richard Henry Lee proposed his resolution for independence in June 1776, he also proposed that a "plan for confederation" be prepared for the colonies. In 1777 a committee appointed by Congress presented a plan called the Articles of Confederation.[1] The Articles basically continued the structure and operation of government as established under the Second Continental Congress. The states wanted a confederation, or "league of friendship," among the 13 independent states rather than a strong national government. By March 1781, all 13 states had **ratified**, or approved, the Articles of Confederation.

Government Under the Articles

Under the Articles, the plan for the central government was simple. It included a **unicameral**, or single-chamber, Congress. It did not include an executive branch or president. A Committee of the States made up of one delegate from each state managed the government when Congress was not assembled. There was no federal court system. Congress settled disputes among states.

Each state had one vote in Congress, no matter what its size or population. Every state legislature selected its own representatives to Congress, paid them, and could recall them at any time.

Congress had only those powers expressed in the Articles—mainly lawmaking. All other powers remained with the independent states. Congressional powers included the powers to: (1) make war and peace; (2) send and receive ambassadors; (3) enter into treaties; (4) raise and equip a navy; (5) maintain an army by requesting troops from the states; (6) appoint senior military officers; (7) fix standards of weights and measures; (8) regulate Indian affairs; (9) establish post offices; and (10) decide certain disputes among the states.

See the following footnoted materials in the ***Reference Handbook:***
1. *Articles of Confederation,* pages 808–811.

Weaknesses of the Articles

Although the Articles of Confederation gave Congress power, they created a weak national government. Because each state had no intention of giving up its sovereignty to a central government, the Articles had weaknesses.

First, Congress did not have the power to levy or collect taxes. It could raise money only by borrowing or requesting money from the states. Each state had to collect taxes from its citizens and turn the money over to the national treasury. Congress could do little, however, if a state refused to provide the money.

Second, Congress did not have the power to regulate trade. Economic disputes among the various states and difficulty in making business arrangements with other countries resulted.

Third, Congress could not force anyone to obey the laws it passed or to abide by the Articles of Confederation. Congress could only advise and request the states to comply.

Fourth, laws needed the approval of 9 of the 13 states. Usually, delegates from only 9 or 10 states were in Congress at any time, making it difficult to pass laws. Also, each state had only a single vote. The votes of any 5 of the smaller states could block a measure that 8 of the larger states wanted.

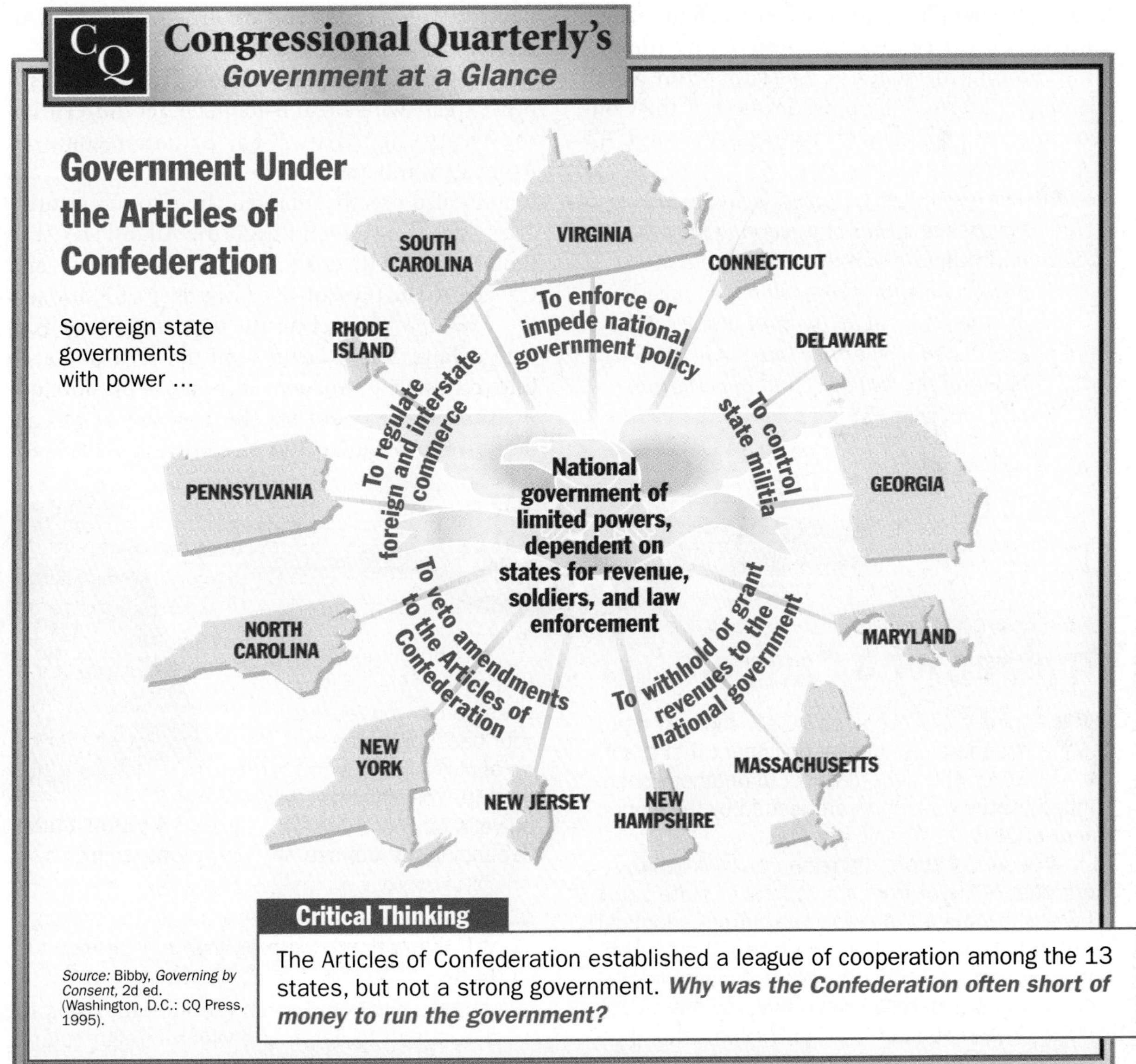

Source: Bibby, *Governing by Consent*, 2d ed. (Washington, D.C.: CQ Press, 1995).

Critical Thinking

The Articles of Confederation established a league of cooperation among the 13 states, but not a strong government. ***Why was the Confederation often short of money to run the government?***

Fifth, amending, or changing, the Articles required the consent of all states. In practice it was impossible to get *all* the states to agree on amendments. As a result the Articles were never amended.

Sixth, the central government did not have an executive branch. The Confederation government carried on much of its business, such as selling western lands and establishing a postal system, through congressional committees. Without an executive, however, there was no unity in policy making and no way to coordinate the work of the different committees.

Finally, the government had no national court system. Instead, state courts enforced and interpreted national laws. The lack of a court system made it difficult for the central government to settle disputes among the states. A legislator from North Carolina addressed the powerlessness of the Confederation in a speech to his state legislature in 1787:

> "*The general government ought . . . to possess the means of preserving the peace and tranquility of the union. . . . The encroachments of some states, on the rights of others, and of all on those of the confederacy, are incontestible [cannot be denied] proofs of the weakness and imperfection of that system.*"
>
> —William Davie, 1787

Achievements

Despite its weaknesses, the Confederation accomplished much. The greatest achievement was the establishment of a fair policy for the development of the lands west of the Appalachians. The individual states **ceded,** or yielded, their claims to these territories to the central government, providing a priceless national asset that became a strong force for national unity. In addition Congress enacted two land **ordinances,** or laws, that provided for the organization of these territories. The **Northwest Ordinance** of 1787, for example, established the principle that the territories owned by the government were to be developed for statehood on an equal basis with the older states.

Another important accomplishment was a peace treaty with Great Britain. Under the terms of the treaty, signed in 1783, Britain recognized American independence. Land acquired from Britain also greatly enlarged the nation's boundaries, including all land from the Atlantic coast to the Mississippi River and from the Great Lakes and Canada to the present-day boundary of Florida.

Congress also set up the departments of Foreign Affairs, War, Marine, and the Treasury, each under a single permanent secretary. This development set a precedent for the creation of cabinet departments under the Constitution of 1787.

GOVERNMENT and You

Applying for a Passport

Planning a trip overseas? If so, you may need a passport—an official document that grants a citizen the right to travel to another country. United States passports are issued by the Department of State in Washington, D.C.

A passport application can be obtained from your post office or from any federal or state court. There is a required fee, and two current, identical photos of your full face are needed to help prove who you are. You will also need a document, such as a birth certificate, to prove that you are a U.S. citizen. Instructions on the application detail the types of proof of citizenship that are acceptable.

It is often the case that several weeks may pass before you receive your passport in the mail, so apply well in advance of the trip. Your passport will be valid for 5 or 10 years, depending on your age.

A United States passport

Investigate Further Search the Internet using the word *passport* to determine which foreign countries have additional requirements for visitors.

Growing Unrest

Past Government authorities often jailed debtor farmers or seized their property. Shays led a mob to attack and close the courts, stopping land confiscations.

Present This marker commemorates Shays's revolt. A private army attacked Shays's mob in this field and killed more than 30 men.

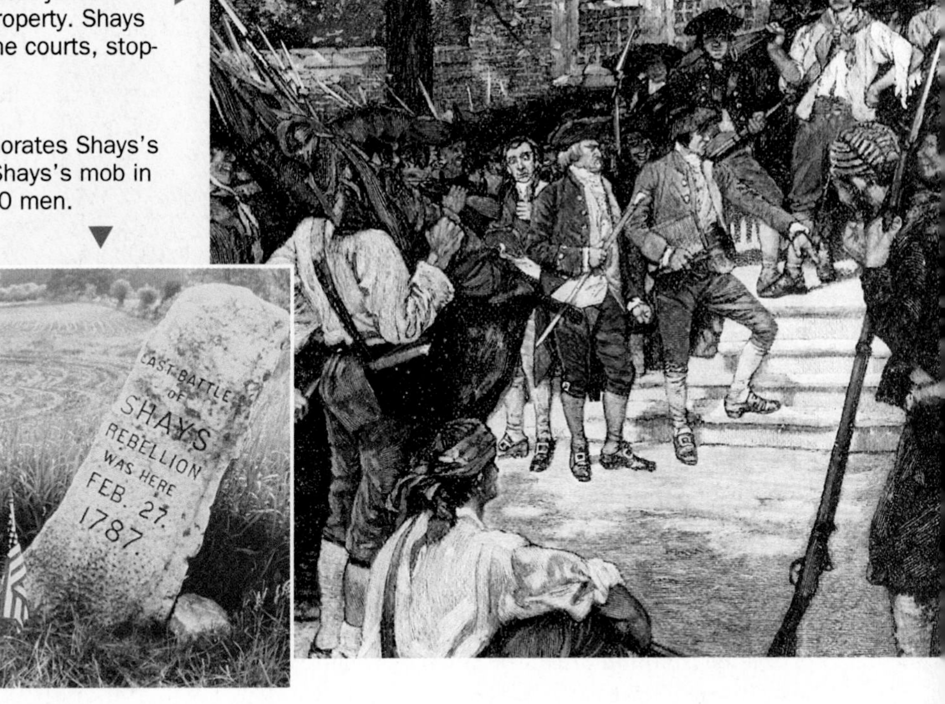

Reaction to Rebellion
How do you think Americans viewed the government after Shays's Rebellion?

To encourage cooperation among the states, the Articles provided that each state give "full faith and credit" to the legal acts of the other states and treat one another's citizens without discrimination. This provision, often ignored, was carried over to the Constitution, under which it could be enforced.

Need for Stronger Government

Despite its achievements, the Confederation faced difficulties in dealing with problems facing the nation. The structure of the central government could not coordinate the actions of the states effectively.

Growing Problems Soon after the war, the states began to quarrel, mainly over boundary lines and tariffs. New Jersey farmers, for example, had to pay fees to sell their vegetables in New York. Some states even began to deal directly with foreign nations. Congress could do little about these matters.

Even worse, the new nation faced serious money problems. By 1787 the government owed $40 million to foreign governments and to American soldiers still unpaid after the Revolutionary War. Without money, the government could not maintain an army for defense of the states.

The states also faced growing financial troubles. By 1786 an economic depression had left many farmers and small merchants angry and in debt.

Shays's Rebellion In 1787 these economic troubles led to armed rebellion. In western Massachusetts several hundred angry farmers armed with pitchforks marched on the Springfield arsenal to get weapons. Daniel Shays, a former captain in the Revolutionary Army, led the farmers. Unable to pay their mortgages some farmers in western Massachusetts were jailed or had their property taken from them. The farmers wanted to prevent the courts from foreclosing on mortgages and taking away their farms. To force the state to pass laws to help them, the farmers threatened to lay siege to Boston.

The Massachusetts militia put down the rebellion, but the unrest frightened American leaders. Henry Knox, later the nation's first secretary of war, echoed the growing number of Americans ready to agree to a strong national government. In a letter to George Washington, Knox wrote:

"This dreadful situation has alarmed every man of principle and property in New England. [People wake] as from a dream and ask what has been the cause of our delusion. What [will] give us security against the violence of lawless men? Our government must be [strengthened], changed, or altered to secure our lives and property."

—Henry Knox

Delegates Alexander Hamilton (above) and James Madison (right)

The Annapolis Convention

The Constitutional Convention was the result of two previous meetings. George Washington, retired and living at his Mount Vernon estate, was concerned about problems that had arisen between Maryland and his home state of Virginia. In 1785 he invited representatives from both states to Mount Vernon to discuss differences over their currencies, import duties, and navigation on the Potomac River and Chesapeake Bay. The meeting was very successful, inspiring Virginia's representatives in 1786 to call all states to another meeting—a convention at Annapolis, Maryland, to discuss commerce. Although all states were invited, only five sent delegates. Among the delegates were Alexander Hamilton of New York and James Madison of Virginia, two leaders who favored a stronger national government. With Shays and his followers threatening the government of Massachusetts, Hamilton persuaded the other delegates to call for another convention in Philadelphia in May 1787. The purpose of this meeting would be to regulate commerce among the states and to propose changes that would make the national government more effective.

After some hesitation, the Confederation Congress gave its consent to hold the Philadelphia convention "for the sole and express purpose of revising the Articles of Confederation." The stage was now set for what has been called the "miracle at Philadelphia."

Section 3 Assessment

Checking for Understanding

1. **Main Idea** In a graphic organizer similar to the one below, list the major weaknesses of government under the Articles of Confederation and its achievements.

Articles of Confederation	
Weaknesses	Achievements

2. **Define** ratify, unicameral, cede, ordinance.
3. **Identify** Northwest Ordinance.
4. How was the original government under the Articles of Confederation organized?
5. Describe two financial problems that could not be resolved under the Articles of Confederation.

Critical Thinking

6. **Identifying Central Issues** What problems did Shays's Rebellion reveal?

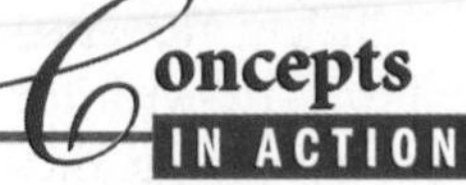

Federalism The plan for confederation that was ratified in 1781 called for a "league of friendship" among 13 independent states. What are some examples of interstate cooperation today? Find a recent example of states cooperating with one another in issues such as curbing air pollution or cleaning up waterways.

Section 4

The Constitutional Convention

Reader's Guide

Key Terms

interstate commerce, extralegal, anarchy

Find Out

- How did the Connecticut Compromise settle the most divisive issue among members of the Constitutional Convention?
- What were the key arguments presented by the Federalists and Anti-Federalists?

Understanding Concepts

Civil Liberties Why do you think many people insisted on a Bill of Rights in the Constitution?

COVER STORY

Massachusetts Approves!

BOSTON, FEBRUARY 1788

By a narrow margin, Massachusetts yesterday became the sixth state to approve the proposed new national constitution. The vote by the special ratifying convention ended nearly a month of heated debate on the issue. Last-minute support by Governor John Hancock and well-known radical leader Sam Adams may have been the key to the Federalist victory. The Federalists seem to have won Adams's endorsement by promising changes to the proposed constitution. Hancock's support is believed to come from the suggestion that he would become the first president if Virginia failed to approve the document, making George Washington ineligible for that office.

John Hancock

The Constitutional Convention began its work on May 25, 1787. All the states except Rhode Island sent delegates. The state legislatures appointed 74 delegates to the Convention, but only 55 attended. Of these, 39 took a leading role.

The Convention Begins

The delegates had great practical experience in politics. Seven had served as governors of their states. Thirty-nine had served in the Confederation Congress. Many had helped write their state constitutions. Eight had signed the Declaration of Independence, and five delegates had signed the Articles of Confederation.

Several men stood out as leaders. The presence of George Washington ensured that many people would trust the Convention's work. Benjamin Franklin, world famous as a scientist and diplomat, now 81 years old, played an active role in the debates.

Two other Pennsylvanians also played key roles. James Wilson often read Franklin's speeches and did important work on the details of the Constitution. Gouverneur Morris, an eloquent speaker and writer, wrote the final draft of the Constitution.

From Virginia came James Madison, a brilliant advocate of a strong national government. His careful notes are the major source of information about the Convention's work. Madison is often called the **Father of the Constitution** because he was the author of the basic plan of government that the Convention eventually adopted.

Organization The Convention began by unanimously choosing George Washington to preside over the meetings. It also decided that each state would have one vote on all questions. A simple majority vote of those states present would make decisions. No meetings could be held unless delegates from at least seven of the 13 states were present.

The delegates decided to keep the public and press from attending the sessions. This was a key decision because it made it possible for the delegates to talk freely.

Key Agreements While the delegates originally came together to revise the Articles, they eventually agreed to abandon the former government and begin again. The delegates reached a consensus on many basic issues. All favored the idea of limited and representative government. They agreed that the powers of the national government should be divided among legislative, executive, and judicial branches. They all believed it was necessary to limit the power of the states to coin money or to interfere with creditors' rights. And all of them agreed that they should strengthen the national government.

The great debates and compromises of the Convention were not over these fundamental questions. Rather, they dealt with how to put these ideas into practice.

Decisions and Compromises

After the rules were adopted, the Convention opened with a surprise. It came from the Virginia delegation who presented a plan for a strong national government.

The Virginia Plan On May 29 Edmund Randolph of Virginia introduced 15 resolutions that James Madison had drafted. They came to be called the Virginia Plan. The plan proposed a government based on three principles: (1) a strong national legislature with two chambers, the lower one to be chosen by the people and the upper chamber to be chosen by the lower. The legislature would have the power to bar any state laws it found unconstitutional; (2) a strong national executive to be chosen by the national legislature; and (3) a national judiciary to be appointed by the legislature.

The introduction of the Virginia Plan was a brilliant political move on the part of the nationalists. By offering a complete plan at the very start, the nationalists set the direction and agenda for the rest of the Convention. Eventually, and after much discussion by delegates who required a number of modifications, the Virginia Plan became the basis of the new Constitution.

The delegates debated the Virginia Plan for the next two weeks. Delegates from the smaller states soon realized that the larger, more populous states would be in control of a strong national government under the Virginia Plan. The smaller states wanted a less powerful government with more independence for the states.

The New Jersey Plan On June 15 the delegates from the small states, led by William Paterson of New Jersey, made a counterproposal. The New Jersey Plan called for government based on keeping the major feature of the Articles of Confederation—a unicameral legislature, with one vote for each state. Congress, however, would be strengthened by giving it the power to impose taxes and regulate trade. A weak executive consisting of more than one person would be elected by Congress. A national judiciary with limited power would be appointed by the executive.

Paterson argued that the Convention should not deprive the smaller states of the equality they had under the Articles. Thus, his plan was designed simply to amend the Articles. The central government was to continue as a confederation of sovereign states. After some discussion the New Jersey Plan was rejected. The delegates returned to considering the Virginia Plan.

As the summer grew hotter, so did the delegates' tempers. Soon the Convention was deadlocked over the question of the representation of states in Congress. Should the states be represented on the basis of population (favored by the large-state delegations) or should they be represented equally, regardless of population (favored by the small-state delegations)? The debate was bitter, and the Convention was in danger of dissolving.

The Connecticut Compromise Finally, a special committee designed a compromise. Called the Connecticut Compromise because Roger Sherman and the delegation from that state played a key role on the committee, this plan was adopted after long debate. The compromise suggested that the legislative branch have two parts: (1) a House of Representatives, with state representation based on population. All revenue laws—concerning spending and taxes—would begin in this house;

and (2) a Senate, with two members from each state. State legislatures would elect senators.

The larger states would have an advantage in the House of Representatives, where representation was to be based on population. The smaller states would be protected in the Senate, where each state had equal representation.

The Three-Fifths Compromise

A second compromise settled a disagreement over how to determine how many representatives each state would have in the House. Almost one-third of the people in the Southern states were enslaved African Americans. These states wanted the slaves counted the same as free people to give the South more representation.

At the same time, the Southern states did not want enslaved persons counted at all for levying taxes. Because they did not have many slaves, the Northern states took the opposite position. They wanted the enslaved persons counted for tax purposes but not for representation.

The Three-Fifths Compromise settled this deadlock. Three-fifths of the enslaved people were to be counted for both tax purposes and for representation.

Compromise on Commerce and the Slave Trade

A third compromise resolved a dispute over commerce and the slave trade itself. The Northern states wanted the government to have complete power over trade with other nations. The Southern states depended heavily on agricultural exports. They feared that business interests in the North might have enough votes in Congress to set up trade agreements that would hurt them. They also feared the North might interfere with the slave trade.

Again, a compromise settled the issue. The delegates determined that Congress could not ban the slave trade until 1808. At the same time, they gave Congress the power to regulate both **interstate commerce,** or trade among the states, and foreign commerce. To protect the South's exports, however, Congress was forbidden to impose export taxes. As a result, the United States is one of the few nations in the world today that does not tax its exports.

The Three-Fifths Compromise

Constitutional Ideals
By accepting the Three-Fifths Compromise, the Framers, in essence, condoned slavery. Leaders, like Thomas Jefferson, (left) accepted slavery as a social norm. Isaac Jefferson, (below) was an enslaved worker at Jefferson's home, Monticello. ***How does slavery clash with the ideals of the Revolution?***

The Slavery Question

The word *slave* does not appear in the Constitution. Beyond the compromises just discussed, the Constitution dealt with slavery only by noting that those escaping to free states could be returned to the slaveholders (Article IV, Section 2).[1] At the time, many of the Northern states were outlawing slavery. Massachusetts had voted to end the slave trade. Delaware had forbidden importing enslaved persons. Connecticut and Rhode Island had decided that all enslaved persons brought into their states would be free. Pennsylvania had taxed slavery out of existence.

Whatever their personal beliefs about slavery, the delegates knew that the Southern states would never accept the Constitution if it interfered with slavery. Thus, in order to create the badly needed new government, the Founders compromised on

See the following footnoted materials in the **Reference Handbook:**
1. *The Constitution,* pages 774–799.

the slavery question. Their refusal to deal with slavery left it to later generations of Americans to resolve this great and terrible issue.

Other Compromises The delegates compromised on several other issues to complete the Constitution. The debate over how to elect the president included the election of the president directly by the people, by Congress, and by state legislatures. The present Electoral College system, in which each state selects electors to choose the president, was finally agreed to as a compromise. Similarly, the president's four-year term was a compromise between those wanting a longer term and those who feared a long term would give the president too much power.

On September 8, 1787, a Committee of Style and Arrangements began polishing the final draft. By September 17 the document was ready. Thirty-nine delegates stepped forward to sign the Constitution. The aging Ben Franklin had to be helped to the table to sign. As others went up to sign, he remarked that during the long debates he had often looked at the sun painted on the back of General Washington's chair and wondered whether it was rising or setting. "[B]ut now at length I have the happiness to know," he said, "it is a rising and not a setting Sun."

Rising sun chair, Constitutional Convention

Ratifying the Constitution

For the new Constitution to become law, 9 of the 13 states had to ratify it. The political debate over ratification lasted until May 29, 1790, when Rhode Island finally voted for approval. The Constitution, however, actually went into effect on June 21, 1788, when New Hampshire became the ninth state to ratify it.

The Federalists and Anti-Federalists

The great debate over ratification quickly divided the people in the states. Fervent debates broke out in the newspapers. One group, known as the Federalists, favored the Constitution and was led by many of the Founders. Their support came mainly from merchants and others in the cities and coastal regions. The other group, called the Anti-Federalists, opposed the new Constitution. They drew support largely from the inland farmers and laborers, who feared a strong national government. The lines of support, however, were not clearly drawn, and many city and business people agreed with the opponents of the Constitution.

The Anti-Federalists criticized the Constitution for having been drafted in secrecy. They claimed the document was **extralegal,** not sanctioned by law, since the Convention had been authorized only to revise the old Articles. They further argued that the Constitution took important powers from the states.

The Anti-Federalists' strongest argument, however, was that the Constitution lacked a Bill of Rights. The Convention had considered including such a bill. However, the delegates decided that the inclusion was not needed because the Constitution did not give the government power to violate the people's rights. Anti-Federalists warned that without a Bill of Rights, a strong national government might take away the human rights won in the Revolution. They demanded that the new Constitution clearly guarantee the people's freedoms. **Patrick Henry** was a strong opponent of the Constitution. He stated:

> "The necessity of a Bill of Rights appears to me to be greater in this government than ever it was in any government before. . . . All rights not expressly and unequivocally reserved to the people are impliedly and incidentally relinquished to rulers. . . . If you intend to reserve your unalienable rights, you must have the most express stipulation; for . . . if the people do not think it necessary to reserve them, they will supposed to be given up."
>
> —Patrick Henry, 1788

The Federalists, on the other hand, argued that without a strong national government, **anarchy**, or political disorder, would triumph. They claimed that only a strong national government could protect the new nation from enemies abroad and solve the country's internal problems. They also claimed that a Bill of Rights was not needed since eight states already had such bills in their state constitutions. To gain the necessary support, however, the Federalists promised to add a Bill of Rights as the first order of business under a new government.

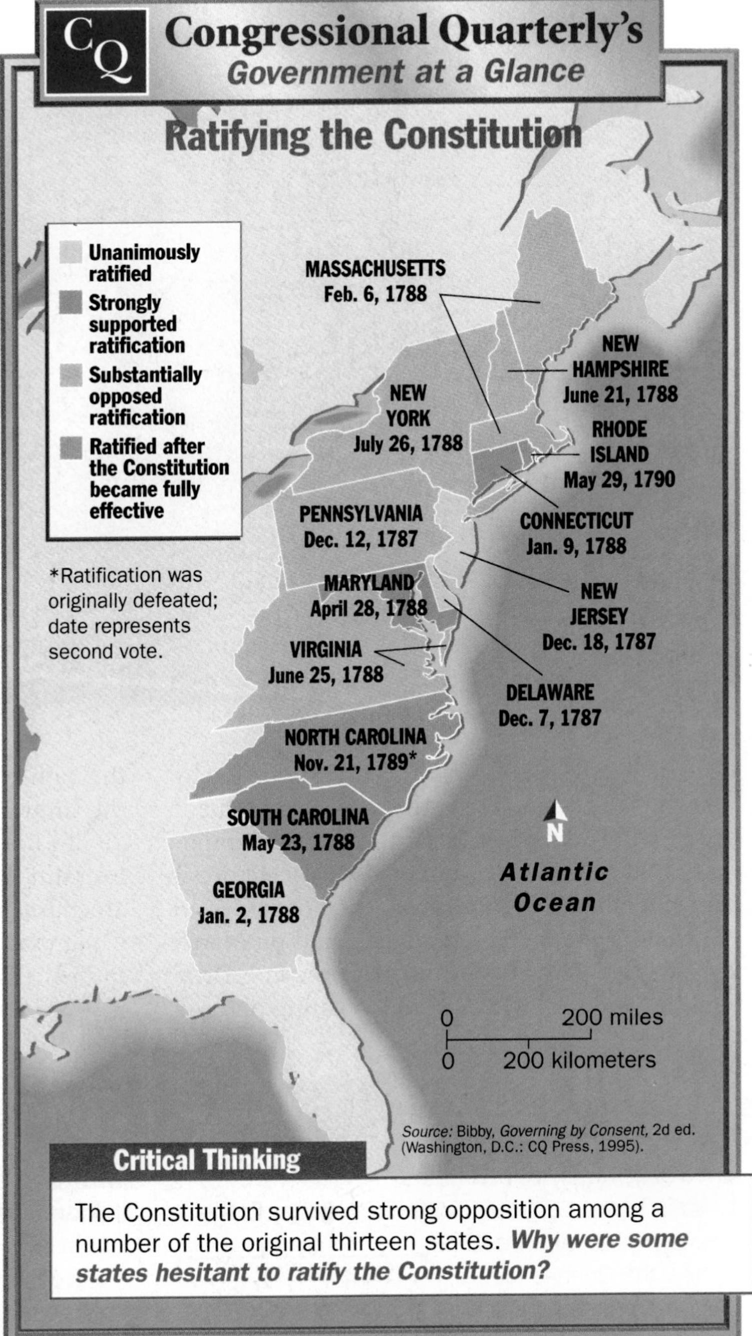

Critical Thinking

The Constitution survived strong opposition among a number of the original thirteen states. ***Why were some states hesitant to ratify the Constitution?***

Progress Toward Ratification

With the promise of a Bill of Rights, the tide turned in favor of the Constitution. Many small states ratified it quickly because they were pleased with equal representation in the new Senate. Although the Constitution went into effect when New Hampshire ratified it, Virginia and New York had not voted for approval. In Virginia, George Washington, James Madison, and Edmund Randolph helped swing a close vote on June 25, 1788. In New York, Alexander Hamilton argued the case for six weeks. Finally, on July 26, the Federalists in New York won by only three votes.

To help win the battle in New York, Hamilton, Madison, and John Jay published more than 80 essays defending the new Constitution. Later they were collected in a book called ***The Federalist.*** 1

See the following footnoted materials in the **Reference Handbook:**
1. *The Federalist, No. 10,* pages 812–814 and *The Federalist, No. 51,* pages 815–816.

The Constitutional Debate

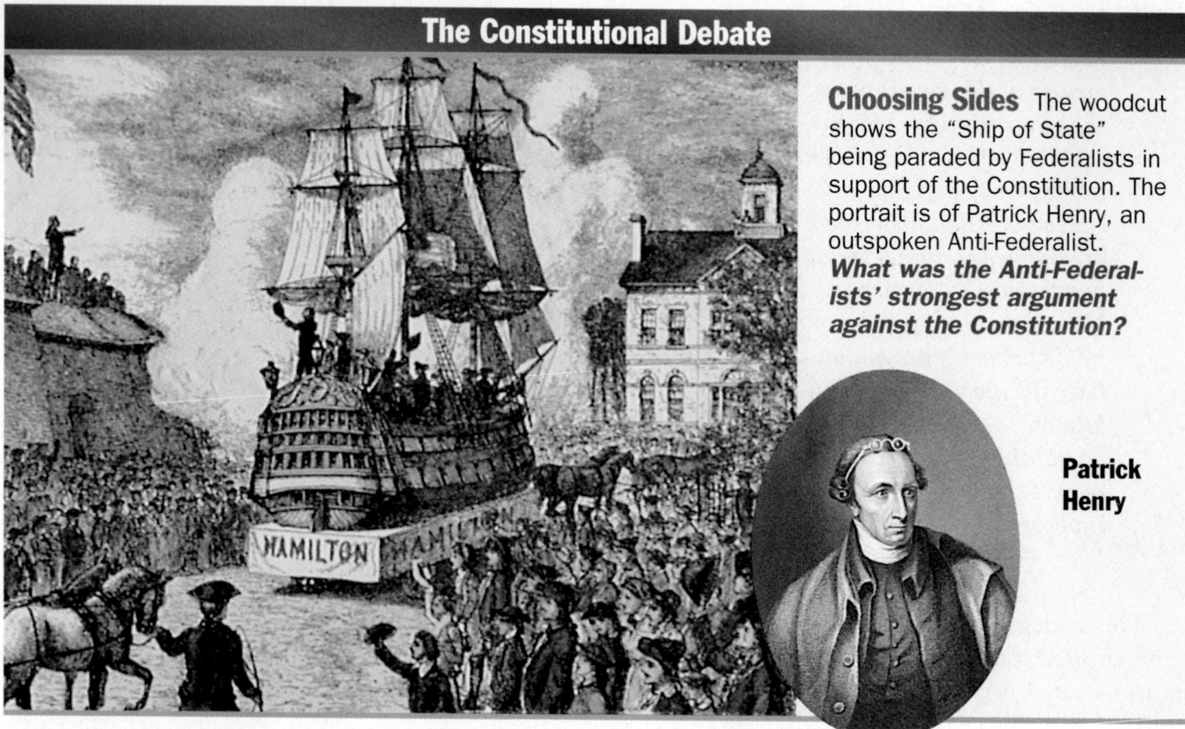

Choosing Sides The woodcut shows the "Ship of State" being paraded by Federalists in support of the Constitution. The portrait is of Patrick Henry, an outspoken Anti-Federalist. ***What was the Anti-Federalists' strongest argument against the Constitution?***

Launching a New State With ratification by Virginia and New York, the new government began, with New York City as the nation's temporary capital. George Washington was elected president and John Adams vice president. Voters elected 22 senators and 59 representatives, and on March 4, 1789, Congress met for the first time in Federal Hall in New York. On April 30 Washington took the oath of office to become the first president of the United States.

To fulfill the promises made during the fight for ratification, James Madison introduced a set of amendments during the first session of Congress. Congress approved 12 amendments and the states ratified 10 of them in 1791. These first 10 amendments became known as the Bill of Rights.

Section 4 Assessment

Checking for Understanding

1. **Main Idea** In a graphic organizer similar to the one at the right, describe how the Connecticut Compromise provided fair treatment for both large and small states.

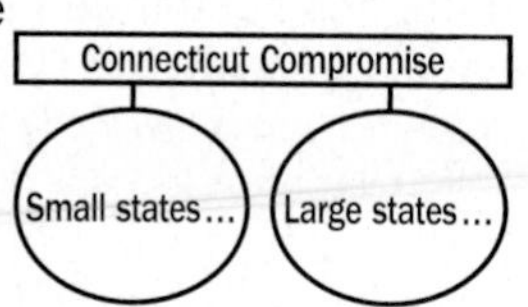

2. **Define** interstate commerce, extralegal, anarchy.
3. **Identify** Father of the Constitution, Patrick Henry.
4. Identify the key issues on which the delegates to the Constitutional Convention agreed.
5. Who were the authors of *The Federalist* and what was the purpose for writing it?

Critical Thinking

6. **Identifying Alternatives** What do you think the outcome of the Constitutional Convention might have been if the public and press had been allowed to attend the sessions?

Concepts IN ACTION

Civil Liberties The Bill of Rights, important in the ratification of the Constitution, continues to be a strong foundation of the American political system. Find examples of civil liberties issues in the news. Write a short news article about why the Bill of Rights is important today.

Using a Computerized Card Catalog

If you want to write a paper on a topic related to the colonial period, you will need to use a variety of reference materials for research. A computerized card catalog can help you narrow your search.

Learning the Skill

Go to the computerized card catalog in your school or local library. Type in the name of an author; the title of a book, videotape, audiocassette, or CD; or a subject heading. The computer will list on-screen the author, titles, or subjects you requested.

The "card" that appears on-screen also lists other important information, such as the year the work was published, who published it, what media type it is, and the language it is written or recorded in. Use this information to determine if the material meets your needs. Then check to see if the material is available. Find the classification and call number under which it is shelved.

Practicing the Skill

Follow the steps below to collect materials on the subject of the Articles of Confederation.

1. Go to the computerized card catalog in your school or local library and conduct a subject search on the Articles of Confederation. Did you have to broaden or narrow your search?
2. A list of subjects should appear on the computer screen. Follow the instructions on-screen to display all the titles under your subject. List four titles that contain information on the Articles of Confederation.

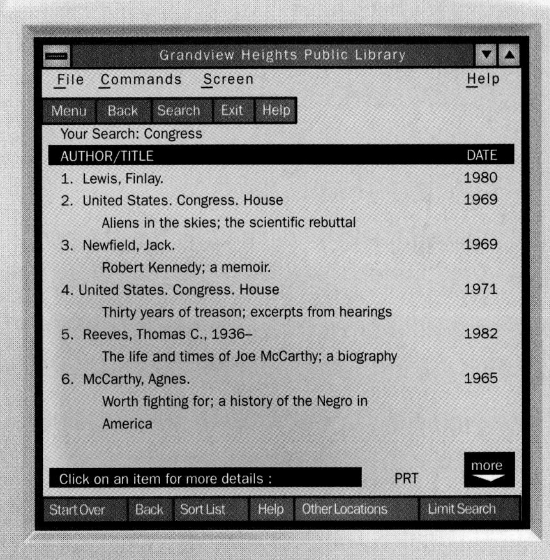

3. Select one title from your list that you want to learn more about. How do you find out more details on this?
4. How many copies of this work are available in the library? Where can you find this work in the library?

Application Activity

Use a library computerized card catalog to research and produce a brochure giving step-by-step directions on how to find background material and commentary on the Declaration of Independence.

Chapter 2

Assessment and Activities

GOVERNMENT *Online*

Self-Check Quiz Visit the *United States Government: Democracy in Action* Web site at gov.glencoe.com and click on ***Chapter 2–Self-Check Quizzes*** to prepare for the chapter test.

Reviewing Key Terms

Write a paragraph that summarizes the key points of this chapter. Use all of the following terms.

1. limited government
2. cede
3. representative government
4. revenue
5. ratify
6. anarchy
7. ordinance
8. interstate commerce

Current Events JOURNAL

Trade Restrictions The colonists used trade restrictions to protest the Stamp Act and the Intolerable Acts. Since that time, nations, groups, and individuals have continued to use trade restrictions as a means to protest unpopular or unfair policies. Use the *Readers' Guide to Periodical Literature* to find magazine articles detailing present-day examples of groups using these methods of protest.

Recalling Facts

1. Identify three key ideas found in the English Bill of Rights.
2. According to John Locke, what fundamental element made government legitimate?
3. Describe the practices established by colonial governments that became a basic part of our system of government.
4. What tasks did the Second Continental Congress accomplish?
5. Why was the Declaration of Independence a revolutionary document?
6. What achievements were made under the Articles of Confederation?
7. State the position of small states in the debate over representation in Congress.
8. What issue did the Convention delegates refuse to settle in 1787?

Understanding Concepts

1. **Growth of Democracy** Explain what the impact of the English political heritage was to the United States and its importance to the development of American government.
2. **Federalism** In your opinion, why was the Articles of Confederation an unworkable or unrealistic plan of government?
3. **Civil Liberties** Why did the Anti-Federalists insist on a Bill of Rights?

Critical Thinking

1. **Understanding Cause and Effect** Use a graphic organizer like the one below to show the cause for each effect listed.

Cause	Effect
	a strong central government
	compromises in the Constitution

2. **Synthesizing Information** How do you account for the contradiction between the constitutional acceptance of slavery and the ideals set forth in both the Declaration of Independence and the Constitution?

Chapter 2

Cooperative Learning Activity

Organizing a Government Organize into groups. Imagine that your group is aboard a space vehicle headed toward a planet that is capable of supporting human life. Once you land on the new planet, the first task is to decide what type of government your community will have. Decide on a model form of government under which you would like to live. Present your model to the class.

Interpreting Political Cartoons Activity

1. What symbol represents the colonies in this 1779 political cartoon?
2. Who do you think the rider on the horse is?
3. What is the message of this cartoon?

Skill Practice Activity

Using a Computerized Card Catalog Use a computerized card catalog to find out more about the British colonial legislation that led to the American Revolution.

1. Type "s/American Revolution."
2. From the list of subjects that appears on-screen, determine which might contain information on acts of Parliament passed immediately before the American Revolution.
3. Follow the instructions on the computer screen to display all the titles under each subject you selected.
4. Which of the books on the screen would you examine to discover more about your subject?

Technology Activity

Using Software Programs Newspaper cartoons were important tools to stir public opinion against Great Britain at the time of the Revolution. Use software clip art to create a political cartoon that might have appeared in a colonial newspaper. The cartoon should illustrate the colonists' feelings toward Britain.

Participating in Local Government

Every community has its unique history. In the course of development, the types of local government often changed. For example, as a village grew to become a city, the government evolved to meet new conditions. How did the structure of your local government change?

Investigate the history of your local government. Visit local government offices to find out when and how your community started, what type of government the community originally adopted, and who the early leaders were. Describe how the government grew and changed over the years. Prepare a brochure about the early governments of your community with the class.

Chapter 3

The Constitution

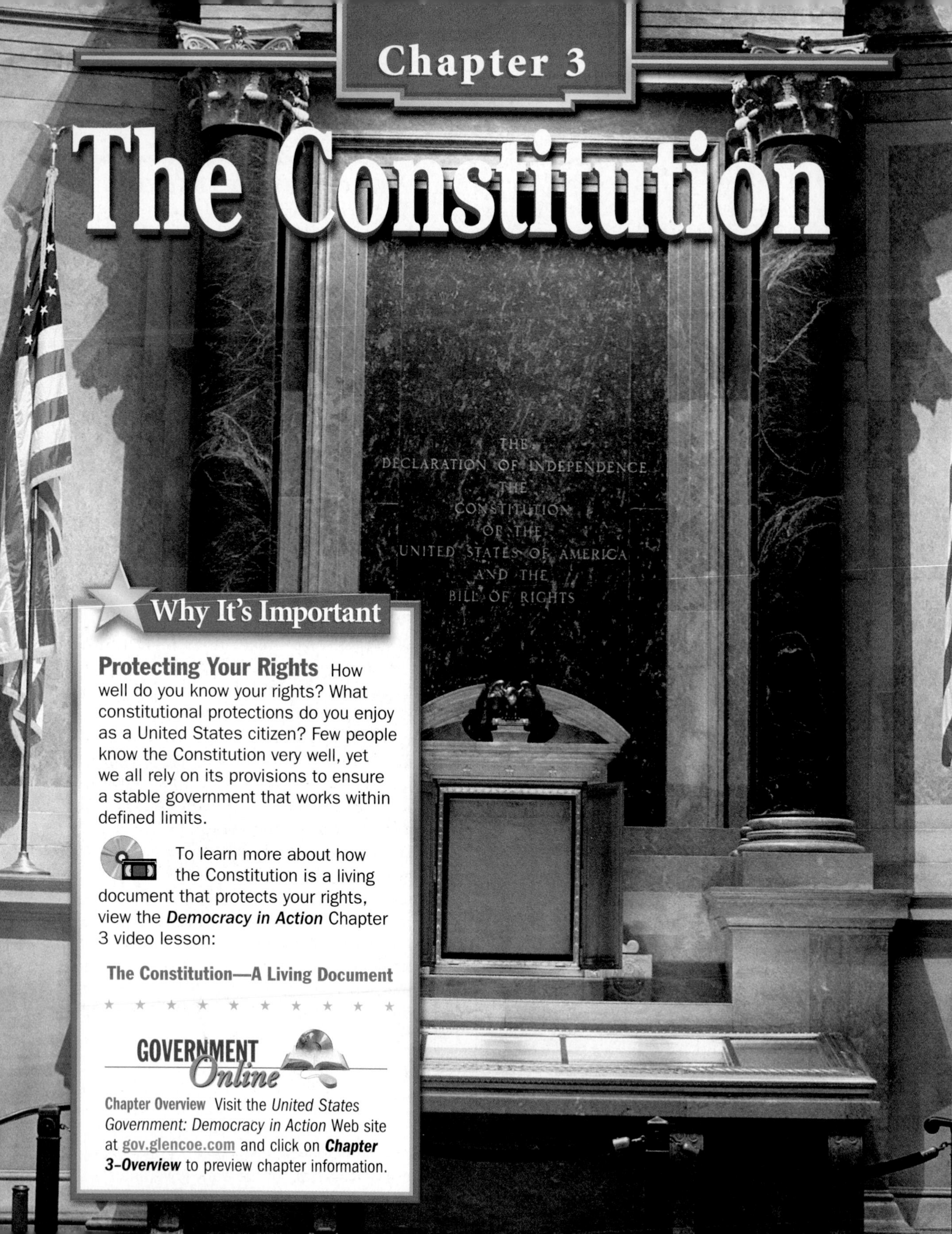

Why It's Important

Protecting Your Rights How well do you know your rights? What constitutional protections do you enjoy as a United States citizen? Few people know the Constitution very well, yet we all rely on its provisions to ensure a stable government that works within defined limits.

To learn more about how the Constitution is a living document that protects your rights, view the ***Democracy in Action*** Chapter 3 video lesson:

The Constitution—A Living Document

GOVERNMENT *Online*

Chapter Overview Visit the *United States Government: Democracy in Action* Web site at gov.glencoe.com and click on ***Chapter 3–Overview*** to preview chapter information.

Section 1

Structure and Principles

Reader's Guide

Key Terms

article, jurisdiction, supremacy clause, amendment, popular sovereignty, federalism, separation of powers, checks and balances, veto, judicial review

Find Out

- What is the basic structure of the Constitution?
- How did the Founders hope to prevent any one branch of government from gaining too much power?

Understanding Concepts

Constitutional Interpretations What are the major principles of the Constitution that represent a social consensus in the United States?

COVER STORY

Book Banned

PARIS, FRANCE, 1751

A book by a French noble is attracting attention and controversy. In *The Spirit of Laws,* published three years ago, Charles-Louis de Secondat, the baron de Montesquieu, proposed dividing political authority into executive, legislative, and judicial powers. Montesquieu argued that assigning each set of powers to a separate branch of government would promote liberty. Although his book has supporters in England and America, it has been harshly attacked throughout Europe.

DÉFENSE DE L'ESPRIT DES LOIX, *A laquelle on a joint quelques* ECLAIRCISSEMENS. Le prix eſt de trente ſols broché. A GENEVE, Chez BARRILLOT & FILS. M. DCC. L.

The Spirit of Laws book

The Founders created the Constitution more than 200 years ago. Like Montesquieu, they believed in a separation of powers. They divided the federal government into legislative, executive, and judicial branches. The Constitution established a republic, in which power is held by voting citizens through their elected representatives. It provides citizens with information about their rights and about what they may reasonably expect of their government. The success of this system of government depends on an informed, participating citizenry. An understanding of the Constitution is key to understanding the structure and daily function of American government.

Structure

Compared with the constitutions of other countries, the United States Constitution is simple and brief. It establishes the structure and powers of government but does not spell out every aspect of how government will function. The Founders wisely left it to future generations to work out such details as the need arose. The Constitution contains about 7,000 words and is divided into three parts—the Preamble, the articles, and the amendments (for the entire text, see the **Reference Handbook,** pages 774–799).

The Preamble The **Preamble**, or introduction, states why the Constitution was written. In the Preamble, the Founders indicated that they wanted a government that would provide stability and order, protect citizens' liberties, and serve the people:

> "*To form a more perfect Union, establish Justice, insure domestic Tranquility, provide for the common defence, promote the general Welfare, and secure the Blessings of Liberty.*"
>
> —The Preamble

◀ **The Constitution on display at the National Archives**

Seven Articles The Constitution contains seven divisions called **articles.** Each article covers a general topic. For example, Articles I, II, and III create the three branches of the national government—the legislative, executive, and judicial branches. Most of the articles are divided into sections.

Article I establishes the legislative branch. Section 1 of Article I creates the United States Congress. Sections 2 and 3 set forth details about the two houses of Congress—the House of Representatives and the Senate. Other sections of Article I spell out the procedures for making laws, list the types of laws Congress may pass, and specify the powers that Congress does not have.

Article II creates an executive branch to carry out laws passed by Congress. Article II, Section 1, begins: "The executive Power shall be vested in a President of the United States of America." This section and those that follow detail the powers and duties of the presidency, describe qualifications for the office and procedures for electing the president, and provide for a vice president.

Article III, Section 1, establishes a Supreme Court to head the judicial branch. The section also gives the national government the power to create lower federal courts. Section 2 outlines the **jurisdiction,** or the authority, of the Supreme Court and other federal courts to rule on cases. Section 3 defines treason against the United States.

Article IV explains the relationship of the states to one another and to the national government. This article requires each state to give citizens of other states the same rights as its own citizens, addresses admitting new states, and guarantees that the national government will protect the states against invasion or domestic violence.

Article V spells out the ways that the Constitution can be amended, or changed. Article VI contains the **supremacy clause,** establishing that the Constitution, laws passed by Congress, and treaties of the United States "shall be the supreme Law of the Land." Finally, Article VII addresses ratification and states that the Constitution would take effect after it was ratified by nine states.

Congressional Quarterly's *Government at a Glance*

Foundations of Personal Liberties

Rights and Freedoms	Magna Carta (1215)	English Bill of Rights (1689)	Virginia Declaration of Rights (1776)	Bill of Rights (1791)
Trial by jury	●	●	●	●
Due process	●	●	●	●
Private property	●		●	●
No unreasonable searches or seizures	●		●	●
No cruel punishment		●	●	●
No excessive bail or fines	●	●	●	●
Right to bear arms		●		●
Right to petition		●		●
Freedom of speech			●	●
Freedom of the press			●	●
Freedom of religion			●	●

Critical Thinking

The above documents granted many liberties at the time they were written; however, these rights were not applied equally to everyone. ***Which three categories of rights were extended by all four documents?***

The Amendments The third part of the Constitution consists of **amendments,** or changes. The Constitution has been amended 27 times throughout the nation's history. The amendment process provides a way this document, written more than two centuries ago, can remain responsive to the needs of a changing nation.

Major Principles

The Constitution rests on six major principles of government: (1) popular sovereignty; (2) federalism; (3) separation of powers; (4) checks and balances; (5) judicial review; and (6) limited government. These principles continue to influence the character of American government.

Popular Sovereignty The Constitution is based on the concept of **popular sovereignty**—rule by the people. United States government is based upon the consent of the governed; the authority for government flows from the people.

Federalism The terms *federalism* and *federal system* describe the basic structure of American government. These terms should not be confused with the term *federal government,* a phrase that simply refers to the national government in Washington, D.C.

The Constitution created a federal system of government. Under **federalism,** power is divided between national and state governments. Both levels have their own agencies and officials, and pass laws that directly affect citizens.

Why did the Founders create such a complex system of government? Why did they choose federalism instead of a unitary form of government in which the central government has all major governing powers? In 1787 there really seemed to be no other choice. The weak union created by the Articles of Confederation[1] had not worked, yet people remained afraid to give all power to a central government. Federalism represented a middle ground—a way to forge a union but limit central power by distributing authority between the states and the national government. Federalism gives the United States a flexible system of government under which the national government has the power to act for the country as a whole, and states have power over many local matters.

See the following footnoted materials in the **Reference Handbook:**
1. *The Articles of Confederation,* pages 808–811.

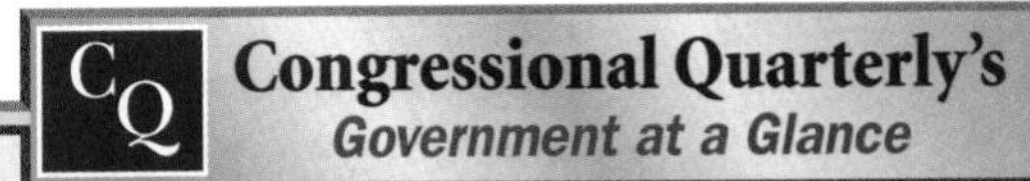

Major Principles of the Constitution

▶ **Popular Sovereignty**

People are the source of government power.

▶ **Federalism**

In this governmental system, power is divided between national and state governments.

▶ **Separation of Powers**

Each of the three branches of government has its own responsibilities.

▶ **Checks and Balances**

Each branch of government holds some control over the other two branches.

▶ **Judicial Review**

Courts have power to declare laws and actions of Congress and the president unconstitutional.

▶ **Limited Government**

The Constitution limits the powers of government by making explicit grants of authority.

Source: Bibby, *Governing by Consent,* 2d ed. (Washington, D.C.: CQ Press, 1995).

Critical Thinking

The principles outlined in the Constitution were the Framers' solution to the complex problems of a representative government. ***What principle allows the president to veto legislation?***

Separation of Powers The Constitution limits the central government by dividing power among the legislative, executive, and judicial branches. Under **separation of powers,** each branch has its responsibilities, a system that the Founders hoped would prevent any branch from gaining too much power.

Checks and Balances To the principle of separation of powers the Founders added a system of **checks and balances,** whereby each branch of government exercises some control over the others. This system works in several ways.

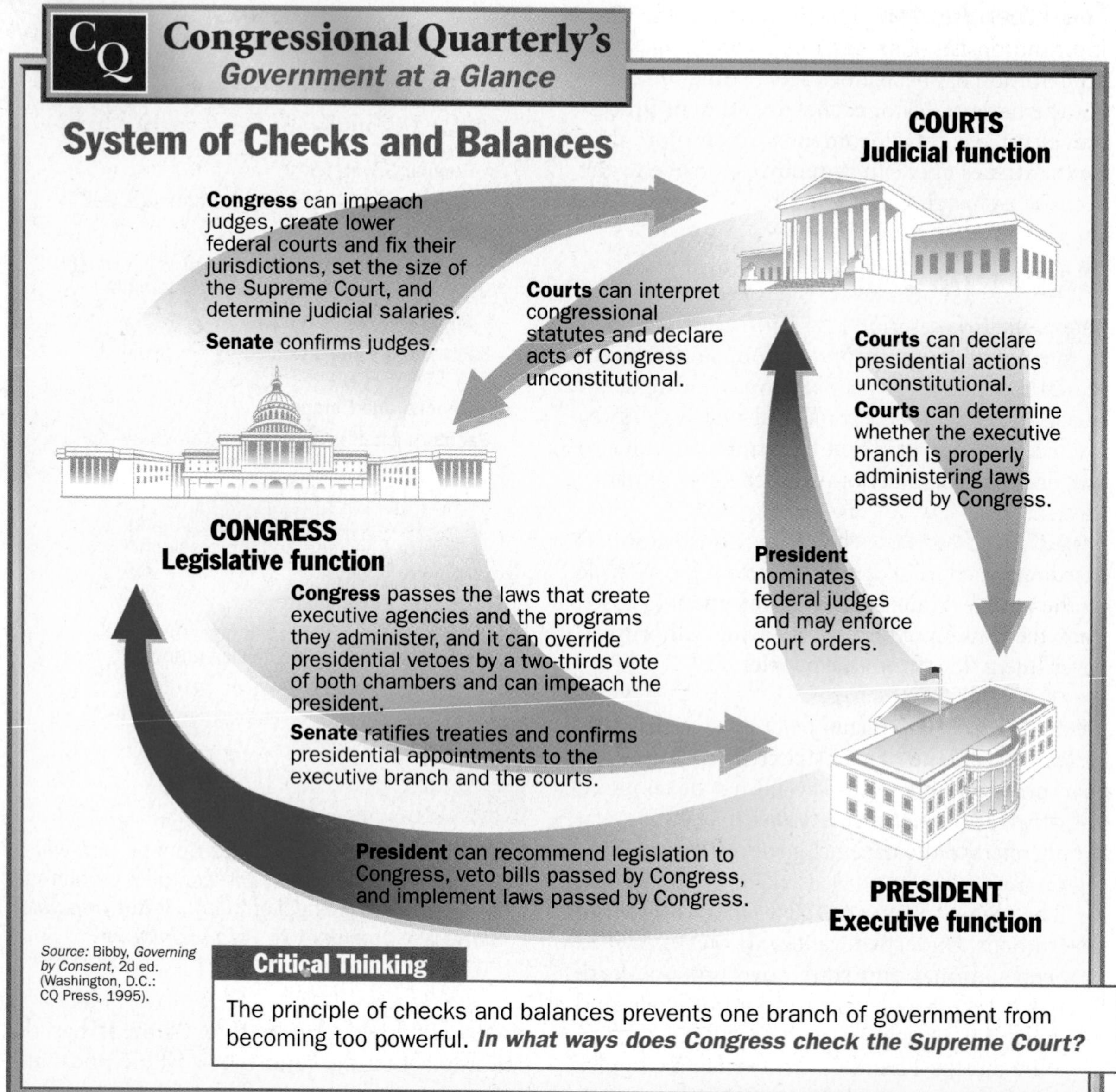

Congress, for example, passes laws. The president can check Congress by rejecting—**vetoing**—its legislation. This veto power is balanced, however, by the power of Congress to override the veto by a two-thirds vote of each house. The federal courts restrain Congress by ruling on the constitutionality of laws. This power of the judicial branch is balanced by the power of the president to appoint federal judges. This presidential power is balanced, in turn, by the Constitution's requirement that the Senate approve appointments. Checks and balances created a system of shared powers.

Judicial Review The power of the courts to declare laws and actions of local, state, or national governments invalid if they violate the Constitution is called **judicial review.** All federal courts have this power, but the Supreme Court is the final authority on the meaning and the interpretation of the Constitution. Because the Constitution is the supreme law of the land, acts contrary to it must be void.

The Founders did not explicitly give such power to the judicial branch. Article III of the Constitution, however, states that "the judicial power shall extend to all cases . . . arising under this Constitution." The Supreme Court in the case of ***Marbury* v. *Madison***[1] in 1803 established the precedent for federal courts to rule on the actions of the government.

The principle of judicial review is important. A Supreme Court decision on the meaning of the Constitution can be changed only if the Court itself changes its views or if an amendment to the Constitution is passed.

Limited Government The principle of limited government means that the Constitution limits the actions of government by specifically listing powers it does and does not have. The first 10 amendments set specific limits in the areas of freedom of expression, personal security, and fair trials.

The Constitution safeguards the nation against abuse of power. In 1974 when President Richard Nixon resigned in the face of evidence that he had acted illegally, President Gerald Ford said:

> *"My fellow Americans, our long national nightmare is over. Our Constitution works. Our great Republic is a government of laws and not of men. Here the people rule."*
>
> —Gerald Ford, 1974

Although the democratic principles that President Ford cited have existed for more than 200 years, the Constitution as it is consistently implemented remains a flexible and dynamic instrument for meeting the changing needs of American government.

Constitutional Safeguards

"It works!"

Checks and Balances The public disclosure of President Nixon's involvement in the Watergate scandal led Congress and the Supreme Court to assert their constitutional powers. ***Explain how the constitutional system of checks and balances supports the theory of separation of powers.***

See the following footnoted materials in the **Reference Handbook:**
1. *Marbury* v. *Madison* case summary, page 761.

Section 1 Assessment

Checking for Understanding

1. **Main Idea** Using a graphic organizer like the one to the right, show how the Constitution divides the powers of the federal government.

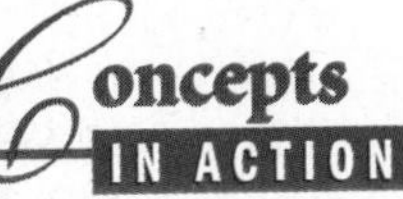

2. **Define** article, jurisdiction, supremacy clause, amendment, popular sovereignty, federalism, separation of powers, checks and balances, veto, judicial review.
3. **Identify** *Marbury* v. *Madison*.
4. What are the six underlying principles of the Constitution?

Critical Thinking

5. **Analyzing Information** What is the relationship between the principles of federalism and the separation of powers as detailed in the Constitution?

Concepts IN ACTION

Constitutional Interpretations One of the major principles of government, as set out in the Constitution, is the principle of checks and balances. Create a diagram showing how a system of checks and balances is provided for in your local government.

Section 2

Three Branches of Government

Reader's Guide

Key Terms

expressed powers, enumerated powers, elastic clause, federal bureaucracy

Find Out

- Why did the Constitution specifically describe the powers of Congress, but remain vague about the powers of the president?
- Which of the three branches of federal government seems to have the most power today?

Understanding Concepts

Separation of Powers What is the chief function of each of the three branches of the federal government?

COVER STORY

Court Says No to Nixon

WASHINGTON, D.C., JULY 1974

The Supreme Court ruled today that President Richard M. Nixon must surrender tape recordings that have long been sought by the House and Senate judiciary committees investigating the 1972 break-in at Democratic Party headquarters. The justices rejected 8-0 the president's argument that recordings of Oval Office conversations are protected by executive privilege and by the doctrine of separation of powers. The Court ordered Nixon to turn over the tapes to Watergate special prosecutor Leon Jaworski. It is widely believed that the tapes contain evidence of the president's involvement in a cover-up of the break-in.

MR. PRESIDENT: RELEASE the TAPES!

A plea for the truth

Article I of the Constitution created a legislature of two houses: the Senate and the House of Representatives. The House was to be the voice of the people, chosen by popular vote. The Senate represented the broad interests of entire states, and senators were originally chosen by their state legislatures. Qualifications for senators were more rigorous than those for members of the House. Yet, in many ways, the House and Senate had equal powers.

Article II created the executive branch of government. The presidency was an entirely new concept in 1787, and the need for the office of the president was hotly debated by the Founders. The provisions for a four-year term, appointment powers, control of the armed forces, and foreign policy decisions were the result of compromises. A president with specified, limited powers was further guarded by an impeachment clause.

Article III established the judicial branch. The Constitution established only one court—the Supreme Court. It gave Congress authority to set up additional courts as the need arose. In recognition of the already operating state courts, the Constitution limited federal jurisdiction to cases arising under the Constitution, the laws of the United States, or to controversies that went outside the jurisdiction of state courts.

The Legislative Branch

The Founders attached great importance to lawmaking and expected Congress to become the most important branch of the national government. At the same time, however, they feared the abuse of power. Their experience with the British Parliament had shown that legislatures with unchecked powers could pass repressive laws and endanger liberty. Consequently, the powers they gave Congress, unlike those enjoyed by the president and the Supreme Court, are **expressed powers,** powers directly stated in the Constitution.

Seats of Governmental Power

Present The U.S. Capitol, located on Capitol Hill, is one of the nation's most familiar landmarks. It contains the current Senate and House chambers. ▶

Past The first seat of Congress contained many symbols, such as an American eagle insignia and 13 arrows and the olive branch united, to mark it as a federal building. ▶

Symbols of Government
What does the U.S. Capitol symbolize to you?

Enumerated Powers

Most of the expressed powers of Congress are itemized in Article I, Section 8. These powers are also called **enumerated powers** because they are numbered 1–18. Five enumerated powers deal with economic legislation—the power to levy taxes, to borrow money, to regulate commerce, to coin money, and to punish counterfeiting. Seven enumerated powers provide for defense—the power to punish piracies, to declare war, to raise and support armed forces, to provide a navy, to regulate the armed forces, to call forth the militia, and to organize the militia. In addition to these powers, Section 8 provides for naturalizing citizens, establishing post offices, securing patents and copyrights, establishing courts, and governing the District of Columbia.

The final enumerated power is the so-called **elastic clause.** This clause gives Congress the right to make all laws "necessary and proper" to carry out the powers expressed in the other clauses of Article I. It is called the elastic clause because it lets Congress "stretch" its powers to meet situations the Founders could never have anticipated.

What does the phrase "necessary and proper" in the elastic clause mean? Almost from the beginning, this phrase was a subject of dispute. The issue was whether a strict or a broad interpretation of the Constitution should be applied. The dispute was first addressed in 1819, in the case of ***McCulloch* v. *Maryland,***[1] when the Supreme Court ruled in favor of a broad interpretation. The Court supported the idea that the elastic clause gave Congress the right to make any laws necessary to carry out its other powers.

Congress Then and Now

The first home of Congress was Federal Hall in lower Manhattan, New York. (It moved to Philadelphia at the end of the first year, 1789.) The House met downstairs; the Senate, on the upper floor. Under the direction of Speaker Fredrick A. Muhlenberg, the House named a committee to establish rules and procedures. As soon as the Senate had its twelfth member—a quorum—it informed the House that it was ready for a joint session to count the electoral votes. House members climbed the stairs and helped count the electoral votes that named George Washington and John Adams president and vice president.

See the following footnoted materials in the ***Reference Handbook:***
1. *McCulloch* v. *Maryland* case summary, page 761.

A Strong Executive

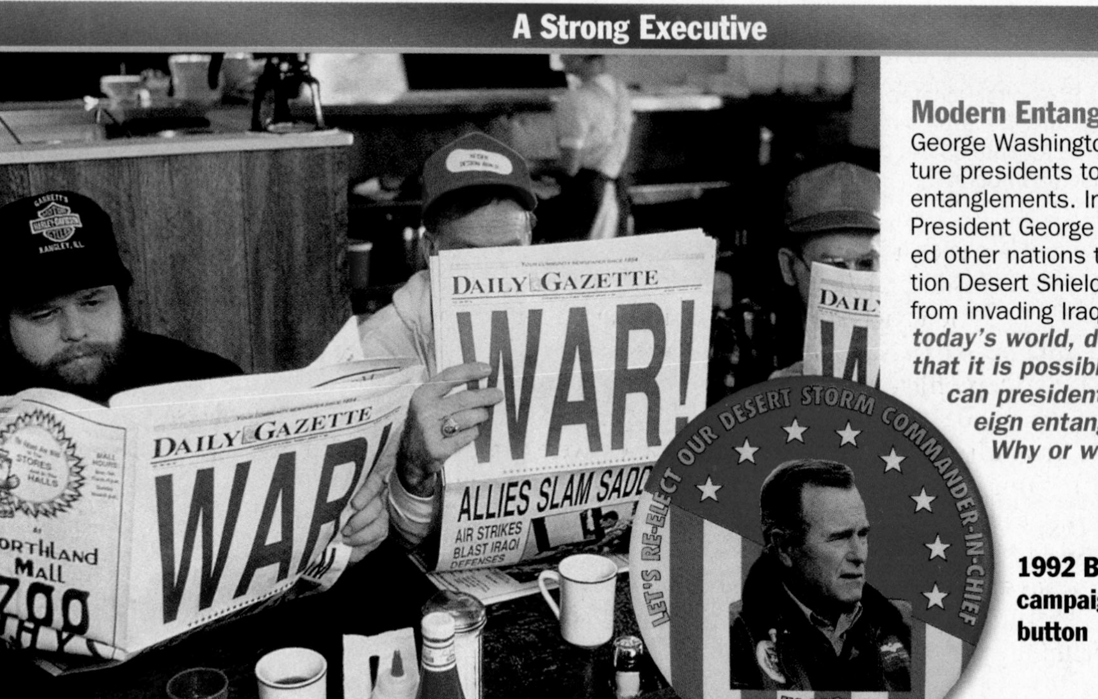

1992 Bush campaign button

Modern Entanglements

George Washington warned future presidents to avoid foreign entanglements. In 1990, though, President George Bush persuaded other nations to join Operation Desert Shield to free Kuwait from invading Iraqi forces. ***In today's world, do you think that it is possible for American presidents to avoid foreign entanglements? Why or why not?***

Once the structure of the House and Senate was in place, each body began to work on legislation. By 1795, four permanent committees were in existence. In the first Congress, the Senate introduced only 5 bills, and the House introduced 26. By comparison, today a total of about 10,000 bills are introduced yearly.

Attendance in legislative sessions was only a part-time job for many years. Members had other jobs or were wealthy enough not to work. Congress did not sit in continuous session until the mid-twentieth century. Today members of Congress live and work nearly year-round in Washington, D.C.

The Executive Branch

The office of the presidency was initiated in response to the weakness of the Articles of Confederation. It was significant that the office was described in the second, not the first, article of the Constitution. Like those of Congress, presidential responsibilities and powers have grown enormously since George Washington took office in 1789.

Vague Constitutional Powers The president is head of the executive branch. The Founders recognized the need for a strong executive to carry out the acts of Congress. They also distrusted direct participation by the people in decision making, fearing that mass democratic movements might try to redistribute personal property. The executive branch, they believed, could protect liberty, private property, and business. The executive branch could also hold the actions of the legislative branch in check.

The Constitution grants the president broad, but vaguely described powers. The exact meaning of the president's power in specific situations is open to interpretation. Article II [1] begins simply by stating: "The executive Power shall be vested in a President of the United States of America." Some scholars call this sentence the "wild card" in the deck of presidential powers. What they mean is that this sentence may be "played," or interpreted, in different ways, like a wild card in a card game. For example, under the executive power, the president can fire officials in the executive branch, make agreements with foreign nations, or take emergency actions to save the nation, even though none of these powers is specifically mentioned in the Constitution.

See the following footnoted materials in the **Reference Handbook:**
1. *The Constitution,* pages 774–799.

Specific Powers Sections 2 and 3 of Article II do define some presidential powers. The president (1) is commander in chief of the armed forces and the state militias (National Guard) when they are called into service; (2) appoints—with the Senate's consent—heads of executive departments (such as the Department of Labor); (3) may pardon people convicted of federal crimes, except in cases of impeachment, or reduce a person's jail sentence or fine; (4) makes treaties with the advice and consent of the Senate; (5) appoints ambassadors, federal court judges, and other top officials, with Senate consent; (6) delivers an annual State of the Union message to Congress and sends Congress other messages from time to time; (7) calls Congress into special session when necessary; (8) meets with heads of state, ambassadors, and other foreign officials; (9) commissions all military officers of the United States; and (10) ensures that the laws Congress passes are "faithfully executed."

The Presidency Then and Now Presidential government was a novel idea in 1789. Much would depend on the character of the person holding the office. Everyone knew, and even discussed openly at the Constitutional Convention, that George Washington was the likely choice. Washington did not seek the office. He wrote his friend, the Marquis de Lafayette:

> "*All that may be necessary to add, my dear Marquis, in order to show my decided predilection [preference], is that (at my time of life and under my circumstances) the [i]ncreasing infirmities of nature and the growing love of retirement do not permit me to entertain a wish beyond that of living and dying an honest man on my own farm.*"
>
> —George Washington

When pressed into service, Washington was very careful about the discharge of his duties, knowing that every act would set a precedent. Inundated with requests for jobs in the executive branch, he refused to show any partiality to friends and relatives. After two terms he retired to private life, stating that two terms were sufficient for anyone.

Early presidents would not recognize the office today. President Washington had so little to do on some days that he advertised in the newspaper the times when he would entertain visitors. He held tea parties for anyone "properly attired" on Friday evenings. Washington had only a handful of advisers and staff. By 1800, when President Adams moved to Washington, D.C., the second president's papers were packed in only seven boxes.

In contrast, modern presidents' schedules are timed minute by minute. Presidents preside over a White House staff numbering in the hundreds, a military force of millions, and a vast **federal bureaucracy** made up of all executive branch employees. The Chief Executive meets with officials on a tight schedule, often working into the night. A fleet of airplanes and helicopters stands ready to carry the president and close advisers to any part of the nation or the world.

A Changing Office

Presidential Leadership George Washington set many precedents as president. Washington, although a brilliant leader, was cautious. During the Civil War, President Lincoln boldly used measures to quiet opposition, even though such measures violated constitutional guarantees of free speech, press, and assembly. ***What outside forces shaped Washington and Lincoln's view of the presidency?***

The Judicial Branch

If judged by the length of Article III, the judicial branch appears to be the weakest of the branches of government. After naming the Supreme Court, the Constitution allows Congress to establish all "inferior" courts. The Framers were not concerned about the power of the justices, allowing them to hold office for life.

Jurisdiction of Federal Courts The judiciary of the United States has two different systems of courts. One system consists of the federal courts, whose powers derive from the Constitution and federal laws. The other includes the courts of each of the 50 states, whose powers derive from state constitutions and laws. Some have described the two-court systems existing side by side as a dual court system.

Every court has the authority to hear only certain kinds of cases. This authority is known as the jurisdiction of the court. Two factors determine the jurisdiction of federal courts—the subject matter of the case and the parties involved in it. Federal courts try cases that involve United States laws, treaties with foreign nations, or interpretations of the Constitution. Cases involving admiralty or maritime law—the law of the sea, including ships, their crews, and disputes over actions and rights at sea—also come under federal court jurisdiction. Federal courts also try cases involving bankruptcy.

Federal Courts Then and Now When the federal government moved to Washington, D.C., in 1800, the capital architects forgot to design a building for the Supreme Court! Two weeks before the start of its term, the Court was assigned a small

We the People

Making a Difference

Sam and Geeta Dardick

Access for those with disabilities

Sam Dardick had polio as a child, resulting in permanent physical disability. Every day he faces obstacles that go unnoticed by most people without disabilities. Climbing stairs, boarding buses, and maneuvering in small public restrooms are a challenge for someone in a wheelchair.

In the 1960s Sam married. His wife, Geeta, who does not have a disability, started to see firsthand some of the challenges her husband faced. At the time there were no national laws requiring businesses to provide access to people with disabilities. "Sam's wheelchair was a problem for both of us. We'd try to rent an apartment and find that 100 percent of them had stairs. We'd go to the movies: stairs again. We'd plan to take the bus . . . more stairs," she said.

When the Dardicks moved to California in the 1970s, they found that the state had wheelchair accessibility laws but needed help to enforce them. Geeta and Sam worked thousands of hours to raise community awareness and to police the construction sites of new buildings to make sure people with disabilities were taken into consideration. "We marched for access to public transportation in San Francisco, testified for accessible apartments in Sacramento, busted inaccessible city council meetings in Nevada City, and started an Independent Living Center in Grass Valley," Geeta said.

The Dardicks helped to bring about the passage of the Americans with Disabilities Act (ADA) in 1990. This was the first national civil rights bill for people with disabilities. The law requires all public places to be wheelchair accessible. It also prohibits job discrimination against persons with physical or mental disabilities.

chamber on the main floor of the Capitol. In the beginning, justices of the Supreme Court were assigned to "ride circuit," meaning that when the Supreme Court was not in session, they had to hear appeals in faraway district courts. John Jay, the first chief justice, who resigned in 1795, later declined President Adams's nomination to serve again because of the strain of such duty.

Congress created the modern federal court system in 1891, but the Supreme Court did not have its own building until 1935. Despite this humble history, the Supreme Court today heads a powerful branch of government. It has carved out power in a number of landmark cases beginning with *Marbury* v. *Madison* in 1803. In that case Chief Justice John Marshall announced that the Judiciary Act of 1789 gave the Court more power than the Constitution allowed. Thus, the act was unconstitutional. The power to declare laws unconstitutional, known as judicial review, elevated the Supreme Court to a status balancing the powers of the other branches.

The Early Presidency

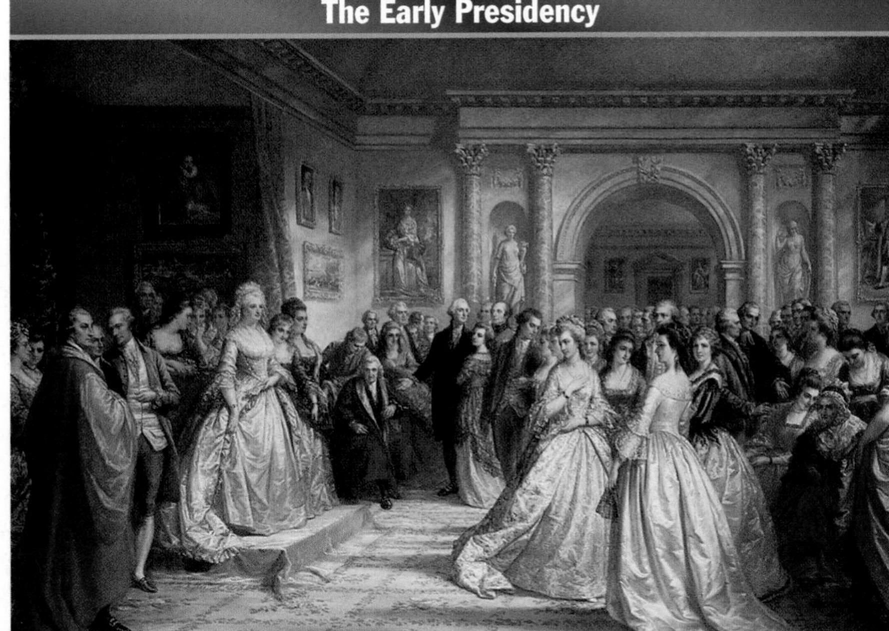

Constitutional Interpretations Shown here in *The Republican Court* by Daniel Huntington, the president held this reception in New York City in 1789 to honor his wife, Martha. In his spare time, Washington often entertained guests. ***Why have the president's duties increased over the past 200 years?***

When it rules on constitutional issues, the Supreme Court cannot be overturned except by a constitutional amendment. But Congress can effectively overturn a Supreme Court decision interpreting a federal statute by enacting a new law.

Shared Power and Conflict

The Constitution created three separate branches of government. It spelled out some specific areas in which those branches would cooperate, such as in passing legislation, conducting war, and spending money. Many of the working relationships among the three branches, however, are not specifically mentioned in the Constitution. These relationships developed over time during the normal ebb and flow of government operation and policy creation.

The President as Legislator The executive and legislative branches must work together closely in order for legislation to become effective policy. Without cooperation among the branches the government can do little, if anything, to address the nation's problems or serve its needs.

In practice, the executive branch provides plans for much of the legislation that Congress considers. The presidential initiative in legislation is mentioned in Article II, Section 3, of the Constitution:

> "*He shall, from time to time, give the Congress information of the state of the Union, and recommend to their consideration such measures as he shall judge necessary and expedient . . . .*"
>
> —Article II, Section 3

The president proposes much of the legislative agenda and spells out the details of programs that are enacted into law. In order for programs to be

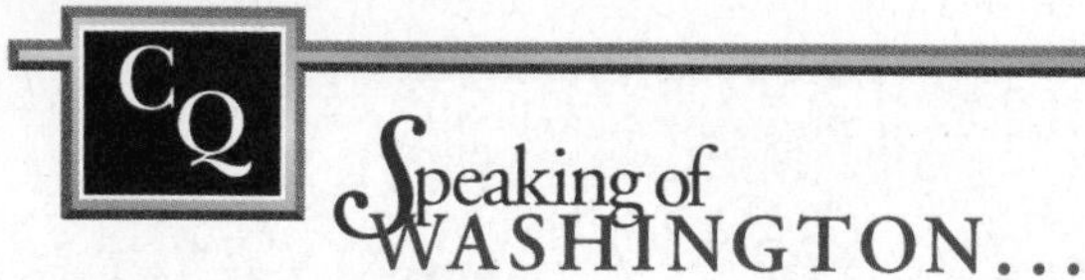

In the Vault **The engrossed (handwritten) original copies of the Declaration of Independence, the Constitution, and the Bill of Rights rest securely on a movable platform at the National Archives in Washington, D.C. Every night after the last visitor has left, these "Charters of Freedom" are lowered 20 feet into a 55-ton vault designed to withstand a nuclear blast.**

effective, the executive branch must have the power to carry out legislative enactments. This often involves creation of a bureaucracy to carry out the details of policy.

The President vs. Congress While cooperation between the executive and legislative branches is necessary, several sources of conflict between these two branches have developed. The expansion of presidential power has changed the structure of the national government without formal changes in the Constitution. The growing power of the executive has, at times, troubled Congress. At other times, presidents have charged Congress with attempts to encroach upon executive power.

Another source of conflict between the branches stems from the responsibility of Congress to monitor the way the executive branch enforces the laws. Sometimes the two branches quarrel over the way the president interprets the will of Congress in bills it has passed. When this happens, the federal courts may be called upon to interpret the intent of Congress on a case-by-case basis.

Occasionally, however, Congress has been accused of yielding too much power to the Chief Executive. For example, in 1935 the Supreme Court nullified the law creating the National Recovery Administration (NRA). In the majority opinion Chief Justice Hughes said:

> "*Congress cannot delegate legislative power to the President to exercise an unfettered discretion to make whatever laws he thinks may be needed or advisable for the rehabilitation and expansion of trade or industry.*"
>
> —Charles Evans Hughes, 1935

Finally, the development of political parties has created a source of conflict. If the executive office is controlled by one party and the legislature by another party, cooperation is unlikely. Each party has a different agenda, different constituents to please, and even a different philosophy of government. At best, different parties in the executive and legislative branches develop carefully studied compromise policies. At worst, they develop gridlock in which nothing productive can be accomplished.

Congress vs. the Courts The Constitution gave Congress power both to create the lower federal courts and to limit the jurisdiction of the Supreme Court. Congress, however, has been

The President and Congress

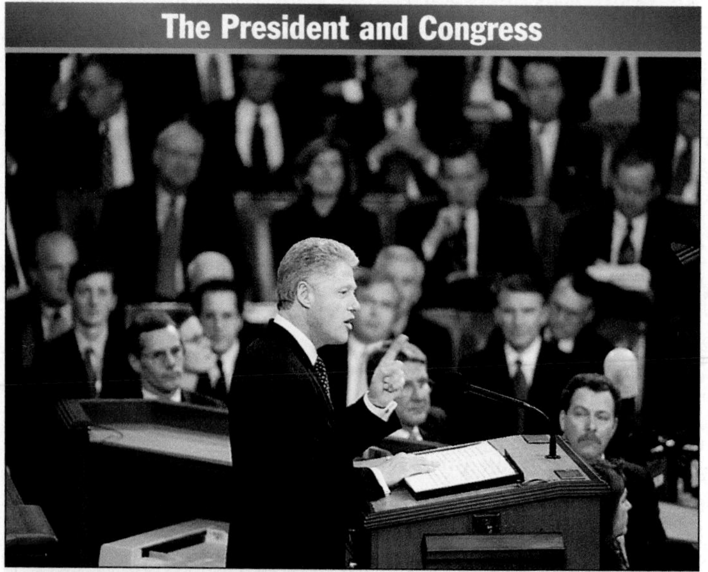

Legislative Proposals President Clinton outlines his legislative proposals to Congress. ***What is the purpose of the president's annual State of the Union Address?***

NRA quilt

A Time of Crisis

Separation of Powers
President Roosevelt's New Deal policies challenged many of the traditional views on the separation of powers. ***How can a time of crisis affect the public's opinion on the role of the national government?***

reluctant to use this authority. When the Supreme Court in 1964 ruled that both houses of state legislatures must be reapportioned on a population basis, the United States House of Representatives passed a bill to strip the Supreme Court and all federal courts of jurisdiction over state legislative redistricting. The Senate, however, killed the bill.

The Supreme Court vs. the President

Some Supreme Court decisions require compliance by the president in order that the decisions may be carried out. Occasionally, a president who disagrees with the Court may refuse to enforce its decision. In the 1830s, the Court upheld the rights of the Cherokee against the state of Georgia. It denied the state of Georgia the power to pass laws affecting Native Americans living there. President Andrew Jackson, however, refused to provide military force to carry out the Court order. In another instance, President Franklin Roosevelt indicated he would not obey adverse decisions in two separate pending cases. In both instances the Court avoided conflict by ruling in favor of the president.

Section 2 Assessment

Checking for Understanding

1. **Main Idea** Using a Venn diagram, show the different functions of the president and Congress in passing legislation and the functions they share.

   President | both | Congress

2. **Define** expressed powers, enumerated powers, elastic clause, federal bureaucracy.
3. **Identify** *McCulloch* v. *Maryland.*
4. Identify five powers of the president.
5. What two systems of courts make up the judiciary of the United States?
6. How can Supreme Court decisions be overturned?

Critical Thinking

7. **Making Comparisons** What information would you need to determine which branch of the federal government has the greatest power? Formulate questions to obtain needed information.

Separation of Powers One of the cases heard by the Supreme Court involved the ruling that televising court proceedings does not necessarily deny defendants the right to a fair trial. Conduct an opinion poll to find out whether people favor or oppose televised trials. Chart the responses and summarize the poll results.

Section 3

Amending the Constitution

Reader's Guide

Key Terms

ratify, petition, balanced budget, impeach, treaty, executive agreement, judicial restraint, judicial activism

Find Out

- How does the amendment process illustrate federalism?
- What are the primary ways that informal changes are made in the Constitution?

Understanding Concepts

Political Processes Why did the Framers make the Constitution difficult to amend?

COVER STORY

Madison's Amendment

WASHINGTON, D.C., MAY 1992

The Twenty-seventh Amendment to the Constitution was ratified by Michigan, the necessary thirty-eighth state today, 203 years after it was proposed. The measure that prevents Congress from voting itself a pay raise stunned government leaders. James Madison offered the amendment in 1789, but it was never adopted. Ten years ago, Gregory Watson, then a 20-year-old student at the University of Texas, discovered the forgotten amendment while doing research for a school paper. Now an aide to a Texas state legislator, Watson made the amendment's passage his crusade. In 1991 the Senate's unpopular pay hike rallied support for his cause.

James Madison

The nation that the Founders wanted to perfect in 1787 consisted of fewer than 4 million people living in 13 agricultural states along the Atlantic coast of North America. More than two centuries later, that same Constitution provides the foundation for governing an industrial and highly technological nation of more than 275 million people in 50 states spread across the continent and beyond. The priceless heritage of the Constitution has been its ability to adapt to new conditions while preserving the basic form of American government. The words of Chief Justice John Marshall in 1819 remain true today:

> "*We must never forget that it is . . . a Constitution intended to endure for ages to come, and, consequently, to be adapted to the various crises of human affairs.*"
>
> —John Marshall, 1819

The Amendment Process

The Founders created a Constitution that could be adapted to a future they could not foresee. One way they provided for change was to describe how Congress and the states could amend the Constitution. As outlined in Article V, amendments may deal with any topic except that no state can lose equal representation in the Senate without the state's consent.

Amendments may be proposed and **ratified,** or approved, in two ways. Regardless of the proposal and ratification methods used, however, the amendment process illustrates the federal system of American government. Amendments are proposed at a national level, but they are ratified on a state-by-state basis.

Proposing Amendments One method of proposing an amendment is by a two-thirds vote of each house of Congress. This is the only method that has been used to date. Dozens of resolutions asking for constitutional amendments are introduced in Congress each year. In recent years, suggestions have been made to put limits on income taxes, to limit the tenure of Supreme Court justices to 12 years, and to give states complete control of oil deposits within their borders. None have won the necessary two-thirds vote.

The other method for proposing amendments is by a national convention called by Congress at the request of two-thirds of the states. This method has never been used, but in recent history it has almost occurred twice. In 1963 states began to **petition**, or appeal to, Congress for a convention to propose an amendment to overturn Supreme Court decisions affecting the election of state lawmakers. By 1967, 33 state legislatures, only 1 short of the required two-thirds, had voted for such a convention. The campaign failed, however, when no other states voted for the convention.

Between 1975 and 1991, 32 state legislatures petitioned Congress for a convention to propose an amendment requiring a **balanced budget**—one in which the federal government's spending never exceeds its income. By 2000 federal revenues exceeded expenses and most Americans lost interest in a balanced budget amendment.

The convention method of proposing amendments is controversial, because such a convention is not required to limit itself to a specific amendment. President Jimmy Carter in the 1970s cautioned that a convention for a federal budget amendment might be "completely uncontrollable." Legal scholars warned that such a convention could propose amendments on any subject.

Ratifying Amendments When an amendment is proposed, Congress chooses one of two methods for states to approve it. One way is for legislatures in three-fourths of the states to ratify the amendment. The other is for each state to call a special ratifying convention. The amendment becomes part of the Constitution when three-fourths of these conventions approve it.

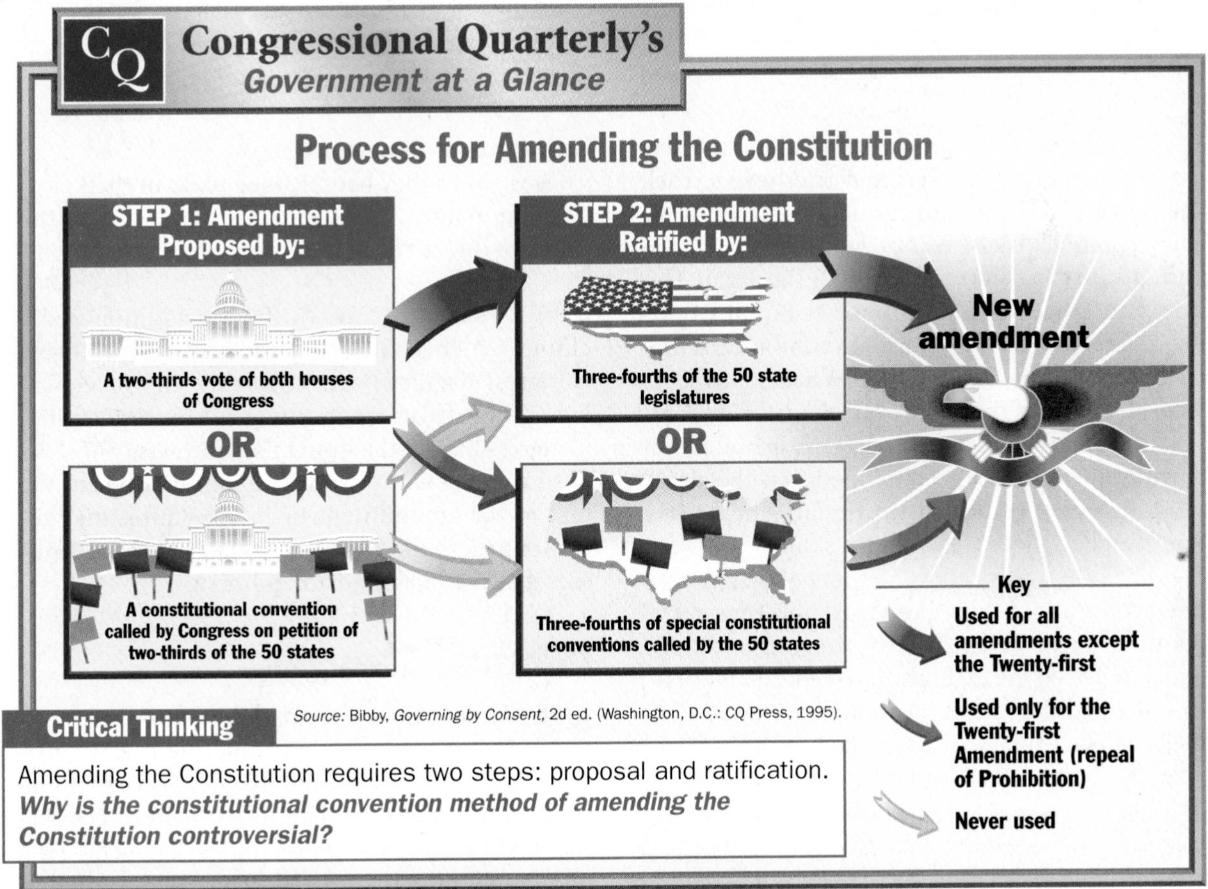

Source: Bibby, *Governing by Consent*, 2d ed. (Washington, D.C.: CQ Press, 1995).

Critical Thinking

Amending the Constitution requires two steps: proposal and ratification. ***Why is the constitutional convention method of amending the Constitution controversial?***

Political Processes Congress approved the ERA in 1972, but it ran into opposition when it was sent to the states for ratification. ***Do you think the Framers of the Constitution made it too difficult to amend the Constitution? Explain.***

ERA button

If a state rejects an amendment in the state legislature method, lawmakers may later reverse their decision and ratify the amendment. Suppose, however, a state legislature approves an amendment and then revokes the ratification. Is this legal? This question arose over the proposed **Equal Rights Amendment (ERA)** that would prohibit discrimination on the basis of gender. When 5 of the 35 state legislatures that approved the ERA later revoked their ratification, questions arose. Many constitutional scholars contended that the states' revocations were unconstitutional. The courts, however, have never resolved the issue.

The other ratification method—by state ratifying conventions—has been used only once. Conventions ratified the Twenty-first Amendment, which repealed the Eighteenth Amendment (1919) that banned the sale of alcoholic beverages. Congress let each state legislature determine how the ratifying conventions would be organized and the delegates elected. Delegates in each state ran for election statewide either on a pledge to support the amendment or on a pledge to reject it. Then, at each state ratifying convention, the elected delegates voted as they had pledged to do in their election campaigns. In effect, this method gave the people a direct voice in the amending process.

Congress Sets the Rules In addition to deciding which ratification method will be used, Congress decides how much time the states will have to ratify an amendment. In modern times, Congress has set the limit at seven years.

Congress can put the time limit either in the text of the amendment or in legislation that accompanies the amendment. Placing a time limit can alter the fate of an amendment.

Informal Changes

Although formal amendments have played an important role in making it a "living" document, the Constitution has kept pace with the times and has grown as an instrument of government through informal change as well. This process does not involve changes in the wording of the Constitution itself. Rather, informal changes occur as government leaders and citizens fill in the details of government on a day-to-day, year-to-year basis to suit the needs of the times.

Changes Through Law Congress has passed laws that have enlarged or clarified many of the Constitution's provisions. The Founders expected Congress to do this, and they gave it authority to spell out many details of the national government.

Article I, for example, gives Congress the power to "lay and collect taxes." But what does this provision mean? Congress has applied the taxing authority of the Constitution and expanded its meaning by passing complex tax laws that fill many volumes.

The same is true of the executive branch that Article II of the Constitution established. Congress has greatly expanded the executive branch by creating the cabinet departments, agencies, boards, and commissions.

In Article III, the Founders created "one Supreme Court" and other courts "as the Congress may . . . establish." Congress completed the judicial branch by passing the Judiciary Act of 1789.

Over the years, Congress has changed the judicial branch many times in response to new conditions. As the nation expanded and the number of court cases increased, Congress created additional federal courts, established new rules of federal court procedure, and provided for court workers such as bailiffs and clerks.

Changes Through Practices Congress has also shaped the Constitution by the way it has used its other powers. Under the Constitution, the House may **impeach,** or accuse, federal officials—including the president—while it is up to the Senate to determine the accused person's guilt or innocence. Article II states that:

> "*The President, Vice-President, and all civil Officers of the United States shall be removed from Office on Impeachment for, and Conviction of, Treason, Bribery, or other high Crimes and Misdemeanors.*"
>
> —Article II, Section 4

The meanings of *treason* and *bribery* are clear, but what about "high crimes and misdemeanors"? This is up to Congress to decide. Congress has investigated more than 60 people on impeachment charges, including three presidents—Andrew Johnson, Richard Nixon, and Bill Clinton.

Proposing an Amendment

More than 10,000 proposals for amendments to the Constitution have been introduced in Congress since 1789. Anyone can initiate an amendment simply by writing a proposal for amending the Constitution to a member of Congress.

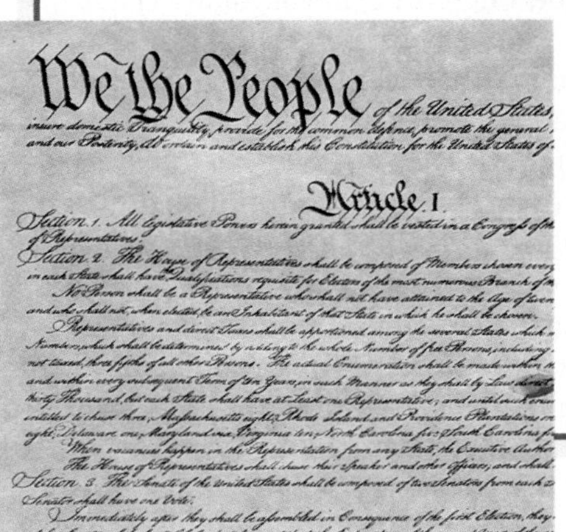

Activity

Select an issue you believe the Constitution needs to address and propose an amendment. Use existing amendments as guides for form and language to write your own amendment. Follow these guidelines when writing your proposal:

- Explain what your proposed amendment will do.
- Explain why you believe it is needed and how the nation will benefit if it is ratified.
- Indicate what opposition you expect there to be to your amendment and why.
- Suggest arguments that could be used to reply to criticism of your amendment.

Submit your proposed amendment in a letter to a member of Congress.

The Constitution

Veto Power

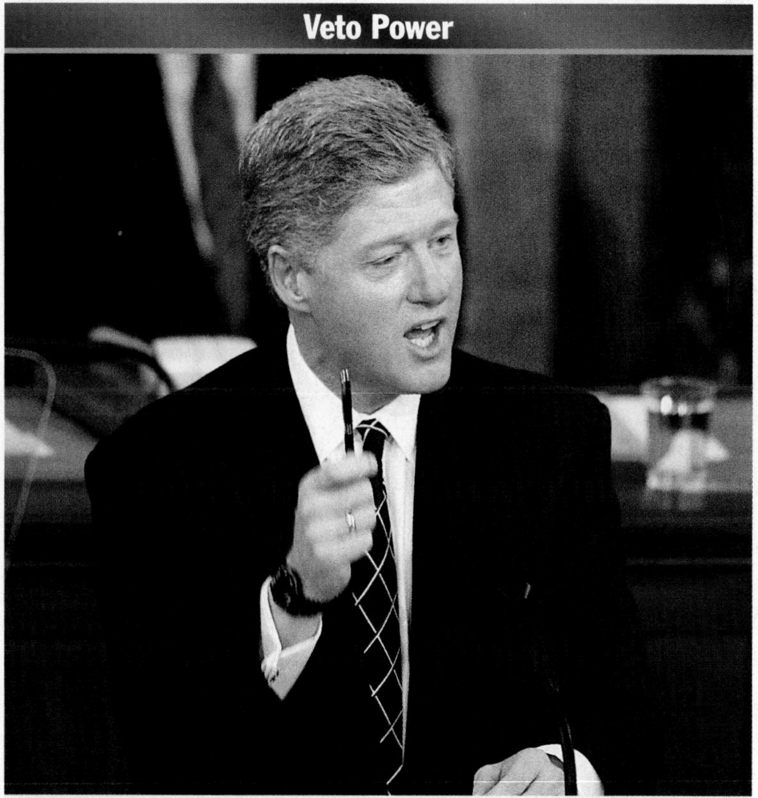

Presidential Influence Clinton warns Congress that if they do not "send me legislation that guarantees every American private health insurance . . . you will force me to take this pen [and] veto the legislation." ***How does the influence modern presidents have on legislation differ from what the Founders intended?***

Informal Presidential Changes

Presidential actions have also added to the Constitution. Many of these additions affect the workings of the modern presidency.

Presidential Succession In 1841 William Henry Harrison became the first president to die in office. As provided in the Constitution, Vice President John Tyler assumed the powers of president. But did Tyler actually become president, or would he merely act as president until the next election?

Tyler took the presidential oath of office. Many officials opposed Tyler's interpretation of the Constitution, but no one successfully challenged him. Not until 1967, when the Twenty-fifth Amendment clarified presidential succession, was Tyler's precedent formally endorsed in the Constitution.

Foreign Affairs Modern presidents usually conduct foreign affairs by executive agreement, instead of using the treaty process specified in the Constitution. While a **treaty** is an agreement between nations, an **executive agreement** is made directly between the president and the head of state of another country; it does not require Senate approval.

Domestic Affairs The Founders thought the executive branch would be concerned mostly with carrying out laws initiated by Congress. Yet in this century, presidents have been aggressive in requesting legislation from Congress.

These practices have become important precedents for building the power of the president. Today the president plays a far greater role in American government and politics than most of the Founders ever imagined.

Court Decisions

As federal courts settle cases involving constitutional questions, they interpret the meaning of the Constitution's sometimes vague words and phrases. The Supreme Court, the nation's highest court, plays a key role in this process.

Judicial Review The most important device the Court uses to interpret the Constitution is judicial review. Although the principle of judicial review is well established, people continue to disagree over how the Court should use this power. Some advocate judicial restraint; others argue for judicial activism.

The philosophy of **judicial restraint** holds that the Court should avoid taking the initiative on social and political questions. The Court should uphold acts of Congress unless the acts clearly violate a specific provision of the Constitution. In other words, advocates of judicial restraint want the Court to leave the policy making to others.

The philosophy of **judicial activism,** on the other hand, holds that the Court should play a role in shaping national policies. The Court should apply the Constitution to social and political questions. The Supreme Court under **Chief Justice Earl Warren**—from 1953 to 1969—accepted cases involving many controversial issues, particularly civil rights and the rights of the accused.

Because the Warren Court is considered an activist Court, people today associate judicial activism with civil rights or social issues. History suggests, however, that the justices' activism may justify their individual choices in any area of policy. Thus, judicial activism may mark either a conservative or liberal court. For example, in the 1920s conservative justices frequently took activist positions against government regulation of the economy.

Since the 1940s, however, most activist policies have been in support of civil liberties. Political liberals have tended to support activism, while conservatives have argued for judicial restraint.

Changing Court Rulings Social and political conditions of the times often affect Court interpretations of the Constitution. The Supreme Court has sometimes ruled that the Constitution means one thing and then, years later, reversed itself. In 1896, for example, the Court ruled that separate public facilities for African Americans were constitutional as long as those facilities were equal. More than a half century later, in 1954, the Court reversed its position when it decided to outlaw racial segregation in public schools.

Changes Through Custom and Usage

The Constitution has been informally enlarged through customs that have developed over time. Political parties are a good example. The Constitution does not mention political parties, but they began soon after the government was organized and have been an important part of American government since then. Today parties help organize government and conduct elections.

The amendments added to the Constitution and the changes achieved through precedent and practice have created a government that can respond to the conditions and needs of the times. Thus, this short, simple document has continued for more than two centuries to serve as the supreme law of the land.

GOVERNMENT Online

Student Web Activity Visit the *United States Government: Democracy in Action* Web site at gov.glencoe.com and click on ***Chapter 3–Student Web Activities*** for an activity about amending the Constitution.

Section 3 Assessment

Checking for Understanding

1. **Main Idea** Using a graphic organizer like the one below, describe at least one way Congress and the Supreme Court each have changed the Constitution.

Changes in the Constitution	
By Congress	
By Supreme Court	

2. **Define** ratify, petition, balanced budget, impeach, treaty, executive agreement, judicial restraint, judicial activism.
3. **Identify** Equal Rights Amendment (ERA), Chief Justice Earl Warren.
4. Identify the two methods of ratifying amendments.

Critical Thinking

5. **Identifying Central Issues** How have the four informal methods of amending the Constitution affected the role of the executive branch in the federal government?

Concepts IN ACTION

Political Processes Do you think the Founders were correct in allowing the Constitution to be amended? Write a letter to the editor of a local newspaper explaining your position on this issue.

Youngstown Sheet and Tube Company v. Sawyer, 1952

Harry S Truman

The Constitution provides for a separation of powers. In 1952 President Harry Truman tested the meaning of this principle. During the Korean War he seized control of the nation's steel mills to prevent a strike by workers even though no law authorized him to do so. The Supreme Court settled the issue in the case of Youngstown Sheet and Tube Company *v.* Sawyer.

Background of the Case

During the Korean War the nation's steelworkers announced they were going to strike. President Truman's advisers warned him that a halt in steel production could endanger the lives of American soldiers. Truman issued Executive Order #10340 directing Secretary of Commerce Charles Sawyer to take control of the country's steel mills. The steel companies attacked the executive order as unconstitutional and went to court. Truman could have dealt with the strike by using the Taft-Hartley Act, but he chose not to do so. This law, passed by Congress over Truman's veto in 1947, authorized the president to get a court order delaying a strike for 80 days. During this "cooling off" period, the companies and workers could try to reach agreement. The president thought the law was antilabor, and he refused to use it.

The Constitutional Issue

Government lawyers argued that the president's authority as chief executive gave him the right to keep steel production going in times of war and national emergency. Further, they argued that under Article II his power as commander in chief of the armed forces allowed the president to take whatever actions were necessary to protect the lives of American troops.

The steel companies claimed the president's order clearly violated the Constitution. In issuing the order, Truman was actually making a law—a power given only to Congress by the Constitution. The Taft-Hartley Act set forth procedures for handling a strike. Nothing in the Constitution or existing laws gave the president power to seize private property. According to the steel companies, the president had clearly exceeded his authority under the Constitution.

Debating the Case

Questions to Consider

1. Do you think the president was, in effect, making law when he issued the executive order?
2. During a grave national crisis such as the Korean War, should a president be allowed to exercise unusual powers?
3. Does the principle of separation of powers limit the powers a president can derive from the Constitution even in times of national emergency?

You Be the Judge

In your opinion, was President Truman's order constitutional? The separation of powers is not absolute. Each branch of government shares in the work and power of the others. There have been numerous examples of presidential lawmaking. Jefferson bought Louisiana and Lincoln freed enslaved persons without waiting for Congress to pass laws. Was Truman's executive order within the powers of the president?

Section 4

The Amendments

Reader's Guide

Key Terms

prior restraint, probable cause, search warrant, arrest warrant, due process of law, eminent domain, lame duck, poll tax

Find Out

- Why is it important in a democratic society that the government follow due process of law when trying suspected criminals?
- How do the amendments to the Constitution show the development of democracy in the United States?

Understanding Concepts

Growth of Democracy How do the amendments reflect changes in society's perception of rights under the Constitution?

COVER STORY

What Bill of Rights?

WASHINGTON, D.C., DECEMBER 1991

Only one in three Americans knows what the Bill of Rights is, according to a poll commissioned by the American Bar Association. The survey offered a series of multiple choice questions to 507 participants. Thirty-three percent correctly identified the Bill of Rights as the first 10 amendments to the Constitution; but 28 percent said it was the Constitution's Preamble. Another 7 percent confused it with the Declaration of Independence, and 10 percent simply didn't know. Fewer than 1 in 10 knew why the Bill of Rights was adopted.

Polling Americans

Despite the difficulty of the amendment process, Americans put it to work almost before the ink was dry on the new Constitution. Because critics attacked the proposed Constitution for not protecting the rights of the people, the Founders promised to add a list of such rights. The first Congress quickly proposed 12 amendments and sent them to the states for ratification. In 1791 the states ratified 10 of the amendments, which became known as the **Bill of Rights.** The first proposed amendment, dealing with representation in the House, was never ratified. The second, dealing with congressional salaries, was not ratified until 1992.

The Bill of Rights

The Bill of Rights limits the powers of government. Its purpose is to protect the rights of individual liberty, such as freedom of speech, and rights of persons accused of crimes, such as the right to trial by jury.

When the Constitution was adopted, some state constitutions had bills of rights. Thus it seemed necessary and reasonable to add similar limits to the new national government. Although the Bill of Rights originally applied only to the national government, almost all its provisions have been applied to the states through a series of Supreme Court decisions.

The First Amendment One of the most important amendments in the Bill of Rights, the First Amendment states:

> "*Congress shall make no law respecting an establishment of religion, or prohibiting the free exercise thereof; or abridging the freedom of speech, or of the press; or the right of the people peaceably to assemble, and to petition the Government for a redress of grievances.*"
>
> —First Amendment, 1791

The First Amendment protects the right of Americans to worship as they please, or to have no religion if they prefer. Thus, unlike many nations, the United States does not have an official religion, nor does the government favor one religion over another. These principles are known as freedom of religion and separation of church and state.

In addition, the First Amendment protects freedom of speech and freedom of the press. The government cannot prevent individuals from freely expressing their opinions. Citizens thus have the right to criticize government officials and decisions, and they are allowed to spread unpopular ideas.

The First Amendment protects not only individual speech, but also extends to the circulation of ideas in newspapers, books, magazines, radio, television, and, to some extent, movies. Unlike the press in some other countries, the American press is not subject to **prior restraint**—that is, government censorship of information before it is published or broadcast.

Freedom Within Limits The freedoms of speech and the press are not unlimited, however. For example, laws prohibit slander and libel. **Slander** is false speech intended to damage a person's reputation. **Libel** is similar to slander, except that it applies to written or published statements. Endangering the nation's safety by giving away military secrets or calling for the violent overthrow of the government also are not protected. In addition, the courts have held that speech should be responsible. For example, no one has the right to cry "Fire!" in a crowded theater just to see what happens.

Another freedom the First Amendment protects is the right to assemble in groups and hold demonstrations. People may pass out pamphlets, hold meetings, and do other things that peaceably call attention to their beliefs. Courts have ruled, however, that the government can require a group to obtain a permit before holding meetings or demonstrations.

Finally, the First Amendment protects the right to criticize government officials and their actions. The rights to sign petitions in support of an idea, to present those petitions to government officials, and to send letters to those officials are all protected.

The Second Amendment This amendment ensures citizens and the nation the right to security. It states:

THE LAW *and You*

Limits to Free Speech

The First Amendment guarantees Americans the right to express their thoughts and opinions. However, this is not an absolute freedom. Some types of speech are not protected by the First Amendment, and engaging in such speech may result in civil or criminal penalties.

For example, you may not make any public statement on private property without the owner's permission, nor can you ever urge listeners to commit a crime. Also, you cannot, either publicly or in private conversations, make damaging statements about a person that you know to be untrue. Obviously, threats of violence and statements that constitute sexual harassment are not protected forms of expression, nor is obscene language in many situations.

Be aware that "speech" involves more than spoken words. Signs, posters, pamphlets, printed T-shirts, and other "writings" are among many modes of expression that the courts consider to be speech.

Practicing free speech

Participating IN GOVERNMENT ACTIVITY

Ask First Would passing out flyers in a store's parking lot to advertise a school event be a First Amendment right? Call a few businesses to find out their policy regarding flyers.

> *"A well-regulated Militia being necessary to the security of a free State, the right of the people to keep and bear Arms shall not be infringed."*
>
> —Second Amendment, 1791

Originally, the Second Amendment was intended to prevent the national government from repeating actions that the British had taken. Before the Revolution, the British tried to take weapons away from colonial **militia,** or armed forces of citizens.

This amendment seems to support the right for citizens to own firearms, but it does not prevent Congress from regulating the interstate sale of weapons, nor has the Supreme Court applied the Second Amendment to the states. States are free to regulate the use and sale of firearms.

A Living Constitution

"Now that's the kind of thing that calls for a constitutional amendment."

Constitutional Amendments Few constitutional amendments survive the ratification process to become part of the Constitution. ***Why do you think the Framers wanted all amendments approved by representatives of the people?***

The Third Amendment This amendment prohibits the government from forcing people to quarter—to provide shelter for—soldiers in their homes, another British practice before the Revolution. In times of war, however, Congress may require a homeowner to house soldiers but only under conditions clearly spelled out by law.

The Fourth Amendment The Fourth Amendment reflects the early Americans' desire to protect their privacy. Britain had used writs of assistance—general search warrants—to seek out smuggled goods. To guard against such searches and seizures, the Fourth Amendment protects the right to privacy. It requires authorities to have a specific reason to search a premises or to seize evidence or people. Police cannot simply conduct a general search or seizure hoping to find damaging evidence, or arrest someone on the chance that he or she might have committed a crime.

To be lawful, a search or an arrest must be based on **probable cause,** meaning that police must have a reasonable basis to believe the person or premises is linked to a crime. A search or an arrest also usually requires a **search warrant** or an **arrest warrant.** These are orders signed by a judge describing a specific place to be searched for specific items or naming the individual to be arrested for a specific crime.

The Fifth Amendment This amendment contains four important protections for people accused of crimes. First, no one can be tried for a serious crime unless a grand jury has decided there is enough evidence to justify a trial.

Second, a person who is found innocent of a crime may not be tried again for the same offense. This clause is designed to prevent continued harassment of individuals in order to convict them of a crime for which they have already been found innocent.

Third, no one may be forced to testify against himself or herself. As a result, people questioned by

Congressional Quarterly's
Government at a Glance

The Bill of Rights

1. Guarantees freedom of religion, speech, assembly, and press, and the right of people to petition the government
2. Protects the right of states to maintain a militia and of citizens to bear arms
3. Restricts quartering of troops in private homes
4. Protects against "unreasonable searches and seizures"
5. Assures the right not to be deprived of "life, liberty, or property, without due process of law," including protections against double jeopardy, self-incrimination, and government seizure of property without just compensation
6. Guarantees the right to a speedy and public trial by an impartial jury
7. Assures the right to a jury trial in cases involving the common law (the law established by previous court decisions)
8. Protects against excessive bail, or cruel and unusual punishment
9. Provides that people's rights are not restricted to those specified in Amendments 1–8
10. Restates the Constitution's principle of federalism by providing that powers not granted to the national government nor prohibited to the states are reserved to the states and to the people

Source: Mitchell, *CQ's Guide to the U.S. Constitution*, 2d ed. (Washington, D.C.: CQ Inc., 1994).

Critical Thinking

The Bill of Rights was not part of the original Constitution. ***Which amendment do you think is the most important? Why?***

the police, on trial, or testifying before a congressional hearing may refuse to answer questions if their answers would connect them with a criminal act. The government must establish a person's guilt by finding independent evidence of the person's involvement with the crime. Individuals cannot be required to convict themselves.

Finally, the Fifth Amendment states that government may not deprive any person of life, liberty, or property without **due process of law.** This means that the government must follow proper constitutional procedures in trials and in other actions it takes against individuals.

The Fifth Amendment also defines government's right of **eminent domain**—the power of government to take private property for public use such as to build a highway, a dam, or a park. The government must pay a fair price for the property taken and must use it in a way that benefits the public.

The Sixth Amendment This amendment protects the rights of individuals charged with federal crimes to defend themselves in a court trial. The Supreme Court, however, has ruled that these rights also apply to people charged with crimes subject to state courts. The Sixth Amendment gives an accused person several important rights.

A basic protection is the right to a speedy, public trial by an impartial jury. Thus, the authorities cannot purposely hold a person for an unnecessarily long time awaiting trial. This protection prevents government from silencing its critics by holding them for years without trials, as often happens under dictatorships. The requirement that trials be conducted in public assures that justice is carried out in full view of the people.

Although the amendment provides for trial by jury, an accused person may ask to be tried by a judge alone. The accused also may ask to have his or her trial moved to another community. A **change of venue,** or new trial location, is sometimes requested when unfavorable publicity indicates that the defendant cannot receive an impartial trial in the original location.

The Sixth Amendment gives accused persons the right to know the charges against them, so that they may prepare a defense. Accused persons also have the right to hear and question all witnesses against them and the right to compel witnesses to appear at the trial and testify in their behalf. These protections allow defendants to respond to the testimony of witnesses. In addition, accused persons have the right to be defended by a lawyer.

The Seventh Amendment The Seventh Amendment provides for the right to a jury trial in federal courts to settle all disputes about property worth more than $20. When both parties in a conflict agree, however, a judge rather than a jury may hear evidence and settle the case.

The Eighth Amendment This amendment prohibits excessive bail—money or property that the accused deposits with the court to gain release from jail until the trial. The judge sets bail in an amount that ensures the accused will appear for trial. When the trial ends, bail is returned. If the accused does not appear, bail is forfeited.

The Eighth Amendment also prevents judges from ordering someone convicted of a crime to pay an excessive fine. Fines for serious crimes may be higher than those for less serious ones. If someone is too poor, he or she cannot be imprisoned for longer than the maximum sentence to "work off" the fine.

Finally, the Eighth Amendment bans "cruel and unusual punishment" for crimes. These are punishments that are out of proportion to the crime committed. For example, 20 years in prison for stealing a candy bar would be cruel and unusual punishment. The Eighth Amendment also has been used to limit the use of the death penalty in some circumstances.

The Ninth Amendment The Ninth Amendment states that all other rights not spelled out in the Constitution are "retained by the people." This amendment prevents government from claiming that the only rights people have are those listed in the Bill of Rights. The amendment protects all basic or natural rights not specifically noted in the Constitution.

The Tenth Amendment The final amendment of the Bill of Rights clarifies the nature of federalism and the relationship of government to the people. It establishes that powers not given to the national government—or denied to the states—by the Constitution belong to the states or to the people.

Other Amendments

The 27 amendments fall into 3 major groups. The first group, which includes the Bill of Rights, was added between 1791 and 1804 to put finishing touches on the original Constitution. The Eleventh and Twelfth Amendments also belong to this group.

Article III, Section 1, of the Constitution gave the federal courts jurisdiction in cases arising between states, between citizens of different states, or between a state and citizens of another state. In 1795 the **Eleventh Amendment** was added to the Constitution to prohibit a state from being sued in federal court by citizens of another state or of another nation.

In 1793 two citizens of South Carolina had sued Georgia in the Supreme Court over property confiscated during the Revolution. The Georgia legislature maintained that a sovereign state could not be summoned into federal court and ordered to defend itself. When Georgia officials refused to appear for the trial, the Supreme Court decided against the state. Although Georgia lost the court case, it won its power struggle with the federal

The Power of the Ballot

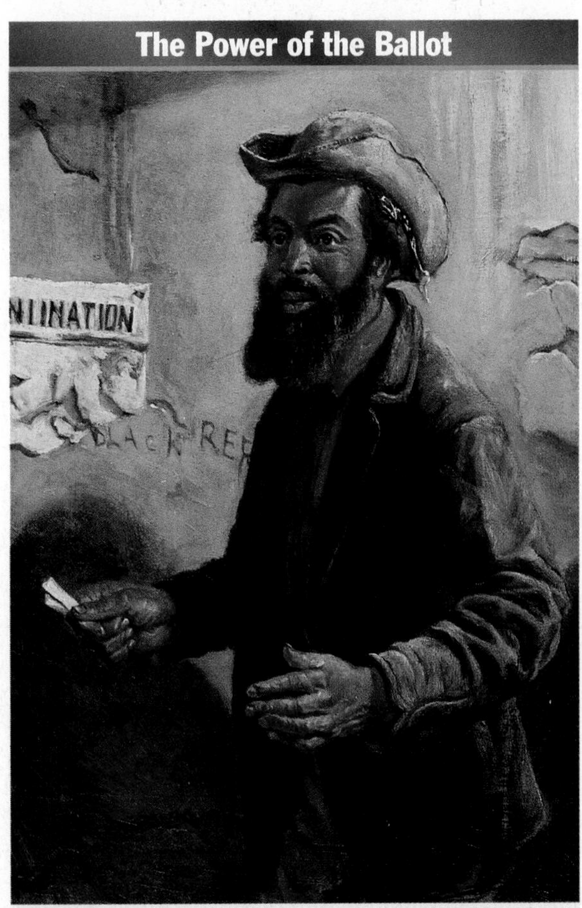

Civil Rights As this painting *His First Vote* by Thomas Waterman Wood shows, African American men won the right to vote when the Fifteenth Amendment became law in February 1870. ***How did the Civil War amendments expand civil rights in the nation?***

judiciary. The day after the Supreme Court announced its decision in ***Chisholm* v. *Georgia***[1] Congress introduced an amendment to limit the jurisdiction of the federal courts.

The **Twelfth Amendment,** added in 1804, corrects a problem that had arisen in the method of electing the president and vice president. This amendment provides for the Electoral College to use separate ballots in voting for president and vice president.

Civil War Amendments The second group of amendments—Thirteen, Fourteen, and Fifteen—often are called the Civil War amendments because they grew out of that great conflict.

The **Thirteenth Amendment** (1865) outlaws slavery, and the **Fourteenth Amendment** (1868) originally was intended to protect the legal rights of

See the following footnoted materials in the ***Reference Handbook:***
1. *Chisholm* v. *Georgia* case summary, page 756.

Congressional Quarterly's
Government at a Glance

Other Constitutional Amendments

Amendments	Date	Purpose
11	1795	Removed cases in which a state was sued without its consent from the jurisdiction of the federal courts
12	1804	Required presidential electors to vote separately for president and vice president
13	1865	Abolished slavery and authorized Congress to pass legislation implementing its abolition
14	1868	Granted citizenship to all persons born or naturalized in the United States; banned states from denying any person life, liberty, or property without due process of law; and banned states from denying any person equal protection under the laws
15	1870	Extended voting rights to African Americans by outlawing denial of the right to vote on the basis of race, color, or previous condition of servitude
16	1913	Empowered Congress to levy an income tax
17	1913	Provided for the election of U.S. senators by direct popular vote instead of by the state legislatures
18	1919	Authorized Congress to prohibit the manufacture, sale, and transportation of liquor
19	1920	Extended the right to vote to women
20	1933	Shortened the time between a presidential election and inauguration by designating January 20 as Inauguration Day; set January 3 as the date for the opening of a new Congress
21	1933	Repealed the Eighteenth Amendment and empowered Congress to regulate the liquor industry
22	1951	Limited presidents to two full terms in office
23	1961	Granted voters in the District of Columbia the right to vote for president and vice president
24	1964	Forbade requiring the payment of a poll tax to vote in a federal election
25	1967	Provided for succession to the office of president in the event of death or incapacity and for filling vacancies in the office of the vice president
26	1971	Extended the right to vote to 18-year-olds
27	1992	Banned Congress from increasing its members' salaries until after the next election

Key
- **Amendments changing the powers of the national and state governments**
- **Amendments changing government structure or function**
- **Amendments extending the suffrage and power of voters**

Critical Thinking

The United States Constitution is the oldest active written constitution in the world, yet it has been amended only 27 times. ***Which amendments are known as the Civil War amendments?***

Source: Mitchell, *CQ's Guide to the U.S. Constitution*, 2d ed. (Washington, D.C.: CQ Inc., 1994).

Amendments in Practice

Present The Fourth Amendment ▶ protects citizens from unlawful searches and arrest by government authorities.

Past The Eighteenth Amendment proved difficult to enforce and led to an illegal trade in alcohol. In *Prohibition Raid,* Thomas Hart Benton depicts police forcing the destruction of illegal alcohol. ▼

Enforcing Laws ***Explain why the Eighteenth Amendment may have been more difficult to enforce than the Fourth Amendment.***

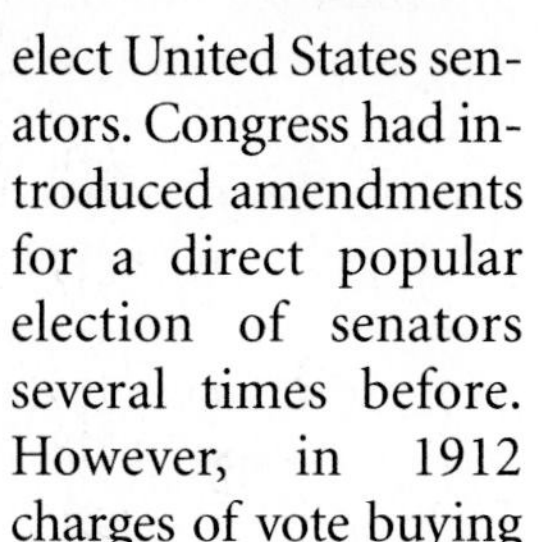

the freed slaves and their descendants. Today it protects the rights of citizenship in general by prohibiting a state from depriving any person of life, liberty, or property without "due process of law." In addition, it states that all citizens have the right to equal protection of the law in all states. The **Fifteenth Amendment** (1870) prohibits the government from denying a person's right to vote on the basis of race.

The Later Amendments The third group of amendments have all been added in the twentieth century. They deal with a range of topics that reflect the changes in modern American society.

The **Sixteenth Amendment** (1913) gives Congress the power to levy individual income taxes. Although the federal government had collected income taxes earlier, in 1895 the Supreme Court reversed a previous decision and held that the basic features of the federal income tax were unconstitutional. This decision prevented passage of another income tax law until after the constitutional amendment. The **Seventeenth Amendment** (1913) states that the people, instead of state legislatures, elect United States senators. Congress had introduced amendments for a direct popular election of senators several times before. However, in 1912 charges of vote buying in state legislatures aided in the passage of this amendment.

The **Eighteenth Amendment** (1919) prohibits the manufacture, sale, or transportation of alcoholic beverages, concluding a crusade to abolish the use of liquor that began in the 1830s. The following year, the **Nineteenth Amendment** (1920) guaranteed women the right to vote. By then women had already won the right to vote in many state elections, but the amendment put their right to vote in all state and national elections on a constitutional basis.

The **Twentieth Amendment** (1933) sets new dates for Congress to begin its term and for the inauguration of the president and vice president. Under the original Constitution, elected officials who retired or who had been defeated remained in office for several months. For the outgoing president, this period ran from November until March.

Such outgoing officials had little influence and accomplished little, and they were called **lame ducks** because they were so inactive. The amendment addressed and in most cases solved this problem by ending the terms of senators and representatives on January 3, and the term of the president on January 20 in the year following their November elections.

The **Twenty-first Amendment** (1933) repeals the unsuccessful Eighteenth Amendment. The Twenty-first Amendment, however, continued to ban the transport of alcohol into any state where its possession violated state law.

The **Twenty-second Amendment** (1951) limits presidents to a maximum of two elected terms. It was passed largely as a reaction to Franklin D. Roosevelt's election to four terms between 1933 and 1945.

The **Twenty-third Amendment** (1961) allows citizens living in Washington, D.C., to vote for president and vice president, a right previously denied residents of the nation's capital. The District of Columbia now has three presidential electors, the number to which it would be entitled if it were a state.

The **Twenty-fourth Amendment** (1964) prohibits **poll taxes** in federal elections—taxes paid in order to vote. Prior to the passage of this amendment, some states had used such taxes to keep low-income African Americans from voting.

The **Twenty-fifth Amendment** (1967) establishes a process for the vice president to take over leadership of the nation when a president is disabled. It also sets procedures for filling a vacancy in the office of the vice president. This amendment addresses a delicate issue—when should a president be considered unable to perform the duties of the office? A few times in the nation's history illness prevented a president from performing his official duties. Should the vice president be considered president during this time? The amendment says that when a president—or vice president with the support of the majority of the cabinet—writes to the president pro tem of the Senate and the Speaker of the House expressing the inability of the president to perform the duties of the office, the vice president immediately becomes the acting president. In a conflict between the president and the vice president over this issue, Congress must decide who will perform the duties of the office.

The **Twenty-sixth Amendment** (1971) lowers the voting age in both federal and state elections to 18.

The **Twenty-seventh Amendment** (1992) makes congressional pay raises effective during the term following their passage. Originally proposed by James Madison in 1789, this amendment lingered in obscurity for more than 200 years until it was discovered by a university student.

Section 4 Assessment

Checking for Understanding

1. **Main Idea** In a table, categorize the 27 amendments into the three major groups described in this section.

Constitutional Amendments		

2. **Define** prior restraint, probable cause, search warrant, arrest warrant, due process of law, eminent domain, lame duck, poll tax.
3. **Identify** Bill of Rights, *Chisholm* v. *Georgia*.
4. What rights are listed in the First Amendment?
5. Identify the twentieth-century amendments that deal with voting rights.

Critical Thinking

6. **Analyzing Information** How do the amendments to the Constitution show that the United States government is more democratic today than it was in 1790?

Growth of Democracy Amendments often reflect a change in society or a need for change in the structure and power of government. Write a report that identifies the reasons and events that led to the adoption of one of the 27 amendments. Present your findings to the class.

Skills

Study and Writing

Taking Notes

Effective note taking involves breaking up the information into meaningful parts so that it can be understood and remembered.

Learning the Skill

When taking notes, you must group facts into a logical order. This order can be chronological—that is, placing facts in order of what happened first, next, and last. Or you may take notes based on relationships between events—for example, causes and effects or problems and solutions.

Before you take notes, skim the material. What are the main points? You can take notes by using any of the organizers listed below.

- Time Line—Notes on sequenced events
- Cause-and-Effect Chart—Identifies connections between events
- Semantic Web—Shows different aspects of a general topic or theme
- Category Chart—Arranges data into specific categories
- Outline—Identifies main ideas with subheads under each main idea

Select an appropriate method; paraphrase your notes in short phrases.

Practicing the Skill

Read Section 2, pages 68–75, then answer the following questions.

1. Complete the web that follows; then state what information it gives you in two or three complete sentences.
2. Complete the outline. What would be a good title for it?
3. What new information does the outline provide that the web did not?

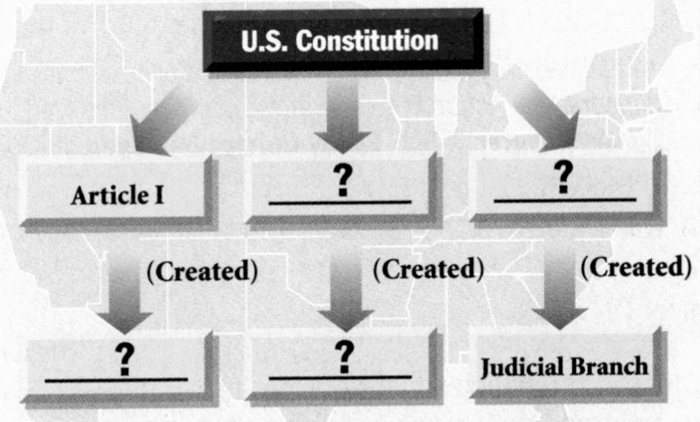

I. ____________
  A. Legislative branch
    1. Senate
    2. ____________
  B. ____________
    1. President
    2. Vast federal bureaucracy
  C. Judicial branch
    1. ____________
    2. ____________

Application Activity

Scan a local newspaper for a short editorial or article about a branch of the national or local government. Take notes by creating an outline or graphic organizer. Summarize the article using only your notes.

The **Glencoe Skillbuilder Interactive Workbook, Level 2** provides instruction and practice in key social studies skills.

Assessment and Activities

Self-Check Quiz Visit the *United States Government: Democracy in Action* Web site at gov.glencoe.com and click on ***Chapter 3–Self-Check Quizzes*** to prepare for the chapter test.

Reviewing Key Terms

Choose the italicized word or phrase that best completes each of the following sentences.

1. The national government is divided into three branches according to the principle of *judicial restraint/separation of powers.*
2. All powers of Congress specifically listed in the Constitution are *expressed powers/enumerated powers.*
3. The idea that the Supreme Court should play an active role in shaping politics reflects the philosophy of *judicial restraint/judicial activism.*
4. According to the principle of *judicial review/eminent domain,* the government can force someone to sell his or her home to make way for a highway.

Recalling Facts

1. What are the six goals of American government as identified in the Preamble to the Constitution?
2. Identify the six major principles of government on which the Constitution is based.
3. What is the constitutional principle illustrated by the division of the national government into three branches?
4. In the Constitution, what right does the final enumerated power give Congress?
5. List five presidential powers as specified in the Constitution.
6. Describe how an amendment to the Constitution is proposed and ratified.
7. In what ways may the Constitution be changed informally?
8. Describe a way in which custom has enlarged the Constitution.

Understanding Concepts

1. **Constitutional Interpretations** How has the system of checks and balances caused the separation of powers among the three branches of government to become less distinct?
2. **Separation of Powers** How did John Marshall help to elevate the Supreme Court to be equal to the other two branches of government?
3. **Growth of Democracy** How do the amendments reflect society's changing perception of who should participate in the political process?

Critical Thinking

1. **Understanding Cause and Effect** Use the graphic organizer below to show two results of having a brief Constitution that is a basic framework, rather than a specific plan, of government.

brief Constitution	result
	result

Current Events JOURNAL

Political Rights Research the status of political freedom in the world. Find articles regarding the fight for freedom in the *Readers' Guide to Periodical Literature* or in the electronic index to periodicals. Compare and contrast political rights in a foreign country you choose with those guaranteed by the U.S. Bill of Rights. Write a press release of your findings.

2. **Predicting Consequences** How would the federal system of government be affected if the Supreme Court did not have the power of judicial review?

Cooperative Learning Activity

Creating an Ad Organize the class into four groups. Group 1 should write a one-minute radio spot supporting the Constitution. Group 2 should write a one-minute spot opposing the Constitution. Group 3 should write a one-minute spot supporting the government under the Articles of Confederation. Group 4 should write a one-minute spot opposing the form of government under the Articles. Each group may time the reading of its ad and record it on an audiocassette. Practice reading several times before recording.

Interpreting Political Cartoons Activity

"Let's never forget that the constitution provides for three equally important branches of government; the legislative and the other two."

1. Which branch of government does the cartoonist imply is the most important?
2. Do you think the writers of the Constitution believed one branch of government was more important? Explain your answer.

Skill Practice Activity

Taking Notes Review the guidelines for taking notes on page 91. Then reread Section 4 about the amendments to the Constitution. Create a time line showing the dates of the amendments discussed in the section.

Technology Activity

Using the Internet Find out about proposed amendments and other legislation that Congress is considering by using the Internet. The home page for the Library of Congress provides information about all legislation facing the House and the Senate.

Participating in Local Government

The First Amendment guarantees freedom of assembly. Contact your local government to find out its rules about holding assemblies, such as political rallies, meetings, or parades. Find out what restrictions the community places on where and when the assemblies take place. Are there certain permits that must be obtained? For what reason might a community not allow an assembly to occur? Present your findings to the class in a short report.

The Federal System

Why It's Important

Federalism According to statistics, Americans move an average of 6 times during their lives, often from state to state. What federal laws protect them wherever they live? If you moved to a new state, how might laws differ?

To learn more about how the powers of the federal and state governments affect your life, view the ***Democracy in Action*** Chapter 4 video lesson:

The Federal System

★ ★ ★ ★ ★ ★ ★ ★ ★ ★

Chapter Overview Visit the *United States Government: Democracy in Action* Web site at gov.glencoe.com and click on ***Chapter 4–Overview*** to preview chapter information.

Section 1

National and State Powers

Reader's Guide

Key Terms

delegated powers, expressed powers, implied powers, elastic clause, inherent powers, reserved powers, supremacy clause, concurrent powers, enabling act

Find Out

- What are the differences between the expressed powers and the implied powers?
- How does the overall power of the national government compare to that of the states?

Understanding Concepts

Federalism In what ways does federalism provide constitutional safeguards for the people?

COVER STORY

Wallace Complies

TUSCALOOSA, ALABAMA, JUNE 1963

With the National Guard on campus, Governor George Wallace reluctantly complied with a request by General Henry Graham to step aside and let African American students register at the University of Alabama.

Wallace attempts to block desegregation

Defying a federal court order, Wallace had stood in a doorway at the university, blocking two African American students. "I denounce and forbid this illegal and unwarranted action by the Central Government," Wallace stated as he refused to move. When President Kennedy responded by federalizing the Alabama National Guard, the governor backed down.

Few confrontations between the state and national governments are as dramatic as the one at the University of Alabama in 1963. Nevertheless, national and state powers have been continually redefined through conflict, compromise, and cooperation since the earliest days of the republic. How do the different levels of government cooperate?

The Division of Powers

The Constitution divided government authority by giving the national government certain specified powers, reserving all other powers to the states or to the people. In addition, the national and state governments share some powers. Finally, the Constitution specifically denied some powers to each level of government.

The Constitution has preserved the basic design of federalism, or the division of government powers, over the years. The American concept of federalism, however, has changed greatly since 1787.

Federalism is not a static relationship between different levels of government. It is a dynamic concept that affects everyday decisions at all levels. An understanding of federalism must begin with the Constitution.

National Powers

The Constitution grants three types of power to the national government: expressed, implied, and inherent powers. Collectively, these powers are known as **delegated powers,** powers the Constitution grants or delegates to the national government.

Expressed Powers The **expressed powers** are those powers directly expressed or stated in the Constitution by the Founders. Most of these powers are found in the first three articles of the Constitution. This constitutional

National and state flags at Monument Valley, Utah

authority includes the power to levy and collect taxes, to coin money, to make war, to raise an army and navy, and to regulate commerce among the states. Expressed powers are also called **enumerated powers.**

Implied Powers Those powers that the national government requires to carry out the powers that are expressly defined in the Constitution are called **implied powers.** While not specifically listed, implied powers spring from and depend upon the expressed powers. For example, the power to draft people into the armed forces is implied by the power given to the government to raise an army and navy.

The basis for the implied powers is the **necessary and proper clause** (Article I, Section 8). Often called the **elastic clause** because it allows the powers of Congress to stretch, it says:

> "*Congress shall have power . . . to make all Laws which shall be necessary and proper for carrying into Execution the Foregoing powers, and all other powers vested . . . in the Government of the United States. . . .*"
>
> —Article I, Section 8

Implied powers have helped the national government strengthen and expand its authority to meet many problems the Founders did not foresee. Thus, Congress has used the implied powers to regulate nuclear power plants and to develop the space program.

Inherent Powers Those powers that the national government may exercise simply because it is a government are its **inherent powers.** For example, the national government must control immigration and establish diplomatic relations with other countries, even though these powers are not spelled out in the Constitution.

The States and the Nation

The Constitution reserves certain powers for the states. These powers belong strictly to the states and are called **reserved powers.** While the Constitution does not list these reserved powers, it grants to the states, or to the people through the Tenth Amendment, those powers "not delegated to the United States by the Constitution, nor prohibited by it to the states." Again, the Founders allowed for states' needs they could not foresee.

GOVERNMENT *and You*

Displaying the Flag

Whether you display the American flag every day, or only on holidays and special occasions, certain laws and customs govern the use of this symbol of national unity.

The flag is usually flown only from dawn to dusk. If displayed at night, it should be lighted. In a group of flags, the U.S. flag should be at the center and higher than the others. Fly the flag at half-staff on the death of a government official and until noon on Memorial Day.

Inside, the flag may hang flat against the wall behind a speaker, with the stars on the left. If on a staff, it should be on the viewers' left. Any other flags should be placed to the right. The flag may be flown upside down only to signal distress.

Remember that, as the symbol of the United States, the flag should be treated with respect.

Never let it touch the ground. When an American flag becomes too worn to display, it should be destroyed in a dignified way, preferably by burning.

Proudly displaying the flag

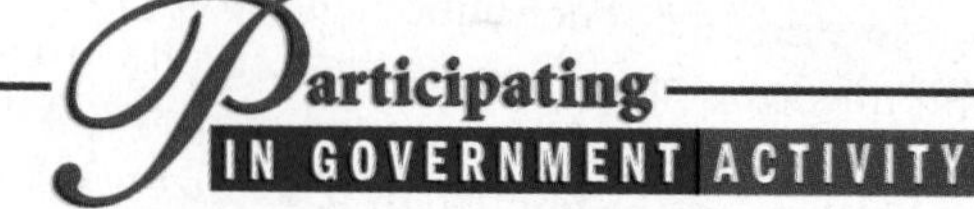

Flag Research What are the rules governing flying the flag at half-staff? When was the last time a flag flew at half-staff over your school?

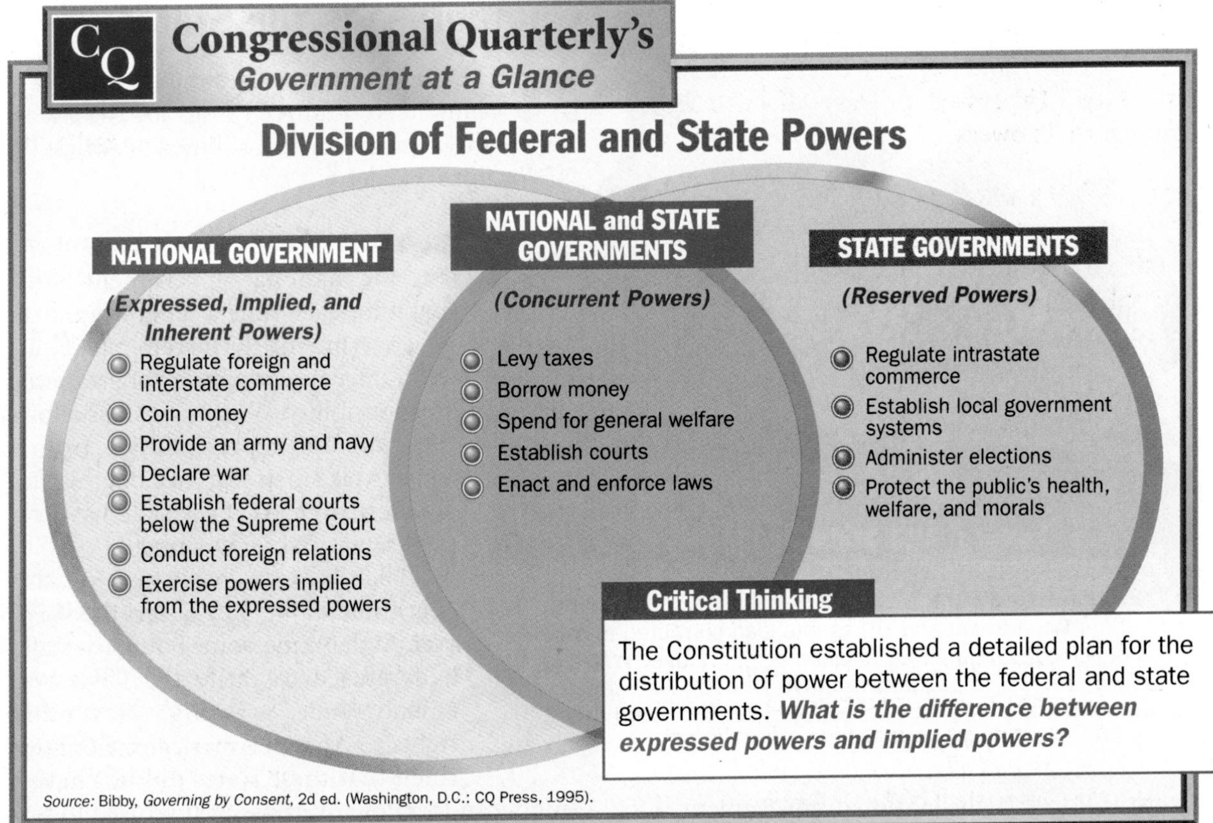

Thus the states may exercise any power not delegated to the national government, reserved to the people, or denied to them by the Constitution. As a result, states regulate public school systems, establish local governments, and require licenses for those who practice certain professions.

The Supremacy Clause What happens when states exceed their reserved powers and pass laws that conflict with national laws? Which law is supreme? Article VI, Section 2, of the Constitution makes the acts and treaties of the United States supreme. For this reason it is called the **supremacy clause.** This clause states:

> "*This Constitution, and the Laws of the United States which shall be made in Pursuance thereof, and all treaties made . . . under the Authority of the United States, shall be the supreme Law of the Land; and the Judges in every State shall be bound thereby.*"
>
> —Article VI, Section 2

No state law or state constitution may conflict with any form of national law. Article VI also requires that all national and state officials and judges be bound to support the Constitution. State officials are not permitted to use their state's reserved powers to interfere with the Constitution.

States create local governments such as those of cities and counties. As such, local governments get their powers from the states. Hence, local governments are also bound by the Constitution's supremacy clause—if a state is denied a certain power, so, too, are the local governments within the state.

Concurrent Powers The federal government and the states also have certain concurrent powers. **Concurrent powers** are those powers that both the national government and the states have. Each level of government exercises these powers independently. Examples of concurrent powers are the power to tax, to maintain courts and define crimes, and to appropriate private property for public use. Concurrently with the national government, the states may exercise any power not reserved by the

Federal and State Cooperation

Concurrent Powers Members of both the Noble County Sheriff's Department and FBI agents lead convicted terrorist Timothy McVeigh out of an Oklahoma courthouse. ***Why did federal and state authorities have to cooperate after the bombing of the federal building in Oklahoma City?***

Constitution for the national government. Of course, state actions must not conflict with any national laws.

Denied Powers Finally, the Constitution specifically denies some powers to all levels of government. Article I, Section 9,[1] enumerates those things the national government cannot do. For example, the national government cannot tax exports, and it cannot interfere with the ability of states to carry out their responsibilities.

The next section of Article I presents a long list of powers denied to the states. No state can make treaties or alliances with foreign governments. Nor can states coin money, make any laws impairing the obligation of contracts, or grant titles of nobility. And states must have congressional permission to collect duties on exports or imports or to make agreements—called compacts—with other states.

Consistent with the belief in the sovereignty of the people, the Constitution applies important limitations to both the national and state governments. These restrictions, designed to protect individual liberties such as free speech and the rights of the accused, are set forth in Article I, Section 9, in the Bill of Rights, and in several other amendments.

Guarantees to the States

The Constitution obliges the national government to do three things for the states. These three obligations are outlined in Article IV, Sections 3 and 4.[2]

Republican Form of Government

First, the national government must guarantee each state a republican form of government. Enforcement of this guarantee has become a congressional responsibility. When Congress allows senators and representatives from a state to take their seats in Congress, it is in effect ruling that the state has a republican form of government.

The only extensive use of this guarantee came just after the Civil War. At that time, some Southern states had refused to ratify the Civil War amendments granting citizenship rights to African Americans. Congress ruled that these states did not have a republican form of government. It refused to seat senators and representatives from those states until the states ratified the Civil War amendments and changed their laws to recognize African Americans' rights.

Protection Second, the national government must protect states from invasion and domestic violence. An attack by a foreign power on one state is considered an attack on the United States.

Congress has given the president authority to send federal troops to put down domestic disorders when state officials ask for help. In the summer of 1967, for example, President Lyndon Johnson sent troops to Detroit to help control racial unrest and rioting. Johnson did so after Michigan's governor declared that the Detroit police and the Michigan National Guard could not cope with the widespread violence.

When national laws are violated, federal property is threatened, or federal responsibilities are interfered with, the president may send troops to a

See the following footnoted materials in the **Reference Handbook:**
1. *The Constitution*, pages 774–799.
2. *The Constitution*, pages 774–799.

state without the request of local authorities—or even over local objections. In 1894, for example, President Grover Cleveland sent federal troops to Chicago to restore order during a strike of railroad workers even though the governor of Illinois objected. During the strike, rioters had threatened federal property and interfered with mail delivery.

During the 1950s and 1960s, Presidents Eisenhower and Kennedy used this power to stop state officials from blocking the integration of Southern schools and universities. Eisenhower sent troops to Little Rock, Arkansas, in 1957 when local officials failed to integrate public schools. Kennedy used troops at the University of Mississippi in 1962 and the University of Alabama in 1963.

The national government has extended its definition of domestic violence to include natural disasters such as earthquakes, floods, hurricanes, and tornadoes. When one of these disasters strikes, the president often orders troops to aid disaster victims. The government also provides low-cost loans to help people repair damages.

Territorial Integrity Finally, the national government has the duty to respect the territorial integrity of each state. The national government cannot use territory that is part of an existing state to create a new state unless the national government has permission from the legislature of the state involved. The admission of West Virginia as a state in 1863 may be considered an exception to this rule.

Admission of New States

Thirty-seven states have joined the Union since the original 13 formed the nation. Most of these states became territories before taking steps to gain statehood. What procedures do these territories then follow to become states?

Congress Admits New States The Constitution gives Congress the power to admit new states to the Union. There are two restrictions on this power. First, as noted earlier, no state may be formed by taking territory from one or more states without the consent of the states involved and of Congress. Second, acts of admission, like all laws, are subject to presidential veto.

The procedure for admission begins when Congress passes an **enabling act.** An enabling act, when signed by the president, enables the people of the territory interested in becoming a state to prepare a constitution. Then, after the constitution has been drafted and approved by a popular vote in the area, it is submitted to Congress. If Congress is still agreeable, it passes an act admitting the territory as a state.

Since the original 13 states formed the Union, Congress has admitted new states under a variety of circumstances. Five states—Vermont, Kentucky, Tennessee, Maine, and West Virginia—were created from existing states. Two states, West Virginia and Texas, were admitted under unusual circumstances.

Federal Troops Enforce the Constitution

Federal and State Struggles
After members of the Arkansas National Guard prevented Elizabeth Ann Eckford from attending Little Rock High School on September 4, 1957, President Eisenhower sent federal troops to forcibly integrate the school. ***What authority did the president have to send federal troops to Little Rock?***

Division of Powers

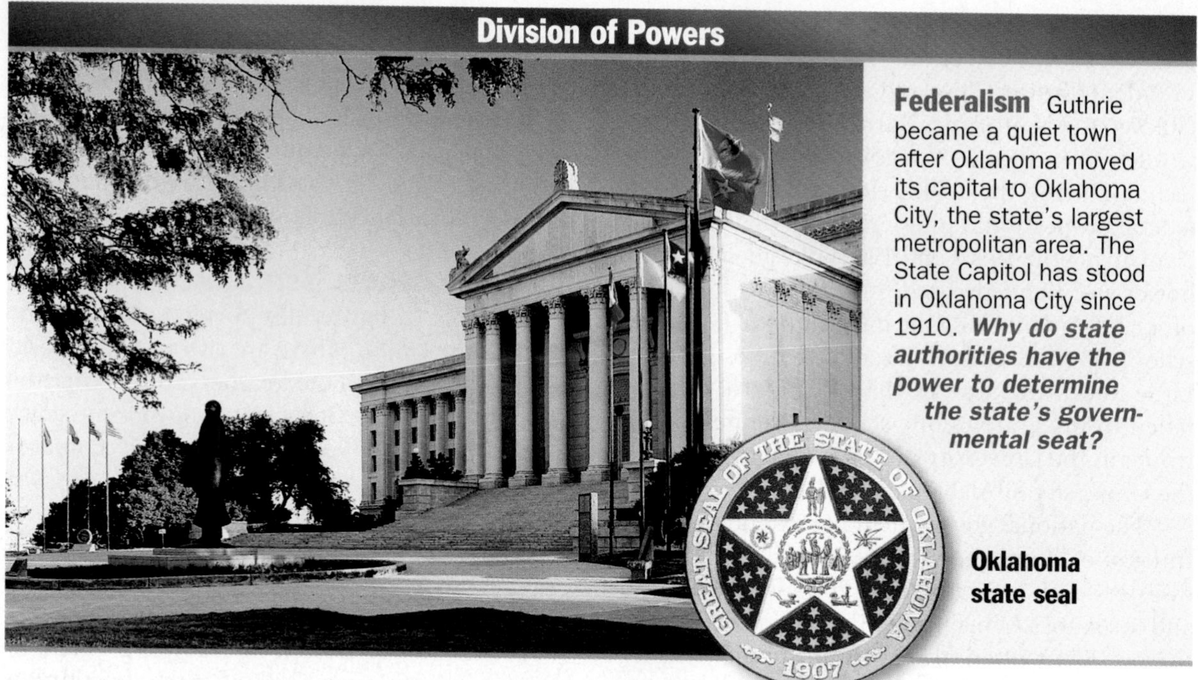

Federalism Guthrie became a quiet town after Oklahoma moved its capital to Oklahoma City, the state's largest metropolitan area. The State Capitol has stood in Oklahoma City since 1910. ***Why do state authorities have the power to determine the state's governmental seat?***

Oklahoma state seal

West Virginia was created from 40 western counties of Virginia that broke away when Virginia seceded from the Union. Some people have argued that the admission of West Virginia was a violation of the Constitution because the Virginia legislature did not give its consent. Congress, however, accepted the decision of the minority of the Virginia legislature that represented the 40 western counties. It held that the western representatives were the only legal acting Virginia legislature at that time.

Texas won independence from Mexico and sought annexation to the United States for several years before being admitted. Antislavery members of Congress opposed creation of a new slaveholding state. Texas was annexed to the United States by a joint resolution of Congress in 1845. The joint resolution provided for immediate statehood, allowing Texas to skip the territorial period. It also stated that Texas could be divided into as many as five states with the approval of both Texas and the United States.

The last two states to be admitted, Alaska and Hawaii, shortened the admission process. They each adopted a proposed constitution without waiting for an enabling act. Both were admitted in 1959.

Puerto Rico has considered statehood over a period of several decades. Puerto Ricans, however, rejected statehood by a vote in 1993.

Conditions for Admission Congress or the president may impose certain conditions before admitting a new state, including requiring changes in the drafted constitution submitted by a territory. In 1911 President Taft vetoed the congressional resolution admitting Arizona because he objected to a section in the Arizona constitution dealing with the recall of judges. Arizona then modified the constitution, and the next year it became the forty-eighth state. When Alaska entered the union in 1959, it was prohibited from ever claiming title to any lands legally held by Native Americans or Aleuts in Alaska. Ohio was admitted in 1803 on the condition that for five years it not tax any public lands sold by the national government within its borders.

The Supreme Court has ruled that the president or Congress may impose conditions for admission of a state. Once a state is admitted, however, those conditions may be enforced only if they do not interfere with the new state's authority to manage its own internal affairs. In the case of Arizona, once it was admitted as a state, it promptly amended its constitution to restore provisions about the recall of judges that Taft had requested be deleted.

When Oklahoma was admitted in 1907, Congress forbade it to move its capital from the city of Guthrie until 1913. The Supreme Court, however, upheld the right of Oklahoma to move the capital to Oklahoma City in 1911. The Court declared:

"The power to locate its own seat of government, and to determine when and how it shall be changed from one place to another, and to appropriate its own public funds for that purpose, are essentially and peculiarly state powers. . . . Has Oklahoma been admitted upon an equal footing with the original states? If she has . . . [Oklahoma] may determine for her own people the proper location of the local seat of government."

—Justice Horace H. Lurton, 1911

Equality of the States Once admitted to the Union, each state is equal to every other state and has rights to control its internal affairs. No state has more privileges or fewer obligations than any other. Each state is also legally separate from every other state in the Union. All states in the Union are bound to support the Constitution.

The National Governors' Association

The National Governors' Association (NGA) supports federalism by helping governors in state policy making and in influencing national policy. In 1908 President Theodore Roosevelt first called the nation's governors together to discuss conservation. After that the governors began to meet regularly as the Governors' Conference to deal with a variety of issues. In the 1960s the governors set up a permanent organization with an office in Washington, D.C.

NGA Helping the Governors In the 1970s the renamed National Governors' Association focused on helping the governors' performance within their own states. The NGA held seminars and published materials on subjects such as organizing the governor's office, dealing with the press, and organizing intergovernmental relations. A series of publications focused on the growing influence of states and governors as innovators. Through the NGA, states shared ideas on how to solve common problems.

NGA Influencing National Policy Beginning in the 1980s, governors focused their attention on national policy concerns. The NGA and its affiliates addressed educational, welfare, and health-care reforms as well as the changing balance in the federal system. Regional governors' associations also became active in policy issues. By joining together, the governors were becoming a big part of the national policy-making process.

Working Within the System

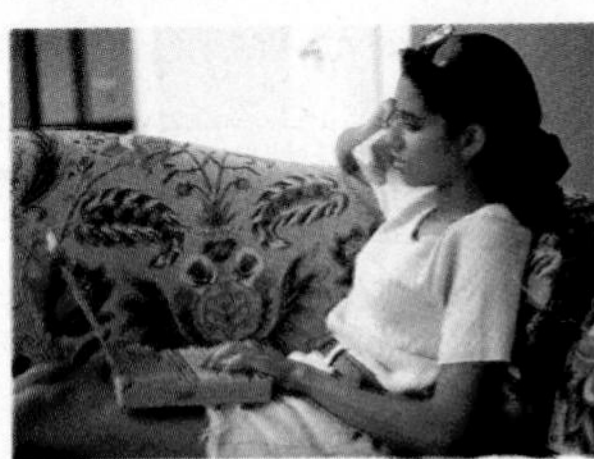

Contacting a legislator

Do we truly have government by and for the people? If so, how can citizens make their opinions known? Can you work within the system to change a law that you believe is unjust?

Your opinion will carry more influence if you join with others. Choose an appropriate means of expressing your views. To question a local ordinance, attend a city council meeting. If you object to a state law, write to your state legislator. Petitions—formal requests for specific action signed by many people—are also effective. You could write letters to the editor or prepare an editorial for a local radio or television broadcast. The Internet also offers an avenue through which citizens can speak out on an issue.

Activity

Choose an issue from an opinion page of the local newspaper. Express whether you strongly agree or disagree in a letter to the newspaper's editor.

In 1989 the NGA hosted President George Bush at an education summit. As a result of this meeting and later interactions, President Bush endorsed a series of educational objectives that the NGA Task Force on Education had established.

When Governor Clinton of Arkansas became President Clinton, the governors seemed ready to have a major impact on national policy. President Clinton's health-care reform proposals, however, became a source of division within the NGA. Disagreement on how to solve the health-care problems began to split the governors along party lines.

The 1994 elections changed the working relationship of governors with the national policy makers. Republicans now controlled Congress, and the NGA had to work with the new congressional leadership. Balancing the budget was the focus of the Republican Congress. The governors lobbied against unfunded mandates that required states to provide programs without federal aid. In 1996 the bipartisanship of the NGA was reborn when 47 governors suggested plans for ending the Medicaid and welfare reform standoff. The effort was an example of the growing strength of the NGA as a supporting pillar of federalism.

Obligations of the States The states perform two important functions for the national government. State and local governments conduct and pay for elections of all national government officials—senators, representatives, and presidential electors. The Constitution gives state legislatures the power to fix the "times, places, and manner" of election of senators and representatives (Article I, Section 4). Under the same provision, Congress has the authority to alter state election laws should it so desire.

In addition, the states play a key role in the process for amending the Constitution. Under the document, no amendment can be added to the Constitution unless three-fourths of the states approve it.

The Supreme Court as Umpire

Because federalism divides the powers of government, conflicts frequently arise between national and state governments. By settling such disputes, the federal court system, particularly the Supreme Court, plays a key role as an umpire for our federal system. The question of national versus state power arose early in our nation's history. In 1819, in the landmark case of ***McCulloch* v. *Maryland*,**[1] the Supreme Court ruled on a conflict between a state government and the national government. In making the decision, the Supreme Court held that in the instance of a conflict between the national government and a state government, the national government is supreme.

See the following footnoted materials in the **Reference Handbook:**
1. *McCulloch* v. *Maryland* case summary, page 761.

Section 1 Assessment

Checking for Understanding

1. **Main Idea** Using a graphic organizer like the one at the right, give an example of each kind of power granted to the national government.

expressed	
implied	
inherent	

2. **Define** delegated powers, expressed powers, implied powers, elastic clause, inherent powers, reserved powers, supremacy clause, concurrent powers, enabling act.
3. **Identify** necessary and proper clause, *McCulloch* v. *Maryland*.
4. What kinds of powers may states exercise?

Critical Thinking

5. **Making Comparisons** How do the obligations of the national government to states compare to obligations of states to the national government?

Concepts IN ACTION

Federalism New states coming into the Union have had to follow a process established by Congress. Beginning with the enabling act passed by Congress, create a flow chart that shows the dates and conditions by which your state was admitted to the Union.

Section 2

Relations Among the States

Reader's Guide

Key Terms

extradite, civil law, interstate compact

Find Out

- What provisions in Article IV of the Constitution attempt to provide for cooperation among the various state governments?
- What are some of the purposes of interstate compacts?

Understanding Concepts

Federalism Why is it necessary that the Constitution require states to cooperate with one another?

COVER STORY

Convict Goes Free

TALLAHASSEE, FLORIDA, OCTOBER 1996

A 64-year-old convict, who escaped from a Florida prison in 1952, but has been a model citizen since, is officially free. When Eddie Brown, of Brooklyn, New York, was stopped for a traffic violation recently, a routine check revealed him to be a long-sought fugitive. Originally Brown had been serving a 5-year sentence for robbery in Florida. When he was caught, Florida officials at first wanted Brown returned to serve his remaining sentence. However, after hearing about the model life Brown had led during his years of freedom, Florida governor Lawton Chiles dismissed the order to extradite him.

No longer needed

The Constitution, in establishing the federal system, defined not only national-state relations but also relations among the states. Conflicts and jealousies among the states had been a major reason for drafting the Constitution in 1787. One way the Constitution dealt with this problem was to strengthen the national government. The second way was to set the legal ground rules, such as extradition, for relations among the states. Because each state retains much power and independence, these rules help to assure cooperation among the states.

Interstate Relations

Article IV of the Constitution requires the states to do the following: (1) give "full faith and credit" to the laws, records, and court decisions of other states; (2) give one another's citizens all the "privileges and immunities" of their own citizens; and (3) **extradite**—that is, return to a state—criminals and fugitives who flee across state lines to escape justice.

Full Faith and Credit The Constitution states that **"full faith and credit"** shall be given in each state to the public acts, records, and judicial proceedings of every other state. In other words, each state must recognize the laws and legal proceedings of the other states. For example, a car registration of one state must be accepted by all the other states. This clause applies only to **civil law**, or laws relating to disputes between individuals, groups, or with the state. One state cannot enforce another state's criminal laws.

The need for this kind of rule in the federal system is obvious. Without it, each state could treat all other states like foreign countries. Further, each state could become a haven for people who decided to move to another state to avoid their legal duties and responsibilities.

The coverage of the "full faith and credit" rule is quite broad. *Public acts* refers to civil

Nonresidents' Rights

Reasonable Discrimination It is often more expensive for residents of one state to attend an out-of-state public college. ***Why do you think states charge out-of-state students higher tuition fees?***

laws passed by state legislatures. *Records* means such documents as mortgages, deeds, leases, wills, marriage licenses, car registrations, and birth certificates. The phrase *judicial proceedings* refers to various court actions such as judgments to pay a debt.

Judicial decisions in civil matters in one state will be honored and enforced in all states. If, for example, a person in Texas loses a lawsuit requiring a specific payment, and moves to Illinois to avoid paying the money, Illinois courts will enforce the Texas decision.

Privileges and Immunities The Founders knew that when citizens traveled between states, they might be discriminated against. A citizen of Delaware, for example, might be treated as an alien in Virginia or Maryland. Therefore, the Constitution provides that "the Citizens of each State shall be entitled to all Privileges and Immunities of Citizens in the several States." As interpreted by the Supreme Court, this clause means that one state may not discriminate unreasonably against citizens of another state. It must provide citizens of other states the same privileges and immunities it provides its own citizens.

The courts have never given a complete listing of **"privileges and immunities."** Included, however, are rights to pass through or live in any state; use the courts; make contracts; buy, sell, and hold property; and marry.

On the other hand, states may make reasonable discrimination against nonresidents. The privileges and immunities clause does not apply to voting, serving on juries, or using certain public facilities. All states require that a person live in a state for a certain amount of time before becoming a voter or public official. States may also require individuals to establish residency before they can practice such professions as medicine, dentistry, or law.

In addition, nonresidents do not have the same right to attend publicly supported institutions such as schools or to use state hospitals as do residents of the state. Nonresidents may be required to pay higher fees for hunting or fishing licenses than residents. State colleges and universities may, and usually do, charge higher tuition fees to students from other states than they do to resident students.

Extradition Because states are basically independent of one another, some means is needed to prevent criminals from escaping justice simply by going from one state to another. For this reason, the Constitution provides:

> "*A person charged in any state with treason, felony, or other crime, who shall flee from justice, and be found in another State, shall, on demand of the executive authority of the State from which he fled, be delivered up, to be removed to the State having jurisdiction of the crime.*"
>
> —Article IV, Section 2

This clause provides for the extradition of fugitives. Congress has made the governor of the state to which fugitives have fled responsible for returning them.

The Supreme Court has softened the meaning of the extradition provision by ruling that a governor is not required to return a fugitive to another state. Although extradition is routine in the vast majority of cases, occasionally a governor will refuse. For example, a Michigan governor once refused to return a fugitive to Arkansas because, the governor said, prison conditions in Arkansas were inhumane. Arkansas officials could do nothing about the governor's decision. In recent years Congress has acted to close the extradition loophole by making it a federal crime to flee from one state to another in order to avoid prosecution for a felony.

Interstate Compacts The Constitution requires the states to settle their differences with one another without the use of force. The principal way in which states may do this is to negotiate **interstate compacts.** Such compacts are written agreements between two or more states. The national government or foreign countries may also be part of an interstate compact.

Congress must approve interstate compacts. This requirement prevents states from threatening the Union by making alliances among themselves. Once a compact has been signed and approved by Congress, it is binding on all states signing it. Its terms are enforceable by the Supreme Court.

Before 1900, only 13 interstate compacts had received congressional approval. Most of them involved boundary disputes between states. As society has become more complex, however, the number of compacts sent to Congress has increased. Today nearly 200 compacts are in force.

States use compacts to deal with such matters as air and water pollution, pest control, toll bridges, and transportation. New Jersey and New York helped start this trend in 1921 when they created the Port of New York Authority to develop and manage harbor facilities in the area. Many compacts today deal with the development and conservation of natural resources. Others deal with the transport and disposal of hazardous waste materials. Interstate compacts have become an important way for the states to deal with regional problems.

Lawsuits Between States Sometimes states are unable to resolve their disputes by these or other methods. When this happens, an interstate lawsuit may result. Since 1789 more than 220 disputes between states have wound up in court. Suits among two or more states are heard in the United States Supreme Court, the only court in which one state may sue another.

States bring one another to court for a variety of reasons. Cases in the West often involve water rights. Arizona, California, and Colorado have gone to the Court in disputes over water from the Colorado River. Other cases have involved sewage from one state polluting the water in another state. Still other cases are disputes over boundary lines. Arkansas and Tennessee had such a dispute as recently as 1970.

Section 2 Assessment

Checking for Understanding

1. **Main Idea** In a chart, list three ways states treat nonresidents differently and the same as residents.

Treated differently	Treated the same
1.	
2.	
3.	

2. **Define** extradite, civil law, interstate compact.
3. **Identify** "full faith and credit," "privileges and immunities."
4. What three constitutional provisions are aimed at promoting cooperation among the states?

Critical Thinking

5. **Understanding Cause and Effect** What environmental problems could interstate compacts address, and what solutions could they achieve?

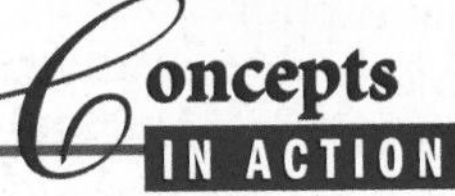

Federalism Imagine you have moved to a new state. Find out if and how a driver's license, automobile registration, and voting registration are changed. Write a report on your findings.

79 4328
SAN MATEO HIGH SCHOOL
San Mateo, California 94401

Section 3

Developing Federalism

Reader's Guide

Key Terms

states' rights position, nationalist position, income tax

Find Out

- Compare the view of the federal government as seen by a states' rightist and a nationalist.
- What events show that federalism has been dynamic rather than static since the 1960s?

Understanding Concepts

Federalism How do national crises, such as war, tend to shift power to the national government?

COVER STORY

Shopping the Net

WASHINGTON, D.C., MARCH 19, 1998

The National Governors' Association (NGA) and other groups representing local officials have decided to support national legislation that temporarily bans sales taxes on Internet transactions. The announcement marks a major policy change for the NGA. Earlier, the group had asked Congress to give states the right to collect sales taxes on Internet commerce based on the tax rates of customers' home states. The NGA agreed to a three-year delay on Internet taxes after negotiating with congressional supporters of legislation banning the taxes. To gain the governors' support, the bill's authors agreed to reduce the length of the delay from six to three years.

Internet User

The roles of state and national government officials have been defined during two centuries of developing federalism. Early Federalists such as John Jay and Alexander Hamilton had to convince the people in the states that the new federalism of the Constitution was better than the old confederacy. While they deeply believed that the United States needed a strong central government to survive, they also knew that many people feared the centralization of power. The colonial experience with the power of British government was still fresh in people's minds.

Alexander Hamilton wrote:

> "*The proposed Constitution, so far from implying an abolition of the State governments, makes them constituent parts of the national sovereignty, by allowing them a direct representation in the Senate, and leaves in their possession certain exclusive and very important portions of sovereign power. This fully corresponds . . . with the idea of a federal government.*"
>
> —Alexander Hamilton, 1787

While Hamilton's basic definition of federalism remains true, interpretations of how federalism affects national-state relationships have changed since 1787 and will no doubt continue to do so.

States' Rightists Versus Nationalists

Throughout American history, there have been two quite different views of how federalism should operate. One view—the **states' rights position**—favors state and local action in dealing with problems. A second view—the **nationalist position**—favors national action in dealing with these matters.

SAN MATEO HIGH SCHOOL
San Mateo, California 94401

The States' Rights Position The states' rights view holds that the Constitution is a compact among the states. States' rightists argue that the states created the national government and gave it only certain limited powers. Any doubt about whether a power belongs to the national government or is reserved to the states should be settled in favor of the states. Because the national government is an agent of the states, all of its powers should be narrowly defined.

States' rights supporters believe state governments are closer to the people and better reflect their wishes than the national government. They tend to see the government in Washington, D.C., as heavy-handed and a threat to individual liberty.

At various points in United States history, the Supreme Court has accepted this view. Under **Chief Justice Roger B. Taney** (1836–1864), the Court often supported states' rights against powers of the national government. The same was true from 1918 to 1936, when the Court ruled new federal laws attempting to regulate child labor, industry, and agriculture in the states unconstitutional. During these times, the Court largely ignored John Marshall's principle of implied powers set out in *McCulloch* v. *Maryland.* Instead, it based its decision on the Tenth Amendment, which says powers not delegated to the national government are reserved to the states or the people.

The Pledge of Allegiance

The pledge to the United States flag has been around so long that many people think it dates back to the beginning of the Republic. Not so. Francis J. Bellamy, a Baptist preacher, wrote the pledge in 1892 for the observance marking 400 years since Christopher Columbus's arrival in the Americas. As originally published, it read: "I pledge allegiance to my Flag and to the Republic for which it stands: one Nation indivisible, with Liberty and Justice for all." The words "my Flag" were changed to "the flag of the United States of America" during the 1920s. Congress added the pledge to the official Flag Code in 1945 and inserted the words "under God" in 1954.

The Nationalist Position The nationalist position rejects the idea of the Constitution as merely a compact among the states. Nationalists deny that the national government is an agent of the states. They argue that it was the people, not the states, who created both the national government and the states. Therefore, the national government is not subordinate to the states.

Nationalists believe the powers expressly delegated to the national government should be expanded as necessary to carry out the people's will. They hold that the "necessary and proper" clause of the Constitution means that Congress has the right to adopt any means that are convenient and useful to carry out its delegated powers. They also claim that the reserved powers of the states should not limit how the national government can use its own powers.

Nationalists believe the national government stands for all the people, while each state speaks for only part of the people. They look to the national government to take the lead in solving major social and economic problems facing the nation.

The Supreme Court established the nationalist position in 1819 in *McCulloch* v. *Maryland,* but it really gained ground in the Court during the late 1930s. At that time, the Great Depression gripped the nation. The national government under President Franklin D. Roosevelt responded by starting new social welfare and public works programs. At first, the Court ruled these programs were unconstitutional. As the Depression grew worse, however, the Court adjusted its views. It supported the expansion of the national government's powers in order to deal with the nation's terrible economic problems.

Growing National Government

A major factor shaping the development of American federalism has been the growth in the size and power of the national government.

Over the years this expansion came largely at the expense of the states.

A key reason for the change is that the Constitution's flexibility has allowed the Supreme Court, Congress, and the president to stretch the government's powers to meet the needs of a modern industrial nation. The expansion of the national government's powers has been based on three major constitutional provisions: (1) the war powers; (2) the power to regulate interstate commerce; and (3) the power to tax and spend.

War Powers The national government has power to wage war. This authority has greatly expanded the federal government's power because, in today's world, national defense involves more than simply putting troops in the field. Such factors as the condition of the economy and the strength of the educational system can affect the nation's military capabilities.

Commerce Power The Constitution gives Congress the authority to regulate commerce. Supreme Court decisions have expanded this power.

The courts today consistently interpret the term *commerce* to mean nearly all activities concerned with the production, buying, selling, and transporting of goods. For example, Congress passed the **Civil Rights Act of 1964** forbidding racial discrimination in public accommodations such as hotels and restaurants. In upholding this law the Supreme Court reasoned: (a) racial discrimination by innkeepers and restaurant owners makes it difficult for the people discriminated against to travel and thus restricts the flow of interstate commerce; (b) Congress has the power to regulate commerce; (c) therefore, Congress may pass laws against racial discrimination.

Taxing Power Congress has no specific constitutional authority to pass laws to promote the general welfare. Congress does, however, have authority to raise taxes and spend money for such purposes.

The Sixteenth Amendment, ratified in 1913, gave Congress the power to tax incomes. The **income tax** levied on individual earnings has become the major source of money for the national government. It has given the national government much greater financial resources than any state or local government has.

Finally, Congress has used its taxing power to increase the national government's authority in two ways. First, taxes may be used to regulate businesses. For example, Congress has put such heavy taxes on certain dangerous products that it is not profitable for companies to make and sell them. Second, Congress may use taxes to influence states to adopt certain kinds of programs. Federal law

Congressional Desegregation

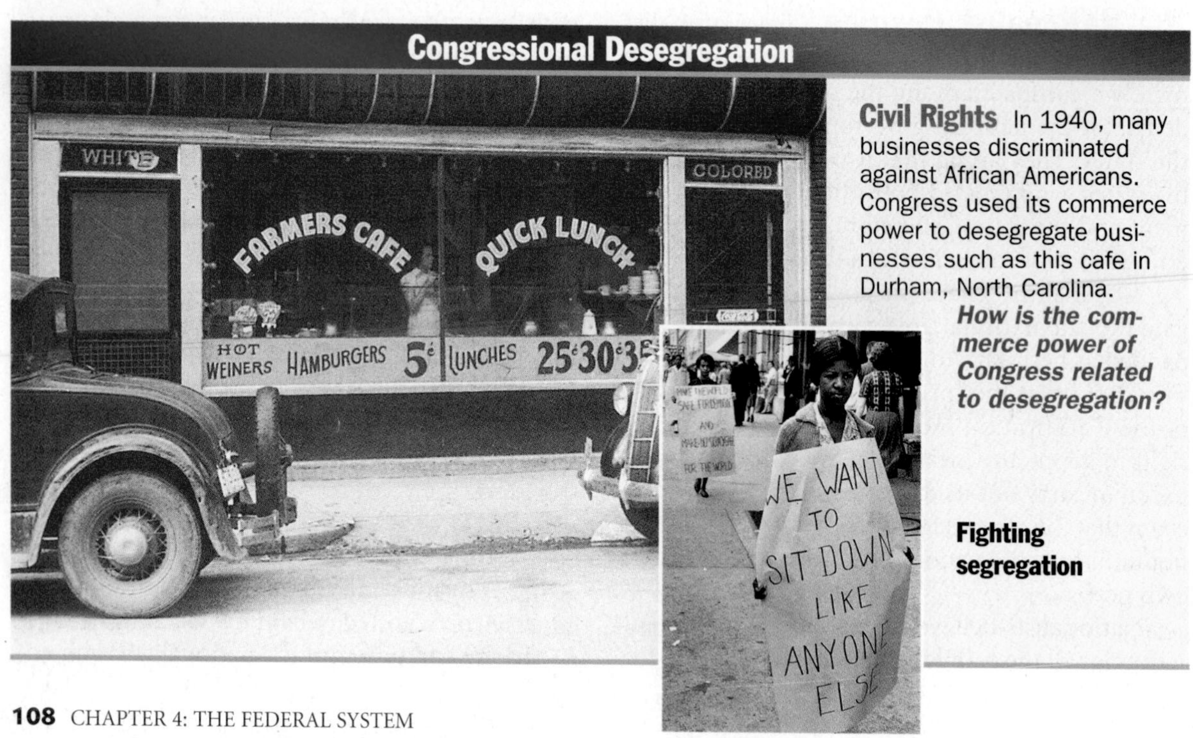

Civil Rights In 1940, many businesses discriminated against African Americans. Congress used its commerce power to desegregate businesses such as this cafe in Durham, North Carolina. ***How is the commerce power of Congress related to desegregation?***

Fighting segregation

allows employers to deduct from their federal taxes any state taxes they pay to support state unemployment programs. This federal tax break helped persuade all the states to set up their own unemployment insurance programs.

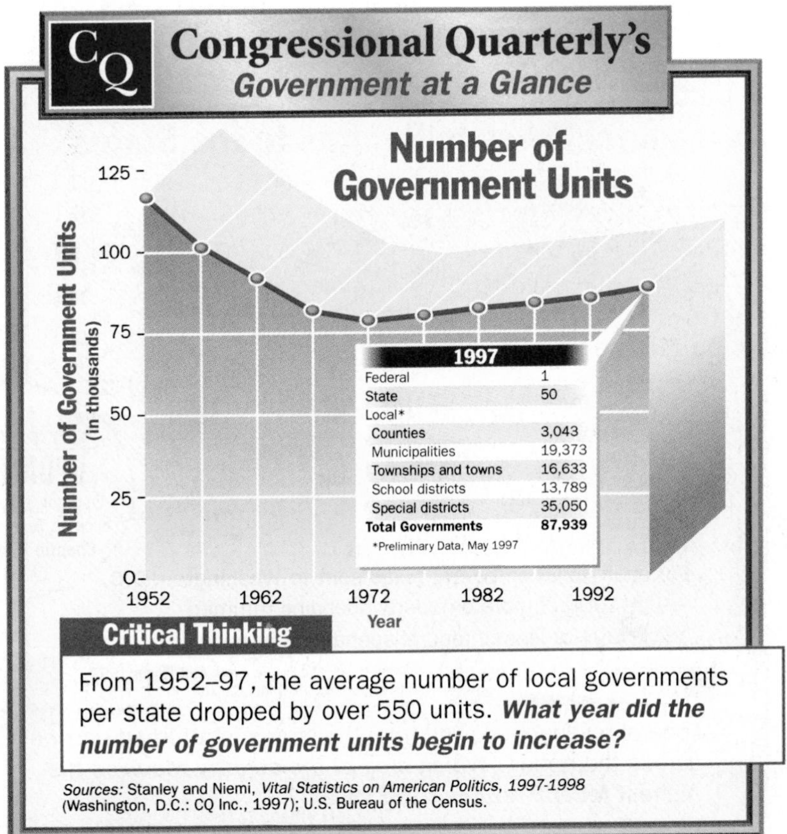

Critical Thinking

From 1952–97, the average number of local governments per state dropped by over 550 units. ***What year did the number of government units begin to increase?***

Sources: Stanley and Niemi, *Vital Statistics on American Politics, 1997-1998* (Washington, D.C.: CQ Inc., 1997); U.S. Bureau of the Census.

Federal Aid to the States

A continuing issue of federalism has been the competition between states for national government spending. Each state wants to get its fair share of national government projects because this spending affects the economies of every state.

Politics and Spending The recent population shift from the states of the Northeast and the Midwest to the states of the South and the Southwest has shifted power in Washington, D.C. More federal government spending has started to go to the Southern states and less to the Northern states.

Direct federal aid to the states is another political issue. The national government has historically provided different types of aid to the states. In 1862 Congress passed a law giving nearly 6 million acres of public land to the states for the support of colleges. Since the 1950s, federal aid to state and local governments has increased tremendously.

State and local offices have learned that along with more federal aid comes greater federal control and red tape. This is because many federal aid programs provide money only if the state and local governments are willing to meet conditions set by Congress.

Shifting Responsibilities In recent years, some presidents and some congressional leaders have wanted to shift the balance of power in the federal system back toward the states. In 1969, for example, President Nixon called for a **"New Federalism"** that would return more authority to state and local governments.

In 1982 President Reagan called for sweeping changes in federal aid policies. These included turning responsibility for dozens of federal programs in areas like education and welfare over to state and local governments. President Bush continued this policy, decreasing federal aid along with federal control. Between 1980 and 1990 federal grants declined dramatically—from $50 billion to $19 billion. Obviously, the relationship between federal and state governments is dynamic and is affected by the policies of the president and of Congress.

President Clinton emphasized the need to "reinvent government," when he came into office. At the same time, the 103rd Congress strongly supported giving the states more authority over spending intergovernmental funds. The House and Senate, however, could not agree on the specific legislation needed. Special interests from both the conservative and liberal sides deadlocked the conference committee that was charged with resolving their differences.

Congressional Quarterly's *Government at a Glance*

Federal Revenue Returns to the States

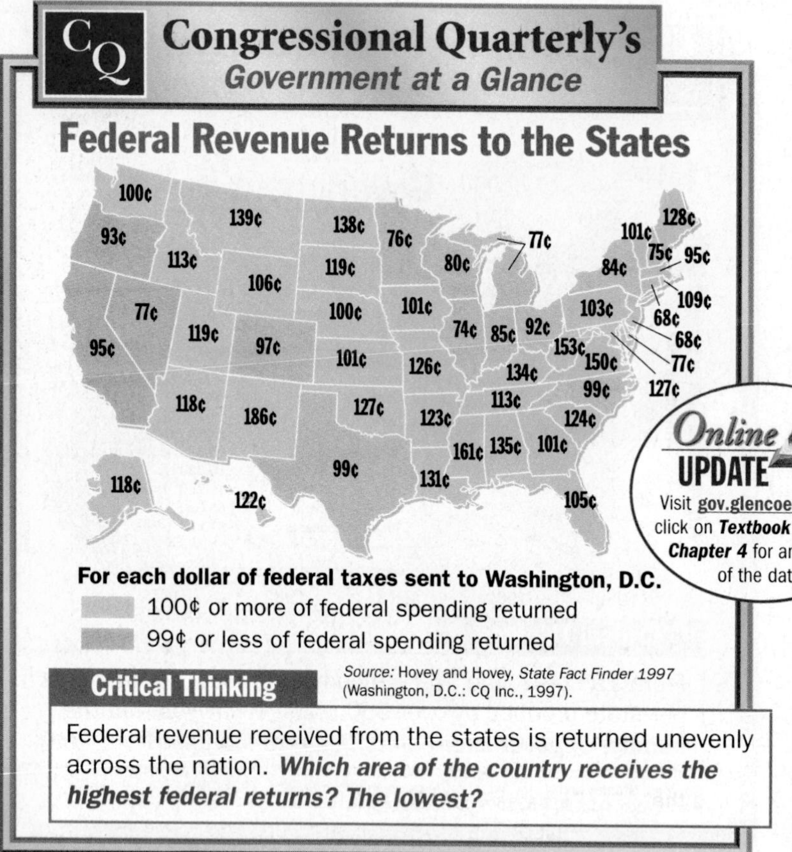

For each dollar of federal taxes sent to Washington, D.C.

- 100¢ or more of federal spending returned
- 99¢ or less of federal spending returned

Source: Hovey and Hovey, *State Fact Finder 1997* (Washington, D.C.: CQ Inc., 1997).

Critical Thinking

Federal revenue received from the states is returned unevenly across the nation. ***Which area of the country receives the highest federal returns? The lowest?***

Online UPDATE Visit gov.glencoe.com and click on ***Textbook Updates–Chapter 4*** for an update of the data.

When the effort to reform the federal system broke down in Congress, the task fell to the executive branch. Governors had long had an interest in obtaining increasing authority and flexibility in using federal funds. The nation's governors, through the National Governors' Association, urged the president to take action.

President Clinton earlier had appointed Vice President Al Gore to head the effort to reinvent government. The administration's National Performance Review drafted the statutory language that could be applied to individual agencies for new regulatory flexibility. It would allow the agencies to set aside federal rules and regulations that were counterproductive to public goals. The idea was not totally new. State requests for waivers of regulations had already been approved in the areas of health and human services, job training and education, the environment, and workplace safety. The Clinton administration seemed willing to extend the same favor in instances where states and localities provided commonsense reasons for sidestepping regulations. Those who were willing to put in the effort to support their case and follow through could now reinvent federalism one small step at a time.

Section 3 Assessment

Checking for Understanding

1. **Main Idea** Using a graphic organizer like the one below, identify three constitutional provisions that have been the basis for the tremendous growth of the national government.

the national government		

2. **Define** states' rights position, nationalist position, income tax.
3. **Identify** Chief Justice Roger B. Taney, Civil Rights Act of 1964, "New Federalism."
4. In what two ways has Congress used its taxing power to increase the national government's authority?

Critical Thinking

5. **Making Comparisons** What is the major difference between the states' rights and the nationalist views of federalism?

Federalism Write an opinion paper stating your position on the following question: Should the national government distribute money to states today with "no strings attached," or should the money be directed toward specific programs? Explain your position.

Supreme Court CASES TO DEBATE

Philadelphia v. *State of New Jersey*, 1978

Landfill in New Jersey

Americans take for granted the right to unrestricted travel from one state to another. If we make a purchase outside our home state, we know we can transport it home without paying a duty or fee. Are there any limits to traffic among the states? The case of City of Philadelphia *v.* State of New Jersey *addressed this question.*

Background of the Case

The disposal of solid and liquid wastes is a problem in urban areas. As the available sites for landfills continue to shrink, some metropolitan areas such as Philadelphia, Pennsylvania, have had to ship their wastes across state lines. In the early 1970s, the volume of waste being shipped into New Jersey was increasing rapidly. The state legislature believed that the treatment and disposal of wastes posed a threat to the quality of the environment in the state.

In 1973 the New Jersey legislature passed laws prohibiting the importation of solid or liquid waste that originated or was collected outside the territorial limits of the state. Operators of private landfills and several cities in other states with whom the collectors had contracts for waste disposal brought suit, attacking the New Jersey law as unconstitutional. They believed that it violated their right to ship materials across state lines under the commerce clause of the Constitution. The Supreme Court heard the case of *City of Philadelphia* v. *State of New Jersey* in 1978.

The Constitutional Issue

In the United States, power is divided among the national government, the state governments, and the people. The Constitution gave the national government power to regulate interstate commerce—trade that crosses state lines. In the New Jersey case, the issue was whether liquid and solid wastes could be defined as interstate commerce according to the Constitution.

Throughout United States history the Supreme Court has expanded the definition of interstate commerce. One early case occurred in 1824. The Court decided in *Gibbons* v. *Ogden* that travel by ship on the Hudson River between New York and New Jersey was interstate commerce. In the 1930s the Court upheld the Wagner Act, a law that extended the meaning of interstate commerce by allowing Congress to regulate business and labor relations. The Court also applied a broad definition of commerce to uphold the Civil Rights Act of 1964, considering the issue of commerce, specifically restaurants, along interstate highways.

Debating the Case

Questions to Consider

1. What caused new legislation to be passed in New Jersey in 1973?
2. Why do waste haulers consider their shipments a form of commerce?
3. What national impact might a decision concerning New Jersey have?

You Be the Judge

Many states are facing the same environmental and commerce issues that faced New Jersey. What could be a far-reaching result if the Court decided in favor of New Jersey? In favor of the landfill owners? In your opinion, does the commerce clause apply in this case? Why or why not?

Section 4

Federalism and Politics

Reader's Guide

Key Terms

sunset law, sunshine law, bureaucracy

Find Out

- How has federalism benefited the two-party system?
- What advantages does federalism provide a person who may be dissatisfied with conditions in his or her home state or area?

Understanding Concepts

Public Policy How does federalism allow for more political participation?

COVER STORY

Term Limits Dead

WASHINGTON, D.C., FEBRUARY 1997

A political reform that started in the states a decade ago came to a halt in Congress today. A proposed constitutional amendment to limit the number of terms a senator or representative could serve failed to pass the House. Not only was the vote well short of the two-thirds majority needed, but the proposal received less support than the last time it was considered, in 1995. Although more than 20 states have passed laws limiting the service of state legislators, the reform now seems unlikely to reach Congress. "Our existing system of term limits works splendidly," claimed Michigan Democrat John Dingell, "it's called elections."

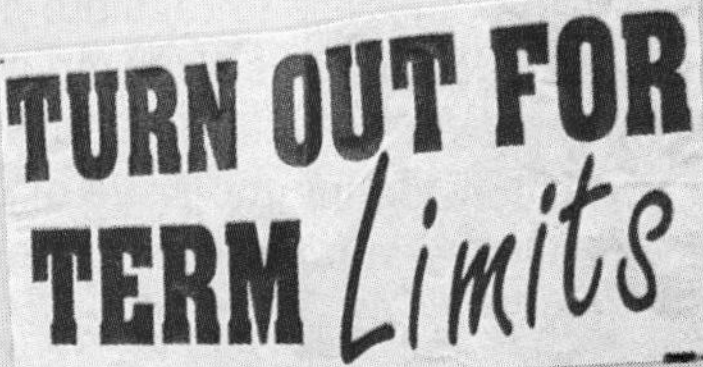

Calls for term limits

The issue of term limits for state and national representatives is just one example of how federalism influences the practice of politics and government. It affects government policy making, the political party system, the political activities of citizens, and the quality of life in the 50 states.

Federalism and Public Policy

A policy is a stated course of action. A high school principal says, "It is our policy that students not park in the teachers' parking lots." A local store announces, "It is our policy to prosecute all shoplifters." In each example, people are defining courses of action they take in response to problems that occur over and over again. Announcing a policy means that a person or an organization has decided upon a conscious, deliberate way of handling similar issues.

The course of action a government takes in response to some issue or problem is called **public policy.** Federalism affects public policy making in two ways. First, it affects how and where new policies are made in the United States. Second, it introduces limits on government policy making.

New Ideas Develop The existence of 50 states and thousands of local governments encourages experimenting with new policies and ideas. Federalism permits states and localities to serve as proving grounds where new policies can be developed and tested. Georgia, for example, was the first state to allow 18-year-olds to vote. That right has since been given to all Americans through the Twenty-sixth Amendment. In 1976 Colorado pioneered the use of **sunset laws.** Sunset laws require periodic checks of government agencies to see if they are still needed. In California local interest groups concerned with the environment were able to get the state to start new air-pollution control programs. California laws became a model for national air-pollution laws.

In 1976 Florida passed a **sunshine law** prohibiting public officials from holding closed meetings.

Policy may also originate at the national level. Sometimes the national government imposes new policies on states in which local pressure groups have resisted change. Some of the great political struggles in the nation's history have occurred over such policies. In the late 1950s and early 1960s, African Americans struggled to win voting and other civil rights in many states. State and local officials resisted these changes. Eventually, African American leaders attracted enough national attention and support to influence the national government to force the states to change civil rights and voting policies.

Federalism and Political Parties

Rival political parties are a key element of democratic government. Politics in the United States, however, is not a desperate all-or-nothing struggle for control of the national government, because federalism makes victories in state and local elections possible. Each political party has a chance to win some elections somewhere in the system. In this way, federalism helps to lessen the risk of one political party gaining a monopoly on political powers.

After the Civil War, for example, the Democratic Party went into a long period of decline on the national level. Yet the party survived because Democratic candidates managed to maintain control of many state and local offices in the Southern states. With such state and local bases, the party developed new policies and new leadership with which to challenge the majority party.

The Democratic Party controlled the White House for only 5 of the 12 presidential terms between 1952 and 2000. Democratic organization at the state and local level, however, enabled the party to win a majority in Congress during most of that period.

GOVERNMENT *Online*

Student Web Activity Visit the *United States Government: Democracy in Action* Web site at gov.glencoe.com and click on ***Chapter 4–Student Web Activities*** for an activity about federalism and politics.

We the People

Making a Difference

David Levitt

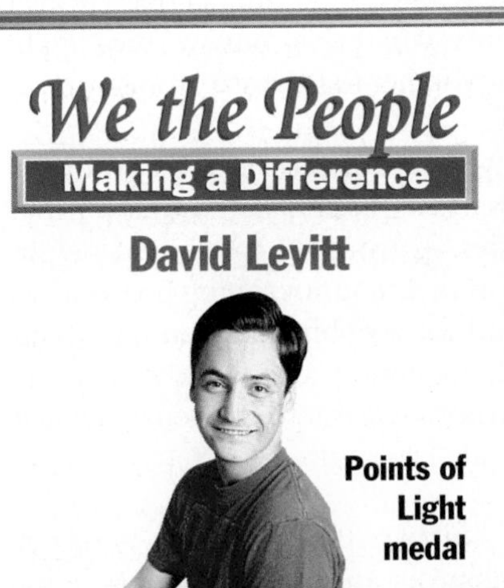

Points of Light medal

David Levitt was only a sixth grader when he decided to do something about the 30 million people in the United States who go to bed hungry every day. He asked his middle school principal whether he could start a program to distribute cafeteria leftovers. The principal pointed out that district health regulations prohibited using previously served food. But encouraged by his mother, David put a plan in motion. First he made his case before the Pinellas County (Florida) school board. After the board gave its approval, he worked to satisfy state health department requirements.

Since its beginnings in 1994, David's food sharing program has distributed more than a quarter of a million pounds of food to county shelters and food banks.

David's efforts to help the people of his state did not stop with the distribution of food. As a high school freshman David worked on state legislation to protect donors of surplus food from liability lawsuits. Most importantly, David's efforts have drawn attention to hunger and the availability of food in his community. David Levitt received recognition for his hard work. When he was awarded a Points of Light medal in a White House ceremony in 1996, David asked Mrs. Clinton what the White House did with its leftovers.

A Balanced Party System

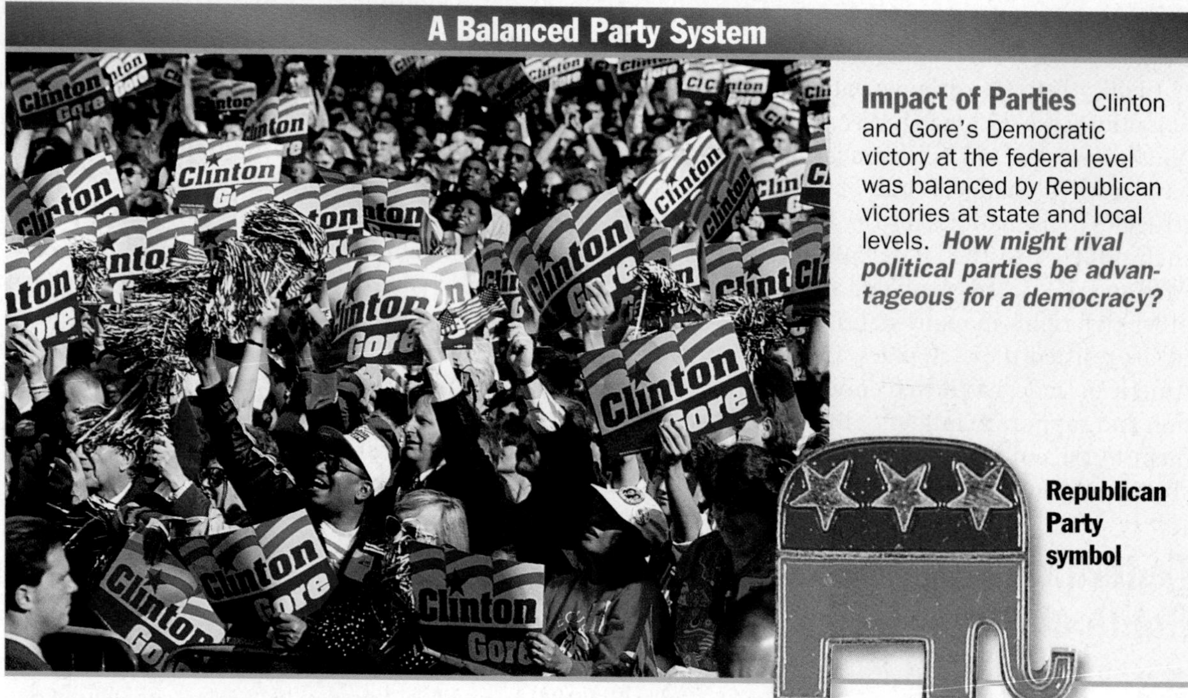

Impact of Parties Clinton and Gore's Democratic victory at the federal level was balanced by Republican victories at state and local levels. ***How might rival political parties be advantageous for a democracy?***

Republican Party symbol

Political Participation

Federalism increases opportunities for citizens of the United States to participate in politics at the national, state, and local levels. It also increases the possibility that a person's participation will have some practical effect at any one of these levels.

Many Opportunities Because federalism provides for several levels of government, people have easier access to political office. The road to national office often begins at the local or state level. This aspect of federalism has tended to preserve political organization from the bottom up.

American federalism gives citizens many points of access to government and increases their opportunities for influencing public policy. Noted political scientist Martin Grodzins believes the two-party system contributes to this access:

> *"The lack of party discipline produces an openness in the system that allows individuals, groups, and institutions (including state and local governments) to attempt to influence national policy at every step of the legislative process."*
>
> —Martin Grodzins, 1985

Americans vote frequently for governors, state lawmakers, mayors, council members, school board members, county prosecutors, and many other state and local officials. They also vote on such local issues as whether to build a mass transit system in their city, whether to outlaw smoking in public places, or whether to increase property taxes for schools.

Citizens may also work with interest groups to influence national policies and state and local government agencies. A group of concerned neighbors may petition their county zoning board to set aside nearby land for a public playground. Members of a local labor union may work together to support their union's efforts to influence passage of a law in the state legislature.

Increasing Chances of Success A related effect of federalism is an increased chance that one's political participation will have some practical impact. Most people are more likely to become involved in political activities if they think there is a reasonable chance their efforts will bear fruit. People working in the campaign of a candidate for city council, for example, need to persuade relatively few voters to elect their candidate. The increased chance for success encourages political participation.

Federalism's Professional Politicians

Since the 1960s more and more public policy has been initiated by people in government service. The great increase in federal programs beginning in the mid-1930s called for a large **bureaucracy,** or organization of government administrators, to carry out legislation. As these bureaucrats gained expertise, they increasingly offered solutions. Political writer Samuel H. Beer describes the results:

> *"In the fields of health, housing, urban renewal, transportation, welfare, education, poverty, and energy, it has been . . . people in government service . . . acting on the basis of their specialized and technical knowledge, who first perceived the problem, conceived the program, initially urged it on president and Congress, went on to help lobby it through to enactment, and then saw to its administration."*
>
> —Samuel H. Beer, 1986

Various political analysts have used the term *technocracy* to describe this kind of decision making which is based on the technical expertise of professionals.

The increase in federal programs also changed the political relationship of state and federal officials. As mayors and state officials sought to take advantage of the new federal programs, they needed to work more closely with federal officials. Organizations such as the United States Conference of Mayors established headquarters in Washington, D. C., to keep up with events and in touch with lawmakers. In time these officials acquired political influence.

Online UPDATE Visit gov.glencoe.com and click on ***Textbook Updates–Chapter 4*** for an update of the data.

Differences Among the States

Federalism contributes to real economic and political differences among the states because it permits each state considerable freedom in arranging its own internal affairs. As a result, some states do more than others to regulate business and industry, while some provide more health and welfare services. Among the individual states, some have stricter criminal laws, some have higher taxes.

Because states can create different economic and political environments, Americans have more choices regarding the conditions under which they want to live. This also means that when people cross a state boundary, they become members of a different political system with its own officials, taxes, and laws.

The Direction of Federalism

Contemporary American federalism has experienced a dramatic shift toward the states. Governors are demanding more responsibility, and budget pressures are acute. In response Congress passed the Unfunded Mandates Reform Act of 1995, limiting the federal government's power to require state and local governments to

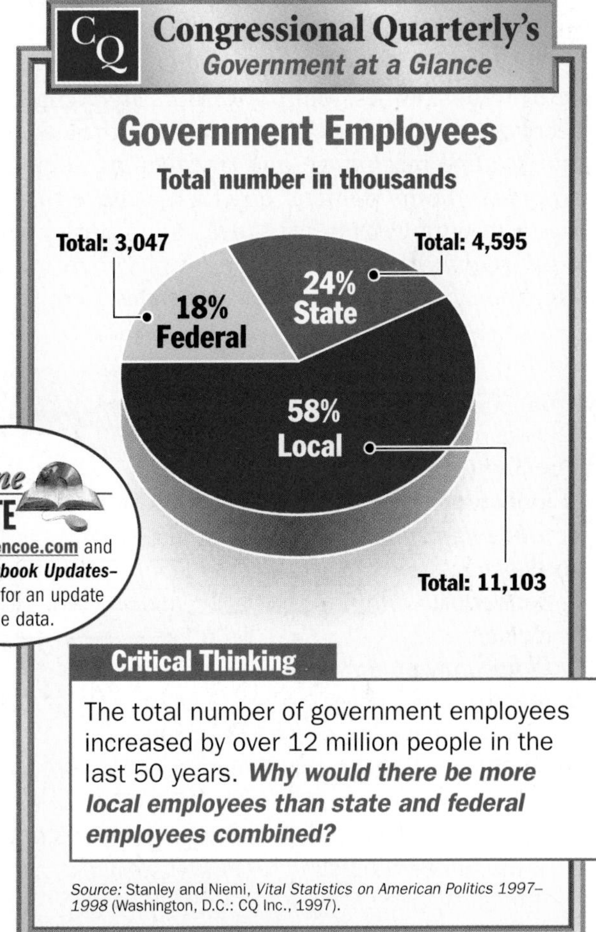

Source: Stanley and Niemi, *Vital Statistics on American Politics 1997–1998* (Washington, D.C.: CQ Inc., 1997).

Accepting New Responsibilities

Federalism at Work
Despite reduced federal aid, Cleveland's mayor Michael White adopted a hard-driving business style of management to help turn around a once-troubled city. ***How are local leaders, like Mayor White, working to reshape federalism?***

Cleveland's city seal

provide services that are not funded from Washington, D.C. At the same time the federal government is loosening regulations, it is tightening the purse strings. This has the effect of shifting the social policy agenda to the states.

The states are ready and willing to accept new responsibilities. Many governors are reengineering state government, modernizing their administrative machinery, and overhauling social programs. Some political observers believe that the shifting power toward states and localities is supported by the need for community identity. Neighborhoods, towns, cities, and states seem to provide more community identity than the national government does. Local governments also feel they more fully understand the needs of their citizens.

For years, people assumed that the national government had the most talented experts and trained executives. Today there is an increasing realization that state governments have talented men and women as nongovernmental advisers who can offer creative innovations in governing. States also have an abundance of expertise in state and local government personnel to guide these innovations. States are using their strengths to reshape American federalism.

Section 4 Assessment

Checking for Understanding

1. **Main Idea** Using a graphic organizer like the one to the right, show two ways that federalism influences public policy making.

   Federalism → [ ] / [ ]

2. **Define** sunset law, sunshine law, bureaucracy.
3. **Identify** public policy.
4. How did African Americans use national attention to change policy in state and local governments in the 1950s and 1960s?
5. How does federalism affect the two-party system in the United States?

Critical Thinking

6. **Making Inferences** How does federalism allow for political and economic diversity among the states?

Public Policy Federalism allows people to have easier access to political office and greater opportunities for influencing public policy. Find out the political offices that a person living in your community can vote for on the state and local levels. Illustrate your findings in a poster display.

Skills

Study and Writing

Writing a Paragraph

Writing a good paragraph involves stating information clearly and in a logical order. A well-organized paragraph helps you express your ideas clearly. You can use this skill for many purposes, from writing a speech to writing the answers to the essay questions on your next test.

Auto impact tests

Learning the Skill

To write a good paragraph, follow these steps:

- Decide on the main idea you want to express and write it in sentence form. This will be the topic sentence of the paragraph.
- Include sentences that add information and explain or expand the main idea expressed in the topic sentence.
- Evaluate your paragraph. Does the topic sentence state the main idea clearly? Do the other sentences support the main idea?

Read the paragraph below. The topic sentence clearly states the main idea. The sentences that follow support the main idea.

Today federalism is more complicated than simply a struggle between nationalists and supporters of states' rights. Sometimes, states' rights supporters and national government supporters switch sides, depending on which view best serves their interests at the time. For example, since 1930 most business groups have supported states' rights. These groups believe state courts and state legislatures are more likely to make decisions favorable to businesses than the national government. In 1966, however, the auto industry supported national auto safety standards. Why? The industry realized that the national standards were likely to be more moderate than the tough state regulations set by California and New York, where automakers sold nearly 20 percent of their cars.

Practicing the Skill

Follow the steps described and organize the sentences below into an effective paragraph.

1. These powers include any powers not reserved for the national government by the Constitution.
2. The Constitution allows for concurrent powers—those shared by the national and state governments.
3. Concurrent powers are exercised separately and simultaneously by the two basic levels of government.
4. An example of a concurrent power is the levying of taxes.

Application Activity

Choose a topic related to this chapter and write an explanatory paragraph about it. Then exchange papers with a classmate. Evaluate the paragraphs according to step three under Learning the Skill.

The **Glencoe Skillbuilder Interactive Workbook, Level 2** provides instruction and practice in key social studies skills.

Assessment and Activities

Self-Check Quiz Visit the *United States Government: Democracy in Action* Web site at gov.glencoe.com and click on ***Chapter 4–Self-Check Quizzes*** to prepare for the chapter test.

Reviewing Key Terms

On a sheet of paper write the headings "National Government" and "State Government." Group the terms below under the appropriate heading.

1. implied powers
2. expressed powers
3. inherent powers
4. reserved powers
5. elastic clause

Recalling Facts

1. Name the clause of the Constitution that resolves conflicts between state law and national law.
2. Which governments are responsible for creating cities and counties?
3. Who provided Americans with a lasting definition of federalism?
4. Describe how Congress gained power to regulate farm production, child labor, wages and hours, and criminal conduct.
5. What is the major source of income for the national government?
6. How did federalism help the Democratic Party survive after the Civil War?
7. How does the federalist system affect political participation?
8. Who pays for elections of senators, representatives, and presidential electors?

Researching Federalism Use the electronic index to periodicals in your library or the *Readers' Guide to Periodical Literature* to find an article that provides a recent example of cooperation between the federal and state governments. Write a brief summary of the article and post it on a bulletin board display.

Understanding Concepts

1. **Federalism** Why does the Tenth Amendment use the term *reserved* to describe the powers that belong to the people and the states?
2. **Federalism** On what historical basis do states' rights supporters argue that the national government is only an agent of the states?
3. **Public Policy** Experts in government agencies initiate many national laws in health, the environment, energy, welfare, education, and business. Why do these bureaucrats have great influence on legislation and decision making?

Critical Thinking

1. **Making Comparisons** Use a graphic organizer like the one below to compare President Ronald Reagan's concept of federalism with President Franklin D. Roosevelt's.

Concepts of Federalism	
Roosevelt	Reagan

2. **Identifying Central Issues** What was the main issue in the case of *McCulloch* v. *Maryland?*

3. **Identifying Assumptions** "Federalism helps lessen the risk of one political party gaining a monopoly on political powers." What assumption about the value of a two-party system does this statement make?

Cooperative Learning Activity

Creating a Front Page Choose an event from this chapter that illustrates the development of the federal system. Work together in groups to produce a newspaper front page that reports the event. The page should include a lead article and several supporting articles. Some students will research the event; others will write about it, edit the articles, and lay out the page. A few students may produce cartoons to illustrate the news event.

Interpreting Political Cartoons Activity

"Look, the American people don't want to be bossed around by federal bureaucrats. They want to be bossed around by state bureaucrats."

1. How does this cartoon demonstrate the states' rights position of federalism?
2. How are the American people "bossed around" by federal bureaucrats?
3. Is the speaker probably a state or federal official? Why?

Technology Activity

Using the Internet Use the Library of Congress World Wide Web home page to find out about several bills that are being considered in the current congressional term. Identify the kind of power—expressed, implied, or inherent—that each piece of legislation illustrates.

Skill Practice Activity

Writing a Paragraph Write a short paragraph for each of the topic sentences that follow. Each paragraph must have at least three sentences supporting the topic and be arranged in a logical way. Use transitional words or phrases to connect your ideas smoothly.

1. The Supreme Court decides conflicts between the national and state governments.
2. States' rights advocates and nationalist position supporters disagree on how federalism should operate.
3. States must compete for funds from the national government.

Participating in Local Government

Congress has the power to add new states to the Union. Find out how and when your state was first settled, developed government, and was admitted to the Union. Use research materials from your school or local library and present your findings in an illustrated report. Create a time line that includes important governmental developments.

UNIT 2

The Legislative Branch

Congressional Voting *How well does your member of Congress represent your interests when he or she votes on bills? Track your representative's vote on important bills during this session of Congress. Post the voting record on a class bulletin board. Write or E-mail your representative regarding how well his or her votes matched your class's positions.*

Electronic Field Trip

The Capitol

Take a virtual tour of the Capitol Building in Washington, D.C., and discover first-hand how the legislative branch works.

Glencoe's Democracy in Action Video Program

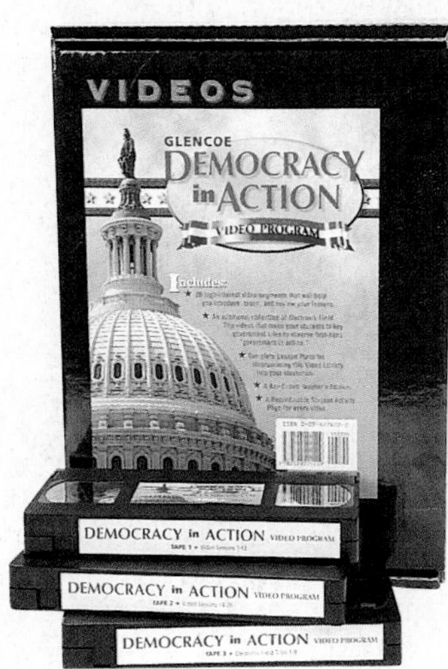

The United States Capitol is a symbol of American government. The **Democracy in Action** video program "The Capitol," referenced below, shows how the Capitol has been the center of decision making throughout America's past and continues to be the focus of the nation's attention.

As you view the video program, try to identify several of the functions that the Capitol serves.

Also available in videodisc format.

View the videodisc by scanning the barcode or by entering the chapter number on your keypad and pressing Search.

Disc 2, Side 1, Chapter 2

Hands-On Activity

Use library or Internet resources to find information about your state capitol, where your state legislature meets. Create an information pamphlet about your state capitol. Incorporate information about historic events, present-day uses, architectural influences, art objects or symbols in the building. Use a word processor to design and compose your pamphlet.

◀ **The statue *Freedom*, cast in bronze with the help of enslaved laborers, stands on top of the dome of the United States Capitol.**

The Organization of Congress

Why It's Important

Your Congress Beginning in January each year, 535 members of Congress come together to determine such things as the safety of your workplace, the amount of taxes you pay, and how medical care will be provided.

To learn more about how Congress works and how it impacts you, view the ***Democracy in Action*** Chapter 5 video lesson:

The Organization of Congress

Chapter Overview Visit the *United States Government: Democracy in Action* Web site at gov.glencoe.com and click on ***Chapter 5–Overview*** to preview chapter information.

Congressional Membership

Reader's Guide

Key Terms

bicameral legislature, session, census, reapportionment, redistrict, gerrymander, at-large, censure, incumbent

Find Out

- How does apportionment of membership in the House of Representatives in districts provide representation to local voters?
- What are the key common characteristics of members of Congress?

Understanding Concepts

Political Processes How well do you think members of Congress represent the people who have delegated legal authority to them?

COVER STORY

Congress Votes Out Perks

WASHINGTON, D.C., 1996

Rank had its privilege, until Congress heard rumblings from the people. Pressured by constituents, senators decided to hand over a few perks. They voted out free lunches, as well as costly gifts and expense-paid junkets to fancy resorts. Was the vote about politics or real reform? Wisconsin Democrat Russell Feingold said, "We in the Senate have to show that we are not fundamentally different from other people." The senators refused to surrender their free parking at the National Airport, however.

Free parking at National Airport

The Founders did not intend to make Congress a privileged group, but they did intend that the legislative branch have more power than any other branch of government. The Constitution emphasized the importance of the lawmaking power by describing Congress in Article I. As James Madison said, Congress is "the First Branch of this Government."

The United States Congress is a **bicameral legislature**—it is made up of two houses: the Senate and the House of Representatives. Most delegates to the Constitutional Convention agreed to a bicameral legislature. Eighteenth-century colonial legislatures had followed the English Parliament with its upper house and a lower house.

Today Congress plays a central role in formulating national policies. Congress initiates and approves laws dealing with everything from health care to tax changes.

Congressional Sessions

Each term of Congress starts on January 3 of odd-numbered years and lasts for two years. For example, the 106th Congress began its term in January 1999; the 107th Congress began in January 2001.

Each term of Congress is divided into two **sessions,** or meetings. A session lasts one year and includes breaks for holidays and vacations. Until about 1933 Congress remained in session generally beginning in December and ending in March. Because of an increasing workload and the Twentieth Amendment, today a session of Congress often lasts from January until November or December.

Congress remains in session until its members vote to adjourn. Neither the House nor the Senate may adjourn for more than three days without the approval of the other house. If Congress is adjourned, the president may call it back for a special session.

◀ **The United States Capitol**

Division of the House

◀ **Past** During sessions of the British House of Commons, "the Government," (shown here) led by Prime Minister William Pitt in the 1790s, sits on one side while the "opposition" sits on the other side. The speaker sits in the center, between the two parties.

Present British procedures influenced the U.S. House of Representatives. Each major political party sits on one side of the chamber, while the Speaker occupies a platform in the front and center.
▼

Political Processes
How does the physical division into political groups help the Speaker of the House to moderate debates?

Membership of the House

With its 435 members, the House of Representatives is the larger body of Congress. The Constitution does not fix the number of representatives in the House. It simply states that the number of House seats must be apportioned, or divided, among the states on the basis of population. Each state is entitled to at least one seat in the House, no matter how small its population.

Qualifications The Constitution sets the qualifications for election to the House of Representatives. Representatives must be at least 25 years old, be citizens of the United States for at least 7 years, and be legal residents of the state that elects them. Traditionally, representatives also live in the district they represent.

Term of Office Members of the House of Representatives are elected for 2-year terms. Elections are held in November of even-numbered years—for example, 1996, 1998, and 2000. Representatives begin their term of office on January 3 following the November election. This means that every 2 years, all 435 members of the House must run for reelection. It also means that the House reorganizes itself every 2 years. Because more than 90 percent of all representatives are reelected, however, there is great continuity in the House. If a representative dies or resigns before the end of the term of office, the governor of the state he or she represented may appoint a temporary replacement until a special election can be called to fill the vacancy.

Representation and Reapportionment

In order to assign representation according to population, the **Census Bureau** takes a national **census,** or population count, every 10 years. The first census was taken in 1790, and each state was apportioned its representatives. The next census will be in 2000. The population of each state determines the new number of representatives to which each is entitled—a process called **reapportionment.** States whose population increases less rapidly than others or whose population decreases may lose representatives, while states whose population grows faster may be entitled to more representatives.

Originally the House had only 64 members. Over the years, as the population of the nation grew, the number of representatives increased. After the 1810 census the House had 186 members. By 1911 the House had 435 members. After the debate sparked by the 1920 census, and concern about the increasing size of the House, Congress passed the Reapportionment Act of 1929 limiting the House to 435 representatives. Now each census determines how those 435 seats will be divided among the 50 states.

Congressional Redistricting After the states find out their reapportioned representation for the next 10-year period, each state legislature sets up congressional districts—one for each representative. Representatives are elected from these congressional districts. If a state is entitled to only one representative, it has one congressional district. In most states the state legislature draws the boundary lines for each congressional election district. The process of setting up new district lines after reapportionment has been completed is called **redistricting.**

Over the years some state legislatures abused the redistricting power. They did so in two ways—by creating congressional districts of very unequal populations and by gerrymandering. During the early 1960s, for example, there were some states in which the largest district in the state had twice the population of the smallest district. In these states a person's vote in the largest congressional districts had only half the value of a person's vote in the smallest districts.

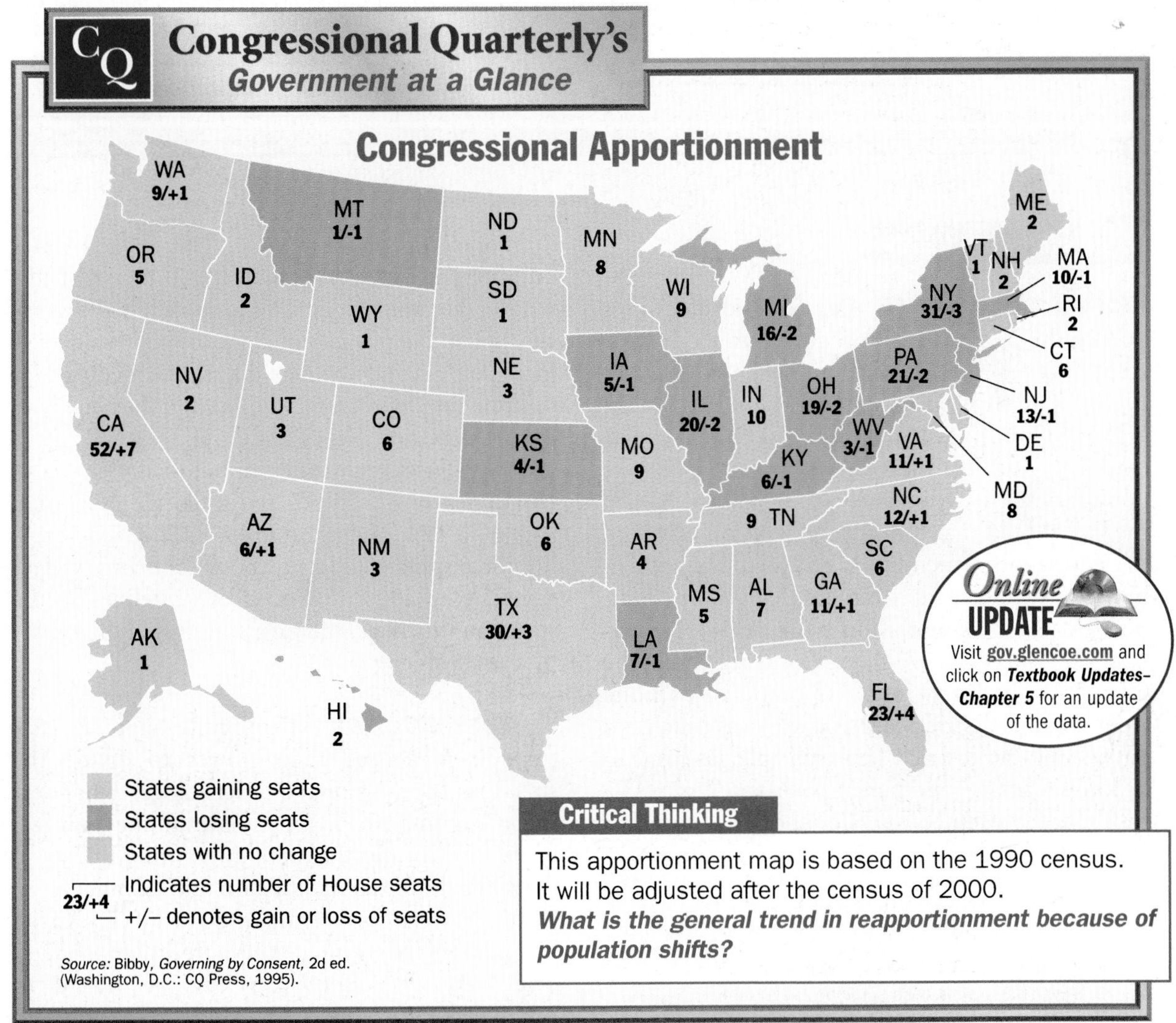

Source: Bibby, *Governing by Consent*, 2d ed. (Washington, D.C.: CQ Press, 1995).

Critical Thinking

This apportionment map is based on the 1990 census. It will be adjusted after the census of 2000.
What is the general trend in reapportionment because of population shifts?

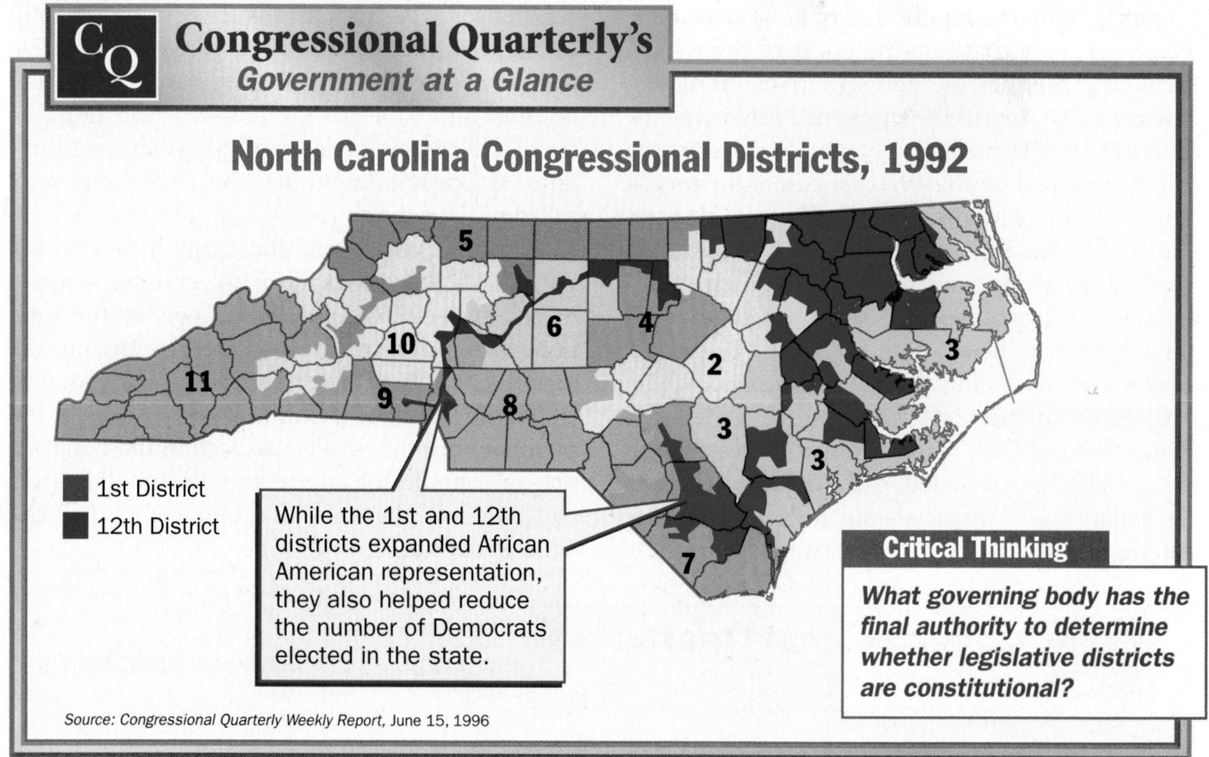

Redistricting Cases In a series of decisions during the 1960s, the Supreme Court addressed reapportionment issues in Tennessee, Georgia, and Alabama. In a case originating in Tennessee, *Baker* v. *Carr*[1] (1962), the Court held that federal courts could decide conflicts over drawing district boundaries. Two years later, in *Reynolds* v. *Sims*[2], the Court held that the equal protection clause of the Fourteenth Amendment required that seats in both houses of the Alabama state legislature be apportioned on a population basis. In *Wesberry* v. *Sanders*[3] (Georgia, 1964), the Court ruled that the Constitution clearly intended that a vote in one congressional district was to be worth as much as a vote in another district. This principle has come to be known as the "one-person, one-vote" rule. As a result, today each congressional district contains about 600,000 people.

Following the census of 1990, several states drew new district lines to increase the power of ethnic or racial minorities. This approach had two results. First, the number of minority representatives increased. Second, the new districts tended to concentrate the Democratic vote, leaving the neighboring districts more Republican.

The Supreme Court upheld challenges to North Carolina's 1992 redistricting (see map above) in 1996 and again in 1998. The second ruling forced the state to postpone its primary elections. Because there are no clear guidelines for the states on this issue, the Court has ruled on a case-by-case basis.

Gerrymandering Historically, state legislatures have abused their power to divide the state into congressional districts by gerrymandering. **Gerrymandering** means that the political party controlling the state government draws a district's boundaries to gain an advantage in elections. Gerrymandering often results in district boundaries that have very irregular shapes. The term *gerrymandering* can be traced to **Elbridge Gerry,** an early Democratic-Republican

See the following footnoted materials in the ***Reference Handbook:***
1. *Baker* v. *Carr* case summary, page 754.
2. *Reynolds* v. *Sims* case summary, page 764.
3. *Wesberry* v. *Sanders* case summary, page 767.

governor of Massachusetts. Gerry had signed a redistricting plan that gave his party a big political advantage over the Federalists. To a map of one particularly irregular district that looked like a salamander, artist Gilbert Stuart added a head, wings, and claws. A newspaper editor published the map as a cartoon and labeled it a "Gerrymander." Federalists popularized the term.

"Packing" and "cracking" are ways to gerrymander. *Packing* a district means drawing the lines so they include as many of the opposing party's voters as possible. Crowding the opposition's voters into one district makes the remaining districts safe for the majority party's candidates. *Cracking* means dividing an opponent's voters into other districts. This division weakens the opponent's voter base.

The Supreme Court has ruled that congressional districts must be compact and contiguous, or physically adjoining. This requirement, plus the one-person, one-vote ruling, has cut down on some of the worst examples of gerrymandering. Nevertheless, the competitive struggle of the two-party system continues to fuel the practice of gerrymandering. Many districts today are still drawn in irregular shapes for political reasons.

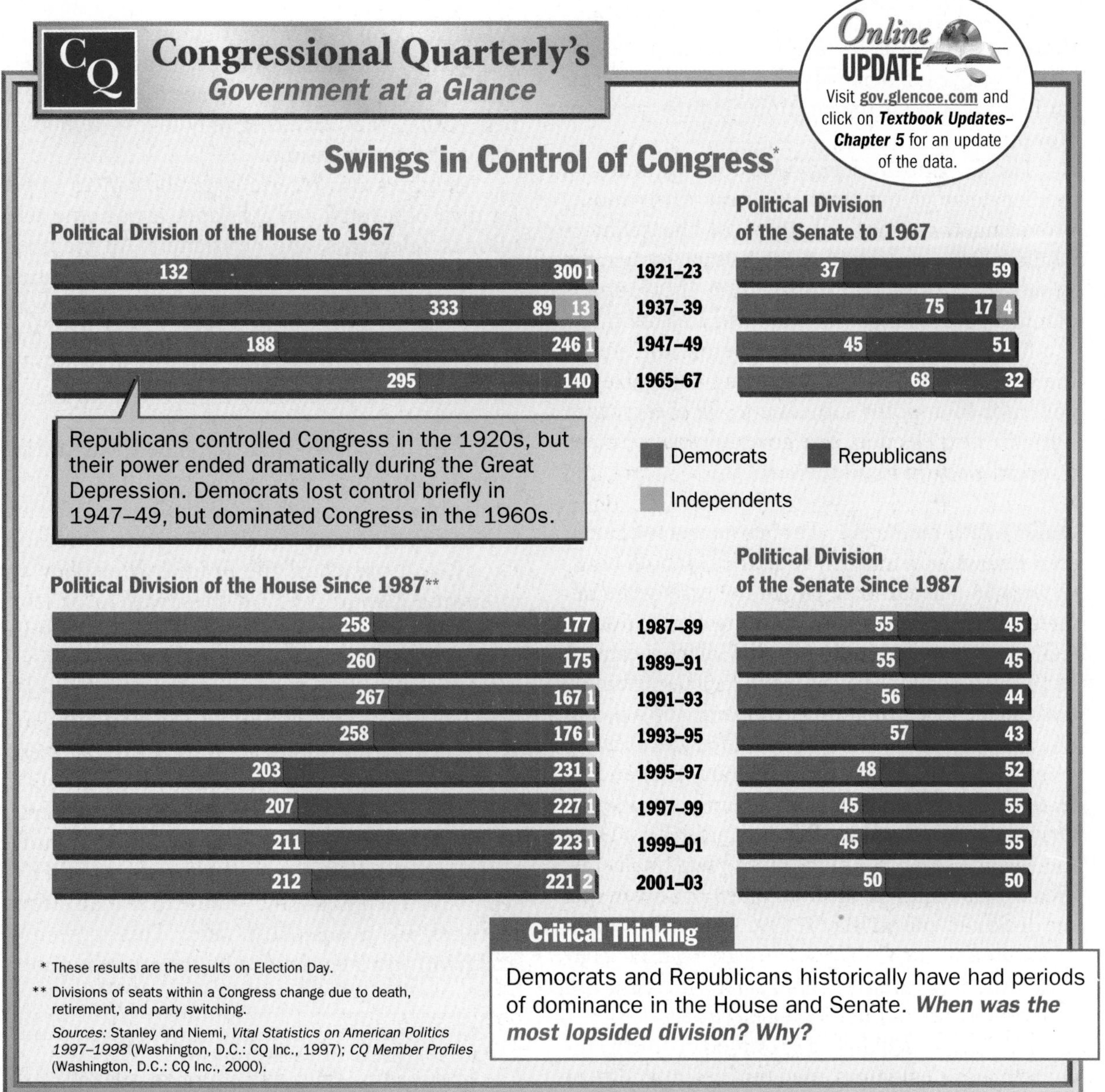

Membership of the Senate

According to the Constitution, the Senate "shall be composed of two senators from each state." Thus, each state is represented equally. Today's Senate includes 100 members—2 from each of the 50 states.

Qualifications The Constitution provides that senators must be at least 30 years old, citizens of the United States for 9 years before election, and legal residents of the state they represent. All voters of each state elect senators at-large, or statewide.

Term of Office Elections for the Senate, like those for the House, are held in November of even-numbered years. Senators also begin their terms on January 3, after the election held the previous November.

The Constitution provided for continuity in the Senate by giving senators 6-year terms and by providing that only one-third of the senators would run for reelection every 2 years. In fact, the Senate has more continuity than the Framers planned because most senators win reelection.

If a senator dies or resigns before the end of the term, the state legislature may authorize the governor to appoint someone to fill the vacancy until the next election. The governor may also call a special election to fill the seat.

Salary and Benefits The Senate and the House set their own salaries. In 1789 salaries for both houses were $6 per day. Low pay in the early years deterred some people from running for Congress. Congress has voted itself periodic salary increases. In 1991 it voted for a pay hike of $23,000, explaining that the increase would be accompanied by a prohibition on honoraria—money paid for speeches.

Meanwhile, a constitutional amendment affecting legislative salaries was being considered. Originally proposed by James Madison in 1789, the **Twenty-seventh Amendment**[1] was finally ratified by the required 38 states when Michigan cast the deciding vote on May 7, 1992. The amendment prohibits a sitting Congress from giving itself a pay raise. Any new congressional salary increase will take effect after an intervening election.

Almost immediately a group of plaintiffs, including some legislators, used the new amendment to challenge a cost-of-living adjustment to raise salaries to $133,600 in January 1993. (Automatic cost of living adjustments raised salaries to $141,300 in 2000.) A United States District Court judge had ruled that:

> "*Automatic annual adjustments to congressional salaries meet both the language and the spirit of the 27th Amendment. . . . One way to maintain high-quality government is to provide our elected officials with a living wage that automatically changes to reflect changed economic conditions.*"
>
> —Judge Stanley Sporkin, 1992

In addition to their salaries, members of Congress enjoy a number of benefits and resources. These include stationery, postage for official business (called the **"franking privilege"**), a medical clinic, and a gymnasium.

Members also receive large allowances to pay for their office staff and assistants, trips home, telephones, telegrams, and newsletters. All members are entitled to an income tax deduction to help maintain two residences, one in their home state and one in Washington, D.C. Moreover, when they retire, senators and representatives may be eligible for pensions of $150,000 or more a year for life.

Privileges of Members The Constitution provides members of Congress certain protections while they carry out their legislative duties. They are free from arrest "in all cases except treason, felony, and breach of the peace," when they are attending Congress or on their way to or from Congress. Members of Congress cannot be sued for anything they say on the House or Senate floor.

This privilege does not extend to what members may say outside of Congress. In *Hutchinson* v. *Proxmire*[2] (1979), the Supreme Court ruled that members of Congress may be sued for libel for statements they make in news releases or newsletters.

The Senate and the House both may judge members' qualifications and decide whether to seat them. Each house may refuse to seat an elected member by a majority vote. This power of **exclusion** was later defined by the Supreme Court

---

See the following footnoted materials in the **Reference Handbook:**
1. *The Constitution*, pages 774–799.
2. *Hutchinson* v. *Proxmire* case summary, page 760.

in the case of *Powell* v. *McCormack* (see Supreme Court Cases to Debate on page 131). Each house may also "punish its own members for disorderly behavior" by a majority vote and expel a legislator by a two-thirds vote. Only the most serious offenses such as treason or accepting bribes are grounds for expulsion. Members who are guilty of lesser offenses may be censured. **Censure** is a vote of formal disapproval of a member's actions.

The Members of Congress

Congress includes 535 voting members—100 senators and 435 representatives. In addition, there are 4 delegates in the House—1 each from the District of Columbia, Guam, American Samoa, and the Virgin Islands—and 1 resident commissioner from Puerto Rico, none of whom can vote. However, they do attend sessions, introduce bills, speak in debates, and vote in committees.

Characteristics Nearly half the members of Congress are lawyers. A large number of members also come from business, banking, and education. Why are there so many lawyers? Because lawyers by profession deal with laws, it is logical for them to serve as legislators. Training in law helps a legislator understand the complex legal issues that may affect legislation.

Senators and representatives typically have been white, middle-aged males. The average age of members of Congress is usually over 50. Slowly Congress has begun to reflect the racial, ethnic, and gender diversity of the general population.

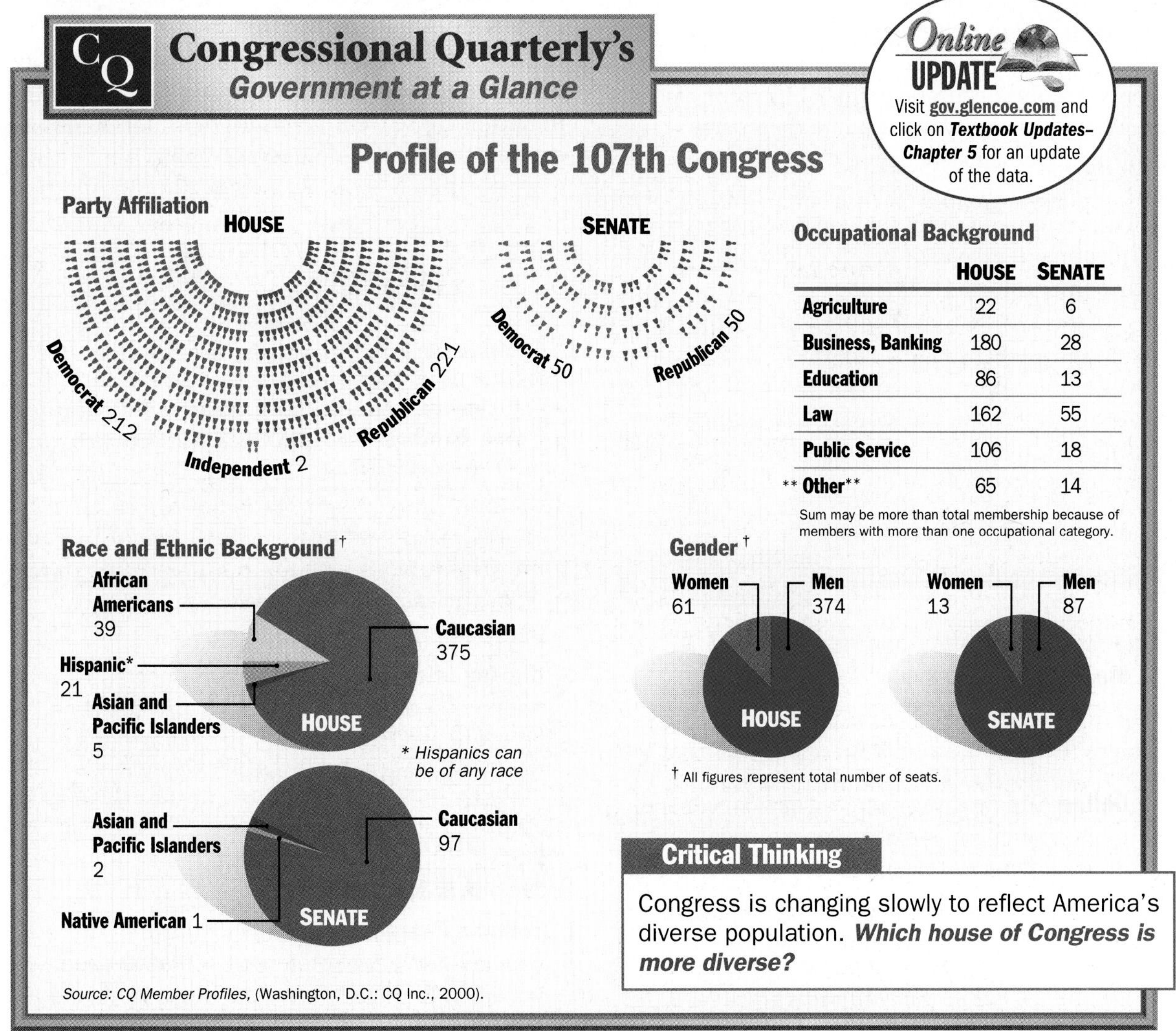

Occupational Background

	HOUSE	SENATE
Agriculture	22	6
Business, Banking	180	28
Education	86	13
Law	162	55
Public Service	106	18
Other**	65	14

** Sum may be more than total membership because of members with more than one occupational category.

Critical Thinking

Congress is changing slowly to reflect America's diverse population. ***Which house of Congress is more diverse?***

Reelection to Congress Membership in Congress has changed very slowly because officeholders seldom lose reelection. One representative put it simply: "All members of Congress have one primary interest—to be reelected." Beginning with Franklin Roosevelt's landslide presidential victories in the 1930s, incumbency helped Democrats dominate Congress in all but a few years.

Between 1945 and 1990, about 90 percent of all **incumbents,** or those members already in office, won reelection. In some elections, many seats went unchallenged because opponents knew that they would have little or no chance of winning. One analyst said that winning an election to Congress for most members was like removing olives from a bottle—"after the first one, the rest come easy."

Why have incumbents been so successful? First, incumbents find it easier to raise campaign funds. **Political action committees** (PACs) provide substantial campaign funds, usually supporting incumbents. Second, incumbents may represent districts that have been gerrymandered in their party's favor. Third, incumbents are better known to voters, who may have met them at rallies or have seen them on television, or read about them in newspapers. Finally, incumbents use their position and office staff to help solve problems for voters.

In the 1990s several factors worked together to boost the chances of challengers in congressional races. First came a growing wave of criticism against the entrenched power that seemed to accompany lengthy terms in office. Then the public targeted government as an institution that had to change. In 1992 voters chose a new Democratic president and 121 new members of Congress.

The Voters Speak In 1994 the tide against incumbents resulted in a big turnabout in Congress, placing Republicans in control of both houses for the first time since 1954. Powerful long-term senators and representatives lost their seats. The standing Speaker of the House, Democrat Thomas Foley, was defeated in that election. Almost half of the freshman members had never held an elected office. In 1996, however, incumbents returned to their winning ways. More than 90 percent of incumbents, both Democrats and Republicans who were running for reelection, won.

House Speaker Newt Gingrich and other Republicans projected gains for their party in the 1998 elections. Democrats, however, won some key House races, cutting the Republican majority to only twelve seats. Gingrich then announced he would resign as speaker and leave Congress. Republicans chose Dennis Hastert of Illinois as speaker when the 106th Congress convened.

GOVERNMENT Online

Student Web Activity Visit the *United States Government: Democracy in Action* Web site at gov.glencoe.com and click on ***Chapter 5–Student Web Activities*** for an activity about the Congressional membership.

Section 1 Assessment

Checking for Understanding

1. **Main Idea** In a graphic organizer similar to the one below, compare the qualifications for representatives and senators.

House	Senate

2. **Define** bicameral legislature, session, census, reapportionment, redistrict, gerrymander, at-large, censure, incumbent.
3. **Identify** Elbridge Gerry, Twenty-seventh Amendment, political action committee.
4. How does Congress reapportion House seats among the states every ten years?

Critical Thinking

5. **Making Inferences** Members of Congress spend part of their time working for reelection. Which house has a greater percentage of its time remaining for legislative work? Why?

Political Processes What percentage of people believe that their representative does not listen to them? Formulate a questionnaire that surveys voters about this issue.

Powell v. *McCormack*, 1969

The Constitution gives Congress the power to be the "Judge of the Elections, Returns and Qualifications of its own Members." It establishes the age, citizenship, and residence requirements for the House and Senate. Does the Constitution allow Congress to judge qualifications beyond these three specific requirements? The case of Powell *v.* McCormack *addressed this question.*

Adam Clayton Powell, Jr.

Background of the Case

Adam Clayton Powell, Jr., was reelected to the House of Representatives in November 1966. However, a congressional investigation had already disclosed questionable activities by Powell and members of his staff during his previous terms. The House refused to seat Powell. In March 1967 Congress declared the seat vacant and notified the governor of New York to order a new election.

Powell charged that he had been unlawfully excluded from his seat in the House and brought suit in the federal courts. Speaker John McCormack and four other officials were named as defendants. They responded that Congress had authority under the Constitution to judge the qualifications of its own members.

The federal district court dismissed the complaint on the grounds that it did not have jurisdiction in this matter. The United States Court of Appeals for the District of Columbia refused to hear the case on the grounds that it was essentially a political question. The Supreme Court heard the case of *Powell* v. *McCormack* in 1969. The 90th Congress, to which Powell had been elected, was no longer in session. In the meantime (1968) Powell had been elected again and seated in the 91st Congress. His lawyers now asked the Court for back salary for the two years he was denied his seat.

The Constitutional Issue

One constitutional question was whether the case was justiciable—could be decided by the Court—under the Constitution. The defendants held that the case was not justiciable by the Court because the Constitution gave Congress, not the Court, power to judge the qualifications of its members.

Further, defendants submitted that the question was "political" and therefore not justiciable by the Court. Finally, defendants asked whether the Court could coerce officers of the House or issue injunctions compelling officers or employees of the House to perform specific acts.

Powell's lawyers believed that Congress did not have the power to judge the moral qualifications of members. The Supreme Court referred to debates at the Constitutional Convention that related to giving Congress power to judge its members' qualifications.

Debating the Case

Questions to Consider

1. What might be a far-reaching result if the Court decided in favor of the Speaker?
2. What might be a far-reaching result if the Court decided in favor of Adam Clayton Powell, Jr.?

You Be the Judge

Must Congress accept a member if he or she meets the three basic tests—age, citizenship, and residency? Does Adam Clayton Powell, Jr., deserve back pay and restoration of his seniority rights?

Section 2

The House of Representatives

Reader's Guide

Key Terms

constituents, caucus, majority leader, whips, bill, calendars, quorum

Find Out

- Why are committees more important in the House than they are in the Senate?
- Why is the Rules Committee one of the most powerful committees in the House?

Understanding Concepts

Growth of Democracy Why does the majority party often get the credit or blame for everything Congress does?

COVER STORY

A Floor Fight in Congress

PHILADELPHIA, PENNSYLVANIA, 1798

Debate on the Sedition Act has reached such a furor that representatives are no longer safe in chambers. In a heated argument yesterday, Mr. Griswold of Connecticut attacked Mr. Lyon of Vermont with a cane. Mr. Lyon defended himself with fire tongs.

Lyon defends himself

Fire tongs cannot remove the hot coals from speeches of Federalists who promote the Sedition Act. Mr. Allen of Connecticut, who supports the Sedition Act, read from the *Aurora*, "Where a law shall have been passed in violation of the Constitution . . . is there any alternative between abandonment of the Constitution and resistance?" Mr. Gallatin addressed the chamber to reveal the real purpose of the Sedition Act: to silence all Republicans.

Political division and debate is unavoidable in democratic government. Legislators must have freedom to express their sometimes inflammatory opinions. Rules are necessary to help ensure fairness, to enable the legislature to conduct business, and to protect the minority.

Article I, Section 5[1], of the Constitution says: "Each House may determine the Rules of its Proceedings." Thomas Jefferson compiled the first parliamentary manual for the Senate when he was vice president. He emphasized the importance of rules:

> "*It is much more material that there be a rule to go by, than what the rule is; that there may be a uniformity of proceeding in business not subject to the caprice [whims] of the Speaker or captiousness [criticisms] of the members.*"
>
> —Thomas Jefferson, 1797

Rules for Lawmaking

The main task of each house of Congress is the same—to make laws. Because the House and Senate differ in many ways, each house has organized itself to carry out its work of making the laws. Complex rules and a structure of leadership enable Congress to carry out its lawmaking duties.

Complex Rules Each chamber has scores of precedents based on past rulings that serve as a guide to conducting business. The House and Senate each print their rules every two years. House rules are generally aimed at defining the actions an individual representative can take, such as limiting representatives to speaking for five minutes or less during a debate.

See the following footnoted materials in the **Reference Handbook:**
1. *The Constitution*, pages 774–799.

The complex rules in the House are geared toward moving legislation quickly once it reaches the floor. House debates rarely last more than one day. Moreover, leaders of the House of Representatives have more power than leaders in the Senate. For example, the rules of the House allow its leaders to make key decisions about legislative work without consulting other House members.

Committee Work Committees do most of the work of Congress. In the House, committee work is more important than in the Senate. Because the membership of the House is so large, its members must organize themselves into smaller groups in order to accomplish their work efficiently. In the committees representatives have more influence than on the House floor, and they have the time to study and shape bills.

In addition, representatives tend to specialize in a few issues that are important to their **constituents**—the people in the districts they represent. For example, Major R. Owens, a representative from Brooklyn, New York, is the only trained librarian in Congress. He emphasizes the importance of libraries in promoting literacy. As an African American, Owens also supports funding for African American colleges and aid for underprivileged students. He explains:

> "*We need more role models who will open new possibilities for those who have been excluded from the dreams that others take for granted.*"
>
> —Major R. Owens

Finally, because House members are elected from districts, much of their time is devoted to serving the interests of their constituents. John J. Duncan, Jr., of Tennessee said:

> "*I have a firm belief we have too many laws on the books now. . . . I've made it pretty clear I believe constituent service is most important and is where a freshman can be most effective.*"
>
> —John J. Duncan, Jr., 1988

We the People: Making a Difference

Vernon Baker

Medal of Honor

In 1944 Vernon Baker, a 25-year-old army second lieutenant serving in World War II, was shot in the wrist by a German sniper. He spent two months in a segregated hospital, then returned to lead his men into battle. On the morning of April 5, 1945, Baker destroyed two enemy bunkers, an observation post, and three machine gun nests. His company was nearly wiped out, but he ordered the seven remaining men to retreat while he drew enemy fire. Somehow, amid exploding shells, Lieutenant Baker escaped.

Although the army segregated African Americans during the war, Baker and his men fought like heroes. Asked why he fought so courageously for a country that treated him as a second-class citizen, Baker replied, "I was a soldier with a job to do, and I did it for the men I was leading."

Presented with the Distinguished Service Cross for his service in Italy, Baker remained in the military after the war. When he retired from the army in 1968, he took a job with the Red Cross, counseling needy military families.

In 1990 Army officials reexamined their records, looking for congressional Medal of Honor candidates among African Americans with outstanding service in World War II. Fifty years after his act of bravery, Vernon Baker accepted the medal in a White House ceremony. "It's a great day. We've all been vindicated," he said.

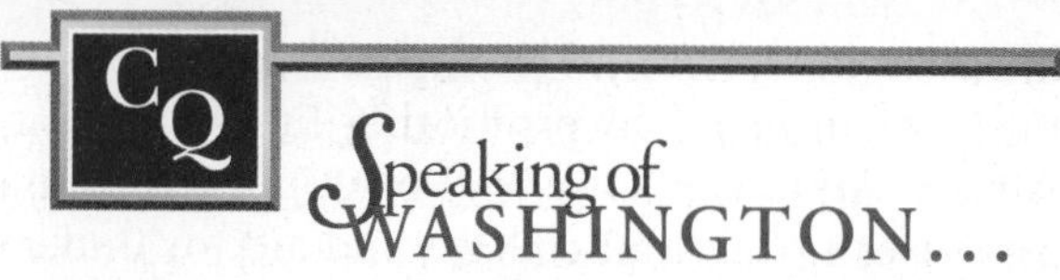

Freedom **The bronze statue on top of the Capitol dome originally was called *Armed Liberty* by its sculptor, Thomas Crawford. He replaced her soft cap, like that worn by freed Roman slaves, with a feathered headdress to please Jefferson Davis, then secretary of war and later president of the Confederacy. Davis feared the cap would inflame antislavery passions.**

Importance of Party Affiliation Many procedures in Congress are organized around the political party affiliation of members. In both the House and Senate, the Republicans sit on the right side of the chamber, the Democrats on the left. In each house the party with the larger number of members, the majority party, selects the leaders of that body, controls the flow of legislative work, and appoints committee chairs. The power to organize the House explains why some conservative Democrats switched to the Republican Party when it became the majority party in Congress after the 1994 election.

The Republican majority began sweeping changes of House rules in 1995, promoted to make the House more accountable. Some changes centralized power in the speakership in order to help Republicans carry out their agenda. The new rules provided for fewer committees, fewer staff members, term limits for chairpersons and the Speaker, and an end to absentee voting in committees. Many Democrats supported the reforms because they were part of a trend begun when the Democrats were the majority party.

House Leadership

Organized leadership coordinates the work of the 435 individual members of the House of Representatives. These leaders serve 6 purposes: (1) organizing and unifying party members; (2) scheduling the work of the House; (3) making certain that lawmakers are present for key floor votes; (4) distributing and collecting information; (5) keeping the House in touch with the president; and (6) influencing lawmakers to support the policies of their political party. The Constitution provides only for the presiding officer of the House. Other than that, the House chooses all its other leaders.

The Speaker of the House The Speaker of the House is the presiding officer of the House and its most powerful leader. The Constitution states that the House "shall choose their Speaker and other officers." A **caucus**, or closed meeting, of the majority party chooses the House Speaker at the start of each session of Congress, and the entire House membership approves the choice of Speaker.

As both the presiding officer of the House and the leader of the majority party, the Speaker has great power. Presiding over the sessions of the House, the Speaker can influence proceedings by deciding which members to recognize first. The Speaker also appoints the members of some committees, schedules bills for action, and refers bills to the proper House committee. Finally, the Speaker of the House follows the vice president in the line of succession to the presidency.

Today, Speakers rely as much on persuasion as on their formal powers to exercise influence. On a typical day, the Speaker may talk with dozens of fellow members of Congress. Often the Speaker does so just to listen to requests for a favor. As former Speaker Thomas P. "Tip" O'Neill once put it, "The world is full of little things you can do for people." In return, the Speaker expects representatives' support on important issues.

House Floor Leaders The Speaker's top assistant is the **majority leader.** The majority leader's job is to help plan the party's legislative program, steer important bills through the House, and make sure the chairpersons of the many committees finish work on bills important to the party. The majority leader is the floor leader of his or her political party in the House and, like the Speaker, is elected by the majority party. Thus, the majority leader is not actually a House official but a party official.

The majority leader has help from the majority whip and deputy whips. These **whips** serve as assistant floor leaders in the House. The majority whip's job is to watch how majority-party members intend to vote on bills, to persuade them to vote as the party wishes, and to see that party members are present to vote.

The minority party in the House also elects its own leaders. These include the minority leader and the minority whips. The responsibilities of these leaders are much the same as those of the majority party's leaders, except they have no power over scheduling work in the House.

Lawmaking in the House

To a visitor, the floor of the House of Representatives may seem totally disorganized. Some representatives talk in small groups or read newspapers. Others constantly walk in and out of the chamber. Most representatives are not even on the floor, because they are in committee meetings, talking with voters, or taking care of other business. Representatives reach the floor quickly, however, when it is time for debate or a vote on proposed bills.

Usually, the House starts its floor sessions at noon or earlier. Buzzers ring in members' offices in the House office buildings, committee rooms, and in the Capitol, calling representatives. The House is normally in session from Monday through Friday. Mondays are for routine work. Not much is done on Friday because many representatives leave to go to their home districts over the weekend. Thus, most of the House's important work is done from Tuesday through Thursday.

How House Bills Are Scheduled All laws start as **bills.** A proposed law is called a bill until both houses of Congress pass it and the

COMPARING *Governments*

Selected National Legislatures

Country	Legislative Chamber(s)	Number of Members	Term of Office	Method of Selection	Date of Last Constitution
Egypt	National Peoples Assembly	454	5 yrs.	popular election	1971
Israel	Knesset	120	4 yrs.	popular election	1949
Japan	Diet			elected by local	1947
	House of Representatives	512**	4 yrs.	and national	
	House of Councillors	252	6 yrs.	constituencies	
Mexico	Chamber of Deputies	400	3 yrs.	popular election	1917
	Senate	64	6 yrs.	popular election	
Russia	State Duma	450	4 yrs.*	popular election	1993
	Federation Council	178	4 yrs.*	local election	
United Kingdom	House of Commons	651**	5 yrs.	popular election	no written constitution
	House of Lords	300***	life	hereditary	
United States	House of Representatives	435	2 yrs.	popular election	1789
	Senate	100	6 yrs.	popular election	

* Initial term was two years; changed to four after second election.
** Number varies.
*** Normal attendance is 300, but many more vote on key decisions.

Source: CIA, *The World Factbook 1996* (Washington, D.C.).

Critical Thinking **Culture and history play large roles in how legislatures are formed around the world. *In what two categories is the United Kingdom unique among the countries shown above?***

Parliamentary Procedure

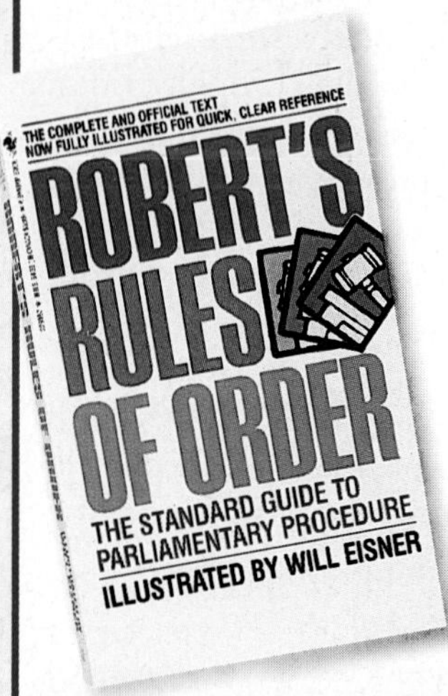

Like Congress, all deliberative assemblies need rules to conduct business in a fair and impartial way. Rules of order had their origin in early British Parliaments. Thomas Jefferson's *Manual of Parliamentary Practice* (1801) provided rules for the new United States government. Many groups use *Robert's Rules of Order,* first published in 1876 by U.S. army officer Henry M. Robert. *Robert's Rules* addresses such issues as:

1. How to make a motion and how to amend a motion
2. What rank or precedence various kinds of motions have
3. How to table or suspend a motion
4. How to close or extend debate
5. How to raise the question of consideration and how to vote
6. What duties and powers the presiding officer has

Activity

1. Obtain a copy of *Robert's Rules of Order.* Appoint a small group to find rules pertaining to the items listed above. Discuss the needs of a small group meeting (about the size of your class). Write rules for such a meeting based on these needs.
2. Choose a presiding officer for a meeting of your government class and a parliamentarian to enforce the rules. Hold a meeting in which the class determines an issue to discuss, hears opinions from the floor, and decides whether to take any action.

president signs it. According to the procedure currently in place, to introduce a bill in the House, representatives drop it into the hopper, a mahogany box that is accessible to all near the front of the chamber.

After a bill is introduced, the Speaker of the House sends it to the appropriate committee for study, discussion, and review. Of the more than 10,000 bills introduced during each legislative term of Congress, only about 10 percent ever go to the full House for a vote. Bills that survive the committee process are put on one of the House calendars. **Calendars** list bills that are up for consideration.

The House has five calendars. Three are used to schedule different kinds of bills for consideration. The Union Calendar lists bills dealing with money issues. Most other public bills are put on the House Calendar. The Private Calendar lists bills that deal with individual people or places. Any bill that the House gives unanimous consent to debate out of regular order is listed on the Consent Calendar. Finally, the Discharge Calendar is used for petitions to discharge a bill from committee.

The House Rules Committee The **Rules Committee** serves as the "traffic officer" in the House, helping to direct the flow of major legislation. It is one of the oldest House committees, and the most powerful. After a committee has considered and approved a major bill, it usually goes to the Rules Committee. The Rules Committee can move bills ahead quickly, hold them back, or stop them completely.

Because the Rules Committee has the power to decide how and when legislation will be considered by the House, it has often been the focus of political battles. From 1858 to 1910, the Speaker of the House, as chair of the Rules Committee, dominated the flow of legislation. In 1911 the House revolted against Speaker Joseph G. Cannon's authoritarian leadership and removed him from the Rules Committee.

In 1975 Democratic majorities in the House once again placed the Rules Committee under control of the Speaker. The Democratic Caucus gave the Speaker the power to appoint, subject to caucus ratification, all majority-party members of the Rules Committee. A former Speaker explained:

> *The Rules Committee is an agent of the leadership. It is what distinguishes us from the Senate, where the rules deliberately favor those who would delay. The rules of the House . . . permit a majority to work its will on legislation rather than allow it to be bottled up and stymied.*
>
> —Speaker Jim Wright, 1987

Republicans became the majority party in the House of Representatives in 1995. Their new Speaker, Newt Gingrich, as minority leader in the previous Congress had sparked an ethics investigation that resulted in Speaker Jim Wright's resignation. Gingrich asserted the power to appoint committee chairpersons, including the leader of the powerful Rules Committee.

Function of the Rules Committee Major bills that reach the floor of the House for debate and for a vote do so by a "rule"—or special order—from the Rules Committee. As major bills come out of committee, they are entered on either the Union Calendar or the House Calendar in the order received. The calendars have so many bills that if they were taken up in that order, many would never reach the floor before the end of the session. To resolve this problem, the chairperson of the committee that sent the bill to the Rules Committee may ask for it to move ahead of other bills and to be sent to the House floor. If the Rules Committee grants the request, the bill moves ahead. The Rules Committee may also include a time limit for debate on the bill and specify how much the bill may be amended on the floor.

Other Purposes of the Rules Committee

The Rules Committee also settles disputes among other House committees. For example, the Armed Services Committee may be considering a bill that involves an area also covered by the Veterans' Affairs Committee. The Rules Committee can help resolve any dispute between the two committees.

Finally, the Rules Committee often delays or blocks bills that representatives and House leaders do not want to come to a vote on the floor. In this way the Rules Committee draws criticism away from members who might have to take an unpopular stand on a bill if it reaches the floor.

A Quorum for Business A **quorum** is the minimum number of members who must be present to permit a legislative body to take official action. For a regular session, a quorum consists of the majority of the House—218 members. When the House meets to debate and amend legislation it may often sit as a Committee of the Whole. In that case, only 100 members constitute a quorum. This procedure helps speed the consideration of important bills. The Committee of the Whole cannot pass a bill. Instead, it reports the measure back to the full House with whatever changes it has made. The House then has the authority to pass or reject the bill.

Section 2 Assessment

Checking for Understanding

1. **Main Idea** In a graphic organizer similar to the one below, show three ways in which the Rules Committee controls legislation.

Rules Committee	

2. **Define** constituents, caucus, majority leader, whips, bill, calendars, quorum.
3. **Identify** Rules Committee.
4. How do committees help the House do its work?
5. How does a representative introduce a bill in the House?

Critical Thinking

6. **Understanding Cause and Effect** Why are changes in House rules more likely to occur when political control of the House shifts to another party?

Growth of Democracy Browse through current newspapers and magazines to find out what legislation the majority party in the House is trying to pass. Make a chart of the key legislation and record its progress for several weeks.

Section 3

The Senate

Reader's Guide

Key Terms

president pro tempore, filibuster, cloture

Find Out

- Why does the Senate have fewer rules and a less formal atmosphere than the House?
- Why does the Senate usually take longer than the House to pass a bill?

Understanding Concepts

Growth of Democracy Why do floor debates in the Senate often include powerful speeches charged with emotion?

COVER STORY

First Lady Elected

NEW YORK, N.Y., NOVEMBER 7, 2000

First Lady Hillary Clinton, the Democratic candidate for senator from New York, defeated Republican Congressman Rick Lazio. At first, Clinton's race seemed an uphill one. The problems of her husband's presidency lingered, and she faced accusations of being a carpetbagger. Clinton campaigned hard, however, and won by a healthy 55-43 percent margin. She was helped by the fact that her first opponent, New York City mayor Rudolph Guiliani, dropped out of the race mid-campaign.

Hillary Clinton

The Senate is a deliberative body. Senators handle issues of specific interest to them in their committees, but they also deal with many other issues on the floor, where there is plenty of time for debate. Senators, who represent entire states, are expected to know something about and deal with many issues—from national defense to social issues to farming.

The Senate at Work

Visitors going from the House to the Senate are often startled by the difference. The Senate chamber is smaller than the House chamber. Usually only a few senators attend sessions. The Senate chamber has 100 desks—one for each senator—facing a raised platform where the president pro tem and another senator preside over sessions. The party leaders or their assistants stay in the Senate chamber at all times to keep the work moving and to look after their party's interests.

Informal Atmosphere In the Senate, the rules are more flexible than in the House. They are designed to make certain that all senators have maximum freedom to express their ideas. For example, the Senate usually allows unlimited debate on proposed legislation. Senate rules are spelled out in fewer than 100 pages. With fewer rules, the Senate has a more informal atmosphere than the House. They may debate a proposal on and off for weeks or even months before taking action on an issue.

Senate Leaders Leadership in the Senate closely parallels leadership in the House, but the Senate has no Speaker. The vice president presides in the Senate, but may not vote except to break a tie. Also, Senate procedures permit individual senators more freedom in their activities. Consequently, party leaders in the Senate may not have as much influence over other senators as their counterparts in the House.

The Vice President The Constitution names the vice president as president of the Senate. The vice president, however, does not have the same role and power as the Speaker of the House. The vice president may recognize members and put questions to a vote. Because the vice president is not an elected member of the Senate, he or she may not take part in Senate debates. The vice president may, if the situation warrants, cast a vote in the Senate, but only in the event of a tie. A vice president may try to influence the Senate through personal contact with senators, however. Many recent vice presidents previously served as senators and thus had close relationships with their former colleagues.

Most vice presidents find Senate duties unchallenging and devote much of their time to executive branch activities, leaving little time to preside over the Senate. In the absence of the vice president, the **president pro tempore** (or president pro tem) presides. The term *pro tempore* means "for the time being." The Senate elects this leader. The president pro tempore is from the majority party and is usually its most senior member.

Majority and Minority Floor Leaders The majority and minority leaders are the most important officers in the Senate. Elected by the members of their political parties, the majority and minority leaders in the Senate are party officials rather than official Senate officers. The majority leader's main job is to steer the party's bills through the Senate. To do this, the majority leader plans the Senate's work schedule and agenda in consultation with the minority leader.

The majority leader is responsible for making certain the majority party members attend important Senate sessions and for organizing their support on key bills. The minority leader develops criticisms of the majority party's bills and tries to keep senators in the minority party working together. As in the House, whips and assistant

The Filibuster—Then and Now

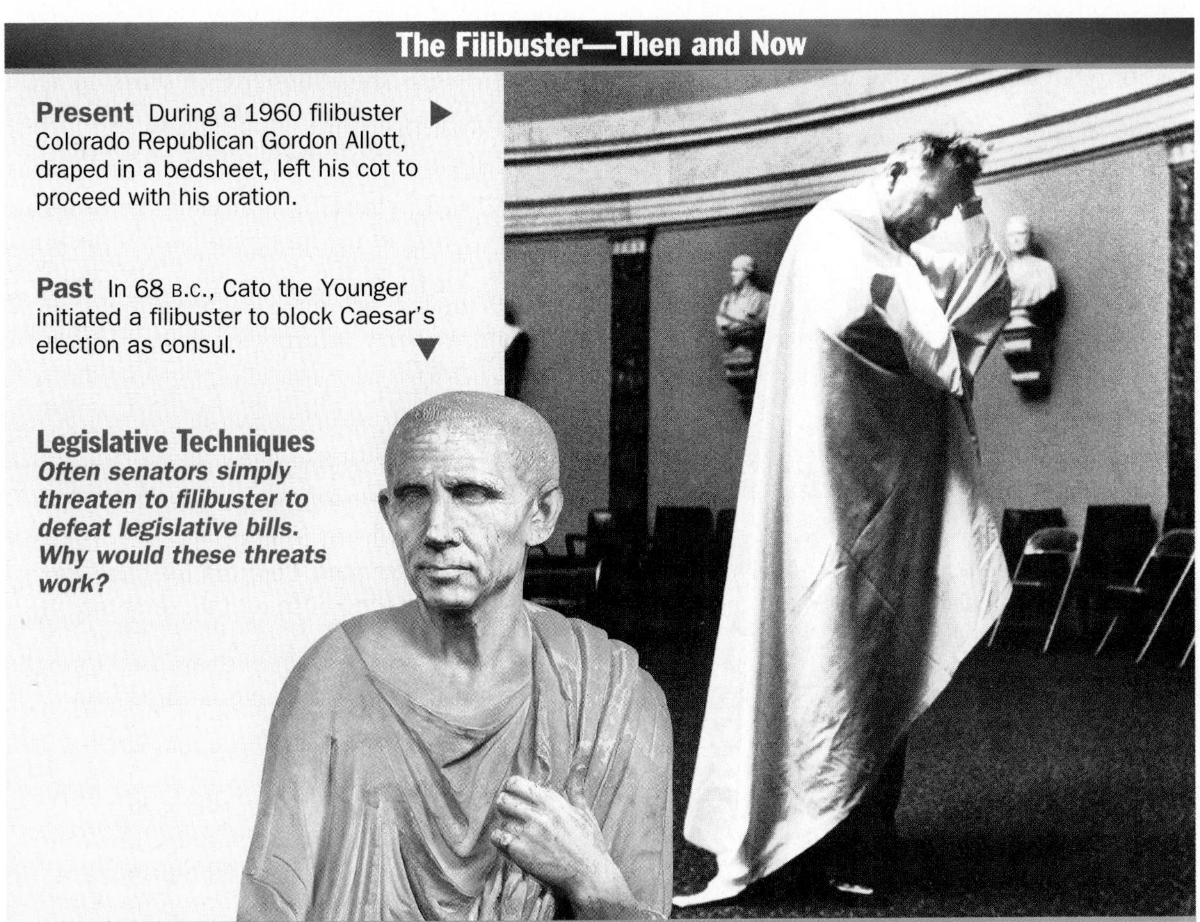

Present During a 1960 filibuster ▶ Colorado Republican Gordon Allott, draped in a bedsheet, left his cot to proceed with his oration.

Past In 68 B.C., Cato the Younger initiated a filibuster to block Caesar's election as consul. ▼

Legislative Techniques
Often senators simply threaten to filibuster to defeat legislative bills. Why would these threats work?

whips assist the majority and minority leaders of the Senate by making sure that legislators are present for key votes.

How Senate Bills Are Scheduled As in the House, any member of the Senate may introduce a bill. Procedures for moving bills through the Senate, however, are more informal than in the House. Because it is smaller, the Senate has never felt the need for a committee like the House Rules Committee. Instead, Senate leaders control the flow of bills to committees and to the floor for debate and vote. They do this by consulting closely with one another and with other senators.

The Senate has only two calendars. **The Calendar of General Orders** lists all the bills the Senate will consider. The Executive Calendar schedules treaties and nominations. The Senate brings bills to the floor by unanimous consent, a motion by all members present to set aside formal rules and consider a bill from the calendar. The procedure has not changed much through the years. In 1913 Massachusetts senator Henry Cabot Lodge explained that the Senate conducted most of its business through unanimous-consent agreements:

> “*Not only the important unanimous-consent agreements which are reached often with much difficulty on large and generally contested measures, but constantly on all the small business of the Senate we depend on unanimous consent to enable us to transact the public business.*”
>
> —Henry Cabot Lodge, 1913

The Filibuster Because the Senate usually allows unlimited debate on a bill, one way for senators to defeat a bill they oppose is to filibuster against it. To **filibuster** means to keep talking until a majority of the Senate either abandons the bill or agrees to modify its most controversial provisions. Senators who have the floor may continue to stand and talk. After the first 3 hours, they may talk about any topic they want or even read aloud from a telephone book or a recipe book.

Senator Strom Thurmond of South Carolina set the record for a filibuster when he spoke against the Civil Rights Act of 1957 for 24 hours and 18 minutes. A filibuster by a group of senators could go on for weeks or even months.

A filibuster can be stopped when three-fifths of the Senate (60 members) votes for cloture. **Cloture** is a procedure that allows each senator to speak only 1 hour on a bill under debate. Obtaining a vote in favor of cloture, however, is usually difficult.

The filibuster is not as strong a weapon as it used to be because the Senate now has a two-track procedural system. If a filibuster starts, the Senate sets aside one time during the day for handling other business. The filibuster then starts up again at the end of such business. However, the threat of a filibuster is often enough to delay or defeat a bill.

Politics As in the House, Senate procedures are organized around the members' party affiliations. Republicans sit on the right side of the chamber, while Democrats sit on the left. More importantly, the majority party controls the flow of legislative work.

Section 3 Assessment

Checking for Understanding

1. **Main Idea** In a graphic organizer similar to the one at the right, show the relationship between the Senate majority and minority leaders, whips, and assistant whips.

majority	minority

2. **Define** president pro tempore, filibuster, cloture.
3. **Identify** Calendar of General Orders.
4. How does the Senate bring bills to the floor?

Critical Thinking

5. **Making Comparisons** Compare the rules and procedures of the House with those of the Senate.

Growth of Democracy Search through a reference work of historic speeches. Use one of the speeches as a model for a persuasive speech of your own.

Section 4

Congressional Committees

Reader's Guide

Key Terms

standing committee, subcommittee, select committee, joint committee, conference committee, seniority system

Find Out

- Why are several different kinds of committees necessary in the House and Senate?
- Why are committee chairpersons considered the most powerful members of Congress?

Understanding Concepts

Political Processes Why have committees become the power centers in Congress?

COVER STORY

Judiciary Committee Looks at Hollywood

WASHINGTON, D.C., SEPTEMBER 18, 2000

Ads for R-rated films shown during television programs with a large percentage of viewers under 17 have sparked a Senate investigation. A federal report also found that underage teenagers are easily sneaking into R-rated movies.

Studio executive testifies.

Many people in Hollywood are suspicious because the hearings are being held less than two months before a national election. "I think it's a bunch of weasels scrambling for votes," said Larry Kasanoff, who heads a company that makes movies based on action-oriented video games like Mortal Kombat and Duke Nukem.

While the subject of R-rated movies makes for a dramatic hearing, much of the detailed day-to-day work of considering proposed legislation takes place in committees that meet in congressional offices. Sometimes the hearings are more exciting and informative than the floor debates that follow.

Purposes of Committees

Both the House and Senate depend upon committees to effectively consider the thousands of bills that are proposed each session. Committees help ease the workload and are the key power centers in Congress.

The committee system serves several important purposes. First, it allows members of Congress to divide their work among many smaller groups. Lawmakers can become specialists on the issues their committees consider. This system is the only practical way for Congress to operate because no lawmaker can possibly know the details of each of the thousands of bills introduced in each term of Congress.

Second, from the huge number of bills introduced in each Congress, committees select those few that are to receive further consideration. Committees are the places in which lawmakers listen to supporters and opponents of a bill. It is in committees where they work out compromises, and decide which bills will or will not have a chance to become law. Most bills never get beyond the committee stage.

Third, by holding public hearings and investigations, committees help the public learn about key problems and issues facing the nation. Congressional committees have called the public's attention to such issues as organized crime, the safety of prescription drugs, hunger in America, airline safety, and many other issues and concerns that have confronted the nation.

Kinds of Committees

Congress has four basic kinds of committees: (1) standing committees; (2) select committees; (3) joint committees; and (4) conference committees. Congress may, however, change the method of committee organization and the number of committees.

Standing Committees Very early in its history, Congress set up permanent groups to oversee bills that dealt with certain kinds of issues. These are called **standing committees** because they continue from one Congress to the next. The House and Senate each create their own standing committees and control their areas of jurisdiction, occasionally adding or eliminating a standing committee when necessary.

The majority party has power to write the rules in Congress. Republicans made changes in the structure and titles of several committees when they became the majority in 1995. They also set six-year term limits for committee chairpersons. The last major realignment of standing committees in the Senate took place in 1977.

Because the majority party in each house controls the standing committees, it selects a chairperson for each from among its party members. The majority of the members of each standing committee are also members of the majority party. Party membership on committees is usually divided in direct proportion to each party's strength in each house. For example, if 60 percent of the members of the House are Republicans, then 60 percent of the members of each House standing committee will be Republicans. Thus, a 10-member committee would have 6 Republicans and 4 Democrats. However, the party in power in the House will often have a super majority on the most important committees.

Subcommittees Nearly all standing committees have several **subcommittees.** Each subcommittee specializes in a subcategory of its standing committee's responsibility. Subcommittees, like standing committees, usually continue from one Congress to the next, although the majority party may make changes. For example, House Republicans in the 104th Congress limited most committees to no more than five subcommittees. The exceptions were Appropriations with 13 subcommittees, Government Reform and Oversight with 7 subcommittees, and Transportation and Infrastructure with 6 subcommittees.

Select Committees From time to time, each house of Congress has created temporary committees. Usually, these committees, called **select committees,** study one specific issue and report their findings to the Senate or the House. These issues

★ ★ ★ THE LAW *and You*

The V-Chip

Troubled by studies that linked TV violence to aggressive behavior in young children, Congress gave parents more control over home television viewing. Use of a V-chip is part of a new communications policy that became law in 1996.

The law requires manufacturers to install a V-chip in new television sets beginning in 1998. This computer chip enables parents to block out shows that have been coded as violent, lewd, or inappropriate for young children.

Legislators know that widespread use of the V-chip will come only after older television sets are no longer in service. However, the device provides politicians a way of taking action on TV violence without stirring up a controversy over censorship. Most children's activists have welcomed the V-chip, although they realize it will not be effective without parents' active participation.

The V-chip

Debate the Issue Do you think the V-chip is a real solution to violence viewed on television? Why or why not?

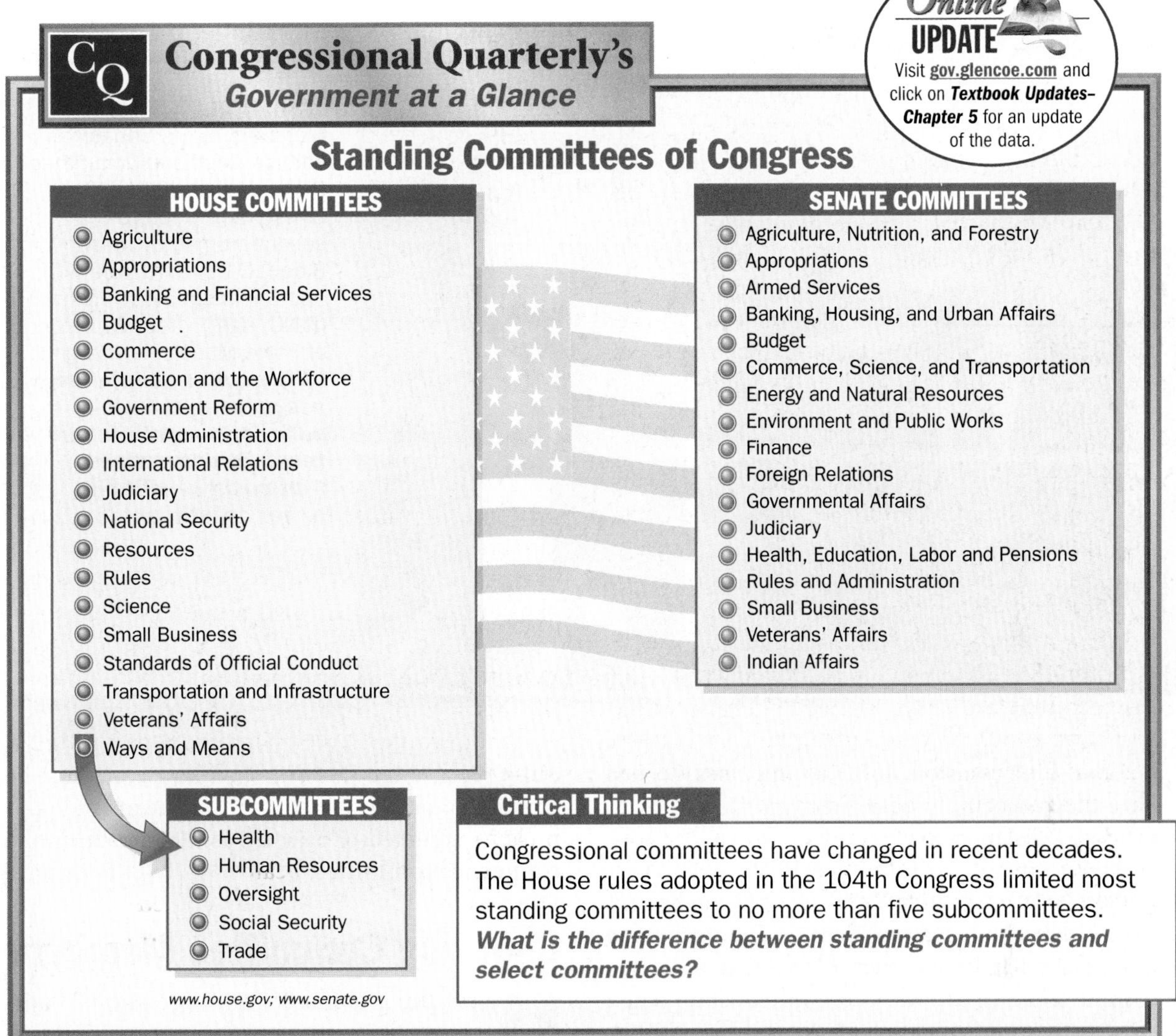

can include: (1) matters of great public concern, such as organized crime; (2) overlooked problems, such as hunger; or (3) problems of interest groups, such as owners of small business, who claim that Congress has not met their needs. Select committees usually cannot report bills to their parent chamber, however.

Select committees were usually set up to last for no more than one term of Congress. In practice, however, select committees may be renewed and continue to meet for several terms of Congress. For this reason, both the House and Senate have reclassified several select committees, such as the **Select Intelligence Committee,** as permanent committees. In 1993 the House terminated four select committees.

Joint Committees Made up of members from both the House and the Senate, **joint committees** may be either temporary or permanent. Like other committees, they have members from both political parties. These committees—such as the Joint Economic Committee—usually act as study groups with responsibility for reporting their findings back to the House and Senate.

In theory, joint committees coordinate the work of the two houses of Congress. In practice, lawmakers usually limit joint committees to handling routine matters such as are handled by the Joint Committee on Printing, and the Joint Committee on the Library of Congress. Some joint committees, however, have been set up to study more volatile matters such as atomic energy,

Legislative Leadership

Committee Leadership
Members of the Senate Foreign Relations Committee, Richard Lugar (R-IN, left), Christopher Dodd (D-CT, second from left), Joseph Biden (D-DE, third from left), and Chairman Jesse Helms (R-NC, right), greet Secretary of State Madeleine Albright. ***Why would a senator seek assignment to foreign policy or budget committees? To committees that could benefit his or her constituents?***

defense, and taxation. Joint committees do not have the authority to deal directly with bills or to propose legislation to Congress.

Conference Committees No bill can be sent from Congress to the president until both houses have passed it in identical form. A **conference committee** is a temporary committee set up when the House and Senate have passed different versions of the same bill. Members of the conference committee, called conferees, usually come from the House and Senate standing committees that handled the bill in question. Democrats and Republicans are represented in the same way here as on other committees.

The job of the conference committee is to resolve the differences between the two versions of the bill. Conference committees play a key role in policy making because they work out a bill that both houses may accept and send to the president. The committee accomplishes this task by bargaining over each section of the bill. A majority of the conferees from each house must accept the final compromise bill—called a conference report—before it can be sent to the floor of the House and Senate. When the conference committee's report—the compromise bill it has finally worked out—reaches the floor of each house, it must be considered as a whole. It may not be amended. It must be accepted or rejected as it comes from the conference committee.

Choosing Committee Members

Assigning members to congressional committees is an extremely important decision in the organization of Congress. Assignment to the right committees can also help strengthen a member's career in several ways. First, membership on some committees can increase a lawmaker's chances for reelection. For freshmen, the best committees may be those that deal with bills that will benefit a lawmaker's state or district.

Second, membership on some committees can mean the lawmaker will be able to influence national policy making. Committees that often help formulate national policies include those dealing with education, the budget, health, the judiciary, and foreign policy. Third, some committees enable a member to exert influence over other lawmakers because they deal with matters important to everyone in Congress. Some of these committees include the House **Rules Committee** and taxation and appropriation committees.

In the House the key committees are Rules, **Ways and Means,** and **Appropriations.** In the Senate the most prestigious committees are Foreign Relations, Finance, and Appropriations. Assignment to the Senate Foreign Relations Committee, for example, will give a lawmaker a chance to directly influence American foreign policy. Senators on this committee usually receive a great deal of publicity.

Assignment to Committees In both the House and Senate, the political parties assign members to the standing committees. Newly elected members of Congress who wish to serve on a particular committee or veteran lawmakers who wish to transfer to another committee may request assignment to the committees on which they want to serve. Each member may only serve on a limited number of standing committees and subcommittees.

The Committee Chairperson's Role Along with party leaders, the chairpersons of standing committees are the most powerful members of Congress. They make the key decisions about the work of their committees—when their committees will meet, which bills they will consider, and for how long. They decide when hearings will be held and which witnesses will be called to testify for or against a bill. In addition, chairpersons may hire committee staff members and control the committee budget. Finally, they manage the floor debates that take place on the bills that come from their committees.

Since the 1970s the powers of committee chairpersons have been limited somewhat. The Legislative Reorganization Act of 1970 made the committee system more democratic by allowing a majority of committee members to call meetings without the chairperson's approval. It also stated that committee members who disagree with the chairperson must have time to present their views and that reasonable notice must be given for all committee hearings. Rule changes in 1995 prohibited the chairperson from casting an absent member's vote and required committees to publish all members' votes.

The Seniority System The unwritten rule of seniority traditionally has guided the selection of chairpersons. The **seniority system** gave the member of the majority party with the longest uninterrupted service on a particular committee the leadership of that committee.

Criticism of the seniority system has resulted in several changes. Beginning in 1971, House Republicans voted by secret ballot to select the highest-ranking Republican on each committee. In 1973 the Democrats, who were the majority party in the House, adopted the same procedure. In a historic action in 1975, House Democrats voted to replace three senior committee chairpersons. In 1995 Republicans also bypassed several senior members up for chairs and ruled that chairpersons of House committees could hold their positions for no more than three consecutive terms.

Section 4 Assessment

Checking for Understanding

1. **Main Idea** In a Venn diagram, show how a conference committee and a joint committee are alike and how they are different.

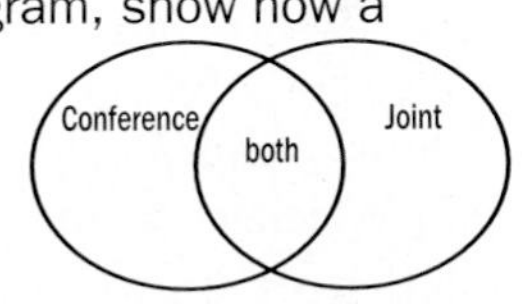

2. **Define** standing committee, subcommittee, select committee, joint committee, conference committee, seniority system.
3. **Identify** Select Intelligence, Rules, Ways and Means, Appropriations Committees.
4. List four important powers of a committee chairperson.

Critical Thinking

5. **Making Inferences** Why did Republicans, when they won control of Congress in 1995, institute many rule changes?

Political Processes Watch coverage of a congressional committee on television, or read about it in a newspaper. Outline the major issues presented in the testimony before the committee. Write a position paper in which you agree or disagree with the witnesses.

Section 5

Staff and Support Agencies

Reader's Guide

Key Terms

personal staff, committee staff, administrative assistant, legislative assistant, caseworker

Find Out

- Why do members of Congress have large personal and committee staffs?
- How could a committee staffer have more influence than a member of Congress over a proposed bill?

Understanding Concepts

Political Processes How do staffs and support agencies help members of Congress carry out their many responsibilities?

COVER STORY

House Audits Books

WASHINGTON, D.C., JANUARY 1995

The new Republican majority wasted no time in "cleaning house." First, they ordered an audit of House records. Then the House Oversight Committee voted to trim staff in the television office and reduce staff in the photography office. Members of Congress would now have to pay the full cost of such services out of their own office funds. The new majority party also cut 96 staff positions that were attached to 28 legislative service organizations. The service organizations dated back to 1959 when Congress certified the Democratic Study Group to analyze legislation.

Republican logo

The work of Congress is so massive and complicated that lawmakers need trained staffs to help them do their work effectively. Staff members also carry out the work of congressional committees. In addition, a number of supporting agencies perform important functions for members.

House rules in 1995 cut the total of committee staff by one-third compared to the levels of the previous Congress. The Senate also made less dramatic cuts—a 15 percent reduction in committee staff. At the same time Congress adopted a resolution to cut the legislative branch budget and reduced the budget of the General Accounting Office. Such staff reductions are rare.

Congressional Staff Role

When Lowell Weicker of Connecticut was in the Senate, a woman wrote to him complaining about the way an airline had handled her dog. The dog, shipped as animal cargo, had died in flight. One of the senator's secretaries mentioned the letter to the press secretary, who thought that perhaps the incident had news value. He phoned the Federal Aviation Agency and other government offices and found that there had been many similar cases. After informing the senator, the secretary wrote a draft of a bill to authorize the Transportation Department to regulate air transport of animals. Senator Weicker later introduced the legislation on the floor of the Senate. The story became headlines in Weicker's home state, and he received many letters of appreciation.

This story illustrates that congressional staff members do much of the important work on legislation. Lawmakers rely on their staffs to help them handle the growing workload of Congress, communicate with voters, help run committee hearings and floor sessions, draft new bills, write committee reports, and attend committee meetings. Congressional staffs also help lawmakers get reelected. Staffers help members of Congress get publicity, keep an eye on political developments back home, and write speeches and newsletters. They also help raise funds for election campaigns and meet with lobbyists and visitors from home.

Congressional Staff Growth

Congress has not always relied on staff to accomplish its work. For almost 100 years, senators and representatives had no personal aides. Occasionally they might hire assistants out of personal funds, but Congress provided no paid staff. Inadequate staffing had become an urgent complaint by the time Congress considered the Legislative Reorganization Act in 1946. After that the number of staff members increased dramatically. The House and Senate employed 2,000 personal staff members in 1947, but more than 11,500 in 1990. Committee staff increased from 400 to more than 3,000 in that same period.

Congressional staffs grew as lawmaking became more complex after the early 1900s. Lawmakers could not be experts on all the issues that came before their committees or upon which they voted in Congress. Having a large staff became one way to get expert help. Also, the demands that constituents placed on lawmakers increased over the years. Members of Congress needed a large office staff simply to deal with the many letters from people in their states or congressional districts. In addition to writing to their senators and representatives, voters in increasing numbers have turned to their lawmakers for help in solving problems. One lawmaker explained, "More than half my total staff time is devoted to resolving individual difficulties that have developed between citizens and their government."

Personal Staff

Congress includes two types of staffs: **personal staff** and **committee staff.** Personal staff members work directly for individual senators and representatives. Committee staff members work for the many House and Senate committees.

The size of senators' personal staffs varies because allowances to pay for them are based on the population of the senator's state and distance from the capital. Senators each receive a yearly budget to operate their offices. Most of this amount is to pay staff salaries. About one-third of personal staff members work in the legislators' home states. The rest work in Washington, D.C. Each member of the House has an allowance to pay for a personal staff. The House and Senate employ thousands of personal staff aides. Lawmakers can hire and fire staff members at will.

Administrative Assistants Lawmakers usually have three types of personal staff members in their offices. The **administrative assistant,** called an AA, is a very important legislative aide. The AA runs the lawmaker's office, supervises the lawmaker's schedule, and gives advice on political matters. A good AA also deals with influential people from the lawmaker's congressional district or state, who may influence the lawmaker's reelection.

An Expanding Government

Public Perceptions Members of Congress must balance the need for large staffs with the need to cut government spending. ***What public perception of Congress does the cartoonist enhance with this cartoon?***

Legislative Assistants Legislative assistants, or LAs, are a second type of personal staff member. An LA makes certain that the lawmaker is well informed about the many bills with which she or he must deal. An LA does research, drafts bills, studies bills currently in Congress, and writes speeches and articles for the lawmaker.

Another important part of the LA's job is to assist the lawmaker in committee meetings and to attend committee meetings when the lawmaker cannot be present. Senators and representatives are members of so many committees and subcommittees that they cannot possibly attend all the committee meetings. When they do attend committee meetings, they often come in at the last minute and briefly talk with their LA to find out what has taken place. The LA, who has followed the meeting and studied the bill in question, may have prepared a short speech for the lawmaker or made up a list of questions for the lawmaker to ask witnesses. Often the senator or representative has not seen the speech or the questions but relies on the LA's judgment.

Aiding Lawmakers

Influencing Congress Members of Congress, like Representative Maxine Waters, depend on their legislative aides. ***How might legislative assistants influence members of Congress?***

LAs also keep track of the work taking place on the floor of Congress, as well as bills that are in committee. While routine legislative business goes on, the lawmaker may be in a committee meeting or talking with voters. When the buzzer rings, signaling time for a vote, lawmakers rush to the floor of the Senate or House from their offices or committee rooms. They may not know what the vote is about unless it involves a major bill that has been scheduled long in advance. As they walk, they look for their LAs. In his book *In the Shadow of the Dome,* former LA Mark Bisnow describes the scene:

> "*As the door of the "Senators Only" elevator opened, their bosses would pour out. . . . If they did not know what they were voting on (votes occurred frequently throughout the day, and it was hard to keep track), . . . they would glance to the side to see if someone were waiting. A staffer might wave and run up for a huddled conference behind a pillar; or if the senator were in a hurry . . . he [or she] might simply expect a quick thumbs-up or thumbs-down gesture.*"
>
> —Mark Bisnow, 1990

Caseworkers Some personal staff members are called caseworkers because they handle the many requests for help from people in a lawmaker's state or congressional district. In addition to their offices in Washington, D.C., lawmakers are likely to have offices in key cities in their home district. Caseworkers usually staff these offices.

Committee Staff

Every committee and subcommittee in Congress has staff members who work for that committee. The larger a committee is, the more staff people it will likely have. The committee chairperson and the senior minority party member of the committee are in charge of these staff members. Committee staffers draft bills, study issues, collect information, plan committee hearings, write memos, and prepare committee reports. They are largely responsible for the work involved in making laws.

Some senior committee staff members are very experienced and are experts in the area their committee covers, whether it be tax policy, foreign affairs, or health care. Laurence Woodworth, who spent 32 years on the staff of the Joint Committee on Internal Revenue Taxation, is a good example of such an expert. As the committee's staff director for 14 years, he was largely responsible for all changes in the tax laws. Later, Woodworth left the committee to become assistant secretary of the treasury.

Supporting Congress

Thomas Jefferson

Congressional Research Congress established the Library of Congress in 1800, and in 1815 purchased Thomas Jefferson's private library of about 6,000 books. The Main Reading Room is the center of the greatest research library in the United States. ***Why would members of Congress require research materials?***

Too Much Power? The people do not elect congressional staffers. Yet they play a key role in lawmaking. Do they have too much influence? Some lawmakers believe they do. Other lawmakers disagree. They say that the staff really collects information and develops alternative courses of action for the lawmakers.

Support Agencies

Several agencies that are part of the legislative branch provide services that help Congress carry out its powers. Some of the services these agencies provide are also available to the other branches of government and to private citizens. Congress has created four important support agencies.

The Library of Congress Congress created the **Library of Congress** in 1800 to "purchase such books as may be necessary for the use of Congress." Today, it is one of the largest libraries in the world. This great center of information contains more than 100 million items, including books, journals, music, films, photographs, and maps. As the administrator of the copyright law, the copyright office in the Library receives two free copies of most published works copyrighted in the United States.

The Library has a Congressional Research Service (CRS) with hundreds of employees. Every year, CRS answers thousands of requests for information from lawmakers, congressional staff, and committees. CRS workers will check out anything, from the number of kangaroos in Australia to the crime rate in urban areas. Members of Congress use the CRS to answer requests for information from voters. They also use CRS for research on matters related to bills before Congress.

Congressional Budget Office (CBO) Congress established the **CBO** in 1974 to coordinate the budget-making work of Congress, study the budget proposals put forward by the president each year, and make cost projections of proposed new programs. The CBO counterbalances the president's elaborate budget-making organization, the Office of Management and Budget. CBO staff members study economic trends, keep track of how much congressional committees are spending, and prepare a report on the budget each April. They also calculate how Congress's budget decisions might affect the nation's economy.

General Accounting Office (GAO) Established in 1921, this agency is the nation's watchdog over the spending of funds Congress appropriates. A comptroller general appointed to a 15-year term directs the **GAO.** The agency has a professional staff of about 5,100 people. They review the financial management of government programs that Congress creates, collect government debts, settle claims, and provide legal service.

Many GAO staff members answer requests for information about specific programs from lawmakers and congressional committees. GAO staff members prepare reports on various federal programs for lawmakers, testify before committees, develop questions for committee hearings, and provide legal opinions on bills under consideration. Almost one-third of the GAO's work now comes from congressional requests for information.

Government Printing Office (GPO) The **Government Printing Office** is the largest multipurpose printing plant in the world. It does the printing for the entire federal government. Every day the GPO prints the *Congressional Record,* a daily record of all the bills introduced in both houses and of the speeches and testimony presented in Congress. Members of Congress can make changes in speeches they have made before they are printed in the *Record.* They can even have speeches they never actually made in the House or Senate printed in the *Record.*

Congressional staff members spend a good deal of time preparing speeches for lawmakers because those words will be inserted in the *Congressional Record.* Thus, when voters ask about the lawmaker's position on a particular issue, the staff can send a copy of the *Record* containing a speech the lawmaker made on that issue to the constituent making the request.

Another valuable publication of the Government Printing Office is the *Statistical Abstract of the United States,* updated and printed every year since 1878. Published by the Bureau of the Census, this volume provides statistical information about population, government finances, personal income, business, agriculture, education, law enforcement, national defense, elections, and many other topics. It is an invaluable source of data used by congressional staff as well as the general public.

The support agencies provide a vital function for Congress. They have helped the legislative branch become less dependent on the executive branch for information. This has helped Congress regain some of the power it held in earlier years.

Section 5 Assessment

Checking for Understanding

1. **Main Idea** In a graphic organizer like the one shown, describe the differences between personal staff and committee staff in Congress.

personal	committee

2. **Define** personal staff, committee staff, administrative assistant, legislative assistant, caseworker.
3. **Identify** Library of Congress, Congressional Budget Office, General Accounting Office, Government Printing Office.
4. Why did the numbers of congressional staff increase rapidly after 1900?

Critical Thinking

5. **Demonstrating Reasoned Judgment** Why do you think the comptroller general who oversees the General Accounting Office is appointed for a 15-year term?

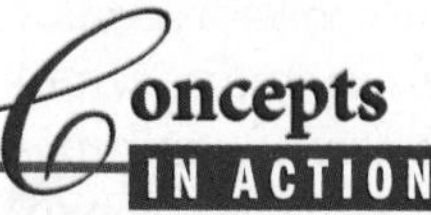

Political Processes Create a political cartoon that includes a caption about the role of committee staff in Congress. Take a position on whether professional staff members have too much power.

Skills

Critical Thinking

Making Generalizations

Generalizations set forth a widely applied principle or rule based on particular facts. "Florida is warmer than Michigan" is a valid generalization based on temperatures recorded over many years.

Learning the Skill

To make a valid generalization, follow these steps:

- Identify the subject matter.
- Gather related facts and examples.
- Identify similarities among these facts.
- Use these similarities to form a general statement about the subject.

Practicing the Skill

Abigail Adams wrote the following letter to her husband, John, who was attending the Second Continental Congress in 1775. Read the excerpt and complete the activity that follows.

> *"The reins of government have been so long slackened that I fear the people will not quietly submit to those restraints which are necessary for the peace and security of the community. If we separate from Britain, what code of laws will be established? How shall we be governed so as to retain our liberties? Can any government be free which is administered by general stated laws? Who shall frame these laws? Who will give them force and energy? It is true your resolutions, as a body, have hitherto had the force of laws; but will they continue to have?"*

Abigail Adams

Identify each following generalization as valid or invalid based on the information presented.

1. There are many issues to answer if America separates from Britain.
2. Some governmental controls are necessary in a community.
3. The colonies should adopt the British code of laws.
4. The Americans should adopt a new constitution.

Application Activity

Over a period of weeks, read the editorials in your local newspaper. Then write a list of generalizations about the newspaper's position on issues such as politics or crime.

The Glencoe Skillbuilder Interactive Workbook, Level 2 provides instruction and practice in key social studies skills.

Congressional Quarterly's

Congress A to Z

Congressional Leadership *The Constitution established a presiding officer for each chamber, but other congressional leaders have little written authority for their roles. Their authority comes from tradition within the parties rather than formal rules that apply to Congress as a whole.*

Duties of Constitutional Leaders

One of the duties of the Speaker of the House and the president of the Senate is to administer the oath of office to newly elected members at the start of each Congress. Because the entire House is up for reelection every two years, all representatives take the oath each time. Members first elect the Speaker of the House, who is sworn in by the most senior member of the House. The Speaker then administers the oath to all other members as they stand together in the chamber. The vice president, the president of the Senate, administers the oath to new senators.

Speaker Dennis Hastert

Senate gavel

Symbols

Both the Senate and the House use a gavel as a symbol of authority. The Senate's cherished symbol is a small, silver-capped ivory gavel. This gavel, retired from active duty in 1954 when it began to disintegrate, is placed on the vice president's desk before the opening of each Senate session. A replica of the old gavel, a gift from the government of India, has been used by the presiding officer of the Senate since 1954.

Senator Lyndon Johnson and Senator Theodore Francis Green

Leadership by Persuasion

Personal style can contribute to or detract from a leader's effectiveness. As Senate majority leader from 1955 to 1961, Lyndon B. Johnson was known for his extraordinary ability to persuade colleagues to support him. In one-on-one encounters, Johnson applied the treatment—cajoling, touching an arm or shoulder for emphasis, leaning closer.

Vice President's Role

The vice president is already a president—of the Senate. A mostly ceremonial position, this part-time responsibility entitles the vice president to a plush office in the Capitol and the singular ability to break a tie vote there. This power is rarely used, but is vital when administration proposals are at stake. During President Clinton's first term, Vice President Al Gore cast three tie-breaking votes in the Senate: In 1993, he twice broke ties to ensure approval of Clinton's deficit reduction package, and in 1994, he voted to uphold a federal rule concerning reformulated gasoline and clean air standards.

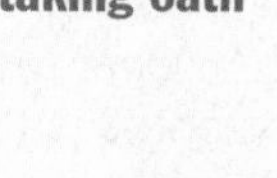

House members taking oath

Vice President Al Gore

Assessment and Activities

Self-Check Quiz Visit the *United States Government: Democracy in Action* Web site at gov.glencoe.com and click on ***Chapter 5–Self-Check Quizzes*** to prepare for the chapter test.

Reviewing Key Terms

Match each term below with one of the following phrases or terms:

a. House **b.** Senate **c.** Both chambers

1. bill
2. majority leader
3. gerrymandering
4. filibuster
5. constituents
6. joint committee
7. redistricting
8. reapportionment
9. censure
10. incumbent

Current Events JOURNAL

Lawmaking Look at the entries under "United States Government, Congress" in the *Readers' Guide to Periodical Literature.* Find articles that refer to a current bill that is moving through Congress. Check previous volumes of the *Guide* to determine how long this bill has been under consideration. Make a time line showing the history of the issue and congressional concern over it.

Recalling Facts

1. What are the qualifications for members of the House and Senate?
2. Identify the most powerful committee in the House of Representatives.
3. How may Congress expel a member?
4. List four advantages incumbents have in running for office.
5. How do House rules differ from Senate rules?
6. What committee serves as the "traffic officer" of the House?
7. What position in the Senate does the vice president serve?
8. When do terms of Congress begin?
9. List eight benefits members of Congress receive in addition to their salaries.

Understanding Concepts

1. **Political Processes** How does the census affect the reapportionment of the House?
2. **Growth of Democracy** Why does the Constitution provide for free and unlimited debate in Congress?
3. **Political Processes** How does the majority party in each house determine the flow of legislation?

Critical Thinking

1. **Making Inferences** Why are bills that minority party members introduce unlikely to be reported out of committee?
2. **Formulating Questions** What questions do you think a new member of Congress considers when requesting committee assignments?
3. **Making Comparisons** In a graphic organizer like the one below, compare the duties of a congressional administrative assistant with those of a legislative assistant.

administrative	legislative

Chapter 5

Cooperative Learning Activity

Writing Your Representative As a class, choose four controversial current issues that concern you and your classmates. Divide the class into four groups. Each group will choose one of the issues and decide what actions Congress should take to deal with the issue.

Have each group assign individuals specific aspects of the issue to research. Then bring the group together to compile its research and write a letter urging support for this position to your member of Congress.

Interpreting Political Cartoons Activity

1. What is the subject of this cartoon?
2. What do the roots of the tree trunk symbolize?
3. According to this cartoon, how difficult is it to unseat an incumbent in Congress?

Skill Practice Activity

Making Generalizations Use the chart on page 129 to answer the following questions:

1. What is the subject of the data presented in the chart?
2. What generalization can you make about the racial makeup of Congress?
3. What generalization can you make about the chances of reelection for incumbent members of Congress?

Technology Activity

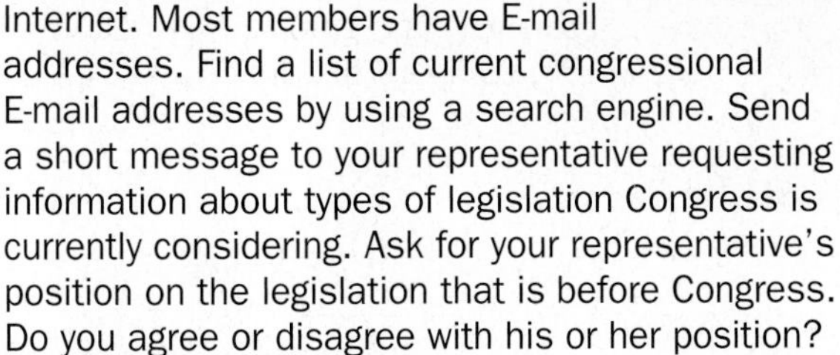

Using E-Mail One of the ways that members of Congress are trying to keep in touch with their constituents is via the Internet. Most members have E-mail addresses. Find a list of current congressional E-mail addresses by using a search engine. Send a short message to your representative requesting information about types of legislation Congress is currently considering. Ask for your representative's position on the legislation that is before Congress. Do you agree or disagree with his or her position?

Participating in Local Government

The idea of having a constitutional amendment requiring term limits for members of Congress has been debated in recent years.

- What are the arguments for and against a constitutional amendment on term limits?
- What is your view?
- What are the views of your friends and relatives?

Research this issue and write a letter to the editor of your local paper expressing your opinion for or against term limits. Be sure to include at least three arguments that support your position in the letter.

Chapter 6

Development of Congressional Powers

Why It's Important

Influencing Congress Congressional staffs read hundreds of letters from constituents every day. These letters help give direction to decisions Congress makes in exercising its powers. In this chapter you will learn what those powers are and, in addition to writing letters, how you can affect those decisions.

Find out more about how Congress impacts your life by viewing the ***Democracy in Action*** Chapter 6 video lesson:

The Powers of Congress

GOVERNMENT Online

Chapter Overview Visit the *United States Government: Democracy in Action* Web site at gov.glencoe.com and click on ***Chapter 6–Overview*** to preview chapter information.

Section 1

Constitutional Powers

Reader's Guide

Key Terms

expressed powers, necessary and proper clause, implied powers, revenue bill, appropriations bill, interstate commerce, impeachment

Find Out

- Why are the money powers granted to Congress by the Founders so important?
- How has the commerce clause enabled Congress to apply a loose interpretation to the Constitution?

Understanding Concepts

Constitutional Interpretations On what types of issues did the Founders restrict congressional actions with the addition of the Bill of Rights?

COVER STORY

Force Approved

WASHINGTON, D.C., JANUARY 1991

The House and Senate averted a potential constitutional crisis over the war powers of the president and Congress today. The House and Senate each adopted resolutions authorizing President Bush to use military force against Iraq, while defeating alternative resolutions that called for a delay. Like previous presidents, Bush has refused to acknowledge Congress's ability to limit his actions as commander in chief. In recent weeks, however, he has lobbied to gain congressional support in his confrontation with Iraq.

Tank from Persian Gulf War

Can a president initiate military action without a declaration of war? The Constitution is silent or unclear on many questions concerning the powers of Congress and the president. Nearly half of the text of the Constitution is contained in Article I—an indication that the Framers intended for Congress to play the central role in governing the nation. The specific nature of that role has developed and changed over time.

Constitutional Provisions

The Constitution describes the legislative powers of Congress in Article I, Section 8, Clauses 1-18.[1] These **expressed powers** of Congress are sometimes called the **enumerated powers.** The last clause (18) of Section 8 gives Congress power to do whatever is "necessary and proper" to carry out its other powers. This **necessary and proper clause** implies that Congress has powers beyond those expressed in the first 17 clauses. Because these **implied powers** have allowed Congress to expand its role to meet the needs of a growing nation, the "necessary and proper clause" has often been called the **elastic clause.**

Conflicting Interpretations Because of the far-reaching implications of the expanding power of Congress, the Supreme Court has often been the site of conflict over what is "necessary and proper" legislation. The first major conflict was between those who believed in a "strict construction," or interpretation, of the Constitution and those who believed in a "loose construction."

When Congress created the Second Bank of the United States in 1816, loose constructionists

See the following footnoted materials in the ***Reference Handbook:***

1. *The Constitution,* pages 774–799.

◀ **Washington Monument and the Capitol**

and strict constructionists engaged in debates. Strict constructionists, who believed that Congress did not have the power to charter such a bank, supported the state of Maryland when it placed a tax on the notes of the federal bank. James McCulloch, a teller at the Second Bank's branch in Baltimore, issued notes on which the tax had not been paid. Maryland filed suit against McCulloch. When Maryland won the suit in its own courts, the United States appealed. The Supreme Court reversed the decision, supporting the loose constructionists. Writing the majority opinion, Chief Justice John Marshall interpreted the necessary and proper clause:

> *"The result of the most careful and attentive consideration bestowed upon this clause is, that if it does not enlarge, it cannot be construed to restrain the powers of Congress or to impair the right of the legislature to exercise its best judgment in the selection of measures to carry into execution the constitutional powers of the government."*
>
> —John Marshall

Powers Denied The powers of Congress, like those of the other branches of the national government, are limited. One important constitutional limit on congressional power is the Bill of Rights. In addition, Article I, Section 9, denies certain powers to Congress. Congress may not suspend the **writ of habeas corpus,** a court order to release a person accused of a crime to court to determine whether he or she has been legally detained. Another important limitation denies Congress the authority to pass **bills of attainder,** laws that establish guilt and punish people without allowing them a trial. Congress is also prohibited from passing **ex post facto laws,** laws that make crimes of acts that were legal when they were committed. Article I, Section 9, also denies several other powers to Congress, among them the power to tax exports.

Legislative Powers

Congress has both legislative and nonlegislative powers. Nonlegislative powers include the power to confirm or deny presidential appointments. Congress has expanded the domain of its legislative powers—the power to pass laws—as the nation has grown. The most significant expansion of congressional legislative power is in its control over the economy—taxing, spending, and regulating commerce.

The Taxing and Spending Power Sometimes called "the power of the purse," the power to levy taxes and provide for the general welfare of the United States is among the most important powers of Congress. It allows Congress to influence national policy in many areas because no government agency can spend money without congressional authorization. Congress may use taxes for many purposes. For example, taxes on narcotics are meant to protect public health.

Article I, Section 7, says "All Bills for raising Revenue shall originate in the House of Representatives." **Revenue bills,** laws for raising money, start in the House and then go to the Senate. This provision was adopted at the Constitutional Convention because the more populous states, such as Virginia and Pennsylvania, insisted on having a greater voice in tax policy than the smaller states. Because representation in the House was to be based on population, the Founders agreed that

Power of the Purse

Government Borrowing Pictured above are a modern United States savings bond and a banknote issued by the First Bank of the United States. ***Why do you think the Founders specified that all revenue bills should originate in the House?***

Congressional Quarterly's
Government at a Glance

The Powers of Congress

Selected Expressed Powers

MONEY POWERS

- Lay and collect taxes to provide for the defense and general welfare of the United States (Clause 1);
- Borrow money (Clause 2);
- Establish bankruptcy laws (Clause 4);
- Coin, print, and regulate money (Clause 5);
- Punish counterfeiters of American currency (Clause 6)

COMMERCE POWERS

- Regulate foreign and interstate commerce (Clause 3)

MILITARY AND FOREIGN POLICY POWERS

- Declare war (Clause 11);
- Raise, support, and regulate an army and navy (Clauses 12, 13, & 14);
- Provide, regulate, and call into service a Militia, known as the National Guard (Clauses 15 & 16);
- Punish acts committed on international waters and against the laws of nations (Clause 10)

OTHER LEGISLATIVE POWERS

- Establish laws of naturalization (Clause 4);
- Establish post offices and post roads (Clause 7);
- Grant copyrights and patents (Clause 8);
- Create lower federal courts (Clause 9);
- Govern Washington, D.C. (Clause 17);
- Provide for laws necessary and proper for carrying out all other listed powers (Clause 18)

Selected Implied Powers

Lay and collect taxes
IMPLIES the power to support public schools, welfare programs, public housing, etc.

Borrow money
IMPLIES the power to maintain the Federal Reserve Board.

Regulate commerce
IMPLIES the power to prohibit discrimination in restaurants, hotels, and other public accommodations.

Raise and support army
IMPLIES the right to draft people into the armed services.

Establish laws of naturalization
IMPLIES the power to limit the number of immigrants to the United States.

Source: Congress A to Z, 2d ed. (Washington, D.C.: CQ Inc., 1993).

Critical Thinking

The powers, structure, and procedures of Congress are defined in detail in the Constitution, whereas the duties of the president and the Supreme Court are not. ***How has Congress used the commerce clause to prevent discrimination in restaurants, hotels, and other public accommodations?***

any revenue bills introduced in Congress would originate there.

The legislative process for **appropriations bills**—proposed laws to authorize spending money—is not spelled out in the Constitution. It has developed through usage. Article I, Section 9, merely requires that "No Money shall be drawn from the Treasury, but in Consequence of Appropriations made by Law." Spending requests generally come from the executive branch. Today, most are presented to Congress in the president's annual budget proposal.

Over the years Congress has used its taxing and spending authority to expand its regulatory powers. For example, when Congress authorizes money for state or local governments, it frequently requires that local officials follow specific federal regulations as a condition of the grant. Moreover, by levying heavy taxes on products such as tobacco that it considers undesirable, Congress may discourage their use.

Congress also uses its money powers to regulate the economy. For example, cutting individual income taxes to stimulate the economy gives taxpayers more money to spend. Conversely, Congress may try to slow economic growth by increasing taxes, leaving taxpayers with smaller paychecks.

Other Money Powers In addition to levying taxes and authorizing that money be spent, Article I allows Congress to borrow to help pay for the cost of government. Congress does this in various ways. The most common method is by authorizing the sale of government securities—bonds or notes. When people buy savings bonds, Treasury bills, or Treasury notes, they are lending the government money. In return, the government promises to repay buyers with interest at the end of a specified period of time—3 months to 30 years, depending on the type of security.

Because it must borrow money to meet its operating expenses, the government has a **national debt**—the total amount of money the government owes at any given time. This debt, almost $1 trillion in 1980 and about $3.2 trillion in 1990, reached almost $6 trillion in 2000. Although the Constitution does not restrict government borrowing, since 1917 Congress has attempted to set an annual limit on the national debt. In recent years, however, it has raised the ceiling time after time so that the government could borrow more money to pay its bills.

As part of Congress's money powers, the Constitution gives the legislative branch the power to coin money and to regulate its value. All currency the federal government issues is legal tender, meaning that it must be accepted as payment. In addition,

THE LAW *and You*

Minimum Wage Laws

What pay should you expect when you look for a job? Generally, employers must pay a standard minimum wage set by federal law. However, many exceptions exist.

If you are a student working for a retail business, in an agricultural job, or for a school's vocational education program, your employer is not required to pay minimum wage. In addition, employers can pay all workers under age 20 less than minimum wage for their first 90 days of employment. Other exceptions include workers who receive tips and seasonal employees. Meals your employer provides, or expenses your employer pays on your behalf, can also reduce your wage rate.

Finally, federal law allows states to pass laws that can be more generous than the minimum wage. Your local employment services office can provide more information about wage laws in your state.

Earning a wage

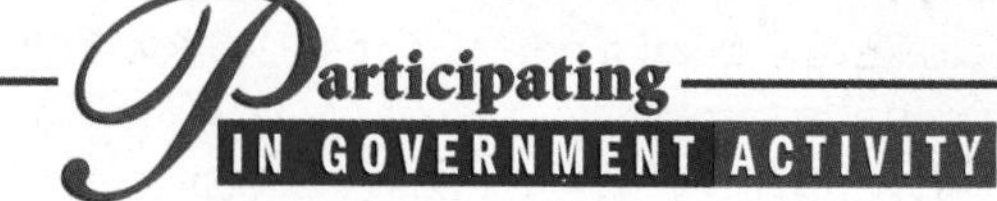

Conduct Research How does the minimum wage affect employment in your community? Gather information and report your findings in a letter to your local newspaper.

Congress has the power to punish counterfeiters—people who print postage stamps, paper money, or government securities illegally—and to establish a system of standard weights and measures.

The money powers of Congress also include the authority to make laws concerning **bankruptcy**—legal proceedings to administer the assets of a person or business that cannot pay its debts. Despite this authority, for more than a century Congress generally left bankruptcy matters to the states. In 1898 Congress passed the bankruptcy law that, with later amendments, remains in force today. Almost all bankruptcy cases are heard in federal courts.

Expanding Interstate Commerce

Constitutional Interpretations The ruling in *Gibbons* v. *Ogden* opened up trade between New York and New Jersey. Within a short time dozens of steamboats ferried passengers and freight across the Hudson River. ***How did this Supreme Court ruling affect states' control of economic activities?***

The Commerce Power

Article I, Section 8, Clause 3,[1] the so-called commerce clause of the Constitution, authorizes Congress to regulate foreign commerce and **interstate commerce,** or commerce among the states. In this clause the Founders provided what has become one of the most sweeping powers of government. The Supreme Court has promoted the expansion of this power by consistently ruling that the meaning of commerce—whether international or interstate—far exceeds the mere buying and selling of goods and services.

Landmark Cases

Gibbons v. *Ogden*

The landmark decision on this subject came in *Gibbons* v. *Ogden* (1824). The state of New York had granted Robert Fulton and Robert Livingston the exclusive right to operate steamboats on New York waters. This monopoly granted Aaron Ogden a permit for steamboat travel across the Hudson River between New York and New Jersey. Thomas Gibbons, operating a competing line, had a coasting license from the federal government. Ogden sued Gibbons, and the state of New York held that Gibbons could not sail in its waters. Gibbons appealed, claiming that Congress, not the state of New York, had the power to regulate commerce. The argument for state control was that commerce involved only products. The Court, however, ruled that all forms of business across state lines come under the commerce clause.

Over the years the Court has expanded its definition of commerce to give Congress even greater power. Any widespread activity that can possibly be considered interstate commerce is subject to federal control. The long list of such activities includes broadcasting, banking and finance, and air and water pollution.

Congress has used its power over interstate commerce to set policy in many other areas, too. For example, Congress requires that businesses engaged in interstate commerce pay their employees a minimum wage. Almost all businesses deal in some way with someone in another state. This power enables Congress to regulate working conditions across the nation.

See the following footnoted materials in the **Reference Handbook:**
1. *The Constitution,* pages 774–799.

Heart of Atlanta Motel v. *United States*

One of the most significant applications of the commerce clause has been in the area of civil rights. In 1964 Congress used its power to regulate interstate commerce to pass the landmark Civil Rights Act. This law prohibited discrimination in places of public accommodation such as restaurants, hotels, and motels. It also prohibited job discrimination.

A Georgia motel owner immediately attacked the law, claiming that the motel was a local business. It was therefore not part of interstate commerce, and the law should not apply. On appeal to the Supreme Court, the justices disagreed. In *Heart of Atlanta Motel* v. *United States* (1964),[1] the Court noted that public places of accommodation served interstate travelers and sold food that had crossed state lines.

> *We, therefore, conclude that the action of Congress in the adoption of the Act as applied here to a motel which concededly serves interstate travelers is within the power granted it by the Commerce Clause of the Constitution, as interpreted by this Court for 140 years.*
>
> —Justice Tom C. Clark, 1964

This decision indicated that the Court was willing to allow Congress broad commerce powers, even in areas that were not economic. Since then the commerce power has even supported federal criminal laws aimed at racketeering and arson.

Foreign Policy Powers Congress has important powers in the areas of foreign policy and national defense. Chief among these are the power to approve treaties, to declare war, to create and maintain an army and navy, to make rules governing land and naval forces, and to regulate foreign commerce.

Congress shares foreign policy and national defense responsibilities with the president. Historically it generally has submitted to presidential leadership in this area. Although Congress has declared war only 5 times, the president, as commander in chief, has used military force in other nations on more than 160 occasions. Most significant of these were the Korean War (1950 to 1953) and the Vietnam War (1965 to 1973). Both conflicts were fought without declarations of war.

See the following footnoted materials in the **Reference Handbook:**

1. *Heart of Atlanta Motel* v. *United States* case summary, page 759.

Establishing Federal Property

Public Policy ***The Grand Canyon of the Yellowstone*** **by Thomas Moran** This painting dramatized the magnificence of the West and inspired Congress to declare Yellowstone a national park in 1872. ***What other types of federal property does Congress have power over?***

After the Vietnam War, Congress acted to reassert its foreign policy powers. Congress held that the Constitution never intended for the president to have the power to involve the nation in undeclared wars. Therefore, in 1973, over President Nixon's veto, Congress passed the War Powers Act. This law forbids the president to commit American forces to combat for more than 60 days without congressional notification within 48 hours. Almost every president since the act's passage has protested its constitutionality. During this period presidents used military force in Cambodia (1975), Iran (1980), Grenada (1983), Lebanon (1983), Libya (1986), the Persian Gulf (1987), Panama (1989), Iraq (1991), and Haiti (1994). Most of these were quick strikes with little warning. Nevertheless, in most cases the president notified Congress of the action.

North Korean flag

Vietnam War hat

Presidents Truman, Kennedy, Johnson, and Nixon challenged congressional powers by expanding U.S. involvement in the Korean and Vietnam Wars without a congressional declaration of war.

Providing for the Nation's Growth

The Constitution also grants Congress power over naturalization, the process by which immigrants to the United States may become citizens. In addition, Article IV, Section 3, authorizes Congress to admit new states and pass laws needed to govern any territories. Today, United States territories such as Guam, the Virgin Islands, and Wake Island fall under this provision. Finally, both Article I and Article IV empower Congress to pass laws to govern federal property. The Founders envisioned such property as military bases and government buildings. Today, however, these provisions establish federal authority over national parks, historic sites, and hundreds of millions of acres designated as public lands.

Other Legislative Powers

Article I, Section 8,[1] gives Congress the power to grant copyrights and patents. A **copyright** is the exclusive right to publish and sell a literary, musical, or artistic work for a specified period of time. Under the present law, this period is the lifetime of the creator plus 50 years. A **patent** is the exclusive right of an inventor to manufacture, use, and sell his or her invention for a specific period, currently 17 years, and may be renewed.

Article I, Section 8, also grants Congress the power to establish a post office and federal courts. Congress also has used its postal power to combat criminal activity. For example, using the mail for any illegal act is a federal crime.

Nonlegislative Powers

In carrying out their legislative powers, both the House and the Senate perform the same basic tasks—considering, amending, and voting on bills. While most of their nonlegislative functions require their cooperation, usually each house performs a different function in exercising these powers.

The Power to Choose a President

The Constitution requires a joint session of Congress to count the Electoral College votes. In modern times this has become a largely ceremonial function.

If no candidate for president has a majority of the electoral votes, the House chooses the president from the three candidates with the most electoral votes. Each state's House delegation has one vote. The Senate, by majority vote, chooses the vice president from the two candidates with the most

See the following footnoted materials in the **Reference Handbook:**
1. *The Constitution,* pages 774–799.

Impeached!

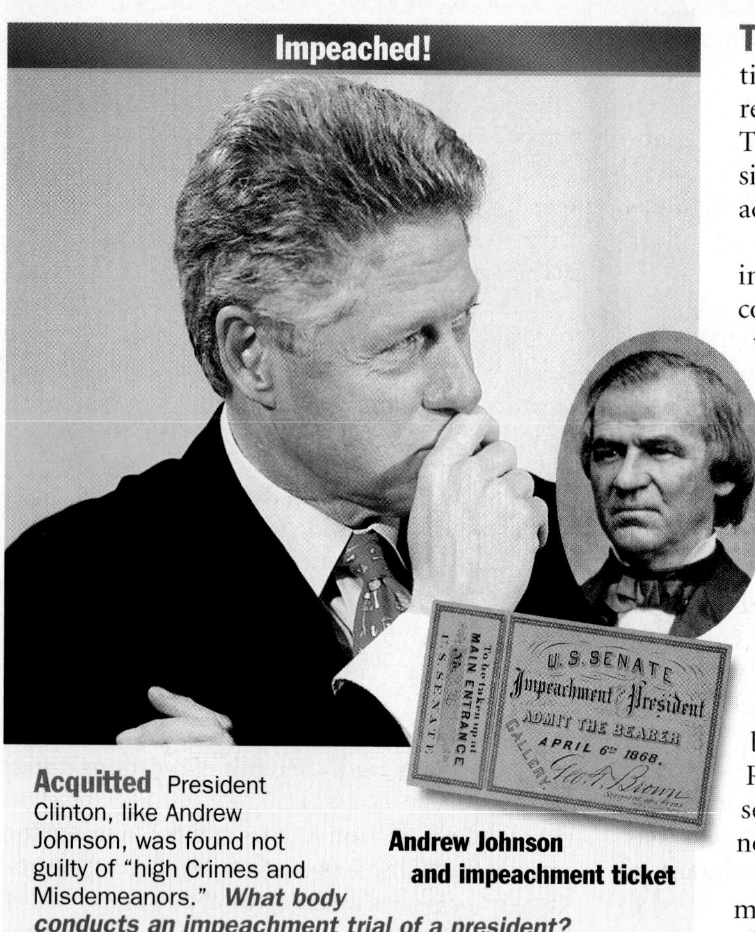

Acquitted President Clinton, like Andrew Johnson, was found not guilty of "high Crimes and Misdemeanors." ***What body conducts an impeachment trial of a president?***

Andrew Johnson and impeachment ticket

electoral votes. It is, therefore, possible that the vice president could be from a different party than the president. Only two times in American history has no presidential candidate captured a majority of the electoral votes. In 1800 the House elected Thomas Jefferson over Aaron Burr, and in 1824 it chose John Quincy Adams over Andrew Jackson.

The **Twentieth** and **Twenty-fifth Amendments**[1] give Congress the power to settle problems arising from the death of elected candidates and from presidential incapacity or resignation. The Twenty-fifth Amendment provides that when the office of vice president becomes vacant, the president appoints a replacement. Both houses of Congress must confirm the appointment. During the 1970s, two vice presidents gained office under this amendment.

The Removal Power The Constitution grants Congress the power to remove any federal official from office. The House of Representatives has exclusive power over **impeachment,** a formal accusation of misconduct in office.

If a majority of the House votes to impeach a public official, the Senate conducts the trial. A two-thirds vote of those Senators present is required for conviction and removal. When the impeachment proceedings involve a president, the Chief Justice of the United States presides.

Since 1789 the Senate has tried several federal judges, a Supreme Court justice, a cabinet secretary, and two presidents on impeachment charges. Many of these cases ended in conviction. However, the Senate acquitted President Andrew Johnson by only one vote in 1868. President Richard Nixon would have been the second president impeached had he not resigned in 1974.

In 1998 the House Judiciary Committee recommended the impeachment of President Bill Clinton. By narrow margins, the House passed two articles of impeachment against the president—for perjury in a grand jury testimony and for obstruction of justice.

The House delivered these two charges against the president to the Senate, and a trial began in January 1999. Article II, Section 4, of the Constitution says that a president (or other civil officer of the United States) "shall be removed from office upon impeachment for and Conviction of, Treason, Bribery, or other high Crimes and Misdemeanors." During the Senate trial, Senators considered whether the charges against President Clinton, if proven, were serious enough to warrant removal from office. In February 1999 the Senate acquitted the president by failing to obtain the two-thirds majority necessary to convict on either charge.

The Confirmation Power The Senate has the power to approve presidential appointments of federal officials. Because most of these appointments involve the promotions of military officers,

See the following footnoted materials in the **Reference Handbook:**
1. *The Constitution,* pages 774–799.

Senate action is usually only a formality. Each year, however, the Senate looks more closely at several hundred nominations to cabinet and subcabinet positions, regulatory agencies, major diplomatic and military posts, and the federal judiciary. Nominees to the Supreme Court receive the most scrutiny. The Senate has rejected about 20 percent of Court nominations.

The Ratification Power Article II, Section 2, of the Constitution gives the Senate the exclusive power to ratify treaties between the United States and other nations. To ratify a treaty, two-thirds of the senators present must vote for it. This power is one of the key ways in which Congress helps shape foreign policy.

In 1980 many senators opposed the second Strategic Arms Limitation Treaty (SALT II) between the United States and the Soviet Union. This opposition prevented a vote, and the treaty was not ratified. With a few exceptions Senate action on treaties has not been a major factor in American foreign policy. Nevertheless, in recent years presidents have often bypassed the treaty ratification process by negotiating executive agreements with other heads of state. These agreements do not require Senate approval.

The Amendment Power Congress shares with state legislatures the power to propose amendments. Amendments may be proposed by a two-thirds vote of both houses or by a convention called by the legislatures of two-thirds of the states. Such a convention has never been called. This method, however, raises important constitutional questions. One significant question is whether a constitutional convention called to propose a certain amendment may then propose amendments on topics other than those contained in the states' original petitions. Some people fear that delegates might propose revisions of long-established constitutional provisions. Congress has considered, but not acted on, measures that would limit constitutional conventions to the issues proposed in state petitions to Congress. Congress also has the power to determine whether state conventions or state legislatures will ratify a proposed amendment.

To date, all of the constitutional amendments added to the Constitution have started in Congress. The states have approved 27 proposed amendments and have failed to ratify only 6. Congress has required all amendments—except the Twenty-first Amendment (1933), which repealed the Eighteenth Amendment on Prohibition—to be ratified by state legislatures. Advocates of the Twenty-first Amendment believed they would have better support in conventions than state legislatures, because many state legislatures were dominated by "Drys," supporters of Prohibition.

Section 1 Assessment

Checking for Understanding

1. **Main Idea** Using a graphic organizer like the one below, list two or more examples of powers the Constitution expresses, implies, and denies to Congress.

expressed	implied	denied

2. **Define** expressed powers, necessary and proper clause, implied powers, revenue bill, appropriations bill, interstate commerce, impeachment.
3. **Identify** Twentieth Amendment, Twenty-fifth Amendment.
4. State the foreign policy powers of Congress.
5. Describe the process by which Congress may remove a member of the executive or judicial branch from office.

Critical Thinking

6. **Drawing Conclusions** Do you think *Gibbons* v. *Ogden* provided a basis for the Court's position in *Heart of Atlanta Motel* v. *United States* that a hotel is a part of interstate commerce? Explain.

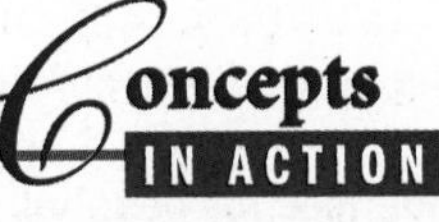

Constitutional Interpretations Research legislation that Congress passed in a recent session. (You may wish to use the *Congressional Quarterly's Weekly Report.*) Identify any bills you believe were based on the power to regulate interstate commerce. Draw a political cartoon supporting or criticizing the legislation.

Flood v. Kuhn et al., 1972

With teams from New York to California, professional baseball is not only a sport but also a business engaged in interstate commerce. Is baseball subject to federal antitrust laws like other businesses? Do baseball players have the right to act as free agents and make their own contracts with the team that will pay the most? The case of Flood *v.* Kuhn *dealt with these questions.*

Curt Flood

Background of the Case

In twelve seasons with the St. Louis Cardinals (1958 to 1969) Curt Flood was a three-time All-Star, played in three World Series, and won seven Golden Glove awards. In 1969, without consulting him, St. Louis traded Flood to the Philadelphia Phillies. He complained to the baseball commissioner that he had earned the right to be treated as more than a piece of property. Flood asked that he be allowed to act as a free agent.

The commissioner refused, stating that baseball's reserve clause meant that each player was tied indefinitely to one club, unless that club wanted to trade the player. This rule saved the owners money because it reduced competition by preventing the players from selling their services to whichever club would pay them the most.

Flood sat out the 1970 season and took his case to the courts. Two lower courts ruled in favor of the owners. Supported by the players' union, Flood appealed. In 1972 the case came to the Supreme Court. By then Curt Flood had left baseball and never played again.

The Constitutional Issue

Under its power to regulate interstate commerce, Congress passed the Sherman Antitrust Act in 1890 as a way to prevent the growth of business monopolies that prevented competition.

In 1922 in *Federal Baseball Club* v. *National League* the Court stated that baseball involved interstate commerce but was not the type of business that the antitrust laws were intended to cover. Some 30 years later in *Toolson* v. *New York Yankees* the Court refused to overrule its earlier decision. Furthermore, it stated that Congress had allowed baseball to develop exempt from antitrust laws rather than subject to them.

Debating the Case

Questions to Consider

1. Where did Congress get the authority to create antitrust laws?
2. What could be the consequences for baseball if the Court ruled in favor of Curt Flood of the St. Louis Cardinals?
3. Should the Supreme Court overrule its own precedents and declare baseball subject to antitrust laws, or should the Court leave the choice to Congress?

You Be the Judge

In fighting the reserve clause, Curt Flood challenged baseball's exemption from the antitrust laws passed by Congress. The reserve clause was clearly a violation of the antitrust laws because it restricted the players' ability to bargain with clubs for their services and thus helped the baseball owners control competition. To rule in Curt Flood's favor the Court would have to overturn its ruling in the earlier cases. How would you rule?

Section 2

Investigations and Oversight

Reader's Guide

Key Terms

subpoena, perjury, contempt, immunity, legislative veto

Find Out

- In what ways are a witness's rights in a congressional investigation similar to and different from a witness's rights in a court?
- By what methods does Congress exercise its power of legislative oversight?

Understanding Concepts

Checks and Balances How does the power of Congress to oversee the carrying out of laws serve as a check on the executive branch?

COVER STORY

Cranston Targeted

WASHINGTON, D.C., MARCH 1991

Senator Alan Cranston is the sole target of a long-delayed Senate Ethics Committee report just released. Four other senators escaped relatively unscathed. The committee found that the 76-year-old senator from California had engaged in "impermissible conduct." The findings followed a 14-month investigation into dealings between a savings and loan (S&L) executive, Charles Keating, and 5 members of the United States Senate. All 5 had helped Keating and accepted campaign contributions from him at the same time. Keating needed protection from the investigations of federal regulators during the S&L crisis.

A defunct S&L

Most congressional powers fall into two of four categories. They are either legislative or nonlegislative powers, and they are either expressed powers or implied powers. Over the years, however, Congress has developed additional powers inherent in governing but not mentioned in the Constitution. These powers are the power to investigate and the power of legislative oversight.

The Power to Investigate

The Founders neither granted nor denied Congress the power to conduct investigations. Nevertheless, in 1792, after Native Americans soundly defeated the United States Army, Congress launched an investigation of the military. This power has played an important role in American politics ever since.

The Investigation Process A standing committee or a select committee may conduct investigations. Investigations may last for several days or go on for months. The committee's staff members may travel around the country collecting evidence and scheduling witnesses. Dozens of witnesses may be called to testify, sometimes under oath, at committee hearings.

Congressional investigations occur for many reasons. Most get little notice, but a few have become media events. In 1998 the Senate Finance Committee opened hearings into the collection methods of the Internal Revenue Service. Witnesses' televised testimony about the strong-arm tactics used by the agency led to a 97 to 0 Senate vote to reform the IRS. In the 1990s Congress investigated allegations against its own members.

In 1995 alone, 20 senators and representatives faced complaints that went to congressional ethics panels. While many of these complaints were politically motivated, several members were indicted, two House members were convicted of crimes, and Senator Robert

Congressional Investigations

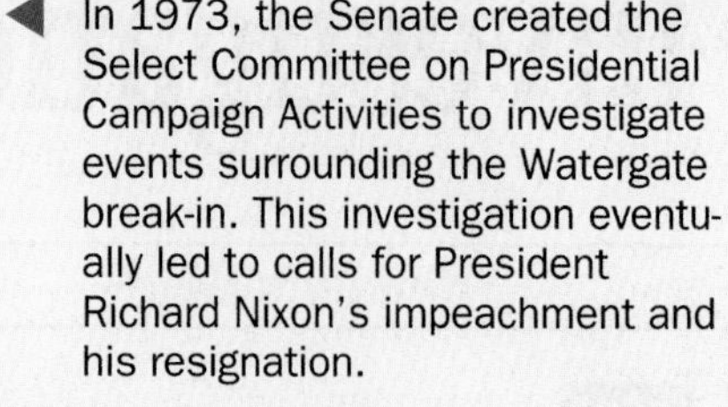

In 1973, the Senate created the Select Committee on Presidential Campaign Activities to investigate events surrounding the Watergate break-in. This investigation eventually led to calls for President Richard Nixon's impeachment and his resignation.

In the early 1950s, Senator Joseph McCarthy, whose accusations proved to be groundless, claimed that Communists had infiltrated educational institutions and high levels of government.

Checks and Balances
How does Congress's power to investigate strengthen the system of checks and balances?

Packwood resigned to avoid being expelled from the chamber. At the same time, a Senate committee probed into inquiries about President Clinton's Whitewater land investments and links to a failed savings and loan company in Arkansas when he was the state's governor.

Investigations may have a variety of consequences. In most circumstances they lead to new legislation to deal with a problem, changes in a government program, or removal of officials from office. Sometimes, however, they damage the reputations of innocent people.

Congressional Powers and Witness Rights

Although congressional investigations are not trials, Congress has several powers that help committees collect evidence. Like courts, congressional committees have the power to subpoena witnesses. A **subpoena** is a legal order that a person appear or produce requested documents. Congress makes great use of this power.

Also like courts, congressional committees can require witnesses to testify under oath. Witnesses who do not tell the truth can be criminally prosecuted for **perjury**, or lying under oath. In addition, committees may punish those who refuse to testify or otherwise will not cooperate by holding them in **contempt**, or willful obstruction, of Congress. Persons found in contempt of Congress may be arrested and jailed. While the Constitution does not grant Congress this power, court decisions have generally upheld it.

Until recent years, witnesses called to testify in person before a congressional committee had few rights. In 1948, for example, the chairperson of a House committee told one hapless witness: "The rights you have are the rights given you by this committee. We will determine what rights you have and what rights you do not have before the committee."

Today this situation has changed, and witnesses have important rights when appearing before a congressional committee. In ***Watkins* v. *United States*** (1957),[1] the Supreme Court ruled that Congress must respect witnesses' constitutional rights just as a court does. The Court stated:

See the following footnoted materials in the **Reference Handbook:**
1. *Watkins* v. *United States* case summary, page 767.

"Witnesses cannot be compelled to give evidence against themselves. They cannot be subjected to unreasonable search and seizure. Nor can the 1st Amendment freedoms of speech, press, religion, or political belief and association be abridged."

—Chief Justice Earl Warren, 1957

One way that congressional committees have sidestepped this requirement is by granting immunity to witnesses. **Immunity** is freedom from prosecution for witnesses whose testimony ties them to illegal acts. Of course, the Fifth Amendment states that people cannot be forced to testify against themselves. Witnesses who are granted immunity, however, can be required to testify about illegal activities in which they are involved. Those who refuse may be held in contempt and jailed.

A 1987 case illustrates the principle of immunity. A Senate committee investigated charges against officials in the Reagan administration. They were charged with selling arms to Iran and using the money to finance a guerrilla war in Nicaragua. The committee granted immunity to Colonel Oliver North, an employee of the president's National Security Council, and compelled him to testify. North implicated the president's national security adviser and others. North was tried and convicted. His sentence was later thrown out and his conviction was overturned on appeal, because evidence used against him was uncovered as a result of his protected congressional testimony.

Legislative Oversight

Many, if not most, congressional investigations are related to another power that Congress has developed. The power of **legislative oversight** involves a continuing review of how effectively the executive branch carries out the laws Congress passes. Under its commerce power and the necessary and proper clause Congress has created a huge bureaucracy. In exercising its oversight power, congressional committees keep watch over these agencies of the executive branch.

The Practice of Legislative Oversight

Legislative oversight is a good example of the constitutional principle of checks and balances. Congress makes the laws. The job of the executive branch is to carry them out. In doing so, the executive branch has the power to decide what legislation means and how it should be put into effect. Through its power of legislative oversight, Congress can check on how the executive branch is administering the law.

Congress has defined its oversight functions in several laws. The Legislative Reorganization Act of 1946 calls for Congress to exercise "continuous watchfulness" over executive agencies. In the Legislative Reorganization Act of 1970, Congress states, "Each standing committee shall review and study, on a continuing basis, the application, administration, and execution" of laws in areas of its responsibility.

Senate Committee Investigations

Government Under Scrutiny Senate Governmental Affairs Committee chairman Fred Thompson (second from right) meets with committee members in 1997 to investigate fund-raising practices by the Democratic National Committee. The committee hearings focused on how American politics and policies may have been inappropriately influenced. ***What investigative powers are assigned to Congress in the Constitution?***

Limits on Legislative Oversight In practice, however, lawmakers exercise the power of legislative oversight in an inconsistent way. Vice President Hubert Humphrey once said that Congress "sometimes gets in the habit of 'pass it and forget it' lawmaking." Very few congressional committees review the actions of the executive branch on a regular basis especially if the president and the majority of Congress are the same party. Instead, legislative oversight usually occurs in bits and pieces as congressional staffs and committees go about their business.

There are several reasons that legislative oversight is not carried out consistently. First, lawmakers do not have enough staff, time, or money to keep track of everything going on in the executive branch. It simply is not possible for Congress to effectively monitor the routine activities of the many executive agencies.

Second, lawmakers know there are not many votes to be gained from most oversight activities. Voters and the news media seldom are interested in oversight activities unless an investigation turns up a scandal or an unusual problem. As one lawmaker aptly put it, "Where there is publicity to be gained, there is oversight to be had."

Third, the language of some laws is so vague that it is very difficult to judge exactly what they mean. Without clear objectives, lawmakers have little basis for judging whether or not the executive branch is carrying out the law's intent.

Finally, committees sometimes come to favor the federal agencies they are supposed to oversee. Lawmakers and the officials who work for a federal agency often become well acquainted, spending long hours working together. In such cases there exists a danger that a committee may not engage in careful, critical oversight of an agency.

Congressional Limits on Executive Activities Congress exercises its oversight power in several ways. One way is for Congress to require executive agencies to submit reports to Congress on their activities. The 1946 Employment Act, for example, requires the president to send Congress an annual report on the nation's economy. During a recent term of Congress, federal agencies submitted more than 1,000 such reports to Capitol Hill.

We the People

Making a Difference

Robin Deykes

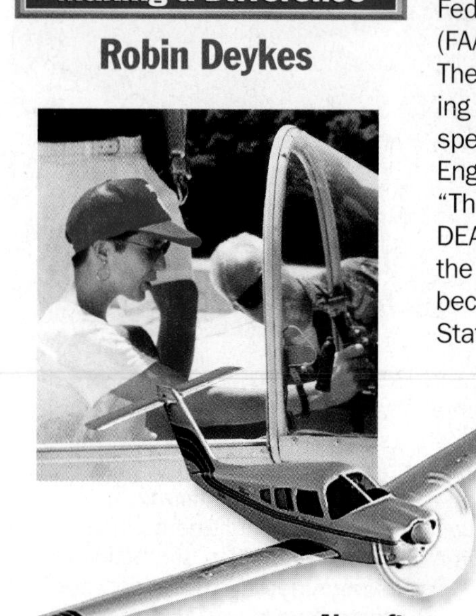

Aircraft

Although Robin Deykes loved to fly, she was nearly grounded in 1995 when the Federal Aviation Administration (FAA) proposed a new set of rules. The rules stated that all pilots flying in the United States must speak and understand spoken English. Robin, who is deaf, said, "They might as well have said NO DEAF PILOTS ALLOWED." Prior to the new rules, deaf people could become pilots in the United States if they used airports that did not require radio contact.

When Robin found out about the FAA's change in rules, she tracked down John Lynch at the FAA who had been involved in developing them. She told him that the new rules would prevent her and other deaf and hearing impaired pilots from flying. "The proposed rules were really the result of a misunderstanding. I thought that most deaf people could speak and read lips," Lynch said. "Robin made me realize that was not always the case." Lynch said the ruling was not intended to keep deaf people from flying.

Robin's efforts helped convince the FAA to change its rules. The rules now state that pilots who are deaf or hearing impaired can continue to fly into airports where no radio contact is required. They also state that if future technology enables deaf and hearing impaired people to communicate by radio, they will also be permitted to fly into radio-controlled airports.

A second oversight technique is for lawmakers to ask one of the congressional support agencies, such as the **General Accounting Office (GAO),** to study an executive agency's work. The GAO monitors the finances of federal agencies to make sure public money has been spent appropriately and legally.

The power of Congress to appropriate money provides another means of oversight. Each year, as part of the federal budget process, the House and Senate review the budgets of all agencies in the executive branch. This review allows Congress to shape public policy by expanding, reducing, or eliminating certain programs.

For years Congress used the legislative veto, in which Congress wrote certain provisions into some laws that allowed it to review and cancel actions of the executive agencies that carried out those laws. This device gave Congress authority over subordinates of the president. In 1983 the Supreme Court ruled in *Immigration and Naturalization Service* v. *Chadha* that the veto was unconstitutional because it violated the principle of separation of powers.

Independent Counsel In 1994 Congress renewed an independent counsel law passed in 1978 authorizing the House or Senate judiciary committee to require the attorney general to investigate charges of crimes by officials. If the investigation finds grounds for further investigation, the attorney general may petition to appoint an independent counsel. In 1994 a three-judge panel named Kenneth W. Starr as independent counsel to investigate real estate investments President Clinton had made while governor of Arkansas. By 1998 Starr had broadened his investigation to include other allegations against the president which led to his being impeached.

Star Makers Congress's authority to investigate conditions in society has produced dramatic hearings and made celebrities of participants. In the 1950s, Wisconsin senator Joseph R. McCarthy drew condemnation from his colleagues for his actions in probing alleged communism in government. His smear tactics added the term *McCarthyism* to the language. In the 1970s, North Carolina senator Sam Ervin gained fame for his judicious handling of the Watergate investigation that toppled the administration of Richard Nixon.

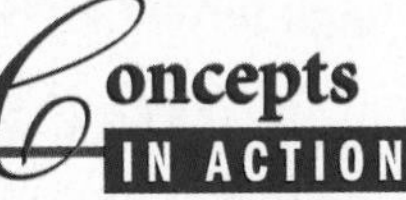

Student Web Activity Visit the *United States Government: Democracy in Action* Web site at gov.glencoe.com and click on ***Chapter 6–Student Web Activities*** for an activity about congressional powers.

Section 2 Assessment

Checking for Understanding

1. **Main Idea** Using a graphic organizer like the one shown, identify the steps Congress can take if a witness at a congressional investigation cites Fifth Amendment protection and refuses to testify.

   1. → 2.

2. **Define** subpoena, perjury, contempt, immunity, legislative veto.
3. **Identify** *Watkins* v. *United States,* GAO.
4. Identify three congressional investigations that focused on the executive branch.

Critical Thinking

5. **Synthesizing Information** How does the use of a subpoena assist legislators in the committee hearing process?

Concepts IN ACTION

Checks and Balances Suppose you are a reporter assigned to cover a recent congressional investigation. Prepare a news broadcast to present to the class in which you identify the purpose of the investigation and its findings. You might want to include interviews as well.

Section 3

Congress and the President

Reader's Guide

Key Terms

national budget, impoundment

Find Out

- How have the characteristics of the American system led to competition and conflict between Congress and the president?
- Why has power shifted back and forth between the president and Congress over the years?

Understanding Concepts

Checks and Balances Why do some people state that deadlock and inaction are built-in features of American government?

COVER STORY

Shutdown Hardship

WASHINGTON, D.C., JANUARY 1996

President Clinton and Congress are searching feverishly for a compromise to end the budget impasse that has brought the partial shutdown of the federal government. Meanwhile, the shutdown is beginning to affect government services. "This is ridiculous," says Dottie Knight, a furloughed employee of the Centers for Disease Control in Atlanta. Knight is working from home without pay, buying stamps to continue mailing CDC materials to the public. In Kansas, the state has suspended unemployment checks because federal funds have stopped.

Government closed until further notice

The Founders probably did not envision a shutdown of the federal government when they established the principle of separation of powers. Nevertheless, they did create a system of checks and balances that can result in a government stalemate. Many of the president's most important executive responsibilities—such as making treaties, appointing federal officials and judges, and paying the expenses of the executive branch—require congressional cooperation. When the Congress refuses to cooperate, the president may be frustrated.

On the other hand, all bills Congress passes require the president's signature before they become law. Overriding a presidential veto requires a two-thirds majority in each house of Congress, which usually is difficult to obtain. Consequently, a veto or even the threat of one is an important legislative power the president exercises. In addition, modern presidents are expected to develop a legislative program and secure its adoption by Congress.

Cooperation and Conflict

The level of cooperation between Congress and the president has varied throughout history. Usually, the best relations exist between the two branches when the president makes few demands on Congress. Less active presidents—such as Dwight D. Eisenhower during the 1950s—who do not take an aggressive role in shaping legislation may get along well with Congress. Those who propose major new programs will almost surely come into conflict with the legislative branch. Recent presidents have frequently found it hard to work with Congress for several reasons.

Constituents and Conflict A large national electorate chooses presidents who promote policies they feel are in the best interests of the entire nation. Individual states and congressional districts, however, elect members of

Congress. Because they represent much narrower interests, members of Congress often have ideas very different from the president about what constitutes desirable public policy.

Gridlock Haunts the Capital

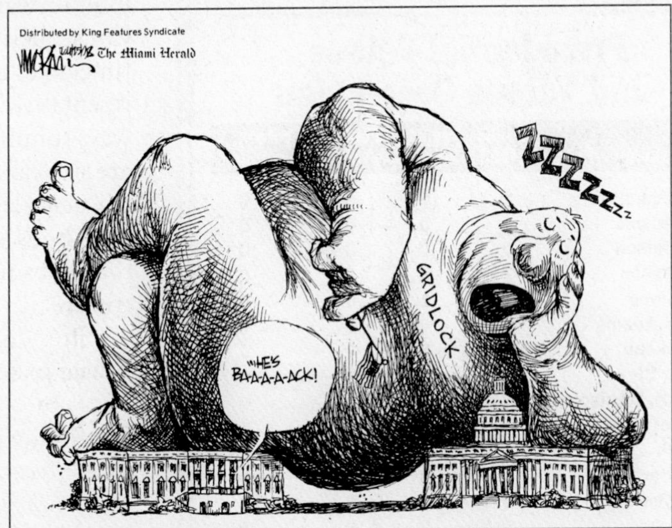

President and Congress Clash Gridlock occurs when the president and Congress cannot agree on legislation. ***According to the cartoon, is gridlock a problem that is quickly or easily resolved? Explain.***

Checks and Balances

The system of checks and balances gives Congress and the president the power to counteract each other. For example, the president may threaten a veto, arguing that a particular bill spends too much money and would spur inflation harmful to the nation. Some members of Congress may cooperate in attempting to amend the bill or override a veto because their states or districts would benefit from the bill.

Political historian James MacGregor Burns contends that the system is "designed for deadlock and inaction." He argues that these checks and balances result in the "President versus Congress."

Party Politics Partisan political differences can affect the relationship between the president and Congress. This is especially evident when the different parties control the White House and Congress. In recent decades the president's party rarely has controlled either house of Congress, so conflict between the branches has increased. The legislative process slowed considerably in 1995 when President Clinton, a Democrat, faced Republican majorities in Congress. When President Clinton won reelection in 1996 and the Republicans again won both houses, one observer anticipated more of what the press had begun to call "gridlock."

> "*The question in the next two years, will be whether that lack of mandate for either side will foster cooperation to get things done or positioning to do battle in the next election.*"
>
> —Curtis B. Gans

Organization as a Cause of Conflict The organization of Congress provides many weapons to those who want to resist a legislative proposal of the president. Rules of procedure, such as the Senate's unlimited debate rule, can be used to block action on legislation. Even when congressional leaders support the president, they may struggle to push presidential initiatives through Congress.

Because the basic shape of legislation is set in committees and subcommittees, the committee system also may be a weapon against the president. Committee chairpersons are powerful members of Congress, and they use their positions to influence bills. Conflicts in government occur when a president wants a major proposal approved and a committee tries to delay, revise, or defeat it.

Differing Political Timetables Conflicts may also occur because the president and Congress have different political timetables. Presidents have a little more than three years to develop, present, and move their programs through Congress before they have to busy themselves running for reelection. At best, they have only eight years to accomplish their agenda.

Congressional Quarterly's
Government at a Glance

Presidential Vetoes and Vetoes Overridden

President	All bills vetoed	Regular vetoes	Pocket vetoes	Vetoes Overridden
Washington	2	2	0	0
J. Adams	0	0	0	0
Jefferson	0	0	0	0
Madison	7	5	2	0
Monroe	1	1	0	0
J.Q. Adams	0	0	0	0
Jackson	12	5	7	0
Van Buren	1	0	1	0
W. H. Harrison	0	0	0	0
Tyler	10	6	4	1
Polk	3	2	1	0
Taylor	0	0	0	0
Fillmore	0	0	0	0
Pierce	9	9	0	5
Buchanan	7	4	3	0
Lincoln	7	2	5	0
A. Johnson	29	21	8	15
Grant	93	45	48	4
Hayes	13	12	1	1
Garfield	0	0	0	0
Arthur	12	4	8	1
Cleveland (1st term)	414	304	110	2
B. Harrison	44	19	25	1
Cleveland (2d term)	170	42	128	5
McKinley	42	6	36	0
T. Roosevelt	82	42	40	1
Taft	39	30	9	1
Wilson	44	33	11	6
Harding	6	5	1	0
Coolidge	50	20	30	4
Hoover	37	21	16	3
F. Roosevelt	635	372	263	9
Truman	250	180	70	12
Eisenhower	181	73	108	2
Kennedy	21	12	9	0
L. Johnson	30	16	14	0
Nixon	43	26	17	7
Ford	66	48	18	12
Carter	31	13	18	2
Reagan	78	39	39	9
Bush	44	29	15	1
Clinton*	25	25	0	2
Total	2,538	1,473	1,065	106

* through 1998

Critical Thinking

Early presidents confined their vetoes to legislation they considered to be unconstitutional. ***What concerns cause modern-day presidents to veto legislation?***

Source: Stanley and Niemi, *Vital Statistics on American Politics 1999-2000* (Washington, D.C.: CQ Inc., 2000).

Online UPDATE
Visit **gov.glencoe.com** and click on ***Textbook Updates–Chapter 6*** for an update of the data.

Senators and representatives are not limited to two terms in office as is the president. Most can look forward to being reelected for many terms. Consequently, members of Congress have political timetables quite different from the president. Representatives, who serve only two-year terms, are always running for reelection. Senators, whose terms are six years, can be more patient in handling controversial legislative proposals. Thus, lawmakers in both houses may not be eager to act on legislation that does not directly benefit their states or districts.

President Lyndon Johnson, who had served as Senate majority leader, complained:

> "*You've got to give it all you can that first year. . . . You've got just one year when they treat you right, and before they start worrying about themselves. The third year, you lose votes. . . . The fourth year's all politics. You can't put anything through when half the Congress is thinking how to beat you.*"
>
> —Lyndon Johnson

The Struggle for Power

For most of the first 150 years of the Republic, Congress dominated policy making. At times, however, strong presidents such as Andrew Jackson and Abraham Lincoln challenged congressional supremacy. They increased presidential powers as they dealt with changing social, political, and economic conditions.

The system of checks and balances makes it likely that the president and Congress will always compete for power. Which branch will dominate in any specific period depends on many factors, including the political issues of the time and the leaders in Congress and the executive branch. Strong presidential leadership during the Depression of the 1930s and the Cold War caused a steady growth in the powers of the presidency at the expense of Congress. During the mid-1970s, however, the trend toward presidential dominance began to stimulate a reaction from Congress. Congressional efforts to reassert lost authority and to gain new influence in public policy led Congress to restrict the president's war-making and budgetary powers and to exercise the legislative veto more often.

Curbing the President's Emergency Powers In times of crisis, Congress has delegated additional powers to the president. Presidents have declared martial law, seized property, controlled transportation and communication, and sent armed forces overseas. President Franklin D. Roosevelt gained vast authority during the Great Depression and World War II. In 1933 Congress empowered the president to close the nation's banks. Legislation during World War II gave Roosevelt even broader control over the nation's economy, including industries, wages and prices, and the rationing of consumer goods. Later presidents continued the emergency powers initially granted to Roosevelt, and technically the United States remained in a state of emergency. In 1971, for example, President Nixon froze wages and prices to combat economic problems stemming from the Vietnam War.

In 1976 Congress passed the National Emergencies Act that ended the 35-year state of emergency as of September 30, 1978. Since that date presidents no longer possess automatic emergency powers. Presidents must notify Congress when they intend to declare a national emergency. A state of emergency now cannot last more than one year unless the president repeats the process. In addition, Congress can end a state of emergency at any time by passing legislation.

The Budget Impoundment and Control Act Over the years presidents have assumed more responsibility for planning the **national budget,** the yearly financial plan for the national government. Because of this, by the early 1970s Congress had slipped into the role of merely reacting to budget proposals.

In 1974 Congress passed the Congressional Budget and Impoundment Control Act in an effort to increase its role in planning the budget. The act established a permanent budget committee for each house and created a **Congressional Budget Office (CBO)** to provide financial experts to help Congress. In addition, the act limited the president's ability to impound funds. **Impoundment** is the president's refusal to spend money Congress has voted to fund a program. The law requires that appropriated funds be spent unless the president requests and both houses of Congress agree that the monies not be spent.

Crisis and Power

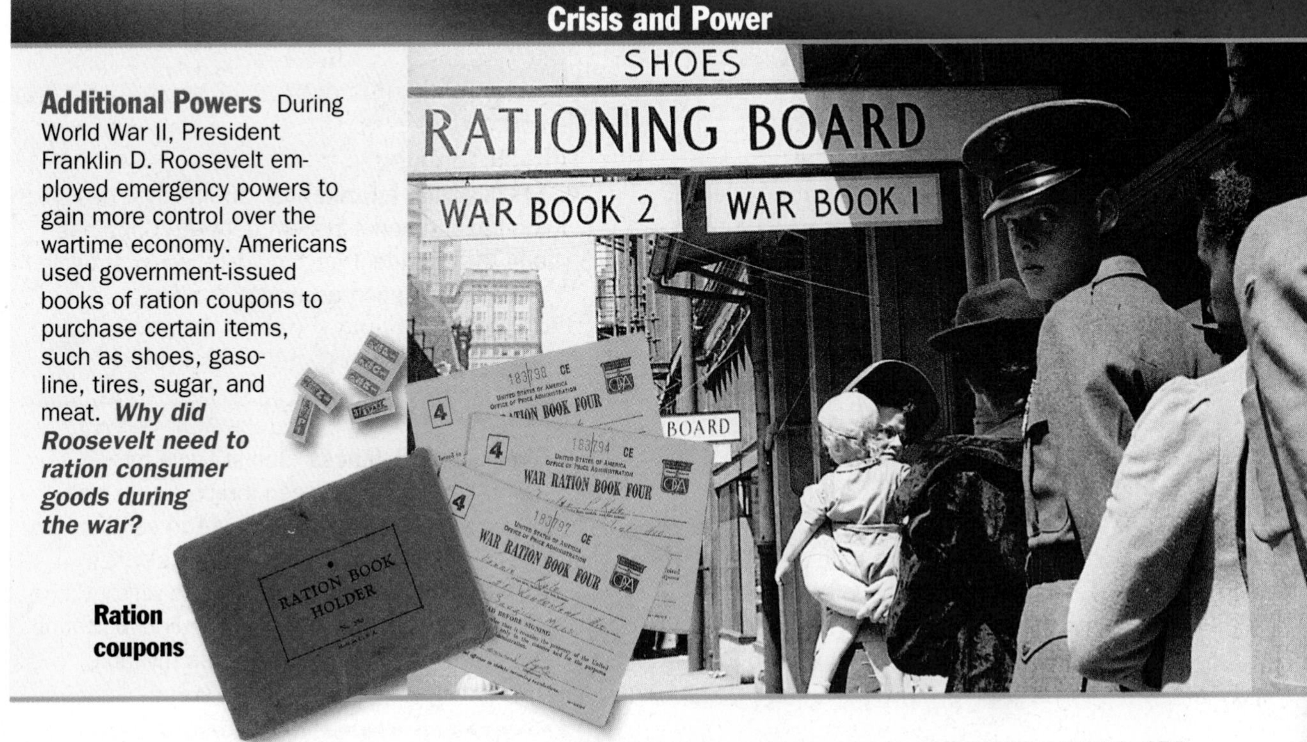

Additional Powers During World War II, President Franklin D. Roosevelt employed emergency powers to gain more control over the wartime economy. Americans used government-issued books of ration coupons to purchase certain items, such as shoes, gasoline, tires, sugar, and meat. ***Why did Roosevelt need to ration consumer goods during the war?***

Ration coupons

Use of the Legislative Veto Between 1932 and 1983—when it was declared unconstitutional—more than 200 laws have contained some form of legislative veto. The veto was not widely used, however, until Congress reasserted its authority in the 1970s. Many members of Congress argued that the device was an effective check on the executive branch.

Presidents have called the legislative veto a challenge to their authority. President Carter complained that its use was "excessive." Others argued that it violated separation of powers. Since the Supreme Court ruling, Congress has searched for a constitutional alternative to the legislative veto.

Line-Item Veto The Constitution provides for a presidential veto of entire bills. Most governors, however, can veto parts of bills, letting the rest become law. Many presidents have asked Congress for a **line-item veto,** enabling them to veto only certain lines or items in a bill.

Sentiment for giving the president such veto power was strong in the mid-1990s. Congress knew, however, that a true line-item veto would require a constitutional amendment. House and Senate Republicans passed a complex version of a line-item veto bill in 1995, calling it an enhanced rescission bill. Signed into law by President Clinton, the bill authorized the president to veto spending items and certain limited tax breaks. In the Line Item Veto Act, Congress attempted to retain some control over such legislation by a provision that it could pass a freestanding bill to reinstate the vetoed spending by a two-thirds vote of both chambers. This act went into effect in 1997.

In the summer of 1997, President Clinton became the first president to exercise the line-item veto. Even after it was passed, however, critics remained vocal about the new law. Supporters believed it would curb excessive spending, but critics said it allowed Congress to shift the responsibility of making spending cuts to the president.

Almost immediately some members of Congress challenged the law in federal court. The Supreme Court threw out this challenge but later ruled on the constitutional merits of the legislation. In 1998, upholding separate challenges by the City of New York and potato growers from Idaho, the Court said that the Line Item Veto Act was unconstitutional.

Justice John Paul Stevens wrote for the majority that the act circumvented the legislative procedures which were clearly spelled out in Article I of the Constitution. "If there is to be a new procedure in which the President will play a different role . . . such change must come not by legislation but through the amendment procedures set forth in Article V of the Constitution," Stevens concluded.

Section 3 Assessment

Checking for Understanding

1. **Main Idea** Using a graphic organizer like the one below, identify three ways in which Congress has gained and lost power.

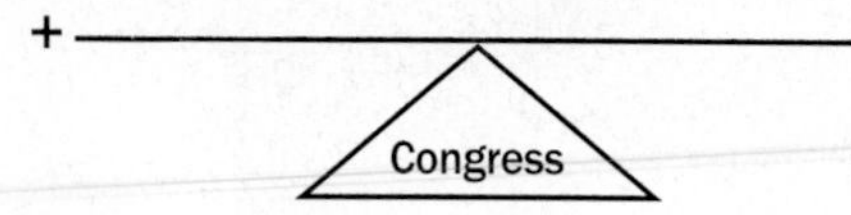

2. **Define** national budget, impoundment.
3. **Identify** Congressional Budget Office.
4. Why do the different constituencies of the president and Congress cause conflict between the executive and legislative branches?
5. How does the political party system contribute to conflict between the president and Congress?

Critical Thinking

6. **Synthesizing Information** One analyst described the constitutional system between Congress and the president as "an invitation to struggle." Is this description accurate? Explain.

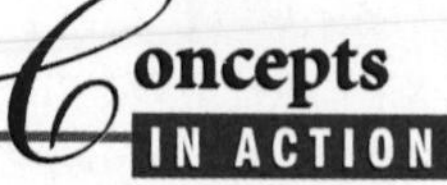

Checks and Balances One struggle for power that exists between the president and Congress is the president's right to send armed forces overseas. When has the president committed military forces overseas without a declaration of war? Create a time line indicating the year and the reason for these military involvements.

Multimedia Presentations

Your government teacher has assigned a presentation about Congress. You want to develop a presentation that really holds your classmates' attention.

Learning the Skill

Most presentations are more dynamic if they include diagrams, photographs, videos, or sound recordings. Equipment you may have at home, plus classroom or library resources, can help you develop interesting multimedia presentations. The equipment can range from simple cassette players, to overhead projectors, to VCRs, to computers, and beyond.

A multimedia presentation involves using several types of media. To discuss Congress's powers, for example, you might show diagrams of congressional powers and play recordings of speeches made in Congress.

Multimedia, as it relates to computer technology, is the combination of text, video, audio, and animation in an interactive computer program. In order to create multimedia presentations on a computer, though, you need to have certain tools. These may include traditional computer graphic tools and draw programs, animation programs, and authoring systems that tie everything together. Your computer manual will tell you which tools your computer can support.

Practicing the Skill

Plan and create a multimedia presentation on a topic found in the chapter, such as the nonlegislative powers. List three or four major ideas you would like to cover. Then think about how multimedia resources could enhance your presentation. Use your school or local library to do a preliminary survey of materials that may be available and list them. Use the following questions as a guide when planning your presentation:

1. Which forms of media do I want to include? Video? Sound? Animation? Photographs? Graphics?
2. Which kinds of media equipment are available at my school or local library?
3. What types of media can I create to enhance my presentation?
4. Which of these media forms does my computer support?

Application Activity

Choose a president from the twentieth century and create a multimedia presentation about his conflict and cooperation with Congress. Use as many multimedia materials as possible, including photographs, drawings, charts, graphs, posters, music recordings, or videotapes. Share your multimedia presentation with the class.

Assessment and Activities

Self-Check Quiz Visit the *United States Government: Democracy in Action* Web site at gov.glencoe.com and click on ***Chapter 6–Self-Check Quizzes*** to prepare for the chapter test.

Reviewing Key Terms

Match each of the descriptions below with the term it describes. Not every term will have a description.

a. appropriations bill
b. impoundment
c. immunity
d. implied powers
e. legislative veto
f. subpoena

1. Powers not specified in the Constitution
2. Grants money to carry out programs
3. Compels a witness to appear
4. Refusing to spend funds
5. Freedom from prosecution

Current Events JOURNAL

Lawmaking Use the *Readers' Guide to Periodical Literature* and other resources to learn about an incident in which the president has used military force since Congress passed the War Powers Act. Write a summary of this event.

Recalling Facts

1. How are expressed powers and implied powers related?
2. Why has the power to regulate interstate commerce become such an important power of Congress?
3. List five nonlegislative powers of Congress.
4. Why does Congress conduct investigations?
5. What are three methods that Congress uses to oversee the executive branch?
6. Identify three powers that Congress and the president share.
7. What are the main causes of conflict between the president and Congress?
8. On what grounds did the Supreme Court declare the legislative veto unconstitutional?

Understanding Concepts

1. **Constitutional Interpretations** Explain how the Constitution's commerce clause has helped African Americans obtain equal rights.
2. **Checks and Balances** What arguments might be made to support a legislative veto power for Congress?

Critical Thinking

1. **Making Generalizations** On what basis might the writers of the Constitution have decided which powers should go only to Congress and which powers Congress should share with the president?
2. **Understanding Cause and Effect** Using a graphic organizer like the one shown, indicate how the power struggle between the President and Congress strengthens or weakens the government.

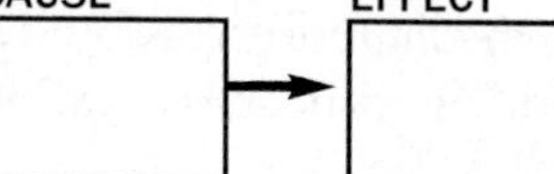

Cooperative Learning Activity

Ranking the Presidents With the class divided into three groups, organize each group to research the relationships that the last five presidents have had with Congress. Each group should rank the presidents according to how effectively they functioned with Congress. Compare the rankings of the three groups.

Interpreting Political Cartoons Activity

"Half full." *"Half empty."* *"Half empty due to congressional inaction and half full due to the tireless efforts of the President."*

1. What is happening in this cartoon?
2. Which side does the administration spokesperson support? Explain.
3. Is the administration spokesperson an objective judge? What biases might he have?

Skill Practice Activity

Multimedia Presentations Study the list of topics below dealing with Congress. Choose one of the topics and explain how you would use at least three types of media in a presentation to best teach the topic to your class.

- The national debt and Congress's attempts to limit it
- The War Powers Act and the relationship between Congress and the president
- The power of Congress to propose amendments
- A congressional investigation

Technology Activity

Using the Internet Most information or news sources can be found on the Internet. Search the World Wide Web for an online newspaper's or newsmagazine's home page to locate current articles regarding congressional actions.

Create a chart that contains the constitutional powers of Congress. Locate each congressional action you found discussed on the Internet in its proper place on the chart. Summarize one article and explain which type of congressional power was exercised.

Participating in Local Government

Because members of Congress represent the interests of individual states and congressional districts, their ideas are often different from the president's, which promote policies that represent the interests of the entire nation. Find out about an important issue in your state that has been reflected in a bill debated in Congress. Find out how your senators and representatives stand on the issue and how they voted on the bill.

Did you agree with the senator's or representative's position on the bill? Write an opinion paper supporting or criticizing your lawmaker's position.

Chapter 7

Congress at Work

Why It's Important

Serving You Congress's primary responsibility is to make law. Members of Congress also make appointments to military academies, provide passes to visit the Capitol and the White House, and help citizens deal with the government bureaucracy.

To learn more about how Congress works and how to access its services, view the ***Democracy in Action*** Chapter 7 video lesson:

Congress at Work

GOVERNMENT Online

Chapter Overview Visit the *United States Government: Democracy in Action* Web site at gov.glencoe.com and click on ***Chapter 7–Overview*** to preview chapter information.

Section 1

How a Bill Becomes a Law

Reader's Guide

Key Terms

private bill, public bill, simple resolution, rider, hearing, veto, pocket veto

Find Out

- Why is it easier to defeat legislation than to pass it?
- What are the positive and negative implications of the lengthy process through which all bills must go before becoming laws?

Understanding Concepts

Political Processes Why does it take so long for Congress to pass legislation?

COVER STORY

Record Filibuster Fails

WASHINGTON, D.C., AUGUST 1957

The Senate passed a major civil rights bill tonight, despite the efforts of South Carolina senator Strom Thurmond to prevent it from coming to a vote. Thurmond took the floor yesterday evening and talked through the night. A glass of orange juice offered by another senator this morning refreshed Thurmond for several more hours, but by late this afternoon, he was leaning on his desk and mumbling. Finally, at 9:12 P.M., he sat down, having held the floor for more than 24 hours, the longest speech in Senate history. A short time later a vote was called, and the bill passed 60 to 18.

Strom Thurmond sets a record

In 1957 the Civil Rights Bill was one of many bills introduced. Unlike a majority of the bills introduced that year, and against the backdrop of a lengthy filibuster, it passed. During each 2-year term of Congress, thousands of bills are introduced—often numbering more than 10,000. Why are so many introduced? Congress, as the national legislature, is open to all Americans who want things from the government. The president, federal agencies, labor unions, business groups, and individual citizens all look to Congress to pass laws favorable to their various interests.

Of the thousands of bills introduced in each session, only a few hundred become laws. Most die in Congress, and some are vetoed by the president. If a bill is not passed before the end of a congressional term, it must be reintroduced in the next Congress to be given further consideration.

In this section you will find out how the lawmaking process actually works. First you will look at the different forms new legislation may take. Then you will learn about the steps a bill must go through in order to become a law.

Types of Bills and Resolutions

Two types of bills are introduced in Congress. **Private bills** deal with individual people or places. They often involve people's claims against the government or their immigration problems. One such private bill waived immigration requirements so that an American woman could marry a man from Greece. Private bills used to account for a large number of the bills introduced in Congress. Lately, however, their numbers have declined. In a recent Congress, only about 230 of the 11,824 bills introduced were private bills.

On the other hand, **public bills** deal with general matters and apply to the entire nation. They are often controversial. Major public bills usually receive significant media coverage. They may involve such issues as raising or lowering taxes, national health insurance, gun control, civil rights, or abortion. Major public bills account for about 30 percent of the bills passed in each term of Congress. They may be debated for months before they become law.

Resolutions Congress may also pass several types of resolutions to deal with unusual or temporary matters. A **simple resolution** covers matters affecting only one house of Congress and is passed by that house alone. If a new rule or procedure is needed, it is adopted in the form of a resolution. Because it is an internal matter, it does not have the force of law and is not sent to the president for signature.

Joint Resolutions When both houses pass a **joint resolution** the president's signature gives it the force of law. Joint resolutions may correct an error in an earlier law, for example, or appropriate money for a special purpose. Congress also uses joint resolutions to propose constitutional amendments, which do not require the president's signature.

Concurrent Resolutions Another type of resolution is a concurrent resolution. **Concurrent resolutions** cover matters requiring the action of the House and Senate, but on which a law is not needed. A concurrent resolution, for example, may set the date for the adjournment of Congress, or it may express Congress's opinion about an issue. Both houses of Congress must pass concurrent resolutions. They do not require the president's signature, and they do not have the force of law.

Riders Bills and resolutions usually deal with only one subject, such as civil rights or veterans' benefits. Sometimes, however, a rider is attached to a bill. A **rider** is a provision on a subject other than the one covered in the bill. Lawmakers attach riders to bills that are likely to pass, although presidents have sometimes vetoed such bills because of a rider they did not like. Sometimes lawmakers attach many unrelated riders simply to benefit their constituents. Such a bill resembles a Christmas tree loaded with ornaments. **"Christmas tree" bills** sometimes pass because of the essential nature of the underlying bill.

Why So Few Bills Become Laws Less than 5 percent of all bills introduced in Congress become public laws. Why so few?

One reason is that the lawmaking process itself is very long and complicated. A congressional

★ ★ ★ POLITICS *and You*

Initiating Legislation

Have you ever said, "There ought to be a law!" when observing an apparent injustice? Some acts of Congress originate with private individuals or groups. If you see a need for a law, you can write a bill and ask a representative or senator to introduce it for consideration.

Rarely, if ever, does a bill begin this way. However, a representative may agree to sponsor your bill. A sponsor will work to put your bill in the proper form for introduction. The sponsor may also make changes in your bill's content to increase its chances for passage.

After your bill is introduced, if you are considered an expert on the subject of the bill you may be asked to testify before a congressional committee. You may also contact other members of Congress to request their support for your legislation. Finally, if Congress passes your bill, be prepared for an invitation to the White House to participate in the president's signing ceremony!

Proposing a law

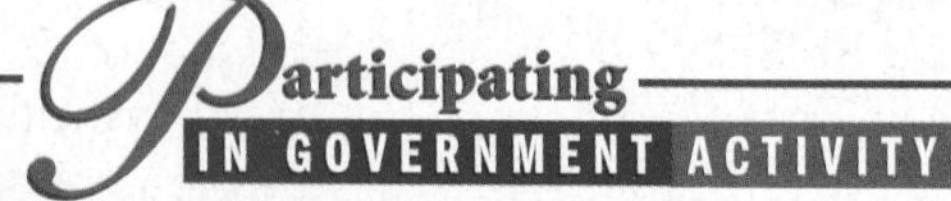

Writing Legislation Most legislation springs from a problem that people cannot resolve themselves. Brainstorm to discover a problem that might be solved by national legislation and write a description of it.

study found that more than 100 specific steps may be involved in passing a law. Thus, at many points in the lawmaking process a bill can be delayed, killed, or changed. This process has two important implications. First, it means that groups that oppose a bill have an advantage over those that support it. Opponents can amend the bill or kill it at many steps along the way.

Second, because the lawmaking process has so many steps, sponsors of a bill must be willing to bargain and compromise with lawmakers and interest groups. Compromise is the only way to get support to move a bill from one step to the next. Without strong support, most major bills have little chance of becoming law. Moreover, bills that powerful interest groups oppose are not likely to be passed.

Another reason so few bills become law is that lawmakers sometimes introduce bills they know have no chance of ever becoming law. Members of Congress may introduce such bills to go on record in support of an idea or policy or simply to attract the attention of the news media. Members may also want to satisfy an important group from their state or district. Still another reason is to call attention to the need for new legislation in an area such as health care or highway safety. Introducing a bill can help lawmakers avoid criticism at reelection time. By introducing a bill, lawmakers can report that they have taken action on a particular problem. When the bill does not move forward, they can blame a committee or other lawmakers.

Introducing a Bill

The Constitution sets forth only a few of the many steps a bill must go through to become law. The remaining steps have developed as Congress has grown in size and complexity and the number of bills has increased.

How Bills Are Introduced The first step in the legislative process is proposing and introducing a new bill. The ideas for new bills come from private citizens, interest groups, the president, or officials in the executive branch. Various people may write new bills, such as lawmakers or their staffs, lawyers from a Senate or House committee, a White House staff member, or even an interest

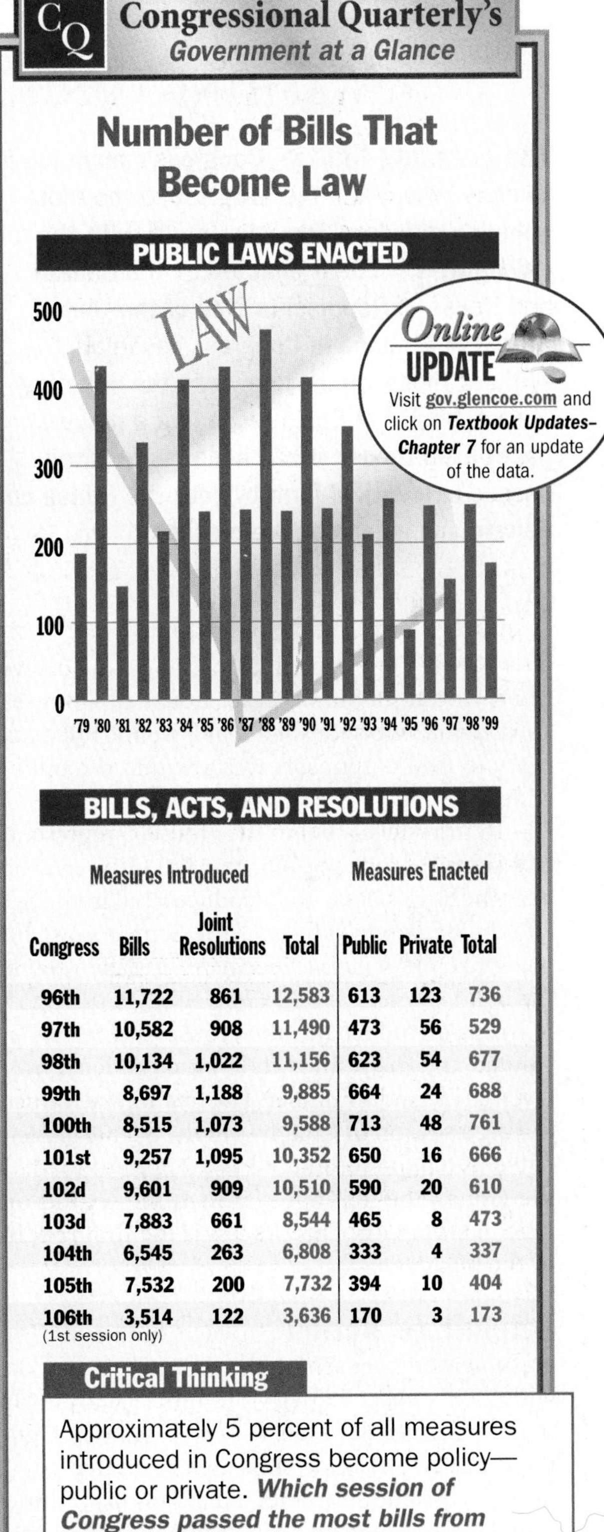

	Measures Introduced			Measures Enacted		
Congress	Bills	Joint Resolutions	Total	Public	Private	Total
96th	11,722	861	12,583	613	123	736
97th	10,582	908	11,490	473	56	529
98th	10,134	1,022	11,156	623	54	677
99th	8,697	1,188	9,885	664	24	688
100th	8,515	1,073	9,588	713	48	761
101st	9,257	1,095	10,352	650	16	666
102d	9,601	909	10,510	590	20	610
103d	7,883	661	8,544	465	8	473
104th	6,545	263	6,808	333	4	337
105th	7,532	200	7,732	394	10	404
106th (1st session only)	3,514	122	3,636	170	3	173

Critical Thinking

Approximately 5 percent of all measures introduced in Congress become policy—public or private. ***Which session of Congress passed the most bills from 1979 to 1999 ?***

Sources: "Resumes of Congressional Activity," Thomas Web site: <thomas.loc.gov>

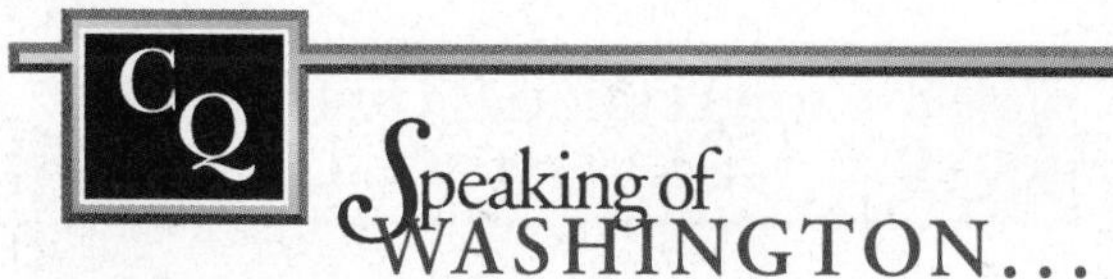

The Enacting Clause **Congress's main job is to pass laws. From the simplest to the most complex, a federal law must begin with the following words: "Be it enacted by the Senate and House of Representatives of the United States of America in Congress assembled . . . ." Without those words, known as the enacting clause, an act of Congress is just a piece of paper even though it has been, as required, passed in identical form by both the House and Senate and signed by the president.**

group itself. Only a member of Congress, however, can introduce a bill in either house of Congress. Lawmakers who sponsor a major public bill usually try to find cosponsors to show that the bill has wide support.

To introduce a bill in the House, a representative simply drops the bill into the hopper, a box near the clerk's desk. To introduce a bill in the Senate, the presiding officer of the Senate must first recognize the senator who then formally presents the bill.

Bills introduced in the House and Senate are printed and distributed to lawmakers. Each bill is given a title and a number. The first bill introduced during a session of Congress in the Senate is designated as S.l, the second bill as S.2, and so forth. In the House, the first bill is H.R. 1, the second bill, H.R. 2, and so on. This process is the **first reading** of the bill.

Committee Action

In each house of Congress, new bills are sent to the committees that deal with their subject matter. Committee chairpersons may, in turn, send the bill to a subcommittee. Under the chairperson's leadership, the committee can ignore the bill and simply let it die. This procedure is called **"pigeonholing."** Most bills die quietly this way. However, the committee also can kill the bill by a majority vote. The committee can recommend that the bill be adopted as it was introduced, make changes, or completely rewrite the bill before sending it back to the House or Senate for further action.

The House and Senate almost always agree with a committee's decision on a bill. Committee members and staff are considered experts on the subject of the bill. If they do not think a bill should move ahead, other lawmakers are usually reluctant to disagree with them. Besides, all members of Congress are also members of various committees. They do not want the decisions of their own committees overturned or questioned, so they usually go along with the decisions other committees make. Time is also a serious factor. Lawmakers have heavy workloads and must depend on the judgment of their peers.

Committee Hearings

When a committee decides to act on a bill, the committee (or subcommittee) will hold hearings on the bill. **Hearings** are sessions at which a committee listens to testimony from people interested in the bill. Witnesses who appear at the hearings may include experts on the subject of the bill, government officials, and representatives of interest groups concerned with the bill.

The hearings on a bill may last for as little as an hour or go on for many months. Hearings are supposed to be an opportunity for Congress to gather information on the bill. Most detailed information about the bill, however, comes from research done by the committee staff.

Hearings can be very important in their own right, though. Skillful chairpersons may use hearings to influence public opinion for or against a bill or to test the political acceptability of a bill. Hearings can also help focus public attention on a problem or give interest groups a chance to present their opinions. In addition, hearings are often the best point in the lawmaking process to influence a bill. It is during hearings that letters and telegrams from interested citizens can have their greatest impact on the bill.

After the hearings are completed, the committee meets in a markup session to decide what changes, if any, to make in the bill. In this type of session, committee members go through the bill section by section adopting changes they deem necessary to make the bill acceptable. A majority vote of the committee is required for all changes that are made to the bill.

Congressional Quarterly's *Government at a Glance*

How a Bill Becomes Law

HOUSE

SENATE

1. Representative hands bill to clerk or drops it in hopper.

2. Bill given *HR* number.

1. Senator announces bill on the floor.

2. Bill given *S* number.

HR1

S1

COMMITTEE ACTION

1. Referred to House standing committee.

2. Referred to House subcommittee.

3. Reported by standing committee.

4. Rules Committee sets rules for debate and amendments.

Bill is placed on committee calendar.

Bill sent to subcommittee for hearings and revisions.

Standing committee may recommend passage or kill the bill.

1. Referred to Senate standing committee.

2. Referred to Senate subcommittee.

3. Reported by standing committee.

FLOOR ACTION

1. House debates, votes on passage.

2. Bill passes; goes to Senate for approval.

OR

A different version passes; goes to conference committee.

1. Senate debates, votes on passage.

2. Bill passes; goes to House for approval.

OR

A different version passes; goes to conference committee.

CONFERENCE ACTION

Conference committee works out differences and sends identical compromise bill to both chambers for final approval.

House votes on compromise bill.

Senate votes on compromise bill.

PASS

APPROVED BILL SENT TO PRESIDENT

President signs bill or allows bill to become law without signing.*

OR

President vetoes bill.

PASS

VETO

Congress can override a veto by a 2/3 majority in both chambers. If either fails to override, the bill dies.

PASS

LAW

* President can keep bill for 10 days and bill becomes law. If Congress adjourns before the 10 days (Sundays excluded) then it does not become law.

Source: *Congress A to Z*, 2d ed.(Washington, D.C.: CQ Inc., 1993).

Critical Thinking

At what point in Congress is the bill most closely examined?

Voting Electronically

Analyzing Votes The electronic voting system in the House displays each representative's name and vote on the wall of the chamber. Representatives insert a plastic card in a box fastened to the chairs to vote "yea," "nay," or "present." ***When do you think a representative would vote "present"?***

Reporting a Bill When all the changes have been made, the committee votes either to kill the bill or to report it. To report the bill means to send it to the House or Senate for action. Along with the revised bill, the committee will send to the House or Senate a written report the committee staff has prepared. This report is important. It explains the committee's actions, describes the bill, lists the major changes the committee has made, and gives opinions on the bill. The report is often the only document available to lawmakers or their staffs as they decide how to vote on a bill. The committee report may recommend passage of the bill or it may report the bill unfavorably. Why would a committee report a bill but not recommend passage? This happens extremely rarely. A committee may believe the full House should have the opportunity to consider a bill even though the committee does not support it.

Floor Action

The next important step in the lawmaking process is the debate on the bill on the floor of the House and Senate. Voting on the bill follows the debate. As you may recall, both houses have special procedures to schedule bills for floor action.

Debating and Amending Bills Usually, only a few lawmakers take part in floor debates. The pros and cons of the bill have been argued in the committee hearings and are already well known to those with a real interest in the bill. The floor debate over a bill, however, is the point where amendments can be added to a bill (unless the House has adopted a closed rule, which means no amendments may be adopted). During the floor debate, the bill receives its second reading. A clerk reads the bill section by section. After each section is read, amendments may be offered. Any lawmaker can propose an amendment to a bill during the floor debate.

Amendments range from the introduction of major changes in a bill to the correction of typographical errors. Opponents of the bill sometimes propose amendments to slow its progress through Congress or even to kill it. One strategy opponents use is to load it down with so many objectionable amendments that it loses support and dies. In both the House and the Senate amendments are added to a bill only if a majority of the members present approves them.

Voting on Bills After the floor debate, the bill, including any proposed changes, is ready for a vote. A quorum, or a majority, of the members must be present. The House or Senate now receives the third reading of the bill. A vote on the bill is then taken. Passage of a bill requires a majority vote of all the members present.

House members vote on a bill in one of three ways. The first is a **voice vote,** in which members together call out "Aye" or "No." The Speaker determines which side has the most voice votes. The second way of voting is by a **standing vote,** or **division vote,** in which those in favor of the bill stand and are counted, then those opposed stand and are counted. The third method is a recorded vote, in which members' votes are recorded electronically. Their votes are flashed on large display panels in the House chamber. This method, used since 1973, saves the House many hours of time that it took for roll-call votes in each session.

Seal of the U.S. Congress

The Senate has three methods of voting. These methods include a voice vote, a standing vote, and a roll call. The voice vote and the standing vote are the same as in the House. In a **roll-call vote,** senators respond "Aye" or "No" as their names are called in alphabetical order. Roll-call votes are recorded and over the years have become increasingly common.

Final Steps in Passing Bills

To become law a bill must pass both houses of Congress in identical form. A bill passed in the House of Representatives often differs somewhat from a bill on the same subject passed in the Senate.

Conference Committee Action Often, one house will accept the version of a bill the other house has passed. At times, however, the bill must go to a conference committee made up of senators and representatives to work out differences between the versions. The members of the conference committee are called **conferees** or managers. They usually come from the House and Senate committees that handled the bill originally.

The conferees work out the differences between the two bills by bargaining and arranging compromises. Conference committees rarely kill a bill. The conference committee is supposed to consider only the parts of a bill on which there is disagreement. In actual practice, however, the members of the committee sometimes make important changes in the bill or add provisions neither the House nor Senate previously considered. A majority of the members of the conference committee from each house drafts the final compromise bill, called a **conference report.** Once it is accepted, the bill can be submitted to each house of Congress for final action.

Presidential Action on Bills Article I[1] of the Constitution states that:

> "*Every Bill which shall have passed the House of Representatives and the Senate, shall, before it becomes a Law, be presented to the President of the United States. . . .*"
>
> —Article I, Section 7

After both houses of Congress have approved a bill in identical form, it is sent to the president. The president may take any one of several actions. First, the president may sign the bill, and it will become law. Second, the president may keep the bill for 10 days without signing it. If Congress is in session, the bill will become law without the president's signature. This rarely happens. Presidents may use this procedure if they approve of most of the provisions of a bill but object to others. By letting the bill become law without a signature, the president indicates dissatisfaction with these provisions. Most of the time, however, presidents sign the bills that Congress sends them.

See the following footnoted materials in the **Reference Handbook:**
1. *The Constitution,* pages 774–799.

Vetoing Bills The president can also reject a bill in two ways. First, the president may veto a bill. In a **veto** the president refuses to sign the bill and returns it to the house of Congress in which it originated. The president also includes reasons for the veto. Second, the president may kill a bill passed during the last 10 days Congress is in session simply by refusing to act on it. This veto is called a **pocket veto.** Because Congress is no longer in session, it cannot override the veto and the bill dies.

Line-Item Veto In 1984, President Reagan suggested a constitutional amendment that would give a president the same veto power that many governors have. These governors may veto specific provisions (lines or items) of a bill while accepting the main part of the legislation. Bill Clinton announced his support of a line-item veto in the 1992 presidential campaign. To sidestep the need for an amendment, Congress passed an enhanced recision bill in 1996. Essentially a line-item veto for spending and tax issues, this bill allowed Congress to override a line-item veto by two-thirds majority vote of both houses.

Clinton* v. *City of New York President Clinton first used the new veto power in August 1997. When the president canceled a provision of the Balanced Budget Act of 1997 and parts of the Taxpayer Relief Act of 1997, two parties filed suit. New York and several local hospitals challenged the veto because it reduced Medicaid funding for New York state. The Snake River Potato Growers of Idaho challenged the veto of a tax break in the Taxpayer Relief Act. On appeal, the Supreme Court ruled in *Clinton* v. *City of New York* (1998) that the Line Item Veto Act was unconstitutional because it "authorizes the president to effect the repeal of laws for his own policy reasons without observing the procedures set out in Article I, [Section] 7."

Congressional Override of a Veto Congress can override a president's veto with a two-thirds vote in both houses. If Congress overrides the veto, the bill becomes law. Congress does not override vetoes very often because it is usually difficult to get the necessary two-thirds vote in both the House of Representatives and the Senate. Opponents of a bill need to have only one-third of the members present and voting plus one additional vote in either the Senate or the House to uphold a veto.

Registering Laws After a bill becomes law, it is registered with the National Archives and Records Service. This process includes identifying it as a public or private law and assigning it a number that identifies the Congress that passed the bill and the number of the law for that term. For example, Public Law 187 under the 105th Congress is registered as PL 105-187. This law is then added to the United States Code of current federal laws.

Section 1 Assessment

Checking for Understanding

1. **Main Idea** Create a flow chart to indicate the major stages by which a bill becomes a law. Which stage do you think is most important?

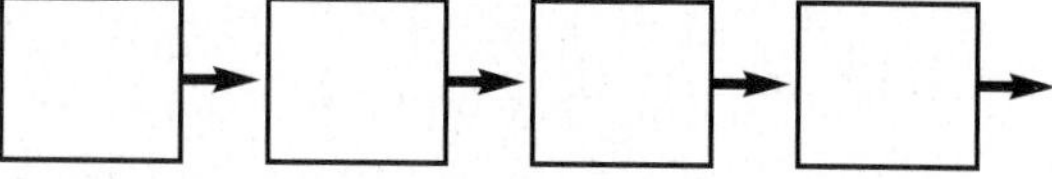

2. **Define** private bill, public bill, simple resolution, rider, hearing, veto, pocket veto.
3. **Identify** voice vote, standing vote, roll-call vote.
4. Why do so few bills actually become laws?

Critical Thinking

5. **Drawing Conclusions** Is it possible for all members of Congress to keep abreast of all bills under consideration? Support your answer.

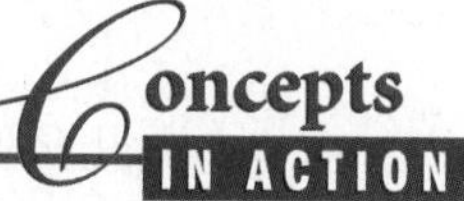

Political Processes Imagine that you are asked to help younger children learn how laws are made in the United States. Create a poster, using cartoonlike illustrations, to show how a bill becomes a law.

Section 2

Taxing and Spending Bills

Reader's Guide

Key Terms

tax, closed rule, appropriation, authorization bill, entitlement

Find Out

- What authority does Congress have over how the national government will raise and spend money?
- What is the procedure whereby Congress provides money to the executive agencies and departments?

Understanding Concepts

Public Policy When Congress votes to begin a government program, what process is followed to fund that program?

COVER STORY

Wasteful Spending!

WASHINGTON, D.C., 1985

Senator William Proxmire awarded the National Institutes of Health his Golden Fleece Award for a grant it gave a Utah researcher to study hexes put on arm wrestlers. "It's $160,000 of the taxpayers' money down the drain," Proxmire maintains. The senator launched the Golden Fleece Award in 1975 to call public attention to wasteful government spending. The first went to the National Science Foundation for spending $84,000 to find out why people fall in love. Other notable past "winners" include the Department of Agriculture for a $46,000 study of the length of time it takes to cook breakfast.

Arm wrestlers

Today, running the national government costs more than $1.2 trillion a year. The Constitution gives Congress the authority to decide where this money will come from and in what ways it will be spent. Passing laws to raise and spend money for the national government is one of the most important jobs of Congress. The government could not operate successfully without money to carry out its many programs and services.

Making Decisions About Taxes

The national government gets most of the money it needs to keep the government functioning from taxes. **Taxes** are money that people and businesses pay to support the government. The Constitution states:

> "*The Congress shall have the power to lay and collect taxes, duties, imposts and excises, to pay the debts and provide for the common defense and general welfare of the United States. . . .*"
>
> —Article I, Section 8

The House's Power Over Revenue Bills

The Constitution gives the House of Representatives the exclusive power to start all revenue measures. Almost all important work on tax laws occurs in the House **Ways and Means Committee.** The Ways and Means Committee decides whether to go along with presidential requests for tax cuts or increases. It also makes the numerous rules and regulations that determine who will pay how much tax. Some of these rulings are very simple while others are more complex. This committee, for example, influences how much of a tax deduction parents are allowed on their income tax for each child living at home. It also decides what kind of tax benefit businesses can claim for building new factories.

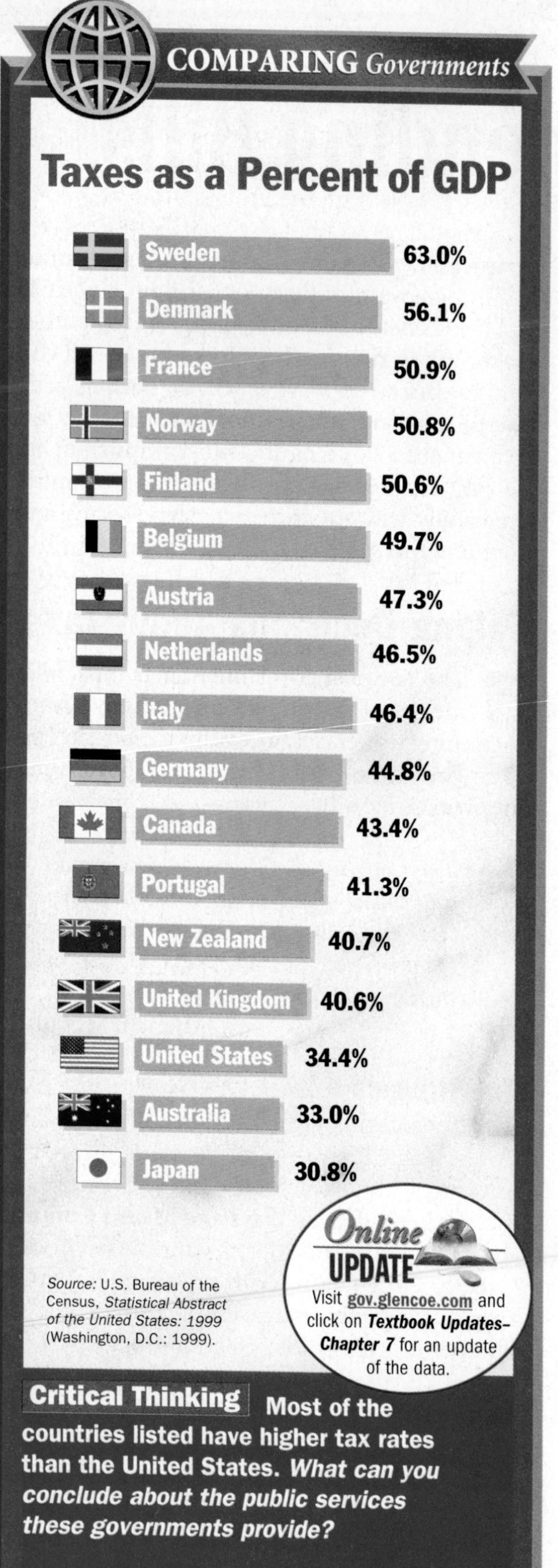

Source: U.S. Bureau of the Census, *Statistical Abstract of the United States: 1999* (Washington, D.C.: 1999).

Critical Thinking **Most of the countries listed have higher tax rates than the United States.** ***What can you conclude about the public services these governments provide?***

For many years the committee's tax bills were debated on the House floor under a closed rule. A **closed rule** forbids members to offer any amendments to a bill from the floor. This rule meant that only members of the Ways and Means Committee could have a direct hand in writing a tax bill.

Other House members accepted this closed-rule procedure on tax bills for several reasons. House leaders claimed that tax bills were too complicated to be easily understood outside the committee. Leaders also warned that representatives could come under great pressure from special interests if tax bills could be revised from the floor. Floor amendments, they argued, might upset the fair and balanced legislation recommended by the committee.

In the 1970s House members revolted against the Ways and Means Committee. In 1973 the House allowed members to amend a tax bill on the floor. In 1974 it forced Chairperson Wilbur Mills to resign following a personal scandal. Critics charged that tax bills soon became a collection of amendments written to please special interests.

In the Senate no closed rule exists, and tax bills often do become collections of amendments. Many tax bills are amended so often on the Senate floor they become "Christmas tree" bills similar to appropriations bills that include many riders.

The Senate's Role in Tax Legislation All tax bills start in the House. Article I, Section 7,[1] of the Constitution, however, says, "The Senate may propose . . . amendments. . . ." Because of this provision, the Senate often tries to change tax bills the House has passed. As a result, many people view the Senate as the place where interest groups can get House tax provisions they do not like changed or eliminated.

The Senate Committee on Finance has primary responsibility for dealing with tax matters. Like the House Ways and Means Committee, the Senate Finance Committee is powerful. Although the Senate Finance Committee has subcommittees, the full committee does most of the work on tax bills. As a result, the chairperson of the Finance Committee is an extremely important figure.

See the following footnoted materials in the **Reference Handbook:**
1. *The Constitution,* pages 774–799.

Appropriating Money

In addition to passing tax laws to raise money, Congress has another important power over government spending. The power of **appropriation,** or approval of government spending, is a congressional responsibility. In Article I, Section 9, the Constitution states, "No money shall be drawn from the Treasury, but in consequence of [except by] appropriations made by law."[1] Thus, Congress must pass laws to appropriate money for the federal government. Congress's approval is needed before departments and agencies of the executive branch such as the Department of Defense or the Federal Communications Commission can actually spend money.

How Congress Appropriates Money

Congress follows a two-step procedure in appropriating money—an authorization bill and an appropriations bill. Suppose the president signs a bill to build recreational facilities in the inner cities. This first step in the legislation is an authorization bill. An **authorization bill** sets up a federal program and specifies how much money may be appropriated for that program. For example, one provision of this law limits the amount of money that can be spent on the program to $30 million a year. The recreation bill also specifies that the Department of **Housing and Urban Development (HUD)** will administer the program. HUD, however, does not yet actually have any money to carry out the program.

The second step in the appropriations procedure comes when HUD requests that Congress provide the $30 million. This kind of bill is an **appropriations bill** and provides the money needed to carry out the many laws Congress has passed. HUD's request for the $30 million for the recreational facilities will be only one small item in the multibillion-dollar budget HUD will send to Congress for that year. HUD's budget, in turn, will be part of the president's total annual budget for the executive branch. Each year the president presents his budget to Congress. There the appropriations committees create their own appropriations bills. Congress might decide to

See the following footnoted materials in the **Reference Handbook:**
1. *The Constitution,* pages 774–799.

Managing the Nation's Purse

Congressional Funding An artist, commissioned by the Works Progress Administration, depicted California's multiethnic workforce. In the mid-1930s, President Franklin D. Roosevelt convinced Congress to appropriate funds to a relief program for the unemployed. WPA artists created hundreds of pieces documenting the times. ***Why must agency heads testify before Congress to receive funding?***

Former head of the National Endowment for the Arts, Jane Alexander, testifies before the Senate Labor Committee.

grant HUD only $15 million to carry out the building program. Next year, HUD would have to ask for another appropriation to continue the program.

The Appropriations Committees The House and Senate appropriations committees and their subcommittees handle appropriations bills. Both the House and Senate appropriations committees have 13 subcommittees that deal with the same policy areas in each house. Thus, the same appropriations subcommittees in the House of Representatives and the Senate would review the HUD budget, including its recreational facility program as presented.

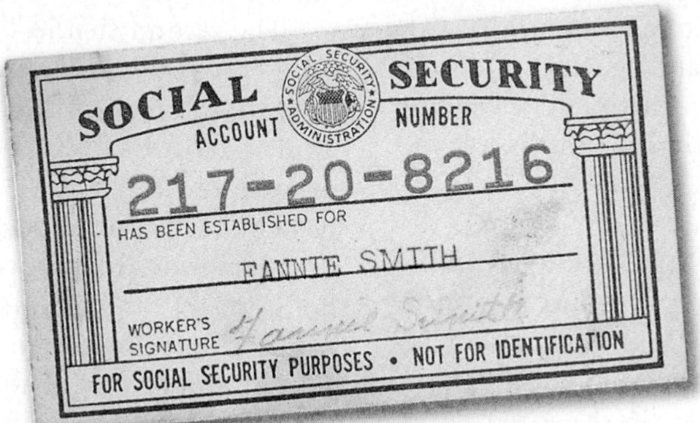

A Social Security card

Every year heads of departments and agencies and program directors testify before the House and Senate appropriations subcommittees about their budgets. During the budget hearings, these officials explain why they need the money they have requested. Each year agency officials must return to Congress to request the money they need to operate in the coming year. In this way lawmakers have a chance to become familiar with the federal agencies and their programs.

Appropriations subcommittees often develop close relationships with certain agencies and projects that they tend to favor in appropriating funds. In addition, powerful interest groups try hard to influence Congress and the appropriations subcommittees to give these agencies all the money they request.

Uncontrollable Expenditures The House and Senate appropriations committees, however, do not have a voice in all the current spending of the federal government. By previous legislation, some of which established many long-standing programs, about 70 percent of the money the federal government spends each year is already committed to certain uses and, therefore, not controlled by these committees. These expenditures are termed **uncontrollables** because the government is legally committed to spend this money. Such required spending includes Social Security payments, interest on the national debt, and federal contracts that already are in force. Some of these expenditures are known as **entitlements** because they are social programs that continue from one year to the next.

Section 2 Assessment

Checking for Understanding

1. **Main Idea** Using a graphic organizer like the one to the right, show the two-step procedure that Congress follows when appropriating money.

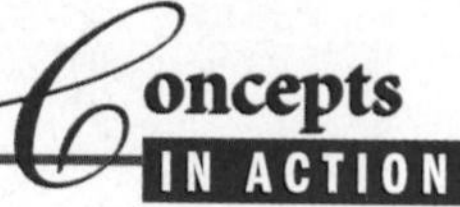

2. **Define** tax, closed rule, appropriation, authorization bill, entitlement.
3. **Identify** Ways and Means Committee, HUD.
4. What control does the House Ways and Means Committee exert over presidential requests for changes in tax laws?

Critical Thinking

5. **Synthesizing Information** Do you think Congress should have the power both to raise and to spend money? Support your answer.

Concepts IN ACTION

Public Policy Using the library or the Internet, research the major categories of revenue and expenditure in the current federal budget. Find out what amounts of money the government plans to raise and spend in each category. Create an illustrated report or series of graphs and charts.

Skills

Critical Thinking

Analyzing Information

To analyze information, you must determine its accuracy and reliability. Biased information may contain factual errors, be incomplete, or be distorted by propaganda techniques.

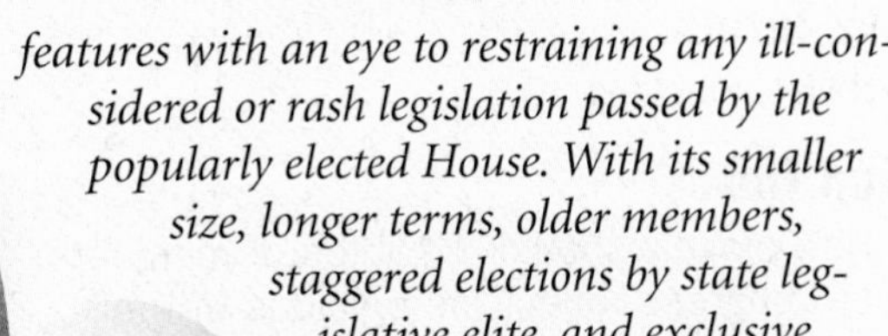

Thomas Jefferson

George Washington

Learning the Skill

To analyze the information you encounter, follow these five steps:

1. Determine the purpose and nature of the information.
2. Determine if the information is from a primary or secondary source.
3. Evaluate the reliability of the source.
4. Determine what evidence the author presents.
5. Compare the information with other sources to see if they support or contradict each other.

Practicing the Skill

Read the excerpt below. It defines the nature of the Senate. Then answer the questions that follow.

> "*In the classic anecdote about the origins of the Senate, Thomas Jefferson—in France during the Constitutional Convention—asked George Washington about the purpose of the new Senate. 'Why,' asked Washington, 'did you pour that coffee into your saucer?' 'To cool it,' Jefferson replied. 'Even so,' responded Washington, 'we pour legislation into the senatorial saucer to cool it.' That the Senate was intended to be the more deliberative and reasoning of the two chambers is well known. In designing the Senate, the Framers chose institutional features with an eye to restraining any ill-considered or rash legislation passed by the popularly elected House. With its smaller size, longer terms, older members, staggered elections by state legislative elite, and exclusive power to advise and consent on treaties and nominations, the Senate was expected to act 'with more coolness, with more system and with more wisdom, than the popular branch.'*"
>
> —from *Politics or Principle*, Sarah A. Binder and Steven S. Smith

1. What subject are the authors addressing?
2. Is it a primary or secondary source?
3. Do you think the source is reliable? Why?
4. What evidence do the authors offer to support their viewpoint?
5. What other places or sources would you check to verify the accuracy of this article?

Application Activity

Look through the letters to the editor in your local newspaper. Prepare a short report analyzing one of the letters. Summarize the context of the article, the writer's motivation, point of view, and possible bias.

The **Glencoe Skillbuilder Interactive Workbook, Level 2** provides instruction and practice in key social studies skills.

Section 3

Influencing Congress

Reader's Guide

Key Terms

lobbyist, lobbying

Find Out

- How closely should the votes of members of Congress reflect the opinions of their constituents?
- What factors must a member of Congress weigh when deciding whether to support the views of an interest group or of the president?

Understanding Concepts

Political Processes What specific groups and individuals influence the legislators' decisions?

COVER STORY

Senator Saves Johnson

WASHINGTON, D.C., MAY 1868

The refusal of Senator Edmund G. Ross to side with other Senate Republicans has saved President Andrew Johnson from being removed from office. Only one vote short of what they needed to convict Johnson of the impeachment charges brought against him, Republicans' pressure on the freshman senator from Kansas had been intense. By refusing to vote with 35 other Republicans, Ross has knowingly put his Senate career on the line. "I almost literally looked down into my open grave," he said of his vote. Political observers agree with the senator's assessment and do not expect him to be reelected to a second term.

Senator Edmund Ross

Like Senator Ross, members of Congress must constantly make difficult decisions. They decide which policies they will support and when to yield or not to yield to political pressures. They must also decide how to vote on controversial issues and when to make speeches explaining their views. In a single session, members may cast votes on a thousand issues. By their speeches and actions they influence the direction of government policies and help shape the public's views about a particular bill or about an issue that is before Congress. Who influences the lawmakers?

Influences on Lawmakers

A great many factors influence a lawmaker's decisions. One factor is the lawmaker's personality. Some members of Congress, for example, are by nature more willing to take risks when making a choice. Sometimes the very nature of the issue determines the factors that will influence lawmakers most. For example, concerning a controversial issue such as gun control, a lawmaker may pay close attention to the voters back home, no matter what his or her own beliefs may be. On issues that have little direct effect on their home states or districts, most lawmakers are likely to rely on their own beliefs or on the advice and opinions of other lawmakers.

Congressional staff members also influence lawmakers' decisions in Congress. They can do this in several ways. One way is by controlling the information on which lawmakers base their decisions. Another way is by setting the agendas for individual lawmakers and for congressional committees that may favor a certain point of view.

Thus, many factors affect a lawmaker's decision on any given issue. Most lawmakers agree that the most important influences on their decision making are the concerns of voters back home, their own political parties, the president, and special-interest groups.

The Influence of Voters

The political careers of all lawmakers depend upon how the voters back home feel about lawmakers' job performance. Only very unusual lawmakers would regularly vote against the wishes of the people in their home states or districts.

Influencing Policy Makers

"Whose conscience are we voting today?"

Influencing Government Lawmakers represent the citizens of their districts and their own political parties. At election time, these groups will hold lawmakers accountable for their votes. ***What does the cartoonist seem to be saying about who influences a legislator's vote?***

What Voters Expect Experienced lawmakers know that their constituents expect them to pay a great deal of attention to their state or district. Most people expect their representatives to put the needs of their district ahead of the needs of the nation. What if a conflict arises between what the lawmaker believes should be done and what the people in the district want? In a national opinion survey, most people said their lawmaker should "follow what people in the district want."

The voting behavior of most members of Congress reflects the results of this survey. On issues that affect their constituents' daily lives, such as civil rights and social welfare, lawmakers generally go along with the voters' preferences. In contrast, on issues where constituents have less information or interest, such as foreign affairs, lawmakers often make up their own minds.

Voters say they want their lawmakers to follow constituents' wishes on the issues and enact laws that reflect their needs and opinions. Most voters, however, do not take the trouble to find out how their senators and representatives cast their votes in Congress. Sometimes voters are not even aware of all the issues lawmakers must decide and vote on. Why, then, is the way lawmakers vote so important to their chance of reelection?

In an election campaign, the candidate from the other party and opposing interest groups will bring up the lawmaker's voting record. They may demand that the lawmaker explain votes that turned out to be unpopular back home. The opposite is also true. A legislator running for reelection may call attention to his or her votes on certain measures in order to attract constituents' support. As a result, voters who might otherwise not know how the lawmaker voted are told how well he or she "paid attention to the folks back home." The margin between a candidate's victory and defeat may be only a few thousand votes. Consequently, a small group of voters on either side—those who were unhappy with a lawmaker's voting record and those who strongly supported that record—could mean the difference between the candidate's victory and defeat. As a result, lawmakers try to find out what the voters back home are concerned about well before an election.

Learning What Voters Want Most lawmakers use several methods to try to keep track of their constituents' opinions. One method is to make frequent trips home to learn the local voters' concerns. Members of the House of Representatives make dozens of trips to their home districts each year. During these trips they will try to speak with as many voters as possible about the issues concerning them.

Voting Along Party Lines

Political Processes Political parties greatly influence legislators' voting decisions. ***How may congressional party leaders persuade lawmakers to support the party position?***

In addition, staff members usually screen the lawmaker's mail to learn what issues concern voters the most. Many lawmakers also send questionnaires to their constituents asking for their opinions on various issues. Near election time lawmakers often hire professional pollsters to conduct opinion surveys among the voters of their districts.

Finally, all lawmakers pay close attention to the ideas of their rain-or-shine supporters—those people who work in candidates' campaigns, contribute money, and help ensure their reelection. As one lawmaker put it, "Everybody needs some groups which are strongly for him." These supporters also help lawmakers keep in touch with what is going on back home.

The Influence of Parties

Almost every member of Congress is either a Republican or a Democrat. Both political parties generally take stands on major issues and come out for or against specific legislation. Political party identification is one of the most important influences on a lawmaker's voting behavior. In most cases knowing which political party members of Congress belong to will help predict how they will vote on major issues. Political party membership often will indicate how a lawmaker votes better than knowing almost anything else about him or her.

Party Voting On major bills most Democrats tend to vote together, as do most Republicans. In the House of Representatives, members vote with their party about two-thirds of the time. Senators, who are generally more independent than House members, are less likely to follow their party's position.

Party voting is much stronger on some issues than on others. On issues relating to government intervention in the economy, party members tend to vote the same way. Party voting is also strong on farm issues and fairly strong on social-welfare issues. Party voting is much weaker on foreign policy issues because the two parties often do not have very fixed positions on international questions. On certain other issues, such as dams and water projects, party position is often less influential than local or regional voter preferences in determining how a legislator votes.

The Importance of Parties One reason Republicans or Democrats vote with their parties is that members of each party are likely to share the same general beliefs about public policy. As a group, Democratic lawmakers are more likely than Republicans to favor social-welfare programs, job programs through public works, tax laws that help people with lower incomes, and government regulation of business. Taken as a group, Republican members of Congress are likely to support less spending for government programs, local and state solutions to problems rather than solutions by the national government, and policies that favor business and higher-income groups.

Another reason for party voting is that most lawmakers simply do not have strong opinions about every issue on which they vote. They do not know enough about every issue to make informed decisions based on all the important details of all the bills on which they must vote. Consequently, they often seek advice on how to vote from other lawmakers who know more about the issue. According to one senator:

> *When it comes to voting, an individual will rely heavily not only on the judgment of staff members, but also on a select number of senators whose knowledge he has come to respect and whose general perspectives [views] he shares.*
>
> —Senator Wendell Ford

On some issues party leaders pressure members to vote for the party's position. Often, party leaders support the president's program if the president is a member of the same party. On the other hand, leaders of the opposing party may vote against the president's program and seek to turn such opposition into a political issue. Congressional party leaders such as the Senate majority leader or the Speaker of the House usually use the power of persuasion. These leaders do not expect to get their way all the time. But they do work hard to influence lawmakers to support the party's position on key issues. Gaining the support of party members is one of the main jobs of a party leader. Very few issues are unaffected by political party affiliation.

Other Influences on Congress

Although voter preferences and political parties strongly influence the decisions of lawmakers, two other influences are often equally strong: the president and interest groups.

The Influence of the President All presidents try to influence Congress to pass the laws that the president and his party support. Some presidents work harder than others at gaining support in Congress, and some are more successful in getting Congress to pass their programs.

Members of Congress have often complained that presidents have more ways to influence legislation and policy than do lawmakers. Presidents can appear on television to try to influence public opinion and put pressure on Congress. In late 1990 and early 1991, for example, President Bush deployed United States troops to Saudi Arabia. Twenty-four weeks of military buildup followed, in which the United States government attempted to force Iraq out of Kuwait. Congress let the president take the lead in responding to Iraq. President Bush took every opportunity to express his views in the press and on television. With growing public support for military action behind the president, Congress voted to approve military action in the Persian Gulf. Presidential influence, in this instance of policy making, had tremendous influence.

Presidents may also use their powers to influence individual members of Congress. They can give or withhold support of lawmakers. In the mid-1960s, for example, Senator Frank Church of Idaho criticized President Lyndon Johnson's conduct of the

We the People

Making a Difference

Arlys Endres

Susan B. Anthony

While she may not be employed as a lobbyist or a member of a political action committee, Arlys Endres of Phoenix, Arizona, has already made her mark in the hallowed halls of Congress. In 1996, when she was 10 years old, Arlys wrote a school report on suffragist Susan B. Anthony. She was later dismayed to discover that a statue honoring Anthony and two other suffragists, Elizabeth Cady Stanton and Lucretia Mott, had been removed from the Capitol Rotunda, and was being stored in the Capitol Crypt. The statue had been given to Congress in 1921. Historical records indicated that it was on display for only a short time before it was whisked away to the Capitol basement.

Arlys wanted to convince Congress to display the statue. She discovered a national effort led by female members of Congress to raise money to reinstall the statue. Arlys mailed at least 2,000 letters to round up supporters and donations. She also went on a door-to-door fund-raising campaign.

In all, Arlys helped raise almost $2,000. Her efforts also took her to Washington, D.C., to see the statue and speak at a "Raise the Statue" rally. Her campaign did not go unnoticed by national legislators. The United States Congress unanimously voted to reinstall the statue in the Capitol Rotunda and promised to leave it on display for at least a year.

Vietnam War. To support his viewpoint, Church showed President Johnson a newspaper column written by journalist Walter Lippmann criticizing the war. "All right," Johnson said, "the next time you need a dam for Idaho, you go ask Walter Lippmann."

Since the early 1900s, many presidents have tried to increase their influence over Congress and the lawmaking process, and they have succeeded. In more recent years Congress has taken steps to limit the president's influence, letting Congress remain a more autonomous legislative body.

The Influence of Interest Groups The representatives of interest groups, called **lobbyists**, are another important influence on Congress. Lobbyists try to convince members of Congress to support policies favored by the groups they represent. Their efforts to persuade officials to support their point of view is called **lobbying**. The largest and most powerful lobbies have their own buildings and full-time professional staffs in the nation's capital.

Lobbyists represent a wide variety of interests such as business organizations, labor unions, doctors, lawyers, education groups, minority groups, and environmental organizations. In addition, lobbyists work for groups that sometimes form to support or to oppose a specific issue.

Lobbyists use various methods to influence members of Congress. They provide lawmakers with information about policies they support or oppose. They visit lawmakers in their offices or in the lobbies of the Capitol and try to persuade them to support their position. They encourage citizens to write to members of Congress on the issues they favor or oppose.

Interest groups and their lobbyists also focus their attention on congressional committees. For example, farm groups concentrate their attention on influencing the committees responsible for laws on agriculture. Labor unions focus their effort on committees dealing with labor legislation and the economy.

Political Action Committees Some observers believe that the importance of individual lobbyists has declined in recent years as political action committees, known as **PACs,** have dramatically increased in number and influence with lawmakers. PACs are political fund-raising organizations established by corporations, labor unions, and other special-interest groups. PAC funds come from voluntary contributions by employees, stockholders, and union members. A PAC uses its funds to support lawmakers who favor the PAC's positions on issues.

GOVERNMENT *Online*

Student Web Activity Visit the *United States Government: Democracy in Action* Web site at gov.glencoe.com and click on ***Chapter 7–Student Web Activities*** for an activity about influencing Congress.

Section 3 Assessment

Checking for Understanding

1. **Main Idea** Using a graphic organizer like the one to the right, identify four ways lawmakers can keep in touch with voters' opinions.

2. **Define** lobbyist, lobbying.
3. **Identify** PAC.
4. On which type of issues do lawmakers tend to pay less attention to voter opinion?
5. What influence does the president have on Congress?

Critical Thinking

6. **Making Inferences** Why do some people think that PACs now have more influence over members of Congress and the process of congressional legislation than do individual lobbyists?

Concepts IN ACTION

Political Processes Contact a special-interest group to request literature on the group's purpose and activities. Summarize how the group attempts to influence legislators. Post the literature and summary on a bulletin-board display.

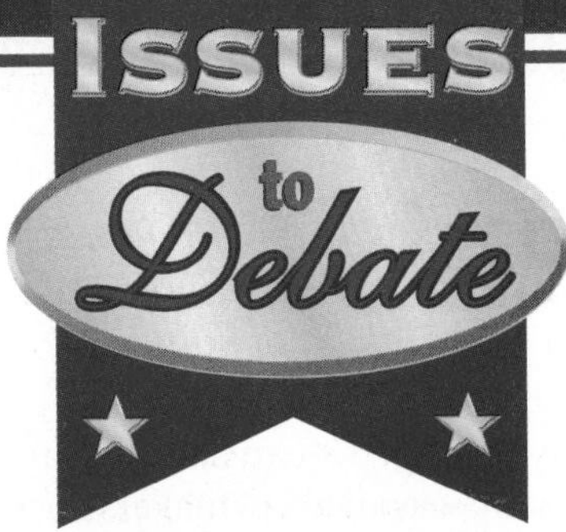

Space Station: What Should Congress Do?

In 1984 the National Aeronautics and Space Administration proposed to build a space station as a long-term project that would provide valuable knowledge and be a way station for trips to other planets or the moon. The project provided additional justification for another major project, the space shuttle.

Cost-Conscious Government

This original vision, as proposed in 1984, was soon questioned because the government had become more cost conscious. By late 1996 President Clinton confirmed that the manned mission to Mars project was dead. Instead, the National Aeronautics and Space Administration began preparing a vast armada of robots to send to the red planet. In 1997, the first robot landed on Mars and sent back dramatic images and extensive data. It collected most of the data that human explorers could collect, at a fraction of the cost. A human mission would have cost $500 billion. NASA builds each of its automated probes for far less money. Some scientists argue that the original plans for a manned space station also should be abandoned because they are no longer relevant.

Humans in Space

Arguments supporting the development of a manned station include the notion that the space station is an inspiring international project that will allow the world's most talented space scientists to keep active until human exploration of space is feasible. Some experts say that it will keep former Soviet scientists away from dangerous employers. The lucrative construction contracts from the United States and other countries further support pursuing a manned station. Scientists also plan to use the station for biological experiments. United States leadership in this area would be questioned if America backed out.

Debating the Issue

Would You Vote For or Against the Funding Bill?

Assume you are a member of Congress who will vote on funding for a manned space station. Your home district has research companies that might benefit from government contracts if the station were built. However, you were elected on a pledge to reduce unnecessary government spending. The proposed budget is for $94 billion over a 15-year period.

Key Issues

✔ What are the benefits and costs of a manned space station?

✔ Could the same benefits be gained at less cost by another method?

✔ How will your decision affect your constituents? Your nation?

Debate Discuss the issue in class. Allow time for two people on either side of the issue to prepare short speeches to present to the class.

Vote Make your decision for or against the funding bill. Then have the class vote and record the results. Discuss the outcome of the vote.

Section 4

Helping Constituents

Reader's Guide

Key Terms

casework, pork-barrel legislation, logrolling

Find Out

- Why do legislators spend much of their time helping their constituents?
- How do the organization and methods of Congress contribute to pork-barrel legislation?

Understanding Concepts

Federalism How does the need to weigh the interests of their constituents affect national policy decisions by members of Congress?

COVER STORY

Chasing Federal Money

WASHINGTON, D.C., MARCH 1997

Displaying a photo of a fiery auto crash on Interstate 35 in downtown Austin, Texas, Representative Lloyd Doggett called for federal help in building a bypass around the city. Doggett wants the House to change the way it distributes federal gasoline taxes among the states. Currently Texas receives just 77 cents of each dollar it contributes in gasoline taxes. Under the Texan's plan, that would increase to 95 cents. The idea angers legislators from northeastern states, which currently receive more of the tax money. New York representative Susan Molinari thinks Texas gets its share of federal money in other areas. "The extra six billion defense dollars that go to Texas, kiss it good-by," she said.

Texas state seal

Representative Doggett's experience mirrors what many seasoned lawmakers have learned—they are expected to do more in Washington, D.C., for their constituents than debate great issues. To be reelected, lawmakers must spend much of their time on two other important tasks. First, they must act as problem solvers for voters who have difficulties with departments or agencies of the federal government. Second, they must make sure that their district or state gets its share of federal money, projects such as new post offices, highways, and contracts.

These two duties are not new to members of Congress, but in recent years these duties have become increasingly important. As the national government has grown, they have become a time-consuming part of the lawmaker's job.

Handling Problems

All lawmakers today are involved with casework. Helping constituents with problems is called **casework.** One House member put it this way, "Rightly or wrongly, we have become the link between the frustrated citizen and the very involved federal government in citizens' lives. . . . We continually use more and more of our staff time to handle citizens' complaints."

Many Different Requests Lawmakers respond to thousands of requests from voters for help in dealing with executive agencies. Typical requests include: (1) A soldier would like the Army to move him to a base close to home because his parents are ill. (2) A local businessperson claims the Federal Trade Commission (FTC) is treating her business unfairly. She would like to meet with top FTC officials. (3) A veteran has had his GI life insurance policy cancelled by a government agency. The agency says the veteran failed to fill out and return a certain form. The veteran says he never got the form, but he wants the life insurance. (4) A new high school graduate would like help finding a government job in Washington.

Many lawmakers complain that although voters say they want less government they demand more services from their members of Congress. Sometimes voters make unreasonable requests or ask for help that a lawmaker is unwilling to deliver. A representative from New York, for example, was asked to fix a speeding ticket. Another member received a call asking what the lawmaker was going to do about the shortage of snow shovels at a local hardware store during a blizzard.

Who Handles Casework All lawmakers have staff members called **caseworkers** to handle the problems of their constituents. In most instances the caseworkers are able to handle the requests for help themselves. Sometimes the problem can be solved with a simple question from a caseworker to the agency involved. At other times, however, the senator or representative may have to get directly involved. One representative explained, "When nothing else is working and the staff feels they've had it with the bureaucracy, then I step in."

Purposes of Casework Why do lawmakers spend so much of their time on casework? Lawmakers are involved in casework because it serves three important purposes. First, casework helps lawmakers get reelected. Lawmakers know that helping voters with problems is part of what they can do for the people in their states or districts. "I learned soon after coming to Washington," a Missouri lawmaker once said, "that it was just as important to get a certain document for somebody back home as for some European diplomat—really, more important, because that little guy back home votes."

As a result, many lawmakers actually look for casework. One lawmaker, for example, regularly sent invitations to almost 7,000 voters in his district asking them to bring their problems to a town meeting his staff runs. Today lawmakers may encourage voters to communicate with them by electronic mail. Many representatives have vans that drive through their districts as mobile offices to keep watch on problems back home.

Second, casework is one way in which Congress oversees the executive branch. Casework brings problems with federal programs to the attention of members of Congress. It provides opportunities for lawmakers and their staffs to get a closer look at how well the executive branch is handling such federal programs as Social Security, veterans' benefits, or workers' compensation.

Third, casework provides a way for the average citizen to cope with the huge national government. In the years before the national government grew so large, most citizens with a problem turned to their local politicians—called ward heelers—for help. One member of Congress explained that:

> "*In the old days, you had the ward heeler who cemented himself in the community by taking care of everyone. Now the Congressman plays the role of ward heeler—wending his way through bureaucracy, helping to cut through red tape and confusion.*"
>
> —Sam Rayburn

Helping the District or State

Besides providing services for their constituents, members of Congress also try to bring federal government projects and money to their districts and states. Lawmakers do this in three ways: (1) through pork-barrel legislation; (2) through winning federal grants and contracts; and (3) through keeping federal projects.

Public Works Legislation Every year, through **public works bills,** Congress appropriates billions of dollars for a variety of local projects. These projects may include such things as post offices, dams, military bases, harbor and river improvements, federally funded highways, veterans' hospitals, pollution-treatment centers, and mass-transit system projects.

Such government projects can bring jobs and money into a state or district. For example, Senator Robert Byrd's pet project, the Appalachian Regional Commission, oversaw more than a billion dollars worth of government spending in its first three years. Beginning in 1989, Byrd used his position as chair of the Appropriations Committee to transplant federal agencies into his home state of West Virginia. For example, agencies or divisions of the FBI, CIA, Internal Revenue Service, and even the Coast Guard were moved from Washington to Byrd's state.

Protecting Their Districts

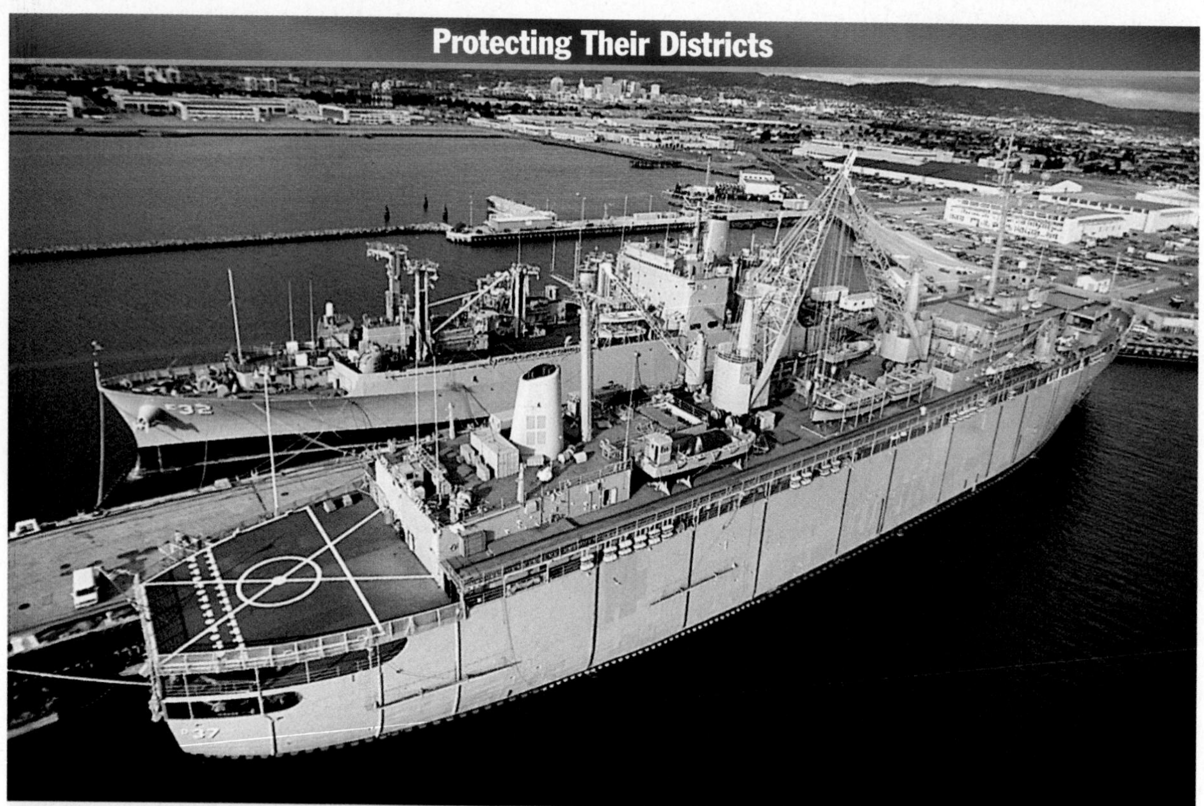

Constituent Services Although Representative Ronald Dellums, who chaired the House Armed Services Commission, maintained that defense funds could be better used to help the disadvantaged, when defense cuts hit close to home, he fought them. In 1993 Dellums challenged the closing of the Alameda Naval Air Station in his California district. ***Why would Dellums oppose the closing of the Alameda Naval Air Station despite his criticism of military spending?***

When Congress passes laws to appropriate money for such local federal projects, it is often called **pork-barrel legislation.** The idea is that a member of Congress has dipped into the "pork barrel" (the federal treasury) and pulled out a piece of "fat" (a federal project for his or her district). Sometimes such legislation draws criticism. Referring to Robert Byrd's project, a Maryland congresswoman claimed she was "afraid to go to sleep at night for fear of waking up and finding another agency has been moved to West Virginia."

More often, lawmakers take the "You scratch my back and I'll scratch yours" approach to public works legislation. Believing that getting federal projects for the home state is a key part of their job, they usually help each other. Such agreements by two or more lawmakers to support each other's bills is called **logrolling.**

Winning Grants and Contracts Lawmakers also try to make sure their districts or states get their fair share of the available federal grants and contracts which are funded through the national budget. A senator from Colorado put it this way, "If a program is to be established, the state of Colorado should get its fair share."

Federal grants and contracts are very important to lawmakers and their districts or states. These contracts are a vital source of money and jobs and can radically affect the economy of a state. Every year federal agencies such as the Department of Defense spend billions of dollars to carry out hundreds of government projects and programs. For example, when the Air Force decided to locate a new project at one of its bases in Utah, almost 1,000 jobs and millions of dollars came into the state. Lawmakers often compete for such valuable federal grants or contracts. For example, several other states wanted the Air Force project, but Utah's lawmakers won the prize for their state.

Behind the Scenes Lawmakers do not have the direct control over grants and contracts that they do over pork-barrel legislation. Instead, agencies of the executive branch such as the Department of Defense or the Department of Labor award federal grants and contracts. Lawmakers, however, may try to influence agency decisions in several ways. They may pressure agency officials to give a favorable hearing to their state's requests. Lawmakers may also encourage their constituents to write, telephone, or E-mail agency officials in order to make their requests or needs known. If problems come up when someone from the state is arranging a grant or contract, congressional members may step in to help.

Many lawmakers assign one or more of their staff members to act as specialists in contracts and grants. These staff members become experts on how individuals, businesses, and local governments can qualify for federal money. They will help constituents apply for contracts and grants. The lawmakers' job is to make sure federal grants and contracts keep coming into their state or district.

Congressional Politics This 1963 cartoon illustrates the pressures for a lawmaker to "bring home the bacon" to his or her congressional district. ***What kinds of projects receive "pork" handouts from Congress?***

Section 4 Assessment

Checking for Understanding

1. **Main Idea** Using a graphic organizer like the one below, explain how allocation of grants and contracts is different from pork-barrel legislation.

grants/contracts	
pork	

2. **Define** casework, pork-barrel legislation, logrolling.
3. **Identify** caseworker, public works bill.
4. Why do lawmakers get involved in casework?
5. List three ways lawmakers bring federal projects to their states.
6. Which branch of government awards federal grants and contracts?

Critical Thinking

7. **Drawing Conclusions** Why do you think the size of the lawmakers' staff has increased in recent years?

Federalism Look through several editions of your local paper to find examples of federal money spent in your state or community. Present your findings in the form of a radio news broadcast. Your broadcast should explain how the pork-barrel legislation benefited your state or local community.

DEMOCRACY WORKSHOP IN ACTION

From a Bill to a Law

In Chapter 7 you learned that thousands of bills are introduced in Congress each year, yet only a handful become law. In this activity, you will take a bill through the process to create your own law. The activity will help you to understand the lawmaking process in both houses of Congress and demonstrate the role that compromise plays in getting a bill passed. You may want to reread pages 181–188 before you begin.

Setting Up the Workshop

1. For this activity you will need pencils, paper, a receptacle for drawing names, and access to a copy machine. If available, you can also use blank transparencies and an overhead projector.
2. Use the lottery method to divide the class into the following three groups:
   Group 1 Witnesses to testify at hearings (six members)
   Group 2 One-half the remainder of the class to be representatives and one-half to be senators
   Group 3 Three students from the Senate group and three students from the House group to act as official recorders to keep track of the wording of bills and alterations to the bills throughout the lawmaking process

STEP 1

Introducing a Bill

Work as a class to develop a list of three proposals for change or improvements in your classroom environment. These proposals might deal with the arrangement of seating, the use of the bulletin board, orderliness of materials on shelves, room decorations, and so on.

Have the recorders from the House and the Senate write down each suggestion in the form of a bill for that house. Number the bills appropriately as explained in the text on page 184.

STEP 2

Moving to Committee

Groups 2 and 3 Senators and representatives should adjourn to separate areas of the classroom. Each house should choose its leader—Speaker of the House, and president pro tem of the Senate. The recorders should then read the text of their three bills out loud. If a copy machine is available, provide a copy of each bill to each member and to the witnesses who were chosen at the beginning of the activity.

The leader of each house should appoint each member to one of three committees. The leader will give each committee one bill for which it will be responsible. Each committee should choose a recorder to keep track of the progress and changes made to the bill. Members of each committee should also select a chairperson for their committee. The chairperson will be responsible for organizing the agenda for the committee meeting, assigning tasks, presiding over the meeting, and conducting votes.

Each committee's task will be to:

1. hold a hearing to hear witnesses in favor of and opposed to the bill
2. make changes to the bill to make it more acceptable
3. prepare a written report on the bill and move it to the floor for a final vote or, if committee members decide that their bill should not be moved to the floor, pigeonhole the bill by a majority vote

A bill must be dropped int‹ the House hopper to be considered for legislative action.

Actor-director Christopher Reeve testified before a Senate Labor subcommittee to increase funding for neurological and communication disorders research.

STEP 3 ★ ★ ★ ★

Calling Witnesses

Groups 1, 2, and 3

The chairperson for each committee should call for a hearing and invite one witness to present his or her opinion on the bill. Committee members should be prepared to ask witnesses questions about their knowledge of the subject and reasons for supporting or opposing the bill.

DEMOCRACY WORKSHOP IN ACTION

Step 3

IB

Union Calendar No. 136

105TH CONGRESS
1ST SESSION

H. R. 2378

[Report No. 105–240]

Making appropriations for the Treasury Department, the United States Postal Service, the Executive Office of the President, and certain Independent Agencies, for the fiscal year ending September 30, 1998, and for other purposes.

IN THE HOUSE OF REPRESENTATIVES

AUGUST 5, 1997

Mr. KOLBE, from the Committee on Appropriations, reported the following bill; which was committed to the Committee of the Whole House on the State of the Union and ordered to be printed

A BILL

Making appropriations for the Treasury Department, the United States Postal Service, the Executive Office of the President, and certain Independent Agencies, for the fiscal year ending September 30, 1998, and for other purposes.

Be it enacted by the Senate and House of Representatives of the United States of America in Congress assembled, That the following sums are appropriated, out of any money in the Treasury not otherwise appropriated, for the

A House bill

Group 1 Before the hearing, the witnesses should meet to divide up the bills being introduced. Each witness should be prepared to support or oppose passage of one bill at the committee hearing.

Committee Action

Groups 1, 2, and 3 After the hearing, the committee should meet in a markup session to go through the bill line by line and decide what changes should be made. Committee members should be prepared to present their suggestions for change in a convincing manner. Votes should be taken on all of the changes.

When all changes have been made, the committee should vote to either kill the bill or report it to Congress. To report the bill, the committee must make a written copy of the final revised bill to send to the House or Senate and prepare a report that includes the following:

1. a description of the bill
2. an explanation of the committee's actions
3. major changes made in committee
4. opinions on the bill

Floor Action

Groups 1, 2, and 3 Once the committees have prepared their reports, the bills are ready for floor action. The members of all three committees should now reconvene as the Senate or House to hold debate on each bill. The leader of each house should preside over the debate, allowing one person at a time to speak. Changes (amendments) can still be made to the bills if a majority of members vote to do so.

Taking a Vote

After the debate on each bill, it is time for the final vote. Each house should take a vote of its members to determine if the bill will pass or be defeated in its amended form. A roll call of each person's vote should be recorded.

Conference Committee

If a different version of a bill passes in both the House and Senate, leaders of Congress should organize a conference committee with three members from each house. This committee should iron out the differences between the House and the Senate versions of the bill and present a compromise to be voted on in both houses.

Presenting the Bill

Each bill that passes through both houses should be forwarded to the president (teacher) for action in written form. If the president vetoes a bill, the House and Senate may vote again to override the veto, or let the veto stand.

Choose a spokesperson to read the bills that have survived. On an overhead projector, display the original form of each bill in each house, along with the final versions. You may want to hold a class discussion on the following questions.

Questions for Discussion

1. What improvements were made by the changes in each bill?
2. If any of the bills were killed in committee, why did this happen?
3. What disagreements in your committee were resolved by compromise?
4. How much effect did the testimony of witnesses have on the final bill?
5. At what point in the lawmaking process is a bill most likely to be changed the most?
6. Could this system be made more efficient? How?

Chapter 7

Assessment and Activities

Self-Check Quiz Visit the *United States Government: Democracy in Action* Web site at gov.glencoe.com and click on ***Chapter 7–Self-Check Quizzes*** to prepare for the chapter test.

Reviewing Key Terms

Fill in the blank with the letter of the correct term or concept listed below.

- **a.** tax
- **b.** rider
- **c.** hearing
- **d.** pocket veto
- **e.** lobbyist
- **f.** closed rule
- **g.** authorization bills
- **h.** entitlements
- **i.** casework
- **j.** pork-barrel legislation

1. A _____ is money that citizens and businesses pay to support the government.

2. _____ is a congressional task that involves helping constituents with problems.

3. A _____ is an often controversial provision tacked on to a bill pertaining to a different subject.

4. Interest on the national debt and Social Security payments are examples of _____.

5. A person who represents a special-interest group to Congress and other government officials is known as a _____.

6. Witnesses usually offer testimony in a committee _____ regarding a specific bill.

7. Under a _____, House members were forbidden to offer amendments to tax bills from the floor.

8. _____ is when Congress passes laws to appropriate money for local federal projects.

9. The president gives a _____ by not signing a bill during the last 10 days Congress is in session.

10. _____ set up federal programs and specify how much money may be appropriated for those programs.

Current Events JOURNAL

Special Interests Look for newspaper or newsmagazine articles about rallies, demonstrations, boycotts, or activities sponsored by special-interest groups. Write a summary of the article and express your opinion about the activity.

Recalling Facts

1. Describe the two types of bills that may be introduced and three types of resolutions that may be passed in Congress.
2. What are four actions a president may take on a bill?
3. What role does the House Ways and Means Committee play in tax legislation?
4. What means do lawmakers use to bring federal projects or money to their states or districts?
5. What factors influence lawmakers when they consider legislation?
6. When are members of Congress most likely to vote with their political party?
7. How do lobbyists influence lawmakers?
8. What key tool do lawmakers use to secure the passage of public works legislation?

Understanding Concepts

1. **Public Policy** What procedure is Congress supposed to use to fund its programs and control its expenses?
2. **Political Processes** Do you think lawmakers' activities would be different if there were no special-interest groups? Explain your answer.
3. **Federalism** In your opinion, what is the most important purpose of casework for constituents in a representative's home state?

Chapter 7

Critical Thinking

1. **Making Inferences** Use the graphic organizer below to show three characteristics that help a bill make its way through the lawmaking process.

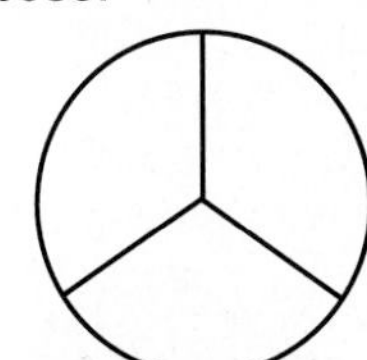

2. **Drawing Conclusions** Why is Congress reluctant to appropriate the full amount of money an agency requests?
3. **Synthesizing Information** Which legislative task is more important—casework or winning federal projects? Support your opinion.

Interpreting Political Cartoons Activity

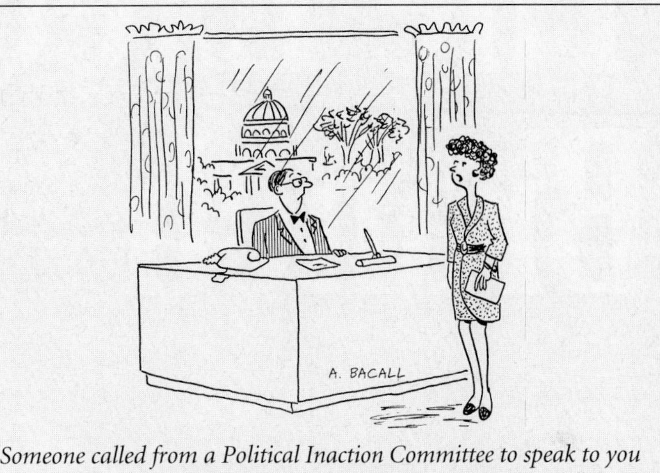

"Someone called from a Political Inaction Committee to speak to you on behalf of apathetic voters. He said he might call back."

1. What is the "Political Inaction Committee" referred to in the cartoon?
2. How is the "Political Inaction Committee" different from other interest groups?
3. Why is this situation unrealistic?

Cooperative Learning Activity

Passing a Bill Organize the class into three groups. Two will be special-interest groups on opposite sides of an issue. The third group will be lawmakers. Each special-interest group should try to persuade the lawmakers to pass a bill favoring its point of view. The lawmakers must then write the bill.

Skill Practice Activity

Analyzing Information Reread the quote from Senator Wendell Ford on page 196 and anwer the questions that follow.

1. What subject is Ford addressing?
2. Is it a primary source?
3. Does Ford offer any evidence that supports his position?
4. Do you think the information is reliable?
5. What evidence would you use to support Ford's position?

Technology Activity

Using the Internet C-Span is a public service that broadcasts daily sessions of the House and Senate. Use the Internet to locate C-Span's World Wide Web home page for a television schedule. Watch one of these congressional proceedings. Summarize what you see for the class.

Participating in Local Government

Obtain a copy of a bill considered in your state from your state representative or senator. Decide what changes you would suggest in the bill. Forward these suggestions to your representative or senator and ask for a response.

UNIT 3

The Executive Branch

Participating IN GOVERNMENT

E-Mailing an Agency

The president is responsible for administration of hundreds of government agencies that affect people's lives in a direct way. From this unit select a federal agency. Find out what its main services are. Then survey people in your community to determine how well the agency serves people. Send the results of your survey to the federal agency via E-mail.

The Lincoln Memorial

Electronic Field Trip

The White House

Take a virtual tour of the Supreme Court Building in Washington, D.C., and see how the judicial branch works.

Glencoe's Democracy in Action Video Program

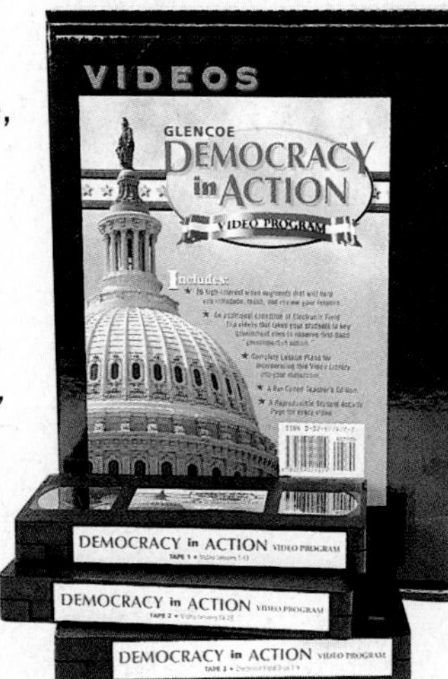

The White House is the site of the president's office, the residence of the First Family, the place where many official social gatherings are held, and a symbol of the presidency. The **Democracy in Action** video program "The White House," referenced below, provides an inside view of the White House and the architectural changes made throughout its history.

Also available in videodisc format.

View the videodisc by scanning the barcode or by entering the chapter number on your keypad and pressing Search.

Disc 2, Side 1, Chapter 3

Hands-On Activity

Use library or Internet resources to find information about the homes of past presidents. Use multimedia tools or software to create a multimedia presentation about historical residences. Incorporate images you find on the Internet. Include information about architectural styles, dates of construction or renovation, unique features, and present condition and use.

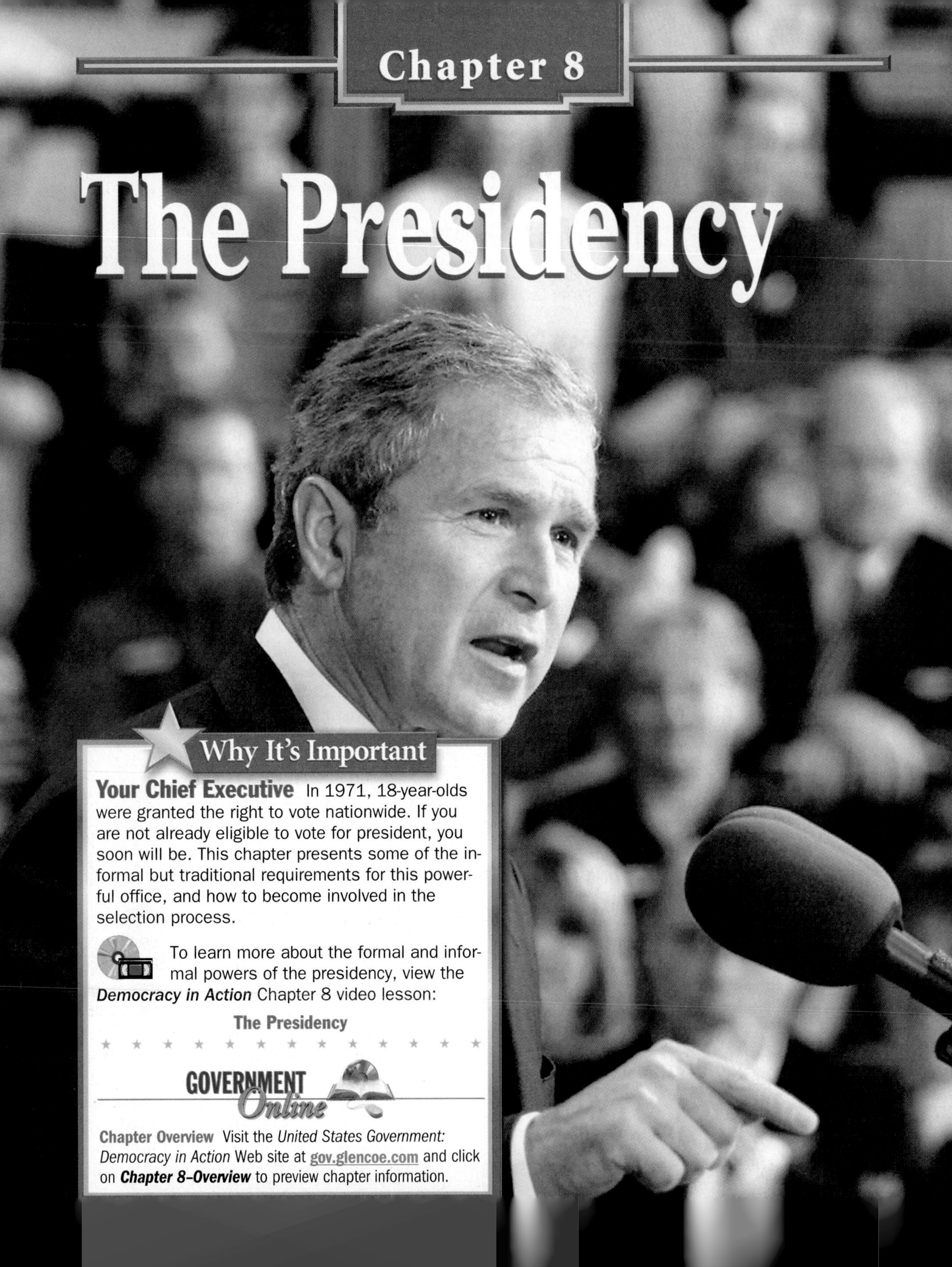

Chapter 8

The Presidency

Why It's Important

Your Chief Executive In 1971, 18-year-olds were granted the right to vote nationwide. If you are not already eligible to vote for president, you soon will be. This chapter presents some of the informal but traditional requirements for this powerful office, and how to become involved in the selection process.

To learn more about the formal and informal powers of the presidency, view the ***Democracy in Action*** Chapter 8 video lesson:

The Presidency

GOVERNMENT Online

Chapter Overview Visit the *United States Government: Democracy in Action* Web site at gov.glencoe.com and click on ***Chapter 8–Overview*** to preview chapter information.

Section 1

President and Vice President

Reader's Guide

Key Terms

compensation, presidential succession

Find Out

- What qualifications for the office of president do you think are most necessary for carrying out the duties of the office?
- What are the constitutional provisions for filling the executive office if the president is unable to perform those duties?

Understanding Concepts

Growth of Democracy Why are personal qualities of candidates for president more demanding than the constitutional qualifications?

COVER STORY

Bush Fills In

WASHINGTON, D.C., MARCH 30, 1981

Vice President George Bush rushed back to Washington from Texas this evening after the shooting of President Ronald Reagan. Bush may be required to assume the responsibilities of the presidency, under the terms of the Twenty-fifth Amendment, if Reagan's wounds prevent him from performing the duties of office. Bush will fill in for the president at tomorrow's functions, including a meeting with leaders of Congress and lunch with the prime minister of the Netherlands. However, no steps have been taken to officially designate him acting president. Reagan is reported to be alert and should be able to make decisions tomorrow.

Vice President Bush

◀ **President George W. Bush**

A vice president, stepping into a president's role, faces a daunting assignment. President Truman, assuming the office when Franklin Roosevelt died, told the press:

> "*I don't know whether you fellows ever had a load of hay fall on you, but when they told me yesterday what happened, I felt like the moon, the stars and all the planets had fallen on me.*"
>
> —Harry S Truman, 1945

The office of the president has been developing for more than 200 years. Just as the nation has grown during that time, the powers of the executive branch have also grown.

Duties of the President

The constitutional duties of the nation's first president, George Washington, and those of a modern president are much the same. However, presidents today have enormous power and responsibility. For example, the Constitution makes the president the commander in chief of the nation's armed forces. In Washington's administration this meant calling out a militia of 15,000 volunteers and getting on a horse and leading the troops to crush a rebellion of whiskey distillers. Today the president oversees a military divided into four major units, makes decisions of how to deploy troops stationed throughout the world, and manages a defense budget of over $270 billion.

In addition to commanding the military, the constitution gives the president responsibility to appoint—with Senate consent—heads of executive departments, federal court judges, and other top officials. In conducting foreign policy, the president makes treaties with the advice and consent of the Senate, meets with heads of state, hosts foreign officials, and appoints ambassadors to represent the United States in other countries.

A Traveling President

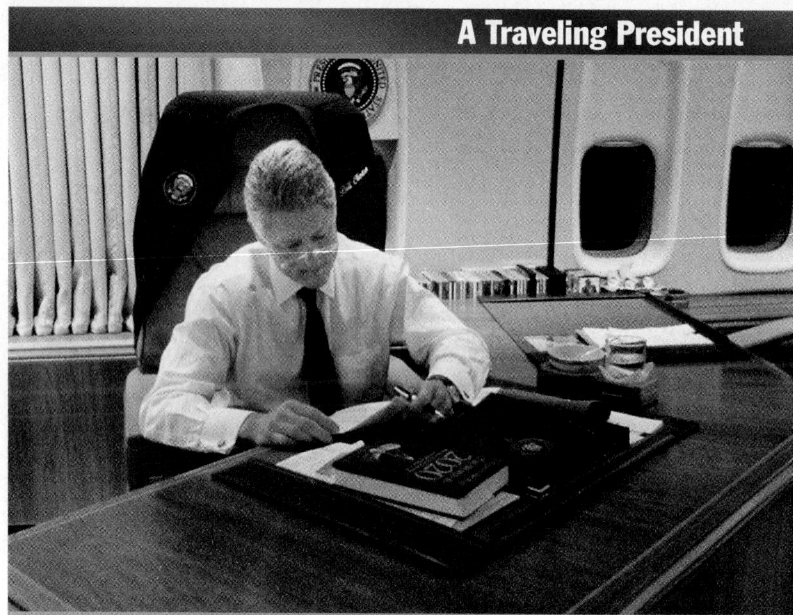

Executive Benefits The president usually flies long distances in *Air Force One.* At other times, the Chief Executive travels in an official car, a private airplane, or a U.S. Navy ship. ***Why does the Secret Service discourage the president's use of public transportation?***

The most important duty of the president may be to ensure that all the laws of the United States are "faithfully executed." A vast bureaucracy assists the president in this task. A president may pardon people convicted of federal crimes, except in cases of impeachment, or reduce a person's jail sentence or fine.

The president has lawmaking power. Each year the president delivers a State of the Union message to Congress, in addition to other messages from time to time. Today Congress expects a president to take some leadership in proposing policy changes.

President's Term and Salary

Originally, the Constitution did not specify how many four-year terms a president may serve. George Washington set a long-held precedent when he served for eight years and refused to run for a third term. However, in 1940 and 1944, Franklin D. Roosevelt broke this tradition when he ran for a third and a fourth term.

The Twenty-second Amendment Reaction to Roosevelt's unprecedented four terms in office and concern over too much executive power led Congress to propose and the states to ratify the **Twenty-second Amendment** in 1951.[1] The amendment secured the traditional presidential limitation of two terms, while allowing a vice president who takes over the presidency and serves two years or less of the former president's term to serve two additional terms. Thus, it is possible for a president to serve up to 10 years.

Salary and Benefits The Constitutional Convention determined that presidents should receive compensation. The Constitution did not specify the amount of **compensation,** or salary, but left the matter for Congress to determine. Between 1969 and 2001, the president received $200,000 a year in taxable salary and $50,000 a year for expenses connected with offical duties. In 1999, Congress raised the president's salary to $400,000, starting with the new president in 2001. The Executive Office of the President also provides a nontaxable travel allowance of up to $100,000 a year. Congress cannot increase or decrease the salary during a president's term.

Other benefits (some that are necessary for security reasons) are provided to the president. For example, *Air Force One,* a specially equipped jet, as well as other planes, helicopters, and limousines are made available to the president and close assistants.

Presidents receive free medical, dental, and health care. They live in the White House, a 132-room

See the following footnoted materials in the **Reference Handbook:**
1. *The Constitution,* pages 774–799.

mansion with a swimming pool, bowling alley, private movie theater, and tennis courts. The White House domestic staff does the cooking, shopping, and cleaning for the president's family.

The government pays the expenses of operating the White House. Items the government does not pay for, however, can amount to thousands of dollars each month. The cost of all personal entertainment, such as receptions and dinners not directly related to government business, is paid by the president.

When presidents retire, they receive a lifetime pension, now $148,400 a year. They also have free office space, free mailing services, and up to $96,000 a year for office help. When presidents die, their spouses are eligible for a pension of $20,000 a year. While these benefits offer financial security to the president and his family, money is not the reason that people seek the presidency.

Presidential Qualifications

The Constitution sets basic qualifications for president. Other qualifications reflect personal qualities expected of presidents. Most Americans over the age of 35 can meet the constitutional requirements for the presidency. Very few can meet the informal requirements.

Constitutional Requirements In Article II, Section 1, the Constitution defines the formal requirements for the office of president.[1] The president must be: (1) a natural-born citizen of the United States; (2) at least 35 years old; and (3) a resident of the United States for at least 14 years before taking office. The same requirements apply to the vice president.

Government Experience Many other qualities are necessary for a person to have a real chance of becoming president. Experience in government is an unwritten but important qualification. Since 1868, for example, only five major-party candidates for the presidency had no previous political experience, with Dwight D. Eisenhower as the most recent example. In this century candidates who have served as United States senators or as state governors have most often won the presidential nomination. For example, Ronald Reagan had served as governor of California and Bill Clinton as governor of Arkansas. A political career provides the opportunity to form political alliances necessary to obtain a party's nomination as well as the name recognition necessary to win votes.

See the following footnoted materials in the ***Reference Handbook:***
1. *The Constitution,* pages 774–799.

Eugene M. Lang

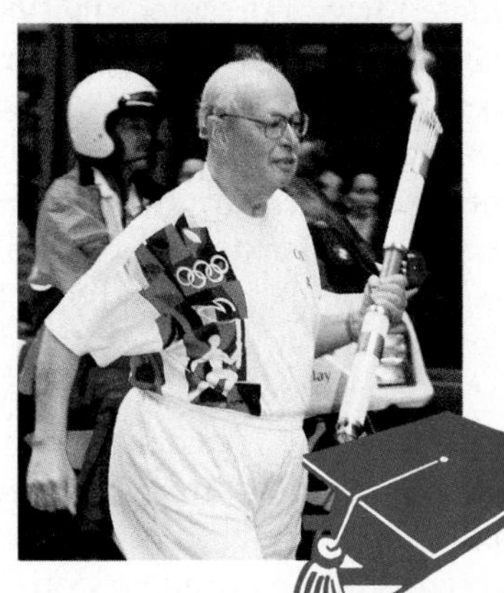

In 1996 Eugene Lang received the nation's highest civilian honor—the Presidential Medal of Freedom. President Clinton presented the award to Lang and 10 other Americans for their outstanding contributions.

Lang received the award for fulfilling dreams. In 1981 Lang went back to his elementary school in East Harlem for a visit. He made the sixth-grade students at the school a promise: if they finished high school, he would pay for their college educations. The motivation worked. Seventy-five percent of the class graduated or received their equivalency certificates.

Lang started the "I Have a Dream" Foundation in 1986. It is a program that provides money to underprivileged children to attend college. The program also offers mentoring and tutoring opportunities for students in need. Today the "I Have a Dream" program has spread to 59 cities and includes more than 15,000 students whose dreams of going to college will become a reality, thanks to Eugene Lang's contributions.

SM

"I Have a Dream"® Foundation

Importance of Money A serious candidate for the presidency must have access to large amounts of money. Even though the federal government provides funds for some aspects of presidential campaigns, running for the presidency means raising money from supporters and using one's own personal finances. Campaigning in the primaries, paying for television time, hiring campaign staff and consultants, and sending out mailings adds up to tens of millions of dollars. Congress has set an upper limit on such spending. In 1992 the law allowed candidates to spend up to $30.91 million before the national nominating convention and an additional $61.82 million between the convention and the election. If candidates spend more than the limit, they lose millions of dollars of public funds that the Federal Election Commission distributes to eligible candidates.

Political Beliefs Because extremely liberal or conservative candidates have little chance of being elected, the major parties usually choose presidential candidates who hold moderate positions on most issues. Exceptions do, however, sometimes occur. In 1964 Barry Goldwater, a very conservative Republican, became his party's presidential candidate. In 1972 a very liberal Democrat, George McGovern, won the nomination. Both of these candidates were soundly defeated in the general election. In the 2000 campaign both candidates, Al Gore and George W. Bush, adopted moderate positions on major issues.

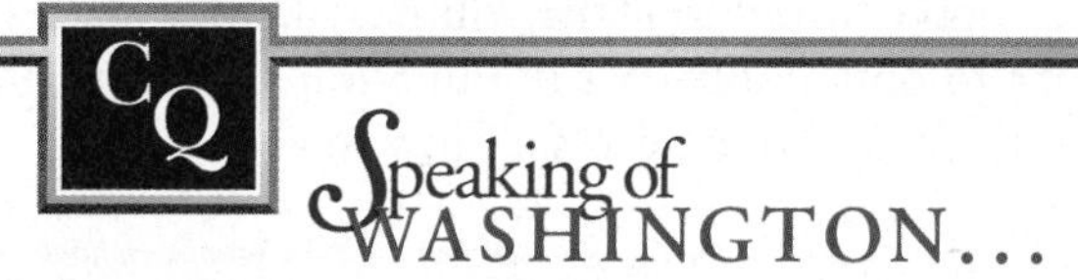

"Constitutionally" Speaking **In the pandemonium after Ronald Reagan was shot in 1981, Secretary of State Alexander M. Haig, Jr., briefed the press in the absence of Vice President George Bush, who was out of town. Asked who was in charge, Haig erroneously replied that he was. "Constitutionally, gentlemen," he said, "you have the president, the vice president, and the secretary of state, in that order...." In fact, the Constitution leaves it to Congress to legislate the line of succession after the vice president. Haig confused the current line, spelled out in a 1947 law, with an earlier law that did have the secretary of state third in line.**

GOVERNMENT Online

Student Web Activity Visit the *United States Government: Democracy in Action* Web site at gov.glencoe.com and click on ***Chapter 8–Student Web Activities*** for an activity about the president and vice president.

Personal Characteristics What personal characteristics does a person need to become president? Most presidents have come from northern European family backgrounds. A few have been from poor families (Abraham Lincoln and Harry S Truman, for example) and a few from wealthy ones (both Theodore and Franklin Roosevelt and John F. Kennedy). Most presidents, however, have come from middle-class backgrounds.

Presidents generally have been white, married, Protestant, financially successful men. No woman, nor any person of African, Hispanic, or Asian ancestry has yet been president or vice president. In 1960 John F. Kennedy became the first Roman Catholic to win the office. Geraldine Ferraro, Democratic candidate for vice president in 1984, was the first woman nominated by a major party for high office. Jesse Jackson, an African American, won the support of many delegates at the 1988 Democratic convention. Another African American, Colin Powell, former chairperson of the Joint Chiefs of Staff, has been sought as a candidate by both major parties.

Personal Growth Holding presidential office tends to underscore a person's inner personal strengths and weaknesses. President Harry S Truman, who had succeeded to the presidency on the death of Franklin Roosevelt, explained the loneliness of the office:

"The presidency of the United States carries with it a responsibility so personal as to be without parallel. . . . No one can make decisions for him. . . . Even those closest to him . . . never know all the reasons why he does certain things and why he comes to certain conclusions. To be President of the United States is to be lonely, very lonely at times of great decisions."

—Harry S Truman

Truman, however, grew into the office and took responsibility for the difficult decisions. One motto on his White House desk read: "The Buck Stops Here."

Presidential Succession

Eight presidents have died in office—bullets struck down four; four died of natural causes. After John F. Kennedy was killed in 1963, the country realized that the rules for **presidential succession** the Constitution established were inadequate.[1] The nation needed a new set of rules to determine who would fill the president's office in case of a vacancy.

Order of Succession Ratified in 1967, the **Twenty-fifth Amendment** established the order of succession to the presidency and spelled out what happens when the vice presidency becomes vacant:

"Section 1. In case of the removal of the President from office or of his death or resignation, the Vice President shall become President.

Section 2. Whenever there is a vacancy in the office of the Vice President, the President shall nominate a Vice President who shall take office upon confirmation by a majority vote of both Houses of Congress."

—Twenty-fifth Amendment, 1967

The amendment was first applied in 1973 after Spiro Agnew resigned as Richard Nixon's vice president. President Nixon then nominated Gerald Ford as vice president, and Congress approved the nomination. A year later, when President Nixon resigned from office, Vice President Ford became president. Ford then nominated Nelson Rockefeller, former governor of New York, to be vice president, and Congress again approved the nomination. This process marked the only time in United States history that both the president and vice president were not elected to these offices.

What would happen if the offices of president and vice president both became vacant at the same time? The Presidential Succession Act of 1947 established the order of succession. According to this

Line of Presidential Succession

- Vice President
- Speaker of the House
- President *pro tempore* of the Senate
- Secretary of State
- Secretary of the Treasury
- Secretary of Defense
- Attorney General
- Secretary of the Interior
- Secretary of Agriculture
- Secretary of Commerce
- Secretary of Labor
- Secretary of Health and Human Services
- Secretary of Housing and Urban Development
- Secretary of Transportation
- Secretary of Energy
- Secretary of Education
- Secretary of Veterans Affairs

Source: Nelson, ed. *The Presidency A to Z* (Washington, D.C.: CQ Inc., 1994).

Critical Thinking

The Presidential Succession Act of 1947 established the order of succession, including the possibility of the offices of president and vice president being vacant at the same time. ***What officer would be next in line if these two top executive offices were vacant at the same time?***

See the following footnoted materials in the **Reference Handbook:**
1. *The Constitution,* pages 774–799.

Next in Line

Presidential Vacancy On March 30, 1981, John Hinckley, Jr., attempted to assassinate President Ronald Reagan. Vice President George Bush took charge during Reagan's subsequent surgery. ***Why is an official presidential line of succession needed?***

law, the next in line for the presidency is the Speaker of the House. The president *pro tempore* of the Senate follows the Speaker. Next in line are the cabinet officers, starting with the secretary of state. The other 13 department heads follow in the order in which Congress created the departments.

Presidential Disability What happens if a president becomes seriously disabled while in office? Several presidents were not able to fulfill their responsibilities. President James Garfield lingered between life and death for 80 days after he was shot in 1881. During that period, no one was officially designated to take on the duties of the president. A stroke disabled President Woodrow Wilson in October 1919. During his recovery, Mrs. Wilson often performed his duties. In 1955 President Dwight D. Eisenhower's heart attack completely disabled him for 4 days. For 20 weeks after that, he could do only a limited amount of work. During his illness Eisenhower's assistants ran the executive branch while Vice President Nixon stood in for him on ceremonial occasions.

The Twenty-fifth Amendment sets forth a series of rules to be followed when a president becomes disabled. The amendment provides that the vice president becomes acting president under one of two conditions. First, the vice president assumes the president's duties if the president informs Congress of an inability to perform in office. Second, the amendment says that the vice president will take over for the president if the vice president and a majority of the cabinet or another body authorized by law informs Congress that the president is disabled. This second provision would take effect if a disabled president was unwilling or unable to inform Congress that he or she could not continue to carry out presidential duties.

Under the terms of the Twenty-fifth Amendment, the president can resume the powers and duties of office at any time simply by informing Congress that a disability no longer exists. If, however, the vice president and a majority of the cabinet or other body authorized by law contends that the president has not sufficiently recovered to perform properly, Congress must settle the dispute within 21 days. Unless Congress decides in the vice president's favor by a two-thirds vote in each house, the president may resume office.

The Vice President's Role

The Constitution gives the vice president only two duties. First, the vice president presides over the Senate and votes in that body in case of a tie. Most vice presidents spend very little time in this job. Second, under the Twenty-fifth Amendment, the vice president helps decide whether the president is disabled and acts as president should that happen.

Standby Work A vice president's work and power depend upon what responsibilities, if any, the president assigns. Hubert Humphrey, Lyndon Johnson's vice president, once said, "The only authority he [the Vice President] has is what the President gives him. He who giveth can taketh away."

Fourteen vice presidents have become president. Of these, nine vice presidents have succeeded to the office upon the death or resignation of the president. Some have done so under difficult circumstances. Harry S Truman became president in 1945, near the end of World War II, when Franklin D. Roosevelt died in office.

Increased Responsibilities The presidents before Eisenhower (1953-1961) usually ignored their vice presidents. Since Eisenhower, however, presidents have tried to give their vice presidents more responsibility. Vice presidents today often represent the president overseas, attending state funerals and other ceremonial functions, serving in a diplomatic role, and visiting with heads of state. In addition, they may make speeches around the country defending the president's policies and decisions. Today vice presidents are members of the National Security Council, the president's foreign and military policy advisers. President Carter made his vice president, Walter Mondale, a member of several groups that advised the president on various issues.

Executive Powers Vice President Cheney represented the president and the nation while making a speech. ***John Adams once said, "I am Vice President. In this I am nothing, but I may be everything." What did he mean?***

More recently, Vice President Al Gore served as a close adviser to President Bill Clinton overseeing areas such as the organization of government and environmental issues. His outspoken support of the North American Free Trade Agreement was credited with helping its approval.

Section 1 Assessment

Checking for Understanding

1. **Main Idea** Using a graphic organizer like the one below, show three constitutional requirements and three informal requirements of a president.

Constitutional	Informal
1.	
2.	
3.	

2. **Define** compensation, presidential succession.
3. **Identify** Twenty-second Amendment, Twenty-fifth Amendment.
4. Who are the first four officers in the line of succession to the presidency?

Critical Thinking

5. **Drawing Conclusions** Why do you think presidential candidates who represent moderate views usually win elections?

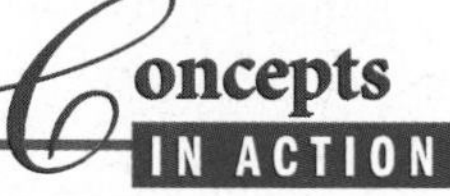

Growth of Democracy Conduct a survey using the following questions: In your opinion, when will the United States have its first female president? Its first minority president? Tabulate the results on graphs and display them in class.

Section 2

Electing the President

Reader's Guide

Key Terms

elector, electoral vote

Find Out

- What evidence suggests that the Founders did not anticipate the effects of political parties on presidential elections?
- Based on the historical record of elections, how well has the Electoral College performed in selecting presidents the nation wanted?

Understanding Concepts

Constitutional Interpretations How has the method of electing a president changed to make the process more democratic?

COVER STORY

House Chooses President

WASHINGTON, D.C., DECEMBER 1824

General Andrew Jackson has won the popular presidential vote, but his 99 electoral votes are not enough to win the highest office. The electors, divided among four candidates, give no one the election. The House of Representatives will now be asked to choose the president. It is likely their choice will be between General Jackson and John Quincy Adams of Massachusetts. Jackson feels confident that the House will make him president. Many observers, however, believe that House Speaker Henry Clay could sway enough votes to give Adams the office.

Jackson campaign box

John Quincy Adams was chosen by the House as the sixth president. Initially, at the Constitutional Convention, the Founders proposed that Congress choose the president without a popular or an electoral vote. They gave up the idea because it violated the principle of separation of powers making it possible for Congress to dominate the presidency.

Direct popular vote was another possible method for electing the president. Many of the Founders, however, feared that citizens could not make a wise choice because they knew little about potential leaders. There was no national news media, radio, or television. In addition, some leaders believed that the most popular candidates might not be the best presidents.

After weeks of debate, the Founders settled on a compromise that Alexander Hamilton introduced. This compromise set up an indirect method of election called the Electoral College. With a few changes, that system is still in use today.

The Original System

Article II, Section 1,[1] established the **Electoral College.** It provided that each state would choose electors according to a method the state legislatures set up. Each state would have as many electors as it had senators and representatives in Congress. At election time, the **electors** would meet in their own states and cast votes for two presidential candidates. This vote was the **electoral vote.** No popular vote was cast for the early presidential elections.

Electoral votes from all the states would be counted in a joint session of Congress. The candidate receiving a majority of the electoral votes would become president. The candidate receiving the second highest number of votes, who also had a majority, would become vice

See the following footnoted materials in the ***Reference Handbook:***
1. *The Constitution,* pages 774–799.

president. In case of a tie, or if no one received a majority, the House of Representatives would choose the president or vice president, with each state having one vote.

As expected, the Electoral College unanimously chose George Washington as the nation's first president in 1789 and 1792. After President Washington retired, however, political parties began to play an important role in national elections. Political parties had an unexpected and profound impact on the Electoral College system.

Fan endorsing Thomas Jefferson in 1800

The Impact of Political Parties

By 1800 two national parties—the Federalists and the Democratic-Republicans—had formed. Each party nominated its own candidate for president and vice president. Each party also nominated candidates for electors in every state. It was understood that if they were chosen, these electors would vote for their party's candidates.

In the election of 1800, the Democratic-Republicans won a majority of electoral votes. As agreed, each Democratic-Republican elector cast one vote for each of the party's candidates—Thomas Jefferson and Aaron Burr. While most electors wanted Jefferson as president, both Jefferson and Burr wound up with 73 votes. Because of the tie, the election went to the House of Representatives.

The opposing party, the Federalists, controlled the House of Representatives. Popular opinion in the nation supported Jefferson, but many Federalists in the House favored Burr. The House debated day and night for six days. Thirty-six ballots were taken before Jefferson was finally elected president and Burr vice president. The 1800 election clearly demonstrated the need for a change in the rules before the next election.

The **Twelfth Amendment** was added to the Constitution in 1804 to solve the problem. It requires that the electors cast separate ballots for president and vice president. The amendment also provides that if no candidate receives a majority of the electoral votes, the House chooses from the three candidates who have the largest number of electoral votes. If no candidate for vice president gets a majority of electoral votes, the Senate chooses from the top two candidates for vice president.

In the 1820s states began to place presidential candidates on the ballot. Since then political parties have chosen electors by popular vote. Parties also changed their method of nominating presidential candidates, giving the people more of a voice. The Electoral College system adapted to the growth of democracy.

The First President

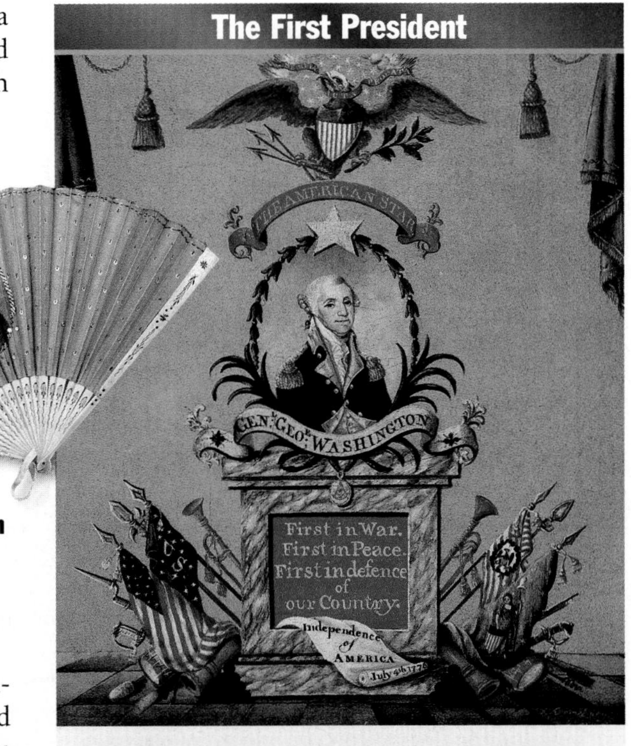

Political Symbols Frederick Kemmelmeyer created this reverential painting to honor Washington, our nation's only unanimously elected president. ***What symbols did the artist use in this painting and how do you think he viewed Washington?***

The Electoral College System Today

The Electoral College is still the method of choosing the president and vice president. Parties choose their nominees for president in conventions held in late summer. Voters cast their

Congressional Quarterly's *Government at a Glance*

Online UPDATE
Visit gov.glencoe.com and click on ***Textbook Updates–Chapter 8*** for an update of the data.

The Electoral College System

Presidential Election Year

Tuesday after first Monday in November
- Voters cast ballots for a slate of electors pledged to a particular presidential candidate.

Monday after second Wednesday in December
- Winning electors in each state meet in their state capitals to cast their votes for president and vice president.
- Statement of the vote is sent to Washington, D.C.

January 6
- Congress counts electoral votes. A majority of electoral votes is needed to win (270 out of 538).

January 20
- Candidate receiving majority of electoral votes is sworn in as president of the United States.

Presidents Elected Who Lost The Popular Vote

President	Electoral Vote	Popular Vote	Opponent	Electoral Vote	Popular Vote
John Q. Adams*	84	113,122	Andrew Jackson	99	151,271
Rutherford B. Hayes**	185	4,034,311	Samuel J. Tilden	184	4,288,546
Benjamin Harrison	233	5,443,892	Grover Cleveland	168	5,534,488
George W. Bush	271	53,692,798	Albert Gore	267	54,056,359

** Clay and Crawford also received electoral votes. The election was determined in the House of Representatives.*

*** Hayes was awarded the disputed electoral votes of three states by a special commission.*

Source: Nelson, ed., *The Presidency A to Z* (Washington, D.C.: CQ Inc., 1994); Cable News Network, 2000 (results as of Dec. 4, 2000).

Critical Thinking

The writers of the Constitution chose the electoral college system as a compromise between selection by Congress and election by popular vote. ***How many weeks pass between a presidential election and inauguration? Is this much time necessary? Why?***

ballots for president every four years (1992, 1996, 2000, etc.) on the Tuesday after the first Monday in November. While the candidates' names are printed on the ballot, the voters are not actually voting directly for president and vice president. Rather, they are voting for all of their party's electors in their state. In December these electors will cast the official vote for president and vice president. Thus, a vote for the Democratic candidate is actually a vote for the Democratic electors, and a vote for the Republican candidate is a vote for the Republican electors.

The Electoral College includes 538 electors—a number determined by the total of House and Senate members plus 3 for the District of Columbia. Each state has as many electors as it has senators and representatives in Congress. Wyoming with 1 representative and 2 senators has 3 electoral votes. California, the most populous state, with 52 representatives and 2 senators, has 54 electoral votes. To be elected president or vice president, a candidate must win at least 270 of the 538 votes. The Electoral College is a winner-take-all system with the exception of Maine and Nebraska. The party whose candidate receives the largest popular vote in any state wins all the electoral votes of that state even if the margin of victory is only one popular vote.

The winning presidential candidate is usually announced on the same evening as the popular election because popular-vote counts indicate who won each state. The formal election by the Electoral College, however, begins on the Monday following the second Wednesday in December when the electors meet in each state capital and cast their ballots. The electoral ballots from each state are sealed and mailed to the president of the Senate for a formal count. On January 6 both houses of Congress meet in the House of Representatives to open and count the ballots. Congress then officially declares the winner president.

Most states do not legally require electors to vote for the candidate who wins the popular vote, but electors usually do so. A few electors, however, have ignored this tradition. In 1976 an elector from the state of Washington voted for Ronald Reagan, even though Gerald Ford had won the majority of popular votes in the state. Similarly, in 1988 an elector from West Virginia switched Democratic candidates and voted for Lloyd Bentsen for president and Michael Dukakis for vice president. Over the years, eight other electors have broken with custom.

Electoral College Issues

The Electoral College system works well in most elections. However, the call for reform is heard after every closely contested election. Critics point to three major weaknesses in the system that could affect the outcome of an election.

Winner Take All If a candidate wins the largest number of popular votes in a state, that person receives all the state's electoral votes. Critics argue that this system is unfair to those who voted for a losing candidate. For example, in 1992 more than 2 million Texans voted for Bill Clinton, but Clinton did not receive any of Texas's electoral votes.

The winner-take-all system makes it possible for a candidate who loses the popular vote to win the electoral vote. This usually happens when a candidate wins several large states by narrow

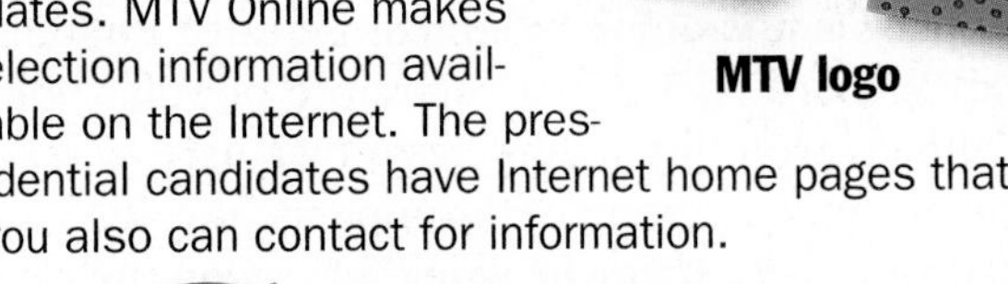

Electing Your President

Young people are less likely to vote than any other age group. However, Music Television (MTV) and Rock the Vote hope to draw more young voters into the political process.

Rock the Vote is a nonprofit organization dedicated to educating and involving young people. It conducts voter registration drives at rock concerts and on rock radio stations. It can even register you to vote over the Internet.

During presidential campaigns, Rock the Vote and MTV distribute a free election guide for young voters at record stores across the nation. MTV also airs a voter education series called *Choose or Lose.* MTV personalities interview the candidates about issues of interest to young voters. Televised MTV forums allow young people to express their concerns directly to the candidates. MTV Online makes election information available on the Internet. The presidential candidates have Internet home pages that you also can contact for information.

MTV logo

Measuring Success How successful was Rock the Vote in the last presidential election? Gather information through magazine articles in *Readers' Guide to Periodical Literature.* Create a graphic using your findings.

25 Electoral Votes at Stake

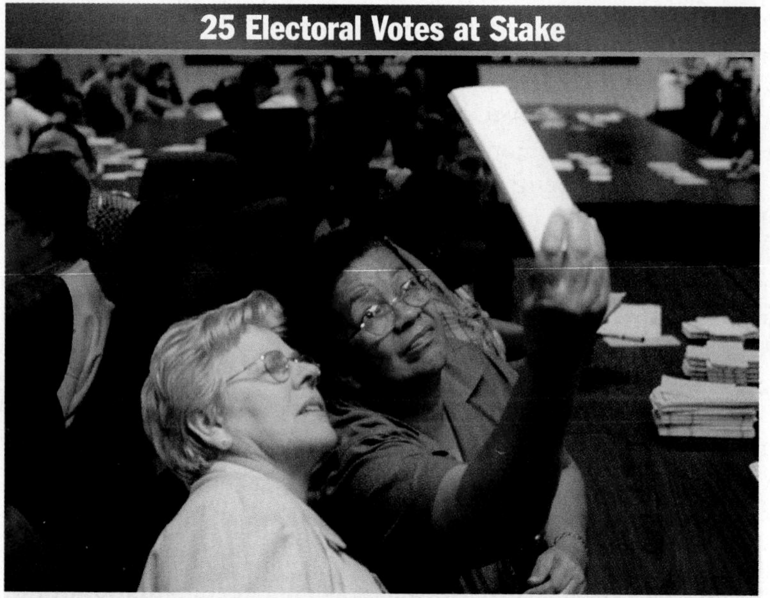

Recounting Ballots Broward County, Florida, election workers scrutinize ballots during the presidential contest of 2000. The race was so close that election officials in several Florida counties manually recounted the ballots to make sure that the count was accurate. ***Who selects the president and vice president if no candidate receives a majority of the electoral votes?***

margins. Four times in American history—in the elections of John Quincy Adams in 1824, Rutherford B. Hayes in 1876, Benjamin Harrison in 1888, and George W. Bush in 2000—the candidate who lost the popular vote won the election. In the 2000 election, for example, Democrat Al Gore won around 300,000 more popular votes than Republican George W. Bush. Bush, however, received 271 electoral votes to 267 for Gore.

The 1960 election almost became another example. Democrat John Kennedy defeated Republican Richard Nixon in a very close popular vote. Kennedy won Illinois and Texas by a narrow margin of about 1 percent of the popular vote. If Nixon had won these states, he would have won the election by winning the electoral vote while narrowly losing the popular vote.

Third-Party Candidates When a third-party candidate is a strong presidential contender, other problems can arise. A third-party candidate could win enough electoral votes to prevent either major-party candidate from receiving a majority of the votes. The third party could then bargain to release electoral votes to one of the two major-party candidates.

Some people say Governor George Wallace of Alabama wanted to use this tactic in the 1968 election. Wallace ran as the American Independent Party's candidate and won 5 states and 46 electoral votes. The election between Republican Richard Nixon and Democrat Hubert Humphrey was very close, with Nixon winning by only about 500,000 popular votes. If Humphrey had beaten Nixon in a few more states, Nixon would not have won a majority of the electoral votes. Then, unless Wallace's electors voted for Nixon, the election would have gone to the House of Representatives.

Election by the House When the House of Representatives must decide a presidential election, each state casts one vote. The candidate who receives 26 or more of the votes is elected.

Election by the House involves three problems: (1) States with small populations such as Alaska or Nevada have as much weight as states with large populations such as New York or California. (2) Under the rules, if a majority of representatives from a state cannot agree on a candidate, the state loses its vote. (3) If some members of the House favor a strong third-party candidate, it could be difficult for any candidate to get the 26 votes needed to win.

Ideas for Reform People usually criticize the Electoral College system whenever problems arise. Many changes to the system have been proposed. One idea is to choose electors from congressional districts. Each state would have two electoral votes, plus one vote for each congressional district in the state. The candidate winning the most votes in a congressional district would win the electoral vote in that district. The candidate winning the most districts in a state would, in addition, receive the two statewide electoral votes.

Another plan proposes that the presidential candidates would win the same share of a state's electoral vote as they received of the state's popular vote. If a candidate captured 60 percent of the popular vote, for example, the candidate would earn 60 percent of the state's electoral vote.

This plan too would cure the winner-take-all problem. Moreover, it would remove the possibility of electors voting for someone that they are not pledged to support. Critics of the plan point out that it could possibly enlarge the role of third parties and complicate the election process. Because third-party candidates could get at least some share of the electoral vote in each election, they might also be able to force a presidential election into the House of Representatives.

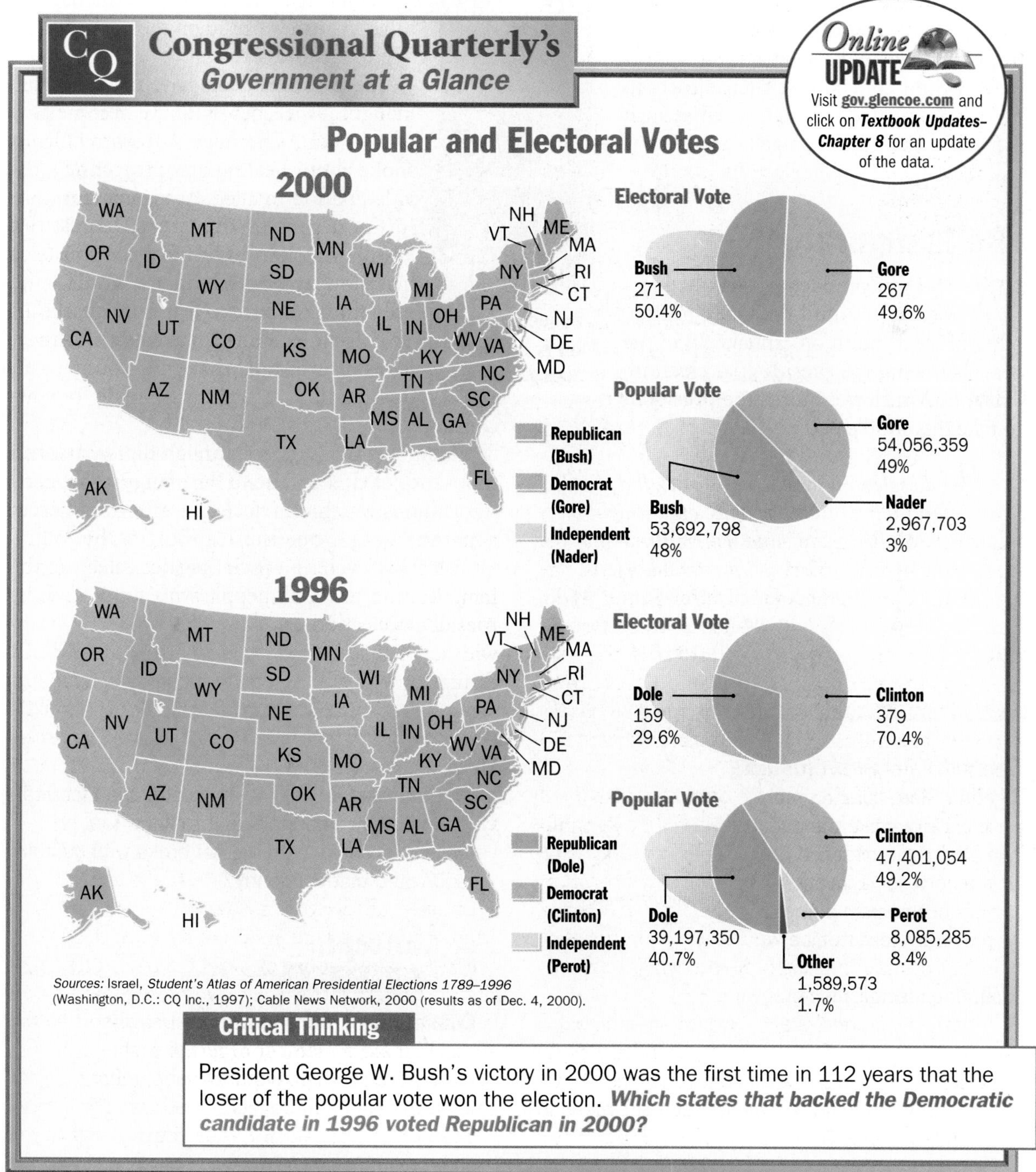

Sources: Israel, *Student's Atlas of American Presidential Elections 1789–1996* (Washington, D.C.: CQ Inc., 1997); Cable News Network, 2000 (results as of Dec. 4, 2000).

Critical Thinking

President George W. Bush's victory in 2000 was the first time in 112 years that the loser of the popular vote won the election. ***Which states that backed the Democratic candidate in 1996 voted Republican in 2000?***

Direct Popular Election Another plan is to do away with the Electoral College entirely. Instead, the people would directly elect the president and vice president. While this alternative may seem obvious, some have criticized it on the grounds that it would greatly change the structure of the federal system. It would undermine federalism because the states would lose their role in the choice of a president. It would also mean that candidates would concentrate their efforts in densely populated areas. Large cities such as New York and Los Angeles could control the outcome of an election.

Souvenir from John F. Kennedy's inauguration

The Inauguration

The new president, called the president-elect until the inauguration, takes office at noon on January 20 in the year following the presidential election. The Constitution requires the president to take this simple oath:

> "*I do solemnly swear (or affirm), that I will faithfully execute the office of President of the United States, and will, to the best of my ability, preserve, protect, and defend the Constitution of the United States.*"
>
> —Article II, Section 8

By custom, an inaugural ceremony is held outside the Capitol in Washington, D.C., weather permitting. The new president rides with the outgoing president from the White House to the Capitol for the inauguration ceremonies. With the outgoing president, family members, government officials, and citizens looking on, the chief justice administers the oath of office. The new president then gives an Inaugural Address.

Several presidents have made notable inaugural speeches that have become part of the nation's heritage. Abraham Lincoln spoke about healing and protecting a divided nation in 1861. At his inauguration in the depths of the Great Depression, Franklin D. Roosevelt lifted the spirits of his fellow Americans with the words, "The only thing we have to fear is fear itself." In 1961 John F. Kennedy called on all Americans to "ask not what your country can do for you—ask what you can do for your country."

Members of Congress, foreign diplomats, and thousands of citizens attend the inaugural ceremony. Millions watch on television. After the speech, a parade goes from the Capitol to the White House. That evening official parties celebrate the inauguration to thank people who supported the president's election campaign.

Section 2 Assessment

Checking for Understanding

1. **Main Idea** Using a graphic organizer like the one to the right, describe the ceremonial events that occur when a new president takes office.

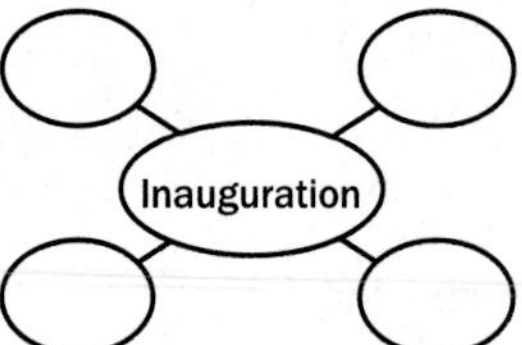

2. **Define** elector, electoral vote.
3. **Identify** Electoral College, Twelfth Amendment.
4. Why do presidential candidates spend more time in states with large populations?
5. What does the phrase "winner take all" mean in presidential elections?

Critical Thinking

6. **Determining Relevance** In judging the Electoral College, how important is it to know that on several occasions an elector broke with custom and voted independently?

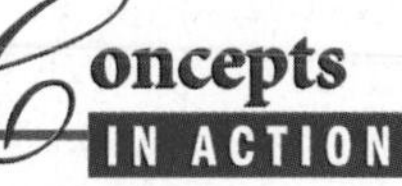

Constitutional Interpretations Imagine that you are a member of an interest group. Choose a position for your group: keep the Electoral College, or abolish it. Then write a persuasive speech explaining your position.

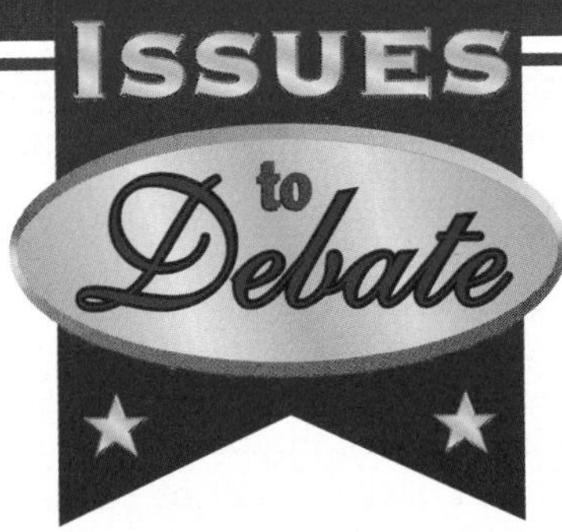

Should the Electoral College be Replaced?

Some Americans think the Electoral College is outdated and ineffective. They want to abolish it and replace it with a system that lets people vote directly for a president. Those who favor the electoral system think it helps to unify the nation, as its creators intended.

Winner Take All

The most common argument against the Electoral College system is that a candidate can win without receiving a majority of the popular vote as George W. Bush did in the 2000 election. Another argument is that a candidate can win a majority of the popular vote and more electoral votes than any other candidate, but still lose. This can happen if a candidate does not receive a majority of electoral votes, and the House of Representatives is called to decide on a winner.

A candidate can also win a large percentage of popular votes in a state, but have no electoral votes to show for it. This is especially true for third-party candidates.

Critics say that the Electoral College system robs voters of their power, because candidates often ignore smaller states with fewer electoral votes.

Guarding Against Tyranny

Supporters of the Electoral College say most people do not understand the merits of the system. James Madison, one of the original creators, believed that if a majority vote was used, the rights of minorities could be compromised. He wanted to guard against "the superior force of an . . . overbearing majority."

Under the Electoral College system, a candidate cannot win without winning in a large number of states. Supporters consider this an advantage because candidates must reach a broad range of people with varying viewpoints to win the vote. Those who focus on narrow segments of the population are less likely to be elected. Supporters also contend that each voter has more clout in an election that involves 51 separate elections than in one large national election.

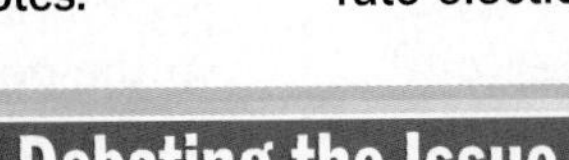

Should Direct Elections Replace the Electoral College System?

Assume that you are a citizen testifying before a congressional committee weighing the advantages and disadvantages of the Electoral College system.

Key Issues

✔ What was the original purpose of the Electoral College? Does it serve that purpose effectively?

✔ What are the advantages and disadvantages of having a direct election?

✔ How would presidential campaigns be affected by direct elections?

Debate Divide the class into two groups—one that supports the system and one that does not. Allow time for each group to prepare and present their arguments to the class.

Vote Make your decision. Then have the class vote for or against replacing the Electoral College system.

Section 3

The Cabinet

Reader's Guide

Key Terms

cabinet, leak

Find Out

- What role does politics play in the appointment of cabinet secretaries?
- How have factors that limit the role of the cabinet as an advisory body affected the relationship between cabinet officers and the presidents they serve?

Understanding Concepts

Political Processes Why are cabinet secretaries who administer large executive departments often not insiders at the White House?

COVER STORY

Jefferson Resigns

NEW YORK CITY, DECEMBER 31, 1793

The bitter feud that has plagued President George Washington's cabinet ended today, as Thomas Jefferson stepped down as secretary of state. The action followed months of tension between Jefferson and Secretary of the Treasury Alexander Hamilton. The contest for influence with the president was settled during the recent crisis with France, when Washington relied on Hamilton instead of his secretary of state. Jefferson recently said of his rival, "I will not suffer my retirement to be clouded by the slanders of a man whose history, from the moment at which history can stoop to notice him, is a tissue of machinations against the liberty of the country."

Thomas Jefferson

Soon after President Washington's election, Congress created a Department of State, a Department of War, a Department of the Treasury, and the Attorney General's office. The president met regularly with his department heads and sought their advice on policy matters. The newspapers of the time called this group Washington's *cabinet,* the general term for the advisers around any head of state. The name stuck.

One of the first responsibilities of a president is to organize and staff the executive branch of government. In fact, the president-elect often has selected most of his nominees for cabinet appointments before taking the oath of office.

Today the president appoints the secretaries that head the 14 major executive departments. Each appointee must be approved by the Senate. The 14 secretaries, the vice president, and several other top officials make up the **cabinet.** Cabinet secretaries are more than advisers; they are also administrators of large bureaucracies.

The Selection of the Cabinet

In selecting their department heads, presidents must balance a great many political, social, and management considerations. Secretaries should have some credible expertise in the policy areas their departments will manage. Appointees must be acceptable to all groups with political power. They should provide geographic balance as well as racial and gender representation. Patronage and party loyalty also are usually important.

Major Factors in Making Appointments

The selection of a president's cabinet is largely a political process. One consideration is that an appointee have a background that is compatible with the department he or she will head. This qualification also can bring some geographic balance to the cabinet. The secretary of the interior, for example, typically is someone from a western state who has experience in land policy and conservation issues. The secretary of housing and urban development (HUD) generally has a big city background. The secretary of agriculture usually is from a farm state.

Equally important is the president's need to satisfy powerful interest groups that have a stake in a department's policies. The secretary of labor, therefore, generally must be someone acceptable to labor unions. The secretary of commerce is expected to have a good reputation with business and industry. The secretary of the treasury is often a banker or someone with close ties to the financial community.

In addition, it is important that appointees have high-level administrative skills and experience. Cabinet officers are responsible for huge departments that employ thousands of people and spend billions of dollars each year. If inefficiency or scandal should result, blame will fall on the secretary—and on the president.

As women and minority groups have gained political power, presidents have considered the race, gender, and ethnic background of candidates when making their appointments. In 1966 Lyndon Johnson named the first African American department secretary, **Robert Weaver,** to lead HUD. Franklin D. Roosevelt appointed the first woman to the cabinet, Secretary of Labor **Frances Perkins,** in 1933. Women in the cabinet remained rare until 1975, when President Ford appointed Carla Hills as HUD secretary. Since then, every president's cabinet has included women and African Americans. President Reagan named the first Hispanic, Lauro F. Cavazos, as secretary of education, in 1988. President Clinton used cabinet appointments as an opportunity to recruit women and minorities to top government posts. The Clinton cabinet became the most gender and racially balanced team in history.

Even after people who satisfy all the requirements are selected, obstacles still exist. It is not always easy to convince them to take the positions. Faced with giving up a secure career for a possible short-term appointment, many qualified candidates find the pay, the work, or life in Washington politics to be unattractive. Almost all modern presidents have been turned down by some of the people they have invited to join their cabinets.

Background of Cabinet Members What kind of person does accept appointment to the cabinet, and why? Almost without exception, cabinet members are college graduates. Many have advanced degrees. Most are leaders in the fields of business, industry, law, science, and education.

Clinton's Chief Diplomat

Interest Groups
Madeleine Albright, the first female secretary of state, shakes hands with Japanese foreign minister Yukihiko Ikeda. Albright is a Washington academic who fled Communist Czechoslovakia as a child. ***What groups of citizens might have felt pride in Albright's appointment?***

Cabinet secretaries earn $151,800 per year, and many cabinet members assume government jobs even though they know that they could have earned more than twice that amount in private employment. Some take their posts out of a deep sense of public service. Typically they move easily in and out of government posts from their positions in private industry or the legal, financial, or educational world.

Nominations and Confirmation The selection process for a new president's cabinet begins long before Inauguration Day. The president-elect draws up a list of candidates after consulting with campaign advisers, congressional leaders, and representatives of interest groups. Key campaign staffers meet with potential candidates to discuss the issues facing the department they may be asked to head. Before making final decisions, members of the president-elect's team may **leak**, or deliberately disclose, some candidates' names to the news media. They do this to test the reaction of Congress, interest groups, and the public.

The Senate holds confirmation hearings on the president's nominees for cabinet posts. The nominee to head each department appears before the Senate committee that oversees the department to answer questions about his or her background and views.

The cabinet is viewed as part of the president's official family. The Senate, therefore, usually cooperates in the appointment process, and most confirmation hearings are routine. Of more than 500 cabinet appointments since the time of George Washington, the Senate has rejected only a handful.

Appointments are not automatic, however. President Clinton had been in office less than a month when his nominee for attorney general, Zoë Baird, had to bow out of the confirmation process. In the midst of Senate hearings, a newspaper reported that Baird earlier had hired illegal aliens for household work. A groundswell of public opinion derailed the nomination.

The Role of the Cabinet

As individuals, cabinet members are responsible for the executive departments they head. As a group, the cabinet is intended to serve as an advisory body to the president. For many reasons, however, most presidents have been reluctant to give the cabinet a major advisory role.

The cabinet meets when the president calls it together. Meetings may be once a week but usually are much less frequent, depending on how a president uses the cabinet. Meetings take place in the cabinet room of the White House and are usually closed to the public and the press.

The First Cabinet

Advising the President Seated next to President Washington are the members of the first cabinet—Henry Knox, Alexander Hamilton, Thomas Jefferson, and Edmund Randolph. ***How has the size and role of the cabinet changed since Washington's first administration?***

Cabinet Members at Work

Influencing Policy Secretary of Labor Alexis Herman (rear center) and Secretary of Health and Human Services Donna Shalala applaud the signing of an executive memorandum on the Americans With Disabilities Act in 1998. ***Should presidents be obligated to make greater use of their cabinets? Why or why not?***

The Cabinet in History From the beginning, the cabinet's role in decision making has depended on how each president wanted to define it. Stronger presidents, such as Jackson, Lincoln, Wilson, and Franklin Roosevelt, have paid the cabinet less attention. Andrew Jackson depended on a small group of friends instead of his cabinet for advice. Since they often met in the White House kitchen, they became known as the "kitchen cabinet." During the Great Depression, Roosevelt relied more on a group of university professors called the "brain trust" and his wife Eleanor than on his cabinet.

Some members of Lincoln's cabinet thought he was weak and that they would run the government. They soon learned otherwise. Secretary of State William Seward acknowledged, "The President is the best of us. There is only one vote in the Cabinet, and it belongs to him." Lincoln's treatment of his cabinet illustrates the role it has played through much of American history. Before issuing the Emancipation Proclamation, he called his cabinet together to inform them of his intention to end slavery. He told them:

> "*I have gathered you together to hear what I have written down. I do not wish your advice about the main matter. That I have determined for myself.*"
>
> —Abraham Lincoln, 1862

The Modern Cabinet Several recent presidents have attempted to increase the role of the cabinet in decision making. In the end, however, most have given up and turned elsewhere for advice. After President Kennedy was assassinated, Lyndon Johnson was anxious to get along with his predecessor's cabinet. He felt he needed them for a smooth transition of power and wanted them to brief him on what was going on in their departments. Soon Johnson, too, was calling on the cabinet less and less. When a meeting occurred, it was generally to give department heads what one presidential assistant called their "marching orders." Johnson's cabinet fared better than Richard Nixon's, however. Some of Nixon's cabinet members did not see him for months at a time.

At the start of his presidency, Ronald Reagan also pledged to make greater use of the cabinet. He stated that his department heads would be his "inner circle of advisers." In an attempt to improve its usefulness, Reagan divided his cabinet into smaller groups. Each group was responsible for a broad policy area such as natural resources or food and agriculture. After only a year in office, however, Reagan began to rely mainly on his White House aides for advice. Presidents Bush and Clinton used their cabinets as sounding boards for their ideas rather than as the advisory body President Washington envisioned.

The Influence of Cabinet Members Some cabinet members who work closely with the president wield influence because they head departments that are concerned with national issues. The secretaries of state, defense, treasury, and the attorney general fill this role in most administrations. These officials are sometimes called an **"inner cabinet."** Other secretaries who head departments that represent narrower interests such as agriculture or veterans' affairs are less influential and have less direct access to the president.

Factors Limiting the Cabinet's Role

Several factors limit the president's use of the cabinet for advice in making key decisions or for help in running the executive branch. Understanding these factors helps to explain why presidents have come to rely on assistants in the Executive Office of the President, a presidential advisory agency established by Congress.

Conflicting Loyalties No president commands the complete loyalty of cabinet members. Even though the president appoints them, cabinet officials have three other constituencies that require loyalty: career officials in their own department, members of Congress, and special-interest groups. Each of these groups has its own stake in the department's programs. Each may push the secretary in directions that are not always in accord with the president's plans and policies.

Disagreements among secretaries may result from loyalty to their department's programs or to its constituent groups. In addition, competition among secretaries for control of a program may cause conflict in the cabinet. President Reagan's secretary of state, George Schulz, and Secretary of Defense Caspar Weinberger battled to influence the president on arms control and foreign policy for almost two years before Weinberger finally resigned in 1987.

Secrecy and Trust A second factor that reduces the usefulness of the cabinet is the difficulty of maintaining secrecy when 14 cabinet secretaries are involved in a discussion of sensitive topics. Presidents sometimes have discovered cabinet debates reported in the press.

Presidents, like anyone else, would prefer to discuss tough problems with people they know and trust. Yet, because of all the factors that must be considered when choosing department heads, presidents generally appoint relative strangers to their cabinets. President Kennedy, for example, had never met his secretary of defense and secretary of the treasury before he appointed them. For these reasons presidents have increasingly turned to the Executive Office of the President and to their own personal White House staffs for help.

Section 3 Assessment

Checking for Understanding

1. **Main Idea** Using a graphic organizer like the one to the right, show which cabinet members often form an "inner circle" closer to the president and which have less direct contact.

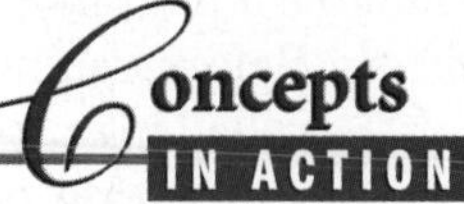

2. **Define** cabinet, leak.
3. **Identify** Robert Weaver, Frances Perkins.
4. What five factors do presidents consider when choosing cabinet officers?
5. Explain how the decline of the cabinet as an advisory body to the president weakens the system of checks and balances.

Critical Thinking

6. **Identifying Alternatives** What could a president do when choosing cabinet members to increase their value as advisers?

Concepts IN ACTION

Political Processes Search library resources for information about the major responsibilities of one of the 14 executive departments. Then prepare a list of interview questions that you think would help to determine the competence of a potential secretary of the executive department you chose.

Interpreting an Election Map

Election maps show various kinds of information about an election. For example, an election map might show the results of a presidential election by identifying the states that voted for each candidate. Another map might show the outcome of a congressional election, district by district.

Learning the Skill

To read an election map, follow these steps:

- Examine the map title or caption to determine what election information is being shown.
- Examine the map key to determine how information is presented.
- Based on this information, decide what kinds of questions the map is intended to answer.

The map below answers some questions about the election of 1948, but not others. It does not, for example, provide the results of the popular vote or the results of the final vote in the Electoral College.

Electoral Votes 1948 Election

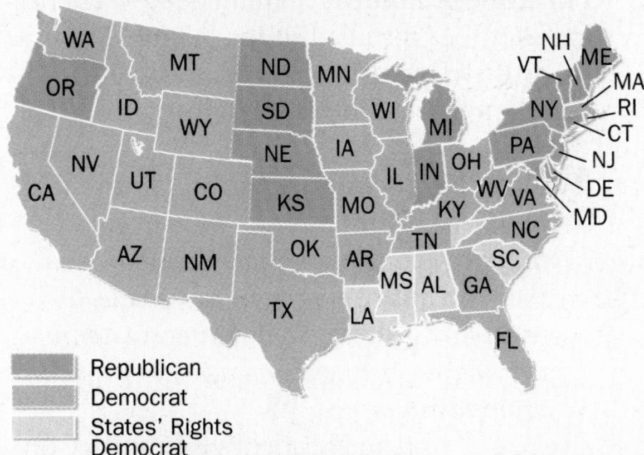

Electoral Votes 1960 Election

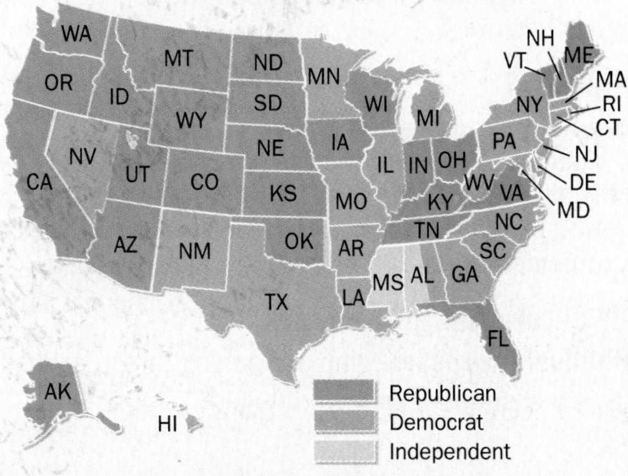

Practicing the Skill

Examine the map above and answer the questions that follow.

1. What does the color red indicate on this map?
2. What does the color blue indicate?
3. How many states voted Republican?
4. Which states split their electoral votes?
5. Compare the two maps. Which states that voted Republican in 1948 voted Democratic in 1960?

Application Activity

In an almanac, newspaper, or other reference work, find the results of a recent city, state, or national election. Draw an election map to present those results. Include a key on your map.

The Glencoe Skillbuilder Interactive Workbook, Level 2 provides instruction and practice in key social studies skills.

Section 4

The Executive Office

Reader's Guide

Key Terms

central clearance, national security adviser, press secretary

Find Out

- What historic changes have made the Executive Office of the President necessary?
- In what ways are the members of the White House Office similar to and different from the president's cabinet?

Understanding Concepts

Political Processes Who are among the president's closest advisers on administration policy?

COVER STORY

Bush Grants Pardons

WASHINGTON, D.C., DECEMBER 24, 1992

President George Bush today pardoned White House aides of former president Ronald Reagan for their involvement in the Iran-contra affair. The pardons closed the legal troubles of those involved in the scandal, which broke in 1986. Two Reagan national security advisers and National Security Council staff were convicted of secret weapons sales to Iran and illegal aid to the Nicaraguan "contra" rebels. In 1987 Reagan accepted a report that blamed the scandal on his "hands-off" attitude toward his advisers. He also accepted responsibility for the actions of his staff.

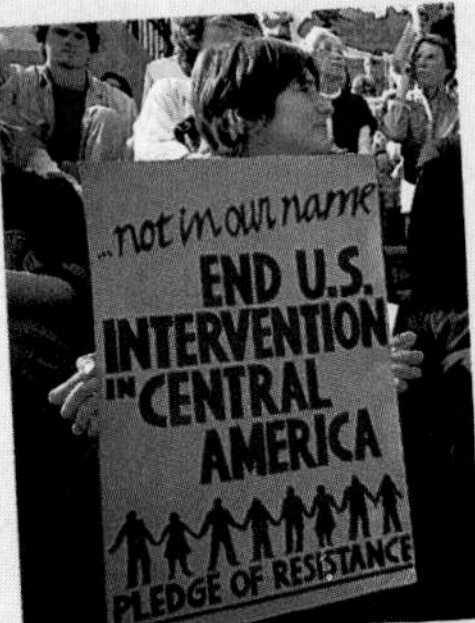

Protesting U.S. intervention in Central America

Not all staff advisers are as high-profile as President Reagan's National Security Council members were in 1987. The **Executive Office of the President (EOP)** consists of individuals and agencies that directly assist the president. Modern presidents rely on the EOP to provide specialized advice and information needed for decision making. They also use it to help them implement presidential decisions and to gain more control over the executive branch.

Executive Office Agencies

Created by President Franklin D. Roosevelt in 1939, the Executive Office of the President has grown to serve the needs of each administration. When Roosevelt took office in 1933 during the Great Depression, he immediately proposed a vast number of federal programs to deal with the country's serious economic problems. As Congress passed one special program after another, the size of the national government began to grow rapidly.

By the mid-1930s, Roosevelt and his few White House assistants felt overwhelmed because they could not coordinate all the new programs and gather all the information the president needed. Consequently, in 1935 Roosevelt appointed the President's Committee on Administrative Management to study the problem. In its report the Committee recommended that a personal staff be "installed in the White House itself, directly accessible to the president." This staff was to assist the president in:

> *"Obtaining quickly and without delay all pertinent information . . . so as to guide him in making responsible decisions, and then when decisions have been made, to assist him in seeing to it that every administrative department and agency affected is promptly informed."*
>
> —The President's Committee on Administrative Management, 1937

In response Congress passed the Reorganization Act of 1939 that created the Executive Office of the President. At the same time, President Franklin Roosevelt moved the Bureau of the Budget out of the Treasury Department into the EOP, where it would be more responsive to his wishes and he could be more aware of its activities. As another part of the EOP, he established the White House Office, which he intended to be a small group of advisers working directly with the president on day-to-day matters.

Organization and Growth Today the EOP consists of the White House Office and several specialized agencies that all report directly to the president. Agency staffs include attorneys, scientists,

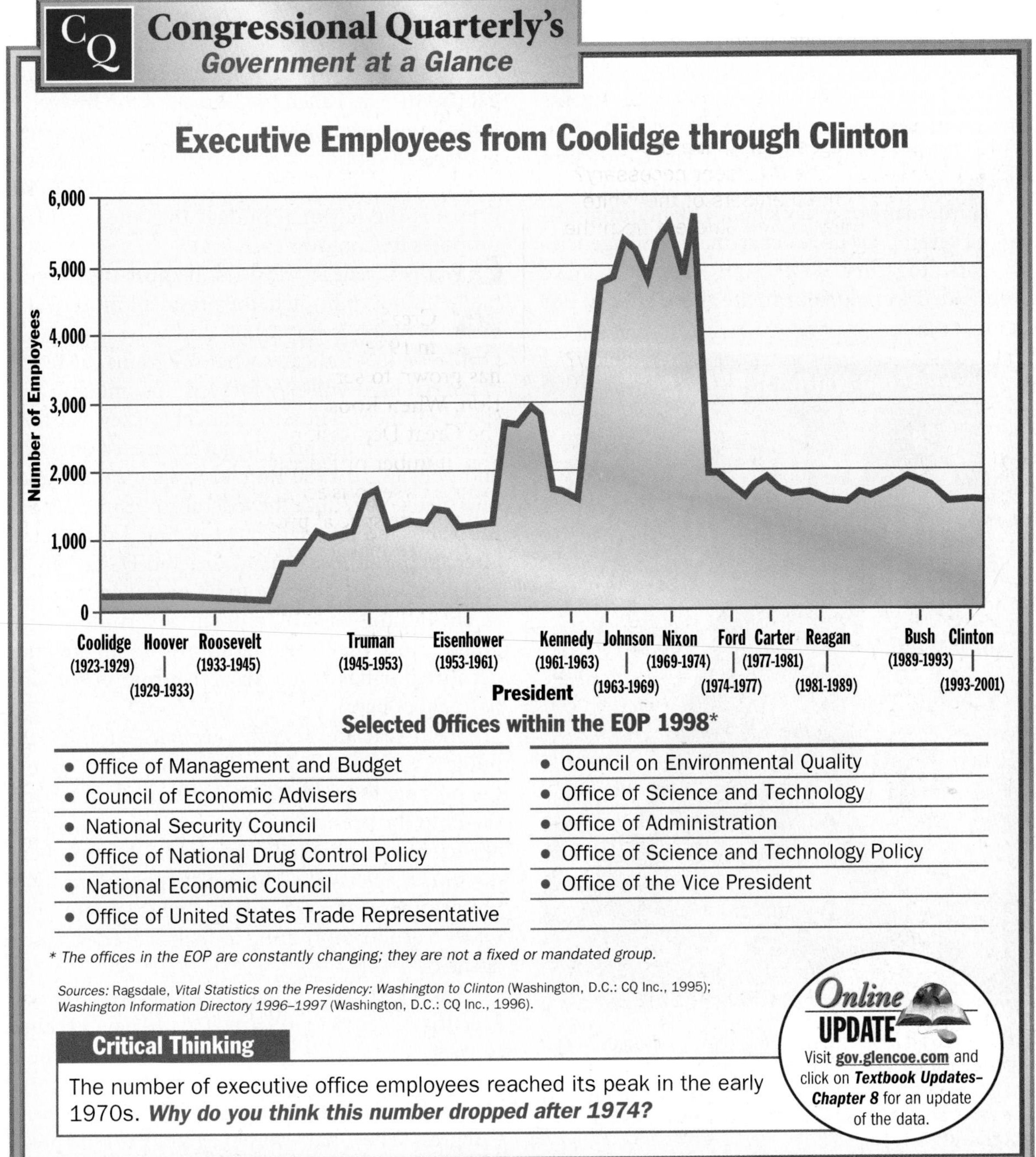

social scientists, and other highly technical or professional personnel. The EOP currently has more than 1,500 full-time employees, many of whom work in the west wing of the White House.

The Executive Office of the President has grown rapidly for three reasons. First, every president has reorganized it, adding new agencies or expanding existing ones in response to the problems of the day. For example, after an American-sponsored invasion of Cuba failed in 1961, President Kennedy enlarged the National Security Council staff.

Second, because some problems facing the nation's industrial society are so complex, presidents have wanted experts available to advise them about issues related to those problems. The Council of Economic Advisers was created for this reason.

Third, many of today's huge federal programs require several executive departments and agencies to work together. EOP staff members have been added to help coordinate these efforts. For example, President Bush created the Office of National Drug Control Policy in 1989. This department coordinated the activities of more than 50 federal agencies involved in the war on drugs.

The three oldest agencies in the EOP have played the greatest role in presidential decision making. They are the Office of Management and Budget, the National Security Council, and the Council of Economic Advisers.

Preparing the National Budget

Budget Priorities Under OMB director Franklin Raines, the 1998 budget ran a surplus. Prior to this, the last balanced budget was in 1969. ***How does the federal budget reflect the administration's priorities?***

The Office of Management and Budget

Before 1970 the **Office of Management and Budget (OMB)** was called the Bureau of the Budget. It is the largest agency in the EOP. Its director, usually a trusted supporter of the president, has become as important as the cabinet secretaries. The OMB prepares the national budget that the president proposes to Congress each year.

Budgets reflect priorities. Because the nation's budget is not unlimited, the president must decide what spending is important and what is not. The OMB's budget indicates what programs the federal government will pay for and how much it will spend on them. Thus, the budget is a key way for a president to influence the government's direction and policies. In 1980 Ronald Reagan campaigned on a pledge to reduce the federal government's role in society and trim federal spending. Immediately after taking office, Reagan ordered David Stockman, his budget director, to prepare detailed plans to cut billions of dollars from government programs. Since the Reagan administration, the budget director has taken an active role in shaping national policy.

Each year all executive agencies submit their budgets to the OMB for review before they go into the president's budget. OMB officials then recommend to the president where to make cuts in each agency budget. To challenge an OMB recommendation, an agency director must appeal directly to the president or a top adviser. This system gives OMB real and continuing influence over executive agencies.

The OMB also reviews all legislative proposals executive agencies prepare. This review is called central clearance. If, for example, the Department of Agriculture drafts a bill on farm price supports, OMB officials will review the bill before it goes to Congress. They make sure it agrees with the president's policy objectives.

The National Security Council Congress created the **National Security Council (NSC)** in 1947 to advise the president and help coordinate American military and foreign policy. Headed by the president, the council also includes the vice president, secretary of state, and secretary of defense. The president may ask other advisers, such as the CIA director or the chairman of the Joint Chiefs of Staff, to participate in NSC meetings.

A special assistant for national security affairs, commonly called the **national security adviser,** directs the NSC staff. Perhaps more than most other advisory groups, the importance of the NSC has varied with the president's use of it. Truman did little with the NSC. Eisenhower held frequent NSC meetings, but he relied more on the advice of his secretary of state, John Foster Dulles, when making key foreign-policy decisions. Under Kennedy the NSC assumed more importance in presidential decision making. Although he did not call many formal NSC meetings, Kennedy relied heavily on his national security adviser.

During President Nixon's first term from 1969 to 1973, National Security Adviser Henry Kissinger and his staff had a great deal of authority. Working closely with Nixon, Kissinger developed the NSC into a kind of alternate State Department in the White House. In 1973 he negotiated the end of the Vietnam War. He negotiated the opening of diplomatic relations with China, an event that then-Secretary of State William Rogers did not learn of until he saw the news on television. Kissinger also coordinated arms-control talks with the Soviet Union. Rogers finally resigned.

President Carter experienced similar overlap in the activities of his national security adviser and his secretary of state. The governments of other nations complained about the confusion this situation created and asked whether the NSC or the State Department spoke for the United States in foreign-policy matters.

During the Reagan administration, the NSC staff conducted a secret operation to sell arms to Iran in exchange for the release of United States hostages. Profits from the arms sales were diverted to Nicaragua to contras, who were fighting the socialist government. The resulting congressional investigation into the Iran-contra affair decreased the power of the NSC to conduct foreign policy.

The National Security Adviser

Checks and Balances Henry Kissinger (right), Nixon's most influential foreign policy adviser, won the 1973 Nobel Peace Prize with Le Duc Tho, the North Vietnamese negotiator, for negotiating a cease-fire in the Vietnam War. Fighting went on, though, until 1975. ***How did Nixon's reliance on Kissinger affect the secretary of state?***

The Council of Economic Advisers Since the Great Depression, the president has been the nation's chief economic planner. Created in 1946, the Council of Economic Advisers helps the president formulate the nation's economic policy. Janet Yellen, named chair of the Council in 1997, had a staff of about 60 other economists, attorneys, and political scientists.

The Council assesses the nation's economic health, predicts future economic conditions, and aids other executive agencies involved with economic planning. It also proposes solutions to specific problems, such as unemployment or inflation. To carry out these functions, it has access to information any federal department gathers having to do with American economic activity. The Council also helps prepare an annual report that is included in the *Economic Report of the President* and transmitted to Congress.

Presenting the President's Views to the World

Press Secretary President Clinton's press secretary, Mike McCurry, answers reporters' questions. The press secretary meets regularly with the media to keep the public informed of the president's views and decisions. ***What other officers are top assistants to a president?***

Other EOP Agencies The number and size of EOP agencies varies from administration to administration, according to the policies each president thinks are important. For example, President Johnson set up an Office of Economic Opportunity to help implement his domestic programs. President Nixon, however, opposed some of Johnson's social policies and eliminated the agency.

Recently the EOP included the following executive agencies in addition to the four agencies already noted: The Domestic Policy Council helps the president plan and carry out long-range policies in domestic areas such as farming and energy. The National Economic Council helps the president carry out long-range economic policy. The Office of Environmental Policy advises the president on environmental issues and policies. It works closely with the Environmental Protection Agency and the departments of Interior, Agriculture, and Energy. The Office of Science and Technology Policy advises the president on all scientific and technological matters that affect national policies and programs. The National Science and Technology Council advises the president about research and development, including the space program. The Office of the United States Trade Representative helps establish United States trade policy and helps negotiate trade agreements with other nations. The Office of Administration provides support services such as data processing and clerical help for the other EOP agencies.

The White House Office

The nation's first presidents had no personal staff. George Washington hired his nephew at his own expense to be his personal secretary. When James Polk was president from 1845 to 1849, his wife Sarah served as his secretary. During the 1890s both presidents Cleveland and McKinley personally answered the White House telephone. As late as the 1920s, Herbert Hoover's personal staff consisted of a few secretaries, several administrative assistants, and a cook.

In its 1937 study of the executive branch, the President's Committee on Administrative Management concluded:

> “*The President needs help. His immediate staff assistance is entirely inadequate. He should be given a small number of executive assistants who would be his direct aides in dealing with the managerial agencies and administrative departments.*”
>
> —The President's Committee on Administrative Management, 1937

Organization and Growth Unlike the selection of cabinet members, the president appoints White House staff without Senate confirmation. Key aides usually are longtime personal supporters of the president. Many are newcomers to Washington. They do not usually have large constituencies, as do some cabinet officers.

The White House Office has become the most important part of the Executive Office of the President. From about 50 people under Roosevelt, the White House staff grew to almost 600 under Nixon. Clinton's White House Office consisted of about 380 people, a small number of whom reported directly to the president. These top assistants became an inner circle around the president. Chief among them were the president's chief of staff, deputy chief of staff, White House counsel, and press secretary.

Duties of the White House Staff White House aides perform whatever duties the president assigns them. Because of the role they perform, some aides become very influential. One former presidential adviser confided to an interviewer, "I had more power over national affairs in a few years in the White House than I could if I spent the rest of my life in the Senate."

One task of the White House Office is to gather information and provide advice about key issues facing the president. Some staffers are policy specialists in specific areas such as foreign affairs or energy problems. Others are political strategists, mainly concerned with the political impact of policy decisions the president makes. The White House counsel advises the president on the legal consequences of those decisions.

Top staff members also act as enforcers, trying to make sure the executive agencies and departments carry out key directives from the president. Bill Moyers, press secretary to President Johnson, explained, "The job of the White House assistant is to help the president impress his priorities on the Administration."

Other key White House staffers present the president's views to the outside world. A press staff headed by the press secretary handles the president's relations with the White House press corps, sets up press conferences, and issues public statements in the president's name. Other staff people work directly with members of Congress. The chief assistant for legislative affairs, for example, advises the president about possible reactions in Congress to White House decisions. These staff members also lobby the lawmakers to gain support for presidential programs.

The executive departments and agencies write the president thousands of reports and memos. In addition, a steady stream of people from inside and outside the government want to see the president. Key aides decide who and what gets through to the president.

Recent presidents have given their top White House staff increased authority over actual policymaking. As a result, more and more policy decisions are being made in the White House rather than in federal agencies.

Section 4 Assessment

Checking for Understanding

1. **Main Idea** Use a Venn diagram to show how the functions of the White House Office and the cabinet are alike and how they are different.

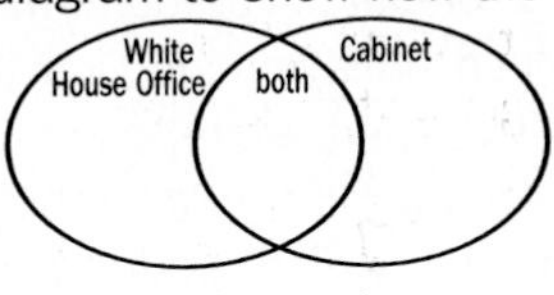

2. **Define** central clearance, national security adviser, press secretary.
3. **Identify** EOP, OMB, NSC.
4. List three reasons why the EOP has grown.
5. What are the three oldest agencies in the EOP, and what roles do they play?

Critical Thinking

6. **Synthesizing Information** How does the influence of key presidential aides affect the checks and balances established by the Constitution?

Concepts IN ACTION

Political Processes Find out who the following presidential advisers are: chief of staff, deputy chief of staff, White House counsel, and press secretary. Research the background of each adviser and present your findings in a chart.

Congressional Quarterly's

Presidency A to Z

Presidential Leadership *Presidents attend historical and artistic exhibits, ethnic festivals, and other symbolic or ceremonial events where they can display their interest in American life, reinforce their image as an average person, promote a cause in which they believe, or represent the nation.*

Ceremonies and Public Appearances

Out of the many types of events they attend, presidents have been especially fond of sporting contests. President William Howard Taft threw out the first baseball of the 1910 major league season on April 14 in Washington, D.C., and most presidents since then have observed the tradition. President Kennedy wanted to make such a good appearance at the event that he secretly practiced his throwing on the White House grounds. Since the Washington Senators baseball franchise moved to Texas in 1971, presidents who have wished to throw out the first baseball have had to travel to nearby Baltimore or other cities.

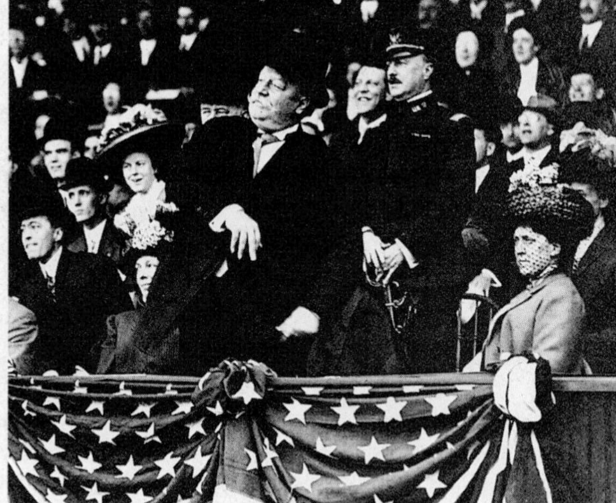

President Taft tosses the first baseball of the season in 1910.

Renowned opera singer Marian Anderson

Presidential Medal of Freedom

Presidents bestow a variety of official awards, the most prominent of which is the Presidential Medal of Freedom, the nation's highest award for civilian achievement. Only the president can award the lustrous red, white, and blue enameled medal, which recognizes significant contributions to American life, the nation's security, or world peace. Recreated by President John F. Kennedy in 1963, the medal remains a rare and highly coveted honor today. Among past winners are singer Marian Anderson, astronaut Neil Armstrong, labor leader César Chávez, anthropologist Margaret Mead, writer E.B. White, and baseball great Jackie Robinson.

National Mourner

When a prominent American dies, the president is expected to lead the nation in mourning. The White House issues statements eulogizing well-known Americans who have died, but presidential attendance at funerals is generally reserved for former presidents, high government officials, or people who had a close personal or political relationship with the president. On April 27, 1994, President Bill Clinton and First Lady Hillary Rodham Clinton attended former president Richard Nixon's funeral. Also attending were all four living former presidents and their wives: George and Barbara Bush, Ronald and Nancy Reagan, Jimmy and Rosalynn Carter, and Gerald and Betty Ford.

Former presidents and their wives honor Nixon at his funeral.

Ceremonial Signing

At times, even the signing of a bill can become a symbolic occasion. On February 8, 1996, President Bill Clinton signed the Telecommunications Act of 1996 at the Library of Congress – and became the first president to sign a bill into law in cyberspace. Lawmakers from both parties hailed the act as a great leap forward, one that cleared out restrictions hindering U.S. companies in the information age. The event featured a high-tech electronic pen for "signing" the bill on the Internet and an appearance by actress Lily Tomlin playing her well-known character, telephone operator Ernestine. Citizens could watch the ceremony unfold in real time over the Internet.

Al Gore looks on as President Clinton signs a bill to revolutionize the way Americans get telephone and computer services.

Assessment and Activities

Self-Check Quiz Visit the *United States Government: Democracy in Action* Web site at gov.glencoe.com and click on ***Chapter 8–Self-Check Quizzes*** to prepare for the chapter test.

Reviewing Key Terms

Define each of the following terms and use it in a sentence that is appropriate to its meaning.

compensation
presidential succession
electoral vote
elector
cabinet
leak
central clearance
national security adviser
press secretary

Recalling Facts

1. List four special benefits that the president receives while in office.
2. How does the winner-take-all system of the Electoral College operate?
3. What is the process by which cabinet members are selected and appointed?
4. Why has the Executive Office of the President grown?
5. What are the two major functions of the Office of Management and Budget?
6. What are the four key positions on the White House Office staff?

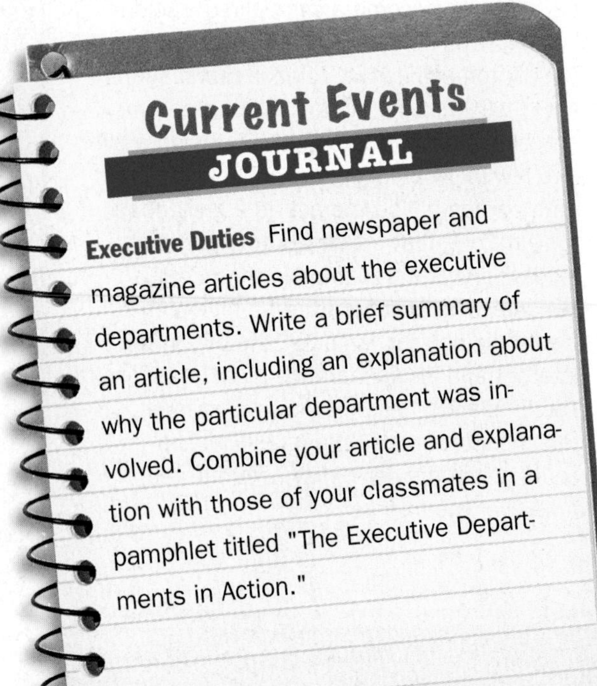

Understanding Concepts

1. **Growth of Democracy** Why do some people criticize plans for the direct popular election of the president?
2. **Constitutional Interpretations** The youngest elected president was John Kennedy at 43. Why do you think the Framers of the Constitution in 1787 set the minimum age for president at 35?
3. **Political Processes** Unlike heads of executive departments, White House staff members are not required to receive congressional approval. What are the advantages and disadvantages of this policy?

Critical Thinking

1. **Drawing Conclusions** Candidates for president are not usually drawn to the office because of the salary. Why do you think these people run for the office?
2. **Identifying Alternatives** Use a graphic organizer like the one below to rank the proposals for reforming the Electoral College system from most to least desirable. Explain your rankings.

proposals	reasons
1.	
2.	
3.	

3. **Synthesizing Information** Will a president who relies on the cabinet for advice be more or less informed than one who depends on close White House advisers? Explain your answer.

Chapter 8

Cooperative Learning Activity

Making a Policy Decision Work together in small groups to research the duties of key members of the White House staff such as chief of staff, deputy chief of staff, White House counsel, and press secretary. Then have each group role-play before the class how each position might be involved in a critical policy decision.

Interpreting Political Cartoons Activity

1. What does the father think is the most important requirement to become president?
2. Does the cartoon make reference to any of the formal qualifications for the office of the president?
3. Do you agree with the statement made in the cartoon? Why or why not?

"This is America, son, where anybody with twenty million bucks to spend could end up being President."

Skill Practice Activity

Interpreting an Election Map Examine the map below and answer the following questions:

1. What does the color blue indicate on this map?
2. How does the map show which states voted for Republican Richard Nixon?
3. Where was the American Independent Party strong?
4. How would you describe the regional distribution of votes in this election?
5. Compare this map with the map of the 1960 election on page 233. Which states that voted Republican in 1960 voted Democratic in 1968?

Electoral Votes 1968 Election

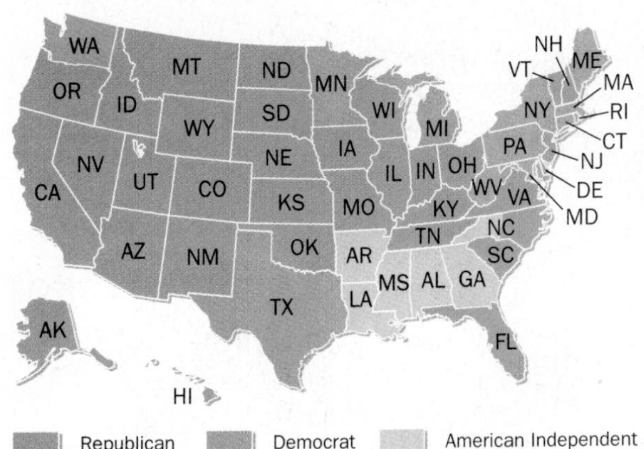

Technology Activity

Using the Internet The White House has its own Web site on the Internet. Find information about current activities or events that are taking place at the White House by accessing this site. Using a word processor, summarize the information you find and format it into a "press release."

Participating in State Government

Contact your state government offices to find out the following information:

- How are the Democratic and Republican electors chosen in your state?
- How and where do the electors cast their ballots for president?

Organize the data chronologically and present your findings in a flowchart or informational brochure.

Chapter 9

Presidential Leadership

Why It's Important

Big Decisions The president of the United States is the most powerful person on earth. The president can determine where our armed forces are sent and who gets pardoned from federal crimes. Presidential appointments in the executive and judicial branches affect our lives every day.

To learn more about how the president makes important decisions and leads our nation, view the ***Democracy in Action*** Chapter 9 video lesson:

Presidential Leadership

GOVERNMENT Online

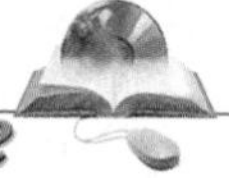

Chapter Overview Visit the *United States Government: Democracy in Action* Web site at gov.glencoe.com and click on ***Chapter 9–Overview*** to preview chapter information.

Presidential Powers

Reader's Guide

Key Terms
mandate, forum

Find Out
- Why do presidential powers tend to grow in times of national emergency?
- What are the sources of and limits to the powers of the president?

Understanding Concepts
Constitutional Interpretations Within the scope of constitutional limitations and powers, why does each president define the office differently?

COVER STORY

Clinton Punishes Senator

WASHINGTON, D.C., MARCH 1993

Democratic senator Richard Shelby of Alabama has learned the cost of refusing a presidential request. President Bill Clinton had asked Democratic legislators to exercise restraint in criticizing his new economic plan. Instead, Shelby blasted the president's proposal and embarrassed Vice President Al Gore on national television. Clinton then moved a $375 million space program, and some 90 jobs, from Huntsville, Alabama, to Houston, Texas. When the White House later honored the University of Alabama's national champion football team, Clinton gave Alabama's other senator 15 free game tickets. Shelby, however, got just one.

A political football

Many presidential powers are not specifically mentioned in the Constitution. They have developed over time, reflecting the changing needs of the nation and personalities of the presidents. The Founders crafted the office with caution, relying on their understanding of human nature and their experience with kings and colonial governors. They also realized that the executive office would reflect the personal characteristics of the person chosen to serve.

The sources and limitations of presidential power have interacted throughout the nation's history. The presidency may have been defined by the Constitution; however, the immediate needs of the nation, the personal energy and influence of each president, and the **mandate,** or expressed will of the people, have shaped the office of the presidency into its modern form.

Constitutional Powers

The Founders made the president the head of the executive branch of the new national government. Having revolted against the hated king of England, the Founders certainly did not want to create their own king. At the same time, and for two major reasons, they did want a national government with a strong executive.

Need for a Strong Executive First, the Founders knew that one of the main weaknesses of the Articles of Confederation was its lack of an independent executive. Without an executive the government had no one to carry out the acts of Congress. Moreover, this lack made it difficult for the government to respond quickly to problems and to enforce laws.

Second, many of the Founders distrusted direct participation by the people in decision making. The Founders feared that mass democratic movements might try to redistribute personal wealth and threaten private property.

◀ President Reagan and Prime Minister Nakasone

Consequently, they wanted a strong executive branch that would protect liberty, private property, and businesses and would hold the legislative branch, which the people could influence, in check.

Presidential Powers in Article II Article II of the Constitution grants the president broad but vaguely described powers, simply stating that "The Executive Power shall be vested in a President of the United States of America."

Sections 2 and 3 of Article II define the president's powers.[1] As commander in chief of the armed forces, the president is mainly responsible for the nation's security. As head of the executive branch, the president appoints—with Senate consent—heads of executive departments. The Chief Executive also conducts foreign policy, making treaties with the advice and consent of the Senate and appointing ambassadors. The president also has judicial powers—to appoint federal court judges, to pardon people convicted of federal crimes except in cases of impeachment, or to reduce a person's jail sentence or fine. Working with

See the following footnoted materials in the **Reference Handbook:**
1. *The Constitution,* pages 774–799.

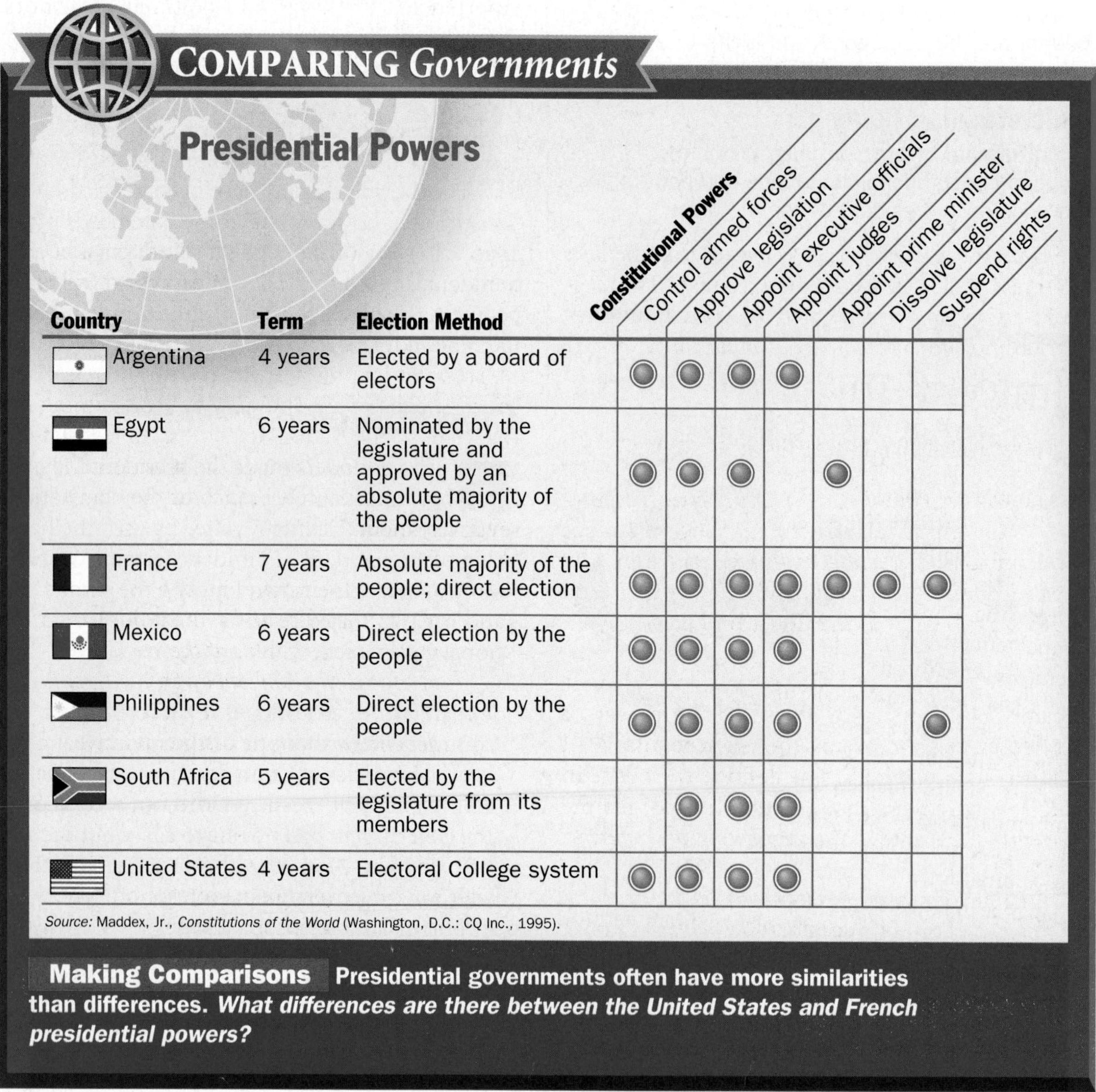

COMPARING *Governments*

Presidential Powers

Country	Term	Election Method	Control armed forces	Approve legislation	Appoint executive officials	Appoint judges	Appoint prime minister	Dissolve legislature	Suspend rights
Argentina	4 years	Elected by a board of electors	●	●	●	●			
Egypt	6 years	Nominated by the legislature and approved by an absolute majority of the people	●	●	●		●		
France	7 years	Absolute majority of the people; direct election	●	●	●	●	●	●	●
Mexico	6 years	Direct election by the people	●	●	●	●			
Philippines	6 years	Direct election by the people	●	●	●	●			●
South Africa	5 years	Elected by the legislature from its members		●	●	●			
United States	4 years	Electoral College system	●	●	●	●			

(Column group heading: **Constitutional Powers**)

Source: Maddex, Jr., *Constitutions of the World* (Washington, D.C.: CQ Inc., 1995).

Making Comparisons Presidential governments often have more similarities than differences. ***What differences are there between the United States and French presidential powers?***

Presidential Decisions

Leadership Style This Currier and Ives lithograph shows the shelling of Fort Sumter in 1861. By sending ships to resupply the federal fort in Charleston harbor, President Lincoln forced the South Carolina militia to take action, thus beginning the Civil War. ***How did Lincoln's actions reveal his view of presidential power?***

the legislature, the president ensures that the laws Congress passes are "faithfully executed." The president delivers an annual State of the Union message to Congress, proposes legislation, and may call Congress into special session when necessary.

Informal Sources of Power

The Constitution's list of presidential powers is brief and simple. Yet, since Washington's time, the president's powers have greatly expanded. Today these powers come from several sources in addition to the Constitution.

Personal Exercise of Power Over the years several presidents have added to the power of the presidency simply by the way they handled the job. Each president has defined the office in unique ways. Several presidents have enlarged the powers of the presidency by their view and exercise of power.

In 1803 Thomas Jefferson made the decision to purchase the Louisiana Territory from France. Nothing in the Constitution, however, stated that a president had the power to acquire territory. Jefferson decided that the presidency had inherent powers, or powers attached to the office itself. These were powers the Constitution did not specifically define but that Article II implied. The Senate agreed with Jefferson and ratified the Louisiana Purchase treaty.

Theodore Roosevelt expressed the broad view of presidential power, explaining that it was both the president's right and duty to "do anything that the needs of the Nation demanded, unless such action was forbidden by the Constitution or by the laws." In a letter to a contemporary historian, Roosevelt explained:

> "*I have used every ounce of power there was in the office and I have not cared a rap for the criticisms of those who spoke of my 'usurpation' of power; . . . I believe that the efficiency of this Government depends upon its possessing a strong central executive. . . .*"
>
> —Theodore Roosevelt, 1908

Immediate Needs of the Nation During the Civil War Abraham Lincoln took action that caused people to call him a dictator. He suspended the writ of habeas corpus and jailed opponents of the Union without a trial or legal authority to do so. He raised an army before getting Congress's approval. He took illegal action against the South by blockading its ports. Lincoln claimed the Constitution gave him the authority to do what was necessary to preserve the Union. In the end, the nation agreed with the president.

Franklin D. Roosevelt used the power of the presidency to expand the role of the federal government in the nation's economy. At a time of severe economic depression, Roosevelt persuaded Congress to create many new social and economic programs and to set up new federal agencies to run them. When Roosevelt became president in 1933, about 600,000 people worked in the federal government. By the time he died in 1945, more than 3 million workers were serving in the federal government.

After Roosevelt's administration, Americans came to expect the president to take a firm hand in directing the nation's economic as well as political life. Today people often measure a president's use of executive power against Roosevelt's. Most modern presidents have tried to act as strong leaders and have taken a broad view of presidential power.

Members of Congress sometimes complain about presidents having too much power. Yet Congress has often granted a president special powers, especially during emergencies. In 1964, for example, President Lyndon Johnson reported that two American destroyers had been attacked in the Gulf of Tonkin. To enable the president to cope with the situation in Vietnam, Congress passed the Gulf of Tonkin Resolution overwhelmingly on August 7, 1964. This resolution gave the president authority to "take all necessary steps, including the use of armed force" to protect Americans in Southeast Asia. Johnson used the powers this resolution granted to enlarge the war in Vietnam as well as other parts of Southeast Asia.

Mandate of the People All presidents like to claim that their ideas and policies represent a mandate from the people. A **mandate**—strong popular support—is one of the greatest sources of power for a president. However, the president's popularity ratings change almost daily. Most modern presidents, therefore, have learned to use the media to communicate their message to the people and gain popular support.

Presidents use all forms of mass media—radio, television, magazines, newspapers, and the White House Web site on the Internet. Franklin D. Roosevelt was the first president to realize that radio had great potential for political use. Roosevelt broadcast "fireside chats" to the American people on the radio. He talked informally about the nation's problems and his proposed solutions for them.

The President and the People

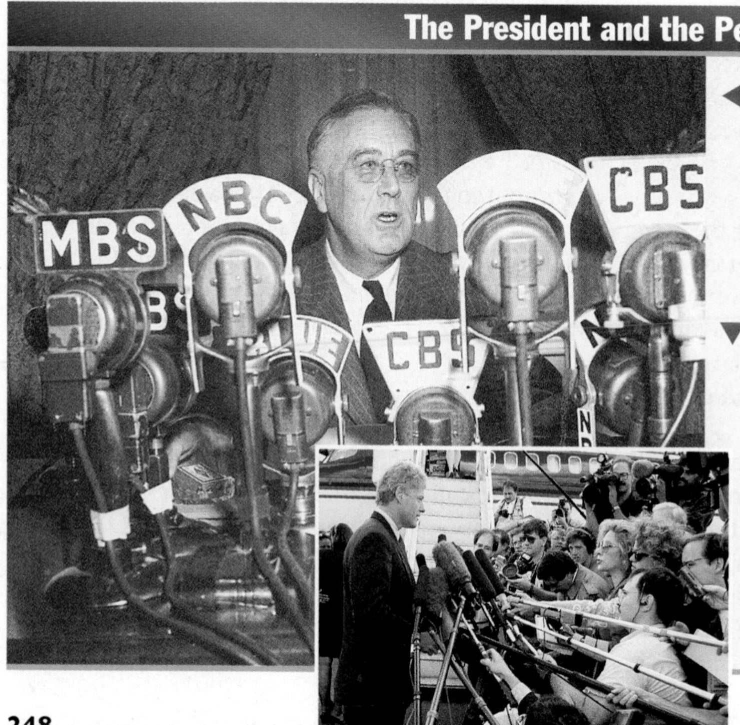

◀ **Past** President Franklin D. Roosevelt exhibited a friendly informality that made Americans feel personally connected to the president. Here FDR speaks to millions of Americans in one of his frequent radio addresses known as fireside chats.

▼ **Present** Presidents hold televised news conferences to communicate their ideas to Americans and maintain the public's support of the presidency and its policies.

Perceptions of the Presidency
What repercussions might arise for a president who does not maintain a good relationship with the media?

Today, television gives presidents even greater power to convey their ideas and personalities directly to the American people. The media called President Ronald Reagan "the Great Communicator" partly because of his ability to deliver his message directly to the people through television. People often judge a president's ideas according to the personal appeal of the president on television, a fact presidents know very well and try to use to their advantage.

Major newspapers and magazines also provide a **forum,** or medium for discussion, for presidential messages. These media, in addition to television and radio networks, assign reporters to cover the president full time. White House staff members make sure the reporters receive a steady flow of information about the president's activities and ideas. One of the staff's objectives is to create the image of a president as an active, personable servant of the people.

Checks and Balances Congress, believing that American involvement in the Vietnam War was an abuse of presidential power, passed the War Powers Act in 1973 over a presidential veto. ***How was the War Powers Act an example of the concept of checks and balances?***

Limits on Presidential Power

The Founders built significant safeguards against the abuse of presidential power into the Constitution. Both Congress and the courts have powers that limit the president's authority. Other factors, not mentioned in the Constitution, also affect the president's actions.

Limitation by Congress The Constitution gives Congress the power to pass legislation over a president's veto. A **congressional override** of a veto may limit a president's effectiveness in carrying out a legislative program or in using executive powers. In 1973 Congress overrode President Nixon's veto of the **War Powers Act** that prevented presidents from committing troops to combat for more than 60 days without congressional approval. Congress felt that Nixon and previous presidents had abused their power as commander in chief. They had done so by involving American soldiers for prolonged periods in an undeclared war in Vietnam.

Other important limitations include the Senate's confirmation power, the power of the purse, and the power to impeach a president. Historically, impeachment proceedings have been initiated against three presidents. The House of Representatives impeached President Andrew Johnson in 1868, but the Senate acquitted him by a margin of one vote. President Richard Nixon resigned in 1974 before the impeachment charges could be brought to the full House. After a short trial in February 1999, the Senate acquitted President Bill Clinton on the two charges that had been brought by the House.

Limitation by the Federal Courts The federal courts have a constitutional power to limit a president. The case of *Marbury* v. *Madison*[1] (1803) established the Supreme Court's right to review legislative actions. During the Great Depression, the Supreme Court ruled some of President Franklin D. Roosevelt's New Deal legislation unconstitutional.

See the following footnoted materials in the **Reference Handbook:**
1. *Marbury* v. *Madison*, page 761.

Landmark Cases

Youngstown Sheet and Tube Company v. Sawyer Does the president have authority to act in areas of authority delegated to Congress if Congress fails to act? Historically, a president's action in such cases was not challenged until Congress passed legislation assuming its authority.

In 1952 President Truman, believing a strike by steelworkers could threaten national security, ordered his secretary of commerce to seize and operate most of the nation's steel mills. The president reported these events to Congress, but Congress failed to take action. Congress had provided procedures for dealing with similar situations in earlier cases.

Opposing the takeover, the steel mill owners sued Secretary Sawyer, and the case eventually reached the Supreme Court. Justice Black, speaking for the majority, said that there was no statute which authorized the president to take possession of the mills. The fact that Congress had not exercised its powers to seize the mills did not mean that the president could do so. He concluded, "The Founders of this Nation entrusted the lawmaking power to the Congress alone in both good and bad times."

Limitation by the Bureaucracy The federal bureaucracy sometimes limits presidential powers. Bureaucrats can obstruct presidents' programs unintentionally by failing to provide needed information, by misinterpreting instructions, and by neglecting to complete a task properly. Bureaucrats have the discretion to interpret as they best see fit. At times their interpretations may not reflect the president's priorities either intentionally or unintentionally.

Limitation by Public Opinion Public opinion can also limit a president. In 1968 public dissatisfaction with President Lyndon Johnson's conduct of the Vietnam War forced him not to run for reelection. Without favorable public opinion, a president cannot succeed in carrying out a political program. One of President Clinton's announced goals in his first administration was to restructure the health-care system. The administration began a major study of health care. Meanwhile, all the interest groups that would be affected began to raise questions. Public opinion eventually derailed the changes.

The American people expect their presidents to be symbolic leaders of the nation. They expect presidents to always act with courage and dignity. If presidents fail to live up to these standards, the nation usually condemns their actions.

The Founders could not build into the Constitution provisions for regulating the moral character of a president. Public opinion, especially through the use of mass media, supports the checks and balances that serve to limit the powers of a president.

Section 1 Assessment

Checking for Understanding

1. **Main Idea** Using a graphic organizer like the one below, list two or more constitutional limits and three other limits on presidential power.

Constitutional limits	Other limits

2. **Define** mandate, forum.
3. **Identify** War Powers Act.
4. In what three ways have former presidents expanded the power of their office?
5. Why, during Lyndon Johnson's presidency, did Congress pass the Gulf of Tonkin Resolution?

Critical Thinking

6. **Distinguishing Fact from Opinion** President Wilson said the president "is at liberty, both in law and conscience . . . to be as big a man as he can." Explain if this statement is fact or opinion.

Constitutional Interpretations Determine if you think there should be greater limits on the president's power. Compose several catchy slogans supporting your view and create signs or buttons that might be used in a rally.

United States v. *United States District Court*, 1972

The Constitution calls upon the president to "preserve, protect and defend the Constitution of the United States." This duty includes protecting the government against subversive actions. Can the president, without a search warrant, order electronic surveillance of people in order to protect against domestic national security dangers? The case of United States v. United States District Court *dealt with this issue.*

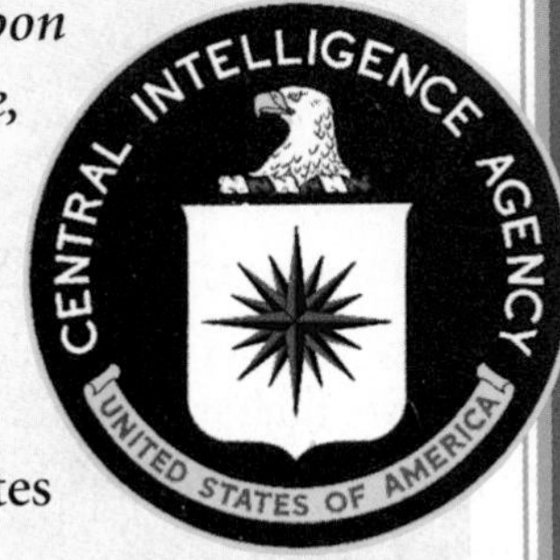

CIA logo

Background of the Case

In the early 1970s several antiwar groups were accused of plotting against the government. President Nixon's administration began using wiretaps, without a search warrant, to monitor citizens whom the administration claimed were engaged in subversive activities. This case arose when a defendant was accused of the dynamite bombing of an office of the Central Intelligence Agency in Ann Arbor, Michigan. The defendant claimed the wiretap evidence used against him had been gathered illegally. The government admitted it had not secured a warrant but claimed the wiretap was lawful under the president's power and duty to protect national security. A United States District Court ruled the evidence was gathered illegally and had to be made available to the defendant before his trial. The attorney general filed suit to set aside the district court's order.

The Constitutional Issue

In reviewing the case the Court said:

> "*Its resolution is a matter of national concern, requiring sensitivity both to the Government's right to protect itself from unlawful subversion and attack and to the citizen's right to be secure in his privacy against unreasonable government intrusion.*"
>
> —Justice Lewis F. Powell, Jr., 1972

The government argued that such surveillance was a reasonable exercise of the president's power to protect domestic security. Further, the government claimed that judges would not have the expertise in such complex situations to determine whether there really was "probable cause." Finally, the government argued that secrecy is essential in domestic security cases; informing a judge in order to get a warrant would create the risk of leaks.

Debating the Case

Questions to Consider

1. Should domestic security cases be handled differently than other types of crimes?
2. What could be the consequences of allowing the wiretapping in such cases without a warrant?
3. Does the government need a search warrant to wiretap in domestic security cases?

You Be the Judge

The Fourth Amendment protects citizens from "unreasonable searches and seizures" by requiring the police to obtain a search warrant from a judge. In order to obtain the search warrant, the police must show "probable cause" for the proposed search. Should the Court make an exception to this warrant requirement, as it has sometimes done in special circumstances? Explain.

Section 2

Roles of the President

Reader's Guide

Key Terms

executive order, impoundment, reprieve, pardon, amnesty, patronage, treaty, executive agreement

Find Out

- How do the presidential roles of head of state, chief diplomat, and commander in chief work together to provide leadership in foreign relations?
- What is the president's role in the growth and stability of the American economy?

Understanding Concepts

Political Processes How have presidents used their political power to increase their policy-making role?

COVER STORY

Nixon Impounds Funds

WASHINGTON, D.C., APRIL 16, 1973

Calling congressional spending wasteful and inflationary, President Nixon has directed cabinet members not to spend moneys appropriated by Congress to fund some government programs he opposes. By executive order, the president has withheld $8.7 billion earmarked for programs he believes are useless. Despite recent court rulings that a president has no power to cut programs mandated by Congress, Nixon claims the right to impound funds because Congress "has not been responsible on money." Congress is considering legislation to block the president's action.

Nixon impounds program funds.

When President Richard Nixon impounded funds, it raised a major issue about the power and duties of a president. What are the roles of the president? There are seven key duties. Five of these duties are based on the Constitution: serving as head of state, chief executive, chief legislator, chief diplomat, and commander in chief. Two of the president's key duties—economic planner and political party leader—are not even implied in the Constitution, but have developed over time.

Head of State

As head of state, the president represents the nation and performs many ceremonial roles. Serving as host to visiting kings, queens, and heads of governments, the president is the nation's chief diplomat. Other ceremonial duties are less vital, but receive much attention. In a tradition that dates back to President Taft, many presidents have thrown out the first ball to begin the major league baseball season. Lighting the national Christmas tree, giving awards and medals, making public service statements on important issues, meeting public figures from musicians to business leaders are all considered a part of the role of president.

The president is both head of state and chief executive. In most countries these two duties are distinct. One person—sometimes a king or queen, sometimes a president without real power—is the ceremonial head of state. Another person—a prime minister or premier—directs the government.

This difference is important. Much of the mystique of the presidency exists because presidents are more than politicians. To millions around the world and to millions at home, the president *is* the United States. As a living symbol of the nation, the president is not just a single individual, but the collective image of the United States.

Chief Executive

As the nation's chief executive, the president sees that the laws of Congress are carried out. These laws range over a great many areas of public concern from Social Security, taxes, housing, flood control, and energy to civil rights, health care, education, and environmental protection.

The executive branch employs more than 2 million people to enforce the many laws and programs Congress establishes.[1] The president is in charge of these employees and the federal departments and agencies for which they work. Of course, no president could directly supervise the daily activities of all these people. At best, presidents can try to influence the way laws are implemented to follow their own philosophy of government.

An Executive Order

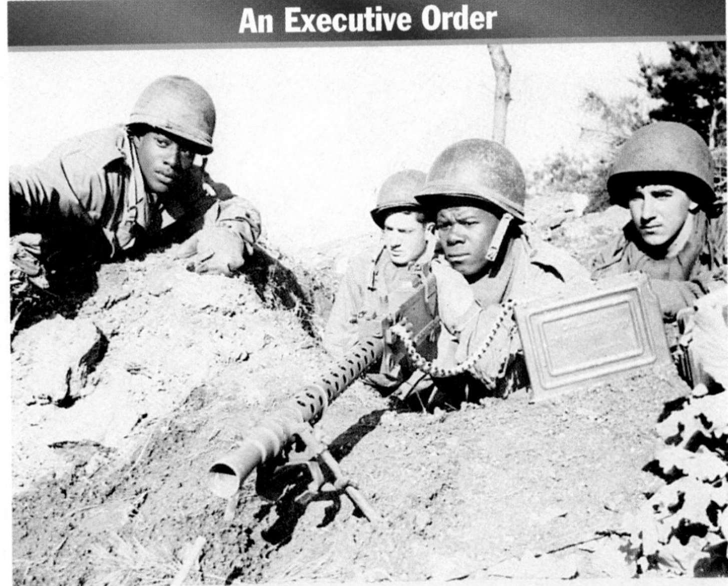

Presidential Power In 1948, by executive order, President Harry S Truman desegregated the armed forces, which affected U.S. troops who later fought in the Korean War. Truman enhanced his presidential powers by taking decisive action without Congress's consent. ***Under which presidential duty does this action fall?***

Tools of Influence Presidents have several tools to influence how laws are carried out. One is **executive orders,** or rules that have the force of law. Presidents issue executive orders to spell out many of the details of policies and programs Congress enacts. For example, President Carter used an executive order to put thousands of acres of land in Alaska under the control of the National Park Service. Carter was exercising power under a law permitting the president to keep certain lands free of commercial development.

Another tool is making presidential appointments. Besides appointing cabinet members, presidents appoint "with the advice and consent of the Senate" about 2,200 top-level federal officials. These officials include agency directors, deputy directors, and their assistants. Presidents try to appoint officials who share their political beliefs because they want these officials to carry out their policies.

A third tool that presidents may use is the right to remove officials they have appointed. President Nixon, for example, fired his secretary of the interior for opposing his conduct of the war in Vietnam. It is not always easy, however, to remove a popular official, who may have congressional and public support. The former director of the FBI, J. Edgar Hoover, was a person with such support. He controlled and directed the FBI for 48 years. Evidence indicates that several presidents had doubts about his capacities and conduct, but Hoover was too popular to fire. Hoover held the office of director of the FBI until his death on May 1, 1972.

A fourth tool, used for a variety of reasons, enables a president to refuse to allow a federal department or agency to spend the money Congress has appropriated for it. This process is known as impoundment of funds. **Impoundment** means that the president puts aside, or refuses to spend, the money Congress has appropriated for a certain purpose. Presidents have practiced impoundment for years. In 1803, for example, President Jefferson did not spend money Congress set aside for new gunboats until less costly designs were found. Most impoundments have been for routine matters. Money is appropriated; the need for spending

See the following footnoted materials in the **Reference Handbook:**
1. For number of employees by department see *United States Data Bank,* pages 827-832.

Presidential Pardon

Reactions to the President Gerald Ford entered the presidency hoping to pull a troubled country together. His pardon of Nixon, though, outraged many Americans who believed the president should be held accountable to the laws of the land. ***Why do you think Ford pardoned Nixon?***

changes. Then the president impounds the money, and Congress agrees.

President Nixon tried to impound funds in the early 1970s to eliminate a number of social programs he did not favor. He impounded huge sums of money—as much as $13 billion in a single year. Groups who stood to benefit from the impounded programs took President Nixon to court in an effort to release the money they had expected to receive. The court ordered the president to spend the appropriated money. Congress passed legislation to prevent such wholesale impounding.

In addition, as chief executive the president appoints, with Senate approval, all federal judges, including the justices of the Supreme Court. Presidents can use this power to influence the course of government. For example, President Clinton appointed Justice Ruth Bader Ginsburg, who generally had more liberal views than the justices appointed by previous Republican administrations.

Reprieves and Pardons As chief executive, the president also can grant "reprieves and pardons for offenses against the United States." A **reprieve** grants a *postponement* of legal punishment. A **pardon** is a *release* from legal punishment. The individuals receiving presidential pardons generally have been convicted of federal crimes. In 1974, however, President Gerald Ford granted "a full, free and absolute pardon unto Richard Nixon" for any crimes the former president might have committed in connection with the Watergate scandal. Nixon had not been indicted or convicted of any crimes at that time.

Amnesty Finally, the president may grant amnesty. **Amnesty** is a group pardon to people for an offense against the government. Amnesty usually applies to military personnel. For example, Presidents Ford and Carter granted amnesty to men who fled the draft during the Vietnam War. Civilians also can be granted amnesty. In the 1890s President Benjamin Harrison granted amnesty to those Mormons who had been accused of practicing polygamy (the practice of having more than one wife at a time) in violation of federal law.

Chief Legislator

Congress expects the executive branch to propose legislation it wishes to see enacted. President Eisenhower once wanted Congress to act on a particular problem he was concerned about. The White House, however, neglected to draft a bill to deal with the situation. A member of Congress scolded the president's staff: "Don't expect us to start from scratch on what you people want. That's not the way we do things here. You draft the bills, and we work them over."

The President's Legislative Program

Usually the president describes a legislative program in the annual State of the Union message to Congress. It calls attention to the president's ideas about how to solve key problems facing the country. A detailed legislative program presented to Congress during the year reflects the president's values and political beliefs.

The president has a large staff to help write legislation. This legislation determines much of what Congress will do each year. The president's office also presents to Congress a suggested budget and an annual economic report.

Taking office after the assassination of President Kennedy, Lyndon B. Johnson called upon Congress to enact Kennedy's programs:

> *I believe in the ability of Congress, despite the divisions of opinions which characterize our nation, to act—to act wisely, to act vigorously, to act speedily when the need arises. The need is here. The need is now.*
>
> —Lyndon B. Johnson, 1963

Congress responded by passing a host of new domestic legislation the administration proposed.

Tools of Presidential Lawmaking

When the president and the majority of Congress are from different political parties, the president must work harder to influence members of Congress to support a particular program. Presidents often meet with senators and representatives to share their views with them, and they appoint several staff members to work closely with Congress on new laws.

Presidents may hand out political favors to get congressional support. They may visit the home state of a member of Congress to support his or her reelection. Or, a president may start a new federal project that will bring money and jobs to a member of Congress's home state or district.

An important presidential tool in lawmaking is the veto power. Each bill Congress passes is sent to the president for approval. The president may sign the bill, veto the bill, or lay it aside. Presidents sometimes use the threat of a veto to force Congress to stop a bill or change it to fit their wishes. The threats succeed because Congress finds it very difficult to gather enough votes to override a veto.

Unlike state governors, the president does not have the power to veto selected items in a bill. Congress did attempt to give the president some power over individual items by the Line Item Veto Act of 1997. President Clinton began to use the new power almost immediately, but the controversial legislation was challenged as soon as it went into effect. While the law survived the intial challenges, the Supreme Court agreed to hear appeals of two cases involving the new veto power in 1998. In *Clinton* v. *City of New York*[1] the Supreme Court struck down the law as unconstitutional.

See the following footnoted materials in the ***Reference Handbook:***
1. *Clinton* v. *City of New York* case summary, page 756.

Presidential Lawmaking

Political Strategy Soon after becoming president, Lyndon Johnson used his 22-year congressional experience and skill as a legislator to persuade Congress to pass his "Great Society" programs. ***How does the cartoonist depict President Johnson's abilities and success as chief legislator?***

Economic Planner

The president's role as chief economic planner has grown rapidly since Franklin D. Roosevelt's New Deal. The Employment Act of 1946 gave new duties to the president. This law directed the president to submit an annual economic report to Congress. The law also created a **Council of Economic Advisers** to study the economy and help prepare the report for the president. In addition, the law declared for the first time that the federal government had the responsibility to promote high employment, production, and purchasing power.

Since 1946 Congress has continued to pass laws giving presidents more power to deal with economic problems. In 1970, for example, Congress gave President Nixon power to control prices and wages. One year later, the president used this power to put a 90-day freeze on all prices, rents, wages, and salaries. The law then expired and was not renewed.

The president also has the duty to prepare the federal budget every year. The president supervises this work and spends many months with budget officials deciding what government programs to support and what programs to cut back. The size of the budget, decisions about the budget deficit, and choices concerning where moneys will be allocated all affect the national economy.

Party Leader

The president's political party expects the chief executive to be a party leader. The president may give speeches to help party members running for office or may attend fund-raising activities to help raise money for the party. The president also selects the party's national chairperson. Often, the president helps plan the party's future election strategies.

Presidents are expected to appoint members of their party to available government jobs. These appointments ensure that supporters will remain committed to a president's programs. Political **patronage**, or appointment to political office, rewards those persons who support the president and the party during an election.

Being a political party leader can be a difficult role for a president. People expect a president, as head of the government, to represent all Americans. Political parties, however, expect presidents

AmeriCorps

Volunteer at work

One way to help society, while earning money to pay for further education or training, is by joining AmeriCorps. AmeriCorps is a federal program that allows young people to earn $4,725 in educational awards in return for a year's service to the nation. Volunteers also receive living allowances, plus health- and child-care services.

In addition to many local projects, AmeriCorps offers two national programs. AmeriCorps-NCCC is a conservation organization for persons ages 18 to 24. Members live at military installations and work in teams on projects lasting one day to six weeks. AmeriCorps-VISTA is a program in which members work individually for other organizations to help them reach more people—by training community volunteers or setting up neighborhood programs, for example. Members live in the communities they serve.

Activity

1. Gather more information about AmeriCorps by writing to the Corporation for National Service at 1201 New York Avenue, NW, Washington, DC 20525, or visit its home page on the Internet.
2. Prepare a report to share your findings with the class.

to provide leadership for their own political party. Sometimes these conflicting roles cause problems. When President Clinton compromised with the Republican Congress to enact legislation in 1996, more liberal members of his own party criticized him. When a president appears to act in a partisan way, however, the media and the public can be critical.

Chief Diplomat

The president directs the foreign policy of the United States, making key decisions about the relations the United States has with other countries in the world. In this role the president is the nation's chief diplomat.

Because Congress also has powers related to foreign policy, there has been a continuing struggle between the president and Congress over who will exercise control of the country's foreign policy. Presidents have an advantage in this struggle because they have access to more information about foreign affairs than do most members of Congress. The administration sometimes classifies this information as secret. The Central Intelligence Agency (CIA), the State Department, the Defense Department, and the National Security Council (NSC) constantly give the president the latest information needed to make key foreign-policy decisions. Skilled presidents use this information to plan and justify actions they want to take. Members of Congress, who lack access to this information, often find it difficult to challenge the president's decisions.

In addition, the ability to take decisive action has greatly added to the power of the presidency in foreign affairs. Unlike Congress, where the individual opinions of 435 representatives and 100 senators must be coordinated, the executive branch is headed by a single person. In a national emergency, the responsibility for action rests with the president.

The Power to Make Treaties As chief diplomat the president has sole power to negotiate and sign **treaties**—formal agreements between the governments of two or more countries. As part of the constitutional system of checks and balances, however, two-thirds of the Senate must approve all treaties before they can go into effect.

The Senate takes its constitutional responsibility about treaties very seriously. Sometimes, the Senate will refuse to approve a treaty. After World War I, the Senate rejected the Treaty of Versailles, the agreement to end the war and to make the United States a member of the League of Nations. More recently, in 1978, only after lengthy debates and strong opposition did the Senate approve two treaties giving eventual control of the Panama Canal to the government of Panama.

The Power to Make Executive Agreements

The president also has the authority to make executive agreements with other countries. **Executive agreements** are pacts between the president and the head of a foreign government. These agreements have the same legal status as treaties, but they do not require Senate consent.

Most executive agreements involve routine matters, but some presidents have used executive agreements to conclude more serious arrangements with other countries. Franklin D. Roosevelt lent American ships to the British in exchange for leases on British military bases. At the time, the British were fighting Nazi Germany, but the United States had not yet entered the war. Roosevelt knew that the strongly isolationist Senate would not ratify a treaty. He therefore negotiated an executive agreement.

Some presidents have kept executive agreements secret. To prevent this, Congress passed a law in 1950 requiring the president to make public all executive agreements signed each year. Some presidents have ignored this law and kept secret those agreements they considered important to national security. In 1969, Congress discovered that several presidents had kept secret many executive agreements giving American military support to South Vietnam, Laos, Thailand, and the Philippines.

Recognition of Foreign Governments As chief diplomat the president decides whether the United States will recognize governments of other countries. This power means the president determines whether the government will acknowledge the legal existence of another government and

GOVERNMENT *Online*

Student Web Activity Visit the *United States Government: Democracy in Action* Web site at gov.glencoe.com and click on ***Chapter 9–Student Web Activities*** for an activity about the roles of the president.

Leading the Armed Forces

◀ **Early President** In this painting attributed to Frederick Kemmelmeyer, President George Washington reviews militia from four states summoned to put down the Whiskey Rebellion in 1794.

Modern President President George Bush had power over the American military operations in Operation Desert Storm. ▼

Presidential Authority Most modern presidents do not directly lead their troops as Washington did. ***How do modern presidents indirectly lead their troops?***

have dealings with that government. Presidents sometimes use recognition as a foreign-policy tool. For example, since 1959, presidents have refused to recognize the Communist government of Cuba. By withholding diplomatic recognition, the United States is indicating its displeasure with the policies of the Cuban government.

Commander in Chief

Presidents can back up their foreign-policy decisions with military force when needed. The Constitution makes the president commander in chief of the armed forces of the United States.

Power to Make War The president shares with Congress the power to make war. President Bush received congressional approval to make war on Iraq before he ordered a massive air strike in January 1991. His actions prevented a serious constitutional question that could have divided the nation if the president had sent troops without congressional approval as he was prepared to do.

Several other presidents have sent American forces into action without a formal declaration of war. For example, Thomas Jefferson used force against the Barbary States of North Africa, and several presidents sent forces into Latin America in the early 1900s. Since 1973, however, no president has officially challenged the constitutionality of the War Powers Act. When President Bush ordered an invasion of Panama to overthrow the dictator Manuel Noriega, he did not seek congressional approval. A constitutional challenge to the War Powers Act did not arise, however, because the operation ended quickly. The issue could become critical in the future if Congress demands withdrawal of troops from an area of actual or threatened combat, and the president refuses to do so.

Military Operations and Strategy Generals, admirals, and other military leaders run the armed forces on a day-to-day basis. The president, however, is responsible for key military decisions. President Washington exercised his constitutional authority over the military in 1794 when defiant whiskey distillers in western Pennsylvania refused to pay the federal tax on their product. Secretary of the Treasury Alexander Hamilton urged the president to take action against the rebels by mobilizing 15,000 state militia. Hamilton himself rode west with the troops; Washington went to Carlisle, Pennsylvania, to inspect them. When the troops arrived in Pittsburgh, there was little opposition to the demonstration of executive strength.

Several presidents have come from a military background. Besides Washington, others have included Andrew Jackson, William H. Harrison, Zachary Taylor, Ulysses S. Grant, Theodore Roosevelt, and Dwight D. Eisenhower.

Some presidents without extensive military experience have had to become involved in military operations. Presidents Johnson and Nixon made the key military decisions in the Vietnam War. President Carter sent a special military force into Iran in 1980 in an effort to free American diplomats who were being held hostage there. In 1991 President Bush decided to give the military more freedom to make strategy decisions when the United States went to war against Iraq. Still, the responsibility for directing overall military strategies remained with the president.

General Eisenhower's military career helped him win the presidency.

As commander in chief, the president has the authority to order the use of atomic weapons, a daunting responsibility. President Nixon said, "I can walk into my office, pick up the telephone, and in twenty minutes 70 million people will be dead."

The president has other duties as commander in chief. During a war the president takes actions at home that will support the war effort. Congress usually grants the president special powers to do this. During World War II, Franklin D. Roosevelt demanded and received from Congress power over price controls, gas and food rationing, and government control of industries needed to produce goods to conduct the war.

The president may also use the military to control serious disorders in the nation. Presidents have used federal troops to put down rioting in American cities. In case of a natural disaster, such as a flood, the president may send needed supplies or troops to help keep order.

The roles as head of state, chief executive, chief legislator, economic planner, party leader, chief diplomat, and commander in chief give the president broad powers. Today, the president of the United States is the most powerful single individual in the world.

Section 2 Assessment

Checking for Understanding

1. **Main Idea** Using a graphic organizer like the one below, describe the different duties of the president's roles as head of state and chief executive.

Head of State	Chief Executive

2. **Define** executive order, impoundment, reprieve, pardon, amnesty, patronage, treaty, executive agreement.
3. **Identify** Council of Economic Advisers.
4. Describe three foreign relations duties of the president that are based on the Constitution.
5. What officials may the president appoint?

Critical Thinking

6. **Understanding Cause and Effect** What decisions by a president affect the direction of the nation's economy?

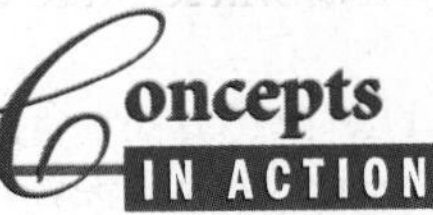

Political Processes Imagine a typical day in the life of a United States president. Prepare an agenda for the president's day. Be sure to keep the seven duties of the president in mind when creating the agenda.

Interpreting Political Cartoons

You have probably heard the saying, "A picture is worth a thousand words." Political cartoonists use pictures to present their opinions about issues.

Learning the Skill

Follow the steps below to interpret the cartoon concerning President Andrew Jackson.

1. Examine the cartoon thoroughly. Read the captions and the labels.
2. Analyze each element in the cartoon. President Jackson is shown dressed as a king holding a "veto." This represents Jackson's liberal use of his veto power to defy the will of Congress. He tramples on the Constitution of the United States, symbolizing the congressional fear that he was trying to impose dictatorial rule.
3. Determine what point the cartoon is making. The cartoonist is comparing the president to a tyrant.

Born to command.

Of veto Memory. **Had I been consulted.**

King Andrew the First.

Practicing the Skill

The cartoon below was published in 1973. It concerns President Richard Nixon's foreign policy. Answer these questions.

1. What is going on in this cartoon?
2. What point is the cartoonist making?
3. Is this a favorable or unfavorable view of the president?

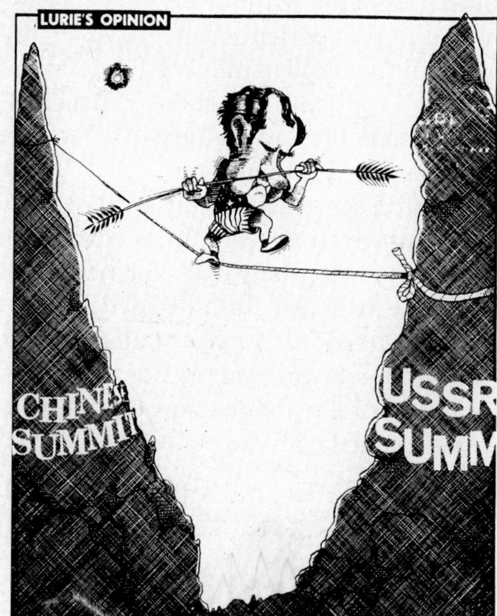

Application Activity

Bring to class a copy of a political cartoon from a recent newspaper or magazine. Explain the cartoonist's viewpoint and the tools used to make the point.

The Glencoe Skillbuilder Interactive Workbook, Level 2 provides instruction and practice in key social studies skills.

Section 3

Styles of Leadership

Reader's Guide

Key Terms

de facto, covert

Find Out

- Why are communication skills so important to being an effective president?
- What leadership quality do you think is most important to the success of a president? Explain why.

Understanding Concepts

Cultural Pluralism Why is it important for the president to be accessible to all of the diverse groups in the country?

COVER STORY

President Promises Aid

GRAND FORKS, NORTH DAKOTA, APRIL 23, 1997

Surveying the damage, a shaken President Bill Clinton promised the people of Grand Forks nearly $500 million to rebuild their city, destroyed by a record flood and fire. "This is not an ordinary disaster, if there is such a thing," the president said. "I've never seen a community this inundated." The entire city, including the downtown business district, was destroyed, leaving some 50,000 people homeless. The president's pledge of aid is more than twice his original request before visiting the scene. "The people here are giving 100 percent, and we should, too," Clinton said. Congress is expected to approve the president's plan.

The Coast Guard assisted Grand Forks.

Every president has a unique style of leadership. In the summer of 1981 President Ronald Reagan and his assistants had prepared complex legislation to cut federal taxes. One day the president's secretary of the treasury, Donald Regan, was working out details of the tax bill with key congressional leaders. At one point the president stopped by to see how things were going. "Would you like to join us?" the secretary asked with a smile. "Heck, no," the president replied, "I'm going to leave this to you experts. I'm not going to get involved in details."

Reagan's response illustrated one aspect of his leadership style. He focused on what his aides called the "big picture." He let others in the cabinet, the EOP, and the White House Office work out the details of his policies. President Carter, Reagan's predecessor, took a different approach. He spent many hours studying the complex details of policies and often became directly involved with his assistants in handling those details. Both presidents had the same tools of power available to them. Each chose to use those tools differently in exercising their leadership responsibilities.

Increased Responsibilities

When they wrote the Constitution, the Founders anticipated that Congress, not the president, would lead the nation. At best, the president was to be the nation's chief administrator and, in time of war, its commander in chief. Instead, over the years the powers and duties of the president have grown steadily. Today the president has the main responsibility for national leadership. Public opinion surveys clearly show that Americans look to the president to exercise strong leadership, to keep the peace, and to solve economic and social problems.

Sometimes presidents demonstrate leadership by introducing bold new ideas. President Truman did this in 1948 when he announced measures to end discrimination against

Styles of Presidential Leadership

Present President Clinton worked closely with key Republican leaders such as House Speaker Newt Gingrich to build consensus across party lines to pass key legislation. ▶

Past President Lyndon Johnson's leadership, called the "Johnson Treatment," involved flattering, cajoling, and threatening others to persuade them. Here Johnson discusses strategy with adviser Abe Fortas. ▶

Presidential Relationships
Which president's leadership style do you think is most effective? Explain.

African Americans. More often, however, presidents demonstrate leadership by responding to crises, problems, or opportunities as they occur. President Nixon took advantage of tensions between the Soviet Union and China to open diplomatic relations between the People's Republic of China and the United States. President Clinton made the difficult decision to intervene in a civil war in Bosnia.

Leadership Qualities and Skills

What kinds of qualities and skills do presidents need to exercise leadership? Several specific leadership qualities common to all good administrators can be identified. Many presidents generally exhibit more than one of these qualities and skills. Several great presidents have had them all.

Understanding the Public A president must know and understand the American people. The most successful presidents have had a genuine feel for the hopes, fears, and moods of the nation they seek to lead. Understanding the people is necessary to gain and hold their support.

Public support, in turn, can give a president real leverage in influencing lawmakers. As a representative body, Congress is very sensitive to the amount of public support a president can generate. When a president is popular, presidential proposals and policies are better received by Congress than when the public holds a president in low regard. When Lyndon Johnson succeeded to the office of president, Congress passed his Great Society legislation. However, when Johnson became unpopular during the Vietnam War, he encountered fierce opposition in Congress. His effectiveness as a leader was almost destroyed.

Failure to understand the public mood can bring disaster to a president. In 1932 when the nation was mired in the Great Depression, President Herbert Hoover believed that the public did not want government to take an active role in confronting the nation's economic problems. Actually, with millions out of work, Americans wanted their problems solved by any means, including federal intervention if necessary. Hoover's failure to understand the mood and fears of the people cost him the 1932 presidential election. He lost to Franklin D. Roosevelt in a landslide.

Ability to Communicate Successful presidents must be able to communicate effectively—to explain their policies clearly and to present their ideas in a way that inspires public support. President Herbert Hoover met infrequently with the press and only answered questions that had been written in advance. In contrast, Franklin D. Roosevelt was a master at communicating. He held weekly press conferences during which he answered all questions. After "fireside chats" on the radio, he sometimes received as many as 50,000 letters of public support a day.

A president who cannot communicate effectively may have difficulty exercising leadership. President Carter, for example, had problems in winning public support for his policies. President Reagan, on the other hand, was a very effective communicator. The press dubbed him "the Great Communicator" because of his ability to sell his ideas to the public.

"First Lady" The first presidential wife to be called "first lady" was Julia Grant. But it was the high visibility of her successor, Lucy Hayes, that raised the term to its current status. She was the first president's wife with a college degree, from Wesleyan Women's College, Cincinnati, Ohio, in 1850. Before the Civil War, the country experimented with other titles for the president's wife. Among the rejects were Lady Washington, Mrs. President, presidentress, and Republican (or Democratic) queen.

Sense of Timing A successful president must know when the time is right to introduce a new policy or to make a key decision as well as when to delay doing so. During the crisis in the former Soviet Union in the early 1990s, President Bush agreed that American economic aid would help encourage democratic reforms there. He decided to delay acting on this policy, however, until the Soviet political situation was clearer and more stable. On the other hand, when some Soviet republics declared independence, Bush was quick to recognize their sovereignty.

Skillful presidents often use their assistants or cabinet secretaries to test a position on a controversial issue. One way is to deliberately leak information to the press. Another device is to have a cabinet secretary or an aide make a statement about the issue or give a speech about it. If public and congressional responses are favorable, the president then supports the position and may implement the policy. If reaction is unfavorable, the idea may be quietly dropped, or the president may begin a campaign to shape public opinion on the issue.

Openness to New Ideas Good leadership also requires the capacity to be flexible and open to new ideas. As events in Eastern Europe and the Soviet Union demonstrated in the early 1990s, situations can change rapidly in the modern world. Consequently, an effective president must be receptive to new solutions to problems.

Presidents who are flexible are willing to engage in informal give-and-take sessions with their advisers. Presidents Franklin Roosevelt and John Kennedy liked to hear their staffs argue differing positions. In contrast, President Ronald Reagan did not tolerate serious dissension among his staff.

Ability to Compromise A successful president must be able to compromise. The nature of politics is such that even the president must often be willing to give up something in order to get something in return. Presidents who are successful leaders are able to recognize that sometimes they may have to settle for legislation by Congress, for example, that provides only part of what they want. Presidents who will not compromise risk accomplishing nothing at all.

Perhaps the most tragic example of a president's unwillingness to compromise is the experience of Woodrow Wilson after World War I. President Wilson favored a League of Nations.[1] The League was to be a global organization that would help prevent future wars. Wilson personally attended the peace conference outside Paris to help draft a peace treaty that included the League.

See the following footnoted materials in the ***Reference Handbook:***
1. *The Fourteen Points*, page 822.

An Inaccessible President

An Imperial Presidency Here President Nixon makes a rare trip to the White House gates to greet citizens. Nixon surrounded himself with aides who usually agreed with him, creating an atmosphere in which all opinions reflected his own. Protected from criticism, Nixon grew increasingly isolated. Nixon thrived on the power of the presidency, and critics dubbed him "King Richard." ***How might Nixon's attitude have limited his ability to govern?***

When the treaty came before the Senate for ratification, several senators raised objections to parts of the plan for the League. President Wilson, however, would not even consider compromise. He refused to make any changes in the plan for the League to satisfy the senators' objections. Instead, he began a speaking tour to build public support for his version of the League plan.

The tour ended suddenly and in disaster. The exhausted Wilson suffered a stroke and was paralyzed. By insisting on everything he wanted, Wilson lost everything. The Senate rejected the treaty, and the United States never joined the League.

Political Courage A successful leader must have political courage. Sometimes presidents must go against public opinion in taking actions they believe are vital to the nation's well-being. To be great leaders, presidents must at times have the courage to make decisions they know will be unpopular with the voters.

President Lincoln made the greatest of such decisions during the Civil War. The early years of the war went very badly for the North. Despite some Union victories, the casualty list was horrendous, and the war's end seemed nowhere in sight. As time passed, the war became increasingly unpopular, and the president came under intense public and political pressure to negotiate a peace with the South. Despite his belief that his decision would cause him to be defeated for reelection in 1864, Lincoln decided to continue the war and to preserve the Union.

Presidential Isolation

Information and realistic advice are key ingredients for successful decision making. As presidents have become more dependent on the White House staff, however, the danger that they may become isolated from the information and advice they need has increased.

Special Treatment Modern presidents get very special treatment. One adviser to President Johnson noted:

> "*The life of the White House is the life of a court. It is a structure designed for one purpose and one purpose only—to serve the material needs and desires of a single man. . . . He is treated with all the reverence due a monarch. . . . No one ever invites him to 'go soak your head' when his demands become petulant and unreasonable.*"
>
> —George Reedy, 1967

In such an atmosphere, it is easy for presidents to see themselves as deserving only praise and to consider their ideas as above criticism.

Voicing Opinions Presidents may discourage staff members from disagreeing with them or giving them unpleasant advice. Lincoln once asked his cabinet for advice on a proposal he favored. Every member of the cabinet opposed it—to which Lincoln responded, "Seven nays, one aye; the ayes have it."

No matter how well they know the president as a person, the *office* of president awes almost all staff advisers. A close adviser and friend of President Kennedy put the feeling this way: "I saw no halo, I observed no mystery. And yet I found that my own personal, highly informal relationship with him changed as soon as he entered the Oval Office." An assistant to President Nixon had similar feelings. He explained that even after working closely with Nixon, "I never lost my reverent awe of the president, or the presidency, which for me were synonymous." Such feelings can make it difficult for staff to present unpleasant news or voice criticism, which may mean that the president sometimes receives one-sided views of an issue.

The Oval Office

Access to the President A veteran political observer once noted that "power in Washington is measured in access to the president." Top members of the White House staff are closer to the president than any other government officials. Presidents have different styles of managing staff. Franklin Roosevelt liked having competitive staff full of differing ideas, but Lyndon Johnson was less open to different ideas or dissent.

William Safire, one of the speechwriters for President Nixon, tells a story that shows what can happen to the careless staffer who happens to disagree with the president. Safire once challenged the accuracy of a statement that Nixon had made. When Nixon insisted that he was correct, Safire produced evidence to show that the president was wrong. As a result, Safire recalls, "For three solid months I did not receive a speech assignment from the president, or a phone call, or a memo, or a nod in the hall as he was passing by."

Woodrow Wilson's closest adviser, Colonel Edward House, admitted that he constantly praised his boss. As for bad news, one presidential adviser explained that the strategy everyone followed was "to be present either personally or by a proxy piece of paper when 'good news' arrives and to be certain that someone else is present when the news is bad."

The Dangers of Isolation Not only do top staffers have easy access to the president, but they also use their closeness to control others' access. Sherman Adams, Eisenhower's chief of staff, had great authority because very few messages of any kind would go to Eisenhower without Adams first seeing them. H. R. Haldeman played a similar role for President Nixon. Few people, including most other White House staff members, got to see Nixon without Haldeman's approval.

President Reagan at first depended heavily on several top advisers. During his second term, however, his new chief of staff, Donald Regan, severely restricted access to the president. One Reagan staffer called Regan the **de facto** president, meaning that although Regan did not legally hold the office, he exercised power as though he was president. Like Nixon before Watergate, President Reagan became increasingly isolated. This isolation may explain why the president apparently was unaware of the **covert**, or secret, activities his National Security Council staff in the Iran-contra affair were conducting.

Perhaps in response to the events of the Nixon and Reagan presidencies, President Bush tried to reverse the trend toward consolidating power in the White House Office, but he had a

We the People
Making a Difference
Jimmy Carter

Habitat for Humanity

Jimmy Carter served as president of the United States from 1977 to 1981. After leaving office, he continued to help mediate and solve international and domestic problems. For his many efforts and dedication, the former president has been nominated seven times for a Nobel Peace Prize.

A year after leaving office Carter founded the Carter Center in Atlanta. The center focuses on global health, human rights, and democracy. Carter's presidential experience, especially in negotiating foreign policy, has helped him resolve conflicts around the world. In 1994 he helped negotiate the return of deposed Haitian president Jean-Bertrand Aristide to office. He has traveled to Ethiopia, Sudan, North Korea, and Bosnia to help the cause of peace.

Carter and his wife Rosalynn are working to eradicate a deadly disease called guinea-worm disease that affects people in India, Pakistan, and 16 African countries. By teaching people to filter their water, the death rate from this disease has decreased.

At home, Carter and his wife are involved in the Habitat for Humanity program. With thousands of other volunteers, they help build houses for the poor. Carter, who is now in his seventies, says, "To work for better understanding among people, one does not have to be a former president. . . . Peace can be made in the neighborhoods, the living rooms, the playing fields, and the classrooms of our country."

very strong chief of staff who restricted access. Although most presidents appoint their close friends to the White House staff, Bush appointed them to the cabinet instead. As one presidential aide explained, "The cabinet has played a very important role in all major decisions. [The president] wants them to be running things—not the White House staff."

Many observers believed that the leadership changes that Bush made were positive moves. Relying more on advice from officials who were not so close to White House operations gave the president access to a greater variety of views.

Staying in Touch Most political observers caution, however, that despite a president's best intentions, power will inevitably drift toward the White House. Keeping in direct touch with the public can be very difficult, if not impossible, for a modern president. The need for cabinet members to protect the interests of their departments and the constituent groups they serve always influences the advice they give.

President Clinton brought plans for major domestic legislation to Washington in 1993. Dealing with White House staff problems became a major distraction, however. The president relied on key staffers for input in frequent brainstorming sessions that often lasted for hours. Many sessions were inconclusive, and the president's agenda lost momentum. To increase efficiency the president found it necessary to reorganize the staff.

The Use of Executive Privilege

Presidents do not want the information from their advisers to become public knowledge. In order to keep White House discussions and policy making confidential, modern presidents have sometimes used executive privilege. **Executive privilege** is the right of the president and other high-ranking executive officers, with the president's consent, to refuse to provide information to Congress or a court.

Although the Constitution does not mention executive privilege, the concept rests on the principle of separation of powers. Presidents since George Washington have claimed that executive privilege is implied in the powers granted in Article II. Congress has disputed executive privilege, claiming that its oversight powers give it the right to obtain necessary information from the executive branch.

Limits of Executive Privilege Presidents have long claimed that executive privilege also protects their communication with other members of the executive branch. They argue that executive privilege is necessary if they are to get frank opinions and advice from their assistants.

Until recently, neither Congress nor the courts had much need to question members of the White House staff. These presidential aides traditionally had little to do with making policy. The various cabinet departments made key policy decisions, and Congress could call department heads to testify as part of its oversight function. Because more policy making has been taking place in the Executive Office of the President, however, the constitutionality and limits of executive privilege have become an important question.

United States* v. *Nixon In 1974 the Supreme Court issued a major decision on executive privilege. President Nixon had secretly tape-recorded his conversations with key aides about the Watergate cover-up. In ***United States* v. *Nixon*,** the Court unanimously ruled that the president had to surrender the tapes to the special prosecutor investigating the scandal.

Although the Court rejected Nixon's claim of executive privilege in this case, it ruled that because executive privilege "relates to the effective discharge of a president's powers, it is constitutionally based." The Supreme Court held the following opinion:

> "*A President and those who assist him must be free to explore alternatives in the process of shaping policies and making decisions; and to do so in a way many would be unwilling to express except privately.*"
>
> —Chief Justice Warren Burger, 1974

The Court's decision did not end the controversy over executive privilege. While many support the view that presidents need such privacy in their communications, others disagree. They argue that by defending the constitutional basis of executive privilege, the Court has opened the way for even more secrecy in the White House. Although the president's right of executive privilege is legally recognized, the question of how far it extends to presidential advisers remains unanswered.

Section 3 Assessment

Checking for Understanding

1. **Main Idea** Using a graphic organizer like the one below, identify six qualities of presidential leadership and give an example of each.

Qualities	Examples

2. **Define** de facto, covert.
3. **Identify** executive privilege, *United States* v. *Nixon.*
4. How do presidents test public opinion before announcing new policies?
5. How do good communication skills help a president gain public support?

Critical Thinking

6. **Synthesizing Information** How can a president's willingness to let staff express disagreements on issues help the president make better decisions?

Cultural Pluralism Suppose that you are the president's chief assistant for legislative affairs. The president has asked for your advice on whether or not the opinions of interest groups should be a factor in making policy decisions. Write a memo supporting your position.

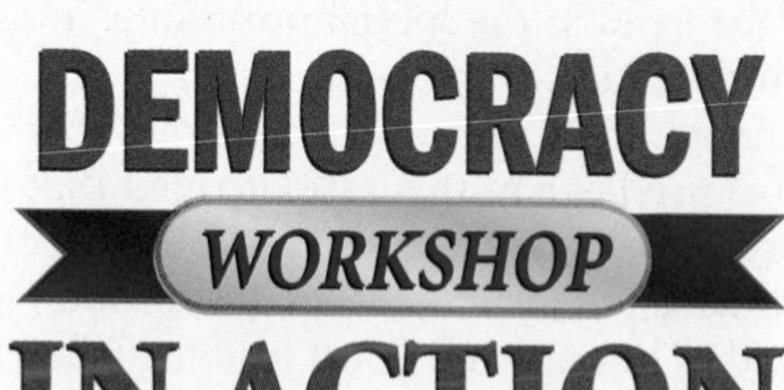

Presidential Debate

In Unit 3 you learned about the office of the president and the enormous responsibility and power granted to the person who holds this office. This activity will help you understand what qualities voters look for in a presidential candidate. By staging a mock presidential debate, you will also see the roles that campaign staffs and the media play in influencing the public's choice of a presidential candidate.

Setting Up the Workshop

1. For this activity you will need a timer or stopwatch, access to research materials such as current magazines and newspapers, and paper and pencils.
2. Divide the class into four work groups:
   Group 1 Presidential candidate #1 and campaign staff (5–10 students)
   Group 2 Presidential candidate #2 and campaign staff (5–10 students)
   Group 3 Presidential candidate #3 and campaign staff (5–10 students)
   Group 4 Representatives from the media to ask questions during the debate (5–8 students)
3. Choose a chairperson to organize your group's activities and a recorder to take notes.
4. If you are in groups 1 through 3, vote to select one person to play the role of your presidential candidate in the debate. The rest of your group's members will make up the campaign staff. The campaign staff's responsibility is to prepare their candidate for the debate.

Identifying Debate Topics

Voters who watch presidential debates want to find out where a candidate stands on issues that affect their lives and the nation's well-being. As a class, decide on four topics that you think are important to the voting public today. Use the categories below to help you narrow your choices. Choose one topic from each category. Sample topics are provided in parentheses. The debate will be limited to the four topics you select.

1. Political issues (campaign reform, campaign financing)
2. Social issues (crime, education, Social Security, welfare)
3. Financial issues (cutting entitlement programs, the budget, housing)
4. Foreign policy issues (the Middle East, terrorism, NATO)

Researching Debate Topics

Groups 1, 2, and 3. Divide your group's campaign staff into four topic teams.

Group 4. Divide your group into four topic teams.

Follow these steps to complete the research needed for the debate:

1. Assign one of the four debate topics to each team.
2. Each team should do research on its topic outside class and bring its written notes to class.
3. Teams should present their findings to their group in an oral summary.

Remember that the presidential candidates will be relying on their group's research to help them come out ahead in the upcoming debate, and the public will be relying on the media to help them choose the best candidate.

Preparing Your Candidate for the Debate

Groups 1–3. To help prepare your candidate, ask him or her questions that you think might be asked during the debate. Think out each response carefully and coach your candidates so they will be well-prepared. Help candidates to make their statements more engaging by suggesting specific gestures, word emphasis, or expressions.

Campaign staffs will want to make sure that their candidates appear "presidential." Make a list of qualities that you would like to see in a presidential candidate and help your candidate to present herself or himself in this manner. Candidates should come across as well-informed, decisive, and confident.

Campaign paraphernalia advertises candidates'. stands on issues.

Vice President Al Gore and George W. Bush shake hands during the 2000 presidential debates.

DEMOCRACY WORKSHOP IN ACTION

The first televised presidential debates occurred in 1960. They pitted a campaign-weary Richard Nixon against a fit and witty John F. Kennedy.

In 1960, for the first time, radio and television played a major role in a presidential campaign. This advertisement for Sylvania television sets focuses on the 1960 televised presidential debates.

Decide before the debate what position your candidate will take on each issue and stick to it. Remember, it is not necessary for everyone in your group to agree on the issues. However, for the purpose of the debate, group members should present a united front. Before the debate, work together to create a name for your candidate's political party and write a brief statement about why your candidate would make the best president based on your group's views and philosophy of leadership.

Group 4. Media representatives should prepare for the debate by first discussing what they think the voters will want to know about the candidates and their stands on each issue. Your responsibility will be to draw out each candidate's knowledge and position on the four issues.

Work as a group to prepare a written list of four questions for each topic and possible follow-up questions. Divide the questions evenly among the group's members. Review the questions to eliminate duplication and to make them as concise as possible. Because of time constraints, choose the most important ones to use first.

Scoring the Debate

Groups 1 through 3 will be awarded points by the teacher based on their knowledge of each issue, how well prepared their candidate is, and how consistent their candidate is in presenting a uniform stand on each issue.

Group 4 will be awarded points by the teacher based on its knowledge of the issues, question relevancy, and the use of follow-up questions where necessary to establish a candidate's stand.

Establishing Debate Ground Rules

1. Work with your teacher to establish the time, date, and rules for the debate.
2. Allow a total of 30 to 45 minutes to stage the debate.
3. Select one student to serve as a debate moderator and one to serve as a timekeeper.
4. Arrange the classroom so the three candidates are at the front of the class. The media should sit facing the candidates.
5. Begin the debate with candidates introducing themselves. Each should give the name of his or her party and a general statement about why he or she would make the best president.
6. Media representatives should direct each question to only one candidate. That candidate will have a maximum of one minute to respond. The other candidates, if they choose, will have 30 seconds to respond to that same question or rebut another candidate's response.

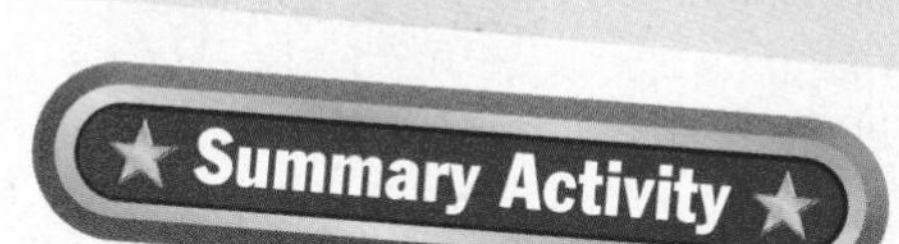

After the debate, work as a class to evaluate each party's performance. Hold a discussion by answering the following questions.

Questions for Discussion

1. What topic seemed to pose the most problems for the candidates? Examine why.
2. Do you think a presidential candidate's personal opinions always have to agree with his or her political stand on an issue? Why?
3. Besides a candidate's stand on an issue, what else do you think voters look for during a debate?
4. How could each of the candidates have been more effective or more persuasive?
5. Based on this debate, which party and candidate would you support and why?

Assessment and Activities

GOVERNMENT Online

Self-Check Quiz Visit the *United States Government: Democracy in Action* Web site at gov.glencoe.com and click on ***Chapter 9–Self-Check Quizzes*** to prepare for the chapter test.

Reviewing Key Terms

On a separate sheet of paper choose the letter of the term defined in each phrase below.

a. executive order
b. reprieve
c. de facto
d. mandate
e. pardon
f. amnesty
g. line-item veto
h. treaty
i. covert
j. forum

1. expressed will of the people
2. medium of discussion of presidential messages
3. the power to accept or reject only parts of a congressional bill
4. a release of a group from legal punishment
5. presidential decree that has the force of law
6. postponement of a person's legal punishment
7. existing "in fact" rather than officially or legally
8. something that is secret

Recalling Facts

1. Identify the five constitutional roles or duties of the president.
2. What are four limits on presidential power?
3. What is the president's role as party leader?
4. Why can failing to understand the public's mood weaken a president's power?
5. How do presidents become isolated?

Understanding Concepts

1. **Constitutional Interpretations** How did President Lincoln's actions during the Civil War violate some people's constitutional rights?
2. **Political Processes** When has Congress allowed expansion of a president's economic power?
3. **Cultural Pluralism** Why is compromise such a vital ingredient for a president to be able to maintain support of the people?

Critical Thinking

1. **Identifying Alternatives** How could Congress have prevented President Jefferson from purchasing the Louisiana Territory?
2. **Understanding Cause and Effect** Use a graphic organizer like the one below to show why President Johnson chose not to run for re-election in 1968.

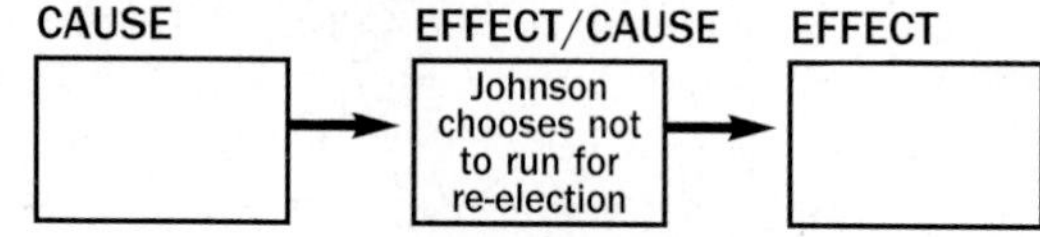

Current Events JOURNAL

Executive Roles Write a heading of each of the president's seven roles at the top of consecutive pages of your journal to form seven sections. For two weeks, find and summarize newspaper articles that illustrate the president's performance in these roles. Determine which role the president engaged in most often. Explain why you think the president devoted so much time to this role.

3. **Drawing Conclusions** What are the dangers in depending only on the cabinet for advice? Only on presidential aides?

Cooperative Learning Activity

Evaluating Presidents Organize the class into groups of six. Each group should choose a different former president and research how well he fulfilled the six qualities of an effective leader. The entire group should then evaluate its president in each area. Each group should present its findings to the class, citing examples and using photos or graphics. Poll the class on which presidents were least effective and most effective in using presidential power.

Interpreting Political Cartoons Activity

1. According to the cartoon, what do the American people expect of their president?
2. How must presidential candidates present themselves to the public?
3. Are the personal qualities of presidential candidates important in an election? Explain your answer.

Skill Practice Activity

Interpreting Political Cartoons Study the cartoon on page 255, then answer the following questions.

1. What is Lyndon Johnson doing in the cartoon?
2. Why do you think Congress is shown as a piano?
3. What does the cartoon suggest about this president's legislative power?
4. What title would you give this cartoon?

Technology Activity

Using E-Mail A president's actions are often limited by public opinion. One way that people communicate their opinions about the president's actions is through E-mail. Find the E-mail address of the White House. Then choose one of the seven roles of the president, and evaluate the president's current performance in the role you chose. Communicate your opinion about his performance to the president by sending E-mail to the White House.

Participating in Local Government

Just like the president, a mayor must be aware of how the people of the community view his or her actions or decisions. Such opinion is often measured through polls of a sample of the population. Design your own poll, using questions about your mayor's recent actions that impact your city. Use the questions to interview friends, family, and neighbors to find out the mayor's popularity in your community. Summarize your results in a chart or graph.

The Federal Bureaucracy

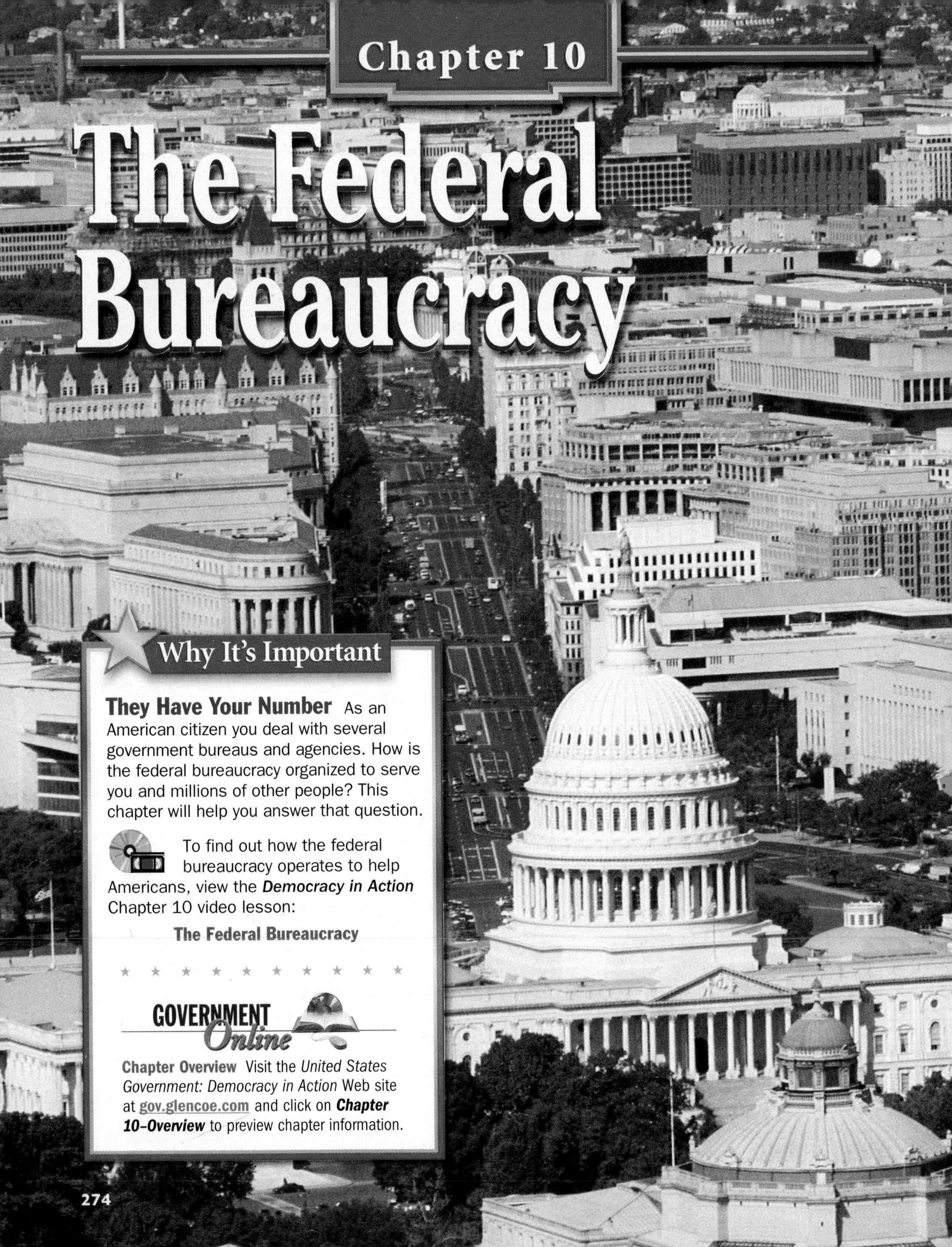

Why It's Important

They Have Your Number As an American citizen you deal with several government bureaus and agencies. How is the federal bureaucracy organized to serve you and millions of other people? This chapter will help you answer that question.

To find out how the federal bureaucracy operates to help Americans, view the ***Democracy in Action*** Chapter 10 video lesson:

The Federal Bureaucracy

GOVERNMENT Online

Chapter Overview Visit the *United States Government: Democracy in Action* Web site at gov.glencoe.com and click on ***Chapter 10–Overview*** to preview chapter information.

Section 1

Bureaucratic Organization

Reader's Guide

Key Terms

bureaucrat, embassy, government corporation, deregulate, procurement

Find Out

- What is the general organizational structure of the 14 cabinet level departments?
- How are independent government agencies different from regulatory commissions?

Understanding Concepts

Public Policy How does government bureaucracy serve the executive branch in carrying out the will of the people's representatives?

COVER STORY

Disaster Causes Tension

WASHINGTON, D.C., NOVEMBER 4, 1996

The May 11 crash of a ValuJet airliner has strained relations between two federal agencies responsible for air safety. The National Transportation Safety Board (NTSB) makes safety recommendations, and the Federal Aviation Agency (FAA) decides whether to implement them. Despite reports of safety violations after the crash, the FAA declared ValuJet to be a safe airline. This was a public relations disaster for the FAA, according to aviation experts. It also served to increase the NTSB's influence with Congress. "The FAA can no longer easily ignore the NTSB," observed one airline executive.

NTSB gains influence

Hundreds of agencies like the FAA help to make up the federal bureaucracy. Most of these departments and agencies are part of the executive branch that carries out the laws passed by Congress. The people who work for these organizations are called **bureaucrats,** or civil servants.

The federal bureaucracy is organized into departments, agencies, boards, commissions, corporations, and advisory committees. Most of these organizations are responsible to the president, although some of them report to Congress. Acts of Congress created almost all of them.

The Constitution provides indirectly for the bureaucracy. Article II, Section 2, states that:

> "*He [the president] may require the Opinion, in writing, of the principal Officer in each of the executive Departments, upon any subject relating to the Duties of their respective Offices, . . .*"
>
> —The Constitution

Article II also gives the president the power to appoint the heads of those departments.

Thus, the Founders anticipated the need for creating federal agencies that would carry on the day-to-day business of government. At the same time they would probably be shocked by the size the federal bureaucracy has grown to today.

In the early years of the Republic, the federal bureaucracy was quite small. When Jefferson became president in 1801, the federal government employed only 2,120 people. These employees were mainly commissioners of Native American affairs, postmasters, customs collectors, tax collectors, marshalls, and clerks.

Today, nearly 3 million civilians work for the federal government. Federal agencies are located in more than 440,000 buildings scattered across the nation and around the world.

◀ Aerial view of Washington, D.C.

The Cabinet Departments

The 14 cabinet departments are a major part of the federal bureaucracy. One of President Washington's first acts in 1789 was to ask Congress to create the Departments of Treasury, State, and War and the office of attorney general. Since 1789, 10 additional departments have been created. A secretary who is a member of the president's cabinet heads each of the departments in the executive branch. Departments usually have a second in command, called the deputy secretary or under secretary. In addition, departments have assistant secretaries. The president appoints all these officials.

The next level under these top officials includes the directors of the major units that make up the cabinet department, along with their assistants. These units have various names, including bureau, agency, office, administration, or division. The top officials in each department—the secretaries, agency directors, deputy directors, and their assistants—set overall department policy. These top leaders rely on ideas and information from career officials who are specialists and business managers in the department. Often, these career workers, who frequently have many years of experience, do the research to provide the alternatives from which the top leaders choose.

Department of State The secretary of state is one of the president's most trusted advisers. The **Department of State** is responsible for the overall foreign policy of the United States. The agency also protects the rights of United States citizens traveling in foreign countries. It staffs **embassies,** or offices of ambassadors in foreign countries, analyzes data about American interests in other countries, and speaks for the United States in the United Nations.

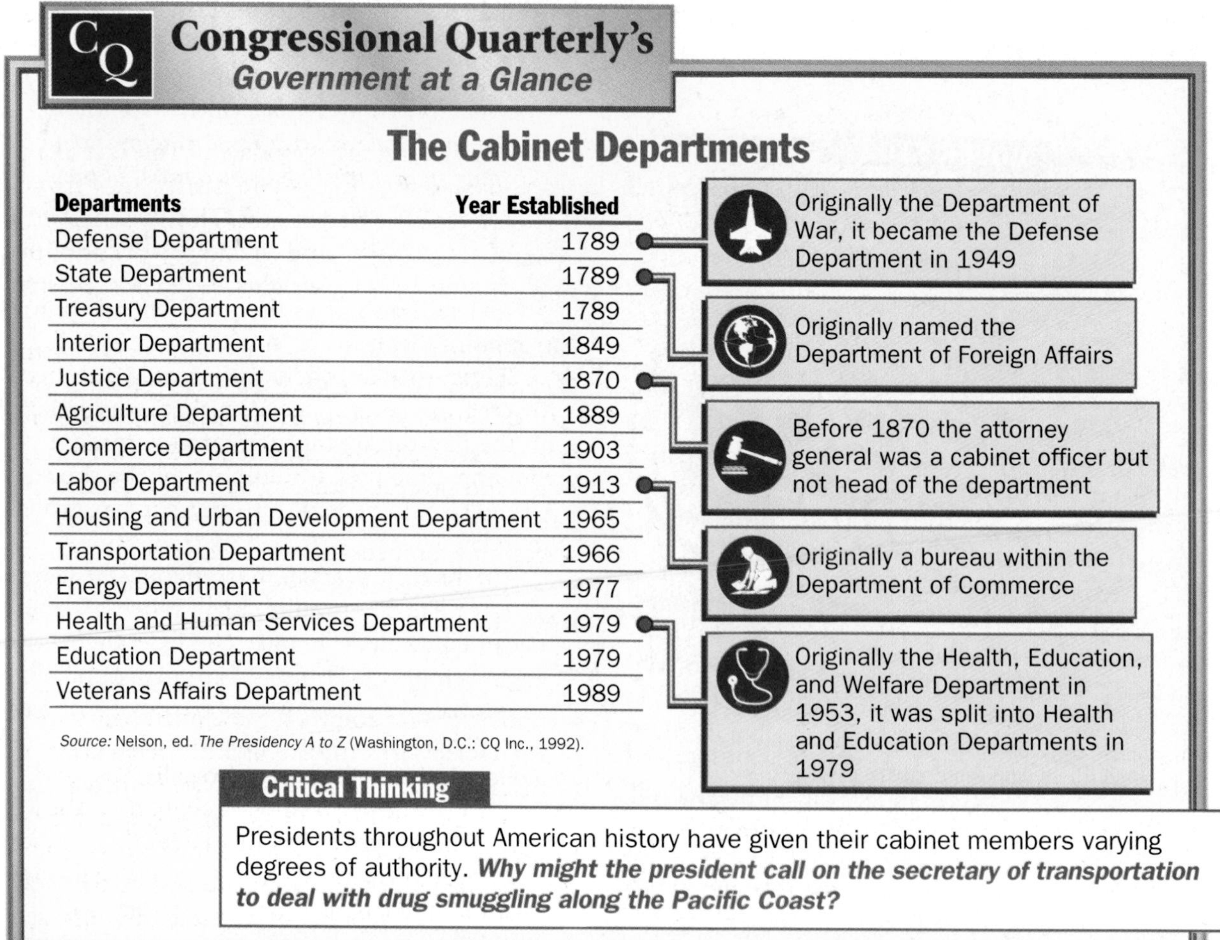

The Cabinet Departments

Departments	Year Established
Defense Department	1789
State Department	1789
Treasury Department	1789
Interior Department	1849
Justice Department	1870
Agriculture Department	1889
Commerce Department	1903
Labor Department	1913
Housing and Urban Development Department	1965
Transportation Department	1966
Energy Department	1977
Health and Human Services Department	1979
Education Department	1979
Veterans Affairs Department	1989

Defense Department: Originally the Department of War, it became the Defense Department in 1949

State Department: Originally named the Department of Foreign Affairs

Justice Department: Before 1870 the attorney general was a cabinet officer but not head of the department

Labor Department: Originally a bureau within the Department of Commerce

Health and Human Services Department: Originally the Health, Education, and Welfare Department in 1953, it was split into Health and Education Departments in 1979

Source: Nelson, ed. *The Presidency A to Z* (Washington, D.C.: CQ Inc., 1992).

Critical Thinking

Presidents throughout American history have given their cabinet members varying degrees of authority. ***Why might the president call on the secretary of transportation to deal with drug smuggling along the Pacific Coast?***

Department of the Treasury Managing the monetary resources of the United States is the primary responsibility of the **Department of the Treasury.** The Bureau of the Mint manufactures coins. The Bureau of Printing and Engraving produces paper money. The Treasury Department also oversees a variety of other duties. One branch—the Internal Revenue Service—collects taxes. The United States Secret Service provides protection for the president, vice president, and other officials. The Bureau of Alcohol, Tobacco, and Firearms administers explosives and firearm laws and regulates the production and distribution of alcohol and tobacco.

Department of the Interior To protect public lands and natural resources throughout the nation and to oversee relations with Native Americans, Congress established the Department of the Interior in 1849. The Bureau of Mines helps oversee the mining of natural resources. The National Park Service manages national monuments, historic sites, recreational areas, and national parks.

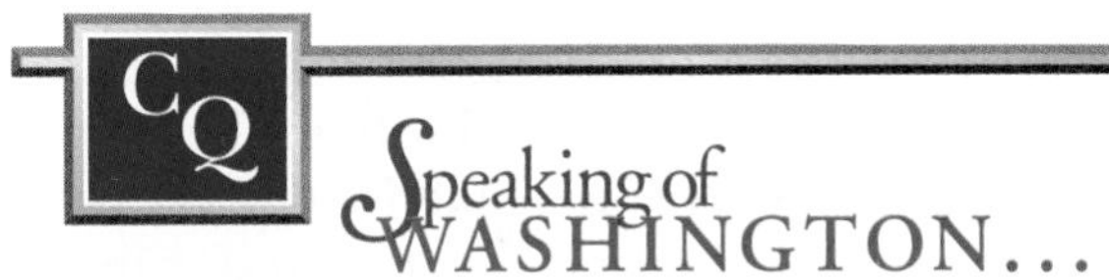

The Bobby Kennedy Law **A 1967 law prevents a president from giving a government job to a family member. The act is called the "Bobby Kennedy law" because it is intended to prevent a repetition of the situation in 1961 when President John Kennedy appointed his brother Robert attorney general of the United States. The law did not prohibit Bill Clinton from appointing his wife, Hillary Rodham Clinton, as head of his health-care reform task force in 1993. There was no challenge to the appointment, presumably because it was unpaid and advisory only.**

Department of Agriculture Created to help farmers improve their incomes and expand their markets, the Department of Agriculture develops conservation programs and provides financial credit to farmers. It also safeguards the nation's food supply.

Department of Justice Congress established the office of attorney general in 1789 to oversee the nation's legal affairs. The Department of Justice was created in 1870. Among its well-known agencies are the Federal Bureau of Investigation (FBI), the Immigration and Naturalization Service (INS), and the Drug Enforcement Administration (DEA). The Antitrust Division of the Department of Justice enforces antitrust laws. The Civil Rights Division helps enforce civil rights legislation.

Department of Commerce To promote and protect the industrial and commercial segments of the American economy, the Department of Commerce was founded in 1903. Three agencies of this department carry out constitutional directives. The Bureau of the Census counts the people every 10 years. Census figures are used to redraw congressional district boundaries. The Patent and Trademark Office issues patents for new inventions and registers trademarks. The National Institute of Standards and Technology provides uniform standards for weights and measurements.

Department of Labor Congress created the Department of Labor in 1913. Charged with protecting American workers, the department ensures safe working conditions, safeguards a minimum wage, and protects pension rights. The Bureau of Labor Statistics analyzes data on employment, wages, and compensation. The Office of the American Workplace encourages cooperation between labor and management.

Department of Defense First called the Department of War and then the United States Military Establishment until 1949, the Department of Defense protects the security of the United States. Through the Joint Chiefs of Staff—the leaders of the Army, Navy, Marines, and Air Force—it oversees the armed forces. With the end of the Cold War, the government began to cut back on the size of this largest cabinet department.

Department of Health and Human Services

Directing programs concerned with the health and social services needs of the American people is the responsibility of this department. It also manages the federal Medicare and Medicaid programs and helps senior citizens and less fortunate Americans through the Social Security Administration. Perhaps the most visible part of the Department of Health and Human Services—particularly since the outbreak of the AIDS epidemic in the early 1980s—

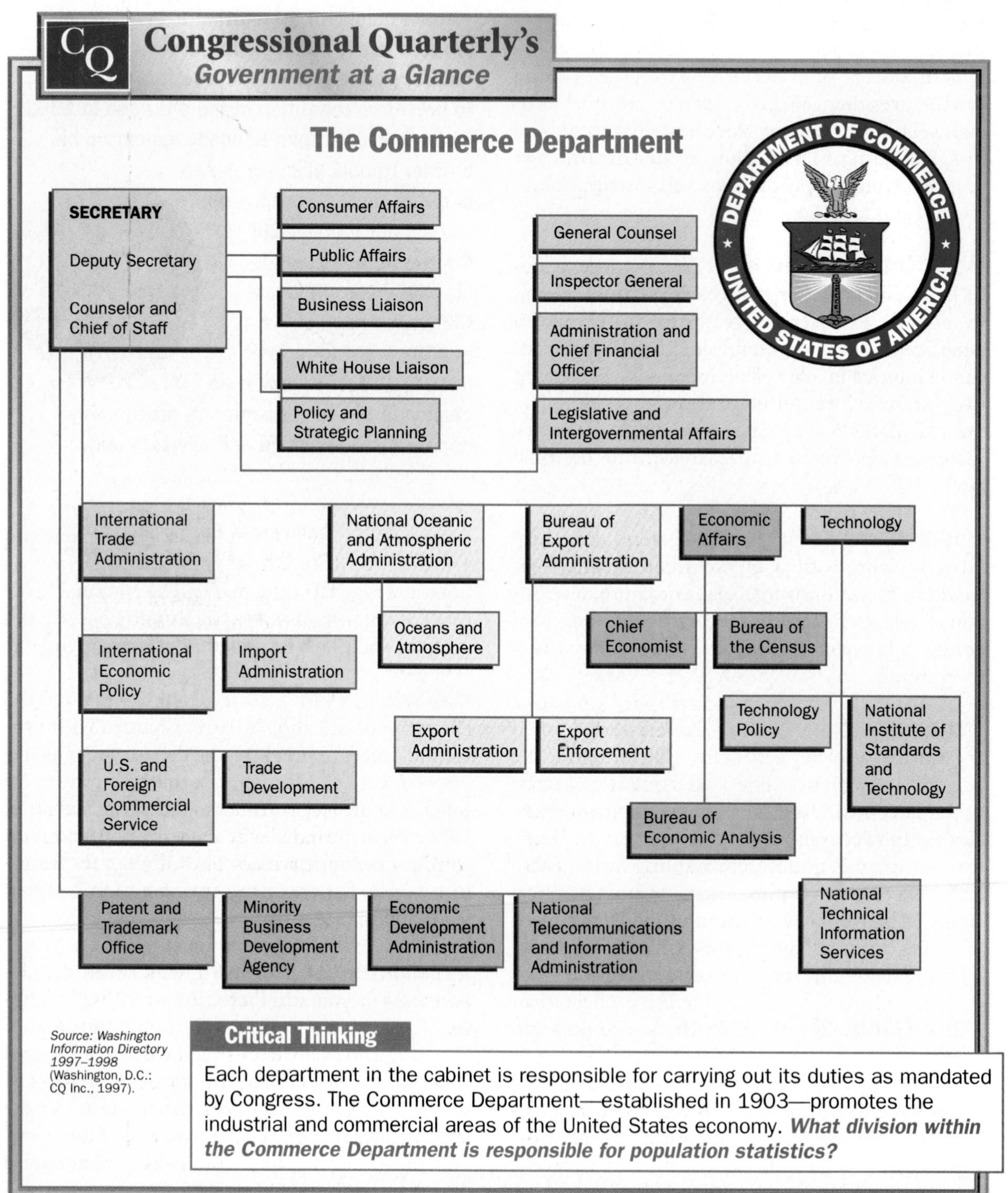

Source: Washington Information Directory 1997–1998 (Washington, D.C.: CQ Inc., 1997).

Critical Thinking

Each department in the cabinet is responsible for carrying out its duties as mandated by Congress. The Commerce Department—established in 1903—promotes the industrial and commercial areas of the United States economy. ***What division within the Commerce Department is responsible for population statistics?***

has been the Public Health Service. This important government agency helps implement a national health policy, conducts medical research, and ensures the safety of food and drugs. The Food and Drug Administration inspects food and drug processing plants and approves new drugs for treatment of diseases.

Department of Housing and Urban Development This department was created in 1965 to preserve the nation's communities and ensure Americans of equal housing opportunities. The Government National Mortgage Association helps make mortgage money available for people to buy homes.

Department of Transportation It is the responsibility of the Department of Transportation to regulate all aspects of American transportation needs, policy development, and planning. This includes regulating aviation, railroads, highways, and mass transit. The department also includes the United States Coast Guard, which assists with search and rescue operations, enforces maritime laws against smuggling, and ensures safety standards on commercial seagoing vessels.

Department of Energy An energy shortage led to the creation of this department in 1977. It plans energy policy and researches and develops energy technology. One of the most important parts of the department, the Federal Energy Regulatory Commission, sets the rates for interstate transmission of natural gas and electricity.

Department of Education An educated population is an essential feature of a democratic form of government. Without informed citizens who are capable of participating in government, a democracy cannot survive. In 1979 Congress created the Department of Education to coordinate federal assistance programs for public and private schools. Today the department oversees programs to help students with limited English proficiency as well as programs for physically challenged students.

Department of Veterans Affairs Founded in 1989, this department was formerly known as the Veterans Administration. It administers several hospitals as well as educational and other programs designed to benefit veterans and their families.

Federal Assistance President Jimmy Carter set up the Department of Education in 1979 to provide advice and assistance to states and school districts. The department helps schools meet the special needs of students who are disadvantaged or have disabilities. ***What might be a national goal of the Department of Education?***

Independent Agencies

The federal bureaucracy also contains more than 100 independent agencies, boards, and commissions that are not part of any cabinet department. The president appoints the heads of these organizations.

A few of these agencies are almost as large and well known as cabinet departments. Two examples are the Environmental Protection Agency (EPA) and the National Aeronautics and Space Administration (NASA). Other agencies such as the Civil Rights Commission and the Small Business Administration are much smaller. Most independent agencies have few employees, small budgets, and attract little public attention. One example of this type of agency is the American Battle Monuments Commission.

Finding A New Path

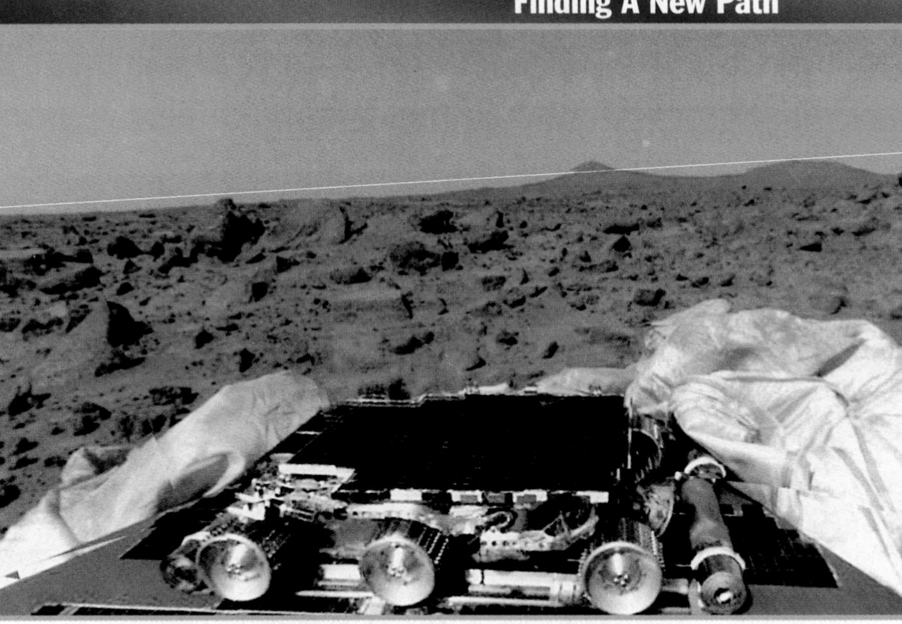

A Bureaucratic Celebrity
NASA, an independent agency, gained further recognition by inaugurating a new era in space exploration with the Mars *Pathfinder*. The *Pathfinder* spacecraft landed on Mars on July 4, 1997, and became the first mobile explorer of another planet. It also sent back to Earth the first high-resolution color images of Mars. ***Why are achievements such as NASA's mission to Mars important to the continued existence of federal agencies?***

Assisting the Executive Branch Some independent agencies perform services for the executive branch. The General Services Administration (GSA) and the Central Intelligence Agency (CIA) are two examples. The General Services Administration is responsible for constructing and maintaining all government buildings. It also supplies equipment for federal offices. The National Archives and Records Administration maintains government records and publishes all rules applying to various federal agencies.

The Central Intelligence Agency provides a very different kind of service. The CIA gathers information about what is going on in other countries, evaluates it, and passes it on to the president and other foreign-policy decision makers. The CIA uses its own secret agents, paid informers, foreign news sources, and friendly governments to collect such information.

Government Corporations Some independent agencies, such as the Small Business Administration, directly serve the public. Many of the major agencies are **government corporations,** or businesses the federal government runs.

Today, the executive branch has at least 60 government corporations. The Tennessee Valley Authority (TVA) is one. The TVA has built dams and supplies electric power for an eight-state area.

The Federal Deposit Insurance Corporation (FDIC) is also a government corporation. It insures bank accounts up to a certain amount. If a bank fails, the FDIC takes it over and repays the depositors.

The best known of the government corporations is the U.S. Postal Service (USPS). Originally an executive department called the Post Office Department, the USPS became a government corporation in 1970. As an executive department, the post office consistently lost money. Since becoming a corporation, the USPS has done a better job of balancing its budget. This is, in part, because Congress passed legislation giving the USPS "the exclusive right, with certain limited exceptions, to carry letters for others." Only the USPS may deliver first-class mail.

Government corporations are organized somewhat like private businesses. Each has a board of directors and a general manager who directs the day-to-day operations. Government corporations are supposed to be more flexible than regular government agencies. They are more likely to take risks and to find innovative solutions to the challenges they are confronting. Most of the corporations earn money that is put back into the "business." Unlike private businesses, however, money from Congress—not funds from private investors—supports government corporations.

Regulatory Commissions

Regulatory commissions occupy a special place in the federal bureaucracy. They are independent of all three branches of the national government. To keep the regulatory commissions impartial, Congress has been careful to protect them from political pressure. Each commission has from 5 to 11 commissioners whom the president appoints with Senate consent. The terms of office of these board members are long—in some cases, as long as 14 years—and the starting dates of the terms are staggered. Unlike other bureaucrats, these commissioners do not report to the president, nor can the president fire them.

Purpose of the Commissions The independent regulatory commissions were created to make rules for large industries and businesses that affect the interests of the public. Commissions also regulate the conduct of these businesses and industries. The regulatory agencies decide such questions as who will receive a license to operate a radio station or to build a natural gas pipeline to serve a large city. The commissions may also act as courts. They may investigate a business for breaking one of the commission's rules. The commission may hold hearings, collect evidence, and set penalties for any business that violates the rules.

Some Problems Decisions of regulatory commissions can involve millions of dollars and greatly affect businesses. As a result, these agencies are often under intense pressure from lobbyists. Lawyers for industries that the commissions regulate have sometimes tried to go in the "back door" to argue their clients' cases in private with agency officials.

Critics of the commissions also charge that the commissions and the industries they are supposed to regulate sometimes have a "revolving door" relationship. Commissioners often are former executives in a regulated industry and sometimes leave the commission for high-paying jobs in the same industry. As a result, critics charge, some commissioners have seemed more interested in protecting regulated industries than in making sure that they serve the public interest.

Others point out that most agencies have had a good record of protecting the public interest. The Securities and Exchange Commission, for example, has protected investors in the stock market from fraud.

GOVERNMENT *and You*

Social Security

If you have a part-time job, 6.2 percent of your pay is probably being deducted for Social Security taxes. The programs funded by such deductions provide important benefits for workers and their families.

Eligibility for Social Security benefits depends on how much you earn and how long you contribute to the Social Security system. For example, to receive monthly payments when you retire, you must accumulate at least 40 work credits. You can receive up to 4 credits a year, based on your earnings. Currently, Social Security retirement benefits provide about 42 percent of a worker's salary.

In addition, statistics show that you have about a 3-in-10 chance of becoming unable to work before you reach age 65. If you are disabled for a year or more, Social Security will pay monthly benefits to help make up for your loss of income. In many cases, minor children of disabled, deceased or retired workers are also eligible for benefits.

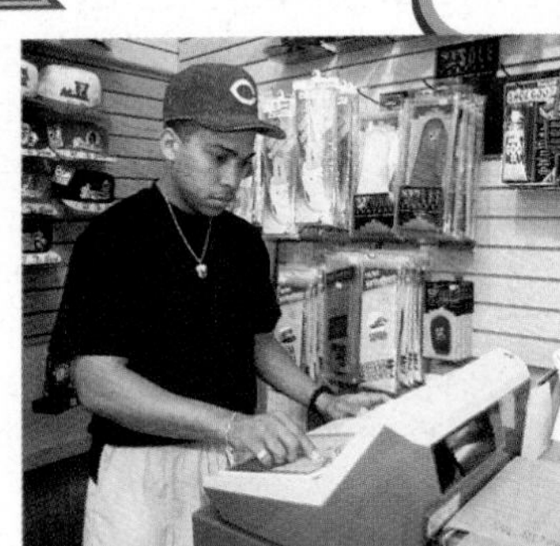

Contributing taxes to Social Security

An Informed Citizen How might the fact that people are living much longer after retirement affect Social Security benefits in the future?

Congressional Quarterly's
Government at a Glance

The Government of the United States

CONSTITUTION

LEGISLATIVE BRANCH

Congress

- Senate
- House
- Architect of the Capitol
- U.S. Botanic Garden
- General Accounting Office
- Government Printing Office
- Library of Congress
- Congressional Budget Office

EXECUTIVE BRANCH

President

- Executive Office of the President
- White House Office
- Management and Budget
- Council of Economic Advisers
- National Security Council
- National Drug Control Policy
- Environmental Policy
- Domestic Policy Council
- National Economic Council
- Vice President
- U.S. Trade Representative
- Council on Environmental Quality
- Science and Technology Policy
- Administration
- National Science and Technology Council

JUDICIAL BRANCH

Supreme Court

- U.S. Courts of Appeals
- U.S. District Courts
- U.S. Court of International Trade
- Territorial Courts
- U.S. Court of Appeals for the Armed Forces
- U.S. Court of Veterans Appeals
- Administrative Office of the U.S. Courts
- U.S. Sentencing Commission
- U.S. Court of Federal Claims
- U.S. Tax Court
- Federal Judicial Center

THE CABINET

- Agriculture
- Commerce
- Defense
- Education
- Energy
- Health and Human Services
- Housing and Urban Development
- Interior
- Justice
- Labor
- State
- Transportation
- Treasury
- Veterans Affairs

SELECTED INDEPENDENT ESTABLISHMENTS AND GOVERNMENT CORPORATIONS

- African Development Foundation
- Central Intelligence Agency
- Commission on Civil Rights
- Consumer Product Safety Commission
- Environmental Protection Agency
- Equal Employment Opportunity Commission
- Export–Import Bank of the U.S.
- Farm Credit Administration
- Federal Communications Commission
- Federal Election Commission
- Federal Emergency Management Agency
- Federal Housing Finance Board
- Federal Maritime Commission
- Federal Reserve System
- Federal Trade Commission
- National Aeronautics and Space Administration
- National Foundation on the Arts and the Humanities
- National Labor Relations Board
- National Science Foundation
- Nuclear Regulatory Commission
- Office of Government Ethics
- Office of Personnel Management
- Office of Special Counsel
- Peace Corps
- Securities and Exchange Commission
- Selective Service System
- Small Business Administration
- Social Security Administration

Source: Washington Information Directory 1997–1998 (Washington, D.C.: CQ Inc., 1997).

Critical Thinking

The lower half of the chart represents the federal bureaucracy, one of the most powerful forces in the government. ***Why do you think it is sometimes called the "fourth branch" of the government?***

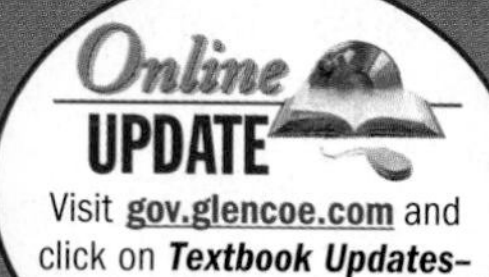

Visit **gov.glencoe.com** and click on ***Textbook Updates–Chapter 10*** for an update of the data.

Deregulation In a 1976 campaign speech, presidential candidate Jimmy Carter called for a reduction in the number of federal agencies. He cited the increasing difficulty of tracking the effectiveness of existing programs in an overregulated society. According to Carter:

> "*We need increased program evaluation. Many programs fail to define with any specificity what they intend to accomplish. Without that specification, evaluation by objective is impossible. . . .*"
>
> —Jimmy Carter, 1976

In recent years Congress has responded to complaints of overregulation by taking steps to **deregulate,** or reduce the powers of regulatory agencies. In 1978, for example, Congress ordered the Civil Aeronautics Board (CAB) to simplify its procedures and cut back on regulation of the airlines. Congress also set a deadline that specified that the CAB was to go out of business in the year 1985.

Deregulation was a major issue in the 1980s and 1990s. As Republicans pushed for regulatory reform, President Clinton proposed to "reinvent government." He signed an executive order that required federal regulations to avoid imposing undue economic burdens on businesses without assessing their costs and benefits. In addition, Congress passed deregulation laws dealing with paperwork reduction, risk assessment, and private-property rights.

Cutting the Federal Workforce One way to cut costs was to reduce the number of workers in federal agencies. After a study by Vice President Al Gore, the administration proposed a reduction of the federal workforce by 252,000 in 6 years. Congress passed a bill requiring the reductions and provided cash incentives for workers to resign. It wrote into law a bill that would reduce the size of the Department of Agriculture, cutting 7,500 jobs by 1999.

In 1994 Congress eliminated much of the federal regulation of the trucking industry and cut back the role of the Interstate Commerce Commission (ICC). Then, before the end of 1995, it passed a bill eliminating the ICC altogether. Some employees were transferred to the Transportation Department. The ICC was the oldest federal regulatory agency, founded in 1887.

Promoting Competition Both the president and Congress seemed to agree on the need to promote competition in traditionally regulated industries. Sweeping legislation rewrote the rules for telecommunications in 1996 as the president and Congress worked together in an effort to make the regulatory agencies themselves more efficient. Congress passed legislation streamlining regulation of the securities industry. Following a 1994 study, Congress also streamlined federal purchasing by repealing 300 laws that had made **procurement,** or purchasing of materials, complicated.

Section 1 Assessment

Checking for Understanding

1. **Main Idea** Using a Venn Diagram like the one to the right, show how regulatory commissions and independent agencies are alike and different.

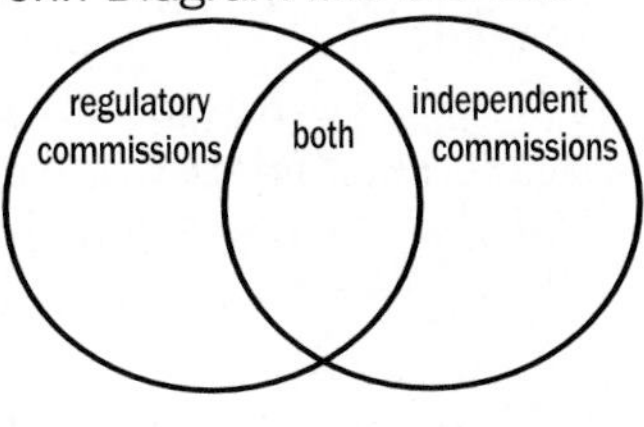

2. **Define** bureaucrat, embassy, government corporation, deregulate, procurement.
3. **Identify** Department of State, Department of the Treasury.
4. How are cabinet departments organized?

Critical Thinking

5. **Making Inferences** Why is it important that regulatory commissions be free from political pressures?

Concepts IN ACTION

Public Policy Imagine that you are on a presidential commission looking into the establishment of a new executive department. Decide on an important issue facing the country today. Think of a new executive department to deal with this issue. Present your suggestion, with reasons, as an oral presentation to the commission.

Section 2

The Civil Service System

Reader's Guide

Key Terms

spoils system, civil service system

Find Out

- How did the civil service system attempt to reform the spoils system?
- What is the difference between a civil servant and a political appointee?

Understanding Concepts

Civic Participation How does the civil service system provide access to government jobs?

COVER STORY

Mail Scandal Spurs Reform

WASHINGTON, D.C., 1881

President James Garfield has released the results of an investigation into allegations against western mail carriers. *The New York Times* had charged the carriers with billing the government unjustified thousands of dollars for mail delivery. The mail carriers claim that delivering to remote areas is very expensive. However, the investigation verified the *Times* claim that many of these highly paid carriers are friends of government officials, and that some deliver mail to places on their routes only three times a year. These revelations have outraged many people and strengthened calls for civil service reform.

19th-century mail carrier

Many people think of a federal bureaucrat as a pencil pusher shuffling papers in Washington, D.C. This image, however, is not accurate for two reasons. First, only 11 percent of all federal government employees work in Washington, D.C. The rest of them work in regional and local offices scattered across the United States and the world. Second, FBI agents, forest rangers, and air-traffic controllers are as much a part of the federal bureaucracy as are secretaries and file clerks. Their activities have little to do with bureaucratic paperwork.

Federal government employees play a vital role in assuring the smooth functioning of the United States government. President Eisenhower addressed this role when he said:

> “*The government of the United States has become too big, too complex, and too pervasive in its influence on all our lives for one individual to pretend to direct the details of its important and critical programming. Competent assistants are mandatory.*”
>
> —Dwight D. Eisenhower

Who are the people who work for the many departments and agencies that make up the federal bureaucracy? The typical man or woman in the federal service is more than 40 years old and has worked for the government for about 15 years. The majority of federal civilian employees earn between $25,000 and $50,000 per year.

About 23 percent of federal workers are members of minority groups, compared with about 14 percent in the private workforce. Women make up about 48 percent of federal workers, roughly the same percentage of women as in the total labor force. A recent survey found that 30 percent of all federal employees had family members who also worked for the government.

Federal workers hold a great variety of jobs. About half of the federal employees are administrative and clerical workers. The government also employs doctors, veterinarians, lawyers, cartographers, scientists, engineers, accountants, and many other professionals.

Origins

Today almost all federal jobs are filled through the competitive civil service system. This system, however, was not in place when our government was established.

A Federal Bureaucrat

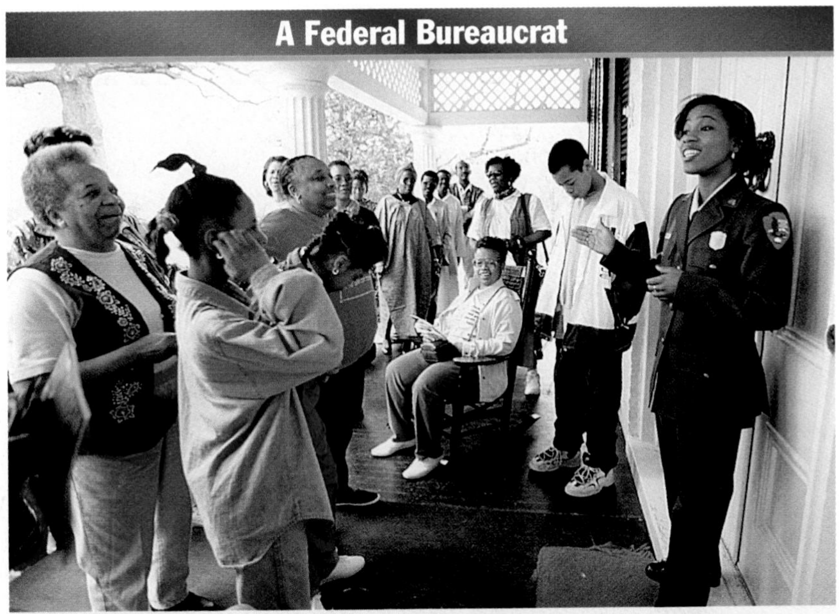

Not Your Typical Office This National Park Service ranger is actually a federal bureaucrat. A ranger's office may be a national park, a national monument, or a national historic site. Park rangers patrol the parklands to protect them from damage and help visitors. ***What other bureaucratic jobs besides park rangers offer people opportunities to work outside the nation's capital?***

The Spoils System

George Washington declared that he appointed government officials according to "fitness of character." At the same time, however, he did favor members of the Federalist Party.

When Thomas Jefferson entered the White House, he found most federal workers opposed him and his political ideas. Consequently, Jefferson fired hundreds of workers who were Federalists. He replaced these workers with people from his own political party, the Democratic-Republican Party.

By the time **Andrew Jackson** became president in 1829, the federal government had begun to grow. Jackson fired about 1,000 federal workers and gave their jobs to his own political supporters. Jackson defended his actions by arguing that it was more democratic to have rotation in office. Long service in the same jobs by any group of workers, he claimed, would only promote tyranny.

A New York senator at the time put it another way. He defended Jackson's actions by stating, "To the victor belong the spoils." The spoils system came to be the phrase that was used for Jackson's method of appointing federal workers. Today, the term **spoils system** describes the practice of victorious politicians rewarding their followers with government jobs.

For the next 50 years, national, state, and local politicians used the spoils system to fill bureaucratic positions. Political supporters of candidates expected to be rewarded with jobs if their candidate won. As the federal government grew larger, the spoils system flourished.

Calls for Reform

The spoils system fostered inefficiency and corruption. Inefficiency grew because, as government became more complex, many jobs required expert staff members. Yet most federal workers were not experts in their jobs. Their special talents lay in working in election campaigns to secure victory for their candidates.

Corruption developed as people used their jobs for personal gain. Government employees did special favors for interest groups in return for political support for their candidates. Jobs were often bought and sold. People made large profits from government contracts. Bureaucrats regularly gave jobs to their friends rather than the lowest bidder.

In the 1850s groups of citizens began to call for reforms. Influential newspapers and magazines pointed out the problems with the spoils system.

A System of Corruption

"PUBLIC OFFICE IS A 'FAMILY SNAP'."

Patronage System Politicians often bestowed federal jobs on friends and family members, as is shown in this 1800s cartoon. Many of these people proved ill-equipped for their jobs and were mainly interested in making themselves rich. ***What does the umbrella in the cartoon symbolize?***

President Grant, whose own administration was filled with corruption, persuaded Congress in 1871 to set up the first Civil Service Commission. By 1875, however, reform efforts faltered as Congress failed to appropriate money for the new commission.

It took a tragedy to restart the reform effort. In 1881 President James A. Garfield ignored Charles Guiteau's requests for a job in the diplomatic service. Infuriated at not being appointed, Guiteau shot President Garfield in the back at a Washington railway station on July 2, 1881. Garfield died 80 days later.

The Pendleton Act The public was outraged. Chester A. Arthur, the new president, pushed hard for reform. In 1883 Congress passed the **Pendleton Act,** creating the present federal civil service system. The **civil service system** is the principle and practice of government employment on the basis of open, competitive examinations and merit. The law set up the Civil Service Commission to administer examinations and supervise the operation of the new system.

The Civil Service Commission operated for 95 years. In 1979, two new agencies replaced it. The Office of Personnel Management handles recruitment, pay, retirement policy, and examinations for federal workers. The Merit System Protection Board settles job disputes and investigates complaints from federal workers.

The Civil Service System Today

Has the present civil service system created new problems while solving those problems linked with the spoils system?

Getting a Job Competition for federal jobs today is stiff. In recent years every job opening has had about 76 applicants. This competition will probably continue. While the federal bureaucracy is huge, the number of federal jobs has not changed much since 1950. Yet the number of people wanting federal jobs keeps on increasing.

The Office of Personnel Management, along with individual agencies, is responsible for filling federal jobs. Job notices are usually posted in post offices, newspapers, and Federal Job Information Centers located in many communities.

Most secretarial and clerical jobs require the applicant to take a written examination. For other jobs such as accountants, social workers, managers, and so on, applicants are evaluated on the basis of training and experience. Veterans are given special preference.

Benefits and Problems Government jobs are attractive because of the many benefits they offer. Salaries are competitive with those in private industry. Federal workers get from 13 to 26 days of paid vacation every year, depending on the length of their service. They have extensive health insurance plans and 13 days of sick leave every year. They may retire at age 55. Government workers who retire after 30 years of service on the job get half pay for the rest of their lives.

Each government job is assigned a certain grade ranging from GS-l, the lowest level, to GS-18, the highest. All civil service workers have job security. They may be fired, but only for specific reasons and only after a very long, complex series of hearings. Many supervisors and top officials find it is easier to put up with an incompetent worker than fire one.

Thus, an ironic situation has developed. On the one hand, the civil service was designed to hire federal workers on merit and protect them from being fired for political reasons. In achieving this goal, however, the system also helps protect a small number of incompetent and inefficient employees.

The Hatch Act The **Hatch Act** limits how involved federal government employees can become in elections. In 1939 Congress passed this law—named after its chief sponsor, Senator Carl Hatch—to prevent a political party from using federal workers in election campaigns. If that happened, it would raise the dangerous possibility that workers' promotions and job security could depend on their support of candidates from the party in power.

The law has been controversial since its passage, and its constitutionality has been the subject of two Supreme Court decisions. Many federal workers dislike the Hatch Act, arguing that the law violates freedom of speech. They also claim the act discourages political participation by people who may be well-informed about political issues.

Supporters of the Hatch Act believe it is needed to keep the federal civil service politically neutral.

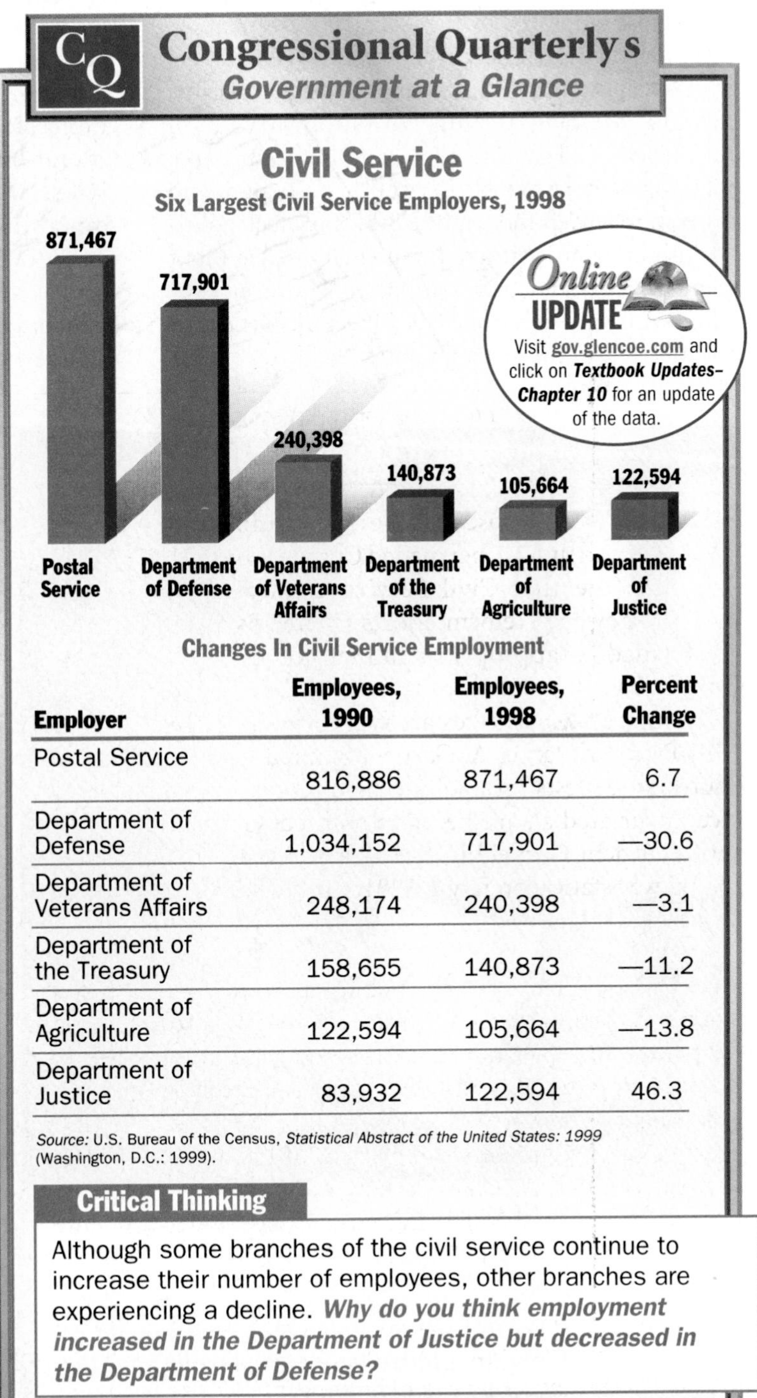

Changes In Civil Service Employment

Employer	Employees, 1990	Employees, 1998	Percent Change
Postal Service	816,886	871,467	6.7
Department of Defense	1,034,152	717,901	—30.6
Department of Veterans Affairs	248,174	240,398	—3.1
Department of the Treasury	158,655	140,873	—11.2
Department of Agriculture	122,594	105,664	—13.8
Department of Justice	83,932	122,594	46.3

Source: U.S. Bureau of the Census, *Statistical Abstract of the United States: 1999* (Washington, D.C.: 1999).

Critical Thinking

Although some branches of the civil service continue to increase their number of employees, other branches are experiencing a decline. ***Why do you think employment increased in the Department of Justice but decreased in the Department of Defense?***

They claim the act protects workers from political pressure from superiors. They also argue it helps prevent employees from using their government positions to punish or influence people for political purposes.

In 1993 Congress revised the act to tighten on-the-job restrictions while loosening up off-duty limits on those employed by the federal government. As amended, the Hatch Act prohibits federal employees from engaging in political activities while on duty, including wearing a campaign button. While off duty, federal workers are allowed to hold office in a political party, participate in political campaigns and rallies, publicly endorse candidates, and raise political funds from within their own government agency's political action committee. However, they cannot run for partisan elective offices or solicit contributions from the general public.

Federal Employees

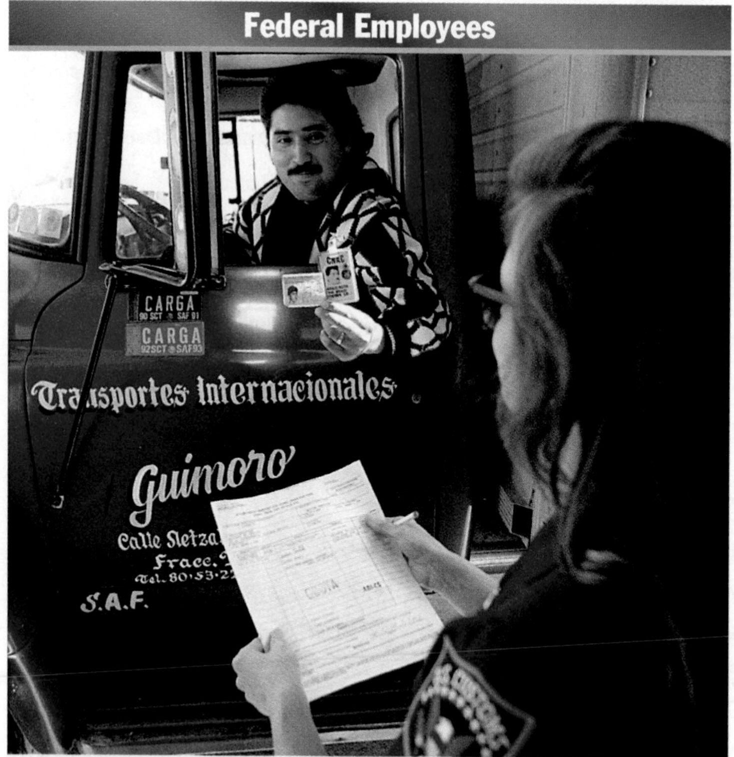

Civil Servants at Work Beginning in the 1800s, civil service staffing has been largely based on merit. President Jimmy Carter urged Congress to pass the Civil Service Reform Act of 1978. This law reorganized and reformed the civil service. ***How do you think the qualifications for a civil servant of today might differ from those for a civil servant from the mid-1800s? Describe the differences.***

Political Appointees in Government

In each presidential election year, the House or Senate publishes a book known by Washington insiders as the *plum book.* The word *plum* stands for *political plum*—a job the new president may fill. The plum book lists all such jobs.

Upon taking office every president has the chance to fill about 2,200 top-level jobs in the federal bureaucracy. These jobs are outside the civil service system. Those who fill these jobs are sometimes called unclassified employees, as opposed to the classified employees hired by the civil service system. About 10 percent of executive branch jobs are appointed by the president. They include 14 cabinet secretaries, about 300 top-level bureau and agency heads, about 150 ambassadorships, and about 1,700 aide and assistant positions.

Filling these jobs gives presidents an opportunity to place loyal supporters in key positions. These political appointees head agencies, offices, and bureaus and make key political decisions. They are expected to try to implement the president's decisions. Unlike career civil service workers, their employment usually ends when a new president is elected. Who are the people with these plum political jobs?

People at the Top The people appointed to the non-civil service positions are first and foremost the president's political supporters. Most are well-educated. Nearly all are college graduates. The great majority have advanced degrees, mostly as lawyers. Others are successful leaders from businesses or professions.

The people holding these types of positions usually are not experts in the work of the agency they head, though they may have served in government before. When the president leaves office, most of them return to other jobs outside the government.

A Ballooning Federal Bureaucracy

Paring Down Government
Historically the federal bureaucracy has expanded to meet the increasing complexities and issues facing the government. ***How do you think the increasing size of the federal bureaucracy affects the president's control of the government?***

A Short Tenure Many new people enter the bureaucracy by presidential appointment. However, these top political appointees hold their positions for only a few years. Because federal agencies are so large and complex, the short tenure makes it difficult for appointees to learn about their jobs. It can take the head of a large agency a year or more to learn all the issues, programs, procedures, and personalities involved in running the agency. One new political appointee discovered, "I was like a sea captain who finds himself on the deck of a ship that he has never seen before. I did not know the mechanism of my ship, I did not know my officers—and I had no acquaintance with the crew."

The result of the short tenures of presidential appointees is that much of the real power over daily operations remains with the career civil service officials. Many of their day-to-day decisions do not make headlines or the nightly newscast, but they do shape the policy of the national government on key problems facing the nation.

Section 2 Assessment

Checking for Understanding

1. **Main Idea** Using a graphic organizer like the one below, note the advantages and disadvantages of the spoils system and the civil service system.

	Advantages	Disadvantages
spoils		
civil service		

2. **Define** spoils system, civil service system.
3. **Identify** Andrew Jackson, Pendleton Act, Hatch Act.
4. What two agencies now make up the former Civil Service Commission?

Critical Thinking

5. **Synthesizing Information** Why do you think political supporters are so eager to fill the plum jobs?

Civic Participation Imagine that you want to obtain employment in a civil service position. You need to evaluate the negative and positive aspects of such employment. Make a list of the pros and cons of a career in the civil service. Discuss your list with your classmates.

Civil Service Commission v. Letter Carriers, 1973

Do First Amendment guarantees of freedom of speech apply to government workers? Should federal employees be free to participate in partisan political activities, or can Congress limit such participation? The case of Civil Service Commission *v.* Letter Carriers *addressed this question.*

A government employee

Background of the Case

The Hatch Act, passed by Congress in 1939, limited federal employees' participation in campaigns or political party activities. The law said federal workers could not campaign for or against a political party, serve as an officer or delegate of a party, raise funds for a party, or run for political office. The purpose of the law was to protect democracy from the influence of partisan government employees. The act did allow workers to vote, join a political party, attend political rallies, and express their opinions.

In 1972, six federal employees, a union, and certain local Democratic and Republican Party committees claimed the act violated the First Amendment. A district court recognized a "well-established governmental interest in restricting political activities by federal employees" but ruled the law was indeed unconstitutional because it was too vague. The court held that free speech was so important that laws limiting speech had to be clear and precise. The Supreme Court ruled on the case in 1973.

The Constitutional Issue

There was no question that the Hatch Act put restrictions on free speech, but were such restrictions justified? Over the years the Court had developed the principle that the right to free speech was not absolute; Congress could put some limits on speech when it was necessary in order to protect the public good. Was this one of those times? The Court also asked whether the restrictions in the law were applied evenly and not aimed at particular political parties, groups, or points of view.

In its 1973 decision the Court referenced the 1947 case of *United Public Workers of America* v. *Mitchell.* In that case George Poole, a federal worker, lost his job for serving as a Democratic ward committeeperson and working as a poll watcher. The Court upheld the law's limitations on political activity, stating that Congress had the power to pass a law "to promote efficiency and integrity in the public service." Justice Hugo Black, in a strong dissent, stated that any law limiting speech must be "narrowly drawn to meet the evil aimed at."

Debating the Case

Questions to Consider

1. What problem did the Hatch Act address?
2. Would allowing government employees to become involved in political campaigns and activities have positive or negative consequences?
3. Did the law's aim outweigh the right to freedom of speech for government employees?

You Be the Judge

Earlier the Supreme Court had found the Hatch Act to be constitutional. In your opinion, should that decision be overturned? Does the Hatch Act violate the First Amendment guarantee of free speech, or is it an acceptable limitation on speech?

Section 3

The Bureaucracy at Work

Reader's Guide

Key Terms

client group, liaison officer, injunction, iron triangle

Find Out

- What are the advantages and disadvantages of bureaucrats taking a greater role in policy making?
- Why do you think people sometimes get frustrated with government bureaucracy?

Understanding Concepts

Separation of Powers What role does the government bureaucracy play in setting policy?

COVER STORY

Ban on Deadly Sweaters

WASHINGTON, D.C., DECEMBER 18, 1996

The Consumer Product Safety Commission (CPSC) today recalled some 32,000 highly flammable women's and girls' sweaters. The sweaters are made of very soft- textured chenille and come in a variety of styles and colors. They sell for up to $130 in department stores and fashion boutiques across the nation. The CPSC surveyed over 100 stores in major U.S. cities to test for the fire hazard. It found that the sweaters burned faster than newspaper. The CPSC urges that consumers immediately stop wearing any sweater they believe may be involved in this recall and return it to the retailer for a refund.

Shopping for chenille

Simply defined, public policy is whatever action the government chooses to take or not to take. The decision of Congress, for example, to provide federal funds for businesses run by disabled persons is a public-policy decision. The decision of the president to refuse to send military aid to a Latin American country is also public policy.

In theory, federal bureaucrats only carry out the policy decisions the president and Congress make. In practice, however, federal bureaucrats today also help make public policy. They often play key roles both in choosing goals the government will try to meet and in selecting programs to achieve those goals. By choosing what or what not to do in various situations, federal bureaucrats are setting policy. Should people who were not elected make policy? Administering federal programs seems to require that they do.

In recent years federal agencies have made key decisions about many policy issues. These include establishing safety requirements for nuclear power plants and deciding the extent to which the nation will depend on oil for energy. Federal agencies are also responsible for setting the eligibility requirements for federal health and welfare programs.

Influencing Policy

Federal bureaucrats help make policy in several ways. The most important of these involves administering the hundreds of programs that have an impact on almost every aspect of national life. Administering these programs requires federal bureaucrats to write rules and regulations and set standards to implement laws Congress passes.

Making Rules When Congress passes a law, it cannot possibly spell out exactly what needs to be done to enforce it. The bureaucracy shapes what the law actually means.

The chief way federal agencies do this is by issuing rules and regulations designed to translate the law into action. One study has shown that, on an average, the bureaucracy formulates 20 rules or regulations to carry out each law.

In 1935, for example, Congress passed the **Social Security Act** establishing the Social Security system. The law makes it possible for disabled workers to receive payments from the government. What does the word *disabled* mean? Are workers disabled if they can work only part-time? Are they disabled if they can work, but not at the same job they once had?

The Social Security Administration in the Department of Health and Human Services has developed 14 pages of rules and regulations describing disability. These regulations even state what blindness means and specifically how it is to be measured. Without such rules, people who are not blind might receive benefits they do not deserve. At the same time, the rules help ensure that anyone who meets the established standard cannot unfairly be denied benefits. It is through thousands of decisions such as these that bureaucrats make federal government policy affecting disabled people.

Often, rule making by federal agencies is the same as lawmaking. For example, the Department of Housing and Urban Development (HUD) has created guidelines for building contractors to follow when hiring minority employees. These guidelines are used to decide whether contractors can work on federally funded construction projects. The HUD guidelines have the force of law. In order to work on the projects, contractors must follow them.

Paperwork For many years the number of rules and regulations federal agencies issued had been growing. Agency regulations totaled more than 50,000 printed pages a year. Along with more regulations came more paperwork. More than 2 billion forms were filled out and submitted to the federal government each year. The Small Business Administration estimated that companies spent at least 1 billion hours per year filling out forms—at a cost of about $100 billion annually.

Congress in 1995 cleared a bill to reduce the amount of federal paperwork. The president signed the bill, requiring the Office of Management and Budget director to set a paperwork reduction goal of at least 10 percent in each of the first 2 years and 5 percent per year to fiscal 2001.

Involvement in Lawmaking The bureaucracy also shapes public policy by helping draft new bills for Congress, testifying about legislation, and providing lawmakers with technical information they may not otherwise have access to. In addition, lawmakers know that it can be difficult to pass major bills without the advice of the federal agencies most concerned with the bills' contents.

Often, the ideas for new laws come from within the bureaucracy itself. Lawyers within the Justice Department, for example, drafted the Safe Streets Act of 1968, which created a new division within the Justice Department—the Law Enforcement Assistance Administration—that existed into the 1980s. In the same way, bureaucrats in what is now the Department of Health and Human Services, along with some hospital administrators and labor unions, worked hard and over a long period of time for the law that set up the Medicare program.

Bureaucratic Policy Making

Federal Policy Decisions made by federal bureaucrats affect the lives of all Americans every day. ***Why do you think the Department of Health and Human Services has 14 pages of rules describing disability?***

Settling Disputes Some federal agencies shape public policy by deciding disputes over the application of a law or set of rules. When agencies do this, they act almost as courts. The regulatory commissions in particular make government policy in this way. They have the authority to hear and resolve disputes among parties that come under their regulatory power. The rulings of these agencies have the same legal status as those of courts.

Providing Advice Bureaucrats also help shape public policy by providing top political decision makers with information and advice. Many career bureaucrats are experts in their areas. In addition, federal agencies collect information on an incredible variety of subjects. These range from the number of bald eagles left in the United States to the effects of secondhand smoking on newborn infants.

Federal agencies may use their information to support or oppose a particular public policy. Several years ago, for example, studies by the Public Health Service on the effects of smoking led to new laws and regulations designed to cut down on the use of cigarettes.

Thus, the federal bureaucracy does more today than simply fill in the details of laws. The bureaucracy plays a role in determining what those policies will be.

Paper Shuffling in the Capital

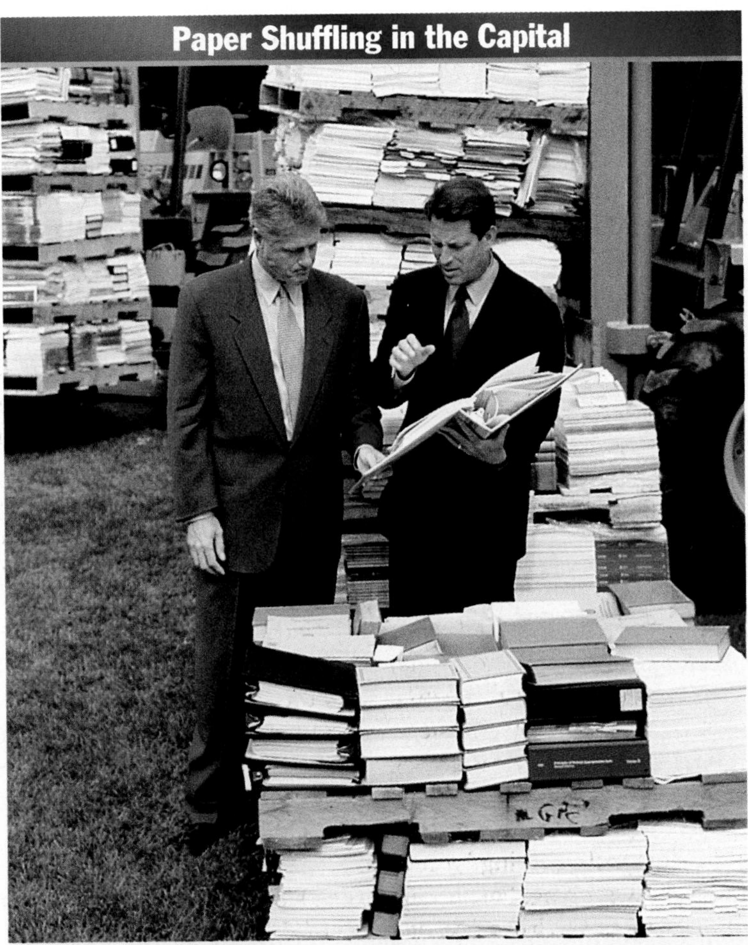

Reducing Government Waste Surrounded by bureaucratic paperwork, Vice President Al Gore presented his proposal "Reinventing Government," also called The National Performance Review, to President Clinton on the White House lawn. Gore attempted to streamline the federal bureaucracy and eliminate waste and duplication. ***Why do you think trimming the bureaucracy and its paperwork is such a difficult task?***

Why the Bureaucracy Makes Policy

The federal bureaucracy has grown and assumed an important role in making public policy for five reasons: (1) growth of the nation, (2) international crises, (3) economic problems at home, (4) citizens' demands, and (5) the nature of bureaucracy itself.

National Growth and Technology The growth of the federal bureaucracy mirrors the growth of the United States. For almost 60 years, the 3 original cabinet departments and the attorney general's office handled the work of the executive branch. As the population grew, so did the government. The same number of officials who ran a country of 50 million people cannot govern a country of more than 250 million.

In addition, rapid advances in technology have made life much more complex. Today, a single president and 535 lawmakers in Congress cannot possibly have all the knowledge and time needed to

The Space Race Expands the Government

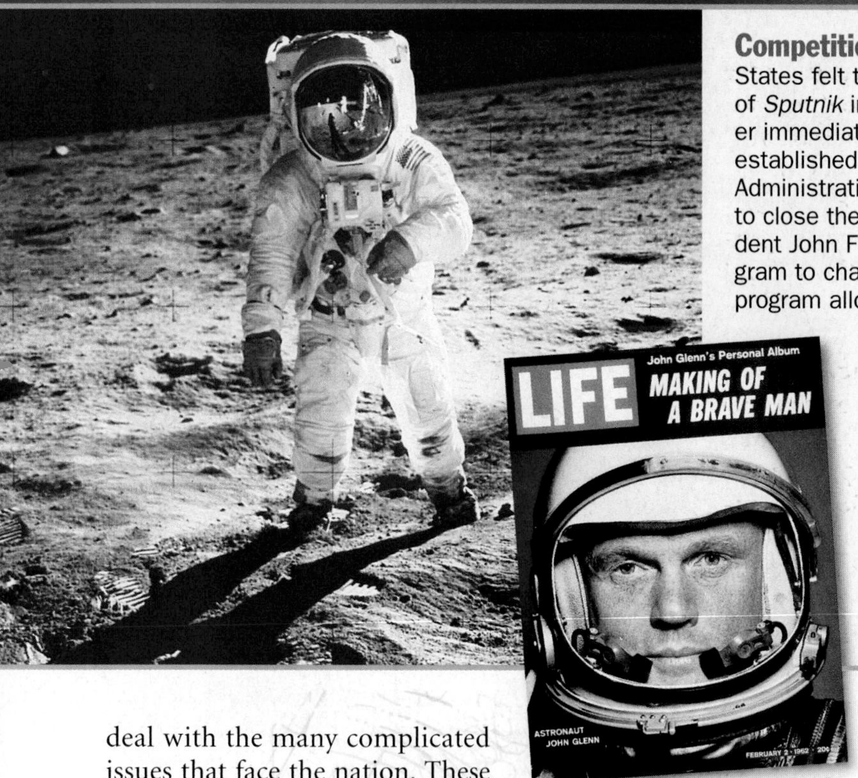

Competition and Expansion The United States felt threatened by the Soviets' launching of *Sputnik* in 1957. President Dwight Eisenhower immediately increased military funding and established the National Aeronautics and Space Administration (NASA), which worked feverishly to close the gap in the space race. Later, President John F. Kennedy authorized the Apollo program to challenge the Soviets in space. This program allowed Edwin E. Aldrin, Jr., (left) and Neil Armstrong to be the first humans to walk on the moon. ***How did the launching of* Sputnik *increase the size of the United States government?***

John Glenn, first American to orbit the earth

deal with the many complicated issues that face the nation. These issues include nuclear power, education reform, space exploration, environmental protection, cancer research, health care, and many others.

Many other tasks such as regulating atomic energy or launching communications satellites also require some government involvement. The president and Congress establish bureaucracies and give them the money and authority to carry out their tasks.

International Crises

Competition with the Soviet Union and international crises following World War II furthered the growth of the federal bureaucracy. During the Cold War from the mid-1940s to the 1980s, the United States and the Soviet Union never fought each other directly. Each country did, however, develop new weapons to defend itself, and both countries gave aid to other countries they wanted as allies. In 1949 the United States created the Department of Defense from the United States Military Establishment. The Defense Department soon grew to be the largest single department in the federal government. With the end of the Cold War, the department began to be reduced.

After the Soviet Union launched *Sputnik I,* the first space satellite, in 1957, the federal government started a large-scale program to improve science and mathematics instruction in the United States. The government established NASA in 1958 to direct the nation's space exploration program. As a further result of the Cold War, the government created several other new agencies. These included the Central Intelligence Agency, the Arms Control and Disarmament Agency, the United States Information Agency, and the Peace Corps.

The Korean War (from 1950 to 1953) and the Vietnam War (from 1964 to 1973) involved millions of American soldiers. Both wars led to the continued need for the Veterans Administration, which was elevated to the cabinet level in 1989, and renamed the Department of Veterans Affairs. It is one of the largest federal agencies.

Economic Problems

President Franklin D. Roosevelt greatly expanded the size of the federal bureaucracy as he attempted to combat the Depression during the 1930s. By 1940 the number of federal workers had almost doubled. Many people accepted the idea that the federal government had a duty to assist the ill, the disabled, the elderly, and the neglected. As a result, the federal government today spends billions of dollars each year on hundreds of assistance programs.

The Depression years also led to the idea that the federal government has a special responsibility both to stimulate the nation's economy and to regulate unfair business practices. Thus, agencies that help businesses, such as the Department of Commerce, have grown along with agencies that regulate businesses, such as the Federal Trade Commission.

Citizen Demands The bureaucracy has also grown in response to issues raised by various interest groups within the country. This is not a new phenomenon. Congress, for example, created the Departments of Agriculture (1862), Commerce (1903), and Labor (1913) in part to meet the increased demands of farmers, businesspeople, and workers.

Once it is established, each agency has client groups that it serves. **Client groups** are the individuals and groups who work with the agency and are most affected by its decisions. The client groups of the Department of Defense, for example, include the defense contractors who make weapons and supplies for the armed forces. The client groups of the Department of Agriculture are largely the farmers and others in the business of agriculture.

Client groups often lobby both Congress and the agency itself for more programs and services. Sometimes competition develops. If business leaders can have "their" people in the Commerce Department, labor leaders want "their" people in the Labor Department to make sure they get their "fair share."

The Nature of Bureaucracy Another reason for the increase in the number of federal agencies is that the country's needs change. Once created, however, federal agencies almost never die. They seem to exist for their own sake. Several years ago Congress created the Federal Metal and Non-Metallic Safety Board of Review. A bureaucrat named Jubal Hale was appointed as its director. The board, however, never received any cases to review. As a result, Hale had no work to do. He spent the next four years reading and listening to phonograph records in his office. Finally, he suggested the agency be abolished, and it was.

Former president Ford put it this way:

> "*One of the enduring truths of the nation's capital is that bureaucrats survive. Agencies don't fold their tents and quietly fade away after their work is done. They find something new to do.*"
>
> —Gerald Ford

These observations are what led to reform. President Clinton's "reinventing government" and the Republican Congress's "Contract With America" both targeted government waste.

Influencing Bureaucratic Decisions

The federal bureaucracy does not make public policy in isolation. The president, Congress, the courts, and client groups influence federal agencies as they conduct business.

Meeting the Country's Needs

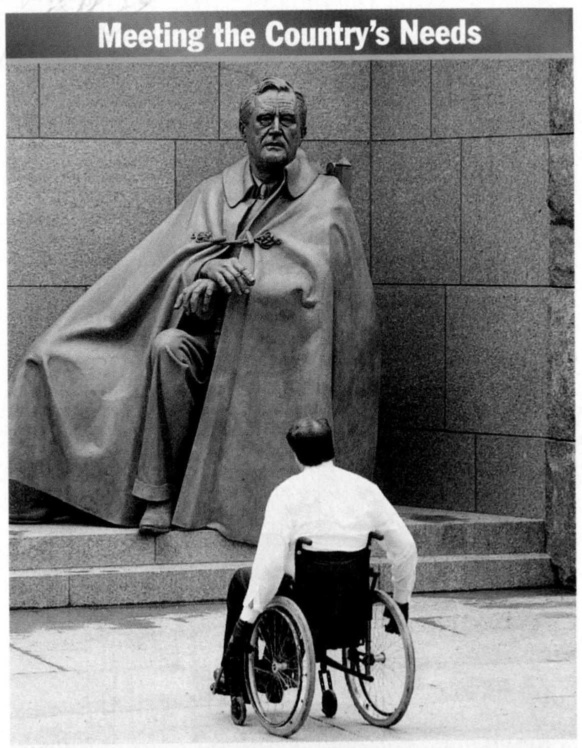

Economics and Expansion Roosevelt's New Deal programs changed the federal government. The FDR Memorial in Washington, D.C., honors the president. ***Why did Roosevelt expand the government during the Depression?***

Influence of Congress Bureaucrats are careful to build support with congressional committees that have authority over the agencies for which the bureaucrat works. Each cabinet department has **liaison officers** who help promote good relations with Congress. Liaison officers keep track of bills moving through Congress that might affect the agency, as well as responding to requests for information from lawmakers.

Congress uses two major tools to influence decision making in federal agencies—new legislation and the budget. Lawmakers can pass laws to change the rules or regulations a federal agency establishes or to limit an agency in some way. Sometimes Congress is successful in these attempts. In 1979, for example, the Internal Revenue Service ruled that donations to private schools were not tax deductible unless the schools enrolled a certain number of minority students. The ruling caused a great deal of controversy, and Congress overturned it with new legislation.

Congress's major power over the bureaucracy is the power of the purse. The nation's lawmakers control each agency's budget. They can add to or cut an agency's budget and, in theory at least, refuse to appropriate money for the agency. What happens more often, however, is that Congress can threaten to eliminate programs that are important to the agency.

Even the power of appropriation has limits as a way for Congress to influence agency decisions. Much of an agency's budget may be used for entitlement expenditures. These expenditures are for basic services already required by law, such as Social Security or pensions for retired government employees. Such services are almost impossible for Congress to cut. Agencies also have developed strategies for getting around possible budget cuts. When the agency sends in its budget, for example, it will underestimate the amount it needs for its entitlement expenditures. At the same time, it will ask for full funding for other parts of its program that it does not want to cut. If the agency runs short of money for entitlements midway through the year, Congress must pass a supplemental appropriation to cover the shortage. If budget cuts must be made, agencies may sometimes target their cuts in the districts or states of key members of Congress who have the power to get budget cuts restored. In 1975, for example, Congress said it

We the People

Making a Difference

Heidi Landgraf

DEA badge

Hearing the words, "My name is Heidi Landgraf. I'm an agent with the DEA," two drug cartel bosses stared in disbelief. This time they were the victims—of a Drug Enforcement Administration sting operation. Heidi Landgraf was at the center of Operation Green Ice, playing the part of a drug lord's daughter. Her two-year performance won Landgraf a 1993 DEA Administrator's Award. As one of more than 100 federal agents involved in the worldwide operation, she helped police in the United States and six other countries arrest a total of 140 suspected criminals and seize about $50 million.

Landgraf's identity as Heidi Herrera was created carefully with tax returns, Visa cards, and a passport. Although she was always under the watchful eyes of fellow agents, she was in constant danger. From a phony business location Landgraf collected cash from major drug dealers across the country and laundered it through banks. After two years of collecting evidence, the DEA scheduled the "take down."

Because her face and name appeared in press accounts of the operation when the news broke, Landgraf had to give up her work as an undercover agent. She continued to work within the DEA, however, in media relations and drug prevention education.

wanted to reduce the budget for Amtrak, the federal agency that operates passenger trains in the United States. Amtrak almost immediately announced plans to comply with the reduced budget by cutting vital passenger service in the districts of key congressional leaders. The announcements had their desired effect: these leaders succeeded in restoring most of the Amtrak funds.

The Influence of the Courts

Federal courts do not actively seek to influence the federal bureaucracy. The courts, however, can have an important impact on policy making. The Administrative Procedures Act of 1946 allows citizens directly affected by the actions of federal agencies to challenge those agencies' actions in court. A federal court may issue an **injunction**—an order that will stop a particular action or enforce a rule or regulation.

Success in Court Cases While the courts can have a real impact on the bureaucracy, citizens have not had much success in court cases against the bureaucracy. One study shows that the courts do not usually reverse the decisions of federal regulatory commissions. For example, the Federal Power Commission and the Federal Trade Commission have won 91 percent of the cases they have argued before the Supreme Court. The National Labor Relations Board and the Internal Revenue Service have won 75 percent of their cases.

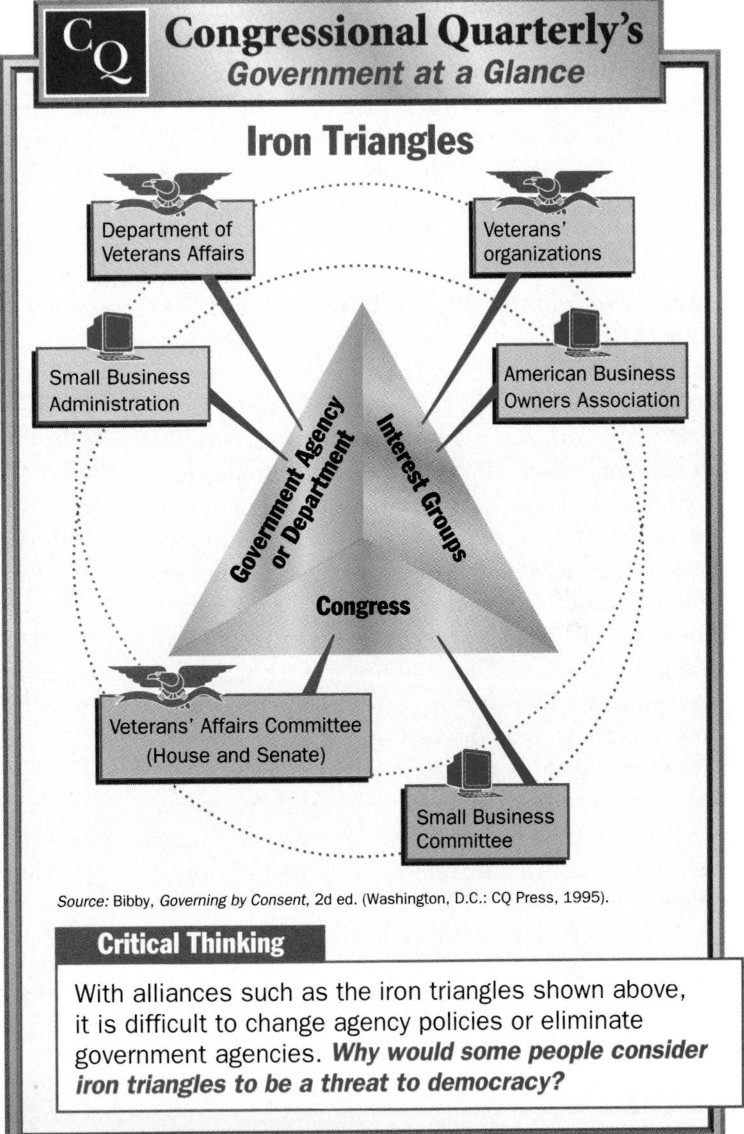

Source: Bibby, *Governing by Consent*, 2d ed. (Washington, D.C.: CQ Press, 1995).

Critical Thinking

With alliances such as the iron triangles shown above, it is difficult to change agency policies or eliminate government agencies. ***Why would some people consider iron triangles to be a threat to democracy?***

The Influence of Client Groups

As stated earlier, each agency has client groups. The Department of Education spends much of its time dealing with state and local school administrators. The Food and Drug Administration works closely with major drug companies. The Commerce Department identifies with and promotes business interests. The Department of Labor has a similar relationship with labor unions.

Client groups often attempt to influence agency decisions through lobbyists in Washington, D.C. These lobbyists work to reach agency officials. Lobbyists may testify at agency hearings, write letters, keep track of agency decisions, and take other steps to support their groups' interests.

Iron Triangles Congressional committees, client groups, and a federal department or agency often cooperate closely to make public policy. When agencies, congressional committees, and client groups continually work together, such cooperation is called an **iron triangle,** because together the three groups have the necessary resources to satisfy each other's needs. The adjective *iron* is used because the relationship is so strong that it is often difficult for other individuals and groups outside the triangle to influence policy in the area.

Public policy toward veterans' affairs is an example of an iron triangle. The **Department of Veterans Affairs (VA)** provides important services such as hospital care, but the VA needs resources to continue offering such services to veterans. Lawmakers on congressional committees responsible for veterans' affairs supply the VA with money but need electoral support to remain in office. Congressional committees also need political support to win internal struggles for power in Congress. Client groups, such as the American Legion, provide the political support that the lawmakers need to remain in office. Client groups in turn need the VA's goods and services to satisfy the demands of their members. It is the working combination of these three groups that basically determines the policy of the national government toward veterans. Similar iron triangles operate in many policy areas such as agriculture, business, labor, and national defense.

People often move from one side of the triangle to another. In the area of national defense, for example, a general in the Department of Defense may retire and become a Washington lobbyist for a defense contractor that sells weapons to the Department of Defense. A staff member of the Senate Armed Services Committee may leave Congress and go to work in the Defense Department. Later, the same person may take a job with a defense contractor.

Many critics believe that because iron triangles allow interest groups undue influence outside the control of the executive branch, Congress should pass laws to regulate them.

Agencies Influence One Another Interactions among agencies also influence decisions and policy making in the bureaucracy. For example, rules made by the Occupational Safety and Health Administration about noise standards in factories may contradict regulations established by the Environmental Protection Agency. Decision makers in each agency may attempt to influence the others to accept their programs or rules. Often, such disputes are settled by interagency task forces or committees.

Student Web Activity Visit the *United States Government: Democracy in Action* Web site at gov.glencoe.com and click on ***Chapter 10–Student Web Activities*** for an activity about the bureaucracy at work.

Section 3 Assessment

Checking for Understanding

1. **Main Idea** Using a graphic organizer like the one below, identify two ways Congress influences federal agencies and two ways federal agencies contribute to legislation.

2. **Define** client group, liaison officer, injunction, iron triangle.
3. **Identify** Social Security Act, Department of Veterans Affairs.
4. What are five reasons that the federal bureaucracy has assumed an important role in making public policy?

Critical Thinking

5. **Making Inferences** Do you think that iron triangles undermine or serve the public interest? Explain your answer.

Concepts IN ACTION

Separation of Powers The government bureaucracy, in theory, carries out the policy decisions of Congress and the president. In practice, however, the bureaucracy also helps influence policy. Create a political cartoon depicting one of the ways in which the federal bureaucracy influences policy.

Using a Word Processor

There are several ways to create a professional-looking printed document. You may use a word processor or a computer word processing software program.

Congress
House of Representatives
Rules
Leadership

Jacklyn Ortez
Work Experience
Education
Organizations

Learning the Skill

After starting your word processing system, a blank document, sometimes called "Document 1," appears on the video screen. To begin composing your document, simply begin typing. To create a new document, click the *New* button on the standard toolbar. The following tips will help you format the document to make it look the way you want.

1. As you type, the word processing program automatically "wraps" the text to the next line when the text reaches the right margin. Press ENTER if you wish to start a new paragraph.
2. You may see paragraph marks (¶) and certain other symbols, called nonprinting characters, on your screen. You may want to turn this function off by clicking the *Show/Hide* button on your toolbar.
3. To insert new text in a line, move the cursor to the point where you want the insertion to go and type the text.
4. To move several lines of text, select the text using the drag method and click the *Cut* button on your toolbar. Then position your cursor in the location that you want to move the cut text and click *Paste.* If you drag or paste text to the wrong place, click the *Undo* button.
5. Use a template to easily create professional documents.
6. To learn about other word processing methods, read the user's manual or click on the *Help* button on the toolbar.

Practicing the Skill

Create a resume using a template. Choose *Style Gallery* from the Format menu and select the resume template. To adapt the resume template into a new document, first choose *New* from the File menu. Then select a template, select the resume option, and press OK. Replace the existing text with your own information. Save your resume.

Application Activity

Create a one- to two-page professional-looking document using the subject of Chester A. Arthur's election or presidency. For example, you might choose to create a campaign brochure for Arthur or a newspaper clipping that details the Pendleton Act.

Assessment and Activities

Self-Check Quiz Visit the *United States Government: Democracy in Action* Web site at gov.glencoe.com and click on ***Chapter 10–Self-Check Quizzes*** to prepare for the chapter test.

Reviewing Key Terms

Choose the letter of the correct term or concept below to complete the sentence.

a. injunction
b. liaison officer
c. government corporation
d. procurement
e. client group
f. iron triangle
g. bureaucrat
h. embassy
i. spoils system
j. deregulate

1. An individual who works for the federal government is a ____.
2. Before the civil service system, many people got government jobs through the ____.
3. Some people work for a _____, such as the Postal Service.
4. Some people lost their jobs when Congress began to _____ the Civil Aeronautics Board and cut down on its procedures.
5. An _____ is the office of an ambassador in a foreign country.
6. A _____, such as a special-interest group, is a key factor in influencing public policy.
7. In some cases, a court will issue an _____ to stop a particular action.
8. To make regulatory agencies more efficient, Congress repealed 300 laws that had made _____, or purchasing of materials, complicated.
9. A _____ helps promote good relations among Congress and cabinet departments.
10. A cooperative effort on the parts of congressional committees, a federal agency, and client groups is called an _____.

Current Events JOURNAL

Bureaucratic Action Choose one of the independent agencies or executive departments discussed in this chapter. Use the *Readers' Guide to Periodical Literature* or other research materials to find out the current activities of the agency or the executive department you chose. Summarize your findings in the form of a newspaper article.

Recalling Facts

1. What three types of agencies make up the federal bureaucracy?
2. What are some independent agencies that are government corporations?
3. What is the special role of independent regulatory commissions in the federal bureaucracy?
4. Why was the civil service system created?
5. To what three job benefits are federal workers entitled?
6. What event led to the practice of government assisting the ill and the neglected?
7. How do client groups attempt to influence the decisions that government agencies make?

Understanding Concepts

1. **Public Policy** Is evaluating existing programs is important in a society with a large bureaucracy? Support your opinion.
2. **Civic Participation** With every new administration, new people are named to hold top management positions within the federal bureaucracy. Explain the advantages and disadvantages of this system.
3. **Separation of Powers** Should bureaucrats be allowed to actually help determine public policy? Support your answer.

Critical Thinking

1. **Making Inferences** Why might strong presidents rely less on their cabinets' advice than weak presidents?
2. **Synthesizing Information** Use a skeleton outline like the one below to organize a paper that would explain why the federal bureaucracy has grown. Use facts from the text and charts in Chapter 10.

The Growth of the Federal Bureaucracy

I. Its size
   A.
   B.
   C.
II. Its Complexity
   A.
   B.
   C.

Interpreting Political Cartoons Activity

1. What is the warning each of these people is giving?
2. How do you think these people's attitudes affect the size of the federal bureaucracy?
3. What governmental dilemma does this cartoon emphasize?

Cooperative Learning Activity

Comparing Agencies Organize into groups. Make a list of the ways in which any four executive departments or agencies of the federal bureaucracy affect your daily life. Rank each of the influences in order of their importance. Rejoin the class and compare lists. Which department or agency was mentioned most often?

Technology Activity

Using Software Search the Internet or your library to find out the increase in the number of people working for the executive departments of the federal government from 1900 to the present. You can use the *Statistical Abstract of the United States* to find these figures. Then use the graphics options of your software to create a bar graph that illustrates the change. Display the completed graphs in the classroom.

Skill Practice Activity

Using a Word Processor Imagine you are a member of a client group that is attempting to influence an agency of the federal bureaucracy. Using a word processor program, create a professional-looking brochure that you would use to publicize your issues and concerns.

Participating in Local Government

You can find jobs within the government bureaucracy in all levels of government. Using your local library or the Internet, research the different types of government jobs in your community. Find out the procedure for applying for these jobs, the qualifications required, and the salaries. Present your findings in an illustrated pamphlet.

The Judicial Branch

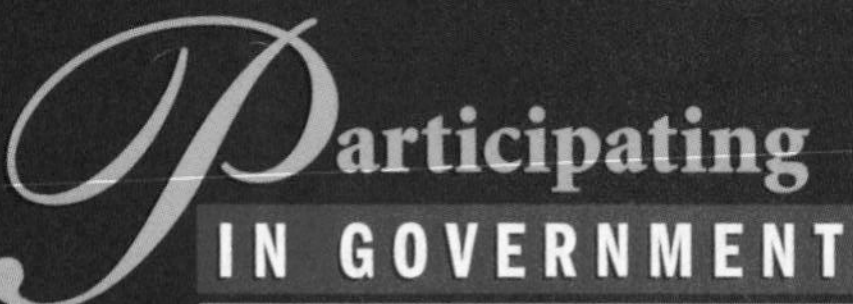

Informing the Citizens *Find out the current cases before the Supreme Court that may be controversial. Watch for information in periodicals and newspapers on the issues in these cases. Write a summary of one of these issues and circulate it among people you know to find out what decision they believe the Court should make. Discuss your findings with the class.*

Electronic Field Trip

The Supreme Court

Take a virtual tour of the Supreme Court Building in Washington, D.C., and see how the judicial branch works.

Glencoe's Democracy in Action Video Program

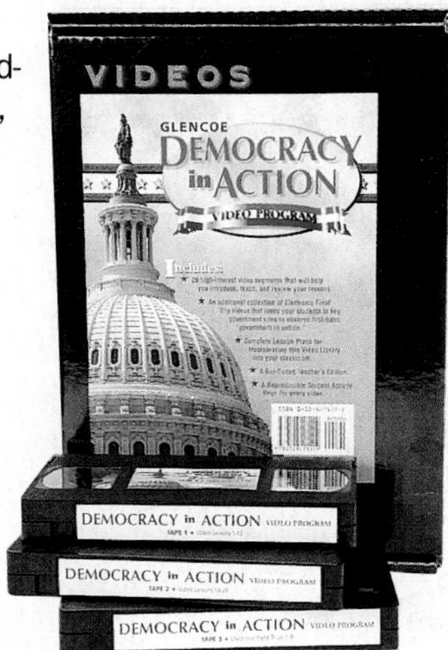

The Supreme Court building is a nearly self-sufficient, structured community. The **Democracy in Action** video program "The Supreme Court," referenced below, describes the Supreme Court's procedures and the administrative support other workers provide for the nine justices.

As you view the video program, try to identify any legal terms you recognize or any words that have a special meaning in a court of law.

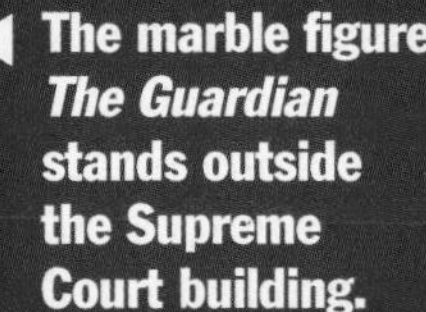

The marble figure *The Guardian* stands outside the Supreme Court building.

Also available in videodisc format.

View the videodisc by scanning the barcode or by entering the chapter number on your keypad and pressing Search.

Disc 2, Side 1, Chapter 4

Hands-On Activity

Use library or Internet resources to research the procedures a case must follow to be heard by the United States Supreme Court. Be sure to include every level of court that hears the case and each appeal prior to the Supreme Court. Use a word processor to create an organizational chart showing the steps in this process with a brief explanation of each one.

Chapter 11

The Federal Court System

Why It's Important

Decisions, Decisions The Supreme Court and lower federal courts decide cases that affect your everyday life, from the air you breathe to the rights you enjoy. In this chapter you will see the relationship of these courts to each other and the powers of each.

To find out more about how the U.S. court system works and how it impacts you, view the ***Democracy in Action*** Chapter 11 video lesson:

The Federal Court System at Work

GOVERNMENT Online

Chapter Overview Visit the *United States Government: Democracy in Action* Web site at gov.glencoe.com and click on ***Chapter 11–Overview*** to preview chapter information.

Section 1

Powers of the Federal Courts

Reader's Guide

Key Terms

concurrent jurisdiction, original jurisdiction, appellate jurisdiction, litigant, due process clause

Find Out

- How does federal court jurisdiction differ from state court jurisdiction?
- How do Supreme Court decisions reflect the attempts of the justices to meet changing social conditions?

Understanding Concepts

Constitutional Interpretations How has the Supreme Court historically increased its power?

COVER STORY

Marshall Is Chief Justice

WASHINGTON, D.C., JANUARY 20, 1801

President John Adams surprised fellow Federalists by nominating Secretary of State John Marshall for chief justice of the United States. Quick Senate confirmation is likely. The nomination follows John Jay's refusal of the position, reportedly because he views the Supreme Court as having too little power. Marshall is thought to favor strengthening the Court and the federal government. Some believe these views could cause conflict between the new chief justice and the probable new president, Marshall's cousin Thomas Jefferson.

John Marshall

The Constitution provided for a Supreme Court of the United States as part of a court system that would balance the powers of the other two branches of government. Unlike the president and Congress, however, the Supreme Court played a very minor role until **Chief Justice John Marshall** was appointed in 1801. He served until 1835 and helped to increase the power of the Court.

Over the years the Court's growing role in American government met serious challenges, as a historian of the Court noted:

> "*Nothing in the Court's history is more striking than the fact that, while its significant and necessary place in the Federal form of Government has always been recognized by thoughtful and patriotic men, nevertheless, no branch of the Government and no institution under the Constitution has sustained more continuous attack or reached its present position after more vigorous opposition.*"
>
> —Charles Warren, 1924

Today the judicial branch of government is well established as an equal with the legislative and executive branches.

Jurisdiction of the Courts

The United States judiciary consists of parallel systems of federal and state courts. Each of the 50 states has its own system of courts whose powers derive from state constitutions and laws. The federal court system consists of the Supreme Court and lower federal courts established by Congress. Federal courts derive their powers from the Constitution and federal laws.

Federal Court Jurisdiction The authority to hear certain cases is called the **jurisdiction** of the court. In the dual court system, state

◀ **U.S. Courthouse in Austin, Texas**

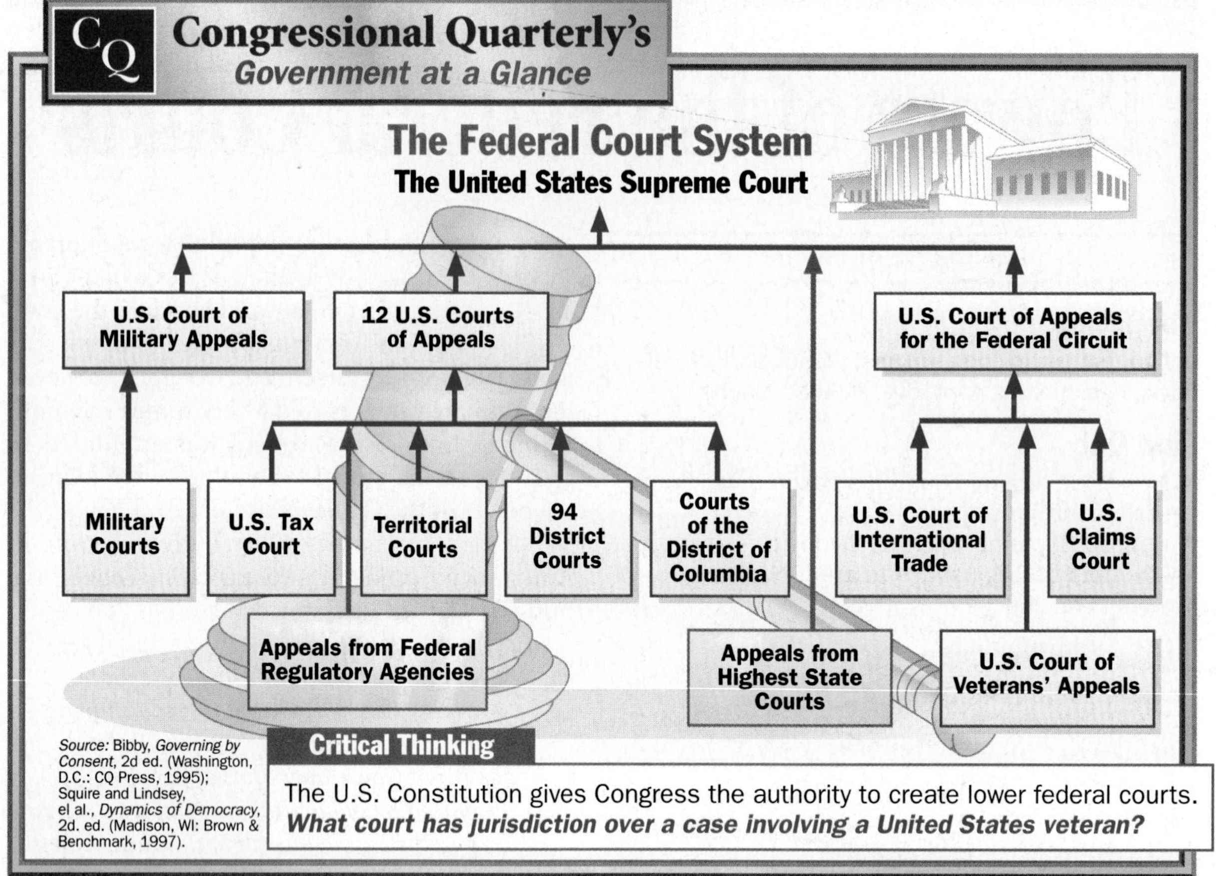

Source: Bibby, *Governing by Consent*, 2d ed. (Washington, D.C.: CQ Press, 1995); Squire and Lindsey, el al., *Dynamics of Democracy*, 2d. ed. (Madison, WI: Brown & Benchmark, 1997).

Critical Thinking

The U.S. Constitution gives Congress the authority to create lower federal courts. ***What court has jurisdiction over a case involving a United States veteran?***

courts have jurisdiction over cases involving state laws, while federal courts have jurisdiction over cases involving federal laws. Sometimes the jurisdiction of the state courts and the jurisdiction of the federal courts overlap.

The Constitution gave federal courts jurisdiction in cases that involve United States laws, treaties with foreign nations, or interpretations of the Constitution. Federal courts also try cases involving bankruptcy and cases involving admiralty or maritime law.

Federal courts hear cases if certain parties or persons are involved. These include: (1) ambassadors and other representatives of foreign governments; (2) two or more state governments; (3) the United States government or one of its offices or agencies; (4) citizens of different states; (5) a state and a citizen of a different state; (6) citizens of the same state claiming lands under grants of different states; and (7) a state or its citizens and a foreign country or its citizens.

Concurrent Jurisdiction In most cases the difference between federal and state court jurisdiction is clear. In some instances, however, both federal and state courts have jurisdiction, a situation known as **concurrent jurisdiction.** Concurrent jurisdiction exists, for example, in a case involving citizens of different states in a dispute concerning at least $50,000. In such a case, a person may sue in either a federal or a state court. If the person being sued insists, however, the case must be tried in a federal court.

Original and Appellate Jurisdiction The court in which a case is originally tried is known as a **trial court.** A trial court has **original jurisdiction.** In the federal court system, the district courts as well as several other lower courts have only original jurisdiction.

If a person who loses a case in a trial court wishes to appeal a decision, he or she may take the case to a court with **appellate jurisdiction.** The federal court system provides courts of appeals that have only appellate jurisdiction. Thus, a party may appeal a case from a district court to a court of appeals. If that party loses in the court of appeals, he or she may appeal the case to the Supreme Court, which has both original and appellate jurisdiction.

Developing Supreme Court Power

Since its creation by the Constitution, the Supreme Court has developed into the most powerful court in the world. It may also be the least understood institution of American government. The role of the Court has developed from custom, usage, and history.

Early Precedents Certain principles were established early in the Court's history. Neither the Supreme Court nor any federal court may initiate action. A judge or justice may not seek out an issue and bid both sides to bring it to court. The courts must wait for **litigants,** or people engaged in a lawsuit, to come before them.

Federal courts will only determine cases. They will not simply answer a legal question, regardless of how significant the issue or who asks the question. In July 1793, at the request of President Washington, Secretary of State Jefferson wrote to Chief Justice John Jay asking the Court for advice. Jefferson submitted 29 questions dealing with American neutrality during the war between France and England. Three weeks later the Court refused to answer the questions with a polite reply:

> *We have considered the previous question stated in a letter written by your direction to us by the Secretary of State. . . . We exceedingly regret every event that may cause embarrassment to your administration, but we derive consolation from the reflection that your judgment will discern what is right. . . .*

 **Landmark Cases**

Marbury* v. *Madison In response to litigation, however, the Court did not hesitate to give an opinion that greatly increased its own power. The case was ***Marbury* v. *Madison,*** the most celebrated decision in American history. As President Adams's term expired in 1801, Congress passed a bill giving the president a chance to appoint 42 justices of the peace in the District of Columbia. The Senate quickly confirmed the nominees. The secretary of state had delivered all but 4 of the

Judicial Review

Constitutional Interpretations On his last night in the White House, Adams stayed up signing judicial commissions for men of his party, the Federalists, defeated in the 1800 elections. The new president, Jefferson, angrily called Adams's appointees "midnight judges." Adams's actions resulted in the landmark case *Marbury* v. *Madison*, which secured the power of judicial review for the Supreme Court. ***Why is judicial review a key feature of the United States governmental system?***

GOVERNMENT Online

Student Web Activity Visit the *United States Government: Democracy in Action* Web site at gov.glencoe.com and click on ***Chapter 11–Student Web Activities*** for an activity about the powers of the federal courts.

commissions to the new officers by the day Thomas Jefferson came into office. Jefferson, in one of his first acts as president, stopped delivery of the remaining commissions. William Marbury, one of those who did not receive his commission, filed suit in the Supreme Court, under a provision of the Judiciary Act of 1789.

The Court heard the case in February 1803. Chief Justice John Marshall announced the ruling that Marbury's rights had been violated and that he should have his commission. However, Marshall said that the Judiciary Act of 1789 had given the Court more power than the Constitution had allowed. Therefore, the Court could not, under the Constitution, issue a writ to force delivery of the commission. Jefferson won a victory, but it was one he did not enjoy. The chief justice had secured for the Court the power to review acts of Congress—the power of **judicial review.**

John Marshall's Influence In several other key decisions under John Marshall, the Court carved out its power. In *Fletcher* v. *Peck*[1] in 1810, the Supreme Court extended its power to review state laws. The Court held that a law passed by the Georgia legislature was a violation of the Constitution's protection of contracts. In 1819 in *Dartmouth College* v. *Woodward*,[2] the Court applied the protection of contracts to corporate charters.

Marshall not only extended the power of the Court, he also broadened federal power at the expense of the states. In *McCulloch* v. *Maryland*[3] the Court declared that states could not hamper the exercise of legitimate national interests. Maryland had attempted to tax the Bank of the United States. In 1824 in *Gibbons* v. *Ogden*,[4] the Court broadened the meaning of interstate commerce, further extending federal authority at the expense of the states. By 1825 the Court had declared at least one law in each of 10 states unconstitutional.

States' Rights Era and the *Scott* Case

President Andrew Jackson nominated **Roger Taney** as chief justice when John Marshall died in 1835. During his eight years in office Jackson named six justices to the Supreme Court. The Court began to emphasize the rights of the states and the rights of citizens in an increasingly democratic society. Then, in the 1840s, states' rights became tied to the slavery issue. In *Dred Scott* v. *Sandford* (1857) an aging Taney read an opinion that declared African Americans were not and could not be citizens, the Missouri Compromise was unconstitutional, and Congress was powerless to stop the spread of slavery. The national furor over the *Scott* case damaged the Court. It also made an objective evaluation of the Taney era nearly impossible.

Due Process

Following the Civil War the Supreme Court issued several rulings on the Thirteenth, Fourteenth, and Fifteenth Amendments.[5] These Reconstruction amendments were intended to ensure the rights and liberties of newly freed African Americans, but the Court refused to apply the **due process clause** of the Fourteenth Amendment when individuals challenged business or state interests. The due process clause says that no state may deprive any person of life, liberty, or property without the due process of law.

Slaughterhouse Cases The first and most significant ruling on the Fourteenth Amendment came down in the 1873 *Slaughterhouse Cases.* Louisiana had granted a monopoly on the slaughtering business to one company. Competing butchers challenged this grant as denying them the right to practice their trade. They claimed that the Fourteenth Amendment guaranteed the privileges and immunities of U.S. citizenship, equal protection of the laws, and due process. The Court ruled for the state of Louisiana. It said that the

See the following footnoted materials in the ***Reference Handbook:***
1. *Fletcher* v. *Peck* case summary, page 758.
2. *Dartmouth College* v. *Woodward* case summary, page 757.
3. *McCulloch* v. *Maryland* case summary, page 761.
4. *Gibbons* v. *Ogden* case summary, page 758.
5. *The Constitution*, pages 774–799.

Protector of Civil Liberties

Fighting Segregation Under the *Plessy* decision, African Americans could be legally barred from using the same public facilities as white Americans. Seven-year-old Linda Brown and her family fought for Linda's right to attend an all-white school. This battle led the Supreme Court, in the *Brown* decision, to overturn the doctrine of "separate but equal" facilities for African Americans and whites. ***In what way was the* Brown *case different from previous segregation cases?***

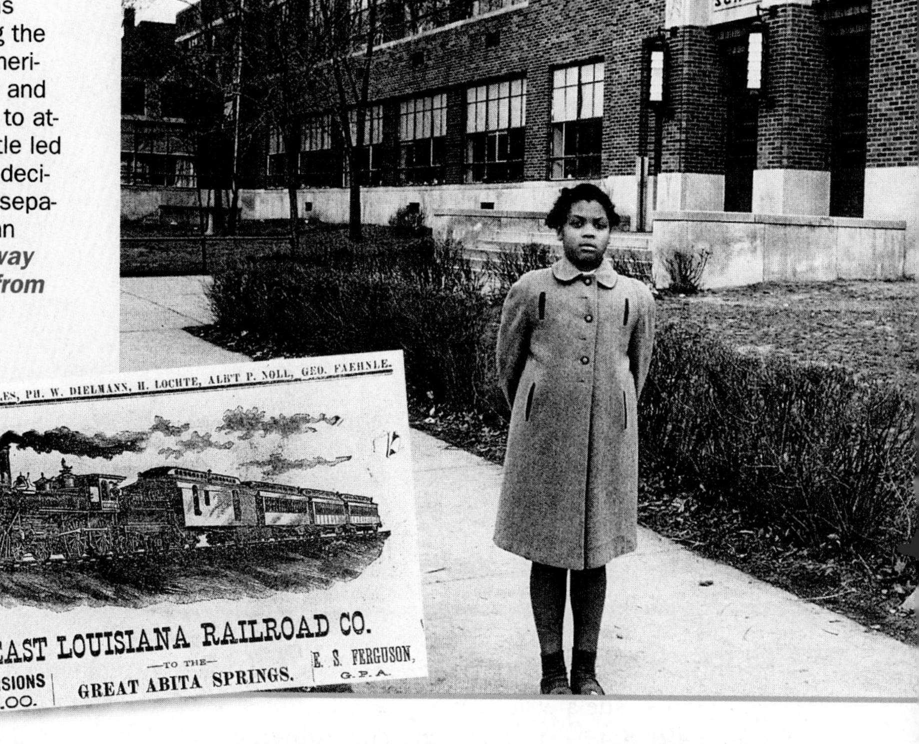

Homer Plessy refused to leave a whites-only railroad coach, leading to the *Plessy* decision.

Fourteenth Amendment did not increase the rights of an individual. It only extended protection to those rights, privileges, and immunities that had their source in federal, rather than state, citizenship.

Landmark Cases

Plessy* v. *Ferguson In 1896 the Court upheld a Louisiana law that required railroads operating within the state to provide separate cars for white and African American passengers. In *Plessy* v. *Ferguson* the Court said that this was a reasonable exercise of state police power to preserve peace and order. "Legislation is powerless to eradicate racial instincts or to abolish distinctions," it concluded. The lone dissenter, Justice Harlan, said this decision was "inconsistent with the personal liberty of citizens, white and black."

The case established the **"separate but equal" doctrine,** which held that if facilities for both races were equal, they could be separate. This ruling would not be overturned until *Brown* v. *Board of Education of Topeka* in 1954.

The Court and Business The Court had refused to broaden federal powers to enforce the rights of individuals. However, it seemed willing to broaden the police power of the states to protect consumers from the growing power of business. In the 1870s, in a group of cases known as the *Granger Cases,* the Court rejected a challenge to state regulatory laws. It held that some private property, such as a railroad, was invested with a public interest. A state could properly exercise its power to regulate such property.

More often, however, the Court sided with business interests as the nation industrialized. In the 1890s, in *United States* v. *E.C. Knight & Co.*[1] and other cases, the Court ruled to uphold the monopoly of business trusts. In *Debs* v. *United States*[2] it upheld the contempt conviction of labor leader Eugene V. Debs, who had disobeyed an order to call off a strike against a railroad company.

See the following footnoted materials in the **Reference Handbook:**

1. *United States* v. *E. C. Knight & Co.* case summary, page 766.
2. *Debs* v. *United States* case summary, page 757.

During the Progressive era the Court upheld several federal and state laws regulating business, but it returned to its support for business by the 1920s.

A major constitutional crisis arose in the 1930s over the question of federal and state regulation of the economy. President Franklin D. Roosevelt, angered by the Court's decision in *Schechter Poultry Corporation* v. *United States*[1] and other cases, proposed to increase the number of Supreme Court justices. He wanted to pack the Court with supportive members. Even though this attempt failed, the Court began to uphold laws that regulated business.

Thurgood Marshall argued the *Brown* case before the Court.

Landmark Cases

Protecting Civil Liberties The Supreme Court emerged as a major force in protecting civil liberties under Chief Justice Earl Warren who served from 1953 to 1969. In *Brown* v. *Board of Education of Topeka,* the Court outlawed segregation in public schools. In several other cases the Court issued rulings that extended equal protection in voting rights and the fair apportionment of representation in Congress and state legislatures. In other cases the Warren Court applied due process requirements and Bill of Rights protections to persons accused of crimes. Although the Court since then has not been as aggressive in advancing these decisions, it has not overruled any major decision of the Warren Court.

As the twentieth century drew to a close, it was apparent that the Supreme Court had carved out considerable power to influence policy in the United States. The legal views of the justices and their opinions on the various cases put before them would determine how the Court would use that power.

See the following footnoted materials in the ***Reference Handbook:***
1. *Schechter Poultry Corporation* v. *United States* case summary, page 765.

Section 1 Assessment

Checking for Understanding

1. **Main Idea** Use a graphic organizer like the one below to show how the Supreme Court extended civil liberties in the 1950s and 1960s.

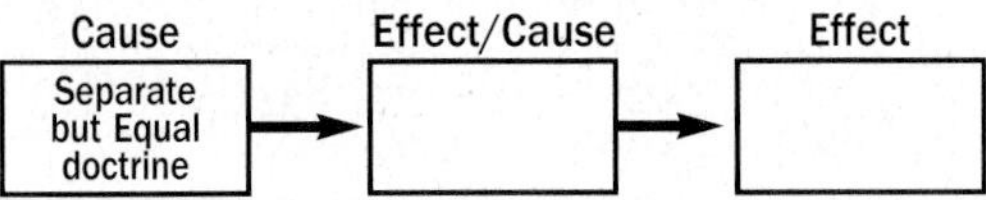

2. **Define** concurrent jurisdiction, original jurisdiction, appellate jurisdiction, litigant, due process clause.
3. **Identify** *Marbury* v. *Madison,* judicial review, "separate but equal" doctrine.
4. Identify the different jurisdictions of federal and state courts.
5. What doctrine was established by the ruling in *Plessy* v. *Ferguson?*

Critical Thinking

6. **Identifying Alternatives** What choice of jurisdiction would be available to a person who was being sued by a citizen of another state for damages amounting to $50,000?

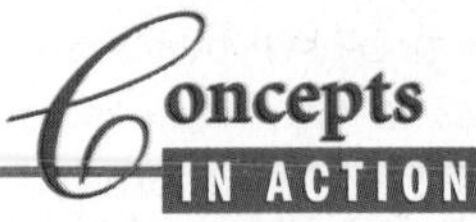

Constitutional Interpretations Choose one of the cases discussed in Section 1 or another case that contributed to the development of the power of the Supreme Court. Research the details of the case, including the background, the ruling, and the reasons for the ruling. Write a newspaper article or tape a news broadcast announcing the effects of the ruling.

United States v. *Virginia,* 1996

Democratic equality means all people are entitled to the same rights before the law. Yet governments often make distinctions among groups of people, such as providing medical benefits only for military veterans. Does a state college's policy of admitting only men violate the constitutional rights of women? A case involving the all-male Virginia Military Institute dealt with this issue.

A female cadet endures VMI traditions.

Background of the Case

Virginia Military Institute (VMI), a state-supported college, was created in 1839 as an all-male institution. Since then, VMI's distinctive mission had been to produce "citizen soldiers," men prepared for leadership in civilian and military life. VMI's "adversative" approach to education required students, called cadets, to wear uniforms, live in spartan barracks, and regularly participate in tough physical training. New VMI students, called "rats," were exposed to a seven-month experience similar to Marine Corps boot camp. In 1990 the U.S. government sued Virginia and VMI at the request of a female high school student seeking admission. After a long process of appeals, the Supreme Court finally took the case in 1996.

The Constitutional Issue

The U.S. government claimed that by denying women the unique educational opportunity offered to men by VMI, the state of Virginia was making a classification that violated the Fourteenth Amendment's guarantee of "equal protection of the law." Under the equal protection clause, governments can treat different groups of people differently only if such a classification serves an important governmental objective such as promoting safety.

VMI explained that its policy should be allowed under the Constitution's equal protection principle because its school for men brought a healthy diversity to the state of Virginia's otherwise coeducational system. Further, VMI claimed that if women were admitted, the school would have to change housing arrangements and physical training requirements. Such changes, VMI claimed, would fundamentally change its distinctive "adversative" approach to education.

Finally, VMI offered to establish a separate program called the Virginia Women's Institute for Leadership (VWIL) at a small, private women's college. Unlike VMI, the women's college did not offer engineering, advanced math, or physics, and its students had SAT scores about 100 points lower than VMI's students. The VWIL program would not involve the tough physical training, uniforms, or barracks life that were key parts of the VMI's "adversative" approach. VMI cited "important differences between men and women in learning and developmental needs" as the reason for the different program.

Debating the Case

Questions to Consider

1. Did VMI's male-only policy violate the equal protection clause?
2. Was VMI's proposed remedy of a separate program a legally acceptable alternative?

You Be the Judge

In your opinion, was VMI's goal of educating citizen soldiers unsuitable for women? Was VMI's men-only policy unconstitutional? If so, what remedy should be offered?

Section 2

Lower Federal Courts

Reader's Guide

Key Terms

grand jury, indictment, petit jury, judicial circuit, senatorial courtesy

Find Out

- How do constitutional courts and legislative courts differ in their jurisdiction?
- How are federal court justices chosen?

Understanding Concepts

Political Processes If federal judges are shielded from direct political influence, why do presidents try to appoint judges who share their views?

COVER STORY

E-Mail Must Be Kept

WASHINGTON, D.C., JANUARY 19, 1989

District Court judge Barrington Parker has temporarily blocked the purging of the White House's E-mail system. Just hours before the Reagan administration was to erase eight years of staff

The National Security Archive logo

computer messages, the judge intervened. In a courtroom exchange, acting Attorney General John Bolton likened deleting E-mail to outgoing officials cleaning out their desks before tomorrow's inauguration of President George Bush. The National Security Archive, a government watchdog group, said that the messages are public documents and are covered under federal records preservation laws. A hearing will determine if E-mail should be treated like other government records.

The Constitution created the Supreme Court. Congress, however, has used its constitutional authority to establish a network of lower federal courts, beginning with the Judiciary Act of 1789. A variety of lower trial and appellate courts handle a growing number of federal cases. These courts are of two basic types—constitutional federal courts and legislative federal courts.

Constitutional Courts

Courts established by Congress under the provisions of Article III of the Constitution are **constitutional courts.** These courts include the federal district courts, the federal courts of appeals, and the United States Court of International Trade.

Federal District Courts Congress created **district courts** in 1789 to serve as trial courts. These districts followed state boundary lines. As the population grew and cases multiplied, Congress divided some states into more than 1 district. Today the United States has 94 districts, with each state having at least 1 district court. Large states—California, New York, and Texas—each have 4 district courts. Washington, D.C., and Puerto Rico also have 1 district court each. There are more than 550 judges who preside over the district courts.

United States district courts are the trial courts for both criminal and civil federal cases. (You will learn more about these types of cases in Chapter 15.) District courts use 2 types of juries in criminal cases. A **grand jury,** which usually includes 16 to 23 people, hears charges against a person suspected of having committed a crime. If the grand jury believes there is sufficient evidence to bring the person to trial, it issues an **indictment**—a formal accusation charging a person with a crime. If the jury believes there is not sufficient evidence, the charges are dropped.

A petit jury, which usually consists of 6 or 12 people, is a trial jury. Its function is to weigh the evidence presented at a trial in a criminal or civil case. In a criminal case, a petit jury renders a verdict of guilty or not guilty. In a civil case, the jury finds for either the plaintiff, the person bringing the suit, or the defendant, the person against whom the suit is brought. If the parties in a civil case do not wish a jury trial, a judge or a panel of three judges weighs the evidence.

District courts are the workhorses of the federal judiciary, hearing hundreds of thousands of cases each year. This caseload represents more than 80 percent of all federal cases. District courts have jurisdiction to hear cases involving federal questions: issues of federal statutory or constitutional law. They can also hear some cases involving citizens of different states. In the vast majority of their cases, district courts render the final decision. Few are appealed. One scholar explained:

> *"Trial judges, because of the multitude of cases they hear which remain unheard or unchanged by appellate courts, as well as because of their fact- and issue-shaping powers, appear to play an independent and formidable part in the policy impact of the federal court system upon the larger political system."*
>
> —Kenneth M. Dolbeare, 1969

Officers of the Court Many appointed officials provide support services for district courts. Each district has a United States attorney to represent the United States in all civil suits brought against the government and to prosecute people charged with federal crimes. Each district court appoints a United States magistrate who issues arrest warrants and helps decide whether the arrested person should be held for a grand jury hearing. A bankruptcy judge handles bankruptcy cases for each district. A **United States marshal** carries out such duties as making arrests, securing jurors, and keeping order in the courtroom. With the help of deputy clerks, bailiffs, and a stenographer, a clerk keeps records of court proceedings.

Rulings of Federal Courts

Settling Disputes Conflicts between the major league players' union and the owners disrupted baseball in 1994 and 1995. Federal District Judge Sonia Sotomayer of New York issued the ruling that ended the baseball strike. ***Why was the baseball strike resolved in a federal court, rather than a state or local court?***

Federal Courts of Appeals Good records are important because a person or group that loses a case in a district court may appeal to a federal court of appeals or, in some instances, directly to the Supreme Court. Congress created the United States courts of appeals in 1891 to ease the appeals workload of the Supreme Court. The caseload of appellate courts has almost doubled every 10 years since 1970, to nearly 50,000 cases annually in recent years.

The appellate level includes 13 United States courts of appeals. The United States is divided into 12 judicial circuits, or regions, with 1 appellate court in each circuit. The thirteenth court is a special appeals court with national jurisdiction. Usually, a panel of three judges sits on each appeal. In a very important case, all of the circuit judges may hear the case.

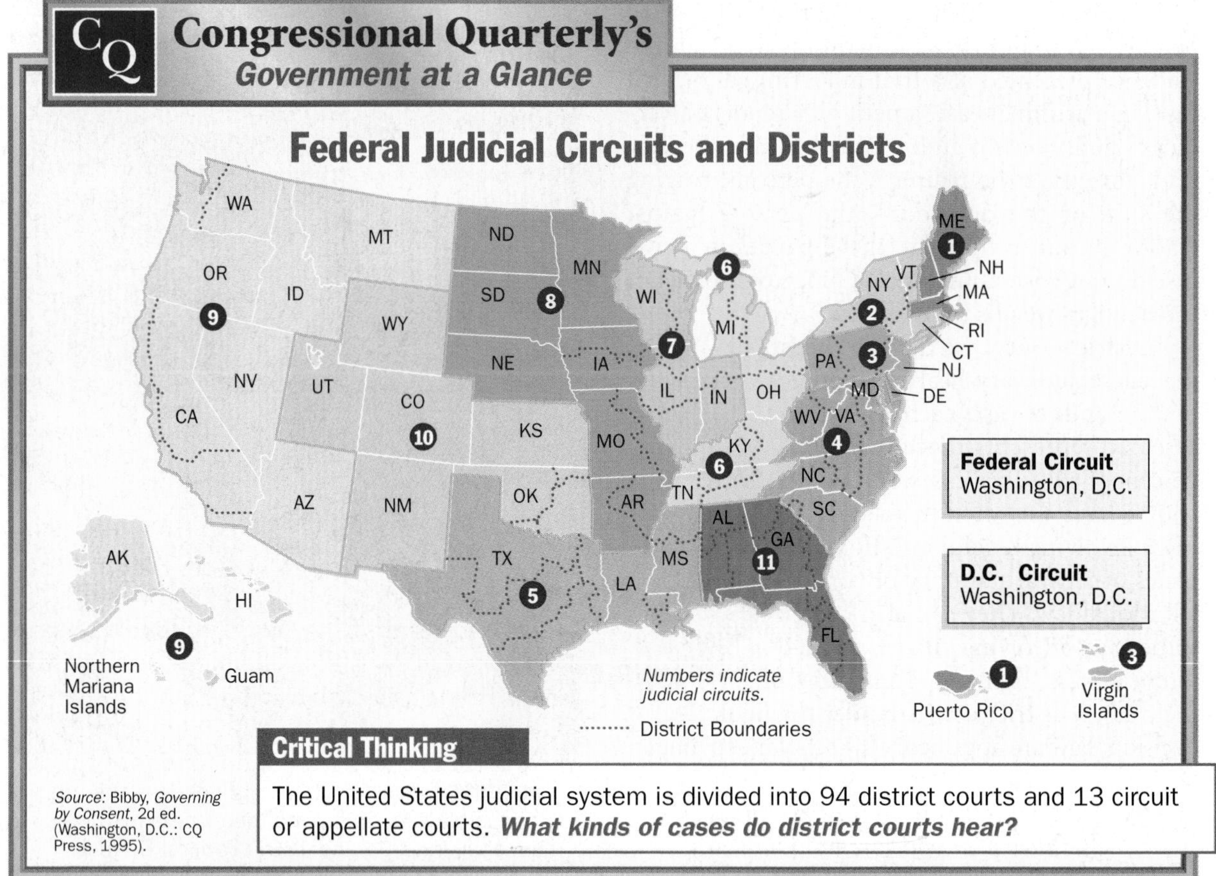

Critical Thinking

The United States judicial system is divided into 94 district courts and 13 circuit or appellate courts. ***What kinds of cases do district courts hear?***

Source: Bibby, *Governing by Consent*, 2d ed. (Washington, D.C.: CQ Press, 1995).

As their name implies, the courts of appeals have only appellate jurisdiction. Most appeals arise from decisions of district courts, the U. S. Tax Court, and various territorial courts. These courts also hear appeals on the rulings of various regulatory agencies, such as the Federal Trade Commission and the Federal Communications Commission.

The courts of appeals may decide an appeal in one of three ways: uphold the original decision, reverse that decision, or send the case back to the lower court to be tried again. Unless appealed to the Supreme Court, decisions of the courts of appeals are final.

In 1982 Congress set up a special court of appeals, called the **United States Circuit Court of Appeals for the Federal Circuit.** This court hears cases from a federal claims court, the Court of International Trade, the United States Patent Office, and other executive agencies. The court's headquarters are in Washington, D.C., but it sits in other parts of the country as needed.

The Court of International Trade Formerly known as the United States Customs Court, this court has jurisdiction over cases dealing with tariffs. Citizens who believe that tariffs are too high bring most of the cases heard in this court.

The Court of International Trade is based in New York City, but it is a national court. The judges also hear cases in other major port cities around the country such as New Orleans and San Francisco. The Circuit Court of Appeals for the Federal Circuit hears decisions appealed from this court.

Legislative Courts

Along with the constitutional federal courts, Congress has created a series of courts referred to as legislative courts. As spelled out in Article I [1] of the Constitution, the **legislative courts**

See the following footnoted materials in the **Reference Handbook:**
1. *The Constitution,* pages 774–799.

help Congress exercise its powers. Thus, it was the power of Congress to tax that led to the creation of the United States Tax Court. The congressional power of regulating the armed forces led to the formation of the Court of Military Appeals. The duty of Congress to govern overseas territories such as Guam and the Virgin Islands led to the creation of territorial courts. Similarly, congressional supervision of the District of Columbia led to the establishment of a court system for the nation's capital.

United States Claims Court Congress established the present Claims Court in 1982. It is a court of original jurisdiction that handles claims against the United States for money damages. A person who believes that the government has not paid a bill for goods or services may sue in this court. The Claims Court's headquarters are in Washington, D.C., but it hears cases throughout the country as necessary. The Circuit Court of Appeals for the Federal Circuit hears any appeals from the Claims Court.

United States Tax Court Acting under its power to tax, Congress provided for the present Tax Court in 1969. As a trial court, it hears cases relating to federal taxes. Cases come to the Tax Court from citizens who disagree with Internal Revenue Service rulings or other Treasury Department agency rulings about the federal taxes they must pay. The Tax Court is based in Washington, D.C., but it hears cases throughout the United States. A federal court of appeals handles cases appealed from the Tax Court.

The Court of Military Appeals Congress established the Court of Military Appeals in 1950. It is the armed forces' highest appeals court. This court hears cases involving members of the armed forces convicted of breaking military law. As its name implies, it has appellate jurisdiction. This court is sometimes called the "GI Supreme Court." The United States Supreme Court has jurisdiction to review this court's decisions.

Territorial Courts Congress has created a court system in the territories of the Virgin Islands, Guam, the Northern Mariana Islands, and Puerto Rico. These territorial courts are roughly similar to district courts in function, operation, and jurisdiction. They handle civil and criminal cases, along with constitutional cases. The appellate courts for this system are the United States courts of appeals.

Courts of the District of Columbia Because the District of Columbia is a federal district, Congress has developed a judicial system for the nation's capital. Along with a federal district court

THE LAW *and You*

Serving on a Jury

If you are registered to vote or have a driver's license, you may be called for jury duty. To serve on a jury, you must be a United States citizen and at least 18 years old. You also must understand English and not have been convicted of a felony. Should you receive a jury summons, be sure to follow its instructions. Failure to do so is a crime.

When you appear for jury duty, you become part of a pool from which jurors are chosen. During the selection process you may be questioned by the judge and by attorneys for each side in a case.

Respond honestly, even if the questions seem embarrassing or irrelevant. If you are not selected, it is not a reflection of you personally. Someone merely felt you were not right for that particular case.

It is possible to be excused from jury duty. However, remember that just as a jury trial is a citizen's right, jury service is a citizen's responsibility.

Citizens on a jury

Interview a Juror Find people from your school or city who have served on a jury. Ask them to recall their impressions of the experience. Report your findings to the class.

and a court of appeals, various local courts handle both civil and criminal cases that need to be heard within the District of Columbia.

The Court of Veterans' Appeals In 1988 Congress created the United States Court of Veterans' Appeals. The new court was to hear appeals from the Board of Veterans' Appeals in the Department of Veterans Affairs. The cabinet-level department was created to deal with veterans' claims for benefits and other veterans' problems. This court handles cases arising from unsettled claims.

Selection of Federal Judges

Article II, Section 2,[1] of the Constitution provides that the president, with the advice and consent of the Senate, appoints all federal judges. The Constitution, however, sets forth no particular qualifications for federal judges. The legal profession regards a position on the federal bench as a highly desirable post, a recognition of a lawyer's high standing in the profession. Federal judges are sometimes described as America's legal elite.

Judges in the constitutional courts serve, as the Constitution prescribes, "during good behavior," which, in practice, means for life. The reason for the life term is that it permits judges to be free from public or political pressures in deciding cases. Thus, federal court judges know that their jobs are safe even if they make unpopular decisions.

Party Affiliation Although presidents often state that they intend to make judicial appointments on a nonpartisan basis, in practice they favor judges who belong to their own political party. In recent years the percentage of appointed federal judges who belong to the president's party has ranged from 81 percent in the case of President Gerald Ford's appointments to a high of 99 percent in President Ronald Reagan's case.

See the following footnoted materials in the ***Reference Handbook:***
1. *The Constitution*, pages 774–799.

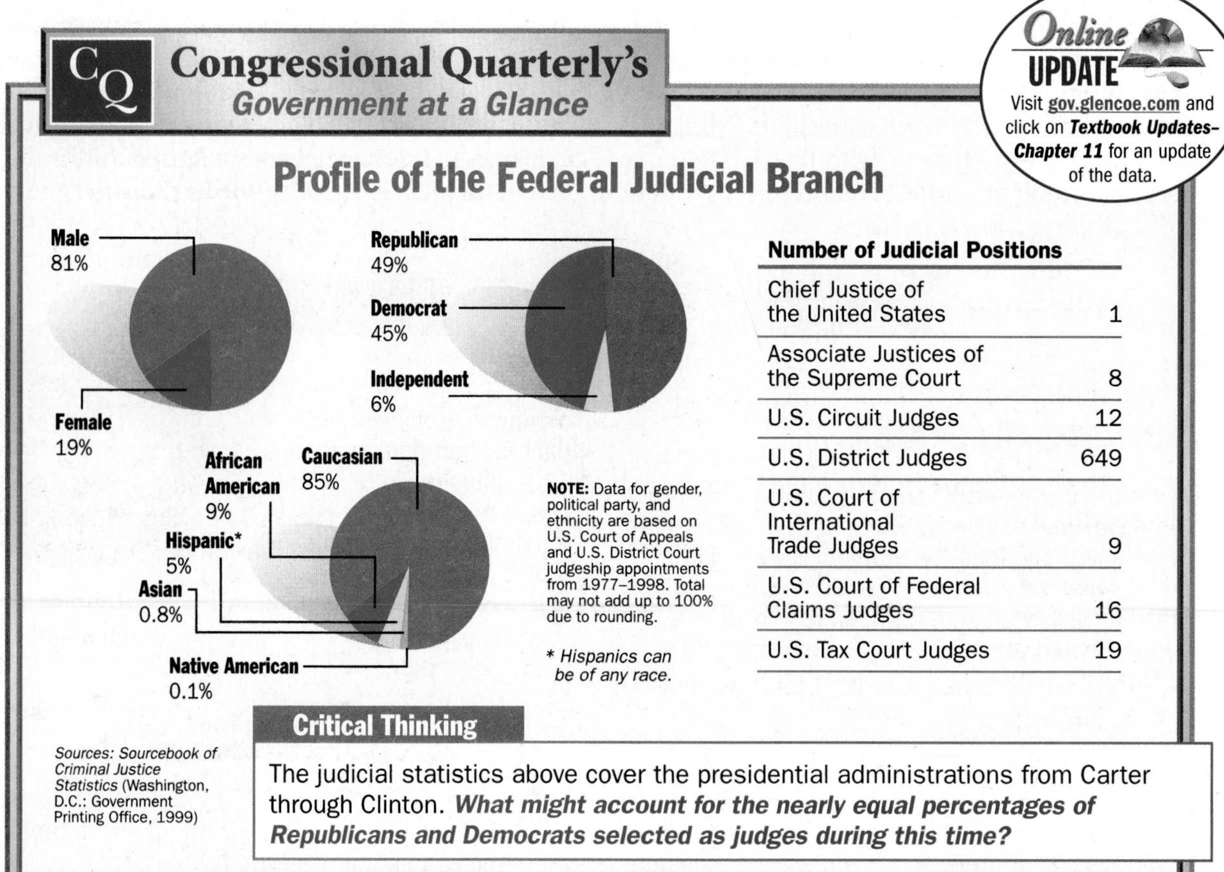

Number of Judicial Positions	
Chief Justice of the United States	1
Associate Justices of the Supreme Court	8
U.S. Circuit Judges	12
U.S. District Judges	649
U.S. Court of International Trade Judges	9
U.S. Court of Federal Claims Judges	16
U.S. Tax Court Judges	19

Critical Thinking

The judicial statistics above cover the presidential administrations from Carter through Clinton. ***What might account for the nearly equal percentages of Republicans and Democrats selected as judges during this time?***

Another significant factor that emphasizes the political nature of court appointments is the power of Congress to increase the number of judgeships. Studies have shown that when one party controls both the presidency and Congress, it is more likely to dramatically increase the number of judicial posts. When President John Kennedy was elected in 1960, the Democratic Congress immediately passed a new omnibus judgeship bill creating 71 new positions for the president to fill.

Judicial Philosophy Presidents often try to appoint judges who share their own points of view. Abraham Lincoln expressed this position when he appointed Salmon P. Chase as chief justice of the United States in 1864: "We wish for a Chief Justice who will sustain what has been done in regard to emancipation [of the slaves] and the legal tenders [money policies]." Studies have shown that presidents have appointed judges who share their judicial philosophy in about 75 percent of the cases.

Presidents follow this practice because they wish to have their own points of view put into effect in the courts. Because judges are appointed for life, presidents view judicial appointments as an opportunity to perpetuate their political ideologies after leaving the White House.

Senatorial Courtesy In naming judges to trial courts, presidents customarily follow the practice of senatorial courtesy. Under the senatorial courtesy system, a president submits the name of a candidate for judicial appointment to the senators from the candidate's state before formally submitting it for full Senate approval. If either or both senators oppose the president's choice, the president usually withdraws the name and nominates another candidate.

The practice of senatorial courtesy is limited to the selection of judges to the district courts and other trial courts. It is not followed in the case of nominations to the courts of appeals and the Supreme Court. Courts of appeals' circuits cover more than one state, so that an appointment to this court is regional in nature. A position on the Supreme Court is a national selection rather than a statewide or a regional one.

The Background of Federal Judges Almost all federal judges have had legal training and have held a variety of positions in law or government including service as law school professors, members of Congress, leading attorneys, and federal district attorneys. About one-third of district court judges have served as state court judges.

Until very recently few women, African Americans, or Hispanics were appointed as judges in the lower federal courts. President Jimmy Carter did much to change this situation in his court appointments. President Lyndon Johnson appointed Thurgood Marshall the first African American justice to the Supreme Court. President Ronald Reagan appointed Sandra Day O'Connor the first female justice to the Supreme Court.

Section 2 Assessment

Checking for Understanding

1. **Main Idea** Use a graphic organizer like the one shown to identify the three options a court of appeals has when deciding a case.

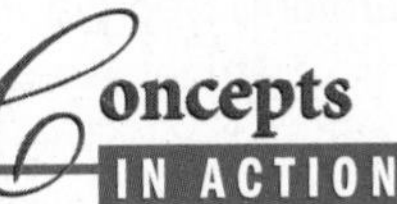

2. **Define** grand jury, indictment, petit jury, judicial circuit, senatorial courtesy.
3. **Identify** United States Circuit Court of Appeals for the Federal Circuit.
4. What two major divisions of federal courts has Congress created?
5. In what two ways do political parties influence the federal court system?

Critical Thinking

6. **Demonstrating Reasoned Judgment** A judge who shares a president's views when first appointed may change views when making decisions on the bench. Why?

Concepts IN ACTION

Political Processes Review the criteria used by presidents to appoint federal judges. Develop any additional criteria that you think should be used for nominating judges. Prepare the criteria in the form of a checklist.

Congressional Quarterly's

The Supreme Court A to Z

Housing the Supreme Court *When the national government moved to Washington in 1801, the Court was such an insignificant branch that those planning the new capital forgot to provide a place for it to meet. Between February 1, 1790, and October 7, 1935, when the justices finally met in the building built especially for the Court, the Court convened in about a dozen different places.*

The Merchant's Exchange building in New York City housed the first Court.

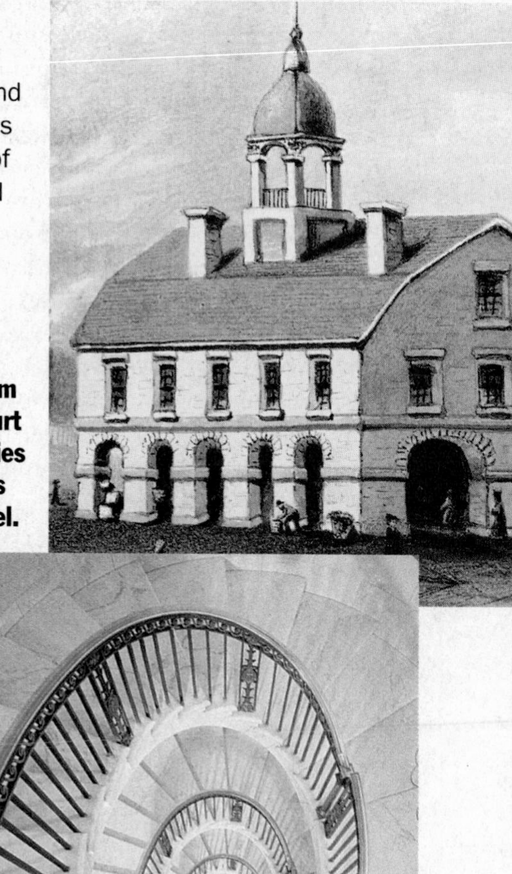

Financing the Court's Permanent Home

President Taft began promoting the idea of a separate building for the Court near the end of his presidency and after becoming chief justice in 1921. In 1929 Congress finally appropriated $9,740,000 for the project. The final cost of the building, including furnishings, was less than the authorized amount. About $94,000 was returned to the U.S. Treasury. It would cost over $100 million to replace the building today.

Taft (third from left), with Court justices, studies architect Cass Gilbert's model.

Marble and Oak

The primary building material is marble, from quarries in Vermont, Georgia, Alabama, Spain, Italy, and parts of Africa. Most of the floors, doors, and walls are made of oak. The building also includes two self-supporting marble spiral staircases rising from the garage to the top floor. The only other such staircases are in the Vatican and the Paris Opera House.

Seldom-used stairs spiral through five floors.

The Courtroom

From the Great Hall, oak doors open into the courtroom, where oral arguments are held and rulings are announced. Measuring 82 by 91 feet with a 44-foot ceiling, the room has 24 columns of Italian marble. Along the upper part of the wall on all four sides are marble panels and tableaux representing historical lawmakers and concepts such as "Majesty of the Law."

The bench at which the justices sit extends across the room. The chairs are black and of varying heights, as each justice may choose his or her own chair. The justices enter the courtroom from behind a red velvet curtain that hangs behind the bench.

Inside the Building

The building has six levels, including a basement, but the public is permitted to see only the ground floor and part of the first floor. The ground floor holds the public information office, the clerk's office, the publications unit, exhibit halls, cafeteria, gift shop, and administrative offices. The first floor contains the Great Hall, the courtroom, the conference room, and all of the justices' chambers except Ruth Bader Ginsburg's. She chose a roomier office on the second floor. The second floor contains the justices' dining and reading rooms, the office of the reporter of decisions, the legal office, and the law clerks' offices. On the third floor is the Court library, and on the fourth floor is a gymnasium.

The building is designed so that the justices need not enter public areas except when hearing oral arguments and announcing opinions. A private elevator connects the underground garage with the corridor, closed to the public, where the justices' offices are located.

Outside the Building

On the steps of the Supreme Court's main entrance is a pair of huge marble candelabra with carved panels representing Justice, holding sword and scales, and the Three Fates of Greek mythology, weaving the thread of life. Inscribed above the entrance is the motto "Equal Justice Under Law." The pediment above the inscription is filled with sculptures representing Liberty enthroned, guarded by Authority and Order.

Supreme Court building pediment

EQUAL JUSTICE UNDER LAW

Section 3

The Supreme Court

Reader's Guide

Key Terms

riding the circuit, opinion

Find Out

- Why does the Supreme Court hear very few cases under its original jurisdiction?
- What political influences affect the selection of Supreme Court justices?

Understanding Concepts

Checks and Balances Why are persons who are nominated as Supreme Court justices subject to close scrutiny?

COVER STORY

Holmes Dies

WASHINGTON, D.C., MARCH 6, 1935

Oliver Wendell Holmes, Jr., who served as an associate justice on the Supreme Court for thirty years, died at his home of pneumonia very early this morning. Appointed in 1902 by Theodore Roosevelt, Holmes wrote 873 opinions for the Court—more than any other justice. Perhaps his most famous opinion was his dissent in *Lochner* v. *New York* (1905), in which he supported the state's right to limit the labor of bakery workers to ten hours per day. His opinion for a unanimous court in *Schenck* v. *United States* (1919) established the "clear and present danger" standard in free speech cases. Holmes, son of the well-known author of the same name, will be remembered for the unique beauty and power of his written opinions.

Oliver Wendell Holmes, Jr.

The Supreme Court stands at the top of the American legal system. Article III of the Constitution created the Supreme Court as one of three coequal branches of the national government, along with Congress and the president.

The Supreme Court is the court of last resort in all questions of federal law. The Court is not required to hear all cases presented before it, and carefully chooses the cases it will consider. It has final authority in any case involving the Constitution, acts of Congress, and treaties with other nations. Most of the cases the Supreme Court hears are appeals from lower courts. The decisions of the Supreme Court are binding on all lower courts.

Nomination to the Supreme Court today is a very high honor. It was not always so. Several of George Washington's nominees turned down the job. Until 1891, justices earned much of their pay while **riding the circuit,** or traveling to hold court in their assigned regions of the country. One justice, after a painful stagecoach ride in 1840, wrote to his wife:

> "*I think I never again, at this season of the year, will attempt this mode of journeying. . . . I have been elbowed by old women—jammed by young ones—suffocated by cigar smoke—sickened by the vapours of bitters and w[h]iskey—my head knocked through the carriage top by careless drivers and my toes trodden to a jelly by unheeding passengers.*"
>
> —Justice Levi Woodbury, 1840

Today the Court hears all its cases in the Supreme Court building in Washington, D.C., in a large, first-floor courtroom that is open to the public. Nearby is a conference room where the justices meet privately to decide cases. The first floor also contains the offices of the justices, their law clerks, and secretaries.

Supreme Court Jurisdiction

The Supreme Court has both original and appellate jurisdiction. Article III, Section 2,[1] of the Constitution sets the Court's original jurisdiction. It covers two types of cases: (1) cases involving representatives of foreign governments and (2) certain cases in which a state is a party. Congress may not expand or curtail the Court's original jurisdiction.

Many original jurisdiction cases have involved two states or a state and the federal government. When Maryland and Virginia argued over oyster fishing rights, and when a dispute broke out between California and Arizona over the control of water from the Colorado River, the Supreme Court had original jurisdiction.

The Supreme Court's original jurisdiction cases form a very small part of its yearly workload—an average of fewer than five such cases a year. Most of the cases the Court decides fall under the Court's appellate jurisdiction.

Under the Supreme Court's appellate jurisdiction, the Court hears cases that are appealed from lower courts of appeals, or it may hear cases from federal district courts in certain instances where an act of Congress was held unconstitutional.

The Supreme Court may also hear cases that are appealed from the highest court of a state, if claims under federal law or the Constitution are involved. In such cases, however, the Supreme Court has the authority to rule only on the federal issue involved, not on any issues of state law. A state court, for example, tries a person charged with violating a state law. During the trial, however, the accused claims that the police violated Fourteenth Amendment rights with an illegal search at the time of the arrest. The defendant may appeal to the Supreme Court on that particular constitutional issue only. The Supreme Court has no jurisdiction to rule on the state issue (whether the accused actually violated state law). The Court will decide only whether Fourteenth Amendment rights were violated.

Supreme Court Justices

The Supreme Court is composed of 9 justices: the chief justice of the United States and 8 associate justices. Congress sets this number and has the power to change it. Over the years it has varied from 5 to 10, but it has been 9 since 1869. In 1937 President Franklin D. Roosevelt attempted to gain greater control of the Court by asking Congress to increase the number of justices. Congress refused, in part because the number 9 was well established.

See the following footnoted materials in the **Reference Handbook:**
1. *The Constitution*, pages 774–799.

The Highest Court in the Land

Judicial Ideals The nine justices meet regularly in the Supreme Court building in Washington, D.C. ***What do you think the motto on the Supreme Court seal means as it applies to the Court?***

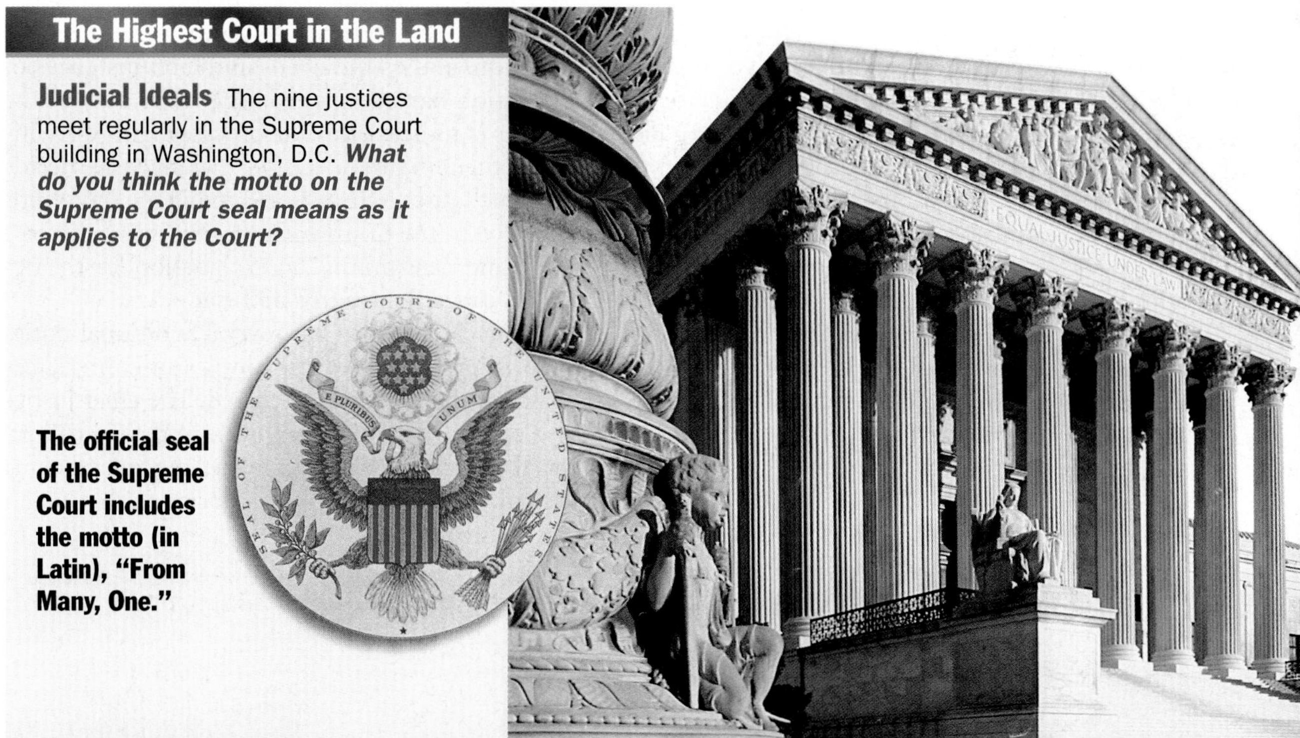

The official seal of the Supreme Court includes the motto (in Latin), "From Many, One."

Supreme Court justices occupy this bench while they hear cases.

Interpreters of the Law The members of the highest court in the land pose for an informal photograph. They are (from left to right) associate justices Sandra Day O'Connor, Anthony Kennedy, Antonin Scalia, Chief Justice William H. Rehnquist, and associate justices David Souter, Ruth Bader Ginsburg, Clarence Thomas, Stephen Breyer, and John Paul Stevens. ***Why is it important that a judge or Supreme Court justice weigh all arguments equally?***

In a recent year the eight associate justices received salaries of $173,600. The chief justice received a salary of $181,400. Congress sets the justices' salaries and may not reduce them.

Under the Constitution, Congress may remove Supreme Court justices through impeachment for and conviction of "treason, bribery, or other high crimes and misdemeanors." No Supreme Court justice has ever been removed from office through impeachment, however. The House of Representatives impeached Justice Samuel Chase in 1804 because of his participation in partisan political activities, but the Senate found him not guilty.

Duties of the Justices The Constitution does not describe the duties of the justices. Instead, the duties have developed from laws, through tradition, and as the needs and circumstances of the nation have developed. The main duty of the justices is to hear and rule on cases. This duty involves them in three decision-making tasks: deciding which cases to hear from among the thousands appealed to the Court each year; deciding the case itself; and determining an explanation for the decision, called the Court's **opinion.**

The chief justice has several additional duties such as presiding over sessions and conferences at which the cases are discussed. The chief justice also carries out a leadership role in the Court's judicial work and helps administer the federal court system.[1]

See the following footnoted materials in the **Reference Handbook:**
1. *Supreme Court Chief Justices,* page 769.

The justices also have limited duties related to the 12 federal judicial circuits. One Supreme Court justice is assigned to each federal circuit. Three of the justices handle 2 circuits each. The justices are responsible for requests for special legal actions that come from their circuit. In 1980, for example, a lower federal court ruled against the federal government's program of draft registration. Lawyers for the federal government then requested the Supreme Court to temporarily set aside the lower court's decision. The Supreme Court justice who was responsible for the federal judicial circuit in which the issue arose heard this request.

Occasionally, justices take on additional duties as their workload permits. In 1945 Justice Robert Jackson served as chief prosecutor at the Nuremberg trials of Nazi war criminals. In 1963 Chief Justice **Earl Warren** headed a special commission that investigated the assassination of President Kennedy.

To maintain their objectivity on the bench, justices are careful not to become involved in outside activities that might prevent them from dealing fairly with one side or the other on a case. If justices have any personal or business connection with either of the parties in a case, they usually disqualify themselves from participating in that case.

Law Clerks In 1882 Justice Horace Gray hired the first law clerk—mainly to be his servant and barber. Today the Court's law clerks assist the justices with many tasks, enabling the justices to concentrate on their pressing duties. Law clerks read all the appeals filed with the Court and write memos summarizing the key issues in each case. When cases are decided, the clerks help prepare the Court's opinions by doing research and sometimes writing first drafts of the opinions.

The justices each hire a few law clerks from among the top graduates of the nation's best law schools. These young men and women usually work for a justice for one or two years. After leaving the Court, many clerks go on to distinguished careers as judges, law professors, and even Supreme Court justices themselves.

Background of the Justices Throughout the Court's history more than 100 men and 2 women have served as justices. What sort of people become the top judges in the land? Although it is not a formal requirement, a justice usually has a law degree and considerable legal experience. Most justices have been state or federal court judges, or have held other court-related positions such as attorney general. One former president, William Howard Taft, served as chief justice. Younger people are not usually appointed to the Court. Most of the justices selected in the twentieth century were in their fifties when they were appointed to the Court. Nine were younger than 50, and the remainder were more than 60 years old.

Justices have not been representative of the general population in social class, background, gender, and race. Most justices have come from upper socioeconomic levels. To date, only two African American justices, Thurgood Marshall and Clarence Thomas, and only two women, Sandra Day O'Connor and Ruth Bader Ginsburg, have been appointed. The Constitution does not require justices to be native-born Americans. Six Supreme Court justices have been born outside the United States. Of these, three were appointed by George Washington.

Related Justices **Several Supreme Court justices have been related. Among them are two with the same name, John Marshall Harlan, who were grandfather (served 1877–1911) and grandson (1954–1971). Stephen J. Field (1863–1897) and a nephew, David J. Brewer (1890–1910), served together for seven years. The two Lamars—Lucius Quintus Cincinnatus Lamar (1888–1893) and Joseph Rucker Lamar (1910–1916)—were cousins.**

Appointing Justices

Justices reach the Court through appointment by the president with Senate approval. The Senate usually grants such approval, but it is not automatic. A respected president is less likely to have a candidate rejected, but the Senate did reject one of President Washington's nominees. During the nineteenth century, more than 25 percent of the nominees failed to win Senate approval. By contrast, during the early part of the twentieth century, the Senate was much more supportive of presidential choices. More recently, the Senate rejected two of President Nixon's nominees and President Reagan's nomination of Robert Bork in 1988. The Senate closely scrutinized Justice Clarence Thomas's nomination in 1991, but finally accepted the nomination by a vote of 52 to 48.

As is the case with lower court judges, political considerations often affect a president's choice of a nominee to the Court. Usually presidents will choose someone from their own party, sometimes as a reward for faithful service to the party. But presidents must be careful to nominate people who are likely to be confirmed by the Senate. President Clinton had to decide among several choices in 1994. Bruce Babbitt was thought to be the likely nominee. However, Babbitt had some powerful enemies among Western senators because of his decisions as secretary of the interior. So the president chose a federal judge, Stephen Breyer, who had friends among Democrats and Republicans. He was a safe choice and was easily confirmed.

Presidents prefer to nominate candidates whose political beliefs they believe are similar to their own. However, several presidents have discovered that it is very difficult to predict how an individual will rule on sensitive issues once he or she becomes a member of the Court. After securing the nomination of Tom Clark, President Truman expressed his displeasure:

> "*Tom Clark was my biggest mistake. No question about it. . . . I don't know what got into me. He was no . . . good as Attorney General, and on the Supreme Court . . . he's been even worse. He hasn't made one right decision I can think of.*"
>
> —Harry S Truman

We the People

Making a Difference

Renée Askins

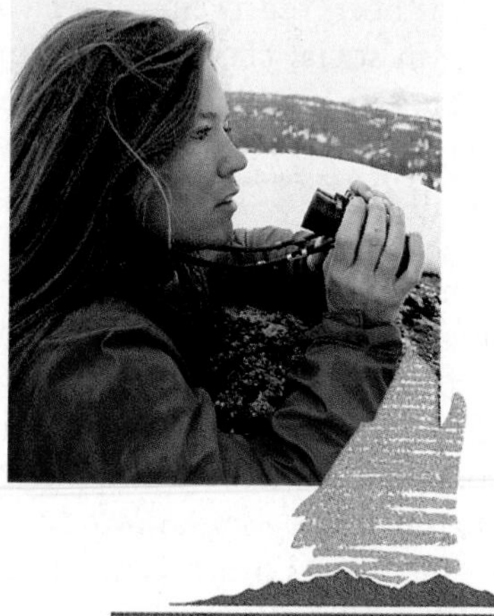

Wolf Fund logo

Wildlife ecologist Renee Askins led the battle to reintroduce the gray wolf into Yellowstone National Park. The struggle lasted almost 30 years, but Askins viewed the issue as righting a wrong. "We exterminated the wolf to take control. I think people are beginning to see we've taken too much control," Askins said.

No wolves had lived in Yellowstone since 1930. The Endangered Species Act of 1973 required that the federal government reintroduce the wolf. However, ranchers and farmers feared that the wolves would kill their livestock and went to federal courts to block the program.

Renee Askins created the Wolf Fund in Moose, Wyoming, to raise money and rally support for reintroducing the gray wolf to the park. Askins pointed out, "Lawyers are costing ranchers more money than they'll ever lose because of the wolf."

In 1995 a federal judge in Wyoming refused ranchers' requests to stop the wolf reintroduction program. As a result, 30 wolves were captured in Canada. Fifteen were released in the park and fifteen in Idaho. Then, in 1997, a district court in Wyoming ordered that the wolves be removed. Supporters of the wolves appealed. Meanwhile, the wolves were allowed to remain in the park until a higher court decided the issue.

On January 13, 2000, the 10th Circuit Court of Appeals in Denver overturned the lower court's ruling. By this time the wolves in Yellowstone and Idaho numbered more than 300. The American Farm Bureau threatened to appeal the decision before the Supreme Court but changed its mind right before the appeal deadline in April 2000. A Farm Bureau attorney stated, "This means the case is closed and the Yellowstone wolves are here to stay."

When President Eisenhower named Earl Warren as chief justice in 1953, he expected Warren to continue to support the rather conservative positions he had taken as governor of California. The Warren Court, however, turned out to be the most liberal, activist Court in the country's history.

In identifying and selecting candidates for nomination to the Court, the president receives help from the attorney general and other Justice Department officials. The attorney general usually consults with the legal community and proposes a list of possible candidates for the president to consider. In making the final selection, the president and the attorney general may also check with leading members of Congress. In addition, they hear from several different groups that have a special interest in the selection of a justice.

In 1932 faculty members of the nation's leading law schools, labor and business leaders, judges, and senators all urged Republican president Herbert Hoover to appoint Democrat Benjamin Cardozo to the Supreme Court. Cardozo was chief judge of the New York Court of Appeals. The support for Cardozo was so great that Hoover nominated Cardozo, who was confirmed without opposition.

Selecting Justices

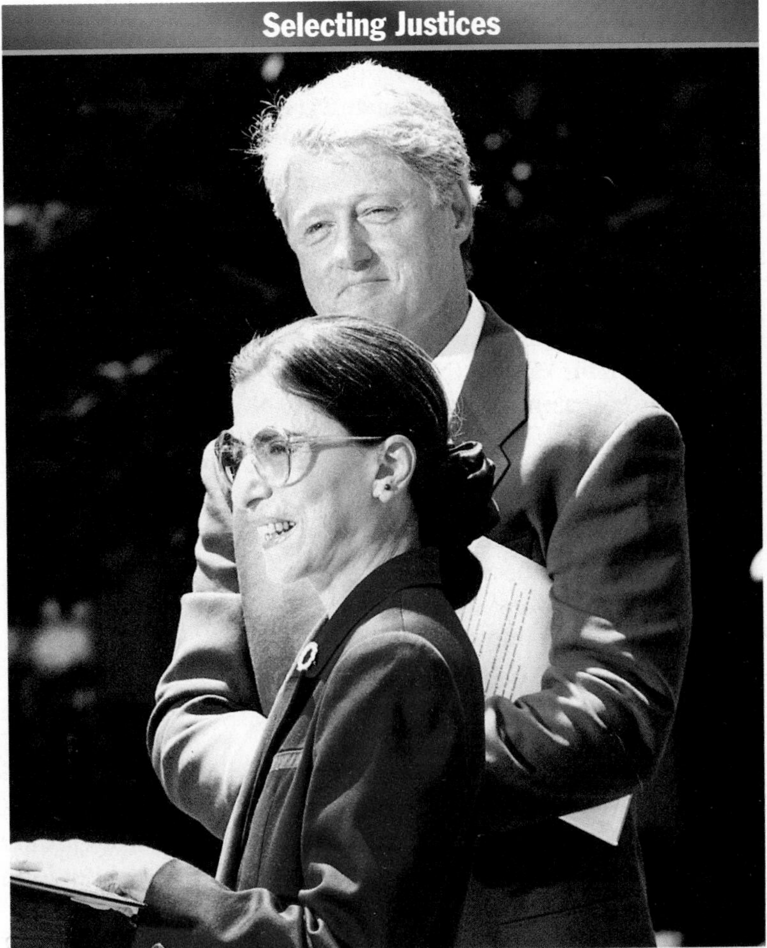

Political Processes President Clinton chose Judge Ruth Bader Ginsburg in June 1993 as his first nominee to the Supreme Court. Ginsburg was active in civil liberties and women's rights issues before going on the federal bench, but has also advocated judicial restraint. ***How do the Supreme Court appointments a president makes have long-term consequences?***

The Role of the American Bar Association The **American Bar Association (ABA)** is the largest national organization of attorneys. Since 1952, the ABA's Committee on the Federal Judiciary has been consulted by every president concerning almost every federal judicial appointment. The role of the ABA is solely to evaluate the professional qualifications of candidates for all Article III judicial positions—the Supreme Court, the United States Courts of Appeals, and the United States District Courts. The committee rates nominees as either "well qualified," "qualified," or "not qualified." The ABA rating is advisory, and neither the president nor the Senate is required to follow it. In instances where the president has nominated someone the ABA has rated "not qualified," the Senate generally has approved that nominee. This does not reflect a lack of confidence in the ABA, but rather that the president and the Senate look at much broader criteria for judicial candidates.

The Role of Other Interest Groups Interest groups that have a stake in Supreme Court decisions may attempt to influence the selection process. Generally, these groups make their positions on nominees known through their lobbyists, or agents, and the media. Strong opposition to a nominee by one or more major interest groups may influence the senators who vote on the nominee.

Labor unions, for example, may oppose a nominee if they believe the nominee is antilabor, based upon his or her previous court decisions, speeches, or writings. Similarly, the **National Organization for Women (NOW)** may oppose a nominee who is considered to be against women's rights. This was the case with President Ford's selection of John Paul Stevens in 1975. Despite NOW's criticism, however, the Senate approved Stevens. More recently, NOW expressed its opposition to the nominations of David Souter in 1990 and Clarence Thomas in 1991. In both instances NOW was concerned that the candidates might cast deciding votes in a case that would overturn *Roe* v. *Wade*.[1]

Stamp celebrates the Court's 200th anniversary.

Civil rights groups are also usually active during the selection process. Groups such as the National Association for the Advancement of Colored People (NAACP) carefully examine nominees' views on racial integration and minority rights.

The Role of the Justices Members of the Supreme Court sometimes have considerable influence in the selection of new justices. As leaders of the Court, chief justices have often been very active in the selection process. Justices who must work with the newcomers often participate in selecting candidates. They may write letters of recommendation supporting candidates who have been nominated, or they may lobby the president for a certain candidate.

Chief Justice William Howard Taft, for example, intervened frequently in the nominating process. He personally led a campaign for the nomination of Pierce Butler, who was named to the Court in 1922. Chief Justice Warren Burger suggested the name of Harry Blackmun, who was also confirmed. Knowing a member of the Court personally helped Sandra Day O'Connor. She received a strong endorsement from former law school classmate Justice William Rehnquist in 1981.

See the following footnoted materials in the ***Reference Handbook:***
1. *Roe* v. *Wade* case summary, page 764.

Section 3 Assessment

Checking for Understanding

1. **Main Idea** Use a graphic organizer like the one below to identify two kinds of cases where the Supreme Court has orginial jurisdiction and two kinds that may be appealed from a state court.

Original	Appeal

2. **Define** riding the circuit, opinion.
3. **Identify** Earl Warren, ABA, NOW.
4. Under what conditions may a case be appealed from a state court to the Supreme Court?
5. In your opinion, should politics influence the selection of Supreme Court justices? Explain.

Critical Thinking

6. **Understanding Cause and Effect** Supreme Court justices have often been active in the selection of new justices. Do you think this is appropriate? Explain your answer.

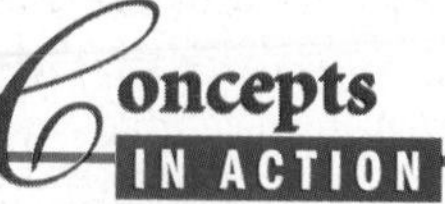

Checks and Balances With a partner, prepare an imaginary interview with a Supreme Court justice. The interview should provide your audience with a biographical sketch of the justice, including information about the person's place of birth, education, and work prior to being appointed.

Skills

Critical Thinking

Distinguishing Fact from Opinion

Facts are statements that can be proved by evidence such as records or historical sources. For example, it is a fact that Lewis Powell, Jr., served on the Supreme Court. Opinions are statements of preferences or beliefs not proven conclusively by evidence. One may hold an opinion that Powell was the greatest Justice ever. Some evidence may support this opinion, but contrary evidence supports other beliefs about Powell as well.

Learning the Skill

The following steps will help you to identify facts and opinions.

1. Study the information carefully to identify the facts. Ask: Can these statements be proved? Where would I find information to verify them?
2. If a statement can be proved, it is factual. Check the sources for the facts. Often statistics sound impressive, but they may come from an unreliable source, such as an interest group trying to gain support for its programs.
3. Identify the opinions. Opinions often contain phrases such as *in my view, I believe, it is my conviction, I think,* and *probably.* Look for expressions of approval or disapproval such as *good, bad, poor,* and *satisfactory.*

Practicing the Skill

The following excerpt concerns Supreme Court justices and their contributions to the Court. Read the excerpt and answer the questions.

Justice Lewis Powell, Jr.

"*I would say that the Court has reached—if not already passed—its capacity to deal with a [growing] caseload. . . . I believe most members of the Court will agree that we are not always able to function with the care, the deliberation, the consultation or even the basic study which are so requisite to the quality and soundness of Supreme Court decisions. In my view, we cannot continue as we are without a gradually perceptible dilution of this quality.*"

—Lewis F. Powell, Jr., 1971

1. Identify facts. Can you prove that the caseload of Supreme Court justices is large and growing?
2. Note opinions. What phrases does Justice Powell use to signal his opinions?
3. What is the purpose of Powell's statement?
4. What action might Justice Powell suggest?

Application Activity

Record a television interview. List three facts and three opinions that were stated. Answer the following questions: Do the facts seem reliable? How can you verify the facts? Was the person being interviewed trying to convince viewers of some position? Explain

The **Glencoe Skillbuilder Interactive Workbook, Level 2** provides instruction and practice in key social studies skills.

Assessment and Activities

GOVERNMENT Online

Self-Check Quiz Visit the *United States Government: Democracy in Action* Web site at gov.glencoe.com and click on ***Chapter 11–Self-Check Quizzes*** to prepare for the chapter test.

Reviewing Key Terms

Define each of the following terms and use it in a sentence.

concurrent jurisdiction
appellate jurisdiction
litigant
grand jury
indictment
petit jury
riding the circuit

Recalling Facts

1. What are the two systems of courts in the United States?
2. What principle resulted from the ruling in *Marbury* v. *Madison?*
3. What are the duties of a grand jury in a criminal case?
4. What kinds of cases are heard by the Court of International Trade?
5. Why do federal judges serve for life?
6. Describe the three decision-making tasks of a Supreme Court justice.
7. What are three duties of the chief justice of the United States?
8. What is the difference between courts with original jurisdiction and courts with appellate jurisdiction?

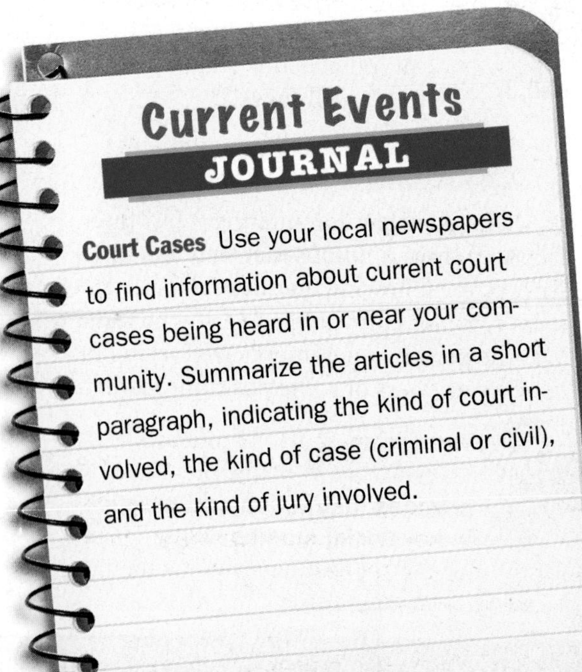

Understanding Concepts

1. **Constitutional Interpretations** If the issue is whether a person's civil rights had been violated in a court decision, through what levels of courts might that person appeal?
2. **Political Processes** Federal district judges generally represent the values and attitudes of the states that they serve. How can a president assure that an appointee meets this criterion?
3. **Checks and Balances** When the Supreme Court rules on an appeal from a state court, what restriction applies to the Court's ruling?

Critical Thinking

1. **Synthesizing Information** What factors determine whether a case will be tried in a state court or a federal court?
2. **Identifying Alternatives** Use a graphic organizer like the one below to identify two alternative solutions for the high case load of the Supreme Court. Explain why you would choose one and not the other.

Alternative 1	Alternative 2

Cooperative Learning Activity

Deciding Issues Organize into nine, seven, or five groups. As a group, list current issues that you think might someday come before the Supreme Court. Develop a persuasive position statement on each issue and present it to another group. Have members of the other group vote individually on paper to support or oppose the statement. Discuss the results with the entire class.

Interpreting Political Cartoons Activity

1. What occurrence is this cartoon calling attention to?
2. Does the cartoonist comment on the qualities or experience of the justice?
3. How does the cartoonist feel about this event?

"Well, it's about time."

Skill Practice Activity

Distinguishing Fact from Opinion Read the following statements. Tell whether each is a fact or an opinion.

1. The Supreme Court's ruling in *Marbury* v. *Madison* greatly increased its power.
2. The *Plessy* v. *Ferguson* ruling was, according to Justice Harlan, "inconsistent with the personal liberty of citizens, white and black."
3. The president should be insulated from the influence of interest groups when making Supreme Court appointments.
4. Presidents prefer to nominate candidates for the Supreme Court that they believe sympathize with their own political beliefs.

Technology Activity

Creating a Multimedia Presentation Work with a partner to create a multimedia presentation about the work of the lower federal courts, including the selection of federal judges. Use the material in Chapter 11 and other reference materials to find information about the different kinds of lower federal courts and the kinds of cases heard in these courts. Incorporate images off the Internet into your presentation. Have the class view the multimedia presentation.

Participating in Local Government

Using your local library or the Internet, research the kinds of courts located in or near your community. Find out the following:

- Are they part of the federal or state system?
- Where are the nearest federal district courts located?
- Where is the nearest appeals court located?

After gathering this information, create a "court directory" map of your community area and share your findings with the class.

Chapter 12

Supreme Court Decision Making

Why It's Important

Everyone's Supreme Court

The Supreme Court of the United States hears cases appealed to it by everyone from prisoners in jail to presidents. What influences the justices' decisions? In this chapter you will learn how the Court makes its judgments.

To learn more about how the Supreme Court works, view the ***Democracy in Action*** Chapter 12 video lesson:

Supreme Court Decision Making

GOVERNMENT Online

Chapter Overview Visit the *United States Government: Democracy in Action* Web site at gov.glencoe.com and click on ***Chapter 12–Overview*** to preview chapter information.

Section 1

The Supreme Court at Work

Reader's Guide

Key Terms

writ of certiorari, per curiam opinion, brief, amicus curiae, majority opinion, dissenting opinion

Find Out

- By what route do most cases from other courts reach the Supreme Court?
- What are the main steps the Supreme Court takes in deciding cases?

Understanding Concepts

Political Processes Why does the Supreme Court decline to hear most of the cases brought to it?

COVER STORY

Justices Do Homework

WASHINGTON, D.C., MAY 18, 1997

Attorneys who practice before the Supreme Court have noticed that the justices are becoming more alert to the oral arguments. They're attacking vague language and unclear legal reasoning. In the past, lawyers have sometimes supported their positions by quoting from a dissenting–or minority–opinion in a prior case. Today, at least one justice is likely to point out that the quote is not from the majority opinion and is thus not the Court's official view. "It's clear to me that they're doing their homework," observes one attorney who recently argued an important case before the Court.

Supreme Court seal

The Supreme Court meets for about nine months each year. Each term begins the first Monday in October and runs as long as the business before the Court requires, usually until the end of June. A term is named after the year in which it begins. Thus, the 1996 term began in October 1996 and ended in July 1997. Special sessions may be called to deal with urgent matters that cannot wait until the next term. Between terms the justices study prospective new cases and catch up on other Court work.

The Court's Procedures

During the term the Court sits for two consecutive weeks each month. At these sittings the justices listen to oral arguments by lawyers on each side of the cases before them. Later they announce their opinions on cases they have heard. The Court hears oral arguments from Monday through Wednesday. On Wednesdays and Fridays the justices meet in secret conferences to decide cases.

After a two-week sitting, the Court recesses and the justices work privately on paperwork. They consider arguments in cases they have heard and study petitions from plaintiffs who want the Court to hear their cases. They also work on **opinions**—written statements on cases they have already decided.

Nearly 8,000 cases were appealed to the Supreme Court in a recent year. However, the Court has time to grant review to only about 5 percent of these cases. The Court may decide several hundred cases, but, for example, it gave full hearings and written opinions in only 129 cases in 1990. That number dropped to 75 cases by 1995. In the opinions that accompany this small number of cases, the Court sets out general principles that apply to the nation as well as to the specific parties in the case. It is mainly through these cases that the Court interprets the law and shapes public policy.

◀ The Supreme Court building

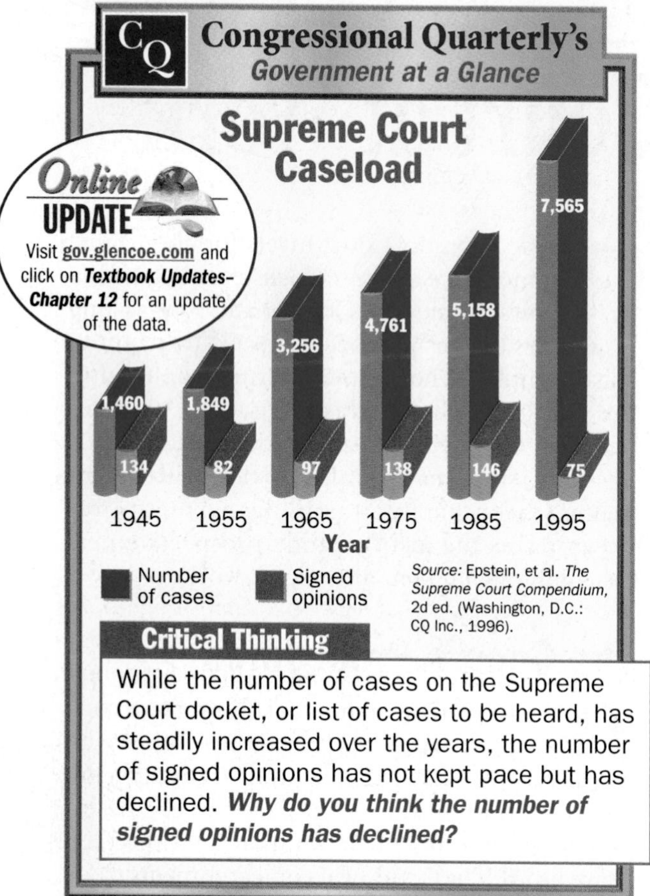

Critical Thinking

While the number of cases on the Supreme Court docket, or list of cases to be heard, has steadily increased over the years, the number of signed opinions has not kept pace but has declined. ***Why do you think the number of signed opinions has declined?***

How Cases Reach the Court

Historically, Congress has set complex and changing requirements for appealing a case to the Supreme Court. A few cases start at the Court because they fall under its original jurisdiction. The vast majority of cases reach the Court only as appeals from lower court decisions. These cases come to the Supreme Court in one of two ways—on appeal or by writ of certiorari.

Writ of Certiorari The main route to the Supreme Court is by a **writ of certiorari** (SUHR·shee·uh·RAR·ee)—an order from the Court to a lower court to send up the records on a case for review. Either side in a civil case may petition the Court for certiorari, or "cert," as lawyers call it. Such petitions must argue that the lower court made a legal error in handling the case, or they must raise some serious constitutional issue.

Whether or not the petition involves the constitutionality of a law, the Court is free to choose which cases it will consider. More than 90 percent of the requests for certiorari are rejected. Denial of certiorari does not necessarily mean that the justices agree with a lower court's decision. They may see the case as not involving a significant public issue. It may involve a question the Court does not want to address, or it may not be the best case for ruling on a specific issue. Regardless of the reason, when the Court denies certiorari, the lower court's decision stands.

On Appeal Certain cases reach the Court on appeal. In most cases, a lower federal or state court has ruled a law unconstitutional. In some cases, the highest court of a state upholds a state law against the claim that it violates federal law or the Constitution.

While the number of cases that arrive on appeal are few, the Court dismisses many of these cases. The Court is not reluctant to dismiss a case if it has procedural defects or does not involve federal law. When a case is dismissed, the decision of the lower court becomes final. Dismissal also has other legal consequences. Lower court judges are supposed to note that the Court believes similar types of cases do not involve a basic conflict with federal laws or the Constitution.

Selecting Cases Justice William O. Douglas once called the selection of cases "in many respects the most important and interesting of all our functions." When petitions for certiorari come to the Court, the justices or their clerks identify cases worthy of serious consideration and the chief justice puts them on a "discuss list" for all the justices to consider. All other cases are automatically denied a writ unless a justice asks that a specific case be added to the list.

Almost two-thirds of all petitions for certiorari never make the discuss list. At the Court's Friday conferences, the chief justice reviews the cases on the discuss list. Then the justices—armed with memos from their clerks, other information on the cases, and various law books—give their views. In deciding to accept a case, the Court operates by the rule of four. If four of the nine justices agree, the Court will accept the case for decision.

When the justices accept a case, they also decide either to ask for more information from the opposing lawyers or to rule quickly on the basis of written materials already available. Cases decided without further information are either returned to the lower court for a new decision or announced with a **per curiam** (puhr KYUR•ee•AHM) **opinion**—a brief unsigned statement of the Court's decision. Only a few of the cases the Court accepts are handled this way. The remaining cases go on for full consideration by the Court.

Steps in Deciding Major Cases

The Supreme Court follows a set procedure in hearing important cases. Much of this activity goes on behind the scenes, with only a small part taking place in an open courtroom.

Submitting Briefs After the Court accepts a case, the lawyers on each side submit a brief. A **brief** is a written statement setting forth the legal arguments, relevant facts, and precedents supporting one side of a case.

Parties not directly involved in the case, but who have an interest in its outcome, may also submit written briefs. Called **amicus curiae** (uh•mee•kuhs KYUR•ee•EYE)—or "friend of the court"—briefs, they come from individuals, interest groups, or government agencies claiming to have information useful to the Court's consideration of the case. In a major civil rights case, 53 amicus curiae briefs were filed—37 for one side and 16 for the other.

Amicus curiae briefs are a subtle way of lobbying, or trying to influence, the Court. Sometimes the briefs present new ideas or information. More often, however, they are most useful for indicating which interest groups are on either side of an issue.

Oral Arguments After briefs are filed, a lawyer for each side is asked to present an oral argument before the Court. Before the twentieth century, counsel was allowed 2 hours for oral argument. Today each side is allowed only 30 minutes to summarize the key points of its case. Justices often interrupt the lawyer during his or her oral presentation, sometimes challenging a statement or asking for further information. The lawyer speaks from a lectern that has a red light and a white light. The white light flashes 5 minutes before the lawyer's time is up. When the red light comes on, the lawyer must stop talking immediately.

The Conference On Fridays the justices meet in conference to discuss the cases they have heard. The nine justices come into the conference room and, by tradition, each shakes hands with the other eight. Everyone else leaves. Then one of the most secret meetings in Washington, D.C., begins.

For the next 6 to 8 hours, the justices debate the cases. No meeting minutes are kept. The chief justice presides over the discussion of each case and usually begins by summarizing the facts of the case and offering recommendations for handling it.

In the past the justices discussed cases in detail. Today the Court's heavy caseload allows little time

Reaching the Supreme Court

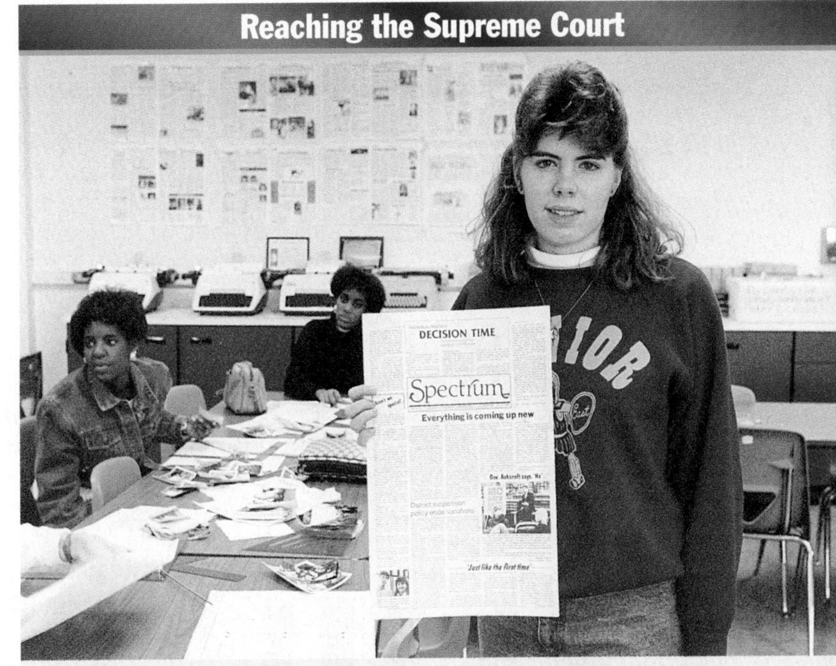

Routes of Justice The principal of Hazelwood East High School censored the student newspaper. The students took him to court. After a federal judge ruled against the students, a federal appeals court overturned that ruling. From there the case went to the Supreme Court in *Hazelwood School District v. Kuhlmeier* (1988). ***Why do you think the process for a case to reach the Supreme Court was set up as it was?***

for such debates. Instead, each decision gets about 30 minutes of discussion. Cases being considered for future review each get about 5 minutes. The chief justice merely asks each associate justice, in order of seniority, to give his or her views and conclusions. Then the justices vote. Each justice's vote carries the same weight.

A majority of justices must be in agreement to decide a case, and at least six justices must be present for a decision. If a tie occurs, the lower court decision is left standing. The Court's vote at this stage, however, is not necessarily final.

Writing the Opinion For major cases the Court issues at least one written opinion. The opinion states the facts of the case, announces the Court's ruling, and explains its reasoning in reaching the decision. These written opinions are as important as the decision itself. Not only do they set precedent for lower courts to follow in future cases, but they also are the Court's way to communicate with Congress, the president, interest groups, and the public.

The Court issues four kinds of opinions. In a **unanimous opinion,** all justices vote the same way. About one-third of the Court's decisions are unanimous. A **majority opinion** expresses the views of the majority of the justices on a case. One or more justices who agree with the majority's conclusions about a case, but do so for different reasons, write a **concurring opinion.** A **dissenting opinion** is the opinion of justices on the losing side in a case. Because the Court does change its mind on issues, a dissenting opinion may even become the majority opinion on a similar issue many years later. Chief Justice **Charles Evans Hughes** expressed this in a frequently quoted defense of dissenting opinion:

> "*A dissent in a court of last resort is an appeal to the brooding spirit of the law, to the intelligence of a future day, when a later decision may possibly correct the error into which the dissenting judge believes the court to have been betrayed.*"
>
> —Chief Justice Hughes

We the People

Making a Difference

Clarence Gideon

One morning in 1961 police officers arrested Clarence Earl Gideon for a burglary the previous night, despite his pleas of innocence. Gideon, a poor man, could not afford to hire a lawyer.

On August 4, Gideon's trial began in the Circuit Court of Bay County, Florida. Gideon addressed the judge, saying, "I request this court to appoint counsel to represent me." The judge explained that the Supreme Court had ruled that states had to provide lawyers for poor people only if they were charged with serious crimes, like murder. Without a lawyer's help, Gideon was found guilty.

Gideon appealed his conviction, claiming, "I knew the Constitution guaranteed me a fair trial, but I didn't see how a man could get one without a lawyer to defend him." The state supreme court refused to review Gideon's case. Gideon appealed his case to the Supreme Court.

Although the jail had no resources, no law library or attorneys to consult, not even a typewriter, Gideon studied law and pursued his goal. The justices finally agreed to let Gideon have his day in court.

In 1963 the Court ruled in Gideon's favor. Justice Hugo Black explained that the Fourteenth Amendment required states to grant citizens those rights considered "fundamental and essential to a fair trial." Those too poor to hire their own attorneys must be provided one by the state. A book was written about Gideon's case.

If the chief justice has voted with the majority on a case, he or she assigns someone in the majority to write the opinion. When the chief justice is in the minority, the most senior associate justice among the majority assigns one of the justices on that side of the case to write the majority opinion. Public policy established from a case may depend in large part on who writes the opinion. For this reason, chief justices often assign opinions in very important cases to themselves or to a justice whose views on the case are similar to their own.

Usually with the help of his or her law clerks, a justice prepares a first draft of an opinion and circulates it among the other justices for their comments. They may accept the draft with minor alterations, or they may find fault with the draft. In that case the writer must make major changes to keep their support.

When the other justices do not accept the initial draft of a majority opinion, a bargaining process often begins. Memos and new versions of the opinion may be written as the justices try to influence or satisfy one another.

Weeks or even months may go by as the justices bargain and rewrite their opinions. Finally, however, the case is settled and the decision is announced during a sitting. All the while, the Court is selecting and hearing new cases.

The Court in Session

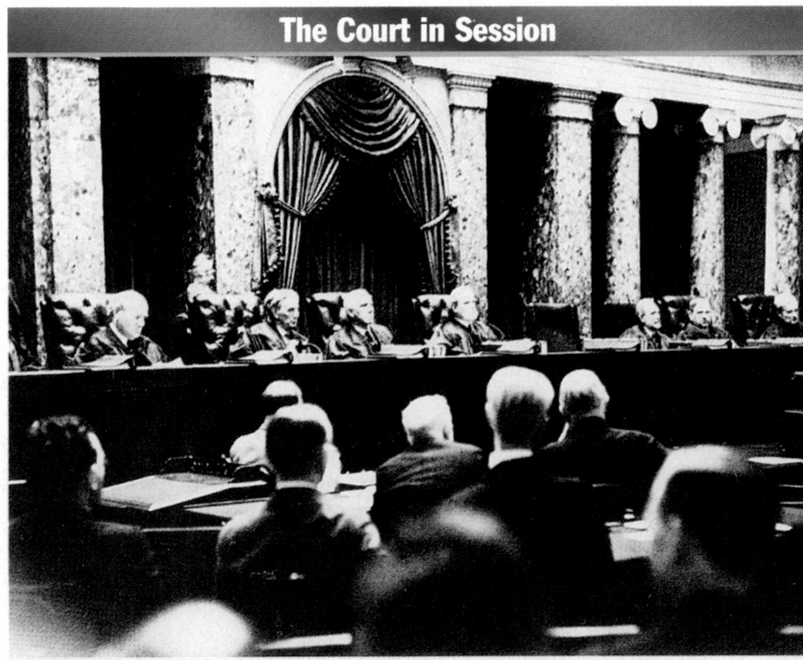

Rules of the Court This clandestine photograph of the Supreme Court in session in 1935 may be the only photo ever taken during a case hearing before the Court. ***Why would Supreme Court sessions be closed to cameras?***

Section 1 Assessment

Checking for Understanding

1. **Main Idea** Use a graphic organizer like the one below to identify the three ways cases reach the Supreme Court.

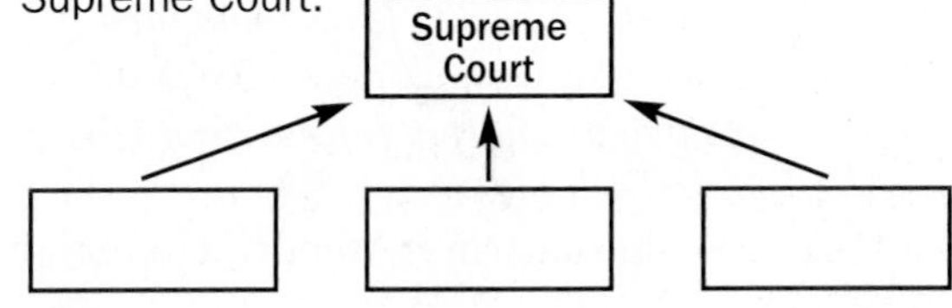

2. **Define** writ of certiorari, per curiam opinion, brief, amicus curiae, majority opinion, dissenting opinion.
3. **Identify** Charles Evans Hughes.
4. What steps does the Supreme Court take in selecting, hearing, and deciding cases?

Critical Thinking

5. **Demonstrating Reasoned Judgment** Do you believe that it is proper that the Supreme Court's deliberations are secret and that no minutes are kept?

Concepts IN ACTION

Political Processes The Supreme Court does not hear all the cases sent to it on appeal. Find out how many cases were sent to the Supreme Court in each of the past 10 years and the number of cases about which an opinion was issued. Present your information in a double bar graph.

Section 2

Shaping Public Policy

Reader's Guide

Key Terms

judicial review, impound, stare decisis, precedent, advisory opinion

Find Out

- Does the Court's use of judicial review give it too much power compared to that of the president and Congress?
- By what means is the Supreme Court limited in its power?

Understanding Concepts

Constitutional Interpretations How do Supreme Court decisions affect laws passed at both the state and national levels?

COVER STORY

Children Work Longer

CHARLOTTE, NORTH CAROLINA, 1918

In a 5-4 decision, the Supreme Court has struck down the federal Child Labor Act of 1916. The action came in a case brought by Roland Dagenhart, whose two young sons work in a local cotton mill. Dagenhart claimed that limiting his children to 8-hour days and a 6-day workweek violates their civil liberties. "All will admit," the Court said, "there should be limitations upon the right to employ children in mines and factories. . . . However, only a state has authority over such matters," the Court concluded. Critics charge that a state's desire to attract industry encourages weak child labor laws.

A 12-year-old spinner in a cotton mill

The Supreme Court is both a political and a legal institution. It is a legal institution because it is ultimately responsible for settling disputes and interpreting the meaning of laws. The Court is a political institution because when it applies the law to specific disputes, it often determines what national policy will be. For example, when the Court rules that certain provisions of the Social Security Act must apply to men and women equally, it is determining government policy.

Tools for Shaping Policy

Congress makes policy by passing laws. The president shapes policy by carrying out laws and by drawing up the national budget. As the Supreme Court decides cases, it determines policy in three ways. These include: (1) using judicial review, (2) interpreting the meaning of laws, and (3) overruling or reversing its previous decisions.

Under Chief Justice Earl Warren in the 1950s, the Court took a stand far in advance of public opinion. The cases seemed to contain more and more public policy. It seemed the Court had become an agent of change that Justice Oliver Wendell Holmes, Jr., had envisioned in 1913:

> "*We too need education in the obvious—to learn to transcend our own convictions and to leave room for much that we hold dear to be done away with short of revolution by the orderly change of law.*"
>
> —Justice Oliver Wendell Holmes, Jr.

Judicial Review The Supreme Court's power to examine the laws and actions of local, state, and national governments and to cancel them if they violate the Constitution is called **judicial review.** The Supreme Court first assumed the power of judicial review and ruled an act of Congress unconstitutional in the case of ***Marbury* v. *Madison*** [1] in 1803. Since then, the Court has invalidated nearly 200 provisions of federal law. This number may seem insignificant when compared to the thousands of laws Congress has passed, but when the Court declares a law unconstitutional, it often discourages the passage of similar legislation for years. In addition, some of these rulings have had a direct impact on the nation's direction. In the *Dred Scott* [2] case (1857), the Court ruled that the Missouri Compromise, which banned slavery in some territories, was unconstitutional. This decision added to the tensions leading to the Civil War.

Impact of Decisions

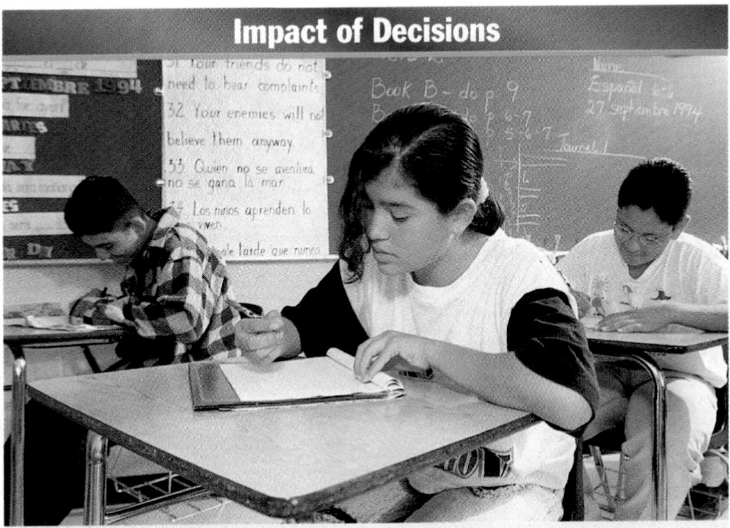

Checks and Balances A decision of the Court affects the entire country. This bilingual classroom is a direct result of the decision in *Lau* v. *Nichols* (1974). ***How is the case of* Lau *v.* Nichols *a good example of checks and balances?***

Judicial Review and Civil Rights The Supreme Court may also review presidential policies. In the classic case of *Ex parte Milligan* [3] (1866), the Court ruled President Lincoln's suspension of certain civil rights during the Civil War unconstitutional. More recently, in the case of *Train* v. *City of New York* [4] (1975), the Court limited the president's power to **impound,** or refuse to spend, money Congress has appropriated.

The Supreme Court exercises judicial review most frequently at the state and local levels. Since 1789 the Court has overturned more than 1,000 state and local laws. In recent years the Court has used judicial review to significantly influence public policy at the state level in the areas of racial desegregation, reapportionment of state legislatures, and police procedures.

Judicial review of state laws and actions may have as much significance as the Court's activities at the federal level. In *Brown* v. *Board of Education of Topeka* [5] (1954), the Court held that laws requiring or permitting racially segregated schools in four states were unconstitutional. The *Brown* decision cleared the way for the end of segregated schools throughout the nation. In ***Miranda* v. *Arizona*** [6] (1966), the Court ruled that police had acted unconstitutionally and had violated a suspect's rights. The *Miranda* decision brought major changes in law enforcement policies and procedures across the nation.

Interpretation of Laws One expert has said that judicial review is "like a boxer's big knockout punch." An equally important but less dramatic way for the Court to shape public policy is by interpreting the meaning of existing federal laws.

Congress often uses very general language in framing its laws, leaving it to others to interpret how the law applies to a specific situation. For example, the Americans with Disabilities Act of 1990 requires that businesses provide "reasonable" accommodations for disabled customers and employees. Disputes over the meaning of such language may wind up in federal court. The Civil Rights Act of 1964 prohibits discrimination on the grounds of "race, color, or national origin" in any program receiving federal aid. In the case of *Lau* v. *Nichols* [7] (1974), the Court interpreted the law to require schools to provide special instruction in English to immigrant students. Equality is not achieved by merely providing the same opportunities

See the following footnoted materials in the ***Reference Handbook:***

1. *Marbury* v. *Madison* case summary, page 761.
2. *Dred Scott* v. *Sandford* case summary, page 757.
3. *Ex parte Milligan* case summary, page 758.
4. *Train* v. *City of New York* case summary, page 766.
5. *Brown* v. *Board of Education of Topeka* case summary, page 755.
6. *Miranda* v. *Arizona* case summary, page 762.
7. *Lau* v. *Nichols* case summary, page 760.

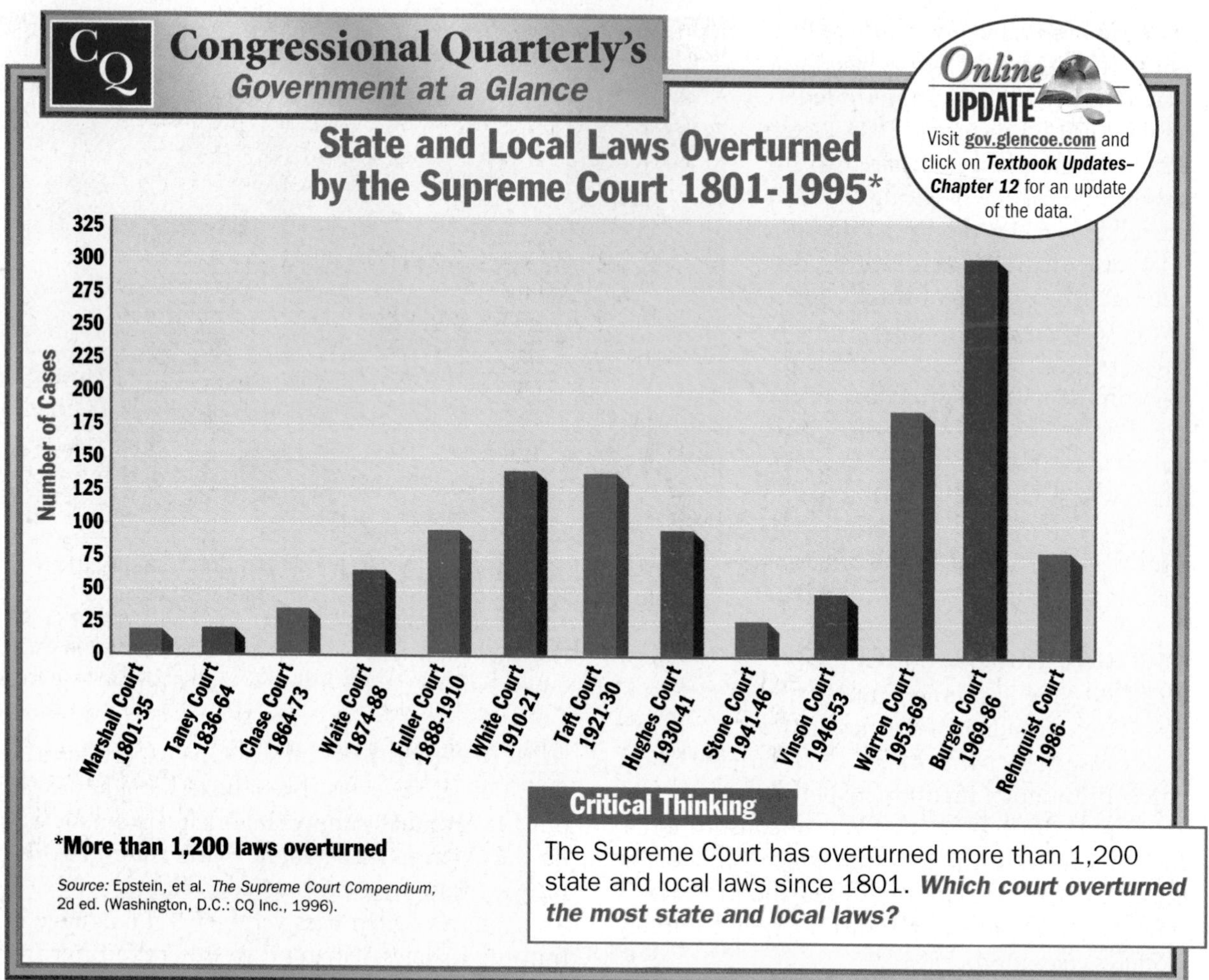

for all, the Court said. Poor English skills prevented these students from fully participating in school.

Because a Supreme Court decision is the law of the land, this ruling's impact was not limited to San Francisco, where the case originated. Local courts and legislatures across the nation, for example, took the Court's decision to mean that classes must be taught in Spanish for Hispanic students who did not speak English well. It is not important whether Congress even considered that teaching Hispanic students in English was a form of discrimination when it wrote the Civil Rights Act in 1964. The Supreme Court nevertheless decided what Congress meant.

Many of the major acts of Congress have come before the Court repeatedly for interpretation in settling disputes. These include the Interstate Commerce Act, the Sherman Antitrust Act, and the National Labor Relations Act. Justice Tom Clark once summarized the Supreme Court's constitutional role as

> "*. . . somewhat of an umpire. It considers what the Congress proposes, or what the executive proposes, or what some individual claims, and rules upon these laws, proposals, and claims by comparing them with the law as laid down by the Constitution . . . and then calls the strikes and the balls.*"
>
> —Justice Tom Clark

Overturning Earlier Decisions One of the basic principles of law in making judicial decisions is **stare decisis** (STEHR·ee dih·SY·suhs)—a Latin term that means "let the decision stand." Under this principle, once the Court rules on a case, its decision serves as a **precedent,** or model, on which to base other decisions in similar cases. This principle is important because it makes the law predictable. If judges' decisions were unpredictable from one case to another, what was legal one day could be illegal the next.

On the other hand, the law needs to be flexible and adaptable to changing times, social values and attitudes, and circumstances. Flexibility exists partly because justices sometimes change their minds. As one noted justice said, "Wisdom too often never comes, and so one ought not to reject it merely because it comes late."

More often, the law is flexible because of changes in the Court's composition. Justices may be appointed for life, but they do not serve forever. As justices die or retire, the president appoints replacements. New justices may bring different legal views to the Court and, over time, shift its position on some issues.

In 1928, for example, the Court ruled in *Olmstead* v. *United States* [1] that wiretaps on telephone conversations were legal because they did not require police to enter private property. Almost 40 years later, however, the Court's membership and society's values had changed. In *Katz* v. *United States* [2] (1967), the Court overturned the *Olmstead* decision, ruling that a wiretap was a search and seizure under the Fourth Amendment and required a court order.

Limits on the Supreme Court

Despite its importance, the Court does not have unlimited powers. Restrictions on the types of issues and kinds of cases the Court will hear, limited control over its own agenda, lack of enforcement power, and the system of checks and balances curtail the Court's activities.

Limits on Types of Issues Despite the broad range of its work, the Court does not give equal attention to all areas of national policy. For example, the Court has played only a minor role in making foreign policy. Over the years most Supreme Court decisions have dealt with civil liberties, economic issues, federal legislation and

See the following footnoted materials in the **Reference Handbook:**
1. *Olmstead* v. *United States* case summary, page 763.
2. *Katz* v. *United States* case summary, page 760.

GOVERNMENT *Online*

Student Web Activity Visit the *United States Government: Democracy in Action* Web site at gov.glencoe.com and click on ***Chapter 12–Student Web Activities*** for an activity about shaping public policy.

regulations, due process of law, and suits against government officials.

Civil liberties cases tend to involve constitutional questions and make up the bulk of the Court's cases. Appeals from prisoners to challenge their convictions, for example, account for about one-fourth of the Court's decisions. Most of these cases concern constitutional issues, such as the right to a fair trial and the proper use of evidence. Many of the Court's other cases deal with economic issues such as government regulation of business, labor-management relations, antitrust laws, and environmental protection. The Court also spends time resolving disputes between the national government and the states or between two states.

Gradual Changes

Judicial Processes Fast-moving national and state governments often "bump up" against the slower-moving, deliberative Supreme Court. ***Why would states want the Court's decision making to move more quickly?***

Limits on Types of Cases The Supreme Court has developed many rules and customs over the years. As a result, the Court will hear only cases that meet certain criteria.

First, the Court will consider only cases where its decision will make a difference. It will not hear a case merely to decide a point of law. Thus, the Court refused to decide whether the state of Idaho could retract its ratification of the Equal Rights Amendment. Not enough states had ratified the amendment, and the deadline had already expired. Whether or not Idaho could change its vote on the ERA made no difference. Further, unlike courts in some countries, the Supreme Court will not give **advisory opinions**—a ruling on a law or action that has not been challenged.

Second, the plaintiff—the person or group bringing the case—must have suffered real harm. It is not enough for people merely to object to a law or an action because they think it is unfair. Plaintiffs must show that the law or action being challenged has harmed them.

Third, the Court accepts only cases that involve a substantial federal question. The legal issues in dispute must affect many people or the operation of the political system itself.

Finally, the Court has traditionally refused to deal with political questions—issues the Court believes the executive or legislative branches should resolve. In the 2000 presidential election, however, the Court for the first time heard two cases involving the recounting of votes in the state of Florida.[1] No clear line separates political questions from the legal issues the Court will hear. In the 1840s two groups each claimed to be the legal government of Rhode Island. The Supreme Court decided the dispute was political rather than legal and that Congress should settle it. In the end, the difference between a political question and a legal question is whatever the Court determines it to be.

Limited Control Over Agenda A third limit on the Supreme Court's power to shape public policy is that with few exceptions it can decide only cases that come to it from elsewhere in the legal system. As a result, events beyond the Court's control shape its agenda. When Congress abolished the draft in the mid-1970s, for example, it ended the Court's ability to decide religious freedom cases involving refusal to serve in the military. On the other hand, passage of the 1964 Civil Rights Act and similar laws created a large volume of civil liberties cases for the Court to decide.

1. *Bush* v. *Gore* case summary, page 756; *Bush* v. *Palm Beach County* case summary, page 756.

Privacy on the Phone

Innovations in telephone technology have made communication much more convenient. Cordless, cellular, and digital phones allow varying degrees of mobility while talking on the telephone. When you use such phones, however, you are transmitting signals through the air that are similar to a radio broadcast. Anyone with a receiver tuned to the right frequency can overhear your conversation. Digital phones offer the most protection against eavesdropping, but special decoders can convert even digital transmissions into voice audio.

Federal laws offer some protection of telephone privacy. While it may not be unlawful to overhear a phone call, it is against the law to divulge the conversation or to use it for someone's benefit. The manufacture or sale of scanning devices that can intercept cellular or digital calls is also illegal. With some exceptions, the recording of telephone conversations without the knowledge or consent of both parties is a violation of federal and state law.

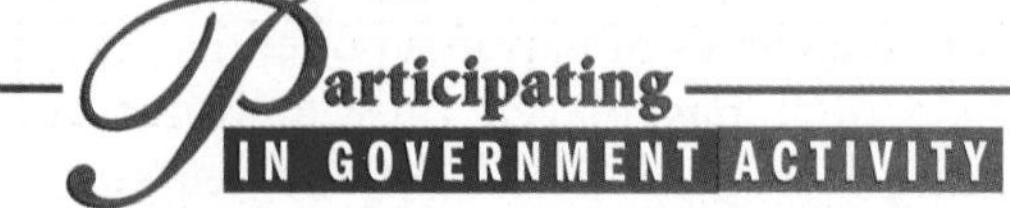

Survey Your Class How many people in the class use a cordless, cellular, or digital phone regularly? How many people are concerned that their conversations may not be private? Contact the Federal Communications Commission to obtain more information about laws protecting telephone use.

Of course, the Court can and does signal its interest in a subject by deliberately taking on a specific case. In 1962, for example, the Court entered the area of legislative apportionment by agreeing to hear *Baker* v. *Carr.* [1] In that Tennessee case, the Court reversed its 1946 position that drawing state legislative districts was a political question. As a result of the *Baker* decision, many cases challenging the makeup of legislative districts were brought to the Court. Still, even when the Court wishes to rule in an area, it may have to wait years for the right case in the proper context to come along.

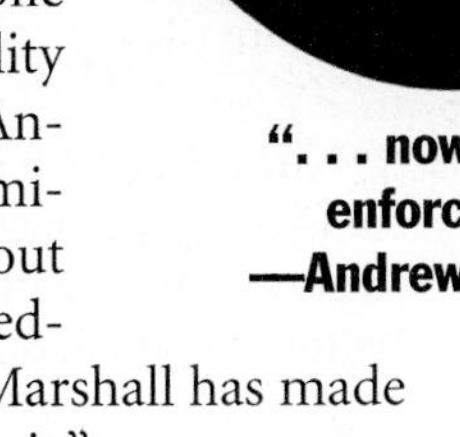

"... now let him enforce it." —Andrew Jackson

Lack of Enforcement Power A fourth factor limiting the Court's power to shape public policy is the Court's limited ability to enforce its rulings. President Andrew Jackson recognized this limitation when he refused to carry out a Court ruling he disliked, reputedly saying: "[Chief Justice] John Marshall has made his decision, now let him enforce it."

See the following footnoted materials in the **Reference Handbook:**
1. *Baker* v. *Carr* case summary, page 754.

Noncompliance may occur in several ways. Lower court judges may simply ignore a Supreme Court decision. During the 1960s many state court judges did not strictly enforce the Court's decisions banning school prayer. During the same period some officials, ranging from school principals to judges to governors, sought ways to avoid Court rulings on integrating schools. Moreover, the Supreme Court simply is not able to closely monitor the millions of trial decisions throughout the United States to make sure its rulings are followed. Nevertheless, most Court decisions are accepted and generally enforced.

Checks and Balances The Constitution provides that the legislative and executive branches of the national government have several ways to try to influence or check the Supreme Court's power. These checks include the president's power to appoint justices and Congress's power to approve appointments or to impeach and remove justices. The system of checks and balances is an ongoing process that the Framers intended would both monitor and protect the integrity of the Court.

Section 2 Assessment

Checking for Understanding

1. **Main Idea** Use a graphic organizer like the one below to compare the power of the Supreme Court with its constitutional limitations.

Power	Limitations

2. **Define** judicial review, impound, stare decisis, precedent, advisory opinion.
3. **Identify** *Marbury* v. *Madison, Miranda* v. *Arizona.*
4. Identify four reasons why the Supreme Court's power to shape public policy is limited.

Critical Thinking

5. **Drawing Conclusions** Do you think the Supreme Court's power would be enhanced or diminished if it would give advisory opinions? Explain your answer.

Constitutional Interpretations Research the supreme courts of Canada and Mexico. Find out how these courts select which cases they will hear. Write a brief summary that compares the selection process of these other supreme courts with that of the United States Supreme Court.

George W. Bush et al. v. Albert Gore, Jr., et al., 2000

George W. Bush

Albert Gore

The Supreme Court sometimes takes a case for review when it wants to clarify the meaning of the Constitution with respect to an important issue. This happened with the presidential election recount in Florida. Disputes over recounting ballots led the Court to address a question involving the Fourteenth Amendment: did all votes being recounted have to be treated equally?

Background of the Case

The outcome of the 2000 presidential election hinged on Florida's 25 electoral votes. When the polls closed November 7, Democrat Al Gore had captured 267 of the 270 votes needed, and Republican George W. Bush had won 246. The vote in Florida was so close – Bush led by 1,784 out of more than 6 million votes cast – that it triggered an automatic recount to ensure an accurate result.

When ballots were again run through tabulation machines, Bush's margin shrank to fewer than 200 votes. Gore requested hand recounts of ballots in four predominantly Democratic counties where thousands of punch-card ballots had recorded no vote for president. Bush asked a U.S. District Court to block any further recounts, and a legal battle for votes began, involving lawyers representing both candidates, the Florida Secretary of State, Florida District Courts, the Florida Supreme Court, and eventually the U.S. Supreme Court.

While the manual recount was still in progress, the Florida Secretary of State certified Bush the winner by 537 votes. Gore appealed first to the Florida circuit court and then to the Florida Supreme Court, which authorized manual recounts of disputed ballots to begin immediately. Bush appealed the ruling to the U.S. Supreme Court, which ordered the recount to stop.

The Constitutional Issue

The Florida Supreme Court ordered any recounts to use a general standard set forth in Florida law to discern "the intent of the voter." The ballots required voters to punch out small squares called "chads." On some ballots, the chad remained attached when punched, resulting in an uncounted vote when tabulated by machine. By what standard would a hand recount judge a voter's intent when a chad is left hanging by one or two corners but has not been cleanly removed?

Lawyers for Gore argued that examining ballots by hand inevitably requires personal judgments about a voter's intent. Lawyers for Bush argued that such a general standard violates the Fourteenth Amendment guarantee of equal protection. Without uniform standards of what constitutes a legal vote, it is impossible to ensure that each person's vote is treated the same.

Debating the Case

Questions to Consider

1. Did the Florida Supreme Court's standard for recounting disputed punch-card ballots result in one person's vote being valued more than another's?
2. What might be the consequences of using a very specific standard to determine which votes count?

You Be the Judge

Review the meaning of the Fourteenth Amendment. In your opinion, did the Florida Supreme Court's method for recounting votes violate the Fourteenth Amendment's guarantee of equal protection under the law? Explain.

Section 3

Influencing Court Decisions

Reader's Guide

Key Terms

bloc, swing vote

Find Out

- How do relationships among the justices affect the Supreme Court?
- What are the various external influences on Supreme Court decisions?

Understanding Concepts

Public Policy How does the power of Congress over the Supreme Court affect public policy?

COVER STORY

Justice Disrupts the Court

WASHINGTON, D.C., 1924

There will be no official photograph of the Supreme Court taken this year. Justice James McReynolds has refused to appear in the photo with Justice Louis D. Brandeis. McReynolds's dislike of Brandeis is well known. In Court conferences, McReynolds will leave the room when it is Brandeis's turn to speak. Such behavior has brought great tension to the Court. It was a major factor in the recent retirement of Justice John Clarke, who describes McReynolds as obnoxious. Chief Justice William Taft also considers McReynolds a problem. "He is a continual grouch," Taft says, and "fuller of prejudice than any man I have ever known."

Justice McReynolds

Why do justices decide cases as they do? What factors influence how each votes on a case? Five forces shape the decisions the Court makes. They are (1) existing laws, (2) the personal views of the justices, (3) the justices' interactions with one another, (4) social forces and public attitudes, and (5) Congress and the president.

Basing Decisions on the Law

Law is the foundation for deciding cases that come before the Supreme Court. Justices, like other people, often hold strong opinions on issues that come before them. In the end, however, they must base their decisions on principles of law, and not simply on their personal opinions.

Laws and the Constitution, however, are not always clear in their meaning. If they were, a Supreme Court would not be needed. The First Amendment, for example, prohibits any law "abridging freedom of speech," but does this right provide absolute freedom or do limits exist? Does freedom of speech mean that a person has the right to falsely cry "Fire" in a crowded theater? The Fourth Amendment prohibits unreasonable searches and seizures, but what is unreasonable? Can tapping a person's telephone be considered an unreasonable search?

Most of the cases the Supreme Court is asked to rule on involve difficult questions like these. Where the meaning of a statute or a provision of the Constitution is not clear, the justices of the Court must interpret the language, determine what it means, and apply it to the circumstances of the case.

In interpreting the law, however, justices are not free to give it any meaning they wish. They must relate their interpretations logically to the Constitution itself, to statutes that are relevant to the case, and to legal precedents. The Court explains, in detail, the legal principles behind any new interpretation of the law.

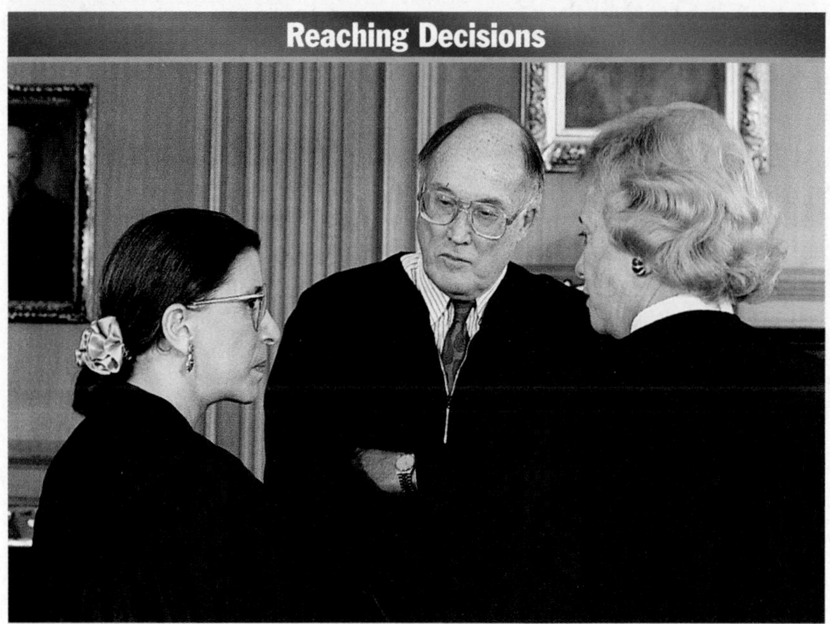

Reaching Decisions

Diverse Views The viewpoints of Supreme Court justices range from conservative to liberal. During frequent discussions such as this one involving Justice Ruth Bader Ginsburg, Chief Justice William Rehnquist, and Justice Sandra Day O'Connor, the justices air their opinions. ***Do you think the judicial branch is as political as the other branches? Why or why not?***

Views of the Justices

Supreme Court justices, like other political figures, are people with active interests in important issues. Some justices, for example, may believe that individual rights must be protected at almost all costs, even if that means a few criminals may go unpunished. Other justices may be more concerned about rising crime rates. They may feel that a little loss of freedom from wiretaps or stop-and-frisk laws is acceptable if it helps curb crime.

Over the years some justices become identified with specific views on certain issues. Justice William O. Douglas, for example, was known as a consistent supporter of the rights of the underprivileged during his 36 years on the Court. Because, like Douglas, most justices take consistent positions in areas of personal concern, voting **blocs,** or coalitions of justices, exist on the Court on certain kinds of issues. In recent years one group of justices has consistently tended toward liberal positions on civil rights and economic issues. A different bloc has consistently tended to take more conservative positions on the same issues.

When justices retire and new appointees take their places, the size and power of each bloc may change. A majority bloc on certain issues may gradually become the minority bloc. If the Court is badly split over an issue, a justice whose views are not consistent with either bloc may represent a **swing vote,** or the deciding vote. When new justices are appointed, the Court sometimes overturns precedents and changes direction in its interpretations.

Relations Among the Justices

In the early years of the Supreme Court, the justices lived and ate together in a Washington boardinghouse during the Court's term. Because the term was fairly short, they did not move their families to Washington, D.C. Justice Joseph Story described life at the boardinghouse:

> "*Judges here live with perfect harmony, and as agreeably as absence from friends and families could make our residence. . . . Our social hours, when undisturbed with the labors of the law, are passed in gay and frank conversation.*"
>
> —Justice Joseph Story, 1812

Today the justices work almost the entire year and live with their families in or near Washington, D.C. In 1976 Justice Lewis F. Powell said, "As much as 90 percent of the time we function as nine small, independent law firms," meeting as a group only for the oral argument sessions and conferences. The justices, he added, communicate with one another mostly in writing: "Indeed, a justice may go through an entire term without being once in the chambers of all the other eight members of the Court."

Harmony or Conflict Despite the lack of frequent interaction, the quality of personal relations among the justices influences the Court's decision making. A Court marked by harmony is more likely to agree on decisions than one marked by personal antagonisms. Justices who can work easily with one another will be more likely to find common solutions to problems.

Even when justices are at odds with one another, they will try to avoid open conflict. A news reporter once asked a justice why he did not complain about certain actions of the chief justice, whom he disliked. The justice replied, "YOU don't have to live here for the rest of your life."

Relatively good personal relations among justices who disagreed strongly on legal issues marked some modern Courts. At other times severe personal conflicts have seriously divided the Court.

Influence of the Chief Justice The chief justice has several powers that can be used to influence the Court's decisions. In presiding over the Court during oral arguments and in conference, the chief justice can direct discussion and frame alternatives. In addition, the chief justice makes up the first version of the discuss list and assigns the writing of opinions to the justices.

These advantages do not necessarily guarantee leadership by a chief justice. Supreme Court chief justices must make skillful use of the tools of influence available to them if they are to be effective leaders and shape the Court's decisions. The chief justice can also influence the amount of personal conflict that might exist on the Court.

The Court and Society

Harold Burton was appointed to the Supreme Court in 1945, after having served in Congress. When asked what the switch was like, he replied, "Have you ever gone from a circus to a monastery?"

Justice Burton's remark illustrates that, unlike Congress, the Court is fairly well insulated from public opinion and daily political pressures. The insulation results from the lifetime tenure of the justices and from rules that limit the way interest groups may try to influence the Court.

Still, the Supreme Court does not exist in a vacuum. The justices are interested in the Court's prestige and in maintaining as much public support as possible. In addition, the justices are part of society and are affected by the same social forces that shape public attitudes.

Concern for Public Support As already noted, the Court relies on the cooperation and goodwill of others to enforce its decisions. The justices recognize that the Court's authority and power depend in part on public acceptance of and support for its decisions. They know that when the Court moves too far ahead or lags too far behind public opinion, it risks losing valuable public support and may weaken its own authority. For example, in one ruling against voter discrimination in the South, Justice Felix Frankfurter, a Northerner, was assigned to write the Court's opinion. After thinking it over, the Court reassigned the opinion to Justice Stanley Reed, a Southerner. The justices hoped this change would ease the resentment that they believed was almost inevitable in the South.

Influence of Social Forces The values and beliefs of society influence Supreme Court justices. As society changes, attitudes and practices that were acceptable in one era may become unacceptable in another. In time the Court's decisions will usually reflect changes in American society, providing another reason why the Court sometimes reverses its earlier decisions. Two major decisions on racial segregation provide an example of how the Court changes with the times.

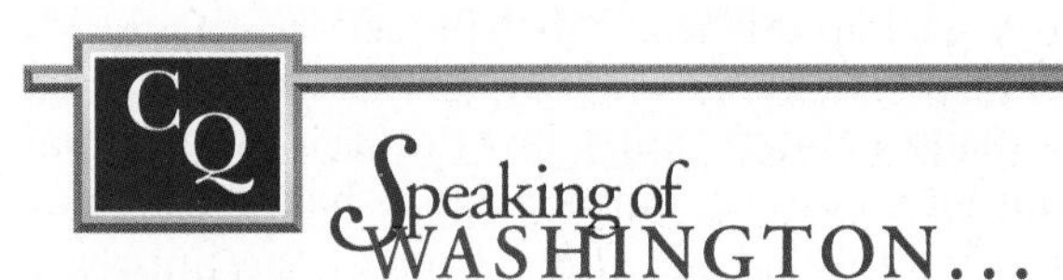

A Handshake Before they enter the courtroom and at the beginning of every private conference, the justices shake hands with one another. This practice began in the late nineteenth century when Chief Justice Melville W. Fuller decided it was a good idea to remind the justices that while they may have had differences of opinion, they did have to get along with one another.

Acknowledging Changes in Society

◀ **Societal Norms** Changes in societal values forced the Supreme Court to declare segregated facilities, like these separate drinking fountains for African Americans and whites at a New Orleans food market, unconstitutional.

▼ **The Military** Soldiers of the 93rd Infantry Division, America's first all–African American combat division, march in formation at Fort Huachuca, Arizona, in the summer of 1943. During World War II, most African American soldiers served in segregated units and were not sent into combat.

Reacting to Change
Why must the Supreme Court react to changes in American values?

Plessy v. *Ferguson*

In the 1890s many restaurants, schools, and trains were segregated. In Louisiana, Homer Plessy had attempted to sit in a section of a train marked "For Whites Only." When he refused to move, Plessy was arrested and convicted of violating Louisiana's segregation law that required "equal but separate accommodations" based on race. Plessy appealed his conviction to the Supreme Court, which in 1896 upheld the Louisiana law as constitutional in the case of ***Plessy* v. *Ferguson.***

The Court ruled that the equal protection clause of the Fourteenth Amendment permitted a state to require separate facilities for African Americans as long as those facilities were equal to the facilities available to whites. In reality, the facilities for African Americans were not truly equal, but few whites at the time were concerned about the needs of African Americans. The *Plessy* decision served as a legal justification for racial segregation for the next half-century.

By the 1950s society's attitudes toward race relations were beginning to change. World War II made it harder to support segregation openly because many African Americans had fought and died for American ideals. In addition, social science research began to document the damaging effects segregation had on African American children. Civil rights groups were demanding an end to racial discrimination.

Reversing *Plessy*

These social forces helped persuade the Supreme Court to overturn the precedent established in the *Plessy* case. During its 1952 term, in ***Brown* v. *Board of Education of Topeka,*** the Court heard a challenge to its 56-year-old interpretation of the Fourteenth Amendment. In 1954 the Court ruled unanimously that separate-but-equal educational facilities were unconstitutional.

In writing the Court's opinion, Chief Justice Earl Warren clearly recognized that social change was important in deciding the case. He reviewed the history of American education in the late 1800s. He then added:

> *Today, education is perhaps the most important function of state and local governments. . . . In these days, it is doubtful that any child may reasonably be expected to succeed in life if he is denied the opportunity of an education. Such an opportunity . . . is a right which must be made available to all on equal terms.*
>
> —Chief Justice Earl Warren, 1954

Chief Justice Warren declared that separate was inherently unequal, and that it violated the equal protection clause of the Fourteenth Amendment. Times had changed, and so had the Court's position.

President's Appointment Power

An Acceptable Nominee President Clinton appointed Stephen Breyer to the Court in 1994. Breyer enjoyed a reputation as a moderate who had an unusual ability to bring about agreement among his colleagues. Breyer's moderate views assured his confirmation. ***Why do particular groups oppose some nominees?***

Balancing the Court's Power

The judicial branch, like the two other branches of the national government, operates within the system of separation of powers and checks and balances. Thus, the powers of Congress and the president affect the Supreme Court's decisions.

The President's Influence A president's most important influence over the Court is the power to appoint justices, with Senate consent. Presidents generally use this appointment power to choose justices who seem likely to bring the Court closer to their own philosophy.

Every full-term president except Jimmy Carter has made at least one Court appointment. President Nixon appointed four justices, including a chief justice, and President Reagan appointed three—all sharing the conservative philosophies of these presidents. The importance of being able to make even a single Court appointment can be decisive when the votes of only one or two justices can swing the direction of Court decisions.

Presidents may also exercise influence with the Court in less formal ways. As head of the executive branch, the president plays a role in enforcing Court decisions. Executive departments and agencies must enforce Court decisions in such areas as integration and equal employment opportunity if they are to have any impact. An administration may enforce such Court decisions vigorously or with little enthusiasm, depending on its views on these issues.

The Influence of Congress The system of checks and balances can also be used to try to shape the Court's decisions. Congress has tried to control the Court's appellate jurisdiction by limiting the Court's ability to hear certain cases. In the late 1950s members of Congress, angry over Court decisions regarding subversive activities, unsuccessfully attempted to end the Court's authority to hear such cases. Congress also can pass laws to try to limit the Court's options in ordering remedies. By the early 1980s, some members of Congress became frustrated by liberal Court rulings on issues ranging from school busing to abortion. They introduced hundreds of bills to limit the Court's remedies in such cases.

After the Court has rejected a law, Congress may reenact it in a different form, hoping that the justices will change their minds. In the 1930s Congress tried to help the nation recover from the Depression by regulating industry. After the Court rejected the National Industrial Recovery Act in 1935, Congress reenacted essentially the same law but limited it to the coal industry. The Court upheld this law in 1937.

Congress also may propose a constitutional amendment to overturn a Court ruling. This strategy has been used successfully several times. For example, in 1793 the Court ruled in *Chisholm* v. *Georgia*[1] that a citizen of another state could sue a state in federal court. To counter this decision, Congress passed and the states approved the Eleventh Amendment that prohibited such action. In an 1895 case, the Court ruled that a tax on incomes was unconstitutional. The Sixteenth Amendment, ratified in 1913, allowed Congress to levy an income tax.

Another way Congress exercises power over the Court is through its right to set the justices' salaries. Although Congress cannot reduce the justices' salaries, at times it has shown its anger toward the Court by refusing the justices raises.

"Thus ended the era of good feeling!"

Packing the Court cartoon, 1937

Congress also sets the number of justices on the Court. In 1937, when President Franklin D. Roosevelt wanted to add six justices to the Court to change its direction and prevent it from declaring New Deal legislation unconstitutional, even lawmakers from the president's own party rejected the proposal.

Finally, in recent years the Senate has used its confirmation power to shape the Court's position. When the president nominates someone to the Court, the Senate scrutinizes the nominee's attitudes about sensitive social issues. Two of President Bush's appointees, David Souter and Clarence Thomas, were questioned intensely in Senate confirmation hearings about their views on abortion. To avoid this kind of questioning, President Clinton chose nominees who had centrist, or moderate, views on sensitive issues. Judging the nominee's stand on selected issues has given Congress increased power to influence the direction the Court will take in shaping public policy.

See the following footnoted materials in the ***Reference Handbook:***
1. *Chisholm* v. *Georgia* case summary, page 756.

Section 3 Assessment

Checking for Understanding

1. **Main Idea** Use a graphic organizer like the one at right to show five forces that shape Supreme Court decisions.

2. **Define** bloc, swing vote.
3. **Identify** *Plessy* v. *Ferguson, Brown* v. *Board of Education of Topeka.*
4. What is the basis for Supreme Court decisions?
5. How do personal relationships among Supreme Court justices affect decision making?

Critical Thinking

6. **Making Inferences** Why did the Supreme Court overturn a precedent in deciding the *Brown* case?

Concepts IN ACTION

Public Policy Although the Supreme Court sets policy, its decisions are affected by the powers of Congress and the president. Create a diagram that illustrates how Congress and the president check the powers of the Supreme Court. Display and discuss your diagram.

Building a Database

A computerized database program can help you organize and manage a large amount of information. Once you enter data in a database table, you can quickly locate a record according to key information.

Learning the Skill

An electronic database is a collection of facts that are stored in a file on the computer. The information is organized into different fields. For example, one field may be the names of your clients. Another field may be the street addresses of your clients.

A database can be organized and reorganized in any way that is useful to you. By using a database management system (DBMS)—special software developed for record keeping—you can easily add, delete, change, or update information. You give commands to the computer telling it what to do with the information, and it follows your commands. When you want to retrieve information, the computer searches through the files, finds the information, and displays it on the screen.

Practicing the Skill

This chapter mentions many landmark Supreme Court cases. Follow these steps to build a database on landmark Supreme Court cases.

1. Determine what facts you want to include in your database and research to collect that information.
2. Follow the instructions in the DBMS that you are using to set up fields. Then enter each item of data in its assigned field. Take as much time as you need to complete this step. Inaccurately placed data is difficult to retrieve.

Supreme Court building

3. Determine how you want to organize the facts in the database—chronologically by the date of the case, or alphabetically by the title of the case.
4. Follow the instructions in your computer program to sort the information in order of importance.
5. Evaluate that all the information in your database is correct. If necessary, add, delete, or change information or fields.

Application Activity

Research and build a database that organizes information on some other aspect of the Supreme Court. For example, you may wish to examine Supreme Court cases that have to do with the Bill of Rights or cases dealing directly with presidential powers. Build your database and explain to a partner why the database is organized the way it is and how it might be used in this class.

Chapter 12

Assessment and Activities

GOVERNMENT *Online*

Self-Check Quiz Visit the *United States Government: Democracy in Action* Web site at gov.glencoe.com and click on ***Chapter 12–Self-Check Quizzes*** to prepare for the chapter test.

Reviewing Key Terms

Match each of the following terms with the description below that correctly identifies it.

amicus curiae, precedent, stare decisis, dissenting opinion, brief, majority opinion, per curiam opinion, writ of certiorari

1. order to lower court for records on a case to be handed up for review
2. lets a decision stand
3. earlier decision on similar cases
4. short unsigned statement of Supreme Court's decision
5. an interested party not directly involved in a case
6. sets forth facts and legal arguments to support one side of a case
7. sets forth reasons for a Supreme Court decision
8. sets forth reasons for disagreeing with a Supreme Court decision

Current Events JOURNAL

Shaping Public Policy Use the *Readers' Guide to Periodical Literature* or the electronic index to periodicals in your library to find articles about recent Supreme Court rulings. Summarize the articles and identify in which of three ways the Court's ruling shaped policy: by using judicial review, by interpreting the meaning of laws, or by reversing the Court's previous decisions.

Recalling Facts

1. Why must the Supreme Court sometimes wait for years before it can rule in an area?
2. What happens when the Supreme Court refuses to hear a case?
3. What procedure do the justices follow in reaching a decision in a case?
4. What is the importance of a Supreme Court majority opinion?
5. What is the importance of a dissenting opinion?
6. Why does the Supreme Court sometimes reverse its earlier decisions?

Understanding Concepts

1. **Political Processes** Why does the Supreme Court refuse to hear so many cases?
2. **Constitutional Interpretations** Chief Justice Charles Evans Hughes once said, "The Constitution is what the judges say it is." Explain the meaning of this statement.
3. **Public Policy** Do you think that the Supreme Court should consider public opinion in deciding cases? Explain.

Critical Thinking

1. **Drawing Conclusions** Some people claim that the Supreme Court actually makes laws. Explain whether you agree or disagree with this assessment of the Court.
2. **Making Inferences** Why do you think President Woodrow Wilson once described the Supreme Court as "a constitutional convention in continuous session"?

3. **Demonstrating Reasoned Judgment** Why are the Supreme Court procedures so rigid?
4. **Synthesizing Information** In a chart, identify factors that affect how the Supreme Court shapes public policy, and name a major case that illustrates each factor.

How the Court Shapes Policy

Factor	Example

Interpreting Political Cartoons Activity

"That's right . . . five-ninths pepperoni and four-ninths sausage."

1. How does this cartoon characterize Supreme Court decision making?
2. What is the joke being made in this cartoon?
3. Is the nature of the Court—as presented in this cartoon—beneficial to American society? Why or why not?

Cooperative Learning Activity

Holding a Forum Organize 10 to 14 people into a group and then divide it into two equal subgroups. Have one subgroup study the Warren Court and the other subgroup the Burger Court. Each subgroup should research its Court, paying particular attention to the Court's decisions on minority rights and criminal justice. Have the entire group compare each subgroup's findings by holding a class forum. Those who researched the Warren Court should sit directly across and facing those who researched the Burger Court. Groups should ask questions of each other while defending the decisions of the Court they researched. Conclude the forum by proposing possible explanations for any differences between the courts.

Technology Activity

Using the Internet Search the Internet for a Web site that has information about recent cases heard by the United States Supreme Court. Write a summary of the ruling, the majority opinion, and the dissenting opinion.

Skill Practice Activity

Building a Database Prepare a database of Supreme Court rulings in the last six months. Use the resources at your local library to find information on the majority opinions, dissenting opinions, and subjects of the rulings.

Participating in Local Government

As you have learned, public opinion does have some influence on the decisions rendered by the Supreme Court. Survey members of your community about a case that is currently being heard or is set to be heard by the Supreme Court. Chart the responses you receive that reflect everyone's opinions about the issues in the case.

UNIT 5

Liberty and Justice for All

Speaking Out for Justice *Providing equal treatment for all is a main goal of the American system of justice. Study a few selected cases that are being tried in your local or state courts. After a thoughtful review of a case, write a summary of what you think the decision in the case should be. Then, after the case has been decided, compare the results to your summary. Did you agree with the court?*

Electronic Field Trip

Ellis Island

Take a virtual tour of Ellis Island in New York City and see America as thousands of immigrants have seen it for the first time.

Glencoe's Democracy in Action Video Program

Before the turn of the century, the United States experienced a flood of new immigrants from all over the world. The **Democracy in Action** video program "Ellis Island," referenced below, presents a photographic documentary of Ellis Island, including narratives of former immigrants' initial experiences upon arriving in America.

As you view the video program, try to picture yourself adjusting to the language, customs, laws, freedom, and responsibilities of citizenship in a new country.

Also available in videodisc format.

View the videodisc by scanning the barcode or by entering the chapter number on your keypad and pressing Search.

Disc 2, Side 1, Chapter 5

Hands-On Activity

Research your own family genealogy as far back as possible. Begin by talking with family members about the ancestors they remember or have heard about. Review photo albums and other family records. Research local offices such as your city hall to find birth, marriage, or death certificates of relatives. Use a word processor to map out your family tree.

The Statue of Liberty stands on Liberty Island in New York Harbor.

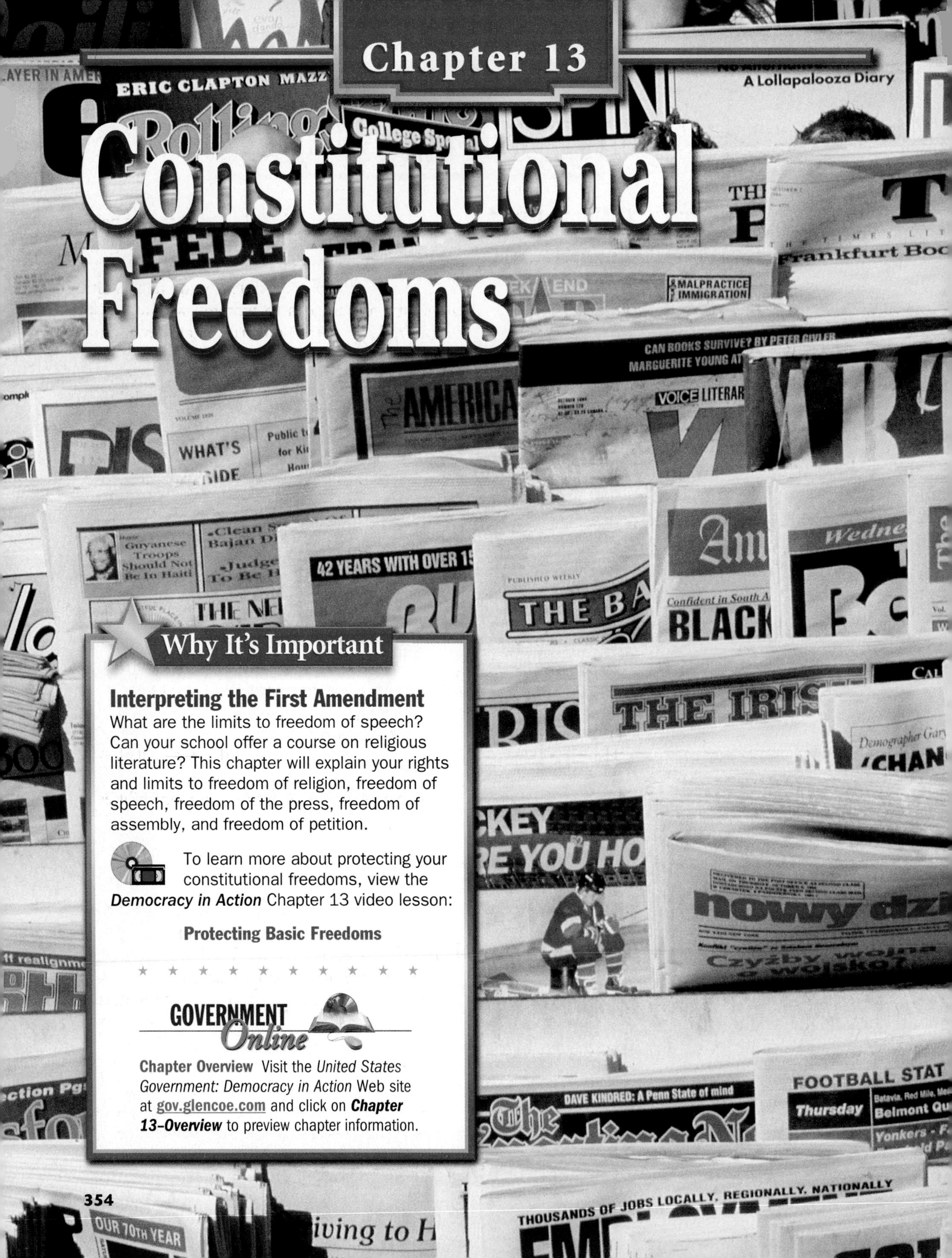

Chapter 13

Constitutional Freedoms

Why It's Important

Interpreting the First Amendment

What are the limits to freedom of speech? Can your school offer a course on religious literature? This chapter will explain your rights and limits to freedom of religion, freedom of speech, freedom of the press, freedom of assembly, and freedom of petition.

To learn more about protecting your constitutional freedoms, view the *Democracy in Action* Chapter 13 video lesson:

Protecting Basic Freedoms

GOVERNMENT Online

Chapter Overview Visit the *United States Government: Democracy in Action* Web site at gov.glencoe.com and click on ***Chapter 13–Overview*** to preview chapter information.

Section 1

Constitutional Rights

Reader's Guide

Key Terms

human rights, incorporation

Find Out

- How did the Supreme Court extend many rights mentioned in the first 10 amendments to the Constitution?
- Why is the Constitution of the United States considered to be a living document?

Understanding Concepts

Civic Participation What general assumptions about its citizens does a democratic government make?

COVER STORY

Censorship Stirs Storm

SNOHOMISH, WASHINGTON, DECEMBER 23, 1996

The refusal of high school officials to allow the student newspaper to cover the firing of a vice-principal has renewed debate over school censorship. Although the Supreme Court's 1988 decision in *Hazelwood School District* v. *Kuhlmeier* expanded the power of school officials to censor student publications, it has been criticized as too limiting of students' First Amendment freedoms. "How can they teach real journalism if students aren't even able to exercise their responsibilities?" says the paper's editor about the Washington controversy. "It's supposed to be the student's voice, not the administrator's voice."

Student journalist at work

All Americans have basic rights. The belief in **human rights,** or fundamental freedoms, lies at the heart of the United States political system and enables citizens and noncitizens to worship as they wish, speak freely, and read and write what they choose.

The Constitution guarantees the rights of United States citizens. Along with the enjoyment of these rights, however, comes a responsibility to ensure their strength and endurance. As the Preamble to the Constitution states, "We, the people" adopted the Constitution, and in many ways, United States citizens remain the keepers of their own rights. Rights and responsibilities cannot be separated. As citizens, people share a common faith in the power they have to steer the course of government. Judge Learned Hand expressed this well when he said:

> "*Liberty lies in the hearts of men and women; when it dies there, no constitution, no law, no court can save it; no constitution, no law, no court can even do much to help it.*"
>
> —Judge Learned Hand

If people do not carry out their responsibilities as citizens, the whole society suffers.

Constitutional Rights

The Constitution of the United States guarantees basic rights in the **Bill of Rights,** composed of the first 10 amendments, and in several additional amendments. The Framers of the Constitution believed that people had rights simply because they were people. In the words of the Declaration of Independence, people "are endowed by their Creator with certain unalienable rights." The Constitution and the Bill of Rights inscribe into law those rights that really belong to everyone. The Bill of Rights, in particular, stands as a written

Freedoms reflected at the newsstand

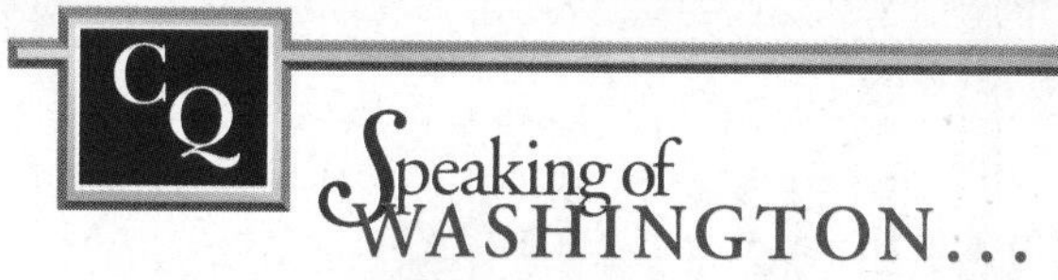

Protecting Basic Freedoms **Writing for the Court in 1833, Chief Justice John Marshall refused to extend provisions of the Bill of Rights to the states in *Barron* v. *Baltimore*, a precedent not reversed until the early twentieth century. A Baltimore wharf owner sued the city because its activities had created shoals and shallows around his wharf. He charged the city with violating the Fifth Amendment by "taking his property without just compensation." The Bill of Rights, Marshall said, was intended to protect citizens against encroachments by the federal government, not by the state and local governments.**

guarantee that government cannot abuse the rights of individuals.

The language of the Bill of Rights is very important, beginning with the words "Congress shall make no law. . . ." Today the Bill of Rights offers protection not only from congressional actions, but also from acts by state and local governments that may threaten people's basic rights.

The Bill of Rights was originally intended as a protection against the actions of the federal government. A process called **incorporation** extended the Bill of Rights to all levels of government. The Constitution drafted in 1787 did not include a bill of rights. Because most of the state constitutions of the time contained bills of rights, the Framers believed it unnecessary to include another such list of rights in the national Constitution.

Many state leaders, however, were suspicious of the new Constitution and when it was submitted to the states for ratification, a number of states refused to approve it unless a bill of rights was added. When the first Congress met in 1789, James Madison introduced a series of amendments that became the Bill of Rights in 1791. These amendments placed certain limitations on the national government to prevent it from controlling the press, restricting speech, and establishing or prohibiting religion, and limiting other areas of personal liberty. The Bill of Rights was not intended to limit state and local governments. An important Supreme Court case, *Barron* v. *Baltimore*[1] (1833), upheld this view. Chief Justice John Marshall, speaking for the Court, ruled that the first 10 amendments "contain no expression indicating an intention to apply them to the state governments."

GOVERNMENT Online

Student Web Activity Visit the *United States Government: Democracy in Action* Web site at gov.glencoe.com and click on ***Chapter 13–Student Web Activities*** for an activity about constitutional rights.

The Fourteenth Amendment

As times changed, so did the Constitution. The addition of the Fourteenth Amendment in 1868 paved the way for a major expansion of individual rights. The **Fourteenth Amendment**[2] not only defined citizenship (a person born or naturalized in the United States is a citizen of the nation and of his or her state of residence), but it also laid the groundwork for making individual rights national. The amendment states in part:

> "*No State shall make or enforce any law which shall abridge the privileges or immunities of citizens of the United States; nor shall any State deprive any person of life, liberty, or property without due process of law. . . .*"
>
> —Fourteenth Amendment, 1868

The Supreme Court has interpreted the due process clause of the Fourteenth Amendment to apply the guarantees of the Bill of Rights to state and local governments. Over the years the Supreme Court has interpreted the word *liberty* in the amendment to include all freedoms the First Amendment guarantees. Thus, no state can deprive any person of freedom of speech, press, religion, or assembly because these freedoms are essential to a person's liberty.

The Supreme Court has also interpreted the words *due process* to include other protections

See the following footnoted materials in the **Reference Handbook:**
1. *Barron* v. *Baltimore* case summary, page 754.
2. *The Constitution*, pages 774–799.

the Bill of Rights guarantees: protection from unreasonable search and seizure; the right of the accused to have a lawyer; and protection from cruel and unusual punishment. These rights have also been applied to the states through the Fourteenth Amendment.

The Supreme Court's interpretation of the Fourteenth Amendment nationalized the Bill of Rights. In the key case of *Gitlow* v. *New York*[1] (1925), the Supreme Court ruled that freedom of speech was a basic right that no state government could deny to any person.

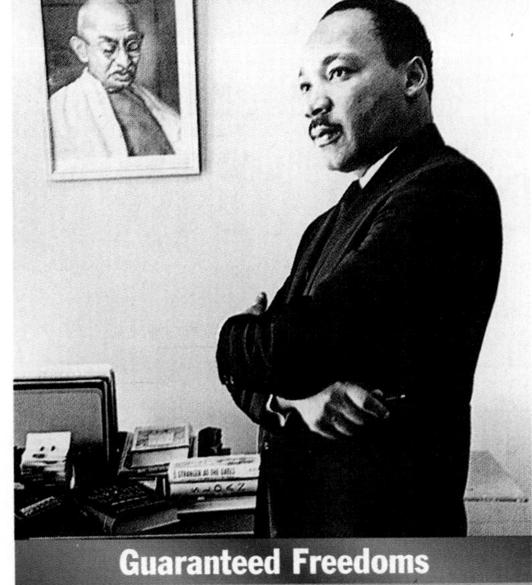

Guaranteed Freedoms

Civil Rights Leader Dr. Martin Luther King, Jr., championed the cause of free speech for all citizens. ***What other freedoms are guaranteed by the Fourteenth Amendment?***

Since the *Gitlow* case, the Supreme Court has incorporated almost all other rights provided for in the first 10 amendments. The only exceptions are the Second, Third, and Tenth Amendments, and two judicial procedures contained in the Fifth and Seventh Amendments. As a result, states are not required to use a grand jury to bring formal charges for serious crimes, nor are they required to have a trial by jury in civil cases involving more than $20.

The Importance of Incorporation The incorporation of the Bill of Rights has meant that United States citizens in every part of the country have the same basic rights. On the face of it, incorporation may not seem significant because state constitutions contain bills of rights. Yet in the past, state governments have ignored individual rights, denied voting rights to minority citizens, and practiced various forms of discrimination. As a result of incorporation, the Bill of Rights becomes a final safeguard when personal rights are threatened, proving that the Constitution is a living document.

In practice, **nationalization** means that citizens who believe that a state or local authority has denied them their basic rights may take their case to a federal court. If the decision of a lower federal court goes against them, they may pursue their claim all the way to the Supreme Court.

See the following footnoted materials in the ***Reference Handbook:***
1. *Gitlow* v. *New York* case summary, page 759.

Section 1 Assessment

Checking for Understanding

1. **Main Idea** Use a graphic organizer like the one below to show the effects of incorporation on the scope of the Bill of Rights.

Cause: incorporation of Bill of Rights	→	**Effect:**

2. **Define** human rights, incorporation.
3. **Identify** Bill of Rights, Fourteenth Amendment.
4. Describe what is meant by the incorporation of the Bill of Rights.
5. Cite the branch of government that has been primarily responsible for the incorporation of the Bill of Rights.

Critical Thinking

6. **Making Inferences** When it came time to submit the new Constitution to the states for ratification, why do you think state leaders insisted on a national Bill of Rights?

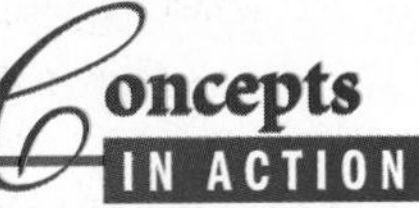

Civic Participation Some people have argued that all Americans should be required to perform some type of compulsory service for the country. Formulate a proposal describing a service that all Americans should perform.

Section 2

Freedom of Religion

Reader's Guide

Key Terms

establishment clause, free exercise clause, parochial school, secular, abridge, precedent

Find Out

- What is the difference between the establishment clause and the free exercise clause of the First Amendment?
- Why did the Court allow state-supported bus transportation for parochial schools but ban their use for field trips?

Understanding Concepts

Cultural Pluralism How does the free exercise clause protect the diverse cultures and religious practices in the United States?

COVER STORY

Hutchinson Banished

BOSTON, MASSACHUSETTS, NOVEMBER 1637

The Massachusetts General Court has found Anne Hutchinson guilty of contradicting the teachings of local ministers and has ordered her banished from the colony. Puritan leaders accused Hutchinson, who had been holding religious meetings in her home twice a week, of undermining their authority as interpreters of scripture. During her trial they established that her beliefs differed from the church's position on salvation. Hutchinson plans to settle in Rhode Island, a colony founded by Roger Williams after he was banished last year for similar religious offenses. Some of Hutchinson's supporters are expected to accompany her.

Anne Hutchinson

Religion has always been and is today a significant aspect of American life. More than 90 percent of Americans identify with a religion. Although religious tolerance developed slowly in the American colonies, by the time of the Constitution the nation incorporated guarantees of religious freedom in the First Amendment.[1] The first clause of the amendment, known as the **establishment clause,** states that "Congress shall make no law respecting an establishment of religion." The second clause, labeled the **free exercise clause,** prohibits government from unduly interfering with the free exercise of religion. The meaning of these clauses, on the surface, may seem clear. Their interpretation, however, underlies a continuing debate in American politics.

The Establishment Clause

By the time of the Constitution, history had taught the Founders that freedom of religion necessarily led to religious diversity. No single church or set of beliefs could predominate. The establishment clause supports this aspect of religious freedom. Thomas Jefferson and others, however, believed that the First Amendment also builds "a wall of separation between Church and State." Just what the "wall of separation" means has been the subject of much controversy in recent years.

Obviously, the establishment clause makes the United States different from countries in the world that have a state-supported religion. In such countries, public tax money goes to support one particular form of religion. How much higher does the "wall of separation" go? Does it mean that the state and any church or religious group should have no contact with each other?

See the following footnoted materials in the **Reference Handbook:**
1. *The Constitution,* pages 774–799.

Religion in Public Life In practice, religion has long been part of public life in the United States. Although Article VI of the Constitution bans any religious qualification to hold public office, most government officials take their oaths of office in the name of God. Since 1864 most of the nation's coins have carried the motto "In God We Trust." The Pledge of Allegiance contains the phrase "one nation under God." Many public meetings, including daily sessions of Congress and most state legislatures, open with a prayer.

Government actually encourages religion in some ways. For example, chaplains serve with each branch of the armed forces. Most church property and contributions to religious groups are tax-exempt.

Attempting to define the proper distance between the church and state often results in controversy. Under the Constitution the task of resolving these controversies falls on the Supreme Court. Although the Supreme Court had ruled on several religious freedom cases, it did not hear one based on the establishment clause until *Everson* v. *Board of Education* (1947). Since the *Everson* decision, the Court has ruled many more times on the establishment clause. Most of these cases have involved some aspect of religion and education.

Everson* v. *Board of Education This case involved a challenge to a New Jersey law allowing the state to pay for busing students to **parochial schools,** schools operated by a church or religious group. The law's critics contended that the law amounted to state support of a religion, in violation of the establishment clause. Writing the Court's decision, Justice Hugo H. Black defined the establishment clause:

> "*Neither a state nor the federal government can set up a church. Neither can pass laws which aid one religion, aid all religions, or prefer one religion over another. . . .*"
>
> —Justice Hugo L. Black, 1947

The Court ruled, however, that the New Jersey law was constitutional. In making the decision, the Court determined that the law benefited students rather than aided a religion directly.

Although this 1947 decision still guides the Court, the *Everson* case illustrated uncertainty over just how high Jefferson's "wall of separation" should be. That uncertainty continues today both in the Court and among the American people.

Constitutional Interpretations

The Establishment Clause An army chaplain leads soldiers in voluntary prayer during the Persian Gulf War. ***Why would this military service not be considered a violation of the establishment clause?***

The motto "In God We Trust" first appeared on U.S. coins in 1864.

Separation of Church and State

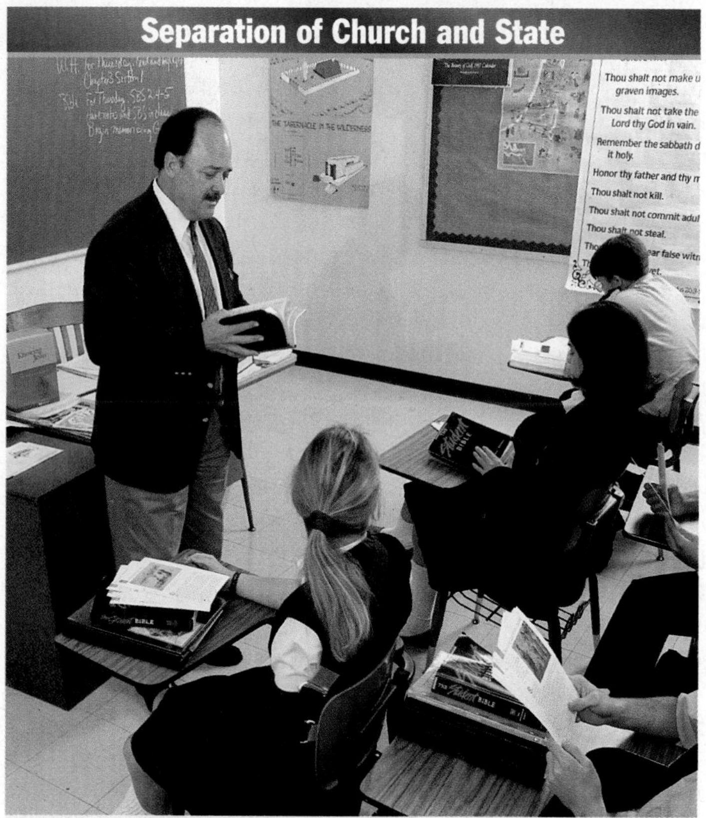

Constitutional Principles The Constitution lays down the principle of church-state separation, so the teaching of religion to students has always been controversial. Yet the House of Representatives opens every session with a prayer. ***Does a constitutional conflict exist in this instance? Explain.***

State Aid to Parochial Schools Some of the most controversial debates over church-state relations have focused on the kinds of aid government can give church-related schools. Since the *Everson* decision, more than two-thirds of the states have given parochial schools aid ranging from driver education to free lunches for students. The Court continues to hear cases arising from these programs, finding some constitutional and others not.

For example, in *Board of Education* v. *Allen*[1] (1968) the Court upheld state programs to provide **secular**, or nonreligious, textbooks to parochial schools. Although the *Everson* decision permitted state-supported bus transportation to and from school, *Wolman* v. *Walter*[2] (1977) banned its use for field trips.

Why are some forms of aid constitutional and others not? The answer is in the so-called *Lemon* test. Since the 1971 case of *Lemon* v. *Kurtzman*,[3] the Court has used a three-part test to decide whether such aid violates the establishment clause. To be constitutional, state aid to church schools must: (1) have a clear secular, nonreligious purpose; (2) in its main effect neither advance nor inhibit religion; and (3) avoid "excessive government entanglement with religion."

In *Levitt* v. *Committee for Public Education*[4] (1973), for example, the Court voided a New York plan to help pay for parochial schools developing testing programs. In *Committee for Public Education* v. *Regan*[5] (1980) the Court permitted New York State to pay parochial schools to administer and grade tests. In the 1980 case the state's department of education prepared the tests. In the 1973 case the tests were teacher-prepared, which the Court considered part of religious instruction.

In *Mueller* v. *Allen*[6] (1983) the Court upheld a Minnesota law allowing parents to deduct tuition, textbooks, and transportation to and from school from their state income tax. Public schools charge little or nothing for these items, because taxes pay for them. Parents whose children attend parochial schools benefited from the deduction. Because the law permitted parents of all students to take the deduction, it passed the Court's three-part test.

In *Mitchell* v. *Helms*[7] (2000) the Court ruled that taxpayer funds could be used to provide religious schools with computers, library books, projectors, televisions, and similar equipment as long as they are not used for religious purposes. This continued the Court's recent pattern of expanding government aid for parochial schools.

See the following footnoted materials in the ***Reference Handbook:***
1. *Board of Education* v. *Allen* case summary, page 755.
2. *Wolman* v. *Walter* case summary, page 768.
3. *Lemon* v. *Kurtzman* case summary, page 761.
4. *Levitt* v. *Committee for Public Education* case summary, page 761.
5. *Committee for Public Education* v. *Regan* case summary, page 756.
6. *Mueller* v. *Allen* case summary, page 762.
7. *Mitchell* v. *Helms* case summary, page 762.

Conflicts over state aid to church schools are not confined to Christian schools. The Court ruled in *Kiryas Joel* v. *Grumet*[1] (1994) that New York State could not create a public school district solely for the benefit of a community of Hasidic Jews.

Release Time for Students Can public schools release students from school to attend classes in religious instruction? The Court first dealt with this question in *McCollum* v. *Board of Education*[2] (1948). The public schools in Champaign, Illinois, had a program in which religion teachers came into the schools once a week and gave instruction to students who desired it. The Court declared this program unconstitutional because school classrooms—tax-supported public facilities—were being used for religious purposes. Justice Black wrote that the program used tax-supported public schools "to aid religious groups to spread their faith."

Four years later in *Zorach* v. *Clauson,*[3] however, the Court accepted a New York City program that allowed religious instruction during the school day but away from the public schools. The Court ruled a release-time program of religious instruction was constitutional if carried on in private rather than public facilities.

 **Landmark Cases**

Engel* v. *Vitale In 1962 and 1963 the Court handed down three controversial decisions affecting prayer and Bible reading in public schools. The first was *Engel* v. *Vitale,* a school prayer case that began in New York State. The New York Board of Regents composed a nondenominational prayer that it urged schools to use: "Almighty God, we acknowledge our dependence upon Thee, and we beg Thy blessings upon us, our parents, our teachers, and our country." In New Hyde Park, parents of 10 students challenged the prayer in court. In 1962 the Court declared the regents' prayer unconstitutional, interpreting the First Amendment to mean the following:

> "*In this country it is no part of the business of government to compose official prayers for any group of the American people to recite as part of a religious program carried on by government.*"
>
> —Justice Hugo H. Black, 1962

In his lone dissent from the *Engel* decision, Justice Potter Stewart argued that the New York prayer was no different from other state-approved religious expression, such as referring to God in the Pledge of Allegiance.

Other School Prayer Cases In 1963 the Court combined a Pennsylvania case—*Abington School District* v. *Schempp*[4]—and one from Maryland—*Murray* v. *Curlett*—for another major decision on school prayer. In these cases the Court banned school-sponsored Bible reading and recitation of the Lord's Prayer in public schools. Because tax-paid teachers conducted the activities in public buildings, the Court reasoned that these acts violated the First Amendment.

In 1985 the Court struck down an Alabama law requiring teachers to observe a moment of silence for "meditation or voluntary prayer" at the start of each school day. The Court ruled that the law's reference to prayer made it an unconstitutional endorsement of religion. In 1992 the Court also prohibited clergy-led prayers at public school graduations.

Then, in *Santa Fe Independent School District* v. *Doe*[5] (2000), the Supreme Court ruled that public school districts cannot let students lead stadium crowds in prayer before football games. According to Justice John Paul Stevens, such prayers "over the school's public address system by a speaker representing the student body" violated the separation of government and religion required by the First Amendment.

Public reaction to the Court's rulings has been divided and heated. Although many people support the Court's stance, others have bitterly protested. About half the states have passed moment-of-silence laws that make no mention of prayer. Congress has considered several constitutional amendments to overturn these Court decisions, but has not yet produced the two-thirds majority needed to propose an amendment.

See the following footnoted materials in the **Reference Handbook:**

1. *Kiryas Joel* v. *Grumet* case summary, page 760.
2. *McCollum* v. *Board of Education* case summary, page 761.
3. *Zorach* v. *Clauson* case summary, page 768.
4. *Abington School District* v. *Schempp* case summary, page 754.
5. *Santa Fe Independent School District* v. *Doe* case summary, page 765.

Practicing Religion A San Marcos, Texas high school football team voluntarily prays before a game. ***On what grounds does the Supreme Court reject schools conducting mandatory prayers?***

Equal Access Act

An exception to the Court's imposed limits on prayer in public schools is the Equal Access Act passed by Congress in 1984. The Act allows public high schools receiving federal funds to permit student religious groups to hold meetings in the school. The bill's sponsors made it clear that they intended to provide opportunity for student prayer groups in public schools, a position that had overwhelming support in both houses of Congress.

The Court ruled the law constitutional in 1990. The case arose from the request of students at Westside High School in Omaha, Nebraska, to form a club for Bible reading and prayer. Student organizers said that membership would be completely voluntary and that it would be open to students of any religion. When school officials refused to let the group meet in the school like other school clubs, the students sued. In *Westside Community Schools* v. *Mergens*[1] (1990) the Court ruled as follows:

> "*Although a school may not itself lead or direct a religious club, a school that permits a student-initiated and student-led religious club to meet after school, just as it permits any other student group to do, does not convey the message of state approval or endorsement of that particular religion.*"
>
> —Justice Sandra Day O'Connor, 1990

Teaching the Theory of Evolution

The Supreme Court also has applied the establishment clause to classroom instruction. In *Epperson* v. *Arkansas*[2] (1968) the justices voided an Arkansas law that banned teaching evolution in public schools. The Court ruled that "the state has no legitimate interest in protecting any or all religions from views distasteful to them."

Some state legislatures passed laws that required teaching the Bible's account of creation with evolution as an alternative point of view. In 1987, however, the Court struck down these laws. In *Edwards* v. *Aguillard*[3] the Court ruled that a law requiring the teaching of creationism violated the establishment clause because its primary purpose was "to endorse a particular religious doctrine."

Other Establishment Issues

Not all establishment clause issues concern education. For example, the Supreme Court has also applied the separation of church and state to public Christmas displays, which have caused controversy in some communities. In *Lynch* v. *Donnelly*[4] (1984) the Court allowed the city of Pawtucket, Rhode Island, to display a Nativity scene with secular items such as a Christmas tree and a sleigh and reindeer. In 1989 the Court ruled that a publicly funded Nativity scene by itself violated the Constitution, in *Allegheny County* v. *ACLU*.[5] The justices upheld placing a menorah—a candelabrum with seven or nine candles that is used in Jewish worship—alongside a Christmas tree at city hall the same year, however.

See the following footnoted materials in the **Reference Handbook:**

1. *Westside Community Schools* v. *Mergens* case summary, page 767.
2. *Epperson* v. *Arkansas* case summary, page 757.
3. *Edwards* v. *Aguillard* case summary, page 757.
4. *Lynch* v. *Donnelly* case summary, page 761.
5. *Allegheny County* v. *ACLU* case summary, page 754.

The Court has also ruled that its ban on school prayer does not extend to government meetings. In *Marsh* v. *Chambers*[1] (1983) the justices noted that prayers have been offered in legislatures since colonial times, and that, unlike students, legislators are not "susceptible to religious indoctrination." Therefore, the establishment clause is not violated by such prayers.

The Free Exercise Clause

In addition to banning an established church, the First Amendment forbids laws "prohibiting the free exercise of religion." But in interpreting this free exercise clause, the Supreme Court makes an important distinction between belief and practice. It has ruled that the right to hold any religious belief is absolute. What about the practice of those beliefs? What if a religion justifies using drugs?

Religious Practice May Be Limited The Supreme Court has never permitted religious freedom to justify any behavior, particularly when religious practices conflict with criminal laws. The Court first dealt with this issue in the case of *Reynolds* v. *United States*[2] (1879). George Reynolds, a Mormon who lived in Utah, had two wives and was convicted of polygamy. Reynolds's religion permitted polygamy, but federal law prohibited it. He appealed his conviction to the Supreme Court, claiming that the law **abridged,** or limited, freedom of religion. The Court, however, upheld his conviction. The *Reynolds* case established that people are not free to worship in ways that violate laws protecting the health, safety, or morals of the community.

Over the years the Supreme Court has consistently followed this principle, upholding a variety of restrictive laws. For example, in *Jacobson* v. *Massachusetts*[3] (1905) the Court upheld compulsory vaccination laws for students, even though some religions prohibit it. In *Oregon* v. *Smith*[4] (1990) the Court denied unemployment benefits to a worker fired for using drugs as part of a religious ceremony.

In 1993 Congress passed and President Bill Clinton signed the Religious Freedom Restoration Act. This law was designed to overturn the principle the Court set forth in the *Smith* case. The act states that people have the right to perform their religious rituals unless those rituals are prohibited by a law that is narrowly tailored and is the "least restrictive means of furthering a compelling [state] interest." The act says Congress has the power to set aside state laws that violate this principle. The act did not survive long. In June 1997 the Court ruled in *City of Boerne, Texas* v. *Flores*[5] that the act was unconstitutional on several grounds.

While government may limit some religious practices, the Court also has ruled that a number of other restrictions violate the free exercise clause. For example, in *Wisconsin* v. *Yoder*[6] (1972), the Court decided that the state could not require Amish parents to send their children to public school beyond the eighth grade. To do so, the Court ruled, would violate long-held Amish religious beliefs that were "intimately related to daily living" and would present "a very real threat of undermining the Amish community."

The Flag Salute Cases Two of the most-discussed free exercise cases concerned whether children could be forced to salute the American flag. The first case began in 1936 when Lillian and William Gobitis, ages 10 and 12, were expelled from school for refusing to salute the flag. As Jehovah's Witnesses, the children and their parents believed saluting the flag violated the Christian commandment against bowing down to any graven image. In *Minersville School District* v. *Gobitis* (1940) the Court upheld the school regulation. The flag was a patriotic symbol, the Court ruled, and requiring the salute did not infringe on religious freedom.

After the *Gobitis* decision, the West Virginia legislature passed an act requiring public schools in the state to conduct classes in civics, history, and the federal and state constitutions. The State Board of Education followed this legislation by directing that all students and teachers in West Virginia's public schools salute the flag and recite the Pledge of Allegiance as part of regular school activities.

See the following footnoted materials in the ***Reference Handbook:***
1. *Marsh* v. *Chambers* case summary, page 761.
2. *Reynolds* v. *United States* case summary, page 764.
3. *Jacobson* v. *Massachusetts* case summary, page 760.
4. *Oregon* v. *Smith* case summary, page 763.
5. *City of Boerne, Texas* v. *Flores* case summary, page 756.
6. *Wisconsin* v. *Yoder* case summary, page 768.

Defending Beliefs

Interpreting the First Amendment Nine-year-old Jana Gobitis, with her hands at her sides, refuses to salute the flag in her third-grade classroom in 1965. Unlike her father, William, Jana never faced expulsion from school for her beliefs. ***How did the Supreme Court, in 1943, change its interpretation of the First Amendment right of free exercise of religion?***

Failure to comply with this requirement constituted insubordination for which a student was to be expelled from school and treated as a delinquent. In addition, the parents of students who failed to comply were liable to prosecution and a penalty of 30 days in jail and a $50 fine.

When a member of Jehovah's Witnesses appealed the state's requirement, the Court overruled the *Gobitis* decision and held such laws to be an unconstitutional interference with the free exercise of religion. The Court concluded in *West Virginia State Board of Education* v. *Barnette* (1943) that patriotism could be achieved without forcing people to violate their religious beliefs:

> "*To believe that patriotism will not flourish if patriotic ceremonies are voluntary and spontaneous instead of a compulsory routine is to make an unflattering estimate of the appeal of our institutions to free minds.*"
>
> —Justice Robert Jackson, 1943

The flag salute cases illustrate how the Supreme Court can change its interpretation of the Constitution. The Court usually follows **precedent,** decisions made on the same issue in earlier cases. As one justice put it, however, "when convinced of former error, this Court has never felt constrained to follow precedent."

Section 2 Assessment

Checking for Understanding

1. **Main Idea** Use a Venn diagram like the one to the right to show the difference between the establishment clause and the free exercise clause of the First Amendment and what they have in common.

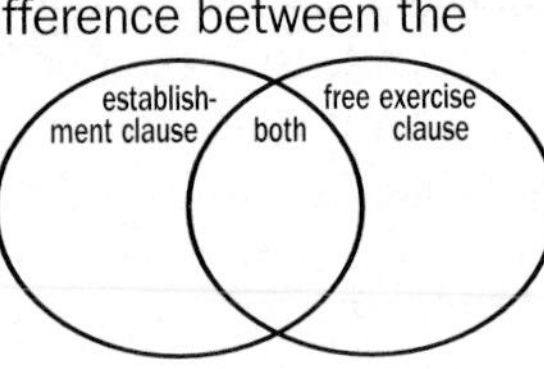

2. **Define** establishment clause, free exercise clause, parochial school, secular, abridge, precedent.
3. **Identify** Equal Access Act.
4. What three tests does the Supreme Court use to determine if government aid to parochial education is constitutional?

Critical Thinking

5. **Recognizing Ideologies** Do you believe that prayer in public schools destroys the separation of church and state as intended in the Constitution? Explain your answer.

Cultural Pluralism Study the free exercise and establishment clauses. Take a position on the following: Government buildings should be allowed to place the motto "In God We Trust" in public view. Outline the reasons for your position, then create a banner or poster stating your position.

Clark v. *Community for Creative Non-Violence,* 1984

Political demonstrations often bring the government's need to maintain order in conflict with the rights of free speech and free assembly. Does the Constitution give groups the right to camp in parks to promote political ideas? The Court dealt with this issue in Clark *v.* Community for Creative Non-Violence.

Lafayette Park statue

Background of the Case

In 1982 a group, the Community for Creative Non-Violence (CCNV), applied to the National Park Service (NPS) for a permit to conduct round-the-clock demonstrations in Lafayette Park and the Mall in Washington, D.C. The CCNV wanted to set up 60 large tents for overnight camping in both parks to call attention to the problems of the homeless. The NPS issued the permit but refused to allow the CCNV to sleep overnight in tents. Camping in national parks is permitted only in campgrounds designated for that purpose, and no such campgrounds had ever been set up in either Lafayette Park or the Mall. The CCNV filed suit claiming a violation of their First Amendment rights. A district court ruled in favor of the NPS; the court of appeals then ruled for the CCNV.

The Constitutional Issue

The Court stated, "The issue in this case is whether a National Park Service regulation prohibiting camping in certain parks violates the First Amendment when applied to prohibit demonstrators from sleeping in Lafayette Park and the Mall." The CCNV argued that sleeping in the tents was essential to convey to people "the central reality of homelessness." Further, the group explained that it would be impossible to get the poor and homeless to participate without the incentive of sleeping space and a hot meal. The CCNV also claimed that while the camping might interfere in some ways with use of the parks by others, the NPS did not have a truly substantial governmental interest in banning camping.

The NPS countered that the regulation against sleeping except in designated campsites was "content neutral;" it was not targeted against the CCNV's message about the homeless. Further, the government did have a substantial interest in keeping the parks attractive and readily available to the millions who wanted to enjoy them. If non-demonstrators were not allowed to camp in the two parks, demonstrators should not be treated any differently, especially since there were other ways to get their political message across to the public.

Debating the Case

Questions to Consider

1. What governmental interest was involved in this case?
2. Was the regulation intended to suppress the CCNV's message about the homeless?
3. What could be the far-reaching consequence of allowing the CCNV to camp in the parks?

You Be the Judge

In your opinion, did the NPS regulation violate the First Amendment? Was a substantial governmental interest served by banning camping as part of the CCNV's demonstration? Did the CCNV have other ways to use the parks to communicate a message about the problems of the homeless?

Section 3

Freedom of Speech

Reader's Guide

Key Terms

pure speech, symbolic speech, seditious speech, defamatory speech, slander, libel

Find Out

- How has the Supreme Court applied the principles of "clear and present danger" and the bad tendency doctrine in determining free speech?
- What speech is protected by the First Amendment, and what speech is not protected?

Understanding Concepts

Civil Liberties What is the intent of the preferred position doctrine?

COVER STORY

License Plates OK

BALTIMORE, MARYLAND, FEBRUARY 26, 1997

A federal judge has ruled that the First Amendment does not allow the government to ban license plates that showcase the Confederate flag. In recent years Maryland has issued special plates to over 300 groups, including the Sons of Confederate Veterans who petitioned for the Confederate flag plates. The group sued when the state recalled the plates after complaints that the flag's ties to slavery made them offensive. "The Court just made it real clear you can't discriminate against this group because of its political viewpoint," an attorney for the group noted. "The government cannot pick and choose the viewpoint it finds to be correct."

A Maryland license plate

Democratic government requires that every person have the right to speak freely. Most people agree in principle with the right of free speech. Everyone wants it for themselves, but they are sometimes tempted to deny it to others whose beliefs differ greatly from their own. The First Amendment exists to protect ideas that may be unpopular or differ from the majority. Popular ideas usually need little protection, but those who support democracy cherish diversity of opinion.

Types of Speech

What exactly is speech? Clearly, talking with neighbors or addressing the senior class in a school assembly is speech. Are students who wear black armbands to protest a school policy engaging in an act of "speech" that the First Amendment protects? Is demonstrating in front of a government building to protest a new law a form of speech? To answer such questions, the Supreme Court has distinguished two general categories of speech that the First Amendment protects.

The verbal expression of thought and opinion before an audience that has chosen to listen, or **pure speech**, is the most common form of speech. Pure speech may be delivered calmly in the privacy of one's home or passionately in front of a crowd. Because pure speech relies only on the power of words to communicate ideas, the Supreme Court traditionally has provided the strongest protection of pure speech against government control.

Symbolic speech (sometimes called expressive conduct) involves using actions and symbols, in addition to or instead of words, to express opinions. During the Vietnam War, for example, protestors burned their draft cards to express their opposition to the war. Other protestors have burned the American flag to express their displeasure with the government. Because symbolic speech involves actions, it may be subject to government restrictions that do not apply to pure speech. For example, the Supreme Court has ruled that the First Amendment does not permit expressive conduct that endangers public safety.

The Supreme Court has generally followed a three-part test when reviewing cases involving expressive conduct. This test was established in 1968 in the case of *United States* v. *O'Brien,*[1] when the government upheld the arrest of four men who burned their draft cards to protest the Vietnam War. In that case the Court ruled that a government can regulate or forbid expressive conduct if the regulation (1) falls within the constitutional power of government, (2) is narrowly drawn to further a substantial government interest that is unrelated to the suppression of free speech, and (3) leaves open ample alternative channels of communication.

Since the *O'Brien* decision the Court has said the First Amendment protected the right to wear black armbands in high schools to protest the Vietnam War (*Tinker* v. *Des Moines School District,*[2] 1969). In 1989 in *Texas* v. *Johnson*[3] it held flag burning was protected symbolic speech. The Court reaffirmed this position in *United States* v. *Eichman*[4] (1990), declaring the federal Flag Protection Act of 1989 unconstitutional. On the other side, in *Frisby* v. *Schultz*[5] (1988) the Court held a city may limit picketing in front of a private residence by protestors. In *Hill* v. *Colorado*[6] (2000) the Court also upheld a Colorado law that prohibits a person from approaching another person without that person's consent in order to speak or offer literature to that person within 100 feet of a health care facility. In these decisions the Court placed the government's interest in protecting the right to privacy ahead of the right of demonstrators to expressive conduct.

Regulating Speech

Because the rights of free speech must be balanced against the need to protect society, some restraints on speech exist. Congress and state legislatures, for example, have outlawed **seditious speech**—any speech urging resistance to lawful

See the following footnoted materials in the ***Reference Handbook:***

1. *United States* v. *O'Brien* case summary, page 767.
2. *Tinker* v. *Des Moines School District* case summary, page 766.
3. *Texas* v. *Johnson* case summary, page 765.
4. *United States* v. *Eichman* case summary, page 766.
5. *Frisby* v. *Schultz* case summary, page 758.
6. *Hill* v. *Colorado* case summary, page 759.

Symbolic Speech

Demonstrative Actions

During the Vietnam War, thousands of defiant young people challenged the idea that citizens have a military obligation to their country. Disabled former Marine Ron Kovic leads protesting Vietnam Veterans Against the War in Miami, Florida, in 1972. Other American men burned their draft cards in protest. ***What methods of symbolic speech are used today?***

authority or advocating the overthrow of the government. How far can government go in limiting free speech? When does speech lose the protection of the First Amendment? Different philosophies about the limits on free speech have emerged as the Supreme Court has wrestled with the issue of where to draw the line.

During the twentieth century the Court has developed three constitutional tests to establish limits on speech. These principles are not precisely defined but are general guidelines that the courts have used when deciding particular cases. They are: (1) the "clear and present danger" rule; (2) the bad tendency doctrine; and (3) the preferred position doctrine.

Justice Oliver Wendell Holmes, Jr.

Clear and Present Danger

When the speech in question clearly presents an immediate danger, the First Amendment does not protect it. If a conflict between free expression and the demands of public safety occurs, the judges frequently rely on the **"clear and present danger"** rule. Justice Oliver Wendell Holmes, Jr., developed the "clear and present danger" test in *Schenck* v. *United States* (1919).

 **Landmark Cases**

Schenck* v. *United States Charles Schenck, the general secretary of the Socialist Party, was convicted of printing and distributing leaflets that urged draftees to obstruct the war effort during World War I. The government claimed his actions violated the Espionage Act of 1917 that made it a crime to "willfully utter, print, write, or publish any disloyal, profane, scurrilous or abusive language" about the government. Schenck argued that the First Amendment protected his actions.

The Supreme Court rejected Schenck's argument and upheld his conviction. Ordinarily the First Amendment would protect Schenck's "speech," the Court said. During wartime, however, his actions threatened the well-being of the nation:

> *"The question in every case is whether the words are used in such circumstances and are of such a nature as to create a clear and present danger that they will bring about the substantive evils that Congress has a right to prevent. . . . When a nation is at war many things that might be said in time of peace . . . will not be endured [and] . . . no Court could regard them as protected by any constitutional right."*
>
> —Justice Oliver Wendell Holmes, Jr., 1919

The Bad Tendency Doctrine

Some Supreme Court justices considered the "clear and present danger" principle insufficient to protect the federal government's substantial interests. They moved to a standard which would restrict even more speech. Several years after the *Schenck* ruling, in the case of *Gitlow* v. *New York*[1] (1925), the Court held speech could be restricted even if it had only a tendency to lead to illegal action, establishing the **bad tendency doctrine.** This doctrine has not generally had the support of the Supreme Court itself since the 1920s. It still, however, reflects the views of many Americans. Supporters of this position acknowledge that it might occasionally lead to laws unnecessarily limiting speech. They believe, however, that society's need to maintain order more than balances any damages done to basic freedoms.

The Preferred Position Doctrine First developed by the Court during the 1940s, the **preferred position doctrine** holds that First Amendment freedoms are more fundamental than other freedoms because they provide the basis of all liberties. Thus, First Amendment freedoms hold a preferred position over competing interests. Any law limiting these freedoms should be presumed unconstitutional unless the government can show it is absolutely necessary.

See the following footnoted materials in the **Reference Handbook:**
1. *Gitlow* v. *New York* case summary, page 759.

Sedition Laws The Espionage Act of 1917 expired at the end of World War I. Later, in the 1940s and 1950s, Congress passed three sedition laws that applied in peacetime as well as during war. One of these, the Smith Act, made it a crime to advocate revolution. In *Dennis* v. *United States*[1] (1951) the Court applied the "clear and present danger" test to uphold the conviction of 11 Communist Party leaders under the act. In later cases, however, the Court sharply narrowed its definition of seditious speech.

In *Yates* v. *United States*[2] (1957) the Court overturned convictions of several other Communist Party members. It decided that merely expressing the opinion that the government should be overthrown cannot be illegal. Thus, the Court distinguished between urging people to believe in an action and urging them to take action.

In *Brandenburg* v. *Ohio*[3] (1969) the Court further narrowed its definition of seditious speech. When Clarence Brandenburg, a Ku Klux Klan leader, refused a police order to end a rally and cross burning, he was arrested. The Court ruled in his favor, however, stating that advocating the use of force may not be forbidden "except where such advocacy is directed to inciting or producing imminent lawless action and is likely to produce such action." The First Amendment does not protect speech intended to advocate immediate and concrete acts of violence.

Other Speech Not Protected

Other forms of speech, less protected than so-called seditious speech, are not protected by the First Amendment. Defamatory speech and "fighting words" fall outside the First Amendment, as do some forms of student speech.

Defamatory Speech The First Amendment does not protect **defamatory speech**, or false speech that damages a person's good name, character, or reputation. Defamatory speech falls into two categories. **Slander** is spoken; **libel** is written. Thus, someone may be sued in a civil court and ordered to pay damages for making false, damaging statements about someone else.

The Court has limited the right of public officials, however, to recover damages for defamation. In *New York Times Co.* v. *Sullivan*[4] (1964) the Court determined that even if a newspaper story about an Alabama police commissioner was false, it was protected speech unless the statement was made with the knowledge that it was false, or with reckless disregard of whether it was false or not.

The Court allowed some defamatory speech about public officials for fear that criticism of government, a basic constitutional right, might be silenced if individuals could be sued for their statements. In later years the justices have extended

See the following footnoted materials in the ***Reference Handbook:***

1. *Dennis* v. *United States* case summary, page 757.
2. *Yates* v. *United States* case summary, page 768.
3. *Brandenburg* v. *Ohio* case summary, page 755.
4. *New York Times Co.* v. *Sullivan* case summary, page 762.

Petitioning for Change

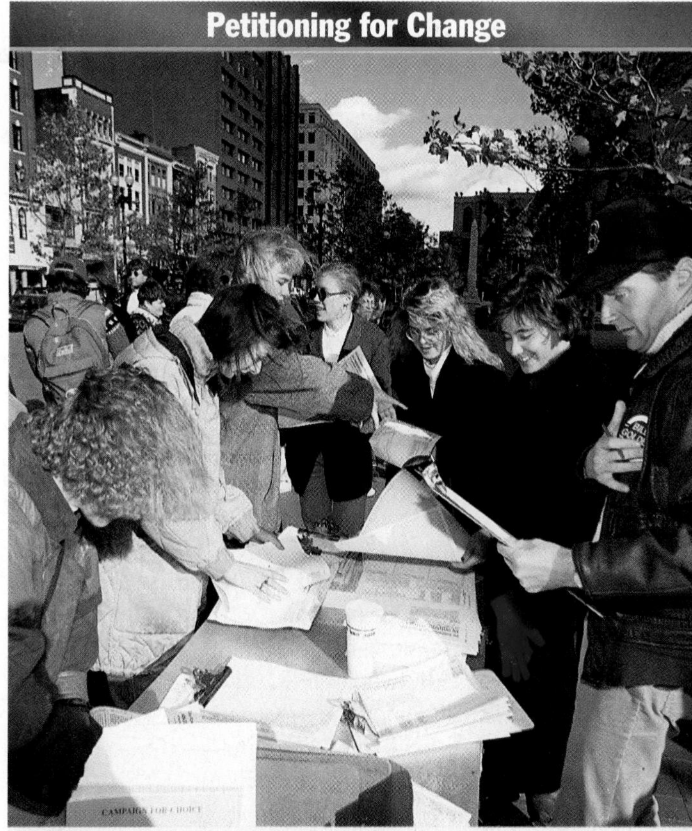

Active Free Speech One way citizens can freely express opinions is by signing petitions concerning public issues they want addressed. ***What did the Supreme Court say about free speech, such as petitioning, in the preferred position doctrine?***

this protection to statements about public figures in general. Political candidates are included, of course, but so are professional entertainers and athletes, and even private citizens who become newsworthy. In *Hustler Magazine* v. *Falwell*[1] (1988), for example, the Court ruled that Reverend Jerry Falwell, a televangelist, could not collect damages for words that might intentionally inflict emotional distress.

"Fighting Words" In 1942 the Supreme Court ruled that words that are so insulting that they provoke immediate violence do not constitute protected speech. The Court upheld a state law that prohibited any person from speaking "any offensive, derisive, or annoying word to any other person who is lawfully in any street or public place." In *Chaplinsky* v. *New Hampshire*[2] (1942) the Court held that:

> *"There are certain well-defined and narrowly limited classes of speech, the prevention of which has never been thought to raise any constitutional problem. These include the lewd and obscene, the profane, the libelous, and the insulting or "fighting" words—those which by their very utterance inflict injury or tend to incite an immediate breach of the peace."*
>
> —Justice Frank Murphy, 1942

Student Speech The Court has limited student speech as well. In the 1969 *Tinker* case, the Supreme Court made it clear that students do not give up all their rights to free speech while in high school. Two Court decisions, however, have greatly narrowed students' First Amendment rights while expanding the authority of school officials.

In *Bethel School District* v. *Fraser*[3] (1986), the Court ruled the First Amendment does not prevent officials from suspending students for lewd or indecent speech at school events, even though the same speech would be protected outside the school building. The Court held that school officials can decide "what manner of speech in the classroom or in school assembly is appropriate."

Two years later, in *Hazelwood School District* v. *Kuhlmeier*[4] (1988), the Court held that school officials have sweeping authority to regulate student speech in school-sponsored newspapers, theatrical productions, and other activities. Justice Byron White drew a distinction between "a student's personal expression," which the First Amendment protects, and speech that occurs "as part of the school curriculum."

See the following footnoted materials in the **Reference Handbook:**

1. *Hustler Magazine* v. *Falwell* case summary, page 759.
2. *Chaplinsky* v. *New Hampshire* case summary, page 756.
3. *Bethel School District* v. *Fraser* case summary, page 755.
4. *Hazelwood School District* v. *Kuhlmeier* case summary, page 759.

Section 3 Assessment

Checking for Understanding

1. **Main Idea** Use a Venn diagram like the one to the right to show the difference between slander and libel and what they have in common.

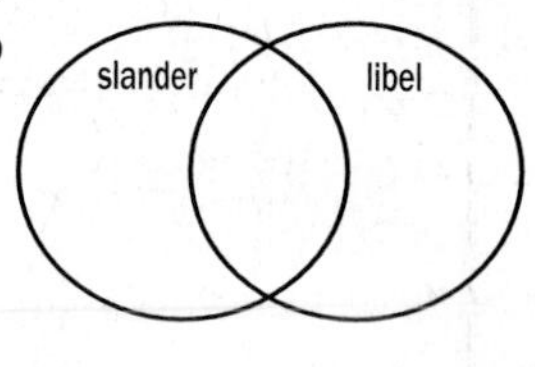

2. **Define** pure speech, symbolic speech, seditious speech, defamatory speech, slander, libel.
3. **Identify** "clear and present danger."
4. What three tests does the Supreme Court use to set limits on free speech?
5. What types of speech does the First Amendment not protect?

Critical Thinking

6. **Making Comparisons** How does freedom of speech in the United States differ in wartime and in peacetime? Refer to Supreme Court decisions in your answer.

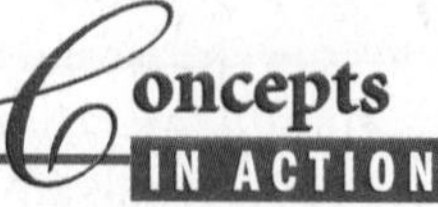

Civil Liberties The Supreme Court has held that First Amendment freedoms are more fundamental than others. Read a Court decision in this chapter and create a political cartoon supporting or opposing the Court's view. Post your cartoon on a bulletin board and challenge other students to guess the case that it identifies.

Section 4

Freedom of the Press

Reader's Guide

Key Terms

prior restraint, sequester, gag order, shield laws

Find Out

- What is the Supreme Court's opinion on prior restraint?
- How has the Supreme Court ruled when the presence of the media could affect a court trial?

Understanding Concepts

Civil Liberties Some people perceive an adversarial relationship between the government and the press. Is this so? Why or why not?

COVER STORY

Judge Won't Lift Gag

DENVER, COLORADO, APRIL 1997

Judge Richard P. Matsch is keeping tight control over the trial of Timothy McVeigh, the government's chief suspect in the bombing of a federal building in Oklahoma City. News organizations asked the judge to lift a gag order he had imposed on trial participants. The journalists claimed the order violated their First Amendment rights. Judge Matsch stood firm, however, and refused to remove the nondisclosure order. He also rejected a media motion to remove a screen installed in the courtroom to conceal jurors from the spectators, and he refused to reveal the names of candidates who had been rejected as jurors.

Weighing justice and freedom of the press

At times, the right of the press to gather and publish information conflicts with other important rights. Judge Richard Matsch's rulings in the 1997 Timothy McVeigh terrorist case were a very high-profile example of such conflict. Most of the time freedom of the press is protected because it is closely related to freedom of speech. It moves free speech one step further by allowing opinions to be written and circulated or broadcast. In today's world the press includes magazines, radio, and television along with newspapers because of their roles in spreading news and opinions.

Prior Restraint Forbidden

In many nations **prior restraint**—censorship of information before it is published—is a common way for government to control information and limit freedom. In the United States, however, the Supreme Court has ruled that the press may be censored in advance only in cases relating directly to national security. Two Court decisions illustrate this principle.

Landmark Cases

Near* v. *Minnesota This 1931 case concerned a Minnesota law prohibiting the publication of any "malicious, scandalous, or defamatory" newspapers or magazines. An acid-tongued editor of a Minneapolis paper had called local officials "gangsters" and "grafters." Acting under the Minnesota law, local officials obtained a court injunction to halt publication.

By a 5-to-4 vote, the Supreme Court lifted the injunction. The Court ruled the Minnesota law unconstitutional because it involved prior restraint. For years the *Near* case defined the Supreme Court's position on censorship. The Court stressed that a free press means freedom from government censorship.

New York Times Co. v. *United States*

The Supreme Court reaffirmed its position in *New York Times Co.* v. *United States* (1971)—widely known as the Pentagon Papers case. In 1971 a former Pentagon employee leaked to the *New York Times* a secret government report outlining the history of United States involvement in the Vietnam War. This report, which became known as the Pentagon Papers, contained hundreds of government documents, many of them secret cables, memos, and plans.

Realizing the Pentagon Papers showed that former government officials had lied to the American people about the war, the *New York Times* began to publish parts of the report. The government tried to stop further publication of the papers, arguing that national security would be endangered and that the documents had been stolen from the Defense Department.

A divided Court rejected the government's claims. The Court ruled that stopping publication would be prior restraint. One justice, Justice William O. Douglas, noted that "the dominant purpose of the First Amendment was to prohibit the widespread practice of governmental suppression of embarrassing information." Justice Hugo L. Black added:

> "*The press [is] to serve the governed and not the governors. . . . The press was protected so that it could bare the secrets of government and inform the people.*"
>
> —Justice Hugo L. Black, 1971

Fair Trials and Free Press

In recent years the First Amendment right of a free press and the Sixth Amendment right to a fair trial have sometimes conflicted. Does the press have the right to publish information that might influence the outcome of a trial? Can courts issue orders that limit news gathering in order to increase the chances of a fair trial and to protect the validity of a jury's deliberations? Do reporters have the right to withhold sources of information that may be important to a trial?

National Security vs. Free Press

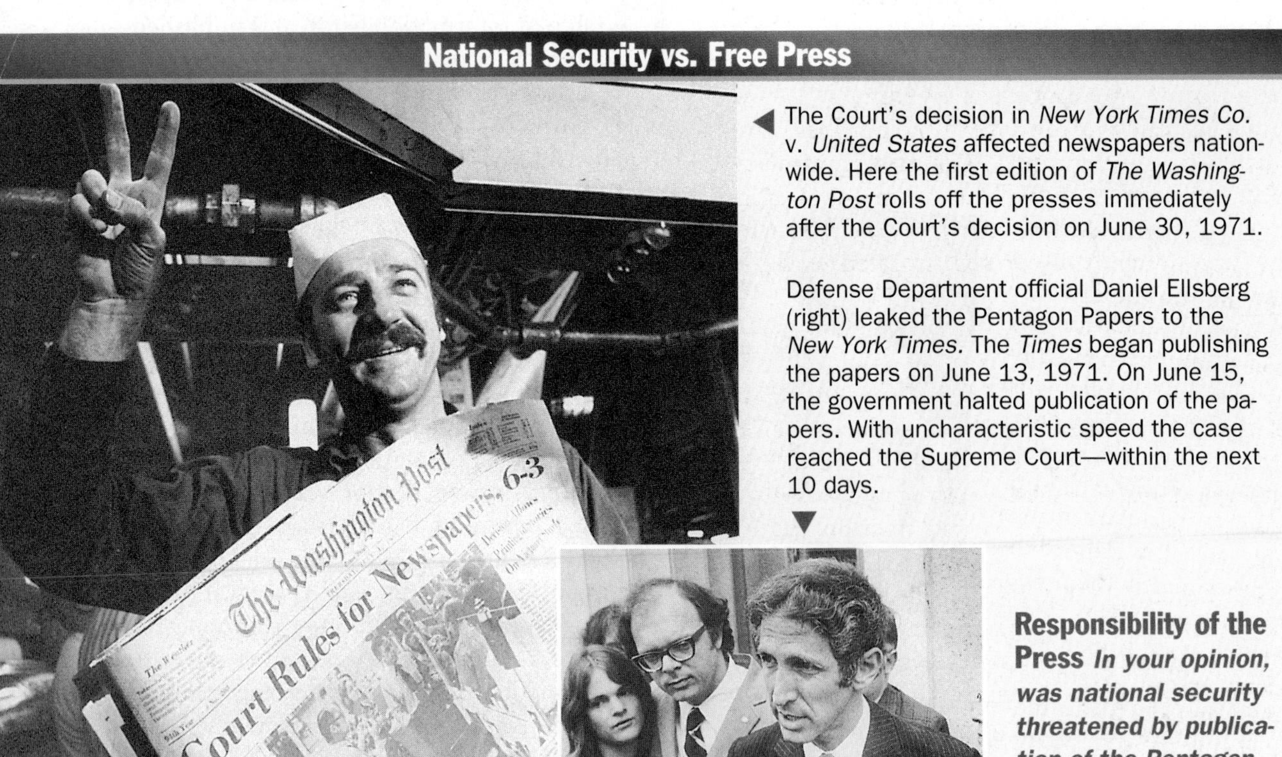

The Court's decision in *New York Times Co.* v. *United States* affected newspapers nationwide. Here the first edition of *The Washington Post* rolls off the presses immediately after the Court's decision on June 30, 1971.

Defense Department official Daniel Ellsberg (right) leaked the Pentagon Papers to the *New York Times.* The *Times* began publishing the papers on June 13, 1971. On June 15, the government halted publication of the papers. With uncharacteristic speed the case reached the Supreme Court—within the next 10 days.

Responsibility of the Press ***In your opinion, was national security threatened by publication of the Pentagon Papers? Explain.***

Landmark Cases

Sheppard v. Maxwell Pretrial and courtroom publicity and news stories about the crime can make it difficult to secure a jury capable of fairly deciding the case. In *Sheppard* v. *Maxwell* (1966) the Supreme Court overturned the 1954 conviction of Samuel H. Sheppard, for just such reasons.

A prominent Cleveland physician, Sheppard was convicted of killing his wife. The case had attracted sensational press coverage. Pretrial news reports practically called Sheppard guilty. During the trial reporters interviewed witnesses and published information damaging to Sheppard.

The Supreme Court ruled that press coverage had interfered with Sheppard's right to a fair trial. Sheppard was later found not guilty. In the *Sheppard* decision, the Court described several measures judges might take to restrain press coverage of a trial. These included: (1) moving the trial to reduce pretrial publicity; (2) limiting the number of reporters in the courtroom; (3) placing controls on reporters' conduct in the courtroom; (4) isolating witnesses and jurors from the press; and (5) having the jury **sequestered**, or kept isolated, until the trial is over.

A Free, but Restricted Press

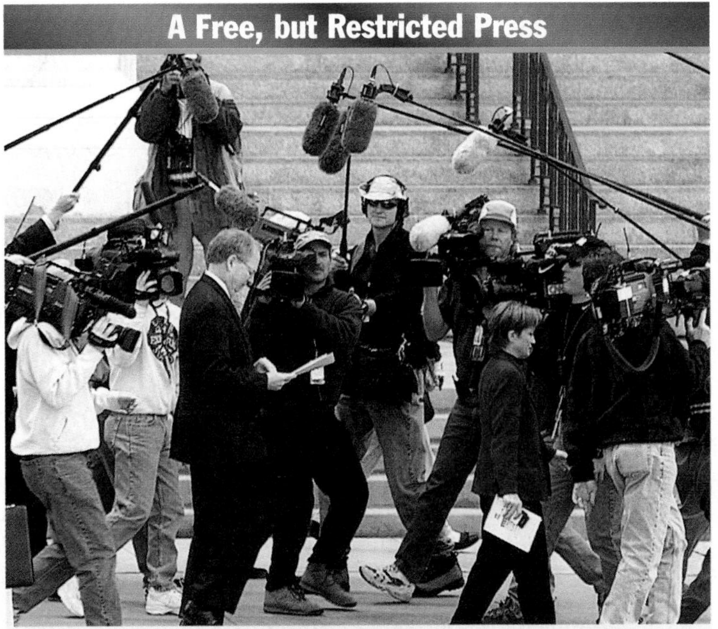

Justice and the Media Press coverage of certain trials is limited by order of the judge. Here members of the press, barred from the courtroom, wait for a chance to interview participants in order to report on court happenings. ***Why would a judge bar the press from a courtroom or have a jury sequestered?***

Gag Orders Unconstitutional

After the *Sheppard* case, a number of trial judges began to use so-called gag orders to restrain the press. A **gag order** is an order by a judge barring the press from publishing certain types of information about a pending court case.

In October 1975 a man killed six members of a Nebraska family. Details of the crime were so sensational that a local judge prohibited news stories about a pretrial hearing. The gag order was challenged and eventually came to the Supreme Court as *Nebraska Press Association* v. *Stuart*[1] (1976). The Court ruled that the Nebraska gag order was too vague and overbroad to satisfy the First Amendment.

Press Access to Trials

In the *Nebraska* case, reporters were permitted in court, even though the trial judge forbade the press to report on the proceedings. In *Gannett Co., Inc.* v. *DePasquale*[2] (1979) the Supreme Court ruled that the public and press could be barred from certain pretrial hearings if the trial judge found a "reasonable probability" that publicity would harm the defendant's right to a fair trial. Since then, the Court has modified the *Gannett* decision, limiting the exclusion of the press only to pretrial hearings dealing with suppression of evidence. In *Richmond Newspapers, Inc.* v. *Virginia*[3] (1980) and later cases, the Court ruled that trials, jury selections, and preliminary hearings must be open to the press and the public except under limited circumstances.

See the following footnoted materials in the **Reference Handbook:**

1. *Nebraska Press Association* v. *Stuart* case summary, page 762.
2. *Gannett Co., Inc.* v. *DePasquale* case summary, page 758.
3. *Richmond Newspapers, Inc.* v. *Virginia* case summary, page 764.

Framers Facing Tomorrow's World

The Constitution and Technology In this artist's rendering, Thomas Jefferson and James Madison ponder the technology of today. The Framers of our government could not have foreseen the complex issues that would accompany technological developments. ***Do you think the Constitution is equipped to resolve the technological issues of today?***

Protecting News Sources Many reporters argue they have the right to refuse to testify in order to protect confidential information and its source. But what if a reporter has information the defense or the government needs to prove its case? Can reporters refuse to surrender evidence? In three cases considered together in 1972, the Supreme Court said that reporters do not have such a right. The Court ruled the First Amendment does not give special privileges to news reporters. Reporters, the Court said, "like other citizens, [must] respond to relevant questions put to them in the course of a valid grand jury investigation or criminal trial." The Court added that any special exemptions must come from Congress and the states.

To date, 30 states have passed **shield laws**—laws that give reporters some means of protection against being forced to disclose confidential information or sources in state courts.

Free Press Issues

In writing the First Amendment, the Founders thought of the press as printed material—newspapers, books, and pamphlets. They could not foresee the growth of technology that has created new instruments of mass communication—and new issues regarding freedom of the press.

Radio and Television Because radio and broadcast television use public airwaves, they do not enjoy as much freedom as other press media. Stations must obtain a license from the **Federal Communications Commission (FCC),** a government agency that regulates their actions.

Although Congress has denied the FCC the right to censor programs before they are broadcast, the FCC can require that stations observe certain standards. In addition, it may punish stations that broadcast obscene or indecent language.

The growth of cable television has raised new questions. For example, to what extent do free speech guidelines apply to cable television? In *Turner Broadcasting System, Inc.* v. *FCC* [1] (1997) the Court ruled that cable television operators should have more First Amendment protection from government regulation than other broadcasters, but not as much as the publishers of newspapers and magazines. Cable operators, the Court said, are not entitled to maximum First Amendment protections because typically only one cable operator controls the video programming market in most communities.

Then in 2000, the Court struck down the part of the Telecommunications Act of 1996 that required cable television operators to block or limit transmission of sexually oriented programs to protect young viewers. In *United States* v. *Playboy*,[2] the Court decided that the cable operators' First Amendment rights were violated because the law was too restrictive.

See the following footnoted materials in the ***Reference Handbook:***
1. *Turner Broadcasting System, Inc.* v. *FCC* case summary, page 766.
2. *United States* v. *Playboy* case summary, page 767.

Motion Pictures In *Burstyn* v. *Wilson*[1] (1952) the Court held that "liberty of expression by means of motion pictures is guaranteed by the First and Fourteenth amendments." The Court has also ruled, however, that movies may be treated differently than books or newspapers.

E-Mail and the Internet Increasing millions of people communicate with each other on the Internet through Web sites and electronic bulletin boards. Should the Internet receive the same freedom of speech safeguards the Constitution gives other media? For example, do people who provide Web sites have the right or obligation to exclude material that is generally considered sexually indecent? Congress passed the Communications Decency Act to try to prevent children from having access to indecency. But the Supreme Court struck down this legislation in *Reno* v. *American Civil Liberties Union*[2] (1997). The Court held that speech on the Internet was entitled to First Amendment protection.

Obscenity The Supreme Court and most other courts have supported the principle that society has the right to protection from obscene speech, pictures, and written material. After many attempts to define obscenity, the Court finally ruled in *Miller* v. *California*[3] (1973) that, in effect, local communities should set their own standards for obscenity. In the *Miller* ruling the Court stated:

> "*It is neither realistic nor constitutionally sound to read the First Amendment as requiring that the people of Maine or Mississippi accept . . . conduct found tolerable in Las Vegas or New York.*"

Since the *Miller* decision, however, the Court has stepped in to overrule specific acts by local authorities, making it clear there are limits on the right of communities to censor.

Advertising Advertising is considered "commercial speech"—speech that has a profit motive—and is given less protection under the First Amendment than purely political speech. In fact, advertisers have long faced strong government regulation and control. In the mid-1970s, however, the Supreme Court began to relax controls. In *Bigelow* v. *Virginia*[4] (1975) the justices permitted newspaper advertisements for abortion clinics. Since then the Court has voided laws that ban advertising medical prescription prices, legal services, and medical services. It has also limited regulation of billboards, "for sale" signs, and lawyers' advertisements.

See the following footnoted materials in the ***Reference Handbook:***

1. *Burstyn* v. *Wilson* case summary, page 756.
2. *Reno* v. *American Civil Liberties Union* case summary, page 764.
3. *Miller* v. *California* case summary, page 762.
4. *Bigelow* v. *Virginia* case summary, page 755.

Section 4 Assessment

Checking for Understanding

1. **Main Idea** Use a graphic organizer like the one shown to analyze the importance of the Supreme Court's ruling on the Communications Decency Act.

Communications Decency Act	
Issue at Stake	Court's Ruling

2. **Define** prior restraint, sequester, gag order, shield laws.
3. **Identify** Federal Communications Commission.
4. When can the government exercise prior restraint on the press?
5. What measures may a court take to restrain press coverage in the interest of a fair trial?

Critical Thinking

6. **Checking Consistency** Are there any circumstances under which reporters should be required to reveal or protect their confidential information or sources? Explain your answer.

Concepts IN ACTION

Civil Liberties The issue of freedom of the press traces back to the *Zenger* case. Research this case and explain how the results of this case relate to freedom of the press issues today. Present your findings in a comparison chart.

Section 5

Freedom of Assembly

Reader's Guide

Key Terms

picketing, Holocaust, heckler's veto

Find Out

- What are the limits on public assembly?
- What constitutional protections are applied to demonstrations by unpopular groups, or to those who might incite violence?

Understanding Concepts

Civil Liberties Why is freedom of assembly subject to greater regulation than freedom of speech?

COVER STORY

Mall Bans Teens

MINNEAPOLIS, MINNESOTA, SEPTEMBER 20, 1996

America's largest mall today became one of the nation's first to restrict teenagers. The Mall of America has barred shoppers under age 16 on weekend nights unless they are with a parent or other adult. Mall officials accuse the teenagers of disturbing other shoppers. On some Saturday nights, 3,000 teens flood the mall, which they say is the coolest spot in Minneapolis. Those interviewed say they will not be caught dead in the mall with their parents. The American Civil Liberties Union, which condemns the ban, will not challenge it, noting previous federal court rulings that First Amendment rights do not apply inside shopping malls.

Mall of America logo

The First Amendment may not guarantee teenagers the right to gather in a shopping mall, but it does guarantee "the right of the people peaceably to assemble, and to petition the Government for a redress of grievances." Freedom of assembly applies not only to meetings in private homes but also to those in public places. It protects the right to make views known to public officials and others by such means as petitions, letters, lobbying, carrying signs in a parade, or marching.

Protecting Freedom of Assembly

Freedom of assembly is a right closely related to freedom of speech because most gatherings, no matter how large or small, involve some form of protected speech. Without this basic freedom, there would be no political parties and no interest groups to influence the actions of government.

Landmark Cases

DeJonge* v. *Oregon One of the Supreme Court's first major decisions on freedom of assembly came in 1937 in the case of *DeJonge* v. *Oregon.* Dirk DeJonge was convicted for conducting a public meeting sponsored by the Communist Party. He claimed he was innocent because he had not advocated any criminal behavior but had merely discussed issues of public concern. In voting unanimously to overturn DeJonge's conviction, the Court ruled Oregon's law unconstitutional. Chief Justice Charles Evans Hughes wrote that under the First Amendment "peaceable assembly for lawful discussion cannot be made a crime."

The *DeJonge* case established two legal principles. The Court determined that the right of assembly was as important as the rights of free speech and free press. Also, the Court ruled that the due process clause of the Fourteenth Amendment protects freedom of assembly from state and local governments.

Assembly on Public Property Freedom of assembly includes the right to parade and demonstrate in public. Because these forms of assembly usually occur in parks, streets, or on sidewalks, it is very possible they could interfere with the rights of others to use the same facilities. Conflicts also arise when parades and demonstrations advocate unpopular causes. Demonstrations, in particular, have a high potential for violence because others, holding conflicting beliefs, often launch counter-demonstrations. The two sides may engage in heated verbal, and sometimes physical, clashes. For such reasons, parades and demonstrations generally are subject to greater government regulation than exercises of pure speech and other kinds of assembly.

Limits on Parades and Demonstrations

To provide for public order and safety, many states and cities require that groups wanting to parade or demonstrate first obtain a permit. The precedent for such regulation was set in *Cox* v. *New Hampshire*[1] (1941). Cox was one of several Jehovah's Witnesses convicted of violating a law requiring a parade permit. He challenged his conviction on the grounds that the permit law restricted his rights of free speech and assembly.

The Court voted to uphold the law, ruling that the law was not designed to silence unpopular ideas. Rather, the law was intended to ensure that parades would not interfere with other citizens using the streets. In part, the decision said:

> "*The authority of a municipality to impose regulations in order to assure the safety and convenience of the people in the use of public highways has never been regarded as inconsistent with civil liberties.*"
>
> —Chief Justice Charles Evans Hughes, 1941

Additional Limits on Public Assembly

Other public facilities such as airports, libraries, courthouses, schools, and swimming pools also may be used for public demonstrations. Here again, however, the Court has set limits. For example, in *Adderly* v. *Florida*[2] (1966) the Court held that demonstrators could not enter the grounds of a county jail without permission. The Court ruled that, while the jail was public property, it was not generally open to public access. The state has the power, the Court reasoned, "to preserve the property under its control for the use to which it is lawfully dedicated."

Other restrictions on peaceable public assembly occur when the right of assembly clashes with the rights of other people. In *Cox* v. *Louisiana*[3] (1965) the Court upheld a law that banned demonstrations and parades near courthouses if

Freedom to Assemble

First Amendment Rights Demonstrators use their right to assemble, rallying against old-growth logging in California. ***Why is the right to assemble fundamental to democracy?***

See the following footnoted materials in the **Reference Handbook:**
1. *Cox* v. *New Hampshire* case summary, page 757.
2. *Adderly* v. *Florida* case summary, page 754.
3. *Cox* v. *Louisiana* case summary, page 756.

How to Find a Supreme Court Decision

Supreme Court gavel

A law library or even the library in your local courthouse may have more than a thousand volumes containing law cases. How can you find information about a particular Supreme Court case? If you know the parties in a case, you can look in a "Digest" of cases. If you look up "Olmstead" for example, you will find "*Olmstead* v. *United States,* 277 U.S. 438." This means that the report of the Olmstead decision begins on page 438 of volume 277 of the *United States Reports.* These reports are published by the Government Printing Office several times each year and date back to the very first year of the Court's history. Possibly an easier way to locate a case is by using the Internet. A federal government home page will allow you to choose a Supreme Court Web site. From there it is simple to locate cases if you know the parties or even the approximate year the case was decided.

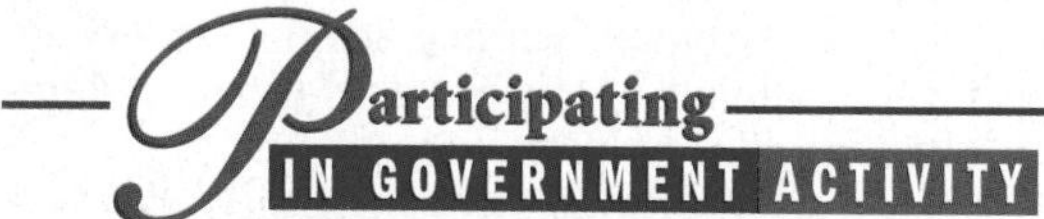

Research a Case Choose an interesting case from this chapter and research it. Take notes and prepare to share what you find with the class.

they could interfere with trials. In *Grayned* v. *City of Rockford*[1] (1972) the justices upheld a ban on demonstrations near schools that were intended to disrupt classes.

Other Supreme Court decisions, however, require that restrictions on freedom of assembly be precisely worded and apply evenly to all groups. In *Police Department of Chicago* v. *Mosley*[2] (1972), the Court voided a city law that banned all demonstrations near school buildings except in the case of **picketing**—patrolling an establishment to convince workers and the public not to enter it—by labor unions.

Assembly and Property Rights The right to assemble does not allow a group to convert private property to its own use, even if the property is open to the public. In *Lloyd Corporation* v. *Tanner*[3] (1972) the Court ruled that a group protesting the Vietnam War did not have the right to gather in a shopping mall.

In recent years some right-to-life groups demonstrating outside private abortion clinics blocked the entrances. The Court appeared unwilling to protect this type of assembly. In *Terry* v. *New York National Organization for Women* (1990) and *Hirsch* v. *Atlanta* (1990), the justices refused to hear appeals of bans on such demonstrations. In 1993, however, the Court ruled that an 1871 civil rights law could not be applied against these demonstrators. In the 1997 case of *Schenck* v. *Pro-Choice Network of Western New York,*[4] the Court upheld parts of an injunction that created a fixed buffer zone around abortion clinics. At the same time the Court struck down "floating buffer zone" laws that attempted to keep a few feet of distance between a demonstrator and a moving person who may be approaching a clinic.

Public Assembly and Disorder

A basic principle of democracy is that people have the right to assemble regardless of the views they hold. Police, however, sometimes have difficulty protecting this principle when public assemblies threaten public safety.

See the following footnoted materials in the **Reference Handbook:**
1. *Grayned* v. *City of Rockford* case summary, page 759.
2. *Police Department of Chicago* v. *Mosley* case summary, page 763.
3. *Lloyd Corporation* v. *Tanner* case summary, page 761.
4. *Schenck* v. *Pro-Choice Network of Western New York* case summary, page 765.

The Nazis in Skokie In 1977 the American Nazi Party, a small group patterned after Adolf Hitler's German Nazi Party, announced plans to hold a rally in Skokie, Illinois, a largely Jewish suburb of Chicago. Skokie residents were outraged. Many were survivors of the **Holocaust**, the mass extermination of Jews and other groups by the Nazis during World War II. Others were relatives of the 6 million Jews killed in the Nazi death camps.

Skokie officials, citizens, and many others argued that the Nazis should not be allowed to march. They claimed that the march would cause great pain to residents and would attract a counter-demonstration.

To prevent the march, the city required the Nazis to post a $300,000 bond to get a parade permit. The Nazis claimed the high bond interfered with their freedoms of speech and assembly. A federal appeals court ruled that no community could use parade permits to interfere with free speech and assembly.

The Skokie case illustrates a free speech and assembly problem some scholars have called the **heckler's veto.** The public vetoes the free speech and assembly rights of unpopular groups by claiming demonstrations will result in violence. Such claims may be effective because government officials will almost always find it easier to curb unpopular demonstrations than to take measures to prevent violence.

This dilemma leads to two related questions. Does the Constitution require the police to protect unpopular groups when their demonstrations incite violence? May the police order demonstrators to disperse in the interest of public peace and safety?

Landmark Cases

Feiner* v. *New York In 1950, speaking on a sidewalk in Syracuse, New York, Irving Feiner verbally attacked President Truman, the American Legion, and the mayor of Syracuse. He also urged African Americans to fight for civil rights. As Feiner spoke, a larger and larger crowd gathered. When the crowd grew hostile, someone called the police. When two officers arrived to investigate, an angry man in the audience told them that if they did not stop Feiner, he would. The police asked Feiner to stop speaking. When Feiner refused, the police arrested him, and he was convicted of disturbing the peace.

The Supreme Court upheld Feiner's conviction, ruling that the police had not acted to suppress speech but to preserve public order. Chief

Demonstrating for Civil Liberties

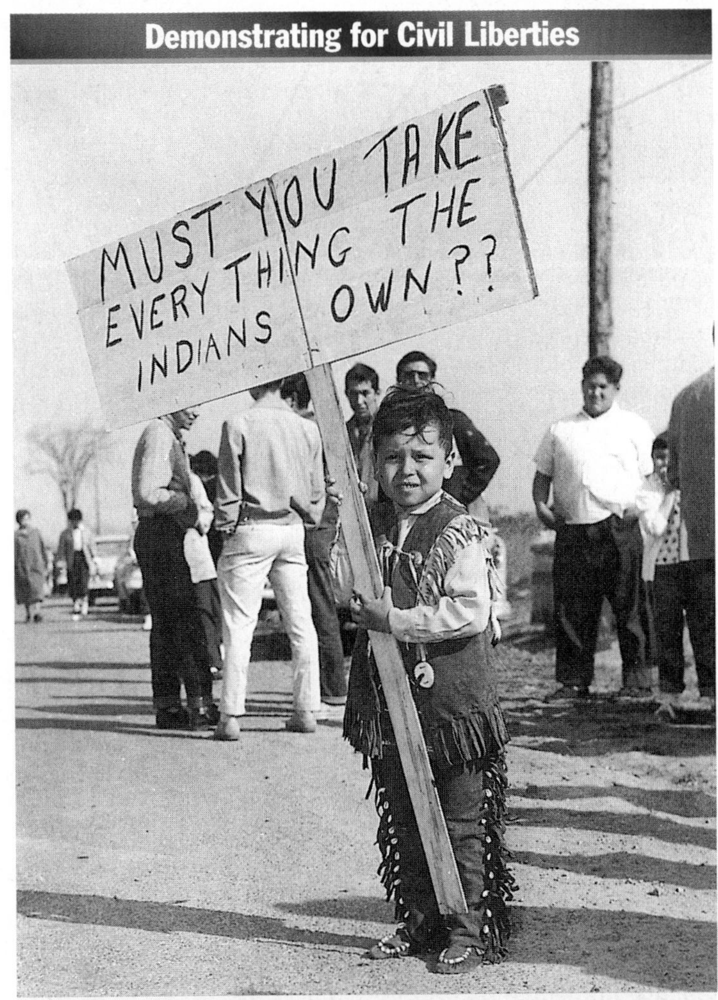

Freedom of Assembly Randy Wegerski, a 4-year-old Tuscarora Native American, joins a picket line in 1958. The protestors gathered to block a state survey of reservation land that had been seized for a power project. ***Do you think government officials should be able to limit demonstrations that interfere in government work?***

Demonstrators and Police Clash

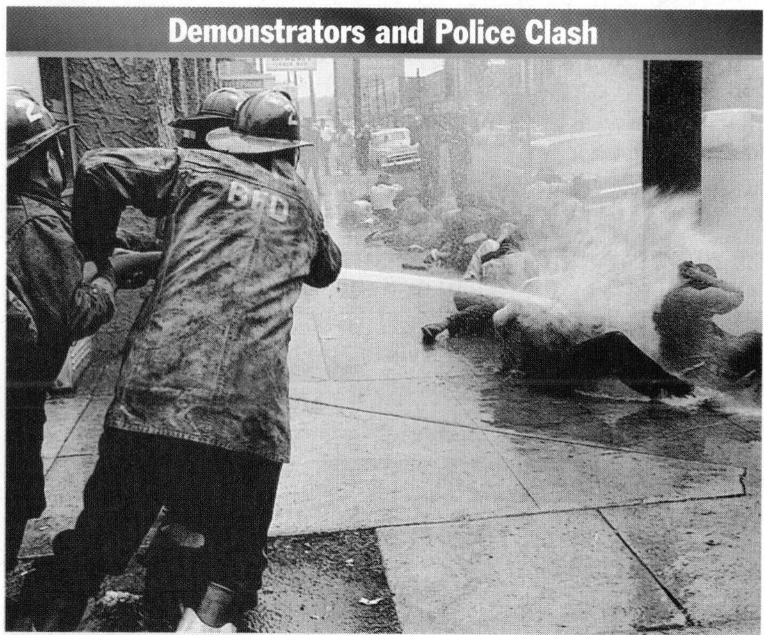

Voices of Protest As a wave of civil rights activity swept across the nation in the 1960s, some government officials and police attempted to preserve laws that held segregation in place by attempting to restrict demonstrations. Police in Birmingham, Alabama, used high-pressure water hoses against marchers in the spring of 1963. ***Why do you think police presence was so great during the civil rights protests of the 1960s?***

Justice Fred M. Vinson spoke for the majority of the Court. He wrote:

> "*It is one thing to say that the police cannot be used as an instrument for the suppression of unpopular views, and another to say that, when as here the speaker passes the bounds of argument and undertakes incitement to riot, they are powerless to prevent a breach of the peace.*"
>
> —Chief Justice Fred M. Vinson, 1951

Gregory* v. *City of Chicago The *Feiner* case stands as a precedent that the police may disperse a demonstration in order to keep the peace. Since then, however, the Court has overturned the convictions of people whose only offense has been to demonstrate peacefully in support of unpopular causes. The case of *Gregory* v. *City of Chicago* (1969) is a good example of the Court's thinking on this matter.

Dick Gregory, an entertainer and African American activist, led a group of marchers from the city hall in downtown Chicago to the mayor's home. Calling city hall a "snake pit" and the mayor "the snake," the demonstrators began parading around the block demanding the ouster of the school superintendent for failing to desegregate schools. About 180 police officers were on hand to provide protection.

A crowd of 1,000 or more hostile onlookers from the all-white neighborhood gathered. They began to heckle and throw rocks and eggs at the marchers.

At 8:30 in the evening, the marchers stopped singing and chanting and paraded quietly. The crowd continued to heckle them. By 9:30 the police concluded that violence was imminent and ordered the demonstrators to disperse. When Gregory and the others refused, they were arrested. Five, including Gregory, were later convicted of disorderly conduct.

In a departure from the *Feiner* case, the Supreme Court overturned the conviction of Gregory and the marchers. The Court ruled that the demonstrators had been peaceful and had done no more than exercise their First Amendment right of assembly and petition. Neighborhood residents, not the marchers, had caused the disorder. The Court concluded that such a march, "if peaceful and orderly, falls well within the sphere of conduct protected by the First Amendment."

Protection for Labor Picketing

Workers on strike or other demonstrators often organize picket lines. For many years the Supreme Court has debated how much protection the First Amendment gives picketers. Picketing conveys a message and is therefore a form of speech and assembly. But labor picketing, unlike most other kinds of demonstrations, tries to persuade customers and workers not to deal with a business. Many people will not cross a picket line, depriving a business of its workers and customers.

Through much of American history, courts have supported many kinds of restraints on labor picketing. Then, in *Thornhill* v. *Alabama*[1] (1940), the Supreme Court ruled that peaceful picketing was a form of free speech. It reflected the growing strength of the labor movement in American life.

In later decisions, however, the Court severely limited the position it took in *Thornhill*. In *Hughes* v. *Superior Court*[2] (1950) the Court refused to overturn a California court's ban on picketing at a supermarket to force it to hire African American workers. The Court wrote:

> *"While picketing is a mode of communication, it is inseparably something more and different. . . . The very purpose of a picket line is to exert influences, and it produces consequences, different from other modes of communication."*
>
> —Justice Felix Frankfurter, 1950

The Court further limited picketing in *International Brotherhood of*

 See the following footnoted materials in the **Reference Handbook:**

1. *Thornhill* v. *Alabama* case summary, page 766.
2. *Hughes* v. *Superior Court* case summary, page 759.

This and other protestors demonstrated during the August 1997 Teamsters–UPS labor dispute which crippled the nation for 15 days.

We the People
Making a Difference
Gladiola Campos

Union Summer logo

In 1996 Gladiola Campos joined 1,000 other college students and activists in a program called Union Summer. The program, which was sponsored by the AFL-CIO, was designed to strengthen the nation's labor movement by encouraging people to join unions and protest unfair labor practices. It was modeled after Freedom Summer, a similar program in 1964 in which students were bussed across the South to register African American voters.

Union Summer participants were paid $210 a week and traveled to various parts of the country to help draw attention to unfair labor practices. Students helped sewage-plant employees protesting in Denver, put pressure on a Washington store to stop selling clothing made in sweatshops, and picketed hotels in South Carolina for their unfair labor practices.

Campos, a University of Texas student, was sent to Los Angeles. One of her projects was distributing leaflets outside a hotel to urge people to boycott the establishment. The owners of the hotel had been blocking their employees' efforts to organize a union for three years. Many of the employees were Hispanic immigrants.

The union issue hits close to home with Campos. Her mother was a maintenance worker when she was growing up in El Paso, Texas. Before the hospital where her mother worked was unionized, Campos said her mother "had to work two jobs, and we couldn't afford health insurance." Campos thinks her summer experience was worthwhile. "I'm finally doing something instead of just talking," she said.

Teamsters, Local 695 v. *Vogt*[1] (1950). The Court upheld a Wisconsin law that prohibited picketing a business unless there was a labor dispute.

Freedom of Association

Does the First Amendment protect an individual's right to join an organization that the government considers subversive? In the *DeJonge* v. *Oregon*[2] (1937) case, the Supreme Court extended the right to freely assemble to protect the right of individuals to freedom of association—to join a political party, interest group, or other organization. Can the government restrict the right of assembly and association to protect national security?

Landmark Cases

Whitney* v. *California In 1927 the Supreme Court reviewed the case of Charlotte Anita Whitney, who had attended a convention where the Communist Labor Party was organized. Because the party advocated workers using violent means to take over control of property, Whitney was convicted of breaking a California law concerning violent actions. The prosecution successfully argued that membership in the party indicated that she had committed a crime. In *Whitney* v. *California* (1927) the Supreme Court decided that:

> "*Although the rights of free speech and assembly are fundamental, they are not absolute. Their exercise is subject to their restriction, if the particular restriction proposed is required in order to protect the state from destruction. . . . The necessity which is essential to a valid restriction does not exist unless speech would produce, or is intended to produce, a clear and imminent danger of some substantive evil which the state constitutionally may seek to prevent.*"
>
> —Justice Louis Brandeis, 1927

The **clear and present danger doctrine** later became a major issue when the government began to arrest and convict accused subversives, primarily Communist Party members during the 1950s. The Alien Registration Act of 1940, known as the Smith Act, contained a section that made advocating forcible overthrow of any government in the United States illegal. The Supreme Court upheld convictions of 12 leaders of the American Communist Party under this act in *Dennis* v. *United States*[3] (1951). In later cases, however, the Court ruled that only actual preparations for the use of force against the government were punishable.

See the following footnoted materials in the ***Reference Handbook:***
1. *International Brotherhood of Teamsters, Local 695* v. *Vogt* case summary, page 760.
2. *DeJonge* v. *Oregon* case summary, page 757.
3. *Dennis* v. *United States* case summary, page 757.

Section 5 Assessment

Checking for Understanding

1. **Main Idea** Use a graphic organizer like the one below to identify two reasons the right to assemble is important to preserve in a democracy and two reasons it can be limited.

to preserve	to limit

2. **Define** picketing, Holocaust, heckler's veto.
3. **Identify** clear and present danger doctrine.
4. What two principles were established by the DeJonge decision?

Critical Thinking

5. **Checking Consistency** Should more restrictions apply if a parade supports an unpopular cause? Support your answer.

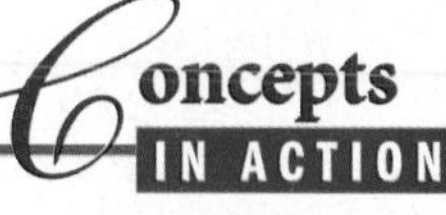

Civil Liberties Imagine that you are the mayor of a town where a citizen is planning a rally to protest the government's environmental policies. Write a letter to the city council explaining the constitutional issues and the public welfare concerns that they should consider before allowing the rally.

Using Library Resources

Your teacher has assigned a major research report, so you go to the library. As you wander the aisles surrounded by books on every topic imaginable, you wonder: Where do I start my research? Which reference works should I use?

Learning the Skill

Libraries contain many reference works. Here are brief descriptions of important reference sources:

Reference Books Reference books include encyclopedias, biographical dictionaries, atlases, and almanacs.

- An encyclopedia is a set of books containing short articles on many subjects arranged alphabetically.
- A biographical dictionary includes brief biographies listed alphabetically by last names.
- An atlas is a collection of maps and charts for locating geographic features and places. An atlas can be general or thematic.
- An almanac is an annually updated reference that provides current statistics and historical information on a wide range of subjects.

Card Catalogs Every library has a card catalog, either on cards or computer or both, which lists every book in the library. Search for books by author, subject, or title. Computerized card catalogs will also advise you on the book's availability.

Periodical Guides A periodical guide is a set of books listing topics covered in magazines and newspaper articles.

Computer Databases Computer databases provide collections of information organized for rapid search and retrieval. For example, many libraries carry reference materials on CD-ROM.

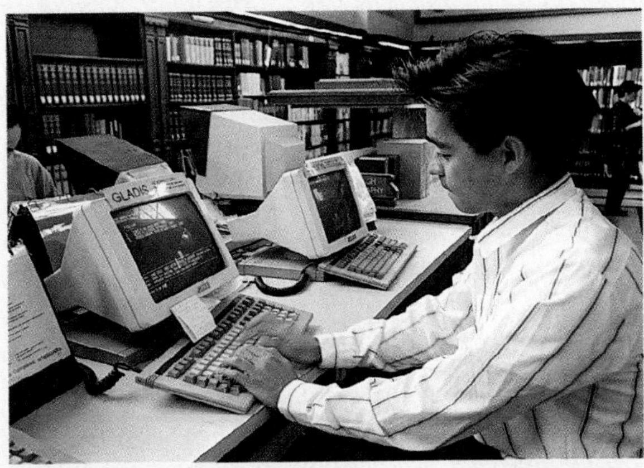

Accessing library resources

Practicing the Skill

Decide which sources described in this skill you would use to answer each of these questions for a report on constitutional freedoms.

1. During which years did Justice Hugo H. Black serve on the Supreme Court?
2. What is the Equal Access Act?
3. How did the public react to the *Tinker* case?
4. Which films have been censored and why?

Application Activity

Using your library, research the following: Is the Federal Communications Commission involved with censorship? What standards does it apply to radio and television programs and why? Present the information you find to the class.

The **Glencoe Skillbuilder Interactive Workbook, Level 2** provides instruction and practice in key social studies skills.

Assessment and Activities

GOVERNMENT Online

Self-Check Quiz Visit the *United States Government: Democracy in Action* Web site at gov.glencoe.com and click on ***Chapter 13–Self-Check Quizzes*** to prepare for the chapter test.

Reviewing Key Terms

From the following list, choose the term that fits each situation described below:

shield laws	**heckler's veto**
pure speech	**seditious speech**
prior restraint	**picketing**
libel	**symbolic speech**

1. Spectators threaten violence against an unpopular demonstration and, in order to keep peace, authorities break up the demonstration.
2. A government official tells a reporter that she cannot publish a story that might compromise national security.
3. A group burns an American flag to show its objection to a government policy.
4. A newspaper publishes an untrue story that damages the reputation of a local resident.
5. Animal rights activists parade outside a store that sells furs and attempt to convince customers not to enter the establishment.
6. An individual urges a group to fight the police rather than obey a police order to disperse.
7. A person stands in front of a group and states her opinion on an issue.
8. A reporter is protected against being forced to disclose a source of information in court.

Identifying Issues Choose one of the freedoms guaranteed by the First Amendment. Use the *Readers' Guide to Periodical Literature* to find articles that focus on current issues and challenges related to that particular freedom. Prepare an oral report, summarizing the issues involved.

Recalling Facts

1. List four freedoms the First Amendment protects.
2. List four examples of how religion remains part of government.
3. What is the significance of *Engel* v. *Vitale?*
4. Identify kinds of speech the First Amendment protects and kinds it does not protect.
5. Under what circumstances would criticism of a public official not be defamatory speech?
6. How might freedom of the press interfere with an individual's right to a fair trial?
7. Why is prior restraint forbidden in the United States?
8. What is the Court's position on obscenity?
9. Why may government require that groups first obtain permits to parade or demonstrate?
10. What is the significance of the *Gregory* case in expanding the right to assemble?
11. What is the Supreme Court's position on picketing?

Understanding Concepts

1. **Civic Participation** How did the Supreme Court's decision in *Gitlow* v. *New York* support the intent of the Fourteenth Amendment to define citizenship and civic participation?
2. **Cultural Pluralism** How does the protection of freedom of religion, as expressed in the Constitution, impact the cultural diversity of the United States?
3. **Civil Liberties** Why did the court treat a Minneapolis newspaper differently than a Hazelwood school newspaper?

Chapter 13

Critical Thinking

1. **Recognizing Ideologies** The Court ruled out laws requiring the teaching of creationism, but not the teaching of creationism itself. Does teaching creationism in public schools serve to "endorse a particular religious doctrine"? Explain.
2. **Making Comparisons** Use a graphic organizer like the one below to compare the three tests for limiting seditious speech.

Limits on Seditious Speech		
relaxes limits	sets standard	toughens limits

3. **Demonstrating Reasoned Judgment** Should the first amendment protect those who publish stolen government documents? Explain your answer.

Interpreting Political Cartoons Activity

1. Whom do you think the person in the cartoon is representing? Why?
2. What is this person doing?
3. What do his thoughts suggest about the nature of an individual's constitutional rights?

Cooperative Learning Activity

Conducting a Survey Form a group of class members and develop a questionnaire to survey other students, teachers, and members of the community about freedom of assembly for teenagers and what limits, if any, they believe should be placed on this right. After the survey is completed, analyze the results. In a short report, indicate the questions asked, the survey's results, and any conclusions that might be drawn.

Skill Practice Activity

Using Library Resources Imagine you are a reporter who was assigned a feature story about pretrial and courtroom publicity. List the various reference materials that could be sources of information on the controversies and history of permitting the press to report on trials. Explain the type of information that you expect to learn from each source.

Technology Activity

Using a Web Site Locate the Web site for the Journalism Education Association. Research the student press rights position of that association. Summarize and discuss these rights with your classmates.

Participating in State Government

Locate a copy of your state's constitution, particularly the Bill of Rights. Compare the rights guaranteed in the First Amendment of the U.S. Constitution with your state's Bill of Rights. Prepare a chart or graphic organizer that identifies the similarities and the differences between the two documents.

Chapter 14

Citizenship and Equal Justice

Why It's Important

Rights and Responsibilities

Your right to vote at age 18 is only one privilege of United States citizenship. What other rights do you have? This chapter will show how responsible citizenship makes everyone's rights more meaningful and effective.

To learn more about your rights and responsibilities as a citizen of the United States, view the ***Democracy in Action*** Chapter 14 video lesson:

Citizenship in the United States

GOVERNMENT Online

Chapter Overview Visit the *United States Government: Democracy in Action* Web site at gov.glencoe.com and click on ***Chapter 14–Overview*** to preview chapter information.

Section 1

A Nation of Immigrants

Reader's Guide

Key Terms

alien, resident alien, non-resident alien, enemy alien, illegal alien, amnesty, private law

Find Out

- How does the United States classify noncitizens?
- How has immigration policy in the United States changed over time?

Understanding Concepts

Cultural Pluralism How has immigration policy contributed to the diversity of cultures in the United States?

COVER STORY

Tactic Saves Refugees

OSWEGO, NEW YORK, JUNE 12, 1944

A government agency has found a way to save some European Jews from the Nazis. Overcoming opposition from within and outside the government, the War Refugee Board has convinced President Franklin Roosevelt to consider 1,000 Jewish refugees as prisoners of war. The Jews will be held for the remainder of World War II at an army base near Oswego. Despite their confinement, the tactic gets around immigration laws and allows the refugees into the United States. The government has come under increasing attack for its restrictions on immigration, as reports of Adolf Hitler's extermination of Europe's Jews have reached the United States.

Jewish refugees check in at Fort Ontario

◀ Statue of Liberty

Oscar Handlin, a well-known American historian, described what immigration has meant to America: "Once I thought to write a history of the immigrants in America. Then I discovered that the immigrants were American history."

Immigrants and Aliens

Throughout American history immigrants have often been referred to as aliens. An **alien** is a person who lives in a country where he or she is not a citizen. Aliens may not intend to become citizens, or they may be in a country only for a short time—conducting business or working for a foreign government, for instance. An immigrant, however, is a person who comes to a new country intending to live there permanently.

Classifying Aliens United States law classifies aliens into five different categories: (1) A **resident alien** is a person from a foreign nation who has established permanent residence in the United States. Thus, immigrants are resident aliens until they become naturalized citizens. Resident aliens may stay in the United States as long as they wish without becoming American citizens. (2) A **non-resident alien** is a person from a foreign country who expects to stay in the United States for a short, specified period of time. A Nigerian journalist who has come to report on a presidential election is an example of a non-resident alien. (3) An **enemy alien** is a citizen of a nation with which the United States is at war. Legally, enemy aliens living in the United States are entitled to the full protection of their lives and property. During wartime, however, the public's feelings often run high, and enemy aliens have sometimes been subjected to discriminatory practices. (4) **Refugees** are people fleeing to escape persecution or danger. In the early 1990s authorized refugee admissions averaged 121,000 per year. (5) An **illegal alien** is a person who comes to the United States without a legal permit, such as a passport, visa, or entry permit. Most enter by illegally crossing United States borders, but many are foreigners who have stayed in the United States after their legal permits have expired. The Immigration and Naturalization Service estimates that between 2 and 3 million "illegals" were living in the United States during the mid-1990s.

Aliens' Rights The protections that the Bill of Rights guarantees, such as freedom of speech and assembly, apply to aliens as well as citizens. In addition, the Supreme Court has repeatedly struck down state government attempts to limit the rights of aliens. In 1982, for example, the Supreme Court ruled that the state of Texas could not deny free public education to children of illegal aliens.

Aliens may own homes, attend public schools, carry on businesses, and use public facilities, just as citizens do. Similarly, aliens are expected to share in many of the responsibilities of American life. They are required to pay taxes, obey the law, and be loyal to the government. They cannot vote, however, and are usually exempt from military and jury duty. Unlike citizens, aliens are not guaranteed the right to travel freely in the United States. This restriction has been applied in times of war. All aliens, even those who have applied for United States citizenship, are required to notify the Immigration and Naturalization Service when they change their residence.

Immigrant's trunk

AMERICA
M. CAMMARATA ARCANGELO
NIAGARA FALLS
N 510 20 STREET N.Y.
AMERICA

Congressional Quarterly's *Government at a Glance*

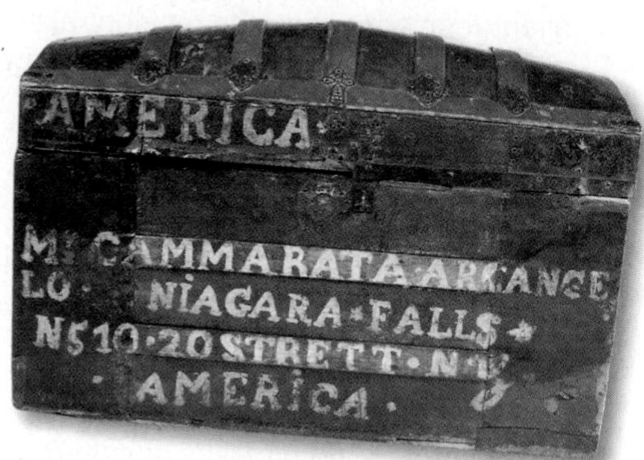

Online UPDATE Visit gov.glencoe.com and click on ***Textbook Updates–Chapter 14*** for an update of the data.

Immigration to the United States

Legal and Illegal Immigration 1989–1998

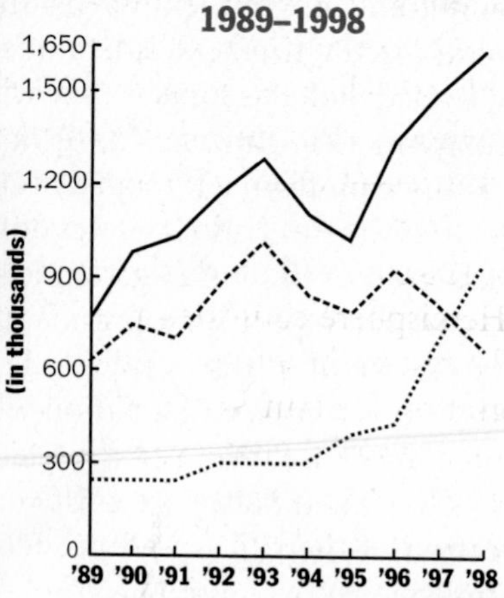
1,650
1,500
1,200
900
600
300
0
(in thousands)
'89 '90 '91 '92 '93 '94 '95 '96 '97 '98
Total Immigration
Legal Immigration
Illegal Immigration

Immigration by Region 1988–1998

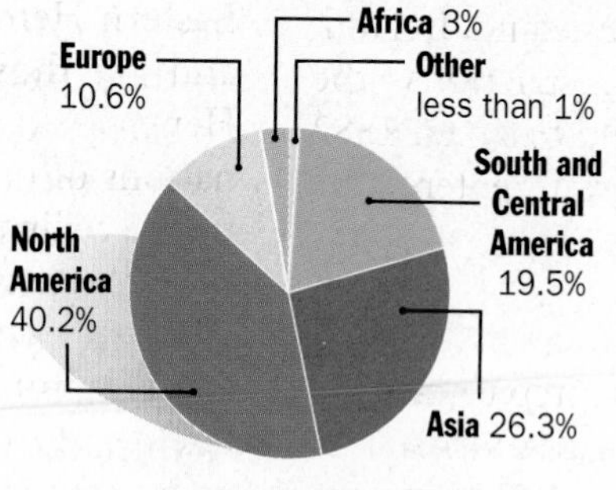
Africa 3%
Europe 10.6%
Other less than 1%
South and Central America 19.5%
North America 40.2%
Asia 26.3%

Sources: U.S. Departments of Justice, *Statistical Yearbook; 1998* (Washington, D.C.: 1998

Top 5 States and Cities for Immigration 1998

State	Number of Immigrants
California	170,126
New York	96,559
Florida	54,965
Texas	44,428
New Jersey	35,091

City	Number of Immigrants
New York, NY	82,175
Los Angeles, CA	59,598
Chicago, IL	30,355
Miami, FL	28,853
Washington, D.C.	24,032

Critical Thinking

In 1996 the total foreign-born population of the United States was approximately 25 million, or 9.3 percent of the total population. ***What was the approximate number of illegal immigrants entering the United States in 1996?***

Immigration Policy

The Constitution clearly assigns Congress the power to control immigration policy. In the years before 1882, however, Congress rarely exercised this power. Since then United States immigration policy has gone through four distinct stages.

Regulating Immigration

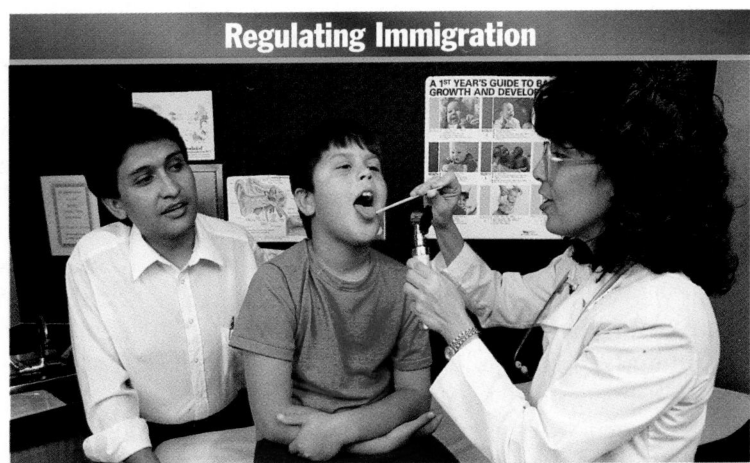

Preferential Treatment The Immigration Reform Act of 1965 granted some immigrants, such as this doctor, high preference for entering the United States. ***Why do you think the current immigration laws give special preference to immigrants who have certain occupations?***

1882–1924: The Growth of Restrictions

In 1882 Congress passed the first major federal immigration law that barred entrance to people such as the mentally handicapped, convicts, and paupers. In that year Congress also passed the Chinese Exclusion Act, which restricted the admission of Chinese laborers. At the same time, the law prevented all foreign-born Chinese from acquiring citizenship. This provision marked the first time a federal law had restricted either immigration or citizenship on the basis of nationality or ethnicity.

The number of restrictions grew steadily in the next three decades. Many Americans feared that immigrants from Asia and southern and eastern Europe would take jobs away from United States citizens. The new immigrants' languages, appearance, customs, and religions were different from those of earlier immigrants from England, Ireland, and Germany. Despite the many restrictions, the number of immigrants soared, and between 1882 and 1924, about 25 million immigrants entered the United States.

1924–1965: National Origins Quotas

In 1924 Congress took a more drastic step toward restricting immigration. The Immigration Act of 1924, also known as the **Johnson Act,** lowered the number of immigrants allowed into the country to less than 165,000 per year—an 80 percent decrease from the years before World War I. It also favored immigrants from northern and western Europe. The national origins system gave countries such as England and Ireland high quotas, because many Americans were of English or Irish descent. The quotas assigned to countries such as Greece and Italy were low because there were fewer Greek or Italian Americans. During the next 40 years, immigration dropped sharply because relatively few people in countries with large quotas were interested in coming to the United States.

Immigration Reform Act of 1965

Congress passed the **Immigration Reform Act of 1965** abolishing the system of national origins quotas. The 1965 law set up two categories of immigrants: (1) those who could come from countries of the Eastern Hemisphere—Europe, Asia, and Africa; and (2) those who could come from Western Hemisphere countries—Canada, Mexico, and the nations of Central and South America. Congress fixed a ceiling of 120,000 total immigrants per year from Western Hemisphere countries and 170,000 per year from the rest of the world.

The Immigration Reform Act of 1965 established preference categories, giving highest preference to persons whose skills would be "especially advantageous to the United States." Next in preference were unmarried adult children of United States citizens; then husbands, wives, and unmarried children of permanent residents; and then professionals such as doctors, lawyers, and scientists. The lowest preference class included refugees from Communist countries or the Middle East and victims of natural disasters.

Immigration Reform and Control Act of 1986

To stem the tide of illegal immigrants, Congress passed the **Immigration Reform and Control Act of 1986.** This law also provided a way for illegal immigrants to become permanent residents and citizens, as well as punishment for employers who hire illegal immigrants.

The major provisions of the act included: (1) Aliens who can show that they entered the United States before January 1, 1982, and have resided continuously in the country since then may apply for amnesty. **Amnesty** is a general pardon the government offers—in this case, to illegal aliens. They would first become lawful temporary residents, then after 18 months they would become permanent residents. (2) After 5 years of permanent residence in the United States, aliens may apply for United States citizenship. (3) Employers are forbidden to hire illegal aliens. Those who do are subject to penalties ranging from $250 to $2,000 for each illegal alien hired. For subsequent and consistent offenses, employers are subject to additional fines and even imprisonment. (4) Employers must ask applicants for documents such as passports or birth certificates to prove they are either citizens or aliens qualified to work in the United States.

The Immigration Act of 1990

By 1990, 85 percent of immigrants to the United States were coming from Asia and Latin America. In 1990 Congress passed a sweeping revision of the 1965 law. The new law was designed to once again take the countries of origin into account and to admit more highly skilled and educated immigrants.

The act established a limit on immigrants from any single country to no more than 7 percent of the annual visas. It also established a "Transition Diversity Program" designed to open immigration to nationals from countries adversely affected by the 1965 law. Europeans, especially Irish immigrants, would benefit from these "diversity visas."

The new law allowed immigration to climb from about 500,000 people to about 700,000 during each of the first 3 years. Then it leveled immigration to about 675,000 people per year. These totals did not include refugees or people who were fleeing persecution from unjust governments in their homelands.

The Immigration Act of 1990 encouraged immigration of workers with "extraordinary abilities," providing 140,000 visas annually for people who had a guaranteed job when entering the United States.

In addition to the immigration quotas, the Immigration Act of 1990 established a category for special immigrants. Special immigrants fall into three groups—refugees displaced by war, close relatives of United States citizens, or those admitted through private laws passed by Congress. A **private law** is one that applies to a particular person. For example, a private law may allow a certain individual to enter the United States regardless of the numerical limits on immigration.

Section 1 Assessment

Checking for Understanding

1. **Main Idea** Use a graphic organizer like the one below to map the purposes of the Immigration Reform and Control Act of 1986.

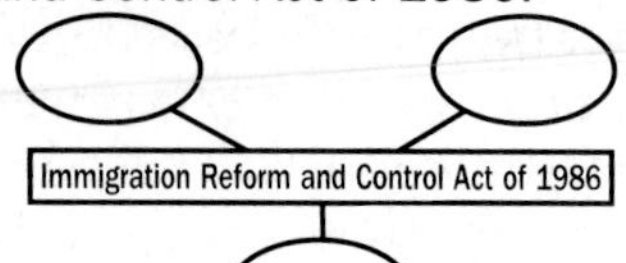

2. **Define** alien, resident alien, non-resident alien, enemy alien, illegal alien, amnesty, private law.
3. **Identify** refugee.
4. What are the five categories of aliens according to United States law?

Critical Thinking

5. **Making Inferences** What changes in attitudes toward immigration does the Immigration Act of 1990 reflect?

Cultural Pluralism Every community has a unique ethnic history. When did people of various ethnic and racial groups begin to come to your community? Research your community's immigration history at the local library. Draw a time line showing how your community grew and when each group began to arrive.

Section 2

The Basis of Citizenship

Reader's Guide

Key Terms

naturalization, jus soli, jus sanguinis, collective naturalization, expatriation, denaturalization

Find Out

- What are the requirements for citizenship in the United States?
- What are the main responsibilities of American citizens?

Understanding Concepts

Constitutional Interpretations What questions about citizenship did the Fourteenth Amendment answer?

COVER STORY

Citizenship at Risk

TALLINN, ESTONIA, AUGUST 2, 1993

Aleksander Einseln, a retired U.S. Army colonel, may have lost a $50,000-a-year pension when he took command of the army of Estonia. And he risks an even greater loss. Citing a law that forbids Americans from serving in a foreign army, the U.S. government has suspended Einseln's military pension and is threatening to revoke his citizenship. Einseln, a combat veteran and dedicated anti-Communist, agreed to command Estonia's army without pay after that nation gained its independence from the Soviet Union. Although upset over the loss of his pension, Einseln's citizenship concerns him more. "I will fight to the end not to lose it," he vows.

Einseln with an Estonian soldier

Citizens are members of a political society—a nation. As such, citizens of the United States have certain rights, duties, and responsibilities. The Declaration of Independence addresses these rights and responsibilities:

> "*We hold these truths to be self-evident, that all men are created equal, that they are endowed by their Creator with certain unalienable Rights, that among these are Life, Liberty, and the pursuit of Happiness. . . . That to secure these rights, Governments are instituted among Men, deriving their just powers from the consent of the governed. . . .*"
>
> —The Declaration of Independence

The United States government, then, draws its power from the people and exists to secure their fundamental rights and equality under the law. Duties of citizens include obeying the law, paying taxes, and being loyal to the American government and its basic principles. As participants in government, citizens have the responsibility to be informed, vote, respect the rights and property of others, and respect different opinions and ways of life. Concerned citizens must be willing to exercise both their rights and their responsibilities.

National Citizenship

Over the years the basis of citizenship has changed significantly in the United States. Today citizenship has both a national and state dimension. This was not always so, however.

The articles of the Constitution mention citizenship only as a qualification for holding office in the federal government. The Founders assumed that the states would decide who was or was not a citizen, and their citizens were also citizens of the United States. The exceptions were African Americans and immigrants who became United States citizens through naturalization, the legal process by which a person is granted the rights and privileges of a citizen.

Landmark Cases

Dred Scott v. Sandford The basis of state citizenship was at stake in the controversial *Dred Scott* v. *Sandford* case in 1857. Dred Scott was an enslaved African American in Missouri, a slaveholding state. Scott had also lived with his slaveholder in Illinois—a free state—and the Wisconsin territory, where the Northwest Ordinance forbade slavery. Scott sued his slaveholder's widow for his freedom, claiming that his earlier residence in a free state and a free territory made him free. A state court ruled in Scott's favor, but the Missouri Supreme Court later reversed the decision, prompting Scott's lawyers to go to the United States Supreme Court.

The Court, led by Chief Justice Roger Taney, ruled that Scott could not bring a legal suit in a federal court. Taney reasoned that African Americans, whether enslaved or free, were not United States citizens at the time the Constitution was adopted. Therefore, they could not claim citizenship. Only descendants of people who were state citizens at that time, or immigrants who became citizens through naturalization, were United States citizens. The Court also stated that Congress could not forbid slavery in United States territories.

The Fourteenth Amendment The *Dred Scott* decision caused great outrage and protest in the North and added to the tensions that led to the Civil War. African American abolitionist Frederick Douglass hoped that the Court's decision would begin a "chain of events" that would produce a "complete overthrow of the whole slave system." In 1868, three years after the end of the war, the Fourteenth Amendment to the Constitution overruled the *Dred Scott* decision. The amendment clearly established what constitutes citizenship at both the national and state levels of government.

The Fourteenth Amendment was clear and forceful about the basis of citizenship:

> *"All persons born or naturalized in the United States, and subject to the jurisdiction thereof, are citizens of the United States and of the state wherein they reside. No State shall make or enforce any law which shall abridge [deprive] the privileges or immunities of citizens of the United States."*
>
> —Fourteenth Amendment, 1868

Citizenship at Stake

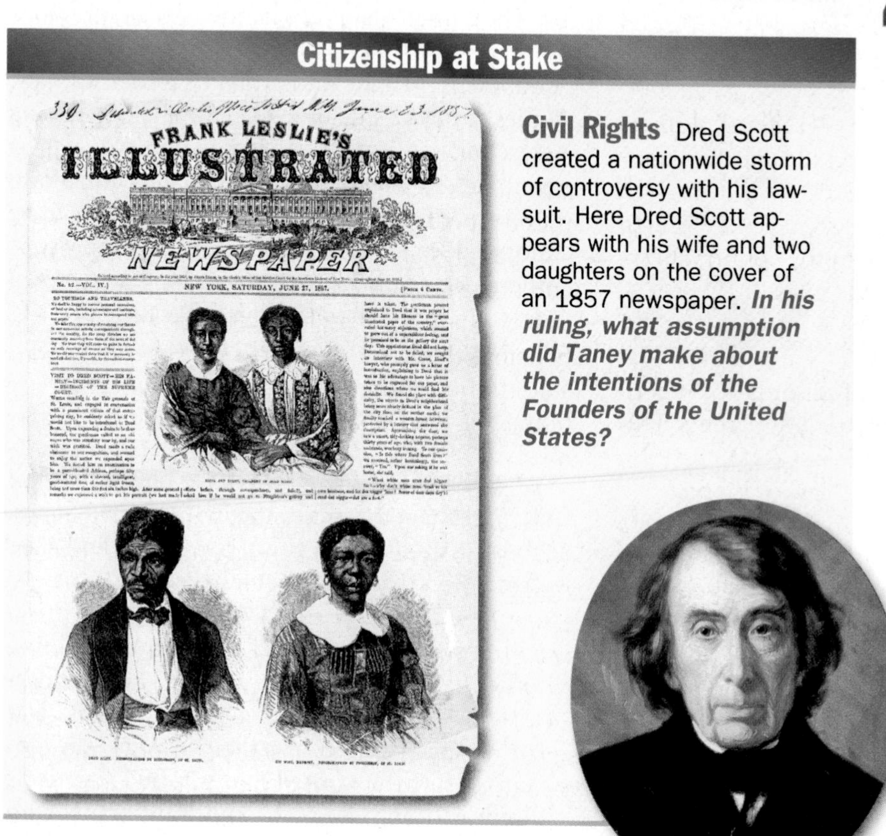

FRANK LESLIE'S ILLUSTRATED NEWSPAPER

NEW YORK, SATURDAY, JUNE 27, 1857.

Civil Rights Dred Scott created a nationwide storm of controversy with his lawsuit. Here Dred Scott appears with his wife and two daughters on the cover of an 1857 newspaper. ***In his ruling, what assumption did Taney make about the intentions of the Founders of the United States?***

Chief Justice Roger Taney

The Fourteenth Amendment guaranteed that people of all races born in the United States and subject to its government are citizens, making state citizenship an automatic result of national citizenship.

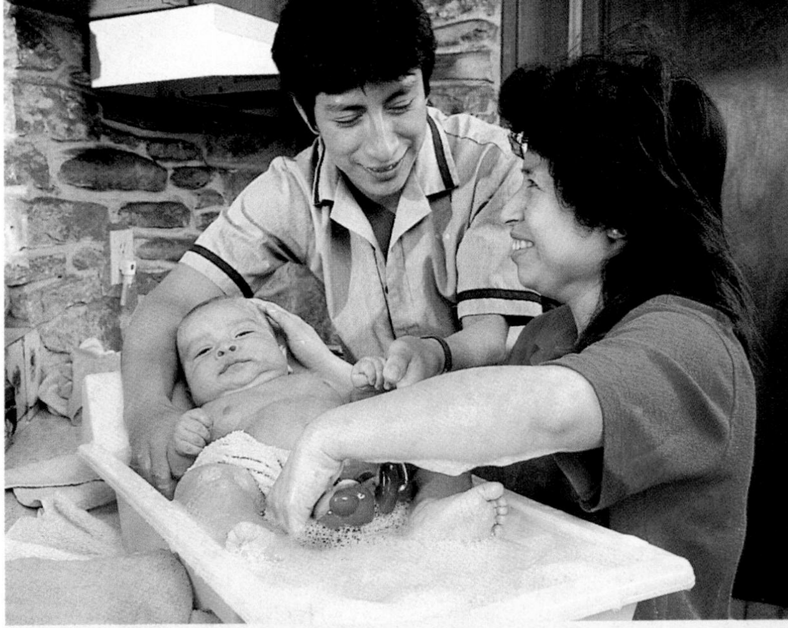

American Citizenship A child born to American parents automatically becomes a citizen of the United States. ***How does the law of jus sanguinis relate to children of Americans working abroad?***

Citizenship by Birth

The Fourteenth Amendment set forth two of the three basic sources of United States citizenship—birth on American soil and naturalization. The third source of citizenship is being born to a parent who is a United States citizen.

Citizenship by the "Law of the Soil" Like most other nations, the United States follows the principle of jus soli (YOOS SOH·LEE), a Latin phrase that means "law of the soil." Jus soli, in effect, grants citizenship to nearly all people born in the United States or in American territories. Birth in the United States is the most common basis of United States citizenship.

Not everyone born in the United States is automatically a citizen. People born in the United States who are not subject to the jurisdiction of the United States government are not granted citizenship. For example, children of foreign diplomats are not American citizens, even though they may have been born in the United States. Children born in this country to immigrant parents or to foreign parents merely passing through the country, however, are citizens of the United States.

Citizenship by Birth to an American Parent Another method of automatic citizenship is birth to an American parent or parents. This principle is called jus sanguinis (YOOS SAHN·gwuh·nuhs), which means the "law of blood."

The rules governing jus sanguinis can be very complicated. If an individual is born in a foreign country and both parents are United States citizens, the child is a citizen, provided one requirement is met. One of the parents must have been a legal resident of the United States or its possessions at some point in his or her life. If only one of the parents is an American citizen, however, that parent must have lived in the United States or an American possession for at least 10 years, 5 of which had to occur after the age of 14.

Citizenship by Naturalization

All immigrants who wish to become American citizens must go through naturalization. At the end of that process, they will have almost all the rights and privileges of a native-born citizen. The major exception is that a naturalized citizen is not eligible to serve as president or vice president of the United States.

Congress has defined specific qualifications and procedures for naturalization. These include a residency requirement that immigrants must satisfy before they can even apply to become citizens. The Immigration and Naturalization Service, a branch of the Department of Justice, administers most of the key steps of the naturalization process.

Qualifications for Citizenship Immigrants who want to become citizens must meet five requirements. (1) Applicants must have entered the United States legally. (2) They must be of good moral character. (3) They must declare their support of the principles of American government. (4) They must prove they can read, write, and speak English. (If applicants are more than 50 years old and have lived in the United States for 20 years, they are exempt from the English-language

Gaining Citizenship

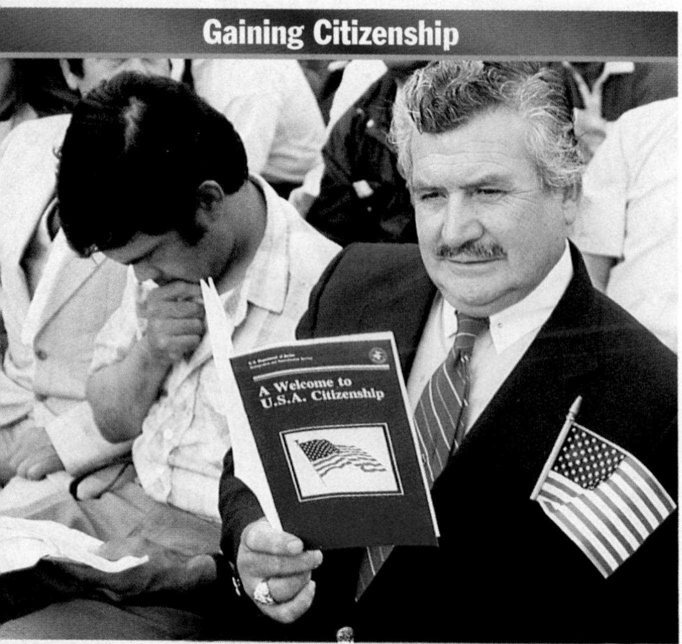

Taking the Oath Immigrants must take an oath of allegiance to the United States when they become citizens. ***Why do you think there are so many steps to becoming a citizen of the United States?***

requirement.) (5) They must show some basic knowledge of American history and government. Draft evaders, military deserters, polygamists, anarchists, Communists, or followers of any other totalitarian system will be denied citizenship.

The Steps to Citizenship

An applicant requesting citizenship must be at least 18 years old, have lived in the United States as a lawfully admitted resident alien for 5 continuous years, and have lived in the state where the petition is filed for at least 3 months. If married to a United States citizen, he or she needs only 3 years of residency before filing.

The key step in the naturalization process is an investigation and preliminary hearing in which the individual is asked questions about his or her moral character. Two witnesses are also asked about the prospective citizen's character and integrity. In addition, applicants may be asked to demonstrate their grasp of the English language and questioned about American government and history. Typical questions include: "What is the highest court in the land?" "How many states are there in the United States?" "What happens if the president dies?" Sometimes applicants are asked to identify certain American presidents.

If an applicant makes it through this step—and most do—he or she will be asked to attend a final hearing. This hearing is usually held in a federal district court and is normally only a formality. Here the judge administers the United States oath of allegiance. The oath requires individuals to renounce loyalty to their former governments, to obey and defend the Constitution and laws of the United States, and to bear arms on behalf of the United States when required by law. The judge then issues a certificate of naturalization that declares the individual a United States citizen. New citizens receive a letter from the president, a short history of the Pledge of Allegiance, and a booklet containing important documents in American history.

Exceptions While naturalization procedures are similar for most people, some exceptions exist. One is **collective naturalization,** a process by which members of a whole group of people, living in the same geographic area, become American citizens through an act of Congress. These individuals do not have to go through the naturalization process.

Congress has used collective naturalization five times. In 1803 people living in the territory gained through the Louisiana Purchase were granted American citizenship. Similarly, when Florida was purchased in 1819, and when the Republic of Texas was admitted to the Union in 1845, people living in these territories received United States citizenship. Likewise, Congress granted citizenship to all people living in Hawaii in 1900 and to the residents of Puerto Rico in 1917.

Other exceptions have occurred. For more than a century, most Native Americans were excluded from citizenship—even after their land was annexed by the United States. A few groups became citizens

GOVERNMENT Online

Student Web Activity Visit the *United States Government: Democracy in Action* Web site at gov.glencoe.com and click on ***Chapter 14–Student Web Activities*** for an activity about the basis of citizenship.

through treaties with the federal government, but in 1868 Congress decided that the citizenship guarantees of the Fourteenth Amendment would not apply to Native Americans. Later Congress offered citizenship to individual Native Americans who gave up their traditional culture. Not until 1924 did Congress make all Native Americans citizens of the United States. On the other hand, citizenship requirements also have been waived under special circumstances. In 1981 a federal judge exempted a 99-year-old Russian immigrant from naturalization requirements because he wanted "to die free as a citizen of this great country."

Losing Citizenship

Only the federal government can both grant citizenship and take it away. State governments can deny a convicted criminal some of the privileges of citizenship, such as voting, but have no power to deny citizenship itself. Americans can lose their citizenship in any of three ways: through expatriation, by being convicted of certain crimes, or through denaturalization.

Expatriation The simplest way to lose citizenship is through **expatriation,** or giving up one's citizenship by leaving one's native country to live in a foreign country. Expatriation may be voluntary or involuntary. For example, a person who becomes a naturalized citizen of another country automatically loses his or her American citizenship. Involuntary expatriation would occur in the case of a child whose parents become citizens of another country.

Punishment for a Crime A person may lose citizenship when convicted of certain federal crimes that involve extreme disloyalty. These crimes include treason, participation in a rebellion, and attempts to overthrow the government through violent means.

We the People

Making a Difference

Irena Sliskovic

Sarajevo road sign

Irena Sliskovic came to the United States in 1995 to escape a war that was tearing her country apart. She was one of 83 Bosnian Muslim students who participated in a program that promised high school students a chance to finish their education in the United States—safely away from the war in Bosnia.

Irena, who was living in Sarajevo, Bosnia-Herzegovina, during the war, lost many friends to the violence that became a part of her everyday life. She and her family were afraid to leave their home for fear of being killed by snipers. When Irena was just 10 months away from her high school graduation, she heard about the American program. Eighty American families offered to open their homes to Bosnian students and help them enroll in schools. Irena applied for the program and was accepted because of her strong academic abilities. She remembers thinking, "I'm going far away to peace and freedom."

Getting to the United States was no easy task. Irena had to sneak out of Sarajevo at night. Shelling near the main road delayed the trip, and she was stopped just 5 minutes from the border and ordered to return to Sarajevo. She escaped, however, and finally crossed the border to Croatia. A few weeks later she flew to the United States.

Irena moved in with a host family in Florence, Kentucky. She attended a nearby high school and graduated a year later. In 1995 the Dayton peace accord helped bring peace to Bosnia—at least temporarily. After high school Irena continued to live in the United States. She attended a college in Kentucky and studied business and computer science.

Responsible Citizens

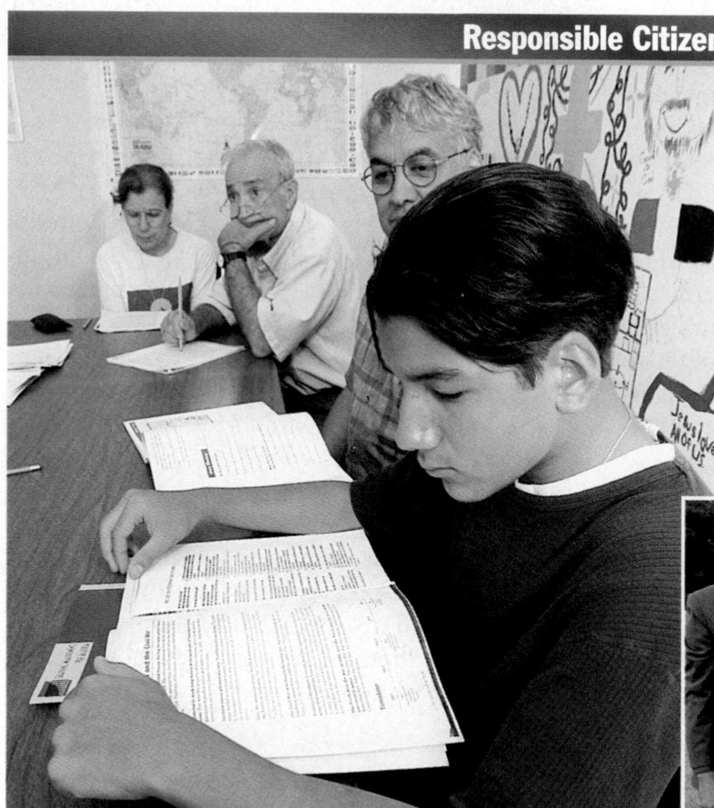

Growth of Democracy Immigrants must learn about American laws to become naturalized citizens. ***Why must citizens know about American laws?***

These immigrants have completed all the naturalization steps to become new citizens.

Denaturalization The loss of citizenship through fraud or deception during the naturalization process is called **denaturalization.** Denaturalization could also occur if an individual joins a Communist or totalitarian organization less than five years after becoming a citizen.

The Responsibilities of Citizens

The ability to exercise one's rights depends on an awareness of those rights. A constitutional democracy, therefore, requires knowledgeable and active citizens.

Knowing About Rights and Laws Responsible citizens need to know about the laws that govern society and to be aware of their basic legal rights. Respect for the law is crucial in modern society, but this respect depends on knowledge of the law.

In addition to schools, a number of organizations help citizens learn more about their rights, laws, and government: legal aid societies, consumer protection groups, and tenants' rights organizations. Moreover, many states now require that government regulations be written in everyday language so that people can understand them.

Citizenship Involves Participation The American ideal of citizenship has always stressed each citizen's responsibility to participate in political life. Through participation, citizens help govern society and themselves and are able to fashion policies in the public interest. Through participation, individuals can put aside personal concerns and learn about one another's political goals and needs. In short, participation teaches about the essentials of democracy—majority rule, individual rights, and the rule of law.

Voting The most common way a citizen participates in political life is by voting. By casting their ballots, citizens help choose leaders and help direct the course of government. Voting therefore affirms a basic principle of American political life that was inscribed in the Declaration of Independence—"the consent of the governed."

Voting is also an important way to express faith in one's political system. When a person casts a vote, he or she is joining other citizens in a common effort at self-government. Voting enables Americans to share responsibility for how their society is governed.

Many people do not vote because they believe they have little effect on political outcomes. Others do not vote because they have little interest in any form of political life.

Voter Participation Counts There have been many close elections over the years at all levels of government. Many seats in the House of Representatives in the 1996 election were decided by very close races. In Pennsylvania Republican Jon D. Fox won by a mere 84-vote margin of victory. Some races were not decided until all absentee votes were tabulated.

Ways of Participating as a Citizen Campaigning for a candidate, distributing leaflets for a political party, and working at the polls on Election Day are all important forms of participation. People can exercise the rights and privileges of citizenship in other ways as well. For example, they can support the efforts of a special interest group to influence legislation or discuss issues with a legislator or another person in government. Writing letters to the editor of a newspaper or newsmagazine, or exercising the right to dissent in a legal and orderly manner are other ways citizens can participate. Exercising these rights is the only way of ensuring their strength and vitality.

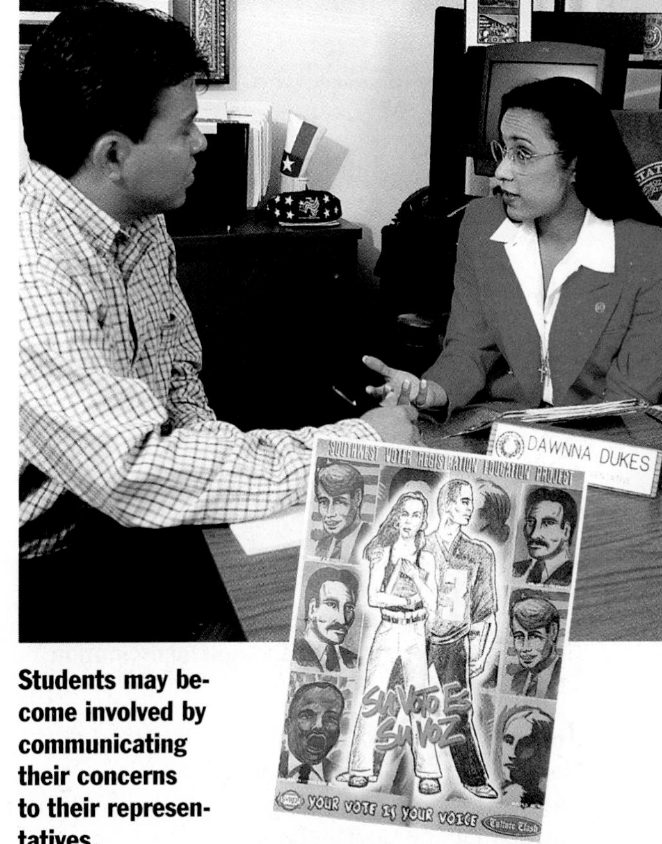

Students may become involved by communicating their concerns to their representatives.

Urging Americans to vote

Section 2 Assessment

Checking for Understanding

1. **Main Idea** Use a graphic organizer like the one below to describe the conditions of American citizenship.

Sources in 14th Amendment	Responsibilities

2. **Define** naturalization, jus soli, jus sanguinis, collective naturalization, expatriation, denaturalization.
3. **Identify** *Dred Scott* v. *Sandford.*
4. What are the five requirements for becoming a naturalized citizen?
5. In what three ways may American citizenship be lost?

Critical Thinking

6. **Synthesizing Information** Why does the United States require citizenship applicants to speak English and have knowledge of the American government?

Concepts IN ACTION

Constitutional Interpretations The Fourteenth Amendment extends the "privileges and immunities" of each state to all American citizens. Make a chart that lists the privileges that you believe your state should provide out-of-state persons and the privileges that should extend only to residents of your state.

Section 3

The Rights of the Accused

Reader's Guide

Key Terms

exclusionary rule, counsel, self-incrimination, double jeopardy

Find Out

- What constitutes unreasonable searches and seizures by the police?
- In the 1960s, how did the Supreme Court rule on the right to counsel and self-incrimination cases?

Understanding Concepts

Civil Rights How have Supreme Court rulings both expanded and refined the rights of the accused as described in the Constitution?

COVER STORY

Seale Bound and Gagged

CHICAGO, ILLINOIS, OCTOBER 29, 1969

Political radical Bobby Seale, charged with conspiracy to incite a riot at last year's Democratic National Convention, had to be restrained during his trial today. Seale's loud outbursts regarding his constitutional rights have repeatedly disrupted court proceedings. Today, federal marshals twice had to wrestle Seale back into his seat. The trial was recessed while marshals tied a gag around Seale's mouth and shackled him to his chair. When Seale's now-muffled shouts continued, Judge Julius Hoffman ordered the gag replaced with strips of tape. While courtroom chains are not uncommon, gagging a defendant is extremely rare.

Bobby Seale

Protest characterized the 1960s. However, in a democracy there will always be citizens who oppose some actions of the government. Indeed, the duty of a citizen is to speak out against injustice—even by an elected authority. How can the government permit dissent and at the same time carry out the will of the majority? Balancing the rights of the individual and the interests of society is not easy.

A related challenge for democratic political systems is dealing with crime and criminals. A crime is an act against a law of the state. It may also harm an individual or a person's property. On the one hand, society must protect itself against criminals. At the same time, individual rights must be preserved. Justice in a democracy means protecting the innocent from government police power as well as punishing the guilty.

To deal with these challenges, the Founders built into the Constitution and the Bill of Rights a system of justice designed to guard the rights of the accused as well as the rights of society. Laws were to be strictly interpreted, trial procedures fair and impartial, and punishments reasonable. Later, the Fourteenth Amendment[1] protected the rights of the accused in the same section that it defined national citizenship.

Searches and Seizures

The police need evidence to accuse people of committing crimes, but getting evidence often requires searching people or their homes, cars, or offices. To protect the innocent, the **Fourth Amendment** guarantees "the right of people to be secure in their persons, houses, papers, and effects, against unreasonable searches and seizures." What constitutes unreasonable searches and seizures? No precise definition has

See the following footnoted materials in the ***Reference Handbook:***

1. *The Constitution*, pages 774–799.

been made, so the courts have dealt with Fourth Amendment issues on a case-by-case basis.

Today the police must state under oath that they have probable cause to suspect someone of committing a crime to justify a search. Generally they must obtain a warrant from a court official before searching for evidence or making an arrest. The warrant must describe the place to be searched and the person or things to be seized.

Before 1980, 23 states had search laws that permitted police to enter a home without a warrant if they had probable cause to believe that the occupant had committed a **felony,** or major crime. In *Payton* v. *New York*[1] (1980) the Supreme Court ruled that, except in a life-threatening emergency, the Fourth Amendment forbids searching a home without a warrant. In *Florida* v. *J.L.*[2] (2000), the Court strengthened Fourth Amendment protections even further by ruling that an anonymous tip that a person is carrying a gun does not give police the right to stop and frisk that person.

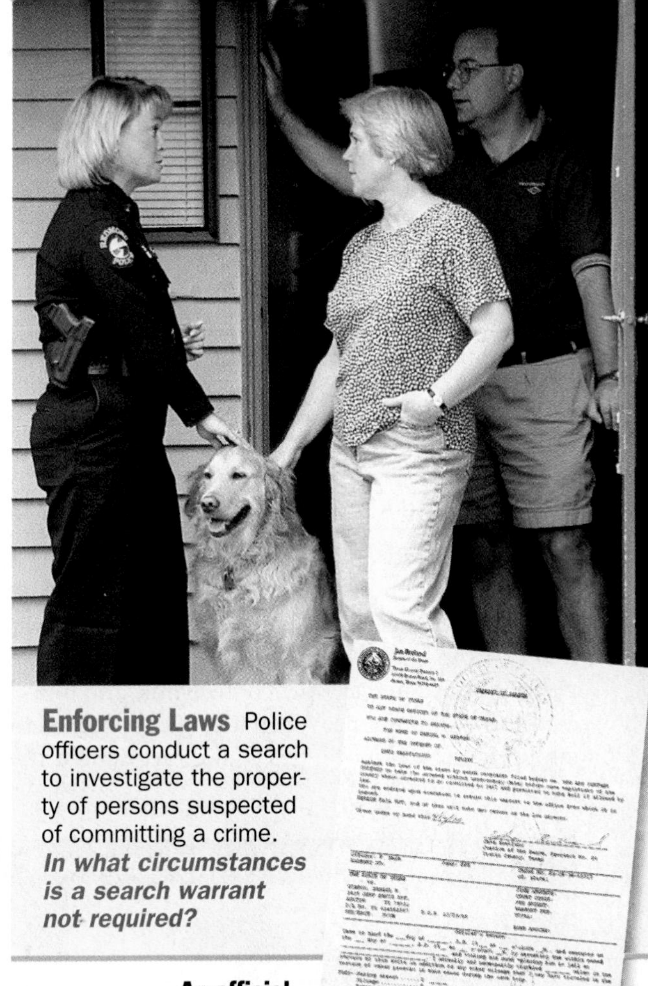

Enforcing Laws Police officers conduct a search to investigate the property of persons suspected of committing a crime. ***In what circumstances is a search warrant not required?***

An official search warrant

Special Situations In many situations, however, police without a warrant may arrest and search anyone who commits a crime in their presence. In the case of *California* v. *Greenwood*[3] (1988) the Supreme Court upheld a warrantless search of garbage outside someone's home. After police found drug paraphernalia in the suspect's trash, they obtained a warrant to search his house. The suspect was later convicted on drug charges. In *Whren* v. *United States*[4] (1996) the Court held that the seizure of drugs made when stopping a vehicle for a minor traffic violation did not violate the Fourth Amendment.

Beginning in the 1980s, the Supreme Court dealt with whether certain kinds of drug tests constitute a search. In 1989 the Court held that drug tests were searches and that it is lawful to conduct such searches among certain workers, even without any individualized suspicion that one or more of the workers uses drugs.

The Exclusionary Rule In *Weeks* v. *United States*[5] (1914) the Court established the exclusionary rule—any illegally obtained evidence cannot be used in a federal court. The *Weeks* decision did not apply to state courts until *Mapp* v. *Ohio*[6] (1961) extended the protection to state courts.

Relaxing the Exclusionary Rule Some people have criticized the exclusionary rule. They ask whether criminals should go free simply because the police made a mistake in collecting evidence. In *United States* v. *Leon*[7] (1984) the Court ruled that as long as the police act in good faith when they request a warrant, the evidence they collect may be used in court even if the warrant is defective. In the *Leon* case, for example, a judge had used the wrong form for the warrant.

See the following footnoted materials in the ***Reference Handbook:***

1. *Payton* v. *New York* case summary, page 763.
2. *Florida* v. *J.L.* case summary, page 758.
3. *California* v. *Greenwood* case summary, page 756.
4. *Whren* v. *United States* case summary, page 768.
5. *Weeks* v. *United States* case summary, page 767.
6. *Mapp* v. *Ohio* case summary, page 761.
7. *United States* v. *Leon* case summary, page 766.

That same year the Court also approved an "inevitable discovery" exception to the exclusionary rule. In *Nix* v. *Williams*[1] (1984) the Court held that evidence obtained in violation of a defendant's rights can be used at trial. The prosecutor, however, must show that the evidence would have eventually been discovered by legal means. The *Nix* case involved a murderer whom police had tricked into leading them to the hidden body of his victim.

Landmark Cases

California* v. *Acevedo In October 1987 police officers observed Charles Steven Acevedo leaving a suspected drug house. He carried a paper bag the size of a package of drugs they knew had been mailed from Hawaii. When Acevedo drove off, the police stopped his car, opened the trunk, and found a pound of marijuana. When the defense moved to suppress the evidence, the trial court denied the motion. Acevedo pleaded guilty but appealed the court's refusal to exclude the marijuana as evidence.

The Supreme Court overruled an earlier decision (*Arkansas* v. *Sanders*, 1979) that had imposed a warrant requirement to search containers or packages found in a lawfully stopped vehicle. The Court established a new precedent to be used in automobile searches. The police are free to "search an automobile and the containers within it where they have probable cause to believe contraband or evidence is contained."

Fourth Amendment in High Schools

Fourth Amendment protections may be limited inside high schools. In the case of *New Jersey* v. *T.L.O.*[2] (1985) the Supreme Court ruled that school officials do not need warrants or probable cause to search students or their property. All that is needed are reasonable grounds to believe a search will uncover evidence that a student has broken school rules.

The New Jersey case arose when an assistant principal searched the purse of a student he suspected had been smoking tobacco in a restroom. The search turned up not only cigarettes but marijuana. The student was suspended from school and prosecuted by juvenile authorities. The Court would probably have ruled in favor of the student if a police officer had conducted the search, but the justices did not place the same restraints on public school officials.

In 1995 the Court further limited Fourth Amendment protections in high schools. In *Vernonia School District 47J* v. *Acton*[3] (1995) the Court upheld mandatory suspicionless drug tests for all students participating in interscholastic athletics.

Wiretapping and Electronic Eavesdropping One observer has said that in Washington, D.C., many important people assume or at least joke that their telephones are tapped. The Supreme Court considers

Limits of the Fourth Amendment

Constitutional Searches School administration officials search school lockers for illegal materials. ***In your opinion, how does the Supreme Court ruling in the case of* New Jersey *v.* T.L.O. *apply to the search of school lockers?***

See the following footnoted materials in the ***Reference Handbook:***

1. *Nix* v. *Williams* case summary, page 763.
2. *New Jersey* v. *T.L.O.* case summary, page 762.
3. *Vernonia School District 47J* v. *Acton* case summary, page 767.

wiretapping, eavesdropping, and other means of electronic surveillance to be search and seizure.

The Court first dealt with wiretapping in *Olmstead* v. *United States*[1] (1928). Federal agents had tapped individuals' telephones for four months to obtain the evidence necessary to convict them of bootlegging. The Court upheld the conviction, ruling that wiretapping did not violate the Fourth Amendment. The Court said no warrant was needed to wiretap because the agents had not actually entered anyone's home.

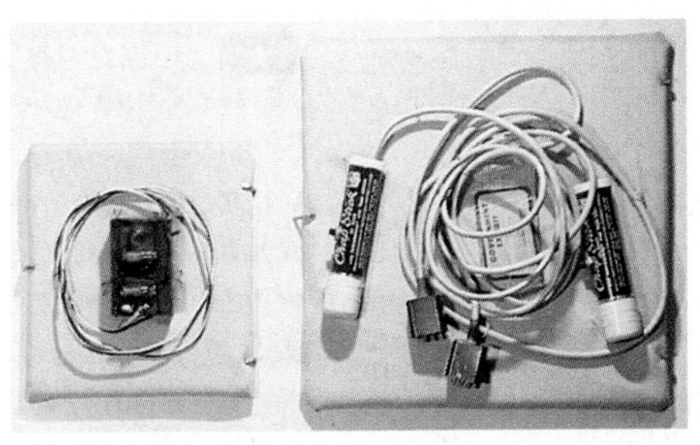

The use of wiretaps, such as this one used to bug the Democratic National Committee headquarters in the Watergate office in 1972, is prohibited without a warrant.

This precedent stood for almost 40 years. Then in 1967, in *Katz* v. *United States,*[2] the Court overruled the *Olmstead* decision. Charles Katz, a Los Angeles gambler, was using a public phone booth to place bets across state lines. Without a warrant, the FBI put a microphone outside the booth to gather evidence that was later used to convict Katz. In reversing Katz's conviction, the Court held that the Fourth Amendment "protects people—and not simply 'areas'" against unreasonable searches and seizures. The ruling extended Fourth Amendment protections by prohibiting wiretapping without a warrant.

Congress and Wiretaps In 1968 Congress passed the Omnibus Crime Control and Safe Streets Act. This law required federal, state, and local authorities to obtain a court order for most wiretaps. Then in 1978 Congress passed the Foreign Intelligence Surveillance Act, requiring a court order even for wiretapping and bugging in national security cases. These two laws virtually prohibit the government from using all electronic surveillance without a warrant.

Guarantee of Counsel

The **Sixth Amendment** guarantees a defendant the right "to have the assistance of counsel for his defense." Generally the federal courts provided counsel, or an attorney, in federal cases. For years, however, people could be tried in state courts without having a lawyer. As a result, defendants who could pay hired the best lawyers to defend them and stood a better chance of acquittal. People who could not pay had no lawyer and were often convicted because they did not understand the law.

Early Rulings on Right to Counsel The Supreme Court first dealt with the right to counsel in state courts in *Powell* v. *Alabama*[3] (1932). Nine African American youths were convicted of assaulting two white girls in Alabama. The Court reversed the conviction, ruling that the state had to provide a lawyer in cases involving the death penalty.

Ten years later, in *Betts* v. *Brady*[4] (1942), the Court held that states did not have to provide a lawyer in cases not involving the death penalty. The Court said appointment of counsel was "not a fundamental right, essential to a fair trial" for state defendants unless "special circumstances" such as illiteracy or mental incompetence required that the accused have a lawyer in order to get a fair trial.

For the next 20 years, under the *Betts* rule, the Supreme Court struggled to determine when the circumstances in a case were special enough to require a lawyer. Then in 1963 Clarence Earl Gideon, a penniless drifter from Florida, won a landmark case that ended the *Betts* rule.

Landmark Cases

Gideon* v. *Wainwright Gideon was charged with breaking into a pool hall with the intent to commit a crime—a felony. Because he was too poor to hire a lawyer, Gideon requested a court-appointed attorney. The request was denied by the court. Gideon was convicted and sentenced to a five-year jail term.

See the following footnoted materials in the ***Reference Handbook:***

1. *Olmstead* v. *United States* case summary, page 763.
2. *Katz* v. *United States* case summary, page 760.
3. *Powell* v. *Alabama* case summary, page 764.
4. *Betts* v. *Brady* case summary, page 755.

While in jail, Gideon studied law books. He appealed his own case to the Supreme Court with a handwritten petition. "The question is very simple," wrote Gideon. "I requested the [Florida] court to appoint me an attorney and the court refused." In 1963, in a unanimous verdict, the Court overruled *Betts* v. *Brady*. Justice Black wrote:

> "*Those guarantees of the Bill of Rights which are fundamental safeguards of liberty immune from federal abridgment are equally protected against state invasion by the Due Process Clause of the Fourteenth Amendment. . . . Reason and reflection require us to recognize that in our adversary system of criminal justice, any person haled into court, who is too poor to hire a lawyer, cannot be assured a fair trial unless counsel is provided for him.*"
>
> —Justice Hugo Black, 1963

Results of the *Gideon* Decision Gideon was released, retried with a lawyer assisting him, and acquitted. More than 1,000 other Florida prisoners and thousands more in other states who had been convicted without counsel were also set free. The Court has since extended the *Gideon* decision by ruling that whenever a jail sentence of 6 months or more is a possible punishment—even for misdemeanors and petty offenses—the accused has a right to a lawyer at public expense from the time of arrest through the appeals process.

Self-incrimination

The **Fifth Amendment** says that no one "shall be compelled in any criminal case to be a witness against himself." The courts have interpreted this amendment's protection against self-incrimination to cover witnesses before congressional committees and grand juries as well as defendants in criminal cases. This protection rests on a basic legal principle: the government bears the burden of proof. Defendants are not obliged to help the government prove they committed a crime or to testify at their own trial.

The Fifth Amendment also protects defendants against confessions extorted by force or violence. Giving people the "third degree" is unconstitutional because this pressure forces defendants, in effect, to testify against themselves. The same rule applies to state courts through the due process clause of the Fourteenth Amendment.

In the mid-1960s the Supreme Court, under Chief Justice Earl Warren, handed down two decisions that expanded protection against self-incrimination and forced confessions. The cases were *Escobedo* v. *Illinois* (1964) and *Miranda* v. *Arizona* (1966).

Sixth Amendment Guarantees

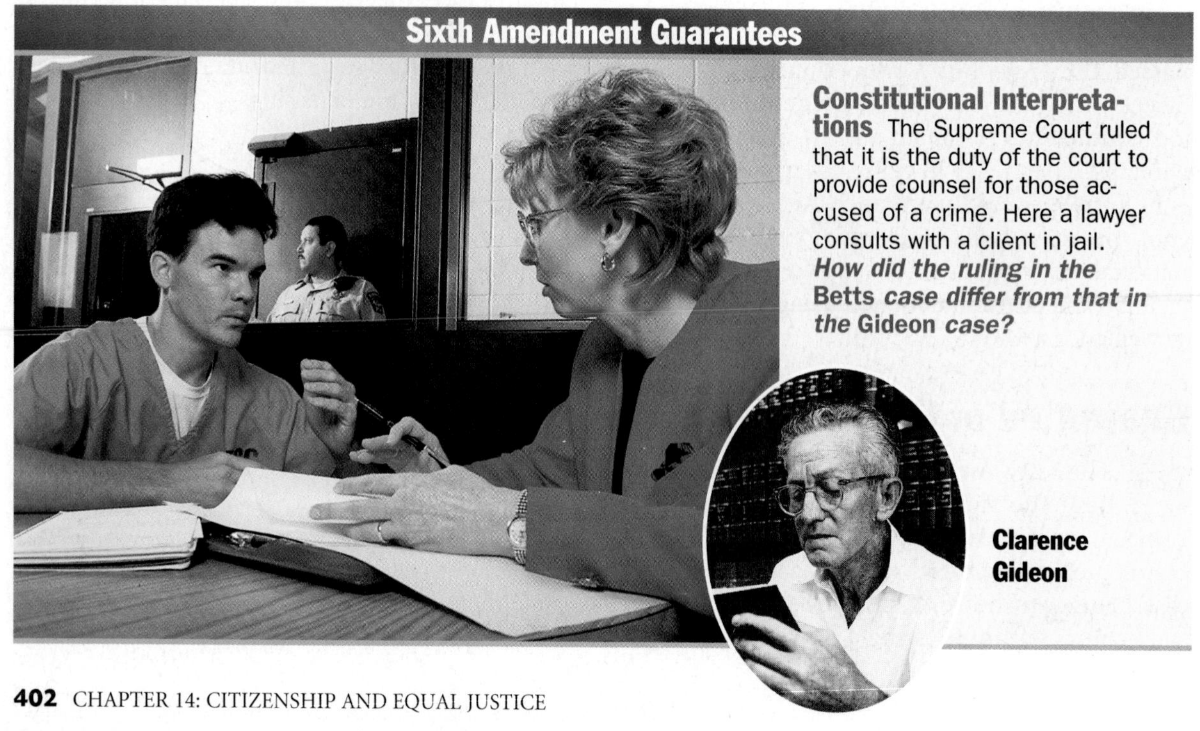

Constitutional Interpretations The Supreme Court ruled that it is the duty of the court to provide counsel for those accused of a crime. Here a lawyer consults with a client in jail. ***How did the ruling in the* Betts *case differ from that in the* Gideon *case?***

Clarence Gideon

Landmark Cases

Escobedo* v. *Illinois In 1960 Manuel Valtierra, Danny Escobedo's brother-in-law, was shot and killed in Chicago. The police picked up Escobedo and questioned him at length. Escobedo repeatedly asked to see his lawyer, but his requests were denied. No one during the course of the interrogation advised Escobedo of his constitutional rights. After a long night at police headquarters, Escobedo made some incriminating statements to the police. At his trial, the prosecution used these statements to convict Escobedo of murder.

In 1964 the Court reversed Escobedo's conviction, ruling that Escobedo's Fifth Amendment right to remain silent and his Sixth Amendment right to an attorney had been violated. The Court reasoned that the presence of Escobedo's lawyer could have helped him avoid self-incrimination. A confession or other incriminating statements an accused person makes when he or she is denied access to a lawyer may not be used in a trial. This is another version of the exclusionary rule.

The Power of Judicial Review

Landmark Decisions In 1966 the Court threw out the felony conviction of Ernesto Miranda, who had confessed while in police custody. ***How did the Miranda decision affect police policies and procedures across the nation?***

Miranda* v. *Arizona Two years later, the Court established strict rules for protecting suspects during police interrogations. In March 1963, Ernesto Miranda had been arrested and convicted for the rape and kidnapping of an 18-year-old woman. The victim selected Miranda from a police lineup, and the police questioned him for two hours. During questioning, Miranda was not told that he could remain silent or have a lawyer. Miranda confessed, signed a statement admitting and describing the crime, was convicted, and then appealed.

In *Miranda* v. *Arizona* (1966) the Supreme Court reversed the conviction. The Court ruled that the Fifth Amendment's protection against self-incrimination requires that suspects be clearly informed of their rights before police question them. Unless they are so informed, their statements may not be used in court. The Court set strict guidelines for police questioning of suspects. These guidelines are now known as the *Miranda* rules. The Court said:

> "*Prior to any questioning, the person must be warned that he has a right to remain silent, that any statement he does make may be used as evidence against him, and that he has a right to the presence of an attorney, either retained or appointed.*"
>
> —Chief Justice Earl Warren, 1966

Since 1966 the Court has qualified the *Miranda* and *Escobedo* rules. For example, in *Oregon* v. *Elstad*[1] (1985) the Court held that if suspects confess before they are informed of their rights, the prosecutor may later use those confessions as evidence. In the 1988 case of *Braswell* v. *United States*,[2] the Court narrowed the protection from self-incrimination in cases involving business crime by ruling that employees in charge of corporate records can be forced to turn over evidence even if it is incriminating.

In 1991 the Court narrowed protection from self-incrimination even further when it ruled that coerced confessions are sometimes permitted. In

See the following footnoted materials in the ***Reference Handbook:***

1. *Oregon* v. *Elstad* case summary, page 763.

2. *Braswell* v. *United States* case summary, page 755.

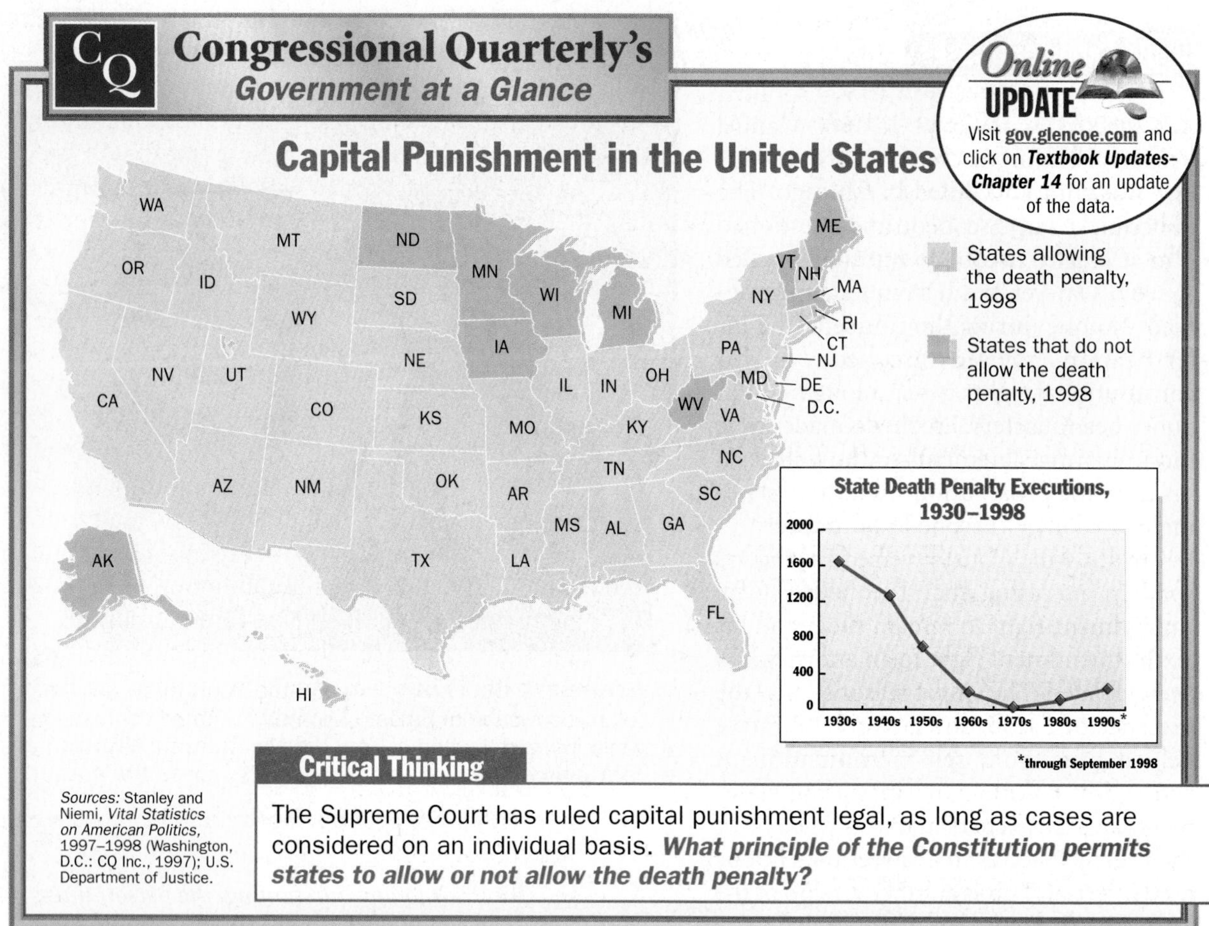

Sources: Stanley and Niemi, *Vital Statistics on American Politics*, 1997–1998 (Washington, D.C.: CQ Inc., 1997); U.S. Department of Justice.

the case of *Arizona* v. *Fulminante*,[1] Oreste Fulminante, who was in prison for illegal possession of a firearm, confessed to a fellow inmate that he had murdered his stepdaughter. The inmate had promised Fulminante protection from other prisoners in exchange for the confession. After the inmate told the authorities about the confession, Fulminante was tried and convicted. Upon appeal the Supreme Court ruled that a forced confession did not void a conviction if other independently obtained evidence sustained a guilty verdict.

In 2000, however, the Court reaffirmed that the *Miranda* rules are deeply rooted in the Constitution and that Congress cannot reverse the requirement to inform arrested persons of their rights. Writing for a seven-to-two majority in *Dickerson* v. *United States*,[2] Chief Justice William Rehnquist stated, "*Miranda* has become embedded in routine police practice to the point where warnings have become part of our national culture."

Double Jeopardy

The Fifth Amendment states in part that no person shall be "twice put in jeopardy of life and limb." **Double jeopardy** means a person may not be tried twice for the same crime, thus protecting people from continual harassment. In *United States* v. *Halper*,[3] (1989) the Supreme Court ruled that a civil penalty could not be imposed after a criminal penalty for the same act. However, the Court ruled in *Hudson* v. *United States*[4] (1997) that people who have paid civil fines for regulatory wrongdoing may also face criminal charges. Also, if a criminal act violates both state and federal law, the case may be tried at both levels.

See the following footnoted materials in the **Reference Handbook:**
1. *Arizona* v. *Fulminante* case summary, page 754.
2. *Dickerson* v. *United States* case summary, page 757.
3. *United States* v. *Halper* case summary, page 766.
4. *Hudson* v. *United States* case summary, page 759.

In addition, a single act may involve more than one crime. Stealing a car and then selling it involves theft and the sale of stolen goods. A person may be tried separately for each offense. When a trial jury fails to agree on a verdict, the accused may have to undergo a second trial. Double jeopardy does not apply when the defendant wins an appeal of a case in a higher court.

Cruel and Unusual Punishment

The **Eighth Amendment** forbids "cruel and unusual punishments," the only constitutional provision specifically limiting penalties in criminal cases. The Supreme Court has rarely used this provision. In *Rhodes* v. *Chapman*[1] (1981), for example, the Court ruled that putting two prisoners in a cell built for one is not cruel and unusual punishment.

There is a controversy, however, over how this protection relates to the death penalty. During the 1970s the Supreme Court handed down several decisions on the constitutionality of the death penalty. In *Furman* v. *Georgia*[2] (1972) the Court ruled that capital punishment as then administered was not constitutional. The Court found the death penalty was being imposed in apparently arbitrary ways for a wide variety of crimes and mainly on African Americans and poor people.

The *Furman* decision, however, stopped short of flatly outlawing the death penalty. Instead, it warned the states that the death penalty needed clarification. Thirty-five states responded with new death penalty laws. These laws took one of two approaches. North Carolina and some other states made the death penalty mandatory for certain crimes. In this way, they hoped to eliminate arbitrary decisions. In *Woodson* v. *North Carolina*[3] (1976), however, the Court ruled mandatory death penalties unconstitutional. The Court held that such laws failed to take into consideration the specifics of a crime and any possible mitigating circumstances.

Georgia and several other states took a different approach. They established new procedures for trials and appeals designed to reduce arbitrary decisions and racial prejudice in imposing the death penalty. In *Gregg* v. *Georgia*[4] (1976) the Court upheld the Georgia law. In the *Gregg* case, the Court ruled that under adequate guidelines the death penalty does not constitute cruel and unusual punishment. The Court stated: "Capital punishment is an expression of society's moral outrage. . . . It is an extreme sanction, suitable to the most extreme of crimes."

See the following footnoted materials in the **Reference Handbook:**

1. *Rhodes* v. *Chapman* case summary, page 764.
2. *Furman* v. *Georgia* case summary, page 758.
3. *Woodson* v. *North Carolina* case summary, page 768.
4. *Gregg* v. *Georgia* case summary, page 759.

Section 3 Assessment

Checking for Understanding

1. **Main Idea** Use a graphic organizer like the one below to compare the significance of the *Gideon, Escobedo,* and *Miranda* cases.

Gideon	*Escobedo*	*Miranda*

2. **Define** exclusionary rule, counsel, self-incrimination, double jeopardy.
3. **Identify** Fourth Amendment, Sixth Amendment, Fifth Amendment, Eighth Amendment.
4. What procedure must police follow in making a lawful search?

Critical Thinking

5. **Identifying Alternatives** What decisions does the accused person have to make at the time he or she hears the *Miranda* rules?

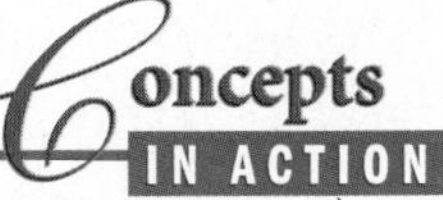

Civil Rights Would you be willing to undergo routine random drug testing or locker searches in your school? Note that the Fourth Amendment right to privacy is at issue here. Create a slogan explaining your position and use it to create a one-page advertisement promoting your position.

Section 4

Equal Protection of the Law

Reader's Guide

Key Terms

rational basis test, suspect classification, fundamental right, discrimination, Jim Crow laws, separate but equal doctrine, civil rights movement

Find Out

- What is the constitutional meaning of "equal protection"?
- How has the Court applied the Fourteenth Amendment's equal protection clause to the issue of discrimination?

Understanding Concepts

Constitutional Interpretations Why do Supreme Court decisions in discrimination cases rest largely on the Fifth and Fourteenth Amendments?

COVER STORY

Pizza Refusal Illegal?

KANSAS CITY, MISSOURI, JANUARY 1997

Is this discrimination in pizza delivery? Paseo Academy, a city magnet school, planned a big mid-day pizza party for honor-roll students. Pizza Hut refused delivery of a $450 pizza order explaining that the area was unsafe—one of its "trade area restrictions" based on crime statistics. A local chain, Westport Pizza, filled the order. Principal Dorothy Shepherd later learned that Pizza Hut had a $170,000 contract to deliver pizzas to 21 Kansas City schools, including Paseo. A school board committee recommended canceling the contract.

The politics of pizza

Many forms of discrimination are illegal. The Declaration of Independence affirmed an ideal of American democracy when it stated "all men are created equal." This statement does not mean that everyone is born with the same characteristics or will remain equal. Rather, the democratic ideal of equality means all people are entitled to equal rights and treatment before the law.

Meaning of Equal Protection

The Fourteenth Amendment forbids any state to "deny to any person within its jurisdiction the equal protection of the law." The Supreme Court has ruled that the Fifth Amendment's due process clause also provides equal protection.

Generally the equal protection clause means that state and local governments cannot draw unreasonable distinctions among different groups of people. The key word is *unreasonable.* In practice, all governments must classify or draw distinctions among categories of people. For example, when a state taxes cigarettes, it taxes smokers but not non-smokers.

When a citizen challenges a law because it violates the equal protection clause, the issue is not whether a classification can be made. The issue is whether or not the classification is reasonable. Over the years the Supreme Court has developed guidelines for considering when a state law or action might violate the equal protection clause.

The Rational Basis Test The **rational basis test** provides that the Court will uphold a state law when the state can show a good reason to justify the classification. This test asks if the classification is "reasonably related" to an acceptable goal of government. A law prohibiting people with red hair from driving would fail the test because there is no relationship

Guaranteeing Equal Rights

Triumph of Civil Rights President Johnson offers the pen used to sign the Civil Rights Act of 1964 to NAACP's Roy Wilkins, as Attorney General Robert F. Kennedy (above right) looks on. ***Senator Everett McKinley Dirksen supported the civil rights bill saying, "No army can withstand the strength of an idea whose time has come." What do you think he meant?***

between the color of a person's hair and driving safely. In *Wisconsin* v. *Mitchell*[1] (1993), however, the Supreme Court upheld a state law that imposes longer prison sentences for people who commit "hate crimes," or crimes motivated by prejudice. Unless special circumstances exist, the Supreme Court puts the burden of proving a law unreasonable on the people challenging the law. Special circumstances arise when the Court decides that a state law involves a "suspect classification" or a "fundamental right."

Suspect Classifications When a classification is made on the basis of race or national origin, it is a **suspect classification** and "subject to strict judicial scrutiny." A law that requires African Americans but not whites to ride in the back of a bus would be a suspect classification.

When a law involves a suspect classification, the Court reverses the normal presumption of constitutionality. It is no longer enough for the state to show that the law is a reasonable way to handle a public problem. The state must show the Court that there is "some compelling public interest" to justify the law and its classifications.

See the following footnoted materials in the **Reference Handbook:**
1. *Wisconsin* v. *Mitchell* case summary, page 768.

Fundamental Rights The third test the Court uses is that of **fundamental rights,** or rights that go to the heart of the American system or are indispensable in a just system. The Court gives a state law dealing with fundamental rights especially close scrutiny. The Court, for example, has ruled that the right to travel freely between the states, the right to vote, and First Amendment rights are fundamental. State laws that violate these fundamental rights are unconstitutional.

Proving Intent to Discriminate

Laws that classify people unreasonably are said to discriminate. **Discrimination** exists when individuals are treated unfairly solely because of their race, gender, ethnic group, age, physical disability, or religion. Such discrimination is illegal, but it may be difficult to prove.

What if a law does not classify people directly, but the effect of the law is to classify people? For example, suppose a law requires that job applicants at the police department take a test. Suppose members of one group usually score better on this test than members of another group. Can discrimination be proven simply by showing that the law has a different impact on people of different races, genders, or national origins?

The Struggle for Equality Under the Law

Protest Strategy Civil rights activists carry out a sit-in in Charlotte, North Carolina, in the early 1960s. They continued their silent protest at the counter, even after the waitresses refused to serve them and left. ***What do you think civil rights activists hoped to accomplish through sit-ins?***

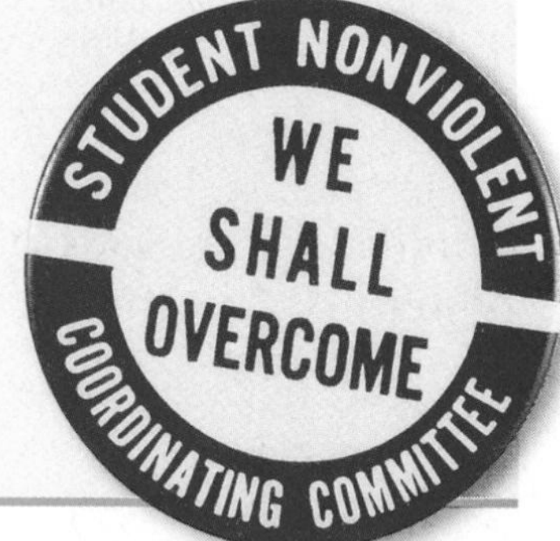

A button expressing a motto of civil rights activists

Showing Intent to Discriminate In *Washington* v. *Davis*[1] (1976) the Supreme Court ruled that to prove a state guilty of discrimination, one must prove that an intent to discriminate motivated the state's action. The case arose when two African Americans challenged the District of Columbia police department's requirement that all recruits pass a verbal ability test. They said the requirement was unconstitutional because more African Americans than whites failed the test.

The Court said that this result did not mean the test was unconstitutional. The crucial issue was that the test was not designed to discriminate. As the Court said in a later case, "The Fourteenth Amendment guarantees equal laws, not equal results."

Impact of the *Washington* Decision Since the *Washington* case, the Court has applied the principle of intent to discriminate to other areas. In one Illinois city, a zoning ordinance permitted only single-family homes, prohibiting low-cost housing projects. The Court ruled the ordinance constitutional, even though it effectively kept minorities from moving into the city. The reason for the decision was that the Court found no intent to discriminate against minorities.

See the following footnoted materials in the **Reference Handbook:**
1. *Washington* v. *Davis* case summary, page 767.

The Struggle for Equal Rights

The Fourteenth Amendment, guaranteeing equal protection, was ratified in 1868, shortly after the Civil War. Yet for almost a century the courts upheld discrimination against and segregation of African Americans. **Racial discrimination** is treating members of a race differently simply because of race. **Segregation** is separation of people from the larger social group.

By the late 1800s, about half the states had adopted **Jim Crow laws.** These laws, most often in Southern states, required racial segregation in such places as schools, public transportation, and hotels.

Landmark Cases

Plessy* v. *Ferguson The Supreme Court justified Jim Crow laws in *Plessy* v. *Ferguson* (1896). The Court said the Fourteenth Amendment allowed separate facilities for different races as long as those facilities were equal. Justice Harlan dissented:

> *I deny that any legislative body or judicial tribunal may have regard to the race of citizens when the civil rights of those citizens are involved. . . . Our Constitution is color-blind, and neither knows nor tolerates classes among citizens. In respect of civil rights, all citizens are equal before the law.*
>
> —Justice John Marshall Harlan, 1896

Nevertheless, for the next 50 years the **separate but equal doctrine** was used to justify segregation in the United States. In the late 1930s and the 1940s the Supreme Court began to chip away at the doctrine in a series of decisions that have had far-reaching implications. The most important decision came in 1954 in a case involving an African American student in Topeka, Kansas.

Brown v. *Board of Education of Topeka*

In the 1950s Topeka's schools were racially segregated. Linda Carol Brown, an eight-year-old African American student, was denied admission to an all-white school near her home and was required to attend a distant all-black school. With the help of the National Association for the Advancement of Colored People (NAACP), Linda's family sued the Topeka Board of Education. The NAACP successfully argued that segregated schools could never be equal. Therefore, such schools were unconstitutional. In 1954 the Court ruled on this case and similar cases filed in Virginia, Delaware, and South Carolina. In a unanimous decision in *Brown* v. *Board of Education of Topeka,* the Court overruled the separate but equal doctrine. This decision marked the beginning of a long, difficult battle to desegregate the public schools.

CQ Congressional Quarterly's *Government at a Glance*

Selected Major Civil Rights Legislation

Year	Act	Major Provisions
1875	Civil Rights Act	Bans discrimination in places of public accommodation (declared unconstitutional in 1883)
1957	Civil Rights Act	Makes it a federal crime to prevent a person from voting in a federal election
1963	Equal Pay Act	Bans wage discrimination based on race, sex, color, religion, or national origin
1964	Civil Rights Act	Bans discrimination in places of public accommodation, federally funded programs, and in private employment; authorizes Justice Department to bring school integration suits
1965	Voting Rights Act	Allows federal registrars to register voters and ensure those registered can exercise their right to vote without qualifications
1967	Age Discrimination Act	Bans discrimination in employment based on age
1968	Civil Rights Act, Title VIII	Bans racial discrimination in sale or rental of housing
1972	Higher Education Act, Title IX	Forbids discrimination based on sex by universities and colleges receiving federal aid
1974	Housing and Community Development Act	Bans housing discrimination based on sex
1990	Americans with Disabilities Act	Bans discrimination in employment, transportation, public accommodations, and telecommunications against persons with physical or mental disabilities

Source: Bibby, *Governing by Consent,* 2d ed. (Washington, D.C.: CQ Press, 1995).

Critical Thinking

The Fourteenth Amendment, ratified in 1868, was passed to protect the rights of former enslaved persons. However, it was not until 1964 that racial segregation in places of public accommodation was made illegal. ***What civil rights act eliminated voting qualifications such as passing a literacy test?***

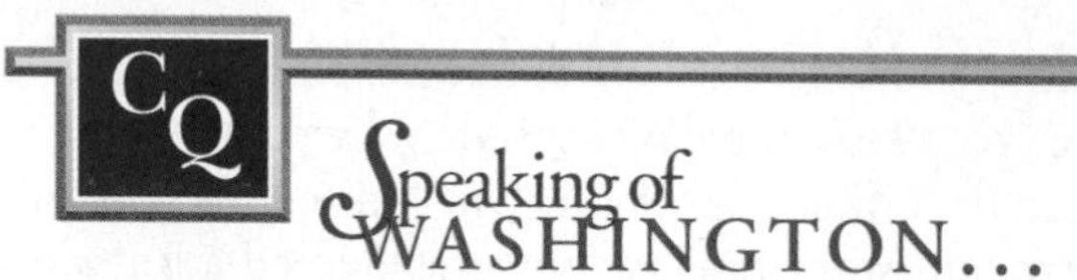

Civil Rights

In 1948 Hubert H. Humphrey, running for the Senate, delivered to the Democrats what might have been the most persuasive convention speech since Bryan's "Cross of Gold." The convention adopted a liberal civil rights plank after hearing Humphrey say, "There will be no hedging . . . no watering down, if you please, of the instruments and the principles of the civil rights program."

By early 1970, public schools were no longer segregated by law. In many areas school segregation continued, however, largely because of housing patterns. Concentration of African Americans in certain areas of cities created school districts that were either largely all African American or all white. Efforts to deal with this situation have involved redrawing school district boundaries, reassigning pupils, and busing students to schools out of segregated neighborhoods. The *Brown* decision established a precedent for Court decisions striking down segregation in public parks, beaches, playgrounds, libraries, golf courses, state and local prisons, and transportation systems.

The Civil Rights Movement

After the *Brown* decision, many African Americans and whites worked together to end segregation through the **civil rights movement.** Throughout the United States, but mostly in the South, African Americans deliberately and peacefully broke laws supporting racial segregation. Some held "sit-ins" at restaurant lunch counters that served only whites. When arrested for breaking segregation laws, they were almost always found guilty. They could then appeal, challenging the constitutionality of the laws.

The most important leader of the civil rights movement was Dr. Martin Luther King, Jr. A Baptist minister, King led nonviolent protest marches and demonstrations against segregation. He understood the importance of using the courts to win equal rights and sought to stir the nation's conscience.

New Civil Rights Laws

Influenced by the civil rights movement, Congress began to pass civil rights laws. The Civil Rights Act of 1964 and other laws sought to ensure voting rights and equal job opportunities. President Lyndon Johnson said, "Passage of this bill and of the 1965 civil rights law . . . profoundly altered the politics of civil rights and the political position of Southern blacks."

Section 4 Assessment

Checking for Understanding

1. **Main Idea** Use the graphic organizer below to show why the Supreme Court overturned the separate but equal doctrine and what effects followed that decision.

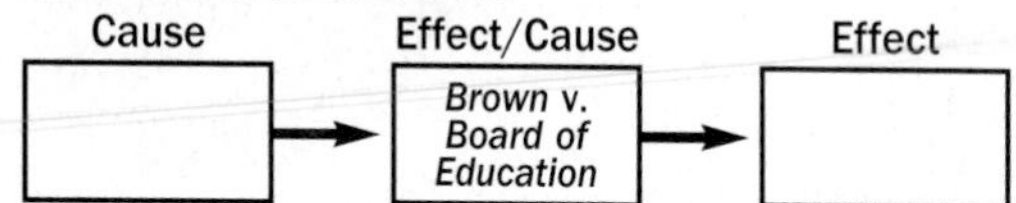

2. **Define** rational basis test, suspect classification, fundamental right, discrimination, Jim Crow laws, separate but equal doctrine, civil rights movement.
3. **Identify** racial discrimination, segregation.
4. List three guidelines or tests the Supreme Court uses in its judgment of cases involving equal protection under the law.

Critical Thinking

5. **Checking Consistency** Was Chief Justice Earl Warren's opinion in *Brown* v. *Board of Education of Topeka* consistent with Justice Harlan's dissenting opinion in *Plessy* v. *Ferguson?* Explain your answer.

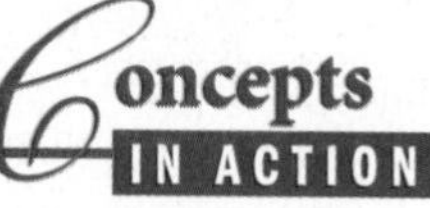

Constitutional Interpretations Find information about the Civil Rights Act of 1964, Voting Rights Act of 1965, Equal Employment Opportunities Act of 1972, Education Amendment of 1972, Voting Rights Act of 1975, and Americans with Disabilities Act of 1990. Prepare an informational brochure that describes these acts.

Apprendi v. *New Jersey,* 2000

The Fourteenth Amendment requires that an accused person receive due process when tried for breaking a state law. How does this affect the enforcement of hate crime laws, which require harsher punishments for crimes motivated by prejudice? The Court faced this issue in the case of Apprendi *v.* New Jersey.

Background of the Case

On December 22, 1994, Charles Apprendi fired several gunshots into an African American family's home in Vineland, New Jersey. Apprendi confessed to the shooting and stated that he did not want the family in the neighborhood "because they are black in color." Later Apprendi took back his statement.

Apprendi was accused of four different shootings and of unlawful possession of weapons. During the plea agreement stage, the state reserved the right to request a harsher sentence for the December 22 shooting on the grounds that it was committed because the victims were members of a minority group. At the evidence hearing, the judge ruled that Apprendi's December 22 shooting was motivated by racial prejudice and sentenced Apprendi to 12 years, which exceeded the usual 10-year maximum for such an offense. Apprendi claimed that the extended sentence violated his rights under the Fourteenth Amendment and argued that the amendment's Due Process Clause requires that bias in a hate crime be proved to a jury beyond a reasonable doubt.

Apprendi's appeal eventually reached the New Jersey Supreme Court, which upheld the decisions of the lower courts. The case was taken before the United States Supreme Court in March 2000.

The Constitutional Issue

During the 1990s, many Americans became increasingly alarmed over violent crimes whose victims were singled out as members of a certain group. State legislatures responded by passing hate crime laws to protect minorities. These laws provide for extended sentences when a court determines that a convicted person committed his or her crime because of prejudice.

Hate crime laws were passed with good intentions. However, establishing that prejudice is a criminal's main motive proved difficult in most cases. The judge in the Apprendi case made his decision based on the "preponderance of evidence." Because judges, not juries, often choose a sentence from a range of punishments prescribed for a certain crime, it seems to be a reasonable way to proceed in determining whether or not a crime is a hate crime.

On the other hand, the crime for which the jury convicted Apprendi was not designated a hate crime in the indictment. The jury did not decide beyond a reasonable doubt that he was motivated by prejudice. Apprendi's case raised the issue of whether a judge has the power under the Constitution to make decisions that greatly increase a sentence.

Debating the Case

Questions to Consider

1. Which amendment specifies trial by jury as part of the due process of law?
2. How might a Supreme Court decision in Charles Apprendi's favor affect other cases in which extended sentences have been handed down?

You Be the Judge

Does the deterrent posed by hate crime laws justify the use of the "preponderance of evidence" standard rather than the "proof beyond a reasonable doubt" standard? Is a defendant denied his or her rights if a judge, not a jury, decides on an extended sentence?

Section 5

Challenges for Civil Liberties

Reader's Guide

Key Terms

affirmative action, security classification system, transcript

Find Out

- What are the issues involved when the Supreme Court deals with affirmative action cases?
- How does the reasonableness standard apply in cases of sex discrimination?

Understanding Concepts

Public Policy How has government addressed the joint responsibilities of citizens' right to know and right to privacy?

COVER STORY

Web Sites Hurt Privacy

NEW YORK, NEW YORK, JUNE 9, 1997

Browsing the Internet

A study has revealed that half of the Internet's 100 most popular Web sites collect personal information from their visitors. Most give visitors no control over how that information is used. The survey was conducted by the Electronic Privacy Information Center, a nonprofit consumer group. According to the survey nearly one-fourth of the sites secretly plant electronic "cookies" in visitors' computers. This could allow a site to track a visitor's other activities on the Internet, data that could be shared without the user's knowledge. The study comes on the eve of government hearings over growing concerns about cyberspace spying and Internet security.

Changing ideas, social conditions, and technology have combined to raise new issues for civil liberties. Today, for example, the government maintains billions of computer records on individual Americans. In addition, private companies collect financial, medical, and legal information on almost everyone. Such record keeping raises important questions about the right to privacy—a right not mentioned in the Constitution but recognized as a constitutionally protected interest. Other important issues involve affirmative action, discrimination against women, and the right to know about government actions.

Affirmative Action

In the 1960s a new approach to dealing with discrimination developed through so-called affirmative action programs. **Affirmative action** refers to government policies that directly or indirectly award jobs, government contracts, promotions, admission to schools and training programs, and other benefits to minorities and women in order to make up for past discrimination caused by society as a whole. Today the national government requires all state and local governments, as well as any institution receiving aid from or contracting with the federal government, to adopt an affirmative action program. Such programs may give special treatment to disadvantaged groups in a variety of ways, including making use of numerical quotas that require, for example, a certain portion of jobs or law school admissions go to minorities or women.

Landmark Cases

Regents of the University of California v. Bakke The Supreme Court first ruled on affirmative action in 1978. Allan Bakke claimed to have been refused admission to the University of California medical school because he was

Remedying Past Discrimination

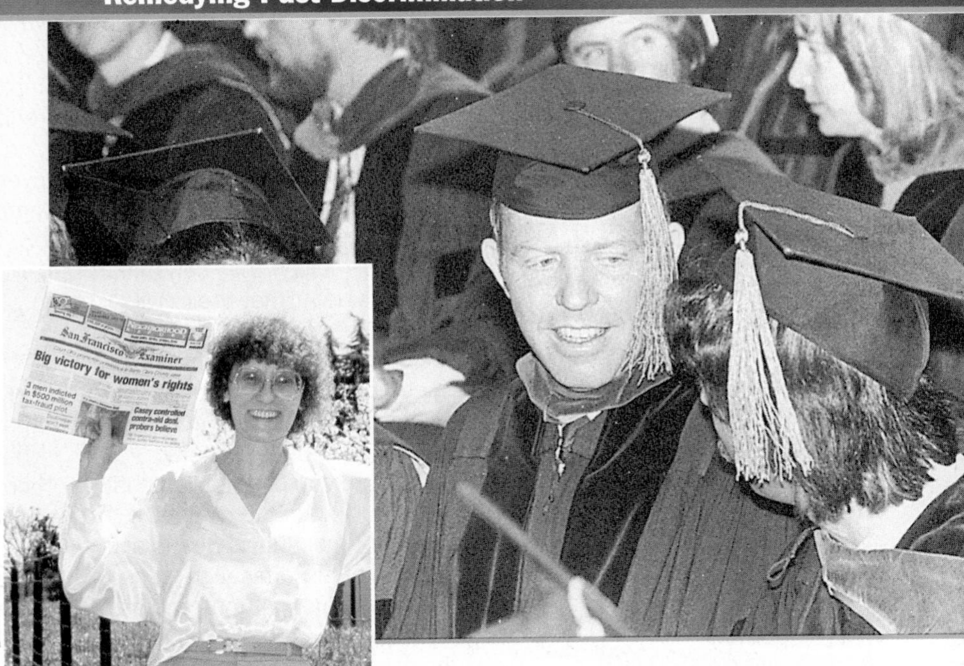

Equality vs. Freedom
Allan Bakke (right) received his degree in 1982, after the Supreme Court ordered the medical school of the University of California to admit him in 1978. Diane Joyce (left) gained a promotion from laborer to road dispatcher by invoking a government affirmative action policy. ***Do you think that fairness in education, hiring, and promotion can be accomplished through the establishment of quotas?***

white. The medical school had set up a quota system that reserved 16 places out of 100 each year for minorities. Minority students with lower test scores than Bakke's were admitted to fill the quota. Bakke sued, claiming he was a victim of reverse discrimination.

The Court ruled 5 to 4 to uphold the basic idea of affirmative action by stating that the university could consider race along with other characteristics when admitting students. The Court, however, went on to explain that a strict quota system based on race was unconstitutional and in violation of the 1964 Civil Rights Act. The Court ordered the university to admit Bakke to its medical school.

Unclear Constitutional Status Since the *Bakke* decision, the constitutional status of affirmative action has become unclear. The Supreme Court has struck down as many affirmative action plans as it has upheld. In 1987, for example, the Court upheld the use of affirmative action in promotions. In the case of *Johnson* v. *Transportation Agency, Santa Clara County, California*[1] (1987) the Court upheld a plan by the transportation department to move women into high-ranking positions. Paul Johnson and Diane Joyce had been competing for the job of road dispatcher. Johnson scored two points higher on the qualifying interview. Because of the county's affirmative action plan, however, Diane Joyce got the promotion. Johnson claimed the plan violated the 1964 Civil Rights Act, but the Court ruled against him.

In *Richmond* v. *J.A. Croson Co.*[2] (1989), however, the Court said that a plan setting aside 30 percent of city contracts for minority companies was unconstitutional. In 1995, in *Adarand Constructors Inc.* v. *Peña*,[3] the Court addressed affirmative action in federal programs. It overturned earlier decisions supporting affirmative action when it held that federal programs classifying people by race are unconstitutional, even when the purpose was to expand opportunities for minorities.

An Ongoing Debate The policy of affirmative action has caused much disagreement. Its supporters argue that African Americans, Hispanics, Native Americans, and women have been so handicapped by past discrimination that they suffer

See the following footnoted materials in the **Reference Handbook:**
1. *Johnson* v. *Transportation Agency, Santa Clara County, California* case summary, page 760.
2. *Richmond* v. *J.A. Croson Co.* case summary, page 764.
3. *Adarand Constructors Inc.* v. *Peña* case summary, page 754.

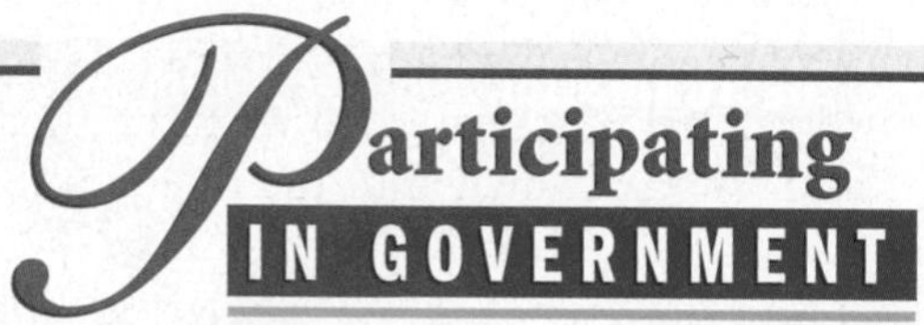

Filing a Civil Rights Complaint

Making a civil rights complaint

If persons believe they have been treated unfairly because of gender, race, color, national origin, religion, or disability, they can make a formal complaint that their civil rights have been violated.

The complaint must be in writing, be signed and dated and include your name, address, and phone number. It must include the name and address of the person or establishment that is the subject of the complaint. The complaint must describe the act and the type of discrimination (gender, race, and so on). It must include the date and place the act occurred and the names, addresses, and phone numbers of any witnesses. No other documents are necessary.

Generally, a complaint must be filed with the appropriate agency within 180 days of the discrimination it alleges. Discrimination in employment, education, housing, credit, and public services are handled by various state or federal government agencies. The Complaints Referral Office of the U.S. Commission on Civil Rights in Washington, D.C., gives advice on where to file a complaint.

Activity

1. Investigate the state or government agencies that handle various civil rights complaints. Use the telephone directory to list which agencies are concerned with the following areas: employment, housing, credit, education, public facilities.
2. Create an imaginary civil rights complaint following the guidelines above. Include the name and address of the agency where you would file your complaint.

from disadvantages not shared by white males. Further, they argue that increasing minorities and women in desirable jobs is such an important social goal that it should be taken into account when judging a person's qualifications for a job, school application, or promotion. Thus, supporters claim that simply stopping discrimination is not enough; government has the responsibility to actively promote more equality for minorities.

Opponents claim that any discrimination based on race or gender is wrong even when the purpose is to correct past injustices. They argue that merit is the only basis for making decisions on jobs, promotions, and school admissions. Opponents are especially against affirmative action programs that use quotas to reserve or set aside a certain number of jobs for minority group members. Some opponents have used the term **reverse discrimination** to describe situations where qualified individuals lose out to individuals chosen because of their race, ethnicity, or gender.

Discrimination Against Women

Women finally won the right to vote with the Nineteenth Amendment in 1920. In recent decades new challenges to discrimination against women have been raised in such areas as employment, housing, and credit policies. Both the Supreme Court and Congress have dealt with these challenges.

The Supreme Court's Position Because the Court treats classifications based on race and national origin as "suspect," it has examined them closely. What about classifications based on gender? Historically, the Supreme Court had ruled that laws discriminating against women did not violate the equal protection clause of the Fourteenth Amendment. In theory, many of these laws were designed to protect women from night work, overtime work, heavy lifting, and "bad elements" in society. In practice, they often discriminated against women. In the 1950s, for example, the Court said an Ohio law forbidding any woman other than the wife or daughter of a tavern owner to work as a barmaid was constitutional.

Landmark Cases

Reed* v. *Reed In 1971 the Supreme Court for the first time held that a state law was unconstitutional because it discriminated against women. In *Reed* v. *Reed,* the Court said a law that automatically preferred a father over a mother as executor of a son's estate violated the equal protection clause of the Fourteenth Amendment:

> "*To give a mandatory preference to members of either sex over members of the other . . . is to make the very kind of arbitrary legislative choice forbidden by the Equal Protection Clause.*"
>
> —Chief Justice Warren Burger, 1971

Reasonableness Standard The *Reed* decision created a new standard for judging constitutionality in sex discrimination cases. The Supreme Court said any law that classifies people on the basis of gender "must be reasonable, not arbitrary, and must rest on some ground of difference." That difference must serve "important governmental objectives" and be substantially related to those objectives.

The substantial interest standard is not as strict a test as the suspect classifications test used to judge racial discrimination. Since 1971, however, the Supreme Court has held that gender classifications are subject to "intermediate" scrutiny. In addition, in 1977 the Court said that treating women differently from men (or vice versa) is unconstitutional when based on no more than "old notions" about women and "the role-typing society has long imposed on women."

Decisions Under Substantial Interest Standard Since the *Reed* decision, courts have allowed some distinctions based on gender, while they have invalidated others. All of the following standards result from Court decisions that bar distinctions based on gender: (1) States cannot set different ages at which men and women become legal adults. (2) States cannot set different ages at which men and women are allowed to purchase beer. (3) States cannot exclude women from juries. (4) Employers cannot require women to take a pregnancy leave from work. (5) Girls cannot be kept off Little League baseball teams. (6) Private clubs and community service groups cannot exclude women from membership. (7) Employers must pay women monthly retirement benefits equal to those paid to men. (8) States cannot bar women from state-supported military colleges.

The following standards are based on Court decisions that allow differences based on gender: (1) All-boy and all-girl public schools are allowed

The Fight for the Right to Vote

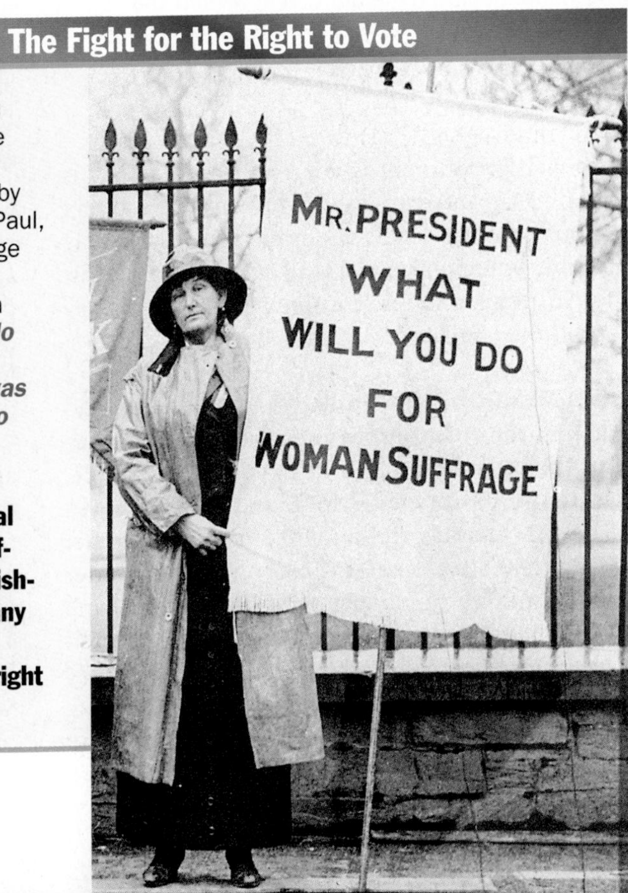

Social Reform A member of the Congressional Union, founded by suffragist Alice Paul, demands suffrage from President Woodrow Wilson in 1919. ***Why do you think the right to vote was so important to women?***

The National Woman Suffrage Publishing Company endorses women's right to vote.

Reasonable Distinctions

Women in the Armed Forces Although many women have enlisted in the armed forces, the Supreme Court ruled in 1981 that Congress could exclude women from the draft. ***Why would the Court allow Congress to exclude women from the draft?***

as long as enrollment is voluntary and quality is equal. (2) A state can give widows a property tax exemption not given to widowers. (3) A state may prohibit women from working in all-male prisons. (4) Hospitals may bar fathers from the delivery room.

Congressional Action Congress has passed many laws protecting women from discrimination. The Civil Rights Act of 1964, for example, banned job discrimination based on gender. In 1972 the Equal Employment Opportunity Act strengthened earlier laws by prohibiting gender discrimination in activities ranging from hiring and firing to promotion, pay, and working conditions. The Equal Credit Opportunity Act of 1974 outlawed discrimination against women seeking credit from banks, government agencies, and finance companies. This law also made it illegal to ask questions about a person's gender or marital status in a credit application.

In 1991 the Civil Rights and Women's Equity in Employment Act required employers to justify any gender distinctions in hiring to job performance and "business necessity."

In 1976 Congress acted to give women equal opportunities in education and school sports. When amending the Omnibus Education Act of 1972, Congress required all schools to give boys and girls an equal chance to participate in sports programs. Schools, however, may maintain separate teams for boys and girls, especially in contact sports.

Citizens' Right to Know

The right of citizens and the press to know what government is doing is an essential part of democracy. Citizens cannot make intelligent judgments about the government's actions unless they have adequate information. Government officials, however, are often reluctant to share information about their decisions and policies.

The national government's **security classification system,** operating since 1917, provides that information on government activities related to national security and foreign policy may be kept secret. Millions of government documents are classified as secret each year and made unavailable to the public.

The Freedom of Information Act In 1966 Congress passed the Freedom of Information Act requiring federal agencies to provide citizens access to public records on request. Exemptions are permitted for national defense materials, confidential personnel and financial data, and law enforcement files. People can sue the government for disclosure if they are denied access to materials.

Congress strengthened the law with several amendments in 1974. Immediately after the amendments went into effect, requests for information began flooding into the government at the rate of 12,500 per month.

The Sunshine Act Before 1976 many government meetings and hearings were held in secret. Such closed sessions made it difficult for the press, citizens' groups, lobbyists, and the public to keep an eye on government decisions. In the Sunshine Act of 1976, Congress helped correct that situation by requiring that many meetings be opened to the public.

The law applies to about 50 federal agencies, boards, and commissions. Meetings these agencies hold must be open to the public, and at least one week's advance notice must be given. Some closed meetings are allowed, but then a **transcript,** or summary record, of the meeting must be made. People may sue to force public disclosure of the proceedings of a meeting, if necessary.

Citizens' Right to Privacy

The Internal Revenue Service, the Census Bureau, state bureaus, and private credit bureaus all collect data about people. Computers make storing and sharing such information easy and routine. Do citizens have a "right to privacy"?

The Constitution and Privacy The Supreme Court has interpreted several rights guaranteed in the Bill of Rights and the Fourteenth Amendment to extend to personal behavior. In cases such as *Pierce* v. *Society of Sisters*[1] (1925), *Roe* v. *Wade*[2] (1973), and *Reno* v. *Condon*[3] (2000), the Court has recognized the right to personal privacy in many areas ranging from child rearing to abortion to sharing personal information without a person's consent. The Court has also held that the right to personal privacy is limited when the state has a "compelling need" to protect society.

Confidentiality What are the limits that a court must observe when seeking to obtain personal information? The Supreme Court ruled in *Jaffee* v. *Redmond*[4] (1996) that communications with mental health professionals, including clinical social workers, are privileged, and ordinarily such professionals cannot be required to disclose the contents of therapy sessions.

Legislation on Privacy In 1974 Congress passed the Family Educational Rights and Privacy Act. These laws allow people to inspect information about themselves in federal agency files and to challenge, correct, or amend the materials they find. The laws also protect access to files from outsiders without proper authorization.

The act also opened school files to parents and to students who are at least 18 years old. They are able to check test scores, reports of guidance counselors, and other information. Any school that refuses to comply can lose federal funding.

See the following footnoted materials in the **Reference Handbook:**
1. *Pierce* v. *Society of Sisters* case summary, page 763.
2. *Roe* v. *Wade* case summary, page 764.
3. *Reno* v. *Condon* case summary, page 764.
4. *Jaffee* v. *Redmond* case summary, page 760.

Privacy and Information Control

What legal recourse does a person have who is the subject of unwelcome publicity that does not involve physical injury or trespass? One of the difficulties that the law has in providing a right to privacy is that it often conflicts with the First Amendment rights of free speech and press. The Supreme Court has not generally supported the right to privacy for public figures. Private citizens have sometimes been successful in recovering damages for invasion of privacy when the press prints false statements about them. Another difficulty in the issue of information control is the failure of the law to keep pace with the electronic revolution that enables a host of data collectors to access and record personal information.

Celebrities sometimes face unwelcome publicity.

Who Knows What? Invite a businessperson, police officer, or government official to class to share information on this topic. Discuss the limits that should apply to protect private citizens.

Privacy and Credit Cards

Personal Privacy Information on this customer may be dispatched through credit card use to various companies. ***In what circumstances might the collection of information about citizens conflict with the individual's right to privacy?***

Sharing Credit Information For many years private credit bureaus have collected information to create reports on consumers' credit. In 1970 the Fair Credit Reporting Act was written to control the collection and distribution of information. Today, however, sophisticated computer-matching projects allow companies and the government to cross-reference data. Commercial information companies sell credit and medical details about individuals to marketing firms that use the information to sell everything from home repairs to life insurance. A growing number of lawmakers believe that the Fair Credit Reporting Act needs to be rewritten. Most agencies must keep a list of anyone who looks at a file. With few exceptions, one agency cannot transfer information about someone to another agency.

Internet Issues Reacting to concerns raised across the country, the Federal Trade Commission oversees business compliance with federal law. The FTC began hearings on Internet privacy beginning in June 1997. A large number of industry representatives testified before the hearing panelists that voluntary compliance was the best approach to handling privacy issues in the online world. Most panelists agreed that privacy will be to the information age what consumer product safety was to the industrial age.

Section 5 Assessment

Checking for Understanding

1. **Main Idea** Use a graphic organizer like the one below to list arguments for and against affirmative action programs.

For	Against

2. **Define** affirmative action, security classification system, transcript.
3. **Identify** reverse discrimination.
4. How does the Supreme Court apply the reasonableness standard in judging discrimination against women?
5. What is the key provision of the Freedom of Information Act?

Critical Thinking

6. **Checking Consistency** Review the lists of decisions barring distinctions based on gender and decisions allowing differences based on gender described on pages 415 and 416. Are there any decisions from the second list that you believe to be inconsistent with the first list? Explain.

Public Policy Find out about the Equal Credit Opportunity Act (1974). Find out the origins, the main purpose, and the basic provisions of both the Fair Credit Reporting Act and the Equal Credit Opportunity Act. Present your information in a chart.

Skills

Study and Writing

Outlining

Outlining may be used as a starting point for a writer. The writer begins with the rough shape of the material and gradually fills in the details in a logical manner. You may also use outlining as a method of note taking and organizing information you read.

Learning the Skill

There are two types of outlines—formal and informal. An informal outline is similar to taking notes. You write only words and phrases needed to remember ideas. Under the main ideas, jot down related but less important details. This kind of outline is useful for reviewing material before an exam.

A formal outline has a standard format. Main heads are labeled with Roman numerals, subheads with capital letters, and details with Arabic numerals. Each level should have at least two entries and should be indented from the level above. All entries use the same grammatical form, whether phrases or complete sentences.

When outlining written material, first read the material to identify the main ideas. Then identify the subheads. Place details supporting or explaining subheads under the appropriate head.

1920s passenger liner ▼

Practicing the Skill

Study this partial outline; then answer the questions that follow.

I. Immigrants and aliens
  A. Classifying aliens
    1. Resident alien
    2. Non-resident alien
    3. Refugee
    4. Illegal alien
  B. Rights of aliens
    1. Bill of Rights guarantees
    2. Cannot vote, travel freely
II. Immigration policy
  A. Growth of restrictions
    1. First federal immigration law, 1882
    2. Immigration restrictions
  B. National origins quotas
    1. Immigration Act of 1924
    2. Immigrants from northern and western Europe favored

1. Is this a formal or informal outline?
2. What are the two main topics in this outline?
3. If you were to add two facts about the Immigration Act of 1924, where would you place them?

Application Activity

Following the guidelines above, prepare an outline for Section 2 of Chapter 14.

The Glencoe Skillbuilder Interactive Workbook, Level 2 provides instruction and practice in key social studies skills.

Assessment and Activities

Self-Check Quiz Visit the *United States Government: Democracy in Action* Web site at gov.glencoe.com and click on ***Chapter 14–Self-Check Quizzes*** to prepare for the chapter test.

Reviewing Key Terms

Match the following terms with the descriptions below.

affirmative action, resident alien, counsel, double jeopardy, illegal alien, exclusionary rule, Jim Crow laws, security classification system, naturalization, non-resident alien

1. a person may not be retried for the same crime
2. the process of gaining citizenship
3. person from a foreign country who establishes permanent residence in the United States
4. person from a foreign country who expects to stay in the United States for a short, specified period of time
5. person who comes to the United States without legal permits
6. an attorney
7. keeps illegally obtained evidence out of court
8. laws that discriminated against African Americans
9. policy giving preference to minorities
10. how government documents are kept secret

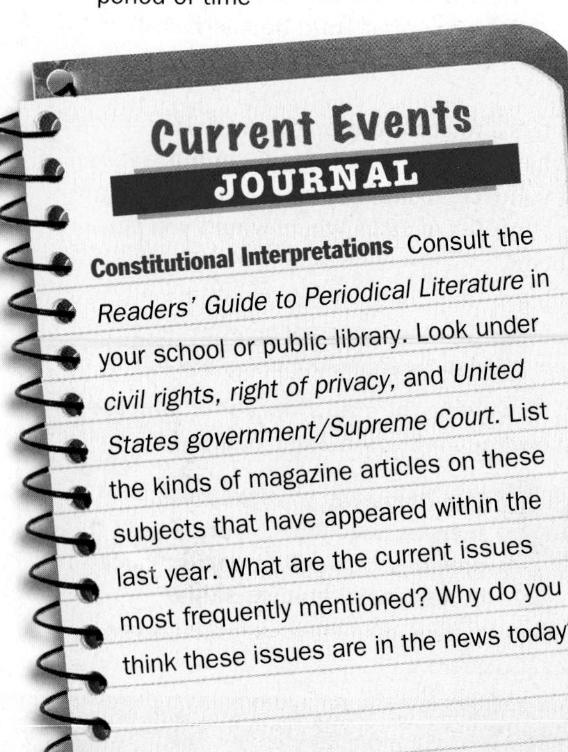

Recalling Facts

1. How did the Constitution address the issue of citizenship?
2. What is the significance of the *Dred Scott* case?
3. What is the difference between an immigrant and an alien?
4. What was the purpose of the national origins system that began in 1924?
5. What are the three basic sources of United States citizenship?
6. What items must be included in a legal search warrant?
7. What is the key protection described in the Fifth Amendment?
8. List the three *Miranda* rules.

Understanding Concepts

1. **Cultural Pluralism** Even after becoming American citizens, many former immigrants and refugees continue to hold on to their customs and traditions. Why do you suppose this is so?
2. **Constitutional Interpretations** How did the Fourteenth Amendment expand citizenship in the United States?
3. **Civil Rights** Why did the Court rule that wiretapping without a warrant was an illegal search and thus a violation of the Fourth Amendment?
4. **Public Policy** What were the provisions of the Family Educational Rights and Privacy Act?

Critical Thinking

1. **Describe** the circumstances in which collecting information about citizens and consumers conflicts with the individual's right to privacy.

2. **Making Generalizations** How did the Escobedo and Miranda cases extend protection against self-incrimination and forced confessions?
3. **Predicting Consequences** Use a graphic organizer like the one below to show what might happen if there were no formal procedures for becoming an American citizen.

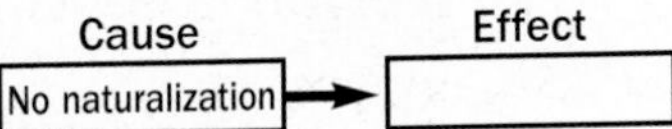

Skill Practice Activity

Outlining On a separate sheet of paper, add supporting details to the outline of Section 3 below.

Searches and Seizures

I. Fourth Amendment guarantees
   A. Exclusionary rule
   B. Fourth Amendment in high schools
   C. Wiretapping

Interpreting Political Cartoons Activity

1. Who are the people grouped on the left of the cartoon?
2. What is the meaning of the comment made by the person on the right?
3. How is "illegal immigrants" being defined by the cartoonist?

Cooperative Learning Activity

Citizenship Organize into groups of five to seven. Imagine that you have just received a new student named Ot in your class. The teacher tells you that Ot is a refugee and has a fairly good command of English. Ot has just come to the United States, and there are many things about American culture that he does not yet understand. Have each group member list two ways that the group could help him adjust to an American high school in particular and American culture in general. Then have the group combine their lists and come up with a step-by-step strategy to help Ot.

Technology Activity

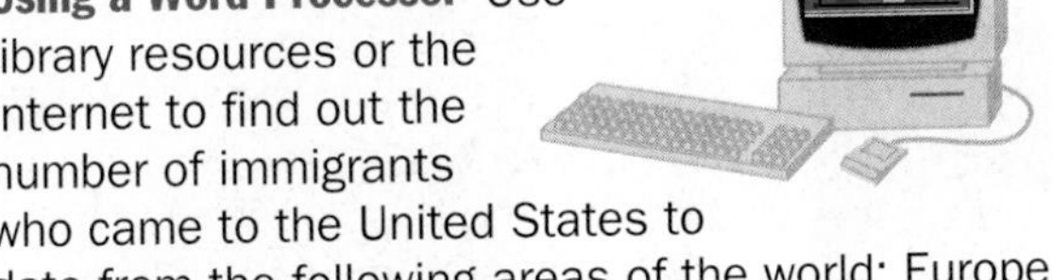

Using a Word Processor Use library resources or the Internet to find out the number of immigrants who came to the United States to date from the following areas of the world: Europe, Asia, Latin America, Africa, and Canada. Calculate what percentage of the total number of people who immigrated each group comprised in the following time spans: 1891–1910, 1911–1930, 1931–1950, 1951–1970, 1971–present. Use the graphic options of your word processor to create a circle graph for each time span, illustrating the percentage of each group of people from each area who immigrated to the United States.

Participating in Local Government

Find out about or visit one of the citizenship classes in your community. Find out what material is covered in courses designed to prepare immigrants for becoming citizens. What obstacles do immigrants have to overcome to be successful in these classes? Who sponsors and pays for these classes? Report your findings to the class.

Chapter 15

Law in America

Why It's Important

Law Made for You When you sign a contract, drive a car, get married, or have a conflict with your neighbor, the law is there to bring about justice. This chapter will explain how civil and criminal laws work to protect you and resolve conflicts in everyday life.

To learn more about civil and criminal law and how they affect you, view the ***Democracy in Action*** Chapter 15 video lesson:

The Law and You

GOVERNMENT Online

Chapter Overview Visit the *United States Government: Democracy in Action* Web site at gov.glencoe.com and click on ***Chapter 15–Overview*** to preview chapter information.

Section 1

Sources of American Law

Reader's Guide

Key Terms

law, constitutional law, statute, ordinance, statutory law, administrative law, common law, equity, due process, substantive due process, procedural due process, adversary system, presumed innocence

Find Out

- What are the four major sources of law in the United States?
- How do the key principles of the legal system provide justice for citizens?

Understanding Concepts

Civic Participation Why is understanding the law an important civic responsibility?

COVER STORY

Famous Lawmaker Dies

BABYLON, MESOPOTAMIA, 1750 B.C.

Hammurabi, who united Mesopotamia's tribes under one rule, is dead. As king, he will be best remembered for his decrees on many aspects of life. He decided disputes involving trade and business, family relations, criminal offenses such as theft and assault, and civil matters such as slavery and debt. In recent years, 282 of these rulings were recorded on stone slabs in the temple. Some requirements, such as an eye for an eye and trial by ordeal, merely continue common practices. Others, such as bans on blood feuds and private revenge, are considered advanced by some Babylonians.

Ancient tablet depicts King Hammurabi

◀ **County courthouse in Rutland, Vermont**

The set of rules and standards by which a society governs itself is known as **law.** Law defines the individual's rights and obligations and specifies the ways citizens and government relate to each other. Law serves several functions in our society. It is used to resolve conflict, protect rights, limit government, promote general welfare, set social goals, and control crime.

Laws affect nearly everything we do—the food we eat, how we drive our cars, how we buy and sell things, and even what happens when we are born and when we die. Laws establish "rules of the game" in business, in our personal lives, and in politics. They can also help us resolve and even avoid conflicts.

While so many laws might seem to limit our freedom, laws also guarantee our individual liberties. Indeed, the rule of law is the principle that both the government and its citizens should be subject to law, and that no person is above the law, regardless of his or her position. This principle is a hallmark of democratic societies because it means government decisions and actions should be made according to established laws rather than by arbitrary actions and decrees.

Early Systems of Law

The earliest known written laws or rules were based on practices in tribal societies. The most well-known of these was the **Code of Hammurabi,**[1] a collection of laws assembled by Hammurabi, king of Babylonia from 1792 to 1750 B.C. This code was made up of 282 legal cases that spelled out relationships among individuals as well as punishments in areas that we would now call property law, family law, civil law, and criminal law.

Another early set of written laws that has influenced our legal system is the Ten Commandments

See the following footnoted materials in the ***Reference Handbook:***

1. *The Code of Hammurabi*, pages 800-801.

found in the Bible. The Bible served as the source of law for the Hebrews living in ancient Palestine. According to Christians and Jews who believe in the Old Testament, Moses received the Commandments from God on Mount Sinai in the thirteenth century B.C. The Commandments proclaim moral rules instructing people on how they should behave toward one another. The Commandment "Thou shalt not steal" is reflected in our laws today.

Our Legal Heritage

The laws that govern our lives and protect our rights are commonly known as constitutional law, statutory law, administrative law, common law, and equity. These laws come from several sources including state and federal constitutions, lawmaking bodies, administrative agencies, and court decisions.

Constitutional Law The Constitution is the most fundamental and important source of law in the United States. The Constitution establishes our country as a representative democracy, outlines the structure of our government, and sets forth our basic rights. The Constitution applies to all Americans and is the supreme law of the land—the standard against which all other laws are judged. Both federal and state courts apply or use provisions of the U.S. Constitution to make decisions.

State constitutions were the first written constitutions in the United States. Eleven of the original 13 states adopted written constitutions between 1776 and 1780. These constitutions spell out governmental arrangements in the states and the rights of citizens that are protected from interference by state governments. Because state constitutions are easier to amend than the United States Constitution, they reflect shifting popular concerns more readily. State constitutions sometimes set forth rights not mentioned in the U.S. Constitution.

State courts decide cases involving state constitutions. State court systems usually adopt the U.S. Supreme Court's rulings on the U.S. Constitution as a guide to interpreting their own constitutions, but they do not have to. Some state courts have ruled that their constitutions protect the right to privacy even though the U.S. Constitution does not. State court rulings on their own constitutions may be appealed to the U.S. Supreme Court if it is claimed that the state constitution or state court violates the U.S. Constitution. In the end, the U.S. Supreme Court has the final word on the meaning of the U.S. Constitution.

The term **constitutional law** applies to that branch of the law dealing with the formation, construction, and interpretation of constitutions. For the most part, cases involving constitutional law decide the limits of the government's power and the rights of the individual. Day-to-day decisions by the president, Congress, and other public officials often involve interpreting the meaning of the Constitution and thus can shape constitutional law. However, the decisions of courts, especially the U.S. Supreme Court, are the main sources of information about the meaning and interpretation of the U.S. Constitution and state constitutions. Constitutional law cases may deal either with civil law or criminal law.

Virginia's Constitutional Convention

State Constitutions Artist George Catlin depicted the delegates involved in creating Virginia's constitution in 1829. Catlin titled his painting *Last Meeting of the Giants.* ***Why is a constitution necessary at the state level?***

Statutory Law Another source of American law is statutory law. A **statute** is a law written by a legislative branch of government. The United States Congress, state legislatures, and local legislative bodies write thousands of these laws. Statutes passed by city councils are called **ordinances.**

Statutes may limit citizens' behavior when, for instance, they set speed limits, specify rules for inspecting food products, or set the minimum age to obtain a work permit. Statutes are also the source of many of the rights and benefits we take for granted, such as the right to get a Social Security check, to enter a veterans' hospital, to get a driver's license, to check your credit record, or return merchandise you have bought but do not like.

Most decisions of federal courts deal with statutory law, and many of the cases decided by the Supreme Court are devoted to interpreting statutory laws. In most of these cases, the courts determine what a statute means or whether it deprives a person of a constitutional right when it is carried out.

Statutory law is sometimes called "Roman law" because it is based on an approach to making laws derived from the ancient Romans. The plebeians, or the common people, of Rome first demanded that the laws of Rome be written down so that everyone might know and understand them. In about 450 B.C. the government of Rome published its laws on 12 tablets. Over the next thousand years, as the Roman Empire spread across Europe to Egypt, Roman leaders kept adding to these written codes until Roman law became very complex. In the A.D. 530s the Roman emperor Justinian had scholars reorganize and simplify all the laws into a final Roman legal code called the **Justinian Code.**

This codification of all its written laws was one of Rome's greatest contributions to civilization. Many countries today have legal systems based on written codes of law that contain ideas from the Justinian Code. The most important of these was the Napoleonic Code, created in 1804 by the French emperor Napoleon Bonaparte. Napoleon's updated version of the Justinian Code is still in force in France today and became the model for the legal systems of many other European countries, parts of Africa, most of Latin America, and of Japan. In addition, both the state of Louisiana and the Canadian province of Quebec—once French colonies—have a system of laws based on the Napoleonic Code.

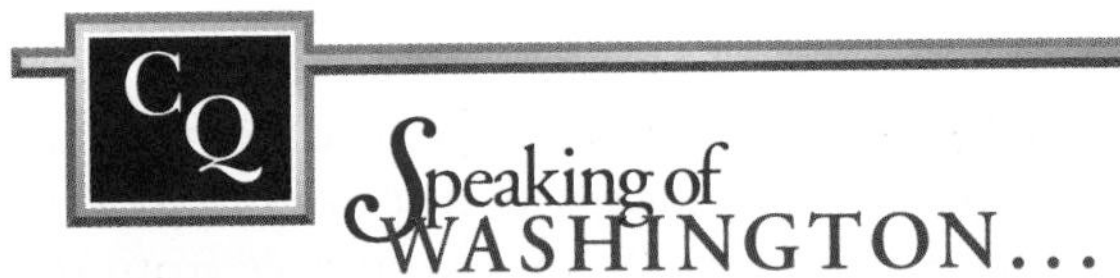

By Order of the President **Martial law, or military rule, has been imposed a few times, but only in certain parts of the country. President Abraham Lincoln declared martial law in several areas during the Civil War, but no president has declared it since that time. Other officials have imposed it in specific locales with presidential approval, though. After the Japanese attacked Pearl Harbor in 1941, for example, the territorial governor proclaimed martial law in Hawaii with President Franklin Roosevelt's approval.**

Administrative Law A significant feature of local, state, and national government in America today is the large number of administrative agencies that run government programs and provide services. These agencies range in size and power from the huge Social Security Administration to the Food and Nutrition Service. **Administrative law** spells out the authority and procedures to be followed by these agencies, as well as the rules and regulations issued by such agencies. Since the Great Depression in the 1930s, law in the United States has been increasingly made through administrative agencies. One legal scholar has stated, "Law promulgated by the agencies now occupies an importance equal to statutory law in regulating every aspect of American society."

Many administrative law cases deal with problems of fairness and due process because most administrative agencies either regulate people's behavior, or provide or deny government benefits such as welfare payments or medical insurance. Thus, disputes constantly arise over whether agencies have acted fairly and given people the opportunity to present facts relevant to their case.

Common Law The single most important basis of the American legal system is the **common law.** This is law made by judges in the process of resolving individual cases. Because it derives from the decisions of judges in settling cases, common law is also called case law.

Common law originated in England. In the eleventh century English monarchs sent judges across the land to hold trials and administer the law. Judges began to record the facts of the cases and their decisions in yearbooks. Over time, judges began to compare the facts and rulings from earlier cases to new cases. When a new case was similar to cases already decided and in the books, the judges followed the earlier ruling, or **precedent.** This was the origin of *stare decisis* (literally, "let the decision stand"), a basic principle used by the U.S. Supreme Court today. In cases that were unique, judges would make their own rulings based on common sense and prevailing customs. These common-law decisions would then become precedents for cases that would follow.

Common Law in America The English colonists brought common law with them to America. By 1776 common law was being used throughout the American colonies along with law created there. After the Revolution, Americans had to choose what parts of English law would remain in force. While many states attempted to resist the influence of English law, common law remained in force throughout the nation. For example, the Delaware constitution of 1776 provided that "The common law of England as well as so much of the statute law. . . shall remain in force." State constitutions today and the federal Constitution are worded in legal terms reflecting English common law. The practice of common law continues across the United States today, except in Louisiana, where legal procedures based on the Napoleonic Code persist.

Equity **Equity** is a system of rules by which disputes are resolved on the grounds of fairness. The principle of equity developed in medieval times as a rival to common law. The office of a royal official, the chancellor, became a court. This court, which represented the king's conscience, developed the theory of equity. Its remedies were much different from those of common law. An equity court could require an action beyond the payment of money or even stop a wrong before it occurred. For example, an equity court could issue an injunction (see page 433) to prevent an action such as a neighbor building a fence across your property. In nineteenth-century America equity and common law merged. Today a single court can administer both systems.

THE LAW *and You*

Choosing a Lawyer

Being sued or having to sign a document you do not completely understand—these are just two reasons that you might need a lawyer. Some lawyers are general practitioners. Others specialize in certain areas, such as personal injury, divorce, or criminal law. Look for an attorney who handles the kind of problem you have.

The best way to find a lawyer is to talk with relatives and friends who have used lawyers. If their legal problems were similar to yours, see if they would recommend their lawyer. Another good source is the *Martindale-Hubbell Law Directory,* found in every courthouse library. This book lists nearly every lawyer in the United States by specialty. Your county bar association can also refer you to a competent attorney. The attorney referral services listed in the Yellow Pages are usually businesses that some attorneys pay for referrals.

If possible, talk with two or more attorneys before hiring your attorney. Many offer a first meeting for free.

Searching an online law directory

Make a List Create an imaginary situation which would require you to hire a lawyer. Prepare a list of topics and questions that you would want to discuss during your first meeting with a lawyer.

A Constitutional Choice

Constitutional Rights
Parents and students are guaranteed a choice between public and private schools because of substantive due process. Here a student completes an art class project at Tabor Academy, a private school in Marion, Massachusetts. ***How is substantive due process different from procedural due process?***

Legal System Principles

Four basic principles underlie the operation of both federal and state courts and the actions of the thousands of men and women who serve in the American legal system. These principles include equal justice under the law, due process of law, the adversary system of justice, and the presumption of innocence.

Equal Justice Under the Law The phrase **"equal justice under the law"** refers to the goal of the American court system to treat all persons alike. It means that every person, regardless of wealth, social status, ethnic group, gender, or age, is entitled to the full protection of the law. The equal justice principle grants all Americans rights, such as the right to a trial by a jury of one's peers. The Fifth through the Eighth Amendments to the Constitution spell out these specific guarantees.

Due Process of Law Closely related to the principle of equal justice is the principle of due process of law. **Due process** has both a substantive part and a procedural part. **Substantive due process** is a kind of shorthand for certain rights, some that are specified in the Constitution (like free speech) and some that are not specified (like the right of privacy in making personal decisions). The Fifth and Fourteenth Amendments contain the due process principle.

Examples of laws that the Supreme Court has found to violate substantive due process include: (1) a law that limits dwellings to single families, thus preventing grandparents from living with their grandchildren; (2) a school board regulation that prevents a female teacher from returning to work sooner than three months after the birth of her child; and (3) a law that requires all children to attend public schools and does not permit them to attend private schools.

Cases about the way a law is administered involve **procedural due process.** Procedural due process prohibits arbitrary enforcement of the law. It also provides safeguards intended to ensure that constitutional and statutory rights are protected by law enforcement. At the most basic level, procedural due process requires (1) notice to a person

Protecting all Americans This police officer reads a suspect his rights. Proper procedures must be followed when police arrest and the courts try suspected offenders. ***Why should the rights of people who may be criminals be protected?***

that he or she has done something wrong and that the government intends to take specific action that will affect the person, and (2) giving the affected person the right to respond or be heard concerning the accusation of wrongdoing.

The Adversary System American courts operate according to the adversary system of justice. Under the current **adversary system,** the courtroom is a kind of arena in which lawyers for the opposing sides try to present their strongest cases. The lawyer for each side is generally expected to do all that is legally permissible to advance the cause of his or her client. The judge in the court has an impartial role and should be as fair to both sides as possible, especially in implementing the essence of the law.

Some observers of the judicial system have attacked the adversary system. They have claimed that it encourages lawyers to ignore evidence not favorable to their sides and to be more concerned about victory than justice. Supporters of the adversary system, on the other hand, maintain that the system is the best way to bring out the facts of a case.

Presumption of Innocence In the United States system of justice, the government's police power is balanced against the presumption that a person, although accused, is innocent until proven guilty. The notion of **presumed innocence** is not mentioned in the Constitution, but it is deeply rooted in the English legal heritage. The burden of proving an accusation against a defendant falls on the prosecution. The defendant does not have to prove his or her innocence. Unless the prosecution succeeds in proving the accusation, the court must declare the defendant not guilty.

Section 1 Assessment

Checking for Understanding

1. **Main Idea** In a graphic organizer, identify the major sources of American law and the key principles of the American legal system.

   sources — American Law — principles

2. **Define** law, constitutional law, statute, ordinance, statutory law, administrative law, common law, equity, due process, substantive due process, procedural due process, adversary system, presumed innocence.
3. **Identify** Code of Hammurabi, Justinian Code, precedent, "equal justice under the law."

Critical Thinking

4. **Identifying Alternatives** Permitting rental agencies to refuse to rent apartments to families with children would violate what kind of due process?

Civic Participation Laws affect nearly everything people do. Laws change to meet the needs of the times. Work with a partner to brainstorm laws that might be needed to meet future challenges. Create and present a skit showing a situation that would require a new law.

Thompson v. *Oklahoma,* 1988

Protesting the death penalty

Nearly every state treats people under the age of 16 as minors. Minors, for instance, cannot drive or get married without their parents' consent, nor can they vote or serve on a jury. Can a person convicted of committing murder when he was 15 years old be given the death penalty? The Court answered this question in the case of Thompson *v.* Oklahoma.

Background of the Case

In January 1983, 15-year-old William Wayne Thompson, along with three older persons, actively participated in the brutal murder of his former brother-in-law. Because Thompson was a "child" under Oklahoma law, the district attorney filed a petition requesting that Thompson be tried as an adult. Each of the four was found guilty, and sentenced to death. Thompson's sentence was appealed on the grounds that his execution would violate the Eighth Amendment's ban on "cruel and unusual punishments" because he was only 15 years old at the time of his offense. An appeals court upheld the conviction and sentence.

The Constitutional Issue

Because the Constitution provides no clear guidance as to the meaning of "cruel and unusual punishments" for minors, the Court would interpret the meaning of the Constitution in terms of whether it thought American society would consider such punishment acceptable to standards of common decency. Would modern society approve of the death penalty for a minor who committed murder?

The Court found that 14 states did not authorize capital punishment at all, and 19 others that approved the death penalty, including Oklahoma, set no minimum age. However, there were 18 states that had set a minimum age of 16 in death penalty cases. Further, the American Bar Association had formally expressed its opposition to the death penalty for minors.

The Court also considered the verdicts of juries in relevant cases. The justices found that about 18 to 20 people under the age of 16 had been executed in the United States up to 1948, but that no such executions had taken place since that time. In a recent period, from 1982 to 1986, 1,393 persons had been sentenced to death, but only 5 were younger than 16 at the time of their offense.

Debating the Case

Questions to Consider

1. Does the evidence suggest that Americans accept the death penalty for minors?
2. Are the differences between minors and older persons significant enough to justify holding minors to a different legal standard than adults?
3. Does the constitutional ban on "cruel and unusual punishments" prohibit the death penalty for people under age 16 at the time of their crime?

You Be the Judge

The question confronting the Court was "whether the youth of the defendant . . . is a sufficient reason for denying the State the power to sentence him to death." Did the evidence from existing state laws, the behavior of juries toward minors, and the very nature of childhood provide sufficient reason to sentence people to death for crimes they committed as minors?

Section 2

Civil Law

Reader's Guide

Key Terms

civil law, contract, expressed contract, implied contract, real property, personal property, mortgage, tort, plaintiff, defendant, injunction, complaint, summons, answer, discovery, mediation, affidavit

Find Out

- What are the various types of civil law that affect people today?
- What are the steps in a civil law case?

Understanding Concepts

Political Processes How does the legal system attempt to provide justice for all?

COVER STORY

Record Holder Sues, Wins Millions

COLUMBUS, OHIO, DECEMBER 14, 1992

Federal judge Joseph Kinneary has ordered the International Amateur Athletic Federation to pay local runner Butch Reynolds nearly $28 million. Reynolds, who holds the world record at 400 meters, sued the IAAF after it suspended him from competition in 1990, alleging steroid use. When a court order allowed Reynolds to compete in the Olympic trials last June, the IAAF responded by extending his suspension. Kinneary ruled that the organization acted with malice toward Reynolds.

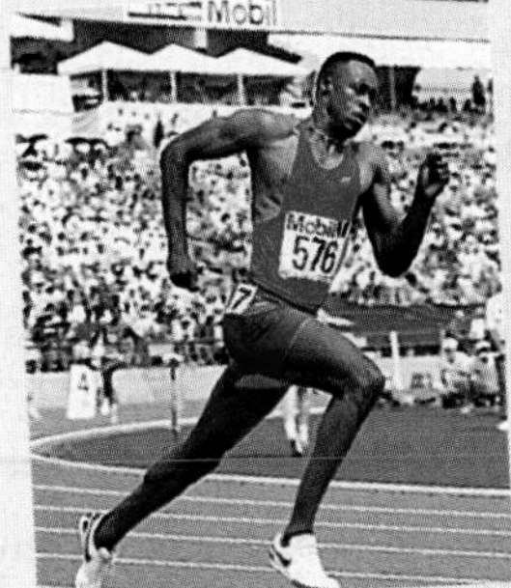

Butch Reynolds

Civil law concerns disputes among two or more individuals or between individuals and the government. Civil cases arise because one party believes it has suffered an injury at the hands of another party or wants to prevent a harmful action from taking place.

Types of Civil Law

Civil law touches nearly every phase of daily life—from buying a house to getting married. About 90 percent of the cases heard in state courts concern civil laws. Four of the most important branches, or types, of civil law deal with contracts, property, family relations, and civil wrongs causing physical injury or injury to property, called torts.

Contracts A contract is a set of voluntary promises, enforceable by the law, between parties who agree to do or not do something. We enter into contracts all the time: when we join a health club, buy a car with credit, get married, or agree to do a job for someone. In an expressed contract the terms are specifically stated by the parties, usually in writing. An implied contract is one in which the terms are not expressly stated but can be inferred from the actions of the people involved and the circumstances.

A valid contract has several characteristics. All parties to a contract must be mentally competent and in most cases must be legal age adults. The contract cannot involve doing or selling anything illegal. The contract's elements must include an offer, acceptance, and in most cases a consideration.

An **offer** is a promise that something will or will not happen. For instance, the auto shop says it will repair your smashed bumper for $500. One party to a contract must then accept the offer made by the other party. If you agree in writing or orally to have the bumper fixed, this constitutes the **acceptance.** Finally, the parties must give some type of **consideration.** They must give, exchange, perform, or promise each other something of value, such as a refinished bumper in return for $500. A very large number of civil suits involve disagreements over contracts.

Property Law An important type of civil law deals with the use and ownership of property. The ability of private individuals to own, buy, and sell property is one feature of a democratic society. **Real property** has been defined by the courts to be land and whatever is attached to or growing on it, such as houses and trees. **Personal property** includes movable things like clothes or jewelry as well as intangible items like stocks, bonds, copyrights, or patents.

Many kinds of legal disputes arise over using, owning, buying, and selling property. Owners of buildings, for example, may fail to repair them or may try to discriminate against others when renting or selling. For many Americans, buying a house is the biggest financial investment they will ever make. This usually involves obtaining a **mortgage**—a loan to pay for the house—as well as a deed, title, and insurance. Both state governments and the federal government have passed many laws dealing with real property. For example, the federal **Fair Housing Act** aims to protect people against discrimination on the basis of race, religion, color, national origin, or gender when they try to buy the home they want or obtain a loan.

Family Law Another branch of civil law deals with the relationships among family members. This includes marriage, divorce, and parent-child relationships, including child custody issues.

In seventeenth-century England family law was strongly influenced by religious law. In the United States there was no established state religion, so family law developed outside the church. Each state developed its individual family law. For example, in America marriage became a civil contract. Two forms of marriage existed in nineteenth-century America—the civil ceremony and the common-law marriage. Because many people lived outside the cities and there was a shortage of clergy, many marriages were simple makeshift ceremonies without official sanction. The law nevertheless tended to recognize these common-law marriages as valid.

Today marriage is a civil contract entered into by both parties. Divorce legally ends a marriage and leaves both parties free to remarry. Legal disputes involving such domestic relations account

Buying a Home

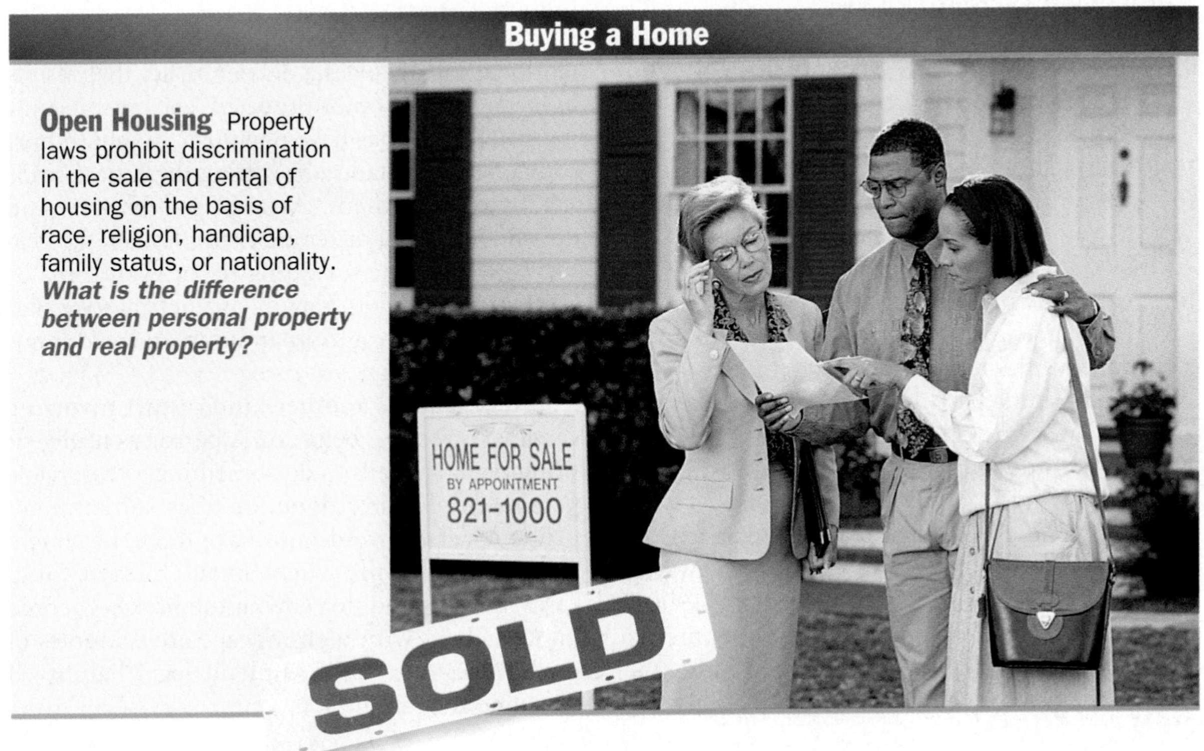

Open Housing Property laws prohibit discrimination in the sale and rental of housing on the basis of race, religion, handicap, family status, or nationality. ***What is the difference between personal property and real property?***

A Heritage of Legal Codes

◀ **Past** A medieval English chancellor followed law codes which might have permitted a creditor to seize a debtor's property and have the person imprisoned for failure to pay a debt.

Present Today judges, like Raul Gonzales in Austin, Texas, also follow law codes; however, punishments for crimes differ from those of earlier times.

▼

Laws Through the Ages
How might the crime of failure to pay a debt be dealt with today?

for a large number of civil cases in state courts. Family law is changing rapidly as the meaning of family changes in American society.

Torts or Civil Wrongs A **tort** is any wrongful act, other than breach of contract, for which the injured party has the right to sue for damages in a civil court. Those responsible for damage caused to someone's property, such as breaking a window, or for injury to someone caused by negligence, such as failing to clear ice from the sidewalk, may be sued by the party suffering the damage or injury. Further, the wronged party may sometimes seek punitive damages—additional money—as a way to punish the party causing the injury.

Tort law was an insignificant branch of law before the Industrial Revolution. Almost every leading case in the late 1800s was connected with railroads. Courts hesitated to award damages to injured workers because they feared such awards would hurt business enterprises. By the 1900s, however, the state and federal governments began to issue safety regulations for industry, and courts established a doctrine of liability for industrial hazards. Today, some would argue that courts are more likely to favor workers claiming injury.

There are two major categories of torts. An intentional tort involves a deliberate act that results in harm to a person or property. The person committing the act may have obviously sought to hurt someone, for instance, by hitting them or spreading lies about them. Assault and battery and defamation of character are examples. Or, the person may be liable for doing harm even if his or her actions, such as playing a practical joke that unintentionally results in an injury, seemed innocent at the time.

Negligence is another kind of tort involving careless or reckless behavior. A person is negligent when he or she fails to do something a reasonable person would have done, or does something a prudent person would not have done. Leaving a sharp kitchen knife where small children could easily reach it and not having the brakes checked on an old car with high mileage are examples of negligence that could result in legal liability if someone is injured.

Steps in a Civil Case

Civil cases are called lawsuits. The **plaintiff** is the person who brings charges in a lawsuit, called the complaint. The person against whom the suit is brought is the **defendant.** The plaintiff in a civil suit usually seeks damages, an award of money from the defendant. If the court decides in favor of the plaintiff, the defendant must pay the damages to the plaintiff. Usually the defendant is also required to pay court costs. If the court decides in favor of the defendant, the plaintiff must pay all the court costs and of course receives nothing from the defendant.

In some lawsuits involving equity, the plaintiff may ask the court to issue an **injunction,** a court order that forbids a defendant to take or continue a certain action. For example, suppose a company plans to build a factory in the middle of a residential area. Citizens believe that the factory would pollute the air. They take the factory owner to court and argue that residents would suffer serious health problems if the factory is constructed. If the citizens win this suit in equity, the judge issues an injunction ordering the company not to build its factory.

Lawsuits are the ultimate method to settle such disputes. However, lawsuits can be time-consuming and expensive with no guarantee that the winner will readily collect any damages that may have been awarded. Lawsuits follow certain steps.

Hiring a Lawyer To start a lawsuit, a person almost always needs a lawyer. Lawyers may work for a contingency fee, typically one-fifth to one-half of the total money won in the lawsuit, or they will work for an hourly fee. If the plaintiff and attorney agree to a contingency fee, no fee is paid if the plaintiff loses the case. The plaintiff, however, pays for the costs of the suit such as copying charges, or fees for investigators or special experts.

Filing the Complaint Most suits go to state courts unless they involve the Constitution or a federal statute or regulation. The plaintiff sets forth the charges against the defendant in a **complaint,** a legal document filed with the court that has jurisdiction over the problem. The complaint tells the defendant what is at issue—that is, what the defendant allegedly did wrong—so that a defense can be mounted. The defendant receives a **summons,** an official notice of the lawsuit that includes the date, time, and place of the initial court appearance. The defendant's lawyer may file a motion to dismiss, asking the court to end the suit. If the court denies this motion, the defendant must then file an **answer,** or formal response to the charges in the complaint, within a certain time, usually 10 to 60 days. Failure to answer means victory by default for the plaintiff. The defendant may also respond by filing a counterclaim, or lawsuit against the plaintiff in which the defendant asserts that the plaintiff also did something wrong.

Pretrial Discovery The next step, called **discovery,** occurs when both sides prepare for trial by checking facts and gathering evidence to support their case. The attorneys and private investigators in major cases may interview witnesses, examine records and photos, and file motions against the other side. This phase can be very expensive as well as time-consuming. In complicated cases discovery may take months or even years.

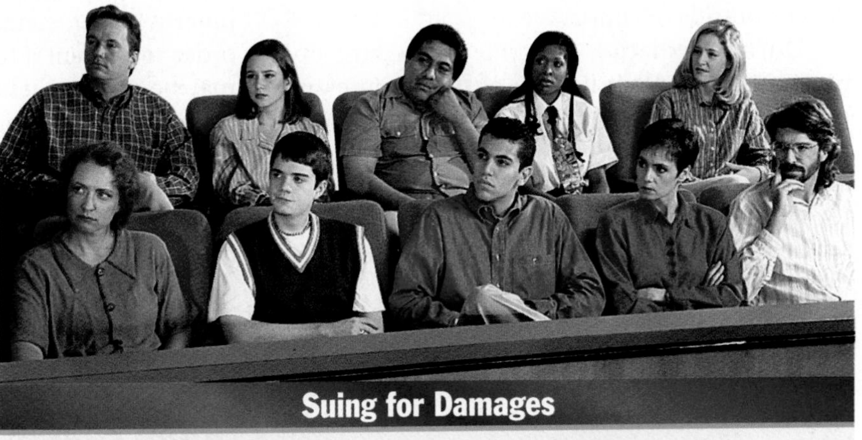

Lawsuits in America Lawsuits involving major sums of money often go to civil court where a jury hears them. ***Do you think that justice would be better served by relying more or less on juries? Explain your answer.***

America's Legal Heritage

◀ **Past** American colonists continued to follow the British traditions of common law in their early courts.

Present Modern civil courts still use common-law principles in all states except Louisiana. ▼

Civil Courtrooms
Why do you think many common-law principles are still in effect today?

Resolution Without Trial Ninety percent of all civil lawsuits are settled before trial through one of several techniques. Either party in a lawsuit may propose a settlement at any time, including during the trial. This often happens during the discovery phase as costs mount and people become more willing to compromise. Judges may encourage people to settle by calling a pretrial conference where the parties talk things over. The court may also require or encourage the parties to settle their dispute outside of court.

During mediation each side is given the opportunity to explain its side of the dispute and must listen to the other side. A trained mediator conducts the sessions by acting as a neutral party and promoting open communication. The mediator does not decide the issue; the parties themselves do that with the mediator's help. The parties may also agree to submit their dispute to arbitration. This process is conducted by a professional arbitrator who acts somewhat like a judge by reviewing evidence and deciding how the problem will be settled. The arbitrator's decision is usually binding on all parties.

Trial If all else fails, lawsuits eventually go to trial, although the courts are so crowded this may take years. Civil trials, like criminal trials, may be heard by a judge only or by a jury of 6 to 12 people. The plaintiff presents its side first, followed by the defendant. Both sides then summarize their cases, and the judge or jury renders a verdict.

The Award Because of the merging of common law and equity, courts have many options in resolving cases, and judges have more power to adjust decisions made by juries. When the plaintiff wins, the court awards damages, injunctive relief, or both. Injunctive relief, stemming from equity, is a court order to prevent a future act. The damages award may be more or less than the plaintiff requested. Occasionally the judge modifies a jury's award if it seems out of line. Even after the award, the case may not be over. The loser may appeal or refuse to pay damages. If the defendant refuses to pay, the plaintiff must get a court order to enforce the payment of damages in one of several ways, such as taking money out of the defendant's paycheck or seizing and selling the defendant's assets.

Small Claims Court

Most states today have provided an alternative to the lengthy trial process by creating **small claims courts.** These courts hear civil cases commonly dealing with collecting small debts, property damage, landlord-tenant disputes, small business problems, and the like. Cases are usually heard by a judge and involve claims ranging up to a maximum of $1,000 to $5,000, depending on the state. Plaintiffs with larger claims can waive the amount of their claim that exceeds the dollar limit and still use these courts, but they cannot recover more than the limit.

Most of these courts have simple forms to complete in order to file a complaint. The forms ask for the defendant's name and address, a description of the dispute, and the amount of damages requested. The defendant is given two to four weeks to respond, and a date for the case is set. No lawyers are required because the idea is to provide ordinary people with a simple and inexpensive means of resolving their disputes. These courts usually charge a $10 to $50 filing fee. Plaintiffs bring evidence of their claim to court and are asked to explain their case in nonlegal terms. The evidence may include testimony from witnesses or their **affidavits**, written statements to verify or prove statements of fact that have been signed by the witness under oath before a magistrate or notary.

Minor Lawsuits Small claims courts, such as this one, conduct proceedings in everyday language and avoid technical legal terms. Almost every state has a court that handles small claims. ***What kinds of cases are heard in small claims courts?***

A judge typically hears the case and gives a decision that is legally binding. When a defendant fails to appear for the hearing, the plaintiff usually wins a default judgment for the amount of the claim. Winning is no guarantee of collecting. If the defendant is unwilling or unable to pay, the plaintiff obtains a written order from the court and then turns the order, along with other information about the defendant, over to the police or sheriff to enforce collection. Usually such judgments are good for five years and may be renewed.

Section 2 Assessment

Checking for Understanding

1. **Main Idea** Use a graphic organizer like the one to the right to show the five steps in a civil lawsuit.

2. **Define** civil law, contract, expressed contract, implied contract, real property, personal property, mortgage, tort, plaintiff, defendant, injunction, complaint, summons, answer, discovery, mediation, affidavit.
3. **Identify** Fair Housing Act.
4. What do four of the most important branches of civil law deal with?
5. What is the difference between intentional tort and negligence tort?

Critical Thinking

6. **Drawing Conclusions** In your opinion should mediation and arbitration be used to settle most civil lawsuits in order to prevent overburdening the court system?

Concepts IN ACTION

Political Processes Interview relatives or a neighbor who has been involved in a lawsuit or in small claims court. Find out the nature of the dispute and the way the lawsuit was resolved. Make sure you get the individual's permission before discussing the case in class. Present a brief documentary of your findings to the class.

Skills

Critical Thinking

Understanding Cause and Effect

Understanding cause and effect involves considering how or why an event occurred. A cause is the action or situation that produces an event. An effect is the result or consequence of an action or situation.

Learning the Skill

To identify cause-and-effect relationships, follow these steps:

1. Identify two or more events or developments.
2. Decide whether one event caused the other. Look for "clue words" such as *because, led to, brought about, produced, as a result of, so that, since,* and *therefore.*
3. Identify the outcomes of events.

Making a graphic organizer can aid in understanding cause and effect. Read the passage below and examine the graphic organizer that follows.

Concern has been raised over a disturbing issue—the chronic truancy of students who have been convicted of crimes. Truancy appears to have a direct impact on the crime rate. Many cities reported a drop of 50 percent or more in shoplifting, daytime burglaries and other crimes in the wake of crackdowns on truants. In addition, virtually all of the youths accused of violent crimes had poor school attendance, according to one judge.

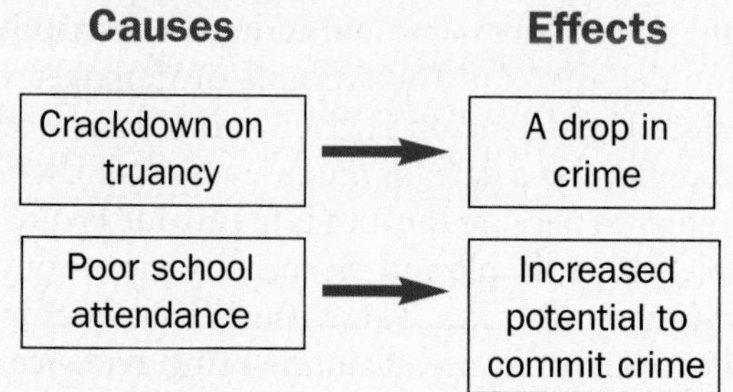

Practicing the Skill

On a separate piece of paper, make a cause-and-effect diagram for each statement below.

1. Under Hammurabi's code a son found guilty of striking his father had his hand cut off.
2. As Roman law became more complex, the task of interpreting it fell to a group of highly skilled lawyers called *juris prudentes.* Since that time, the science of law has been known as jurisprudence.
3. Congress and state legislatures pass thousands of laws every year, and as the number of laws grows, more and more aspects of life become regulated by government.

Application Activity

Read an account of a recent criminal or civil trial in your community as reported in a local newspaper. Determine at least one cause and one effect of that event. Show the cause-and-effect relationship in a chart.

The Glencoe Skillbuilder Interactive Workbook, Level 2 provides instruction and practice in key social studies skills.

Section 3

Criminal Law

Reader's Guide

Key Terms

criminal law, criminal justice system, petty offense, misdemeanor, felony, arrest warrant, grand jury, indictment, information, plea bargaining, jury, verdict, hung jury, sentence

Find Out

- How are the types of crime identified according to severity?
- What are the main steps in a criminal case?

Understanding Concepts

Political Processes How does the criminal justice system attempt to balance the rights of the accused and the rights of society?

COVER STORY

Pizza Thief Sentenced

REDONDO BEACH, CALIFORNIA, JANUARY 1995

California's mandatory sentencing law for repeat offenders, commonly known as the "three-strikes law," has attracted attention in the local case of Jerry Williams involving a stolen slice of pizza. Ordinarily, Williams's crime would be a misdemeanor. However, Williams has two previous felony convictions. Under California's three-strikes law, the judge was required to sentence Williams to 25 years to life in prison. Opponents of the three-strikes law point to the Williams case as an example of how such laws require sentences that may be out of proportion to the crime. To date, 13 other states have passed sentencing laws similar to California's.

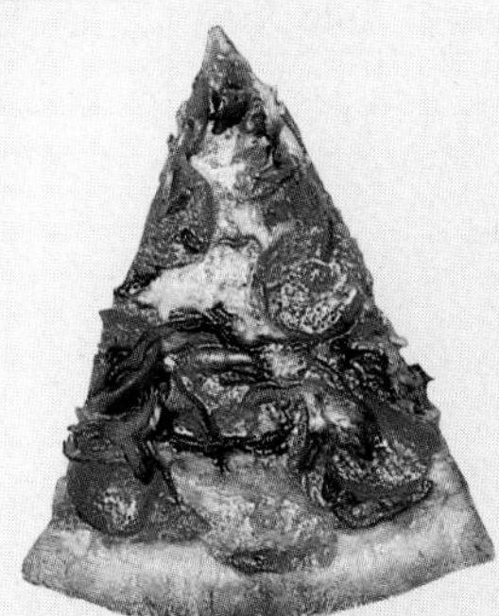

Stolen property

In criminal law cases, the government charges someone with a crime and is always the prosecution. The defendant is the person accused of a crime. A **crime** is an act that breaks a criminal law and causes injury or harm to people or to society in general. Not doing something may also be considered a crime. For example, in some states it is a crime for doctors who suspect that one of their young patients is being abused to fail to report the case to the authorities.

By far, most crimes committed in the United States break state laws and are tried in state courts. In recent years, however, there have been an increasing number of federal criminal cases. A federal criminal case might involve such crimes as tax fraud, counterfeiting, selling narcotics, mail fraud, kidnapping, and driving a stolen car across state lines. If a criminal court finds a person guilty, the judge may order the defendant to serve a term in prison, to pay a fine, or both.

The criminal justice system is the system of state and federal courts, judges, lawyers, police, and prisons that have the responsibility for enforcing criminal law. There is a separate juvenile justice system with special rules and procedures for handling cases dealing with juveniles, who in most states are people under the age of 18.

Types of Crime

State governments have jurisdiction over most crimes. Each state has its own penal code, written laws that spell out what constitutes a crime and the punishments that go with it. Crimes may be classified as petty offenses, misdemeanors, or felonies.

Petty Offenses Minor crimes such as parking illegally, littering, disturbing the peace, minor trespassing, and driving beyond the speed limit are petty offenses. When people commit a petty offense, they often receive a ticket, or citation, rather than being arrested.

If they do not challenge the citation, they may only have to pay a fine. Ignoring a petty offense, such as not paying a fine, may itself constitute a more serious crime.

Misdemeanors More serious crimes like vandalism, simple assault, stealing inexpensive items, writing bad checks for modest amounts, being drunk and disorderly, and so on are **misdemeanors.** A person found guilty of a misdemeanor may be fined or sentenced to jail, usually for one year or less.

Felonies Serious crimes such as burglary, kidnapping, arson, rape, fraud, forgery, manslaughter, or murder are considered **felonies.** These crimes are punishable by imprisonment for a year or more. In the case of murder, the punishment could be death. People convicted of felonies may also lose certain civil rights such as the right to vote, possess a firearm, or serve on a jury. Further, they may lose employment opportunities in some careers such as the military, law, teaching, or law enforcement. Misdemeanors may sometimes be treated as felonies. Drunk driving, for instance, is often a misdemeanor. However, if a person has been arrested for drunk driving and has been convicted of the same offense before, that person may be charged with a felony.

Steps in Criminal Cases

There are several steps which nearly every criminal case follows, although the exact procedures often vary from state to state. At each step defendants are entitled to the protections of due process guaranteed in the Bill of Rights. The prosecutor, a government lawyer with the responsibility for bringing and proving criminal charges against a defendant, must prove beyond a reasonable doubt to a judge or jury that the defendant violated the law.

Investigation and Arrest Criminal cases may begin when police believe a crime has been committed and start an investigation to gather enough evidence to convince a judge to give them a warrant to arrest someone. A valid **arrest warrant**

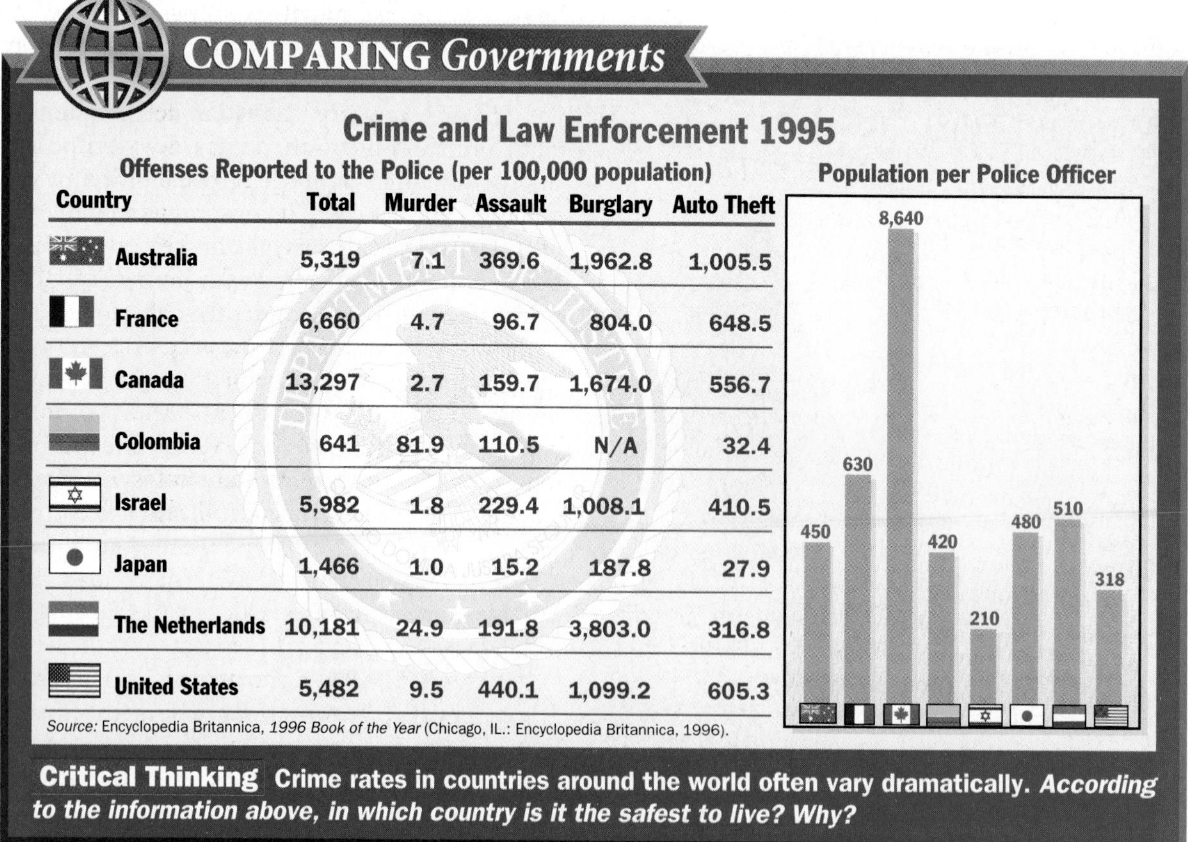

COMPARING *Governments*

Crime and Law Enforcement 1995

Country	Total	Murder	Assault	Burglary	Auto Theft
	Offenses Reported to the Police (per 100,000 population)				
Australia	5,319	7.1	369.6	1,962.8	1,005.5
France	6,660	4.7	96.7	804.0	648.5
Canada	13,297	2.7	159.7	1,674.0	556.7
Colombia	641	81.9	110.5	N/A	32.4
Israel	5,982	1.8	229.4	1,008.1	410.5
Japan	1,466	1.0	15.2	187.8	27.9
The Netherlands	10,181	24.9	191.8	3,803.0	316.8
United States	5,482	9.5	440.1	1,099.2	605.3

Source: Encyclopedia Britannica, *1996 Book of the Year* (Chicago, IL.: Encyclopedia Britannica, 1996).

Critical Thinking Crime rates in countries around the world often vary dramatically. *According to the information above, in which country is it the safest to live? Why?*

Driving Under the Influence of Alcohol

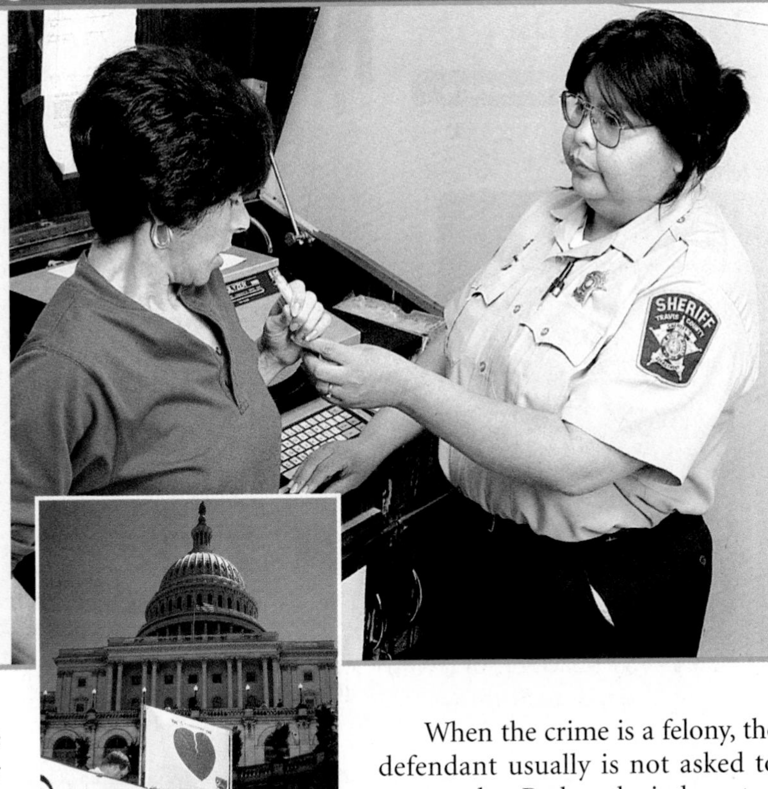

Rights on the Road Drunk driving is a serious national problem. Here a police officer administers a test to determine the alcohol content of a breath sample. Mothers Against Drunk Driving, or MADD, is an interest group that encourages the public to become actively involved in the fight against drunk driving. ***Do you think that it is constitutional for a police officer to test someone for drunk driving?***

MADD display in front of the Capitol ▶

must list the suspect's name and the alleged crime. An arrest may occur without a warrant if the police catch someone in the act of committing a crime or, in some cases, if they have reasonable suspicion to believe that a person has broken the law.

The arrested person is taken to a police station where the charges are recorded or "booked." At this point the suspect may be fingerprinted, photographed, or put in a lineup to be identified by witnesses. Police may (often with a court order) administer a blood test, or take a handwriting sample. These procedures do not violate a person's constitutional rights, and lawyers do not have to be present. However, suspects have the right to ask for a lawyer before answering questions.

Initial Appearance Whenever someone is arrested, he or she must be brought before a judge as quickly as possible, usually within 24 hours, to be formally charged with a crime. The judge explains the charges to the defendant and reads the person's rights. If the charge is a misdemeanor, the defendant may plead guilty and the judge will decide on a penalty. If the defendant pleads not guilty, a date is set for a trial.

When the crime is a felony, the defendant usually is not asked to enter a plea. Rather, the judge sets a date for a preliminary hearing, and a process aimed at determining the merits of the charges begins. The judge may also decide whether the suspect will be released or "held to answer." A suspect may be released on his or her "own recognizance" if the judge thinks the person is a good risk to return to court for trial, or the judge may require bail, a sum of money the accused leaves with the court until he or she returns for trial. According to the Eighth Amendment,[1] the amount of bail required should fit the severity of the charge but cannot be excessive. In some cases bail may be denied, as when a defendant is likely to flee.

Preliminary Hearing or Grand Jury The next step in the criminal justice process also varies from state to state and between state and the federal governments. In federal courts and in many state courts, cases will go to a **grand jury**, a group of citizens who review the prosecution's allegations in

See the following footnoted materials in the ***Reference Handbook:***
1. *The Constitution,* pages 774–799.

We the People
Making a Difference
Mary Ellen Beaver

Mary Ellen Beaver has developed a reputation that has earned her the nickname "Fighting Grandma." Since 1969 Beaver has been working hard to help migrant workers understand their legal rights and improve their working conditions.

Beaver, now in her sixties, began her campaign after seeing groups of poorly dressed tomato pickers pass by her Pennsylvania farm each day in run-down buses. "I was outraged. They had no rights and were being exploited," she said.

Beaver collected clothing to take to the workers and organized a group of churches to help provide support. Her work helped to convince Pennsylvania legislators to pass the state's 1978 Farm Labor Law. She also created a support group for workers called Friends of Farm Workers. For her dedication and hard work, she earned a humanitarian medal from Pope John Paul in 1984.

Other states have benefited from Beaver's efforts. After leaving Pennsylvania she worked with the Neighborhood Legal Assistance Program in South Carolina to monitor migrant working conditions in the state's peach orchards. She also worked for the Florida Rural Legal Services, which provides legal support to Florida's migrant workers. In a lawsuit filed against a sugarcane company, Florida cane workers were awarded $51 million in back wages.

Beaver says the reward for her work is "when a worker comes up to me and says, 'No one has ever treated me with respect before.'"

order to determine if there is enough evidence to "hand up" an **indictment,** or formal criminal charge.

Grand jury hearings are conducted in secret and may consider types of evidence not allowed in trials. Defendants are not entitled to have an attorney represent them, although their attorney may be able to observe the proceedings.

If a preliminary hearing is used instead of a grand jury indictment, the prosecution presents its case to a judge. The defendant's lawyer may also present certain kinds of evidence on behalf of the defendant. If the judge believes there is a probable cause to believe the defendant committed the crime, the case moves to the next stage. If the judge decides the government does not have enough evidence, the charges are dropped. In some states the prosecuting attorney is allowed to try to obtain a grand jury indictment if a judge dismisses a case at the preliminary hearing.

Convening a grand jury is time-consuming and expensive. Today, in misdemeanor cases and in many felony cases, courts use an information rather than a grand jury indictment. An **information** is a sworn statement by the prosecution asserting that there is sufficient evidence to go to trial. Because grand juries most often follow the recommendations of the prosecution, many people believe that a grand jury is an unnecessary expense.

Plea Bargaining In about 90 percent of all criminal cases, the process comes to an end with a guilty plea because of **plea bargaining.** In this pretrial process the prosecutor, defense lawyer, and police work out an agreement through which the defendant pleads guilty to a lesser crime (or fewer crimes) in return for the government not

GOVERNMENT *Online*

Student Web Activity Visit the *United States Government: Democracy in Action* Web site at gov.glencoe.com and click on ***Chapter 15–Student Web Activities*** for an activity about criminal law.

prosecuting the more serious (or additional) crime with which the defendant was originally charged. In many courts the judge also participates in the process, especially if the length of the sentence is part of the negotiation. Plea bargaining has become very widely used as a way to handle the tremendous volume of criminal cases the courts must process every year.

Supporters of the process claim it is efficient and saves the state the cost of a trial in situations where guilt is obvious, as well as those where the government's case may have weaknesses. Some opponents argue "copping a plea" allows criminals to get off lightly. Others say that it encourages people to give up their rights to a fair trial. The Supreme Court in several decisions has approved the process as constitutional. In *Santobello* v. *New York*[1] (1971) the Court said plea bargaining was "an essential component of the administration of justice. Properly administered, it is to be encouraged."

See the following footnoted materials in the **Reference Handbook:**
1. *Santobello* v. *New York* case summary, page 765.

Arraignment and Pleas After the indictment by a grand jury, a preliminary hearing, or an information, the next step is the arraignment. At the **arraignment** the judge reads the formal charge against the defendant in an open courtroom. The defendant is represented by an attorney. During this process the judge may ask the defendant questions to ensure the person understands the charges and the process. A copy of the charges is given to the defendant, and the judge asks if the defendant pleads guilty or not guilty.

The defendant then enters one of four pleas responding to the charges. It could be: (1) not guilty, (2) not guilty by reason of insanity, (3) guilty or, in some states, (4) no contest *(nolo contendere)*. By pleading *nolo contendere* the defendant indirectly admits guilt by saying, "I will not contest it;" however, this does not go on the records as a guilty plea. If the defendant pleads guilty or *nolo contendere*, he or she has given up the right to a defense, the judge then decides a punishment, and the defendant may be sent to prison immediately. If the plea is not guilty, there must be a trial, and a court date is set.

Right to a Fair Trial

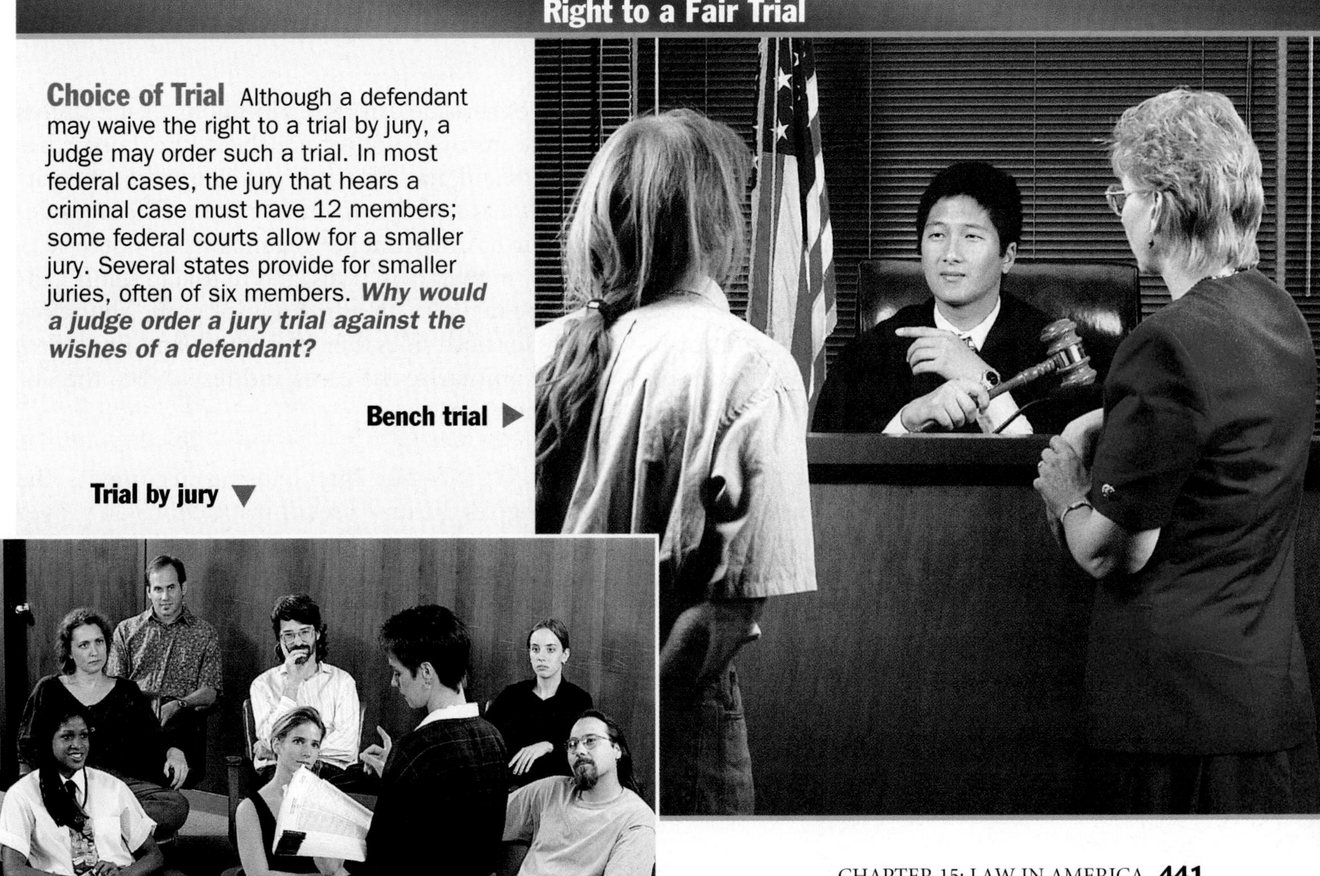

Choice of Trial Although a defendant may waive the right to a trial by jury, a judge may order such a trial. In most federal cases, the jury that hears a criminal case must have 12 members; some federal courts allow for a smaller jury. Several states provide for smaller juries, often of six members. ***Why would a judge order a jury trial against the wishes of a defendant?***

Bench trial ▶

Trial by jury ▼

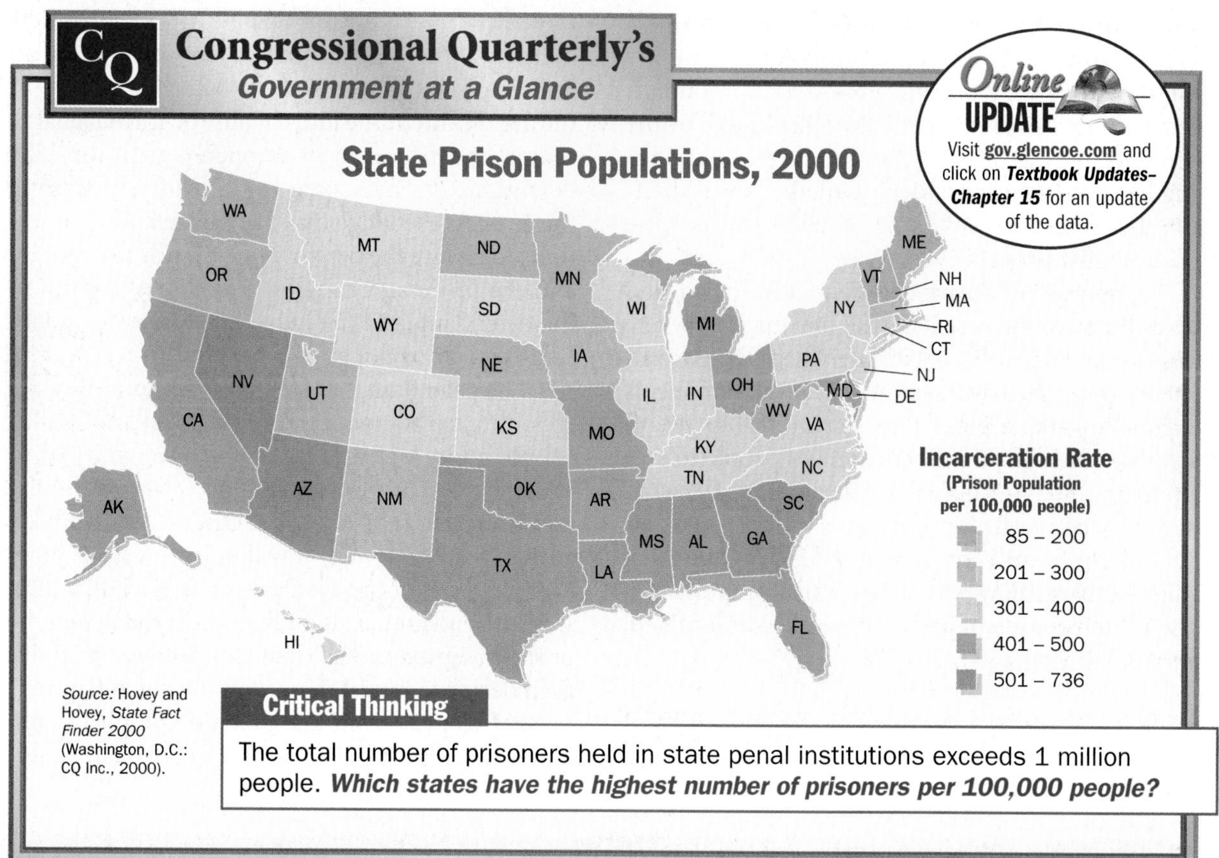

Source: Hovey and Hovey, *State Fact Finder 2000* (Washington, D.C.: CQ Inc., 2000).

Critical Thinking

The total number of prisoners held in state penal institutions exceeds 1 million people. ***Which states have the highest number of prisoners per 100,000 people?***

The Trial The **Sixth Amendment** [1] guarantees that defendants should not have to wait a long time before their trial starts. However, the courts are so crowded that long delays are common. Defendants accused of a felony have a right to choose between a jury trial or one heard only by a judge, known as a bench trial. In a bench trial the judge hears all the evidence and determines guilt or innocence. Experience has shown that judges are more likely to find defendants guilty than are juries. A **jury** is a group of citizens who hear evidence during a trial in order to decide guilt or innocence. The prosecuting and defense attorneys select jurors from a large pool of residents within the court's jurisdiction. Both sides try to avoid jurors who might be unfavorable to their side and often challenge potential jurors.

When the jury and alternate jurors have been selected, the prosecution presents its case against the defendant. Witnesses are called, and evidence is presented. The defense attorney has the right to cross-examine prosecution witnesses, and at any time either side can raise objections to statements or actions by the other side. Next, the defense has its turn and may call witnesses. The prosecuting attorney has the right to cross-examine them. Under the **Fifth Amendment** [2] defendants do not have to testify in their own trials, and refusal to testify cannot be taken as an admission of guilt. The attorneys for both sides then present closing arguments that summarize the cases and respond to the opposition's case.

The Decision After closing arguments the judge gives the jury a set of instructions on proper legal procedures for the case, and explains the law that the jury is required to apply to the facts brought out at trial. The jury members then go to a jury room to decide if the defendant is guilty or not guilty. The jury selects a foreperson to lead

See the following footnoted materials in the **Reference Handbook:**
1. *The Constitution,* pages 774–799.
2. *The Constitution,* pages 774–799.

their discussions and serve as their spokesperson. Jury deliberations are secret and have no set time limit. During its deliberations the jury may ask questions of the judge or ask to review evidence. To decide that a person is guilty, the jury must find the evidence convincing "beyond a reasonable doubt." In nearly all criminal cases the **verdict,** or decision, must be unanimous. If a jury is unable to reach a decision, it is called a **hung jury** and dismissed, and the trial ends in a mistrial. A new trial with another jury may be scheduled at a later date.

Hearing Cases Bertina Lampkin is a supervising judge in Cook County, Illinois, assigned to Night Narcotics Court. She claims, "I don't think there is a better job. I love to hear the arguments. If the lawyers come prepared and give good arguments, it is the best day I can have." Lampkin takes the bench at 4 P.M., sometimes working until 1 A.M. ***Why do you think court is held at night?***

Sentencing When the verdict is "not guilty," the defendant is released immediately and with very few exceptions cannot be tried again for the same crime. If the verdict is "guilty," the judge usually determines the **sentence,** the punishment to be imposed on the offender. Sentences often specify a period of time to be spent in prison. However, a sentence may involve payment of a fine or a number of hours to be spent in community service. In a few states jurors may play a role in sentencing, particularly in cases in which the death penalty is a possible sentence. Today, victims of the crime are often allowed to make statements about the sentence, and judges may take those statements into account. The law usually sets minimum and maximum penalties for various crimes, and the judge chooses a punishment from within those ranges. With a serious crime the judge may hold hearings in order to consider how the defendant's background and other circumstances of the crime might affect the sentence. This type of hearing is constitutionally required in death penalty cases. People convicted of misdemeanors and felonies have the right to appeal their cases to a higher court, although this right to appeal is not a constitutional one.

Section 3 Assessment

Checking for Understanding

1. **Main Idea** Use a Venn diagram like the one here to show the differences and similarities between the steps in criminal and civil lawsuits.

2. **Define** criminal law, criminal justice system, petty offense, misdemeanor, felony, arrest warrant, grand jury, indictment, information, plea bargaining, jury, verdict, hung jury, sentence.
3. **Identify** Sixth Amendment, Fifth Amendment.
4. **Identify** three classifications of crimes.

Critical Thinking

5. **Demonstrating Reasoned Judgment** Do you think people charged with violent crimes should be allowed to raise bail? Why?

Concepts IN ACTION

Political Processes Create a political cartoon that illustrates the way the criminal justice system tries to balance the rights of the accused against the rights of society.

Classroom Courtroom

In Chapter 15 you learned that most laws that affect people in their everyday lives are state and local laws. People who violate those laws are tried in state courts. This activity will help you to understand the criminal trial process and the steps that someone must go through if he or she has been charged with committing a felony.

Setting Up the Workshop

1. Select volunteers to play the following roles in the courtroom trial:
   - **defendant**
   - **judge**
   - **bailiff**
   - **three-member prosecution attorney team**
   - **three-member defense attorney team**
   - **witnesses**
   - **jury**
2. Gather props to use in court to represent the evidence that exists in the case. You will also need paper and pencils to take notes.
3. Rearrange the classroom to make it resemble a courtroom.

Gathering the Facts of the Case

Your trial is based on the following incident:

On the evening of December 22, a person wearing a ski mask and carrying a gun robbed a convenience store. The person entered the store at approximately 1 A.M. when only the clerk and one other customer were present. The suspect held the gun on the clerk and demanded the contents of the cash register. The clerk gave him $78 in cash, and the suspect left the store without noticing the customer hiding in the rear of the store. According to the clerk, the suspect drove off in a light-colored pickup truck. The clerk was able to provide a partial license plate number.

At 1:05 A.M. the clerk called 911 to report the crime. A police cruiser responded to take information from the clerk (Sara Mason) and the customer (Jason Allen) and to gather evidence. Ten minutes later a second cruiser responded. The second officer reported he had just pulled someone over in a light-colored truck for speeding. The partial license plate number given by the clerk matched some of the numbers on that vehicle's plate.

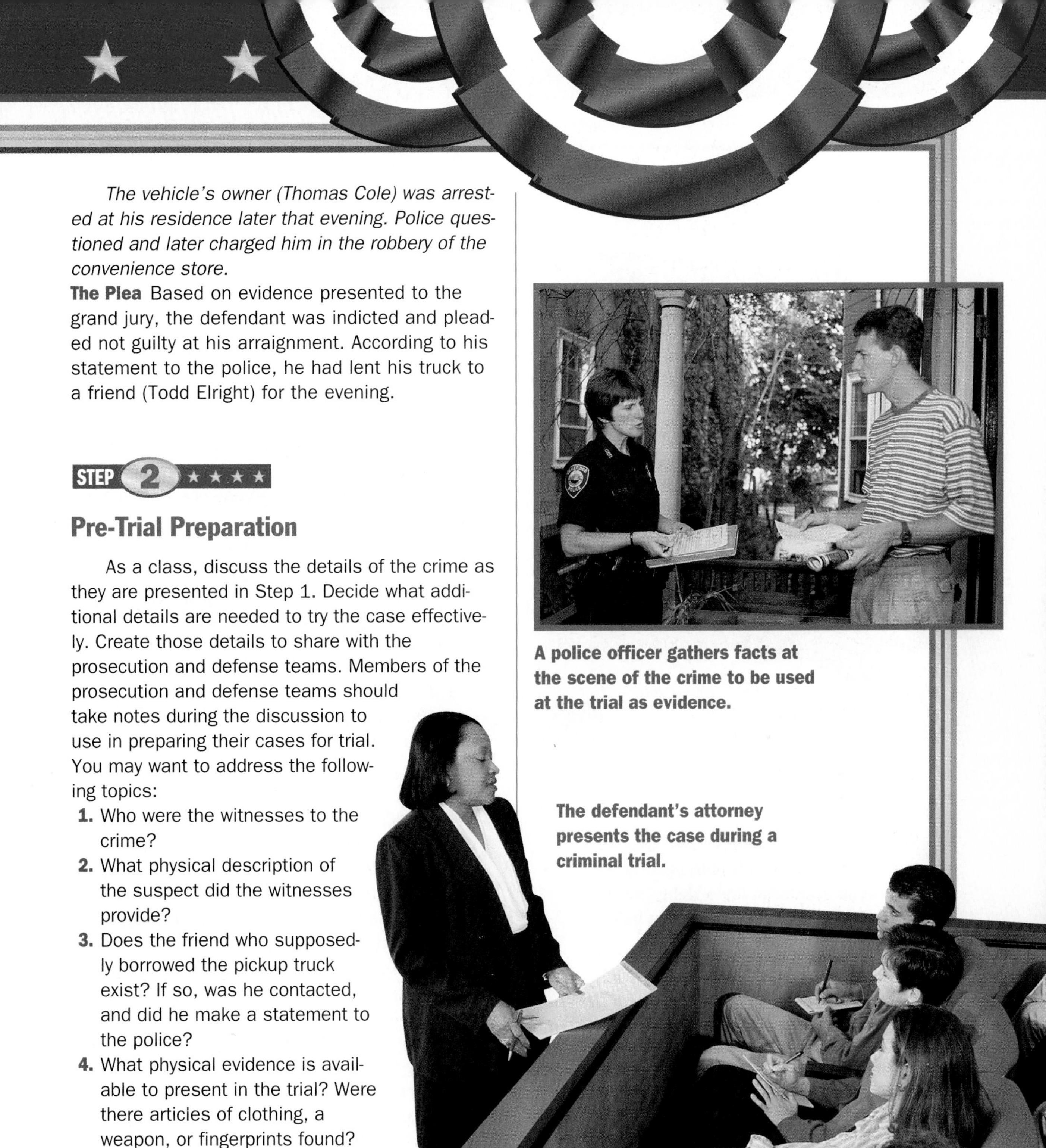

The vehicle's owner (Thomas Cole) was arrested at his residence later that evening. Police questioned and later charged him in the robbery of the convenience store.

The Plea Based on evidence presented to the grand jury, the defendant was indicted and pleaded not guilty at his arraignment. According to his statement to the police, he had lent his truck to a friend (Todd Elright) for the evening.

STEP 2

Pre-Trial Preparation

As a class, discuss the details of the crime as they are presented in Step 1. Decide what additional details are needed to try the case effectively. Create those details to share with the prosecution and defense teams. Members of the prosecution and defense teams should take notes during the discussion to use in preparing their cases for trial. You may want to address the following topics:

1. Who were the witnesses to the crime?
2. What physical description of the suspect did the witnesses provide?
3. Does the friend who supposedly borrowed the pickup truck exist? If so, was he contacted, and did he make a statement to the police?
4. What physical evidence is available to present in the trial? Were there articles of clothing, a weapon, or fingerprints found?
5. Was the stolen money recovered?

A police officer gathers facts at the scene of the crime to be used at the trial as evidence.

The defendant's attorney presents the case during a criminal trial.

DEMOCRACY WORKSHOP IN ACTION

Step 4

"Justice" is often portrayed as a mythic goddess whose blindfolded eyes symbolize impartiality when the scales of justice are held in balance.

STEP 3

Attorney Preparation

Members of the prosecution and defense teams should work separately to prepare their individual strategies for trying their cases. The burden of proof falls on the prosecution team; however, each side will need to be prepared to do the following:

1. share its witness list and evidence list with the opposing team,
2. present an opening statement when the trial begins,
3. call witnesses to the stand and ask them questions,
4. present physical evidence to the court,
5. deliver a closing statement to convince the jury of the guilt or innocence of the defendant.

STEP 4

Conducting the Trial

1. **Beginning the Proceedings** The **bailiff,** who is responsible for maintaining order in the courtroom, should announce that the trial is about to begin and order those present in the courtroom to rise as the judge enters. The **judge** will oversee the proceedings. The role of the judge will be to decide on the appropriateness of the actions of the **attorneys** and to respond to objections from both sides. To the best of his or her ability, the judge will need to make sure that the trial is carried out in a manner that is fair to both sides without infringing on the rights of the defendant.
2. **Presenting Their Cases** The trial should begin with an opening statement by the **prosecution** and **defense teams.** The prosecution will then present its case first by calling and questioning its **witnesses.** After the prosecution questions

each witness, the defense has an opportunity to cross-examine each of the prosecution's witnesses. After the prosecution rests, the defense presents its case by calling its own witnesses to the stand. The prosecution can also cross-examine the defense's witnesses. The **bailiff** calls and swears in each witness before he or she begins testimony.

After the defense rests, the prosecution and defense attorneys will present closing statements summarizing the case and urging a conclusion of guilt or innocence.

3. **Reaching a Verdict** The **judge** will then charge the jury, or explain its responsibilities. The **jury's** duty is to decide on the guilt or innocence of the defendant based on the evidence and whether he is guilty "beyond a reasonable doubt." The jury will then adjourn to discuss the case. Jury members should elect a foreperson to lead the proceedings and to announce their verdict to the court.
4. **Sentencing** Once the verdict has been announced, the judge will sentence the defendant if he is found guilty or dismiss him if the verdict is not guilty. If a unanimous verdict cannot be reached, the jury will be considered a hung jury.

After the trial, members of your class may want to evaluate the effects of the trial's outcome on those people who were involved in the crime. Write a paragraph explaining what your feelings might have been after the trial if you were:

- the convenience store clerk
- the defendant
- a member of the jury

Questions for Discussion

1. Do you think the trial was fair? Why or why not?
2. Does determining guilt "beyond a reasonable doubt" favor the defendant or the prosecution in this particular case?
3. Was there vital information that was knowingly withheld by either side that could have affected the jury's decision? Explain.
4. Should the defendant have testified on his own behalf? Why or why not?
5. How might the outcome of the trial have changed if the case had been heard by a judge only, and not by a jury?

Chapter 15

Assessment and Activities

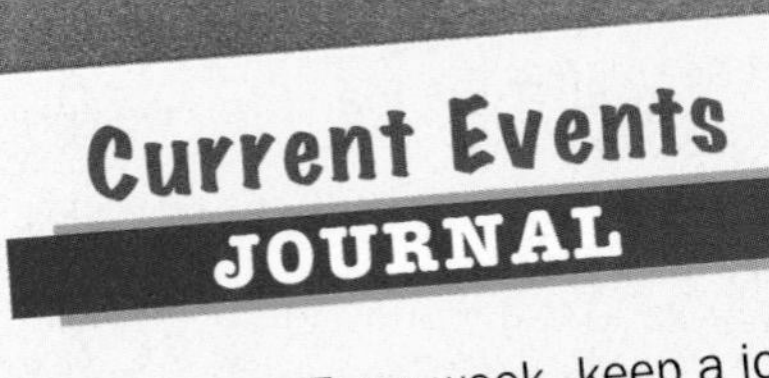

Self-Check Quiz Visit the *United States Government: Democracy in Action* Web site at gov.glencoe.com and click on ***Chapter 15–Self-Check Quizzes*** to prepare for the chapter test.

Reviewing Key Terms

On a separate sheet of paper, choose the letter of the term identified in each statement below.

a. due process
b. verdict
c. indictment
d. contract
e. statute
f. misdemeanor
g. common law
h. tort
i. adversary system
j. injunction
k. administrative law

1. a minor or less serious crime
2. the procedures of and rules issued by government agencies
3. any wrongful act, other than breach of contract, for which the injured party has the right to sue for damages in a civil court
4. law made by judges in resolving individual cases
5. decision of a jury in a criminal case
6. a judicial system in which lawyers for the opposing sides present their cases in court
7. a law written by a legislative branch
8. a charge by a grand jury that a person committed a particular crime
9. a set of voluntary promises, enforceable by the law, between parties to do or not to do something
10. a court order that forbids a defendant to take or continue a certain action

Current Events JOURNAL

Unwritten Laws For a week, keep a journal of the activities in your home, paying special attention to the unwritten rules established by your family, such as "Don't leave your things on the stairs." Make a list of these rules. Then classify them according to the purpose of the rules, such as rules for safety or rules for keeping order. Present your legal code to your family.

Recalling Facts

1. What two early systems of laws have influenced the development of the United States legal system?
2. In the United States, what is the standard against which all other laws are judged?
3. Why is a statutory law sometimes called "Roman law"?
4. When does a court rule that a law violates substantive due process?
5. What two kinds of cases do courts in the American legal system hear?
6. What is the first step in a criminal case?
7. Why has plea bargaining become widely used in criminal cases?
8. What does family law deal with?
9. What happens during the discovery phase of a lawsuit?
10. Who hears cases in small claims court?

Understanding Concepts

1. **Civic Participation** How may the principle of "equal justice under law," applied in federal court cases, benefit minorities, poor people, or young people?
2. **Political Processes** How does the idea of "guilty beyond a reasonable doubt" protect the rights of defendants?

Chapter 15

Critical Thinking

1. **Making Comparisons** What is the difference between procedural due process and substantive due process?
2. **Demonstrating Reasoned Judgment** Use a graphic organizer like the one below to identify reasons for and against plea bargaining.

Plea Bargaining	
For	Against

Interpreting Political Cartoons Activity

1. What is occurring in this cartoon?
2. How do you think the cartoonist feels about the reliability of witnesses' testimonies during court trials?
3. Do you feel that the current trial system ensures justice? Explain.

"Do you swear to tell your version of the truth as you perceive it, clouded perhaps by the passage of time and preconceived notions?"

Cooperative Learning Activity

Role Playing Work in a small group to create a skit in which you role-play the steps involved in trying a civil case. Work with the group to create the situation. Then assign a specific role to each member of your group, such as plaintiff, defendant, attorneys, judge. Present your skit to the class.

Skill Practice Activity

Understanding Cause and Effect Each sentence below illustrates a cause-and-effect relationship. On a separate sheet of paper, identify the cause and effect in each sentence.

1. The witness identified the man as the bank robber, leading to an arrest.
2. Many citizens avoid lengthy trials and high expenses by going to small claims courts. Small claims courts aim to solve disputes speedily and cheaply.
3. Police officers patrol streets and parks on foot, in automobiles, on motorcycles, or on horses to prevent crime.
4. If one party believes it has suffered an injury at the hands of another or wants to prevent a harmful action from taking place, that party may file a civil case.

Technology Activity

Using the Internet Locate a Web site on the Internet that deals with criminal law. Find out about pending federal criminal cases and the issues involved in these cases. Write a short report summarizing the main issues of one case.

Participating in Local Government

The government must provide a lawyer for defendants in criminal cases who cannot afford one. This is not true of civil cases. Thus, many lawyers donate their time to help poor people with lawsuits. Find out about the work of a legal aid society in your community. Report your findings to the class.

UNIT 6

Participating in Government

Voter Profile *Age, gender, racial background, occupation, and many other factors may influence a person's political choices. Survey more than 100 adults, identifying several characteristics such as those mentioned above. Include questions such as: "Do you consider yourself a Democrat, Independent, or Republican?" "Did you vote in the last presidential election?" Analyze the results. For example, what percentage of people ages 18-25 voted?*

Electronic Field Trip

Court TV

Step inside a television courtroom and see the judicial system in action.

Glencoe's Democracy in Action Video Program

Court TV brings the judicial process into thousands of homes, helping people understand how the civil and criminal justice system works. The **Democracy in Action** video program "Court TV," referenced below, includes a discussion with a teen participant who stresses how much the justice system affects us.

As you view the video program, imagine yourself as an attorney arguing a case for your client, or as a judge hearing the opposing arguments of a court case.

Also available in videodisc format.

View the videodisc by scanning the barcode or by entering the chapter number on your keypad and pressing Search.

Disc 2, Side 1, Chapter 6

Hands-On Activity

The Supreme Court allows no cameras for still pictures or for television. Most other courts restrict the media in some way. Do you believe that news media should have more access to trials, or do you think this would subject court decisions to too many public pressures? Construct a short poll on this topic and use e-mail to survey friends.

◀ **A copper eagle flagpole ornament in Boston, Massachusetts**

Chapter 16

Political Parties

Why It's Important

Political Awareness Political parties play a large role in the decisions made by government. This chapter will help you understand the function of political parties. It may also help you identify your own political beliefs.

To find out more about how political parties influence policy and how you can get involved in the political process, view the ***Democracy in Action*** Chapter 16 video lesson:

Political Parties

GOVERNMENT Online

Chapter Overview Visit the *United States Government: Democracy in Action* Web site at gov.glencoe.com and click on ***Chapter 16—Overview*** to preview chapter information.

Development of Parties

Reader's Guide

Key Terms

political party, theocracy, ideologies, coalition government, third party, single-member district, proportional representation

Find Out

- What is a multiparty system and how does it affect governing?
- Why have third parties played only a minor role in American politics?

Understanding Concepts

Growth of Democracy Could Americans have participated as effectively in government without political parties?

COVER STORY

No Government in Italy

ROME, ITALY, NOVEMBER 4, 1974

Resistance to authority is spreading as Italy enters its 21st week without a national government. Political chaos is nothing new to Italians. Italy has had 36 governments in the past 31 years. However, the current crisis is the nation's worst since World War II. It began in June, when a coalition of 3 political parties collapsed after only 3 months in power. Last week another effort failed to forge a ruling majority from among Italy's more than 12 political parties. Most Italians accepted the news calmly. Few believe that their 37th government, whenever it is formed, will be better than the 36th.

An Italian demands a government

Unlike Italy, the structure of the government in the United States does not need a coalition of political parties for the government to operate. That does not mean, however, that political parties do not exist in the United States. In a nation as large and diverse as the United States the voice and will of the individual citizen can easily be lost.

Parties and Party Systems

A **political party** is a group of people with broad common interests who organize to win elections, control government, and thereby influence government policies. Although most nations have one or more political parties, the role that parties play differs with each nation's political system.

One-Party Systems In a one-party system the party, in effect, is the government. The decisions of party leaders set government policy. In some one-party nations, political differences arise only within the party itself because the government tolerates no other opposition. In elections in such nations, only the party's candidates appear on the ballot.

One-party systems are usually found in nations with authoritarian governments. Such parties often come into power through force. For example, a revolution in 1917 brought the Communist Party to power in Russia. Today Cuba, Vietnam, North Korea, and China are among the few nations that remain one-party Communist governments.

One-party systems also exist in some non-Communist countries such as Iran where religious leaders dominate government. A government dominated by religion is known as a **theocracy.** The Muslim clergy controls the Islamic Republican Party. All major opposition parties have been outlawed or are inactive. Mexico has also had a one-party government for many years. As in Iran, minor party candidates

◀ The Democratic National Convention in Los Angeles, 2000

appeared on the ballot. Mexico's Institutional Revolutionary Party (PRI) never lost a major election, and its leaders dominated Mexico's government. In 1997 voters began to shift to rival parties, and in 2000 a non-PRI candidate was elected president.

Multiparty Systems In nations that allow more than one political party, the most common political system today is the multiparty system. France, for example, has 5 major parties, and Italy has 10. In such countries voters have a wide range of choices on election day. The parties in a multiparty system often represent widely differing **ideologies**, or basic beliefs about government.

In a multiparty system, one party rarely gets enough support to control the government. Several parties often combine forces to obtain a majority and form a **coalition government.** When groups with different ideologies share power, coalitions often break down when disputes arise, requiring new elections. Thus, many nations with multiparty systems are politically unstable.

Two-Party Systems Only about a dozen nations have systems in which two parties compete for power, although minor parties exist. In the United States, the major parties are the Republican Party and the Democratic Party.

Growth of American Parties

Many of the Founders distrusted "factions," or groups with differing political views. In *The Federalist, No. 10*[1] James Madison observed:

> *"The public good is disregarded in the conflicts of rival parties, and . . . measures are too often decided, not according to the rules of justice and the rights of the minor party, but by the superior force of an interested and overbearing majority."*
>
> —James Madison, 1787

In his Farewell Address of 1796,[2] President George Washington warned against the "baneful [very harmful] effects of the spirit of party." Even so, by the end of President Washington's second term, two political parties had arisen. The Federalists called for a strong central government. The Democratic-Republicans believed that the states should have more power than the central government.

Student Web Activity Visit the *United States Government: Democracy in Action* Web site at gov.glencoe.com and click on ***Chapter 16–Student Web Activities*** for an activity about political parties.

Parties Before the Civil War After the Federalists elected John Adams president in 1796, their power quickly declined. Thomas Jefferson won the presidency under the Democratic-Republican banner in 1800 and 1804. The Democratic-Republicans dominated politics into the 1820s. Then conflicts over banking, tariffs, and slavery shattered the party. By 1828, when Andrew Jackson won the presidency, the Democratic-Republicans were splitting into two parties. Jackson aligned with the group called Democrats. The other group called itself National Republicans, or Whigs.

By the 1850s the debate over slavery had created divisions within both parties. The Democrats split into Northern and Southern factions. Many Whigs joined a new party that opposed the spread of slavery—the Republican Party.

Parties After the Civil War By the Civil War's end, two major parties dominated the national political scene. The Republicans remained the majority party from the Civil War until well into the twentieth century. Democrats held the presidency for only 4 terms between 1860 and 1932.

Parties in the Great Depression and After In 1932 the Democratic Party won the White House and assumed control of Congress. For the next 50 years, Democrats remained the majority party. Beginning in 1968, Republicans controlled the White House for 5 of the next 8 presidential terms. After losing the White House to Bill Clinton in 1992, Republicans won the 1994 mid-term elections, taking both houses of Congress for the first

See the following footnoted materials in the **Reference Handbook:**
1. *The Federalist, No. 10,* pages 812–814.
2. *Washington's Farewell Address,* page 817.

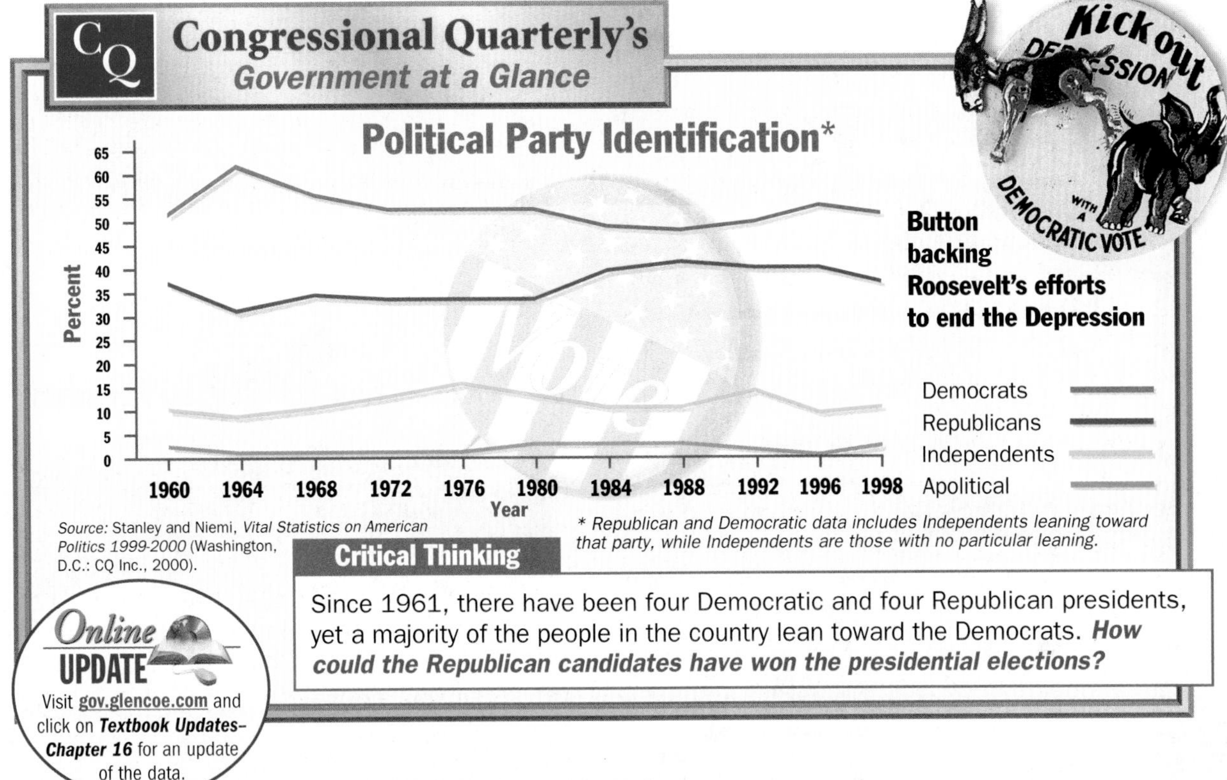

Button backing Roosevelt's efforts to end the Depression

Source: Stanley and Niemi, *Vital Statistics on American Politics 1999-2000* (Washington, D.C.: CQ Inc., 2000).

* *Republican and Democratic data includes Independents leaning toward that party, while Independents are those with no particular leaning.*

Critical Thinking

Since 1961, there have been four Democratic and four Republican presidents, yet a majority of the people in the country lean toward the Democrats. ***How could the Republican candidates have won the presidential elections?***

Online UPDATE Visit gov.glencoe.com and click on ***Textbook Updates–Chapter 16*** for an update of the data.

time in 40 years. Beginning in 1995, for the first time since Truman, a Democratic president worked with a Republican Congress.

The Role of Minor Parties

Despite the dominance of the two major parties, third parties have been part of the American political scene since the early days of the Republic. A **third party** is any party other than one of the two major parties. In any election there may be more than one party running against the major parties, yet each of them is labeled a "third" party. Because they rarely win major elections, third parties are also called minor parties.

Although a variety of reasons motivates them, third parties have one thing in common. They believe that neither major party is meeting certain needs. A third party runs candidates who propose to remedy this situation.

Types of Third Parties Although there may be some exceptions and overlapping, minor parties generally fall into one of three categories. The **single-issue party** focuses exclusively on one major social, economic, or moral issue. For example, in the 1840s the Liberty Party and the Free Soil Party formed to take stronger stands against slavery than either the Democrats or the Whigs had taken. A single-issue party generally is short-lived. It may fade away when an issue ceases to be important, or a party with a popular issue may become irrelevant if one of the major parties adopts the issue.

Another type of third party is the **ideological party,** which focuses on overall change in society rather than on an issue. Ideological parties such as the Socialist Labor Party and the Communist Party USA advocate government ownership of factories, transportation, resources, farmland, and other means of production and distribution. The Libertarian Party calls for drastic reductions in government in order to increase personal freedoms.

The third type of minor party is the **splinter party,** which splits away from one of the major parties because of some disagreement. Such disputes frequently result from the failure of a popular figure to gain the major party's presidential nomination. The most notable occurrence was in 1912, when former president Theodore Roosevelt led a group out of the Republican Party to form the Progressive, or Bull Moose, Party. Splinter

Congressional Quarterly's
Government at a Glance

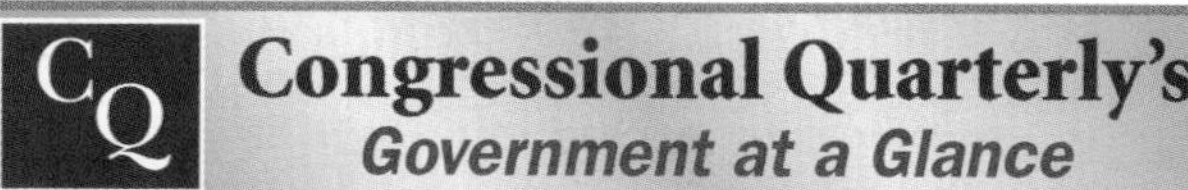

American Political Parties Since 1789

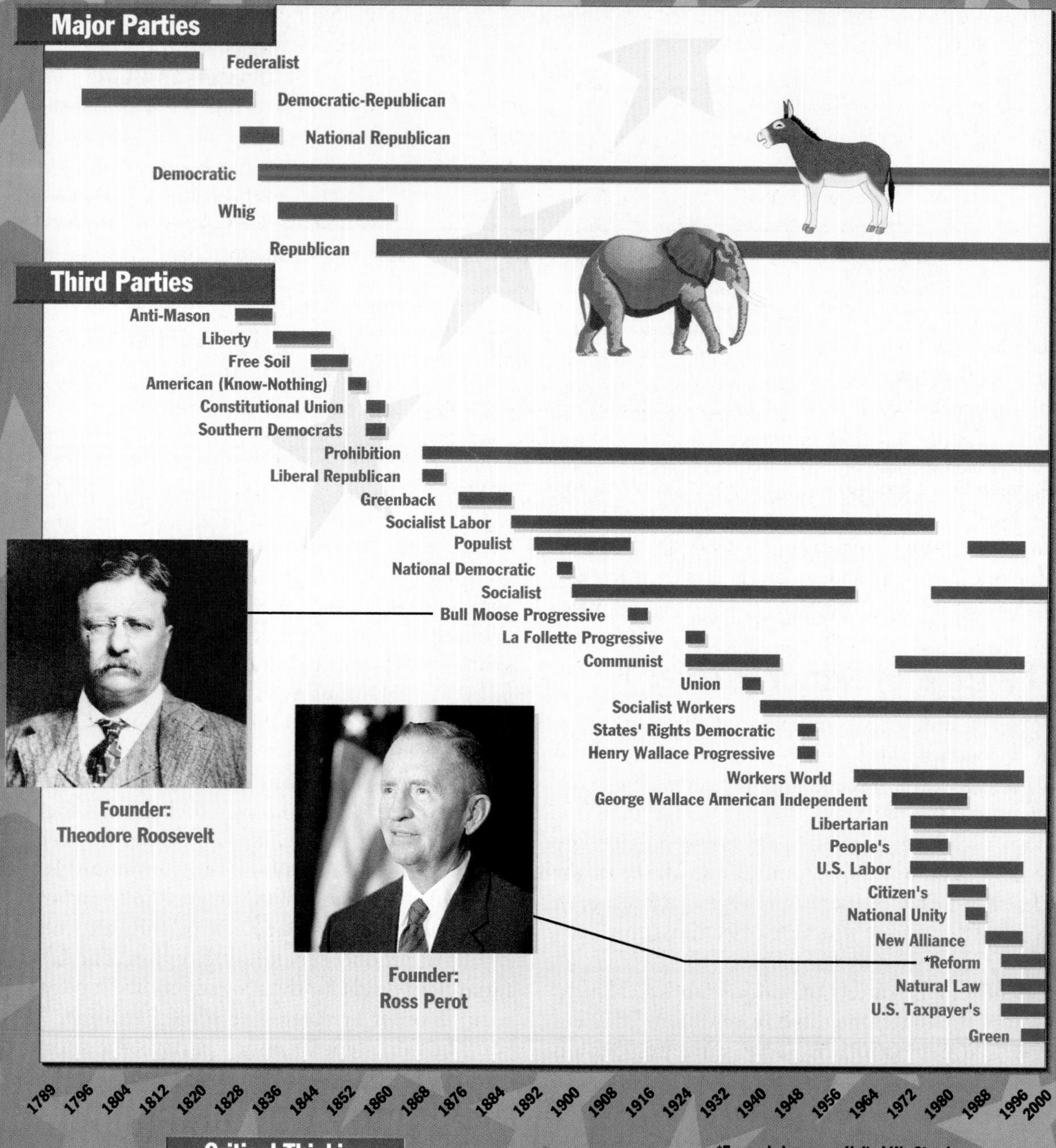
Major Parties
Federalist
Democratic-Republican
National Republican
Democratic
Whig
Republican
Third Parties
Anti-Mason
Liberty
Free Soil
American (Know-Nothing)
Constitutional Union
Southern Democrats
Prohibition
Liberal Republican
Greenback
Socialist Labor
Populist
National Democratic
Socialist
Bull Moose Progressive
La Follette Progressive
Communist
Union
Socialist Workers
States' Rights Democratic
Henry Wallace Progressive
Workers World
George Wallace American Independent
Libertarian
People's
U.S. Labor
Citizen's
National Unity
New Alliance
*Reform
Natural Law
U.S. Taxpayer's
Green
Founder:
Theodore Roosevelt
Founder:
Ross Perot
1789 1796 1804 1812 1820 1828 1836 1844 1852 1860 1868 1876 1884 1892 1900 1908 1916 1924 1932 1940 1948 1956 1964 1972 1980 1988 1996 2000

*Formerly known as United We Stand

Critical Thinking

Many political parties throughout American history have challenged the Democrats and Republicans, yet none have been very successful. ***Which third party has made the most recent attempt at the presidency?***

Source: **Cook, Rhodes. *How Congress Gets Elected* (Washington, D.C.: CQ, Inc. 2000)**

parties typically fade away with the defeat of their candidate. The **Bull Moose Party** disappeared after Roosevelt lost in 1912, for example.

The Impact of Third Parties Minor parties have influenced the outcome of national elections. Theodore Roosevelt's Bull Moose Party drew so many Republican votes from President William Howard Taft in 1912 that Democratic candidate Woodrow Wilson was elected. In 1968 the **American Independent Party** won 13.5 percent of the vote, and some believe this swayed the narrow election of Republican candidate Richard Nixon. Some believe Ross Perot's independent candidacy may have helped Bill Clinton win in 1992.

Bull Moose Party button

Third parties often have promoted ideas that were at first unpopular or hotly debated. Major parties later adopted many of their issues. For example, third parties first proposed a minimum wage for workers, the five-day workweek, unemployment insurance, and health insurance.

Obstacles to Third Parties As a result of the two-party tradition, minor parties face difficulties in getting on the ballot in all 50 states. The names of Republicans and Democrats are automatically on the ballot in many states, but third-party candidates are required to obtain a large number of voter signatures in a short time.

Another difficulty for third-party candidates is that nearly all elected officials in the United States are selected by **single-member districts.** Under this system no matter how many candidates compete in a district, only one will win. Because most voters support a major party, the winner will almost always be a Democrat or a Republican.

By contrast, many nations use an election system based on **proportional representation.** In this system several officials are elected to represent voters in an area. Offices are filled in proportion to the votes that each party's candidates receive. Such a system encourages minor parties.

A related problem is financing third-party campaigns. Political campaigns require a great deal of money. Americans, convinced that a third-party candidate cannot win, are reluctant to contribute to such a campaign.

In the past, third parties have appealed mainly to voters in certain regions of the country or to certain groups in society. To survive, a third party must plant political roots in all parts of the country. Few third parties have demonstrated this kind of staying power.

Section 1 Assessment

Checking for Understanding

1. **Main Idea** Use a graphic organizer like the one below to identify three types of political party systems and how they affect governing.

Party System	Effects

2. **Define** political party, theocracy, ideologies, coalition government, third party, single-member district, proportional representation.
3. **Identify** Bull Moose Party, American Independent Party.
4. Identify three obstacles facing third parties.

Critical Thinking

5. **Making Inferences** Why might the National Organization for Women want to choose and run a third-party candidate?

Growth of Democracy Imagine you have been named to a committee to plan a new government for a former colony. The structure of this government will influence the development of political parties. Consider the advantages and disadvantages of no parties, one-party, two-party, and multiparty systems. Write a speech explaining your choice.

Section 2

Party Organization

Reader's Guide

Key Terms

independent, precinct, precinct captain, ward, state central committee, national convention, national committee, patronage

Find Out

- How are parties organized on the national, state, and local levels?
- How do political parties assist in educating the public?

Understanding Concepts

Political Processes What role do the Republican and Democratic Parties play in the day-to-day operations and processes of the government?

COVER STORY

Teen Youngest Delegate

SALT LAKE CITY, UTAH, AUGUST 13, 1996

A local teenager has become one of the most visible delegates at the Republican National Convention in San Diego this week. Among the speakers at yesterday's opening session was 18-year-old Jason Brinton, a June graduate of West High School. Brinton's election last spring to be part of Utah's 28-member delegation makes him the youngest delegate at the Republican gathering. " I campaigned vigorously at the Utah Convention as a voice for the young people of our party," he said. Brinton also heads the state chapter of Teen Age Republicans, a political action group headquartered in Manassas, Virginia.

Jason Brinton

In order to succeed, a political party must have a dedicated core of willing volunteers like Jason Brinton of Utah. Both major parties employ small paid staffs in permanent party offices at county, state, and national levels. Between elections these employees carry out the day-to-day business operations of the party. At campaign time, however, political parties also use volunteers to perform a wide range of tasks. Volunteers obtain campaign contributions, publicize candidates, send out campaign literature, canvass voters, and watch at the polls on Election Day. Parties also seek the help of various professionals to win elections. These professionals include media experts to prepare television commercials, pollsters to take public opinion polls, and writers to prepare speeches for the candidates. In addition, to be successful, a party needs strong leadership and good organization at every level.

Membership and Organization

Democrats and Republicans are organized into 50 state parties and thousands of local parties that operate independently of the national organization. Although the 3 levels generally cooperate, separate authority exists at each level. Local, state, and national parties select their own officers and raise their own funds.

Party Membership How does a voter join a political party, and what does it mean to belong? In many states citizens must declare their party preference when they register to vote or when they vote in certain kinds of elections. Joining a political party, however, is not required in the United States. A voter may declare that he or she is an **independent,** not supporting any particular party.

People who belong to a political party generally do so because they support most of its ideas and candidates. Both the Republican and Democratic Parties do everything they can to attract supporters. In this sense, the two major parties are open parties, welcoming whoever wishes to belong and accepting whatever degree of involvement these individuals choose. Party membership involves no duties or obligations beyond voting. Members do not have to attend meetings or contribute to the party if they choose not to do so. Most people who consider themselves Democrats or Republicans do nothing more than vote for the party's candidates.

Organizing for VICTORY

A Hand Book for PRECINCT LEADERS

Paper handbook distributed to local Democratic leaders in 1936

Some citizens, however, become more involved in the political process. They may support a party by contributing money or by doing volunteer work for the party or its candidates. In most states, one must be a party member in order to hold an office in a party or to be its candidate for a public office. Thus, party membership provides a way for citizens to increase their influence on government. The parties, in turn, depend on citizen involvement, especially at the local level, to carry out activities and accomplish goals.

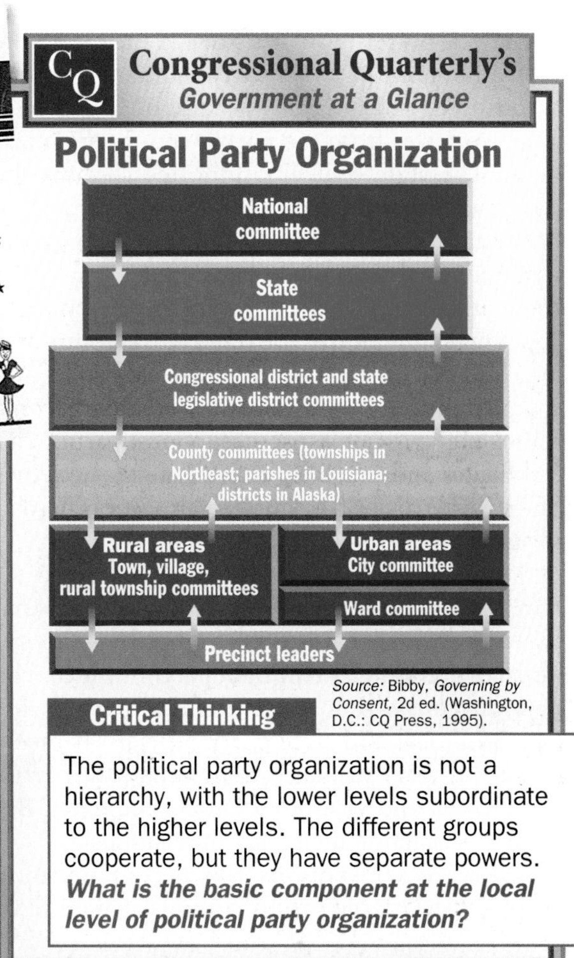

Local Party Organization The basic local unit is the **precinct,** a voting district ranging in size from just a few voters to more than 1,000 voters, all of whom cast their ballots at the same polling place.

In a precinct each party has a volunteer **precinct captain,** who organizes party workers to distribute information about the party and its candidates and to attract voters to the polls. Several adjoining precincts comprise a larger district called a **ward.** Party members in each ward select a person, also unpaid, to represent the ward at the next level of party organization—the party's county committee.

The county committee selects a chairperson to handle the county party's daily affairs. The **party county chairperson** usually has a great deal of political power in the county. He or she is very often the key figure in determining which candidate receives the party's support. If the state's governor, or a United States senator, is from the same party, they may seek recommendations from the county chairperson when appointing judges and administrative officials.

At the same time, however, local parties, because of the nature of their membership, are the weakest link in the organizational chain. One study of political parties concluded the following:

> "*The vast majority of local parties are essentially voluntary organizations. . . . They have the least influence and the fewest resources. The combination of . . . reliance on volunteers in an era when volunteers are hard to find, complex campaign finance regulations, and the general low regard in which parties are held combine to discourage the best leadership or the greatest participation.*"
>
> —Xandra Kayden and Eddie Mahe, Jr., 1985

State Party Organization In each state the most important part of a party is the **state central committee,** which usually is composed largely of representatives from the party's county organizations. The state central committee chooses the **party state chairperson.** In selecting this person, however, the committee generally follows the wishes of the governor, a United States senator, or some other party leader powerful in state politics.

A main function of the state central committee is to help elect the party's candidates for state government offices. In addition, the state central committee may provide assistance to local parties and candidates and may help coordinate the activities of the local parties. Of course, it also works hard at raising money.

National Party Organization The national party organization has two main parts—the national convention and the national committee. The **national convention** is a gathering of party members and local and state party officials. It meets every four years, primarily to nominate the party's presidential and vice-presidential candidates. Beyond this function it has very little authority.

Between conventions the party's **national committee,** a large group composed mainly of representatives from the 50 state party organizations, runs the party. Some members of Congress and some state and local elected officials also may sit on the national committee, as may other selected party members.

The **party national chairperson,** elected by the national committee, manages the daily operation of the national party. Usually the person selected is the choice of the party's presidential candidate. The national chairperson also raises money for the party, touts its achievements, and promotes national, state, and local party cooperation.

Both the Democrats and the Republicans also have independent campaign committees for Congress. These committees provide assistance to senators and representatives who are running for reelection. Each party's committee also provides resources to help challengers defeat senators and representatives from the other party.

Political Party Functions

The Constitution does not provide for political parties or even mention them. Yet political parties are an essential part of the American democratic system. Through the election process, the people select the officials who will

POLITICS *and You*

Running for Office

The most direct way of being involved in government is to hold elected office. The procedures and requirements for becoming a political candidate vary somewhat from state to state. However, in most cases to do so you must file an official petition, signed by the required number of registered voters, with the appropriate local or state election board before a specified deadline. If other members of your political party have filed petitions for the same office, you may have to win a primary election to become the candidate.

Among the resources you will need in your campaign are time, money, and volunteers. Running for political office takes a great deal of personal time. Loans and donations from supporters will pay for brochures, TV and radio spots, and other devices to promote your candidacy. Volunteers can help get your message out to voters by distributing your materials. You may also need expert volunteer help to file the campaign finance reports required under state and federal law.

GRANDY FRED! ...instead... GOVERNOR '94

Campaign button

Candidate Qualifications Contact your local board of elections to determine the qualifications, requirements, and procedures for running for office in your community.

govern them. As part of this process, political parties perform several important functions. No other body or institution in American government performs these tasks.

Recruiting Candidates Political parties seek men and women who seem to have a good chance of being elected. Selecting candidates for public office and presenting them to the voters for approval is the major function of political parties. It is often said that political parties are election-oriented rather than issues-oriented. This characteristic helps the Republicans and the Democrats maintain their status as major parties. Although members within each party share a general ideology about government and society, wide differences often exist on specific issues, even among the party's elected officials. Republicans in the Senate may refuse to support a Republican president's request for legislation, for example, and House Democrats may vote on both sides of a bill. To maintain broad appeal, each party tries to avoid disagreements and unite behind its candidates.

Educating the Public Despite efforts to avoid division, political parties do bring important issues to the attention of the public. Each party publishes its position on the issues of the day, such as inflation, military spending, taxes, pollution, energy, and the environment. Candidates present these views in pamphlets, press conferences, speeches, and television, radio, and newspaper advertisements. These devices help citizens form opinions on controversial topics and give voters a choice between differing positions on issues.

Sometimes major party candidates feel safer attacking their opponent's views than stating their own. Important issues can become lost in a sea of personal attacks. When major party candidates fail to address issues, a minor party candidate may force debate on these subjects. In 1992 and 1996 Ross Perot brought his concern for the national debt and the nation's economic problems to the campaign agenda. In 2000 Ralph Nader championed consumer and environmental issues as leader of the Green Party.

Unfortunately, many Americans are not well-informed about important issues or the background of candidates. Political parties simplify elections by helping such people decide how to vote. By supporting a candidate just because he or she is a Democrat or a Republican, the voter knows generally how the candidate stands on key issues. Political party affiliation helps voters assess which candidate will be more acceptable.

Third Parties Sway Elections

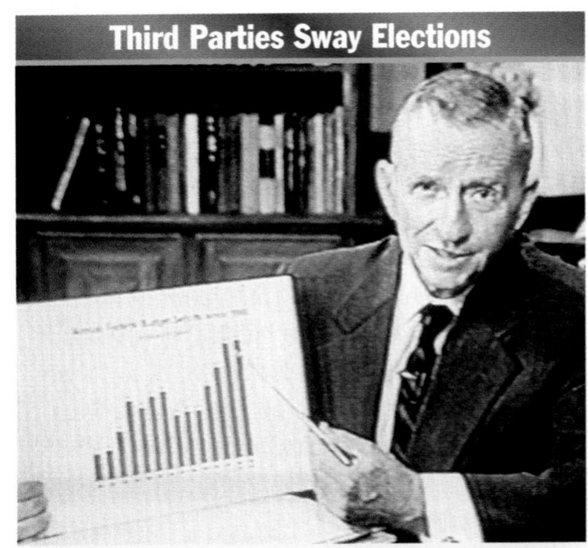

Appealing to Voters Independent candidate Ross Perot filmed "infomercials" during his presidential campaigns. Here he holds a chart depicting the economic decline of the nation, and declares that he can put the nation's finances in order. ***What do you think Perot's strong support in the 1992 election revealed about the American people?***

Operating the Government Political parties also play a key role in running and staffing the government. Congress and the state legislatures are organized and carry on their work on the basis of party affiliation. Party leaders in the legislatures make every effort to see that their members support the party's position when considering legislation.

A party also acts as a link between a legislature and a chief executive. A chief executive works through his or her party leaders in the legislature to promote the administration's program. For most of the past 30 years, however, one party has controlled the White House and the other has controlled one or both houses of Congress. In recent years the same situation has developed between governors and legislatures in more than half the states.

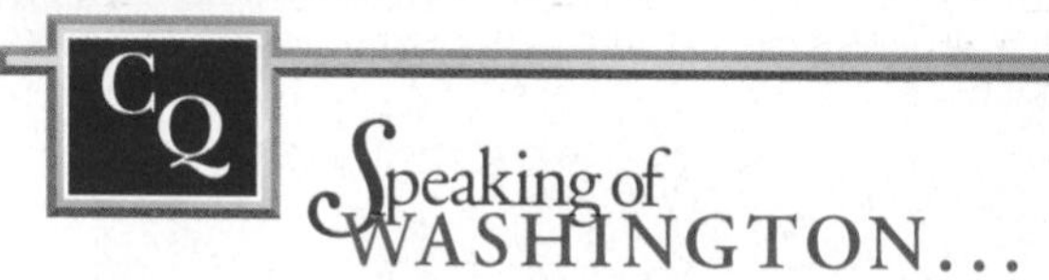

Chairwomen **The first woman to chair a national party committee (the Democratic National Committee) was Jean Westwood of Utah in 1972. She was chosen by presidential nominee George McGovern. At the bidding of President Gerald R. Ford, Mary Louise Smith of Iowa was the first woman to serve as chair of the Republican National Committee, from 1974 to 1976. Both Westwood and Smith had been state organizational leaders.**

Dispensing Patronage Political parties also dispense **patronage**, or favors given to reward party loyalty, to their members. These favors often include jobs, contracts, and appointments to government positions. Business executives or labor unions that contribute heavily to a political party, for example, may expect government to be sympathetic to their problems if that party comes to power. They may be awarded contracts to provide government with goods or services. Loyal party workers may be placed in government jobs. Although laws and court decisions have limited patronage in recent years, the practice remains a major way that parties control and reward their supporters.

The Loyal Opposition The party out of power in the legislative or executive branch assumes the role of "watchdog" over government. It observes the party in power, criticizes it, and offers solutions to political problems. If the opposition party does this successfully, public opinion may swing in its favor and return it to power in a future election. Concern about this makes the party in power more sensitive to the will of the people.

Reduction of Conflict In a complex society, conflict among groups with differing interests is inevitable. To win an election, a political party must attract support from many different groups. To accomplish this, a party encourages groups to compromise and work together. A key outcome of this process is that parties encourage government to adopt moderate policies with mass appeal.

Parties contribute to political stability in another way, too. When one party loses control of the government, the transfer of power takes place peacefully. No violent revolutions occur after elections, as they do in some nations. In the United States, the losing party accepts the outcome of elections because it knows that the party will continue to exist as the opposition party and someday will return to power.

Section 2 Assessment

Checking for Understanding

1. **Main Idea** Use a graphic organizer like the one to the right to show the three levels at which each major political party functions.

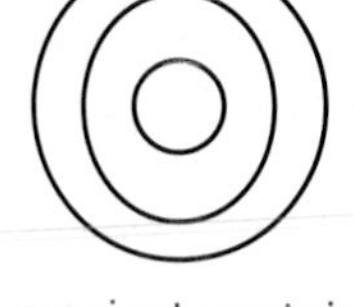

2. **Define** independent, precinct, precinct captain, ward, state central committee, national convention, national committee, patronage.
3. **Identify** party county chairperson, party state chairperson, party national chairperson.
4. What are the methods a political party uses to educate the public?

Critical Thinking

5. **Understanding Cause and Effect** What are the advantages and the disadvantages of the system of patronage?

Political Processes Prepare for a debate on the following statement: The two-party system has outlived its usefulness. Choose either the pro or con side of the issue and prepare arguments for the side you chose. Pair up with a classmate who has prepared arguments opposing yours and debate the issue.

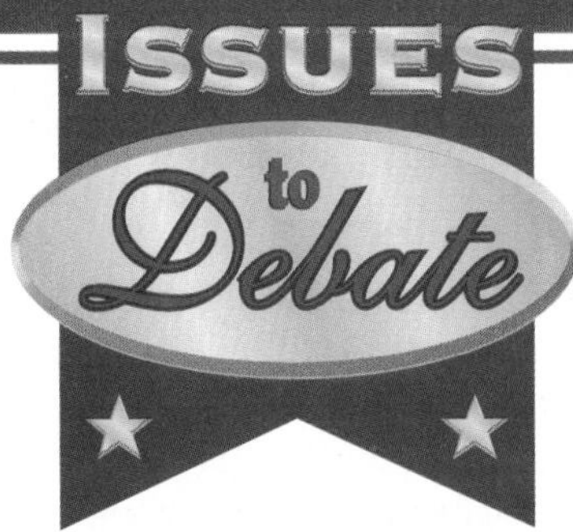

Should There Be Limits on Campaign Spending?

Although there are limits to how much individuals and groups can contribute to a federal candidate, there are no limits on how much money a candidate can raise or spend. In the presidential election of 2000, candidates spent at least $2 billion on their campaigns.

Money and Influence

Fund-raising abuses and a disgruntled public have forced Congress to take a closer look at what can be done to limit campaign spending. In 1997 the Senate proposed a constitutional amendment to put a cap on spending. It was voted down. Currently, there are several bills up for consideration that deal with campaign-finance reform. However, insiders say the chance of these bills passing is slim.

Those who favor reform argue that large corporations and other special interest groups have more money to spend on contributions, which gives them more influence over the candidates. With the costs of campaigning dramatically increasing in every election, many people are concerned that only the wealthy or someone backed by one of the two major parties can be a candidate for president or Congress.

Protecting Free Speech

In 1976 the Supreme Court considered the issue of putting a cap on campaign spending. It ruled that setting limits on an individual's campaign spending was unconstitutional because it violated the right of free speech. The Court said that money is necessary for a candidate to reach voters.

Others who balk at limits say that if campaign spending is controlled, incumbents will have an edge because of name recognition. To compete, opponents need to be able to spend large amounts of money to generate the same kind of name recognition. One bill in Congress proposed that free television time and reduced mail rates be offered to candidates who voluntarily adhere to spending limits.

Debating the Issue

Should the Government Establish a Cap on Federal Campaign Spending?

Assume you are a member of Congress who will vote on a constitutional amendment to limit campaign spending. Spending limits would hurt your next campaign, but you are receiving pressure from your district to curb campaign spending.

Key Issues

✔ Do you think unlimited campaign spending can lead to political corruption?

✔ Is the threat to free speech a valid argument for not limiting campaign spending?

✔ Are the wealthy favored in the campaign process?

Debate Discuss the issue in class. Select three people on each side of the issue to hold a debate in front of the class.

Vote Vote for or against limited campaign spending. Those on each side of the issue should work together to draft a letter to Congress expressing their viewpoint.

Section 3

Nominating Candidates

Reader's Guide

Key Terms

caucus, nominating convention, boss, direct primary, closed primary, open primary, plurality, runoff primary, ticket, platform, planks

Find Out

- How are primaries conducted as a method of choosing candidates?
- What are the processes followed at a national nominating convention?

Understanding Concepts

Political Processes Primaries and nominating conventions are democratic methods of selecting candidates. What are some drawbacks?

COVER STORY

Hard to Choose

CHICAGO, ILLINOIS, JUNE 12, 1920

After failing in four tries to nominate a presidential candidate, the Republican National Convention recessed last night. When the delegates went to bed, General Leonard Wood and Illinois governor Frank Lowden were the front-runners for the nomination. This morning the delegates found the situation had changed. Exhausted Republican leaders emerged at 6 A.M. from an all-night meeting in the Blackstone Hotel, after settling on Ohio senator Warren Harding to be the candidate. Harding finished a distant fourth in yesterday's voting. After six more ballots today, the delegates finally agreed to the choice of Harding.

1920 Republican candidates

Party nominations are often hard-fought contests. In the summer that Harding was selected, the Democrats later required 44 ballots to choose their candidate, Ohio governor James Cox. To win elections, a party must first offer appealing candidates and conduct expensive campaigns.

How Candidates Are Selected

Historically, individuals have sought nomination for public office in one of four ways: (1) caucus; (2) nominating convention; (3) primary election; or (4) petition. Although election laws vary greatly from state to state, all candidates have reached the ballot through one or more of these methods.

Caucuses Early in our nation's history, **caucuses**—private meetings of party leaders—chose nearly all candidates for office. The caucus became widely criticized as undemocratic, however, because most people had no say in selecting the candidates.

In modern caucuses, party rules require openness with the selection process starting at the local level. Selecting delegates starts at the neighborhood level and then moves to the county, congressional district, and finally the state level. Twelve states use caucuses today.

Nominating Conventions As political caucuses came under attack, the **nominating convention,** an official public meeting of a party to choose candidates for office, became popular. Under this system, local party organizations send representatives to a county nominating convention that selects candidates for county offices and chooses delegates who will go to a state nominating convention. The state convention, in turn, selects candidates for statewide office and chooses delegates who will go to the national convention.

In theory, the convention system was more democratic than party caucuses because power would flow upward from the people. As the convention system developed, however, it became increasingly undemocratic. Powerful party leaders, called **bosses,** chose delegates and controlled conventions. Public reaction against the bosses in the 1900s led to primary elections as the method of selection at the state and local levels.

Primary Elections The method most commonly used today to nominate candidates is the **direct primary,** an election in which party members select people to run in the general election. Two types of primary elections are held. Most states hold a **closed primary,** in which only members of a political party can vote. Thus, only Democrats pick Democratic candidates for office, and only Republicans can vote in the Republican primary. In an **open primary,** all voters may participate, even if they do not belong to the party, but they can vote in only one party's primary.

Primary elections are conducted according to state law and are held at regular polling places just as general elections are. Each state sets the date of its primary, provides the ballots and the people to supervise the election, and counts the votes. In most states a primary candidate does not need a majority of the votes to win, but only a **plurality,** or more votes than any other candidate. In a few states, however, if no candidate receives a majority, a **runoff primary** is held. The runoff is a second primary election between the two candidates who received the most votes in the first primary. The person who wins the runoff becomes the party's candidate in the general election.

In most states today, candidates for governor and for the House, Senate, other state offices, and most local offices are selected in primary elections. In many states, however, party caucuses and nominating conventions continue to exist alongside primaries.

Petition Under the petition method, a person announces his or her candidacy and files petitions that a specified number of voters have signed in order to be placed on the ballot. Some states require that all candidates file petitions.

We the People

Making a Difference

J.C. Watts, Jr.

City sign

J.C. Watts, Jr., grew up in Eufaula, Oklahoma, where the railroad tracks divided the town into African American and white communities. Watts recalls those days: "I remember I had to sit in the balcony of the movie theater." In 1973 Watts became the Eufaula High School Ironheads' first African American quarterback. Now Watts is the only African American Republican in the United States House of Representatives.

When the Eufaula city council renamed a street after the football hero, historians and citizens resisted, claiming that renaming a street that already happened to be named after President Andrew Jackson would desecrate the memory of the president. The Eufaula city council declared, "We felt J.C. Watts would be more important to the history of Eufaula than Jackson ever was."

As a former star football player at the University of Oklahoma, Watts enjoyed name recognition. He used that name recognition to launch his congressional career. Watts traveled to Washington with a conservative Republican message and the charisma to deliver it well. Following the 1998 elections, House Republicans elected Watts chair of the Republican Conference—a House majority leadership position—for the 106th Congress.

Those who know Watts describe him as a man on a mission. Watts's father, J.C. "Buddy" Watts, explains, "I've had a lot of people say that he'd be the first [African American] president."

In a primary contest, the party-backed candidate has an advantage because party workers will circulate petitions. The party will also use its financial and organizational resources to back its choice. Candidates without caucus or convention support have serious obstacles to overcome. If such a candidate poses a serious threat, however, party leaders frequently are willing to make a deal. They might offer the challenger party support for another office, or appointment to a government post, to avoid a primary. Political analyst Theodore H. White once explained why:

> *Established leaders hate primaries for good reason; they are always, in any form, an appeal from the leaders' wishes to the people directly. Primaries suck up and waste large sums of money from contributors who might better be tapped for the November finals; the charges and countercharges of primary civil war provide the enemy party with ammunition it can later use with blast effect against whichever primary contender emerges victorious.*
>
> —Theodore H. White, 1961

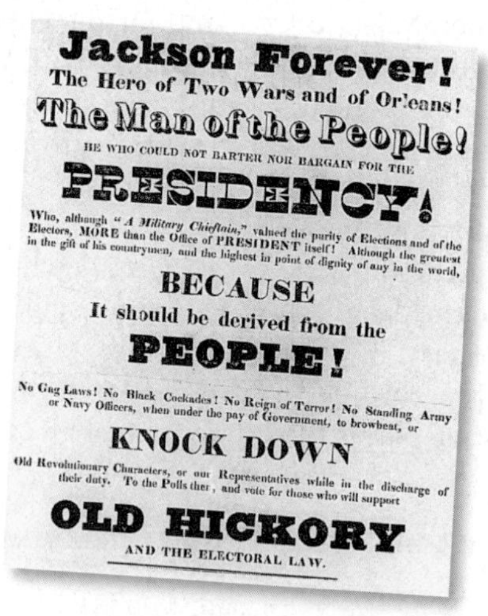

Andrew Jackson presented himself to voters as the hero of the "common man."

Presidential Nominations

The most exciting and dramatic election in American politics is the presidential election. Every 4 years, each major party gathers during July or August in a national convention. Elected or appointed delegates representing the 50 states, Guam, Puerto Rico, the Virgin Islands, American Samoa, and the District of Columbia attend the convention. The task of the delegates is to select a **ticket**—candidates for president and vice president—that will win in the November general election. Because this ticket, if elected, can change history and affect every American's life, millions of Americans watch the televised coverage of the conventions. The drama and spectacle of a convention, however, have not always been so open to the public's view. Likewise, presidential nominations have not always been as democratic as they are today.

The History of Presidential Nominations

Before national nominating conventions, congressional caucuses chose presidential candidates. From 1800 to 1824, congressional leaders from each party met in secret and selected their party's ticket. In the presidential election of 1824, Andrew Jackson made the caucus system an issue, declaring that a small group of representatives did not speak for the nation. Although Jackson lost the election, his revolt against "King Caucus," as he called it, discredited the caucus system and led to the eventual adoption of the nominating convention.

A minor political party, the Anti-Masons, held the first national convention in 1831, and the two major parties quickly copied the idea. Since 1832 a convention of party members has chosen major party presidential candidates. To make these conventions more democratic, by 1916 almost half the states were choosing **convention delegates** in presidential primary elections.

For years, when citizens voted in a presidential primary, they really were choosing among groups of party members pledged to support specific candidates. The group pledged to the winning candidate became that state's delegation to the national convention.

In the 1970s, however, both major parties provided a more democratic nomination process. For example, new party rules encouraged that women, minorities, and young people be included as convention delegates. By 1988, presidential primaries existed in 38 states and were part of the selection process for three-fourths of the delegates to the two national conventions.

Presidential Primaries Today Like other primary elections, presidential primaries operate under a wide variety of state laws. In addition, each party frequently changes its rules regarding delegate selection. Even in the same state, each party's primary may operate under different procedures. The following three generalizations, however, can be made about presidential primaries: (1) They may be a delegate selection process or a presidential preference poll, or both. (2) Either the candidate who wins the primary gets all the state's convention delegates (called "winner-take-all"), or each candidate gets delegates based on how many popular votes he or she receives in the primary. (3) Delegates selected on the basis of the popular vote may be required to support a certain candidate at the national convention, or they may be uncommitted.

Many presidential primaries were originally winner-take-all. The Democrats now use **proportional representation.** Under this system a state's delegates must represent the candidates in proportion to the popular vote each receives in the primary once a certain threshold is reached. The Republicans allow both winner-take-all and proportional systems.

Although proportional representation was intended to make a party's nomination process more democratic, in many states it had an unanticipated result. Combined with the other rules for state delegations, proportional representation made delegate selection almost impossibly complicated. Consequently, today more than half the states with presidential primaries hold "beauty contests." These are preference polls in which voters indicate which candidate they would like to be the nominee. Caucuses later choose the actual delegates.

Criticisms of Presidential Primaries

While most people agree that the presidential primary system is a great improvement over the previous method of selecting convention delegates, it has its critics. A major criticism is that the primaries extend over too long a time in an election year. With the first primary held in February and the last in June, seeking a party's nomination is a very long, costly, and exhausting process.

Another criticism is that the primaries seem to make the image of the candidates more important than the issues. The news media's coverage of primary campaigns tends to play up candidates' personalities rather than their positions on important questions. Also, relatively few people vote in primaries. Thus, the winner of a primary may not be as popular as the victory would indicate.

Candidates who win the early primaries capture the media spotlight. Often the other candidates are saddled with a "loser" image that makes it difficult for them to raise campaign contributions. Some are forced to drop out before the majority of voters in either party have the chance to pick their choice for the nominee.

Some states have joined forces to create regional primaries. Fourteen Southern states, from Texas to Maryland, held their 1988 Democratic presidential primaries on March 8. Candidates who did not do well in this "Super Tuesday" election lost almost all chance of becoming their party's nominee.

Getting to the National Convention

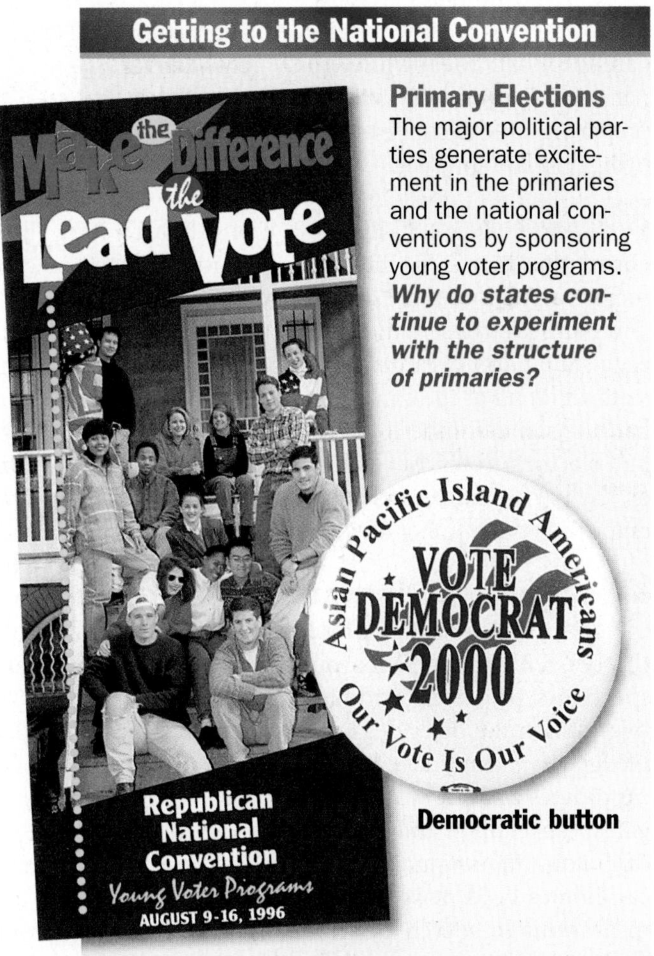

Primary Elections
The major political parties generate excitement in the primaries and the national conventions by sponsoring young voter programs. ***Why do states continue to experiment with the structure of primaries?***

Democratic button

Because primaries eliminate many opponents, they often result in one-sided convention victories for particular candidates. Some observers believe that the nominating convention itself has become simply a rubber-stamp operation. If the primary winners come to the convention with enough delagate votes to win the nomination, they ask, why hold the nominating convention at all? Of course, it is possible that in the future, primary election support for contenders will be more equally divided, in which case the convention will once again be an arena of debate over and real battles for the presidential nomination.

The National Convention

From February to June, the candidates crisscross the country competing for delegate support. Meanwhile, the national committee staff is preparing for the convention to be held in late summer.

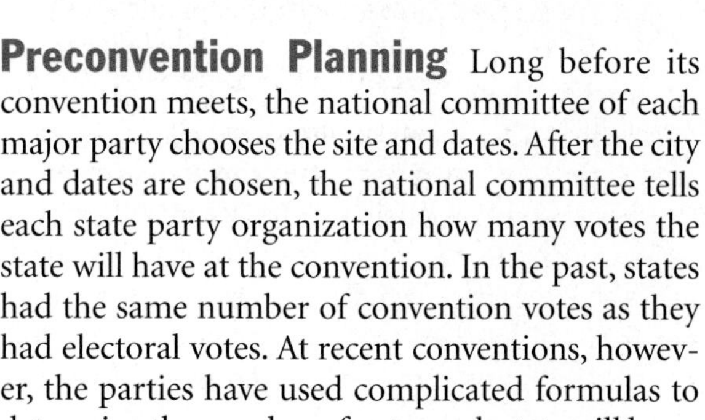

Supporting presidential candidates

Preconvention Planning Long before its convention meets, the national committee of each major party chooses the site and dates. After the city and dates are chosen, the national committee tells each state party organization how many votes the state will have at the convention. In the past, states had the same number of convention votes as they had electoral votes. At recent conventions, however, the parties have used complicated formulas to determine the number of votes each state will have.

Assembling the Convention From across the country, thousands of delegates assemble in the convention city, accompanied by a mass of spectators, protesters, and news media representatives. When the delegates arrive, many are already pledged to a candidate, but others are not. All the candidates actively woo these uncommitted delegates, especially if the presidential nomination is still in doubt. As rumors of political deals circulate, candidates hold news conferences, and reporters mill about in search of stories. One writer described a national convention as:

> "*. . . an American invention as native to the U.S.A. as corn pone or apple pie. . . . It has something of the gaiety of a four-ring circus, something of the sentiment of a class reunion, and something of the tub-thumping frenzy of a backwoods camp meeting.*"
>
> —Theodore H. White

The noise and confusion subside as the party chairperson calls the opening session to order. The evening of the opening day marks the keynote speech, an address by an important party member intended to unite the party for the coming campaign. The delegates then approve the convention's four standing committees—rules and order of business, credentials, permanent organization, and platform and resolutions—that have been at work for several weeks.

Because in recent conventions there has been little suspense about who would be either party's candidate, the only real conflict has involved committee reports. The convention spends the second and third days, or even longer, listening to these reports and to speeches about them.

The Rules Committee Each party's **rules committee** governs the way its convention is run. The committee proposes rules for convention procedure and sets the convention's order of business. The delegates must approve any proposed changes in the rules of the last convention. Although the rules committee report is usually accepted, at times real battles have developed over it. The outcome of a rules fight can be vital to a candidate for the presidential nomination. For example, at the 1980 Democratic convention, Senator Edward Kennedy was eager to capture the nomination, even though President Jimmy Carter had won a majority of the delegates in the primaries.

Thinking that many of the Carter delegates were not strong supporters of the president, Kennedy sought to defeat a rule binding delegates to vote for the candidate who had won their state primary. If the rule were defeated, the Carter delegates would be free to support whomever they wished. Kennedy felt that many of the Carter delegates would then switch to him. When Kennedy lost this rules vote, he also lost whatever chance he had for the nomination.

The Credentials Committee The credentials committee must approve the delegations from each state. Sometimes disputes arise over who the proper delegates are. Candidates who trail in delegate support may challenge the credentials of their opponents' delegates. Two entire rival delegations may even appear at the convention, each claiming to be a state's official delegation. It is up to the credentials committee to determine which delegates should be seated. Although the committee's decisions may be appealed on the convention floor, the delegates generally accept its report without changes.

Fights over credentials often have been livelier than rules fights at national conventions. In 1964, for example, African Americans at the Democratic convention charged that an all-white Mississippi delegation had excluded them, giving the African American citizens of Mississippi no representation at the convention. The credentials committee allowed some African Americans to be seated in the Mississippi delegation. In 1968 the same situation occurred. The committee refused to seat another all-white Mississippi delegation, and this time replaced it with an integrated rival delegation.

The Committee on Permanent Organization This committee selects the permanent chairperson and other officials for the convention. After it reports, the delegates elect the permanent convention officials who take the day-to-day control of the convention from the temporary officials.

The Platform Committee The platform committee, as its name suggests, is assigned an important task—the writing of the party's **platform,** a statement of its principles, beliefs, and positions on vital issues. It also spells out how the party intends to deal with these issues. The party must try to adopt a platform that appeals to all factions, or divisions, at the convention—not always an easy task.

Part of the difficulty in getting platforms accepted is that individual parts of the platform, called **planks,** may divide the delegates. In 1968, for example, a pro-Vietnam War plank angered Democrats who wanted the United States to withdraw from that conflict. In 1980 the Republican platform contained a plank opposing the Equal Rights Amendment. Although this plank was controversial, the platform passed.

Because the party's presidential candidate must support the party platform, all contenders try to get their viewpoints into the platform. Rival candidates with opposing views often will create a fight within the party over the platform. The danger is that a platform fight may divide the party. If the fight is bitter, as it was for Democrats in 1968, the party may become so divided that it loses the election.

Party Conventions Some first-timers at the Republican National Convention in Philadelphia in 2000 were astounded by the excitement and energy of the crowd. ***Why do the major political parties strive to hold entertaining national conventions?***

Nominating the Candidates After each committee's reports are adopted, the highlight of the convention occurs. It is time to select the party's candidate for president. From the opening day, the leading contenders have been working to hold onto their delegates and to gain as many uncommitted delegates as possible.

In recent years, however, the front-runners have won enough committed delegates in the primaries to take the suspense out of the nominating process. Even so, the nominating speech for each candidate sets off a demonstration, as supporters parade around the convention hall. After the nominating speeches and all the seconding speeches that follow are made, the balloting starts.

The convention chairperson now instructs the clerk to read the alphabetical roll call of the states, and the chairperson of each state delegation calls out the delegates' votes. The candidate who receives a majority of the votes becomes the party's nominee. If no candidate does, then further roll calls must be taken until one candidate wins a majority.

In recent conventions most candidates have been selected on the first ballot. This is partly because television has helped to narrow the field of candidates in the primaries. Candidates who win few delegates in the early primary states quickly drop out, knowing that they will not be able to raise the large sums of money needed to keep the campaign going. By convention time, there may be no mystery about who will be the presidential nominee.

Party leaders benefit from the early victory of one candidate, having more time to plan the convention and unify the party. The convention can then become a scripted television event. However, with the mystery removed from the nominating process, a convention may not be able to attract a large television audience. This is one reason that the major television networks have reduced their coverage to a few hours of prime time.

Walter Mondale chose Geraldine Ferraro as his running mate.

The Vice-Presidential Nomination The vice-presidential nomination, which normally takes place on the last day of the convention, may create some suspense. Usually, the party's presidential nominee selects a running mate, and the convention automatically nominates the person chosen. A vice-presidential candidate is generally selected to balance the ticket, meaning that he or she has a personal, political, and geographic background different from the presidential nominee. This balance is designed to make the ticket appeal to as many voters as possible.

In 1960 John F. Kennedy, a young Catholic senator from Massachusetts, chose Lyndon B. Johnson, an older Protestant senator from Texas, as his running mate. In 1984 Minnesota senator Walter F. Mondale made New York representative Geraldine Ferraro the first female vice-presidential major party candidate.

Adjournment With the nomination of the presidential and vice-presidential candidates, the convention is almost over. These major nominees appear before the delegates and make their acceptance speeches. These speeches are intended to bring the party together, to attack the opposition party, to sound a theme for the upcoming campaign, and to appeal to a national television audience. The convention then adjourns.

Section 3 Assessment

Checking for Understanding

1. **Main Idea** Use a graphic organizer like the one below to show four ways candidates for office can get on the ballot and why each method has drawn criticism.

Method	Criticism

2. **Define** caucus, nominating convention, boss, direct primary, closed primary, open primary, plurality, runoff primary, ticket, platform, plank.
3. **Identify** convention delegates, rules committee.
4. How do states deal with the situation in which no primary candidate wins a majority of votes?
5. How is each major party's presidential candidate chosen at its national nominating convention?

Critical Thinking

6. **Making Generalizations** What historical and political changes in society have influenced presidential nominating methods?

Political Processes Create a poster that presents a democratic and cost-efficient system for selecting nominees for president.

Using an Electronic Spreadsheet

People use electronic spreadsheets to manage large groups of numbers quickly and easily. You can use an electronic spreadsheet and allow the computer to perform the mathematical functions with any data that involves numbers that can be arranged in columns and rows.

Learning the Skill

A spreadsheet is an electronic worksheet. It is made up of numbered cells that form rows and columns. Each column (vertical) is assigned a letter or number. Each row (horizontal) is assigned a number. Each point where a column and row intersect is called a *cell.* The cell's position on the spreadsheet is labeled according to its corresponding column and row—Column A, Row 1 (A1); Column B, Row 2 (B2) and so on. See the diagram below.

A1	B1	C1	D1	E1
A2	B2	C2	D2	E2
A3	B3	C3	D3	E3
A4	B4	C4	D4	E4
A5	B5	C5	D5	E5

Spreadsheets use *standard formulas* to calculate the numbers. By entering a simple equation into the computer, you command the computer to add, subtract, multiply, or divide the numbers in specific cells, rows, or columns.

To make changes in a spreadsheet, use a mouse or the cursor keys to move to the cell you choose. That cell will be highlighted or have a border around it. If you change a number in any cell, the computer will automatically change the totals to reflect the new number. The computer will even copy a formula from one cell to another.

Practicing the Skill

Suppose you wanted to chart the number of votes the Republican, Democratic, and third-party candidates received in the last five presidential elections. Use these steps to create a spreadsheet that will provide this information:

1. In cells B1 and C1, respectively, type the name of the political party; in cell D1 type in *Third Party*. In cell E1, type the term *total.*
2. In cells A2-A6, type the year of a presidential election. In cell A7, type the word *total.*
3. In row 2, enter the number of votes each party received in the year named in cell A2. Repeat this process in rows 3-6.
4. Create a formula to calculate the votes. The formula for the equation tells which cells (B2 + B3 + B4 + B5 + B6) to add together.
5. Copy the formula to the right in the cells for the other parties.
6. Use the process in steps 4 and 5 to create and copy a formula to calculate the total number of votes all parties received in each year.

Application Activity

Use a spreadsheet to enter your test scores and your homework grades. At the end of the grading period, input the correct formula and the spreadsheet will calculate your average grade.

Chapter 16

Assessment and Activities

GOVERNMENT *Online*

Self-Check Quiz Visit the *United States Government: Democracy in Action* Web site at gov.glencoe.com and click on ***Chapter 16–Self-Check Quizzes*** to prepare for the chapter test.

Reviewing Key Terms

Insert the correct terms into the sentences below. Some terms will be used more than once.

bosses	**ticket**
plank	**national convention**
ideology	**platform**
caucus	

1. A political party's (1) is expressed in each (2) of the (3) that it adopts at the (4) to select its (5).
2. Although the (6) replaced the party (7) in choosing its (8), the party's (9) continued to influence the nomination process.

Recalling Facts

1. Identify the pairs of major parties that have existed in American history.
2. What is the function of the rules committee?
3. What is the main function of the two major political parties?
4. What are the responsibilities of a precinct captain within a political party?
5. What role does the political party out of power assume?
6. What is the difference between open and closed primaries?
7. Identify the three types of third parties and identify a party of each type.
8. What is the purpose of the credentials committee?

Understanding Concepts

1. **Growth of Democracy** Why have third parties had so little success in the United States?
2. **Political Processes** Why are many Americans uninformed about the issues in a campaign?
3. **Political Processes** Why is a primary election better than a party caucus for selecting candidates?

Critical Thinking

1. **Understanding Cause and Effect** The two major parties are criticized as being out of touch with the needs of many Americans. How might a successful third party affect the two major parties?
2. **Predicting Consequences** Use a graphic organizer like the one below to identify the advantages and disadvantages of a national primary to nominate each party's presidential candidate.

Advantages	Disadvantages

Current Events JOURNAL

Multiparty Systems Use newsmagazines to research the political events of the past year in countries that have multiparty systems, such as Japan, Italy, Israel, and France. Find out about an election or an event that had an impact on the government of one of these countries, and how the existence of several parties affected the outcome of the election or the event. Present your findings in a brief written report.

Chapter 16

Cooperative Learning Activity

Political Parties Research the history of American political parties. Organize into groups of three or four, and choose a leader to coordinate the project. Have your group choose a political party—either a major party or a third party, and prepare a brief history of it. Create an illustrated time line showing major events in the party's history to accompany your report. Divide research, writing, and illustrating tasks among your group members. Display the report and time line in the classroom.

Interpreting Political Cartoons Activity

1. What event is this cartoon documenting?
2. What symbols does the cartoonist use?
3. Why does the elephant seem so jubilant?

Skill Practice Activity

Using an Electronic Spreadsheet Use a spreadsheet to record the frequency of news about political parties. Scan a local or national newspaper every day for two weeks to find out how many times political parties are mentioned, which political parties are mentioned, and why the party is in the news. Print out your spreadsheet and use it to analyze the impact of political parties on Americans' daily lives.

Technology Activity

Using the Internet Find current information about the Democratic and Republican Parties on the Internet. Use a search engine to find the sites for the Democratic and Republican Parties. Some states include sites that provide information about events of the respective parties at the state level. After compiling your information, write an information pamphlet about ways that citizens can participate in state political parties. Share your findings with the class.

Participating in State Government

The method by which delegates are selected to national nominating conventions depends on party rules and on the laws of each state. Work with a partner to determine the process in your state. Contact each party's county and state organizations and local board of elections to find out the following information:

- How many delegates your state sends to each party's national convention
- How this number is determined
- How the delegates to the national convention are selected
- Any special laws or rules that apply to the processes

When all information is gathered and analyzed, present your findings to the class.

Chapter 17

Elections and Voting

Why It's Important

Every Vote Counts A successful democracy is built on an informed electorate that is influenced by many factors. You are—or soon will be—part of that electorate.

To find out more about how to cast your vote and to learn about its impact, view the ***Democracy in Action*** Chapter 17 video lesson:

Elections and Voting

GOVERNMENT Online

Chapter Overview Visit the *United States Government: Democracy in Action* Web site at gov.glencoe.com and click on ***Chapter 17—Overview*** to preview chapter information.

Section 1

Election Campaigns

Reader's Guide

Key Terms

campaign manager, image, political action committee, soft money

Find Out

- What are the basic elements of a presidential campaign?
- Why were the Federal Election Campaign Acts passed?

Understanding Concepts

Political Processes What strategic decisions must political parties and candidates make during each campaign?

COVER STORY

Presidential Standoff

WASHINGTON, D.C., NOVEMBER 20, 2000

Nearly two weeks after the election, Democrat Al Gore and Republican George W. Bush are still battling to win the presidency. Disputed votes in Florida make it impossible to declare a national winner. Although Gore appears to have won the nationwide popular vote by some 300,000 votes, Florida's electoral votes are needed for either candidate to reach the winning number of 271. At issue were vote counts in four populous counties. Hand recounts could not be completed by the Secretary of State's deadline, and Gore asked the Florida Supreme Court to rule. When the court altered the Secretary of State's deadline, Bush then turned to the U.S. Supreme Court, asking it to rule that the Florida judicial branch could not interfere with the state's legislature.

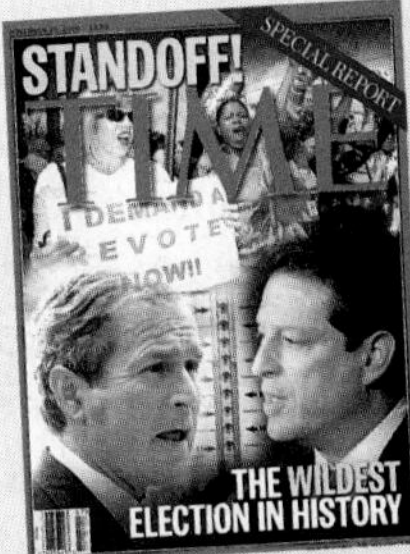

TIME Cover

Running for political office is expensive. National elections to select all representatives and one-third of the senators are held every two years. Senators and representatives spend considerable time and effort raising campaign funds. Presidential elections are held every four years. Candidates for the highest office must have access to hundreds of millions of dollars to run their campaigns. The presidential campaign is not only expensive, but also is a lengthy and complex process. The reward for the winner, however, is the most powerful position in government.

Electing the President

Candidates for president begin organizing their campaigns almost one year before the election. Primary races in the spring help to narrow the field of candidates. Following the national conventions in late summer, the presidential campaigns become intense by early September. They end on Election Day—the first Tuesday after the first Monday of November. During the final eight weeks of the campaign, the candidates spend long, frenzied hours traveling from state to state. Taping television messages, shaking hands, making speeches, giving interviews, and many other campaign activities are exhausting. Candidates may forget where they are and greet the people of Denver with a "Hello, Dallas." The slipup will be on the nightly news.

Electoral Votes and the States To be elected president, a candidate must win at least 270 of the 538 available electoral votes. The total electoral vote is equal to the number of representatives and senators from all the states, plus 3 votes from Washington, D.C. Each state's electoral vote is the total number of its senators and representatives in Congress.

The candidate who wins the greatest number of popular votes in any state usually receives all of that state's electoral votes. To win the

◀ **Students support an election campaign.**

"Faithless Electors" **The electors in the electoral college system almost always vote as expected, so that the nominee of the party that carried the popular vote wins all of the state's electoral votes (according to the winner-take-all system, used in all states but Maine and Nebraska). Exceptions are rare, with only 9 so-called "faithless electors" among the more than 17,000 electors chosen since 1789. In 1988, for example, Democratic nominee Michael Dukakis was denied 1 of his 112 electoral votes when a West Virginia elector cast her ballot for Dukakis's running mate, Lloyd Bentsen. She gave her vice-presidential vote to Dukakis.**

presidency, a candidate must pay special attention throughout the campaign to those states with large populations such as California, New York, Texas, and Pennsylvania. The larger a state's population, the more electoral votes it has. A presidential candidate who won the electoral votes of the 10 or 11 largest states would obtain the 270 votes necessary to win the presidency.

It makes sense, therefore, for a presidential candidate to pay attention to the states with large electoral votes. These states will be visited more by the candidate during the campaign and its citizens will also see and hear more advertisements promoting the candidate. When these largest states appear to be divided between the contenders, however, other states with smaller electoral votes become vital to the candidates.

Campaign Strategy Planning how to capture key states is only one of many decisions a presidential candidate must make. For example, should the candidate wage an aggressive, all-out attack on an opponent, or would a more low-key campaign be a better strategy? What should be the theme or slogan of the campaign? What issues should be stressed? How much money should be spent on television commercials, radio advertising, and newspaper ads?

Campaign Organization A strong organization is essential to running a presidential campaign. Heading the organization is a **campaign manager,** who is responsible for overall strategy and planning. In the national office, individuals handle relations with television, radio, the print media, and manage finances, advertising, opinion polls, and campaign materials.

On the state and local levels, the state party chairperson usually coordinates a campaign. Local party officials and field workers contact voters, hold local rallies, and distribute campaign literature. The field workers, who are usually volunteers, ring doorbells, canvass voters by telephone, and do whatever they can do to make sure voters turn out to vote on Election Day.

Television and the Candidate's Image

The **image,** or mental picture, that voters have of a candidate is extremely important. The candidate who is perceived as more "presidential" has a decided advantage on Election Day. The mass media are extremely powerful in any campaign because they can create both positive and negative images for the candidates.

The most important communication tool for a presidential candidate is television. Studies have shown that people are more likely to believe what they see and hear on television than what they read in the newspapers or hear on the radio. A candidate's organization spends a great deal of time and effort on "packaging" its candidate. Political commercials create the candidate's presidential image.

Just as important as candidates' appearances on television commercials are their appearances on the news programs. Television is now the single most commonly used source of news for most Americans. Television coverage is the main way millions of citizens have of knowing how a campaign is progressing.

Another way in which candidates use television in presidential campaigns is to participate in debates. Televised debates were first held in 1960 and have been held in every campaign since 1976. Because they come late in the campaign, debates often affect voters who are undecided. Both parties know that these voters may determine the winner of the election. Preparing for a debate has become very serious business.

Financing Campaigns

Running for political office is expensive. Spending for each seat in Congress in 1996 cost about $1.5 million. Presidential candidates spent an estimated $400 million. Republicans and Democrats spent more than $1.6 billion in the 1996 election cycle, more than 37 percent higher than in 1992. The 1996 election made campaign finance reform a political issue, both because of the amount of money spent and questionable fund-raising methods.

Campaign Finance Rules Until the 1970s, candidates for public office relied on contributions from business organizations, labor unions, and interested individuals. This system of financing political campaigns tended to give wealthy individuals and groups the opportunity to wield a great deal of political power. It also cast suspicion on successful candidates—perhaps they owed special favors or treatment to the people who contributed to their campaigns. Under this system, political figures with greater access to money stood a better chance of reaching the voters than those who did not command such support.

The Federal Election Campaign Act of 1971 (and its amendments in 1974, 1976, and 1979) provided for a new system of campaign financing for federal elections based on three principles: (1) public funding of presidential elections, (2) limitations on the amounts presidential candidates could spend on their campaigns, and (3) public disclosure of how much candidates spend to get elected.

Under these laws, business organizations and labor unions were prohibited from making any direct contributions. Individuals, however, could contribute up to $1,000 to any candidate's primary or general election campaign.

Political Action Committees The new election campaign laws encouraged the growth of political action committees (PACs). A **political action committee** is an organization designed to support political candidates with campaign contributions.

An individual may contribute up to $5,000 to a PAC. While a PAC may not contribute more than

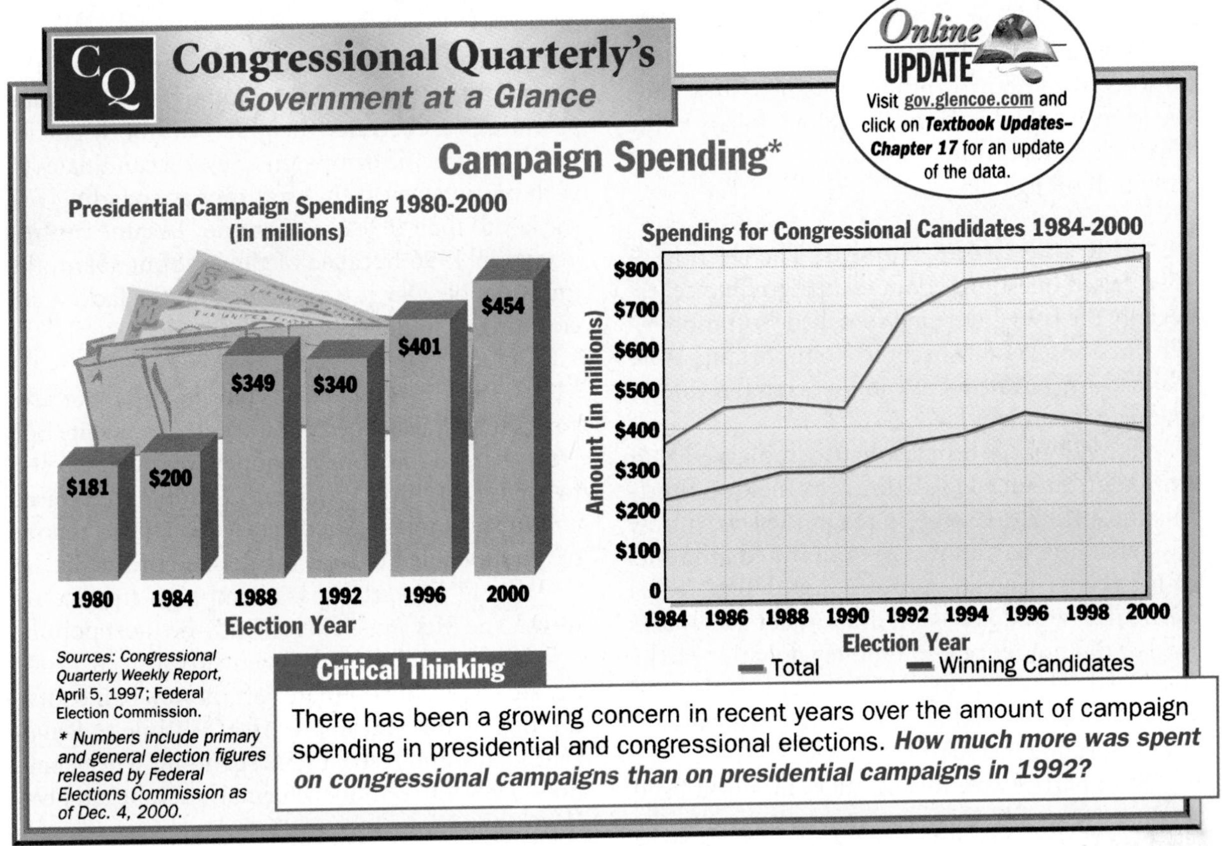

Sources: Congressional Quarterly Weekly Report, April 5, 1997; Federal Election Commission.

** Numbers include primary and general election figures released by Federal Elections Commission as of Dec. 4, 2000.*

Critical Thinking

There has been a growing concern in recent years over the amount of campaign spending in presidential and congressional elections. ***How much more was spent on congressional campaigns than on presidential campaigns in 1992?***

Working in a Campaign

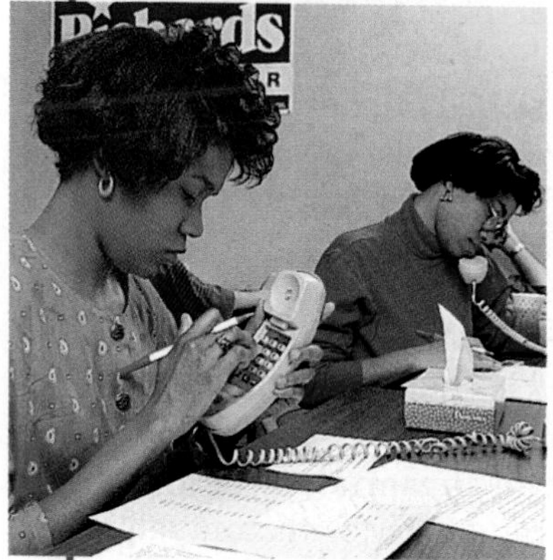

Campaign workers

Even if you are not eligible to vote, you can still support the candidate of your choice by becoming a volunteer in his or her campaign. A phone call or a visit to the candidate's local headquarters will sign you up as a campaign worker.

Volunteers perform many routine campaign activities. On one occasion you might stuff envelopes with campaign literature. On another, you may go door to door in a neighborhood to distribute brochures and talk to people about the candidate. You could help staff a phone bank that is calling voters with a prepared message about the candidate. On Election Day, your job might be to call selected voters to remind them to vote or to ask if they need a ride to the polls.

Volunteering in a campaign helps the candidate you favor, as well as gives you a good look at election politics from the inside.

Activity

1. Call the local branch of the Democratic Party or Republican Party to obtain more information on volunteering for the party. Share this information with the class.
2. Find the candidate of your choice in an upcoming election. Focus on a race and gather information on the candidates involved. Then create a summary of each candidate's position on issues. Which candidate do you support? Why?

$5,000 to a single candidate, it may make contributions to as many candidates as it wishes. PAC spending climbed from a few million dollars in the 1975–76 election cycle to about $430 million in 1995–96.

Serious Questions Raised The election of 1996 raised questions about campaign finance, especially the laws governing so-called "soft money." Why had soft money become so important? Were major contributors merely influencing the vote or buying government favors?

In 1979 party officials had complained that campaign finance legislation was making fund-raising difficult. Congress responded with new laws enabling parties to raise unlimited amounts of money for general purposes, not designated to particular candidates—**soft money.** For a few years the law did not require soft money donations to be disclosed. Then, a suit filed by the organization Common Cause resulted in a rule requiring disclosure beginning in 1991.

Both parties were raising huge amounts of soft money. Generally, business donated more to the Republican Party, while labor supported the Democrats. In the 1996 campaign soft money spending reached new heights, with both parties targeting specific campaigns. Several candidates in each party believed that soft money spending was the key to their defeat. Soft money became controversial in 1996 because of the amount spent, the questionable way it was raised, and the lack of accounting as to how it was spent.

The Road to Reform? During the 1996 campaign, fund-raising became an issue. Candidate Bob Dole charged that foreign money was buying access to the Oval Office. President Clinton called for an end to soft money. After the election, news reports of questionable fund-raising flooded the media.

Would Congress pass campaign finance reform? The McCain-Feingold bill, the most popular alternative, had already been introduced in the Senate. It would eliminate soft money, ban contributions by foreigners, give free TV time to Senate candidates, and restrict PAC spending. The Senate, however, wanted more information. It began hearings in the summer of 1997.

Why is campaign finance reform so difficult? The political stakes are high. PACs generally give incumbents the lion's share of their contributions. Why should incumbents willingly vote for reforms to make it easier for challengers to unseat them? In 1993, when Democrats controlled Congress and the White House, they found ways to avoid passing a reform bill. Republicans, who controlled Congress after 1995, did no better.

Ceiling on Campaign Spending

Presidential candidates may accept federal funding for their campaigns. If they do—and all major party presidential candidates since 1976 have accepted—they are limited in how much they may spend. In 2000 the Republican, Democratic, and Reform Party candidates received $155 million from the government.

Presidential candidates of third parties qualify for federal funding if their party received more than 5 percent of the popular vote in the previous presidential election. Ross Perot accomplished this feat in 1996 for the Reform Party, and so the 2000 Reform Party candidate, Pat Buchanan, qualified for federal funding in the 2000 election.

Disclosure Under the federal election laws, candidates, political action committees, and political parties must keep records of contributions and report to the **Federal Election Commission** (FEC) all contributions over $100. The FEC, an independent agency in the executive branch, administers the federal election laws. The FEC's records are open to public inspection.

Money and Ethics

Campaign Reform Questionable campaign funding has dominated partisan battles on Capitol Hill. ***According to the cartoonist, how has the high cost of running for public office affected the ethics of campaign fund-raising?***

Section 1 Assessment

Checking for Understanding

1. **Main Idea** Use a graphic organizer like the one below to show the effects the Federal Election Campaign Acts had on campaign financing.

CAUSE		EFFECTS
Federal Election Campaign Acts	→	

2. **Define** campaign manager, image, political action committee, soft money.
3. **Identify** Federal Election Commission.
4. How can third party candidates qualify for federal funds for a presidential campaign?

Critical Thinking

5. **Synthesizing Information** PACs can contribute to as many political candidates as they wish. Why might they contribute to all major candidates in a presidential campaign?

Political Processes Imagine that you are running for political office. Prepare a campaign strategy for your election. Explain what campaign tools you would use and how you would finance your campaign. Create an illustrated poster outlining your strategy.

Synthesizing Information

Synthesizing information involves integrating information from two or more sources. The ability to synthesize, or combine, information is important because information gained from one source often sheds new light upon other information. If you can synthesize information, you will get more out of everything you read.

Learning the Skill

To synthesize information, follow these steps:

- Decide whether the two sources are comparable. Ask: Can Source A give me new information or new ways of thinking about Source B?
- If you decide that the two are comparable, put into your own words what you can learn or what new hypotheses you can make.

Following are a chart and a bar graph giving information on votes by major political parties and political party identification of the adult population. The first step in synthesizing information is to examine each source separately. The bar graph shows the votes cast for president in 1988 and 1992. The chart details what political party adults claimed to support.

The next step is to ask whether the information given in the two sources is comparable. The answer is yes. Finally, we ask: what can the chart tell us about the bar graph? The bar graph indicates whether adults voted in 1988 and 1992 according to the political party they claimed to support.

Practicing the Skill

Use what you have learned to examine the graph and the chart, and answer the questions that follow.

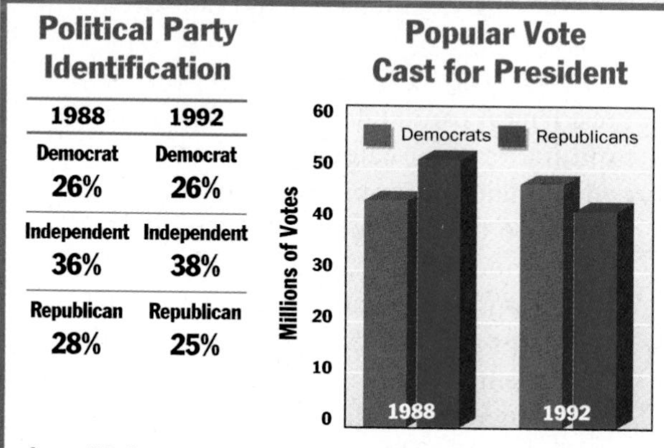

Political Party Identification

1988	1992
Democrat 26%	Democrat 26%
Independent 36%	Independent 38%
Republican 28%	Republican 25%

Source: U.S. Bureau of the Census, *Statistical Abstract of the United States: 1996* (Washington, D.C.: 1996).

1. What percentage of Americans identified themselves as Independent in 1988? How did this change in 1992? How did this change affect the presidential election of 1992?
2. Did more Americans identify themselves as Democrats or Republicans in 1992? Did this match the way people voted? Explain.
3. What conclusions can you draw from the graph and chart together?

Application Activity

Find two sources of information on a topic dealing with political parties and write a short report. In your report, answer these questions: What are the main ideas in the sources? How does each source add to your understanding of the topic? Do the sources support or contradict each other?

The **Glencoe Skillbuilder Interactive Workbook, Level 2** provides instruction and practice in key social studies skills.

Expanding Voting Rights

Reader's Guide

Key Terms

suffrage, grandfather clause, poll tax

Find Out

- Why did it take so long for African Americans and for women to win voting rights?
- What did each of the voting rights acts achieve?

Understanding Concepts

Growth of Democracy What were the steps in the process of extending the right to vote to all adult citizens?

COVER STORY

Videotaping of Polls OK?

MONTGOMERY, ALABAMA, OCTOBER 1994

The U.S. Department of Justice has advised state officials in Mississippi and Alabama that to allow private videotaping at polling places on Election Day may be a violation of federal law. Some largely white citizens' groups in these states have formed so-called "ballot security" forces to police certain polling places. These groups claim that their videotaping helps to combat voting fraud. However, Justice Department attorneys worry that the taping makes some African Americans uncomfortable and may prevent them from voting. "We will not countenance any thinly veiled attempts to intimidate black voters at the polls," warned Assistant Attorney General Deval Patrick.

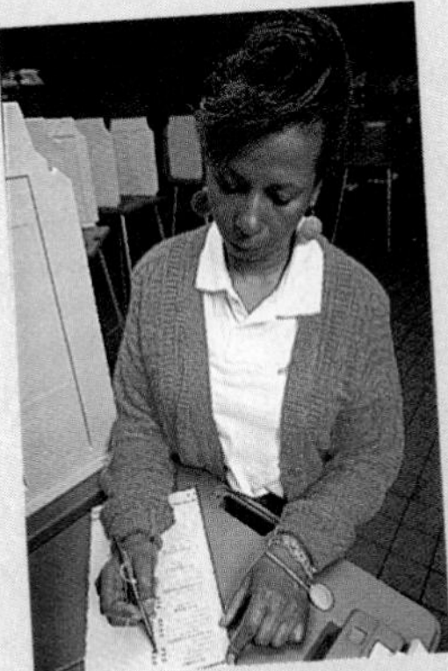

Not intimidated by "security"

Voting is not a privilege, it is a right. Voting is absolutely vital to the success of American democracy. After all, democracy means rule by the people. Through their votes, Americans have the power to select more than 500,000 government officials at all levels of government.

The right to vote, or **suffrage,** is the foundation of American democracy. Today almost all United States citizens 18 years old or older may exercise this right. Like other rights, however, the right to vote is not absolute. It is subject to regulations and restrictions. Unlike today, the right to vote for all citizens over the age of 18 did not always exist. During various periods in the history of the United States, law, custom, and sometimes even violence prevented certain groups of people from voting.

Early Limitations on Voting

Before the American Revolution, the colonies placed many restrictions on the right to vote. Women and most African Americans were not allowed to vote; neither were white males who did not own property or pay taxes. Also excluded in some colonies were people who were not members of the dominant religious group. As a result, only about 5 or 6 percent of the adult population was eligible to vote.

Why did these restrictions exist? Educated men of the time did not believe in mass democracy in which every adult could vote. Many believed voting was best left to wealthy, white, property-owning males. As John Jay, first chief justice of the United States, put it: "The people who own the country ought to govern it."

During the first half of the 1800s, state legislatures gradually abolished property requirements and religious restrictions for voting. By the mid-1800s the country had achieved universal white adult male suffrage. The issue of woman suffrage, however, had not been addressed.

We the People
Making a Difference
Christine Todd Whitman

New Jersey State seal

Kate Whitman is proud that her mother is Governor Christine Todd Whitman. She's also proud that her mother supports equal rights and equal pay and knows about the plight of working mothers. She knows that her mother wants to make the streets "safe from assault weapons and drunk drivers." Kate saw her mother rise, in just a few years, from Somerset County freeholder to become the governor of New Jersey. Now Christine Todd Whitman is considered to be a potential vice-presidential or even presidential candidate in the future.

During the gubernatorial race in New Jersey, Whitman acknowledged her obstacles. She knew that voters would be hard on a female candidate. She spent years of hard campaigning, fund-raising, and shaking more hands than she could count. Although self-confidence comes naturally to Whitman, in the world of politics she required a renewed sense of determination. Her hard work paid off but did not end after she won the election.

Whitman initiated bold proposals to rebuild New Jersey's economy. She reduced taxes, cut government spending, and made New Jersey's government smaller and more efficient. Whitman's victories have made her a rising star in the Republican Party. Becoming the first female in state history to win the governor's seat in New Jersey may have been just the first step in a life of campaigns and political victories.

Woman Suffrage

The fight for woman suffrage dates from the mid-1800s. Woman suffrage groups grew in number and effectiveness in the last half of the century, and by 1914 they had won the right to vote in 11 states, all of them west of the Mississippi. Not until after World War I, when the Nineteenth Amendment was ratified, was woman suffrage put into effect nationwide. The Nineteenth Amendment states:

> *"The right of citizens of the United States to vote shall not be denied or abridged by the United States or by any State on account of sex."*
>
> —Nineteenth Amendment, 1920

African American Suffrage

When the Constitution went into effect in 1789, African Americans, both enslaved and free, made up about 10 percent of the United States population. Yet nowhere were enslaved persons permitted to vote, and free African Americans who were allowed to vote could do so in only a few states.

The Fifteenth Amendment The first effort to extend suffrage to African Americans nationwide came shortly after the Civil War, when the Fifteenth Amendment[1] was ratified in 1870. The amendment provided that no state can deprive any citizen of the right to vote "on account of race, color, or previous condition of servitude." In addition to extending suffrage to African Americans, this amendment was important because for the first time the national government set rules for voting, a power that only the states had previously exercised.

Grandfather Clause Although the Fifteenth Amendment was an important milestone on the road to full suffrage, it did not result in complete voting rights for African Americans. Southern states, for example, set up a number of roadblocks

See the following footnoted materials in the **Reference Handbook:**
1. *The Constitution*, pages 774–799.

designed to limit and discourage the participation of African American voters.

One such roadblock was the so-called grandfather clause incorporated in the constitutions of some Southern states. The **grandfather clause** provided that only voters whose grandfathers had voted before 1867 were eligible to vote without paying a poll tax or passing a literacy test. Because the grandfathers of most African American Southerners had been enslaved and had not been permitted to vote, this clause effectively prevented most of them from voting. The Supreme Court declared the grandfather clause unconstitutional in 1915.

Literacy Test Until recent years many states required citizens to pass a literacy test to qualify to vote. Some Southern states used the literacy tests to keep African Americans from the polls. While in many cases white voters were judged literate if they could write their names, African American voters were often required to do much more. For example, they were frequently asked to explain a complicated part of the state or national constitution. The Voting Rights Acts of 1965 and 1970 and later additions to these laws outlawed literacy tests.

Poll Tax Another device designed to discourage African American suffrage was the poll tax. A **poll tax** was an amount of money—usually one or two dollars—that a citizen had to pay before he or she could vote. Because the poll tax had to be paid not only for the current year, but also for previous unpaid years as well, it was a financial burden for poor citizens of all ethnic backgrounds. In addition, the tax had to be paid well in advance of Election Day, and the poll-tax payer had to present a receipt showing payment before being permitted to enter the voting booth. Voters who lost their receipts were barred from voting. Thousands of African Americans in the states with poll taxes were excluded from the polls.

Ratified in 1964, the Twenty-fourth Amendment outlawed the poll tax in national elections. The use of the poll tax in state elections, however, was not eliminated until a 1966 Supreme Court decision.

The Voting Rights Acts Despite the elimination of many discriminatory practices by the early 1960s, African American participation in elections, particularly in the South, was still limited. The civil rights movement of the 1960s resulted in national

Overcoming Obstacles

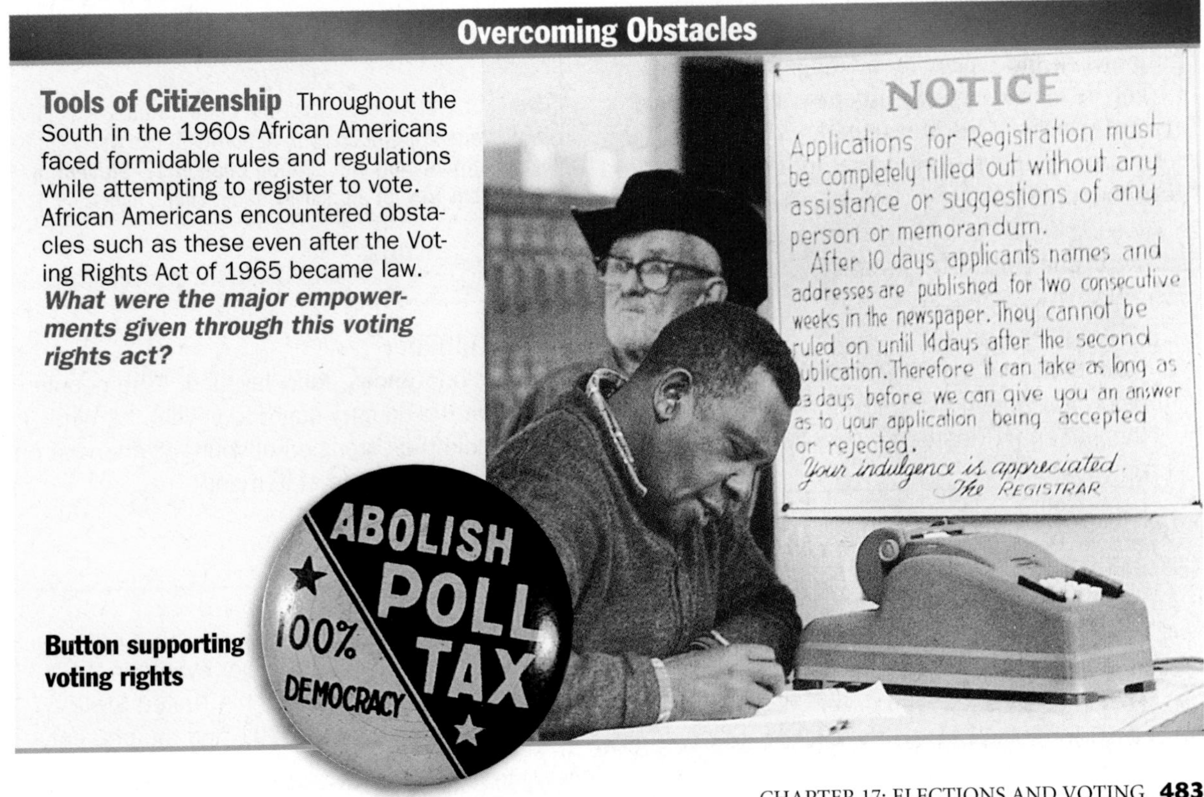

Tools of Citizenship Throughout the South in the 1960s African Americans faced formidable rules and regulations while attempting to register to vote. African Americans encountered obstacles such as these even after the Voting Rights Act of 1965 became law. ***What were the major empowerments given through this voting rights act?***

Button supporting voting rights

legislation that enabled larger numbers of African Americans to participate in the electoral process. The 1965 **Voting Rights Act** was one of the most effective suffrage laws ever passed in this country.

The Voting Rights Act of 1965 and later voting rights laws of 1970, 1975, and 1982 brought the federal government directly into the electoral process in the states. The 1965 law empowered the federal government to register voters in any district where less than 50 percent of African American adults were on the voting lists. The government could also register voters in districts where it appeared that local officials were discriminating against African Americans.

The voting rights laws also forbade the unfair division of election districts in order to diminish the influence of African American voters or of other minority groups. The laws provided for the appointment of poll watchers to ensure that the votes of all qualified voters were properly counted. Literacy tests of potential voters were abolished. The laws also required that ballots be printed in Spanish for Spanish-speaking communities. Other minority language groups—Native Americans, Asian Americans, Aleuts—were given the same right.

The Voting Rights Acts resulted in a dramatic increase in African American voter registration. In 1960 only 29 percent of all African Americans in the South were registered. By the early 1990s, the figure had risen to more than 60 percent.

The increased opportunity to vote meant that African American Southerners could now play a more important role in political life in the South. More than 1,000 African Americans were elected to political office within a few years of the passage of the Voting Rights Act of 1965. In the North the election of African American mayors in cities such as Cleveland, Detroit, Chicago, New York, and Newark could be traced to the Voting Rights Acts as well.

Twenty-sixth Amendment

For many years the minimum voting age in most states was 21. In the 1960s, when many young Americans were fighting in Vietnam, a movement to lower the voting age to 18 began. The basic argument for lowering the voting age was that if individuals were old enough to be drafted and fight for their country, they were old enough to vote. This debate ended with the ratification of the Twenty-sixth Amendment, which states:

> "*The right of citizens of the United States, who are eighteen years of age or older, to vote shall not be denied or abridged by the United States or by any State on account of age.*"
>
> —Twenty-sixth Amendment, 1971

Thus more than 10 million citizens between the ages of 18 and 21 gained the right to vote.

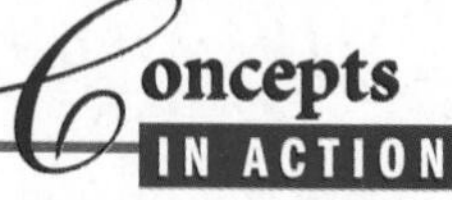

GOVERNMENT Online

Student Web Activity Visit the *United States Government: Democracy in Action* Web site at gov.glencoe.com and click on ***Chapter 17–Student Web Activities*** for an activity about voting rights.

Section 2 Assessment

Checking for Understanding

1. **Main Idea** Use a graphic organizer like the one below to explain the changes brought about by the Fifteenth, Nineteenth, and Twenty-sixth amendments.

15th	19th	26th

2. **Define** suffrage, grandfather clause, poll tax.
3. **Identify** Voting Rights Act.
4. What did the Twenty-fourth Amendment outlaw?
5. Why were the provisions of the Voting Rights Acts important?

Critical Thinking

6. **Making Inferences** John Jay said, "The people who own the country ought to govern it." What impact did the extension of voting rights have on the meaning of Jay's statement?

Concepts IN ACTION

Growth of Democracy Create an illustrated time line that focuses on major events in the extension of voting rights in the United States. Include events between 1791 and the present.

Oregon v. *Mitchell*, 1970

Before the Twenty-sixth Amendment gave 18-year-olds the right to vote, many people questioned whether Congress had the power to set the voting age in state and local elections. The issue came to the Supreme Court in the case of Oregon *v.* Mitchell.

A new voter

Background of the Case

In 1970 Congress passed the Voting Rights Act Amendments (not amendments to the Constitution). These laws changed residency and literacy test requirements and lowered the voting age for federal, state, and local elections to 18 years. President Richard Nixon signed the bill into law, but strongly objected to the provision on the voting age. Nixon stated that he approved lowering the voting age, but believed "along with most of the nation's leading constitutional scholars—that Congress has no power to enact it by simple statute, but rather it requires a constitutional amendment." The states of Oregon, Arizona, Texas, and Idaho also opposed the law. Both the Nixon administration and the states filed suits against the law. Since the presidential election of 1972 was rapidly approaching, the Supreme Court quickly accepted the cases. The Supreme Court wanted to hear the case and render a decision since it would impact the national election.

The Constitutional Issue

The major question was whether Congress had the authority to lower the voting age in state and local elections. Congress argued that Article I, Section 4, and Article II, Section 1, clearly gave it the authority to set conditions in the states for electing the president, vice president, and members of Congress. Further, Congress claimed the Fourteenth and Fifteenth Amendments allowed Congress to forbid states from excluding citizens 18 to 21 years of age from voting, just as they had allowed Congress to eliminate other restrictions on voting in the states.

The states raised the issue of federalism. Article I, Section 2 of the Constitution reserved to the states the power to set qualifications to vote in elections for their own officials such as governors, state lawmakers, and so on. Further, the Tenth Amendment reserved to the states all powers not expressly given to the national government.

Debating the Case

Questions to Consider

1. Did the Constitution intend for the states or Congress to have the authority to regulate age limits for voting in national elections?
2. Did the Constitution intend for the states or Congress to have the authority to regulate state and local elections?
3. How should the two levels of government—national versus state and local—relate to each other under the Constitution?

You Be the Judge

Review the parts of the Constitution cited by each side. Based on your interpretation of the Constitution, which side's reading of the Constitution do you agree with? What could be the consequences of letting Congress set the voting age for state and local elections? In your opinion, did the Constitution give Congress the power to lower the voting age to 18 in national elections and in state and local elections as well?

Voter's Handbook

Voting is a basic political right of all citizens in a democracy who meet certain qualifications set by law. Voting allows citizens to take positive actions to influence or control government.

Reader's Guide

Key Terms

canvass, register, polling place, precinct, office-group ballot, ticket-splitting, party-column ballot, canvassing board, absentee ballot

Find Out

- How does a person register to vote?
- What are the procedures for voting?

Understanding Concepts

Civic Participation How can a person prepare to vote?

Qualifications to Vote

Today you are qualified to vote if you are not a convicted felon or legally insane, and you are (1) a citizen of the United States and (2) at least 18 years old. Most states also require that you be a resident of the state for a specified period and that you register or enroll with the appropriate local government.

Who Sets the Qualifications to Vote?

Originally, under Article I, Section 2, the Constitution left voting qualifications entirely to the states. The Constitution gave to Congress only the power to pick the day on which presidential electors would gather and to fix "the Times, Places, and Manner of holding elections" of members of Congress.

Since the end of the Civil War, Congress and the federal courts have imposed national standards on state-run elections. A series of constitutional amendments, federal laws, and Supreme Court decisions forced the states to conduct elections without discrimination because of race, creed, color, or gender. Even with such federal requirements, however, the registration of voters and regulation of elections are primarily state powers.

Will My Vote Count?

Each person's vote counts. If you doubt it, think about how many elections have been decided by one or just a few votes. In 1976 more than 81 million votes were cast for president. Gerald Ford rather than Jimmy Carter would have won that election if about 9,000 voters in key states had voted for Ford instead of Carter.

When Milton R. Young, a Republican, ran for the Senate in North Dakota, he led his challenger by fewer than 100 votes out of more than 236,000 cast. The official **canvass**, the vote count by the official body that tabulates election returns and certifies the winner, finally confirmed Young's victory. Sometimes victory hinges on a single vote. In a Cincinnati, Ohio, suburb a candidate for the town council was suddenly hospitalized and unable to vote. When the votes were counted, he had lost by 1 vote.

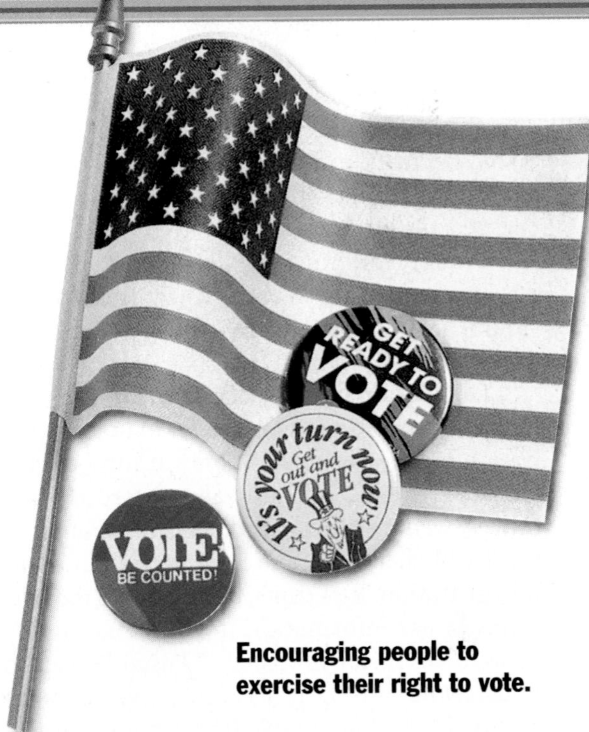

Encouraging people to exercise their right to vote.

Registering to Vote

Americans must take the initiative if they want to vote. Unlike in many countries, in the United States you must **register**, or enroll with the appropriate local government.

Why Do You Have to Register to Vote?

Registration became common in the late 1800s as a way to stop voting fraud. In those days the slogan "Vote Early and Often" was not a joke. In Denver in 1900, for example, one man confessed to having voted 125 times on Election Day! Reformers saw registration as a way to stop such abuses and clean up elections by giving officials a list of who could legally vote. In the South, registration laws came to be used to stop African Americans and poor whites from voting.

How Can I Register to Vote?

Registration requirements are set by state law and differ from state to state. Telephone your local board of elections, or county or city government to check on your state's requirements.

Registration forms typically ask for your name, address, place and date of birth, gender, Social Security number, and party. You must also sign your name so your signature can be checked at the time you vote.

Usually, you must register to vote by 15 to 30 days before an election. Only three states (Maine, Minnesota, and Wisconsin) allow you to register on Election Day.

The **National Voter Registration Act** that took effect in 1995 requires states to make registration forms available not only at motor vehicle departments but also at numerous state offices, welfare offices, and agencies that serve the disabled. It also requires states to allow mail-in registration. It permits, but does not require, states to use information from change-of-address forms filed with the U. S. Postal Service to update voter lists. Driver's license applicants are required to fill out a separate form for registering to vote. Public agencies must make it clear to beneficiaries that registering to vote is optional and that not registering will not affect the amount of assistance they receive.

Supporters of the National Voter Registration law believed that it would add 50 million citizens to the voting rolls when the changes went into effect. Many more citizens did register. However, the ease of registration did not help voter turnout in the 1996 election. Less than half the voting age population participated, one of the lowest turnouts in history.

Voting Procedures

You vote at a **polling place** in your home **precinct.** A precinct is a voting district. Each city or county is usually divided into precincts containing from 200 to 1,000 voters.

What Happens at the Polling Place?

Generally, before the date of the election you will receive notification of where you are to vote. Procedures will vary slightly at different polling places. Look over the sample ballot posted on a wall near the entryway. Then: (1) Go to the clerk or election judge's table and sign in by writing your name and address on an application form. (2) The clerk will read your name aloud and pass the application to a challenger, a local election official representing a political party. (3) The challenger compares your signature with your voter registration form. If they match, the challenger initials your form and returns it to you. (4) Give your form to one of the judges and enter the booth to vote.

CQ **Congressional Quarterly's**
Government at a Glance

Impact of the National Voter Registration Act

	1992	1994*	1996	1998*
Total Voting Age Population	**189,529,000**	**193,650,000**	**196,511,000**	**200,929,000**
Total Registered	**133,821,178**	**130,292,822**	**146,211,960**	**141,850,558**
Turnout	**104,405,155**	**75,105,860**	**96,456,345**	**73,117,022**
% Turnout	**55.09%**	**38.78%**	**49.08%**	**36.4%**

- During the first two years of the National Voter Registration Act (NVRA) there were a total of 41,452,428 registration applications processed nationwide.

** 1994 and 1998 were not a presidential election years.*

Source: Federal Election Commission, *Executive Summary of the Federal Election Commission's Report to the Congress on the Impact of the National Voter Registration Act of 1993 on the Administration of Federal Elections.* (Washington, D.C.; 1997). Federal Election Commission, *National and State Voter Registration & Turnout in the Congressional Election 1998.*

Online **UPDATE**

Visit gov.glencoe.com and click on ***Textbook Updates–Chapter 17*** for an update of the data.

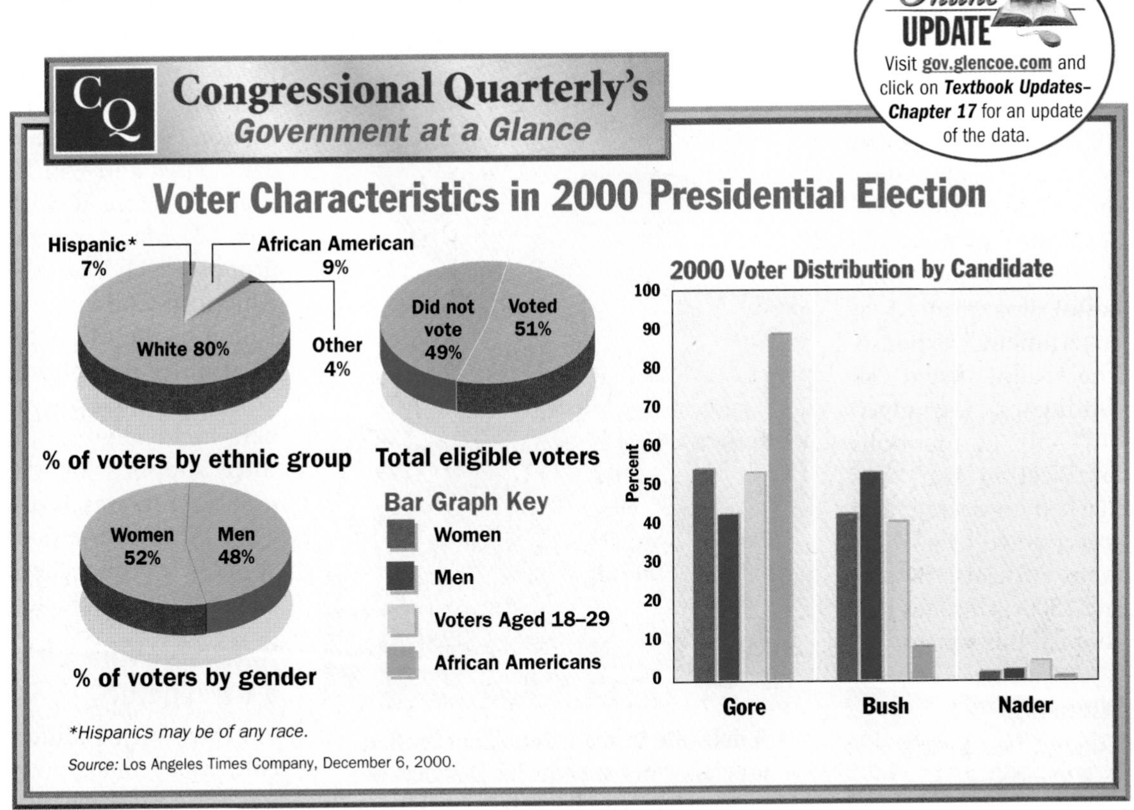

Can My Right to Vote Be Challenged?

You cannot be stopped from voting because of your race, gender, religion, income, or political beliefs. You can be challenged, however, if your registration or identification is in question.

What Will the Ballot Look Like?

Two forms of ballots are generally used. An **office-group ballot** lists the candidates of all parties together by the office for which they are running. Their political party affiliation is listed beside their name. Many believe this form of ballot encourages **ticket-splitting,** voting for candidates from different parties for different offices.

The **party-column ballot** lists each party's candidates in a column under the party's name. There is usually a square or circle at the top of each party's column. By putting one mark in the square or circle, you can vote a straight ticket for all the party's candidates. You may also vote for each office individually by marking one box in each column. You may also write in the name of someone not listed on the ballot for any office.

How Do I Use the Voting Machine?

Voting machines are used in many polling places to count votes more quickly and accurately. The two most common types are the punch-card machine and the lever machine.

If you are given a punch-card as your ballot, enter the private booth and insert your card in the voting machine. Your punch-card will then be lined up with the names of the candidates. To vote, use the stylus provided to punch holes in the appropriate places on the ballot. Put your card in its envelope and give it to the election judge as you leave the booth.

To use the lever machine, enter the booth and pull the large lever to one side to close a curtain around you. The ballot is part of the machine and will face you. To vote, pull down the small levers by the names of the candidates you prefer. You can change your vote or correct a mistake by resetting any small lever. Once you have pulled all the small levers you want to, pull the large lever again to record your vote and reset the machine for the next voter.

Will My Vote Be a Secret?

The law entitles you to a secret ballot. Borrowed from a procedure developed in Australia in 1856, the **Australian ballot** was printed at government expense. The ballot listed all candidates, was given out only at the polls on Election Day, was marked in secret, and was counted by government officials. By the late 1800s, all states had adopted this system.

A delegate to the national convention proclaims her support for Democratic candidates.

Who Actually Counts the Votes and Certifies a Winner?

A canvassing board, or official body that is usually bipartisan, counts votes. As soon as the polls close, the ballots from each precinct are forwarded to city or county canvassing boards. These boards put all the returns together and send them on to the state canvassing authority. Within a few days of the election, the state canvassing authority certifies the election of the winner. Each winner gets a certificate of election from the county or state canvassing board.

Through television and radio, people usually know the winners before canvassing boards certify them. In close elections the result may depend upon the official vote count and certification.

How Can I Prepare to Vote?

The best way to prepare to vote is to stay informed about candidates and public issues. As Election Day nears, newspapers, TV, radio, and newsmagazines will carry useful information. You might also try the following: (1) The local League of Women Voters may publish a *Voters' Information Bulletin,* a fact-filled, nonpartisan rundown on candidates and issues. (2) Each political party has literature and other information about their candidates and will be eager to share it with you. (3) Many interest groups such as the American Conservative Union or the AFL-CIO Committee on Political Education rate members of Congress on their support for the group's programs. If you agree with the views of an interest group, check its ratings of candidates.

How Can I Choose a Candidate?

Everyone has different reasons for supporting one candidate over another. Asking these questions may help you decide: (1) Does the candidate stand for things I think are important? (2) Is the candidate reliable and honest? (3) Does the candidate have relevant past experience? (4) Will the candidate be effective in office? Look for the resources the person will bring to the job. Does the candidate have good political connections? (5) Does the candidate have a real chance of winning? You have a tough choice to make if it appears that your favorite candidate has a slim chance of winning. You may want to vote for a losing candidate to show support for a certain point of view. You may also want to vote for someone having the greatest chance of beating the candidate you like the least.

Special Circumstances

With more than 190 million potential voters, special circumstances always affect some voters. Over the years, special procedures and protections have been developed to help ensure that despite such circumstances all eligible Americans may vote.

What Is an Absentee Ballot?

An absentee ballot allows you to vote without going to the polls on Election Day. You must obtain an **absentee ballot** within a specified time before an election, fill it out, and return it (usually by mail) to the proper election official. The deadlines to apply for and return absentee ballots vary by state. Check with local election officials for details.

When Can I Use an Absentee Ballot?

Rules vary from state to state. Generally you may vote by absentee ballot if: (1) you will be out of town on Election Day; (2) you will be hospitalized on Election Day; (3) you have a physical disability or special illness that makes it difficult to get to the polling place (in such cases a doctor's certificate may be needed); (4) you cannot vote on Election Day because of religious observances; or (5) you will be in jail for a misdemeanor or are awaiting trial.

In an effort to increase voter turnout, some states have relaxed rules on absentee ballots. Texas, for example, allows anyone who wishes to do so to cast an absentee ballot. The voter must simply request one.

How Do I Apply for an Absentee Ballot?

Request an absentee ballot (in person or by mail) from your local board of elections or other appropriate office. In order to receive your ballot, you will need to give your name, voting residence, and reason for being absent from the polls on Election Day.

Can Disabled Voters Receive Special Assistance?

Any voter who needs help in voting because of a disability is entitled to receive it. Some states allow you to pick the person to assist you. Other states require that only officials at the polling place can help. To protect disabled voters from pressure, some states require that two election officials from opposite parties be present during voting. Election officials may not disclose any information about how you voted.

Do Non-English-Speaking Voters Receive Special Help?

Under the Voting Rights Act of 1975, ballots and related election materials must be printed in the language of voting minorities as well as in English. This provision applies only in areas where illiteracy in English is high or recent voting turnout was unusually low.

Election materials, for example, are available in Spanish and English in many parts of Florida, Texas, California, and other states. In Hawaii, election materials have been put into Cantonese, Ilocano, and Japanese as well as English.

Handbook Assessment

Checking for Understanding

1. **Main Idea** Use a graphic organizer like the one to the right to show the circumstances under which a voter can use an absentee ballot.

If		then
	→	absentee ballot

2. **Define** canvass, register, polling place, precinct, office-group ballot, ticket-splitting, party-column ballot, canvassing board, absentee ballot.
3. **Identify** Australian ballot.
4. What are two requirements to vote in the United States?

Critical Thinking

5. **Making Inferences** Why do you think the secret ballot was adopted?

Concepts IN ACTION

Civic Participation Citizens must prepare to vote. Walking into a voting booth without preparation makes voting a meaningless activity. What should a person know in order to vote meaningfully? Create a pamphlet describing the kinds of things voters should know in order to make their vote count.

Section 3

Influences on Voters

Reader's Guide

Key Terms

cross-pressured voter, straight party ticket, propaganda

Find Out

- What personal background factors do you believe will influence your decision as a voter?
- What outside influences affect how a person votes?

Understanding Concepts

Civic Participation How does a citizen overcome obstacles to voting and voter apathy?

COVER STORY

Motor Voter Law Works

ATLANTA, GEORGIA, JULY 12, 1995

Nearly three times more Georgians registered to vote in the six months since the National Voter Registration Act took effect than registered in all of 1994. The new law has been labeled "Motor Voter" because it requires states to offer voter registration with driver's license applications, renewals, or address changes. Registration opportunities at certain social service agencies are also required, and states can register voters in schools and libraries. Twenty million Americans are expected to register now that the process has been simplified. The United States currently has the lowest voter participation of any Western democracy.

A registered voter

Five major factors influence voter decisions: (1) personal background of the voter; (2) degree of voter loyalty to one of the political parties; (3) issues of the campaign; (4) voters' image of the candidates; and (5) propaganda. Perhaps the biggest decision, however, is whether to vote on Election Day.

Personal Background of Voters

Voters' personal backgrounds affect their decisions. A person's background includes such things as upbringing, family, age, occupation, income level, and even general outlook on life.

Age Consider, for example, how an individual's age might affect a voting decision. A 68-year-old senior citizen would probably favor a candidate who promised an increase in Social Security payments, provided, of course, that positions the candidate took on other issues did not offend that voter. On the other hand, a 23-year-old voter might resent the prospect of having more money deducted from her paycheck to pay for increased Social Security payments. This young voter might then decide to vote against the candidate.

Other Background Influences Voters' education, religion, and racial or ethnic background also affect their attitudes toward the candidates. For example, an African American might favor a candidate who supports strong antidiscrimination measures in education and employment. A Jewish voter might not vote for a candidate who has expressed strong reservations about American support of Israel.

It is important to understand that people's backgrounds tend to influence them in particular ways. However, individuals do not always vote the way their backgrounds might lead one to believe. Will labor union members always vote for the Democratic presidential candidate, as they historically have? The large number of union members who voted for Republican Ronald Reagan in 1980 confirms that they do not. Will college-educated voters, most of whom usually vote Republican, always give their votes to the Republican candidate? The landslide vote by which Lyndon Johnson, a Democrat, defeated Republican Barry Goldwater in 1964 indicates that this has not always been the case.

The Cross-Pressured Voter One reason why voters' backgrounds do not always forecast how they will vote is that many voters are cross-pressured. A cross-pressured voter is one who is caught between conflicting elements in his or her own life such as religion, income level, and peer group. For example, Catholics are generally more inclined to vote Democratic than Republican. Yet, suppose an individual Catholic voter is also a wealthy business executive. Well-to-do businesspeople are usually Republicans. Furthermore, many of this voter's close friends are Democrats. They will no doubt have some influence on this voter's thinking.

How will this person vote? Such a voter's personal background, like that of millions of other voters, has conflicting elements. For this voter, other areas important to voter decision making—such as campaign issues and the personalities of the candidates—will probably play an equally influential role in determining how he or she will vote.

Loyalty to Political Parties

Another influence on voters' decisions is their loyalty (or lack of it) to one of the political parties. Because the majority of American voters consider themselves either Republicans or Democrats, most vote for their party's candidates.

Strong Versus Weak Party Voters Not all voters who consider themselves Republicans or Democrats support their party's candidates with the same degree of consistency. Strong party voters are those who select their party's candidates in election after election. Strong party voters tend to see party as more important than the issues or the candidates. In the voting booth, they usually vote a straight-party ticket—they select the candidates of their party only.

Loyal Voters

Traditions of Voting A person's affiliations with family, coworkers, and friends is just one of the factors that influences how and how often that person votes. ***What practice of regular voters does this cartoon illustrate?***

Unlike strong party voters, weak party voters are more likely to switch their votes to the rival party's candidates from time to time. In 1980, as an example, 27 percent fewer Democrats voted for Carter than had voted for him in 1976. Weak party voters are more influenced by issues and the candidates than they are by party loyalty.

Independent Voters Another important group of voters is the **independent voters,** who think of themselves as neither Republicans nor Democrats. Even when independents tend to lean toward one party, their party loyalty is weak.

The number of independent voters has increased over the years. Because of this increase, independent voters have become an important element in presidential elections. Along with weak party voters, independent voters may help determine who wins the right to occupy the White House every four years. In 1992 Ross Perot, an independent candidate, won many of these votes.

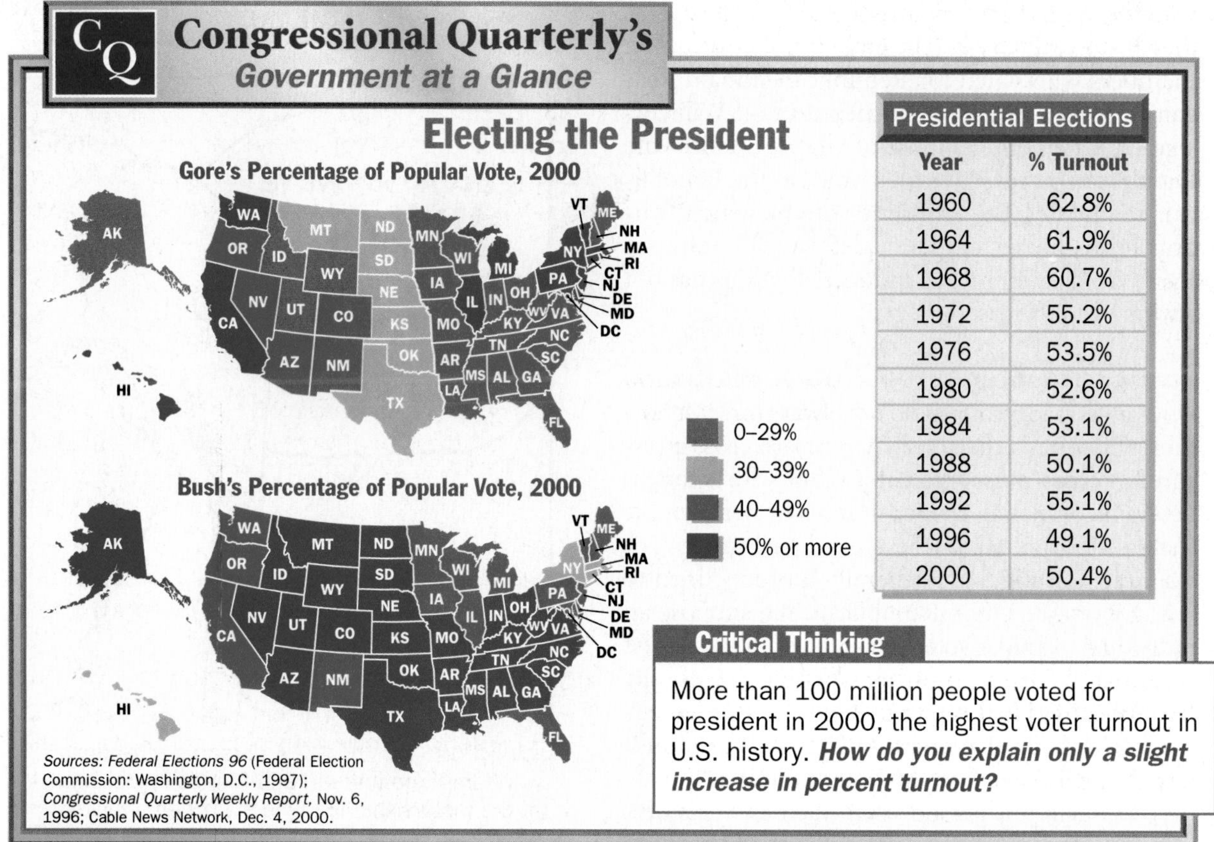

Presidential Elections

Year	% Turnout
1960	62.8%
1964	61.9%
1968	60.7%
1972	55.2%
1976	53.5%
1980	52.6%
1984	53.1%
1988	50.1%
1992	55.1%
1996	49.1%
2000	50.4%

Critical Thinking

More than 100 million people voted for president in 2000, the highest voter turnout in U.S. history. ***How do you explain only a slight increase in percent turnout?***

Both President Bill Clinton and Republican Bob Dole adjusted their message and strategy to appeal to these voters in 1996. Eventually, Perot's support declined to less than half its 1992 level.

Experts believe that the number of weak party voters and independent voters will increase in the future. Presidential candidates will no longer be able to rely on party loyalty for victory. Analysts predict that the issues of a campaign and the candidates' images will influence more and more voters.

Issues in Election Campaigns

Many voters are not well-informed about all the issues discussed in election campaigns. Still, today's voters are better informed than the voters of earlier years. Several reasons account for this shift.

First, television has brought the issues into almost every home in the country. Second, voters today are better educated than were voters of the past. A third reason is that current issues seem to have a greater impact on the personal lives of many more voters than at any time since the Great Depression of the 1930s. These issues include pollution, the energy crisis, inflation, school busing, gun control, crime, unemployment, and women's rights.

A presidential election that demonstrated the importance of issues was the election of 1980. For example, many Americans blamed President Jimmy Carter for the high cost of living, the high rate of inflation, and the high rate of unemployment. In his four years in office the economy had worsened, and Carter seemed unable to turn it around. Carter's opponent, Republican Ronald Reagan, used the economic issue to attack the president's administration.

At the end of the televised debate between the two candidates, Reagan asked the millions of Americans watching, "Are you better off than you were four years ago? Is it easier for you to go and buy things in the stores than it was four years ago?"

For most Americans the answer to these questions was "No." Reagan's tactic was effective. Because Reagan made such a strong issue of the economy, millions of voters who had voted for Carter four years earlier switched to the Republican challenger.

The Candidate's Image

Just as important as the issues themselves is the way the voters perceive the issues. If, for example, they believe that an administration is dealing effectively with the economy, they may reward the president with their votes. Conversely, if they believe an administration's measures are ineffective, voters may punish the president by voting for the other candidate.

Certainly, most Americans want a president who appears to be someone they can trust as a national leader. All candidates try to convey this image to the public, but not all are successful in doing so. Gerald Ford, running for president in 1976, struck many voters as well-meaning but dull. Adlai Stevenson, who lost to Dwight D. Eisenhower in 1952 and 1956, was perceived by many voters as too intellectual to be president.

Many voters select candidates on image alone—for the personal qualities they perceive them to have. In 1964 President Lyndon Johnson had the image of a peacemaker, while his opponent, Barry Goldwater, was viewed as more willing to lead the nation into war. At the very least, a candidate must be viewed as competent to handle the problems of the day. Many voters rejected Michael Dukakis in 1988 because they believed he was unqualified to deal with the nation's problems. President Harry S Truman cited the danger of getting this image when he said:

> "*Being a president is like riding a tiger. A man has to keep riding it or be swallowed. . . . A president is either constantly on top of events or, if he hesitates, events will soon be on top of him.*"
>
> —Harry S Truman

A candidate, then, must convey the impression of having the qualities voters expect in a president.

Propaganda

Political parties, interest groups, and businesses need to convince people of the value of their candidates, ideas, goods, or services. Americans are used to hearing hundreds of such messages every day. Many of these messages could be classified as "propaganda." **Propaganda** involves using ideas, information, or rumors to influence

POLITICS and You

Knowing your Political ID

Perhaps you have not thought much about whether you are a liberal (left), conservative (right), or moderate (center); a Democrat, Republican, or an Independent. You can measure your "political ID" by how you feel about certain issues. Democrats are generally more liberal and Republicans generally more conservative. Independents may fall in between on some issues and lean left or right on others. Liberals tend to be "loose constructionists" and conservatives "strict constructionists" of the Constitution. A liberal generally believes that government has more social responsibility for providing education, health, welfare, and civil rights. A conservative generally believes that individuals and voluntary associations should be given more responsibility to make choices in these areas.

Participating IN GOVERNMENT ACTIVITY

Check Some Issues Research some recent controversial political issues. With which side do you agree? Place yourself on a chart of the political spectrum between the far left and far right side.

Congressional Quarterly's
Government at a Glance

Propaganda Techniques

Technique	How to Recognize it
Labeling	Name calling; identifying a candidate with a term such as "un-American"
Glittering Generality	Vague or broad statements containing little substance
Card Stacking	Giving only one side of the facts to support a candidate's position
Transfer	Associating a patriotic symbol with a candidate
Plain Folks	Identifying the candidate as "just one of the common people"
Testimonial	A celebrity endorses a candidate
The Bandwagon	Urging voters to support a candidate because everyone else is

Critical Thinking

Campaigns use different techniques to promote the best interests of their candidates. ***Which techniques would an incumbent candidate more likely use? Why?***

opinion. Propaganda is not necessarily lying or deception; however, neither is it objective. Propaganda uses information in any way that supports a predetermined objective.

Propaganda techniques were initially used on a mass scale by commercial advertisers. As political campaigns adapted to television, campaign managers developed sophisticated messages using seven propaganda techniques.

"Plain folks" has been a popular technique since Andrew Jackson won the White House in 1828. The technique that asks a person to "jump on the bandwagon" followed close behind. When a party's convention is all decked out in patriotic symbols, it is using "transfer" to influence viewers. A Hollywood actor or popular musician who speaks for a candidate is giving a "testimonial," or endorsement. Republicans used the term "liberal" as a negative label for Democrats beginning in the 1980s. Democrats often refer to conservative Republican candidates as "right-wing" politicians. A debate is a good place to identify "card stacking," as each candidate quotes only those statistics that support his or her position.

When political propaganda becomes obviously misleading, people become skeptical of politicians. Name calling can override the important issues of a campaign. Voters say they do not appreciate that approach, and some analysts believe the result can be reduced voter participation.

Profile of Regular Voters

Citizens who vote regularly have certain positive attitudes toward government and citizenship.

Investigators have found that education, age, and income are important factors in predicting which citizens will vote. The more education a citizen has, the more likely it is that he or she will be a regular voter. Middle-aged citizens have the highest voting turnout of all age groups. Voter regularity also increases with income—the higher a person's income, the more regularly that person votes.

Profile of Nonvoters

The struggles over the extension of suffrage have resulted in more Americans having the right to vote than ever before. Nevertheless, for several reasons many Americans do not vote.

Some citizens do not vote because they do not meet state voting requirements. Almost all states have three basic requirements—United States citizenship, residency, and registration. A voter who does not fulfill all of these requirements is not permitted to vote.

All states limit the voting right to American citizens. Even people who have lived in this country for many years but who have not formally become United States citizens cannot vote in American elections.

Most states require voters to be residents of the state for a certain period before they are allowed to vote. When a voter moves to a new state, he or she needs time to become informed about local and state issues and candidates. Before 1970 the period of required residence ranged from 3 months to 2 years. The Voting Rights Act of 1970, however, along with two Supreme Court decisions, created a residence period of 30 days in all elections. In a few states this period may be extended to 50 days. Some states have no required residence period at all.

All states, with the exception of North Dakota, require voters to register or record their names officially with local election boards. On Election Day an election official must check voters' names. Voters whose names are on the list sign in by writing their names on a form. Registration is a way to prevent voter fraud or dishonest elections. All voter registration is permanent if a voter, once registered, remains on the list unless he or she dies, moves, or fails to vote within a certain number of years.

One problem in meeting residency and registration standards is that American society is highly mobile. Experts estimate that almost one-fifth of Americans move to a new location every five years. A new resident may forget to register or find that the registration offices are open at inconvenient times. Also, complicated registration procedures and residency requirements affect voter participation. In recent years, however, these requirements have been made less burdensome, and voter turnout is still low.

Decline in Participation The percentage of Americans voting in presidential elections has declined from about 62 percent in 1960 to less than 50 percent in 1996. In fact, the 1996 turnout was the lowest since 1924. In the presidential election of 1960, about 41 million citizens of voting age did not vote. In the 2000 presidential election, the number had grown to about 100 million. Even fewer Americans vote in congressional elections. The voting rate is lower still in state and local elections.

Ways of Increasing Voter Turnout Political experts who are concerned about the high rate of nonvoting in the United States have suggested a number of ways to get more citizens to the polls on Election Day. For example, shift Election Day from Tuesday to Sunday, so that citizens are free to vote without having to take time off from work. Another idea would be to allow voters to register on Election Day. Some favor a national registration system, so that voters' registration follows them to a new state when they move. Making it easier to vote, however, has not been effective in getting more people to the polls in recent years.

Section 3 Assessment

Checking for Understanding

1. **Main Idea** Use a graphic organizer like the one below to show how parties try to influence voters.

2. **Define** cross-pressured voter, straight party ticket, propaganda.
3. **Identify** independent voter.
4. Identify factors in a voter's personal background that influence that individual's vote.

Critical Thinking

5. **Demonstrating Reasoned Judgment** What qualities of competence and leadership would you think are important for a presidential candidate to have?

Civic Participation Voter apathy is an issue in the United States today. Draw a political cartoon that depicts a reason people give for not voting.

Congressional Quarterly's

Elections A to Z

Elections in the United States *The United States has a long and colorful history of elections. The federal government and the states establish the election environment, but the people determine the winners and losers.*

The First Election: Unanimous

In the first election the American people had no problem selecting a president. George Washington was the unanimous choice, winning 69 electoral votes—the maximum possible in 1789. No other president has matched that feat, although Franklin D. Roosevelt came close in 1936 with 98.5 percent of the electoral vote. Most other presidential elections have been more competitive, sometimes creating issues the Founders did not foresee.

Nineteenth century sheet music honoring the first president

First Campaign Button

Campaign buttons first appeared in the 1896 William McKinley–William Jennings Bryan race for president. (Bryan also began the tradition of backbreaking campaign travel and speeches from the back of a train.) The first campaign buttons were made of celluloid, a tough plastic invented in 1870 and better known for its use in early movie films. Later buttons were made of stamped, enameled metal.

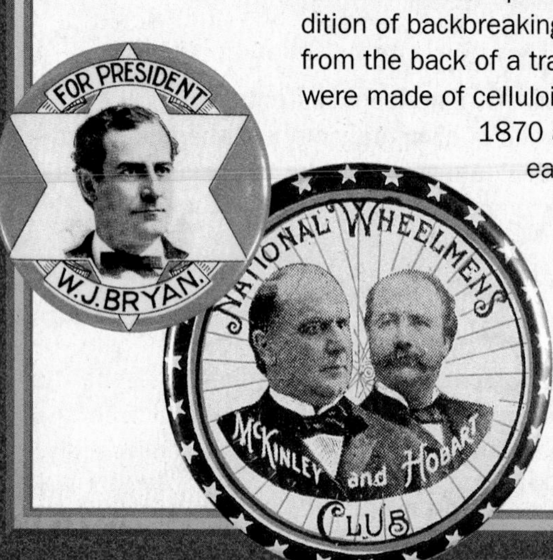

Celluloid buttons endorsing contenders in the 1896 presidential race

Firsts in Senate Elections

Mel Carnahan became the first dead person elected to the U.S. Senate in November, 2000. Carnahan, Governor of Missouri, was killed in a plane crash on October 16, but it was too late to remove his name from the ballot. Carnahan won more votes than the Republican incumbent, John Ashcroft, and after the election the new governor appointed Carnahan's widow Jean to serve as senator.

Hillary Rodham Clinton became the first first lady to win public office when she was elected senator from New York in November, 2000.

Strom Thurmond of South Carolina was the first and only person to be elected to the Senate on a write-in vote. In 1954, former governor Thurmond, then a Democrat, received 143,442 write-in votes to defeat his party's endorsed candidate. He has been in the Senate ever since, but as a Republican since 1964.

Senator Strom Thurmond admires a bust of himself on Capitol Hill in 1997.

E.L. Henry portrayed some of the people Congress considered when choosing a day for national elections in *Electioneering in a Country Town.*

Picking the Date

In January 1845, Congress considered several factors before setting Election Day as the Tuesday after the first Monday in November in even-numbered years. November was chosen because, with the harvest over, farmers would be more likely to vote. As to the question of the best weekday, Congress ruled out Monday (the first day) and Friday (the last day), bypassed Saturday and Sunday (shopping and religious days), and eliminated Thursday (British election day). With just Tuesday and Wednesday remaining, Congress chose Tuesday. But which Tuesday would be best? Congress recognized that scheduling Election Day on November 1 would disrupt accountants and shopkeepers who had to close out the October books. Therefore, it settled on the Tuesday after the first Monday. Prior to 1845, elections had been held in the first week of December, with the day varying between December 1 and December 7.

Chapter 17

Assessment and Activities

GOVERNMENT Online

Self-Check Quiz Visit the *United States Government: Democracy in Action* Web site at gov.glencoe.com and click on ***Chapter 17–Self-Check Quizzes*** to prepare for the chapter test.

Reviewing Key Terms

Write the term that best completes each sentence.

political action committees
soft money
straight-party ticket
cross-pressured voter
suffrage
grandfather clause

1. Political candidates often receive campaign contributions and support from _____.
2. Women in the United States gained ____ in 1920.
3. Most independent voters do not vote a _____.
4. Political parties can raise unlimited amounts of money for general purposes, not designated to particular candidates through _____.
5. The _____ was a roadblock to voting for most African American Southerners.
6. One cannot be sure how a _____ will vote because that person has conflicting interests.

Current Events JOURNAL

Campaign Financing Find recent newspaper and magazine articles that report on issues of campaign financing and/or campaign finance reform. Pay special attention to pending legislation, if any. Summarize the articles, and share the articles and summaries with your classmates.

Recalling Facts

1. How does the number of electoral votes of a state affect presidential campaigning?
2. Describe presidential campaign organizations.
3. What were the three devices used after 1870 to prevent African Americans from voting?
4. Which group of Americans gained the right to vote under the Twenty-sixth Amendment?
5. What effects has television had on presidential elections?
6. What factors are important in predicting which citizens will vote?
7. Describe the current voter registration system.

Understanding Concepts

1. **Political Processes** Individuals have suggested extending public financing of election campaigns to include congressional campaigns. Explain the advantages and disadvantages of this idea.
2. **Growth of Democracy** Why were the Voting Rights Acts necessary?
3. **Civic Participation** The right to vote belongs to every United States citizen. In your opinion, what do citizens forfeit if they do not exercise their right to vote?

Critical Thinking

1. **Predicting Consequences** Identify at least three consequences that could result from limiting the amount of money any individual could give to a political campaign.

2. **Making Inferences** The Twenty-sixth Amendment enabled 18-year-olds to vote. In terms of percentage, however, far fewer members of this age bracket actually exercise their right to vote than is the case with any other age group. How might you explain this?
3. **Making Inferences** Use a graphic organizer like the one below to list three ways of increasing voter turnout.

1.
2.
3.

Interpreting Political Cartoons Activity

1. According to the cartoonist, why don't some people vote?
2. How does the cartoonist exaggerate campaign advertising?
3. Should Americans rely on television advertisements to gather information on candidates? Why or why not?

Cooperative Learning Activity

Ranking Candidates Organize into groups of five or six. Within your group agree on eight qualities that you think are important for an officeholder whether for president or other lower-level office. Arrange the qualities in their order of importance, from most important to least important. How can you find out about the qualifications of those seeking public office? Have a spokesperson share your list with the class and present strategies for discovering the qualifications of political candidates.

Technology Activity

Using a Word Processor Find out the percentage of eligible voters (those who were registered) who voted in the most recent presidential election. Organize the eligible voters into specific age groups. Use the table option of your word processor to design a table illustrating this information.

Skill Practice Activity

Synthesizing Information Synthesize information from Sections 1, 2, and 3 and from outside sources to complete a one- to two-page report on an aspect of a modern or historical presidential election.

Participating in Local Government

Find out what the voter registration laws are in your community. Contact your local election board for this information. Present the information on an illustrated poster. Include information about local residency requirements, the procedure for registering, the time and location in which people can register, and the types of identification needed to register.

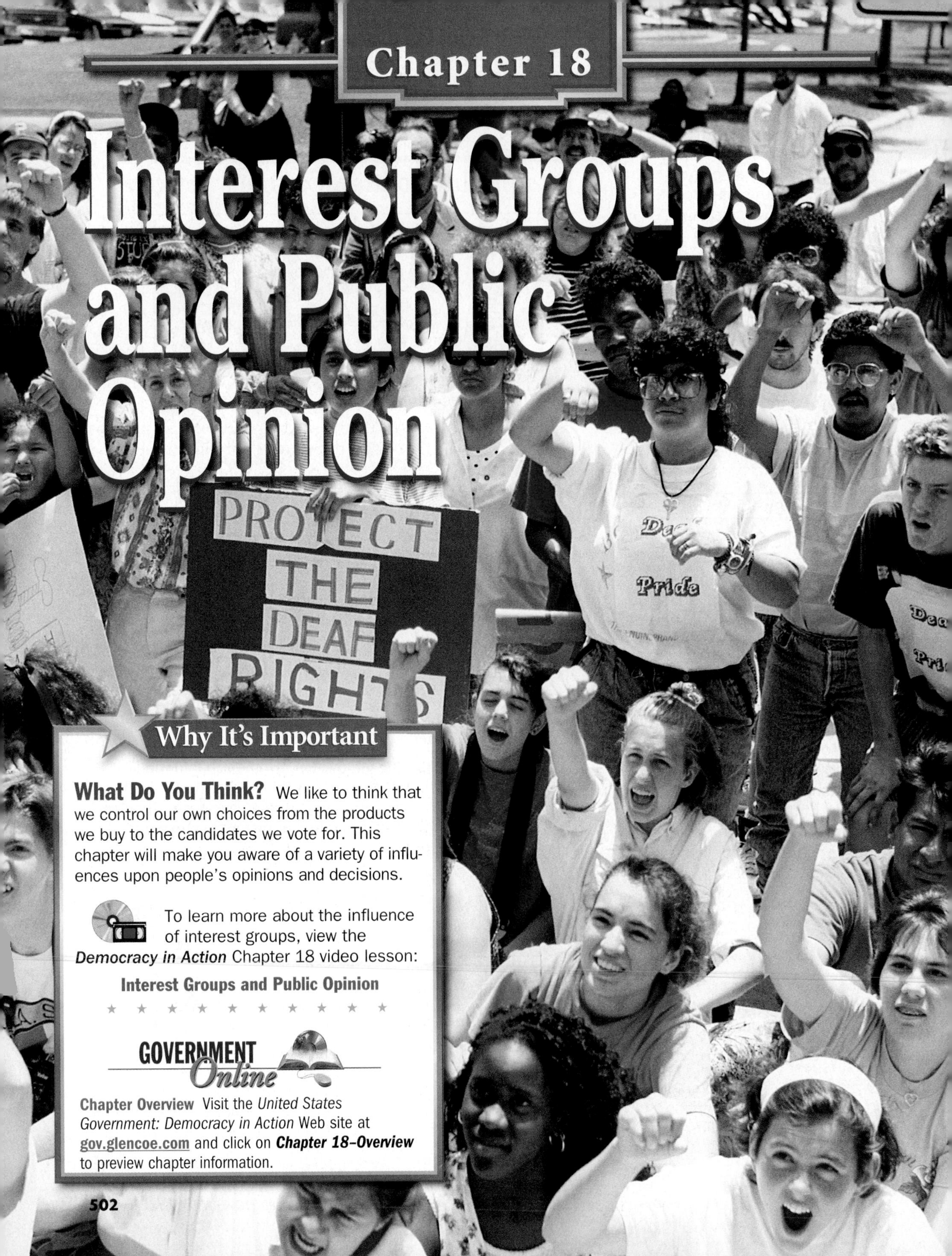

Chapter 18

Interest Groups and Public Opinion

Why It's Important

What Do You Think? We like to think that we control our own choices from the products we buy to the candidates we vote for. This chapter will make you aware of a variety of influences upon people's opinions and decisions.

To learn more about the influence of interest groups, view the *Democracy in Action* Chapter 18 video lesson:

Interest Groups and Public Opinion

GOVERNMENT *Online*

Chapter Overview Visit the *United States Government: Democracy in Action* Web site at gov.glencoe.com and click on ***Chapter 18–Overview*** to preview chapter information.

Section 1

Interest Group Organization

Reader's Guide

Key Terms

interest group, public-interest group

Find Out

- Why are interest groups powerful agents in influencing public policy?
- What are the main categories of interest groups?

Understanding Concepts

Civic Participation Why do you think many people choose not to participate in an interest group?

COVER STORY

MADD Issues Grades

DALLAS, TEXAS, NOVEMBER 23, 1993

Mothers Against Drunk Driving (MADD), a group based in nearby Irving, today released a long-awaited report card on the nation's fight against drunk drivers. At a carefully timed news conference in Washington, D.C., MADD officials announced a letter grade for each state's efforts in the fight. To make sure its message got out, MADD sent tapes of the event to radio and TV stations nationwide. Later, MADD leaders in each state held press conferences to announce the grade received by that state. It is estimated that, on the eve of the Thanksgiving holiday, MADD's tactics have reminded some 62 million Americans of the dangers of drunk driving.

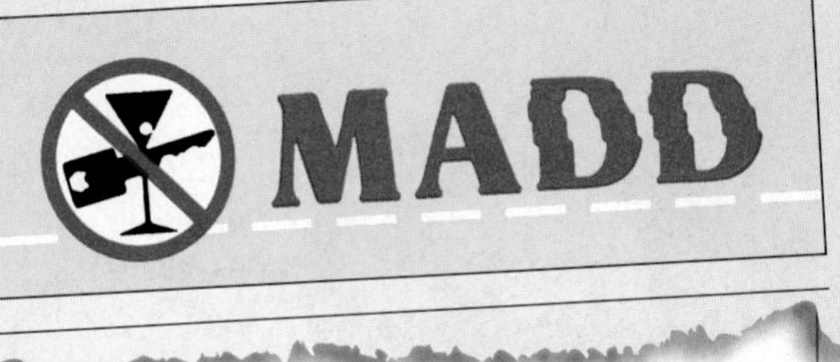

In addition to political parties, Americans have historically formed a wide variety of special-interest groups. An **interest group** is a group of people who share common goals and organize to influence government. MADD is one special-interest group in the United States.

Many early leaders in the United States believed that interest groups could be harmful to the function of government. In *The Federalist,* No. 10[1] James Madison referred to **"factions"** as groups of people united to promote special interests that were "adverse to the rights of other citizens, or to the permanent and aggregate interests of the community." Madison explained that removing the causes of factions was not as acceptable as removing their effects. He believed that the Constitution would be a sufficient safeguard against the potential abuses of these interest groups.

Whether the Constitution has served to eliminate the harmful effects of interest groups is still a current issue. Today Americans have organized to pressure all levels of government through interest groups. These groups spend much time and money in organized efforts to influence officeholders to support laws that the groups feel will be beneficial. Are the activities of these groups "adverse to the rights of other citizens," as Madison believed they could be? Or do interest groups serve an important role in helping people interact with their government?

Power of Interest Groups

Alexis de Tocqueville, a French traveler in the United States in the early 1800s and author of *Democracy in America,*[2] recognized the Americans' tendency toward group membership:

See the following footnoted materials in the **Reference Handbook:**

1. *The Federalist,* No. 10, pages 812–814.
2. *Democracy in America,* page 818.

> *In no country of the world has the principle of association been more successfully used, or applied to a greater multitude of objects, than in America. . . . In the United States associations are established to promote the public safety, commerce, industry, morality, and religion.*
>
> —Alexis de Tocqueville, 1835

Defining Interest Groups Political parties nominate candidates for office and try to win elections to gain control of the government. Interest groups may support candidates who favor their ideas, but they do not nominate candidates for office. Instead, interest groups try to influence government officials to support certain policies.

Another difference between interest groups and political parties is that interest groups usually are concerned with only a few issues or specific problems. They do not try to gain members with different points of view. Political parties, on the other hand, are broad-based organizations. They must attract the support of many opposing groups to win elections. They also must consider conflicting issues and problems that affect all Americans, not just certain groups.

Finally, most interest groups are organized on the basis of common values, rather than on geographic location. Political parties elect officials from geographic areas to represent the interests of people in those areas. National interest groups unite people with common attitudes from every region of the country.

The Purpose of Interest Groups Interest groups help bridge the gap between the citizen and the government. Through interest groups, citizens communicate their "wants," or policy goals, to government leaders—the president, Congress, city council, or state legislators. When lawmakers begin to address the vital concerns of an interest group, its members swing into action.

Political Power Interest groups follow the old principle, "There is strength in numbers." By representing more than one individual, an interest group has a stronger bargaining position with leaders in government, but only proportionally. Officials in a small community, for example, will listen to a 100-member group of citizens organized into a "Local Safety Association," while a large city would not.

On the state and national levels, an interest group draws from the financial resources and expertise of its many members. Organized and equipped with sufficient resources, an interest group can exert influence far beyond the power of its individual members.

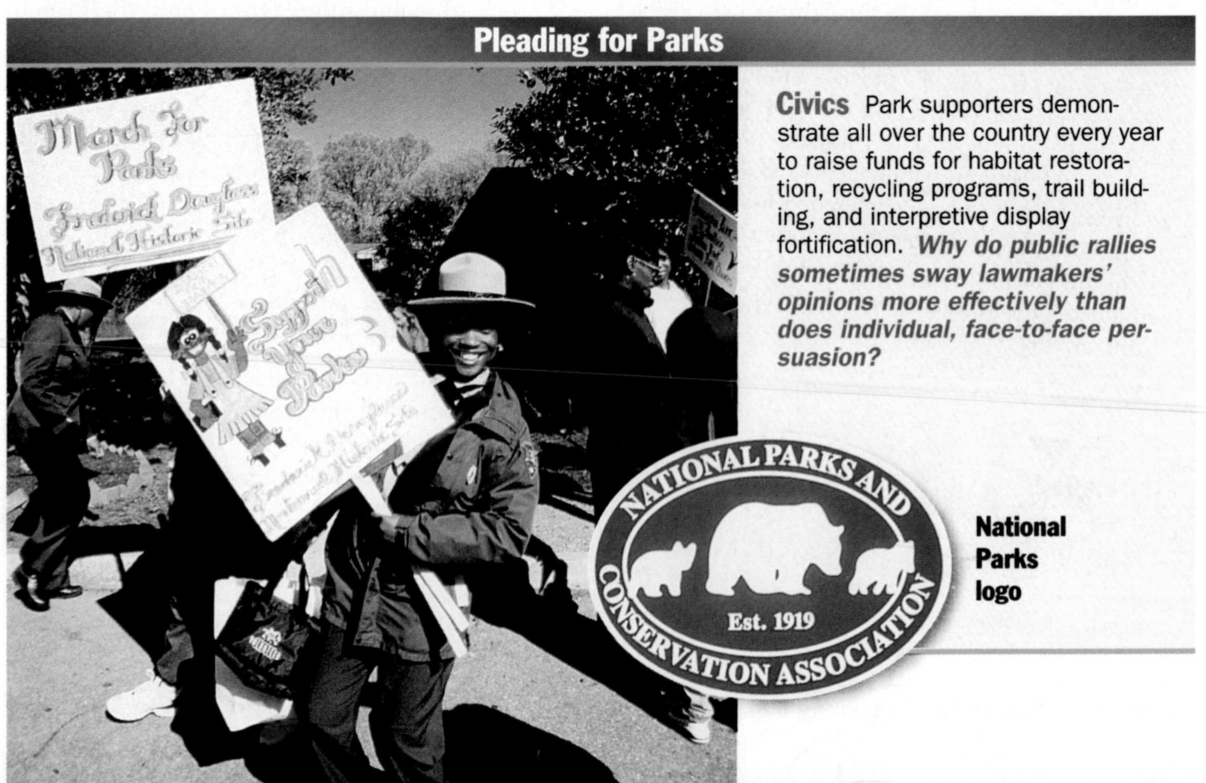

Pleading for Parks

Civics Park supporters demonstrate all over the country every year to raise funds for habitat restoration, recycling programs, trail building, and interpretive display fortification. ***Why do public rallies sometimes sway lawmakers' opinions more effectively than does individual, face-to-face persuasion?***

National Parks logo

Leadership and Membership

Interest group leaders strengthen the political power of the group by unifying its members. They keep members informed of the group's activities through newsletters, mailings, and telephone calls. They act as speakers for their group and try to improve its image in the media. They plan the group's strategy, raise money to run the organization, and oversee all financial decisions of the group.

Why do people belong to interest groups? First, a group may help promote an individual's economic self-interests. For example, a labor union works to gain higher wages and other benefits for its members. Business groups try to get the government to pass laws and make decisions that will help them increase profits. A senior citizens' group, such as the American Association of Retired Persons (AARP), works for higher Social Security benefits.

A second reason for joining a group centers on an individual's beliefs, values, or attitudes. Many citizens believe in certain ideas or political principles that they wish to see passed into law. For example, Sierra Club members work to conserve national resources and protect the environment from pollution. Members want laws passed requiring clean air and water.

Other reasons are nonpolitical. A person who joins a farm organization may simply like the company of other farmers. This social function also helps create group unity, a vital element in attaining the group's political goals.

Many people, however, do not belong to any interest group. Studies have shown that people on lower socioeconomic levels are less likely to join such groups. Studies of business organizations and other interest groups also show that membership tends to come from upper income levels. So, while the opportunity to join together to influence government is a right of all, the people who might benefit most do not often exercise that right.

Business and Labor Groups

Nearly all Americans have economic interests and concerns about taxes, food prices, housing, inflation, unemployment, and so forth. As a result, many interest groups are concerned with economic issues. These business and labor interest groups seek to convince lawmakers of policies that they feel will strengthen the economy.

Business-Related Interest Groups Business interest groups are among the oldest and largest in the United States. The National Association of Manufacturers (NAM) works to lower individual and corporate taxes and limit government regulation of business. Another business group—the United States Chamber of Commerce—tends to speak for smaller businesses. A third group is the Business Roundtable, composed of executives from almost 200 of the country's largest and most powerful corporations.

Labor-Related Interest Groups The largest and most powerful labor organization today is the **AFL-CIO.** Among the many unions in the AFL-CIO are the United Auto Workers (UAW), United Mine Workers (UMW), and the International Brotherhood of Teamsters. A separate organization called The Committee on Political Education (COPE) directs the AFL-CIO's political activities. COPE's major goals include fund-raising, voter registration drives, and support for political candidates.

Agricultural Groups

Three major interest groups represent almost 4 million American farmers. The largest of these groups is the American Farm Bureau Federation, which speaks for the larger, more successful farmers and is closely associated with the federal Department of Agriculture.

The National Farmers' Union (NFU) draws its membership from smaller farmers and favors higher price supports for crops and livestock. The group has also supported laws protecting migrant farm workers. The oldest farm group is the Patrons of Husbandry, known as the Grange. Although this group is more of a social organization than an interest group, it has been very outspoken in advocating price supports for crops.

Just as important are commodity associations representing groups such as dairy farmers and potato growers. Congressional subcommittees dealing with agriculture are organized around commodity lines.

Other Interest Groups

Besides purely economic interest groups, there are countless other kinds of interest groups. These range from professional and environmental organizations to governmental and public interest groups.

Professional Associations The American Bar Association (ABA) and the American Medical Association (AMA) are two examples of interest groups that include members of specific professions. Basically, these two groups influence the licensing and training of lawyers and doctors. Both groups, however, are actively involved in political issues. Professional associations also represent bankers, teachers, college professors, police officers, and hundreds of other professions. While these associations are concerned primarily with the standards of their professions, they also seek to influence government policy on issues that are important to them.

Environmental Interest Groups The concern for ecology and the environment has led to the formation of about 3,000 environmental interest groups. Their goals range from conserving natural resources to protecting endangered wildlife. One key environmental organization is the Sierra Club. Other environmental groups include the National Wildlife Federation, Friends of the Earth, and Environmental Action, Inc.

Public-Interest Groups Groups concerned about the public interest seek policy goals that they believe will benefit American society. These **public-interest groups** are not concerned with furthering the interests of a narrow group of people. Instead, they claim to work for the interests of all Americans. For example, Ralph Nader's Public Citizen, Inc., devotes itself to consumer and public safety issues affecting the general population. Common Cause, founded in 1970, is a public-interest group that has tried to reform various aspects of the American political system.

Interest Groups in Government Organizations and leaders within American government may also act as interest groups. Two powerful organizations today are the **National Conference of**

GOVERNMENT and You

Contributing to Interest Groups

Membership dues to labor organizations, trade and professional associations, and certain other groups that influence government may be deductible expenses on your federal income tax return. To a lesser extent, contributions made by you to such organizations may also be tax deductible. In addition, some expenses that result from volunteer work you do for such groups may be tax deductible.

The federal tax code allows deduction of cash contributions and other donations to groups that are tax-exempt organizations. Generally, these are nonprofit organizations that exist primarily for educational, charitable, scientific, or religious purposes. However, such groups are allowed to do a limited amount of lobbying.

On the other hand, groups that devote a substantial portion of their activities to influencing the government do not qualify as tax-exempt organizations, and contributions to such groups usually are not tax deductible. If you want to know the tax status of a group, the Internal Revenue Service Publication 78 lists all tax-exempt organizations.

IRS Publication 78 on the Web

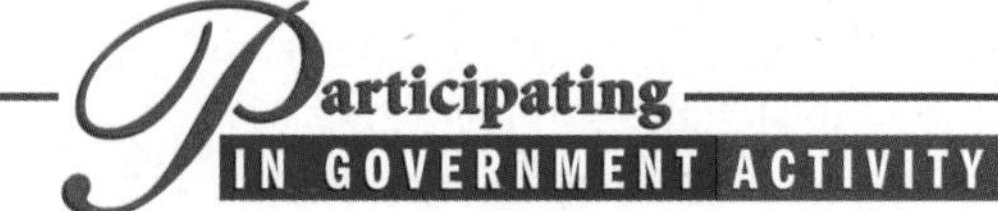

Research Find out the tax status of a nonprofit organization in your community. Is the organization tax exempt? Why do you think it qualifies or does not qualify as a tax-exempt organization?

State Legislators and the **National Governors' Association.** State and local government officials may seek to influence members of Congress or the executive branch because they want a greater share of federal aid. Interest groups such as the National Association of Counties, the Council of State Governments, or the National League of Cities seek support for policies to benefit cities and states.

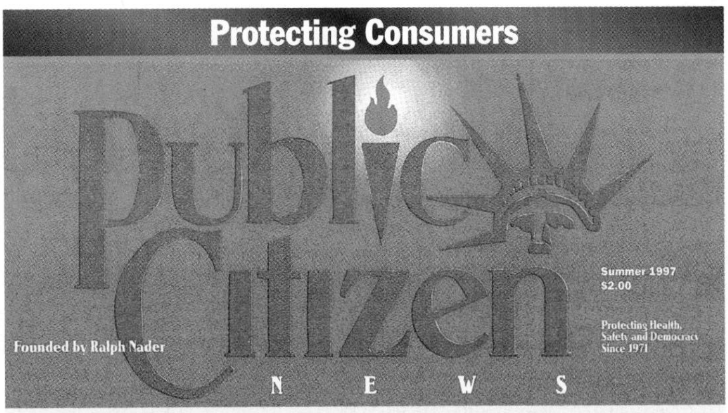

Civic Participation Ralph Nader's Public Citizen, Inc., is a consumer advocacy group. Its activities have resulted in a number of consumer protection laws. ***What difficulties might an activist like Nader face in influencing lawmakers?***

Additional Groups

Thousands of interest groups have been formed for other reasons. Any list would be inadequate to illustrate the diverse interests. Some are formed to promote a particular cause. Some groups seek to influence public policy while others organize into groups to support the aims of large segments of the population and to protect civil rights.

Foreign governments and private interests of foreign nations also seek to influence government in the United States. Foreign-interest groups may seek military aid, economic aid, or favorable trade agreements. They may make political donations in an effort to sway political decisions. All foreign agents must register with the United States government.

The possible influence of foreign donations on the 1996 presidential election was one target of congressional hearings on campaign finance in 1997. Committee members, led by committee chairperson Senator Fred Thompson, heard allegations concerning instances of individuals buying access to top leaders, money laundering of campaign donations, and attempts by foreign nationals to influence the 1996 elections. Both the Democratic National Committee and the Republican National Committee returned some questionable donations—most of them solicited by agents who had connections to interests in Asia.

Section 1 Assessment

Checking for Understanding

1. **Main Idea** Use a Venn diagram like the one to the right to compare the goals of an interest group and a political party.

2. **Define** interest group, public-interest group.
3. **Identify** factions.
4. Why are interest groups more effective in influencing the government than are individual citizens?
5. List six categories of interest groups.
6. What are three reasons why citizens join interest groups?

Critical Thinking

7. **Expressing Problems Clearly** Do interest groups help make representative government truly "government by the people"? Explain.

Concepts IN ACTION

Civic Participation Create a promotional brochure describing an interest group that you would like to see formed to address some interest or concern that you have. Include a description of the concern or interest, goals of the group, the kinds of people likely to be members of the group, and the methods your group would use to attain its goals.

Section 2

Affecting Public Policy

Reader's Guide

Key Terms

lobbying, lobbyist

Find Out

- By what methods do interest groups' lobbyists influence policymakers?
- How do political action committees influence elections?

Understanding Concepts

Public Policy Why do members of Congress rely on lobbyists to provide them with information?

COVER STORY

Too Many Amendments?

NEW YORK, NEW YORK, NOVEMBER 26, 1996

The present practice of turning causes into constitutional amendments is a troubling development, says political analyst John Leo. The Framers established a difficult amendment process, Leo notes, because they wanted amendments to be well-founded, necessary, and rare. However, an explosion of proposals to change the Constitution has come from interest groups who use the process to call attention to their cause, he says. Proposed amendments on school prayer, the budget, an official language, term limits, flag burning, abortion, victims' rights, and campaign finance are currently before Congress. These are all important issues, but few are legitimate constitutional necessities, Leo observes.

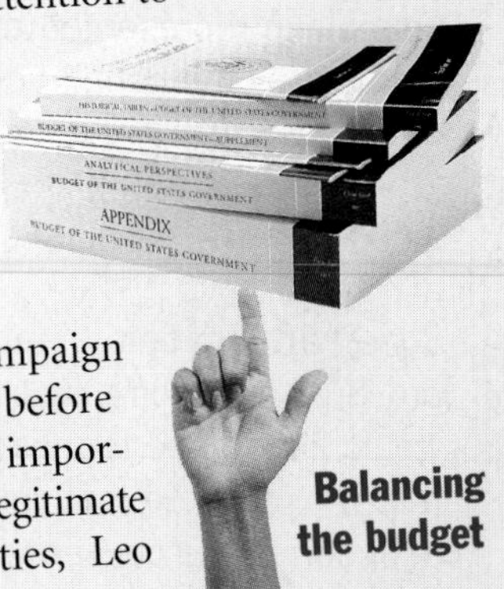

Balancing the budget

Most interest groups use a variety of methods to try to influence public policy. Representatives of the group contact government officials directly in Washington, D.C., or a state capital. Interest or pressure groups may also use television, radio, magazine, and newspaper advertising to create public support for their policies. They may even resort to court action or seek a constitutional amendment to achieve their goals.

The Work of Lobbyists

Most interest groups try to influence government policy by making direct contact with lawmakers or other government leaders. This process of direct contact is called **lobbying** because of the practice of approaching senators and representatives in the outer room or lobby of a capitol. The representatives of interest groups who do this kind of work are called **lobbyists.** Lobbying is one of the most widely used and effective techniques available to interest groups.

Who Are Lobbyists? In 1995 Congress redefined lobbyists to mean anyone who was employed or retained by a client, made more than one contact on behalf of the client, and spent more than 20 percent of his or her time serving the client. Why was such a specific definition necessary? The new Lobbying Disclosure Act of 1995 was intended to close loopholes in the 1946 Federal Regulation of Lobbying Act that had enabled most lobbyists to avoid registering with Congress. Before the new legislation only about 6,000 of the more than 13,600 lobbyists were registered. Unregistered lobbyists avoided the close scrutiny needed to prevent illegal influence upon members of Congress.

Currently registered lobbyists must file semiannual reports with the Clerk of the House and the Secretary of the Senate. These reports must disclose the issues or legislation being addressed, the government branches and agencies contacted, and an estimate of the amount of money paid by the client.

What kinds of people are lobbyists? Many lobbyists are former government officials. They usually have friends in Congress and the executive branch and know the intricacies of Washington politics. Lobbying has indeed been attractive to members of Congress:

> "*Tempted by the staggering fees that lobbyists can command, lawmakers and their aides are quitting in droves to cash in on their connections. For many, public service has become a mere internship for a lucrative career as a hired gun for special interests.*"
>
> —*Time,* March 3, 1986

Congress did ban former members from becoming lobbyists within one year of leaving office.

Many other lobbyists are lawyers or public relations experts. Understanding the government and how it works is vital for a lobbyist to be successful and effective.

White House Lobby

Presidents perhaps have the biggest stakes in influencing legislation. But not until the administration of Dwight D. Eisenhower was there a formal White House lobbying operation. Eisenhower's congressional liaison officers were retired general Wilton B. Persons, a deputy to Chief of Staff Sherman Adams, and Bryce N. Harlow, a former House committee staffer who replaced Persons when he succeeded Adams in 1958. Harlow was the first full-time presidential lobbyist. Presidents, of course, hold the ultimate lobbying weapon—the veto.

Providing Useful Information One of a lobbyist's most important methods of persuasion is to provide policymakers with useful information that supports an interest group's position. Lobbyists often try to meet personally with members of Congress or other government officials. Meetings may occur in a lawmaker's office or home, or in a more casual location such as at a favorite restaurant or on a golf course.

In order to gain support from members of Congress, lobbyists provide legislators with pamphlets, reports, statistics, and other kinds of information. House and Senate rules, however, restrict the gifts lobbyists may give lawmakers. Senators and their staff cannot accept any gift (including meals and entertainment) of more than $50 from a lobbyist. The Senate also has a $100 limit on gifts from any single source. The House has banned all gifts from lobbyists.

How much do members of Congress rely on information presented by lobbyists? Legislators realize that lobbyists can be biased in presenting their cases. A lobbyist who intentionally misrepresents the facts, however, may lose access to the lawmaker permanently.

Lobbyists also provide information by testifying before congressional committees. Usually when Congress is considering a bill, lobbyists are invited to testify. For example, lobbyists representing the oil industry may testify before a committee considering legislation to tax oil profits. Finally, when a bill comes to the floor in either house of Congress, lobbyists continue to work hard to influence lawmakers' votes.

Drafting Bills Besides providing information to lawmakers, lobbyists and interest groups may actually help write bills. Many well-organized interest groups have research staffs that help members of Congress draft proposed laws. Studies have shown that interest groups and their lobbyists draft parts of or entire bills for almost 50 percent of all legislation.

Interest Groups Seek Support

Interest groups run publicity campaigns to win support for their policies. A wide range of techniques is available to interest groups in their effort to influence policy makers.

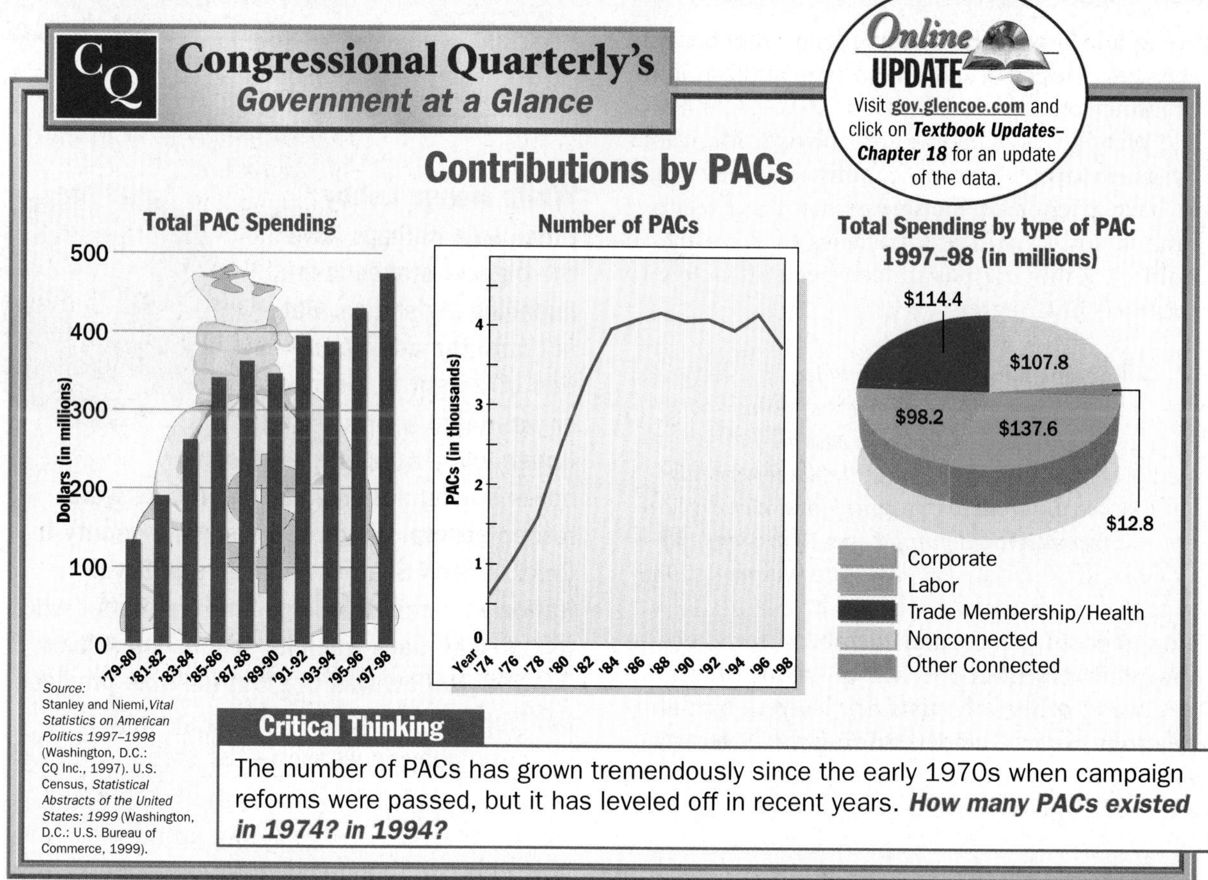

Source: Stanley and Niemi, *Vital Statistics on American Politics 1997–1998* (Washington, D.C.: CQ Inc., 1997). U.S. Census, *Statistical Abstracts of the United States: 1999* (Washington, D.C.: U.S. Bureau of Commerce, 1999).

Critical Thinking

The number of PACs has grown tremendously since the early 1970s when campaign reforms were passed, but it has leveled off in recent years. ***How many PACs existed in 1974? in 1994?***

Media Campaigns Interest or pressure groups use the mass media—television, newspapers, magazines, and radio—to inform the public and to create support for their views. For example, when Congress considered changes to the nation's health-care system in the 1990s, the American College of Surgeons used advertising to explain its position on patient choice. Environmentalists have run television and magazine ads to dramatize pollution and the hazards it poses.

Letter Writing Many interest groups urge their members to write letters to government officials to demonstrate broad support for or against a public policy. For example, the National Rifle Association can deliver hundreds of thousands of letters from its members. While members of Congress and other public officials understand that these letters may not represent the opinion of the entire nation, writing letters is one method to make officials aware of an issue that is important to the group.

Limitations The public's perception of interest groups is that they are financially and politically powerful. How important are these groups in determining public policy?

Interest groups do provide representation for Americans in addition to the representation they have in Congress. They allow Americans to be represented according to their economic, social, or occupational interests. Pressure groups also act as watchdogs and protest government policies that harm their members.

Several factors limit the effectiveness of interest groups. Different interest groups compete for power and influence, keeping any single group from controlling lawmakers and other public officials. Generally, the larger the group, the more diverse are the interests of its members. This diversity has meant that nationally organized interest groups may be unable to adopt broad policy goals. As a result, smaller interest groups or those that unite people who have narrower aims have been most effective in shaping policy.

While large interest groups have membership that provides an impressive financial base, most organizations struggle to pay small staffs. In recent years, however, the greatest concern about the power of interest groups has been their financial contributions to political campaigns.

The Rise of Political Action Committees

Lobbying is just one method interest groups use to influence lawmakers. These groups also provide a large percentage of the funds used in candidates' election campaigns. Most of these funds come from **political action committees** (PACs), or organizations specifically designed to collect money and provide financial support for a political candidate. A Washington lobbyist admitted, "I won't even take a client now unless he's willing to set up a political action committee and participate in the [campaign contribution] process."

How PACs Began Before 1974, wealthy individuals gave large sums to finance political campaigns. Then the federal government passed laws to reform campaign finance. The new laws limited the amounts that individuals could contribute to federal candidates. While federal law prevented corporations and labor unions from making direct contributions to any federal candidate, it permitted their political action committees to do so.

Laws Governing PACs At the beginning of this period the government set rules regulating political action committees. The main federal laws governing PACs are the Federal Election Campaign Act (FECA) of 1971; the amendments to it passed in 1974, 1976, and 1979; and the Revenue Act of 1971. Under these laws a PAC must register with the government 6 months before an election. It must raise money from at least 50 contributors and give to at least 5 candidates in a federal election. PACs must also follow strict accounting rules.

PACs can give $5,000 directly to each candidate per election. The government, however, has not limited the total amount a PAC can spend on a candidate's campaign as long as the PAC does not work directly with the candidate.

In 1976 the Supreme Court ruled that any independent group may give money to a political candidate as long as the group does not have legal ties to that candidate. PAC spending climbed from a few million dollars in the 1975–76 election cycle to about $358 million in 1999–2000. PACs provided about $42 million to Senate candidates and $123 million to House candidates.

Federal Election Commission The Federal Election Commission (FEC) issues regulations and advisory opinions that control PAC activities. In 1975, for example, the FEC ruled that corporations can use their own money to administer their PACs and may also use payroll deductions to raise money from employees of a PAC. The FEC's decision stimulated the growth of PACs among business interests.

The Power of Money

Influence of PACs Recently Americans have questioned the implications of huge financial contributions by PACs to legislators. ***According to the cartoonist, where do legislators' loyalties lie?***

We the People

Making a Difference

David Laughery

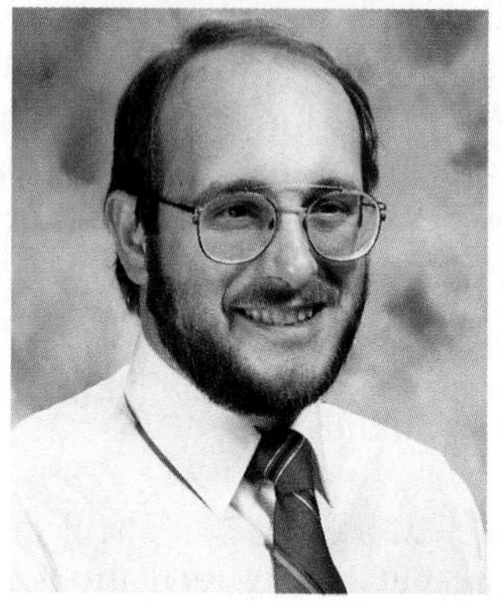

Pennsylvania teacher David Laughery believes that people of any age can make a difference if they make their voices heard. "My students first made their voices heard when they decided to . . . lobby for the adoption of a citywide helmet ordinance," Laughery said.

With encouragement from Laughery, the students in his class joined five other classes to develop a plan to lobby their township's Board of Supervisors. Students gathered statistics on bike-related injuries and deaths.

Armed with their research data and a prepared speech, the students presented their recommendation to their local township board. The board agreed to review their request for a helmet law in the Hershey, Pennsylvania, community.

Just a few weeks later, Pennsylvania state legislators passed a statewide helmet law. Students' efforts at a local level were no longer needed. However, the students believed they had performed a valuable service by educating the people of their community about the importance of a bike helmet law. "For the first time in their lives, these kids realized that they, too, are citizens who not only have rights, but also responsibilities," Laughery said.

In the decade after the ruling, the number of corporate PACs increased by more than 1,000 percent.

Supreme Court Decisions The Supreme Court has also affected the growth and operation of PACs. For example, in the case of *Buckley* v. *Valeo*[1] (1976) the Court ruled that different divisions of a corporation or different union locals can set up as many PACs as they wish. In 1996 the Court held that national, state, and local committee spending in support of federal candidates was a form of free speech. There could be no spending limit. Spending for federal campaigns soared to more than $1.6 billion.

PACs and the Groups They Serve

PACs can be classified into two categories, according to the groups they serve. They are either affiliated or independent.

Affiliated PACs PACs tied to corporations, labor unions, trade groups, or health organizations are called affiliated PACs. Comprising about 70 percent of all PACs, they raise funds through voluntary contributions from corporate executives, union officials, workers, and stockholders. Examples of affiliated PACs are the Sun Oil Corporation's SunPAC, the Realtors' Political Action Committee, and the Cattlemen's Action Legislative Fund (CALF).

Nonconnected PACs Groups interested in a particular cause such as free trade may set up PACs that are not connected to any existing interest group. Some nonconnected PACs are organized primarily to participate in elections. These nonconnected or independent PACs make up about 25 percent of all PACs. Examples of such PACs and their varied interests include Americans for Free International Trade, Council for a Livable World, The House Leadership Fund, National Abortion Rights Action League PAC, National Right to Life PAC, and Republicans for Choice.

Nonconnected PACs raise money largely through direct-mail appeals to people across the nation. They are very successful and usually raise more money than business or labor PACs. Independent PACs, however, spend less on candidates and elections than do the affiliated PACs because massive direct-mail fund-raising is very costly.

See the following footnoted materials in the ***Reference Handbook:***
1. *Buckley* v. *Valeo* case summary, page 755.

Most of the money raised must be used to pay postage and staff workers and to buy mailing lists of potential contributors.

Strategies for Influence

Political action committees generally follow two strategies to influence public policy. They use their money to gain access to lawmakers and to directly influence election outcomes.

Trading Support for Access Interest groups can promise campaign support for legislators who favor their policies, or they can threaten to withhold support. (Campaign contributions were exempted from the 1995 Lobbying Disclosure Act restricting gifts to members of Congress.) Loss of a sizable contribution could affect a candidate's chances of winning. Other interest groups with comparable political strength who support opposite goals, however, might back the candidate.

Interest groups, especially PACs, raise much of the money used in political campaigns. They realize that making a campaign contribution does not guarantee that a candidate, if elected, will always vote the way they wish. Such groups, however, know that campaign contributions will at least assure access to the officials they help elect.

Busy lawmakers are more likely to set aside time in their crowded schedules to meet with a group that has given money than to meet with a group that has not. As a result, PACs may give donations to lawmakers who do not always support the views of the PACs.

PACs generally support incumbents, or those government officials already in office. In recent elections 88 percent of corporate and trade PAC donations went to incumbents in House campaigns and more than 65 percent to incumbents in Senate elections.

Influencing Elections The decision to support incumbents has the expected result. Incumbents in both the House and Senate have a good chance of winning reelection. In some cases the task of challenging an incumbent for a seat in Congress is so difficult that there are no challengers. Joan Claybrook, president of Public Citizen, Inc., an interest group Ralph Nader founded, said, "That these PACs feel compelled to contribute to lawmakers who have no opponent shows that what is being sought is access and influence."

How Much Influence Some members of Congress acknowledge the power of the PACs. Representative Barney Frank once said, "We are the only human beings in the world who are expected to take thousands of dollars from perfect strangers and not be affected by it." Other members of Congress disagree. Representative Dan Glickman has claimed, "I do not think any member of Congress votes because of how a PAC gives him money on El Salvador, or the MX missiles, or . . . broader, abstract national issues."

Section 2 Assessment

Checking for Understanding

1. **Main Idea** Use a graphic organizer like the one below to list two methods lobbyists and PACs use to influence public policy.

	Lobbyists	PACs
1.		
2.		

2. **Define** lobbying, lobbyist.
3. **Identify** political action committee.
4. What kinds of backgrounds do people who become lobbyists often have?

Critical Thinking

5. **Making Generalizations** What qualities of a lobbyist would make that person successful in furthering the goals of democratic government?

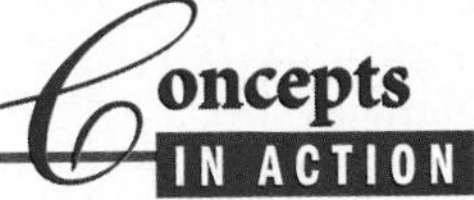

Public Policy Members of Congress rely on lobbyists to provide them with information. Write a job description for a professional lobbyist. Include the skills and experience required for the position and the list of duties the position will involve.

Section 3

Shaping Public Opinion

Reader's Guide

Key Terms

public opinion, peer group, mass media, political culture

Find Out

- What are the patterns of political ideology in the United States?
- Which of the forces in political socialization are most influential?

Understanding Concepts

Cultural Pluralism By what process does American democracy begin with diverse opinions and end with acceptable public policy?

COVER STORY

Channel One Is Big

LOS ANGELES, CALIFORNIA, DECEMBER 18, 1995

After five years on the air, Channel One News continues to grow. The 12-minute newscast is seen in 12,000 schools by some 8 million viewers. That's 40 percent of the nation's teens and roughly 5 times the number who watch ABC, CBS, CNN, and NBC news combined. Young Channel One crews—some anchors are still in school—cover stories on location throughout the world. Although many educators are sharply critical of the program's commercials, one study found that Channel One viewers have more knowledge of current issues and events than students in schools that do not carry the broadcast.

Channel One News correspondent

Every elected official wants to know what the public is thinking. "What I want," Abraham Lincoln once declared, "is to get done what the people desire to have done, and the question for me is how to find that out exactly." Lincoln did not have television. Today the president watches the same news as everyone else. To a large extent the media in the United States both reflect and direct what the American people are thinking about.

The Nature of Public Opinion

Most Americans have opinions or preferences about many matters that affect their lives. These range from preferences about the best baseball players to favorite television programs. Few such opinions, however, have much effect on government. Yet one form of opinion, public opinion, has an enormous influence on government. **Public opinion** includes the ideas and attitudes a significant number of Americans hold about government and political issues. Three factors characterize the nature of public opinion.

Diversity Public opinion is varied. In a nation as vast as the United States, it is unlikely that all citizens will think the same way about any political issue. Because of the diversity of American society, different groups of people hold different opinions on almost every issue.

Communication People's ideas and attitudes must in some way be expressed and communicated to government. Unless Americans make their opinions on important issues clear, public officials will not know what people are thinking. Accordingly, officials will not be able to weigh public opinion when making decisions. Interest groups communicate the opinions of many individuals. Officials also rely on opinion polls and private letters and telegrams to know what people are thinking.

Significant Numbers The phrase "a significant number of Americans" in the definition of public opinion means that enough people must hold a particular opinion to make government officials listen to them. For example, perhaps the most important reason why President Lyndon Johnson decided not to run for reelection in 1968 was that so many people opposed his conduct of the Vietnam War.

Political Socialization

Personal background and life experiences exert important influences on opinion formation. Individuals learn their political beliefs and attitudes from their family, school, friends, and coworkers in a process called **political socialization.** This process begins early in life and continues through adulthood.

Family and Home Influence Political socialization begins within the family. Children learn many of their early political opinions from their parents. In most cases, the political party of the parents becomes the party of their children. A study of high school seniors showed that only a small minority differed in party loyalty from their parents. As adults, more than two-thirds of all voters continue to favor the political party their parents supported.

Schools School also plays an important part in the political socialization process. In the United States, all students learn about their nation, its history, and its political system. Democratic values are also learned in school clubs and through school rules and regulations.

Peer Groups An individual's close friends, religious group, clubs, and work groups—called peer groups—are yet another factor in the political socialization process. A person's peer groups often influence and shape opinions. For example, a member of a labor union whose closest friends belong to the same union is likely to have political opinions similar to theirs.

Social Characteristics Economic and social status is another aspect of political socialization. Whether a person is young or old, rich or poor, rural or urban, Easterner or Southerner, African American or white, male or female may affect personal political opinions.

Polarity of Public Opinion

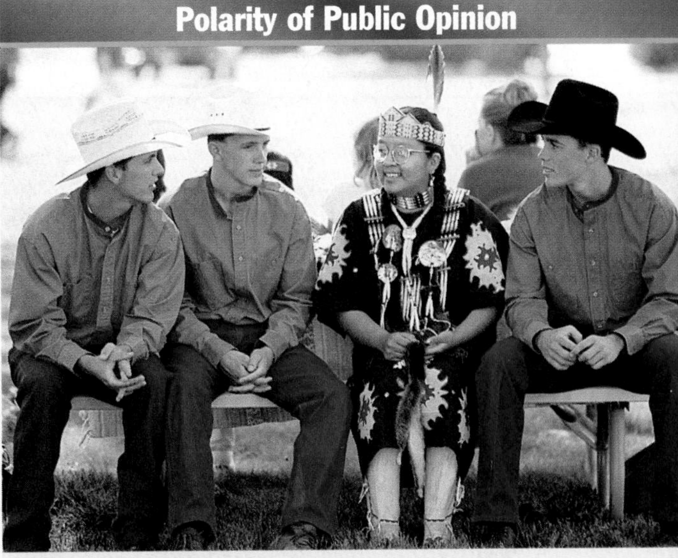

Diverse Opinions Americans' differing opinions on political issues spring from the diversity of Americans themselves. This diversity is reflected during a Native American festival in Delta, Utah. ***How do you think this diversity affects public opinion?***

The Mass Media Television, radio, newspapers, magazines, recordings, movies, and books—the mass media—play an important role in political socialization. The media, especially television, provide political information and images that can directly influence political attitudes. For example, broadcasts of a rally against a Supreme Court decision or a riot outside an American embassy can help shape viewers' opinions.

Movies, recordings, novels, and television entertainment can also affect opinions. Showing police as heroes or as criminals, for example, can shape attitudes toward authority. The way the media depict different groups of people such as women, African Americans, Asian Americans, Hispanics, or immigrants can help discredit stereotypes—or create them.

Other Influences Government leaders also play an important role in political socialization. The president especially has a tremendous influence on

Rallying for Support

Influential Actions Students support the G.R.E.A.T. (Gang Resistance Education and Training) program in central Texas and rally against drugs and crime. ***How do rallies, such as this one, help shape public opinion?***

people's opinions. The news media provide almost continuous reports on the president's activities and policy proposals.

Like the president, members of Congress try to influence opinions. They frequently go back to their home states or home districts and talk to their constituents. Many legislators send newsletters or write personal letters to voters. They also appear on television programs and give newspaper interviews on timely issues. Lawmakers who come across as sincere, personable, and intelligent are particularly effective in influencing opinions on major issues. At state and local levels, lawmakers also use the media to gain public support for their views.

At the same time, interest groups try to shape public opinion. If an interest group can win enough support, public opinion may pressure legislators to accept the group's goals. Churches and other religious organizations also affect people's political opinions.

Political Efficacy Most individuals are unaware that political socialization occurs in their lives because it is a slow process that happens over their lifetimes. Simultaneously, many people do not realize that this socialization has a direct effect upon their feelings of political efficacy. **Political efficacy** refers to an individual's feelings of effectiveness in politics. Some people are socialized to believe that they cannot impact the "system." Other people are socialized to trust that their actions can be effective and lead to changes important to them. Feelings of political efficacy are vital in a democracy. Without citizen participation, democracies would be unable to realize the concept of government "of the people, by the people, and for the people."

Political Culture

Every nation in the world has a **political culture,** a set of basic values and beliefs about a nation and its government that most citizens share. For example, a belief in liberty and freedom is one of the key elements of American political culture. Ralph Waldo Emerson expressed this value when he wrote:

> "*The office of America is to liberate, to abolish kingcraft, priestcraft, castle, monopoly, to pull down the gallows, to burn up the bloody statute-book, to take in the immigrant, to open the doors of the sea and the fields of the earth.*"
>
> —Ralph Waldo Emerson

Additional examples of widely shared political values include support for the Constitution and Bill of Rights, commitment to the idea of political equality, belief in the virtue of private property, and an emphasis on individual achievement. The American political culture helps shape public opinion in the United States in two ways.

A Context for Opinion The political culture sets the general boundaries within which citizens develop and express their opinions. Public opinion on any issue or problem almost always fits within the limits the political culture sets. For example, Americans will disagree over just how much the federal government should regulate the airline industry. Very few Americans, however, would urge that government eliminate regulations altogether or that it take over and run the industry.

Screening Information A nation's political culture also influences how its citizens interpret what they see and hear every day. Put another way, an American and a Russian citizen might interpret the same event quite differently. If shown a photo of people in line outside a grocery store, the Russian might attribute it to a food shortage. The American citizen would likely think there was a sale.

Ideology and Public Policy

An **ideology** is a set of basic beliefs about life, culture, government, and society. One's political ideology provides the framework for looking at government and public policy. However, Americans tend to determine their positions issue by issue rather than follow a strict ideology. Polls show that many people express inconsistent opinions on issues. For example, most people favor lower taxes, but they also want better schools and increased government services. American political values tend to fall into two broad but distinct patterns of opinions toward government and public policies—liberal and conservative.

Liberal Ideology A **liberal** believes the government should actively promote health, education, and justice. Liberals are willing to curtail economic freedom to increase equality, for example, by regulating business to protect consumers. In social matters, however, liberals believe the government should not restrict most individual freedoms.

Conservative Ideology A **conservative** believes in limiting the role of government, except in supporting traditional moral values. Conservatives believe private individuals, not the government, should solve social problems. They oppose government limitations on businesses and believe free markets ensure the best economic outcomes.

Moderates and Libertarians **Moderates** fall somewhere between liberals and conservatives. For example, a moderate may want the government to regulate business and support traditional values. Libertarians support both economic and social freedoms—free markets and unrestricted speech.

GOVERNMENT *Online*

Student Web Activity Visit the *United States Government: Democracy in Action* Web site at gov.glencoe.com and click on ***Chapter 18–Student Web Activities*** for an activity about shaping public opinion.

Section 3 Assessment

Checking for Understanding

1. **Main Idea** Use a graphic organizer like the one below to contrast liberal and conservative ideologies.

	social policy	economic policy
liberals		
conservatives		

2. **Define** public opinion, peer group, mass media, political culture.
3. **Identify** political socialization, political efficacy, liberal, conservative, moderate.
4. What five social characteristics can influence the opinions a person holds?

Critical Thinking

5. **Demonstrating Reasoned Judgment** Do you think that the mass media have too much influence on American public opinion? Explain why or why not.

Cultural Pluralism Use library resources or the Internet to find examples of situations in which public opinion has caused an elected official to change his or her position on an issue. Present your findings in the form of a poster to your classmates.

Supreme Court CASES TO DEBATE

Bennett et al. v. Spear et al., 1996

Fish without water

Since the passage of the Endangered Species Act (ESA) in 1973, environmental groups have used the law to file suits to stop actions they believed threatened the environment. Would the ESA also allow lawsuits by those who believed the government was doing too much to protect the environment? The Supreme Court faced this issue in the case of Bennett et al. *v.* Spear et al.

Background of the Case

The ESA requires federal agencies to ensure that any action they undertake is not likely to hurt an endangered species or adversely modify the species' critical habitat. During a drought in 1992, the federal Fish and Wildlife Service decided to cut off irrigation water normally sent to farmers and ranchers in Oregon and California to protect two endangered species of fish, the Lost River Sucker and the Shortnose Sucker. The federal agencies had determined that lowering water levels in federal reservoirs to provide irrigation water used by farms and ranches could possibly hurt the fish. The lack of water for irrigation caused farmers' crops to die and forced ranchers to sell their cattle because they could not feed or water them, resulting in losses of $75 million. Two ranchers and irrigation districts filed suit under the ESA against the federal government. A court of appeals ruled that only people who wanted to preserve an endangered species fell within the "zone of interests" protected by the ESA, and therefore were allowed, or had "standing," to file suit under the ESA. The ranchers appealed to the Supreme Court.

The Constitutional Issue

The Supreme Court is sometimes called upon to interpret the meaning of federal laws such as the ESA. In this instance, a key argument centered on the meaning of the citizen suit provision of the ESA. The provision stated "any person may commence a civil suit" challenging the way the Secretary of the Interior carries out the law. Since the ESA was created to protect endangered species, did the phrase mean that only people who wanted to use the law to preserve endangered species came within the "zone of interest" protected by the law and could start lawsuits? Or did it mean people who had recreational or commercial interests also fell within the reach of the law and could therefore sue?

Debating the Case

Questions to Consider

1. What two requirements did the ESA put on federal agency actions?
2. On what grounds were ranchers using the ESA allowed to sue the federal government?
3. Why did the court of appeals rule that the ranchers could not sue under the ESA?
4. What specific question was the Supreme Court asked to resolve?

You Be the Judge

What could be the long-term consequences of letting the ranchers sue the government under the ESA? In your opinion, do all persons have an equal interest in the environment? Does the ESA permit lawsuits from those who say they have lost money or property because the government has gone too far in protecting endangered species? Explain your decision.

Section 4

Measuring Public Opinion

Reader's Guide

Key Terms

biased sample, universe, representative sample, random sampling, sampling error, cluster sample

Find Out

- By what methods is public opinion measured?
- Why is the phrasing of the questions in an opinion poll so important?

Understanding Concepts

Cultural Pluralism In conducting a national poll, why is it important to have a variety of racial, ethnic, and religious groups represented in the sample?

COVER STORY

What Do Polls Show?

WASHINGTON, D.C., MARCH 1996

A study by the Pew Research Center for the People and the Press has found that Americans pay attention to news stories about wars and disasters, but ignore just about everything else. Only 21 percent of people surveyed knew at least three of four well-reported facts about national issues. Such findings undermine the value of opinion polls, some journalists suggest, because polls assume that participants have some knowledge of the subject. "Pollsters are asking people questions they aren't equipped to handle but are too embarrassed not to answer," writes Virginia Postrel, editor of *Reason* magazine. "Then both reporters and politicians are making a big deal of the response."

Gulf War soldier

Americans express their opinions at the ballot box. In between elections, officials want to know what the public is thinking. The methods of accessing and the technology for tabulating public opinion have changed and expanded over the years.

Traditional Methods

In the past elected officials relied on several methods of gauging public opinion. Reading newspapers, meeting leaders of interest groups, and talking with voters helped them to determine the public mood.

Political Party Organizations Through much of American history, local and state party organizations were a reliable source of information about the public's attitudes. Party leaders were in close touch with voters in their home towns, cities, counties, and states. National leaders, in turn, communicated regularly with Republican and Democratic Party bosses in such cities as New York, Chicago, Philadelphia, and Detroit. When the two major parties did not respond to issues quickly, support for third parties increased registering public disapproval. In the early 1900s, however, political reforms designed to curb the abuses of the big city party organizations began to weaken the role of parties in daily political life. As a result, their ability to provide reliable information on voters' attitudes declined.

Interest Groups Elected officials have always tried to stay in touch with the leaders of various interest groups. These groups also seek such contact to make sure public officials know the opinions of their members. Interest groups, however, often represent the attitudes of a vocal minority concerned with specific issues such as gun control, health care, or auto safety. They are not a good measure of broader public opinion.

The Mass Media The mass media can be a measure of public attitudes because it speaks to a broad audience. The audience, by its response, helps determine the content of media information. For example, if a news program gets higher audience ratings because of coverage of a certain issue, it is an indication of public interest in that issue. To know what the public is thinking about, politicians keep an eye on newspaper headlines, magazine cover stories, editorials, radio talk shows, and television newscasts.

These sources of information, however, may give a distorted view of public opinion for several reasons. The mass media's focus on news that has visual appeal or shock value, such as stories about violent crime, distorts the public perception of reality. People who watch television news as their only source of news, for example, tend to be more pessimistic about the nation than those who also use other sources for information. People who write letters to the editor and call radio talk shows tend to have stronger opinions than those of the general audience.

Letter Writing One time-honored form of expressing opinion in a democracy is to write letters to elected officials. The first major letter-writing campaign convinced George Washington to seek a second term as president in 1792. Letter writing increases in times of national crisis or major government decisions. The president may even request letters from the public to indicate support for a new policy or to provide the White House with ammunition for a battle with Congress. In the same way, lawmakers may ask their supporters to write to the president.

Today interest groups often stage massive letter-writing campaigns using computerized mailings to generate thousands of letters on an issue. Officials, however, may give such letters much less attention than they do more personal ones from individual constituents.

Electronic Access Members of Congress and the White House may now be reached by E-mail or by fax. This allows citizens to react almost immediately to events and government decisions. Another way to respond quickly to speeches, press conferences, and other events is by telephone or telegram.

Straw Polls Unscientific attempts to measure public opinion are made through **straw polls.** Some newspapers, as well as radio and television stations, still use straw polls. Newspapers may print "ballots" in the paper and ask people to "vote" and mail their "ballots" to the editor. Television and radio stations ask questions—"Should the mayor run for reelection?"—and give the audience telephone numbers to call for *yes* or *no* answers. Members of Congress often send their constituents questionnaires.

Straw polls are not very reliable indicators of public opinion because they do not ensure that the group, or **sample,** of people giving opinions accurately represents the larger population. Straw polls always have a **biased sample**—the people who respond to them are self-selected. They choose to respond.

Scientific Polling

Almost everyone involved in politics today uses scientific polls to measure public opinion. Scientific polling involves three basic steps: (1) selecting a sample of the group to be questioned; (2) presenting carefully worded questions to the individuals in the sample; and (3) interpreting the results.

Sample Populations In conducting polls, the group of people that are to be studied is called the **universe.** A universe might be all the seniors in a high school, all the people in the state of Texas, or all women in the United States. Since it is not possible to actually interview every person in Texas or every woman in the United States, pollsters question a **representative sample,** a small group of people typical of the universe.

Most pollsters are able to use samples of only 1,200 to 1,500 adults to accurately measure the opinions of all adults in the United States—about 183 million people. Such a small group is a representative sample because pollsters use **random sampling,** a technique in which everyone in the universe has an equal chance of being selected.

Sampling Error A **sampling error** is a measurement of how much the sample results may differ from the sample universe. Sampling error decreases as the sample size becomes larger. Most national polls use 1,200 to 1,500 people; this number represents the characteristics of any size population, with an error of only plus or minus 3 percent. If a poll says that 65 percent of Americans favor tougher pollution laws, with a 3 percent sampling error, between 62 and 68 percent of the entire population favor such laws.

Knowing the sampling error is important when poll data is interpreted. During the 1976 presidential race, for example, one poll said Jimmy Carter was behind Gerald Ford 48 percent to 49 percent. With a sampling error of 3 percent, Carter could have been ahead. As it turned out, Carter won the election.

Sampling Procedures How do pollsters draw random samples of the whole nation? There are various ways that they accomplish this. One method, a **cluster sample,** organizes, or clusters, people by geographical divisions. The clusters may be counties, congressional districts, or census tracts (regions established by the Census Bureau).

At times pollsters adjust or weight the results of a poll to overcome defects in sampling. Pollsters may adjust a poll to take into account variations in race, gender, age, or education. For example, if pollsters found that not enough Americans over the age of 65 had been interviewed, they might give extra weight to the opinions of the senior citizens who were interviewed.

Poll Questions The way a question is phrased can greatly influence people's responses and, in turn, poll results. In 1971 the Gallup Poll asked whether people favored a proposal "to bring home all American troops from Vietnam before the end of the year." Two-thirds of those polled answered *yes.* Then the Gallup Poll asked the question differently: "Do you agree or disagree with a proposal to withdraw all U.S. troops by the end of the year regardless of what happens there [in Vietnam] after U.S. troops leave?" When the question was worded this way, less than half agreed with the proposal, a big difference from the first response.

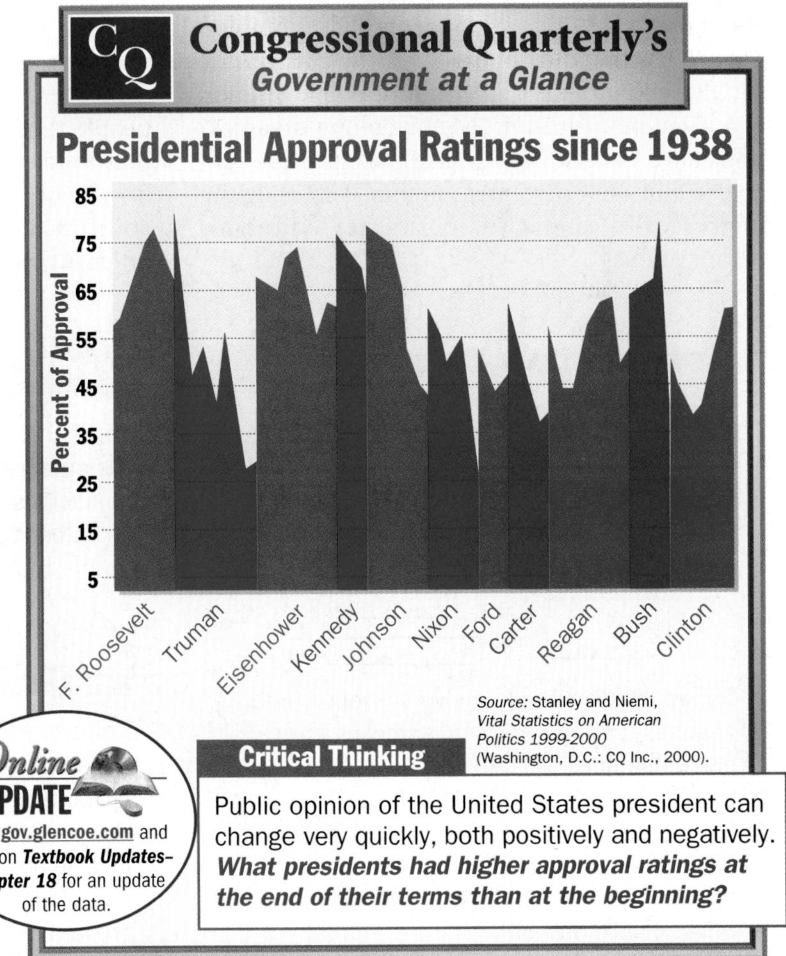

Source: Stanley and Niemi, *Vital Statistics on American Politics 1999-2000* (Washington, D.C.: CQ Inc., 2000).

Critical Thinking

Public opinion of the United States president can change very quickly, both positively and negatively. ***What presidents had higher approval ratings at the end of their terms than at the beginning?***

Online UPDATE Visit gov.glencoe.com and click on ***Textbook Updates–Chapter 18*** for an update of the data.

Mail and Phone Polls In recent years many public opinion polls have been conducted by mail or by telephone, largely because interviewing people in their homes is expensive. Although the mail questionnaire method is cheaper and more convenient than personal interviews, it has two disadvantages. One is that relatively few questionnaires are returned—usually only about 10 to 15 percent. Second, pollsters cannot control respondents' careless or confusing replies.

Telephone interviews are now used in many national polls. To be reliable a telephone poll, like other polls, should select a representative sample of the population. Most pollsters use a method called random digit dialing. They select an area code and the first three local digits. Then a computer randomly chooses and dials the last four digits. Although telephone polls are more reliable than mail questionnaires, problems do exist. Pollsters may fail to reach the person being called. In addition, some people refuse to answer the questions or are confused by or are inattentive to the interviewer.

Interpreting Results The methods pollsters use have improved markedly since the beginnings of scientific polling in the 1930s. Nevertheless, a number of problems still exist. First, the interviewer's appearance or even the tone of his or her voice can influence answers. Second, individuals sometimes give what they believe is the correct or socially acceptable answer. For example, many people will say they voted in an election when they did not. Third, there is no guarantee that the respondent knows anything about the subject; the person being interviewed may only pretend to have an informed opinion. One poll found that about one-third of its respondents had an opinion about a law that did not exist.

Polls do provide a snapshot of public opinion at a given point in time. Major polling organizations have learned how to take polls that are reliable within a few percentage points. Poll results are important to candidates, businesses, and many organizations.

Public Opinion and Democracy

The Framers of the Constitution sought to create a representative democracy that would meet two goals. The first was to provide for popular rule—to give the people an active voice in government. The people were to have control over the lawmakers who represented them.

The Framers' second goal was to insulate government from the shifting whims of ill-informed public opinion. The Framers would have understood modern journalist Walter Lippmann, who said that the people

> "*. . . can elect the government. They can remove it. They can approve or disapprove its performance. But they cannot administer the government. They cannot themselves perform. . . . A mass cannot govern.*"
>
> —Walter Lippmann

The system the Framers created has worked well. Research shows that the government is responsive to public opinion—to the wishes of the people. At the same time, public opinion is not the only influence on public policy. Interest groups, political parties, the mass media, other institutions of government, and the ideas of activists and public officials themselves also help shape public policy.

Section 4 Assessment

Checking for Understanding

1. **Main Idea** Use a graphic organizer like the one below to identify two goals the Framers of the Constitution wanted to meet by creating a representative democracy.

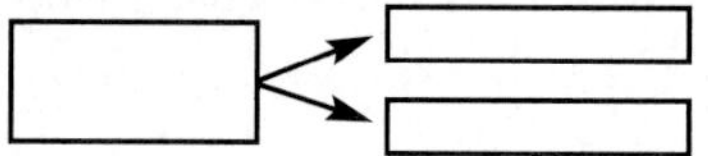

2. **Define** biased sample, universe, representative sample, random sampling, sampling error, cluster sample.
3. **Identify** straw poll, sample.
4. Identify seven sources that public officials use to determine public opinion.
5. List reasons that poll results may not accurately reflect public opinion.

Critical Thinking

6. **Demonstrating Reasoned Judgment** Why do politicians pay closer attention to the results of polls conducted through personal interviews rather than through the mail?

Cultural Pluralism Find a public opinion poll in a newspaper or newsmagazine. Analyze the poll by focusing on the following questions: How many people were contacted? Does the poll include a random or representative sampling? What is the sampling error? Are the questions presented in an unbiased, effective way? Present your answers in an analytical report.

Interpreting Opinion Polls

Well-designed public opinion polls give us accurate "snapshots"of how Americans are thinking at a given time. Knowing how to read data from a public opinion poll will help you to understand what your fellow citizens are thinking.

Learning the Skill

To analyze a poll, follow these steps:

- Look at the title and the date of the poll to determine a context for what you read.
- Note who was interviewed. Ask: How large was the sample? Sample sizes should be as large as possible for higher reliability.
- Ask: What was the sampling error? Margins of error are critically important for determining whether differences shown in the poll are significant.
- Note what questions were asked and whether they are phrased in an unbiased way.
- State the results in sentence form.

A Balanced Budget

In your opinion, if the federal budget is balanced in five years, will this help you and your family financially, hurt you and your family financially, or not affect you and your family too much?

Help	33%
Hurt	19%
Not much affect	40%
Don't know	8%

This poll was conducted in February 1997. The sample was 1,228 Americans, with a margin of error of plus or minus 4.5 percent. We can therefore assume that the poll is fairly accurate.

It is important that questions be phrased neither to encourage nor discourage a given answer. Note that by giving interviewees options (help, hurt, or not affect your family financially), the pollsters avoid suggesting an answer.

When you state the results of the poll in sentence form, indicate how the poll data reflects Americans' thoughts about the poll topic.

Practicing the Skill

Use what you have learned about analyzing poll data to examine the data about the poll results above and to answer the questions that follow.

1. What is this poll about?
2. What was the size of the polling sample and what was the margin of error?
3. State the results of the poll in sentence form.
4. Compose a nonbiased question to poll Americans on their approval or disapproval of Congress's work.

Application Activity

Select an issue of concern to you and decide what you want to know about it. Develop a nonbiased question to poll opinions on that issue. Randomly select a sample group from the population you have decided to poll. Record your answers. Present your results in a chart. Include your sample size and a brief summary.

The Glencoe Skillbuilder Interactive Workbook, Level 2 provides instruction and practice in key social studies skills.

Assessment and Activities

Self-Check Quiz Visit the *United States Government: Democracy in Action* Web site at gov.glencoe.com and click on ***Chapter 18–Self-Check Quizzes*** to prepare for the chapter test.

Reviewing Key Terms

Match the following terms with each of the descriptions given below:

interest group	**political culture**
peer group	**universe**
lobbyist	**sampling error**
random sampling	**mass media**
public opinion	**representative sample**

1. representative of an interest group
2. everyone in the group sampled has an equal chance of being selected
3. close friends, church, social, or work groups
4. people who share common policy goals and organize to influence government
5. basic values and beliefs about a nation and its government that most citizens share
6. small group of people typical of the universe
7. the ideas and attitudes a significant number of Americans hold about certain issues
8. television, radio, newspapers, movies, books
9. measurement of how much the sample results may differ from the universe being sampled
10. group of people from which samples are taken for polls or statistical measurements

Current Events JOURNAL

Interest Groups Bring several recent issues of national newsmagazines to class. Choose one of the following special interests: business, labor, environment, or education. Find any articles in which an interest group is mentioned. Report the news items to the class.

Recalling Facts

1. Identify three reasons or concerns that cause people to join interest groups.
2. What is the largest and most powerful labor union in the United States?
3. How do interest groups try to influence public opinion to support their policies?
4. What seven forces influence a person's political socialization?
5. What is the relationship between political culture and public opinion?
6. For what reasons may the results of scientific polls not be accurate?

Understanding Concepts

1. **Civic Participation** How can an interest group influence local government? Include examples.
2. **Public Policy** Why would it be undemocratic for the federal government to pass a law forbidding interest groups or lobbyists to contact members of Congress?
3. **Cultural Pluralism** Explain the relationship between voting, public opinion, and public policy.
4. **Cultural Pluralism** How do people's ethnic backgrounds affect opinions on issues?

Critical Thinking

1. **Understanding Cause and Effect** Studies have shown that people in lower socioeconomic levels are less likely to contribute to, lead in, or even join special-interest groups. Why do you think that this is so?

2. **Making Comparisons** Use a graphic organizer like the one below to compare the AFL-CIO with an environmental interest group in the areas of size, composition of membership, and methods used to accomplish their goals.

	AFL-CIO	*Other*
Size		
Members		
Methods		

Cooperative Learning Activity

Taking a Poll Identify an issue that concerns your school and then organize the class into four groups. Have each group formulate questions for an opinion poll on that issue. Have the four groups randomly select respondents from the same universe. Representatives of each group should ask questions of their sample population and record their answers. Compare the results of each poll as a class.

Interpreting Political Cartoons Activity

1. What do the oxen's words suggest about politicians?
2. What is about to happen in the cartoon?
3. What does the choice of a wagon and oxen suggest about the cartoonist's viewpoint?

Skill Practice Activity

Interpreting Opinion Polls Use the Internet or scan a newsmagazine or newspaper to find a report of a recent public opinion poll. Then use what you have learned about analyzing public opinion polls to answer the following questions on a separate sheet of paper.

1. What is the poll about, and when was it taken?
2. What specific questions were asked? Can you think of a way that these questions might be phrased that would be less biased?
3. State the results of the poll in sentence form.

Technology Activity

Using E-mail Research an interest group that you might like to join. Locate an E-mail address for the group and compose a letter requesting information about the group—its purpose, activities, dues, and number of members. Produce a class pamphlet titled "Interest Groups to Join."

Participating in Local Government

Arrange an interview with a public official in your local government. Ask how that official finds out what issues are important to the public, and how he or she measures public opinion on those issues. Present your findings in class.

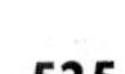

Chapter 19

The Mass Media

Why It's Important

I Heard It on the News We depend on mass media for news, entertainment, and even information about the products we buy. This chapter will explain the power and influence of the mass media as they relate to individuals, to interest groups, and to the government.

To find out more about how the media influence your decision making, view the ***Democracy in Action*** Chapter 19 video lesson:

The Mass Media

GOVERNMENT Online

Chapter Overview Visit the *United States Government: Democracy in Action* Web site at gov.glencoe.com and click on ***Chapter 19–Overview*** to preview chapter information.

Section 1

Structure of the Mass Media

Reader's Guide

Key Terms

mass media, newspaper chain, wire service, ratings

Find Out

- What are the major forms of print and electronic media?
- What is news? What is the major purpose of news reporting?

Understanding Concepts

Free Enterprise Television advertising dollars depend on the size of the viewing audience. How has cable TV with additional networks affected incomes of the ABC, CBS, and NBC networks?

COVER STORY

Politicians Online

WASHINGTON, D.C., AUGUST 30, 1996

The Internet is rapidly becoming a hot media tool for political candidates. Among the first to venture into cyberspace was Republican presidential challenger Bob Dole, who established his Web site earlier this year. In 7 weeks, the site had more than 500,000 visitors. Dole strategists know that young people are the most frequent travelers on the information superhighway. They also realize that President Bill Clinton's biggest victory in 1992 was among young voters. Some political experts compare the Internet to TV before candidates fully realized its value for getting a message out. The "Net" is growing like 1950s television, they observe, only at a faster rate.

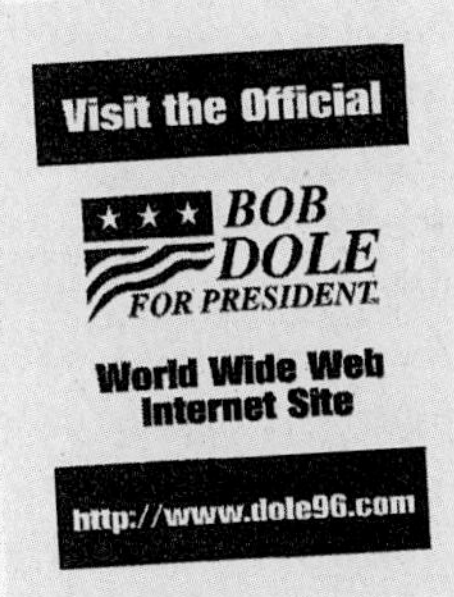

Bob Dole's Web site

Playing a crucial role in government, the mass media include all the means of communication that bring messages to the general public. Because of new technologies, the electronic media—including television, radio, and online services—are growing and changing rapidly. The growth of the electronic media, in turn, affects the print media—newspapers, magazines, newsletters, and books. While these changes provide increasing access to information, they also challenge the social and political institutions that have the responsibility to ensure traditional rights and freedoms.

Supreme Court justice Lewis F. Powell explained the vital contribution of media to a democratic society:

> *An informed public depends upon accurate and effective reporting by the news media. No individual can obtain for himself the information needed for the intelligent discharge of his political responsibilities. For most citizens the prospect of personal familiarity with newsworthy events is hopelessly unrealistic. In seeking out the news the press therefore acts as an agent of the public at large. It is the means by which the people receive that free flow of information and ideas essential to intelligent self-government.*
>
> —Lewis F. Powell, 1974

Print Media

The mass media has been called "the fourth branch" of government. Equating the media with the executive, the legislative, and the judicial branches of the national government indicates the powerful role of mass communications in the United States today. The flow of information has always played a vital part in our democracy. Newspapers have conveyed political information since colonial times.

◀ **President Clinton leaves a press conference.**

Newspapers In the early 1800s few Americans subscribed to a newspaper, but newspapers were shared and read in public. Taverns were a customary meeting place to hear the news. Having read their personal paper, subscribers usually mailed it to someone else. Much of the mail in the 1830s was newspapers.

These early newspapers provided a sense of a national community. Circulation boomed in the late 1800s as papers sold for a penny or two—affordable to those who earned only a dollar per day. Publishers expanded circulation, believing that democracy needed informed citizens. By 1900, an average of one newspaper was published for each United States household. This ratio continued until the 1960s, when daily newspaper circulation failed to keep pace with population growth for the first time. What caused the decline of the daily paper?

Many people believe that the daily newspaper's decline was primarily caused by television. Blaming television for declining newspaper subscriptions overlooks other important factors. Following the lead of magazines, many dailies actually discouraged subscriptions among readers who they believed were not good targets for upscale advertisers. Rather than reinvesting profits in news gathering and in promoting readership, many local papers simply became vehicles for slick advertising. Their resulting step away from complete news coverage opened the door for national newspapers such as *USA Today.*

In the late 1800s Americans bought newspapers on street corners for the reduced rate of one cent a day.

Concentration of Newspaper Ownership

Many American cities used to have two or more daily newspapers. As a result of mergers, however, daily local newspapers today have no competitors in 98 percent of American cities. In addition, national chains have bought many independent newspapers. The Gannett **newspaper chain,** for example, owns more than 100 daily and weekly newspapers across the country, including *USA Today.* Another chain, Park Communications, also owns more than 100 newspapers. Newspaper chains now account for 77 percent of daily newspaper circulation, a large increase since 1960. The increasing trend toward mergers raises questions. Does concentration of ownership limit the variety of views and opinions that reach the reader? Is discussion narrowed by the lack of competitors in many cities?

Magazines and Books

More than 10,000 magazines are published every year in the United States. The major weekly national newsmagazines—*Time, Newsweek,* and *U.S. News & World Report*—have become important vehicles for setting the agenda for discussion of national issues. Other magazines such as *Business Week* focus on economic news. Some journals publish essays and stories representing political opinions on current issues. These include the *National Review,* which favors conservative points of view, and *The New Republic,* which presents liberal ideas. Many highly specialized magazines such as *Oil and Gas Weekly* and *Aviation Week & Space Technology* carry news about political issues and government actions of interest to their readers.

Approximately 40,000 book titles are published every year in the United States. Many have political themes, ranging from memoirs by former presidents to issues such as foreign policy.

Wire Services A **wire service** is an organization that employs reporters throughout the world to collect news stories for subscribers. The two major wire services are the Associated Press (AP) and United Press International (UPI). Wire services send the news electronically to subscriber newspapers and to radio and television stations.

These organizations are not considered mass media in themselves because they do not communicate directly with the public. They are, however, a vital source of news stories.

Electronic Media

Radio, television, and the Internet make up the electronic media. As several political scientists have noted, the continued development and use of electronic media affect political life in the United States:

> *In today's technological world, the media . . . are everywhere. The American political system has entered a new period of high-tech politics, a politics in which the behavior of citizens and policymakers, as well as the political agenda itself, is increasingly shaped by technology.*
>
> —George C. Edwards III, Martin P. Wattenberg, Robert L. Lineberry

Radio Radio brought Americans closer to their government—the voices of politicians came into homes from Maine to California. Radio had served only one generation by the 1950s, when television brought the whole family into one room to watch an event. The growth of television, however, did not displace radio, as some had predicted it would. Nearly all Americans (99.9 percent) have radios in their cars or homes, totaling more than 500 million radios. Thousands of AM and FM radio stations specialize in different formats.

Radio continues to communicate political messages through political programming and advertisers who buy time on specific stations to reach the voting audience they most want to reach. "Talk radio" emerged in the 1980s as a forum for opinion and even candidates. During the 1992 presidential campaign, Bill Clinton took part in a series of talk radio interviews that allowed him to discuss many of the frustrations that the radio audience was experiencing. Michael Harrison, an industry insider, said of Clinton, "He played talk radio like a piano."

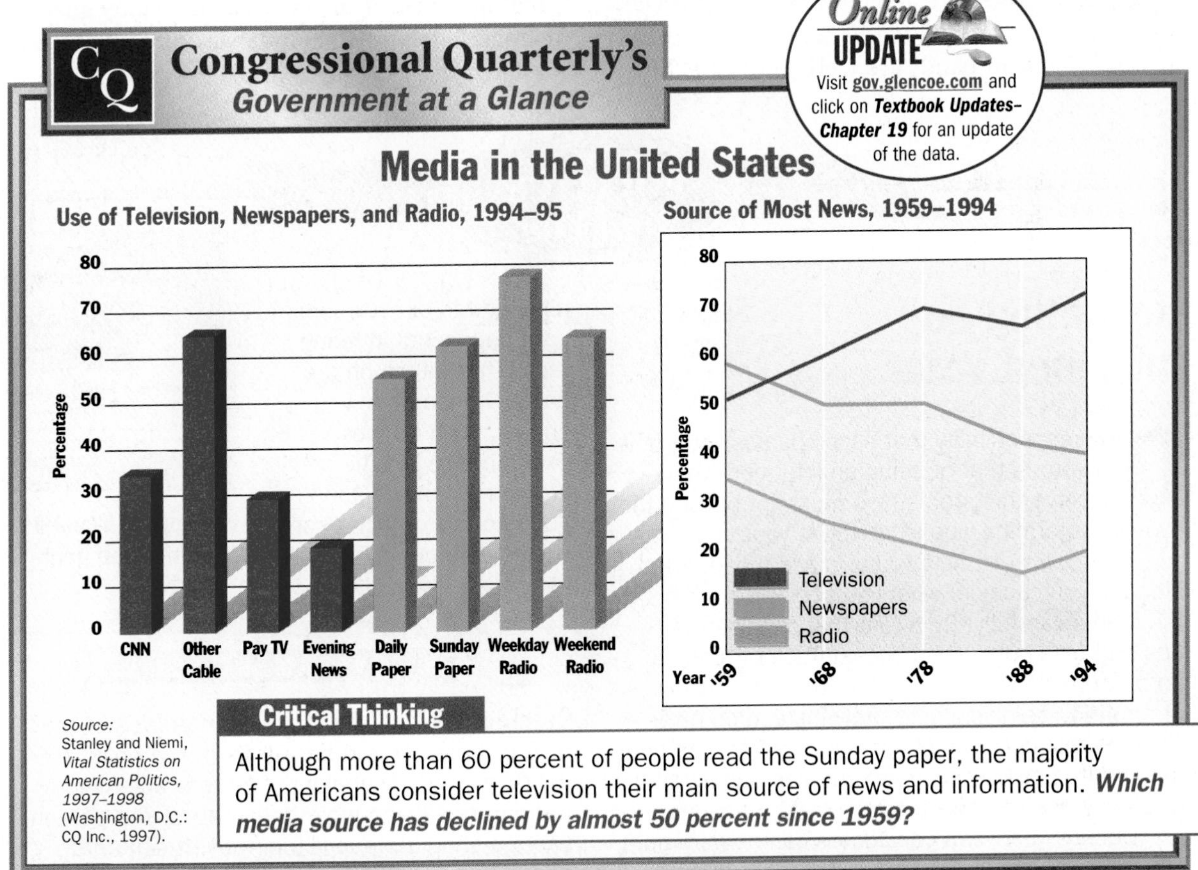

Television In one generation television replaced the newspaper as Americans' main source of news. By the 1960s television had become a powerful force in American politics. Three major networks—ABC, NBC, and CBS—divided most of the television audience. The first televised presidential debates took place between Democrat John F. Kennedy and Republican Richard Nixon in 1960. Later in the decade, television brought the Vietnam War directly into American living rooms every evening during the nightly news, considerably affecting public opinion about the war. No political leader could ignore the impact of television on public opinion.

By 1951 TV stations broadcast entertainment, news, special events, and sports contests throughout the nation.

Broadcast Licensing The **Federal Communications Commission (FCC)** regulates and licenses private owners of broadcast stations in two categories: commercial and noncommercial. Radio licenses are divided between AM and FM bands. Television bands are UHF and VHF. Most commercial TV stations are network-affiliated, but more than 400 operate as independents.

FCC rules aim to prevent a few sources from controlling the flow of information. Networks are limited in the number of AM and FM radio stations and TV stations they may own.

Cable Television With the growth of cable television, the major television networks began to lose their dominant position in providing news and entertainment in the late 1980s. Cable reached only 18 percent of all households in 1980. By 1995 the cable companies served more than 60 percent of American homes. New networks, videocassette recorders (VCRs), and cable options reduced the share of the big three networks' audience to only 50 or 60 percent. Cable News Network (CNN) began to challenge the national networks in news coverage. Many government agencies, foreign embassies, and lobbyists in Washington, D.C., stayed tuned to CNN to keep up

★ ★ ★ POLITICS *and You*

Becoming an Informed Voter

One responsibility that accompanies your right to vote is that of being an informed voter. To achieve this status, you must get beyond the hype to determine who is worthy of your support.

The media can help you to make these decisions, if you consider what you see and hear in the media carefully. Be aware that candidates' ads and paid political broadcasts do not present an objective look at the issues. They are merely attempts to gain your vote. Rely instead on news stories and interviews of candidates. Also, the print media often provide more information about candidates and issues than the broadcast media do.

Debates between candidates can be informative. In addition, "meet-the-candidates" nights allow you to directly compare opponents in many races that will be on the ballot. Nonpartisan voters' guides, such as those published by the League of Women Voters, are another good source of factual and objective information.

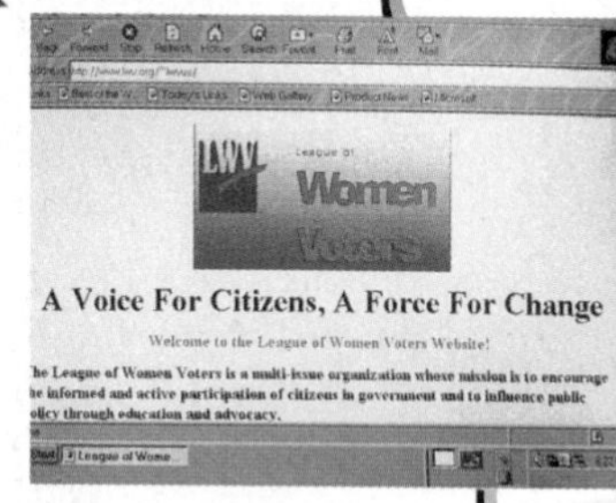

League of Women Voters' Web page

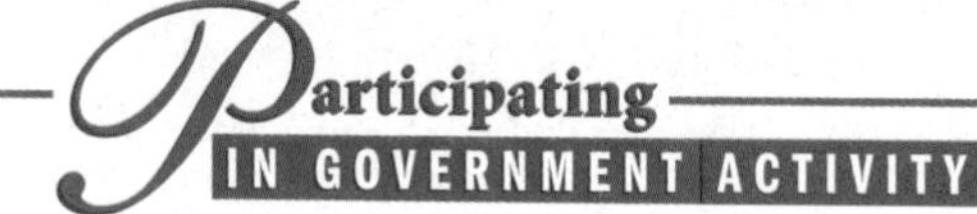

Create a Political Ad Working in groups of four or five, research the background of a political candidate or officeholder. Create a one-minute radio or television advertisement for the person. Groups should present their advertisements. As a class, analyze whether each ad is objective.

Bringing the News to You

Directing Politics
The CNN newsroom is the heart of the organization's news-gathering operation. The network uses modern technology to transmit information around the world almost instantaneously. ***Do networks like CNN maintain too much influence over politicians and public policy? Why or why not?***

with late-breaking news. CNBC, C-SPAN, and an increasing array of choices further splintered the news audience.

Public Broadcasting Not all radio and television stations in the United States are commercial—operated for profit. The Public Broadcasting Act of 1967 created the **Corporation for Public Broadcasting** (CPB) to distribute federal money for noncommercial, or nonprofit, radio and television. CPB set up the Public Broadcasting System (PBS) in 1968. PBS schedules, promotes, and distributes programs to television stations that are part of the system. In 1970 CPB set up National Public Radio (NPR), the radio counterpart of PBS.

NPR and PBS programs provide alternatives to the commercial networks' programs. Public broadcasts focus on cultural offerings such as classical music, opera, ballet, educational programs, academic lectures, documentaries, and nature shows. These programs generally attract small but loyal audiences.

Public radio and television stations depend on three sources of money: funds from the national government that CPB distributes; grants from private foundations such as the Ford Foundation or the Rockefeller Foundation; and donations from individuals and businesses. The Corporation for Public Broadcasting does not tell stations what programs to broadcast. CPB does influence programming, however, by paying for some programs and not others.

Government Broadcasting The national government owns and directly operates a few radio and television stations for two purposes. First, the government creates and sends radio and television programs to American personnel stationed at military posts throughout the world through the Armed Forces Radio and Television Network. Second, the government sends out general news and information through shortwave, medium wave, and FM broadcasts throughout the world. Over the years the former Soviet Union, Cuba, and other Communist nations often jammed the signals to prevent these broadcasts from reaching their citizens.

The International Broadcasting Act of 1994 reorganized all U.S. nonmilitary broadcasts, placing the network under the United States Information Agency. The four branches—Voice of America, Radio Martí, Radio Free Europe, and Radio Liberty—are all now operated by the agency's board of governors.

Online Services In 1995 Nielsen Research reported that only about 11 percent of Americans used the Internet. Rapid growth in Internet use, however, is affecting politics. By 1996 the major parties, leading presidential contenders, and some minor party candidates had established home pages on the World Wide Web. Web sites allowed candidates direct access to the voters and even interaction with them via E-mail. Today many people use the Internet for information and to access government at all levels—local, state, and national.

Media Ownership Who owns the mass media in the United States? Since owners can influence the messages the media present, the question of ownership is important especially for television, radio, and newspapers.

In many democratic countries such as Britain, France, Israel, and Sweden, newspapers are privately owned; the government, however, controls the broadcast media. With the exception of Britain, broadcast programming tends to support the policies of the political parties in power.

In the United States, the print and nearly all the broadcast media are privately owned, profit-seeking businesses. Until recently, many different owners have controlled the nation's newspapers and radio and TV stations. Currently, however, media ownership is much more concentrated.

Because media has an obligation to serve the public interest, national, state, and local governments set the rules. Broadcasters, cable owners, and telephone companies all operate under government regulation. Governments grant private companies monopolies to serve people within defined areas. Until the 1996 Telecommunications Act, competition among these services was very limited. One aim of this act was to broaden competition in order to lower costs to consumers.

What Makes News

In a democracy the media also have a duty to present news that will inform citizens and promote the public interest. What is news? Generally news events must be current or recently discovered, quickly communicated, and relevant to the audience. The news should enable citizens to understand the key decisions being made by government, business, interest groups, and individuals that will affect their lives.

News or Entertainment? News has entertainment value, and news reporting has commercial value. Because of their need to make a profit, the mass media need to deliver a large audience to the advertisers. The larger the audience, the more the media can charge for each commercial advertising spot. Ratings services provide the statistics that show audience size. These **ratings** help determine who gets the advertisers' dollars. News stories that include personal drama, conflict, and violence attract more viewers. Complex issues that have greater meaning may be overlooked when the media place main emphasis on winning the ratings wars.

When the media are deciding exactly what to report, the need to entertain and the duty to inform often conflict. Responsible editors and journalists are aware of

A Mass Medium

Talking to the World America Online (AOL) technology experts monitor millions of online connections 24 hours a day in this modem control room. On a typical day AOL subscribers log on millions of times. ***Does the Internet interfere with the duty of the media to responsibly inform the public? Explain.***

this dilemma and usually try to meet both needs. Some argue that by presenting entertaining news they reach large numbers of citizens who might not otherwise pay attention to current events.

International News Americans learn about events in the world primarily from the mass media. Mass media research shows that when given a choice, however, Americans do not seek out world news. For example, when NBC broadcast a prime-time, one-hour interview with then-Soviet leader Mikhail Gorbachev, only 15 percent of the national television audience watched. Public opinion polls show that two-thirds of Americans are usually not aware of foreign news events.

Because Americans are not as interested in foreign news as they are in domestic events, foreign news usually gets brief space and time compared with major domestic news stories. Foreign affairs often must involve violence and disaster or include celebrities in order to compete with national news. During a war or other international crisis involving American lives, however, foreign news may replace almost all other news.

Most of the foreign news in American newspapers comes from one of four news-gathering organizations: Associated Press (AP), United Press International (UPI), Reuters of Britain, and Agence France-Presse of France. The American mass media employ about 670 full-time overseas correspondents, two-thirds of whom are Americans. About 75 percent of these correspondents are stationed in Western Europe or Asia.

A Technological Revolution

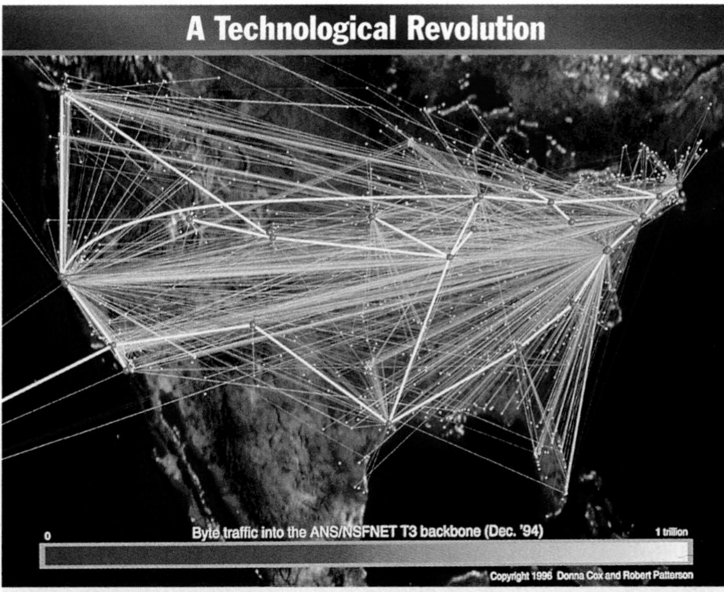

Modern Developments This enhanced satellite photograph displays the vast telecommunications network in the United States. ***How has the modern revolution in communications technology impacted the political process in the United States?***

Section 1 Assessment

Checking for Understanding

1. **Main Idea** Use a graphic organizer like the one below to classify six major forms of media.

print	electronic
1.	4.
2.	5.
3.	6.

2. **Define** mass media, newspaper chain, wire service, ratings.
3. **Identify** Federal Communications Commission, Corporation for Public Broadcasting.
4. For what reasons does the federal government own and operate television and radio stations?

Critical Thinking

5. **Formulating Questions** Write three questions that should be asked in order to determine whether the media are serving our democracy well.

Concepts IN ACTION

Free Enterprise Find out the most recent ratings for the top three television networks. Read media analysts' explanations of how and why each network received the rating it did. Explain the analyses in a report to your class that includes graphs and charts.

Section 2

How Media Impact Government

Reader's Guide

Key Terms

news release, news briefing, leak, media event, front-runner, spot advertising

Find Out

- Why do the media and government need each other?
- How has television influenced the campaigns for major political offices?

Understanding Concepts

Political Processes How do the media help set the public agenda?

COVER STORY

Talk Show Power

BOSTON, MASSACHUSETTS, FEBRUARY 8, 1993

A man on a CNN talk show states that cellular phones cause cancer. The government announces a study of the issue, while the stock of cellphone maker Motorola drops 20 percent. At the urging of a local radio host, 2,000 Bostonians gather to protest taxes. These events illustrate the growing popularity—and power—of TV and radio talk shows. As audiences call in their opinions, government officials are listening. They know that audiences tend to be voters. For example, an amazing 98 percent of C-SPAN viewers voted in 1992. "It's a political early-warning sign," says pollster Harrison Hickman of the shows, "like radar in Greenland."

C-SPAN logo

The mass media and United States government officials often have an uneasy relationship. They need to work together, but their jobs often place them in adversarial positions. Politicians want to use the mass media to help them reach their goals, such as convincing the public that their policies are worthwhile and getting reelected. Politicians also want the media to pass on their messages just as the politicians present them.

The President and the Media

The president and the mass media, especially television, have a mutually beneficial relationship. As one of the most powerful government officials in the world, the president is a great source of news. Almost 80 percent of all United States television coverage of government officials focuses on the president. The mass media, in turn, offer presidents the best way to "sell" their ideas and policies to the public.

Franklin D. Roosevelt was the first president to master the broadcast media. Broadcast television did not exist at the time, and most newspaper owners did not support FDR. Therefore, he presented his ideas directly to the people with "fireside chats" over the radio. FDR had an excellent speaking voice. Journalist David Halberstam later describes the impact of an FDR fireside chat:

> "*He was the first great American radio voice. For most Americans of this generation, their first memory of politics would be of sitting by a radio and hearing that voice, strong, confident, totally at ease. . . . Most Americans in the previous 160 years had never even seen a President; now almost all of them were hearing him, in their own homes. It was literally and figuratively electrifying.*"
>
> —David Halberstam, 1980

The era of television politics really began with the 1960s presidential debates. All presidents since that time have paid great attention to their television image and their use of that medium. In 1970 Senator J. William Fulbright of Arkansas told Congress:

> *Television has done as much to expand the powers of the President as would a constitutional amendment formally abolishing the co-equality of the three branches of government.*
>
> —J. William Fulbright, 1970

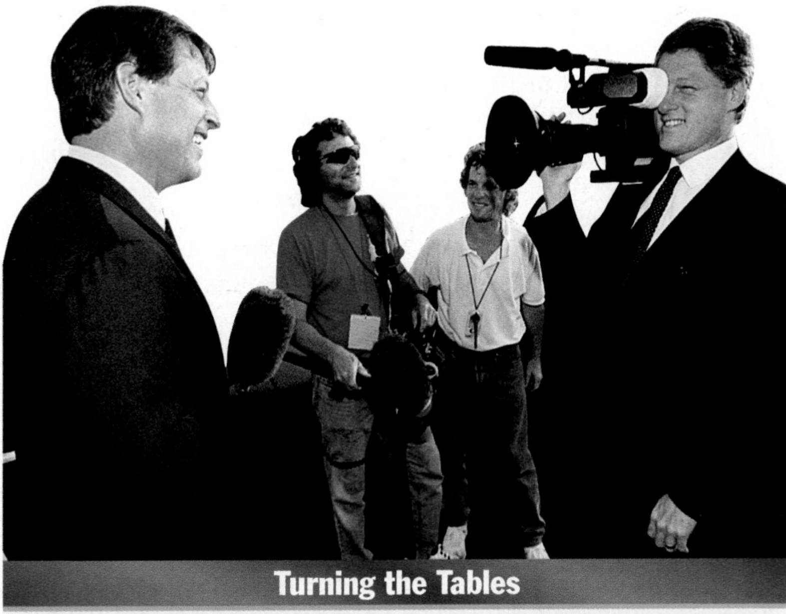

Turning the Tables

Political Processes Bill Clinton and Al Gore have fun with the media as the real television crew looks on. ***How valuable is a presidential media event?***

The White House staff media advisers try to manage relations with the mass media by controlling the daily flow of information about the president. To do so, they use news releases and briefings, press conferences, background stories, leaks, and media events.

News Releases and Briefings

A government news release is a ready-made story officials prepare for members of the press. It can be printed or broadcast word for word. A news release usually has a dateline that states the earliest time it can be published.

During a news briefing a government official makes an announcement or explains a policy, decision, or action. Briefings give reporters the chance to ask officials about news releases. The president's press secretary meets daily with the press to answer questions and provide information on the president's activities.

Press Conferences

A **press conference** involves the news media's questioning of a high-level government official. Presidents have held press conferences since the days of Theodore Roosevelt.

Over the years most presidential press conferences have been carefully planned events. In preparation for a press conference, the president often studies briefing books that identify potential questions. The White House may limit questions to certain topics. Aides may have friendly reporters ask certain questions they want the president to answer.

Other Means of Sharing Information

Sometimes the president or another top official, such as the secretary of state, will give reporters important information called **backgrounders.** Reporters can use the information in a story, but they cannot reveal their source. Reporters will make this kind of information public by saying, "Government sources said. . . ." or "A senior White House official said. . . ."

Backgrounders give government officials the opportunity to test new ideas or send unofficial messages to other policy makers, or even foreign governments. The media can, in this manner, make information public without making it official.

When officials give the media information totally off the record, reporters cannot print or broadcast the information. Off-the-record meetings can be useful both to government officials and the media. Officials often establish valuable connections with newspapers. Journalists may

"What Hath God Wrought?" **Modern presidents might be asking themselves the same thing. That four-word question, telegraphed from Washington to Baltimore on May 24, 1844, by Morse code inventor Samuel F. B. Morse, revolutionized news reporting and marked the beginning of the end of presidential privacy. Morse's message began the era of instantaneous delivery of words by wire, which soon stretched across oceans and linked the world as never before. Almost at once, the cables were crackling with a steady flow of stories about public figures, leading to today's age of mass communications.**

receive some tips to assist them with their news coverage.

Another way top officials try to influence the flow of information to the press is through a **leak**, or the release of secret information by anonymous government officials to the media. These officials may be seeking public support for a policy that others in the government do not like. Sometimes low-level officials may leak information to expose corruption or to get top officials to pay attention to a problem.

Media Events Modern presidents often stage a **media event**, a visually interesting event designed to reinforce a politician's position on some issue. A president who takes a strong stand against pollution, for example, makes a stronger statement when he stands in front of a state-of-the-art, administration-supported manufacturing plant than in the Oval Office.

Media events show how much politicians and the press rely on each other. The politicians want media exposure; the press wants a story. George Reedy, press secretary to Lyndon Johnson, observed:

> *"I'd like just once to have the courage to go on the air and say that such and such a candidate went to six cities today to stage six media events, none of which had anything to do with governing America."*
>
> —George Reedy, 1985

Media and Presidential Campaigns

Television impacts presidential campaigns. The first televised political advertisements appeared in the 1952 presidential campaign between Dwight Eisenhower and Adlai Stevenson. Since then, television has greatly influenced who runs for office, how candidates are nominated, how election campaigns are conducted, and how political parties fit into the election process.

Identifying Candidates Television has influenced the types of candidates who run for office in several ways. First, candidates for major offices must be telegenic—they must project a pleasing appearance and performance on camera. John F. Kennedy and Ronald Reagan were good examples of candidates for the television age. They were handsome, had good speaking voices, and projected the cool, low-key style that goes over well on television.

Second, television has made it much easier for people who are political unknowns to quickly become serious candidates for major offices. Bill Clinton was not well known when he addressed a national television audience at the Democratic convention in 1988. Four years later, as governor of Arkansas, he ran successfully for the Democratic nomination. In 1992 his campaign organization made skillful use of television. By the time the nominating convention met, Clinton had won enough primary elections to capture his party's nomination.

Third, television has encouraged celebrities from other fields to enter politics. In recent years actors, astronauts, professional athletes, and television commentators all have run successfully for Congress. Such people have instant name recognition with voters. They do not have to work their way up through their political party's local and state organizations.

The Presidential Nominating Process

The mass media have fundamentally changed nominations for president through **horse-race coverage** of elections, especially primaries. This approach focuses on "winners" and "losers," and "who's ahead," nearly as much as on issues or policy positions. One study of the ABC, CBS, and NBC evening newscasts during the 1996 primary campaign found that 45 percent of the stories were horse-race coverage, while 39 percent focused on policy issues and 16 percent focused on campaign issues.

Early presidential primaries are critically important to a candidate's chances even though the voters in these primaries represent only a small fraction of the national electorate. The media declare a candidate who wins an early primary, even if by a very small margin, a **front-runner,** or early leader. The press largely determines the weight attached to being a front-runner. The label carries great significance, however. It is generally only the front-runners who are able to attract the millions of dollars in loans and campaign contributions, as well as the volunteer help needed to succeed in the long, grueling nominating process.

The last time a party gathered for its nominating convention without knowing its nominee for certain was in 1976, when incumbent president Gerald Ford narrowly won a first-ballot nomination over Ronald Reagan. The 2000 candidates were identified by April. George W. Bush's victories in early primaries assured him enough delegates to win the Republican nomination. Al Gore, the vice president, had no serious challenger after Bill Bradley withdrew in March.

With the nominees in place, convention planners have time to produce a huge made-for-television production. In 2000, Democrats and Republicans ran carefully scripted convention programs with celebrities, music, and video presentations. Because the drama of choosing a nominee was missing, however, television audience ratings fell. The networks decided to carry less convention coverage, because the convention was "not news."

Campaign Advertising Television has also affected how candidates communicate with the voters. The first candidates in American history did little campaigning; they left such work to political supporters. Andrew Jackson's election started the "torchlight era," in which candidates gave stump speeches, parades, and expensive entertainment for voters and supporters. Around

Convention Coverage

Civic Responsibility The major political parties carefully craft exciting convention programs to attract the media and the American public's attention. Here reporter Sam Donaldson conducts an interview as the media gather at the Democratic National Convention in 2000. ***Why does each citizen have a responsibility to look beyond the images of candidates presented by the media?***

We the People

Making a Difference

Lloyd Newman and LeAlan Jones

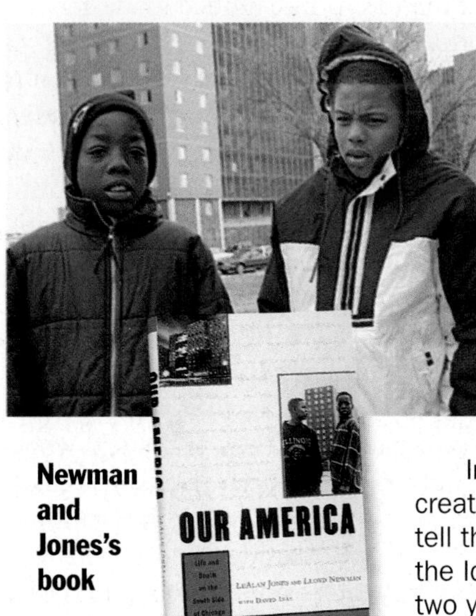

Newman and Jones's book

When LeAlan Jones and Lloyd Newman were both 13 years old, a producer approached them from National Public Radio (NPR) and asked them to document what it was like to live among the poverty and violence of Chicago's South Side. Armed with tape recorders, the two friends interviewed people who lived in and around the Ida B. Wells housing project, and also recorded their own experiences. The result was a 30-minute radio documentary titled "Ghetto Life 101." The documentary won many national and international awards.

In 1994 Lloyd and LeAlan created another documentary to tell the tragic story of a murder in the Ida B. Wells housing project: two young boys threw Eric Morse, a 5-year-old boy, out of a 14-story window when he refused to steal candy for them. LeAlan said their goal was "to expose how violence has spread to younger age groups and to find ways to prevent this kind of crime from recurring." In the documentary, titled "Remorse: The 14 Stories of Eric Morse," the two teens interviewed friends and neighbors who knew the victim and the suspects. They also recorded an interview with Eric Morse's mother, who refused to talk to anyone in the media except them. Their second documentary won another series of awards, including the prestigious Robert F. Kennedy Journalism Award and the Peabody Award.

The two teens have given a voice to the people of Chicago's projects. In 1997 they published their first book, *Our America: Life and Death on the South Side of Chicago.*

1900, candidates began using advertisements in newspapers and magazines and mass mailings of campaign literature. In 1924 candidates began radio campaigning. Television campaigning began with Eisenhower in 1952.

Television campaigns use **spot advertising,** the same basic technique that television uses to sell other products. Spot advertisements are brief (30 seconds to 2 minutes), frequent, positive descriptions of the candidate or the candidate's major themes. Advertisements may also present negative images of the opposing candidate.

Financing TV Advertising Candidates today must spend huge sums of money for sophisticated television advertising campaigns. One 30-second commercial in a medium-size market can cost several thousand dollars. It has been estimated that a senator must raise more than $7,500 per week for 6 years to pay for a reelection campaign. Most of the money goes to television ads. Reed Hundt, Chairman of the Federal Communications Commission, summed up the problem:

> "*The cost of TV time-buys makes fund-raising an enormous entry barrier for candidates for public office, an oppressive burden for incumbents who seek reelection, a continuous threat to the integrity of our political institutions, and a principal cause of the erosion of public respect for public service.*"
>
> —Reed Hundt, 1995

Political Parties Television has weakened the role of political parties as the key link between politicians and the voters in national politics. It has also made candidates less dependent on their political party organization. Today it is television, rather than the political parties, that provides most of the political news for people interested in politics. Voters can get the information they need to decide how to vote without depending on the party organization. Television also lets candidates appeal directly to the people, bypassing party bosses. Should a candidate do well in the primary elections, the political party has little choice but to nominate him or her even if party leaders do not agree. Finally, television advertising requires so much money that candidates cannot depend solely on their party to provide needed campaign funds. They must approach other donors if they are to run a competitive campaign and win election.

The need for large donations compromises candidates and parties. In 1996 candidates for the Senate, the House, and the presidency accepted large sums from donors that had interests in government policy. While only a small percentage of the donations was illegal, many people questioned a campaign finance system that seemed to encourage conflicts of interest.

Congress and the Media

Thousands of reporters have press credentials to cover the House and Senate. Several hundred spend all their time on Congress. Most congressional coverage focuses on individual lawmakers and is published mainly in their home states. The news stories usually feature the local angle of national news stories.

Nearly every member of Congress has a press secretary to prepare press releases, arrange interviews, and give out television tapes. Congress, however, gets less media coverage than the president because of the nature of its work. Most important congressional work takes place in committees and subcommittees over long periods of time. Congress's slow, complicated work rarely meets television requirements for dramatic, entertaining news.

Additionally, no single congressional leader can speak for all 535 members of Congress. Nationally known lawmakers often are seen as spokespersons for their own political parties rather than for Congress. When the legislature is in the news, the mass media tend to report on the most controversial aspects of Congress: confirmation hearings, oversight activities, and the personal business of members.

Confirmation Hearings The Constitution requires Congress to confirm presidential appointments to high government posts. The Senate usually holds hearings to review such nominations. The most controversial hearings attract wide media coverage.

Sometimes the media will uncover damaging information about an appointee. In 1989, for example, President George Bush nominated former senator John Tower to be his secretary of defense. Media investigations contributed to harsh criticism of Tower's alleged alcoholism and marital problems. Despite having a solid legislative record, Tower became the first cabinet nominee the Senate had rejected in 30 years.

In 1993 President Clinton nominated Lani Guinier to head the Civil Rights Division of the Justice Department. When newspaper columnists criticized Guinier's writings on racial preferences as too radical, Senate support for her nomination eroded. The White House tried to shore up support among members of the Judiciary Committee, but when none of these members offered verbal support, Clinton withdrew the nomination.

Oversight Activities In its role of legislative oversight, Congress has the power to review how the executive branch enforces laws and carries out programs. Oversight is handled through routine hearings, but sometimes lawmakers uncover a major scandal. Such investigations have become some of the biggest stories in American politics.

In 1987, for example, Congress created a committee to investigate the secret sale of arms to Iran by Reagan White House aides and the use of money from the arms sale to support a group in Nicaragua called the contras. Millions of viewers watched the nationally televised hearings.

Personal Business The media also look for scandal in the personal lives of members of Congress. Until recently the media usually overlooked

Student Web Activity Visit the *United States Government: Democracy in Action* Web site at gov.glencoe.com and click on ***Chapter 19–Student Web Activities*** for an activity about how media impact government.

Congressional Coverage

Political Processes C-SPAN presents live and taped coverage of a broad range of events, including major floor debates and committee hearings in Congress, presidential and other news conferences, and speeches by political figures. ***How do you think C-SPAN coverage has impacted Congress?***

personal problems of lawmakers. Now, however, even powerful lawmakers may not escape media attention. For example, under media scrutiny, Speaker of the House Newt Gingrich returned to the publisher a large cash advance on a book he was writing.

C-SPAN Television By the late 1970s, congressional leaders realized that they were losing to presidents in the never-ending struggle for more media coverage. In 1979 the House allowed closed-circuit television coverage of floor debates. In 1986 the Senate allowed television coverage of Senate debates. The floor proceedings of the House and Senate are now regularly broadcast to lawmakers' offices and to cable television subscribers across the nation via C-SPAN (Cable-Satellite Public Affairs Network).

Congressional Recording Studios Both the House and Senate have extensive recording studios, where lawmakers prepare radio or television messages for the voters in their home districts. Tapes are mailed to hometown stations for use in local news or public affairs programs.

The Court and the Media

Most Americans depend upon the mass media to learn about Supreme Court decisions. Yet the Supreme Court and lower federal courts receive much less media coverage than Congress or the president. During a recent Supreme Court term, for example, *The New York Times* reported on only three-fourths of the Court's decisions. Other newspapers covered less than half of the Court's cases.

Major newspapers and television and radio networks do assign reporters to cover the Supreme Court. However, the judicial branch gets less coverage because of the remoteness of judges and the technical nature of the issues with which the Court deals. Broadcast media are less likely to report court decisions than newspapers, because broadcast news does not allow time to explain issues in depth and television news must be highly visual.

Remoteness of Judges As appointed officials, Supreme Court justices and other federal judges almost never seek publicity and rarely appear on radio or television. Judges must remain unbiased and fear publicity may interfere with their ability to decide cases fairly.

Technical Issues The Court handles complex issues, many of which interest only a small number of people. In addition, the Supreme Court maintains the tradition that the Court's opinions must speak for themselves. Thus, justices do not hold news conferences to explain major decisions or to answer questions.

In reality, how much does the media really influence Americans? This question is not easy to answer. So many different factors influence people's knowledge, attitudes, and behavior toward politics.

Experts agree, however, that the mass media have a huge impact on defining the public agenda and on voting and elections.

Setting the Public Agenda

The public agenda is a list of societal problems that both political leaders and citizens agree need government attention. Aid to the homeless, long-term health care for the elderly, teenage substance abuse, and high crime rates are all problems that are part of the public agenda.

The mass media play an important role in setting the public agenda. They highlight some issues and ignore others. They define some conditions as problems and let other conditions go unnoticed. They help determine which political issues people and their leaders will be discussing.

Awareness of Issues The media's greatest power is to define reality for the American people. The media cover some issues more thoroughly than others. Coverage largely determines which issues people think to be important. A foreign policy expert explains:

> "*The mass media may not be successful in telling their audience what to think, but the media are stunningly successful in telling their audience what to think about.*"
>
> —Bernard Cohen, 1963

Thus, issues or problems that get the greatest attention in the media are the ones people think are most important. A study of media coverage of the Vietnam War, for example, found that the content of news stories about war-related events had less impact on people than the total amount of attention given to the war.

Attitudes and Values The media also have an impact on public opinion toward government and issues of the day by influencing people's attitudes and values. The media play an important role in political socialization, the learning process through which children and adults form their basic attitudes and values toward politics. The media, especially television, convey messages about war and peace, crime, environmental problems, voting, elections, foreign countries, and many other topics.

The media also affect people's general orientation toward politics. Media stories may give people a sense of a world out of control. They may reassure people that all is going well. The media's focus on bad news—scandals, violence, or power struggles between Congress and the president—has led to what some experts call television malaise. This uneasiness is a general feeling of distrust and cynicism. For example, studies have shown that people who rely on television as their main source of news generally have more negative feelings toward government and the political system.

Section 2 Assessment

Checking for Understanding

1. **Main Idea** Use a graphic organizer like the one below to show how television coverage of elections has affected parties and their candidates.

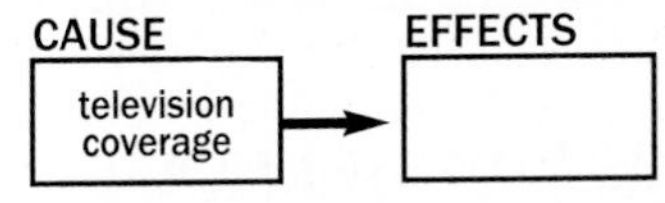

2. **Define** news release, news briefing, leak, media event, front-runner, spot advertising.
3. **Identify** backgrounders, horse-race coverage.
4. Explain government and media's "mutually beneficial relationship."
5. How do the mass media help set the public agenda in the United States?

Critical Thinking

6. **Demonstrating Reasoned Judgment** Examine the following statement: "The media's greatest power is in the way they define reality for the American people." Do you agree or disagree with this statement? Explain.

Political Processes Create a political cartoon that describes the role of the mass media in forming your basic ideas about government, politicians, and national and international events. Consider both broadcast and print media.

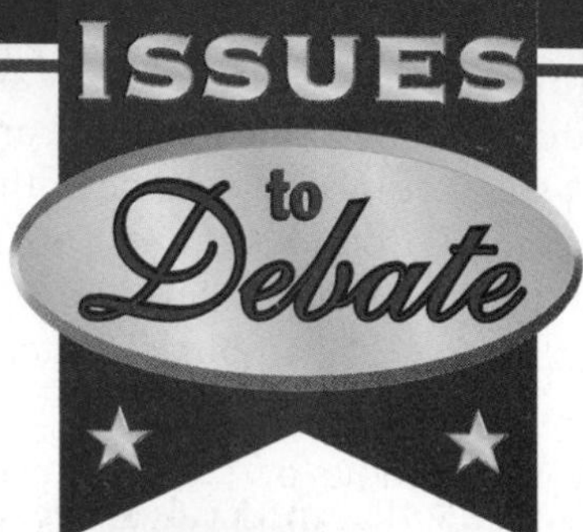

Should News Also Be Part Entertainment?

Today it is sometimes difficult to tell the difference between news and entertainment. Some journalists are even paying for dramatic stories. "Checkbook journalism" is what some journalists are calling stories like that of convicted sex offender Mary Letourneau, who is serving an eight-year prison sentence. In April 2000 a Washington court ruled that Letourneau can keep earnings from television movies or other media that tell her story.

The Role of the Press

Historically, the role of the press has been to inform the public to help them govern themselves intelligently. Framers of our government believed a responsible press and an informed public were necessary to protect democracy. In general, "checkbook journalism" and news as entertainment have been frowned upon by the mainstream press.

Today, even the local nightly television news may be driven by the ratings game to cover stories that entertain more than they inform. News organizations may not be as blatant as "checkbook journalists," but they may pay travel expenses, "consulting" fees, or promote a person's book or movie in exchange for a story.

The increase in media outlets, such as cable television and online computer services, creates greater competition for a share of the audience. Those outlets with the highest ratings earn the most money because advertisers pay more to reach a larger share of the audience.

Entertainment Versus Information

Drama, violence, and celebrity coverage attract a larger audience than discussions of city government problems or foreign policy debates. However, some people think that the scramble for ratings compromises the role of the press, and that fairness and accuracy are sacrificed in the process.

Some members of the media point out that they are only giving the people what they demand. The media argue that people are free to choose the kind of news they want. Critics of this attitude respond that the press sets the public agenda. These critics believe the news publishers and broadcasters decide what is important for the public to think about. Because of this, critics believe the publishers and broadcasters should act responsibly.

Debating the Issue

Should the News Media's Role Include Entertainment?

Assume that you are a news producer at a local television station. How would you instruct your news team on this issue? Would you be concerned about ratings and advertising dollars that support your station?

Key Issues

✔ How can paying for a story affect news quality?

✔ In today's society, does the press still have a responsibility to keep the public informed?

Debate Choose volunteers to represent station owners and serious journalists in debating the issue.

Vote After the debate, all class members should vote on the issue and discuss the results.

Regulation of the Media

Reader's Guide

Key Terms

prior restraint, libel, shield law, equal time doctrine, fairness doctrine

Find Out

- Why does the federal government have more power to regulate the broadcast media than the print media?
- What five issues did the Telecommunications Act of 1996 address?

Understanding Concepts

Civil Liberties Should all the liberties that are extended to the print media be also extended to the broadcast media? Explain your answer.

COVER STORY

Radio Pirates Shut Down

BERKELEY, CALIFORNIA, APRIL 12, 1996

The Federal Communications Commission hauled Stephen Dunifer into court today for operating Free Radio Berkeley, an unlicensed station. Like many "guerrilla" broadcasters, Dunifer began by transmitting music and radical messages from various secret locations. "Pirate radio" has grown steadily since 1988, when the FCC shut down a station transmitting from a boat off Long Island. FCC officials charge that pirate broadcasts interfere with the signals of licensed stations. Many pirates claim their politics is the real reason for their troubles.

Headquarters of Free Radio Berkeley

Despite the limitations on radio pirates, the mass media in the United States have more freedom than anywhere else in the world. The First Amendment protects free speech, and private individuals own the media. Such freedom has given rise to many diverse avenues of expression. Radio and television talk shows and Internet communications are among the fastest-growing forums. Government regulations are aimed at providing order, fairness, and access to media.

Protecting the Media

The First Amendment[1] says in part that "Congress shall make no law . . . abridging the freedom . . . of the press." The guarantee of this freedom is fundamental to democracy. Thomas Jefferson described the importance of a free press when he argued:

> "*The people are the only censors of their governors. . . . The only safeguard of the public liberty . . . is to give them full information of their affairs through the channel of the public papers & to contrive that those papers should penetrate the whole mass of the people.*"
>
> —Thomas Jefferson, 1787

Free Press Guaranteed In the United States, the First Amendment means that print media are free from **prior restraint,** or government censorship of information before it is published. Over the years the Supreme Court has struck down attempts to give government prior restraint powers. These decisions mean that editors and reporters have freedom to decide what goes in or stays out of their publications.

See the following footnoted materials in the **Reference Handbook:**

1. *The Constitution,* pages 774–799.

Media Megamerger

Massive Media The CEO's of America Online and Time Warner announce their companies' plans to merge. Such large business reorganizations require approval by federal regulators. This merger involved ownership of publishing, music, Internet, and film assets. ***Why do you think there is more federal regulation of broadcast media than of print media?***

Libel Freedom of the press, however, is not absolute. False written statements intended to damage a person's reputation constitute **libel.** People who believe a published story has damaged their careers or reputations may sue for libel. However, it is almost impossible for a public official to win a libel suit. The reason is in part that there is no law against criticizing government officials.

Public figures who believe they have been libeled may file a libel suit to discourage the press from continuing to do stories about them. If taken to court, publishers must prove that they intended to tell the truth. Defending against a libel suit can be very expensive. Also, public officials who file libel suits may win sympathy from the public who resent the way reporters report the news.

The Right to Gather Information Freedom for the media to publish whatever they want means little if they cannot collect information about government actions and decisions. If government officials tell lies, hold secret meetings, or try to limit reporters' access to information in other ways, the media may not be able to provide the information citizens need. Does the First Amendment give the media special rights of access to courtrooms or government offices? Further, does it give reporters special protection for their news sources—the people they consult to get information?

The Right of Access The press has gone to court many times to fight for the right of access. The results have been mixed. Generally, the Supreme Court has rejected the idea that the media have special rights of access. In 1965, for example, in *Zemel* v. *Rusk*[1] the Court ruled that "the right to speak and publish does not carry with it the unrestrained right to gather information." A similar ruling came down in 1972 in *Branzburg* v. *Hayes*[2] when the Court decided that "the First Amendment does not guarantee the press a constitutional right of special access to information not available to the public generally."

The lower courts have been more supportive of the right of access. In the last decade the media filed more than 200 right-of-access lawsuits. They won access in about 60 percent of these cases.

Despite such victories in the lower courts, authorities do not have to give the media special right of access to crime or disaster sites if the general public is excluded, although they usually do. Reporters may be kept out of legislative sessions that are closed to the general public. Neither do reporters have special access to grand jury proceedings.

Protection of Sources Reporters often need secret informants when investigating government officials, political radicals, or criminals. Success in gathering news may depend on getting information from people who do not want their names made public. If the courts, the police, or legislatures force reporters to name their sources, these sources of information may vanish. On the other hand, criminals may go unpunished if reporters do not give police information about them.

See the following footnoted materials in the ***Reference Handbook:***
1. *Zemel* v. *Rusk* case summary, page 768.
2. *Branzburg* v. *Hayes* case summary, page 755.

The press and the United States government have fought many battles over the media's right to keep sources secret. More than half the states have passed **shield laws** to protect reporters from having to reveal their sources. While no federal shield law exists, the Privacy Protection Act of 1980 prevents all levels of government from conducting surprise searches of newsrooms, except in a few special circumstances.

Regulating the Media

The federal government has more power to regulate the broadcast media than to regulate the print media, for two reasons. First, a limited number of radio and television airwaves exist. During the 1920s when radio was first popular, stations drowned out each other's signals. As a result, the Radio Act of 1927 created the Federal Radio Commission to divide channels among broadcasters. Then in 1934 Congress created the Federal Communications Commission (FCC) to manage all types of electronic communications.

FCC logo

Second, the airwaves are a public resource and should be regulated like other public utilities such as the electric company or water company. Herbert Hoover helped plan federal regulation of radio when he was secretary of commerce in 1924:

> *Radio communication is not to be considered merely a business. . . . It is a public concern impressed with the public trust and to be considered primarily from the standpoint of public interest to the same extent and upon the same general principles as our other public utilities.*
>
> —Herbert Hoover, 1924

The Federal Communications Commission The FCC is the government agency with authority to regulate over-the-air and cable television, AM and FM radio, telephones, satellites, telegraph, and CB radio. The FCC has five commissioners that the president appoints and the Senate approves. Each commissioner serves a five-year term.

The FCC has broad powers to make rules that require stations to operate in the public interest. The most important power is to grant licenses to all radio and television stations in the country. The FCC's two most important regulatory activities deal with the content of broadcasts and with ownership of the media.

Content Regulation The FCC cannot censor broadcasts. It can influence the content of broadcasts, however, by fining stations that violate rules and by threatening not to renew a station's license.

One FCC rule is the **equal time doctrine,** which requires stations to give equal airtime to candidates for public office. If one major candidate is allowed to buy commercial time, then other candidates must have the same chance to buy an equal amount of time. This rule does not apply to news stories, but it does include "free time" broadcasts or interview shows.

The FCC took many steps to deregulate broadcasting during Ronald Reagan's presidency. The most controversial change was removal of the **fairness doctrine.** This doctrine required broadcasters to provide "reasonable opportunities for the expression of opposing views on controversial issues of public importance." The doctrine was supposed to discourage one-sided coverage of issues and encourage stations to present a range of views.

Some broadcasters claimed the fairness doctrine was actually censorship. In reality, they argued, it caused stations to avoid reporting on any type of controversy. The Supreme Court had upheld the doctrine in 1969 in *Red Lion Broadcasting Co.* v. *FCC.*[1] The Court stated that the doctrine protected "an uninhibited marketplace of ideas in which truth will ultimately prevail." The Court added that a regulation such as the fairness doctrine was justified in the broadcast media because the airwaves are scarce. If print media such as newspapers are presenting one-sided coverage, the Court said, anyone could start another paper.

See the following footnoted materials in the **Reference Handbook:**
1. *Red Lion Broadcasting Co.* v. *FCC* case summary, page 764.

When the FCC wanted to drop the fairness doctrine in 1987, Congress passed a law requiring the FCC to keep it. But President Reagan vetoed the bill, saying:

> "*This type of content-based regulation by the Federal Government is, in my judgement, antagonistic to the freedom of expression guaranteed by the First Amendment.*"
>
> —Ronald Reagan

Reagan said the growth of cable television had added so many new outlets for different ideas that the scarcity argument no longer mattered.

Telecommunications Act of 1996

President Reagan's observation about the effects of the growth of cable television was an early indication that the old rules governing communications needed to be reviewed. By the mid-1990s many people in the electronic media agreed that the government policy regulating their industry was outdated. Broadcast owners and many other communications interests pressured Congress to review communications policy.

Emerging technologies had made new business relationships in telecommunications possible. Telephone lines could carry the same signals that cable companies carried, and cable companies might eventually offer phone service. Both could offer Internet hookups, videoconferencing, and other services. Voice, data, video, and images could be transmitted via broadcast, narrowcast, or point-to-point services. Phone companies realized that if government policy permitted, their lines could carry many additional information services. Broadcasters had already invested in cable and wanted to expand. They also wanted Congress to grant free use of additional spectrum to shift from analog to digital TV. Congress agreed that the time had come to review telecommunications regulations.

Early in 1996, Congress passed a new Telecommunications Act. Vice President Al Gore expressed enthusiastic optimism: "The Berlin walls of the telecom industry are going to be brought down as this legislation is implemented."

COMPARING *Governments*

Media Access

Country	Televisions: Total number*	Televisions: Number per 1,000 people	Radios: Total number*	Radios: Number per 1,000 people	Newspapers: Total circulation*	Newspapers: Circulation per 1,000 people
China	400,377	319	244,745	195	NA	NA
Iraq	1,788	82	4,970	228	436	20
Israel	1,717	291	3,127	530	1,717	291
Mexico	25,866	270	31,039	324	9,293	97
Russia	59,616	405	50,537	344	15,456	105
United States	220,409	805	579,087	2,115	58,046	212
Thailand	11,264	189	12,158	204	3,874	65
United Kingdom	3,259	516	84,099	1,445	19,322	332

* *Total in thousands* *NA = not available*

Sources: U.S. Census Bureau, *Statistical Abstract of the United States: 1999* and *The New York Times 2000 Almanac*

Critical Thinking **The United States leads the world in the number of media available for one country.** ***Which country has the largest number of televisions? Which country has the largest number of televisions per 1,000 people?***

Congress Addresses Key Issues

When the debate over new communications policy began in Congress, most members were aware of the need to address several key issues. First, because information is a commodity that benefits all Americans, it should be delivered at low cost. About 6 percent of the people remained unconnected to phone service because they could not afford it. Lower rates would make this service available to more people. Congress believed competition would be the key to lower rates.

Second, the use of the broadcast spectrum needed review. The **broadcast spectrum** is the range of frequencies over which electronic signals may be sent. Television and radio broadcasters, private radio such as that used by police and taxi drivers, wireless telephones, and satellite communications all use parts of the broadcast spectrum. Television broadcasters wanted additional spectrum allocation in order to broadcast digital TV—images with sharper pictures and CD-quality sound. Utility companies, Internet providers, and wireless computer networks all wanted new spectrum allocation.

Third, Congress voted to allow the FCC to make decisions about spectrum allocation. The act permitted broadcast owners to purchase more stations even within the same market. It allowed cross-ownership of cable and broadcast stations. These provisions were all aimed at increasing the competition.

Congress addressed a fourth related issue. Telephone companies wanted to compete with cable companies in delivering television programming. The FCC had prevented cross-ownership of telephone and cable. The act opened local markets to competitors. It dropped some of the old cable rate regulations, believing competition would reduce costs to consumers.

Finally, Congress addressed obscene and violent programming. The Telecommunications Act contained the "Communications Decency Act of 1996." The new law extended provisions of the Communications Act of 1934, prohibiting obscene or harassing conversation on any telecommunications facility. It amended the federal criminal code to apply current obscenity statutes to computer users and ordered the broadcast industry to establish ratings for objectionable programming. Parents could use the "V-chip" to program their televisions to block programs with objectionable content. All new televisions sold in the United States were to include the V-chip by 1998. However, the Supreme Court struck down this act in 1997.

Congress knew that telecommunications policy could not be finalized in one law. Ongoing decisions were left to the FCC. Congress charged the FCC to work with each state's telecommunications commissions to carrry out a broad range of policy issues. Part of this responsibility was to find ways to provide increasing communications access to public elementary and secondary schools and to libraries.

Empowerment vs. Censorship

Parental Rights Supporters and opponents of the V-chip met at the White House to discuss its implications. In February 1996, President Clinton signed into law the requirement that all new television sets be equipped with the V-chip device by 1998. ***Do you think the V-chip constitutes a governmental intrusion into Americans' homes, or is it an empowerment of the television viewer?***

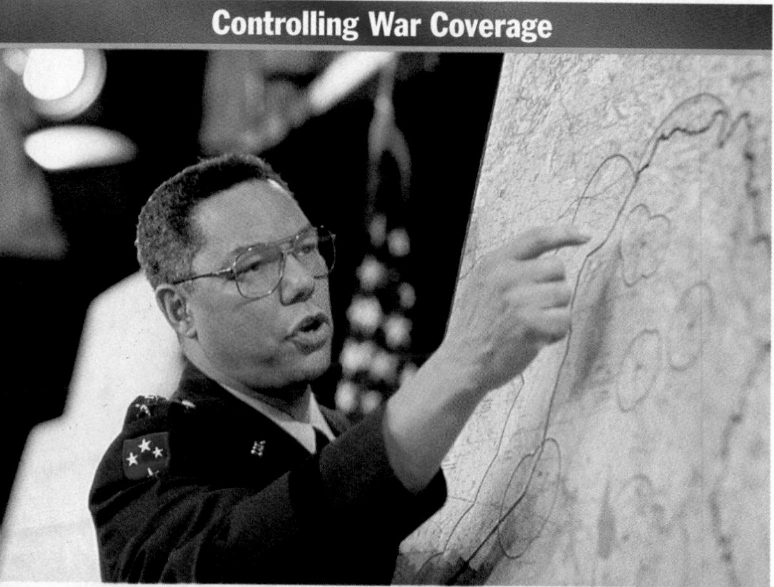

Controlling War Coverage

Freedom of the Press General Colin Powell briefs the media. During the Persian Gulf War the government controlled access to both the area of active combat and military personnel. ***Do you think the government should have the right to limit information during times of war?***

Media and National Security

Tension between the need for the government to keep secrets to protect national security and the citizens' need for information will always exist in a free society. Tensions are especially evident in foreign affairs where intelligence information and military secrets are involved. The government attempts to control information about national security by classifying information as secret and by limiting press coverage of military actions.

The federal government gives a "secret" security classification to many government documents. During the Vietnam War, *The New York Times* published a secret Defense Department study describing how the United States became involved in the war. The government tried to stop publication. In *New York Times Co.* v. *United States*[1] (1971), however, the Supreme Court ruled that the publication did not harm national security.

When controversy about a military action arises, however, the media may criticize the government and try to dig up secret information. Additional tension between the military and the media was created during the 1991 Persian Gulf War. Throughout the military buildup and the actual war, the Defense Department limited the media to a small group of reporters who were permitted to visit battlefields. These reporters would collect stories to share with all other reporters left behind in press headquarters. Most reporters covering the war had to depend upon official briefings to gain information about military progress.

See the following footnoted materials in the **Reference Handbook:**
1. *New York Times Co.* v. *United States* case summary, page 763.

Section 3 Assessment

Checking for Understanding

1. **Main Idea** Use a graphic organizer like the one below to explain why broadcast media are more heavily regulated than print media.

2. **Define** prior restraint, libel, shield law, equal time doctrine, fairness doctrine.
3. **Identify** broadcast spectrum.
4. Why did Congress review communications policy in 1996?

Critical Thinking

5. **Synthesizing Information** Why might the need for national security conflict with the First Amendment protections given the media?

Concepts IN ACTION

Civil Liberties Interview, write, or E-mail a local newspaper editor to find out what precautions the newspaper takes to prevent libel suits. Share the information you obtain with your classmates.

Skills

Study and Writing

Conducting Interviews

Interviews allow you to gather information about interesting people such as Jesse Jackson, a civil rights leader, political leader, and Baptist minister. As a candidate for the Democratic presidential nomination in 1984 and 1988, Jackson focused attention on the problems of African Americans and other minority groups and stressed the economic problems of farmers and workers. Jackson continues the fight for Americans today.

Learning the Skill

To interview Jesse Jackson or anyone else, you would want to follow these steps.

a. Make an appointment Contact the person, and explain why you want the interview, what kinds of things you hope to learn, and how you will use the information. Discuss where and when you will conduct the interview, and ask if you may use a tape recorder.

b. Gather background information Find out about the early life, education, career, and other accomplishments of the person you will interview. Familiarize yourself with books or articles that the interviewee has published. Then do research on the topics you will discuss.

c. Prepare questions Group questions into subject categories, beginning each category with general questions and moving toward more specific questions. Formulate each question carefully, phrasing it in a way that encourages a well-developed answer. If the answer could simply be *yes* or *no,* rephrase the question.

d. Conduct the interview Introduce yourself and restate the purpose of the interview. Ask questions and record responses accurately. Ask follow-up questions to fill gaps in information.

e. Transcribe the interview Convert your written or tape-recorded notes into a transcript, a written record of the interview presented in a question-and-answer format.

Jesse Jackson

Practicing the Skill

Answer the following questions based on an interview you might do with Jesse Jackson.

1. What kind of background information might you gather?
2. What are some broad categories of questions you might ask?
3. What are some specific questions you might ask?
4. What would you do if you ran out of prepared questions and there was a lull in the interview?
5. How would you deal with keeping an accurate record of direct quotes from Jackson?

Application Activity

Interview an interesting family member or friend about an important or unique experience. As you transcribe the interview, be aware of common themes and interesting facts. Present your transcription to the class.

Chapter 19

Assessment and Activities

Self-Check Quiz Visit the *United States Government: Democracy in Action* Web site at gov.glencoe.com and click on ***Chapter 19–Self-Check Quizzes*** to prepare for the chapter test.

Reviewing Key Terms

Choose the letter of the correct answer below to complete each sentence.

a. wire service
b. equal time doctrine
c. prior restraint
d. news releases

1. Government officials prepare ____, ready-made stories for the press.
2. The _____ requires stations to give the same amount of airtime to major candidates.
3. The First Amendment frees the United States print media from ____.
4. A ____ employs reporters internationally to collect news for subscribers.

Current Events JOURNAL

The *Congressional Record* The *Congressional Record* is a printed account of the daily events and speeches of members of Congress that is made available to government officials and private citizens alike. Review a copy of the *Congressional Record.* Try to find a speech by or reference to your local member of the House of Representatives or a senator from your state. Summarize your findings in a paragraph.

Recalling Facts

1. What are "the four branches" of government?
2. What amendment protects the media?
3. What caused the decline of newspapers as Americans' main source for news?
4. What government agency limits the number of radio and television stations a single company can own?
5. What steps does the federal government take when attempting to control sensitive national security issues?
6. In recent years who has been responsible for picking a front-runner?
7. What aspects of Congress does the media tend to cover?
8. What are the benefits of congressional recording studios?

Understanding Concepts

1. **Free Enterprise** Why is free enterprise a key tool in safeguarding freedom of the press?
2. **Political Processes** Why does the media have a major impact on voting and elections in the United States?
3. **Civil Liberties** The FCC cannot censor broadcasts and the government may not exercise prior restraint over print media. Why is freedom of the press under the First Amendment fundamental to democracy?

Critical Thinking

1. **Synthesizing Information** What two characteristics or features of the mass media have the greatest impact on American government and politics?
2. **Demonstrating Reasoned Judgment** Should the media have been limited in its coverage of the 1991 Persian Gulf War? Support your answer.

3. **Synthesizing Information** Use a graphic organizer like the one below to list two or more arguments for and against this statement: "The media's greatest power is in the way they define reality for the American people." Then explain why you agree or disagree with the statement.

For	Against
1.	1.
2.	2.
Conclusion:	

Interpreting Political Cartoons Activity

'Okay, bring in the new guy . . .'

1. Who is the "new guy"?
2. According to the cartoon, how is the new guy treated by the press and Congress? Explain.
3. What does the television camera symbolize?

Cooperative Learning Activity

Mass Media and You The mass media have at least some connection to most people's everyday lives. How much does television influence your thinking about the relative importance of events? Organize into groups of five or six students. Each group should independently create a list of five to ten of the most important political events they can remember learning about or seeing on television within the last two years. Compare the lists from each group. How many of the events listed were national? How many were international? Did the events concern the environment, foreign affairs, local or federal laws or policies, crime, trade, or other topics? On the chalkboard create a table from these categories to analyze your findings.

Skill Practice Activity

Conducting Interviews Select a famous political or media figure. Gather biographical information that would help you prepare for an interview with that person. Use what you find to develop a list of 10 questions to ask the person you selected to interview if you had the opportunity.

Technology Activity

Using the Internet Search the Internet to find Web sites that provide information about reactions to the Telecommunications Act of 1996. Find out which groups opposed the legislation and the reasons for their opposition. Write a short report summarizing your findings.

Participating in Local Government

Interview local government officials and find out how and what type of media are involved in your local politics. Also find out how the media influence the public policy of the local government. Design a diagram to present your findings.

UNIT 7

Public Policies and Services

E-mailing Your Senators *Promoting a stable, growing economy is a major goal of the federal government. Decisions by Congress, the president, and the Federal Reserve Board affect our economic lives every day. As you read Chapters 20 and 21, list the specific ways in which the government affects you economically. At the end of the unit, write an essay on whether the government has an overall positive or negative impact on your economic well-being. E-mail your essay to your senators in Washington, D.C.*

Electronic Field Trip

The FBI Training Academy

Step inside the school where agents of the Federal Bureau of Investigation (FBI) receive their training.

Glencoe's Democracy in Action Video Program

One of the services that governments provide is the training of a professional law enforcement agency. The **Democracy in Action** video program "The FBI Training Academy," referenced below, shows the depth and variety of training required of FBI agents.

As you view the video program, try to identify the character traits that help a person become a professional law enforcement agent.

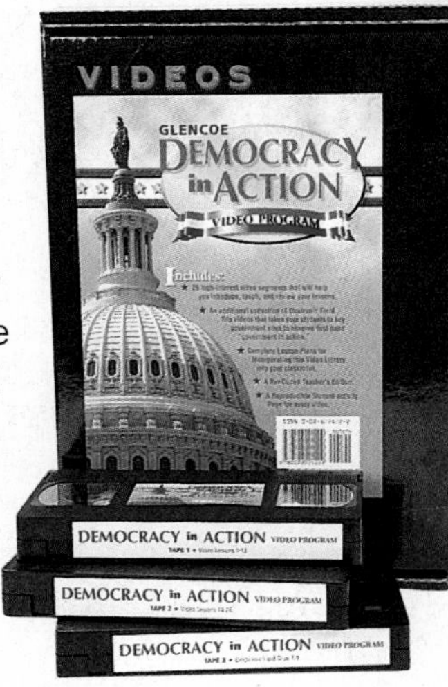

◀ The Washington Monument

Also available in videodisc format.

View the videodisc by scanning the barcode or by entering the chapter number on your keypad and pressing Search.

Disc 2, Side 1, Chapter 7

Hands-On Activity

Think about the wide range of abilities an FBI agent should have. List the skills involved in carrying out the duties of the Bureau. Use a word processor to create a job description for a new special agent position in the FBI. Include qualifications of applicants, responsibilities of the job, and the types of training provided by the Academy.

★ ★ ★ ★ ★ ★ ★ ★

Chapter 20

Taxing and Spending

Why It's Important

Paying for Government The services provided by government cost money. You and almost everyone else pay taxes to support government spending. What are the effects of government spending? In this chapter you will learn how government policy affects prices, jobs, and your economic decisions.

To better understand why taxes are necessary, view the ***Democracy In Action*** Chapter 20 video lesson:

Taxing and Spending

Chapter Overview Visit the *United States Government: Democracy in Action* Web site at gov.glencoe.com and click on ***Chapter 20–Overview*** to preview chapter information.

Section 1

Raising Money

Reader's Guide

Key Terms

taxes, taxable income, dependent, withholding, securities, national debt

Find Out

- How does the income tax compare with other sources of federal revenue in terms of the amount collected?
- How does the federal government use tax laws to affect economic decisions?

Understanding Concepts

Civic Participation How are income taxes collected from citizens of the United States?

COVER STORY

Income Tax Coming

CHEYENNE, WYOMING, FEBRUARY 1913

Wyoming has become the 36th and final state needed to ratify the Sixteenth Amendment. First proposed in 1909, the constitutional amendment authorizes Congress to levy an income tax on many Americans. Approval of the amendment concludes a long struggle to enact a permanent income tax after an emergency tax on incomes during the Civil War expired in 1872. Calls for the amendment began in 1895, when the Supreme Court declared an income tax law passed the previous year to be unconstitutional. Congress is expected to act quickly to pass a new tax bill, which President-elect Woodrow Wilson has promised to sign.

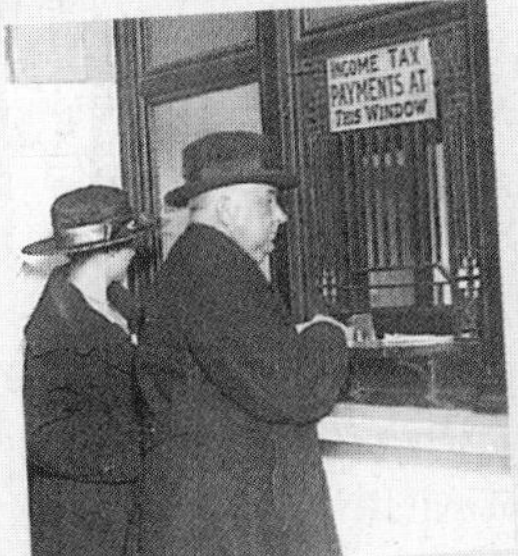

Americans paying income taxes

Collecting taxes is one way the federal government plays a role in the United States economy. The amount of money the government collects in revenues and the government's budget are calculated in figures too large for most people to comprehend. In a recent year the national government took in almost $1.5 trillion in revenues. That figure represents an average of nearly $6,000 for each person in the nation. What are the sources of all this money? Two major sources are taxes and borrowing.

Taxes as a Source of Revenue

Benjamin Franklin once said, "In this world, nothing is certain but death and taxes." **Taxes** are payments by individuals and businesses to support the activities of government. The Constitution states that Congress

> "*. . . shall have power to lay and collect taxes, duties, imposts, and excises, and to pay the debts and provide for the common defense and general welfare of the United States. . . .*"
>
> —Article I, Section 8

Today taxes are the chief way the federal government raises money.

Individual Income Tax The individual income tax is the federal government's biggest single source of revenue. About 44 cents of every dollar the government collects comes from this source. In a recent year, the individual income tax produced more than $630 billion.

The federal income tax is levied on a person's **taxable income**, or the total income of an individual minus certain deductions and personal exemptions. People may elect to take deductions for contributions made to charity, for state and local income taxes paid, for home mortgage interest, and for other expenses.

◀ **Republicans celebrate tax cuts on Capitol Hill.**

Taxes in America

Government Processes Paying taxes often requires filling out complex tax forms. Congress has been asked to review and simplify the taxpaying process.

Citizen Processes By and large, most Americans no longer violently protest government taxes. Here a couple fills out income tax forms.

Taxes and Public Opinion ***Do you think public opinion places any limits on the government's ability to tax?***

Or, people may take a standard deduction that the government calculates. The government also permits personal exemptions that reduce the amount of income that is taxable. Such exemptions are based on the number of people who are dependent on the wage earner who pays the income tax. A **dependent** is one who depends primarily on another person for such things as food, clothing, and shelter.

The income tax is a **progressive tax,** one based on a taxpayer's ability to pay. The higher a person's taxable income, the higher the tax rate. People with higher incomes, however, can often take advantage of certain deductions not as available to those in lower tax brackets. These deductions may make the tax system less progressive.

The deadline for filing income tax returns each year is April 15. Nearly everyone with taxable income in the preceding calendar year must file income tax returns by that date. During the year employers withhold a certain amount of money from the workers' wages. This **withholding** pays the anticipated taxes ahead of the April 15 filing date. Self-employed people—including business owners, tradespeople, and professionals—who do not receive regular salaries are expected to file estimates of their income four times a year and make payments with each estimate. In this way those taxpayers avoid having to make one large annual payment on April 15. At the same time, the government receives a steady flow of income throughout the year.

The **Internal Revenue Service (IRS),** a bureau of the United States Treasury Department, collects these taxes through its regional centers. The IRS receives and processes about 200 million returns and supplemental documents each year. IRS staff members use computers to quickly check each return. They **audit,** or check more closely, a small percentage of returns each year. The IRS also investigates many suspected criminal violations of the tax laws each year.

Corporate Income Tax Corporations, as well as individuals, must pay income taxes. The federal government taxes all the earned income of a corporation beyond its expenses and deductions. Corporate income taxes represent about 12 percent of federal government revenues. Nonprofit organizations such as colleges, labor unions, and churches are exempt from this tax.

Social Insurance Taxes The federal government collects huge sums of money each year to pay for Social Security, Medicare, and unemployment compensation programs. The taxes collected to pay for these major social programs are called **social insurance taxes.** Employees and employers share equally in paying the tax for Social Security and Medicare. Employers deduct it directly from each worker's paycheck, add an equal amount, and send the total to the federal government. The unemployment compensation program is a combined federal-state operation financed largely by a federal tax on the payrolls of businesses. All these social insurance taxes are often called payroll taxes.

Social insurance taxes are the fastest-growing source of federal income. In 1950 they amounted to only $4 billion. In fiscal year 1998, these taxes brought in about $525 billion. As the second-largest source of federal tax income, social insurance taxes contribute about 35 cents of each dollar collected.

Unlike other taxes, social insurance taxes do not go into the government's general fund. Instead, they go to Treasury Department special trust accounts. Congress then appropriates money from these accounts to pay out benefits. These taxes are **regressive taxes** because people with lower incomes usually pay a larger portion of their income for these taxes than do people with higher incomes.

Excise Taxes Taxes on the manufacture, transportation, sale, or consumption of goods and the performance of services are called **excise taxes.** The Constitution permits levying excise taxes, and since 1789 Congress has placed taxes on a variety of goods. Some early targets for excise taxes were carriages, snuff, and liquor. Today the government imposes excise taxes on gasoline, oil, tires, cigars, cigarettes, liquor, airline tickets, long-distance telephone service, and many other things. Some excise taxes are called luxury taxes because they are levied on goods such as cigarettes and liquor not considered to be necessities. Excise taxes contribute about $50 billion a year to the federal government, with taxes on liquor and tobacco bringing in the most income.

Customs Duties Taxes levied on goods imported into the United States are called **customs duties,** tariffs, or import duties. The federal government imposes customs duties to raise revenue or to help protect the nation's industries, businesses, and agriculture from foreign competition. A high customs duty is called a **protective tariff.** Many business, labor, and farm groups support protective tariffs because they raise the price of foreign goods, making them less competitive compared to American goods on the domestic market.

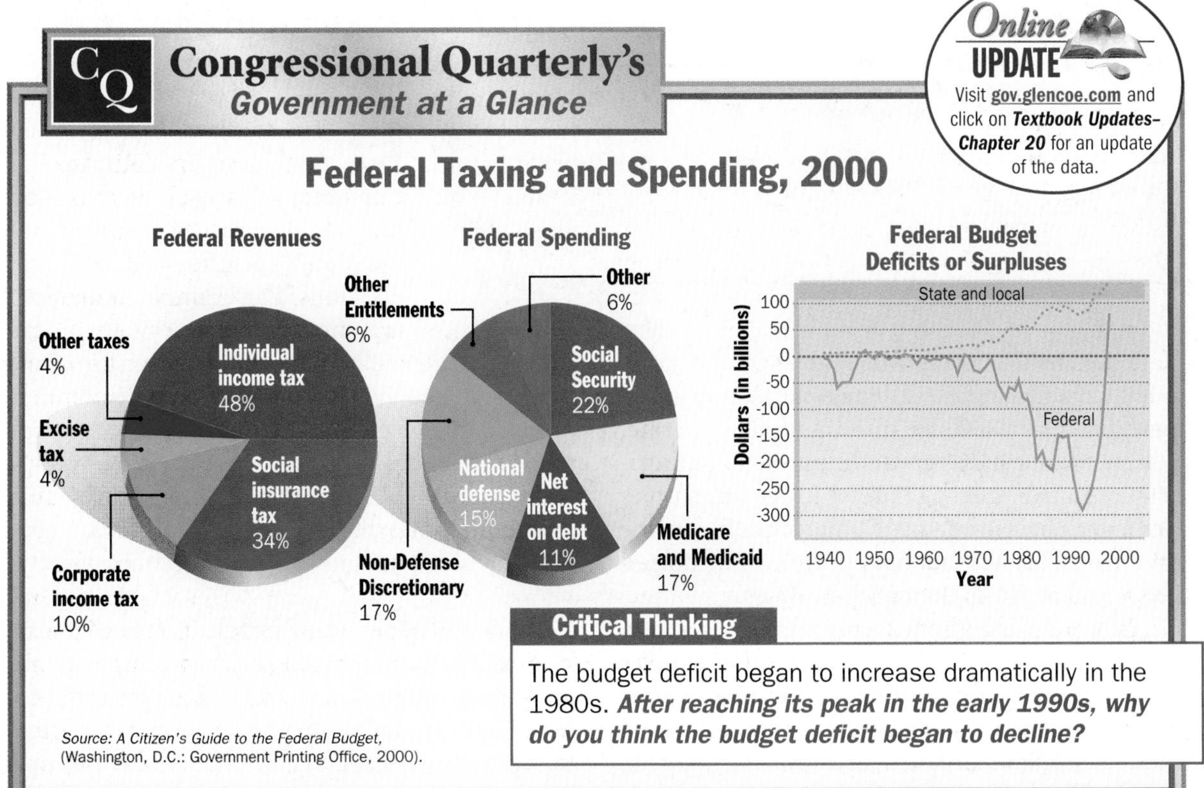

Critical Thinking

The budget deficit began to increase dramatically in the 1980s. ***After reaching its peak in the early 1990s, why do you think the budget deficit began to decline?***

Source: A Citizen's Guide to the Federal Budget, (Washington, D.C.: Government Printing Office, 2000).

GOVERNMENT and You

Why We Pay Taxes

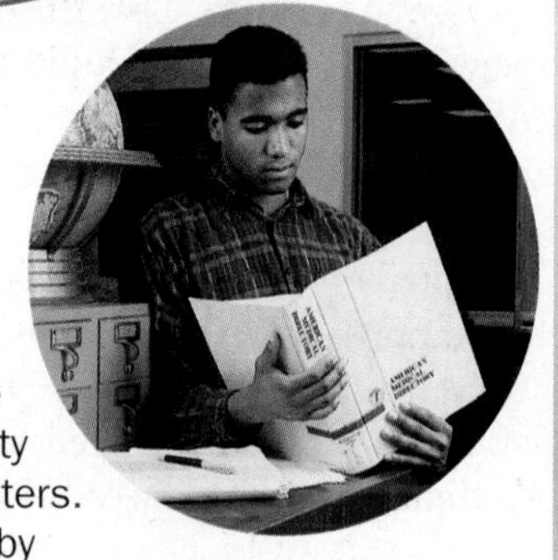

Using books paid for by taxes

Government makes life better in many ways. If you are an average teen, you probably drive on area roads and highways, attend public schools, and use the local library. Your safety and property are protected by police and firefighters. You do not expect to be poisoned by the food you eat and the water you drink, or that products you use will harm you. You live free from fear of foreign invasion or guerrilla attack.

No one charges you for these and many other services, benefits, and protections that you enjoy. However, as the old saying goes, "there is no such thing as a free lunch." Taxes on gasoline maintain highways. Sales, property, and income taxes finance local and state services. Federal income taxes also support many programs and services. In fact, most government activities that enhance the quality of life in the United States are made possible by the taxes we pay.

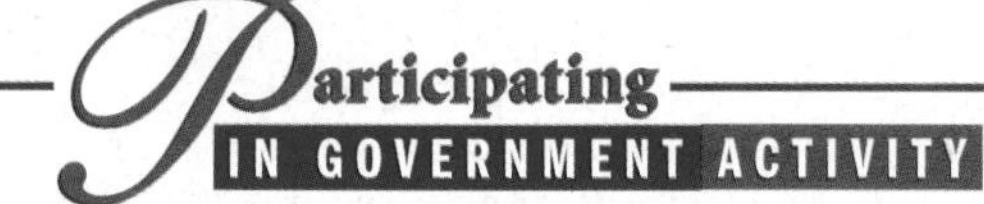

Investigate Determine the role of government in providing and paying for some facility, program, or service you enjoy in your community.

The Constitution gives Congress the authority to levy customs duties. Congress can decide which foreign imports will be taxed and at what rate. Congress, in turn, has given the president authority by executive order to raise or lower the existing tariff rates by as much as 50 percent. Today, the government levies customs duties on imported items, ranging from diamonds to shoes.

Before the income tax, customs duties were a major source of federal income. As other sources of taxes grew, customs duties declined as a share of federal revenue. In a recent year they produced about $19 billion, or less than 2 cents of every tax dollar collected.

Estate and Gift Taxes The federal government collects an **estate tax** on the assets (property and money) of a person who dies and a gift tax on gifts of money from a living person. First levied in 1916, the estate tax today is assessed on large amounts (estates of more than $675,000 in 2000). The gift tax is charged on gifts of more than $10,000 given in one year to another individual. These taxes redistribute the wealth of families and individuals as well as raise revenue. The gift tax prevents people from avoiding an estate tax by giving money to relatives and friends before death—money given to a spouse is exempt.

The estate tax and the gift tax are progressive taxes—the larger the estate or gift, the higher the tax rate. In a recent year these two taxes brought in about $16 billion to the federal treasury.

Taxes and the Economy

The tax laws in the United States are very complex and can affect actions of citizens. The federal government sometimes uses taxes to influence economic decisions. For example, individual income tax deductions for home mortgage interest provide an incentive for home ownership and aid the construction industry.

Groups affected by tax increases have sometimes influenced Congress to pass special exemptions in order to reduce the taxes they have to pay. The result is that the tax system contains many special provisions designed to benefit certain groups.

Tax Loopholes Many people believe that provisions, or tax exemptions, favoring certain groups are unfair. These exemptions are often referred to as **tax loopholes.** Some people can afford to hire attorneys and tax specialists who can find loopholes in the complicated tax laws. People in high-income brackets have used strategies such as declaring business losses or investing in tax shelters to avoid paying taxes. Other exemptions represent government efforts to encourage an activity. A tax exemption on oil exploration encourages people to invest their money in businesses searching for new energy sources.

Tax Reforms In 1985 President Reagan proposed tax changes to eliminate what he termed "an endless source of confusion and resentment." After much debate, Congress passed the Tax Reform Act of 1986. The act reduced a variety of tax deductions, tax credits, and tax shelters. It also reduced the number of tax brackets or rates. Depending on their income, individuals were taxed at rates between 15 percent and 28 percent. President Clinton's proposal in 1993 increased the top marginal rate to 36 percent. A new 10 percent surtax on higher incomes made the effective top rate 39.6 percent.

Tax Credits The federal government today provides tax credits generally to people in lower income brackets. **Tax credits** allow taxpayers to reduce their income tax liability. Each dollar of tax credit offsets a dollar of tax liability. The earned-income credit enables many families with lower incomes to receive refunds. Workers who must pay for the care of their children or other dependents receive a tax credit for that expense. Certain elderly and retired people may be entitled to a tax credit, depending on the amount of their income.

Borrowing for Revenue

In addition to collecting taxes, the federal government borrows money. In 1996, borrowing amounted to about $146 billion, or about 10 cents for every dollar the government raised.

Bonds and Other Securities The government borrows by selling federal **securities**—financial instruments that include bonds, notes, and certificates. Federal government securities are popular with investors because they are safe and interest may not be taxable. The most popular bonds for small investors are savings bonds. In return for lending the government money, investors earn interest on their bonds. The federal government pays a huge amount of interest.

The National Debt When the government's spending is greater than its income, it goes into debt. Government borrowing to fund annual budget deficits over time creates the **national debt.** The size of the national debt affects the federal budget and the economy.

Student Web Activity Visit the *United States Government: Democracy in Action* Web site at gov.glencoe.com and click on ***Chapter 20–Student Web Activities*** for an activity about raising money.

Section 1 Assessment

Checking for Understanding

1. **Main Idea** Use a graphic organizer like the one below to show the steps in collecting federal income tax.

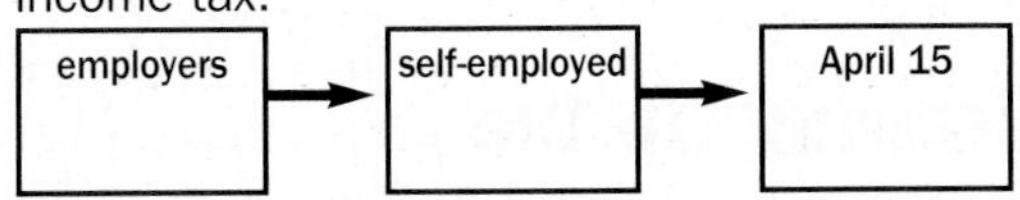

2. **Define** taxes, taxable income, dependent, withholding, securities, national debt.
3. **Identify** progressive tax, IRS, social insurance taxes, regressive tax, tax loophole.
4. What is the federal government's biggest single source of tax revenue?

Critical Thinking

5. **Identifying Alternatives** Why does the government raise most of its revenues through taxing rather than borrowing?

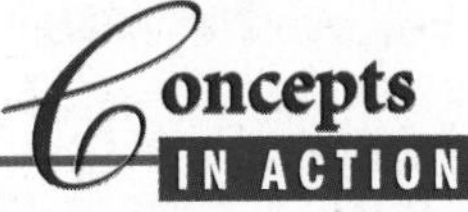

Civic Participation Obtain a paycheck stub—yours or a family member's. Note the categories and amounts of money deducted for city and state taxes, FICA, and Social Security. Create a graph that shows the percentage of the earned wages deducted in each category.

Section 2

Preparing the Federal Budget

Reader's Guide

Key Terms

fiscal year, uncontrollables, entitlement, incrementalism

Find Out

- How do the executive and legislative branches work together to produce an annual budget for the federal government?
- Why is it so difficult for the federal government to reduce spending or raise taxes in order to balance the budget?

Understanding Concepts

Public Policy What factors prevent the budget from changing very much from year to year?

COVER STORY

Washington Retires

PHILADELPHIA, PENNSYLVANIA, SEPTEMBER 1796

George Washington announced today that he will not seek a third term as president. In a statement released to the press, he also expressed his concerns for the nation. Washington urged government leaders to avoid unnecessary spending. "Cherish public credit," the president advised, "avoiding likewise the accumulation of debt." He admonished that "toward the payment of debts there must be revenue," which will mean taxes. "No taxes can be devised which are not more or less inconvenient and unpleasant," Washington said. He warned that the alternative would be a national debt that will unfairly burden future generations of Americans.

George Washington

From Washington's day to the present, the nation has always accounted for its revenues and expenditures. Today, the federal budget enables the government to predict and control revenue and spending for each year. The federal budget operates in a **fiscal year**—a 12-month accounting period that extends from October 1 of one year to September 30 of the next year.

The budget is an important policy document. It reflects the federal government's view of the nation's needs and priorities. By showing how much will be spent on various national concerns such as defense and social welfare, it serves as a blueprint for the federal government's spending.

George Washington was able to put all the figures for the national government's expenditures for one year on one large sheet of paper. Today the federal budget consists of more than 1,000 pages of small type.

Preparation of the budget involves the efforts of thousands of people and goes on continually. Work on a budget starts a full 19 months before a fiscal year begins. Thus, before one year's budget is completed, work on the next year's budget is already under way.

The executive and legislative branches share in the preparation of the budget—an example of checks and balances at work. Under the president's leadership, the executive branch draws up a proposed budget. Congress uses the president's budget as a basis for preparing a tax and spending plan to submit back to the president.

Drawing Up the President's Budget

During much of American history, presidents have traditionally played a limited role in researching and drawing up the budget. Various federal agencies usually sent their budget requests directly to the secretary of the treasury, who passed them on to Congress.

The Budget and Accounting Act of 1921 changed this procedure in an effort to streamline the process. As a result of this law, the president is responsible for directing the preparation of the budget and making the major decisions about national budget priorities. The law requires the president to propose to Congress the budget for the entire federal government each fiscal year. This budget must be delivered within 15 days after Congress convenes each January.

The actual day-to-day preparation of the budget is the responsibility of the **Office of Management and Budget (OMB).** The OMB, along with the president's Council of Economic Advisers (CEA), confers with the president on budgetary matters.

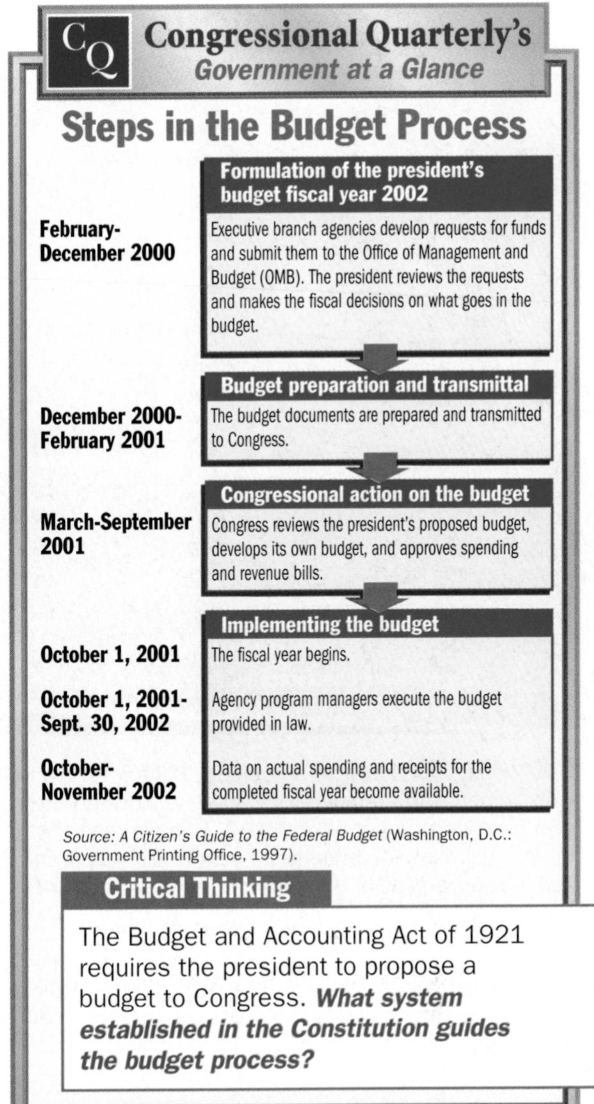

Source: A Citizen's Guide to the Federal Budget (Washington, D.C.: Government Printing Office, 1997).

Critical Thinking

The Budget and Accounting Act of 1921 requires the president to propose a budget to Congress. ***What system established in the Constitution guides the budget process?***

Start of the Process Budget making begins in early spring for the budget that is to go into effect a year from the following October. Each federal agency draws up a list of its own spending plans and sends these requests to the OMB.

The Director of the OMB takes the first set of figures to the president, along with OMB's analysis of the nation's economic situation. At this point the president, assisted by the secretary of the treasury and the CEA, makes key decisions about the impact of the preliminary budget on the administration's general economic policy and goals. They discuss such questions as: Will the budget increase or reduce federal spending? Which federal programs will be cut back and which will be expanded? Will the federal government need to borrow more money? Should taxes be raised or lowered?

Agencies Review Their Budgets The White House returns its decisions on the budget to the agencies and departments with guidelines to help them prepare their final budgets. The Department of Defense, for example, may be told to cut its budget by $5 billion, and the Transportation Department may be told it can increase its budget by $1 billion.

Over the next few months, the executive departments and agencies work on detailed budget plans fitting the president's guidelines. During this time OMB officials and agency heads negotiate cuts and additions to bring each agency's budget in line with the president's decisions.

Final Presidential Review During the fall, the OMB submits a complete budget document to the president for final review and approval. Some last-minute juggling always takes place. Agency heads may make last-ditch efforts to convince the president to overrule an OMB decision and save a particular program. The president may order changes in parts of the budget in response to pressure from interest groups or political party members.

Finally, the administration rushes the president's budget to the printer—often only days or perhaps hours before the January deadline. The president formally sends the budget to Congress

Bipartisan Celebration

Balancing the Budget President Clinton and Vice President Gore joined with members of Congress to celebrate passage of a balanced-budget bill in 1997. This was the first balanced-budget bill passed in nearly 30 years. ***Do you think an unbalanced budget is a problem? Why or why not?***

along with an annual budget message. Congress then takes the next steps in working out the federal budget.

Uncontrollables Despite having a key role in the budget process, the president does not have complete freedom in making budgetary decisions. About 70 percent of the federal budget consists of what are called uncontrollables. **Uncontrollables** are expenditures required by law or resulting from previous budgetary commitments.

A large portion of the uncontrollables are called **entitlements,** or benefits that Congress has provided by law to individuals, and which they have an established legal right to receive. Entitlements include Social Security, pensions for retired government employees, Medicare, Medicaid, and veterans' benefits.

Another largely uncontrollable item in the budget is the interest that must be paid on the national debt. As yearly budgets have forced the federal government to borrow more and more money, the interest on the debt has grown. In fiscal 1996, interest on the debt amounted to more than 15 percent of the federal government's total expenses.

Congressional Budget Action

Article I, Section 9, of the Constitution requires that Congress approve all federal spending. Thus, the president draws up budget proposals, but only Congress has the power to raise revenue and pass appropriations. No money may be spent and no taxes may be collected until Congress approves.

Congress may revise the president's budget proposals as it sees fit. Conflict between Congress and the president over the budget is inevitable. If the opposing party, not the president's party, controls either house of Congress, that house will loudly criticize the president's budget. Even if the president's own party controls Congress, lawmakers may have different ideas than the president as to how money should be allocated. Key lawmakers and the president often must negotiate over different parts of the budget. Compromises are usually necessary on both sides before a budget is passed.

Congressional Budget Act of 1974 For years separate subcommittees of the Senate and House handled each agency's requested expenditures. This separation made it difficult for Congress to keep track of the total annual budget. To remedy this situation, Congress passed the Congressional Budget Act in 1974. This law set up House and Senate Budget Committees and the **Congressional Budget Office (CBO).**

The CBO's job is to carefully evaluate the overall federal budget for Congress. The CBO has its own professional staff of experts. They report to Congress and act as a counterbalance to the OMB in the executive branch.

Gramm-Rudman-Hollings Act By the mid-1980s the size and growth of the national debt worried economists. In 1985 Congress enacted the Balanced Budget and Emergency Deficit Control Act, known as Gramm-Rudman-Hollings (GRH) after the senators who designed it. This law was aimed at forcing the president and Congress to work together to reduce budget deficits.

GRH and later amendments required the OMB and CBO to issue a joint report each year estimating how much the proposed budget would exceed income and how much it should be cut to meet deficit-reduction targets. The federal budget deficit continued to grow because the president and Congress could not agree on budgetary priorities. The failure to meet deficit-reduction targets prompted Congress to search for another remedy.

Budgetary Enforcement Act of 1990 After lengthy negotiations President Bush and the Democratic Congress agreed on the Budgetary Enforcement Act (BEA). The BEA divided the budget into three areas: domestic policy, defense, and international affairs. Spending that exceeded the budgeted limit in any area would come out of the next year's funding for that area.

A recession in 1991–1992, however, temporarily derailed the deficit-cutting plan. When the economy improved beginning in 1993, tax receipts increased, making the job of reducing the deficit easier. Some members of Congress called for a balanced budget. President Clinton and other members of Congress, however, were satisfied that the annual deficits had been reduced from more than $300 billion to about $145 billion. In 2000 the national debt equaled more than $5.5 trillion. The debt represented 57 percent of the nation's gross domestic product.

Key Steps in Congressional Budget Making The budget-making process generally follows three steps. First, House and Senate Budget Committees review the major features of the president's budget proposals. On April 15 these committees prepare a concurrent resolution. With the president's proposals as a starting point, this resolution sets forth the total federal spending and tax plan for the coming fiscal year.

The next step, called reconciliation, occurs between April 15 and June 15. During reconciliation various House and Senate committees reconcile, or fit, the spending and taxing plans set out in the

We the People

Making a Difference

Leonard Sanders

Taxes pay for many community services, but a private citizen can also step in to meet a need. Leonard Sanders, a retired mine worker in the tiny town of Elkville, Illinois, won the state lottery in 1995. Sanders had plenty of uses for the money. After dividing up his winnings with his wife and children, however, he decided to direct some of his extra cash to improving his hometown. Sanders helped restore the 90-year-old church where his wife worshiped as a child. Then he bought and refurbished an empty grocery store to convert into a community center. He purchased two new pool tables, exercise equipment, furniture, and a television set for the center. Friends pitched in to build a small kitchen. The kitchen is stocked with free food and drinks which are paid for by a trust. Sanders set up the trust to fund the operation for future generations. The new community center provides a place for Elkville residents to gather for recreation and conversation. Sanders's additional plans for his town include a pavilion for the baseball park.

"Money will never change my attitude toward life," he said. "Elkville is really a nice place with a nice bunch of intelligent people. I've known most of them for 20 or 30 years, and we have always gotten along."

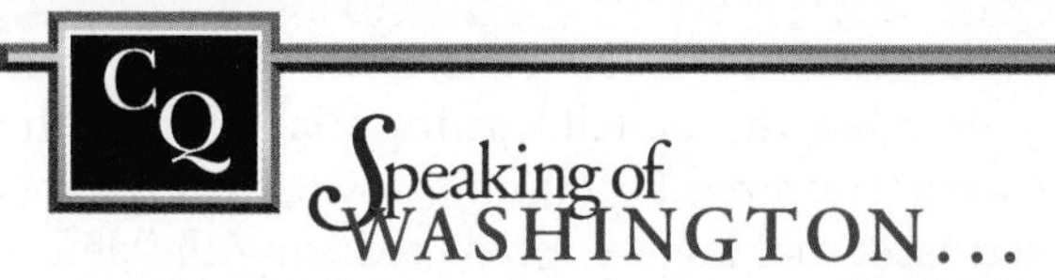

The First Budget In the nation's early years Congress handled appropriations in a haphazard way. By the close of World War I the government had grown far too complex for the old system. In 1921 Congress passed the Budget and Accounting Act, setting up the Bureau of the Budget to oversee the budget-making process and the General Accounting Office to improve congressional oversight of spending. The Bureau of the Budget was reorganized as the Office of Management and Budget in 1970.

concurrent resolution with existing programs. The committees put the changes made during this process into a reconciliation bill that both the House of Representatives and Senate must vote on and approve. The House then passes an appropriations bill, officially setting aside money for all expenditures approved through the reconciliation process. Congress is supposed to complete this bill by June 30, but the bill is often delayed because of the complexity of the details that must be approved by both houses.

The final step in the budget process involves the procedures spelled out in the GRH Act. The fiscal year begins on October 1. On October 15 the OMB issues a final report and may make cuts in the budget to fit deficit-reduction targets.

Incremental Budget Making

Some analysts use the term *incrementalism* to explain the budget-making process. **Incrementalism** means that generally the total budget changes only a little (an increment) from one year to the next. Thus, the best forecaster of this year's budget is last year's budget, plus a little more.

Incrementalism means that usually federal agencies can assume they will get the same amount of money they received in the previous year. Incrementalism also means that most budget debates focus on a proposed increment or reduction for an agency. For example, budget battles rarely center on whether the FBI should continue to exist, but rather on how much of an increase or decrease the FBI should get for that particular year.

A budget may reflect a president's specific policy. President Reagan's budgets in 1981 and 1982 called for slower growth in spending for some social programs and increases in defense spending. Congress approved the first of these budgets but passed the second with modifications. After relations with the Soviet Union improved, the federal government began to reduce defense spending.

Section 2 Assessment

Checking for Understanding

1. **Main Idea** Use a graphic organizer like the one below to show how the budget process is affected if Congress and the president are from different political parties.

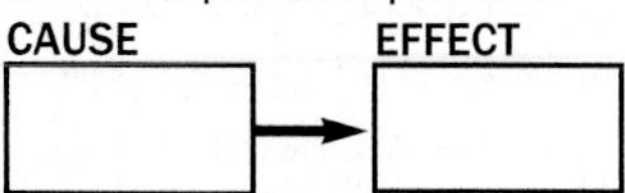

2. **Define** fiscal year, uncontrollables, entitlement, incrementalism.
3. **Identify** Office of Management and Budget, Congressional Budget Office.
4. Identify four entitlements that are a part of the federal budget.

Critical Thinking

5. **Expressing Problems Clearly** Why does the federal government find it difficult to raise taxes or reduce spending to balance the budget?

Public Policy Imagine that you are a part of a presidential committee set up to decide the spending priorities for next year's government budget. Your job is to list the four top areas that you think should have the greatest share of the budget. Prepare a supporting argument for the four areas you have chosen.

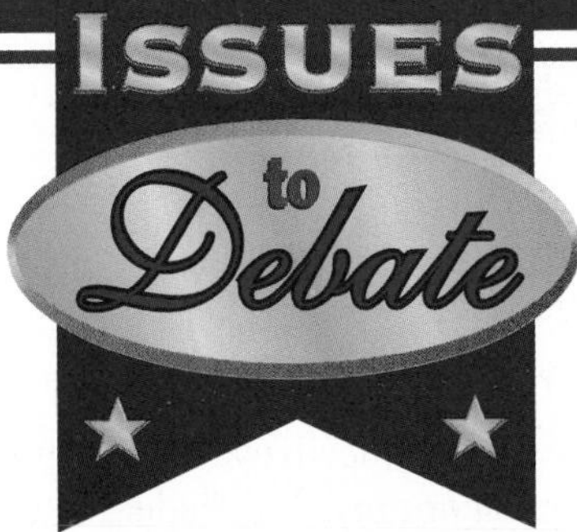

Should the Federal Income Tax Be Replaced?

For decades the income tax has provided the bulk of federal government revenue. The system operated by the IRS has been reliable in generating consistent federal tax revenues for many years. Despite this record, many people believe that the income tax should be replaced or undergo a major overhaul.

Taxpayer Complaints

American taxpayers provide the Internal Revenue Service (IRS) with information about their earnings each year. By filing their income tax returns, taxpayers save the government millions of hours of work. The tax withholding system works well to help people pay in advance so that they do not owe the government a large sum of money in April. However, some people complain that the system is too complicated. Others report that the IRS is either unresponsive to taxpayer questions or that it aggressively targets taxpayers who complain.

A Political Issue

Some politicians have suggested that the whole tax structure should be replaced. Steve Forbes, a former presidential candidate, suggested replacing the income tax with a flat tax. Another alternative would be a national sales tax. A sales tax, unlike the income tax, would not require an army of IRS agents to enforce the tax and check taxpayer returns. Tax loopholes that have developed with the current income tax would all be eliminated if the income tax were replaced.

IRS logo

Supporters of the income tax, however, point out that it is a progressive tax, collecting a larger percentage from more wealthy taxpayers than from poorer ones. The income tax can be used to redistribute wealth by giving tax credits to the poorest citizens. Making the system more efficient, not abandoning it, is the answer, they argue.

Debating the Issue

Would You Support or Replace the Federal Income Tax?

Assume that you are a taxpayer testifying at a congressional committee hearing, weighing the advantages and disadvantages of the income tax.

Key Issues

- ✔ How much time and effort does it take for the average person to complete and file his or her income tax returns?
- ✔ Is the IRS responsive to taxpayer questions?
- ✔ What are the advantages and disadvantages of this system of collections?
- ✔ What other form of taxation would provide fairer taxation with less effort?

Debate Prepare a statement in support of or against the income tax. Allow time for two people on each side of the argument to present their statements to the class.

Vote Make your decision. Then have the class vote for or against replacing the current income tax with another tax.

Section 3

Managing the Economy

Reader's Guide

Key Terms

fiscal policy, monetary policy, gross national product (GNP), discount rate, reserve requirement, open-market operations

Find Out

- What is the difference between fiscal policy and monetary policy?
- What are the four major categories of federal government spending?

Understanding Concepts

Public Policy Why must the Fed operate free of pressures from Congress or the president?

COVER STORY

Rate Hikes Near End

WASHINGTON, D.C., SEPTEMBER 11, 2000

Under the guidance of Federal Reserve chairman Alan Greenspan, the Fed has boosted interest rates six times since June 1999. Its goal was to slow the economy and keep inflation under strict control.

Cartoon depicting Chairman Greenspan

The hikes appear to have worked. Economists now forecast only small inflation gains—3.3 percent for 2000 and 2.7 percent for 2001. At the same time, they predict continued gains in productivity. How? Computers, satellites, and other technological advances have helped increase workers' efficiency in what has come to be called the "New Economy."

Federal government policy has a significant bearing on the economy. The Federal Reserve Board's decisions affect the money supply. Officials in both the executive and the legislative branches make difficult decisions to try to promote a healthy economy.

Where the Money Goes

The federal government was spending about $3 billion a year when Franklin D. Roosevelt became president in 1933. Today, that amount would pay for less than one day of the federal government's expenditures. The government currently spends more than $1.5 trillion a year.

How can a person imagine such a large amount of money? Perhaps it is more meaningful to break the total amount down into its four major components. Besides interest on the national debt, the main spending items are direct benefit payments to individuals, national defense, and discretionary spending.

Direct Benefit Payments Spending for Social Security, social-welfare, and health-care programs has become one of the biggest items in the federal budget. Almost half of every dollar spent goes for such items. In a recent budget, the federal government allocated about $960 billion for direct benefit payments of one kind or another.

Uncontrollable expenditures account for a large portion of this budget item. The biggest entitlement program is Social Security. In a recent year Social Security benefits totaled $350 billion.

National Defense Spending for national defense was one of the biggest items in the budget beginning with World War II. When Ronald Reagan became president in 1981, he made a bigger Defense Department budget a major objective of his administration. He felt that the world situation called for further increases in spending for military equipment and training.

When sweeping changes in the Soviet Union and Eastern Europe signaled an end to the Cold War, President Bush announced major changes in United States defense. He said he would eliminate some nuclear weapons and end the round-the-clock alert posture of strategic bombers. The president said:

> *"We can now take steps to make the world a less dangerous place than ever before in the nuclear age. I have asked the Soviets to go down this road with us—to destroy their entire inventory of ground-launched theater nuclear weapons."*
>
> —President George Bush, September 27, 1991

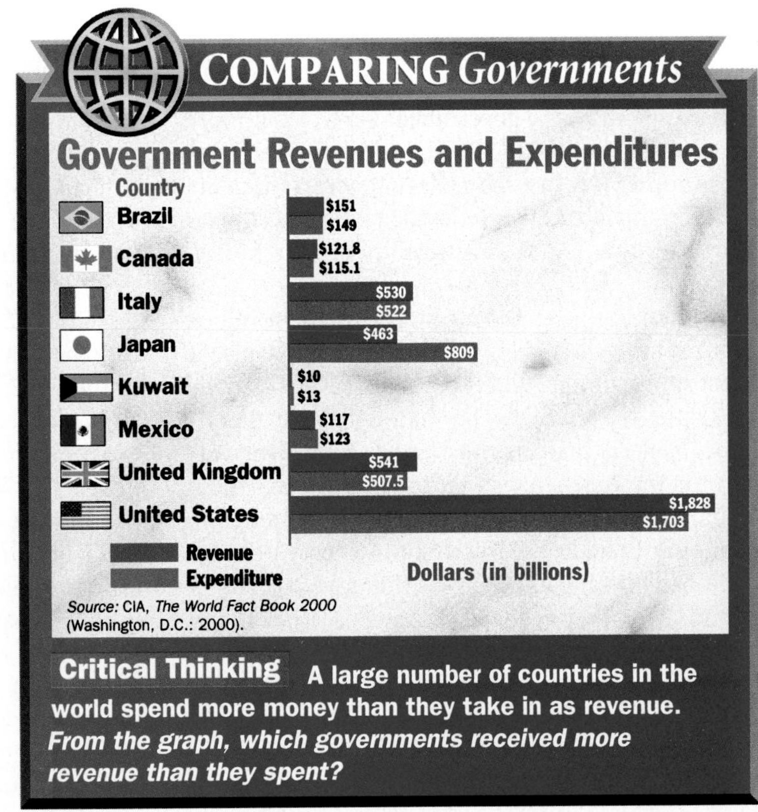

Critical Thinking A large number of countries in the world spend more money than they take in as revenue. *From the graph, which governments received more revenue than they spent?*

Since then, the federal government has gradually reduced the share of the budget that goes to defense. In 1996 defense spending represented about 16 percent of total outlays, down from about 21 percent in 1992.

Discretionary Spending The federal government spends a sizable portion of tax revenues on the environment, transportation, criminal justice, and other areas. Much of this discretionary spending is in the form of grants to states and localities. State and local governments use federal grants for road repair, public housing, police training, school lunch programs, flood insurance, and so on.

States and communities have come to rely on this intergovernmental revenue for an increasing share of their total revenue. Between 1980 and 1989, however, federal grants to state and local governments declined. More recent federal budgets have increased federal aid to states while shifting federal grants away from infrastructure investments and toward public-welfare programs.

Fiscal and Monetary Policy

Beginning with the Great Depression of the 1930s, the federal government has taken an increasing role in managing the nation's economy. Arguments continue over just how large a part the government should play. Debates arise because, in the modified free-enterprise system, control over the economy is divided between government and the private sector—individuals and businesses. Yet most Americans expect the federal government to play a significant role in moderating the economy's ups and downs, while promoting steady economic growth.

The government uses two primary devices to influence the direction of the economy: (1) fiscal policy and (2) monetary policy. **Fiscal policy** involves using government spending and taxation to influence the economy. **Monetary policy** involves controlling the supply of money and credit to influence the economy. This control is exercised through the Federal Reserve System.

Fiscal Policy The federal budget is a major tool of fiscal policy because it shapes how much money the government will spend and how much it will collect through taxes and borrowing. The president and Congress can use the budget to pump money into the economy to stimulate it, or to take money out of the economy to slow it down.

To stimulate the economy, the government may spend more money than it takes in. Through increased spending the government aims to put more people back to work and increase economic activity.

Another way that the government can stimulate the economy is through reducing taxes. Lower taxes give consumers and investors more purchasing power.

When the government increases spending or reduces taxes, it is likely to run a deficit because it must spend money that it does not have. Since the 1930s the United States has had deficit, or unbalanced, federal budgets most of the time. One reason for these deficits is that for many years these unbalanced budgets were thought to benefit the economy. In addition, this policy was very popular politically because it allowed the government to spend heavily on social programs that many Americans were demanding.

This policy of deficit spending led to increasingly large budget deficits and a growing national debt. During the 1970s and early 1980s, economists began to worry about the effects this would have on the nation's future.

Demands for cutting the deficit and even balancing the budget grew. Many economists, however, argued that a balanced budget would mean the federal government could not use fiscal policy to shape the economy. Some said that the deficit as a percentage of the **gross national product (GNP)** was more important than the deficit alone. The GNP is the sum of all goods and services produced in the nation in a year. They pointed out that the deficit still represented only 5 to 6 percent of the GNP.

Other economists disagreed. They pointed to the rapid growth of the deficit and of the national debt itself. When Congress promised to balance the budget in 1981, the gross federal debt was $995 billion. In 2000 it reached $5,653 billion ($5.7 trillion). Interest payments on the debt nearly equaled spending for defense.

Monetary Policy The United States economy is a money economy. Americans exchange goods and services through a vast system of money and credit. The Constitution gives the national government authority to "coin money [and] regulate the value thereof." Today, the federal government tries to regulate the economy through its monetary policy.

Monetary policy involves controlling the supply of money and the cost of borrowing money—credit—according to the needs of the economy. The government controls the money supply through the Federal Reserve System.

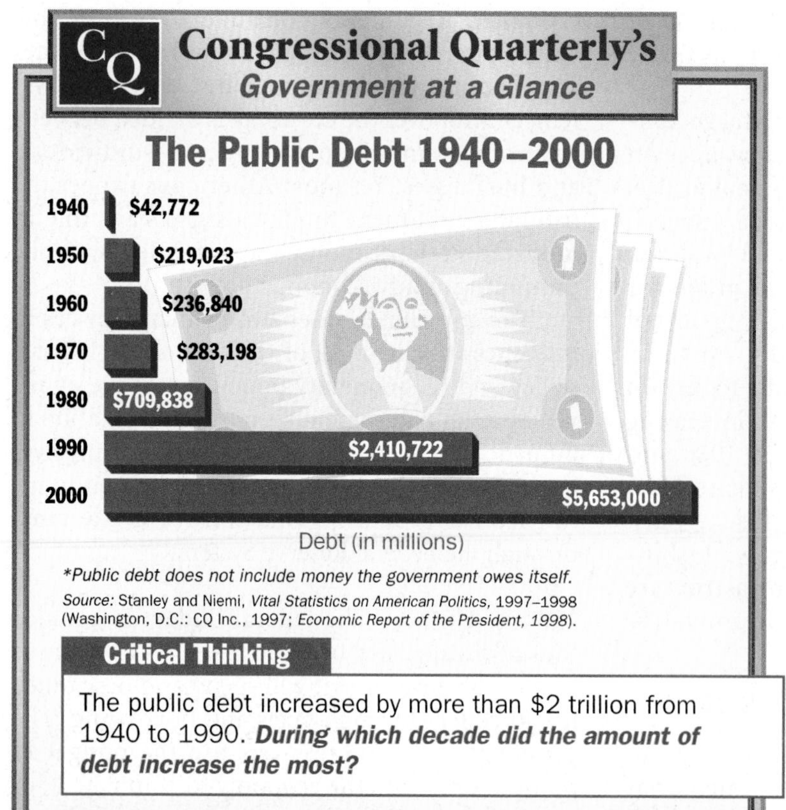

*Public debt does not include money the government owes itself.

Source: Stanley and Niemi, *Vital Statistics on American Politics, 1997–1998* (Washington, D.C.: CQ Inc., 1997; *Economic Report of the President, 1998*).

Critical Thinking

The public debt increased by more than $2 trillion from 1940 to 1990. ***During which decade did the amount of debt increase the most?***

The Federal Reserve System

The Federal Reserve System, known as **the Fed,** is the central banking system of the United States. When people or corporations need money, they may borrow from a bank. When banks need money, they may go to the Fed. Thus, in reality, the Federal Reserve System is a banker's bank.

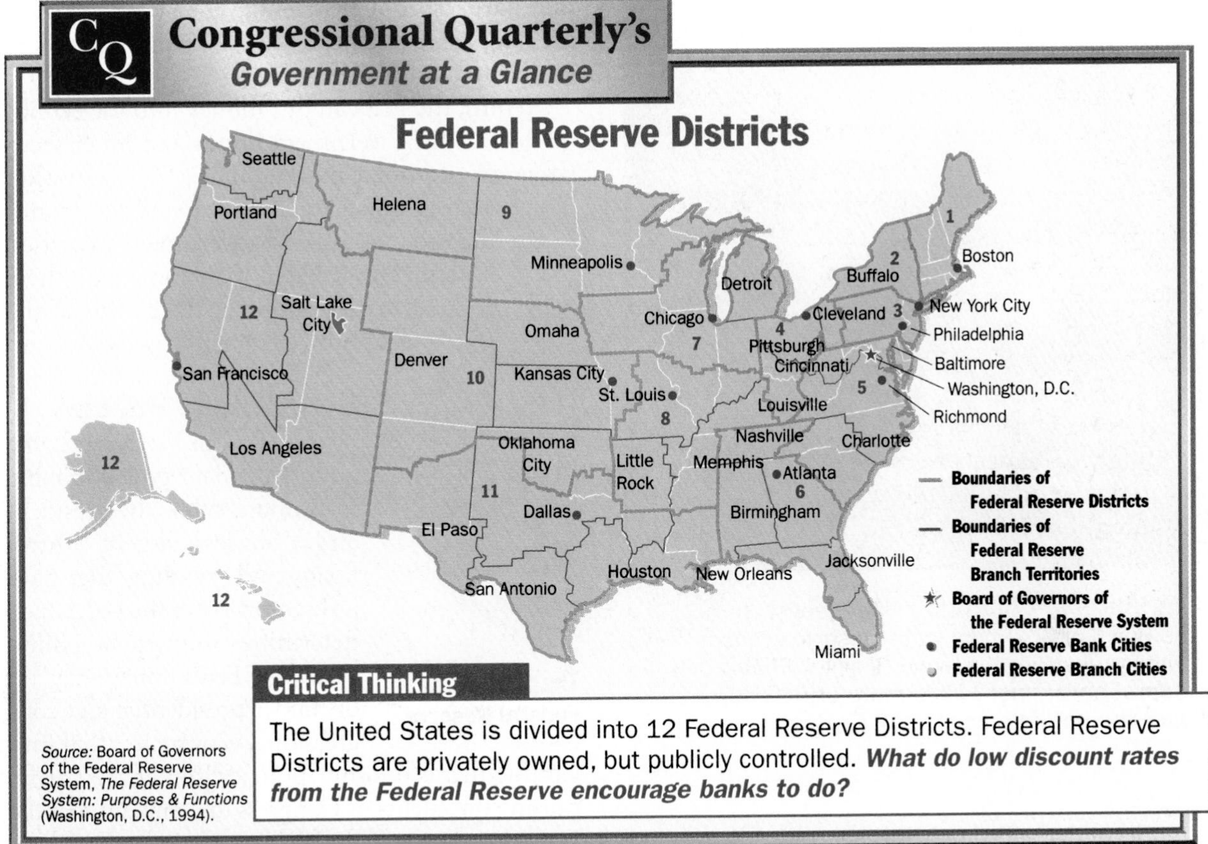

Critical Thinking

The United States is divided into 12 Federal Reserve Districts. Federal Reserve Districts are privately owned, but publicly controlled. ***What do low discount rates from the Federal Reserve encourage banks to do?***

Source: Board of Governors of the Federal Reserve System, *The Federal Reserve System: Purposes & Functions* (Washington, D.C., 1994).

Organization of the Fed The United States is divided into 12 Federal Reserve Districts. Each district has 1 main Federal Reserve Bank. In addition, most Federal Reserve Banks have branch banks within their districts.

About 5,700 of the approximately 13,600 banks in the United States are members of the Federal Reserve System. These include all the large banks in the country. These member banks control the largest share of total bank deposits in the United States.

Board of Governors A 7-member **Board of Governors** in Washington, D.C., supervises the entire Federal Reserve System. The president selects these members whose appointments must be ratified, or approved, by the Senate. The president selects one of the board members to chair the Board of Governors for a 4-year term.

Once appointed, board members and the chairperson are independent of the president. Even Congress exercises little control or influence over the board, since the board does not depend on Congress for an annual appropriation for operating expenses. This allows the Board of Governors to make economic decisions independent of political pressure.

Making Monetary Policy The Board of Governors has two major responsibilities in forming monetary policy. First, it supervises the operations of the Federal Reserve Banks in the 12 districts across the country. Second, and most important, it determines the general money and credit policies of the United States.

The Fed uses three main tools to control the financial activities of the nation's banks and, through them, the nation's monetary policy. First, the Fed can raise or lower the discount rate. The **discount rate** is the rate the Fed charges member banks for loans. Low discount rates encourage banks to borrow money from the Fed to make loans to their customers. High discount rates mean banks will borrow less money from the Fed.

Controller of the Money Supply

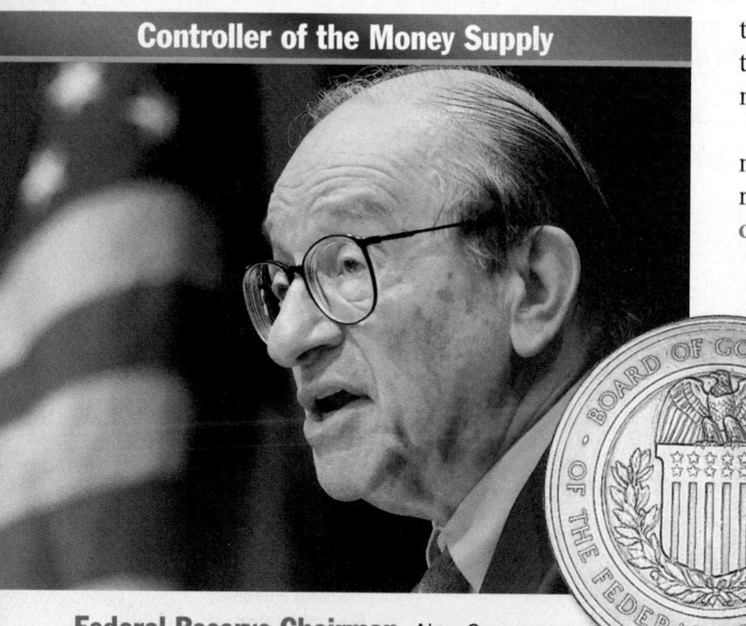

Federal Reserve Chairman Alan Greenspan and the Board of Governors try to preserve economic growth by regulating the money supply. ***Should the federal government have more or less control over the nation's economy? Explain.***

The seal of the Federal Reserve

Second, the Fed may raise or lower the **reserve requirement** for member banks. Member banks must keep a certain percentage of their money in Federal Reserve Banks as a reserve against their deposits. If the Fed raises the reserve requirement, banks must leave more money with the Fed. Thus, they have less money to lend. When the Fed lowers the reserve requirement, member banks have more money to lend.

Third, the Fed can put money into the economy by buying government bonds and other securities on the open market. These **open-market operations** stimulate and help expand the economy. The Fed may also sell government securities. As investors spend their money on these securities, money is taken out of the economy, causing it to slow down.

Conflicting Policies In recent years the Fed has become an independent policy-making institution. While the president and Congress largely control taxing and spending, they have little control over the Fed, which determines monetary policy. Thus, the Fed's policy may aid or hinder presidential and congressional economic programs. Conflicting economic policies sometimes arise, causing presidents or Congress to complain that the Fed is interfering with their economic programs.

Because of such conflicts, some people would like to limit the Fed's role and make it less independent. Others maintain that the nation needs an institution removed from political pressures to watch over monetary policy.

Section 3 Assessment

Checking for Understanding

1. **Main Idea** Use a graphic organizer like the one below to compare recent federal grants with those in the 1980s.

Federal Grants	
1980s	Recently

2. **Define** fiscal policy, monetary policy, gross national product (GNP), discount rate, reserve requirement, open-market operations.
3. **Identify** the Federal Reserve System, Board of Governors.
4. What are the four main spending categories of the federal government?

Critical Thinking

5. **Identifying Alternatives** What methods could the federal government use to stimulate the economy during a time when people were opposed to deficit spending?

Public Policy Research several back issues of *The Wall Street Journal* or selections from the *Readers' Guide to Periodical Literature* to identify instances when Federal Reserve Board decisions affected the economy. Create a poster of headline captions showing the Fed's actions.

Using the Internet

To learn more about almost any topic imaginable, use the Internet. The Internet, often referred to as the "Net," is a global network of computers. The Internet provides a medium in which one can research and share information, and collaborate with others on a variety of fronts. Many features, such as E-mail, interactive educational classes, and even shopping services, are offered on the Net. To get on the Internet you will need three things:

1. A personal computer
2. A modem—a device that connects your computer to a telephone line
3. An account with an Internet Service Provider (ISP). An Internet Service Provider (such as AOL or a local Internet Service Provider) is a company that enables you to log on to the Internet, usually for a fee.

Learning the Skill

Once you are connected, the easiest way to access Internet sites and information is to use a "Web browser." A Web browser is a program that lets you view and explore information on the World Wide Web. The World Wide Web consists of documents called Web pages, and each page on the Web is referred to as a site. Each Web page has its own address, or URL. Many URLs start with a *http://* prefix.

Practicing the Skill

This chapter focuses on the tax and spending policies of our government. Follow these steps to learn more about government finances.

1. Log on to the Internet and access a World Wide Web search engine, such as Yahoo, Lycos, or WebCrawler.

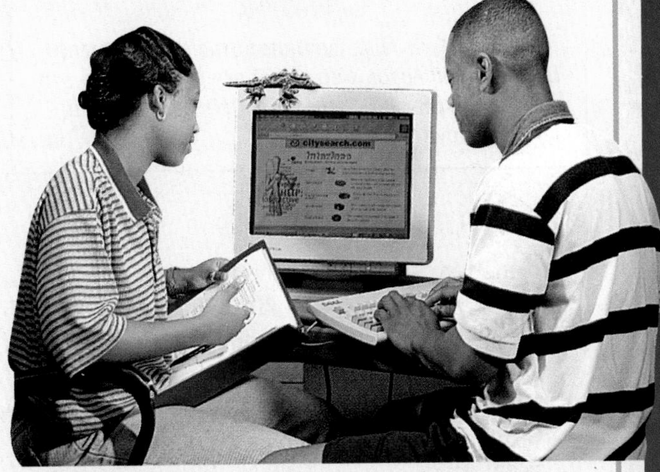

Surfing the Net

2. Search by selecting one of the listed categories or by typing in the subject you want to find, such as *government finances.*
3. Continue your search by scrolling down the list that appears on your screen. When you select an entry, click on it to access the information. Sometimes the information you first access will not be exactly what you need. If so, continue searching until you find the information that you want. Use what you find to create a graph or chart on some aspect of local, state, or national government finances.

Application Activity

Follow this procedure to locate information about the budget of the federal government. Use the information you gather to create a chart or graph depicting how the government allocates its funds.

Chapter 20

Assessment and Activities

GOVERNMENT Online

Self-Check Quiz Visit the *United States Government: Democracy in Action* Web site at gov.glencoe.com and click on ***Chapter 20–Self-Check Quizzes*** to prepare for the chapter test.

Reviewing Key Terms

Insert the terms below into the following paragraph to describe how the federal government regulates the economy. Do not use a term more than once.

withholding	**securities**
national debt	**taxes**
taxable income	**incrementalism**
fiscal policy	**GNP**
monetary policy	**fiscal year**
entitlements	**uncontrollables**

The federal government collects more than $1 trillion in (1) each year. Through (2) wage earners pay taxes on their (3) during the year. The government's (4) begins on October 1. Because of (5) such as (6) in the budget, government spending often exceeds revenue, which enlarges the (7). Some economists are not alarmed because deficits are only about 5 percent of the (8). Others would like to see changes in (9) to control spending or raise taxes. By its (10) the Fed may stimulate economic growth to relieve some of these concerns.

Recalling Facts

1. What is the deadline for filing individual income tax returns?
2. Identify three institutions that are exempt from the federal income tax.
3. What are three responsibilities of the Internal Revenue Service?
4. What are four types of taxes that the federal government collects?
5. What executive agency is charged with preparing the federal budget?
6. Why are federal securities such as bonds popular with investors?
7. What is the goal of the Gramm-Rudman-Hollings Act?
8. What factors make it difficult for Congress to cut spending?
9. Identify state and local uses of intergovernmental revenues.

Understanding Concepts

1. **Civic Participation** How do self-employed people provide withholding of their income taxes?
2. **Public Policy** Why has the United States been unable to balance the national budget most of the time beginning in the 1930s?
3. **Public Policy** What kinds of banks are members of the Federal Reserve System?

Critical Thinking

1. **Making Generalizations** Why would business or labor groups support protective tariffs?
2. **Analyzing Information** What budgetary decisions would the federal government face if an international development threatened world peace?

Current Events JOURNAL

Tax Record Keep track of and list the types of taxes that you and your family pay over a one-week period. Use your information to create a table identifying the types of taxes you pay, and compare your information with that of your classmates.

3. **Identifying Alternatives** Use a graphic organizer like the one below to show two measures the federal government could take if the national debt seemed to be growing too fast.

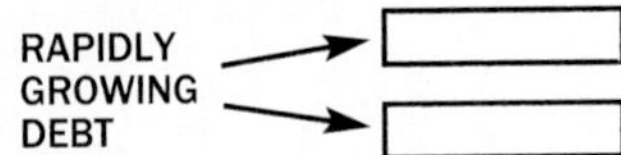

4. **Analyzing Information** Why must the Federal Reserve Board of Governors operate free of pressure from the president or Congress?

Interpreting Political Cartoons Activity

1. What is this man doing?
2. How does he seem to feel about this?
3. Do you think this man's feelings are representative of the general feeling of taxpayers? Explain.

Cooperative Learning Activity

Visualizing the Debt Organize the class into five equal groups. Each group should make a poster to illustrate the national debt—currently about $5 trillion. Use photos, illustrations, symbols, or other art pieces to show various but concrete representations of how large this debt is. For example, the debt represents 1 billion sports cars valued at $50,000 each.

Technology Activity

Using Software One of the ways the Federal Reserve System controls the financial activities of the nation's banks is by raising and lowering the discount rate, the rate of interest it charges on its loans to other banks. Banks base the interest rates they charge on the Fed's discount rate. On the Internet or at your library research the Federal Reserve System's discount rate from 1990 to the present. Use the graphing options of your software to design a line graph illustrating this information. Based on the information on your graph, identify the best periods for people to borrow money from banks.

Skill Practice Activity

Using the Internet Go through the steps described in the Skill to search the Internet for information on the IRS. Write an article for the school newspaper or magazine based on the information you retrieve about your topic.

Participating in Local Government

Review the various kinds of taxes that are sources of revenue for local governments. Working in groups of three, complete the following tasks:

1. Identify three needs that your community has.
2. Estimate the amount of taxes that would need to be raised to meet these needs.
3. Determine whether any current tax rate may be increased to meet one or more of these needs.
4. Decide on any additional fair tax to raise money to benefit the needs that you have identified.
5. Discuss whether people will be in favor of additional taxes to meet these needs.

Chapter 21

Social and Domestic Policy

Why It's Important

Impact of Policy National policy affects your economic decisions, your education, your health, and much more. This chapter describes the important policy choices that your government makes. It also examines how political issues affect social and domestic policy.

To learn more about how social and domestic policy is established, view the ***Democracy In Action*** Chapter 21 video lesson:

Social and Domestic Policies

GOVERNMENT Online

Chapter Overview Visit the *United States Government: Democracy in Action* Web site at gov.glencoe.com and click on ***Chapter 21–Overview*** to preview chapter information.

Section 1

Business and Labor Policy

Reader's Guide

Key Terms

mixed economy, laissez-faire, trust, monopoly, interlocking directorate, oligopoly, securities, collective bargaining, injunction

Find Out

- What are the overall aims of United States business policy regarding competition and consumers?
- How did the federal government help unions to organize and grow?

Understanding Concepts

Free Enterprise Are government regulations consistent with the principle of free enterprise? Explain your answer.

COVER STORY

Scholarship Scams

WASHINGTON, D.C., SEPTEMBER 1996

The Federal Trade Commission (FTC) has issued a consumer alert about crooked scholarship offers. The FTC cautions that fraudulent companies are promising students scholarships in return for an up-front fee. Most offer a money-back guarantee but make it difficult to get a refund. Some companies ask for a checking account number, "to confirm the student's eligibility," and then debit the account without the student's consent. Many scholarship services charge a fee, but the FTC advises that a legitimate company will never guarantee a scholarship.

Successful recipient of legitimate scholarship

◀ Yosemite Valley is preserved by the government.

The Federal Trade Commission is just one of many government agencies involved in regulating the American economy. Although free enterprise is the foundation of the American economic system, ours is a **mixed economy**—a system in which the government both supports and regulates private enterprise.

Promoting and Protecting Business

Regulating business is a relatively recent function of the federal government, dating back slightly more than 100 years. The active promotion and protection of business, however, has been a major activity of United States government since George Washington was president. Washington's secretary of the treasury, Alexander Hamilton, claimed that emerging American manufacturers needed protection from foreign competition. He first proposed a protective tariff in 1791, but Congress shelved the request. After the War of 1812, British goods flooded American markets, threatening to destroy newly created industries. A member of Parliament in 1816 explained Britain's advantage:

> *"It was well worth while to incur a loss upon the first exportation, in order, by the glut, to stifle in the cradle, those rising manufactures in the United States, which the war has forced into existence, contrary to the natural course of things."*
>
> —Henry Brougham, Esq., 1816

The United States responded to this threat with higher tariffs.

Free Trade In recent years the federal government has emphasized lower tariffs and promoted free trade for many items. The North American Free Trade Agreement (NAFTA),

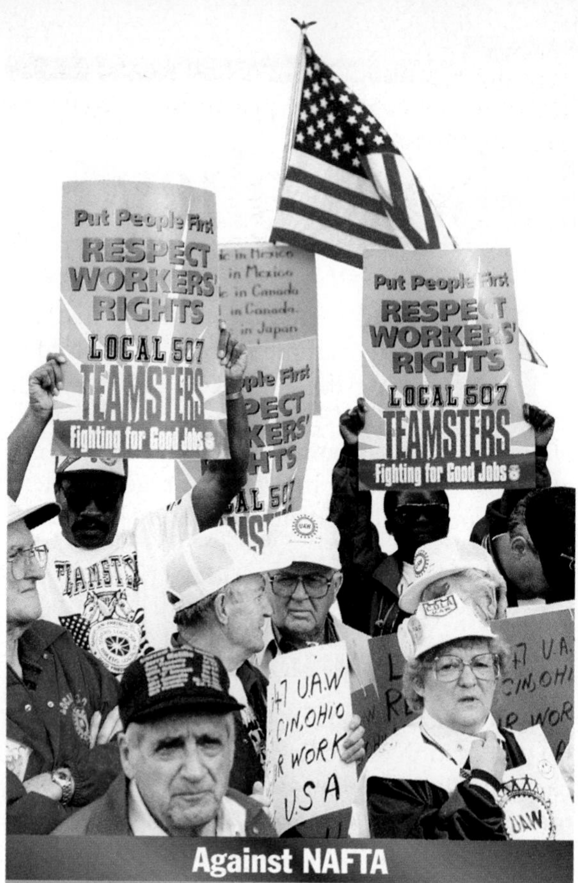

Against NAFTA

Trade Policy Many Americans, especially supporters of labor unions, have strongly opposed NAFTA. Supporters of NAFTA, however, believe that the agreement will lower costs for consumers and expand U.S. markets. ***Why are labor unions opposed to NAFTA?***

signed by Canada, Mexico, and the United States in 1994, was designed to gradually eliminate trade restrictions among the trading partners. The United States plays a leading role in promoting free trade around the world.

Consumers benefit from the lower cost of many imported goods. Although current rates are at an all-time low, tariffs are still used to protect American industries from foreign competition. The government also restricts some products through quotas, or limits on the number that may be imported.

Types of Federal Subsidies Today the federal government provides four types of subsidies, or aids to business. One is tax incentives that allow businesses to deduct certain expenses from their annual tax returns. A second is government loans, or credit subsidies, that provide funds for businesses at low interest rates. A third type of subsidy is free services, such as weather information, census reports, and other information valuable to businesses across the nation. Finally, the government provides direct cash payments to businesses whose products or services are considered vital to the general public. Businesses in the field of transportation often receive this type of subsidy.

Commerce Department Aid to Business

A separate department of the executive branch, the Department of Commerce, was formed in 1913 for the sole purpose of promoting business interests. Congress mandated that the department "foster, promote, and develop the foreign and domestic commerce of the United States."

The main functions of the Commerce Department are to provide information services, financial assistance, and research and development services. Several agencies within the Commerce Department supply businesses with valuable information and subsidies, particularly the Bureau of the Census, which provides important economic data to businesses.

Help for Small Businesses Because competition is important to the free-enterprise system, the federal government tries to help small businesses. An important independent executive agency outside the Commerce Department that aids businesses is the Small Business Administration (SBA). In addition to offering credit subsidies, the SBA gives free advice and information to small business firms.

Regional offices of the SBA offer government-sponsored classes on sound management practices for owners of small businesses. Businesses may also seek advice from the SBA on how to overcome their problems, and the SBA also conducts programs to help women and minorities in business.

Regulating Business

Some Americans believe that government regulation of the economy is at best a mixed blessing. These people usually agree with the following sentiments expressed by economist Arthur B. Laffer:

> *Those who advocate, in their desperation, more government to solve the problems of our society are demonstrably wrong. . . . The solution rests in less—not more—government!*
>
> —Arthur B. Laffer

Writer Victor Kamber expressed the opposite point of view. In Kamber's opinion:

> *Many Americans have forgotten that we set up regulatory agencies in the first place to protect the public interest. Industries considered vital to the public—such as transportation, food, finance, communications, and nuclear power—were regulated in order to provide the public a steady flow of safe products in a stable environment.*
>
> —Victor Kamber, July 1984

Whether a person agrees with one point of view or the other sometimes depends upon whether the person is being regulated or is benefiting from the regulation. Nevertheless, federal regulation of economic activity springs from a constitutional provision.

Constitutional Basis of Regulation The Constitution grants Congress the power to "lay and collect taxes" for the general welfare and to "regulate commerce . . . among the several states." Most regulatory laws enacted in the twentieth century are based upon these two powers.

The commerce clause in Article I, Section 8,[1] provides the primary constitutional basis for government regulation of the economy. The Founders designed this clause to allow the federal government to control interstate commerce, eliminating one major deficiency of the Articles of Confederation. Over the years the Supreme Court has broadened the interpretation of interstate commerce to include a wide variety of economic activities. For example, interstate commerce today covers the

See the following footnoted materials in the **Reference Handbook:**
1. *The Constitution,* pages 774–799.

We the People
Making a Difference
Henry B. Gonzalez

Texas state seal

After serving for 36 years, 81-year-old Democratic representative Henry B. Gonzalez retired in 1997. Gonzalez arrived on Capitol Hill in 1961 where he quickly earned a reputation as an unpredictable maverick who often refused to work within established traditions. In his hometown, however, he is celebrated as a defender of the downtrodden. Raul Yzaguirre, president of the National Council of La Raza, summarized Gonzalez's character: "He was a pioneer. In the bad old '40s and '50s, political courage to stand up to segregation and racism was not real evident. Henry B. stood out like a giant."

Gonzalez is credited with crafting tough savings-and-loan bailout legislation and pushing an overhaul of banks' deposit insurance system. His passionate commitment, though, was in ensuring affordable housing for the poor.

When some Democratic leaders tried to topple Gonzalez from his ranking spot on the Banking and Finance Committee, Gonzalez's supporters rallied. Joseph Kennedy of Massachusetts pronounced, "What are we going to do, take away a ranking membership from a guy who is a folk hero among Democrats?" Gonzalez made a masterful speech in his own defense, saying, "I say to you, I have served with honor and integrity and success. I have never failed myself and I have never failed you." Gonzalez received two standing ovations and retained his seat.

production and transportation of goods, communications, mining, and the sale of stocks and bonds. Citing the commerce clause, Congress has passed many laws regulating these activities. Moreover, the meaning of regulation has changed over the years. Besides restricting certain activities, regulation now includes prohibiting, promoting, protecting, assisting, and establishing standards for many aspects of interstate commerce.

Demand for Reform Until the late 1800s, the federal government for the most part took a hands-off, or laissez-faire, approach to the economy. The states passed the few regulations that limited business activities. Businesses were generally small, locally owned, and primarily served local markets.

By the late 1800s, the American economy had changed. Huge corporations dominated American industry. Rapid industrialization was accompanied by many abuses. Business combinations consolidated control of several industries in the hands of a few giant corporations that squeezed smaller companies out of business. Americans questioned the fairness of a system that allowed railroads to charge higher rates for farmers than for manufacturers. Because of these abuses, Americans began to demand government regulation of business.

Congress responded by passing the Interstate Commerce Act in 1887. This act established the first federal regulatory agency, the Interstate Commerce Commission (ICC), and placed certain limits on the freight rates railroad companies charged. Congress later passed two measures to control corporations that threatened to destroy competition.

The Sherman and Clayton Antitrust Acts

In the late 1800s, the trust became a popular form of business consolidation. In a trust several corporations combined their stock and allowed a board of trustees to run the corporations as one giant enterprise. The trustees could set production quotas, fix prices, and control the market, thereby creating a monopoly. A monopoly is a business that controls so much of a product, service, or industry that little or no competition exists.

The Standard Oil Trust organized by John D. Rockefeller was an example of such a trust. In 1879 it controlled the production and sale of 90 percent of the oil refined in the United States. The Standard Oil Trust consisted of several oil companies whose stock was held by a single board of trustees. The chief stockholder and trustee was Rockefeller himself. At the time, monopolistic trusts like Rockefeller's dominated many industries.

Congress's first attempt to halt monopolies came in 1890 with the passage of the **Sherman Antitrust Act.** The first two sections of the act stated the following:

> *"Every contract, combination in the form of trust or otherwise, or conspiracy, in restraint of trade or commerce among the several states, or with foreign nations is hereby declared illegal.*
>
> *Every person who shall monopolize, or attempt to monopolize, or combine or conspire with any other person or persons to monopolize any part of the trade or commerce among the several states . . . shall be guilty of a misdemeanor."*
>
> —Sherman Antitrust Act, 1890

Today, violating the second section of the Sherman Antitrust Act is a felony.

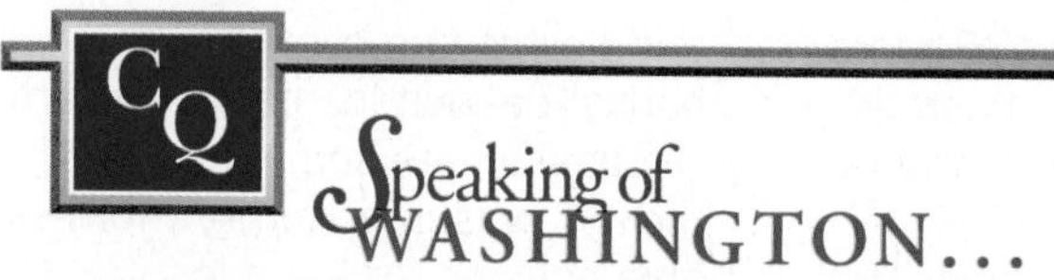

Deregulation Beginning with the administrations of Jimmy Carter and Ronald Reagan, regulation of businesses was eased in the 1970s and 1980s. On the theory that more competition would lower prices and improve efficiency, many industries were partly or completely deregulated, including the airline, banking, bus, cable television, railroad, and trucking industries. One measure of bureaucratic red tape and regulation is the number of pages in the *Federal Register,* where all new regulations are published. From 5,307 pages in 1940, the *Register* grew to 87,012 pages in 1980. By 1990, the total was down to 53,618 pages, with most of the decrease in economic regulation.

The language of the act did not specify what restraint of trade meant. The Sherman Antitrust Act, therefore, proved difficult to enforce. It was, however, successfully enforced in one notable case. In 1906 the federal government charged the Standard Oil Company with violating the first two sections of the act. Convicted, the company ultimately appealed to the Supreme Court, which upheld the conviction and ordered the company to be split into a number of smaller companies. For the first time in the nation's history, the government declared a major trust illegal.

Despite the conviction, the trend toward larger and larger business combinations continued. Then in 1914 Congress passed the **Clayton Antitrust Act** to clarify the Sherman Act. The Clayton Act prohibited charging high prices in an area where little competition existed, while at the same time charging lower prices in an area with strong competition. The act also said businesses could not buy stock in other corporations in order to reduce competition. Finally, the act addressed the control of companies by outlawing **interlocking directorates**—a circumstance in which the same people served on the boards of directors of competing companies.

Enforcing the Antitrust Laws

In the same year that Congress passed the Clayton Act, it established the Federal Trade Commission (FTC), an independent regulatory agency, to carry out the provisions of the Clayton Act. The commission may define unfair competitive practices, issue orders to halt these practices, examine corporate purchases of stock, and investigate trade practices. Since its creation the FTC's duties have expanded. Today the FTC has many responsibilities in addition to enforcing the Clayton Act. These include enforcing laws that prohibit false advertising and requiring truthful labels on textiles and furs. The FTC also regulates the packaging and labeling of certain consumer goods, requires full disclosure of the lending practices of finance companies and retailers who use installment plans, and checks consumer credit agencies.

Despite additional antitrust legislation passed since the Clayton Act, a few large corporations dominate several industries. Today, instead of trusts and monopolies, economic power belongs to oligopolies. An **oligopoly** exists when a few firms dominate a particular industry. By the 1990s about 50 multibillion-dollar companies controlled approximately one-third of the manufacturing capacity in the United States.

Enforcing the country's antitrust laws is the responsibility of the Antitrust Division of the Department of Justice. Working with the Federal Trade Commission, this division has the power to bring suit against suspected violators of antitrust laws.

Consumer Protection

Besides antitrust laws, Congress has passed other regulatory laws protecting consumers and ensuring fair product standards. Congress has also established independent regulatory agencies that protect consumers or regulate certain economic activities. These regulatory agencies are independent in the sense that they are largely beyond the control of the executive branch.

To maintain this independence, Congress decided that each agency would have from 5 to 11 members, each appointed by the president and confirmed by the Senate. Normally the term of each of the commissioners is long enough to prevent a president from appointing enough new members to control the agency. The president may remove a member only for certain reasons specified by Congress.

The types of independent regulatory agencies vary widely. Such agencies range from the Federal Reserve System, established in 1913, to the Consumer Product Safety Commission, established in 1972.

Consumer Protection Laws

Before 1900 many corporations were not overly concerned about whether their products were healthful or safe. Some truly deplorable practices were common in the food processing and drug industries. Some companies mislabeled foods and sold foods contaminated by additives. Other foods such as meat were tainted because of the unsanitary conditions in processing plants. Consumers were duped into buying medicines that were often worthless and sometimes dangerous.

Shortly after the turn of the century, Upton Sinclair, in his book *The Jungle,* described conditions in a meatpacking house. He wrote:

Disability and the Workplace

Free from discrimination

Today disabled people have recourse against discrimination in education, housing, transportation, and employment. The Americans with Disabilities Act (ADA) says that remedies under the Civil Rights Act of 1964 apply to ADA employment cases. The ADA bans inquiries about disabilities for job applicants. Also, employees are to be provided "reasonable accommodations" necessary to assist them in doing their jobs. The act also forbids employers to pay workers with disabilities less than nondisabled persons who do the same work and forbids discrimination in promotions.

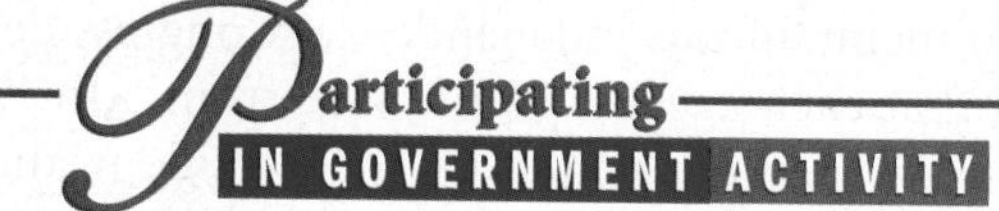

Make a List What would be "reasonable accommodations" for a person in a wheelchair working in a tall office building?

> *There would be meat stored in great piles in rooms; and the water from leaky roofs would drip over it, and thousands of rats would race about it. . . . These rats were nuisances, and the packers would put poisoned bread out for them; they would die, and then rats, bread, and meat would go into the hoppers together.*
>
> —Upton Sinclair, 1906

In addition to Sinclair's stinging condemnation, magazine articles about similar conditions aroused public indignation. As a result, Congress passed the Pure Food and Drug Act in 1906 to make it illegal for a company engaged in interstate commerce to sell contaminated, unhealthful, or falsely labeled foods or drugs. The Meat Inspection Act, also passed in 1906, provided for federal inspection of all meatpacking companies that sold meats across state lines.

The Food and Drug Administration (FDA) is responsible for protecting the public from poorly processed and improperly labeled foods and drugs. Scientists at FDA laboratories inspect and test prepared food, cosmetics, drugs, and thousands of other products every year. Agents from the FDA inspect factories, food processing plants, and drug laboratories. They also check labels for accuracy. If a product fails to meet FDA standards, the FDA may force it off the market.

Protection Against False Advertising The Federal Trade Commission (FTC) protects consumers from misleading and fraudulent advertising. The FTC has the power to review the advertising claims made about all products sold in interstate commerce. It may determine whether an advertisement for a product is false or unfair. If it is, the FTC can order a company to change the ad to comply with FTC standards. As a result of one FTC ruling, cigarette manufacturers must place a health warning on cigarette packages. According to another FTC regulation, all manufacturers must clearly list the contents of packaged products on the label.

Consumers and Product Safety Books and articles about the ways in which consumers are cheated and deceived in the marketplace have always been popular. One such book accelerated consumer activism in the 1960s. In 1965 Ralph Nader warned about poorly designed automobiles that were "unsafe at any speed." Nader became a leader in the consumer movement.

As a result of this movement, Congress created the Consumer Product Safety Commission (CPSC) in 1972. Its purpose was to protect consumers against "unreasonable risk of injury from hazardous products." To reduce consumer risks, the CPSC investigates injuries caused by merchandise, such as lawn mowers, kitchen appliances, toys, and sports equipment. It then establishes standards of safety for each type of consumer product. If any product fails to meet these standards, the CPSC can order it off the market.

Regulating the Sale of Stocks Another form of government regulation protects small investors from being misled about the value of stocks and bonds. Since 1934 the Securities and Exchange Commission (SEC) has regulated the trading of **securities**, or stocks and bonds.

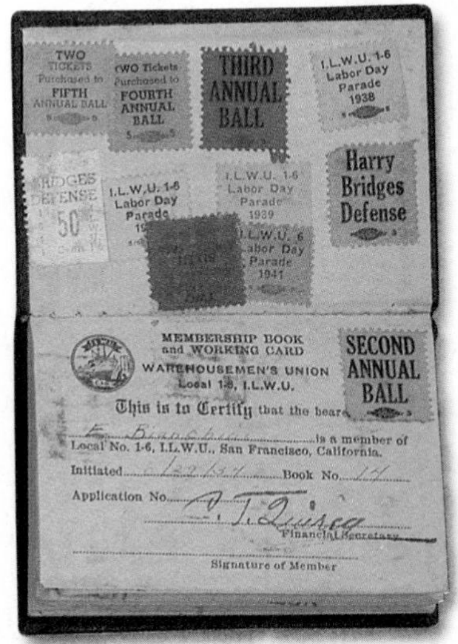

A warehouse worker's union membership material

The origins of the SEC go back to the stock market crash of October 1929. After the crash a congressional investigation uncovered many examples of fraud and unsound financing schemes in the nation's stock markets and brokerage houses. As a result, Congress created the SEC.

Today the SEC licenses people who sell securities in the national market, investigates cases of suspected fraud in the sale of securities, and regulates the nation's stock markets. It also regulates the securities issued by public utility companies and requires all corporations that issue public stock to file regular reports on their assets, profits, sales, and other financial data. These reports must be made available to investors so that they may judge the true value of a company's stock offerings.

Government and Labor

Federal law regulates the relationship between employers and employees. As large corporations multiplied in the late 1800s, the relationship between employer and employee first became impersonal, then deteriorated. Some businesses failed to provide a safe, clean work environment and fair wages. Employers used several methods to break up labor unions and fired workers who joined these organizations.

Protecting Unions and Workers Labor unions in the United States date back to the early 1800s. It was not until the 1850s, however, that the first nationwide union was organized. Under pressure from employers, and without support from the federal government, early unions failed to survive for very long. The first successful national union, the American Federation of Labor, was founded in the 1880s.

Workers organized unions and elected leaders to represent them in negotiations with employers for labor contracts that specified wages, hours, and working conditions. This practice of negotiating labor contracts is known as **collective bargaining.**

Employers generally refused to negotiate with unions. As a result, unions often resorted to strikes to try to obtain concessions. Between 1881 and 1905, American unions called about 37,000 strikes.

For many years, the government favored business at the expense of labor unions. Federal troops and state militia broke up some strikes. The courts even used the Sherman Antitrust Act, originally intended to regulate business, to prohibit union activities as being in "restraint of trade."

The government's attitude toward labor began to change in the early 1900s. The Clayton Antitrust Act, passed in 1914, included a provision that labor unions were not to be treated as "conspiracies in restraint of trade." Before the 1930s employers were often successful in challenging laws that regulated wages and working conditions. In 1937, however, the Supreme Court heard an appeal of a case in which a state had written a minimum wage law to protect women and children.

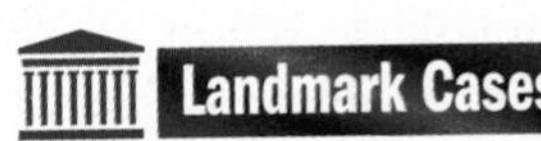

West Coast Hotel* v. *Parrish Elsie Parrish, a hotel employee, brought suit to recover the difference between the wages paid her and the minimum wage. The hotel owner claimed that the law deprived the employer of freedom of contract. The Supreme Court, however, upheld the minimum

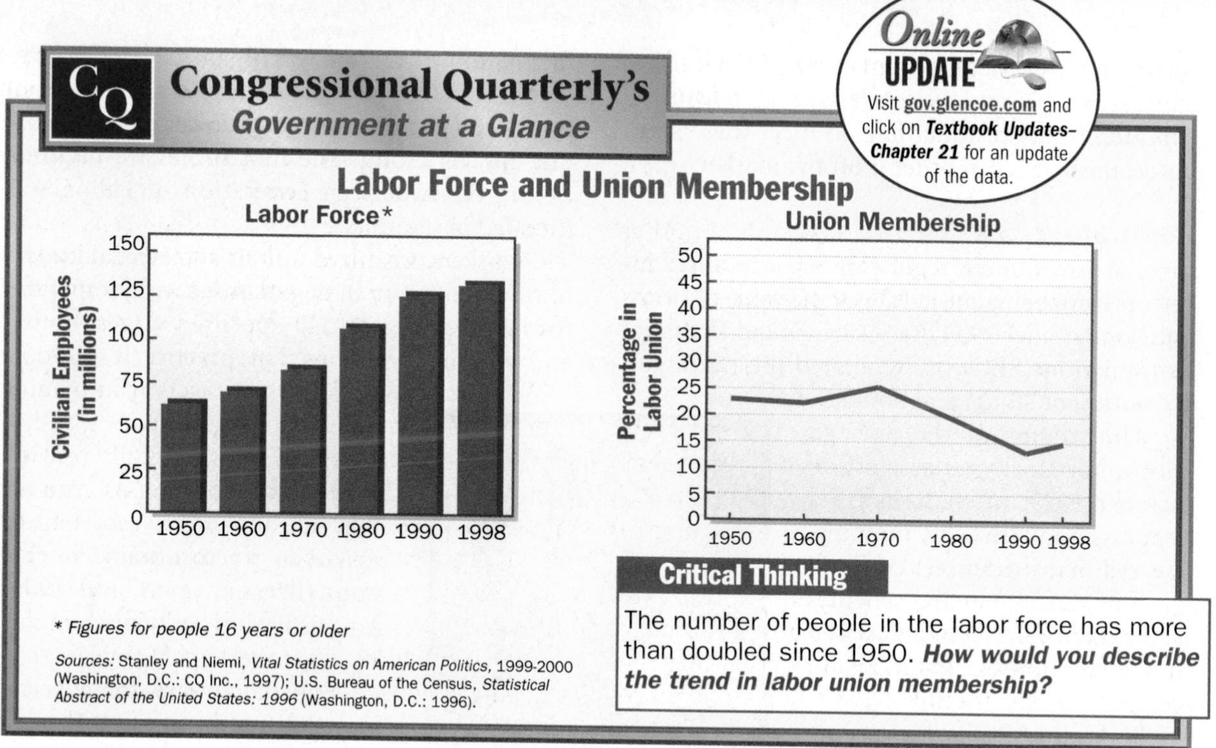

* *Figures for people 16 years or older*

Sources: Stanley and Niemi, *Vital Statistics on American Politics, 1999-2000* (Washington, D.C.: CQ Inc., 1997); U.S. Bureau of the Census, *Statistical Abstract of the United States: 1996* (Washington, D.C.: 1996).

wage set by the Industrial Welfare Committee of the state of Washington, saying:

> "*The exploitation of a class of workers who are in an unequal position with respect to bargaining power and are thus relatively defenseless against the denial of a living wage is not only detrimental to their health and well-being, but casts a direct burden for their support upon the community. . . . The community may direct its lawmaking power to correct the abuse.*"
>
> —Chief Justice Charles Evans Hughes, 1937

Today laws set minimum wages and maximum working hours and prohibit child labor. In addition, the Department of Labor, established in 1913, provides employment offices and job-training programs for people in search of a job, collects helpful data, and offers unemployment insurance.

Labor Laws of the 1930s The greatest gains of organized labor occurred during the Great Depression of the 1930s with the passage of revolutionary labor laws. These laws, passed under President Roosevelt's New Deal, are often called "labor's bill of rights." They guaranteed labor's right to bargain collectively and strike, and generally strengthened labor unions.

In 1932 Congress passed the Norris-La Guardia Act that gave workers the right to join unions and to strike. It outlawed yellow-dog contracts, which forced workers to sign contracts agreeing not to join a union. The act also restricted the use of federal court injunctions against labor unions. **Injunctions**—court orders to prevent an action from taking place—were often issued to force striking unions back to work.

In 1935 Congress passed the **Wagner Act,** guaranteeing the right of all workers to organize and bargain collectively. To achieve this goal, the law prohibited employers from engaging in certain "unfair labor practices." According to the Wagner Act, employers could not refuse to bargain collectively with recognized unions, interfere in union organization, or discharge or otherwise punish a worker because of union activities.

To enforce these prohibitions, the Wagner Act created the National Labor Relations Board (NLRB). The board had power to supervise elections to determine which union a group of workers wanted to represent it. The NLRB could also hear labor's complaints and issue "cease and desist" orders to end unfair labor practices. Under the Wagner Act, unions gained tremendously in membership and strength.

Regulating Unions Soon after the passage of the Wagner Act, business leaders began to protest that labor unions were growing too powerful. Critics of the Wagner Act claimed that it was one-sided and too favorable to labor. They complained that many workers were being forced to join unions against their wills. Also, employers were being forced to hire only union workers. To avoid strikes employers had to agree to establish a closed shop. In a **closed shop,** only members of a union may be hired. Responding to these criticisms, Congress passed the **Taft-Hartley Act** in 1947.

The purpose of the Taft-Hartley Act was to restore the balance between labor and management. It was the federal government's first attempt to regulate certain practices of large unions. The act required unions to give 60 days' notice before calling a strike. This "cooling-off period" was intended to provide additional time for labor and management to settle their differences. The act also restored limited use of injunctions. In strikes that endanger the nation, the president may obtain an injunction to stop the strike for 80 days. According to the Taft-Hartley Act, employers may sue unions for damages inflicted during a strike.

While the act prohibited the closed shop, it did permit the union shop. In a **union shop,** workers are required to join a union soon after they have been hired (but not before). Under the law, union shops can be formed if a majority of workers vote for them. They cannot be formed, however, in any state that has passed a "right-to-work" law. Right-to-work laws are state labor laws that prohibit both closed shops and union shops. They provide that all workplaces be **open shops** where workers may freely decide whether or not to join a union.

Protecting Union Members Labor unions have not always acted in the best interests of their members. In 1957, for example, a Senate investigating committee found that some leaders of the powerful Teamsters Union had misused and, in some cases, stolen funds. The same leaders were accused of associating with gangsters and racketeers and of having used bribery, threats, and violence against those who tried to challenge them.

These widely publicized labor scandals led to the passage of the Landrum-Griffin Act of 1959. This law made misusing union funds a federal crime. The Landrum-Griffin Act also protected union members from being intimidated by their leaders. It was also helpful in eliminating fraud in union elections. The act included a "bill of rights" for union members. This guaranteed the right of members to nominate and vote by secret ballot in union elections, to participate and speak freely at union meetings, to sue their union for unfair practices, and to examine union records and finances.

Section 1 Assessment

Checking for Understanding

1. **Main Idea** Use a graphic organizer like the one below to identify three laws passed by Congress that resulted in the growth of labor unions.

	growth of labor unions

2. **Define** mixed economy, laissez-faire, trust, monopoly, interlocking directorate, oligopoly, securities, collective bargaining, injunction.
3. **Identify** Sherman Antitrust Act, Clayton Antitrust Act, Wagner Act, Taft-Hartley Act.
4. What are the government's main goals regarding competition and consumers?

Critical Thinking

5. **Identifying Central Issues** What general problem do the Federal Trade Commission, the Securities and Exchange Commission, and the Consumer Product Safety Commission address?

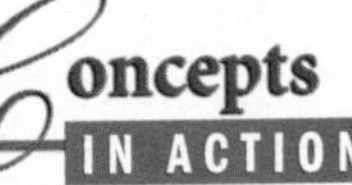

Free Enterprise Interstate commerce depends on an adequate transportation system funded by the federal government. Find out about highway construction plans in your area. Create a bulletin board display with a map of the planned construction and pertinent financial information.

Section 2

Agriculture and Environment

Reader's Guide

Key Terms

price supports, acreage allotment, marketing quotas

Find Out

- How does American farm policy attempt to stabilize farm prices?
- What is the working relationship between the federal government and localities in carrying out environmental policy?

Understanding Concepts

Civic Participation What can citizens do to help protect the environment?

COVER STORY

More School Cheese

WASHINGTON, D.C., DECEMBER 16, 1996

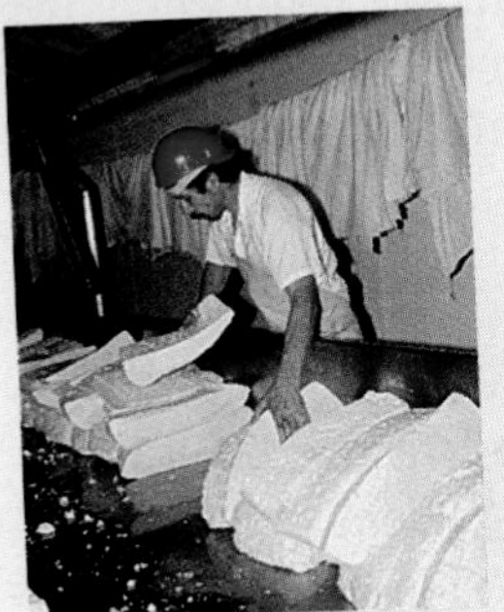

Supported by the government

The U.S. Department of Agriculture (USDA) will buy additional cheese to supplement the 73 million pounds it annually provides to the National School Lunch Program. The expanded order is intended to aid dairy farmers, who have seen milk and cheese prices tumble more than 30 percent. The action marks the second time this year the USDA has made a food purchase to bail out an industry. To help ranchers, the department recently ordered 74.6 million pounds of ground beef for federal food programs. A spokesperson for the lunch program noted "members are always happy to receive commodity products that enable them to keep school meal prices manageable."

The federal government has always encouraged American agriculture. In 1790 about 95 percent of the American people lived in rural areas, and most Americans were farmers. Farming remained the major occupation until after the early 1900s. Today, however, less than 5 percent of the American people are farmers. The United States is an urban nation with more than 75 percent of the people residing in towns and cities.

From 1935 to the present, the number of farms in the United States has declined from 6.8 million to about 2 million because small family farms are disappearing. The average farm today is just under 500 acres, more than twice as large as the average farm of 30 years ago. Large corporate farms are making agriculture big business.

While the total number of farms has decreased, farm output per work hour has increased almost every year. In 1900 one farmer could feed about 7 people. Now the average farmer can feed approximately 80 people.

The Federal Government and the Farmer

Despite the transition from a rural to an urban nation, the federal government has strongly encouraged American agriculture. Because farming is so vital to the nation, governments at the federal, state, and local levels provide support and assistance to farmers.

Early Agricultural Legislation In 1862 Congress passed three acts that were important to farmers. One law created the **Department of Agriculture.** In the beginning the chief purpose of this department was to show farmers how to improve and modernize their agricultural methods. In 1889 the Department of Agriculture was elevated to cabinet-level status.

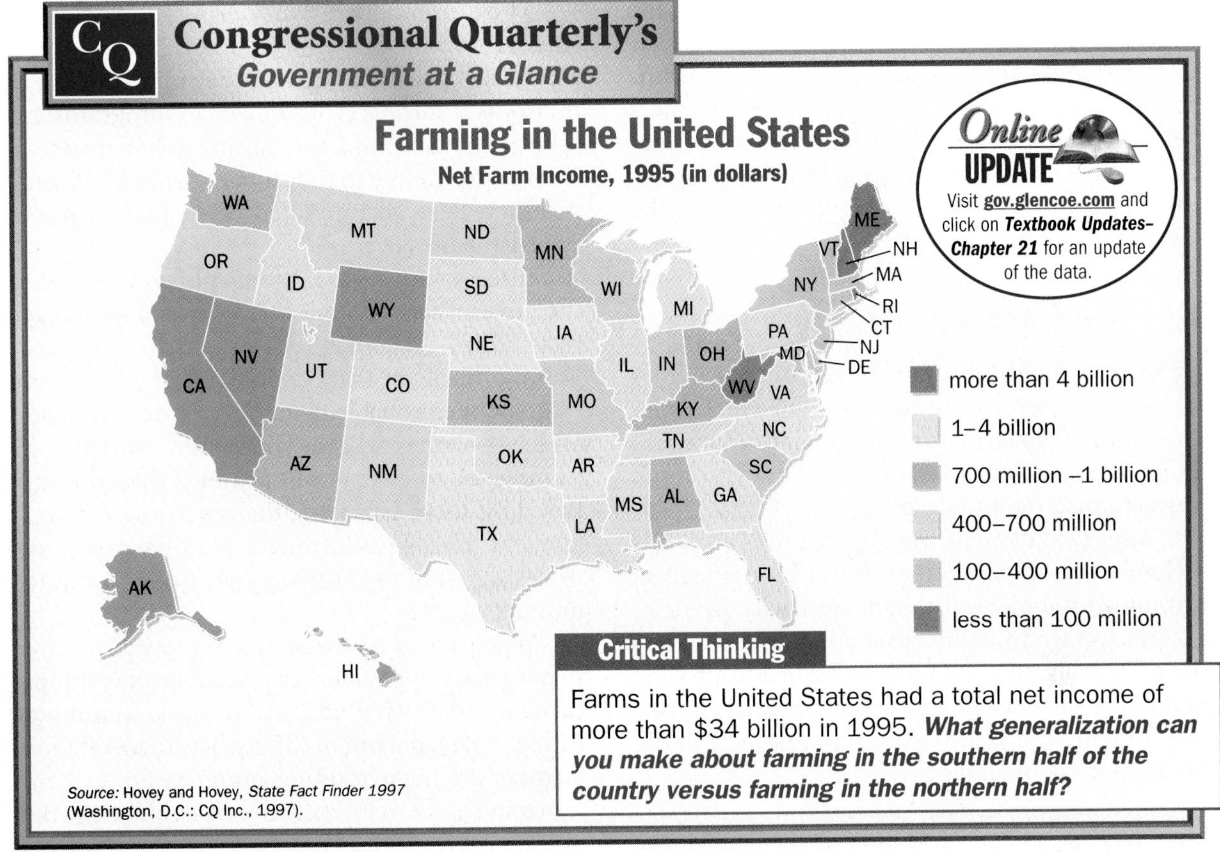

Critical Thinking

Farms in the United States had a total net income of more than $34 billion in 1995. ***What generalization can you make about farming in the southern half of the country versus farming in the northern half?***

The second law, the Morrill Act, aided Northern states by granting them millions of acres of federal land to establish state-operated colleges of agriculture. The third law, the Homestead Act, gave land to those willing to farm it.

Farm Problems In the 1920s the nation's farms faced serious problems. A historian's view creates a bleak picture:

> *"The high tariff enacted by the Republicans after World War I helped destroy the farmer's European market; the changing diet of the American family and immigration restrictions curtailed the farmer's market at home. Low crop prices, threats of foreclosures, an inadequate credit supply, soil erosion, locusts, droughts, sharecropping, tenant farming and migrant farming complete the dismal picture of farm conditions in the United States prior to the New Deal."*
>
> —John H. Cary, 1981

As farm prices continued to decline, thousands of farmers lost their land. During the first years of the Great Depression, conditions became worse. Then in 1933 a huge dust storm swept across the Great Plains and carried the area's soil across the Midwest, even darkening the sky in New York. One account in the *Saturday Evening Post* described the scene in South Dakota:

> *"When the wind died and the sun shone forth again, it was a different world. There were no fields, only sand drifting into mounds. . . . In the farmyard, fences, machinery, and trees were gone, buried. The roofs of sheds stuck out through drifts deeper than a man is tall."*
>
> —R.D. Lusk, November 1933

Responding to this disastrous situation, President Roosevelt's New Deal legislation set out to raise the price of farm products by limiting the production of certain crops that were in oversupply.

Under the Agricultural Adjustment Act (AAA), the government paid farmers for not producing their usual amount of corn, wheat, hogs, and other commodities. It also provided loans to help farmers keep their land. Although the Supreme Court declared the AAA unconstitutional in 1936, Congress quickly passed a similar act that overcame the Court's objections.

Aid for Farmers Today

The Department of Agriculture provides many services to farmers. The chief functions are to help farmers market their produce, stabilize farm prices, conserve land, and promote research in agricultural science.

The Department of Agriculture also has helped develop rural areas. Rural Electrification Administration loans brought electricity and telephone service to many rural areas. The Farmers Home Administration was established to provide loans for farmers to buy land, livestock, seeds, equipment, and fertilizer, to build homes, to dig wells, and to obtain disaster relief.

Marketing Services Several agencies of the Department of Agriculture are concerned with helping farmers find buyers for their crops. The Agricultural Marketing Service advises farmers on the demand for crops, current prices, and transportation methods. It also performs market research to help farmers know when and where to sell their products. The Foreign Agricultural Service promotes the sale of American farm goods in foreign markets.

Programs for Stabilizing Prices The federal government has tried several methods for preventing farm prices from falling below a certain level. The current approach involves the coordination of three programs—price supports, acreage allotments, and marketing quotas. The Commodity Credit Corporation (CCC) administers these programs.

Under the program of **price supports,** Congress establishes a support price for a particular crop. The CCC then lends the farmer money equal to the support price for the crop. If the actual market price falls below the support price, the farmer repays the loan with the crop.

The Commodity Credit Corporation holds the surplus crops in government storage facilities until the market price goes up and the crop can be sold. It also uses surplus crops in welfare programs, for school lunches, and for famine relief overseas. Even so, from time to time, huge surpluses of some products have accumulated when market prices stayed at a low level.

In order to avoid large surpluses every year, the government has adopted the idea of acreage restriction, or **acreage allotment.** In this program, officials in the Department of Agriculture estimate the probable demand for a crop in world and national markets. Then they estimate the number of acres that will produce that amount. Based on these estimates, the government assigns farmers acreage allotments and pays support prices for only the crops grown on the assigned number of acres.

When a crop has been overproduced and large surpluses threaten to lower prices, the government turns to **marketing quotas,** or marketing limits. Aided by Department of Agriculture officials, farmers set up marketing quotas among themselves and agree to market only an assigned portion of their overproduced crop.

Not all observers agree with the government practices of having price supports and farm subsidies. In the early 1990s critics said the Department of Agriculture was overgrown and its overlapping agencies were not efficient. In 1994 Congress responded to Agriculture secretary Mike Espy's proposal to reorganize the department. The resulting reorganization created the Farm Service Agency that consolidated conservation programs and reduced the department's budget. The same legislation that created the Farm Service Agency also made participation in a federal crop insurance program mandatory for farmers who took part in federal price supports.

Promoting Conservation Conserving the nation's land and forests is a vital responsibility of agencies in the Department of Agriculture. The Forest Service has restored millions of acres of forests used for outdoor recreation, timber, and for wildlife habitat. The Soil Conservation Service works through 3,000 soil conservation districts and with farmers to manage conservation problems.

Protecting the Environment

For many years the federal government did not set environmental policy. State and local governments developed few controls over air, water, land, and other natural resources.

Beginning in the 1950s, the federal government reacted to public concern over the deteriorating environment. The federal government passed legislation to clean up the air and water. In 1970 Congress issued a series of sweeping environmental laws. The **Environmental Protection Agency** (EPA) was created and charged with enforcing a host of regulations. Most of the regulations mandated changes in business and operations to comply with the law, but Congress provided no federal funds to states, localities, and businesses to pay for the improvements.

Air Pollution Policies Congress first expressed concern about air pollution as early as 1955 when it passed the Air Pollution Act. This act, however, was limited to promoting research on air quality and to providing technical assistance to states and communities.

In the 1960s Congress passed stronger laws requiring states to set clean-air standards and to prepare plans for their enforcement. The 1970 Clean Air Amendments established the Environmental Protection Agency (1970), giving the federal government power to enforce air quality standards.

The 1990 Clear Air Act mandated reductions in emissions. As a result, air quality in the United States improved between 1990 and 1999. Smog decreased four percent. Lead concentrations decreased ten percent. Sulfur dioxide concentrations, which cause acid rain, were down 36 percent. Carbon monoxide from car exhausts also decreased by 36 percent. In December 1999, the government announced tailpipe standards designed to reduce emissions even more—up to 95 percent in new cars. Furthermore, in 2000 the EPA developed rules for cleaner buses and heavy duty trucks.

Water Pollution Policies The Water Pollution Control Act of 1948 first provided for federal technical assistance to the states, but, as with the early pollution laws, the act was weak. Congress passed stronger measures. The Water Quality Improvement Act of 1970 prohibited the discharge of harmful amounts of oil and other dangerous materials into navigable waters. The law concerned such pollution sources as ships, onshore refineries,

Toxins in the Air

Past In the post-World War II era, the automobile became an indispensable part of Americans' lives. Cars waited in a traffic jam on a Pasadena, California freeway in 1958.

Present For many decades automobiles and factories have spewed pollutants into the air. In 2000 the EPA reported that nearly 62 million Americans lived in areas where the air was considered unhealthy as opposed to 150 million in 1990.

Environmental Protection
The nation's chief source of air pollution is the automobile. Do you think more laws should be enacted to force Americans to use public transportation? Explain.

Polluting America's Waterways

Regulating Pollution Polystyrene booms float on a pond near Moonstone Beach, Rhode Island, in an effort to contain oil spilled from a barge. Environmentalists worry that the oil spill and resulting pollution will upset the delicate ecosystem in the area. ***Do you think the power to regulate air and water quality should belong to the federal or state governments? Why?***

and offshore oil drilling platforms. It also provided for extensive control over pesticide drainage into the Great Lakes.

The major legislation to end water pollution was the Water Pollution Control Act of 1972. It set the goal of completely eliminating the discharge of pollutants into the nation's waterways. Under the act all polluters dumping waste into waterways—cities, industries, or farmers—needed a permit. The EPA's responsibility was to study each dumping location to monitor the dumper's compliance with regulations. Many lawsuits involving the EPA resulted. On the one hand, environmentalists sued because they thought the EPA was too permissive about dumping. On the other hand, industries sued the EPA, arguing that the agency was unreasonable in its standards.

In 1987 Congress updated the law, giving communities until 1994 to remove toxins from sewage and to dispose of sludge more carefully. The EPA projected that communities needed to invest about $111 billion in sewage-handling facilities. In addition, public water systems would have to spend about $1.4 billion to comply with 84 EPA standards. New equipment needed to bring the nation's community water supply systems into compliance would cost another $10 billion.

Unfunded Mandates The EPA issued hundreds of regulations to implement environmental laws. As costs grew each year, state and local leaders began to complain about these **unfunded mandates,** programs ordered but not paid for by federal legislation. The local share of environmental costs escalated from 76 percent of $35 billion in 1981 to a projected 82 percent of nearly $48 billion in 2000. Steven Walker, air quality chief in Albuquerque, New Mexico, said, "It seems like every November from now to [forever] there's some deadline we have to meet."

Pressured by state and local governments and by businesses, Congress reviewed unfunded mandates in 1996. New laws restricted the ability of the federal government to impose additional requirements on state and local governments without providing funds to pay for them. Cost-benefit analyses were required for most federal mandates imposed on businesses.

Energy and the Environment

In the 1950s most Americans were not familiar with terms like *energy crisis, environmental pollution,* and *ecology.* In the 1970s the declining quality of the environment and the diminishing supply of cheap energy forced the national government to place these important matters high on its policy agenda.

The Native Americans living in this land and the settlers who came later found abundant natural resources—unending forests, clear lakes and rivers, rich deposits of metals. As the country grew, Americans developed increasingly sophisticated technologies to use these resources to build a strong industrial nation. They gave little thought to the possibility that these resources might be depleted or that the careless exploitation of resources could have a serious impact on the environment.

By the early 1960s, however, the costs became obvious. Many rivers and lakes were dirty, fouled by sewage and chemical wastes. Smog engulfed major cities, oil spills polluted the beaches, and the heavy use of pesticides endangered wildlife.

In the winter of 1973–1974, Americans found themselves in an energy crisis. Arab countries cut off shipments of oil because the United States had supported Israel during an Arab-Israeli war. Industries dependent on oil laid off workers. Many gas stations closed, and long lines formed at the ones that were open. States lowered speed limits, and people set thermostats lower to save energy.

The federal government responded with emergency legislation, but many people called for a long-term solution. As the government fashioned a new energy policy in the mid-1970s to meet future energy crises, people began to recognize the costs of a cleaner environment and conflicts among interest groups with different goals. Americans discovered that preserving clean air might require them to drive cars with pollution-control devices that made the cars more costly to buy and operate. Oil companies wanted to drill for more offshore oil, while environmentalists believed that such drilling posed too great a risk to the marine environment.

Competing interest groups such as energy companies, conservation organizations, and consumer advocates struggled to shape new policies and programs that reflected their concerns. The head of the Department of Energy outlined the goals of a national energy strategy:

> “*We want to chart a course of diplomatic, commercial, regulatory, and technological policy that will reduce U.S. vulnerability to future disruptions in oil markets, improve the environment, and increase economic efficiency.*”
>
> —James D. Watkins, 1991

Just four years later, policy changed as fear of shortages evaporated. By 1995 increased supplies had created a glut of oil on the international market. This led to lower oil prices and the use of more foreign oil in the United States. By 2000 the United States was importing 55 percent of its oil. Then in the summer of that year, gasoline prices rose dramatically. In response, Congress appropriated funds for the research and development of biofuels—fuel made from organic wastes—to replace a large part of the gasoline made from imported oil.

GOVERNMENT Online

Student Web Activity Visit the *United States Government: Democracy in Action* Web site at gov.glencoe.com and click on ***Chapter 21–Student Web Activities*** for an activity about agriculture and environment.

Section 2 Assessment

Checking for Understanding

1. **Main Idea** Use a graphic organizer like the one below to compare clean air legislation of the 1950s, 1960s, and 1990s.

1950s	1960s	1990s

2. **Define** price supports, acreage allotment, marketing quotas.
3. **Identify** Department of Agriculture, Environmental Protection Agency, unfunded mandates.
4. How does the federal government attempt to stabilize farm prices?

Critical Thinking

5. **Predicting Consequences** What will be the economic and environmental effects of recent air and water pollution legislation?

Concepts IN ACTION

Civic Participation Choose a conservation project that you can do in your community. You might “adopt” a park, a pond, or a roadside to clean up and to keep attractive. Share your ideas with the class in the form of a proposal presentation.

Section 3

Health and Public Assistance

Reader's Guide

Key Terms

social insurance, public assistance, unemployment insurance

Find Out

- What is the purpose of Social Security, and how does it operate?
- What are the most recent changes in federal public assistance programs?

Understanding Concepts

Federalism How do the states and federal government work together to provide unemployment insurance and public assistance?

COVER STORY

Drug Use Down Among Youth

WASHINGTON, D.C., AUGUST 21, 2000

The Substance Abuse and Mental Health Administration released its annual National Household Survey on Drug Abuse today. According to Dr. Donna E. Shalala, the secretary of health and human services, the study's most important finding is that drug use has dropped among young people aged 12 to 17. "Most of our young people are getting the message that drugs are not the stuff of dreams, but the stuff of nightmares," Dr. Shalala said. More discouraging were the study's revelations about tobacco use. In 1998 about 800,000 people under 18 started smoking cigarettes. "We have a long way to go—miles to go—in our journey to a drug free America," commented Dr. Shalala.

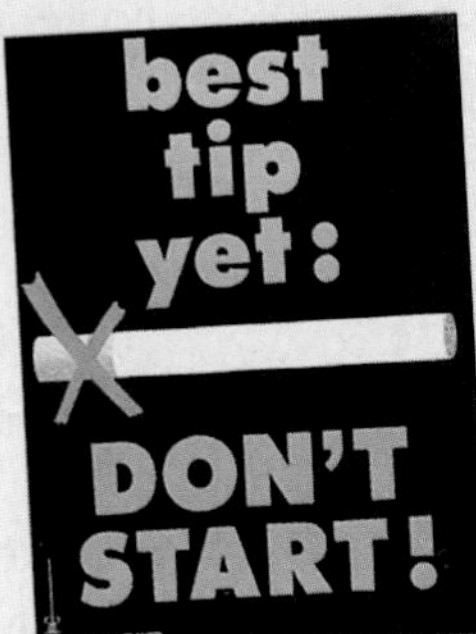

Promoting an anti-smoking message

Today the government is interested in Americans' health. Well into the 1900s the hardships of ill health, old age, poverty, and physical disability were private matters. For needy Americans local and state governments provided very limited help in the form of orphanages, almshouses, and poor farms. Most people in need depended on themselves and on churches and private charitable organizations.

The Great Depression of the 1930s changed public attitudes. During that decade the national government started two types of programs: social insurance and public assistance.

The Impact of the Depression

After the stock market crash of 1929, the American economy continued to slump badly month after month for the next several years. Unemployment increased from about 3 percent of the nation's workforce in 1929 to almost 25 percent in 1933. The song "Brother, Can You Spare a Dime?" expressed the mood of the early 1930s. Almost overnight, unemployment, hunger, and poverty became massive national problems.

New Deal Programs As the Depression deepened, private charities and local and state governments could not cope with the problems of the poor. To ease the nation's suffering, President Franklin D. Roosevelt proposed and Congress passed the Social Security Act in 1935. This act was the first of many government-supported social insurance, public assistance, and health-care programs. The government envisioned these programs as long-term ways to provide some economic security for all citizens.

Today the United States has two kinds of social programs. **Social insurance** programs are designed to help elderly, ill, and unemployed citizens. **Public assistance** programs distribute public money to poor people. The government

COMPARING *Governments*

Social Spending

Country	Old age, invalidity, and death	Sickness and maternity	Work Injury	Unemployment	Family Allowances	Percent of total government spending, 1992
Australia	✓	✓	✓	✓	✓	**29.6**
Colombia	✓	✓	✓		✓	**16.4** (1)
Israel	✓	✓	✓	✓	✓	**20.9**
Mexico	✓	✓	✓			**12.3** (2)
Thailand		✓	✓			**3.8**
United Kingdom	✓	✓	✓	✓	✓	**29.6**
United States	✓		✓	✓		**22.2**
Zimbabwe	✓		✓			**2.5** (3)

Source: Encyclopedia Britannica, *1996 Book of the Year* (Chicago: Encyclopedia Britannica, 1996). (1) 1986 (2) 1993 (3) 1989

Critical Thinking **The large majority of governments around the world provide some kind of social benefits for their citizens. *Which two countries provide the fewest number of programs?***

uses general tax revenues to pay for these programs. Unlike social insurance, public assistance does not require recipients to contribute to the cost of the programs.

Social Insurance Programs

The Social Security Act and its later amendments created a social insurance system with three main components. The first component is Social Security, or **Old Age, Survivors, and Disability Insurance (OASDI).** The second component is a health-insurance program called Medicare, and the third is unemployment insurance.

The Social Security Administration administers OASDI from its huge headquarters in Baltimore and from 1,300 local offices around the country. The Health Care Financing Administration manages the Medicare program. Both of these agencies are important units within the Department of Health and Human Services. The Department of Labor runs the unemployment insurance program.

Social Security More than 90 percent of American workers participate in the Social Security system. Employers and employees contribute equally, while self-employed persons pay their own Social Security tax. Retirees, survivors, disabled persons, and Medicare recipients are eligible for benefits. Survivors are spouses and children of deceased people covered by Social Security. Medicare provides health insurance for persons 65 or older.

Changing the System In 1981 the Social Security system faced a severe cash shortage as outgoing payments rose faster than incoming payroll taxes. In 1983 Congress passed a law that included a gradual rise in the retirement age from 65 to 67 by the year 2027. It also required that Social Security benefits of some retired people with higher incomes be subject to federal income tax. The law required federal workers to join Social Security, increased the Social Security payroll tax, and deferred cost-of-living increases to retirees.

Many experts believe that despite the changes

Congress made in 1983, social security will face even worse cash shortages within a few decades as increasing numbers of older Americans retire. How to reform the system became a major issue in the 2000 presidential election. Republican candidate George W. Bush proposed allowing people to invest a portion of their social security payroll taxes in stocks and bonds. Democratic candidate Al Gore called for maintaining the current level of guaranteed benefits by supplementing the social security payroll taxes with money from the general income tax. Any major changes in the system will require Congressional action. Peter G. Peterson, who served on a bipartisan commission on entitlements, said:

> "*The costs of Social Security and Medicare alone are projected to rise to between 35 and 55 percent of taxable payroll by 2040. . . . Balancing the budget by 2002 is a low-impact warm-up exercise compared with the grueling iron-man challenge that lies ahead when 76 million boomers retire.*"
>
> —Peter G. Peterson

Henry J. Aaron, an economist at the Brookings Institution, expressed a different point of view:

> "*Social Security does have a projected deficit over 75 years, but it can be easily managed. . . . Modest benefit reductions and small tax increases imposed gradually can bring revenues and expenditures into balance. The main factor driving up the combined cost of Medicare and Social Security is . . . growth in per capita medical costs.*"
>
> —Henry J. Aaron

Medicare Health Insurance In 1965 Congress added **Medicare** to the Social Security program. The basic Medicare plan pays a major share of the total hospital bills for more than 30 million senior citizens.

A second portion of the Medicare program is voluntary. For those who choose to pay an extra amount, Medicare also helps pay doctors' bills and costs of X rays, surgical dressings, and so on. Nearly all the people covered by the basic plan are enrolled in the voluntary portion of the Medicare plan.

Unemployment Insurance The 1935 Social Security Act also set up **unemployment insurance** programs for people who are out of work. Under these programs, federal and state governments cooperate to provide the needed help.

Workers in every state are eligible to receive unemployment payments if their employers dismiss them from their jobs. To fund the program, employers pay a tax to the federal government. Then, when workers are involuntarily laid off, they may apply for weekly benefits from a state, not a federal, employment office.

Public Assistance Programs

Federal government public assistance programs began during the Depression. Although the federal government provides most of the money for these programs from general tax revenues, state and local welfare agencies actually run the programs. The major public assistance programs are: Supplemental Security Income (SSI), food stamps, Medicaid, and the Job Opportunities and Basic Skills program (JOBS). A program called Aid to Families with Dependent Children ended in 1996 with the passage of a major welfare-reform bill.

Supplemental Security Income (SSI) Set up by Congress in 1974, Supplemental Security Income brought together under federal control all state programs for the aged, the blind, and the disabled. Under the original Social Security Act, the states had administered these programs, and benefits and procedures varied greatly from state to state. SSI sought to simplify these programs and streamline the administration of benefits.

The Social Security Administration runs the program. The federal government makes a monthly payment to anyone who is 65 or older, who is blind or disabled, or who has little or no regular income.

Food Stamps President Kennedy started the food stamp program by executive order in 1961. Congress created a food stamp system by law in 1964. The purpose of the food stamp program was to increase the food-buying power of low-income families and help dispose of America's surplus agricultural production. When the program started, approximately 367,000 people received food stamps. By 1999 more than 18 million Americans received food stamps at a cost to the government of nearly $16 billion.

Medicaid Congress established the Medicaid program in 1965 as part of the Social Security system. **Medicaid** is designed to help pay hospital, doctor, and other medical bills for persons with low incomes. General federal, state, and local taxes fund this program that aids more than 35 million people at a cost of about $108 billion each year.

Some observers have noted that both Medicaid and Medicare contribute to rising hospital and medical costs. Because the government pays the medical bills, neither the patients nor doctors or hospitals have an incentive under this program to try to keep costs down.

Aid to Families with Dependent Children

Aid to Families with Dependent Children was designed during the Depression. It helped families in which the main wage earner died, was disabled, or left the family. A family with dependent children was eligible for AFDC assistance if its income was too low according to criteria set by the state.

In its early years, about 75 percent of those receiving aid were children of fathers who had died or been disabled. By the 1990s more than 80 percent of the children receiving aid had fathers who had either deserted their families or who had never married the mothers of the children. The 1994 Census Bureau report on poverty showed that more than 21 percent of the nation's children under the age of 18 were living in poverty despite the government's efforts under AFDC.

The AFDC program was sharply criticized. Some critics argued that the program promoted having babies outside of marriage. They also claimed that it promoted fatherless families by encouraging men to leave their families in order to make their children eligible for aid. Over the years Congress attempted to modify the program, but it remained controversial.

The Need for Reform Few people denied that society had a responsibility to help care for its disadvantaged, sick, and disabled. At the same time, for many different reasons few political leaders and citizens were happy with the public assistance system. After more than 30 years of rapidly increasing program costs, the level of poverty remained high in the United States. In a recent year more than 38 million people, or 14.5 percent of Americans, were living in poverty.

Much of the public frustration over the welfare system stemmed from reports of welfare fraud and the cycle of dependence that developed among many welfare recipients. Many single parents on welfare had few strong incentives to work. Minimum-wage jobs provided less income than the welfare system, and working often meant paying additional day care expenses. Disadvantaged people were trapped in a cycle of joblessness, inadequate education, and welfare.

Fighting for Support

Federally Funded Programs A New Yorker demonstrates to show his support for federally funded health-care programs. ***Why would some citizens feel it was necessary to actively show their support for Medicaid?***

JOBS Congress first responded to calls for welfare reform in the Family Support Act of 1988. The act created a Job Opportunities and Basic Skills program (JOBS). It required states by 1990 to implement welfare-to-work programs aimed at helping people get off the welfare rolls. The federal government promised to pay a share of the costs of education and job training.

Transforming the Welfare System

Changes in Administrative Agencies President Clinton signed a tough welfare-reform bill in 1996 that requires more welfare recipients to find work. Clinton stated that government has a role in creating opportunities for employment of citizens through education and job training. ***How do you think the welfare-to-work bill affected administrative agencies?***

Patterned after successful state reforms, the 1988 JOBS program included a provision that welfare recipients who took jobs and got off the welfare rolls would continue to be eligible for subsidized child care and health benefits for one year. In addition, it provided that no parent would be required to accept a job that would result in a reduction in the family's net cash income.

Sweeping Changes in Welfare In the 1992 election campaign President Clinton vowed to "end welfare as we know it." In the 1994 elections, Republicans proposed broad welfare changes in their "Contract With America." Although the president and Congress supported reform, it took two years to enact compromise legislation. After vetoing two previous Republican-sponsored bills and despite objections by liberals in his own party, the president signed a major welfare overhaul. On July 31, 1996, he announced:

> "*Today we have an historic opportunity to make welfare what it was meant to be: a second chance, not a way of life. . . . I believe we have a duty to seize the opportunity it gives us to end welfare as we know it.*"
>
> —President Bill Clinton

The bill ended Aid to Families with Dependent Children (AFDC), a cash welfare program. It replaced AFDC with lump-sum payments to the states. States were given authority to design and operate their own welfare programs. The bill, however, placed several restrictions on the states' use of federal welfare funding. It established work requirements for welfare recipients and placed time limits on families' eligibility for welfare assistance. The bill authorized a reduction in the food stamp program spending and placed limits on food stamp benefits available to people without children. The federal government agreed to provide $14 billion over the following six years for child-care services to families on welfare.

Reaction to welfare reform was swift and sharply divided. A leading Democratic senator warned:

> "*If you think things can't be worse, just you wait until there are a third of a million children in the streets. That's what we're talking about.*"
>
> —Senator Daniel Patrick Moynihan

At the same time, House Speaker Newt Gingrich, a Republican, expressed a different point of view when he stated:

> *"I think that welfare reform is very important. I think it's particularly important for children who are currently trapped in poverty. . . . Creating the natural expectation that people will be busy working is a big step."*
>
> —House Speaker Newt Gingrich

Promoting Public Health

In 1792 Secretary of the Treasury Alexander Hamilton urged Congress to provide hospital care for "sick and disabled seamen." Congress responded by establishing the United States Public Health Service in 1798. Ever since that time, the federal government has been concerned with public health.

Health Programs Today the largest percentage of federal government spending on health goes for the Medicare and Medicaid programs. In addition to these, however, the government operates several programs designed to promote and protect public health. The Department of Defense, for example, provides hospital and other medical care for active and retired American military personnel and their families. In addition, the Veterans Administration (VA) operates medical, dental, and hospital care programs for needy veterans.

The Public Health Service, which is now a part of the Department of Health and Human Services, operates research, grant, and action programs designed to promote the health of all citizens. Federal agencies, such as the Centers for Disease Control (CDC), work to control diseases such as AIDS, diphtheria, measles, and many different strains of flu. The CDC is also concerned with insect-spread diseases such as malaria and typhus.

There has been a recurring debate over a national health care system, a prominent point of discussion in recent elections. Several alternative health care proposals have been introduced into Congress, but no consensus has been reached.

Food and Drug Protection The Food and Drug Administration (FDA) tests samples of food and drug products in its laboratories. The agency has the power to ban or withdraw from distribution drugs it finds unsafe or ineffective. As a result, the FDA often finds itself involved in controversy. Some doctors, for example, claim FDA policies make it almost impossible for the public to receive the benefits of certain drugs. Sometimes people suffering from a particular disease, such as cancer or AIDS, will travel outside the United States to obtain drugs permitted elsewhere.

In contrast, some consumer protection groups believe the FDA is not tough enough in banning drugs and food additives that may be harmful. Clearly, the FDA has a difficult job. It must protect the public from dangerous substances while not denying them the drugs they need.

Section 3 Assessment

Checking for Understanding

1. **Main Idea** Use a graphic organizer like the one below to show who is eligible for Social Security benefits and Supplemental Security Income.

Social Security	Supplemental Security

2. **Define** social insurance, public assistance, unemployment insurance.
3. **Identify** Medicare, Medicaid.
4. How did the welfare overhaul in 1996 affect Aid to Families with Dependent Children (AFDC)?

Critical Thinking

5. **Predicting Consequences** How would consumers' use of medicine be affected if the federal government discontinued the Food and Drug Administration?

Federalism Interview three senior citizens who have used Medicare. Ask the following: How does the Medicare system benefit you? What problems have you had with the system? What improvements could be made to Medicare? Compare your answers with your classmates.

South Dakota v. Dole, 1987

Drinking and driving is a serious national problem. Congress tried to deal with this problem when it required states to raise their legal drinking age to 21 as a condition for getting federal highway funds. Does the Constitution allow Congress to set such restrictions on federal grants to the states? The Court addressed this in South Dakota *v.* Dole.

SADD

Students Against Driving Drunk

Background of the Case

In the mid-1980s Congress concluded that a lack of uniformity in the minimum drinking age among the states was contributing to a national highway safety problem. A Presidential Commission on Drunk Driving appointed to examine alcohol-related accidents on the nation's highways had concluded that the lack of uniformity in the minimum drinking ages set by the states created "an incentive to drink and drive" because "young persons commute to border states where the drinking age is lower." Congress passed a law in 1984 directing the secretary of transportation to withhold 5 percent of federal highway funds from those states that did not adopt 21 years old as the minimum drinking age. South Dakota, a state that permitted 19-year-olds to purchase alcohol, challenged the law as a violation of the Constitution.

The Constitutional Issue

Article I, Section 8, of the Constitution gives Congress the authority to "lay and collect Taxes, Duties, and Excises to pay the Debts and provide for the common Defence and general Welfare of the United States." In carrying out this spending power the Supreme Court had ruled in a 1936 case, *United States* v. *Butler,* that Congress could attach conditions on the receipt of federal funds.

South Dakota recognized Congress could set some conditions on those who received federal dollars. However, South Dakota argued that the Twenty-first Amendment barred Congress from requiring the states to raise the drinking age to 21 years old. The amendment, South Dakota claimed, "grants the states virtually complete control over whether to permit importation or sale of liquor and how to structure the liquor distribution system." South Dakota also argued that setting a minimum drinking age was clearly within the "core powers" reserved to the states by the amendment. The secretary of transportation conceded that the amendment did give the states authority to impose limits on the sale of alcohol. However, he argued, it did not give states the power to allow sales Congress wanted to stop in order to promote the important national goal of safety on interstate highways.

Debating the Case

Questions to Consider

1. Did the congressional requirement to raise the drinking age contribute to a national goal?
2. Would South Dakota violate anyone's constitutional rights by making the drinking age 21 in order to get the federal funds?

You Be the Judge

In your opinion, was the Twenty-first Amendment an "independent constitutional bar" that prevented Congress from putting the condition of a minimum drinking age on federal highway funds given to the states? Explain your answer.

Section 4

Education, Housing, and Transportation

Reader's Guide

Key Terms

urban renewal, public housing, mass transit

Find Out

- What steps has the federal government taken since 1980 to support public education?
- Why has federal housing policy been a political battleground for many years?

Understanding Concepts

Federalism How do the states and the federal government work together to carry out transportation and housing policies?

COVER STORY

Female Coaches Lose

BROOKLYN, NEW YORK, APRIL 1997

Female coaches have not fully shared in the women's sports boom, charge two Brooklyn College professors following a recent study. In the 25 years that the government has required equal opportunity in school sports, the percentage of women coaches of girls' teams has fallen from nearly 100 percent to less than 40 percent. The study suggests that this is one consequence of the law's requirement of more equal funding for boys' and girls' sports. As pay for girls' coaches has increased, the jobs have become more appealing to male coaches.

Coached by a female?

Providing for public education was one of the main powers the Constitution reserved for the states. For many years the states left the primary responsibility of providing for public education with local governments. Connecticut created the first school fund in 1795 with money from the sale of public lands. Indiana set up the first modern public school system in 1816.

Public Education Programs

Today public education in the United States is a huge enterprise. In most states elementary and high school education remains a local responsibility under state guidelines. The basic administrative unit for public schools is the local school district.

Federal Aid to Education While public education remains under local control, the federal government plays an ever-increasing role, providing aid to local schools in several forms. In a recent year, the federal government contributed more than $1.3 billion in direct aid to local public schools and almost $12 billion of additional funds to be distributed through the states. The federal government provides even more support for higher education—about $17.6 billion to institutions of higher learning in a recent year.

Aid to Public Schools Congress began to provide aid for specific educational activities in the schools with the Smith-Hughes Act of 1917. This act set up matching grants to the states for teaching courses in agriculture and home economics. Since then Congress has passed several laws directed toward other aspects of elementary and secondary education.

During the mid-1960s, President Lyndon Johnson made improved education in the United States a major goal of his Great Society program. In 1965, during the height of public support for Johnson's ideas, Congress passed the first general aid-to-education law—the Elementary and Secondary Education Act. This act and later amendments provided federal aid to most of the nation's school districts.

Aid to Higher Education Until 1862 higher education was a private undertaking. In that year Congress passed the Morrill Act, giving a major boost to higher education in America. This law granted the states more than 13 million acres (about 32 million hectares) of public land for the endowment of colleges to teach "agriculture and the mechanical arts." States established 69 of these so-called land-grant colleges under the Morrill Act and a second similar law.

In recent years Congress has provided a number of specific programs to aid higher education. The best known are the various G.I. Bills of Rights that provided funds for veterans of World War II, the Korean War, and the Vietnam War to gain a college education. In addition the Office of Postsecondary Education makes available many student financial assistance programs.

Education Issues The government's policy of providing general federal aid to public schools and colleges has been controversial. Opponents of such aid argue that education should be a state and local concern. They say federal aid leads to federal control of the curriculum and school systems. The president of a major university put it this way: "Federal spending power is used indirectly to control colleges in ways the government could not use directly."

In 1983 the National Commission on Excellence in Education, appointed by President Ronald Reagan, issued its report. On a series of international tests, United States students generally ranked below their European and Asian peers. The commission called for many reforms. The excellence movement that sprang from the report had mixed results. Barbara Lerner was one of the first to explain the gap in test scores:

Promoting Learning

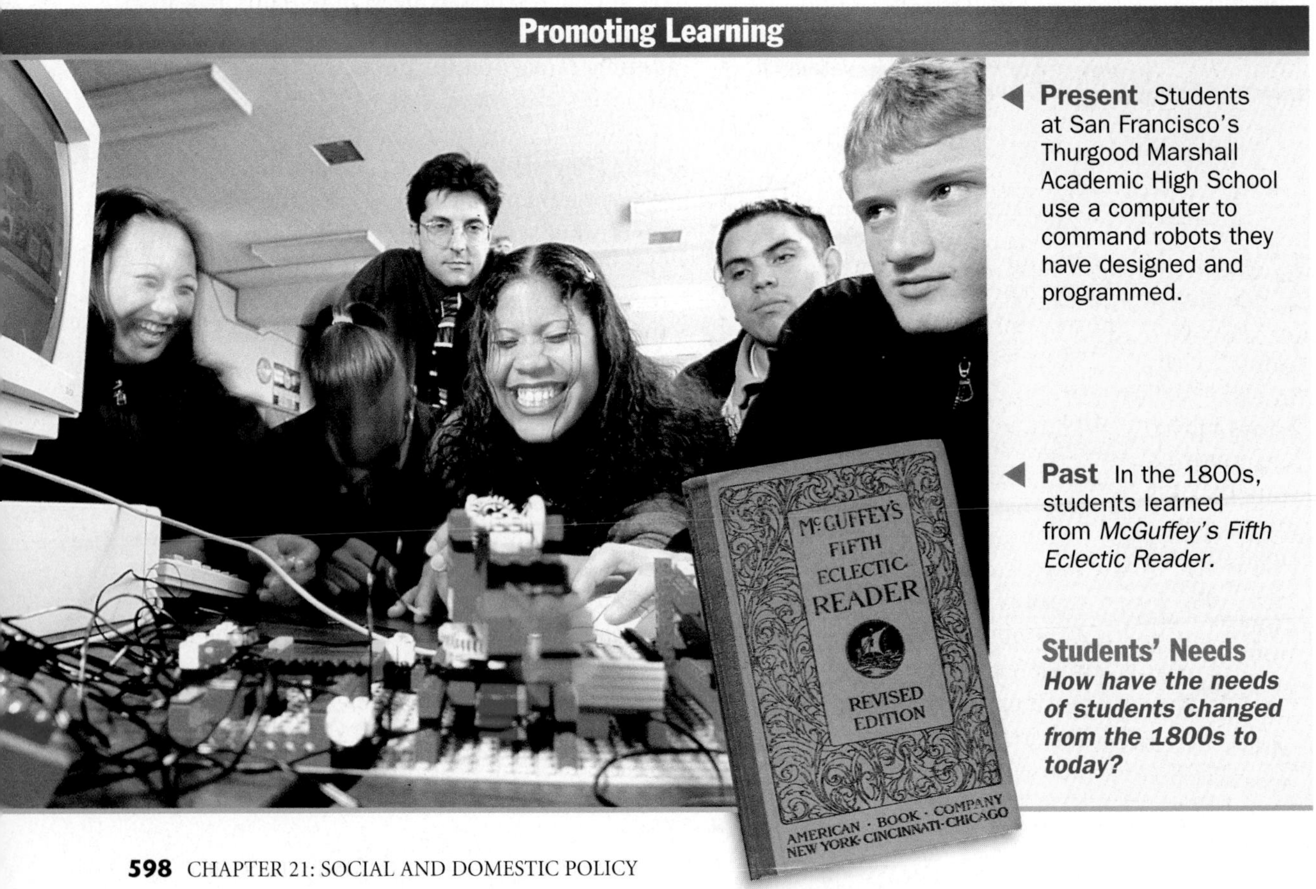

◀ **Present** Students at San Francisco's Thurgood Marshall Academic High School use a computer to command robots they have designed and programmed.

◀ **Past** In the 1800s, students learned from *McGuffey's Fifth Eclectic Reader.*

Students' Needs
How have the needs of students changed from the 1800s to today?

> *"Data from good domestic tests . . . show that in an absolute sense we did not really get worse in the 1980's as we had done in the 1960's and 70's, but neither did we get much better. For the most part we stood still. . . . Our foreign competitors, however, did not stand still; they surged ahead. . . ."*
>
> —Barbara Lerner, 1991

Concerned about the relative decline in student scores, President Bush declared education a top priority of his administration. In 1991 he unveiled a "Choice" program that allowed students to attend any school—even private and parochial schools—at the states' expense. In addition, the federal government would provide $30 billion in grants to the states to help them design "Choice" programs and another $200 million to enable disadvantaged children to participate in them.

In 1994 Congress passed the Goals 2000: Educate America Act. The government adopted eight educational goals such as improving graduation rates. It also required states to develop academic standards in order to be eligible for grants. In 1995 Congress provided $6 million to underwrite some start-up costs for charter schools that states were developing. President Clinton favored such state initiatives to develop public schools that set benchmarks for performance.

Housing and Urban Programs

Adequate housing is an important part of the general welfare of any society. The federal government has developed several programs to ensure adequate housing for all citizens.

Housing Policy The government first became involved in housing policy during the Great Depression. Millions of Americans were losing their homes or farms because they could not meet their mortgage payments. Housing construction almost came to a halt. The government responded to this catastrophe with a series of federally-funded loan and housing support programs.

After World War II, Congress assured the government's continuing role in housing policy by passing the Housing Act of 1949. In this law Congress declared its goal to be "a decent home and a suitable living environment for every American family."

Promoting Home Buying and Building

The federal government has developed several programs to promote building and purchasing houses. The best known program is the **Federal Housing Administration (FHA).** The FHA, a part of the **Department of Housing and Urban Development (HUD),** guarantees banks and other private lenders against losses on loans they make to those who wish to build or buy homes. By acting as an insurer for these mortgages, the FHA has allowed many low- and middle-income families who might not have qualified for private loans to purchase their own homes.

The FHA program almost completely supports itself and costs the taxpayers very little. The money gained from interest and other charges, along with income from investments, provides funds to run the program. In addition HUD offers rent assistance to low-income families.

The majority of the federal housing programs that HUD administers are targeted on cities. The federal government has addressed urban problems with two types of programs: urban renewal and public housing.

Urban Renewal To arrest the decline and assist the rebuilding of central cities, the federal government supports urban renewal programs. Cities can apply for federal aid to clear deteriorating areas and to rebuild. Most renewal projects begin by removing run-down properties. Private developers may then buy the land at a reduced price and rebuild according to plans approved by the city and HUD. As part of urban renewal, federal mortgage insurance is available to the private developers.

The goal of urban renewal policies has been to restore slum areas and make cities more attractive places in which to live. Critics charge, however, that urban renewal neglects new lower-income housing. Instead, urban renewal has forced lower-income people from their homes to make way for more affluent housing and commercial centers. As one spokesperson for the disadvantaged said of urban renewal, "We're already living nowhere, and now they're going to move us out of that." In addition, critics charge urban renewal has destroyed some of the social fabric of the city by dispersing residents of ethnic neighborhoods and uprooting local businesses.

Rebuilding Cities In Houston, Texas, public housing stands in the shadow of the city. ***How can urban renewal help lower-income families?***

Supporters of urban renewal argue that the policy has represented a useful effort on the part of the national government to get local governments and private investors to work together to save the cities. They also point to the Housing and Community Development Act of 1974, which requires cities to demonstrate that they are actually serving the needs of the disadvantaged when redeveloping areas.

Public Housing Programs Since 1937 and especially after the 1949 Housing Act, the federal government has given aid to local governments to construct and operate **public housing** for low-income families. To implement the program, a city first sets up a "public housing authority" to which the federal government can make low-interest loans that may cover up to 90 percent of the housing construction costs. The government also grants subsidies to these agencies to allow them to operate by charging very low rents. Income from the rents is used to repay the federal loan. About 4 million Americans live in public housing, largely concentrated in the major cities.

Over the years public housing projects have faced serious problems and opposition from many groups. Local authorities have mismanaged some public housing projects. Many such projects have turned into high-rise slums and centers of crime. The situation had grown so grave by 1973 that President Nixon halted federal aid for public housing projects. In doing so, Nixon stated, "All across America, the federal government has become the biggest slumlord in history."

The government has yet to find a truly effective public housing policy. In 1976 Congress resumed federal aid for public housing projects on a limited scale. At the same time HUD has experimented with rent subsidies as one alternative to public housing. Under this plan lower-income families pay a percentage of the rent—normally 30 percent—for private housing, and the government pays the rest of the rent directly to the landlord.

For many years federal housing policy was a political battleground. Republicans wanted to get the government out of the housing business. Democrats wanted the government to provide more low-income housing. In 1994 both parties agreed to give state and local officials more control over housing policies. HUD Secretary Henry G. Cisneros recommended the HOME program. Through matching grants to states and localities, public housing funding was redirected into assistance for the homeless and subsidized private housing.

Transportation Programs

In 1632 the Virginia legislature proclaimed: "Highways shall be layed out in such convenient places . . . as the parishioners of every parish shall agree." Governments at all levels in the United States have been concerned about improving transportation ever since.

The national government's first direct entry into the field of transportation began in 1811 with construction of the National Road that ultimately ran from Maryland to Illinois. The federal government continued to contribute, usually through some form of subsidy, to the building of channels, locks, dams, canals, ports, highways, railroads, and airports.

In 1966 Congress created the Department of Transportation (DOT) to coordinate national transportation policies and programs. This department brought together more than 30 agencies dealing individually with transportation policies. These agencies had been scattered throughout the government. Today the DOT operates through 7 major agencies that reflect the various forms of transportation.

Other Agencies Numerous agencies within the Department of Transportation provide important services. The Federal Aviation Administration (FAA) works to ensure safety in aviation. It licenses pilots and enforces safety rules for air traffic. The Federal Highway Administration (FHWA) oversees the vast network of federal roads. The Federal Railroad Administration promotes and regulates the nation's railroad transportation. The National Highway Traffic Safety Administration is responsible for enforcing laws to protect drivers and promote highway safety.

Building and Maintaining Highways The Federal Road Aid Act of 1916 set the pattern for the development of federal highway programs. Under this law the federal government provided yearly grants for road building to the states and required each state to match this aid on a dollar-for-dollar basis. These grants-in-aid, administered by the FHWA, form the basis of today's federal highway programs.

Under the Federal Aid Highway Act of 1956 and subsequent amendments, states receive billions of dollars every year to build and improve the Interstate Highway System that crisscrosses the nation. This system, begun in 1956, consists of more than 45,000 miles of 4-to-8-lane superhighways connecting nearly all of the nation's major cities. Federal funds cover 90 percent of the cost of the Interstate Highway System. The money for federal highway grants comes from the Highway Trust Fund. This fund is a special account that receives federal excise taxes on gasoline, tires, truck parts, and related items.

Roads West

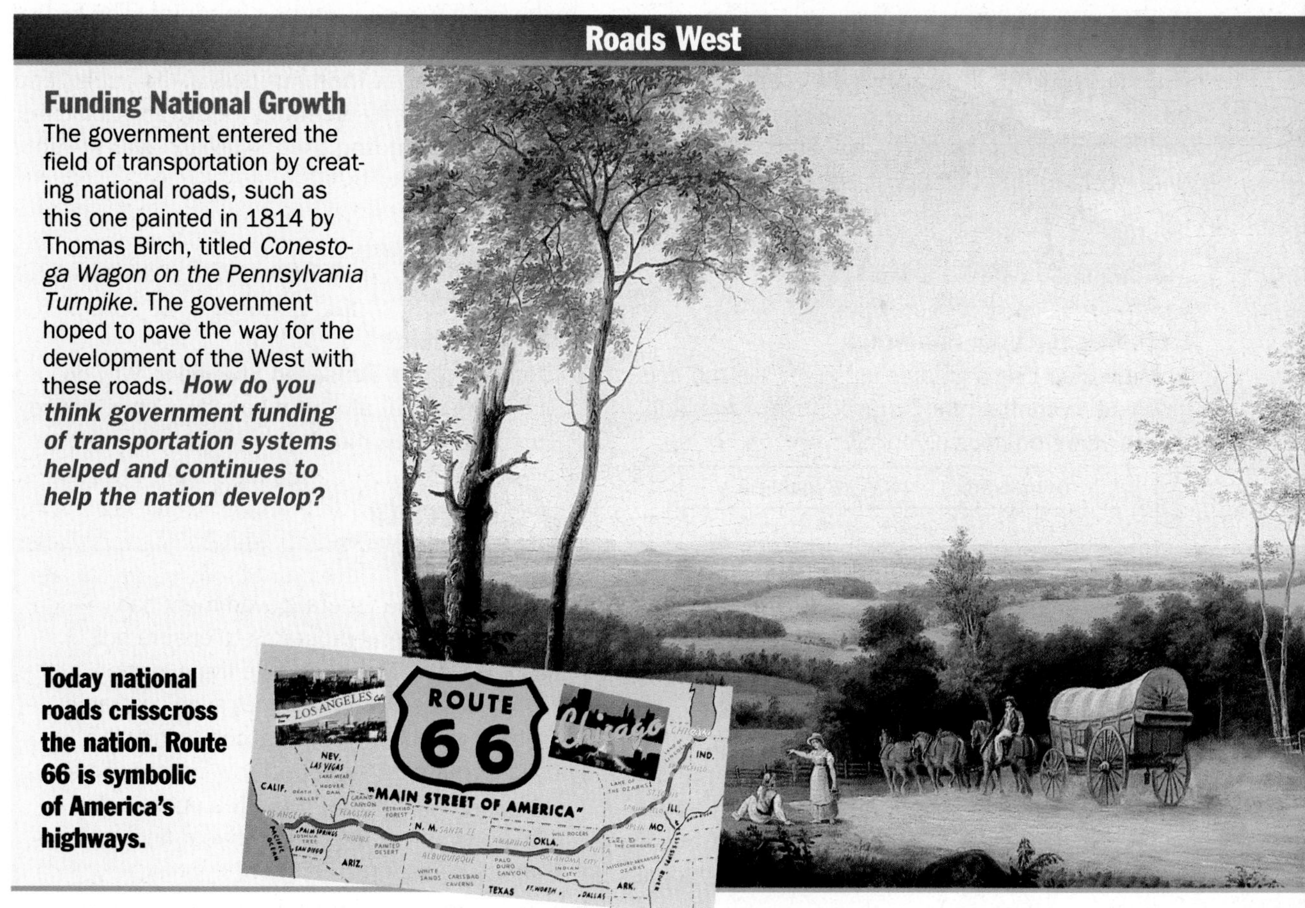

Funding National Growth
The government entered the field of transportation by creating national roads, such as this one painted in 1814 by Thomas Birch, titled *Conestoga Wagon on the Pennsylvania Turnpike*. The government hoped to pave the way for the development of the West with these roads. ***How do you think government funding of transportation systems helped and continues to help the nation develop?***

Today national roads crisscross the nation. Route 66 is symbolic of America's highways.

While the federal government provides the financial aid, the states do the work of constructing and improving the interstate highways. Once the work has been completed, the interstate roads belong to the state or local governments, which have the responsibility of maintaining them.

Today the Federal Highway Administration oversees federal highways and their funding. The FHWA also applies federal safety standards to trucks and buses and does planning and research on highway construction and maintenance. The FHWA's main job, however, is to administer the massive federal-aid highway program that supports the construction and upkeep of about 25 percent of the nation's roads.

National Highway System Congress reexamined the nation's transportation system and adopted several changes in National Highway System (NHS) legislation in 1995. The new legislation designated 161,000 miles of highways as NHS routes, repealed the federal maximum speed limits and motorcycle-helmet laws, and gave states more control over highway spending and policies.

Mass Transit The traffic helicopter seldom broadcasts good news for city dwellers. The streets and highways of large and small cities are clogged daily with automobile traffic, and urban planners warn of future gridlock, where traffic hardly moves. Still, many people prefer to drive their own vehicles when traveling in and around cities.

Could the urban transportation problem be solved with better **mass transit** systems such as subways, commuter railroads, and bus lines? When properly operated, mass transit can transport more people than individual automobiles and help to reduce congestion and air pollution. Beginning in the 1970s, the Urban Mass Transit Administration (UMTA) administered federal grant programs aimed at improving such transit systems in urban areas. The federal government continues to help cities cope with the growing need for better mass transit systems as a substitute for the automobile. The government also helps fund improvements in present transportation systems.

Efforts are underway to upgrade existing bus service, promote car and van pooling, and think of ways to make use of existing rail systems in and around cities.

The Intermodal Surface Transportation Efficiency Act (ISTEA) of 1991 authorizes the federal highway and transit funding program. The Federal Transit Administration oversees programs designed to integrate local businesses, the public, and the government in planning local transit systems. Most federal funding goes to urban areas of more than 200,000 people.

Section 4 Assessment

Checking for Understanding

1. **Main Idea** Use a graphic organizer like the one below to contrast the Democratic and Republican views on housing policy.

Democrats	Republicans

2. **Define** urban renewal, public housing, mass transit.
3. **Identify** Federal Housing Administration, Department of Housing and Urban Development.
4. Describe three programs the government initiated to aid education in the 1990s.
5. What was the role of the FHA in helping individual families afford housing?

Critical Thinking

6. **Demonstrating Reasoned Judgment** Why do governments at all levels spend so much money to support education?

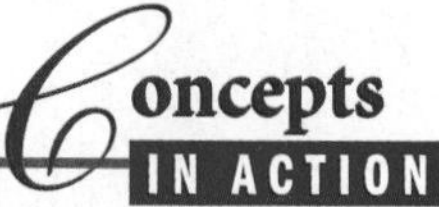

Federalism The federal government has developed several programs to ensure adequate housing for the people living in the United States. Find out about such programs that are established in your community that build or remodel homes for low-income families. Find out how the programs operate and who administers them. Share your findings with the class.

Skills

Critical Thinking

Making Comparisons

When making comparisons, you identify the similarities and differences among two or more ideas, objects, or events. You might compare two or more things in terms of some attribute—for example, the money spent by New York and Texas on education in one year. Or you could compare the same entity at different times—for example, the money spent by Illinois on education in 1995 and 2000.

Learning the Skill

Follow these steps to make comparisons:

a. Identify or decide what will be compared.
b. Determine a common area or areas in which comparisons can be drawn.
c. Look for similarities and differences within these areas.
d. If possible, find information that explains the similarities and differences.

Practicing the Skill

The Clinton administration's Goals 2000: Educate America Act, passed in 1994, has met with controversy. Read the passages below. Then answer the questions that follow.

Passage A

"Goals 2000 imposes a myriad of new federal dictates. It increases federal control of state education spending, requires national standards, issues intrusive federal 'skills certificates' that undermine parents' rights efforts, and influences state and local assessments. . . . [P]oliticians who partake of this hoax should be scorned for misusing taxpayer funds and undermining real education reform efforts."

—Natalie Williams and Lance Izumi, Claremont Institute

President Clinton visits a school.

Passage B

"Just as Oregon's school improvement law changed the relationship between the Oregon Department of Education and local school districts, Goals 2000 is changing the relationship we have with U.S. Department of Education. Federal officials do not tell us what to do but do offer assistance so we can achieve our goals."

—Norma Paulus, Oregon State Superintendent of Public Instruction

1. What is the topic of these passages?
2. How are the passages similar? Different?
3. What conclusions can you draw about the opinions of the writers?

Application Activity

Survey your classmates about an issue in the news. Summarize the opinions and compare the different results in a paragraph.

The Glencoe Skillbuilder Interactive Workbook, Level 2 provides instruction and practice in key social studies skills.

Assessment and Activities

Self-Check Quiz Visit the *United States Government: Democracy in Action* Web site at gov.glencoe.com and click on ***Chapter 21–Self-Check Quizzes*** to prepare for the chapter test.

Reviewing Key Terms

Choose the letter of the correct term or concept below to complete the sentence.

a. mixed economy
b. public assistance
c. social insurance
d. laissez-faire
e. urban renewal
f. marketing quota
g. securities
h. oligopoly
i. mass transit
j. acreage allotment

1. The government tries the _____ method to avoid storing overproduced grain.
2. A small number of powerful companies controlling a market is called an _____.
3. A hands-off government approach to the economy is called _____.
4. Stocks and bonds are forms of _____.
5. A _____ is an agreement among farmers to sell only aportion of an overproduced crop.
6. A federal program of _____ provides a certain minimum standard of living to those who do not earn enough income.
7. Federal _____ programs are designed to provide insurance against such social problems as old age, illness, and unemployment.
8. A _____ is one in which the government both supports and regulates private enterprise.
9. The federal government supports _____ in cities to help replace old buildings.
10. Cities build _____ systems to provide a substitute for automobiles.

Current Events JOURNAL

Researching Look through newspapers and magazines to find examples of ways that government and private citizens attempt to solve the issues of education and housing. You might also look for examples in the activities of local community organizations. Share your findings with the class.

Recalling Facts

1. Describe the business environment that led to the Sherman and Clayton Antitrust Acts.
2. What commission was created in 1972 to protect consumers against hazardous products?
3. What was the purpose of the 1947 Taft-Hartley Act?
4. What three programs does the federal government use to prevent low farm prices?
5. Why did the government enact the Social Security Act of 1935?
6. What are the four major public assistance programs of the federal government?
7. How is the federal government involved in education?
8. When did the federal government first become involved in housing policy?

Understanding Concepts

1. **Free Enterprise** How does the federal government attempt to preserve competition among business enterprises today?
2. **Civic Participation** What debated issues have prevented the United States from having a clear and consistent energy policy?
3. **Federalism** Which clause of the U.S. Constitution underlies federal regulation of the economy?

Critical Thinking

1. **Identifying Assumptions** What underlying assumptions about social problems can you identify in Arthur B. Laffer's assertion that "The solution rests in less—not more—government" and in Victor Kamber's view that ". . . we set up regulatory agencies in the first place to protect the public interest"?
2. **Predicting Consequences** Use a graphic organizer like the one below to show how a rapid rise in the elderly population and slower growth for the population under 30 could affect the Social Security system.

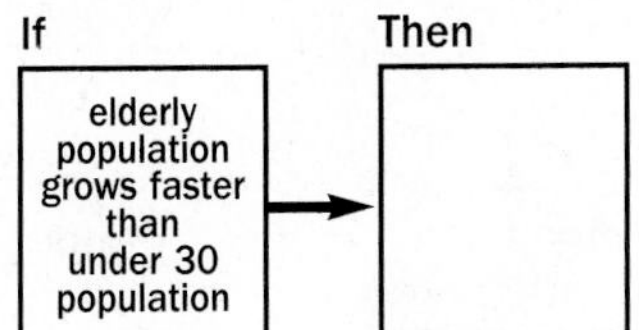

Interpreting Political Cartoons Activity

1. How does the cartoonist present the difficulties of Social Security reform?
2. How does the cartoonist portray baby boomers?
3. According to the cartoon, who will financially support retired baby boomers?

Technology Activity

Creating a Multimedia Presentation In recent years the federal government has involved itself in protecting the nation's environment. Work in small groups; create a multimedia presentation for a public service announcement on ways that your school can conserve natural resources.

Cooperative Learning Activity

Current Issues Divide the class into six groups. Have each group choose two topics from the following list: Medicare, Public Housing, Transportation, Education, Energy, Social Security, Public Assistance, Business Regulations, Conservation. Have each group collect news articles related to their topics for two weeks, then report to the class on significant developments.

Skill Practice Activity

Making Comparisons Reread the quotations concerning Social Security by Peter Peterson and Henry Aaron on page 592. Then answer the following questions.

1. In what ways are the passages similar?
2. On what point do the experts disagree?
3. Which expert do you agree with? Why?

Participating in Local Government

Find out how your local government protects consumers' rights. Find out what legislation protects consumers and how consumer complaints are handled. Also, find out what private community organizations work to protect consumers' rights. Prepare an oral report to share with the class.

Chapter 22

Foreign Policy and Defense

Why It's Important

A Global Society You are part of a global community. Increasingly, governments make choices about how their citizens will be affected by interaction with other nations. A democracy relies on informed citizens for direction in these decisions.

To learn more about how our foreign policy is established, view the ***Democracy in Action*** Chapter 22 video lesson:

Foreign Policy and National Defense

GOVERNMENT Online

Chapter Overview Visit the *United States Government: Democracy in Action* Web site at gov.glencoe.com and click on ***Chapter 22–Overview*** to preview chapter information.

Section 1

Development of Foreign Policy

Reader's Guide

Key Terms

foreign policy, national security, isolationism, internationalism, containment, détente

Find Out

- What are the major objectives of United States foreign policy?
- Why has a reevaluation of foreign policy been necessary since the end of the Cold War?

Understanding Concepts

Public Policy How did United States foreign policy contribute to winning the Cold War?

COVER STORY

China Policy Attacked

WASHINGTON, D.C., JUNE 24, 1997

A request by President Bill Clinton to extend China's status as a favored trading partner has aroused strong feelings in Congress. Opponents of the extension cite China's poor human rights record, including its persecution of political dissenters and Christians. Some call for trade sanctions to punish China. U.S.–China relations have also suffered from China's selling of nuclear materials to other nations. While critical of China's behavior, House majority leader Dick Armey reluctantly supports the trade extension. "Normal trade relations are best for the people of China today and offer the best prospect for liberating them in years to come," Armey said.

China's flag

China is one of the few Communist nations remaining in the world today. For nearly a half century after World War II, the global competition between communism and anticommunism known as the Cold War shaped American foreign policy. With the collapse of the Soviet Union and the fall of Communist governments in Eastern Europe in the early 1990s, it was clear the Cold War was over. The West, led by the United States, had won. Speaking to the U.S. Congress in 1992, the president of Russia stated:

> "*The idol of communism, which spread everywhere social strife, animosity and unparalleled brutality, which instilled fear in humanity, has collapsed. . . . I am here to assure you that we will not let it rise again in our land.*"
>
> —Boris Yeltsin, 1992

Today the United States confronts a global environment that is rapidly changing and marked by new challenges, such as increased economic and trade competition and the spread of international terrorism. At the same time, there is reason for optimism. George Kennan, one of America's most distinguished diplomats, recently described the post–Cold War period this way: "It is an age which, for all its confusions and dangers, is marked by one major blessing: for the first time in centuries, there are no great power rivalries that threaten immediately the peace of the world."

Goals of Foreign Policy

Foreign policy consists of the strategies and goals that guide a nation's relations with other countries and groups in the world. The specific strategies that make up United States foreign policy from year to year and even decade to decade change in response to changes in the international environment,

◀ **President Clinton in China**

such as the collapse of communism. However, the long-term goals of that policy remain constant. These goals reflect both the nation's ideals and its self-interest.

National Security The principal goal of American foreign policy is to preserve the security of the United States. National security means protection of a nation's borders and territories against invasion or control by foreign powers. This goal is basic because no nation can achieve other aims such as improving its educational system or providing better health care if it is under attack.

The goal of national security helps determine how the United States deals with other nations. Every part of American foreign policy—from maintaining an ambassador in a small Latin American country to signing a mutual assistance treaty with allied nations in Europe—is related to the nation's security.

Free and Open Trade In today's global economy national security means more than military defense. A nation's vital economic interests must also be protected. Thus, maintaining trade with other nations and preserving access to necessary natural resources have also been basic goals of American foreign policy. Trade is an absolute necessity for the United States. Highly productive American factories and farms need foreign markets in which to sell their goods. The United States also is in need of a number of natural resources, including oil. Generally, the United States supports trade that is free from both export and import restrictions.

World Peace One of the important goals of American foreign policy has been world peace. American leaders have worked for world peace because they believe it is another way to guarantee national security. If other nations are at peace, the United States runs little risk of being drawn into a conflict. To achieve this vital goal, the United States government has cooperated with other governments to settle disputes. The United States has also supplied economic aid to other countries, in part to prevent uprisings and revolutions. The desire for world peace was the main reason the United States helped organize the United Nations after World War II.

Attempting to Ensure National Security

Threats to Security
President Clinton, Russian President Boris Yeltsin, and Ukrainian President Leonid Kravchuk seal a disarmament pact in 1994. Clinton and his advisers were concerned about destabilizing forces in Ukraine and the long-range missiles and warheads there pointed at the United States. ***How do disarmament agreements such as this fulfill the foreign policy goals of the United States?***

Democratic Governments Throughout its history the United States has been an example of democracy. In addition, the United States aids democratic nations and helps others create democratic political systems. With the help of the United States, many of the formerly Communist nations in Europe began to form democratic political systems in the 1990s.

Concern for Humanity The United States has often demonstrated its concern for others. Victims of natural disasters or starvation have looked to the United States for help. In such times of crisis, the United States has responded by providing food, medical supplies, and technical assistance for humanitarian reasons. At the same time, this aid serves the strategic interests of the United States by maintaining political stability in the world.

Development of Foreign Policy

Until the late 1800s, American foreign policy was based on **isolationism**—avoiding involvement in world affairs, especially in the affairs of Europe. During the twentieth century, presidents and their foreign policy advisers shifted toward a policy of **internationalism.** Internationalists believed that involvement in world affairs was necessary for national security. A look at the history of American foreign policy since 1789 will reveal how these approaches to foreign policy developed.

Isolationism When George Washington became president in 1789, the United States was a small nation, deeply in debt and struggling to build a new government. For this reason American leaders believed that the United States should not become involved in the politics and wars of Europe. Before leaving office President Washington urged Americans to follow a path of isolationism.

President Thomas Jefferson also warned against forming "entangling alliances" with foreign nations. He stated that "Americans should never ask for privileges from foreign nations, in order not to be obliged to grant any in return."

The Monroe Doctrine In 1823 President James Monroe announced a new foreign policy doctrine that extended the meaning of isolationism. Later known as the Monroe Doctrine, it stated:

A Victim of War

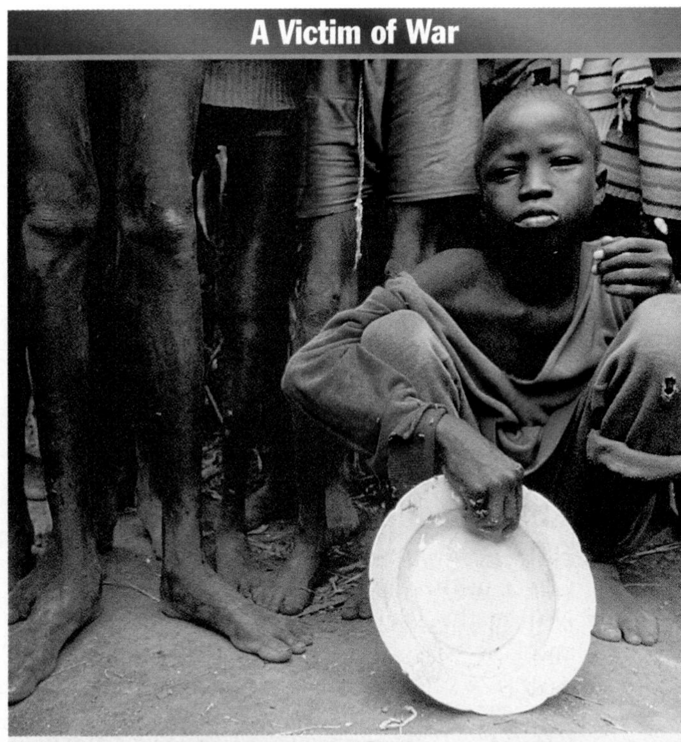

Humanitarian Policies A Sudanese refugee from the country's long civil war between northern Muslims and southern Christians waits to receive food donated by the United States and its allies. Self-interest is usually the basis of a nation's foreign policy. ***How would feeding Sudanese refugees serve United States interests?***

> "*The American continents, by the free and independent condition which they have assumed and maintain, are henceforth not to be considered as subjects for future colonization by any European powers. . . . We owe it . . . to candor, and to the amicable relations between the United States and those powers to declare that we should consider any attempt on their part to extend their system to any portion of this hemisphere as dangerous to our peace and safety. . . .*"
>
> —James Monroe, 1823

The United States as a World Power By the 1890s the United States was rapidly becoming one of the great industrial nations of the world. Accordingly, the United States began to look for world markets for its products and for new sources of raw materials. For some government leaders, isolationism no longer fit the United States's role as an economic power. These leaders believed the United States should play a more active role in world affairs. In their minds the nation needed to expand and acquire a colonial empire.

In 1898 the United States fought the Spanish-American War, in part to free Cuba from Spanish rule. As one result of that war, the United States acquired the Philippine Islands, Guam, and Puerto Rico. Hawaii was then annexed in 1898 and Samoa in 1900. Although isolationist sentiments survived, the United States was now a major power in the Caribbean as well as the Pacific region and East Asia.

Fearing communism as depicted in this comic book (left), Americans launched the Marshall Plan to help the economies of Western Europe rebuild after WW II.

Involvement in Two World Wars

When World War I broke out in Europe in 1914, isolationist sentiment in the United States was still strong. After Germany used unrestricted submarine warfare against neutral ships—including those of the United States—President Wilson asked Congress to declare war against Germany in 1917. For the first time in United States history, American troops went overseas to fight in a European war.

Disillusioned by the terrible cost in human lives and the failure to achieve the ideals of democracy worldwide after the war, Americans eagerly returned to isolationism. Throughout the 1920s and 1930s, most Americans wanted to avoid again becoming involved in European political affairs. During these years, however, ruthless dictators came to power—Mussolini in Italy, Hitler in Germany, and military leaders in Japan. By the 1930s, dramatic changes were taking place around the globe as these nations used military force to overtake other nations.

When World War II broke out in 1939, the United States officially remained neutral. The Japanese attack on Pearl Harbor in 1941, however, brought the United States into the war. Since then, the United States has based its foreign policy on internationalism.

The Cold War

The United States emerged from World War II as the leader of the free nations of the world. The United States's new role soon brought it into conflict with the Soviet Union, which had also emerged from the war as a world power. American government leaders viewed the power and ambitions of the Soviet Union as a threat to national security. Between 1945 and 1949, the Soviet Union established its dominion over the governments of Eastern European countries. Winston Churchill referred to the division between the Communist-controlled Eastern Europe and the free nations of Western Europe as an "iron curtain." Churchill warned that the Soviets would eventually look beyond Eastern Europe and try to gain control of other parts of the world. Meanwhile, in 1949 the Chinese Communists seized control of China. The Communist takeovers in these nations convinced American leaders that they must do something to halt Communist aggression.

As the rivalry between the United States and the Soviet Union intensified, it became clear that a "cold war" had begun. The **Cold War** was a war of words and ideologies rather than a shooting war.

Containment and the Truman Doctrine

Faced with the threat of expanding communism, the United States formulated a policy aimed at keeping the Soviet Union from spreading its power beyond Eastern Europe. In developing the policy President Truman drew upon the ideas of George F. Kennan, an American diplomat and an expert on Soviet history and culture. This policy, known as **containment,** in part involved responding to any action taken by the Soviets with a countermove by the United States.

American leaders also wanted to halt the spread of communism by giving economic aid to nations they said were threatened by totalitarian regimes. In keeping with the containment policy, President

Harry S Truman announced what later became known as the Truman Doctrine in a speech in 1947:

> "*I believe that we must assist free peoples to work out their own destinies in their own way. I believe that our help should be primarily through economic and financial aid which is essential to economic stability and orderly political processes. . . .*
>
> *The free peoples of the world look to us for support in maintaining their freedoms. If we falter in our leadership, we may endanger the peace of the world—and we shall surely endanger the welfare of this nation.*"
>
> —Harry S Truman, 1947

Three months later the Marshall Plan provided badly needed economic aid for war-torn Europe. Within four years the United States gave nations of Western Europe more than $13 billion.

Cold War tensions and fears also led the Soviet Union and the United States to engage in a costly arms race. At the end of World War II, the United States was the world's only nuclear power. However, by the late 1950s the Soviet Union had developed nuclear weapons and large rockets that could deliver nuclear warheads. From this point until the end of the Cold War, both nations began creating more weapons of increasingly greater destructive power.

The Korean and Vietnam Wars During the Cold War era the United States fought two wars that were the consequence of the policy of containment. In the Korean War (1950–1953) the United States came to the aid of pro-American South Korea when that country was invaded by Communist North Korea. The Korean War put the idea of containment into practice. President Truman said, "We've got to stop the Russians now." He saw the invasion of South Korea as part

We the People

Making a Difference

Douglas Engelbart

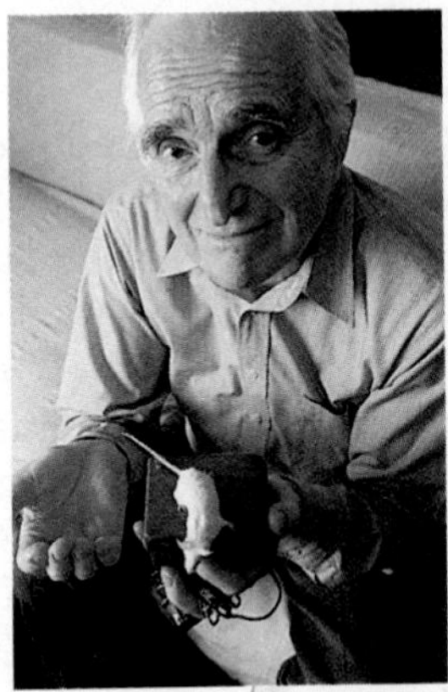

A mouse

As technology develops, the world becomes a smaller place and the management of United States foreign policy becomes more critical. Some of the credit for expanding technology and shrinking the world belongs to Douglas Engelbart. In 1963 Engelbart invented what he called an "X-Y Position Indicator for a Display System." You probably know his invention by another name—a mouse. Engelbart claims, "No one remembers who first called it that, but we all agreed that it looked like a mouse."

The mouse brought a point-and-click ease to computing and is essential for surfing the World Wide Web, but Engelbart did not profit from the invention. He explains, "I made a conscious decision at age 25 that money would be secondary." The engineer chose research over wealth. Instead, Engelbart's employer, Stanford Research Institute, reaped the financial rewards.

Since his contribution to modern technology, Engelbart has enjoyed other victories. In 1989 he overcame lymphoma and retired from his job to start his own research organization. He and his daughter, Christina, formed the Bootstrap Institute, a think tank located in office space donated by Logitech. Incidentally, Logitech manufactured its 100 millionth mouse in 1996.

Today, in his 70s, Engelbart lectures to software and technology leaders and sells the benefits of another invention—his five-button, one-handed keyboard. Many people ask him if he is frustrated that others have made billions on his invention. Engelbart answers, "I feel frustrated in not having had more of an effect on the world."

Foreign Policy Motives
President Reagan and Soviet leader Gorbachev shake hands at a 1988 summit meeting in Moscow. Gorbachev initiated the meetings to convince Reagan that the Soviets wanted to end the arms race. The talks resulted in the signing of the first Soviet–U.S. agreement to reduce the number of existing nuclear missiles. ***Why do you think Gorbachev sought to establish closer ties with the United States?***

of expansionism by the Soviet Union and sent American troops to Korea under the sponsorship of the United Nations.

In the Vietnam War (1964–1973) the United States committed troops for many years to fight on the side of the South Vietnamese government against Communist North Vietnam. Many American policy makers and Presidents Lyndon Johnson and Richard Nixon said American involvement in the conflict was justified by the need to contain Communist expansion. In 1970, for example, President Nixon stated, ". . . if the United States leaves Vietnam . . . it will be ominously encouraging to the leaders of Communist China and the Soviet Union who are supporting the North Vietnamese."

The Policy of Détente Because of their hopes for peace and their fears of nuclear war, United States leaders in the 1970s began to explore possibilities for easing the tensions of the Cold War. President Nixon and his national security advisor, Henry Kissinger, spoke of a new policy called **détente,** or a relaxation of tensions. The key idea of this policy was to look for ways to improve relations between Communist nations and free nations. One consequence was that in 1972 President Nixon visited the People's Republic of China in order to open communications with the Communist leaders there. By 1978 cultural and diplomatic ties between the United States and China had grown enormously, and the United States under President Jimmy Carter extended diplomatic recognition to China.

A second consequence of détente was the Strategic Arms Limitations Treaty, called SALT. These arms-control negotiations took place over a number of years. The SALT talks were aimed at limiting defense costs and reducing the risk of nuclear war for both the United States and the Soviet Union. President Nixon and Soviet leader Leonid Brezhnev signed the first SALT agreement in 1972, and many additional talks and agreements followed.

A Harder Line In 1979 Soviet troops invaded Afghanistan. President Jimmy Carter responded by imposing an embargo on the sale of grain to the Soviet Union, and the United States boycotted the Summer Olympic Games held in Moscow. Tension between the Soviet Union and the United States mounted.

In November 1980, Americans elected Ronald Reagan, a strong anti-Communist, as president. He took office determined to challenge the Soviet Union in every way. He adopted a harder line against communism. Referring to the Soviet Union as an "evil empire," Reagan asked Congress for the largest peacetime defense-spending increase in United States history.

End of the Cold War By the late 1980s decades of competition with the United States as well as the basic flaws of communism as a political system finally took their toll on the Soviet empire. Deteriorating economic and political conditions forced Soviet leader Mikhail Gorbachev to begin making major changes in policy in an effort to reduce military spending, reform the Soviet economy, and create a new openness. Called **perestroika,**

these reforms were too little, too late. By 1989 the Soviet Union had begun to collapse. Late that year the symbol of the Cold War, the Berlin Wall dividing Communist East Germany from West Germany, was torn down by demonstrators, and a year later the two Germanys were reunited. Poland, Czechoslovakia (soon to divide into the Czech Republic and Slovakia), and Hungary overthrew their Communist governments and established more democratic governments. Hard-line Communist leaders were also overthrown in Romania and Bulgaria, and by 1992 the former Soviet Union itself had begun changing its government, splitting into Russia and 14 other separate nations. The Cold War that had begun shortly after the end of World War II was over.

Toward a New Political Order The end of Communist governments in Eastern Europe and the breakup of the Soviet Union changed the world political environment. President George Bush referred to this as "a new world order." How would the United States reshape its foreign policy to deal with the new reality? Some leaders spoke of a **"peace dividend"**—the release of funds from military use to serve domestic needs. Few leaders wanted to return to a policy of isolationism.

Former secretary of state James A. Baker III identified three developments that would affect American foreign policy in the next century:

> *"One such transformation is the emergence of a truly global economy based on free market principles. The second is the geopolitical shift associated with the end of the Cold War. And the third is the rise of culture, broadly defined, as an important but often misunderstood international force."*
>
> —James A. Baker III, November 1995

The United States is a major force in the global economy. President Bill Clinton led an effort to promote global free trade. He signed the North American Free Trade Agreement (NAFTA), which committed Canada, Mexico, and the United States to lowering trade restrictions. He also signed the General Agreement on Tariffs and Trade (GATT), which broadened worldwide business opportunities and created the World Trade Organization (WTO).

These international economic relationships following the Cold War have placed corporations in a position to affect foreign policy. The government, in turn, must balance eagerness to open world markets with concerns over environmental problems, labor practices, and consumer protection.

The emergence of the European Union, China, and other Asian nations as major players, as well as regional conflicts and nationalist movements, has led to a new American foreign policy, increasingly focused on the entire globe.

Section 1 Assessment

Checking for Understanding

1. **Main Idea** Use a graphic organizer like the one to the right to show the three developments that James A. Baker III said would affect future United States foreign policy.

   U.S. foreign policy

2. **Define** foreign policy, national security, isolationism, internationalism, containment, détente.
3. **Identify** Cold War, "peace dividend."
4. What are the basic aims of American foreign policy?
5. How did the United States carry out its policy of containment?

Critical Thinking

6. **Drawing Conclusions** Do you believe the United States could follow a policy of isolationism at this time? Support your answer.

Concepts IN ACTION

Public Policy Today's new political order resulted in a reassessment and a smaller defense budget for the United States, thereby leaving extra money available for domestic needs. Create a political cartoon about this topic and how this "peace dividend" could be utilized by the American public. Be sure to include a caption for your cartoon.

Section 2

Shared Foreign Policy Powers

Reader's Guide

Key Terms

ambassador, treaty, executive agreement, bipartisan

Find Out

- How is the executive branch structured to carry out United States foreign policy?
- What are the constitutional foreign policy powers of the president and Congress?

Understanding Concepts

Checks and Balances What powers of Congress act as a check upon the president's power to conduct foreign policy?

COVER STORY

U.S. Supports Revolt

WASHINGTON, D.C., NOVEMBER 6, 1903

President Theodore Roosevelt today recognized the independent nation of Panama, four days after ordering warships into the region and only three days after Panamanian rebels declared the province's freedom from Colombia. Roosevelt's action is believed to be the fastest U.S. recognition of another nation in history. The revolt and diplomatic maneuver clear the way for the United States to construct a canal across Panama, a proposal to which Colombia refused to agree. U.S. officials have long favored a canal across Central America to provide a shorter water route from the Atlantic to the Pacific. The rebels in Panama also support such a canal.

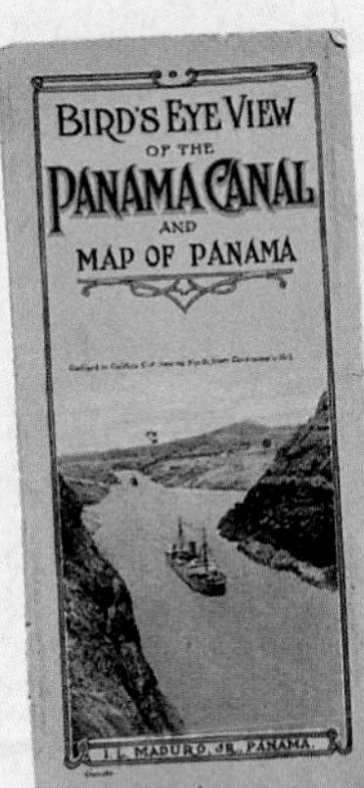

A map of the Panama Canal

The Framers of the Constitution attempted to divide the responsibility for foreign affairs between the president and Congress. They did not, however, clearly outline the boundaries of power of each branch. As a result, on many occasions the president and Congress have vied for power.

Over the years events have enabled the president to assume more responsibility in foreign policy. Today, according to one political scientist, "Any discussion of the making of United States foreign policy must begin with the President. He is the ultimate decider."

Presidential Powers and Responsibilities

The president derives power to formulate foreign policy from two sources. First, the Constitution lists certain presidential powers related to foreign policy. Second, as the head of the world's superpower, the president functions as an important world leader.

Constitutional Powers of the President

President Bill Clinton addressed the American people on September 15, 1994:

> *My fellow Americans, tonight I want to speak to you about why the United States is leading an international effort to restore democratic government in Haiti. Haiti's dictators, led by [Lt.] General Raoul Cedras, control the most violent regime in our hemisphere. . . . In the face of this continued defiance and with atrocities rising, the United States has agreed to lead a multinational force to carry out the will of the United Nations. . . . No president makes decisions like this without deep thought and prayer.*
>
> —Bill Clinton, 1994

President Clinton's speech illustrates the president's ability to commit the nation to involvement in foreign affairs.

Brokering Peace

Peace Agreement With President Clinton looking on, Israel's Prime Minister Yitzhak Rabin (left) and PLO leader Yasir Arafat (right) signed a peace agreement in 1993. ***What presidential role did Clinton fulfill in the Israeli-PLO agreement?***

Commander in Chief

The Constitution grants the president the power to be the commander in chief of the nation's military forces. As commander in chief, the president may send troops, ships, and planes or may even use nuclear weapons anywhere in the world, without congressional approval. For example, President Bush decided to send military forces to Saudi Arabia soon after Iraq had invaded Kuwait.

Head of State In addition to giving powers as commander in chief, Article II, Section 2,[1] grants the president certain diplomatic powers. The president appoints **ambassadors,** officials of the United States government who represent the nation in diplomatic matters. The president also receives ambassadors from foreign governments. By receiving an ambassador or other diplomat from a certain country, the president gives formal recognition to that government. Conversely, by refusing to receive an ambassador, the president can withhold diplomatic recognition of a foreign government. Formal recognition of a government is vital because it qualifies that government to receive economic and other forms of aid. Article II, Section 2, also gives the president power to make treaties. A **treaty** is a formal agreement between the governments of two or more nations.

As head of state, the president plays an important part in controlling foreign policy. The president represents the United States and symbolizes the leadership and policies of the nation to the world. In an international crisis, Americans also look to their president for leadership.

See the following footnoted materials in the ***Reference Handbook:***
1. See *The Constitution,* pages 774–799.

Foreign Policy Advisers

The president has the final responsibility for establishing foreign policy. Before making foreign policy decisions, however, presidents usually consult advisers. Generally, chief executives rely upon the information and advice of the cabinet members, the White House staff, and officials in specialized agencies dealing with foreign policy. At times presidents also go outside the government and seek advice from private individuals who have specialized knowledge in foreign affairs.

The Secretaries of State and Defense In their specialized fields, all cabinet members bring international problems to the president's attention and recommend how to deal with them. For two cabinet departments, however—the Department of State and the Department of Defense—foreign affairs are a full-time concern.

The **secretary of state** supervises all the diplomatic activities of the American government. In the past most presidents have relied heavily on their secretaries of state. In the early years of the

Republic, four secretaries of state—Thomas Jefferson, James Madison, James Monroe, and John Quincy Adams—went on to become president.

Normally, the secretary of state carries on diplomacy at the highest level. The secretary frequently travels to foreign capitals for important negotiations with heads of state and represents the United States at major international conferences.

The **secretary of defense** supervises the military activities of the United States government. The president receives information and advice from the secretary of defense on the nation's military forces, weapons, and bases.

The National Security Adviser In recent administrations the **national security adviser**—who is also the director of the National Security Council (NSC)—has played a major role in foreign affairs. Under President Nixon, for example, the national security adviser, Henry Kissinger, not only presented options but also recommended policies. He was the president's closest adviser.

The Central Intelligence Agency In order to make foreign policy decisions, the president and his advisers need information about the governments, economies, and armed forces of other nations. The task of gathering and coordinating this information is primarily the responsibility of the **Central Intelligence Agency** (CIA).

The National Security Act established the CIA and defined its duties in 1947. Today the CIA, under the direction of the National Security Council, coordinates the intelligence activities of other agencies. The organization also safeguards top-secret information and conducts intelligence operations that the council authorizes.

Although it does use foreign agents, or spies, to obtain information, such undercover operations are only a small part of the CIA's function. Most of the agency's employees simply gather and evaluate information, much of it available from news media coverage of foreign officials and from official publications in foreign countries.

Recently critics of the CIA have questioned the agency's efficiency. Inefficiency was most evident after the CIA failed to predict Iraq's invasion of Kuwait in 1990. In addition, the collapse of the Soviet Union during 1991 caught the CIA by surprise. With the end of the Cold War, one prominent newsmagazine carried a lead article titled "Is the CIA Obsolete?"

★ ★ ★ GOVERNMENT *and You*

Volunteering for the Armed Forces

By volunteering for the military, you can serve your country, learn a skill, and provide for your future at the same time. Each branch of the armed forces has its own requirements. In general, you must be at least 17 years old to enlist, have a high school diploma, have no criminal record, and be a U.S. citizen or legal alien. You also must meet certain physical requirements, pass a drug test, and take a multiple-choice test to identify your academic and vocational strengths. The results are used to qualify you for certain training programs, some of which can pay up to a $12,000 bonus.

In addition to the skills you gain from your training, you can often take college or technical courses in your off-duty time. The military will help pay for these courses. When you complete your full-time military commitment, you can receive as much as $40,000 to continue your education.

Looking for recruits

Participating IN GOVERNMENT ACTIVITY

Research Investigate your opportunities in a specific branch of the military. Contact a nearby recruiting station to find out information about the branch you choose. Present your findings to the class in the form of an advertising brochure.

Making Foreign Policy The government employs hundreds of foreign policy experts whom the president may consult before making a decision. In some cases family members and trusted political friends have had more influence on a president than the secretary of state. A mild-mannered Texan named Colonel Edward House was President Woodrow Wilson's most trusted adviser, especially during World War I, even though he held no cabinet post.

In recent years, however, each president has taken a different approach to foreign policy. President Eisenhower relied heavily on Secretary of State John Foster Dulles for foreign policy advice. President Kennedy, on the other hand, put together a team of foreign affairs experts who worked together in the basement of the White House. A group of advisers who lunched with the president in the White House every Tuesday often influenced President Johnson's decisions on the Vietnam War. Included in this "Tuesday Cabinet" were the director of the CIA and the White House press secretary. In contrast, the opinions of National Security Adviser Henry Kissinger were the major influence on President Nixon.

In the final analysis, however, it is the president who determines what policies are to be followed. As President Ronald Reagan wrote, only the president can "respond quickly in a crisis or formulate a coherent and consistent policy in any region of the world."

Encouraging Peace

Diplomatic Moves In 1997 Secretary of State Madeleine Albright (left) visited the Middle East and met with Yasir Arafat (right) and Israeli leaders to revitalize the peace process. Albright's trip was not successful. She remarked, "I am a realist and not a magician. I cannot pull a rabbit out of a hat if there aren't the makings of it there." ***Why might Albright make such a statement about her efforts?***

Powers of Congress

Although the president directs United States foreign policy, Congress plays an important role. The basis for this role lies in the Constitution. The Constitution gives Congress significant foreign policy powers, including the power to declare war and appropriate money. The Senate must ratify treaties and confirm diplomatic appointments. Even though Congress has these powers, some people believe it has seldom used them effectively. Instead, Congress has, in the words of former senator Barry Goldwater, revealed its "inability to act decisively in time of need."

Power to Declare War The Constitution balances the president's powers as commander in chief by granting Congress the power to declare war. Although the president may send troops anywhere in the world, only Congress may declare war. Yet Congress has exercised its power to declare war only five times in our nation's history. It declared war in 1812 against Britain, in 1846 against Mexico, in 1898 against Spain, in 1917 against Germany, and in 1941 against Japan, Germany, and Italy. In these five cases the United States was officially at war with a foreign government. In each instance the president asked Congress for a declaration of war. Then, in accordance with the Constitution, both houses of Congress adopted the war resolution by a majority vote.

In other instances, instead of requesting a formal declaration of war, presidents have asked Congress to pass a joint resolution concerning the use

Transporting Aid to Somalia

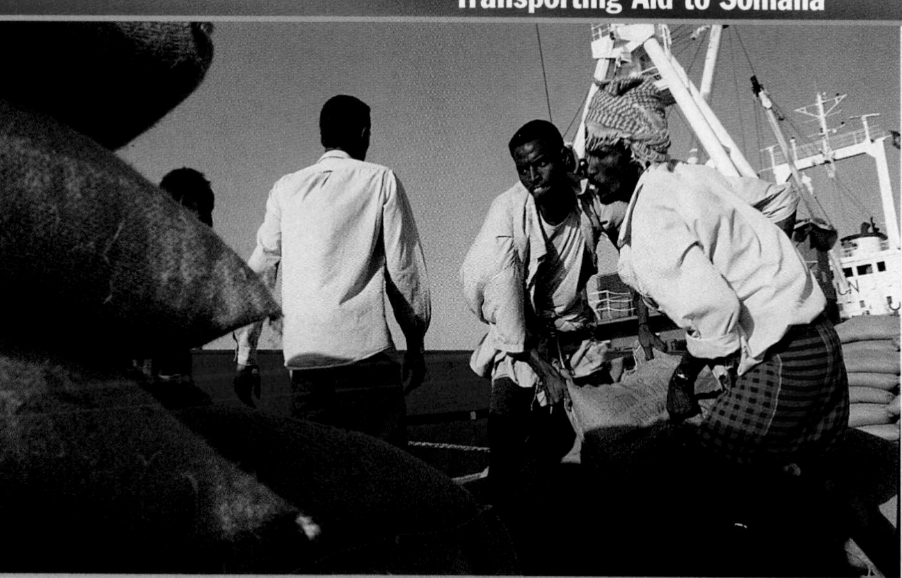

Presidential Actions The United States sent food to war-torn Somalia in Operation Restore Hope. The U.S.–led United Nations mission, although a humanitarian one, suffered casualties. President Clinton faced pressure from both Congress and the American public to recall American troops, but he refused, believing that Somali lives and American credibility were at stake. ***Do you think presidents should have the power to keep American troops in foreign countries, ignoring pressure from Congress?***

of American troops. In 1964, for example, President Lyndon Johnson asked Congress for authority to use troops in Vietnam. In response to an alleged North Vietnamese attack on United States ships that occurred in the Gulf of Tonkin off Vietnam's coast, Congress passed the Gulf of Tonkin Resolution.**1** The resolution authorized the president "to take all necessary measures to repel any armed attack against the forces of the United States."

Dismayed by the results of the Gulf of Tonkin Resolution, Congress tried to check the president's power to send troops into combat by passing the War Powers Act in 1973. The act declared that the president could not send troops into combat for more than 60 days without the consent of Congress. Seventeen years later, after the 1990 Iraqi invasion of Kuwait, some members of Congress questioned President Bush's commitment of troops in the Middle East. The War Powers Act was not invoked, however. Instead, Congress authorized the use of force against Iraq. With this Congressional approval, President Bush authorized Operation Desert Storm that easily defeated the Iraqi forces.

Former senator Jacob Javits explained the dilemma facing members of Congress who support the War Powers Act in this way:

> "*The reluctance to challenge the president is founded in an awareness that he holds, in large degree, the fate of the nation in his hands. We all wish to assist and sustain the presidency. But I have come to the conclusion that the awesome nature of the power over war in our time should require us to withhold, in relevant cases, that unquestioning support of the presidency.*"
>
> —Jacob Javits, 1985

Power to Appropriate Money By far the greatest source of congressional power in foreign policy derives from Congress's control over government spending. Only Congress can appropriate the funds to equip American armed forces and to build new weapons. Congress must authorize funds for defense and foreign aid each year. If Congress disapproves of a president's action, such as committing troops to a limited war, it can refuse to provide the funds to maintain the force.

In a similar fashion, Congress may refuse to provide funds for aid to other nations. Congress also may decide not only the sum to be granted, but also the conditions that a foreign country must meet to be eligible for aid.

Power in Treaty Making The Constitution also gives the Senate the power of "advice and consent" on all treaties. The president may make

See the following footnoted materials in the **Reference Handbook:**
1. *Gulf of Tonkin Resolution,* page 826.

treaties with foreign governments, but a two-thirds vote of the Senate must ratify them. In reality, then, Congress is called upon for its consent, not its advice—a practice that actually began with President Washington.

The Senate's power in treaty making is real, however. The Senate has voted down or refused to consider more than 130 treaties since 1789. In 1978 President Jimmy Carter faced strong opposition from Senate conservatives regarding his proposed Panama Canal treaties. After much debate, the Senate did eventually ratify both treaties.

Increasingly presidents have turned to another tool for making binding commitments with foreign governments. **Executive agreements** are pacts between the president and the head of a foreign government that have the legal status of treaties but do not require Senate approval. Today executive agreements make up more than 90 percent of all United States international agreements.

Most Favored Nation

Presidents have relied on executive agreements to enhance their foreign policy powers. Although there is little difference between a treaty and an executive agreement, Congress has not strongly objected to these presidential decisions. In fact Congress has authorized that all trade agreements be handled as executive agreements, requiring only a simple majority vote of both houses. Under United States law the president may grant **most-favored-nation (MFN)** status to trading partners. Such agreements reduce tariff rates on all exports from that nation to the United States. By a two-thirds majority vote Congress may overturn the president's decision to grant MFN status. In 1997, for example the House voted to kill a bill that would have ended renewal of most-favored-nation status for China.

Power to Confirm Appointments

The Senate must also confirm presidential appointments to diplomatic posts. This power was intended to give the Senate an opportunity to screen applicants for foreign policy positions and thus help determine foreign policy. Usually the Senate is willing to accept the persons the president appoints to diplomatic posts.

The President and Congress

Congress's powers could enable the legislature to block some of a president's foreign policies and even initiate policies of its own. Congress, however, waits for the president to set a direction in foreign policy. On most issues Congress passes the foreign policy bills and treaties the president and his advisers propose.

Over the past several decades, especially in times of war and severe crisis, the president's foreign policies have enjoyed **bipartisan**, or two-party, congressional support. For example, Republican and Democratic members of Congress readily supported President Wilson in World War I and President Roosevelt in World War II. During the Persian Gulf War in 1991, President Bush also received bipartisan support from Congress. During

A Historical Double Take

A Change of Policy In 1978 President Jimmy Carter won Senate ratification of the Panama Canal treaties, which transferred control of the canal from the United States to Panama by the end of the century. Many Americans were outraged at the Panama "giveaway." ***Why were Americans outraged and what do you think motivated the United States to make such a treaty?***

the Vietnam War, however, bipartisan support began to unravel when Congress and the public were deeply divided about the nation's role in the long and costly war.

Presidential Advantages The president has advantages over Congress in conducting foreign policy. One is the president's position as the leader of the nation. Only the president—or a chosen spokesperson such as the secretary of state—can speak for the nation in dealings with other governments. It is the president to whom Americans look for leadership in foreign affairs.

A second advantage is that the president controls those agencies, such as the Department of State and the National Security Council, that help formulate and carry out foreign policy on a day-to-day basis. Consequently, the president has greater access to vital secret information about foreign affairs. Such information often is not available to members of Congress.

A third advantage is that the president is able to take quick decisive action. Today it is often necessary to respond to events rapidly, and at times extreme secrecy is essential. The House and Senate must discuss, vote, and take into consideration the opinions of many members. Congress simply cannot act as quickly as the president or maintain secrecy with so many people involved.

Finally, by using executive agreements, the president can bypass the Senate when making agreements with other nations. As a result of these advantages there has been a steady increase in the president's power over foreign policy matters.

Influence of Public Opinion

Though the president and Congress have the major responsibility for making foreign policy, their decisions are often influenced by the opinions of the American people. Public opinion, for example, directly influenced the Vietnam War. Mass protests and demonstrations in the 1960s and the early 1970s had a direct impact on foreign policy. Early on, most Americans supported the fighting in Vietnam. But as the number of Americans wounded and killed grew and media coverage heightened public awareness of the situation, public opinion slowly began to turn against the war. As the war dragged on, other groups joined the protests. The growing discontent contributed heavily to President Lyndon Johnson's decision not to seek reelection in 1968 and later influenced President Richard Nixon's decision to begin pulling American troops out of Vietnam.

Besides public opinion, pressure from interest groups can also affect foreign policy. The votes of Congress on foreign policy questions are subject to the influence of organized interest groups. These groups whose concerns range from trade to human rights issues can have a substantial impact on legislation that affects their areas of interest.

Section 2 Assessment

Checking for Understanding

1. **Main Idea** Use a Venn diagram like the one below to compare executive agreements and treaties.

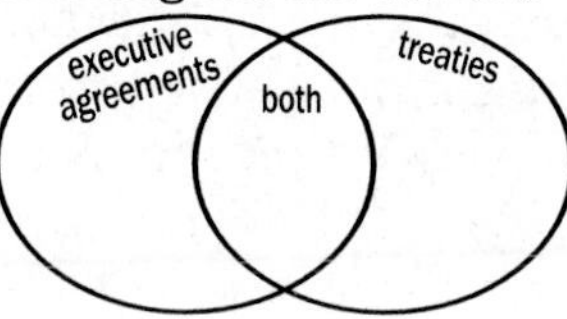

2. **Define** ambassador, treaty, executive agreement, bipartisan.
3. **Identify** secretary of state, national security adviser, Central Intelligence Agency.
4. Which cabinet members generally work most closely with the president on foreign policy?
5. What are the foreign policy powers of Congress?

Critical Thinking

6. **Forming an Opinion** Do you think the president has too much power in making foreign policy? Explain your answer.

Checks and Balances Use library resources to find specific examples of how public opinion changed U.S. policy in Vietnam in the 1960s and 1970s. Prepare a poster that illustrates the public's reaction to the war and the government's responses. Be sure to include pictures, captions, and headlines in your poster.

Section 3

State and Defense Departments

Reader's Guide

Key Terms

embassy, consulate, consul, passport, visa, conscription

Find Out

- How is the State Department structured to carry out United States foreign policy?
- What constitutional powers do Congress and the president have over the military?

Understanding Concepts

Separation of Powers What constitutional provisions separate the powers of Congress and the president in developing and carrying out foreign policy?

COVER STORY

Troops in Somalia

WASHINGTON, D.C., DECEMBER 4, 1992

President George Bush ordered 28,000 U.S. troops into Somalia to protect relief workers in their efforts to distribute aid to that nation's starving people. A civil war in the East African nation has prevented supplies from reaching much of the population. Bush stressed that the intervention is for humanitarian, not strategic reasons.

U.S. soldier hugs a Somali child.

"I understand that the United States alone cannot right the world's wrongs," the president declared. "But we also know that some crises in the world cannot be resolved without American involvement." Analysts see Bush's action as defining a new role for the U.S. military in the post–Cold War world.

It is the duty of the president and Congress to make American foreign policy. Appointed officials in the executive branch, however, carry out foreign policy on a day-to-day basis.

Two departments in the executive branch are primarily responsible for foreign policy and for national security. The Department of State, one of the smallest cabinet-level departments in terms of employees, carries out foreign policy. The Department of Defense is the largest of all the executive departments both in terms of money spent and people employed. It looks after the national security of the United States.

The Department of State

Created by Congress in 1789, the Department of State was the first executive department. Originally known as the Department of Foreign Affairs, it was soon renamed the Department of State. The secretary of state, head of the State Department, is generally considered to be the most important member of the cabinet, ranking just below the president and vice president.

The State Department advises the president and formulates and carries out policy. Officially, the Department of State's "primary objective in the conduct of foreign relations is to promote the long-range security and well-being of the United States." The Department of State carries out four other important functions: (1) to keep the president informed about international issues, (2) to maintain diplomatic relations with foreign governments, (3) to negotiate treaties with foreign governments, and (4) to protect the interests of Americans who are traveling or conducting business abroad.

Organizational Structure Five assistant secretaries direct the five geographic bureaus of the State Department. These bureaus are the Bureaus of African Affairs, European and Canadian Affairs, East Asian and Pacific Affairs,

Inter-American Affairs, and Near Eastern and South Asian Affairs. Other bureaus analyze information about specific foreign policy topics. One such bureau deals with educational and cultural affairs, another with political-military problems, and another with intelligence and research. The work of the State Department, therefore, is organized both by topics and regions.

The Foreign Service More than half of the employees of the State Department serve in other countries. The officials who are assigned to serve abroad in foreign countries belong to the **Foreign Service.**

College graduates who seek a career in the Foreign Service must pass an extremely demanding civil service exam. Successful applicants then receive training in special schools. Foreign Service Officers (FSOs) usually spend several years abroad in a diplomatic post. Then they may be recalled to Washington, D.C., to participate in foreign policy discussions at the State Department.

For many FSOs, an overseas assignment is valued, but for others it may be a life of hardship. As one observer of the State Department noted:

> "*Working at State demands far more than the usual 40-hour week. . . . Officers stationed overseas are almost never off duty. Not only may they be called on at any hour of the day or night, they also represent the government in every aspect of their lives and personal encounters. Even socializing is work. Attending parties, seemingly an attractive way of making a living, pales after weeks of mandatory and boring appearances following an intensive workday.*"
>
> —Barry Rubin, 1985

In their service abroad, Foreign Service Officers are normally assigned either to an American embassy or to an American consulate.

Guarding United States Interests

Representing a Nation Guards patrol the United States embassy in Riyadh, Saudi Arabia. ***Why do you think embassies have been a target for political protests and terrorist activities in recent years?***

Embassies The United States maintains embassies in the capital cities of foreign countries—such as Tokyo, Japan; Paris, France; and Nairobi, Kenya. An **embassy** includes the official residence and offices of the ambassador and his or her staff. The primary function of an embassy is to make diplomatic communication between governments easier. Currently, the State Department directs the work of about 150 American embassies.

Embassy officials keep the State Department informed about the politics and foreign policies of the host government. They also keep the host government informed about American policies.

An ambassador heads each American embassy. Most ambassadors today come from the ranks of the Foreign Service as experienced and highly qualified professional diplomats. Some ambassadors, however, may be political appointees, selected for reasons other than their diplomatic knowledge or experience. In every case, however, an ambassador is appointed by the president and must be confirmed by the Senate.

Each embassy includes specialists who deal with political and military matters, trade, travel, and currency. The specialists help resolve disputes

The Commander in Chief

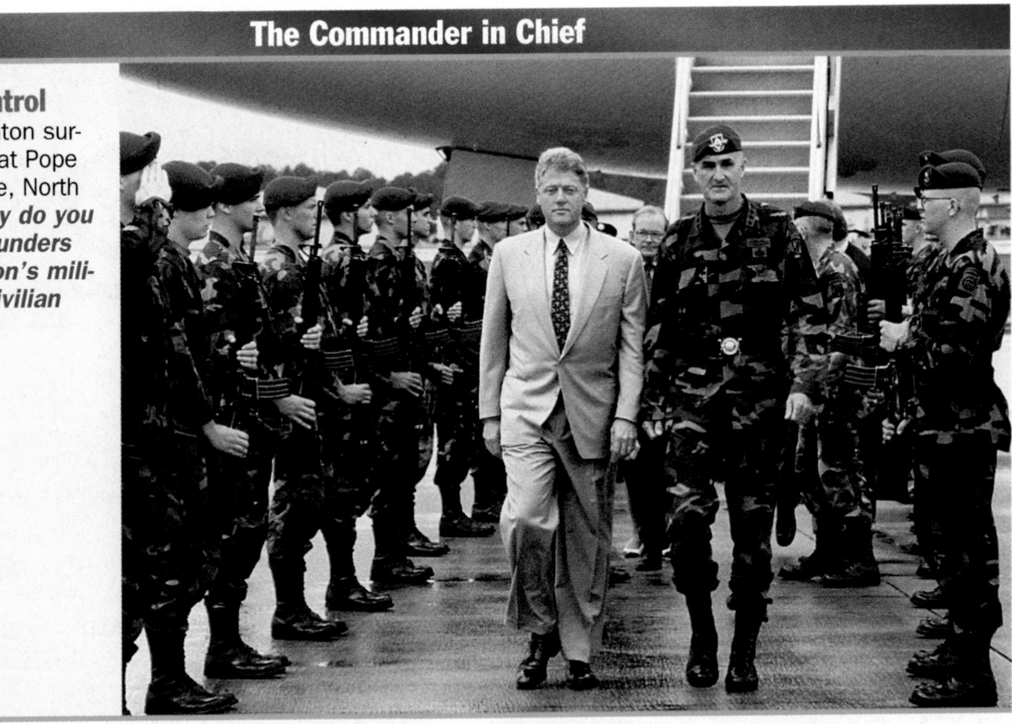

Military Control President Clinton surveyed troops at Pope Air Force Base, North Carolina. ***Why do you think the Founders put the nation's military under civilian control?***

that arise between the host country and the United States. Most disputes are minor enough to be settled by the embassy staff. In the case of major disagreements, governments may break off diplomatic relations by closing their embassies. Such action represents the strongest sign of displeasure that one government can show toward another.

Consulates The United States also maintains offices known as **consulates** in major cities of foreign nations. Consulates are not normally involved in diplomatic negotiations with foreign governments. They function primarily to promote American business interests in foreign countries and to serve and safeguard American travelers in the countries where consulates are located.

Heading each consulate is a Foreign Service Officer called a **consul.** In the course of a routine day, the consul and staff handle individual problems and inquiries about such matters as shipping schedules, business opportunities, and travel needs.

Passports and Visas For Americans traveling abroad, the State Department issues a document called a **passport.** The traveler whose photograph and signature appear on the passport is entitled to certain privileges and protection established by an international treaty. With a passport, an American citizen can expect to be granted entry into many countries.

In some cases, however, to be granted the right to enter another country it is necessary to obtain another document called a visa. A **visa** is a special document issued by the government of the country that a person wishes to enter. If a citizen of Kenya wishes to visit the United States, for example, he or she must apply for a visa at an American embassy or consulate in one of the major Kenyan cities.

American immigration laws require nearly all foreign visitors to obtain visas prior to entering the United States. The countries of Western Europe, however, do not require American travelers to carry visas, only passports.

The Department of Defense

To protect national security, the Department of Defense (DOD) supervises the armed forces of the United States and makes sure these forces are strong enough to defend American interests. The Department of Defense assists the president in carrying out the duties of commander in chief.

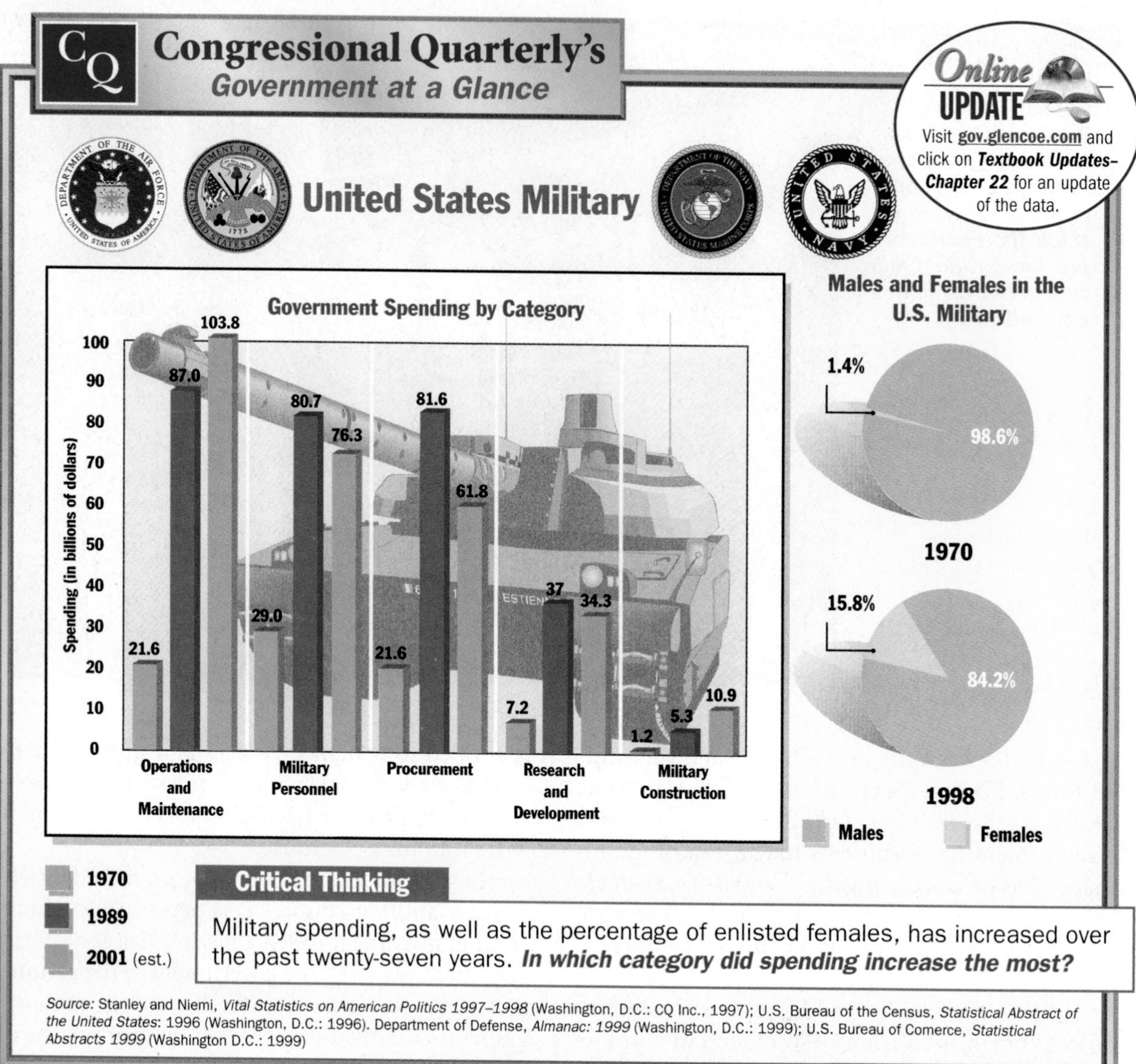

Establishing the Department of Defense

Before 1947 the Departments of War and the Navy were responsible for the nation's defense. The country's experiences in coordinating military forces in World War II, however, prompted a military reorganization. The result was the National Security Establishment, which two years later became the Department of Defense. From the outset, the secretary of defense was a member of the president's cabinet.

Civilian Control of the Military The Founders wanted to ensure that the military would always be subordinate to the civilian leaders of the government. As a result, the ultimate authority for commanding the armed forces rests with the civilian commander in chief, the president of the United States.

Congress also exercises considerable authority over military matters. Because of its constitutional power over appropriations, Congress determines how much money the Department of Defense will spend each year.

Congress also has the power to determine how each branch of the armed forces will be organized and governed. In order to maintain civilian control of the military, the top leaders of the Department of Defense all are required to be civilians.

Size of the Department of Defense With more than 800,000 civilian employees and about 1 million military personnel on active duty, the Defense Department is the largest executive department. It is headquartered in the Pentagon in Arlington, Virginia, near Washington, D.C.

Army, Navy, and Air Force Among the major divisions within the Department of Defense are the Departments of the Army, the Navy, and the Air Force. A civilian secretary heads each branch. The United States Marine Corps, under the jurisdiction of the Navy, maintains its own leadership, identity, and traditions.

The Joint Chiefs of Staff The president, the National Security Council, and the secretary of defense rely on the **Joint Chiefs of Staff** (JCS) for military advice. This group is made up of the top-ranking officers of the armed forces. Included are the Chief of Staff of the Army, Chief of Staff of the Air Force, and the Chief of Naval Operations. The Commandant of the Marine Corps also attends meetings of the Joint Chiefs of Staff. The fifth and sixth members are the Chairman and Vice Chairman of the Joint Chiefs of Staff. The Chairman is appointed for a two-year term by the president.

A Volunteer Military The United States has used two methods of staffing its armed forces—by conscription, or compulsory military service, and by using volunteers. Conscription was first used during the Civil War and was implemented during World War I and world War II.

By executive order President Richard Nixon suspended conscription, or the draft, in 1973. Since then membership in the military has been voluntary. Nixon's order, however, did not repeal the law that created the Selective Service System that administered the draft. For that reason, males between the ages of 18 and 25 could be required to serve if conscription is reinstated.

Military Registration Since 1980 all young men who have passed their eighteenth birthdays have been required to register their names and addresses with local draft boards. Though women are not eligible to be drafted, they may volunteer to serve in any branch of the armed services. All military services are now committed to the goal of increasing the number of female recruits.

GOVERNMENT Online

Student Web Activity Visit the *United States Government: Democracy in Action* Web site at gov.glencoe.com and click on ***Chapter 22–Student Web Activities*** for an activity about the State and Defense departments.

Section 3 Assessment

Checking for Understanding

1. **Main Idea** Use a graphic organizer like the one below to show the organizational structure of the State Department.

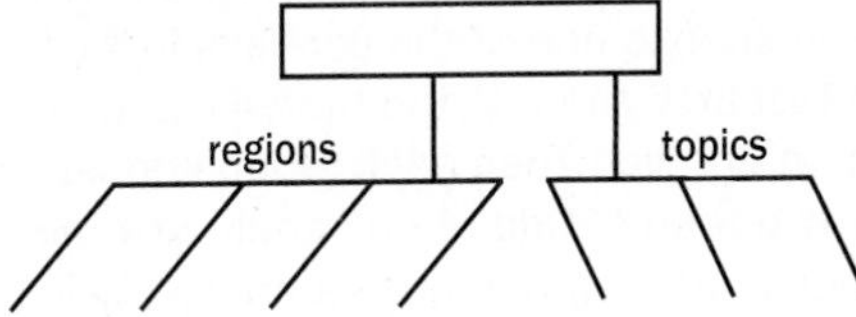

2. **Define** embassy, consulate, consul, passport, visa, conscription.
3. **Identify** Foreign Service, Joint Chiefs of Staff.
4. What are the powers of Congress in military matters?

Critical Thinking

5. **Demonstrating Reasoned Judgment** Do you think an armed forces of volunteers will perform better or worse than one of draftees?

Concepts IN ACTION

Separation of Powers What foreign policy goals do you think the State Department should carry out today? Review the major foreign policy goals of the United States outlined in Section 1. Choose the two goals that you think are most important today. Present a two-minute speech outlining why you think these goals are the most important.

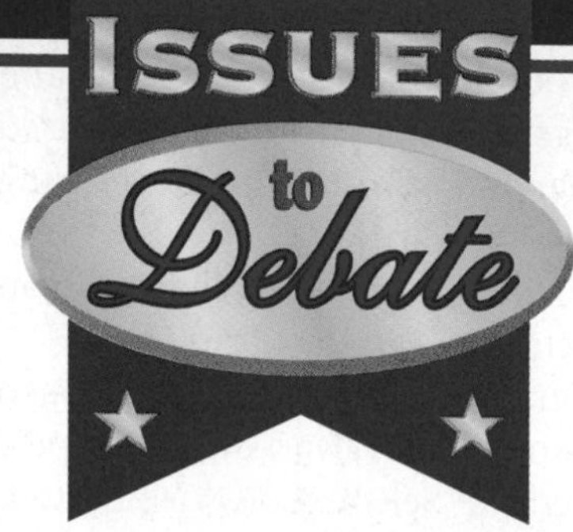

When Should Military Force Be Used?

The goals of United States foreign policy are to maintain national security and world peace, protect free trade, support democratic governments, and promote the humane treatment of people in other nations. When national security is threatened, most people support the use of military force. Should military force be used to promote other goals such as intervening in a civil war to support a democratic government?

Post–Cold War Intervention

Since the end of the Cold War the United States has faced many different situations that have required specific policy decisions and actions. These actions have involved advising, negotiating, and policing conflicts throughout the world. The scope of actions has ranged from sending troops into Somalia in 1992 to protect deliveries of food during a devastating civil war, to a full-blown war in the Persian Gulf after Iraq invaded Kuwait in 1990. Since 1989 the United States has sent troops to intervene in such areas as Panama (1989), the Persian Gulf (1990), the Balkans (1991), Somalia (1992), Haiti (1994), and Bosnia-Herzegovina (1995).

Solving Problems

Diplomacy is always the first choice when trying to resolve a conflict. However, if diplomacy fails, the United States has resorted to other means. Economic and political sanctions placed on a conflicting country have been used in some instances. Forging alliances with other nations through the United Nations can also place pressure on a nation. If those methods fail, the show or use of military force is usually a final option.

Debating the Issue

Is Military Force Justified when National Security Is Not at Stake?

Was national security at stake in each intervention listed above? How do you think the United States should have dealt with those conflicts?

Key Issues

✔ What foreign policy goals do you think prompted the United States to get involved in each of the conflicts?

✔ What would the probable outcome of each of the conflicts have been if the United States had not intervened?

✔ What are the possible consequences if a world power, such as the United States, does not get involved in international conflicts?

Debate Divide the class into five groups. Each group should choose one of the conflicts listed above and research the role the United States played in that conflict. Then each group should divide into two teams. One team should use the facts that each of the groups has gathered to justify the United States's actions in the conflict. The other team should prepare an alternative policy that the United States could have implemented to handle the situation.

Vote Team members should vote on each issue to see what percentage of the class favors military intervention.

Foreign Policy In Action

Reader's Guide

Key Terms

mutual defense alliance, regional security pact, multilateral treaty, bilateral treaty, collective security, sanction

Find Out

- What are the main alliances of the United States today?
- What are some ways the United States can influence the policies of other nations?

Understanding Concepts

Growth of Democracy What changes in the role of NATO are consistent with the promotion of democracy in Europe?

COVER STORY

Playing Chicken

BRUSSELS, BELGIUM, APRIL 2, 1997

Target of controversy

A dispute between the United States and the European Union over chickens and turkeys is threatening to erupt into a trade war. At the center of the controversy are differences in each side's meat-inspection system. EU officials contend that poultry processed in U.S. plants does not meet European health standards and cannot be imported. An EU import ban would cost U.S. industry $50 million to $86 million annually. American officials say they will respond by blocking $300 million in EU meat exports to the U.S. The EU denounced the threat as counterproductive to an agreement. Neither side is optimistic that a deal is near.

The desire to preserve national security and economic well-being often can lead to conflicts between nations. To minimize the danger to national security, the United States tries to settle such conflicts peacefully and to negotiate agreements with foreign governments. The tools that are available include alliances, programs of foreign aid, economic sanctions, and, in extreme circumstances, military action.

Alliances and Pacts

Throughout history, when nations felt a common threat to their security, they negotiated **mutual defense alliances.** Nations that became allies under such alliances usually agreed to support each other in case of an attack.

Through such alliances the United States has committed itself to defending the regions of Western Europe and the North Atlantic, Central and South America, and the island nations of the South Pacific. The United States has signed mutual defense treaties with nations in these three regions. The treaties that protect these areas are referred to as **regional security pacts.**

The North Atlantic Treaty Organization

After World War II, the United States and several nations in Western Europe wanted to defend themselves against the Soviet Union. The leaders of the free world developed a regional security pact to guarantee the security of Western Europe and other nations. This pact created the **North Atlantic Treaty Organization (NATO).** This mutual defense treaty stated: "The parties agree that an armed attack against one or more of them in Europe or North America shall be considered an attack against them all."

Under NATO, hundreds of thousands of troops were stationed on military bases in Western Europe. Troops from the United States, West Germany, Great Britain, and other NATO

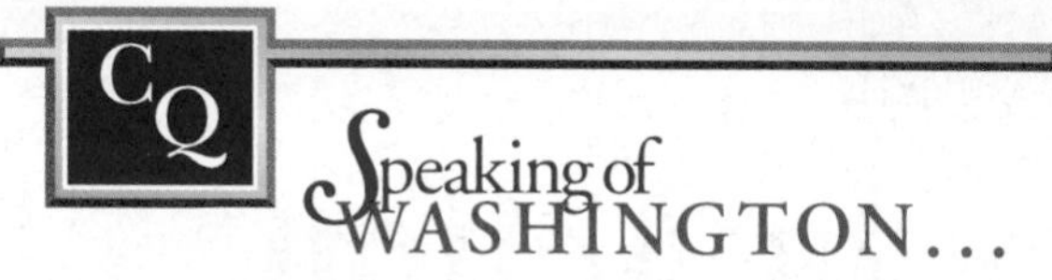

A Little Diplomacy, Please. **Theodore Roosevelt's adage "Speak softly and carry a big stick" has served presidents well in foreign affairs. No matter how softly presidents speak as the nation's chief diplomat, the world listens because they are also the commander in chief of a powerful military force. Roosevelt's own sallies into diplomacy made possible the building of the Panama Canal and helped to end the Russo-Japanese War in 1905, a feat that earned him the Nobel Peace Prize.**

nations served under a common command: the Supreme Allied Command Europe (SACEUR). France, though still a member of NATO, withdrew its armed forces from the NATO command.

For more than 40 years, NATO countered the military might of the Warsaw Pact nations led by the Soviet Union. As the Cold War ended, however, the rivalry lost momentum. In November 1990, the *International Herald Tribune* reported:

> "*Leaders of the 22 members of the North Atlantic Treaty Organization and the Warsaw Pact abandoned more than four decades of military confrontation on Monday by signing an arms treaty that will dramatically reduce non-nuclear arsenals in Europe.*
>
> *In a companion pledge disavowing any future aggression against each other, the leaders declared that the end of the Cold War era meant that they are no longer adversaries, will build new partnerships and extend to each other the hand of friendship.*"
>
> —*International Herald Tribune,* 1990

NATO After the Cold War What would be the role of NATO after the major military threat to its members ended? When war broke out in southeastern Europe among former republics of Yugoslavia in 1991, NATO intervened. The United States persuaded its NATO allies to stage air strikes against Bosnian Serb military sites—the first time NATO had ever launched a military offensive.

Some people, however, believed that NATO had served its purpose and should be dismantled. Then-Secretary of State Warren Christopher saw a continuing role for NATO:

> "*NATO remains the central security pillar for Europe, and core institution for linking the security of North America and Europe. In the last five years, NATO has undertaken sweeping changes to match the sweep of Europe's transformation.*"
>
> —Warren Christopher, June 2, 1995

One key question was how NATO would relate to Russia and the former Soviet satellite nations. When NATO opened membership to these eastern European nations, Russia felt threatened. The alliance then opened talks with Russian leaders, hoping to persuade Russians to see the West differently. In 1997 NATO and Russia signed an agreement giving Russia a seat on a joint council of NATO. While not offering full NATO membership, the document pledged that Russia would continue its transformation to democracy and NATO would review its own doctrine to bring it in line with post–Cold War reality.

Latin America and the Pacific In 1947 the United States and its Latin American neighbors signed the Rio Pact. Among its provisions is this statement:

> "*An armed attack by any State against an American State shall be considered as an attack against all the American States, and, consequently, each one of the . . . contracting parties undertakes to assist in meeting the attack. . . .*"
>
> —Rio Pact, 1947

Since 1947 most Latin American nations and the United States have participated in the Rio Pact.

Following its revolution, Cuba withdrew from the pact in 1960. In 1948 the United States signed a related treaty, establishing the **Organization of American States (OAS).** Unlike the Rio Pact, the OAS is primarily concerned with promoting economic development.

The United States also has a regional security pact with Australia and New Zealand. The ANZUS Pact, signed in September 1951, obliged Australia, New Zealand, and the United States to come to one another's aid in case of attack. In 1984 the government of New Zealand adopted a policy that excluded nuclear weapons and nuclear-powered ships from the nation's ports and waters. In response to this policy, the United States announced in 1986 that it would no longer guarantee New Zealand's security under the ANZUS treaty.

Online **UPDATE**

Visit gov.glencoe.com and click on ***Textbook Updates–Chapter 22*** for an update of the data.

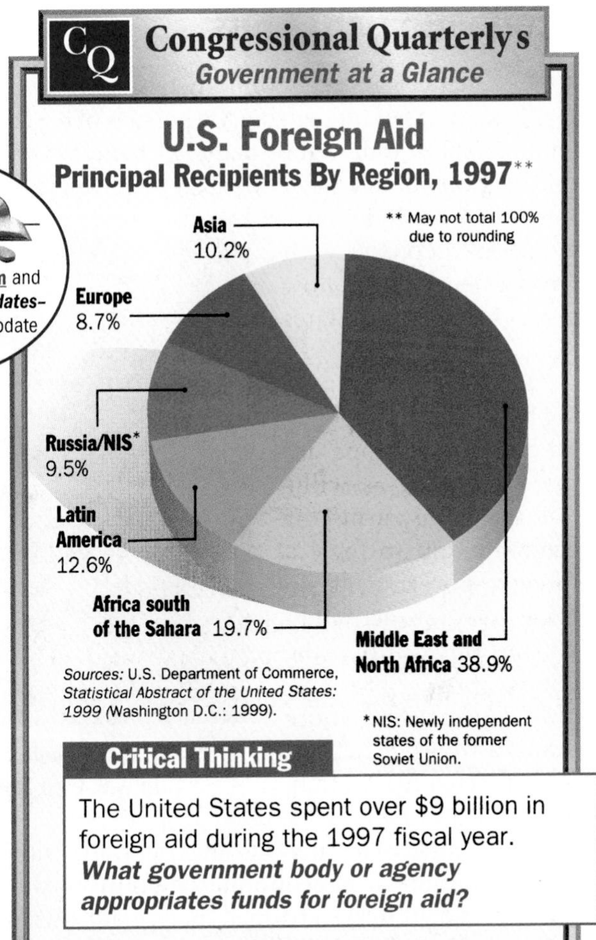

Critical Thinking

The United States spent over $9 billion in foreign aid during the 1997 fiscal year. ***What government body or agency appropriates funds for foreign aid?***

Bilateral Treaties of Alliance

NATO, the Rio Pact, OAS, and ANZUS are all examples of multilateral treaties. **Multilateral treaties** are international agreements signed by several nations. The United States has also signed bilateral treaties of alliance. A **bilateral treaty** involves only two nations.

One bilateral treaty, signed in 1951, makes the United States an ally of Japan. A similar treaty, also signed in 1951, pledges the United States to the defense of the Philippines. A third bilateral treaty, signed in 1953, makes the United States an ally of South Korea.

The United States has alliances with almost 50 nations. These nations can count on the military support of the United States in case of an attack. The objective of these treaties is to provide collective security for the United States and its allies. **Collective security** is a system by which the participating nations agree to take joint action against a nation that attacks any one of them.

Foreign Aid Programs

Military alliances are one benefit that the United States may offer to friendly nations. American leaders can also offer military support in the form of grants or loans to purchase American armaments. Economic aid is another benefit American leaders can offer. Economic aid has long been used to forge closer ties between the United States and the world's developing nations. Since the end of World War II, this aid has had two purposes. One purpose has been to establish friendly relations with these nations. The second purpose has been to help these nations emerge as eventual economic partners.

Many developing nations have problems satisfying even the minimum needs of their people for food, housing, and education. They urgently need loans and technical assistance. Since 1946 the United States has provided more than $300 billion in economic aid worldwide and about $160 billion in military aid. Today the Agency for International Development (AID), an agency of the State Department, administers American programs of economic aid. AID has considerable independence, however, and dispenses loans and technical assistance with very little direction from the secretary of state.

Economic Sanctions

Alliances and economic benefits are two methods of influencing the policies of other nations. The withdrawal or denial of benefits is a third diplomatic strategy. American policy makers sometimes use this strategy when they deal with governments that follow policies the United States dislikes.

One way of withdrawing benefits is by applying sanctions. **Sanctions** are measures such as withholding loans, arms, or economic aid to force a foreign government to cease certain activities. During this century, the United States has employed sanctions more than 75 times. Sanctions were directed against Iraq, beginning in 1990.

A U.S. soldier with children in war-torn Bosnia-Herzegovina

The United States may also restrict trade with another nation as an economic sanction. In the 1980s President Reagan banned the use of American technology in building a natural gas pipeline in the Soviet Union. He did this to protest the Soviet Union's role in suppressing a trade union in Poland.

The Use of Military Force

Those who believe that military force is a necessary tool of foreign policy argue that many times in recent history limited military action might have preserved peace. In 1938, for example, rather than risk war Great Britain and France agreed to allow the German dictator Adolf Hitler to take over part of Czechoslovakia. Thus emboldened, Hitler went on to swallow the rest of that country, a move that eventually led to World War II.

The United States government has, upon occasion, had to use military force to settle disputes with other nations. In addition to the five times the United States declared war, American troops have been used abroad on a number of occasions. Since World War II, the United States has committed troops abroad for various reasons without a declaration of war in Korea, Vietnam, Grenada, Panama, the Persian Gulf region, and in war-torn Bosnia-Herzegovina. President Clinton also sent 2,000 troops into Haiti to preserve democratic government.

Section 4 Assessment

Checking for Understanding

1. **Main Idea** Use a graphic organizer like the one below to show the results that the United States tries to achieve through foreign aid.

   CAUSE → EFFECTS

2. **Define** mutual defense alliance, regional security pact, multilateral treaty, bilateral treaty, collective security, sanction.
3. **Identify** NATO, OAS.
4. What is the purpose of NATO?
5. List two mutual defense alliances, besides NATO, in which the United States is a partner.

Critical Thinking

6. **Making Inferences** Why would the stipulation of "an attack against one shall be considered as an attack against all" create a sense of security?

Concepts IN ACTION

Growth of Democracy Research the requirements needed to be Peace Corps volunteers and the kinds of work they perform. Imagine that you are a Peace Corps volunteer who was invited to speak to your class and present the information you have researched.

Sending E-Mail

World leaders and ordinary citizens communicate across great distances all the time. *Telecommunications* refers to communicating at a distance through the use of a telephone, video, or computer. A standard computer is ready for telecommunication after two items are added to it. The first piece of equipment is a *modem.* A modem is a device that enables computers to communicate with each other through telephone lines. The second necessary item is *communications software,* which lets your computer prepare and send information to the modem. It also allows your computer to receive and understand the information it receives through the modem.

Learning the Skill

Electronic mail, or E-mail, enables users to send and receive messages and data worldwide, to and from anyone connected to the Internet. Simply by clicking a button, a user immediately sends a message. The computer (called a server because it serves several other computers) for the *Internet Service Provider* (ISP) receives the message and stores it in an electronic "mailbox." The message is available whenever the recipient chooses to receive it. If you are on an E-mail network, you have a specific address. This address identifies the location of your electronic "mailbox"—the place where you receive your E-mail. To send E-mail, you must include the address of the recipient.

Practicing the Skill

To send an E-mail message, complete the following steps:

1. Select the "Message" function from your communications software.

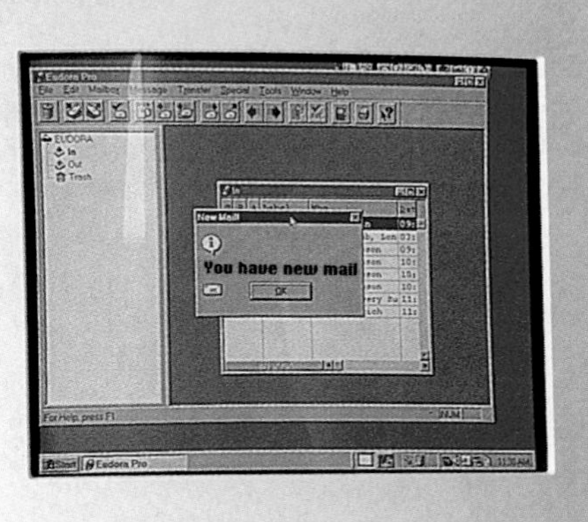

Your E-mail system may notify you of incoming mail.

2. Type in your message—and proofread it for errors.
3. Type in the E-mail address of the recipient and select the "Send" button. Some E-mail systems allow you to also select a receipt option before you send your message. The ISP will then send you a receipt notice when your message has been delivered and opened.

The E-mail system places the message in the receiver's mailbox. He or she may read the message at any time, and send you a return message.

Application Activity

Select a current foreign policy issue to research. Then browse the Internet or call the government to obtain the E-mail address of a federal official concerned with the foreign policy issue. E-mail the federal official, sharing opinions about the issue, asking questions about the issue, and requesting information.

Chapter 22

Assessment and Activities

GOVERNMENT Online

Self-Check Quiz Visit the *United States Government: Democracy in Action* Web site at gov.glencoe.com and click on ***Chapter 22–Self-Check Quizzes*** to prepare for the chapter test.

Reviewing Key Terms

Choose the letter of the correct term or concept below to complete the sentence.

a. executive agreement	**f.** consulate
b. internationalism	**g.** détente
c. foreign policy	**h.** isolationism
d. bipartisan	**i.** multilateral treaty
e. sanction	**j.** ambassador

1. In the 1800s the United States avoided involvement in world affairs, a policy known as _____.
2. The highest-ranking diplomat one nation sends to represent it in another nation is an _____.
3. Imposing an economic _____on another nation restricts trade with that nation.
4. A pact between the president and the head of a foreign government, called an _____, does not require the Senate's approval.
5. Located in major cities of foreign nations, a _____ promotes American business interests and safeguards American travelers.
6. A nation's _____ guides its relations with other countries and groups in the world.
7. An international agreement signed by a group of several nations is called a _____.
8. The United States now follows a policy of _____ regarding world affairs.
9. The Nixon administration put the policy of _____ into effect to ease the tensions of the Cold War.
10. The president's foreign policies often have enjoyed _____ congressional support.

Current Events JOURNAL

Foreign Policy Goals Check current newspapers and newsmagazines for articles about United States relations with foreign nations. Clip the articles and build a table categorizing these relations under these headings: Maintaining national security, Promoting world peace, Protecting free trade, Supporting democratic governments, and Promoting humane treatment of people.

Recalling Facts

1. What have been the major characteristics of American foreign policy since 1945?
2. Who, in addition to the cabinet, advises the president on foreign policy?
3. For what foreign policy purposes does Congress appropriate money?
4. What four advantages does the president have over Congress in conducting foreign policy?
5. Describe the organization of the Department of State.
6. What is the Foreign Service?
7. What is the responsibility of the Department of Defense in foreign policy?
8. What three regions of the world has the United States committed itself to defending through multilateral treaties?
9. What is the purpose of the Agency for International Development (AID)?

Understanding Concepts

1. **Public Policy** Many American presidents have achieved more success in foreign policy than in domestic affairs. Explain why this might be so.

2. **Separation of Powers** Should Congress play a greater role in the formation of American foreign policy? Why or why not?

Critical Thinking

1. **Drawing Conclusions** With the changes in world politics after the Cold War, do you believe the role of the CIA will change? Give reasons for your answers.
2. **Synthesizing Information** Use a Venn diagram like the one below to show how the responsibilities of the Departments of State and Defense overlap.

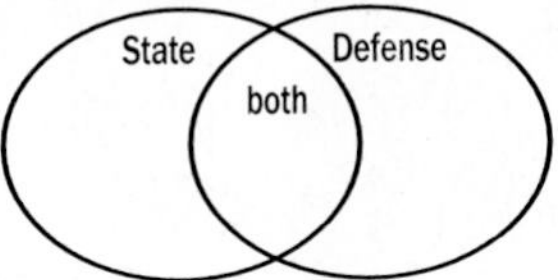

Interpreting Political Cartoons Activity

1. What do the cacti in this cartoon represent?
2. How does this cartoon characterize United States foreign policy?
3. How does this cartoon characterize a president's role in foreign policy?

Cooperative Learning Activity

Listing Criteria Organize into groups of five or six students and consider the following issue: American attitudes concerning foreign aid are much more negative today than they were years ago. As a group, make a list of criteria that you would impose upon a nation being considered for aid. Why, for example, would you choose some countries and not others? When finished, meet as a class and discuss the groups' lists.

Skill Practice Activity

Sending E-Mail Scan the Internet to find the E-mail addresses of a foreign policy interest group. Using your communications software, send a message to the group concerning United States foreign policy today. You may want to ask:

(1) How have the United States foreign policy goals been affected by the collapse of communism? (2) What are the chief concerns of United States foreign policy today?

Technology Activity

Using E-mail The United States Congress plays an important role in directing United States foreign policy. Public opinion sometimes influences these decisions. E-mail your senators or representative the results of the **Issues to Debate** votes in your class.

Participating in National Government

Providing foreign aid is a way for the United States to maintain good relationships with foreign nations. Find out how you can contribute to an international relief effort. Outline the results of your research.

UNIT 8

State and Local Government

Participating IN GOVERNMENT

Your Government in Action

The best way to understand government is to see it in action. Visit a branch of your state government—the state capitol, a state agency, or a court in your community. Make arrangements by calling ahead, especially if you are going as a group. Do some research before the visit and plan where you will go, whom you will see, and what questions you might ask.

Electronic Field Trip

Statuary Hall

View statues of each state's honored citizens in a historical art exhibit located in the Capitol building in Washington, D.C.

Glencoe's Democracy in Action Video Program

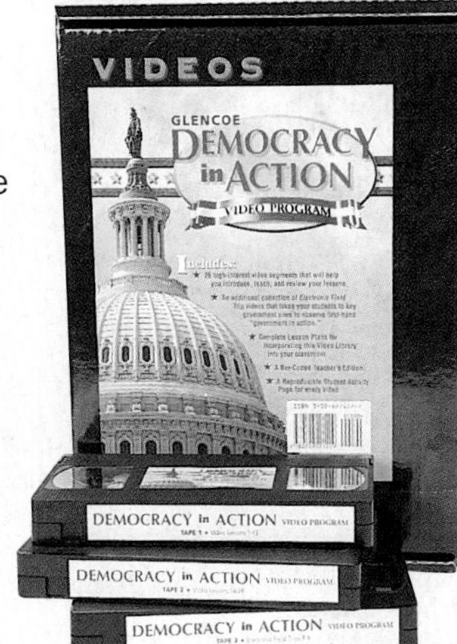

Congress established Statuary Hall to give every state the opportunity to honor two significant people in the form of statues. The **Democracy in Action** video program "Statuary Hall," referenced below, provides an opportunity to view important people who have contributed to our nation's history.

As you view the video program, try to notice any regional, cultural, or other differences between different statues and between the people they honor.

Also available in videodisc format.

View the videodisc by scanning the barcode or by entering the chapter number on your keypad and pressing Search.

Disc 2, Side 1, Chapter 8

Hands-On Activity

Use a computerized card catalog or the Internet, to research information about statues that are located in Statuary Hall at the Capitol. Create a short report about the statues representing your state. Be sure to include the artist who created the statue, the birthplace of the individuals represented, and the historical significance of each person.

◀ State capitol of New Hampshire

Chapter 23

Structure and Function of State Government

Why It's Important

State Government and You

Your state government has more influence over the lives of its citizens than any other government. From driver's license requirements to the money available for education, state government touches your life every day.

To learn more about the operation of state governments and how they impact your life, view the Chapter 23 ***Democracy In Action*** video lesson:

The State and You

Chapter Overview Visit the *United States Government: Democracy in Action* Web site at gov.glencoe.com and click on ***Chapter 23–Overview*** to preview chapter information.

Section 1

State Constitutions

Reader's Guide

Key Terms

initiative, constitutional convention, constitutional commission

Find Out

- What are the four most important functions of state constitutions?
- What are the basic common characteristics of state constitutions?

Understanding Concepts

Federalism Why are state constitutions lengthy documents compared to the nation's Constitution?

COVER STORY

War in Rhode Island?

PROVIDENCE, RHODE ISLAND, MAY 18, 1842

A force led by elected governor Thomas Dorr tried to seize the state arsenal. The state militia, controlled by sitting governor Samuel King, scattered the attackers. The incident caps a controversy that began in October over the state constitution's severe limitations on voting rights. The current government's rejection of a new, more liberal constitution, drafted by Dorr supporters and ratified by the voters, escalated the dispute. King's refusal to accept Dorr's election as the new governor precipitated the present crisis. The federal government has declined to intervene, despite appeals from both sides.

Governor Dorr

As Governor-elect Dorr found out, changing a state constitution is not always easy. Constitutional government in America began with colonial charters, long before the United States Constitution. When the colonies declared their independence in 1776, some states kept their old colonial charters as their state constitutions. Other states, like Virginia and Pennsylvania, drew up new constitutions. Since 1776 the 50 states have had a total of 146 constitutions. Only 19 states have kept their original documents, and all the states have added many amendments.

Importance of Constitutions

State constitutions are important for several reasons. First, **state constitutions** create the structure of state government. Like the federal Constitution, every state constitution provides for separation of powers among three branches of government—legislative, executive, and judicial. State constitutions outline the organization of each branch, the powers and terms of various offices, and the method of election for state officials.

Second, state constitutions establish the different types of local government, such as counties, townships, municipalities, special districts, parishes, and boroughs. State constitutions usually define the powers and duties as well as the organization of these different forms of local governments.

Third, state constitutions regulate the ways state and local governments can raise and spend money. In many states, for example, the state constitution limits the taxing power of local governments. The state constitution usually specifies the kinds of taxes that state and local governments may impose. It may also specify how certain revenues must be used. In some states, for example, the constitution requires that money taken in through a state lottery must be earmarked for education.

◀ Statehouse, Boston, Massachusetts

Governmental Transitions

State Constitutions Citizens celebrated the inauguration of each new government as colonies adopted state constitutions. John L. Krimmel captures the excitement of a new state government in *Election Day in Philadelphia,* 1815. ***Do you think every state needs its own constitution? Why or why not?***

Finally, state constitutions establish independent state agencies, boards, and commissions that have power in areas that affect citizens' lives directly. These include, for example, public utility commissions that regulate gas and electric rates, and state boards of education that help administer public schools throughout the state.

As the basic law of the state, the state constitution is supreme above all other laws made within the state. At the same time, the state constitution cannot contain provisions that clash with the United States Constitution.

Constitutional Characteristics

Throughout the 50 states, constitutions vary widely. At the same time, most state constitutions share some basic characteristics that make them similar in many ways.

Bill of Rights Besides a provision for separation of powers among the three branches of state government, all state constitutions contain a bill of rights. This section includes all or most of the protections of the Bill of Rights in the Constitution of the United States. In addition, many state constitutions contain protections not provided for in the national Constitution. These protections include the workers' right to join unions, a ban on discrimination based on gender or race, and certain protections for the physically challenged, among others.

Length Originally, state constitutions were about the same length as the United States Constitution. Over the years additions to state constitutions in many states have resulted in very long documents. While the national Constitution has about 7,000 words, the average state constitution today has more than 28,000 words. Very long constitutions are found in such states as Texas, with 62,000 words, and Alabama, with about 174,000 words—equal to about 200 pages of a textbook.

Detail Long state constitutions are filled with details, often covering many varied and unusual aspects of life in a state. Such constitutions might include any of the following: a special tax to help veterans of the Civil War; a requirement that public schools teach agricultural subjects; fixed salaries for certain state and local officials; or a declaration of state holidays.

Critics of state constitutions claim that such detailed, specific provisions are not needed in a constitution, but rather should be handled in state laws. Chief Justice John Marshall once wrote that a constitution "requires only that its great outlines should be marked, its important objects designated."

A major reason for the development of lengthy and detailed state constitutions has to do with politics. State constitutions are sometimes very detailed because certain groups and individuals have lobbied hard to include provisions that are to their advantage. Including such provisions in the state constitution protects against their being changed by a simple vote of the legislature.

Amendments and Changes

Changing a constitution may be necessary because society itself changes over time, and new conditions require new actions or policies. In recent years, for example, some state constitutions have been amended to provide greater powers for the governor. Many people believe that modern conditions require stronger executive leadership than most early state constitutions allowed. The governor of New Mexico received expanded powers regarding the removal of certain state officials. The governor of Oregon was granted more time to veto bills after a legislative adjournment. Some amendments to state constitutions provide for very specific policies. Thus, some state constitutions have an enormous number of amendments. These usually only add to the length and detail of the constitution. As of 2000, for example, Alabama had 596 amendments.

Proposing Amendments The amendment process has two steps: proposal and ratification. Constitutions of the 50 states provide four different methods of proposing amendments. These include methods by state legislatures, by popular initiative, by a constitutional commission, or by a constitutional convention.

In every state the state legislature has the power to propose an amendment to the state constitution. This method is the most commonly used. The actual practice of proposing a legislative amendment varies somewhat from state to state. In 17 states a majority vote of the members of each house of the legislature must propose an amendment to the state constitution. In 18 states a two-thirds vote of all members of each house is required. In 9 states a three-fifths majority vote of the legislature is required. Finally, a few states require the legislature to vote for an amendment in two different sessions before the proposal is official.

Seventeen states also allow the people to propose constitutional amendments by popular initiative. An **initiative** is a method by which citizens propose an amendment or a law. The initiative process begins when an individual or group writes a proposed amendment. People in favor of the amendment then circulate it as part of a petition to obtain the signatures of a required number of eligible voters. The number of signatures required varies from state to state. Constitutional initiatives account for only about 5 percent of the proposed amendments to state constitutions.

The third method of proposing amendments to a state constitution is by convening a state constitutional convention. A gathering of citizens, usually elected by popular vote, a **constitutional convention** meets to consider changing or replacing a constitution.

Finally, many states have used a fourth method, the constitutional commission, to propose constitutional amendments. A **constitutional commission** is a group of experts appointed to study the state constitution and recommend changes. Eight states established constitutional commissions in the 1980s, but few of their recommendations resulted in amendments. Kentucky's commission recommended 77 changes in 1987. Only one was referred to the voters by 1988.

Governor Supports Controversial Issue

State Initiatives In 1996 Governor Pete Wilson of California supported an initiative called Proposition 209, a state constitutional amendment to abolish race and gender preferences in state and local programs. ***What do you think are the advantages and disadvantages of the initiative method of proposing constitutional amendments?***

Methods of Ratification All states except Delaware require ratification of amendments by popular vote. The kind of majority necessary to approve an amendment varies. Forty-four states require a simple majority of those who vote on the proposed amendment. Three other states require a majority of all voters who cast ballots in the election. Illinois requires either a majority of all voters who cast ballots in the election or three-fifths of those voting on the amendment. New Hampshire requires a two-thirds majority. In Delaware two consecutive sessions of the state legislature must vote to ratify an amendment. Studies show that once an amendment is placed on the ballot, it has a good chance of being ratified.

Criticism and Reform

Over the years people have criticized state constitutions for being too long and too full of needless detail. What are the procedures by which new state constitutions could be enacted?

Constitutional Convention In order to replace existing state constitutions, most states require a constitutional convention. In a few states, a special commission may also draft a new constitution that must be reviewed by the state legislature, followed by ratification by the people.

In every state the process of calling a constitutional convention begins when the state legislature proposes the convention, which is usually put to the voters for approval. If the people agree, the state holds an election to choose delegates. Once they convene, the delegates may write a new constitution or suggest changes in the existing document. The voters then must ratify the changes or the new constitution.

Although 14 states require that a popular vote be held periodically on the question of calling a convention, the voters in recent years have opposed the idea. Only five were held in the 1980s.

Although many people have called for reform, most states have kept their existing constitutions. Twenty-eight states have constitutions that are more than 100 years old. Many, including Massachusetts (1780), Wisconsin (1848), and Oregon (1857), still have their original constitutions.

Judicial Interpretation In the 1980s the number of formal amendments and revisions to state constitutions declined. More and more state judges, however, began to interpret state constitutions independently of the United States Constitution. Added to the formal amendment process, **judicial review** has become an important means of constitutional change in the states as well as the national government.

Section 1 Assessment

Checking for Understanding

2. **Main Idea** Use a graphic organizer like the one below to identify the purposes served by state constitutions.

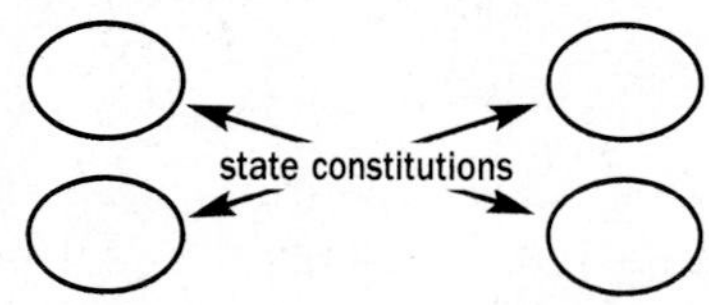

2. **Define** initiative, constitutional convention, constitutional commission.
3. **Identify** state constitution.
4. In what ways are most state constitutions alike?
5. Why are state constitutions amended more frequently than the federal Constitution?

Critical Thinking

6. **Identifying Central Issues** Why do you think so many amendments to state constitutions have been adopted, when the people have been reluctant to approve of constitutional conventions for reform?

Federalism Many state constitutions contain historic provisions that are no longer applicable, such as a tax to help veterans of the Civil War. Examine your state constitution. Identify provisions in the constitution that may no longer be applicable. Do you think that states should take the time to eliminate these provisions? Why?

Section 2

The Three Branches

Reader's Guide

Key Terms

bicameral, lieutenant governor, plurality, item veto, civil case, criminal case

Find Out

- How do state legislatures and governors work together to pass laws and carry out policies that affect citizens of a state?
- How do states differ in their methods of selecting qualified people to serve as judges?

Understanding Concepts

Separation of Powers How does the principle of separation of powers in state government compare with that of the federal government?

COVER STORY

Bill-Signing Race

AUSTIN, TEXAS, JUNE 20, 1997

Governor George W. Bush put his signature on nearly 100 bills Thursday, leaving him 480 more to decide in the next three days. The Texas legislature sent 1,487 bills to the governor during its 140-day session, which ended on June 2. Many were passed in the closing hours of the session. In a bill-signing marathon, through Thursday afternoon Bush had approved 1,002 bills, vetoed 4, and allowed 1 to become law without his signature. Sunday is the deadline for the governor to act. However, a spokesperson for Bush said that the governor planned to get through most of the remaining legislation on Friday.

Governor Bush

Passing of new laws depends on the cooperation of the governor and the legislature. Like the United States government, the states divide power among three branches—legislative, executive, and judicial.

The Legislative Branch

The state legislature passes laws that deal with a variety of matters, including health, crime, labor, education, and transportation. The state legislature has the power to tax and the power to spend and borrow money. Finally, the state legislature acts as a check on the power of the governor and the bureaucracy.

State legislatures are known by various names. In 19 states the state legislature is called the general assembly. In New Hampshire and Massachusetts, the legislature is known as the general court. In North Dakota and Oregon, it is called the legislative assembly.

Almost every state has a **bicameral** state legislature—one with two houses, like the United States Congress. The upper house is always called the senate, and the lower house is usually called the house of representatives. In some states, the lower house is called the general assembly, the legislative assembly, or the general court. Nebraska has the only **unicameral,** or one-chambered, state legislature in the country.

The Road to the Legislature

Members of the state legislature are elected from legislative districts of relatively equal population. Until 1964 many state voting districts were based on area rather than population. Most state constitutions made the county the basic voting district for the state senate. Because of differing rates of population growth, this system often resulted in striking differences in representation. A county with a population of 1,500 was entitled to elect 1 senator, as was a county with a population of 800,000.

In 1964 the Supreme Court ruled that voting districts for both houses of state legislatures had to be based on roughly equal populations. Chief Justice Earl Warren stated the Court's position in the case of *Reynolds* v. *Sims*[1] (1964): "Legislators are elected by voters, not farms or cities or economic interests." In most states voting districts were redrawn to comply with the Court's **"one person, one vote"** ruling. While cities gained from voting districts based on equal population, the suburbs gained many seats in the legislatures of states such as Illinois, New York, and New Jersey.

Qualifications and Term of Office The state constitutions define the legal qualifications for state legislators. In most states a person must be a resident of the district he or she wishes to represent. To serve as a senator, a person usually must be at least 25 years old and a resident of the state for some specified time. To serve in the lower house, a person usually must be at least 21 years old and meet residency requirements.

Legal qualifications aside, the office of state legislator seems to attract certain kinds of professional people. Many state legislators are lawyers. A sizable number of state legislators also come from professions that state laws directly affect, such as real estate and insurance. Unlike members of the United States Congress, the majority of state legislators work part-time and are not well paid. In 11 states legislators are paid only when the legislature is in session. In most states members of the senate serve four-year terms, while members of the lower house serve two-year terms. In Alabama, Maryland, Louisiana, and Mississippi, members of both the senate and the lower house serve four-year terms of office.

Legislative Sessions In the past, a typical state legislature met for one or perhaps two months of the year. Some state legislatures met as infrequently as every other year. To handle a growing workload, the length and frequency of legislative sessions have increased. In more than three-fourths of the states, the legislature now holds annual sessions. Only seven states have legislatures that still meet every other year.

See the following footnoted materials in the **Reference Handbook:**
1. *Reynolds* v. *Sims* case summary, page 764.

Organization of Legislatures Most state legislatures are organized like the United States Congress. The size and population of a state does not determine the size of its legislature as one might expect. A populous state like California has 80 members in its lower house, while New Hampshire has 400 members in its lower house. On the average, membership in the lower house of a state legislature is about 100. State senates, on the other hand, average only about 40 members.

In the lower house, the presiding officer is called the **speaker of the house**—a position similar to that of the Speaker in the House of Representatives. The majority party in the lower house usually chooses the speaker. The speaker has the power to appoint the chairpersons along with all other members of house committees.

In 27 states the presiding officer of the upper house is the **lieutenant governor.** He or she serves very much like the vice president of the United States, who presides over the United States Senate. In those states that do not have a lieutenant governor, senators usually elect their presiding officer.

The Committee System In most state legislatures, more than 1,000 bills are introduced each session. Having an organized system for doing this work is vital. Just as in Congress, committees conduct much of the work.

The Course of Legislation As in Congress, a member of the state legislature introduces each bill. However, unlike Congress many legislative bills actually originate in the executive branch of state government.

Interest groups such as labor unions, business organizations, or even an association of bird-watchers may propose a bill and submit it to a legislator to introduce. These groups may also provide experts to testify for the bill in committee hearings.

Student Web Activity Visit the *United States Government: Democracy in Action* Web site at gov.glencoe.com and click on ***Chapter 23–Student Web Activities*** for an activity about state constitutions.

A bill may begin in either house of the state legislature. The presiding officer of that house sends the bill to a committee that specializes in the subject matter of the bill. The committee discusses the bill and may hold public hearings. It may rewrite the bill or modify it. It then sends the bill back to the full house along with its recommendation that the bill be passed or not passed.

Once a bill is on the agenda of the full house, it is ready for discussion and vote. If one house passes a bill, it must go through a similar process in the other house. Sometimes the second house changes a bill it has received. In this case the legislature creates a conference committee from both houses to resolve the differences. Both houses then must vote on the conference committee's bill.

If passed, bills go to the governor for signature or veto. Of the bills that are introduced, less than one-fourth become laws.

Where the Work Is Done

Lawmaking Processes Members of the Texas legislature meet in committee. The committee is the basic work unit of state legislatures. ***What are some legislative areas normally dealt with by committees?***

The Executive Branch

Every state has an executive branch of government headed by a governor. The office of governor, in a sense, was created to be weak. Because of their bad experience as colonies with royal governors, the early states limited the powers of their governors. This practice continued through the nation's history, as most state constitutions severely restricted the governor's powers. Until 1965 most governors had short terms of office, a one-term limit on their service, and weak executive powers. Like the office of president, the office of governor has generally become more powerful in recent years. Because of the great differences in the area and population of states, however, a vast difference in the power and influence of the 50 governors exists.

Becoming a Governor State constitutions spell out the few legal or formal qualifications for becoming governor. In most states a governor must be at least 30 years old, an American citizen, and a state resident for 5 or more years. Citizenship and residency requirements vary widely.

In addition to these legal qualifications, however, a person must usually meet certain political qualifications. Most governors, for example, have served in state and local government before running for governor. Many have served as state lieutenant governor or state attorney general. One-half of the governors recently elected are lawyers who have practiced in their own or other states.

Election In most states the process for electing a governor has two basic steps. First, an individual must gain the nomination of a major political party, usually by winning a party primary. Only three states—Connecticut, Utah, and Virginia—still use the older convention method to nominate candidates for governor. Second, once chosen, the party nominee then runs in the general election.

In most states the candidate who wins a plurality vote is elected governor. A **plurality** is the largest number of votes in an election. In five states, however, a majority is required for election. In Arizona, Georgia, and Louisiana, if no one receives a majority, a run-off election is held between the two candidates who receive the most votes in the general election. In Mississippi the lower house of the state legislature chooses the governor if no candidate obtains a majority in the general election. In Vermont the house and senate choose.

Term of Office and Salary Most governors serve four-year terms. In two states—Vermont and New Hampshire—the term of office is only two years. Many states also limit the number of terms a governor may serve in office. Twenty-four states have a two-term limit. Kentucky, Mississippi, and Virginia forbid their governors successive terms in office. Governors' salaries range from $179,000 in New York to $60,000 in Arkansas. Most states also pay a governor's official expenses and provide state vehicles for transportation. In addition, 45 states provide an official residence for the governor.

The Roles of the Governor The governor's activities range from proposing and signing legislation to visiting foreign countries to seek business for the state. The executive branch of state government carries out laws the state legislature passes. The governor's responsibilities may include budgeting, appointing officials, planning for economic growth, and coordinating the work of executive departments. The amount of control that a governor has over the executive branch varies widely from state to state.

People look to the governor for leadership. Therefore, the governor is expected to play an important legislative role. Theodore Roosevelt, who served as governor of New York State, said, "More than half of my work as governor was in the direction of getting needed and important legislation."

Governors are usually looked upon as the leaders of the party in their states. The governor attends political-party dinners, speaks at party functions, and may campaign for party candidates in local elections. In addition, governors participate in events such as the Democratic or Republican Governors' Conference.

Frequently governors attempt to negotiate grants from the national government in such areas as aid to schools, urban aid, or highway construction. Governors may also represent their states in seeking cooperation from other states in such areas as transportation and pollution control. More recently, governors have even represented their states internationally as they have tried to encourage foreign businesses to locate in their states or sought outlets for trade of products their states produce.

Managing the Executive Branch The governor's executive powers include two basic components: the power to carry out the law and the power to supervise the executive branch of state government.

The constitutions of many states created a divided executive branch, making many executive officials politically and legally independent of each other. In more than half the states, for example, the people elect the governor, the lieutenant governor, the attorney general, and the secretary of state. In addition, they often serve for different terms of office and have specific and separate responsibilities that the state constitution defines.

As a result, officials from different political parties who have different ideas and conflicting political ambitions may head executive offices. Cooperation is often difficult, leaving the governor limited control over the executive branch.

Some states, such as Tennessee and New Jersey, give the governor considerable control over the executive branch. The constitutions of these states have created an executive branch with only one elected official or only a few such officials.

In all but eight states, the governor has full responsibility for preparing the state budget. Once prepared, this budget will be submitted to the state legislature for approval. The power to make up the budget allows a governor to push certain programs and policies.

All governors can exercise military powers through their role as commander in chief of the state **National Guard.** The National Guard can be used in a national emergency, such as a war, if the president calls it into action. Normally, however, the National Guard serves as a state militia, under the governor's control. State constitutions allow the governor to use the National Guard to maintain law and order in case of state emergencies.

Executive Reform Since 1965 more than half the states have reformed their constitutions to give the governor greater executive power. In addition to lengthening the governor's term of office, many states have provided that the lieutenant governor must run on a joint ticket with the governor. Other changes that have strengthened the governor's powers include giving the governor more control over appointments to departments and agencies.

Legislative Powers As does the president, a governor has legislative power without being part of the legislative branch. A governor can propose legislation to the state legislature. He or she can send legislative messages to the state legislature and can present new programs as part of the state budget. In addition, a governor can arouse public opinion to support these legislative proposals.

Today all governors have a veto power over legislation the state legislature passes. North Carolina was the last state to grant this power to its governor (1996). In all but a few states the governor possesses an item veto. An **item veto** is the power to turn down a particular section or item in a piece of legislation without vetoing the entire law. The use of the item veto has led to a controversy. Two Wisconsin legislators sued their governor over his veto of "individual sentences, words, parts of words, single letters," and other minor details in a legislative bill. A federal appeals court sided with the governor. A state legislature can override a governor's veto under certain conditions. Usually a two-thirds vote of all the legislators in each house is required to override a veto.

A third legislative power of the governor is the ability to call a special session of the state legislature. Legislatures meet at regularly scheduled times, but the governor can call a special session to deal with legislation he or she feels is vital to the state's best interests and well-being.

Judicial Powers A governor normally has some limited powers over the state court system and the administration of justice. Governors appoint almost one-fourth of all state judges throughout the country. In addition, a governor may have one or more of the following powers over people convicted of crimes: the right to grant pardons, shorten sentences, waive fines, and release prisoners on parole.

The Women of Kansas **In 1991 Kansas became the first state to have a woman governor (Joan Finney, Democrat), a woman senator (Nancy Landon Kassebaum, Republican), and a woman representative (Jan Meyers, Republican) at the same time.**

Other Executive Officers In all but three states—Maine, New Hampshire, and New Jersey—other elected officials are part of the executive branch. Less visible than the governor, these executives often hold important positions.

Forty-three states have a lieutenant governor, a position similar to that of the vice president of the United States. The lieutenant governor becomes governor when the office is vacated. The lieutenant governor also usually presides over the state senate.

In all but seven states the people elect the top legal officer in the state government, the attorney general. In the remaining states the governor usually appoints the attorney general. The **attorney general** supervises the legal activities of all state agencies, gives legal advice to the governor, and acts as a lawyer for the state in cases in which it is involved. Probably the most significant power of the attorney general is the power to issue **opinions,** or written interpretations of the state constitution or laws. These opinions carry legal authority unless a court overturns them.

At the federal level, the secretary of state deals with foreign relations. In state government, the position of **secretary of state** is very much what its name describes—the chief secretary or clerk of state government. The secretary of state is in charge of all state records and official state documents, including all the official acts of the governor and the legislature.

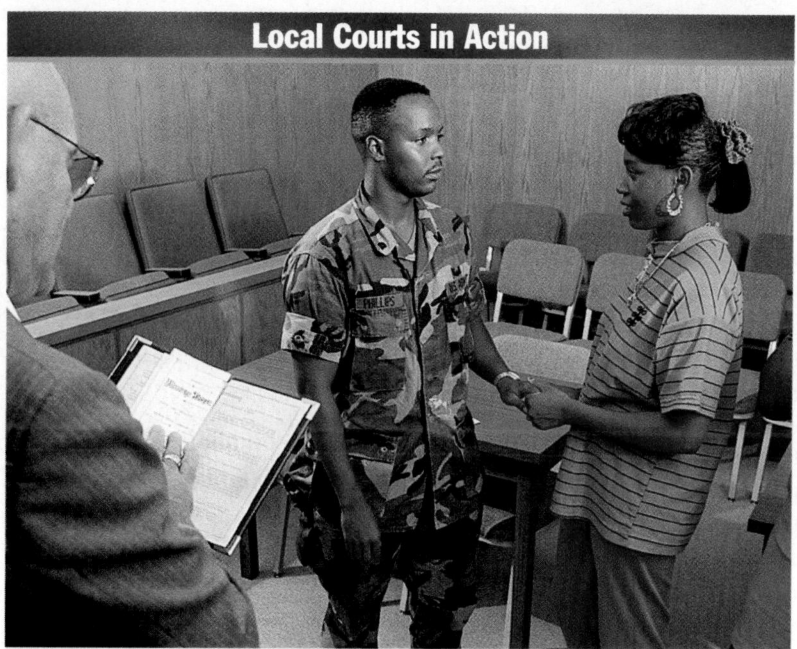

Local Courts in Action

Elected Justices A justice of the peace performs a wedding ceremony. Such justices are commonly elected. ***What are the arguments for and against electing justices?***

The **state treasurer** manages the money that a state government collects and pays out. He or she pays the bills of state government and often serves as the state tax collector. In most states the state treasurer also has the power to invest state funds.

Many other executive officers work in state governments. Most states have a state comptroller or auditor, a superintendent of public instruction, and other agencies, boards, and commissions.

The Judicial Branch

Vital to the operation of state governments, the judiciary interprets and applies state laws. In doing so, state courts help resolve conflicts like business disagreements and grievances that citizens may have against each other. State courts also punish crimes that violate state laws.

The Importance of State Courts State courts interpret and apply state and local laws. State courts decide most cases of murder, assault, and reckless driving, which are usually violations of state laws. State courts also decide cases that involve local laws, like littering or illegal parking. All local courts are part of a state court system. The local municipal court in which a person challenges a traffic ticket is also part of a state court system.

State courts deal with two general types of legal disputes: civil and criminal cases. A **civil case** usually involves a dispute between two or more private individuals or organizations. In a **criminal case,** the state brings charges against a citizen for violating the law. Criminal cases involve either a misdemeanor or a felony. The state is always the prosecution in criminal cases, while it is usually not involved in civil cases.

State Court Systems State court systems vary in their structure. They also vary in the names the states give the courts. In general, state court systems include three types of courts: minor courts, general trial courts, and appeals courts.

The best-known minor court, especially in small towns and rural areas, is the justice court, presided over by a justice of the peace. The justice of the peace performs marriages, handles minor civil and criminal cases, and legalizes documents. In many cities police courts, municipal courts, or magistrate courts handle minor legal matters like petty crimes or property disputes. These courts are also known as minor courts of limited jurisdiction, local trial courts, and inferior trial courts.

States include a whole range of minor courts. Small claims courts hear civil arguments that involve small amounts of money. Juvenile courts hear cases involving people under the age of 18. Domestic relations courts handle disputes between husbands and wives and other family members. Traffic courts hear cases dealing with traffic and parking violations. Probate courts handle cases involving the inheritance of property.

General trial courts, known from state to state by such different names as county courts, circuit courts, courts of common pleas, superior courts, and district courts, stand above minor courts in the state court system. These courts may hear any type of case, civil or criminal. Cases involving serious crimes like murder, arson, and robbery are heard in these courts.

Appeals courts review cases that a lower court has already decided. The highest state court is usually called the supreme court. The supreme court is the state court of final appeal. In Maryland and New York this court is called the court of appeals. The state's supreme court performs another significant function. It interprets the state's constitution and laws. Three-fourths of the states have additional appeals courts, called intermediate appellate courts. These courts were created to relieve the state supreme court of the large number of cases that were being appealed.

Selecting State Court Judges State judges are selected in four different ways. Some are elected in a popular election; others, in an election by the legislature. Some judges are appointed by the governor. Still others are selected through a method called the **Missouri Plan** that combines appointment by the governor and popular election.

Many people have disagreed about the wisdom of electing judges. Those who favor popular election believe that if government is "of the people, by the people, and for the people," then the people must choose their judges. Critics argue that popular election may make state judges too concerned about the effect of their decisions on the public. They fear that judges who are thinking about re-election might be tempted to please the voters more than to administer the law impartially. Further, voters often know little or nothing about the candidates for judicial posts and have no way of discriminating among candidates. Despite these concerns, popular election is still a common method of selecting judges in 21 states. In 8 states, the governor appoints all or nearly all state judges.

Removal of Judges A judge must demonstrate a minimum level of competence, skill, and knowledge. The judge often makes the final ruling in a case and has the last word about very critical decisions in people's lives. If judges are so important, it should be possible to evaluate their performance and remove those who are unqualified. How is this done?

One method of removing judges is through impeachment. Impeachment is a procedure through which charges are brought against a judge or any public official accused of misconduct. Impeachment of judges, however, has proved to be inefficient and time-consuming.

In recent years most states have created disciplinary boards or commissions to investigate complaints about judges. These judicial conduct organizations are usually made up of both lawyers and nonlawyers. If a disciplinary board finds that a judge has acted improperly or unethically, it makes a recommendation to the state's supreme court. The court then may suspend or remove the judge.

Section 2 Assessment

Checking for Understanding

1. **Main Idea** Use a graphic organizer like the one below to show how the roles of president and governor differ in at least two ways.

president	governor

2. **Define** bicameral, lieutenant governor, plurality, item veto, civil case, criminal case.
3. **Identify** National Guard, attorney general, secretary of state, Missouri Plan.
4. Why do some people question the wisdom of electing state court judges?

Critical Thinking

5. **Making Comparisons** How is the path a bill takes to become a law similar in a state legislature and the national Congress?

Concepts IN ACTION

Separation of Powers Look through local newspapers and find articles about the governor of your state. For each article, describe what role or roles your governor is playing. Attach your article and role description on a class bulletin-board display titled "The Roles of the Governor."

Section 3

State Government Policy

Reader's Guide

Key Terms

corporate charter, public utility, workers' compensation, unemployment compensation, conservation, mandatory sentencing, victim compensation, extradition, parole, shock probation, shock incarceration, house arrest

Find Out

- What are four major objectives of state economic policy?
- Why does each state have its own criminal laws?

Understanding Concepts

Public Policy What are the major areas in which states write and enforce public policy?

COVER STORY

Freedom for Cats

SPRINGFIELD, ILLINOIS, APRIL 23, 1949

Governor Adlai Stevenson has rejected a leash law for cats. "It is in the nature of cats to do a certain amount of unescorted roaming," stated the governor in his veto message. The bill declared prowling cats a danger to the state's bird population. "The problem of cat versus bird is as old as time," Stevenson observed. "If we attempt to resolve it by legislation, who knows but what we may be called upon to take sides as well in the age-old problems of dog versus cat, bird versus bird, or even bird versus worm." The governor added that the legislature has more important concerns than cat delinquency.

Roaming Springfield

While a leash law for cats may not seem like an important area of concern for a state, it does represent the variety of areas in which state governments legislate. The major areas of concern for most states include the regulation of business, the administration and control of natural resources, the protection of individual rights, and the implementation of education, health, and welfare programs.

State Regulation of Business

In the United States, every business corporation must have a charter issued by a state government. A **corporate charter** is a document that grants certain rights, powers, and privileges to a corporation. A charter is important because it gives a corporation legal status.

Before 1860 state charters greatly restricted the powers of corporations. By the 1890s, however, courts and legislatures, influenced by business interests and aware that giant corporations were becoming indispensable, had relaxed controls over business. States that continued to restrict corporations found their major businesses moving to other states where the laws were more lenient.

Types of Regulation In the twentieth century, various consumer groups demanded regulation of giant corporations. In response, federal and state governments passed stronger regulations. State laws regulated interest rates that banks could charge. States helped set insurance companies' rates, administered licensing exams, and generally protected consumer interests. Legislation regulated all kinds of corporations, but laws regulating banks, insurance companies, and public utilities were especially rigorous. A **public utility** is an organization, either privately or publicly owned, that supplies such necessities as electricity, gas, telephone service, or transportation service. In the United States private stockholders own most public utility companies. States may give public utility companies the right to supply service in the state or part of the state. In return for granting the right to supply a service, the state assumes the right to regulate the company. Recently states have reduced regulations in order to encourage competition.

Protecting Consumers Since the 1950s states have acted to protect consumers from unfair and deceptive trade practices such as false advertising. Three-fourths of the states have laws regulating landlord-tenant relations. Most states also regulate health-care industries. State governments have enacted legislation dealing with consumer sales and service—everything from regulating interest charges on credit cards to setting procedures for estimating the cost of automobile repairs. Most states also try to protect consumers in a number of housing-related areas, such as home-repair costs and home mortgages. Several states also require consumer education in the schools.

Protecting Workers Nearly all states have laws that regulate the safety and sanitary conditions of factories. Federal child-labor rules limit the number of hours that 14- and 15-year-olds may work and place other restrictions on work for those under age 18. In addition to the federal rules, many states regulate the hours that 16- and 17-year-olds may work. Most states require minors to have work permits.

The state governments also provide **workers' compensation**—the payments people unable to work as a result of job-related injury or ill health receive. Workers who lose their jobs may receive **unemployment compensation** under programs that state governments set up and regulate.

Workers in all states have the right to belong to labor unions, but some states protect workers from being forced to join unions. More than one-third of the states have passed laws, often called "right-to-work" laws, that prohibit the union shop. The **union shop** is an agreement between a union and an employer that all workers must join a union—usually within 30 days of being hired.

Business Development State governments have been very active in trying to attract new business and industry. Governors often travel throughout the country or even to foreign countries to bring new business to their states. Television advertising, billboards, brochures, and newspaper advertisements promote travel or business opportunities.

Beginning in the 1930s, state governments sold **industrial development bonds** to people or institutions and used the money to help finance industries that relocated or expanded within the state. The state paid off the bond within a specified

GOVERNMENT *and You*

Licenses

Some activities, if practiced by unqualified persons, can be a danger to society. Licensing allows the government to make sure that people who perform specific activities meet certain standards. If you work as a doctor or teacher, you will have to be licensed by the state. For public safety, anyone who operates a motor vehicle must have a driver's license. You probably had to complete a driver education course and pass a test to get your driver's license. In the professional world education and testing assure that, like licensed drivers, licensed professionals possess a minimum level of competence.

Other licenses control everyday activities that could also be harmful. For example, hunting and fishing licenses protect wildlife populations. Because most licenses require a fee and must be periodically renewed, licensing also raises money for the state.

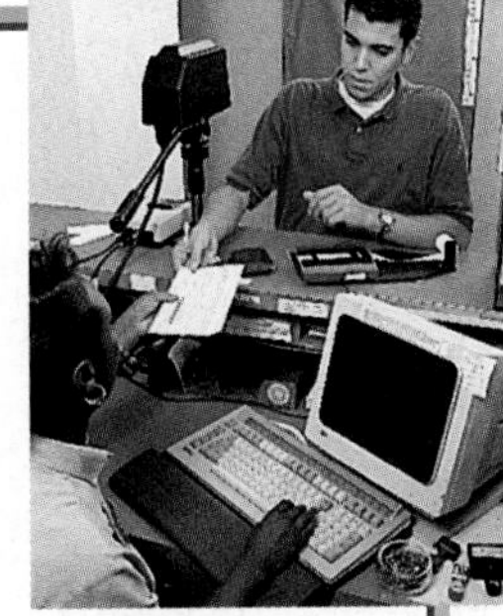

Obtaining a driver's license

Investigate Find out what activities or occupations require licenses in your state.

We the People
Making a Difference

Elizabeth Wright-Ingraham

Wright-Ingraham's architecture

Elizabeth Wright-Ingraham was the first female architect to be licensed in the state of Illinois. The granddaughter of the famous architect Frank Lloyd Wright, Elizabeth had an impressive legacy, but it has been difficult to move out of the shadow of her legendary grandfather. In 1970 she founded the Wright-Ingraham Institute, a think tank for graduate study and public education in Colorado. Its purpose was to introduce a broad core base for educational systems. Twenty different universities participated.

Wright-Ingraham believes that all things in nature are interconnected. She has built more than 130 structures employing an economy of resources. Her Vista Grande Community Church (1987) was the first building in the nation to use the Thermo-mass System—insulation contained within the structural concrete. It is now used throughout the nation. Today Wright-Ingraham is a respected champion of Western architecture and environmentalism. She also chairs her town planning commission, sits on the advisory board of a medical research laboratory, lectures, and writes papers.

time period from money that the industry paid back to the state in the form of taxes. Today a state may offer an incentive such as a tax credit, or a reduction in taxes, in return for the creation of new jobs or new business investment.

States and the Environment

State governments are concerned about two goals that sometimes clash: economic growth and environmental protection. A thriving economy brings money, jobs, and business to a state. Economic growth can, however, cause environmental problems. Factories provide jobs but they can also produce air and water pollution.

Environmental Concerns In recent years the quality of the physical environment has become a major concern of the public. Scientists have warned that air and water pollution endanger public health.

The states' reaction to environmental issues has been mixed. In conservation and land use, the states took a leading role. In the 1940s California was the first state to pass an antipollution law. Most state governments acted to combat pollution, however, only after the federal government had passed stringent environmental laws.

Not until the 1980s, when the federal government took less regulatory action, did the states reclaim many regulatory powers from Washington, D.C. States passed new laws regulating everything from roadside billboard advertising to the labeling of food products, assuming some of the functions of the Federal Trade Commission.

Business seemed threatened from a new direction. Once fearful of federal regulation, it now turned to the national government for protection from the states' new restrictions. One observer of this turnaround noted:

> *"California, for example, passed a law in 1986 requiring food processors to warn consumers about any food containing carcinogenic chemicals. Processors and grocers are not asking the state to change its mind; they are trying to get Congress to pass legislation preempting all such state laws."*
>
> —David Rapp, October 1990

Influenced by a giant oil spill off the coast of Alaska in 1989, however, Congress actually strengthened state power with a law that allows states to impose any liability standards on business that they choose.

Pollution Control Pollution is one of the painful by-products of modern life. Before 1964 only nine states had enacted regulations to control air pollution. In the 1960s, however, the federal government passed a number of pollution curbing laws including the Clean Air Act (1963), the Water Quality Act (1965), the Air Quality Control Act (1967), and the National Environmental Policy Act (1969). These laws set up federal standards for air and water quality and also provided federal money. The 1970 Clean Air Amendments gave the federal government enforcement power and the 1990 Clean Air Act required emission reductions.

The states have more recently taken steps to control pollution. Most states now require environmental impact statements for major governmental or private projects, describing how the project is likely to affect the environment. Many states require industries to secure permits if their wastes pollute the air or water. Often such permits are so costly that the industry finds it cheaper to install antipollution devices. Most have developed waste-management programs. Most also regulate the disposal of radioactive wastes.

Costs of Pollution Control Federal and state interest in pollution control remains strong. This is especially evident in the Brownfields initiative, begun in 1993. By 2000 this federally sponsored program had awarded more than $140 million in grants to almost 400 communities from New Bedford, Massachusetts, to Metlakatla, Alaska. The money was used to clean up abandoned, lightly polluted areas and to make them productive parts of surrounding communities. These grants have created thousands of jobs and attracted $2.50 in private investment for every dollar spent by federal, state, and local governments.

Conservation The care and protection of natural resources including the land, lakes, rivers, and forests; oil, natural gas, and other energy sources; and wildlife is called **conservation.** In recent years state governments have increased their efforts to conserve these resources.

A number of states have laws that allow the state government to plan and regulate land use. Through a land-use law, for example, a state government can preserve certain land from industrial development and set aside other land for parks. Hawaii was the first state to enact a land-use law. Wyoming, Idaho, and Florida soon followed.

Other states have taken action to protect land and water resources. Oregon, for example, has taken steps to protect 500 miles of rivers and ban billboards and disposable bottles. Nearly half of the states have passed laws to control strip-mining, a form of mining that removes the topsoil.

These actions only touch the surface of what states have done in the area of conservation. More action is likely to follow as the environment remains an important public issue.

Protecting Life and Property

For the most part, protecting life and property is the responsibility of state and local governments. These governments provide more than 90 percent of all employees in the criminal justice system. Laws dealing with most common crimes come directly from state government. The federal government has only limited jurisdiction over most crimes. Local governments usually do not make criminal laws, but they enforce state laws that protect life and property.

State Criminal Laws Laws regulating such crimes as murder, rape, assault, burglary, and the sale and use of dangerous drugs are all part of the state criminal code. Local governments can only enact laws dealing with crime that their state governments allow them to pass.

The federal system allows for great variety in the ways states deal with crime, permitting the states to experiment with new programs and techniques. Each state sets its own system of punishment. Several states have introduced mandatory sentencing for drug-related crimes. **Mandatory sentencing** is a system of fixed, required terms of imprisonment for certain types of crimes. In most other states, a judge has greater flexibility in imposing sentences on drug offenders. To take another example, about four out of five states have passed **victim compensation** laws, whereby state government provides financial aid to victims of certain crimes.

Problems of Decentralized Justice Because criminal justice is usually a state responsibility, the justice system has often been described as decentralized, or even fragmented. Generally, however, decentralization has been regarded as an advantage. Different crime rates, along with different living conditions, may call for criminal laws specifically geared to a particular state.

Decentralized justice does create some problems, however. For example, **extradition** is a legal procedure through which a person accused of a crime who has fled to another state is, on demand, returned to the state where the crime took place. While Article IV[1] of the United States Constitution does specifically require extradition, sometimes governors have been reluctant to extradite people.

State Police Forces The well-known Texas Rangers were formed in 1835 as a border patrol force. The first actual state police force, however, was the Pennsylvania State Constabulary, organized in 1905. As the automobile became more widely used, many states turned to mobile police forces. State police are normally limited in the functions they perform—most are basically highway patrol units. The state police have investigative powers in many states, but in only a few states do they possess broad police responsibilities.

See the following footnoted materials in the **Reference Handbook:**
1. *The Constitution,* pages 774–799.

Criminal Corrections State courts handle the great majority of all criminal cases in the United States. State prisons, county and municipal jails, and other houses of detention throughout a state make up a state's correction system. Recently state spending for corrections has been growing faster than for education, public welfare, hospitals, or highways. A California criminal justice official explained the trend:

> *"As crime continued to grow, as violence continued to grow, and there was an incarcerative response, then there was a necessity to build. Of course, building prisons is extremely expensive. And when you build them, you must staff them, and that's extremely expensive."*
>
> —G. Albert Howenstein, 1990

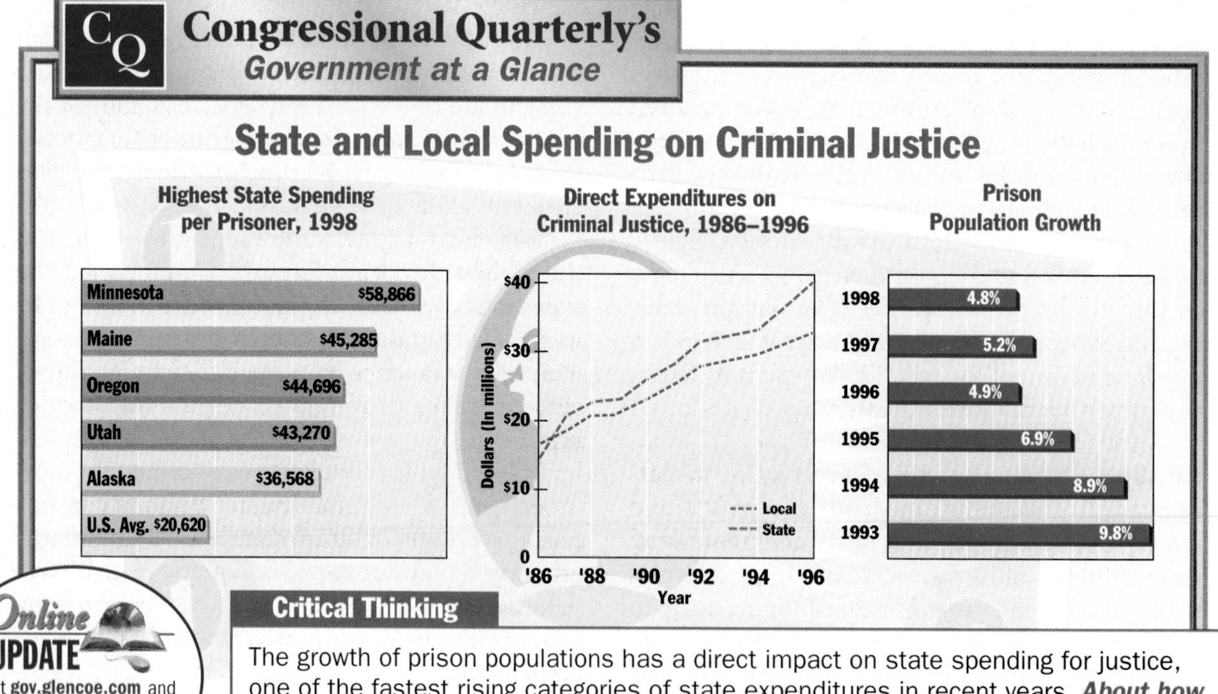

Judges, aware of the strains on the system, often choose probation as a sentence. Today more than 2 million people are on probation. Hundreds of thousands are on parole. **Parole** means that a prisoner serves the rest of the sentence in the community under the supervision of a parole officer. Because of probation and parole, three out of every four offenders who might otherwise be in prison are in the community.

Sentencing Options Many states are giving judges more sentencing options, such as shock probation, shock incarceration, intensive supervision probation or parole, and house arrest. Several states introduced **shock probation** in the 1960s. It was designed to show young offenders how terrible prison life could be through a brief prison incarceration followed by supervised release. **Shock incarceration,** a relatively new program, involves shorter sentences in a highly structured environment where offenders participate in work, community service, education, and counseling.

Intensive supervision probation or parole keeps high-risk offenders in the community, but under close supervision that involves frequent home visits or even nightly curfew checks. The offender often wears an electronic device that continually signals his or her location.

A related alternative sentence is **house arrest,** which requires an offender to stay at home except for certain functions the court permits. Several states are using this approach to incarceration.

Providing for Education, Health, and Welfare

Health, education, and welfare programs combined make up the largest part of state spending. In a recent year, for example, more than 60 percent of all state expenditures were in these three areas. Education accounted for the largest share; welfare was the next largest.

Education For many years the control and financing of public schools was almost entirely in local hands. In 1900, for example, state governments contributed only 17 percent of all the costs of public education. Today states contribute about 45 percent of public school revenues.

Vast differences among the states in terms of public school financing exist. Hawaii has no local school districts, and the state contributes about 90 percent of all public school funds. In New Hampshire, Oregon, and South Dakota, the state contributes less than 30 percent of public school funds. Local funds in these states account for the largest share of school revenues.

There are also differences in the total amount of spending per pupil among the states and among localities within each state. The differences between rich and poor school districts within some states are so great that recently state courts have struck down some funding systems as unconstitutional.

State governments establish local school districts and give these districts the power to administer public schools. State governments regulate the taxes that school districts may levy and the amount of money they may borrow. They set forth many of the policies that school districts must administer. For example, nearly half of the states require a minimum competency test for graduation. In addition, states stipulate the number of days schools must stay open, the number of years a student must go to school, the number of grades that must be taught, the types of courses a school must offer, the number of course credits required for graduation, the minimum salaries of teachers, and general teacher qualifications. Some state governments also establish detailed course content, approve textbooks, and create statewide examinations that all students must take.

While state expenditures have increased for education in general, they have skyrocketed in the area of higher education. During the 1980s state spending for higher education almost doubled, outpacing federal and local support for colleges and universities by a wide margin.

Public Health In the area of health, the state's police power allows the state to license doctors and dentists, regulate the sale of drugs, and require vaccination for schoolchildren. State governments also provide a wide range of health services. States support hospitals, mental health clinics, and institutions for the disabled.

State health agencies serve five broad areas: personal health, health resources, environmental health, laboratories, and aid to local health departments.

State health agencies provide care for mothers and their newborn children, treatment of contagious diseases and chronic illnesses, mental health care, public dental clinics, and immunization against communicable and other diseases. Personal health expenditures make up more than two-thirds of all state public health costs.

State governments are also now involved in a number of environmental health activities, including air and water quality control, radiation control, and hazardous waste management. State health agencies provide laboratory services to local health departments that often cannot afford to maintain their own facilities. State governments often pay the bill for public health services that local authorities deliver and administer.

Public Welfare Government efforts to maintain basic health and living conditions for those people who have insufficient resources of their own are called **public welfare,** or human services. Public welfare programs have grown at every level of government in the twentieth century. In 1900 welfare functions were few; local governments and private charitable organizations provided those that did exist. By 1934 more than half the states had public welfare programs. By the 1990s all three levels of government were spending billions of dollars on welfare programs from food stamps to cash payments.

Under the Social Security Act of 1935, the federal government created three areas of public assistance to provide financial help to state governments. These were Aid to Families with Dependent Children (AFDC), Aid to the Blind, and Old Age Assistance. Congress added Aid to the Permanently and Totally Disabled in 1950. The federal government passed welfare reform legislation in 1996, ending AFDC. Then AFDC was replaced with lump-sum payments to the states. Subject to some restrictions, states were given authority to operate their own welfare programs.

Medicaid, another federal-state welfare program, provides money to the states to help people who cannot afford necessary medical services. The program covers elderly people with insufficient funds, the blind and disabled, and low-income families with dependent children. State governments administer Medicaid, set certain conditions for eligibility, and provide almost 45 percent of the total cost.

State Welfare Programs Most states have programs of general assistance for people who do not fall into any of the federally mandated categories. States administer and finance general assistance programs, with some help from local governments. Their benefits vary from state to state. Urbanized states like New York, California, Michigan, and Massachusetts tend to have more generous programs than do less urbanized states. Since the early 1930s, state government expenditures have increased dramatically because of expansion in public health, education, welfare, and environmental protection spending.

Section 3 Assessment

Checking for Understanding

1. **Main Idea** Use a graphic organizer like the one below to show the four major policy areas in which state governments enact legislation and an example of each.

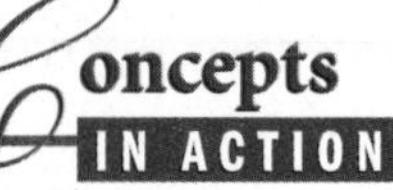

policy area	example

2. **Define** corporate charter, public utility, workers' compensation, unemployment compensation, conservation, mandatory sentencing, victim compensation, extradition, parole, shock probation, shock incarceration, house arrest.
3. **Identify** industrial development bonds, Medicaid.
4. Why is a decentralized system of justice an advantage in the United States?

Critical Thinking

5. **Expressing Problems Clearly** What factors must a state legislature weigh when considering taxing or regulating large business corporations?

Concepts IN ACTION

Public Policy Each state writes and enforces public policy in areas such as education, environment, housing, and welfare. Create a poster that illustrates serious problems related to one of these areas and possible policy solutions.

Supreme Court Cases to Debate

Shelton v. *Tucker*, 1960

A public school teacher at work

State and local governments have the primary responsibility for governing education in the United States. Thus, states pass many laws related to schools, teachers, and curriculum. Is a state law that requires teachers to publicly report every organization to which they belong or regularly give money constitutional? The Supreme Court dealt with this question in the case of Shelton v. Tucker.

Background of the Case

In 1958 the Arkansas state legislature passed a law called Act 10 that required every teacher in a public school to annually file a report listing without limitation "all organizations . . . to which he has belonged during the past five years, and also listing all organizations to which he at the time is paying regular dues or is making regular contributions." The law did not say the information collected from each teacher had to be kept confidential, and it allowed local school boards to make use of the information in any way they wanted. Arkansas's teachers were not covered by a civil service system. Rather, they were hired on a year-to-year basis and thus had no job security beyond the end of each school year. B.T. Shelton, a teacher in the Little Rock Public Schools for 25 years, refused to comply with the new law and lost his teaching job. Shelton sued on behalf of teachers across the state, claiming that Act 10 was unconstitutional. Both state and federal courts ruled against Shelton.

The Constitutional Issue

Neither the Constitution nor the Bill of Rights explicitly protects the right of individuals to associate with others who share similar beliefs. However, starting in the 1920s the Supreme Court began making decisions based on the idea that freedom of association was an important part of the freedom of speech and assembly guaranteed in the First Amendment, as well as the concept of liberty contained in the Fourteenth Amendment. In 1958, in the case of *NAACP* v. *Alabama,* the Court formally recognized this right. Justice Harlan wrote: "Effective advocacy . . . is undeniably enhanced by group association;" thus, "state action which may have the effect of curtailing the freedom to associate is subject to the closest scrutiny." The Court developed the idea of freedom of association because it recognized that laws requiring people to disclose their organizational memberships could easily become a way for governments to punish people who joined unpopular or minority organizations.

Debating the Case

Questions to Consider

1. Did Act 10 serve a legitimate governmental purpose, or did it collect more information than the state government needed to judge the fitness of teachers?
2. How could a law like Act 10 be used to restrict individual liberties?

You Be the Judge

In your opinion, did the Arkansas law violate teachers' freedom of association? How do the concepts of freedom guaranteed in the First and Fourteenth Amendments apply in this case? Would a government ever be justified in keeping track of its citizens' activities to this degree?

Section 4

Financing State Government

Reader's Guide

Key Terms

excise tax, regressive tax, progressive tax, proportional tax, bond, intergovernmental revenue, federal grant, block grant, mandate

Find Out

- What are the major sources of state tax revenue?
- Under what kinds of programs does the federal government provide aid to states?

Understanding Concepts

Public Policy How does state tax policy attempt to distribute the burden of taxes among different people and groups?

COVER STORY

This Cut Is Tasty

ATLANTA, GEORGIA, 1996

By a nearly unanimous vote, the legislature has removed all sales tax on food bought in Georgia. With this action, Georgia joins a growing trend. Twenty-five years ago, 29 states taxed food purchases. Today only 18 do so. Healthy state revenues encouraged the $500 million Georgia tax break. "We wanted to do something to get money back to taxpayers," said the bill's sponsor, Representative Tom Buck. However, critics suggest that the legislature's action may actually result in tax increases in order to maintain revenue levels. They point out taxation's basic principle: the broader the tax base, the lower the rates, and the smaller the increase over time.

No longer taxed in Georgia

State taxes raise nearly half of the general revenue of state governments. In addition, states receive money from the federal government, lotteries, and license fees. States may also raise revenue by borrowing money.

Tax Revenue

Individual state constitutions limit state taxing powers. The federal Constitution also limits a state's taxing powers in three ways: (1) A state cannot tax goods or products that move in or out of the state or the country. These imports and exports make up interstate and foreign commerce that only Congress can tax or regulate. (2) A state cannot tax federal property. (3) A state cannot use its taxing power to deprive people of "equal protection of the law." A state also cannot use its taxing power to deprive people of life, liberty, or property without "due process of the law."

State constitutions may also prevent states from taxing property used for educational, charitable, or religious purposes. Some state constitutions specifically prohibit or limit certain taxes such as the sales tax and the income tax. In other states voters have approved constitutional amendments limiting property taxes.

The Sales Tax State governments began using the sales tax during the Great Depression in the 1930s. Today almost all states have some type of sales tax, which accounts for about half the total tax revenue of state governments. Two types of sales tax exist. The general sales tax is a tax imposed on a broad range of items people buy—cars, clothing, household products, and many other types of merchandise. In some states, food and drugs are not subject to this tax. The selective sales tax is a tax imposed on certain items such as gasoline, liquor, or cigarettes. The selective sales tax is also called an **excise tax**.

People have strongly criticized the sales tax as a regressive tax. A **regressive tax** is a tax that affects people with low incomes more than those with higher incomes. Because everyone buys necessary items such as clothing, the sales tax represents a higher percentage of the poorer person's income.

The State Income Tax

Today most states have individual income taxes and corporate income taxes. Despite much opposition, the state income tax now accounts for more than 30 percent of all state tax revenues, compared to 10 percent in 1956. The state imposes the income tax on the earnings of individuals and corporations.

When this tax varies with a person's ability to pay, it is called a **progressive tax**. Some states assess income taxes at the same rate for every wage earner. For example, each person's income might be taxed 10 percent. In this case it is called a **proportional tax.**

Other Taxes

States require license fees for a wide variety of businesses and professions—doctors, realtors, lawyers, electricians, and others. Likewise, many states issue licenses for bus lines, amusement parks, and other businesses. Fees for motor vehicle registration and driver's licenses by far bring in the most license tax revenue that states collect.

States impose severance taxes on the removal of natural resources such as oil, gas, coal, uranium, and fish from state land or water. Severance taxes are especially good sources of revenue in oil- and gas-producing states, such as Oklahoma and Texas. Kentucky brings in considerable revenue from a severance tax on coal.

Most states have numerous taxes that are less well known. Many still use the state property tax, which is a tax on certain kinds of property such as jewelry and furniture. Every state except Nevada has inheritance or estate taxes. These are taxes that states collect on the money and property inherited when a person dies.

Other Sources of Revenue

States differ widely in their sources of revenue. Taxes pay only a part of state government expenses. To finance the rest, states turn to borrowing, lotteries, and the federal government.

Financing the State

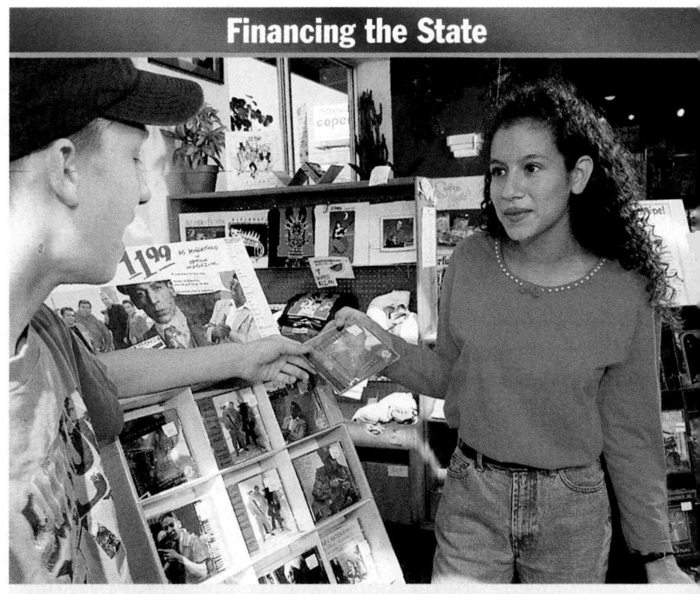

Responsibilities of Taxpayers State sales taxes are easy to administer because the person who sells the item, like the employee at this music store, collects the tax. ***Why might the state sales tax be a little less painful for the taxpayer than other types of state taxes?***

Borrowing

States usually borrow money to pay for large, long-term expenditures such as highway construction or other building projects. State governments borrow by selling bonds. A **bond** is a contractual promise on the part of the borrower to repay a certain sum plus interest by a specified date. In most states voters must be asked to approve new bond issues.

Lotteries

Nearly three-fourths of the states run public lotteries to raise revenue. Lotteries, once outlawed, emerged again after Congress passed legislation permitting state lotteries in 1963. Lotteries became the fastest-growing source of state revenues in the 1980s. The states spend about half the lottery income on prizes and 6 percent on administration.

Intergovernmental Revenue

The federal government, with its vast revenue and taxing power, provides about 20 percent of all state revenues. **Intergovernmental revenue,** or revenue distributed by one level of government to another, may come in the form of a **federal grant.** These grants, also called grants-in-aid, are sums of money given to the states for a variety of specific purposes.

Federal grants not only supply funds, but, by stipulating how the grants are to be used, also influence the states in a number of ways. Grants supply funds for programs that states may not otherwise be able to afford. Grants also stimulate programs and goals that the federal government believes are necessary. Finally, grants set certain minimum standards in the states. For example, the federal government provides grants to make sure that all states provide a minimum public welfare program.

Under **categorical-formula grants,** federal funds go to all the states on the basis of a formula. Different amounts go to different states, often depending on the state's wealth. These grants usually require states to provide matching funds. Under project grants state or local agencies, or even individuals, may apply for funds for a variety of specific purposes: to fight crime, to improve a city's subway system, to control air and water pollution, among other things.

State governments usually prefer block grants over categorical grants as a form of federal aid. A **block grant** is a large grant of money to a state or local government to be used for a general purpose, such as public health or crime control. Block grants have fewer guidelines, and state officials have considerably more choice over how the money will be spent.

Federal Mandates In the 1980s and 1990s federal government's share of state and local government revenue declined, but federal regulatory mandates increased. A **mandate** is a formal order given by a higher authority, in this case by the federal government. Between 1980 and 1990, the federal government increased the number of mandated programs for which state and local governments had to raise their own revenue. State and local officials complained about the increasing number of unfunded and underfunded federal mandates in areas such as health and the environment. Some people believed that the federal government had intruded on areas of state sovereignty.

In 1995 Congress responded to increasing criticism of unfunded mandates. New legislation curbed many of the unfunded requirements that federal agencies imposed on state and local governments. For example, the law required any congressional committee that approved a bill containing a federal mandate to describe its direct cost to the state, local, or tribal governments, or private companies. The authorizing committee was also required to submit an estimate of the mandate's total cost to the Congressional Budget Office. For any mandate on private business costing more than $100 million yearly, federal agencies were required to conduct cost-benefit analyses of new regulations. They were also directed to consult with state and local government officials about all requirements before imposing new unfunded mandates.

Section 4 Assessment

Checking for Understanding

1. **Main Idea** Use a graphic organizer like the one below to show why state officials prefer block grants as a form of federal aid.

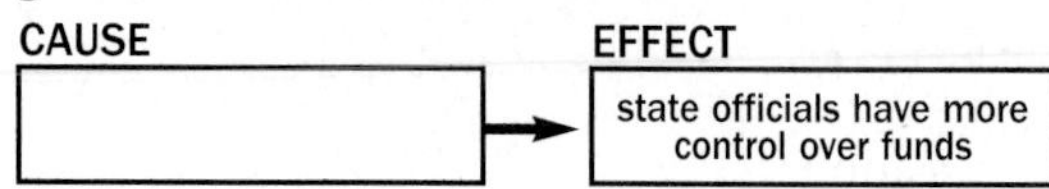

2. **Define** excise tax, regressive tax, progressive tax, proportional tax, bond, intergovernmental revenue, federal grant, block grant, mandate.
3. **Identify** categorical-formula grant.
4. What are the two main categories of state tax revenue?

Critical Thinking

5. **Understanding Cause and Effect** How does Congress influence state policies through its distribution of federal grants?

Public Policy Contact your state offices or use library reference materials to find out the major areas of your state's spending and the major sources of your state's revenue. Summarize your information and present the data in two circle graphs.

Writing a Report

Researching and writing a report allows you to use skills you have already learned, such as taking notes and outlining.

Learning the Skill

Use the following guidelines to help you in writing a report.

- Select an interesting topic. As you identify possible topics, focus on resources that would be available. Do preliminary research to determine whether your topic is too broad or too narrow.
- Write a thesis statement that defines what you want to prove, discover, or illustrate in your report.
- Prepare and do research on your topic. First formulate a list of main idea questions, and then do research to answer those questions. Prepare note cards on each main idea question, listing the source information.
- Organize your information by building an outline or another kind of organizer. Then follow your outline or organizer in writing a rough draft of your report.
- A report should have three main parts: the introduction, the body, and the conclusion. The introduction briefly presents the topic and gives your topic statement. In the body, follow your outline to develop the important ideas in your argument. The conclusion summarizes and restates your findings.
- Revise the draft into a final report. Wait for a day, and then reread and revise it.

Practicing the Skill

Suppose you are writing a report on policies proposed to the legislature by a state governor.

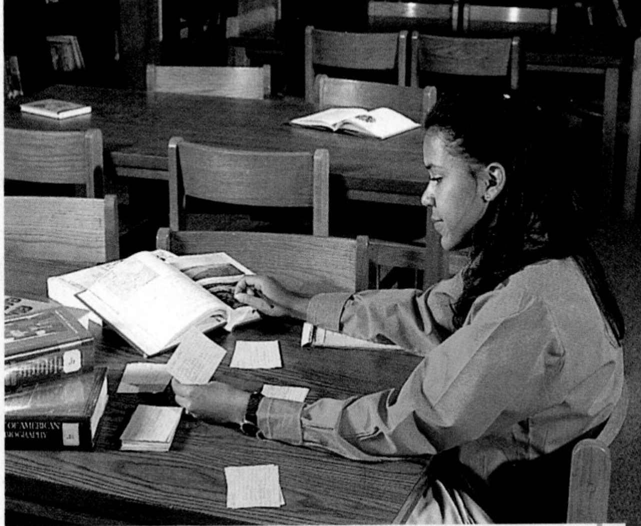

Researching a topic

Answer the following questions about the writing process.

1. How could you narrow this topic?
2. What are the three main idea questions to use?
3. Name three possible sources of information.
4. What are the next two steps in the process of writing a report?

Application Activity

In the Chapter 13 skill lesson, you used research resources in your library to find information on the FCC. Continue your research on this topic and write a short report.

The Glencoe Skillbuilder Interactive Workbook, Level 2 provides instruction and practice in key social studies skills.

Assessment and Activities

Self-Check Quiz Visit the *United States Government: Democracy in Action* Web site at gov.glencoe.com and click on ***Chapter 23–Self-Check Quizzes*** to prepare for the chapter test.

Reviewing Key Terms

Define each of the following terms.

1. public utility
2. mandate
3. criminal case
4. initiative
5. civil case
6. item veto
7. regressive tax
8. intergovernmental revenue
9. bicameral
10. workers' compensation

Recalling Facts

1. What is the method most states use to ratify an amendment to a state constitution?
2. Why were voting districts in many states before 1964 unequal in population?
3. What are the political qualifications that a person must meet to become governor?
4. What are four methods that states use to appoint state judges?
5. How do states regulate public utilities?
6. Compare the goal of workers' compensation with that of unemployment compensation.
7. What are five functions of state-supported health agencies?
8. What kind of tax accounts for about half the total tax revenue of state governments?
9. In what three ways do federal grants influence the states?

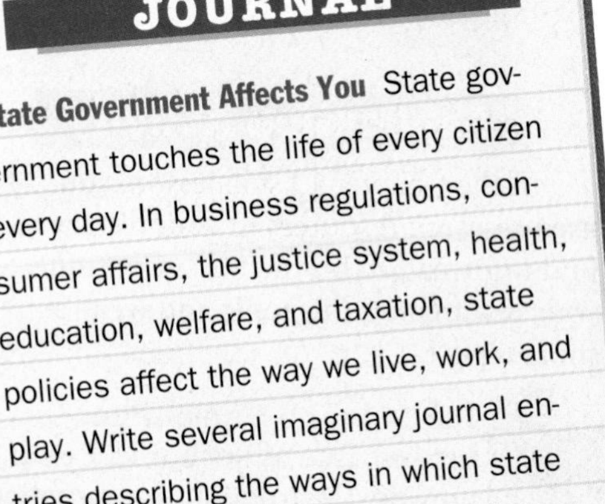

State Government Affects You State government touches the life of every citizen every day. In business regulations, consumer affairs, the justice system, health, education, welfare, and taxation, state policies affect the way we live, work, and play. Write several imaginary journal entries describing the ways in which state government has affected your life in one recent week.

Understanding Concepts

1. **Federalism** In the federal system, how is sovereign power divided among state and federal laws and constitutions?
2. **Separation of Powers** What legislative policy-making role is a governor expected to fill?
3. **Public Policy** Why are most criminal cases heard in state courts rather than in federal courts?
4. **Public Policy** Why do you think most people prefer a state sales tax to a state income tax?

Critical Thinking

1. **Making Comparisons** How do state constitutions compare in length and detail to the United States Constitution?
2. **Understanding Cause and Effect** Use a graphic organizer like the one below to show why there is a great difference in the level of spending for education among local districts.

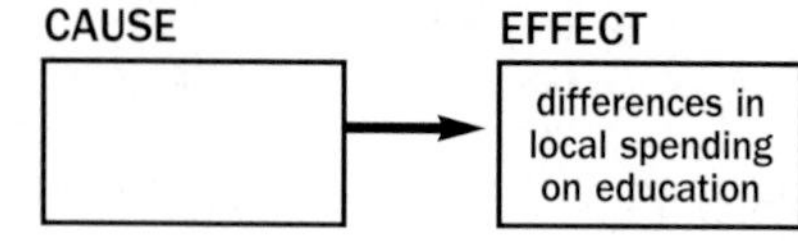

Chapter 23

Cooperative Learning Activity

Present a News Broadcast
Work with a group of three or four. Imagine that your group is covering the state government beat for a local television station. Work with your group to present an imaginary news report from your state capitol for an upcoming newscast. Include information about your state's legislature, governor, courts, policy issues, and finances. Present your newscast to the class.

Interpreting Political Cartoons Activity

1. What is the subject of this cartoon?
2. As depicted here, how are state funds allocated to schools?
3. How does the cartoonist feel about the current funding system?

Skill Practice Activity

Writing a Report Exchange with another student the reports you completed in the "Application Activity" for the skill lesson in this chapter. Critique the reports using the following questions. For each question, find examples in the report and present them to the author.

1. Does the report have an introduction, body, and conclusion?
2. Does the introduction define the writer's thesis or main point of the report?
3. Is the body of the report organized in a logical sequence of information?
4. Are there clear transitions between ideas? Give an example of a good transition and a weak one.
5. Does the conclusion restate and summarize the thesis of the report?

Technology Activity

Using E-Mail Locate a Web site for your state's government on the Internet. Find out about current bills that your state legislature is considering. Using E-mail, compose a letter to your legislator requesting his or her opinion about current bills of interest to you that are being considered.

Participating in State Government

The area in which state government makes decisions that may affect you most is education. As a person directly affected by the educational system, you are likely to have suggestions for improving it. Together with members of your class, brainstorm ideas for improving education in your state. Conduct research or do a survey, if necessary, to gather more information. Write a few of the best ideas from the brainstorming session and your research into a coherent plan. Draft a letter to your state representative suggesting a bill that addresses your concerns.

Structure and Function of Local Government

Why It's Important

Local Government Serves You

Local governments provide citizens with basic services such as education, fire and police protection, water, and sewage and sanitation. They are the governments closest and most accessible to you.

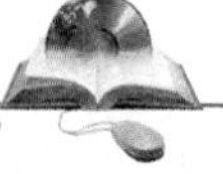

To learn more about how local governments affect you, view the ***Democracy in Action*** Chapter 24 video lesson:

Local Government

★ ★ ★ ★ ★ ★ ★ ★ ★ ★

GOVERNMENT Online

Chapter Overview Visit the *United States Government: Democracy in Action* Web site at gov.glencoe.com and click on ***Chapter 24–Overview*** to preview chapter information.

Section 1

Structure of Local Government

Reader's Guide

Key Terms

county, county board, township, municipality, special district, incorporation, referendum

Find Out

- What are the four basic types of local government according to the areas they serve?
- What are the similarities and differences among the three major structural forms of municipal government?

Understanding Concepts

Federalism What is the relationship between a state government and local governments?

COVER STORY

Governor Now Mayor

DES MOINES, IOWA 1997

Governor Ray

Fifteen years after leaving public service, former governor Robert Ray has agreed to fill in as mayor of Des Moines. Mayor Arthur Davis will not be able to complete his four-year term because of illness. The decision puts an end to a month of bickering among city council members, who could not decide whether to hold a special election or appoint an interim mayor. Ray says he will return to private life when the term ends. "I've never heard of anyone doing this," he jokes. While it may be unusual for a former governor to run city hall, Des Moines may benefit from his years at the state capitol. He asks, however, that people not call him "governor."

Many people are served by smaller units of local government than that of Des Moines. Approximately 86,000 units of local government serve the people of the United States. Local government assumes many forms. Counties, townships, municipalities, and special districts are the most common. Today three of every four people in the United States live in an urban area, either in a central city or a surrounding suburb. Nearly half of the population lives in metropolitan areas of a million or more people. The rest of the people are served by smaller units of local government.

Created by the State

Although the United States has a strong tradition of local self-government, local governments have no legal independence. Established by the state, they are entirely dependent on the state governments under which they exist. The state may assume control over or even abolish them. For example, a state may assume control over a local school district that is in financial trouble.

State constitutions usually set forth the powers and duties of local governments. A state constitution may also describe the form of government a locality may adopt, depending on its size and population. State laws may regulate even the kinds of taxes that local communities may levy.

Types of Local Government

The United States has four basic types of local government—the county, the township, the municipality, and the special district. All four do not exist in every state, and their powers vary from state to state.

The County The **county** is normally the largest territorial and political subdivision of a state. The county form of government is found

◀ Milwaukee, Wisconsin parade

in every state except Connecticut and Rhode Island. In Louisiana counties are called **parishes,** and in Alaska they are called **boroughs.**

Counties of the United States display tremendous variety. First, the number of counties within a state varies from state to state. Texas has 254 counties, while Delaware has only 3 counties. Second, counties also differ in size and population. Los Angeles County in California covers an area of more than 4,000 square miles (10,360 square kilometers) with a population exceeding 7 million people. In contrast, Howard County in Arkansas has an area of only 574 square miles (1,477 square kilometers) and a population of about 13,500.

County governments also vary considerably in power and influence. In rural areas and in the South, county government has been vital. In these places early settlements were spread out over large areas, with few towns and villages. One town in each county became the seat of county government. The county courthouse became a popular political gathering place.

On the other hand, county government has never been very important in New England. In this region people settled in towns, and each township, rather than the county, became the significant unit of local government.

Recently in some metropolitan areas, county governments have grown in importance as they assumed some of the functions that municipalities once handled. For example, the government of Dade County, Florida, now administers transportation, water supply, and other services for the Miami area. In many other places, however, county governments have declined in importance but continue to exist in spite of attempts to change or even abolish them.

Structure of County Governments

States provide county governments with a variety of organizational structures. A **county board** has the authority to govern most counties. The name of this board varies from state to state. It may be called the county board of supervisors, the board of county commissioners, or the board of freeholders. Board members are almost always popularly elected officials. State law strictly limits the legislative powers of county boards. For the most part, county boards decide on the county budget, taxes, and zoning codes.

In many counties the county board has both executive and legislative powers. Board members often divide executive power, with each member responsible for a different county department, such as public welfare, roads, or recreation. In many counties the county board shares executive power with other officers who are usually elected. These officials may include the county sheriff, attorney, clerk, coroner, recorder of deeds, treasurer, auditor, assessor, surveyor, and superintendent of schools. County governments supervise elections, issue certain licenses, keep records of vital statistics, and administer many services, including hospitals, sports facilities, and public welfare programs.

The Township

Townships exist as units of local government in fewer than half the states. In the 1600s the early settlers in New England established the first townships in America. In New England the township is another name for the town, a fairly small community with a population usually fewer than 5,000. Today 20 states—mostly in New England and the Midwest—have townships. In many states counties are subdivided into townships. The size and jurisdiction of townships vary greatly from one state to another. In New Jersey the township covers a large area that may include several municipalities.

The activities that township governments undertake vary from state to state as well. In states such as Nebraska and Missouri, the primary function of township government is road building and road maintenance. In Pennsylvania, townships provide a wide array of government services, including police and fire protection.

In many rural areas townships have lost population and power in the last few decades. For example, many townships in Kansas have lost power to county governments. In some other areas of the Midwest, such as Indiana, control over education has passed from the township to either the county or the local school district.

In some urban areas, however, township government has taken on increased importance. In areas of rapid metropolitan growth, townships have assumed some functions of city government such as providing water, sewage disposal, and police protection. Urban townships in states such as Michigan and New Jersey have also become increasingly important.

The New England Town Thomas Jefferson once described politics in the typical New England town as "the perfect exercise of self-government." With the strong community spirit fostered by their founders, these towns became models of citizen participation in local government.

The **town meeting** served as the centerpiece of town government in New England. In the past, town meetings were open to all voters. Those who attended could express their opinions or just mingle and socialize with their neighbors. At the town meeting citizens participated in the lawmaking process, decided on taxes, and appropriated money for any public projects they thought necessary. They elected town officials, called selectmen. Selectmen were responsible for administering the local government between town meetings.

Over the years, as New England towns grew and their governments became more complex, the town meeting form of direct democracy became impractical. Today, in some very small towns, the town meeting still operates much as it used to. In larger towns and cities, however, the voters elect representatives to attend the town meetings in their stead. In addition, selectmen now have the power to make some of the decisions that citizens once made. Finally, some towns have hired town managers to perform duties similar to those of county administrators.

The Municipality A **municipality** is an urban unit of government—a town, borough, city, or urban district that has legal rights granted by the state through its charter. The first charters were much like charters for private corporations, except that towns and cities were much more narrowly controlled. Each municipality had an individual special charter until state legislatures began to pass general laws after 1850. These early charters and statutes contained powers that today seem curious. For example, Ohio gave its cities power to regulate the transportation of gunpowder; to prevent the immoderate riding of horses; to provide for measuring hay, wood, coal, or other articles for sale; and to suppress riots, gambling, bowling, and billiards.

By the twentieth century, most states divided municipalities into classes depending on their population. In this way they could provide each class a more standard type of charter.

The Special District The **special district** is a unit of local government that deals with a specific function, such as education, water supply, or transportation. Special districts are the most common type of local government, and they deal with a wide variety of special services. The local school district is the most common example of a special district.

THE LAW *and You*

Teen Courts

Authorities have long sought ways to reduce teen crime. One approach that many communities have adopted is to establish teen courts. In teen courts, teenagers serve as jurors, defense attorneys, and prosecutors. The courts hear the cases of teens who have committed a minor, first-time offense. These offenders get a chance to avoid the record that would result from a juvenile court proceeding. They also learn a valuable lesson in how the law works.

Teen courts got their start in Texas in the 1970s and have since spread to more than 30 states. They often are supported by funds from school districts and traditional courts, or by civic groups that hope to reach young offenders before they become hardened criminals. Statistics show that teen crime is generally down in communities where such programs exist.

Teens conduct a trial.

Research Call or write municipal governments in your area to find out whether they have teen courts and how they work.

Forms of Municipal Government

A municipal government may be formed when a group of people asks the state legislature to permit their community to incorporate, or set up a legal community. This process, called **incorporation,** is different from state to state. Generally a community must meet certain requirements for incorporation. These requirements usually include having a population of a certain minimum size and petitions signed by a specified number of residents requesting incorporation. At times a **referendum,** or special election, may be held to determine whether the people want incorporation.

Once a community is incorporated, the state issues it a charter. The charter allows the community to have its own government and gives the municipal corporation legal status. The municipality now has the right to enter into contracts, to sue and be sued in court, and to purchase, own, and sell property. The state legislature can change the powers granted to a municipal government at any time.

Every municipal charter provides for the type of government the community will have. Today urban areas in the United States use one of three basic forms of municipal government: the mayor-council form, the commission form, or the council-manager form.

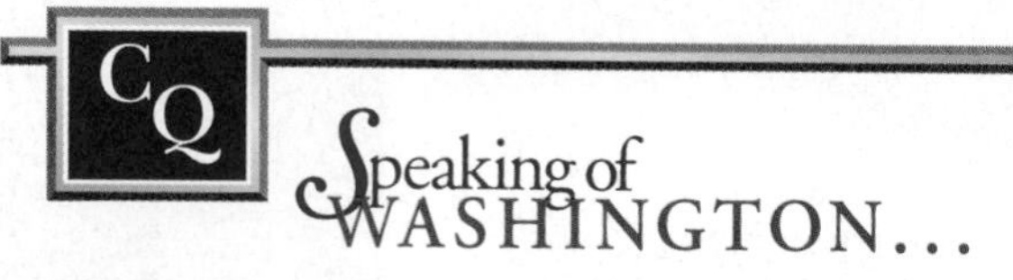

Name Recognition George Washington leads in the number of American places bearing presidents' names. Besides the nation's capital and the state of Washington, there are Washington counties in 31 states. Twenty-two cities and towns throughout the country are known to be named for the first president, as is Mount Washington in New Hampshire.

The Mayor-Council Form

The most widely used form of municipal government is the **mayor-council form.** It is also the oldest type of municipal government in the United States. Until the 1900s it was used in most American cities, regardless of their size. Today about half the cities in the United States use this form. It is the form of government preferred by the largest cities.

The mayor-council form follows the traditional concept of separation of powers. Executive power belongs to an elected mayor, and legislative power to an elected council. All cities except one have unicameral, or one-house, councils.

Most city councils have fewer than 10 members, who usually serve 4-year terms. Some larger cities, however, have larger councils. For example, Chicago has a 50-member council, the largest in the nation. In most cities, council members are elected from the city at large. In some cities, however, citizens of individual wards or districts of the city elect council members.

Two main types of mayor-council government exist, depending upon the power given the mayor. These two types are the strong-mayor system and weak-mayor system. In the **strong-mayor system,** the municipal charter grants the mayor strong executive powers. A strong mayor usually has the power to veto measures the city council passes, and many of his or her actions may not require council approval. The mayor can appoint and fire department heads and high-ranking members of the municipal bureaucracy. In addition, a strong mayor can prepare the municipal budget, subject to council approval, and propose legislation to the city council. The mayor usually serves a four-year term. The strong-mayor system is most often found in large cities.

Many small cities, especially in New England, use the **weak-mayor system** of municipal government. In this form the mayor has only limited powers. The mayor has little control over the budget or the hiring and firing of municipal personnel. The city council makes most policy decisions, and the mayor's veto power is limited. The mayor usually serves only a two-year term. In some small municipalities, the office of the mayor is only a part-time position.

The success of the mayor-council form of government depends to a large extent on the individual who serves as mayor. In the strong-mayor system, a politically skillful mayor can provide effective leadership. Under the weak-mayor plan, because official responsibility is in many hands, success depends upon the cooperation of the mayor and the council.

The Commission Form The **commission form** of municipal government combines executive and legislative power in an elected commission, usually composed of five to seven members. Each commissioner heads a specific department and performs executive duties related to that department. The most common departments are police, fire, public works, finance, and parks. The commissioners also meet as a legislative body to pass laws and make policy decisions. One of the commissioners usually has the title of mayor. The mayor has no additional powers, however, and usually carries out only such ceremonial functions as greeting important visitors and officiating at the dedication or opening of hospitals and other public institutions.

The commission form of municipal government developed after a devastating tidal wave struck Galveston, Texas, in 1900. As the citizens of Galveston tried to rebuild their city, they found their mayor-council government unable to handle the many urgent problems stemming from the disaster. Consequently, the Texas state legislature permitted Galveston to elect five leading citizens to oversee the city's reconstruction. The commission form proved so successful in Galveston that other municipal leaders adopted the commission form in their communities. By 1920 more than 500 cities had the commission form of government.

Despite its early success, today only 3 percent of American cities use the commission form. Over the years municipal leaders discovered that this form of government had serious defects. First, in the absence of a powerful leader, the commission form can lead to a lack of cooperation and planning in government. This form of government has no strong executive to persuade or force the commissioners to act as an effective group. When commissioners disagree, it may be very difficult to make decisions or establish policies. Second, when commissioners do agree, it may be simply to support one another's budget requests. As a result, the municipal budget may be far more generous than it should be.

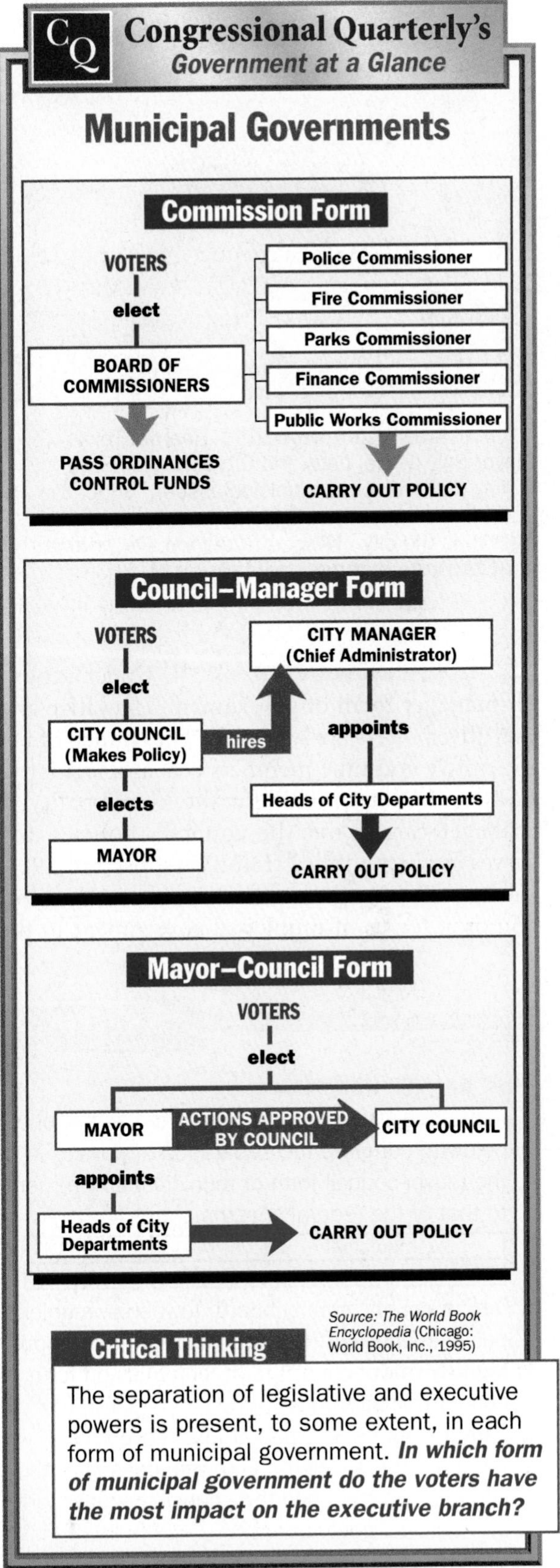

Source: *The World Book Encyclopedia* (Chicago: World Book, Inc., 1995)

Critical Thinking

The separation of legislative and executive powers is present, to some extent, in each form of municipal government. ***In which form of municipal government do the voters have the most impact on the executive branch?***

Professional Administrator Hearne, Texas Mayor Billy Daniel (left) and City Manager Floyd Hafley (right) discuss municipal issues. Under the council-manager form of government, the city manager runs the city. ***Who establishes the policies that the city manager administers?***

The Council-Manager Form Under a **council-manager form** of government, legislative and executive powers are separated. The council of between five and nine members acts as a legislative body and makes policy for the municipality. A manager carries out the council's policies and serves as chief administrator. First used in 1908, the council-manager form is now one of the most common forms of municipal government in the United States. More than 40 percent of cities, mostly in the West and the South, use this form.

The office of city manager is the key feature of the council-manager plan. Appointed by the council, the city manager is the chief executive. He or she appoints and fires municipal workers, prepares the budget, and runs the day-to-day affairs of the city. The city manager may also make policy recommendations to the council. Most city managers are professionals trained in public administration. They must answer to the council and are subject to dismissal by the council.

The council-manager form usually includes a mayor with limited powers. In most cases the mayor is a council member whom the council elects for a two-year term.

Political experts believe the council-manager form brings better management and business techniques into government. Executive and legislative powers are clearly separated, and it is easy for the voters to assign praise or blame for what the government has done.

Some critics, however, point out disadvantages associated with council-manager government. Citizens do not elect the city manager. Many managers are not even residents of the city at the time of their appointment. Also, the council-manager plan may not provide the strong political leadership that is necessary, especially in large cities with ethnically and economically diverse populations.

Section 1 Assessment

Checking for Understanding

1. **Main Idea** Use a graphic organizer like the one below to compare the separation of powers in the mayor-council form of municipal government to that of the federal government.

municipal	federal

2. **Define** county, county board, township, municipality, special district, incorporation, referendum.
3. **Identify** mayor-council form, commission form, council-manager form.
4. Identify four basic types of local government.
5. What are the strengths and weaknesses of the commission form and the council-manager form of municipal government?

Critical Thinking

6. **Drawing Conclusions** Why do many large cities prefer the council-manager form of municipal government?

Federalism The four basic types of local government that exist in the United States are the county, the township, the municipality, and the special district. Choose one type of local government that exists where you live. Create a diagram that shows how it is organized. The diagram should indicate the officials that make up the government and their functions.

Section 2

Serving Localities

Reader's Guide

Key Terms

zoning, mass transit, metropolitan area, suburbs, real property, personal property, assessment, market value

Find Out

- What are the major issues surrounding the services local governments provide?
- How do special districts and regional arrangements help local governments serve the needs of communities?

Understanding Concepts

Political Processes What are some examples of changes in local government structure or function that helped address issues of concern to citizens?

COVER STORY

Fights Fire for a Fee

ROME, ITALY, 79 B.C.

Marcus Licinius Crassus has found a way to profit while providing a public service. Recognizing the city's need for fire protection, Crassus established a first-rate firefighting company that boasts its own horse-drawn water tank. Crassus accompanies his workers to the fires and negotiates his fee with the building's owner before they battle the blaze. A hard bargainer, Crassus usually demands the property as the price for saving it, and also that the owner agree to pay him rent for life. His success as both firefighter and businessman has made Crassus one of Rome's biggest landlords.

Protected by Crassus

Firefighting is just one of many services of local government. Today most of these services are provided by taxes levied on everyone, rather than by fees from individuals.

Local Government Services

Local governments provide education, fire and police protection, water, sewage and sanitation services, trash collection, libraries, and recreation.

Education Providing education is one of the most important functions of government. In many states a large share of local tax revenues goes to pay for public schools. Some states pay a large percentage of local public school costs, but local school districts generally provide most of the money and make the key decisions regarding the operation of the public schools. Local funding and local control of schools go hand in hand. However, local funding also contributes to inequality of education across the many districts of a state. Wealthier districts can provide much better educational opportunities. As a result, some states and the state courts have recently begun to address this issue, raising questions about the way education is financed.

Zoning Local governments use **zoning** to regulate the way land and buildings may be used. Through zoning, a local government can shape the way in which a community develops. Zoning boards can plan for regulated growth, preserve the character of neighborhoods, and prevent the decline of land values. A zoning board may rule that certain districts (zones) can be used only for homes, others only for businesses, and others only for parks.

Some people criticize zoning. They claim that zoning is an excessive use of government power because it limits how people can use their property. Some criticize zoning laws that make it difficult for certain people, often minorities or families with children, to move into particular neighborhoods. Critics call this restrictive zoning. Advocates of zoning claim that without zoning, a community might develop in ways that would lower property values and make it an unpleasant place to live.

Police and Fire Protection Police and fire services are expensive and make up a large part of the local budget. Police protection, for example, is the second-largest expense of many American cities, after public education.

Fire protection is a local function that varies with the size of the community. In small towns volunteers usually staff the fire department. In large cities professional, full-time fire departments provide the necessary protection. Professional fire departments also serve some small towns that have many factories and businesses.

Water Supply Local governments make the vital decisions regarding water service. In smaller communities they may contract with privately owned companies to supply water. The threat of water pollution and water shortages has prompted some local governments to create special water district arrangements. In case of a water shortage, such districts or local governments may attempt to limit the amount of water consumed.

Sewage and Sanitation Local government is responsible for sewage disposal. Untreated sewage, if allowed to return to the natural water supply, can endanger life and property. Many local governments maintain sewage treatment plants to deal with this problem.

Sewage and sanitation disposal are very expensive local services. For cities with populations of less than 50,000, sewage and sanitation combined comprise the second-highest local governmental expenditure after police and fire protection. These costs have forced some smaller communities to contract with private companies to provide their sewage and sanitation services.

Because of environmental concerns, landfills are no longer the simple solution to sanitation that they once were. Some local governments use garbage-processing plants to dispose of the community's solid wastes.

Sewage and sanitation issues also often require that officials make difficult political decisions. For example, where should sewage treatment plants be located? Although such plants are necessary, people often oppose having them near their homes. Another difficult decision involves how to pay for these services. Although people want a clean and healthy community, they often object to paying taxes that are used for improved sewage and sanitation services.

Trekking Through the City

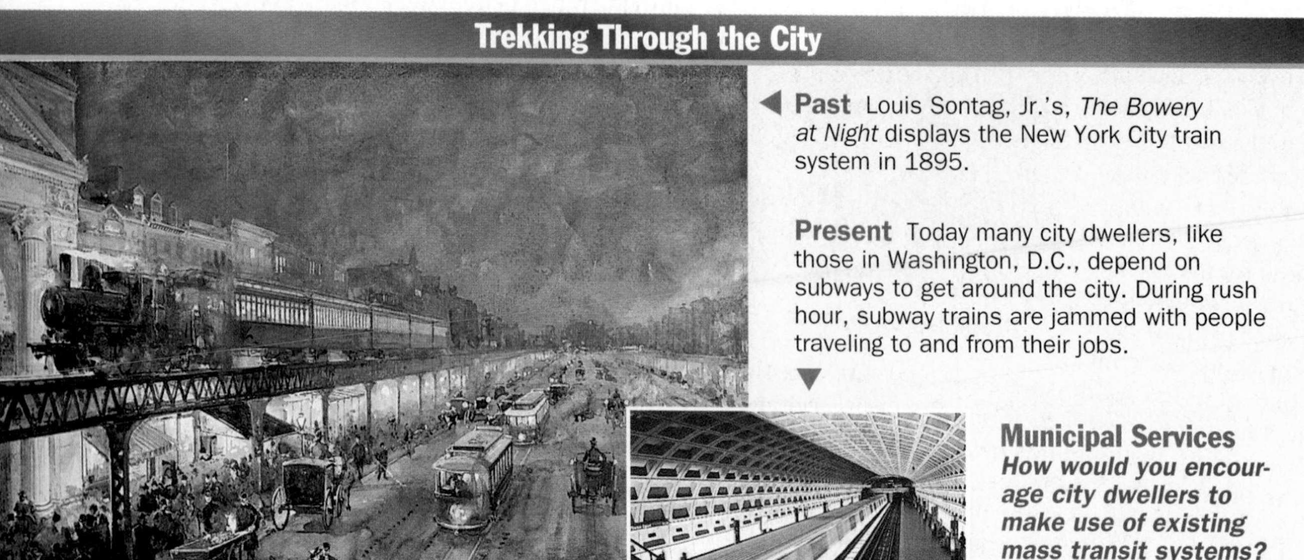

◀ **Past** Louis Sontag, Jr.'s, *The Bowery at Night* displays the New York City train system in 1895.

Present Today many city dwellers, like those in Washington, D.C., depend on subways to get around the city. During rush hour, subway trains are jammed with people traveling to and from their jobs. ▼

Municipal Services
How would you encourage city dwellers to make use of existing mass transit systems?

Transportation As more people choose to live in suburban areas but continue to work in cities, transportation becomes a real concern of city government. In addition, shopping centers are located beyond walking distance from people's homes. To get to work and to shop, millions of Americans rely on either the automobile or **mass transit** facilities such as subways, trains, and buses.

Local governments spend millions of dollars each year to maintain some 650,000 miles of streets. In recent years local governments have tried to encourage people to use mass transit rather than their own automobiles for three important reasons. First, mass transit is usually more efficient than the automobile. A high-speed rail system, for example, can transport about 10 times more people each hour than a modern expressway. Second, mass transit causes less pollution than automobiles. Third, mass transit uses less energy per person than automobiles. Still, many people prefer the independence of driving their own vehicles.

Social Services Many local governments offer important services to citizens who cannot afford them. Normally, local governments provide services to people who have special needs that may result from unemployment, low income, ill health, or from permanent handicaps.

One type of social service provides aid to people who are temporarily unemployed. This aid consists of cash payments and help in finding new jobs. A second program is hospital care for people who need medical attention and cannot afford the expense. The third is direct assistance to needy people in the form of cash payments. This third type of social service is often referred to as "welfare."

Local governments, especially cities, have a huge fiscal responsibility for social services. Paying for these programs is one of the biggest single expenditures for many large cities in the United States today. Although the federal and state governments pay part of the cost, the share that local governments pay toward these programs continues to rise.

Recreation and Cultural Activities As the leisure time of Americans has increased, local governments have responded with recreation and cultural programs. Many local communities offer programs in swimming, dancing, puppetry, and arts and crafts. In addition, many localities provide programs in baseball, football, and other sports. The maintenance of parks, zoos, and museums is also a function of local government. Many cities and counties have helped build stadiums, arenas, and convention centers that are used for sports and entertainment.

Metropolitan Communities

Cities, towns, and villages are metropolitan communities. These urban communities differ greatly in size, ranging from a few thousand to millions of people.

The Census Bureau classifies any community with 2,500 people or more as an urban community. Whether an urban community is called a city, a town, or a village depends on local preference or sometimes on state charter classifications. What is called a city in one state may be called a town or a village in another. The Office of Management and Budget has classified large urban areas as **Metropolitan Statistical Areas.** A **metropolitan area** or metropolis is a large city and its surrounding suburbs. This area may also include small towns that lie beyond the suburbs.

Cities Cities are densely populated areas with commercial, industrial, and residential sections. They are chartered by the state as municipal corporations.

Most cities in the United States became major urban centers during the Industrial Revolution of the 1800s. They attracted African Americans, Americans from rural areas, and immigrants who sought jobs and better living conditions. After World War I, many more African American families migrated to large cities throughout the country in search of better opportunities. Since 1945 newcomers from Puerto Rico, Mexico, Cuba, and other Spanish-speaking regions, as well as immigrants from many countries in Asia, have contributed to rapid urban growth.

Beginning in the 1970s, cities in the South and West became the growth leaders. Census statistics revealed a shift in urban population away from the Northeast and Midwest to cities in the region known as the Sunbelt. New industries attracted people to Sunbelt cities such as Jacksonville, Florida; Houston, Texas; and San Diego, California.

Expansion in the Sunbelt San Diego, California, is located in the Sunbelt and enjoys great growth in industry and population. ***What types of city services would be stressed by fast population growth?***

Meanwhile, the 10 largest cities in the Northeast and Midwest all lost population. In many of these older cities, job opportunities and financial resources dried up. Detroit's population was 1.67 million in the 1960 census; by 1990 it was 1.03 million. Chicago lost 7.4 percent of its population in the 1980s alone. While the population of some Northeastern and Midwestern cities stabilized in the 1990s, 8 of the 10 largest cities continued to lose population. With the exception of Los Angeles, however, major Sunbelt cities continued to grow.

Towns Early in the United States's history, most Americans lived in small towns and villages. After the 1860s large cities grew faster than towns and villages. Between 1970 and 1990, as cities faced problems, several factors made rural areas and small towns once again attractive to Americans. Many towns and villages experienced growth, but the fastest-expanding areas were the suburbs.

Suburbs After the 1990 census the Census Bureau classified 396 areas of the United States as urbanized areas. Each of these concentrations of people contains 50,000 or more residents. These areas are made up of one or more central cities plus the adjacent densely settled territory—the **suburbs.** Today more Americans live in suburbs than in cities or rural areas. A suburb may be called a village, a town, or a city, and it usually has its own form of government.

Many people began to move to the suburbs after World War II. Between 1950 and 1990, middle-class families seeking to buy homes flocked to new residential suburbs. By 1970 an important population shift had occurred—most people living in urban areas resided in the suburbs. Even in the South, cities lost population to suburban areas. Atlanta, Georgia, experienced a 20.7 percent decline, while the surrounding metropolitan area increased 173.1 percent.

The first rapid suburban growth took place close to the edge of cities in the 1950s and 1960s. Federal money for highways and home loans induced families to move to the suburbs, as the federal Urban Renewal Program demolished hundreds of thousands of low- and middle-income urban housing units in the cities. Federal Housing Administration and Veterans Administration programs subsidized homes for nearly 14 million families, with the majority being built in the suburbs.

By the 1980s older suburbs close to cities' edges began to take on the character of the city. Once again people moved, this time to an outer suburban ring. These new suburban communities, 15 to 50 miles from the city center, attracted middle-class workers and professional people.

The growth of suburbia signaled political change. In an article titled "The Empowering of the Suburbs," Rob Gurwitt predicted:

> " *Politics in the outer reaches of suburbia—the land of mega-malls and endless commuting—will soon attract the attention of a lot of people who never really had to think about it before. . . . In several legislatures, the suburbs as a whole will be the new heavyweights, outnumbering the urban or rural delegations that once held unquestioned sovereignty.* "
>
> —Rob Gurwitt, February 1991

Special Districts

Local governments often face such problems as providing a safe water supply and adequate transportation. From time to time, to solve these problems, local governments establish special districts that are better able to respond to solving specific problems than other units of local government.

The second reason for special districts derives from the financial limitations states impose on other units of local government. Most state governments limit the taxing and borrowing powers of local municipal governments. Some states also have laws that limit how much these local governments may spend. Creating a new special district not subject to such limitations becomes a practical solution for local leaders whose budgets are strained to meet local needs. Most special districts may make their own policies, levy taxes, and borrow needed money.

The water commission and the port authority are two common types of special districts in the United States. The local school district is another such special unit. Other special districts are responsible for administration of airports, sewage disposal, and roads. As the most common unit of local government, the special district is found in every state except Alaska. Counting school districts, more than 47,000 special districts exist, comprising more than half of all the local governmental units in the country.

The School District The school district is usually governed by an elected local body, the school board. The **school board** is responsible for setting school policies, hiring a superintendent of schools, and overseeing the day-to-day workings of schools. It also makes up the school budget, decides on new school programs and facilities, and often has the final decision about hiring teachers and supervisory staff. In some places the school board may also decide on the amount of school taxes to be levied.

Citizens often have strong feelings about how their schools should be run. In many communities, however, less than one-third of the eligible voters actually vote in school board elections. Turnout is usually higher when citizens vote on issues dealing with money, such as school bond referendums and school tax levies.

Regional Arrangements

In the 1990s local governments joined to develop creative approaches to regional issues. Cooperative efforts addressed everything from waste management to law enforcement.

Five rural counties in Alabama formed a waste management authority. Officials realized that they would have more bargaining power with the company that operates the landfills local governments use if they joined together. City police departments and county sheriffs' offices in some areas share crime laboratories, keep joint records, operate joint radio bands, and share the cost of training personnel. Fire departments have made agreements that require the fire station closest to answer the first alarm, ignoring political boundaries. Perhaps the most venturesome regional arrangement is Portland, Oregon's, Metropolitan Service District (Metro). As the nation's only regional authority with multiple responsibilities run by elected officials, Metro covers three counties. Its main task is controlling growth under Oregon's land-use laws. Metro also does all the transportation and water-quality planning for the area, runs the zoo, manages the convention center and coliseum, and deals with solid waste disposal and recycling.

Financing Local Government

Local governments are the governments that are charged with providing costly services such as mass transit, airports, parks, water, sewage treatment, education, welfare, and correctional facilities. The costs for these services are enormous. Taxes provide the revenues necessary to do all this.

The Property Tax One of the oldest taxes, property taxes once provided revenue for all levels of government. Today property taxes are the most important source of revenue for local governments, accounting for more than two-thirds of all their tax revenues.

Property taxes are collected on real property and personal property. **Real property** includes land and buildings. **Personal property** consists of such things as stocks and bonds, jewelry, furniture, automobiles, and works of art. Most local governments now tax only real property. If personal property is taxed at all, the rate is usually very low.

Congressional Quarterly's *Government at a Glance*

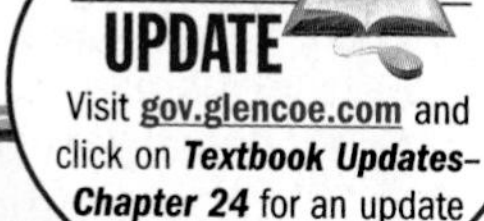

State and Local Government Income and Expenditures

Fiscal Dependency Among Levels of Government*

Year	State from Federal	Local from Federal	Local from State
1952	13.9%	1.2%	26.0%
1962	18.9%	1.8%	25.2%
1972	23.8%	4.0%	30.6%
1982	20.0%	6.7%	30.2%
1992	21.4%	3.1%	30.3%
1995	22.3%	3.5%	30.7%

**Intergovernmental revenue as percentage of total*

Source: Stanley and Niemi, *Vital Statistics on American Politics 1999–2000* (Washington, D.C.: CQ Inc., 2000). U.S. Bureau of Census, *Statistical Abstracts of the United States: 1999* (Washington D.C.: U.S. Bureau of Commerce: 1999).

State and Local Government Expenditures by Function**

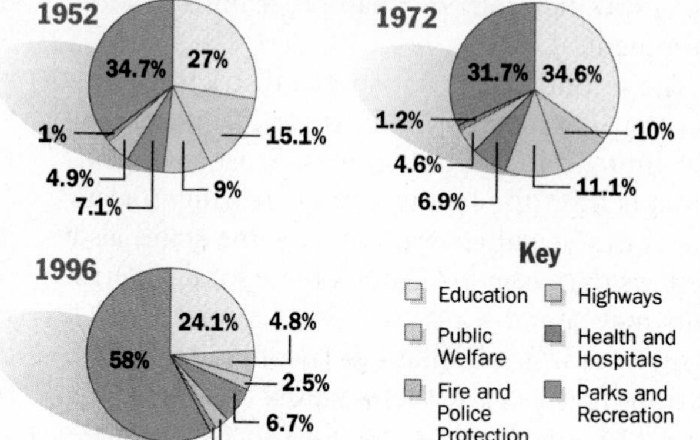

***May not total 100% due to rounding*

Critical Thinking

In addition to taxes, the state and federal governments are a source of income for local governments, which use state and federal money to fund local programs. ***In which areas were there decreases in spending from 1952 to 1996? Increases?***

How do local governments determine what the property tax will be? The process of calculating the value of the property is called **assessment.** It begins when the tax assessor appraises the market value of the homes and other real property in the community. The **market value** of a house or a factory is the amount of money the owner may expect to receive if the property is sold.

Most local governments do not tax property on its market value but on its assessed value, which is usually only a percentage of its market value. For example, a house that has an appraised worth of $80,000 may have an assessed value of 30 percent of that figure, or $24,000.

Public opinion surveys indicate that most Americans view the property tax as unfair. The major charge against the property tax is that it is regressive—placing a heavier burden on people with lower incomes than on those with higher incomes. The property tax also weighs heavily on retired home owners with fixed incomes who cannot afford constantly rising taxes.

The second criticism of the property tax is that it is often very difficult to determine property values on a fair and equal basis. Standards may vary with each tax assessor. Tax assessors are elected officials, often underpaid and inadequately trained.

A third criticism is that reliance on the property tax results in unequal public services. A wealthy community with a large tax base can afford better public services than a less wealthy community with a small tax base. Based on this criticism, some state supreme courts have ruled against using the property tax to pay for local schools. They have held that using property taxes to support schools is a violation of the Fourteenth Amendment's guarantee of equal protection of the law.

Finally, property used for educational, religious, or charitable purposes and government property is exempt from the property tax. Some communities give tax exemptions to new businesses and industries to encourage them to relocate there. As a result, the nonexempt property owners must bear a heavier share of the tax burden.

Other Local Revenue Sources Local governments must have other revenue sources. These include local income taxes, sales taxes, fines and fees, and government-owned businesses.

The local income tax is a tax on personal income. If the state and the local community both have an income tax, the taxpayer pays three income taxes: federal, state, and local.

The sales tax is a tax on most items sold in stores. Many states allow their local governments to use this tax. In some places it is a selective sales tax, one that is applied to only a few items.

Fines paid for traffic, sanitary, and other violations, and fees for special services provide part of the income for local governments. Special assessments are fees that property owners must pay for local services that benefit them. For example, a city may impose a special assessment when it improves a sidewalk that benefits home owners or shopkeepers. Some cities also earn revenue through housing projects, markets, and parking garages.

States permit local governments to borrow money in the form of bonds—certificates that promise to repay the borrowed money with interest by a certain date. Some investors consider local government bonds to be good investments because their earned interest is not subject to federal income taxes. Municipal bonds raise money for large, expensive projects such as a sports stadium, school buildings, or government office buildings.

Intergovernmental Revenue In addition to local sources of revenue, most local governments receive economic aid from state and federal governments. This aid often comes in the form of grants.

When local governments carry out state laws or administer state programs such as constructing highways or matching welfare payments, they receive state aid. State governments also grant funds for specific purposes such as recreation and education. Today states provide more than one-third of the general revenue of local governments. Most state aid consists of **categorical-formula grants**—support for specific programs—used for education, highways, public welfare, and health and hospitals.

Federal financial aid has come in two forms: categorical grants and block grants. Usually Congress includes guidelines with categorical grants, for example, to help pay for a new highway, for police training programs, or to aid in sewage control. Local officials prefer **block grants,** or unrestricted aid to community development or social services.

GOVERNMENT Online

Student Web Activity Visit the *United States Government: Democracy in Action* Web site at gov.glencoe.com and click on ***Chapter 24–Student Web Activities*** for an activity about serving localities.

Section 2 Assessment

Checking for Understanding

1. **Main Idea** Use a graphic organizer like the one below to compare the advantages of using mass transit with those of driving personal automobiles.

mass transit  personal auto

2. **Define** zoning, mass transit, metropolitan area, suburbs, real property, personal property, assessment, market value.
3. **Identify** Metropolitan Statistical Areas.
4. What are three goals of zoning?
5. Why is the property tax considered by some people to be an unfair tax?

Critical Thinking

6. **Analyzing Information** Why do local governments, with state and federal assistance, provide social services to residents?

Political Processes Obtain a copy of the most recent budget of your local government. Write an article identifying the services that account for most of the budget. Also, identify the main sources of your local government's revenue. Include your suggestions for change, either in spending priorities or in sources of revenue.

Skills

Critical Thinking

Demonstrating Reasoned Judgment

Judgments involve using criteria to assess the worth of something such as an election candidate or a public policy. Criteria are standards for making judgments. Criteria may be derived from experience, history, ethics, or other sources. For instance, honesty is one criteria for judging a political candidate.

Learning the Skill

To make a reasoned judgment you need to follow these three steps:

1. Review the facts to understand the problem. Examine all the proposed solutions.
2. Use your knowledge to decide whether each proposed solution is likely to be effective.
3. Examine information that both supports and contradicts your conclusion.

Practicing the Skill

Suppose that you are the mayor of a city in which vandalism is a major problem.

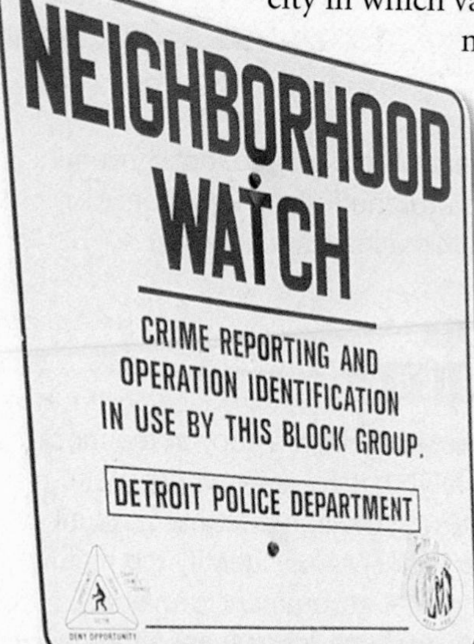

Guarding the neighborhood against crime

Most of the illegal activity is centered in three neighborhoods that also have high unemployment rates. Read the lettered proposals below for dealing with the problem. Answer the questions that follow.

A. Civic education programs should be created for grades 1–12.
B. Police should walk rather than drive around the areas they patrol.
C. Job training programs for unemployed young people should be started in these neighborhoods.
D. Neighborhood crime watch programs should be organized.
E. The city should enlist the help of churches and community groups to provide recreational activities and counseling services for teenagers.

1. Write a sentence explaining how each proposal might help to alleviate the problem.
2. On a scale of 1 (low) to 10 (high), indicate how effective you consider each proposal.
3. Write a paragraph explaining how proposals you support would work together.

Application Activity

Read a newspaper article about a local issue or problem. Use the facts in the article to draw a conclusion about the effectiveness of proposed solutions to the problem. Write a paragraph explaining your opinion.

The Glencoe Skillbuilder Interactive Workbook, Level 2 provides instruction and practice in key social studies skills.

Section 3

Challenges of Urban Growth

Reader's Guide

Key Terms

urban renewal, infrastructure, revitalization, gentrification, metropolitan government

Find Out

- How have shifts in the population affected cities and their governments in recent years?
- What large problems do metropolitan governments face today and in the future?

Understanding Concepts

Federalism What is the financial relationship between local governments and state and federal governments?

COVER STORY

New Yorkers Assess Police

NEW YORK CITY, SEPTEMBER 15, 2000

According to a poll released today, 8 out of 10 New Yorkers believe their police are doing a good job of fighting crime. Steven M. Fishner, the mayor's criminal justice coordinator, explained that the New Yorkers' vote of confidence is no accident. Crime in the city has declined 55 percent since 1993, and homicides are down by 65 percent. The poll also reveals a downside to citizens' perception of the police department. Many people suspect that police use racial profiling when making arrests and are lax in disciplining brutal and corrupt officers. For example, 42 percent of the African Americans and 36 percent of the Hispanics who responded indicated that they would be "fearful" or "somewhat concerned" if an officer approached them.

Concentrating many people in limited space creates problems. Today many urban areas in the United States confront housing shortages, inadequate transportation, pollution, poverty, and crime. Although these problems are most acutely experienced in big cities, they also exist in the surrounding suburbs and small towns.

Population and Housing

Recall the kinds of population shifts that have taken place in recent years. Cities in the Northeast and Midwest lost population as those in the South and West grew rapidly. The population of small towns and rural areas increased, and many people moved from cities to nearby suburban areas.

What are the causes and results of these changes? What challenges have these changing growth patterns presented for local communities? Studying the changes in housing is a key to understanding many urban problems.

Managing Decline As the population in an area increases, available land becomes more scarce and, hence, more costly. Local governments often have to decide whether available land should be used for new housing, industry, stores, or office buildings.

Municipal governments attempt to manage land use to provide an environment for orderly growth. What action should be taken when an area begins to deteriorate?

In the 1950s some inner cities showed signs of decline. People who could afford new housing left the inner cities and moved to the suburbs; poorer people remained. Jobs became scarce as industries moved out—either to attractive suburban areas or to new locations in the South and West. Inner-city housing deteriorated, and slums multiplied. Residents had to endure inadequate heating, leaky pipes, poor sanitary conditions, and rising crime rates.

Refurbishing Communities

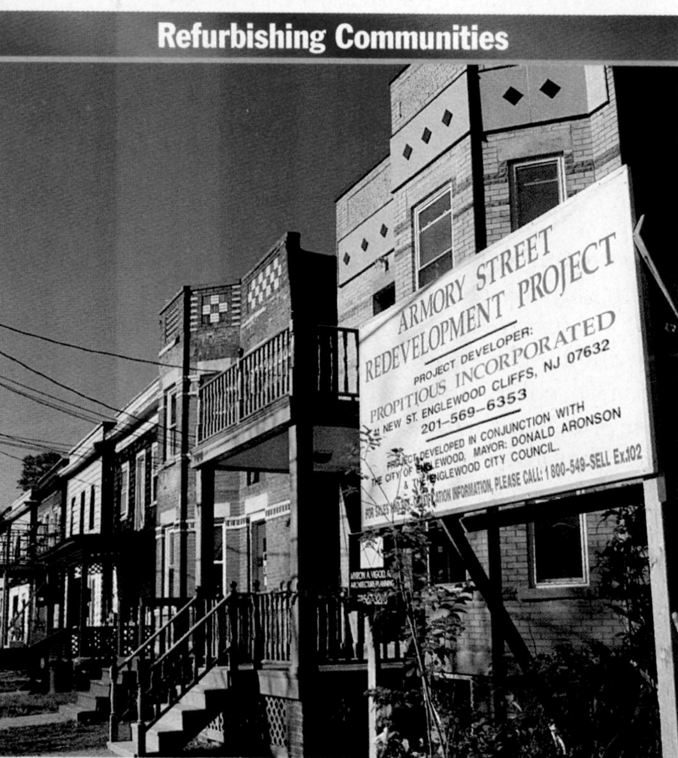

Local Issues Through this redevelopment project in Englewood, New Jersey, local officials hope to transform older housing units into more functional and affordable housing. ***Which local issue do you think is the most urgent in your community?***

Urban Renewal Mayors of large cities, aware of the growing inner-city problems, appealed to the federal government for help. The federal government offered an **urban renewal** program as a solution. Spending hundreds of millions of federal dollars for new construction in the 1950s and 1960s, cities attempted to address their housing problems. Generally the approach was to tear down existing housing and build giant apartment complexes. Cities uprooted millions of people in an effort to renew blighted areas. In some cases urban renewal forced residents out of their old neighborhoods and replaced older buildings with new luxury apartment houses that the original residents could not afford.

After years of massive spending, the results were not encouraging. Fewer affordable new housing units were created than were needed. Unemployment remained a problem. New Haven, Connecticut, was typical:

> *"The most important effect of the first core area projects and then those in the next ring was to produce a continuous flow of displaced persons, as much as one-fifth of the entire population of the city was uprooted between 1956 and 1974. Community social networks were in part destroyed by the very officials who sought to stop decay and make New Haven slumless."*
>
> —Susan F. Fainstein and Norman L. Fainstein, 1986

Urban renewal added new low-rent public housing, but slowed production of other types of housing. Low-rent units under construction increased from 14,000 in 1956 to 126,800 in 1970. However, low-rent or subsidized government housing discouraged private investment in apartment units. The construction of new rental units declined from about 750,000 in 1972 to 297,000 in 1980. The construction of privately owned new housing units peaked at 1.6 million in 1955 and leveled off to about 1.4 million by 1970. Fewer total housing units available meant higher costs overall for rent.

Housing Discrimination To make matters worse, some Americans suffered the effects of discrimination in housing, especially in the rental market. For many years smaller communities and suburban areas excluded African Americans and other minorities. Meanwhile, inner-city living developed a cycle of low pay, poor housing, inadequate education, and unemployment.

Suburbs at times kept out the poor, the elderly, and people with children. Some apartment owners were unwilling to rent to people with children. A 1981 study in Los Angeles found that owners excluded families with children from 71 percent of the apartments surveyed.

The courts have consistently ruled against discrimination in housing. Moreover, in 1968 Congress passed a federal Open Housing Act that bars discrimination in the sale and rental of housing. Nevertheless, housing discrimination is sometimes difficult to prove, and the government has not always enforced laws against it.

Coping with Housing Shortages Many major cities, including Atlanta, New Orleans, and Philadelphia, responded to the housing shortage by renovating older housing units. Renovation projects rewired homes, installed new plumbing, and rebuilt floors and walls. In cities such as Baltimore and Des Moines, funds from the city government along with federal, state, and private funds made some highly successful renovation programs possible.

The federal government also provided low-interest loans to local housing authorities through public housing programs. These loans helped to build housing projects for low-income residents. Local housing authorities received federal aid to help maintain rents at affordable levels.

Social Problems

Large cities face serious social problems. The concentration of poverty, homelessness, crime, and drug and alcohol abuse is easily identified in large cities. The local and national media often report on these problems, raising the national awareness of their seriousness. City governments, however, must be more than aware of these social conditions. They must try to alleviate them.

Homelessness Housing shortages are only one side of the housing problem in major cities. The other side is the human issue—homelessness. Hundreds of thousands of people spend their nights in shelters or on the streets. Unemployment and the housing shortage contribute to this problem. In addition, two-thirds of the homeless have a serious personal problem that contributes to their plight—alcoholism, drug addiction, or a criminal record. About one-third are mentally ill. The average homeless adult has been out of work for four years. Housing alone will not solve this problem. Rehabilitation programs are needed to address the personal problems that caused people to be homeless.

Private and religious charitable organizations contribute the most to relieve homelessness. The federal government provides a very small portion of assistance. In a recent year, the federal government provided about the same amount of assistance for the whole nation that the city of New York spent for its own homeless people.

Drug Abuse Closely associated with homelessness in many cities is drug abuse and addiction. Crack, a stronger form of cocaine, became the scourge of the cities in the 1980s. Street gangs built a network for selling the drug in most of the nation's cities before the federal **Drug Enforcement Administration** realized the extent of the problem.

Inner-city teenagers, unable to find low-skill jobs, rationalized crack selling as a gateway to prosperity. Many worked long, hard hours in the drug trade and hoped to escape the poverty cycle. The rewards, however, did not match the danger. Many crack dealers earned no more than the minimum wage, and the earnings were often consumed in drug use.

The national media focused on drugs as a major problem in the United States. Some called it a $25 billion drain on the national wealth and implicated drugs in the renewed rising crime rates in the cities. One national magazine that made a commitment to cover drug abuse said:

> “*We plan accordingly to cover it as a crisis, reporting it as aggressively and returning to it as regularly as we did the struggle for civil rights, the war in Vietnam, and the fall of the Nixon presidency.*”
>
> —*Newsweek,* June 16, 1986

In November 1988, Congress responded to President Reagan's request for new antidrug legislation. The new law created the office of federal drug "czar" and increased spending for drug treatment and law enforcement. By 1991 the Justice Department's budget reached $10 billion, much of it targeted for fighting drug trafficking. There was some evidence that federal intervention was having an effect. A survey released in January 1990 reported a decline in the number of high school seniors who said they had tried illegal drugs. Use of crack showed the sharpest decline—a 50 percent drop from the 1985 figure.

However, the problem of drug abuse resurfaced in the media just a few years later. Teenage use of marijuana doubled between 1993 and 1996. While the number of hard-core drug users remained steady at about 3 million, the addicts were using an increasing amount of drugs. President Clinton responded to the news by appointing Barry R. McCaffrey, a retired army general, as head of the **Office of National Drug Control Policy.** At confirmation hearings McCaffrey promised the Senate renewed efforts, especially in the treatment of drug users:

"Specifically, let me underscore my conviction that drug testing and then the treatment of convicted criminals prior to and following release from prison is vital. We simply must provide treatment to these people if we expect to protect the American people from violence and property crimes."

—Barry R. McCaffrey, 1996

A federal survey released in August 2000 showed that teenage drug use is again on the decline.

Meeting Future Challenges

In the years ahead municipal governments face problems that demand imagination, citizen involvement, and good leadership. In most cases solving these problems will take large investments of money. Municipalities continue to depend on help from state and federal governments. The level of aid may not satisfy big cities, however.

Large cities have special problems that add to their financial burdens. They usually have higher rates of poverty, crime, and unemployment than smaller localities. In 1979, for example, about one-third of all people living below the federally defined level of poverty resided in large cities.

Infrastructure Paved streets and sidewalks, pipes that bring water to homes, and sewers that dispose of liquid wastes make up what is known as the **infrastructure** of a city. Also included in the infrastructure are bridges, tunnels, and public buildings. In America's older cities, the infrastructure shows severe signs of wear. Much of it is in dire need of repair or replacement. An economist who is an expert on the subject has warned, "Much of our infrastructure is on the verge of collapse."

Repairing the infrastructure will mean huge expenditures for local governments well into the future. All levels of government together spent about $10 billion in 1960 for airports, highways, railroads, and transit. By the 1990s government spending for these forms of transportation surpassed $100 billion a year.

Cities face mounting costs for cleanup of polluted water, sewer system replacement, and waste

We the People

Making a Difference

Gillian Kilberg

What would you do if you inherited $20,000? Seventeen-year-old Gillian Kilberg decided to start a summer camp to help underprivileged children. Kilberg, from McLean, Virginia, received the inheritance when her grandmother died. "I wanted to do something with the money so people would remember my grandmother," she said.

Kilberg's plan was to create a "special trips" camp for children ages 5 to 12. The camp would give children from the Washington, D.C., area an opportunity to visit places that they could probably never visit on their own. Although $20,000 seemed a large sum of money, Gillian soon realized she had to raise more. She worked with a local sheriff to create her program, and sent letters to friends and relatives explaining her project. "We ended up raising about $30,000, which was amazing," she said.

Gillian's summer camp, which she called Grandma Rita's Children, sent 47 children on 15 different day trips to places like the National Air and Space Museum and a Baltimore Orioles baseball game. They went backstage at a Motown concert and even paid a visit to Supreme Court justice Clarence Thomas.

Gillian believed "one summer is not enough to make a permanent difference" in [the children's] lives." So she donated the $5,000 Prudential Spirit of Community Award that she won and raised additional funds in 1997 for another camp. In its second summer Grandma Rita's Children hosted 52 children on 19 day trips.

treatment plants. Infrastructure costs are so enormous that local governments cannot do the job alone. State and federal aid is available for road building, water and sewage systems, bridge construction, and many other public works.

Mass Transit Maintaining a sound transportation network is a serious challenge for local governments. Chronic traffic jams and air pollution have resulted from the millions of Americans using their automobiles to commute to work. As noted earlier in this chapter, an alternative to automobile use in urban areas is mass transit—buses, subways, and rail lines. Mass transit moves large numbers of people, produces less pollution, and consumes much less fuel than automobiles. Despite these advantages of mass transit, however, most Americans prefer to drive to work alone in their automobiles.

Development Trinity College's groundbreaking ceremony opens The Learning Corridor in Hartford, Connecticut. The Learning Corridor is a neighborhood revitalization program to create a central hub of educational and economic development. ***How do projects like The Learning Corridor help eradicate social and economic problems in cities?***

Many local leaders believe that more people would use mass transit facilities if they were cleaner, faster, and more efficient. Elaborate mass transit systems have been built in Washington, D.C., Atlanta, and in the San Francisco–Oakland area. San Francisco's Bay Area Rapid Transit system (BART) cost twice its original estimate to build. High costs discourage planners in other cities from taking on such projects.

The Need for Economic Development

Cities have struggled with different solutions to their financial problems. These solutions have included state and federal aid, loans, budget cuts, and layoffs of city workers. Many cities have also tried to deal with their financial woes by stimulating greater economic development. Economic development is especially critical for cities that have lost businesses over the past 30 years.

How can municipal governments stimulate economic development? One approach is revitalization. **Revitalization** means that local governments make large investments in new facilities in an effort to promote economic growth. In recent years a number of major cities have attempted to revitalize their downtown areas. Baltimore built a $170-million office and residential complex. Detroit invested more than $200 million in a regional shopping mall and two giant office buildings. Funds usually come both from local government and private investors. State and federal aid may also be available for revitalization projects.

The second major approach to economic development is tax incentives to industries that relocate in a community. Tax incentives may take a number of forms. Local governments, especially in suburban areas, often try to attract new business by offering lower property tax rates. Some states, such as Connecticut and Indiana, offer tax reductions to businesses that relocate in areas of high unemployment. Similarly, the federal government also offers tax reductions, or credits, to businesses that move into areas of poverty and unemployment.

Gentrification One of the most debated issues of the revitalization movement concerns gentrification. Also called "displacement," **gentrification** is the phenomenon of new people moving into a neighborhood, forcing out those who live there and changing the area's essential character.

Beginning in the 1980s some middle-income suburbanites and recent immigrants moved into the cities, often into areas where they could restore old houses and other buildings and take advantage of the lower housing costs while enjoying the benefits of city life.

The positive side of gentrification is that it restores vitality to the city by reclaiming deteriorating property and bringing new business to decayed areas. It also has a negative effect, however. It accelerates property sales, inflating property values and increasing taxes. Property becomes too expensive for poorer residents who live in these neighborhoods to stay. If the displaced residents are largely from a minority group, the issue may become a heated one. Some cities have defused this issue by passing legislation that slows or prevents displacement. For example, Savannah, Georgia, preserved much of its social diversity by providing its limited-income residents help in restoring their properties.

New Federal and State Priorities The federal government, acting to reduce budget deficits, eliminated programs such as Urban Development Action Grants and the Comprehensive Employment Training Act. Why were federal and state governments less responsive to city problems? Perhaps these governments had changed their priorities. A federal commission, "Urban America in the Eighties," suggested that social and economic migration to the suburbs was a natural, even an advantageous, development that should not be discouraged. It added that federal aid to the cities should not try to stop this trend. The suburbs were becoming powerful economic and political entities. After the census of 1990, new district lines gave suburbs additional seats in Congress and state legislatures. The nation's focus seemed to be shifting from city problems to suburban opportunities. To survive as healthy communities, perhaps cities would have to solve their own problems.

Metropolitan Government One way to address urban problems is by reorganization into a **metropolitan government** that serves a larger region. Most problems do not affect just one local community. Instead, they are problems of an entire region. Air pollution created in a city spreads to nearby suburbs and rural towns. Suburban residents use city services, but they do not help to pay taxes for these services. Because a metropolitan area is an interdependent region, those who favor metropolitan government feel that one government for an entire metropolitan area would be better equipped to handle regional problems.

Many people feel that a metropolitan government would reduce government waste and duplication of services. For example, one metropolitan sewage treatment plant might just as easily serve many communities. This would save each local government the cost of creating its own sewage treatment facility. Other services, such as water supply and transportation, might also be provided more economically on an area-wide basis.

Section 3 Assessment

Checking for Understanding

1. **Main Idea** Use a graphic organizer like the one below to compare challenges that municipal governments faced in the 1950s to those they face today.

1950s	Today

2. **Define** urban renewal, infrastructure, revitalization, gentrification, metropolitan government.
3. **Identify** Drug Enforcement Administration, Office of National Drug Control Policy.
4. What are the positive and negative outcomes of gentrification?
5. How would a metropolitan government address urban problems?

Critical Thinking

6. **Predicting Consequences** What additional problems will cities face if governments are unable to fund replacement of urban infrastructures?

Federalism Mayors of large cities must present strong arguments to get federal funds to address city problems. What could a mayor say to the president and Congress to support the cities' cause? Research the types of projects that would benefit your community. Write a proposal explaining the need for federal money to support that project for your community.

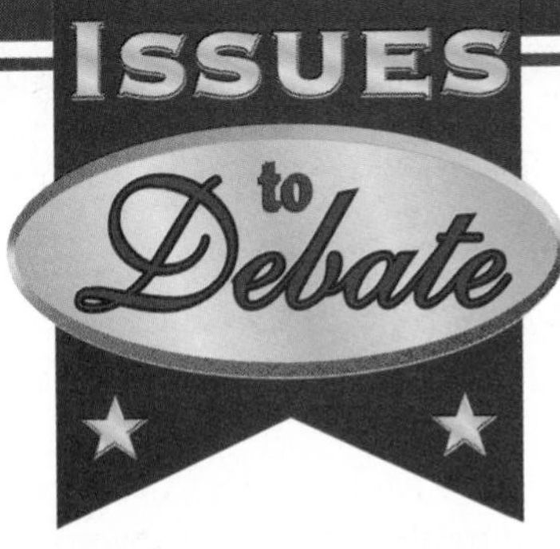

Should Cities Improve Mass Transit to Solve Traffic Congestion?

In 1991 Congress passed the Intermodal Surface Transportation Efficiency Act (ISTEA). ISTEA's goal was to balance the growing needs of transportation with the quality-of-life issues, such as clean air. Yet, the nation's transportation system is under stress. Congestion continues to get worse. ISTEA may be credited with declining pollution levels in several major cities, but in truth, the gains have come from improved technology and cleaner-burning fuels.

Cars Rule

Despite the flexibility that ISTEA gave to states to use road money for alternative transportation, the United States remains a car-dominated country. States spent almost the entire $23.9 billion ISTEA provided in its Surface Transportation Program for roads. Because of heavy spending from ISTEA funds, from states, and from local governments, pavement conditions have improved steadily. Meanwhile many senior citizens, persons with disabilities, and people living on limited incomes need mass transit services.

Better Roads or a Better Environment?

Trucking and auto interests lobby for improved highways. Alternative-transportation advocates, however, believe that a better environment and less congestion would result if money were channeled to projects aimed at reducing vehicular traffic and improving air quality.

Debating the Issue

Should Your Community Use Federal Funds for Mass Transit?

The Federal Transit Administration (FTA) works together with metropolitan areas to develop transportation plans. Assume you live in a city where the FTA has offered $30 million to the community for transportation improvements. This would be enough to build an elevated walkway and to extend the city's transit railway into its growing Central Market, a shopping complex. Truckers and people living in a rapidly developing residential area, however, want most of the money to be used to widen a congested two-lane road into a four-lane highway leading downtown.

Key Issues

✔ Will people use mass transit to avoid congested highways?

✔ Should the city spend funds to benefit the Central Market at the expense of other shopping areas?

Debate Select seven class members to represent an urban commission to study this issue. Select several people to testify on each side of the issue.

Vote Have the commission vote whether to use the funds for a highway or to improve mass transit.

Chapter 24

Assessment and Activities

GOVERNMENT Online

Self-Check Quiz Visit the *United States Government: Democracy in Action* Web site at gov.glencoe.com and click on ***Chapter 24–Self-Check Quizzes*** to prepare for the chapter test.

Reviewing Key Terms

From the list below, write the term that best completes each sentence.

county	**real property**
municipality	**infrastructure**
special district	**revitalization**
zoning	**gentrification**
market value	**metropolitan government**

1. Basic facilities such as streets, water lines, and public buildings make up what is known as the _____ of a city.
2. Sometimes called "displacement," _____ has often changed the character of an urban area.
3. To promote economic growth, local governments have tried _____ through large investments in new facilities.
4. In the South and in rural areas _____ government is important.
5. Local governments may use _____ to control growth.
6. Local governments rely on _____ taxes as a main source of revenue.
7. Some people feel that the best way to address urban problems is reorganization using _____ that serves a large region.
8. Originally, a charter for a _____ was much like one that states granted to corporations.
9. A public school district is a _____ established by local government.
10. The government does not tax property on the _____, or the amount of money the owner may expect to receive if the property is sold.

Current Events JOURNAL

Recognize Local Action Find recent examples of local government and private citizens attempting to solve problems of homelessness, education, housing, or crime in your community. You might look through your local newspapers or find out about activities of local church and community organizations. Share your findings with the class.

Recalling Facts

1. What document specifies the powers and duties of local government?
2. What are the main functions of a municipal charter?
3. What are the three main forms of municipal government?
4. What is the single largest public service provided by local tax revenues?
5. How may zoning laws make it difficult for minorities or families with children to move into a certain area?
6. What is the biggest government expenditure for many large American cities?
7. Describe four kinds of population shifts in metropolitan areas since 1950.
8. What are the major causes of homelessness in the nation's cities?
9. What is the main reason that many cities have not built mass transit systems?

Understanding Concepts

1. **Federalism** What is the relationship between a state and a municipality within that state?
2. **Political Processes** Why did some state supreme courts rule against using the property tax to pay for local schools?

Chapter 24

Critical Thinking

1. **Making Comparisons** Use a Venn diagram like the one below to compare a local government's charter to a state constitution.

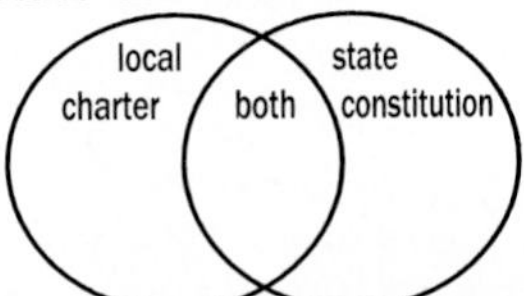

2. **Identifying Central Issues** In your view, which of the federal government's goals in dealing with the illegal drug problem is the most important? Why?

Interpreting Political Cartoons Activity

1. Whom do the two figures represent?
2. What statement is the cartoonist making about the state of cities?
3. According to the cartoonist, what can the government do to help cities?

Cooperative Learning Activity

Interest Groups Organize into small groups. Each group should research a problem such as traffic congestion that it wants the municipal government to address. Have the class hear the arguments of each group.

Skill Practice Activity

Demonstrating Reasoned Judgment Suppose you are the mayor of a city that has a growing population of homeless people with no health care, or access to schools. Existing shelters are crime-ridden and overcrowded. Read the following proposed measures and then answer the questions that follow.

A. The city should buy abandoned warehouses and turn them into temporary shelters.
B. The city should assign police to keep order in existing shelters.
C. The city should open a free clinic to provide medical care for the homeless.
D. The city should build low-rent housing.

1. How would each of the measures above alleviate the problems of the homeless?
2. If you had to choose only two proposals, which would you choose, and why?

Technology Activity

Using the Internet Search the Internet for your state's Web site. Note information on state and local governments. Based on your findings, create a pamphlet on your state's government. Include the name of your governor, an organizational chart of the government, and a state map labeling major cities.

Participating in Local Government

Attend a county, township, village, or special district meeting. Obtain copies of the agenda. Take notes on what you hear at the meeting and whether the agenda was followed, and report on what happened to the class.

UNIT 9

Political and Economic Systems

Participating IN GOVERNMENT

Comparing Governments *One of the most interesting ways to learn about political systems in other countries is to talk directly with a person from another country. Investigate your community to find out whether there is a foreign exchange student, visiting businessperson, or recent immigrant from another country. With the teacher's permission, invite that person to class for a time of sharing information.*

Electronic Field Trip

The United Nations

Step inside the United Nations building in New York City by way of a video tour of this hub of world diplomacy.

Glencoe's Democracy in Action Video Program

The United Nations was created after World War II to support global cooperation and world peace. The **Democracy in Action** program "The United Nations," referenced below, provides information about the basic functions of the United Nations and how decisions are made in a collaborative effort.

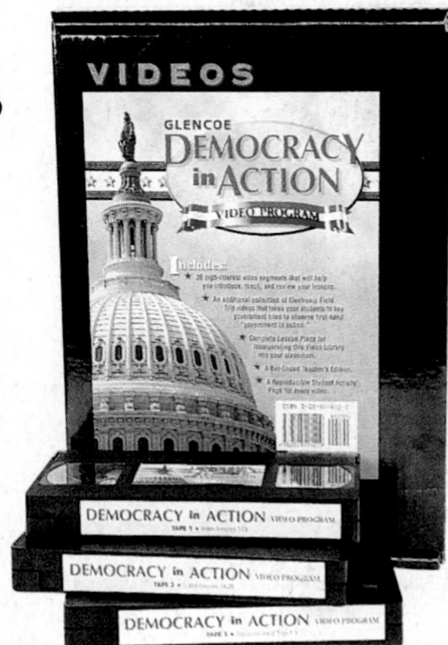

Also available in videodisc format.

View the videodisc by scanning the barcode or by entering the chapter number on your keypad and pressing Search.

Disc 2, Side 1, Chapter 9

Hands-On Activity

Use the Internet to locate the Web site for the United Nations. Research the United Nations databases for information about the status of developing nations, such as life expectancy, and per capita income. Create a short report comparing two developing nations' statistical data. Incorporate charts and graphs to illustrate your comparison.

Present your findings to your classmates.

The statue *Victory* is a memorial to the soldiers who lost their lives in World War I and World War II.

Chapter 25

Political Systems in Today's World

Why It's Important

Political Systems Americans often take democracy for granted. By comparing political systems, we can develop an appreciation for those that provide a large degree of personal freedom and opportunity.

To learn more about the advantages and disadvantages of two specific political systems, view the ***Democracy in Action*** Chapter 25 video lesson:

Parliamentary vs. Presidential Systems

★ ★ ★ ★ ★ ★ ★ ★ ★ ★

GOVERNMENT Online

Chapter Overview Visit the *United States Government: Democracy in Action* Web site at gov.glencoe.com and click on ***Chapter 25–Overview*** to preview chapter information.

Section 1

Consolidated Democracies

Reader's Guide

Key Terms

consolidated democracies, abdicate, oligarchy, parliamentary government, life peers, presidential government, *kanyro*

Find Out

- What are the key differences between parliamentary and presidential governments?
- What are the challenges for democracy in Western Europe and Japan?

Understanding Concepts

Comparative Government How does parliamentary government differ from presidential government?

COVER STORY

Japanese Teens Rebel

MITAKA CITY, JAPAN, APRIL 6, 1987

"Young people in Japan today have no desire to work as hard as our parents," observes Junko Kotohda, as she dines with her family. Like her parents and sisters, Kotohda is seated on the floor in traditional Japanese fashion. However, there's Western food on the table—tonight it's fried chicken. "Our parents are workaholics," she continues. "We want entertainment too." But Kotohda, a high school senior, will not join teens at Tokyo's Yoyogi Park where, dressed like 1950s American rock 'n' rollers, they dance to boom boxes. "I have my own individuality," she insists.

A modern Japanese teen

Japan is one of the leading industrialized democratic nations of the world. Along with the United States and the countries of Western Europe, Japan shares leadership in world trade and political influence. These nations also share common democratic values that can be traced back for many centuries.

Origins of Democracy

The earliest origins of democratic ideas are found in ancient Greece and Rome. Democratic ideas developed in Europe and were brought to the Americas by the English colonists who settled here. The principles of representative government developed over many centuries in England. Core values of democracy were still developing in the Western world during the 1800s. Today some nations are in transition to democracy. Political scientists call other nations **consolidated democracies.** These nations have democratic elections, political parties, constitutional government, an independent judiciary, and usually a market economy. While Great Britain, France, and Japan share common democratic principles, the development of each nation's political system is unique.

Reform in Great Britain Great Britain was a limited constitutional monarchy in the early 1800s. While the monarch still held some powers, most political decisions were made by Parliament. All British people were, in theory, represented in the House of Commons. In practice, however, political power remained with the landed aristocracy. The middle class and working class had no voting rights. Reforms that were proposed—voting rights for all adult men, elimination of property qualifications for voting, a secret ballot, and equal electoral districts—were at first rejected by Parliament. However, most of these reforms were enacted before 1900. By 1928 women in Britain over the age of 21 had won the right to vote in national elections.

◀ Elderly South African casts first ballot.

Rulers and Figureheads

The British System Prime Minister Tony Blair, not the British monarch, exercises the real power of government. ***Why do you think Great Britain continues to have a monarchy?***

Political Struggles in France The French Revolution set out to win basic rights for all citizens in 1789. It ended in dictatorship, followed by a return to monarchy. In July 1830 angry Parisian workers again took to the streets. They forced King Charles X to **abdicate**, or formally renounce the throne, and set up a new constitutional monarchy.

Discontent with the new monarch, King Louis Philippe, led to the Revolution of 1848. Only briefly did the people enjoy the freedoms won in this revolt, however. Voters elected Louis-Napoleon Bonaparte, the nephew of Napoleon I. Louis-Napoleon drafted a new constitution for the Second French Republic and later took the title Emperor Napoleon III. When Napoleon III was defeated in war in 1870, France took steps toward becoming a republic. The French Constitution of 1875 finally provided for a president elected by the legislature and a cabinet of ministers that was responsible for government policy.

Japanese Democracy Japan took a later and more direct route to democracy than did the United States and Western Europe. In 1945, following Japan's surrender in World War II, American forces under General Douglas MacArthur set up an occupation government. One of the major tasks of this government was to prepare a democratic constitution for Japan which was written in 1946 and went into effect in 1947.

For many years Japan had been an authoritarian **oligarchy**, with government by a few—in this case, powerful military and industrial leaders. The new constitution, however, states that political power rests with the people. Echoing the words of the Preamble to the United States Constitution, it begins:

> "*We, the Japanese people, acting through our duly elected representatives in the National Diet [legislature] . . . do proclaim that sovereign power resides with the individual people and do firmly establish this Constitution.*"
>
> —Japanese Constitution, 1947

With the new constitution, Japan ended the period when the emperor held all governing power. The nation set up a parliamentary system in many ways similar to that of Great Britain.

Parliamentary Systems Today

Democratic governments may take several forms. One of the most widespread forms is **parliamentary government**. In this form of government, executive and legislative functions both reside in the elected assembly, or parliament. Often the parliament selects the leaders of the executive branch of government, who are known as the cabinet. Parliamentary governments around the world are largely patterned on the British model.

British Parliament In Great Britain **Parliament,** the national legislature, holds almost all governmental authority. Parliament is a bicameral (two-house) legislature, consisting of the House of Commons and the House of Lords. Both have a role in enacting legislation, but the House of Commons has much greater power than the House of Lords.

The British legislative body of elected representatives is the **House of Commons.** The people elect members of the House of Commons, known as Members of Parliament (MPs), for five-year terms. Their terms may be shorter, however, if Parliament is dissolved for new elections before the end of the five-year period.

The House of Commons meets in a small chamber in Westminster, an ancient majestic Parliament building located on the Thames River in London. Five rows of benches line each side of the chamber. The front row on each side is reserved for the leading members of each major party. Behind them sit the rank-and-file MPs, who are called backbenchers. The members of the party in power sit on one side of the chamber. The opposition party members sit on the other side.

The House of Commons determines Great Britain's legislative and financial policies. While any MP may introduce legislation, most bills are introduced by the majority party. Members debate bills on the floor of the Commons and then send them to one of eight standing committees to work out final details of all bills. Committees must report out every bill to the House of Commons for a vote. A majority vote is needed for passage.

The **House of Lords,** as its name implies, has historically been an aristocratic body. Until recently, the body included about 1,200 members, most of whom had inherited titles. In 1999, a reform law removed the right of all except 92 hereditary peers to sit and vote in the House. The House of Lords is now dominated by about 540 **life peers,** people who have been awarded a title for outstanding service or achievement.

At one time the House of Lords was a powerful branch of Parliament. Today, however, the House of Lords has very limited power. Money bills, for example, must originate in the Commons. The House of Lords also may amend legislation or vote down bills passed by the Commons. In both cases, however, the Commons may overrule the upper chamber and make its own bill a law.

The Prime Minister Great Britain has no separation of powers between the executive and legislative branches of government. The leader of the majority party in the House of Commons becomes the **prime minister** and chooses other ministers to head executive departments and serve as a cabinet.

GOVERNMENT Online

Student Web Activity Visit the *United States Government: Democracy in Action* Web site at gov.glencoe.com and click on ***Chapter 25–Student Web Activities*** for an activity about consolidated democracies.

Most ministers are members of the majority party in the House of Commons.

A prime minister who loses support of his or her own party resigns from office. The party then chooses another prime minister. If the majority party should lose a vote on an important issue, it is said to have "lost the confidence of the House" and must resign. Parliament is then dissolved, and new general elections are held to determine what party will control the House of Commons.

Japanese Diet Japan has a parliament of two houses, called the **National Diet.** The upper house is the House of Councillors, and the lower house, the House of Representatives. The Japanese constitution states that the National Diet shall be the "sole lawmaking organ of the state." In addition, the Diet has authority over the nation's fiscal policies. The House of Councillors has only a limited power to delay legislation.

The House of Representatives has members chosen from election districts. Each district, with a single exception, elects three to five representatives. Each member of the lower house serves for 4 years unless the parliament is dissolved before the term expires.

The House of Representatives elects the prime minister and has the power to vote "no confidence" in the prime minister or chief executive and the cabinet. When this happens, the prime minister may dissolve the House of Representatives and call for new elections. Although both houses consider legislative measures, the House of Representatives may override a negative vote in the House of Councillors by a two-thirds majority.

Members of the House of Councillors are chosen for 6-year terms. Because the House of Councillors may not be dissolved, its members usually serve their full terms of office. Similar to the upper houses of other governments, the House of Councillors provides a calmer, more detached form of deliberation than the House of Representatives. In this way, it helps moderate any hasty actions taken by the lower house.

Committees carry on much of the work of both houses of the Diet. Cabinet ministers often testify before committees where they face penetrating questions from members of the opposition party. Committee proceedings tend to be very lively, and they are often televised. In contrast, the proceedings of the full Diet tend to be dull. Unlike the United States Congress or the British Parliament, no colorful politicians play to the gallery or the press corps.

When voting on legislation, members of the majority party are expected to vote with the government. If they do not agree with the legislation, they simply abstain. Because the opposition parties are rarely strong enough to do more than delay legislation, most legislation is passed.

Function of the Cabinet In parliamentary government, members of the cabinet preside over departments or ministries. These include ministries such as justice, foreign affairs, finance, education, health and welfare, agriculture, and labor. In Japan the remaining cabinet members are so-called "ministers of state." They include the deputy prime minister and heads of various agencies, such as the Economic Planning Agency and the Science and Technology Agency.

The existence of factions or interest groups within Japan's political parties causes a high rate of turnover in the cabinet. Members of these factions often receive cabinet posts to gain political experience or as a reward for their support and service to the factions. The powerful factions within the majority party also serve as a check against the cabinet or the prime minister assuming too much power.

Dissolving the Government In Great Britain and other parliamentary systems, the prime minister and the cabinet together are referred to as the Government, a word equivalent to the American use of the word *administration.* The Government is responsible to the elected representatives. If the Government should lose a vote on an important issue, it must resign. The legislature is then dissolved, and new general elections are held.

Sometimes the government dissolves Parliament even while it still has a majority in the House of Commons. This dissolution may happen if a government senses that public support for it is so strong that it will elect more members of its party than it currently has. Then, at the prime minister's request, Parliament is dissolved and a general election is held to select members of the Commons.

Presidential Government

Another way to organize democracy is by **presidential government.** The United States created the office of the president to carry out the laws. The Constitution separated the executive from the legislative and judicial branches. Many nations have presidents with powers similar to those of the United States. The president of France has additional powers, unique to that nation.

French Presidents The 1958 constitution helped transform the office of president into the most powerful position in the government of France. Today the French president, who serves a seven-year term, is the only member of the government directly elected by voters of the nation at large. As the only nationally elected official, the French president often claims to speak for the entire nation. The first president of the Fifth Republic, for example, was the national World War II hero **General Charles de Gaulle.** He summed up the position and power of the presidency in 1964, explaining that "the indivisible authority of the state is completely delegated to the president by the people who elected him."

Much like chief executives in other democracies, the president of France is responsible for negotiating treaties, appointing high officials, and acting as chair of the high councils of the armed forces. In addition, the French president has two special powers—the right to appeal directly to the people by means of a referendum and dictatorial powers in times of national emergency. In 1962 President Charles de Gaulle ordered a referendum to approve a constitutional amendment providing for the direct election of the president, rather than by an electoral college. Voters approved the referendum with a 62 percent majority.

Working with the Assembly The president maintains contact with the legislative branch of the French government through a premier, whom the president appoints. (*Premier* is the French word for "first" and is the name given to the French equivalent of prime minister.) The premier, in turn, names ministers, who form the cabinet. Together they conduct the day-to-day affairs of the government. Theoretically, the premier and the cabinet are responsible to the National Assembly—the lower house of the French Parliament. Without the support of the majority of the National Assembly, the cabinet must resign and the president appoints a new premier. In the parliamentary system in Great Britain, however, the premier and the ministers are not members of the Assembly.

In practice, the premier and the cabinet answer to the president rather than the National Assembly. In regular meetings with the premier and the cabinet, the president makes sure that they continue to guide the president's program.

Under the constitution the president also has the authority to dissolve the National Assembly and call for new elections. This power may be used if the president loses the support of a majority of the Assembly. With this power, even the threat of dissolving the Assembly may be enough to force the deputies to accept the president's leadership.

Challenges for Consolidated Democracies

Western democracies rejoiced at the collapse of communism in the Soviet Union and Eastern Europe. After years of tension, the ideals of democracy had triumphed. Both the economic and the political systems in many Communist countries had failed. With the end of the Cold War, nations in Eastern Europe and many other areas around the world were moving toward democratic institutions. How would the new realities in the era following the Cold War affect democratic institutions in Western Europe and Japan?

Challenges for Western Europe The basic structure of competition that existed between Germany and other European powers gave way to cooperation and unity during the Cold War. Following the collapse of the Soviet Union and the retreat of the United States, Western Europe was at a crossroads. Would nationalism revive and lead to distrust, tension, and military reaction? Or would

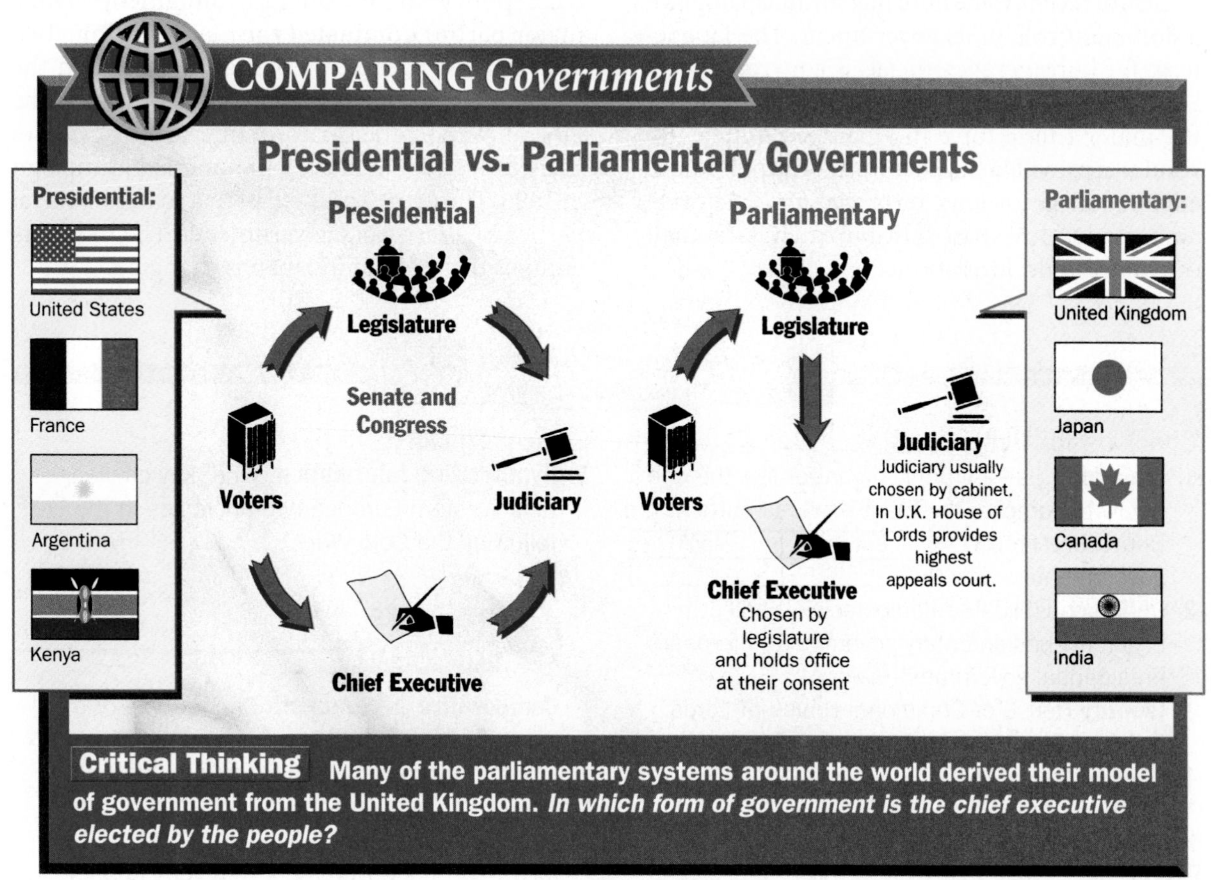

Critical Thinking Many of the parliamentary systems around the world derived their model of government from the United Kingdom. ***In which form of government is the chief executive elected by the people?***

Western Europe take advantage of the opportunity to build a structure for cooperation and stability?

The European Union has largely been achieved by political and economic leadership rather than by popular movements. Agreements reached at high levels of government have moved slowly toward the distant goal of European federalism. Political parties, however, consider national politics more important than European politics. What goal will parties support—nationalism and self-interest, or European federalism? Ethnic and cultural regions within states desire to maintain their distinctions—the right to be different. What political structures will allow such differences with cooperation?

Challenges for Japan The Cold War security alliance between the United States and Japan was the foundation for Japan's relations with the Western world. With the end of the Cold War the ground began to shift under this alliance, and Japan began transformations that still affect the development of its democracy today.

Until recently, the bureaucracy in Japan played a dominant role in its government. The Japanese term for bureaucratic officials is **kanyro.** One political scientist observed that the *kanyro* "represent the major ruling force in Japanese politics." Bureaucrats provided the Diet with the expert knowledge required for long-term planning. A former ambassador to Japan said bureaucrats actually originated most legislation:

> "*Most laws, including all important bills, are drafted not by the Diet but by the bureaucracy in behalf of the cabinet. They are presented . . . to the Diet and are then passed by the same Diet majority that has chosen the prime minister in the first place.*"
>
> —Edwin O. Reischauer, 1988

Popular pressure for political reform in Japan resulted in the transformation of Japan's electoral system in 1996. The old system had elected 511 legislators from multiple-seat districts. Under the old system smaller parties won a number of Diet seats, but the Liberal Democratic Party had dominated politics since the 1950s. Under the new electoral law, 300 legislators were elected from single-seat, winner-take-all districts. The remaining 200 representatives were elected from party slates in 11 nationwide districts. The new system allowed more powerful national parties to emerge, with greater member loyalty. It also reduced the influence of the bureaucracy.

Today Japan's political parties no longer entrust policy to bureaucratic judgment. Three major parties dominated the 1996 election. Two new centrist parties, the Renewal Party and the Democratic Party, emerged from a feud within the Liberal Democratic Party. All three centrist parties bashed the bureaucrats in the political campaign in 1996. The *kanyro* must be prepared to serve rival parties in alternating governments. The only certainty is that politics in Japan is changing.

Section 1 Assessment

Checking for Understanding

1. **Main Idea** Use a graphic organizer like the one below to compare the most powerful parts of the British and French governments.

British	French

2. **Define** consolidated democracies, abdicate, oligarchy, parliamentary government, life peers, presidential government, *kanyro*.
3. **Identify** House of Commons, House of Lords, National Diet, General Charles de Gaulle.
4. What happens when the Government in Britain loses a vote in Parliament?
5. What role do bureaucrats play in Japan?

Critical Thinking

6. **Synthesizing Information** What key challenges face Western European democracies in the era following the Cold War?

Comparative Government Choose one of the countries with a parliamentary system of government discussed in this section. Draw a diagram that compares the organization of the United States government with the parliamentary system of government that you choose.

Afroyim v. *Rusk*, 1967

Chief Justice Earl Warren once explained, "Citizenship is man's basic right for it is nothing less than the right to have rights. Remove this priceless possession and there remains a stateless person, disgraced and degraded in the eyes of his countrymen." Can Congress take away the citizenship of an American who violates a law? Afroyim *v.* Rusk *dealt with this issue.*

Polish and American flags

Background of the Case

Beys Afroyim from Poland became a naturalized American citizen in 1926. In 1950 Afroyim went to Israel, and while there he voted in an election for the Israeli Parliament. In 1960 Afroyim wanted to renew his U.S. passport, but the U.S. State Department refused to grant him a new passport. The State Department informed Afroyim that under the terms of the Nationality Act of 1940, he had lost his American citizenship. The law stated that U.S. citizens shall "lose" their citizenship if they vote "in a political election in a foreign state." Afroyim appealed and lost in both a federal district court and an appeals court.

The Constitutional Issue

Afroyim's case raised the question of whether the Nationality Act's penalty for voting in foreign elections, the loss of citizenship, was constitutional. The Court stated, "The fundamental issue before this Court . . . is whether Congress can . . . enact a law stripping an American of his citizenship which he has never voluntarily renounced or given up." Afroyim argued that neither the Fourteenth Amendment nor any other provision of the Constitution expressly grants Congress the power to take away a person's citizenship once it has been acquired. Thus, the only way he could lose his citizenship was to give it up voluntarily.

In 1958, in *Perez* v. *Brownell,* the Supreme Court upheld the Nationality Act, ruling that Congress could revoke citizenship because it had implied power to regulate foreign affairs. Further, Justice Felix Frankfurter rejected the argument that the Fourteenth Amendment denied Congress the power to revoke citizenship. Afroyim urged the Court to overturn its earlier decision and rule in his favor.

Debating the Case

Questions to Consider

1. What might be the consequences of allowing the government to determine if a person can keep his or her citizenship?
2. Could voting in a foreign election be considered the same as voluntarily giving up one's citizenship?
3. Should Congress have the power to take away a person's citizenship if the person violates a law against voting in a foreign election?

You Be the Judge

The Court had to determine whether to overrule the *Perez* decision. The choice depended on its interpretation of the so-called citizenship clause of the Fourteenth Amendment, which states: "All persons born or naturalized in the United States . . . are citizens of the United States. . . ." Did that imply citizenship could be temporary? Or did the amendment mean citizenship is permanent until a person voluntarily gives it up? State your opinion.

Emerging Democracies

Reader's Guide

Key Terms

apartheid, sanctions

Find Out

- What are some of the difficulties Poland faces in transition to democracy?
- How are changes in South Africa and Mexico making those nations more democratic?

Understanding Concepts

Growth of Democracy Why is democracy the most preferred government in the world and the most difficult to establish?

COVER STORY

Democracy Changes Little

PORT-AU-PRINCE, HAITI, SEPTEMBER 19, 1997

Three years ago on this date, millions of Haitians rejoiced as U.S. troops ousted a military dictator and restored their elected president. While today they are no longer terrorized by the dictator's brutal hit squads, most Haitians can point to little other improvement in their lives. Plans to privatize state-controlled industries, a move seen as key to Haiti's economic growth, have been stalled in the legislature, where no party controls a majority. Meanwhile, prices are higher, jobs fewer, and foreign investment down. Many Haitians are sending money out of the country, a sign of declining confidence in the democracy that they so recently welcomed to their shores.

Haitians rejoice, temporarily.

A wide variety of political systems can be found in the world today. At one extreme, several authoritarian states permit few rights and freedoms to their peoples. On the other side, a growing number of democracies endeavor to uphold human rights and to provide their citizens freedom and opportunities that Thomas Jefferson called the "pursuit of happiness."

Recently democracy seems to be spreading across the world. With the collapse of communism, a new opportunity for nations to create democratic institutions has emerged. Vast differences still exist, however, in what people believe to be democratic principles. The term "democracy" seems to give an aura of legitimacy to governments that continue to repress basic freedoms. Nations whose governments range from the left to the right of the political spectrum want to be called democratic. In some nations the gap between the stated adherence to democracy and the actual practice of government is very wide.

Among the emerging democracies since World War II are Poland, Mexico, and South Africa. Each of these countries represents a set of conditions that may be studied in order to understand the challenges that face emerging democracies. Democracies need to develop constitutional governments and free elections with multiparty systems. While governing by the will of the majority, they must also protect the rights of minorities.

Constitutional Government in Poland

In 1989 the people of Poland, East Germany, Czechoslovakia, Hungary, Romania, and Bulgaria threw out Communist governments imposed on them at the end of World War II. Poland led the way in these Revolutions of 1989 when a trade union emerged from an underground resistance movement to sweep the first democratic elections since World War II. The collapse of communism in the region, however, did not ensure the development of democracy.

Lech Walesa casts his vote in Gdansk.

Solidarity in Poland

Labor unrest was the catalyst for Poland's transition to democracy. A strike in the shipyards in 1980 spread to other industries and produced a victory for the workers. When **Solidarity**, a free union founded by **Lech Walesa**, launched a national strike in 1981, the government declared martial law. Walesa and other leaders were arrested. Increasing economic trouble led to a new wave of strikes in 1988. The Communist government, unable to quell dissent and stop the workers from striking, legalized Solidarity and allowed it to compete in national elections.

Solidarity won nearly all the contested seats. Walesa received 74 percent of the vote in the 1990 presidential election. In 1992 the parliamentary election resulted in representation for 29 political parties. The two major challenges Poland now faced were the need to create a written constitution that supported democratic values and the need to decentralize political power by building local governments.

Creating a New Constitution Reformers who took office in Poland in the early 1990s wanted to establish free elections, a market economy, and the rule of law. To do this, they had to have a written constitution that would place clear limits on the powers of those who governed.

In 1992 Poland's President Walesa signed a so-called "Little Constitution." This document defined the division of power among parliament, the prime minister, and the president. It was intended as a temporary measure until a new constitution could be written and approved by the people.

Over the next several years, preparing a constitution turned out to be a difficult task. New political parties, including some composed of former Communist officials, emerged and struggled to gain political advantage. The second free legislative election in September 1993 returned power to a coalition of ex-Communists. In the 1995 presidential election, Alexander Kwasniewski, a former Communist, narrowly defeated Lech Walesa. Kwasniewski projected the image of a man with moderate social democratic views who supported free enterprise.

Poland's ability to hold elections that transferred power to new government leaders was a sign of its developing democracy. However, Poland had still not resolved the vital issue of a permanent constitution. The National Assembly finally adopted the new Constitution of the Republic of Poland on April 2, 1997, and the voters approved it in May.

Building Local Governments The leaders of Poland's Solidarity movement, along with other reformers in Eastern Europe, saw the need for strong local governments. Reformers believed that effective local governments would give citizens a chance to get directly involved in issues—such as schools, roads, and trash collection—that immediately concerned them. Under communism all these matters were centrally controlled by national ministries.

An important step toward local government in Poland was the Local Self-Government Act in 1990. This act created autonomous local governments responsible for such matters as education, public libraries, municipal housing, local public transport, waste collection, local law enforcement, and fire protection. The law also laid the basis for insuring the place of autonomous local governments in the 1997 Polish constitution. Chapter VII

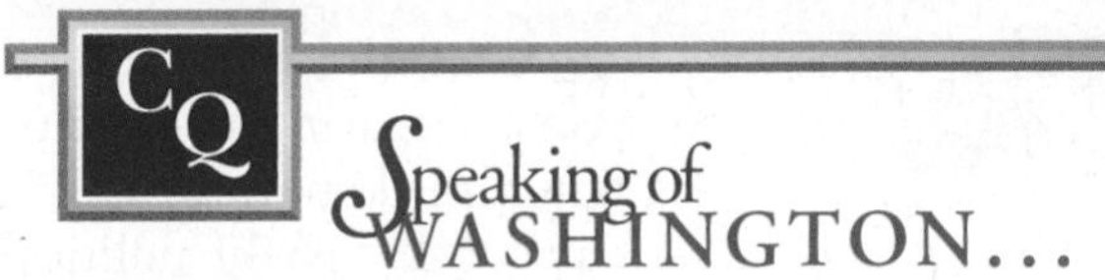

Recognizing Foreign Leaders **The Presidential Medal of Freedom, the U.S government's highest civilian honor, is awarded only at the president's discretion. Although the vast majority of recipients have been American citizens, a few foreign dignitaries and political leaders have been honored for important contributions to world peace.**

of the constitution states: Local governments perform public duties that are not reserved by the Constitution or legislation for the agencies of other public authorities . . . Local governments are legal entities . . . The autonomy of local governments is protected by the courts.

Like Poland nearly every Eastern European country has a post-communist constitution that sets up local governments and guarantees their autonomy. However, many obstacles remain in Poland and elsewhere to the development of truly effective local governments. But progress is being made Polish reformer Joanna Regulska recently said, "despite difficulties and shortcomings, local government reform remains one of the few unquestionable successes of the Polish transition."

Democracy in South Africa

Since 1990, most of the countries in Africa south of the Sahara have attempted transition from authoritarian government to democracy. The chief obstacles to democracy in the region—long-standing ethnic rivalries and economic inequality—have been difficult problems to overcome. The region has experienced a wide range of outcomes. While Rwanda's leaders presided over massacres and other horrors, Nelson Mandela was inaugurated as the first president of a democratic South Africa. That nation had finally ended its practice of **apartheid**, or the strict segregation of the races. Rwanda, however, failed to resolve ethnic differences, as its Hutu military leaders attempted to eliminate the country's Tutsi population, rather than to negotiate with them.

Apartheid and Sanctions Under apartheid, beginning in 1948 the South African population of Blacks (Africans), Whites, Coloreds (mixed European and African descent), and Asians was strictly separated. Blacks suffered the worst under this legalized segregation. Apartheid laws defined whom Blacks could marry, and where they could travel, eat, and go to school. Blacks could not vote or own property, and could be jailed indefinitely without cause.

As worldwide opposition to apartheid mounted, South Africa became increasingly isolated from the global community. In the 1980s the United States and the European Economic Community nations ordered economic **sanctions**, or coercive measures, against South Africa, and United States businesses began to withdraw investments. Over time, these sanctions placed some pressure on South Africa's economy.

Apartheid Breaks Down In the last half of the century Black nationalist groups such as the **African National Congress (ANC)** had pressed for reforms, but the government had repeatedly crushed the resistance. By the 1960s ANC leader Nelson Mandela had formed a military operation. In 1962 South African officials charged Mandela with treason and jailed him for life. From his prison cell Mandela became a world-famous symbol for freedom in South Africa.

By the late 1980s, mounting pressure from the anti-apartheid movement and from foreign countries brought a gradual end to apartheid. In 1990 President Frederik de Klerk released Mandela from prison. During the next few years the South African government repealed the remaining apartheid laws.

First Free Elections In April 1994 South Africa held its first nonracial national election. Nineteen parties offered candidates for the National Assembly. The election went smoothly, and foreign observers declared that it was free and fair. The African National Congress won about 63 percent of the vote and 252 of the 400 seats in the National Assembly, which then chose **Nelson Mandela** as president without opposition.

Directions for Democracy Removing the legal structure of apartheid was an essential first step toward democracy. A second major challenge for the new democratically elected government in South Africa was raising the standard of living of disadvantaged South Africans while maintaining economic growth.

The 1994 democratic election created high popular expectations that were difficult to fulfill. The personal cooperation between Mandela and de Klerk at first kept the transition period smooth. The ANC agreed to form a government of national unity, allowing other parties including the Zulu Inkatha Freedom Party and the Afrikaner Nationalist Party to have some cabinet offices. The minority parties were, however, critical of the ANC and in June 1996 the Nationalists withdrew from the government.

Despite these political differences South Africa's accomplishments have surpassed expectations. The difficult task will be to keep diverse groups working together to implement a reconstruction and development plan, expand the economy, reduce crime and violence, and create jobs.

Calling for Democracy

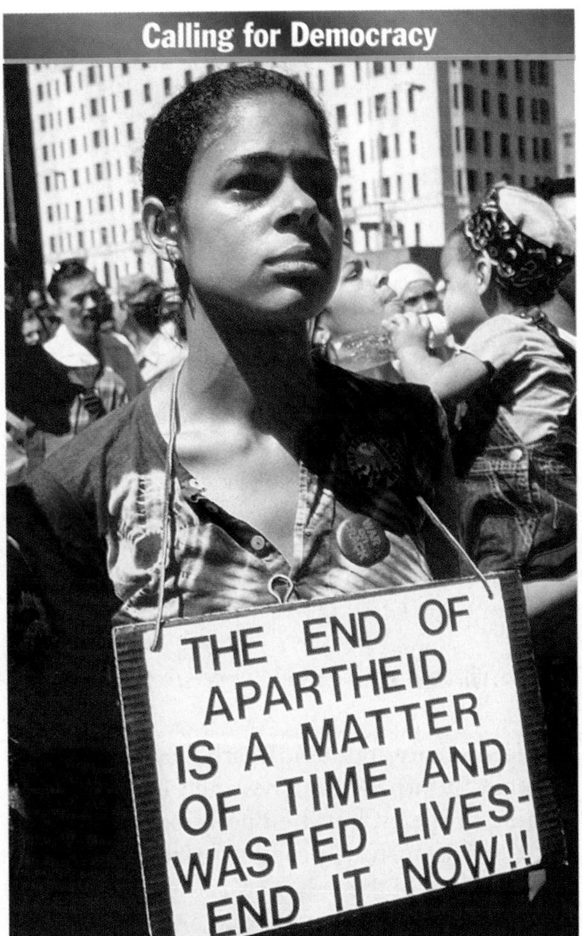

Transforming a Nation In the 1980s, many Americans demanded that United States corporations end their investments in South Africa. Many antiapartheid demonstrations were held on college campuses. ***How might the restriction of U.S. corporate investment in South Africa affect the average citizen of that country?***

Democracy in Mexico

Competing political parties are a characteristic of consolidated democracies. Rival parties make elections meaningful by giving voters a choice about policies. In July 2000 Mexico took a major step towards becoming a multi-party democracy when **Vicente Fox**, the candidate of the National Action Party, or PAN, was elected Mexico's president. Fox defeated the Institutional Revolutionary Party, or PRI, the political machine that had ruled the country virtually unchallenged since 1929.

History of Constitutional Government

After Mexicans rose up to depose the dictator Porfirio Díaz in 1910, various factions warred with each other to determine the direction of the country and who would govern. When civil war ended, the constitution of 1917 established a national government that provided a variety of individual, social, and economic rights for citizens. However, the president's power and the control of the government by one political party for more than 60 years led political opponents to describe the Mexican government as authoritarian rather than democratic.

Like the United States, Mexico is a federal republic. The United States of Mexico is made up of 31 states and a single federal district, Mexico City, the nation's capital. Each of the states exercises political power through a state governor and a state legislature. As in the United States the Mexican constitution of 1917 divided the national government into three branches: executive, legislative, and judicial.

Unlike the Constitution of the United States, the Mexican constitution is lengthy and very specific about certain matters. This has made frequent amendments necessary. For example, it said that religious groups cannot take part in any type of

Mexican Politics

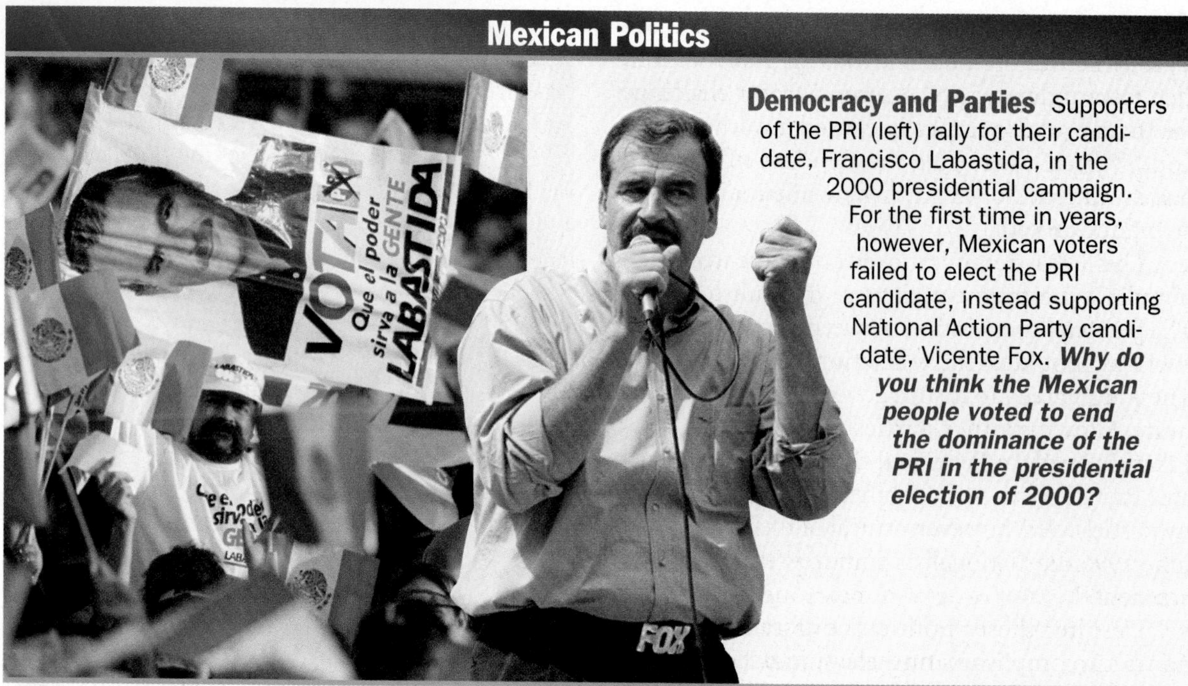

Democracy and Parties Supporters of the PRI (left) rally for their candidate, Francisco Labastida, in the 2000 presidential campaign. For the first time in years, however, Mexican voters failed to elect the PRI candidate, instead supporting National Action Party candidate, Vicente Fox. ***Why do you think the Mexican people voted to end the dominance of the PRI in the presidential election of 2000?***

political activity and clerical garb may not be worn in public. It forbade churches and foreigners from owning property, but it empowered the government to seize private property, particularly land, and to redistribute it.

The constitution of Mexico also protects the rights of workers and peasants to strike and provides for a minimum wage, equal pay for equal work, and an eight-hour workday. One political scientist described the 1917 constitution as the "most advanced labor code in the world at its time."

Strong Executive Branch The president, who exercises strong control over the government, heads the executive branch. Directly elected for one six-year term, the president derives power from several sources. One source is the 1917 constitution that allows the president to appoint cabinet ministers, supreme court justices, ambassadors, and high military officers. The constitution also names the president as the commander in chief of the armed forces. In addition, the president, through the cabinet, has the power to recommend legislation that takes precedence over all other legislation when it reaches the bicameral Congress.

Another source of presidential power has been leadership of the dominant political party, the PRI. Presidential power stems from the vast array of patronage positions, or government jobs that are awarded to loyal party supporters.

Weak Legislative Branch Mexico's legislative branch, or Congress, is composed of two houses, the Senate and the Chamber of Deputies. Each state, including the federal district, elects 2 senators. The lower house, the Chamber of Deputies, in contrast, is made up of 500 deputies. The people elect 300 of the deputies. The remaining 200 are drawn from the competing political parties based on the proportion of the popular vote each party receives in the election. Deputies serve for three years and, like the senators, cannot immediately run for reelection. Although the constitution provides for a separation of powers between the executive and legislative branches, in reality the president dominates Congress.

Judicial Branch Consistent with Mexico's federal system of government, the nation's judicial system is composed of federal and state courts. At the highest federal level is the Supreme Court with 26 justices divided into 6 divisions to handle criminal, civil, labor, and administrative cases. The president selects the justices—all have been members of the PRI. Below the Supreme Court are circuit courts and district courts.

State and Local Government The constitution of 1917 established Mexico as a "representative, democratic, and federal republic formed by free and sovereign states in all matters which concern their internal government, but united in a stabilized federation." At the same time, the constitution also limited the powers of the federal government to only those powers specifically granted to it by the constitution. It reserved all other powers to the states.

The people of each state elect their governor to a single six-year term. Reelection is not permitted. The people elect members to the states' unicameral legislatures for three-year terms.

New Politics, New Policies For decades massive organizational resources, political patronage, and the support of the major media served to keep the PRI in power. In some cases the PRI was accused of manipulating elections. In the 1991 election, for example, a correspondent from the *Wall Street Journal* reported an occurrence in one town:

> "*The ruling Institutional Revolutionary Party (PRI) organized a big musical festival . . . which culminated with the local candidate distributing thousands of toys to the children of those attending. Meanwhile parents were reminded to vote for the PRI.*"
>
> —*Wall Street Journal,* August 23, 1991.

In 1994, however, PRI candidate **Ernesto Zedillo Ponce de León** won the presidency and introduced nationwide electoral reforms that did much to end the PRI's long tradition of ballot box fraud. These reforms helped set the stage for victory for Vicente Fox's PAN party six years later in 2000.

Leadership of the PAN When the PAN victory was announced in Mexico City, thousands of voters chanted: "Don't fail us! Don't fail us!" Fox has promised to institute major new policies during his six-year term. He wants to double education spending, reduce income gaps between rich and poor, crack down on the narcotics trade, clean up the corrupt police system, and boost the nation's economy by tax reform and increasing exports to the United States.

Fox and his reform-minded supporters face may obstacles. Even though PAN won enough seats in the Mexican Congress to replace the PRI as the dominant party, it did not get enough votes to gain an outright majority. Thus, Fox's party will have to form coalitions with other parties in the Congress to pass legislation. Another hurdle could be corruption within the national government's huge bureaucracy—all of its million workers were appointed by the defeated PRI. The United States, which shares a 2000 mile border with Mexico, has a big stake in its neighbor's effort to become a fully consolidated democracy.

Section 2 Assessment

Checking for Understanding

1. **Main Idea** Use a graphic organizer like the one below to list the similarities of the federal systems in the United States and Mexico.

United States	Mexico

2. **Define** apartheid, sanctions.
3. **Identify** Solidarity, Lech Walesa, African National Congress (ANC), Nelson Mandela, Vicente Fox, Ernesto Zedillo Ponce de León.
4. What economic issue must Poland resolve?
5. What have been the chief obstacles to democracy in Africa south of the Sahara?

Critical Thinking

6. **Understanding Cause and Effect** What recent events in Mexico have contributed to making the country more democratic?

Growth of Democracy Research the past 50 years of history of either Poland or South Africa. Focus on events that have contributed to making those nations more democratic. Create an illustrated time line of these events. Highlight the event you think was most critical in making the nation more democratic.

Section 3

Authoritarian States

Reader's Guide

Key Terms

cadre, shah, *faqih*

Find Out

- How does China's Communist Party control the government?
- What role has religion played in the formation of the government of Iran?

Understanding Concepts

Comparative Government What are the differences and similarities among the governments of Cuba, Iran, and Iraq?

COVER STORY

Jail for Teen Hustlers

HAVANA, CUBA, NOVEMBER 1, 1996

Every day the streets of this city fill with teenagers in search of an income. Called *jinoteros*, these young street hustlers will sell nearly anything—a cigar, a place to stay, a night on the town—to foreign tourists. Alarmed at their growing numbers, Havana police have begun throwing *jinoteros* in jail. Many of them express resentment because of the meager job outlook in Cuba's poor economy. "I have to earn a living," complains Miguel Angel Iglesias, a 19-year-old *jinotero*. "I used to like it in Cuba," Iglesias explains. "Now I have nothing. Before, there was hope. Now it's all gone."

Iglesias hustles for money.

While democracy enjoys unprecedented allegiance in the world today, authoritarian governments are still in the majority. Some nations have tried and failed to achieve democracy; others have rejected democracy altogether. In some nations, like Nigeria, attempts at democracy have failed because political, military, and civilian elite groups have retained power. Ethnic and religious strife persist in nations like Afghanistan, Liberia, and Sri Lanka. Other nations, such as the People's Republic of China and Cuba, remain committed to communism. Finally, the influence of a dominant religion or leader underlies the government of states such as Iran and Iraq.

The People's Republic of China

In a speech delivered to the Russian parliament, Boris Yeltsin said that the socialist experiment had left the people of the former Soviet Union at the "tail end of world civilization." Even as Russian leaders acknowledged the triumph of market economies and political democracy, Chinese Communists held fast to their control of China's government. However, they did initiate some economic reforms that opened certain areas of the rigidly controlled economy to free enterprise. In 1989 the Chinese Communist leadership suppressed a growing pro-democracy movement but continued the current economic reforms.

China's Political Background After China became a republic in 1912, rival factions divided the country. In 1929 the Nationalist Party, under the leadership of Chiang Kai-shek, defeated the Communists and gained partial control of the nation. When Japan invaded China in the 1930s, the Nationalists and Communists came together to defend their country. After Japan's defeat in World War II, a civil war broke out between the two rival parties.

In 1949 Communist revolutionaries led by Mao Zedong seized power in the world's most heavily populated nation. The Nationalists fled to safety on the offshore island of Taiwan, where they remain today.

As a guide to establishing a Communist economy and government, the People's Republic of China turned to the Soviet Union:

> *We must learn . . . from the advanced experience of the Soviet Union. The Soviet Union has been building socialism for forty years, and its experience is very valuable to us. . . . Now there are two different attitudes towards learning from others. One is the dogmatic attitude of transplanting everything, whether or not it is suited to our conditions. . . . The other attitude is to use our heads and learn those things which suit our conditions, that is to absorb whatever experience is useful to us. That is the attitude we should adopt.*
>
> —Mao Zedong, 1957

Controlling the Government Red Guards, or young radical Communists, honored Mao Zedong in the 1960s. ***How does the Chinese Communist Party ensure that it will control the government today?***

Following the Soviet Union's example, the Chinese leaders proceeded to establish a totalitarian government strictly controlled by the Chinese Communist party (CCP), in much the same way that the Soviet Communist Party once controlled the Soviet Union.

Communist Party Government Despite upheavals in Eastern Europe and the former Soviet Union, in the People's Republic of China the Chinese Communist party (CCP) and its leaders remain firmly in control of the government. Although the CCP is not an official organ of the government, it determines governmental policies and ensures that the government carries out the party's policies and decisions. At every level, officials referred to as cadre hold key posts. Most of these are party members, even though only about 4 percent of the Chinese people belong to the Communist Party.

In 1982 China adopted two new constitutions, one for the party and another for the national government. Under its new constitution, theoretically at least, the Communist Party's highest governing body is the National Party Congress, composed of between 1,500 and 2,000 delegates. Members of party organizations across the nation select these delegates. In practice, however, the National Party Congress merely serves as a rubber stamp for policies of the party's leaders.

The National Party Congress does, however, elect the party's Central Committee, which serves in place of the Congress when it is not in session. The number of members of the Central Committee runs between 200 and 300 full and alternate members. Its major responsibility is to elect the members of the party's Political Bureau—the **Politburo.** The Politburo usually is composed of about 20 top party leaders.

The Politburo's Standing Committee, which functions when the full Politburo is not meeting, is even more elitist and is composed of the top six CCP leaders. The Politburo's Standing Committee appoints members of the Secretariat. The Secretariat then implements party policies by supervising the daily activities of the party. In addition, the CCP has various other organizations that carry out special functions under the direction of the Secretariat.

Mark, Dennis, and David Richard

Wheels for Humanity logo

In 1988 Mark Richard saw a disabled woman crawling along a roadside in Guatemala. He made up his mind to bring the woman a wheelchair. When he returned to the United States, Mark contacted the local chapter of the Spinal Cord Injury Association. Together they delivered 20 wheelchairs to Guatemala. Twice a year after that Mark repeated the trip, distributing 2,000 wheelchairs. His older brother Dennis helped until he died in 1994. In July 1995 David Richard, another brother, began collecting wheelchairs throughout southern California. He created a nonprofit organization called Wheels for Humanity. In a California warehouse, volunteers restore battered wheelchairs to be distributed to disabled children in Vietnam, Guatemala, Bosnia, Costa Rica, Nicaragua, and other countries. In just 18 months the Richards improved 987 lives with the gift of a wheelchair. "Once you put your hand on a used wheelchair, you're hooked," David says.

The work of Wheels for Humanity continues. Various sources estimate that more than 21 million people worldwide are in need of wheelchairs.

At the top of the CCP, and probably the most powerful party leader, is the General Secretary who may or may not be a prominent government official as well. Many members of the Politburo hold top government posts. Politburo member Jiang Zemin, for example, also serves as China's president. From the late 1970s to the 1990s, however, the unquestioned leader of China was Deng Xiaoping, who held no official government or party position. It is important to understand that leadership in China often may rest upon background rather than upon position.

China's National Government The People's Republic of China operates under a constitution adopted in 1982. The new constitution is designed to enable China to achieve a stable and relatively advanced industrialized nation by the end of the century. The 1982 constitution calls the Chinese Communist Party the "core of the leadership of the whole Chinese people," while it describes the nation as "led by the Communist Party." It adds, "The Chinese people will continue to uphold the people's democratic dictatorship and socialist road."

Established by the constitution, the National People's Congress (NPC) is identified as "the highest organ of state power." In theory, legislative power in China rests with the NPC and its Standing Committee that serves when the NPC is not in formal session. The Chinese NPC and its Standing Committee, however, have little independent legislative power. A large number of the leaders of the Standing Committee do hold important leadership posts in the Communist Party, which actually decides on the government's actions and policies. The NPC serves as a symbol of citizen participation in the nation's government when it selects the country's ceremonial president and vice president and the premier who actually presides over the body called the State Council.

In China the State Council carries out the same functions that a cabinet or council of ministers carries out in other nations. Although the State Council is supposed to be responsible to the National People's Congress and its Standing Committee, it answers in fact to the CCP's Politburo. Most of the leaders in the State Council also hold high posts in the CCP.

The State Council, which meets about once a month, operates as the executive branch of the government. It makes decisions, prepares legislation for the National People's Congress, determines the nation's budget, and ensures the Communist Party's policies are followed. The State Council's Standing Committee, headed by the premier, carries out most of these functions, however.

Political Parties Although the Chinese Communist Party dominates the government in China, it permits eight minority parties to exist. These are largely made up of people from China's middle class or of intellectuals—a term that often also includes students. These parties are expected to work under the leadership of the CCP. An opposition party—the Federation for a Democratic China (FDC)—was formed in Paris following the Chinese government's massacre of protesters at **Tiananmen Square** in Beijing, China in 1989.

Tiananmen Square Historically, the Chinese Communist Party has tolerated little opposition. In April 1989 resentment against low pay for professional workers, restrictions on students studying abroad, and growing inflation brought thousands of demonstrators to Tiananmen Square. One student said the demonstrations were "for democracy, for freedom." Soon, protesters began a hunger strike in the square. Coming at the time of Soviet leader Mikhail Gorbachev's visit to China, the protest embarrassed China's leaders.

On May 20 Premier Li Peng sent unarmed troops to clear the square. When that failed, armed troops moved in. On June 3, 1989, they began firing on demonstrators. On the following day news of the Tiananmen Square massacre shocked the world. Government and civilian estimates of deaths differ. An eyewitness, upon visiting one hospital, described the tragedy:

> "*The doctors were crying, and took me to the morgue. They didn't have enough drawers for the bodies, so they had to stack them. All of the victims were young men, all of them were bare-chested, and none of them had any shoes. Many had writing on their chests and were wearing headbands. They were just piled up in there, half-way to the ceiling.*"
>
> —Margaret Herbst, 1989

Since the massacre at Tiananmen Square, the Chinese government has imposed strict controls on the nation's younger generation.

Appeals for Democracy

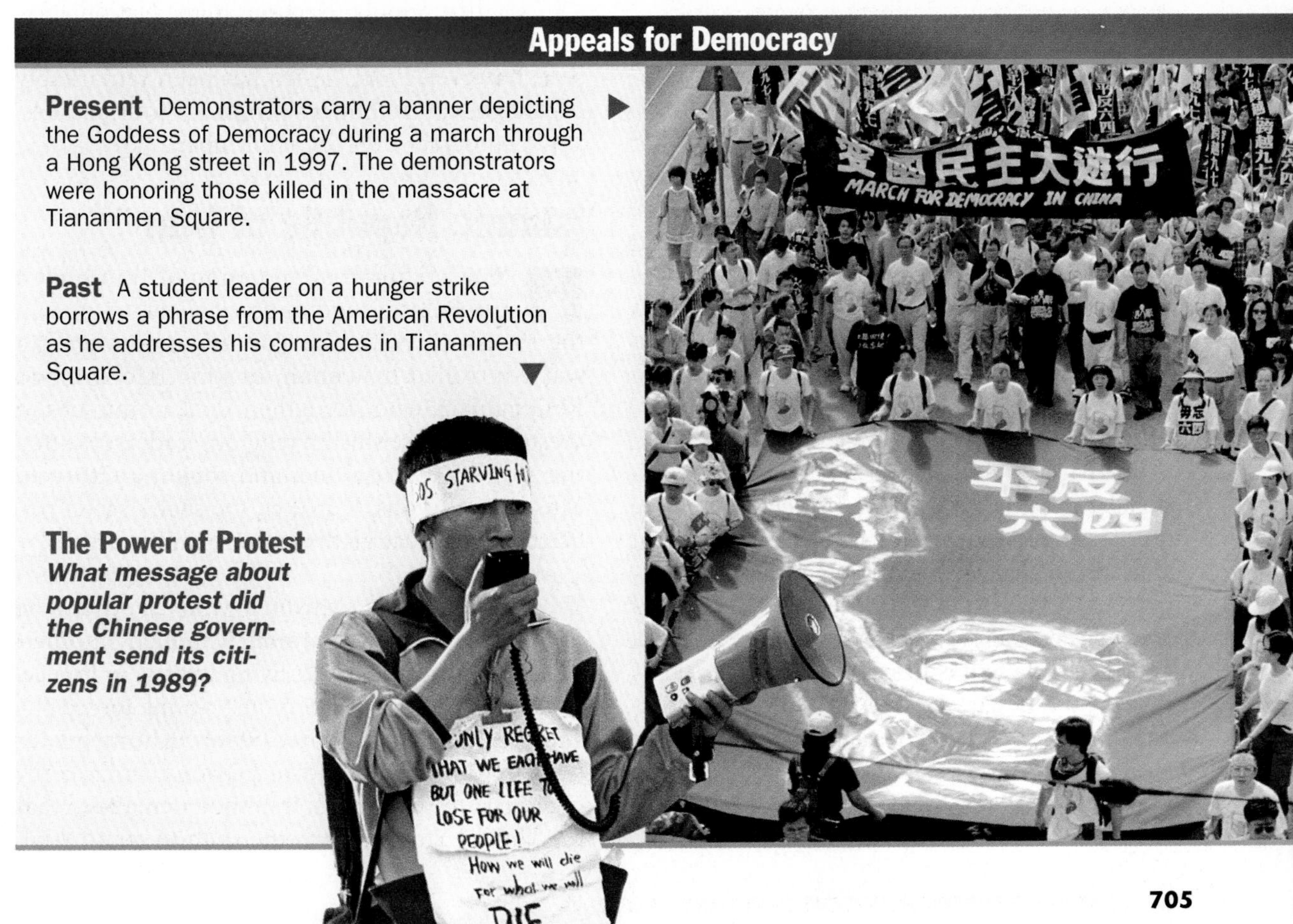

Present Demonstrators carry a banner depicting the Goddess of Democracy during a march through a Hong Kong street in 1997. The demonstrators were honoring those killed in the massacre at Tiananmen Square.

Past A student leader on a hunger strike borrows a phrase from the American Revolution as he addresses his comrades in Tiananmen Square.

The Power of Protest
What message about popular protest did the Chinese government send its citizens in 1989?

Castro's Staying Power

Opposition to Castro Since Fidel Castro aligned himself with the Soviet bloc in the early 1960s, Cuba has been perceived as a threat to the United States and to the security of the region. ***What is this cartoonist saying about Castro's government?***

Communism in Cuba

Fidel Castro led Cubans in a revolt that ousted dictator Fulgencio Batista in January 1959. When Castro promised democratic reforms, he did not mean holding elections. He did begin a program to redistribute ownership of land and nationalize industries. This angered Americans who lost property they owned in Cuba. When the United States cut off sugar imports from Cuba, Castro turned to the Soviet Union for help.

Communist Dictatorship Under **Fidel Castro** Cuba became a Communist dictatorship. He supported revolutionary movements in Latin America and Africa while maintaining strict control over Cuba's political and economic institutions. Tensions and disagreement between Cuba and the United States led to two crises. In 1961 anti-Castro exiles, trained by the United States, invaded Cuba at the **Bay of Pigs.** The failed invasion left Castro in power and embarrassed the United States. One year later the United States discovered that Soviet missiles were being installed in Cuba. Tense negotiations with the Soviet Union brought the crisis to an end, but U.S.–Cuban relations were strictly limited after this event that had nearly brought the world to the brink of nuclear war.

Economic Crisis The end of the Cold War left Cuba isolated in the early 1990s. The loss of Soviet aid and low prices for sugar exports caused a deep economic crisis. The United States maintained its trade embargo against Cuba, hoping that Fidel Castro would agree to a greater respect for human rights and move to a democratic system in exchange for better relations and economic aid. To put pressure on Castro, the United States Congress passed and President Clinton signed the Cuban Democracy Act in 1992. However, the administration believed that this law failed to move Castro toward democratic reforms.

Cuba's Future In 1993 Cuba held its first popular elections to the National Assembly. There was only one candidate for each seat, however. Fidel Castro has been remarkably capable of controlling his people for four decades. Will democracy ever come to Cuba?

Islamic Republic of Iran

The Middle Eastern nation of Iran built a capitalistic economy based on oil revenues in the 1960s and 1970s. A major military power, Iran was controlled by a **shah,** or king, Mohammed Reza Pahlavi, who strengthened economic ties to Western nations. Muslim religious leaders resented the shah's Western values and sought a return to Muslim traditions. However, the shah's secret police helped silence all dissent for many years.

Islamic Revolt Muslims who opposed the shah rallied around **Ayatollah Ruhollah Khomeini,** a Shiite Muslim leader living in exile in France. In early 1979 massive demonstrations forced the shah to flee to the United States. Khomeini returned from France to form a government according to Islamic principles. Iran soon demanded that the United States return the shah to stand trial.

When the United States refused and the shah took refuge in Egypt, anti-American sentiment heightened in Iran. In November 1979 Iranians stormed the U.S. Embassy, took American diplomats hostage, and held them for more than a year.

Institutions of Government The establishment of the Islamic Republic of Iran began a process of increasing state power. Khomeini and his Islamic followers established a regime in which Iran's religious leaders had the veto power over the actions of political leaders. The state used perceived and real threats from Iraq and America's trade embargo to consolidate power. Since the death of Khomeini in 1989 the government has centralized functions in the *faqih* (the top religious-political leader), the presidency, and the judiciary. The office of prime minister was eliminated, and its power was transferred to the president.

Republic of Iraq

Beginning with its emergence as a national state in 1921, Iraq has been ruled by strong military leaders. The most powerful is the current dictator, **Saddam Hussein.** In 1980 Hussein kept Shiite Muslims from gaining influence in Iraq by invading Iran. The eight-year war killed about 1 million people in the two countries.

Hussein, needing to boost oil reserves and seeking to shift the blame for Iraq's deteriorating economy, invaded neighboring Kuwait in 1990. When Iraqi troops headed toward the border of Saudi Arabia, the Saudis asked the United States for protection. The Persian Gulf War broke out between Iraq and coalition forces from seven nations in January 1991. After his forces set fire to several oil fields, Hussein quickly withdrew them from Kuwait. Defeated in war, he focused on crushing opposition within Iraq and rebuilding his military strength.

After the Persian Gulf War, the United Nations (UN) required Iraq to disclose and destroy all of its chemical and biological weapons. The UN also imposed economic sanctions on Iraq to force compliance. The sanctions placed severe economic hardships on Iraq and threatened to weaken Hussein's hold on the country. Hussein tried to break the sanctions by capitalizing on the differences among UN Security Council members. In 1997, Iraq refused to allow UN teams that included Americans to inspect its weapons plants. Under intense international pressure, the Iraqis backed down; but doubts remained about Hussein's willingness to cooperate with the UN.

The existence of authoritarian governments, such as those in Iran and Iraq, presents a major challenge to American diplomacy. "Hot spots" around the world could erupt at any time. Although the UN has responded to some crises, the United States has relied on separate military alliances when its interests and those of its allies are threatened.

Section 3 Assessment

Checking for Understanding

1. **Main Idea** Use a graphic organizer like the one below to profile each of the countries covered in this section, and indicate whether the country is moving toward or away from democracy.

Authoritarian States

country	controlled by	+/- democracy

2. **Define** cadre, shah, *faqih.*
3. **Identify** Tiananmen Square, Fidel Castro, Bay of Pigs, Ayatollah Ruhollah Khomeini, Saddam Hussein.
4. Why is China not a democratic nation?
5. What events in 1979 returned Iran to Muslim control?

Critical Thinking

6. **Recognizing Ideologies** Why did Mao Zedong believe China should study the Soviet Union's experience?

Comparative Government Choose a country discussed in this section. Research recent political developments in this country. Imagine that you are traveling to the country that you chose. Write a letter to a friend describing the country, its government, and the extent to which the government affects people's lives.

Section 4

Global Security

Reader's Guide

Key Terms

national security, international security, global security, nuclear proliferation, trading blocs

Find Out

- What are the different levels and types of international conflict?
- What are the various kinds of security agreements that nations have established to promote peace and economic progress?

Understanding Concepts

Political Processes How do UN agencies work to maintain peace in the world?

COVER STORY

Nuke Dumping Feared

PYONGYANG, NORTH KOREA, JANUARY 18, 1997

A plan by a Taiwan power company to ship up to 200,000 barrels of nuclear waste for disposal in this nation has rekindled old fears. Although the North Koreans refuse comment, Taiwanese officials insist the deal is merely a commercial contract. However, others worry that the world's last hard-line Communist nation may be hoping to resume its nuclear weapons development program. In 1994 North Korea agreed to stop converting exhausted fuel from its own power plants into weapons-grade plutonium. While the Taiwan deal does not appear to jeopardize this agreement, U.S. and Asian officials are not eager to see North Korea have any part in nuclear trade.

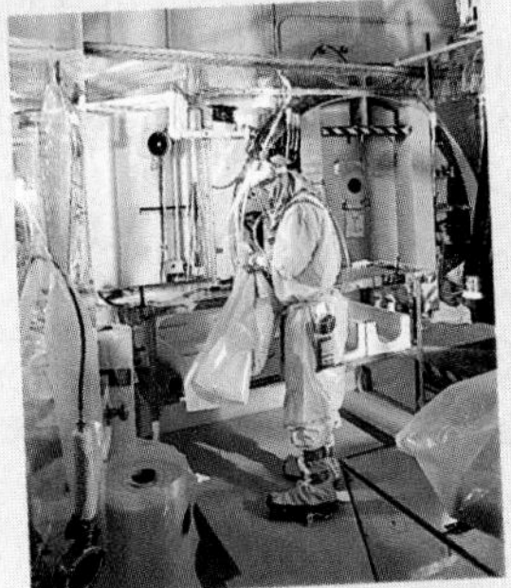

Power plant worker

Democracy thrives in peaceful conditions. The struggle for democracy, however, takes place in an international environment that is not always conducive to democracy. Many troubled areas of the world could ignite into war at any time.

Basically, **national security** means protection of a nation's borders and territories against invasion or control by foreign powers. However, national security means more than military defense. A nation's vital international economic interests must also be protected.

Many policy makers and scholars today also talk about **international security.** By this they mean the creation of world stability as a result of the interaction of many nations' policies. They argue that today no nation can ensure its own security in isolation.

Finally, some observers have begun to talk about **global security.** They believe that the key issue today is the safety of the entire world, not simply agreements that preserve the security of several nations.

Types of International Conflict

Many types of conflict have threatened the security of the nations of the world—nuclear war, limited war, regional war, and civil wars. This is true because nations have been arming with weapons at a rapid rate. More than 75 percent of the worldwide arms sales has gone to developing nations. In recent years many countries have purchased sophisticated, high-technology weapons such as fighter jets, tanks, and precision-guided missiles, substantially increasing the danger of war.

Concerned over the growing threat to peace, the leading military powers have taken some steps to limit such sales. In 1987, for example, the United States, Canada, Britain, France, Italy, Germany, and Japan adopted a common policy to limit the export of technology that could

Terrorist Attack

Bombing of an American Embassy

Rescue workers and medical personnel attend to the wounded after a bomb destroys the United States embassy building in Nairobi, Kenya. Hearing of the bombing, President Clinton responded in a brief statement: "I have said many times that terrorism is one of the greatest dangers we face in this new global era." ***Do you think such incidents help terrorists achieve their objectives? Why or why not?***

help other countries build missiles. At the same time, however, these same nations increased other weapons sales.

The Nuclear Threat The world faces a major security problem because of the spread of nuclear weapons. Six nations—the United States, Russia, Great Britain, France, China, and India—have had nuclear weapons for several years. In addition, Israel, South Africa, Argentina, Taiwan, and Pakistan are believed to possess nuclear weapons or to be able to assemble them very quickly. Iraq has been trying to develop such weapons since at least 1980. World leaders became concerned about Soviet nuclear weapons when the Soviet Union dissolved in 1991.

The international community uses three strategies to contain the spread of nuclear weapons, sometimes called **nuclear proliferation.** The first is to strictly limit the export of plutonium-processing technologies needed to build weapons. Countries buying such exports must agree they will not use them to make weapons and must follow safeguards set up by the International Atomic Energy Agency (IAEA). Unfortunately, without the permission of countries that purchase nuclear technologies, the IAEA cannot carry out inspections.

A second strategy has been the **Nuclear Nonproliferation Treaty (NPT).** Countries with nuclear weapons that signed the treaty agreed not to provide nuclear weapons to other countries. Non-nuclear powers that signed agreed not to develop such nuclear weapons. A third strategy is for the nuclear powers to use diplomacy to try to eliminate the underlying causes that drive smaller countries to acquire nuclear weapons. In 1988 the United States successfully pressured Saudi Arabia to sign the NPT.

Limited War A war in which the more powerful nation or nations will not go beyond certain limits has been called **limited war.** In June 1950 North Korea invaded South Korea with the permission and military support of the Soviet Union. The United States came to the aid of South Korea. During the Korean War, which lasted until a cease-fire agreement was signed in 1953, about 50,000 American soldiers were killed. Even though American leaders held the Soviet Union responsible, however, the United States limited fighting to the Korean Peninsula and did not use nuclear weapons.

Regional Wars Regional wars are conflicts in a particular area or region of the world that do not involve the major powers. The Arab-Israeli wars in 1948–1949, 1956, 1967, and 1973 are examples, as are the India-Pakistan wars of 1965 and 1971, and the Iran-Iraq War of the 1980s. Regional wars usually occur near or along national borders. Third parties do not usually get involved in the fighting, but they often aid the combatants.

Civil Wars Civil wars result from struggles for power within a nation. Civil wars are a matter of international concern because they often draw in other nations and could escalate. For example, China, Syria, Cuba, South Africa, Turkey, and Vietnam have all intervened in civil wars.

Security Agreements

Each nation is responsible for its own security. Governments often seek to protect the interests of their people by signing treaties or agreements. These agreements may be military, economic, or both. The North American Free Trade Agreement, and the European Union are examples of economic cooperation. NATO was initially an agreement to protect European nations from military aggression.

GATT To promote international trade, 90 countries subscribed to a **General Agreement on Tariffs and Trade (GATT)** in 1947. A new GATT was signed in 1994, which included many additional countries. Under the provisions of this agreement, member nations continue to meet to remove or reduce trade barriers such as tariffs. In addition, emerging regional trading blocs are removing barriers to trade among participating nations. Groups of nations in Europe, Asia, and North America are developing regional economic cooperation.

The European Union In 1957 six Western European nations—France, West Germany, Italy, Belgium, the Netherlands, Luxembourg—agreed to move toward a common trading market called the **European Economic Community (EEC).** In 1967 the EEC merged with two other organizations to become the European Community. The goal was to remove all economic restrictions, permitting workers, capital, goods, and services to move freely throughout the member nations. In 1985 the European Community set 1992 as the target date for completion of the union and began the EC 92 program. Its principal aim was to sharpen Europe's economic competitiveness. It would also prepare the way for the complete monetary and political union of Europe.

Project 1992 brought some political unity to the European Community, which became the **European Union (EU)** in November 1993. The economic success of the EU, however, is responsible

GOVERNMENT *and You*

Your Rights Overseas

If you visit another country, be aware that its laws may be very different from ours. Things that are no problem at home can cause you trouble overseas. For example, attempting to use a credit card that has exceeded your limit can get you arrested in some countries. Photographing police, military installations and personnel, and other subjects may also result in your detention.

If arrested, you have the right under international law to contact the U.S. consulate. Consular officials cannot get you out of jail, but they can recommend attorneys and will try to see that you are treated humanely. Since most countries do not permit bail, you may have to spend months in solitary confinement awaiting trial.

Remember that when you leave the United States, although you are a United States citizen,the Bill of Rights stays behind. The best way to protect your freedom overseas is to learn about a country's laws and customs before you visit.

American students tour France.

Be Informed Visit the State Department's Web site on the Internet for travel advice about a country you would like to visit.

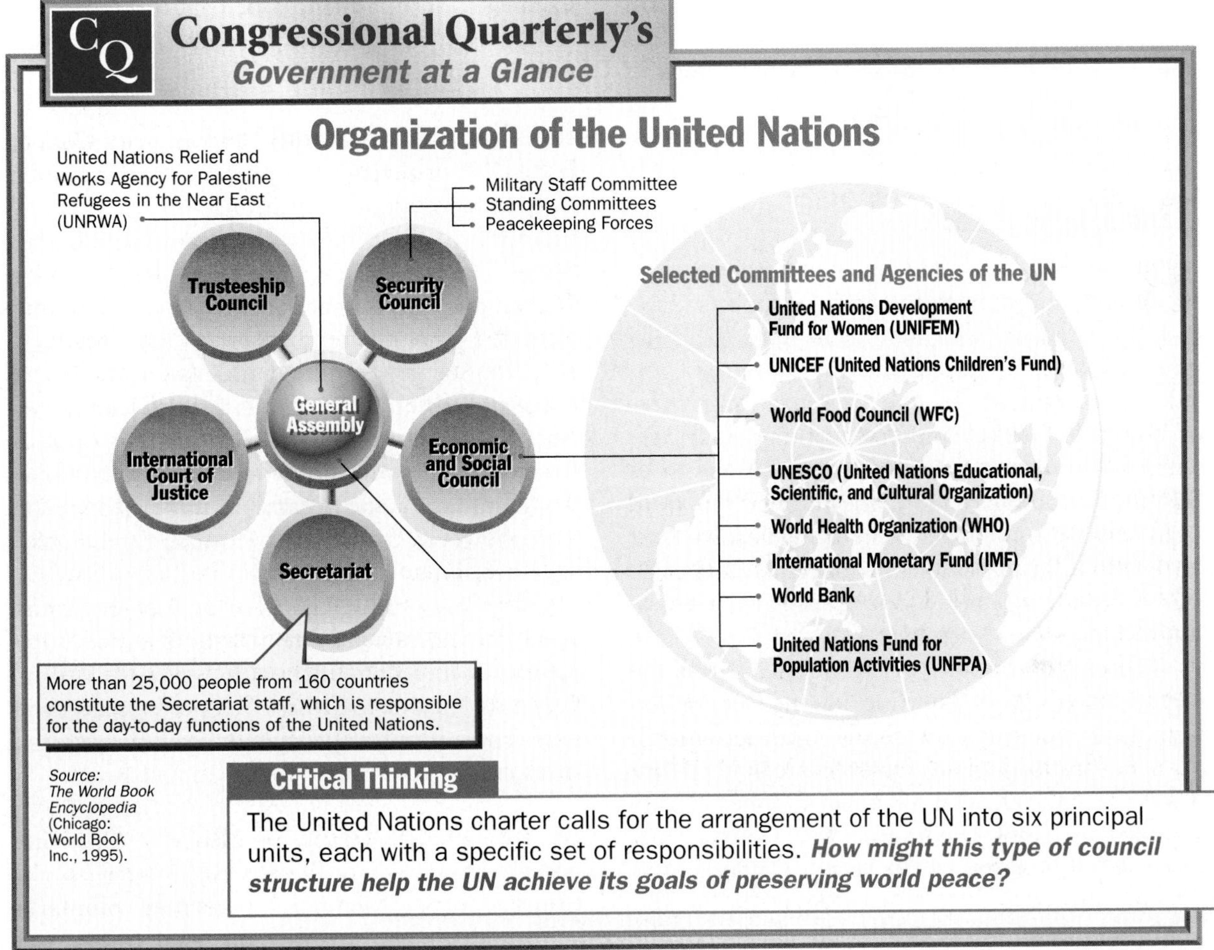

for its attractiveness to potential members. Since the early 1970s the admission of Britain, Ireland, Denmark, Greece, Portugal, Spain, Austria, Finland, and Sweden increased the EU's population to 370 million. Eastern European nations likewise wish to join their emerging free economies with the European Union.

North American Trade Agreement Long an advocate of free trade, the United States has negotiated with Canada and Mexico to eliminate most trade restrictions. In 1991 President Bush began trade negotiations with Mexico, and President Clinton concluded the **North American Free Trade Agreement (NAFTA),** effective January 1, 1994. Visiting Mexico in 1997, Clinton reaffirmed his commitment to expanding NAFTA and eliminating trade barriers in the Western Hemisphere.

North Atlantic Treaty Organization Perhaps the world's best-known defense treaty, the **North Atlantic Treaty Organization (NATO)** was formed after World War II. NATO had a well-defined role—maintaining security in Europe against the threat of Soviet communism. When the Cold War ended, however, many people wondered whether NATO was necessary. The issue was partly addressed when civil war broke out in southeastern Europe in 1991. The United States persuaded its NATO allies to launch air strikes against Bosnian Serb military sites.

Another issue was how NATO would relate to Russia and the former Soviet satellite nations. When NATO opened membership to Eastern European nations, Russia felt threatened. The alliance then opened talks with Russian leaders. In 1997 NATO and Russia signed an agreement giving Russia a seat on a joint council of NATO. While not offering full NATO membership, the document pledged that Russia would continue its transformation to democracy and NATO would review its doctrine to bring it in line with post-Cold War reality.

The United Nations

In 1945 the United States and other nations helped establish the United Nations (UN) to provide a forum for nations to settle their disputes by peaceful means. The Charter of the United Nations identifies the organization's three major goals. One is to preserve world peace and security. The second is to encourage nations to be just in their actions toward one another. The third is to help nations cooperate in trying to solve their problems. United Nations membership is open to all "peace-loving states." More than 165 nations of the world are now members.

Three major bodies in the UN help fulfill the organization's goals. They include the General Assembly, the Security Council, and the International Court of Justice. UN headquarters are in New York City, where the General Assembly and the Security Council are based. The International Court of Justice holds its sessions in The Hague, Netherlands.

The General Assembly The largest of the UN's peacekeeping bodies is the General Assembly. It discusses, debates, and recommends solutions for problems presented to the United Nations. Each member may send a delegation of 5 representatives to the General Assembly, but each nation has only one vote.

The Security Council The Security Council is the UN's principal agency for maintaining peace. It is composed of 15 nations. The permanent members of the Security Council are the United States, Russia, the People's Republic of China, France, and Great Britain. The General Assembly elects the other 10 members for 2-year terms.

The Security Council has the authority to make peacekeeping decisions for the United Nations. The Council may call for breaking off relations with a nation, ending trade with a nation, or using military force. Because of its rules of procedure, however, the Security Council rarely makes such decisions.

According to the UN Charter, 9 of the Council's 15 members must vote in favor of any course of action. On important matters, however, the 9 members must include the votes of all permanent members. Thus, if only 1 permanent member vetoes a measure, the Security Council is unable to act.

International Court of Justice The third peacekeeping body of the UN is the International Court of Justice. Member nations may voluntarily submit disputes over international law to this court for settlement. The General Assembly and the Security Council select the 15 judges that sit on the International Court of Justice.

Section 4 Assessment

Checking for Understanding

1. **Main Idea** Use a graphic organizer like the one below to summarize the various international security agreements.

Organization	Membership	Goals

2. **Define** national security, international security, global security, nuclear proliferation, trading blocs.
3. **Identify** General Agreement on Tariffs and Trade (GATT), European Union (EU), North American Free Trade Agreement (NAFTA).
4. Identify four types of international conflict.

Critical Thinking

5. **Predicting Consequences** What could result if the major powers totally abolished their nuclear weapons?

Political Processes Identify and find out about the duties, responsibilities, and programs of the specialized agencies of the United Nations. Create a poster that illustrates the work of these agencies. Display completed posters in the classroom.

Skills

Study and Writing

Preparing a Bibliography

In Chapter 23 you learned how to write a report. To complete your report, you need to prepare a bibliography that lists all the sources you used.

Learning the Skill

A bibliography should follow a definite format. Each entry must contain author, title, publisher information, and publication date. Arrange entries alphabetically by the author's last name. The following are accepted formats for bibliography entries.

Books

Author's last name, first name. Full Title. Place of publication: publisher, copyright date.

Hay, Peter. Ordinary Heroes: The Life and Death of Chana Szenes, Israel's National Heroine. New York: Paragon House, 1986.

Articles

Author's last name, first name. "Title of Article." Periodical in which article appears, Volume number (issue date): page numbers.

Watson, Bruce. "The New Peace Corps in the New Kazakhstan." Smithsonian, Vol. 25 (August 1994): pp. 26–35.

Other Sources

For other kinds of sources, adapt the format for book entries.

Practicing the Skill

Review the sample bibliography, then answer the questions that follow.

Castañeda, Jorge G. The Mexican Shock: Its Meaning for the United States. New York: The New Press, 1995.

Politics in Mexico

Marquez, Viviane Brachet de. The Dynamics of Domination: State, Class, and Social Reform in Mexico, 1910–1990. Pittsburgh, Penn., University of Pittsburgh Press, 1994.

Cockburn, A., "The Fire This Time." Condé Nast Traveller, Vol. 30 (June 1995): pp. 104–113.

1. Are the bibliography entries in the correct order? Why or why not?
2. What is incorrect in the second book listing?
3. What is incorrect in the article listing?

Application Activity

Compile a bibliography for the research report you completed in Chapter 23. Include at least five sources.

The Glencoe Skillbuilder Interactive Workbook, Level 2 provides instruction and practice in key social studies skills.

Assessment and Activities

GOVERNMENT *Online*

Self-Check Quiz Visit the *United States Government: Democracy in Action* Web site at gov.glencoe.com and click on ***Chapter 25–Self-Check Quizzes*** to prepare for the chapter test.

Reviewing Key Terms

Insert the correct terms from the following list into the sentences below.

life peers	**national security**
oligarchy	**apartheid**
global security	***faqih***
kanyro	**cadre**
shah	**sanctions**

1. For many years Japan was ruled by an _____, a government led by a few powerful military and industrial leaders.
2. Britain's House of Lords is partially made up of _____, people who have been awarded a title for outstanding service or achievement.
3. The 1996 electoral reform in Japan reduced the influence of bureaucrats, known as _____.
4. Until recently, the South African government supported _____, or the strict segregation of the races.
5. To force the end of apartheid, the United States ordered economic _____, or coercive measures, against South Africa.
6. Chinese government officials, usually members of the Communist Party, are called a _____.
7. In the late 1970s Muslims in Iran revolted against the _____, or king.
8. The top religious-political leader in Iran is the _____.
9. The protection of a nation's borders and territories against invasion is known as _____.
10. The safety of the entire world is known as _____.

Research Issues For one week, find newspaper or magazine accounts of one of the countries discussed in the chapter. Find out what issues face that country today. Summarize the issues in a short written report.

Recalling Facts

1. Where are the earliest origins of democratic ideas to be found?
2. Who holds almost all governmental authority in Great Britain?
3. What did Poland's "Little Constitution" provide for?
4. What are the challenges facing South Africa's government today?
5. From what sources does Mexico's executive branch derive its power?
6. What governing body operates as the executive branch of the Chinese government?
7. What was the first limited war in the post–World War II era?
8. What are the three major goals of the United Nations?

Understanding Concepts

1. **Comparative Government** How are the powers of the president of France similar to and different from those of the president of the United States?
2. **Growth of Democracy** How does term limitation such as is found in Mexico support broader participation in government?

Critical Thinking

1. **Expressing Problems Clearly** Use a graphic organizer like the one below to identify the challenges that Poland faced once its people had overthrown their communist leaders.

2. **Recognizing Ideologies** How does the role of the Communist Party illustrate its importance in the government of China?

Cooperative Learning Activity

Comparing Governments Working in small groups, research a nation whose government was not described in this chapter. Is it authoritarian or democratic? Presidential or parliamentary? Does it have legislative representatives? Do political parties compete for offices? Compile your findings in a pamphlet.

Skill Practice Activity

Preparing a Bibliography Review the sample bibliography below. Then answer the questions that follow.

Firestein, David J. Beijing Spring 1989: An Outsider's Inside Account. Banner Press, 1990.

Bell, Gertrude Lowthian. The Letters of Gertrude Bell. New York: Boni and Liveright, 1928.

J.F. Hage, "Fulfilling Brazil's Promise: a Conversation with President Cardoso," Foreign Affairs, Vol. 74, July–August 1995: pp. 62–75.

1. Put the entries above in the correct order.
2. What is incorrect in the Firestein book listing?
3. Rewrite the J.F. Hage article listing correctly.

Interpreting Political Cartoons Activity

1. How is the United Nations portrayed in this cartoon?
2. How are various countries portrayed in this cartoon?
3. According to the cartoonist, does the UN seem equipped to effectively handle the world's crises? Explain your answer.

Technology Activity

Using the Internet Use the Internet to find a Web site of an embassy of one of the countries discussed in Chapter 25. Find information about the country, its government, and its political system. Report your findings in an oral report to the class.

Participating in Local Government

Take a poll of adults you know in your community. Find out their opinion about the work of the United Nations. Also find out what they think about United States involvement in that organization.

Chapter 26

Development of Economic Systems

Why It's Important

Economic and Political Connections

The world's people function in a variety of economic systems. Understanding the relationship between economic decisions and political freedom will enable you to make better choices as a citizen.

To learn more about world economic systems and how they affect citizens, view the ***Democracy In Action*** Chapter 26 video lesson:

Comparing Economic Systems

GOVERNMENT Online

Chapter Overview Visit the *United States Government: Democracy in Action* Web site at gov.glencoe.com and click on ***Chapter 26–Overview*** to preview chapter information.

Section 1

Capitalist and Mixed Systems

Reader's Guide

Key Terms

scarcity, traditional economy, command economy, market economy, factors of production, entrepreneur, monopoly, profit, mixed economy

Find Out

- What are the characteristics of capitalism that differentiate it from socialism and communism?
- Why can the economy of the United States be called a mixed economy?

Understanding Concepts

Free Enterprise What kinds of economic choices do individuals make in a free enterprise system?

COVER STORY

More Millionaires

WASHINGTON, D.C., AUGUST 4, 1997

In 1979 fewer than 14,000 Americans earned $1 million or more a year. Today the number tops 70,000. The newly rich defy the traditional stereotypes of affluence. Many are average folks who spend their days toiling for wages. The secret of their wealth is that they work for a growing number of businesses that reward employees with company stock in addition to paychecks. "We told them, 'If we make it, you're going to get the rewards,'" says Home Depot cofounder Bernie Marcus of his workers. Marcus estimates that his company's success has made about 1,000 of its employees millionaires. "We should be a model for the free enterprise system," he says.

Home Depot employees

Americans benefit from an economic system that provides great opportunities. However, like all other nations, we must deal with the problem of limited resources. Economic systems have developed in the world to deal with this fundamental economic problem—scarcity. **Scarcity** is a condition that exists because society does not have all the resources to produce all the goods and services that everyone wants. In dealing with this problem, economic systems address the questions "What should be produced?" "How should it be produced?" and "For whom should it be produced?"

All economic systems can be classified into three major types—traditional, market, and command. In a **traditional economy** habit and custom dictate the rules for all economic activity, determining what, how, and for whom goods and services are produced. A **command economy** has a central authority—usually the government—that makes most of these economic decisions. State planning commissions or other agencies determine the needs of the people and direct resources to meet those needs. A **market economy** allows buyers and sellers acting in their individual interests to determine what, how, and for whom goods and services are produced. In a market economy the individual's decisions are like votes. Consumers "vote" for a product when they purchase it, thus helping producers determine what to produce. Producers determine the best method for producing goods and services.

Factors of Production

The resources of an economic system are called **factors of production** because economies must have them in order to produce goods and services. They may be grouped into four categories: land, capital, labor, and entrepreneurs.

Land includes all natural resources such as soil, water, and air. Minerals such as copper or

◀ Worker surveys industries in Beijing, China.

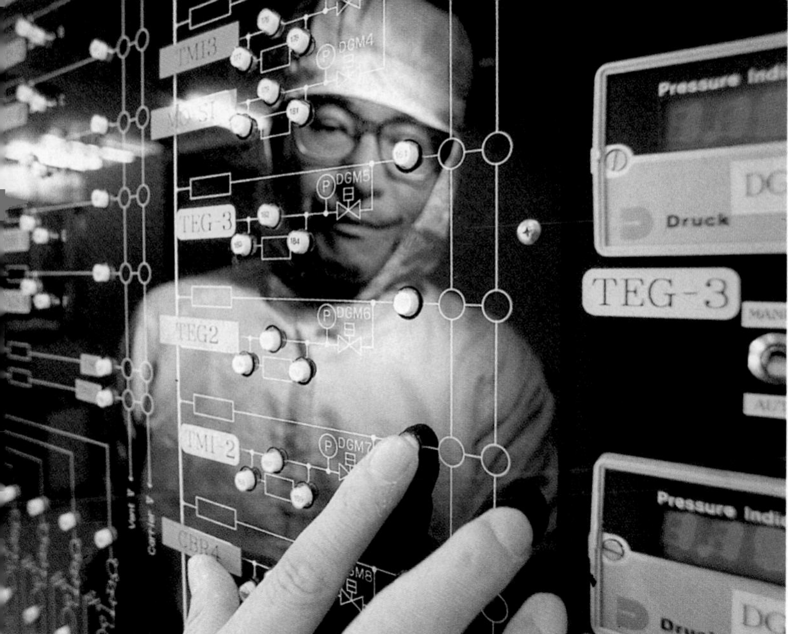

Factors of Production A researcher at Fujitsu—a Tokyo-based company—checks data on the control board of a machine used to grow crystals. Fujitsu specializes in creating communications and electronic devices. ***Using a product that is familiar to you, explain how each of the factors of production was used in its production.***

iron ore are land resources. Rich soil for farming is a land resource, as are forests that yield timber. **Capital** is the means of production—money, factories, heavy machinery—used to produce other products and goods. The furnaces in a steel mill that convert iron ore to steel are capital. **Labor** is human resources—people who produce goods and services. Factory workers, farmers, doctors, plumbers, teachers, and everyone else who is employed are part of an economy's labor force. Finally, **entrepreneurs,**—risk takers who organize and direct the other factors of production to produce goods and services in search of profit—are the fourth factor of production.

Forms of Economic Organization

Three major forms of economic organization—communism, socialism, and capitalism—represent the range of economic systems that determine how the factors of production are allocated. **Communism** is a command system in which the central government directs all major economic decisions. **Socialism** is a partial command system in which the government influences many economic decisions. Under **capitalism,** people make the economic decisions in free markets.

People have strong opinions about the strengths and weaknesses of the three principal economic systems. The authors of *Comparative Economic Systems* said:

> "*In evaluating the strengths and weaknesses of capitalism, one is confronted with the possibility that the capitalist system may best sustain the fundamental human values of liberty and freedom of the individual. Indeed, it may even be the only context within which Western democratic political institutions can flourish.*"
>
> —William Loucks and William Whitney, 1969

Although people refer to national economies as communist, socialist, or capitalist, most countries in the world today have mixed economic systems. Moreover, at any given time a nation may be moving in the direction of a command economy or a market economy.

Characteristics of Capitalism

In the United States and several industrial countries, capitalism is the economic system. Capitalism is based on private ownership of the means of production—the capital—and on individual economic freedom. A capitalist economic system is often called a **free enterprise system.**

In the free enterprise system, people who own the means of production are called capitalists. The owner of a small corner grocery store, the person who owns a few shares of stock in a huge corporation, industrialists who own large factories or coal mines, and those who own financial institutions are all capitalists.

Most capitalist economies today have five main characteristics. These include private ownership, individual initiative, competition, freedom of choice, and profit (or loss).

Private Ownership Capitalist economies depend on the right of private ownership of property and control of economic resources. Government provides some public services such as road building, water and sewers, parks, and libraries. In addition, the government may own land, as in the case of national parks.

Capitalism also emphasizes respect for personal property not used in production. The Fifth Amendment to the United States Constitution states that the government shall not deprive people of their property "without due process of law; nor shall private property be taken for public use, without just compensation." The right to inherit property is another feature of private ownership in a capitalist system. In a pure capitalist system there would be no limit on this right. In the United States, inheritance taxes limit this feature.

Individual Initiative In a capitalist system, the law does not prevent anyone from trying to be an entrepreneur. Each year thousands of Americans go into business for themselves. In a recent year, for example, Americans started more than 230,000 new businesses. Many of these start-ups were in such fast-growing fields as microcomputers, bioengineering, robotics, electronic communication, and energy.

Competition Another essential aspect of capitalism is competition. Competition exists when there are a number of sellers of a product or service, and no one seller can exercise control over the market price. For example, competition exists when a neighborhood has several different supermarkets that compete with one another for business. The supermarket that offers the best combination of price, quality, and service is likely to get the largest share of the business. Competition helps assure that the consumer will get products of good quality at low prices.

A monopoly is the opposite of competition. Monopoly exists when an industry includes only one seller resulting in no competition at all. **Oligopoly,** a situation where there are only a few large firms in an industry, is more common.

Congressional Quarterly's *Government at a Glance*

Economic Systems

	COMMUNISM	SOCIALISM	CAPITALISM
Ownership of Resources	All productive resources are government owned and operated.	Basic productive resources are government owned and operated; the rest are privately owned and operated.	Productive resources are privately owned and operated.
Allocation of Resources	Centralized planning directs all resources.	Government plans ways to allocate resources in key industries.	Capital for production is obtained through the lure of profits in the market.
Role of Government	Government makes all major economic decisions.	Government directs the completion of its economic plans in key industries.	Government may promote competition and provide public goods.

Critical Thinking

The table shows economic systems in theory. In practice there are no pure capitalist or communist systems, and socialist systems vary from nation to nation. ***Who or what authority allocates the factors of production in each of the three systems?***

We the People

Making a Difference

Food From the 'Hood

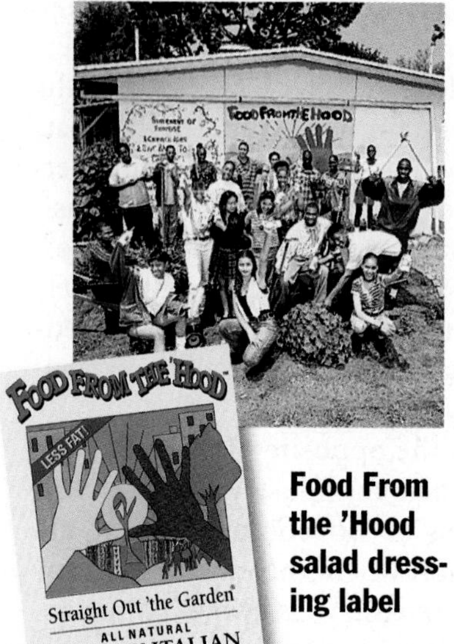

Food From the 'Hood salad dressing label

When biology students at Crenshaw High School planted a small garden next to their football field, they had no idea they were also planting the seeds for a successful business. The first year's harvest of herbs and vegetables, sold at local farmers' markets, generated $600 for college scholarships. The rest of the produce went to the neighborhood's homeless people.

After a successful first year, students at the Los Angeles high school decided to create their own business. They called it Food From the 'Hood. Using herbs and produce from their garden, they concocted their own all-natural salad dressing called Straight Out 'the Garden. The dressing was a hit and is now found on the shelves of more than 2,000 natural-food stores throughout the nation.

The company is run just like any other successful company. Students who want to work for the company must apply for jobs just as with any other job. The screening process is rigorous. Applicants must write essays and participate in an internship program to obtain a position.

Profits from the salad dressing are used to run the business and establish scholarships. One-fourth of the vegetables grown each year are donated to the homeless. The student-run company has earned an achievement award from *Newsweek* magazine, and has been visited by such well-known dignitaries as Britain's Prince Charles.

Businesses in such an industry often compete fiercely with each other, but there are also times when they are tempted to limit competition by dividing the market or agreeing to raise prices. To ensure competition in free enterprise economies, governments pass laws against monopolies that try to control their markets.

Freedom of Choice Buyers, sellers, and workers all have freedom of choice in a capitalist system. Consumers can buy the products they can afford from whatever companies they choose. At the same time, businesses are free to provide whatever legal goods and services they think people want. Workers can decide where they will work and what they will do. When new jobs open up at better pay, workers may move from one job to another.

Profit or Loss The capitalist system is based on the profit motive. **Profit** is the difference between the amount of money used to operate a business and the amount of money the business takes in. Profits are the fuel that keeps a free enterprise economy running.

Profits are part of the reward to the entrepreneur for assuming the risk. They also pay for future expansion and provide for unexpected events. Business owners use some profits for their own income. In addition, they may reinvest some of these profits in their business or in some other company.

In a capitalist economy, the risk of loss accompanies the potential for profits. Entrepreneurs must be willing to take chances and risk losses to be successful in a capitalist system.

Changing Face of Capitalism

The economic system of the United States is based on capitalism, but it includes elements of a command economy. In the United States, government has played a growing role in the economy as a protector, provider of goods and services, consumer, and regulator.

Regulation and Social Policies For its first 100 years, the United States government played a limited role in the national economy, and business was largely unregulated. By the late 1800s powerful industrialists began to dominate the economy, squeezing out competitors. Because immigration brought an abundance of laborers, wages fell. Families with low incomes were forced to allow their children to work long hours in terrible conditions.

As a result of these conditions, public attitudes toward business changed. Both the states and the national government began to adopt regulatory legislation to ensure competition and promote public safety. Today the government plays an important role in regulating business, labor, and agriculture.

In the 1930s the federal government began to take responsibility for the well-being of individuals and for the financial condition of the nation through fiscal and monetary policy. Since then the government has assumed increasing responsibility for social policies in housing, transportation, health, education, and welfare. As a result, the United States today has what economists call a **mixed economy**, or modified capitalism.

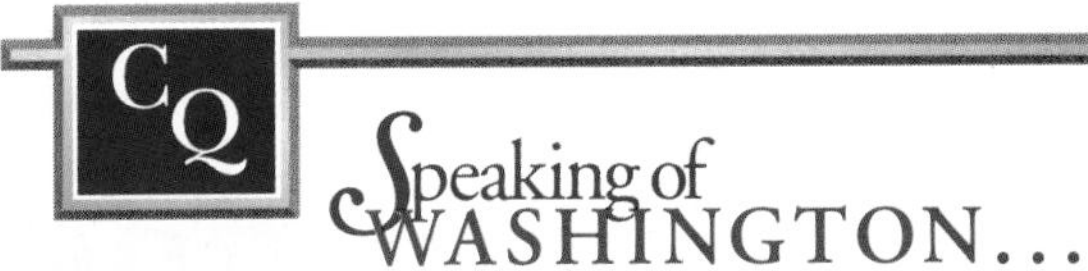

Emperor **The word *emperor* and its feminine form, *empress,* have come to refer to a sovereign who rules more than one kingdom or territory. In the nineteenth century Victoria was queen of England but empress of India. Today Japan is the only major country that still refers to the ceremonial head of state or monarch as "emperor."**

Capitalism Around the World In Japan government works closely with business to limit foreign competition in the domestic market. The government of Japan spends relatively little on welfare, and taxes are low.

Singapore, Taiwan, and South Korea are three other Asian capitalist countries that have made remarkable progress in the last 20 years. The governments of Singapore and Taiwan also have a close relationship with private business. Government planning redirects resources into target industries.

Generally Western European economies are more controlled and regulated than that of the United States. However, many Western European governments have moved away from central planning toward more free markets in recent years. Eastern European countries have privatized a large percentage of their industries.

Section 1 Assessment

Checking for Understanding

1. **Main Idea** Use a graphic organizer like the one on the right to identify five characteristics of capitalist economies.

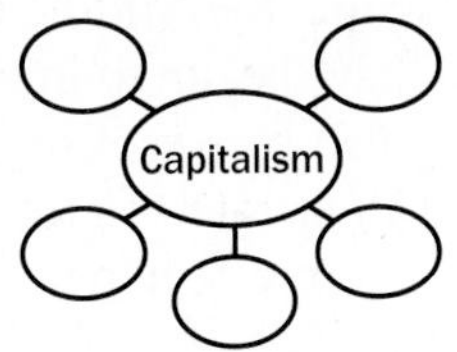

2. **Define** scarcity, traditional economy, command economy, market economy, factors of production, entrepreneur, monopoly, profit, mixed economy.
3. **Identify** communism, socialism, capitalism, free enterprise system.
4. What are the three forms of economic organization that have emerged in the world?
5. How has the U.S. government played a growing role in the nation's economy since the late 1800s?

Critical Thinking

6. **Making Inferences** How does the free market system promote freedom of choice for consumers in the United States?

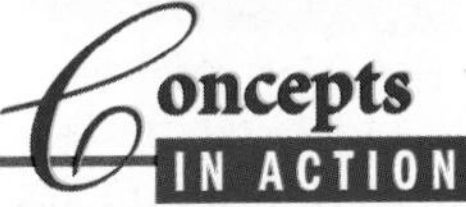

Free Enterprise One of the issues debated by advocates of a planned economy and those who support a free market economy is whether there can be democratic freedoms such as freedom of speech without having economic freedom. Write an essay explaining the connection between economic freedom and civil liberties.

Section 2

Emerging Economies

Reader's Guide

Key Terms

developing nations, newly developed nations, welfare state, nationalization

Find Out

- What are the important economic choices that developing and newly developed nations must make?
- How have economic choices affected the development of nations in Latin America and Africa?

Understanding Concepts

Comparative Government What are the differences and similarities of socialist governments and communist governments?

COVER STORY

Turkish Schools Fall Short

YENIDOGAN, TURKEY, SEPTEMBER 12, 2000

This week 14 million children started the school year in Turkey. But 1 million more went to work or stayed home instead. Why? The World Bank reports that schools in most Turkish villages only go to the fifth grade. Poor village families cannot afford to bus their children to urban schools. Even in urban areas such as Istanbul or Ankara, school expenses are daunting. Mandatory school uniforms cost up to $80 each, and parents must pay for textbooks and supplies as well. Those who can pay get overcrowded classrooms and underpaid teachers. Education union president Alaatin Dincer says, "Turkey needs 190,000 more teachers and 106,000 more classrooms and only then can we have 30 kids to a class."

Turkish children work in the fields.

By the late twentieth century many developing countries were moving toward industrialization. As these nations developed industry and trade, they faced similar problems but dealt with them in a variety of ways. Turkey, for example, increased its defense spending instead of its spending for education. In 2000 Turkey allotted $90 per student, far below the level spent by developed countries such as Greece ($240 per student) and Germany ($817 per student). Such gaps between rich and poor nations continued to be a concern to world leaders.

Developing and Newly Developed Nations

Developing nations are states with little or no industry. The majority of these countries are largely agricultural. A few, such as Saudi Arabia and Kuwait are rich, usually because of oil. Many developing nations are former colonies of Western European nations that gained independence after World War II. Much of the world's population is in developing nations.

Newly developed nations are states that have had significant or rapid industrial growth in recent years. These countries, mostly in Eastern Europe, the Middle East, Asia, and South America, have begun to influence the world economy. They also face economic choices that will determine their rate of growth and the shape of their economic systems.

The Economic Choices

Some developing and newly developed nations have chosen to rely on free markets, trade, and contacts with the West to develop their economies. Their economic systems lean toward capitalism. The free market determines what goods and services are produced and at what prices. They are open to investment from capitalist countries.

COMPARING *Governments*

Developing Countries

Country	Percent Urban	GDP per Capita (U.S. $)	External Debt (billions of U.S. $)	Adult Literacy Rate	Population Growth Rate
Bangladesh	19	$1,470	$16.5	38.1%	1.59%
Bulgaria	69	$4,300	$10	98%	1.16%
Chile	84	$12,400	$39	95.2%	1.17%
Ethiopia	16	$560	$10	35.5%	2.76%
Ghana	36	$1,900	$6	64.5%	1.87%
Honduras	44	$2,050	$4.4	72.7%	2.52%
Malaysia	54	$10,700	$43.6	83.5%	2.10%
Turkey	71	$6,200	$104	82.3%	1.27%

Sources: CIA, *The World Factbook 2000* (Washington: 2000); *The World Almanac and Book of Facts 2000* (Mahwah, NJ: 2000).

Critical Thinking **Changes in development indicators are apparent as countries work toward developing industrial economies. *Which measures of development increase as countries become more industrial?***

Online **UPDATE**
Visit **gov.glencoe.com** and click on ***Textbook Updates–Chapter 26*** for an update of the data.

Other developing and newly developed nations have chosen socialism as a model for their economies. Under socialism, government owns some factors of production. As a result, the government controls the production and distribution of some products. Under communism, the government owns all factors of production and takes a much more direct role in deciding what, how, and for whom to produce. Other important differences distinguish the command elements in democratic socialist economies and communist economies.

One difference is that under democratic socialism the voters can replace those in command of the economy and the government. In a communist country there is only one party, and the people have no control over those who lead the economy.

Another difference is that most socialist countries use the command system to control only parts of their economy. The governments in these countries operate such important industries as mining and transportation. They may not operate industries that produce food, clothing, or household items. In contrast, in communist economies, government planners control every part of the economy.

Socialists believe that wealth should be distributed as equally as possible. In practice, they have tried to achieve this goal by making basic goods and social services equally available to everyone. Modern socialist governments also provide a wide array of so-called "cradle-to-grave" benefits for their citizens. Usually these benefits include free hospital, medical, and dental care; tuition-free education through college; generous retirement benefits; and low-rent public housing. Other government-provided services may include maternity allowances, free treatment for alcohol and drug abuse, and generous unemployment payments.

Critics of socialism claim such policies create a **welfare state.** They believe that having many welfare programs makes people overly dependent on government. Socialists answer that every person should be able to receive such basic necessities as food, shelter, clothing, and medical care. Cradle-to-grave services do not come free, however.

Socialist governments require citizens to pay very high taxes to pay for social services. Businesses in socialist economies are also heavily taxed.

Searching for Economic Answers

Many developing and newly developed nations have sought economic progress by adopting socialist economic policies. These policies, often with little success, aim to raise the standard of living of the large masses of poor people. Socialist governments in these countries often use **centralized planning,** or government control of the economy, to an even greater extent than developed socialist nations do. They believe only centralized planning can achieve rapid industrial growth. In many of these nations, authoritarian governments take over economic planning. Many of these governments focus on welfare and education programs for the poor.

These socialist governments often turn to nationalization of existing industries, redistribution of land or establishment of agricultural communes, and a welfare system.

Socialist governments often take control of industry—usually selecting the country's most important industries—through a process called **nationalization.** When nationalization occurs in democratic countries, the government pays private owners of the businesses that it takes over. In less democratic countries, socialist governments have taken over private property with little or no compensation to the owners.

Nationalization in Latin America Because of their colonial history or their reliance on foreign investment, many developing nations have had industries that are foreign-owned. This is especially true in Latin America. Nationalization of these industries by the government has been both an economic policy and a gesture of anticolonialism. In addition to foreign ownership of business, many developing countries have been ruled by wealthy elites. In these states, the poverty of masses of people could ignite revolution and civil war at almost any time.

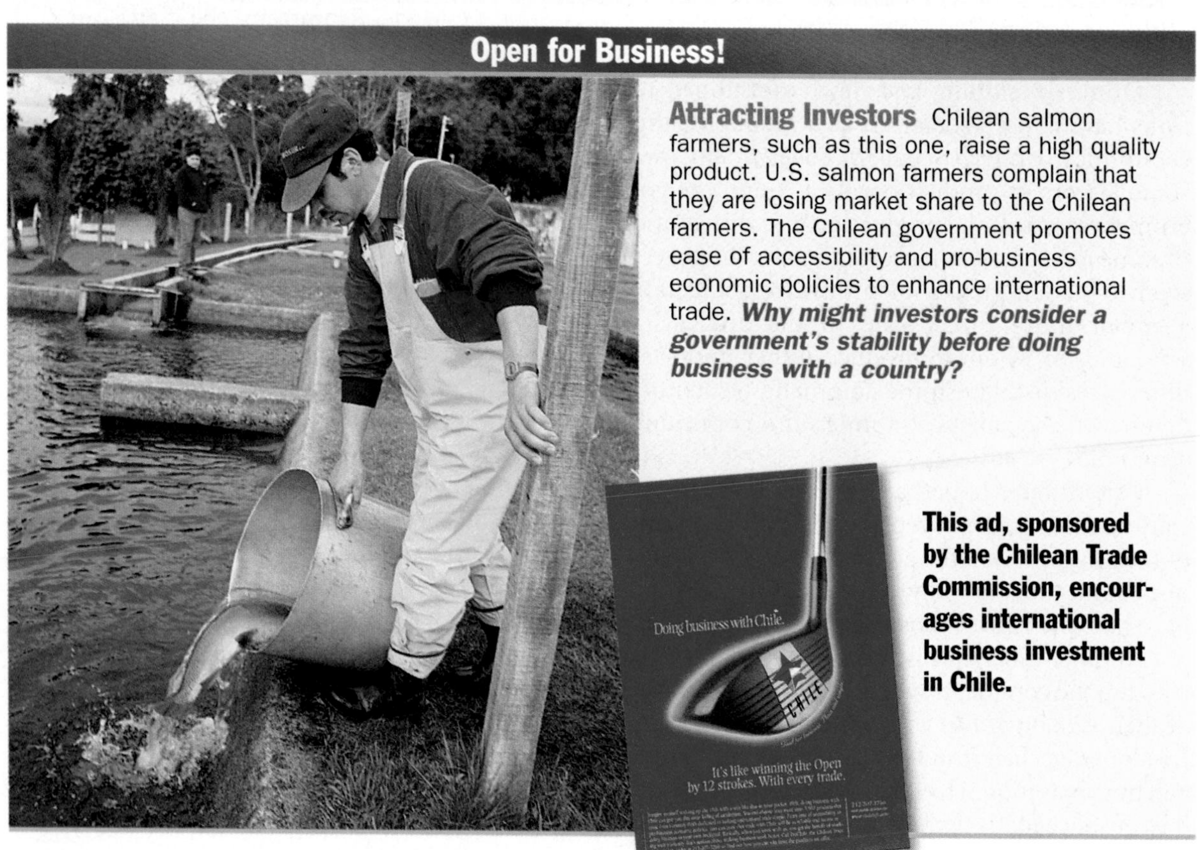

Open for Business!

Attracting Investors Chilean salmon farmers, such as this one, raise a high quality product. U.S. salmon farmers complain that they are losing market share to the Chilean farmers. The Chilean government promotes ease of accessibility and pro-business economic policies to enhance international trade. ***Why might investors consider a government's stability before doing business with a country?***

This ad, sponsored by the Chilean Trade Commission, encourages international business investment in Chile.

The nation of Chile reflects the difficulties of a developing nation attempting to build a socialist democracy. In 1970 Chileans elected Salvador Allende as president. Allende, a Marxist socialist, took quick steps to nationalize businesses, including American copper mining companies. Wealthy Chileans, frightened by Allende's ties to Castro's Cuba and the government's efforts to nationalize industries, withdrew their money from Chile and invested it in other countries. As a result, the Chilean economy spiraled downward. In 1973 Chilean military leaders working with the CIA led a coup against Allende.

After Allende was found dead, a new government, led by General August Pinochet, took over. Pinochet dissolved the congress, canceled civil liberties, and issued a new constitution. He also encouraged foreign investment. Inflation fell, consumer goods became available again, and the economy prospered. Mounting popular pressure against Pinochet, however, forced him to hold elections in 1988. The new leaders since then have increased government spending on education, health, and housing. The economy of Chile has improved, and the nation is interested in joining the North American Free Trade Agreement (see Section 4).

Restructuring and Profiting

Modernization A liberalization of many African economies has opened up those countries to private foreign capital investment. Foreign investors press those African countries, like Nigeria, to establish more efficient financial institutions. ***How does modernization of economic infrastructure, such as banks, help African countries to develop?***

Agricultural Communes Until recent government moves toward free enterprise, Israel had a moderately socialist economy. In the early 1900s, Jewish immigrants brought many European socialist ideas to the area that is now Israel. They built collective agricultural communes, or **kibbutzim.** In these communes, wealth was held in common and profits were reinvested in the settlement after members had been provided with food, clothing, shelter, and medical services. Since Israel's founding in 1948, the communes have allowed some private property. Today, the kibbutzim still contribute to Israel's economy, although their members make up a small share of the country's population.

Economic Development in Africa After independence, many African nations tried to develop economies based on one cash crop or one resource for trade. Promoting the export of cash crops and raw materials while trying to industrialize did not produce sufficient capital. Seeking more funds for development, African nations turned to foreign governments and banks for loans. Some governments in Africa followed a capitalist model and developed close ties to the West. Others organized socialist economies.

During the Cold War era, African leaders in such lands as Tanzania, Ghana, Senegal, and Guinea, turned to socialism because they viewed western capitalism as another form of colonialism. In accepting socialism, they adapted it to African traditions. African varieties of socialism combined Marxism, nationalism, communal land ownership, and group decision making.

Beginning in the 1970s, droughts, growing populations, lack of capital, and falling world prices for their exports weakened most African economies. Relying on foreign help to remedy these problems, African countries south of the Sahara took on $130 billion worth of debt by the 1980s. African leaders increasingly realized that they would have to find answers to Africa's problems without much outside help. To break their

An Ailing Economy

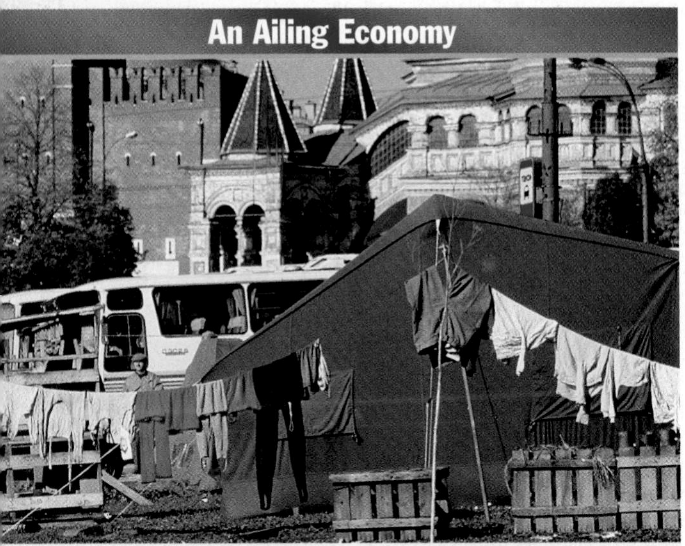

Seeking Investment Moscow's homeless citizens erected tattered tents on the lawn of the Rossia Hotel near Red Square in 1990. Government leaders appealed to the West to save the sinking Russian economy. Western investors hesitated, not knowing how far the Russian officials would move toward free markets. ***Why do investors prefer free market economies?***

reliance on foreign countries, some African nations formed regional associations to promote trade and economic cooperation. Governments that had once adapted socialist policies increasingly encouraged free enterprise.

Socialism's Practical Problems

Socialist ideology remains a popular and widely held political belief in the developing world. However, several practical problems have caused socialism to fail to live up to its promises. First, a primary need for developing economies is capital investments. The quickest route to capital is through foreign investors. Yet banks and private investors have been cautious when investing in developing nations. A major concern is whether the emerging economy will honor its obligations. Free market economies without a threat of nationalization of businesses attract capital. Economies based on a Marxist model do not.

Second, the failure of large-scale state planning to meet the needs of the consumers in Eastern European nations raises concern about socialism's ability to do so in other regions. Developing nations have large populations with basic consumer needs. Failure to meet these needs would risk revolt.

Finally, Western governments, particularly the United States, have exercised influence and pressure in favor of a combination of free markets and democracy in developing nations. The growing interdependence of nations in a global economy and a global communications network have made resistance to the West's economic leadership difficult, if not futile. Meanwhile, governments in industrialized nations have been willing to accept some government planning.

Section 2 Assessment

Checking for Understanding

1. **Main Idea** Create a graphic organizer like the one below. In the left box, identify the economic issues facing developing countries. In the right box, list policies some have adopted to promote economic progress.

2. **Define** developing nations, newly developed nations, welfare state, nationalization.
3. **Identify** centralized planning, kibbutzim.
4. Why have many Latin American industries been foreign-owned?
5. What factor contributes to socialism in Africa?

Critical Thinking

6. **Making Comparisons** Analyze the economic choices that developing and newly developed nations must make in an increasingly interdependent global economy.

Concepts IN ACTION

Comparative Government Review the characteristics of economies under socialist governments and under communist governments. Create an organizational chart that illustrates decision making under each of these types of government.

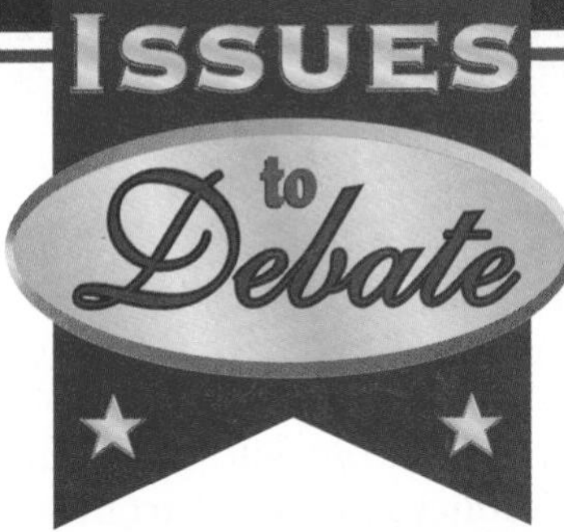

Should the United States Increase Foreign Aid?

Foreign aid is a very small percentage of the federal budget. However, most Americans believe that we spend too much on foreign aid. When the nation is in an economic recession, foreign aid comes under strong criticism.

Foreign Aid Policies

United States foreign aid policies began in 1947 with the Marshall Plan, designed to help Western Europe recover from World War II and to build strong U.S. trading partners that supported democracy.

Most recently the newly free nations of Eastern Europe began to receive American aid. When Russia struggled after the collapse of communism, many believed that the United States had an opportunity to influence the growth of democracy by economic support of that country. Others believed that aid should be given according to Russia's commitment to establishing a free enterprise economy.

Today most people believe that foreign aid is a significant portion of the federal budget, yet it represents about 1 percent of total federal spending.

Recent Aid Arguments

Some opponents of foreign aid say that it often goes to foreign governments that provide little relief for the poor. Other critics point out that aid may actually hinder foreign economic development. For example, food aid may depress the prices of agricultural products, thus ruining the developing nation's farmers. Finally, some critics argue that the United States is no longer an economic giant that can afford foreign aid.

Defenders of foreign aid believe that the problem is the misconception that foreign aid "represents a massive outflow of dollars from the United States." Actually, most of the money appropriated for foreign aid returns to the United States as foreign nations purchase American products. Another argument for foreign aid is that it contributes to the stability of developing nations, thereby protecting the security of the United States.

Debating the Issue

What Percentage of the Federal Budget Should Be Foreign Aid?

How much should Americans be willing to invest in the development of foreign economies? Is foreign aid a necessary investment for world stability?

Key Issues

✔ Should foreign aid be an important part of national security policy?

✔ How should the nation determine when and for whom foreign aid should be spent?

Debate Divide the class into three to five teams. Have the first team research a recent U.S. foreign aid budget and serve as a panel to decide aid to be given. Each of the other teams should represent a nation seeking aid and present their cases to the panel.

Vote The first team should consider each request individually. After deciding the amount of aid on a case-by-case basis, add up the total assistance.

Section 3

Collapse of Soviet Communism

Reader's Guide

Key Terms

gross national product, state farm, collective farm, coup

Find Out

- What were the causes of Soviet economic troubles in the 1980s?
- How did economic problems lead to the collapse of the Soviet Union?

Understanding Concepts

Comparative Government How did the Communist Party control the government and economy of the Soviet Union?

COVER STORY

Fast Lane for Russia

MOSCOW, RUSSIA, OCTOBER 2, 1995

A Jeep for sale in Moscow

Russians are readily embracing the middle-class lifestyle of Western democracies. Nothing better symbolizes the changes sweeping this nation than the flea market that has taken over Moscow's Exhibition of Economic Achievements park. Built as a shrine to the Soviet system, it is now the center of free enterprise in the city. Muscovites swarm here to get deals on all sorts of goods. A park pavilion once housed an exhibit celebrating the Soviet space program. It has now become an auto showroom. A few space capsules remain, scattered among the used cars. But the crowds are here to see the new Fords and Jeeps.

Beginning in 1917 the Soviet Union built the world's leading communist economic system, calling itself a socialist economy. However, the Soviet Union used the term *socialism* in a different sense from the democratic socialist countries. The Soviet Union saw its socialism as an intermediate stage in the transformation from capitalism to pure communism.

A major difference between noncommunist socialist systems and the Soviet economy was that it was closely controlled by an authoritarian political party—the Communist Party. In the Soviet Union the government, meaning in actual practice the Communist Party, made nearly all economic decisions. With few exceptions, all enterprises were state owned and operated. The Soviet government also controlled labor unions, wages, and prices.

Soviet Economic Problems

The Soviet Union built one of the world's largest economies and came to rival the United States as a superpower. Its defense industries were strong, yet the rest of the Soviet economy faced very serious problems.

Beginning in the mid-1980s, the Soviet **gross national product** (GNP), the sum of all the nation's goods and services, grew by only 2 or 3 percent a year. Development of heavy industry slowed. Soviet products could not compete in world markets. The huge, oppressive state bureaucracy that managed every detail of Soviet production bred economic stagnation. Mikhail Gorbachev, Soviet leader at the time, described the situation this way:

> "*At some point the country began to lose momentum. Economic failures became more frequent. Difficulties began to accumulate. . . . Elements of stagnation began to appear in the life of society.*"
>
> —Mikhail Gorbachev

Soviet central planning created four main problems. First, it encouraged producers to meet targets with goods that were easy to produce rather than with goods that were the most needed. Second, the system failed to produce badly needed consumer goods and services. Third, the quality of goods suffered. Finally, the system discouraged new ideas.

Few Consumer Goods and Services Central planning directed most Soviet resources into heavy industry and military hardware. In an era that stressed consumer goods, the Soviet economy was not able to deliver the goods and services consumers needed. Items such as potatoes, onions, toothpaste, well-made clothing, coffee, and sugar were hard to find in state stores. People had money, but there was little or nothing to buy.

To meet their production targets, factory managers often turned out those goods that were easiest to produce. For example, a factory that made nails was told to produce 100 tons of nails. The factory manager produced large nails because fewer such nails were needed to reach the 100-ton target. Builders and carpenters in another part of the economy, however, really needed small nails.

Little Concern for Quality Economic planners made few provisions for quality. Instead, they focused on quantity. As a result, the quality of goods produced suffered because the Soviets had, in effect, created a system that valued the production of 100 clunking, low-quality tractors more highly than the production of 10 smoothly running ones.

Consumer goods in the Soviet Union acquired a reputation for shoddiness. Soviet economists reported that only 10 percent of their finished products could compete with those made in the West.

Resistance to New Ideas Hard-pressed Soviet plant managers trying to meet production targets often resisted efforts to install new machines or new methods. The managers believed interruption would slow down production and cause them to miss their production quotas.

Agriculture in the Soviet Union

About 98 percent of all Soviet farmland was under government control. As a result, farming, like industry, had to follow government production plans. About two-thirds of Soviet farmland consisted of state farms. **State farms** were owned by the government and run like factories, with the farmworkers being paid wages. The remaining one-third of Soviet farmland consisted of collective farms. On a **collective farm**, the government owned the land but rented it to families.

Farmworkers had little incentive to work hard on vast state-run farms. Inefficiency was widespread. For example, 20 percent of the grain and

Shortage of Consumer Goods

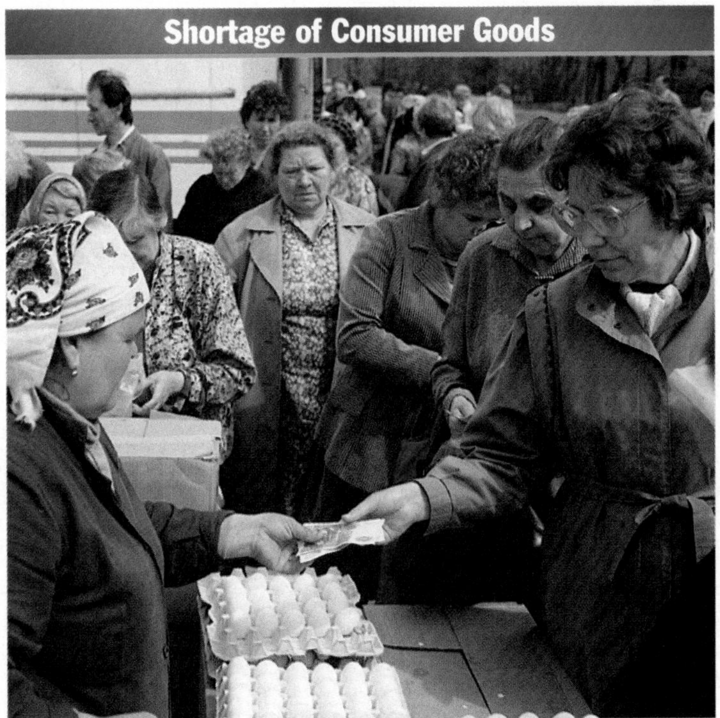

Central Planning The small quantity of eggs for sale shrank as many Soviet citizens lined up to buy them. Under central planning Soviets had money, but nothing to buy. More recently Russians produced consumer goods, but inflation soared to incredible heights. ***How might the scene above be different today?***

fruit harvest and 50 percent of the potato crop were wasted each year because of either late harvesting or inadequate storage facilities.

Attempts at Reform

Under **Mikhail Gorbachev**, who came to power in 1985, Soviet officials adopted hundreds of new economic policies. These measures were called *perestroika,* or economic restructuring.

Examples of Restructuring The government legalized some small service industries in such areas as plumbing, auto repair, and dressmaking. The new law allowed people to run their own businesses by registering with officials. Another law put more than 76,000 small factories and farms on a self-financing basis.

Soviet planners also merged five different farm ministries, gave greater freedom to state-run farms, and permitted a number of crops to be sold at uncontrolled prices. Farmworkers were given incentives. Small teams of workers contracted to manage individual farms. Each team's income depended on how much the farms produced.

Results of Perestroika

Despite the restructuring, the Soviet economy continued to falter. After six years of reform efforts, Soviet citizens called for Gorbachev's resignation.

Breakup of the Soviet Union In 1991 several republics threatened to secede from the Soviet Union. Then a group of Communist hard-liners attempted to overthrow the government. Such a planned but sudden grab for power is called a **coup.** The president of the Russian Republic, Boris Yeltsin, called for nationwide resistance to the coup. The Soviet people responded in support of Yeltsin and Gorbachev, and the coup failed.

As demonstrations broke out in the streets, angry crowds toppled statues of Communist leaders. Gorbachev resigned as Communist Party leader but remained Soviet president. Several Soviet republics seized the opportunity to declare their independence.

The Soviet economy remained lifeless. Gorbachev seemed unwilling to replace central planning with a free market. When inflation reached an

GOVERNMENT *and You*

Hosting a Foreign Exchange Student

Does your school participate in a student exchange program? Has your family or anyone whom you know ever hosted a high school student from another country?

Families who support or participate in intercultural exchange programs believe that the experience promotes understanding and respect among the world's people. Hosting an exchange student provides your family with a chance to learn firsthand about another country, its government, and its culture. It also allows you to share your way of life with the visiting student.

Intercultural programs vary; families may host a student for a summer, a semester, or a year. Visiting students generally are members of the junior or senior class in high school. Some communities, however, participate in exchange programs for college students, teachers, or elementary school students. Host families may have members who are the same age as the visiting student. Families with young children, couples with no children, and single people, however, also host exchange students.

A foreign exchange student with his host family

Organizations that sponsor exchange programs provide orientation meetings and staff to help make the experience valuable for everyone.

Participating IN GOVERNMENT ACTIVITY

Conduct an Interview Ask a foreign exchange student about his or her experiences in the United States and at home. Also discuss differences in forms of government the students have experienced.

annual rate of 200 percent and production fell dramatically, Gorbachev appealed for help from the United States and other Western nations. These nations' leaders criticized the Soviets for retreating from plans to develop a market economy.

Several Soviet republics that had declared their independence formed a loose confederation called the Commonwealth of Independent States. This move effectively ended the Soviet Union. Each republic, including Russia, would now carve out its own future.

Economic Problems

The West applauded when Russia held democratic elections in 1996, in which Russians reelected President Boris Yeltsin, and in 2000, in which they elected Vladimir Putin. Both presidents faced huge economic problems, however. Bureaucrats used inside knowledge of policy changes to buy state properties at bargain rates and strip their assets. These insiders took over the big banks, newspapers, television, and more.

Concerned with these and other problems, foreign and domestic investors began to withdraw their funds from Russia. Lacking capital for improvements, obsolete factories turned out shoddy goods that no one wanted. Sales declined, and workers went unpaid. A barter system replaced cash. Terrorism and street crime increased. A shrinking tax base provided meager government revenues. Russia borrowed from the International Monetary Fund (IMF), creating a debt it could not repay.

Last leader of the Soviet Union, Mikhail Gorbachev

An Uncertain Future

Do capitalism and democracy have a future in Russia? Despite the changes since 1991, the Russians have been unable to push through political and economic reforms to correct problems that plagued the country under Communism. Even with periodic elections the country is run much as it was during the communist years—and by many of the same people. A key reason may be the lack of social consensus in Russia on democratic values and the main characteristics of capitalism. Economist Robert Samuelson explains the importance of such beliefs:

> "*Market capitalism is not just an economic system. It is also a set of cultural values that emphasizes the virtues of competition, the legitimacy of profit and the value of freedom.*"
>
> —*Newsweek,* September, 1998

Section 3 Assessment

Checking for Understanding

1. **Main Idea** Use a graphic organizer like the one here to identify four problems that Soviet centralized planning created.

   Soviet centralized planning

2. **Define** gross national product, state farm, collective farm, coup.
3. **Identify** Mikhail Gorbachev, perestroika, Boris Yeltsin.
4. What was the main source of agricultural problems in the Soviet Union?
5. What events in 1991 led to the collapse of the Soviet Union?

Critical Thinking

6. **Analyzing Information** How did perestroika help reshape the Soviet economy?

Concepts IN ACTION

Comparative Government Before the 1980s, the Soviet economy was under the control of government planners from the Communist Party. Create a political cartoon that illustrates one of the problems that centralized planning created for the Soviet economy. Share your cartoon with your classmates.

Section 4

The Global Economy

Reader's Guide

Key Terms

comparative advantage, tariffs, quotas, trading blocs

Find Out

- Why are nations developing trading blocs and regional trade agreements?
- What economic choices and problems face developing nations in the global economy?

Understanding Concepts

Global Perspectives How is the global economy making nations interdependent?

COVER STORY

Global Generation X

BEIJING, CHINA, SEPTEMBER 5, 1997

American young people have been going abroad for as long as Mom and Dad have been able to send them. But today's young travelers are unlike earlier generations. Instead, they are drawn by the opportunities available in fast-growing foreign economies. Typical is 24-year-old Rachel DeWoskin, who went to China three years ago to pursue a public relations career. "You're part of a system," DeWoskin says of America. "But in China, you're setting up a system. It's like being a cowboy, a pioneer." Breaux Walker, who left New York to start a computer business in Shanghai, agrees. "This is so worth it," he says. "This is the real deal."

An American student working in Hong Kong

Americans contribute in many ways to the rapidly changing global economy. All nations of the world, however, have a stake in the world's economy. Whether rich or poor, large or small, every nation must find some way to compete in an interconnected system of markets throughout the world. Two of the most important factors affecting stability in the global economy are the free flow of international trade and the continued economic development of the poorer nations of the world.

International Trade

Trade among nations is a major aspect of global interdependence. International trade allows consumers to buy imported goods at lower prices than similar products on the national market. Creating lower-priced products is possible because some nations produce certain goods more efficiently or have cost advantages.

The principle of **comparative advantage** says that each country should produce those goods it can make more efficiently and purchase those that other nations produce more efficiently. When nations specialize in goods they can produce most efficiently, the total world production is greater. This means that the total cost of all products is less, and therefore, the average cost of any product is less, benefiting all consumers.

Since World War II, industrial democracies have promoted free trade or the removal of trade barriers through the formation of regional associations. Even though it favors efficient production, unrestricted international trade is not supported by everyone. It can displace selected industries, and groups of workers may lose their jobs because of foreign competition. For this reason trade often has been restricted by tariffs or quotas. **Tariffs** are taxes placed on imports to increase their price in the domestic market. **Quotas** are limits on the quantities of a product that may be imported.

COMPARING *Governments*

Trade in the Global Economy

Country	Trading Partners (3 largest import and export trading partners): Imports	Exports	Value of Imports (billions of U.S. dollars)	Value of Exports (billions of U.S. dollars)
United States	Canada, Japan, Mexico	Canada, Mexico, Japan	$912	$663
Japan	United States, China, South Korea	United States, Taiwan, China	$306	$413
South Korea	United States, Japan, China	United States, Japan, China	$116	$144
China	Japan, United States, Taiwan	United States, Hong Kong, Japan	$165.8	$194.9
Russia	Germany, Belarus, Ukraine	Ukraine, Germany, United States	$48.2	$75.4
Brazil	United States, Argentina, Germany	United States, Argentina, Germany	$48.7	$46.9
Jamaica	United States, European Union, Caricom*	United States, European Union, Canada	$2.7	$1.4
Cote d'Ivoire	France, United States, Italy	France, Netherlands, United States	$2.6	$3.9

*Caribbean Community and Common Market Countries

Critical Thinking The global economy is expanding as more middle- and low-income countries participate in international trade. *What generalizations can you make about the main trading partners of the countries shown here?*

Online **UPDATE** Visit gov.glencoe.com and click on ***Textbook Updates–Chapter 26*** for an update of the data.

Trade Agreements

The United States, Germany, Japan, Great Britain, and France are the world's leading trading nations. The United States imports raw materials, foods, and manufactured products. United States exports include agricultural and high-technology products and various manufactured goods.

GATT To promote international trade, 90 countries subscribed to the **General Agreement on Tariffs and Trade (GATT)** in 1947. Under the provisions of this agreement and a new GATT negotiated in 1994, member nations continue to meet to reduce or remove barriers on trade, such as tariffs. The new GATT set up a regulatory body—the World Trade Organization. In addition, emerging regional trading blocs are removing barriers to trade among participating nations. Groups of nations in Europe, Asia, and North America are developing regional economic cooperation. Two of the leading regional economic groups are the European Union (EU) and the North American Free Trade Agreement (NAFTA).

The European Union In 1957 six Western European nations—France, West Germany, Italy, the Netherlands, Belgium, and Luxembourg—agreed to move toward a common trading market called the European Economic Community (EEC). In 1967 the EEC merged with two other organizations to become the **European Community (EC).** By the late 1980s Great Britain, Ireland, Denmark, Greece, Spain, and Portugal had joined.

The goal of the EC was to remove all economic restrictions throughout the member nations. In 1985 the EC set 1992 as the target date for completion of the trading union and began the EC 92 program. Its principal aim was to sharpen Europe's economic competitiveness and to prepare for the complete monetary and political union of Europe.

In January 1993 the EC became the world's largest unified market. On November 1, 1993, the EC became the **European Union (EU).** Two years later Austria, Finland, and Sweden joined the organization. The next steps for the EU would be enlargement and economic and monetary union (EMU). When Eastern European nations began to break free of Communist governments, their new leaders recognized the value of belonging to a unified European market. Almost immediately they began negotiations to join their emerging free market economies with Western Europe. In 1996 the European Commission dispatched questionnaires to 10 applicant countries that wanted to join the EU.

Many believed that the launching of a single currency was the EU's most important political project. The "euro," the new monetary unit, was introduced in 1999. The euro would be a measure of value rather than a form of paper currency. Economic and monetary union (EMU) was viewed as a major step in European integration.

North American Trade Agreements Another large trading bloc is North America. Long an advocate of free trade, the United States negotiated with Canada and Mexico to take steps toward greater economic cooperation. The United States and Canada completed an agreement to reduce tariffs, which went into effect in 1989. During the next 10 years, this pact would eliminate most trade restrictions between the two nations.

In 1991 then-Mexican president Carlos Salinas de Gortari, seeking to improve his nation's finances, suggested talks to establish a free trade agreement with the United States. President Bush opened negotiations in 1991, and President Clinton and the leaders of Canada and Mexico concluded the North American Free Trade Agreement (NAFTA) in 1993. Trade among the three North American partners expanded rapidly. Some Americans, however, feared the loss of jobs as some businesses moved from the United States to Mexico.

Growth Leaders in Asia

Economic growth depends on several factors. Emerging economies need investment capital, stable markets, and economic freedom.

Japan's Leadership in Asia After World War II, with aid from the United States and the World Bank, Japan emerged as the dominant economy of Asia. From 1953 to 1966, Japan was an active borrower from the World Bank. By 1970 Japan reversed roles and became a major lender.

Japan's growth was the envy of the industrialized world in the 1980s. A favorable balance of trade, especially with the United States, fueled the expansion of many industries. Japan became a leader in the growth of East Asia, investing in several other nearby economies.

Japan's growth rate slowed dramatically in 1990. The nation's property and stock markets crashed, leaving banks with bad debts. Japan failed to adequately address the problem for years and eventually faced financial difficulties affecting banks, securities firms, and life-insurers.

Developing Asian Economies Several Asian countries with free market economies have rapidly industrialized in the 1990s. South Korea, Thailand, Malaysia, and Indonesia produced the world's most dynamic growth—yearly rates of more than 8 percent. By 1997, however, these nations also faced economic trouble. Unhealthy financial systems and incompetent governments scared away international investors. In South Korea the government had guided banks to make loans to strategic industries, in effect crowding out smaller businesses. As a result, bad debt threatened the country's entire banking system. South Korea as well as Indonesia turned to the International Money Fund, the World Bank, the United States, and Japan for billions of dollars of loans.

China recognized in the 1970s that private incentives were necessary for economic growth. Since 1978 its average annual per capita growth has exceeded 8 percent. By the late 1990s industrial production was growing at more than 13 percent per year. As China developed its economy, the democracies watched with cautious optimism. Economic progress seems to strengthen pressures on governments to allow greater political freedom.

At the same time, the World Bank estimates that 350 million Chinese still live in poverty. China's major cities are flooded with people from the provinces in search of jobs. Human rights violations and great income disparities are problems that China must face as it seeks to become a world economic power.

GOVERNMENT *Online*

Student Web Activity Visit the *United States Government: Democracy in Action* Web site at gov.glencoe.com and click on ***Chapter 26–Student Web Activities*** for an activity about development of economic systems.

Multinationals and the World Economy

Multinational corporations—those having divisions in more than two countries—are playing and will continue to play a role in the developing global economy.

Five Views of Multinationals How much will multinational corporations affect people around the world? One view is that corporations will be increasingly able to demand tax, regulatory, and wage concessions by threatening to move to another country. Only highly educated people or those with skills will benefit as wages remain low.

A second view is that multinationals are less attracted by low wages than by a highly educated workforce and healthy economies. Competition for foreign direct investment will lead countries to try to provide those attractions. A third view is that the mobility of multinationals will benefit all countries. The transfer of capital and technology will actually raise the standard of living in the poorer countries faster than in the wealthier ones.

The fourth view predicts uneven development. One region of the world will grow at the expense of another. The fifth view is that multinationals are not as significant a factor in world economic development as the experts believe.

Developing Nations in the World Economy

According to the Worldwatch Institute, the world economy produced $41 trillion of goods and services in 1999. However, not all nations have benefitted from global wealth. Forty-five percent of the income from this production went to only 12 percent of the world's people who live in Western industrial nations.

Uneven population growth is a factor in the growing gap between rich and poor areas. Rapid population growth in poor countries leads to overusing natural resources. It also results in the rapid expansion of cities, as people migrate from rural areas to find jobs. A world divided between rich and poor nations leads to political instability.

Developing nations look to highly industrialized countries such as the United States for models of economic growth. The industrialized countries, however, are the largest consumers of natural resources and the largest producers of wastes. Would such a model for growth be sustainable for the entire world? In 1996 the President's Council on Sustainable Development defined what **sustainable development** meant:

> *[an activity] that can be continued indefinitely without harming the environmental, economic, or social basis on which it depends and without diminishing the opportunities of future generations to enjoy the resources and a quality of life at least equal to our own.*
>
> —President's Council on Sustainable Development, 1996

International Business The reach of some multinational corporations is far and wide. Here students in Beijing enjoy an American soft drink while relaxing. ***What evidence of multinational corporations exists in your community?***

Traditional Economic Goals From the 1950s through the mid-1970s the goal of most leaders was to increase the gross domestic product (GDP) of developing nations by 5 to 7 percent each year. The idea was that big gains in GDP would "trickle down" to the poorest people.

By the mid-1990s many developing nations had achieved regular increases in their GDP. Living conditions for the poor in most countries, however, did not improve much. International organizations and developing nations had to rethink the goals of international development policy.

Today, basic human needs have become a focus of development policies. Those needs include food, shelter, health, protection, the chance to develop self-esteem, and the freedom to make choices about one's life. According to one economist:

> *"Economic development came to be redefined in terms of the reduction or elimination of poverty, inequality, and unemployment within the context of a growing economy."*
>
> —Michael Todaro

Obstacles to Development

Major obstacles to achieving the goals of development include lack of national unity, military rule, rapid population growth, poor health, and lack of capital. Until the end of World War II, developing nations were colonies of one of the great industrial powers. When the colonial rulers left, old fears and hatreds suppressed during colonial years surfaced. People's lives and loyalties in these new nations were tied to their ethnic groups, regions, or religious, racial, or language groups rather than to the new country.

Military control of national governments has slowed development. During the 1970s and 1980s, military governments controlled more than half the nations of Africa. More than two-thirds of the nations of Asia, the Middle East, and Latin America have had military governments at some time since 1945.

While the people accepted military leaders as reformers who helped end colonial rule, under military rule the portion of the national budget going to the military often increased at least 50 to 70 percent, using up money that might have gone to economic development.

A third obstacle to development is rapid population growth. More than 75 percent of the world's people live in the poorest countries, and the number is growing. The fast expansion of urban areas increases the number of difficult challenges that these governments will have to face.

In the least developed nations, life expectancy averages only 49 years compared to 75 years in many industrialized countries. Three sources of poor health in developing nations are hunger, poor water, and lack of medical care. The poorest nations have only 9 doctors per 100,000 people. Developing nations believe that the world community should initiate policies to ensure a more fair distribution of the world's resources to encourage development. Most industrialized nations believe governments should adopt free market economies and solve internal problems rather than depend on aid from the industrialized nations.

Section 4 Assessment

Checking for Understanding

1. **Main Idea** Using a graphic organizer like the one below, identify factors that affect the stability of the global economy.

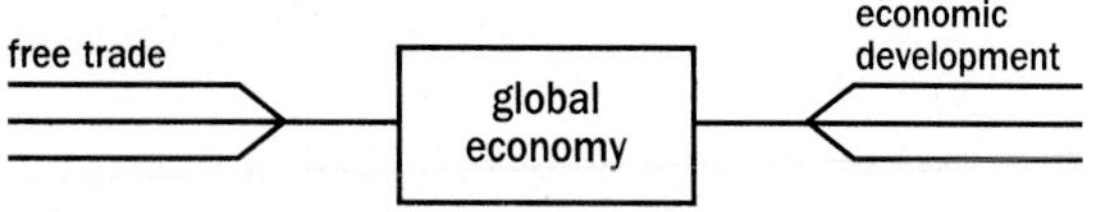

2. **Define** comparative advantage, tariffs, quotas, trading blocs.
3. **Identify** General Agreement on Tariffs and Trade (GATT), European Community (EC), European Union (EU).
4. Why do nations trade with one another?

Critical Thinking

5. **Drawing Conclusions** Which obstacle to development do you believe to be the most significant? Why?

Global Perspectives Developing nations often look to industrialized nations for models of economic growth. However, developing nations face obstacles to their economic development. Review these obstacles. Then prepare a plan for helping developing nations to overcome these obstacles and build their economies.

Making Decisions

A decision is a choice from among two or more alternatives. Decision making is a key part of citizenship. When choosing which candidate to vote for or whether to attend a public hearing, thoughtful decision makers take into account the impact of their choices on themselves and others. Following the steps below will help you make more thoughtful decisions.

Learning the Skill

1. State the situation or define the problem. Gather all the facts. Ask: Why do I have to make a decision on this matter? Whom will my decision affect?
2. List the options. Ask: What are the alternatives? How can I deal with this situation in a different way?
3. Weigh the possible outcomes. What are the positive or negative effects of each?
4. Consider your values. Values are the beliefs and ideas that are important to you. Your values should serve as your guidelines in making all decisions.
5. Make a decision and act. Use all the information gathered to make a decision. Then act on your decision.
6. Evaluate the decision. Ask: How did the outcome affect you and others? Would you make the same decision again? Why or why not?

Practicing the Skill

Answer the following questions about decision making.

1. Why should you consider more than one option when making a decision?

International economic decisions were made at a 1997 Denver, Colorado summit.

2. How will using the six steps help lessen the possible risks involved in acting on a decision?
3. What might be the result of making a decision that conflicts with your values and beliefs?

Application Activity

Read newspapers for articles about an event that affects your community, such as a decision whether to tear down a historic landmark to build a new shopping mall. Make an educated decision about the event. Explain your reasoning.

The Glencoe Skillbuilder Interactive Workbook, Level 2 provides instruction and practice in key social studies skills.

Assessment and Activities

Self-Check Quiz Visit the *United States Government: Democracy in Action* Web site at gov.glencoe.com and click on ***Chapter 26–Self-Check Quizzes*** to prepare for the chapter test.

Reviewing Key Terms

Match the following terms with each of the descriptions given below.

factors of production	**trading blocs**
newly developed nations	**coup**
command economy	**tariffs**
gross national product	**market economy**
developing nations	**quotas**

1. an economy in which the government makes most of the economic decisions
2. an economy in which consumers make most of the economic decisions
3. the resources that an economic system needs to produce goods and services
4. nations with little or no industry
5. nations recently having significant or rapid industrial growth
6. the sum of a nation's goods and services
7. a planned but sudden grab for power
8. taxes placed on imports to increase their price in the domestic market
9. limits on the quantities of a product that may be imported
10. a group of nations that trade without economic barriers

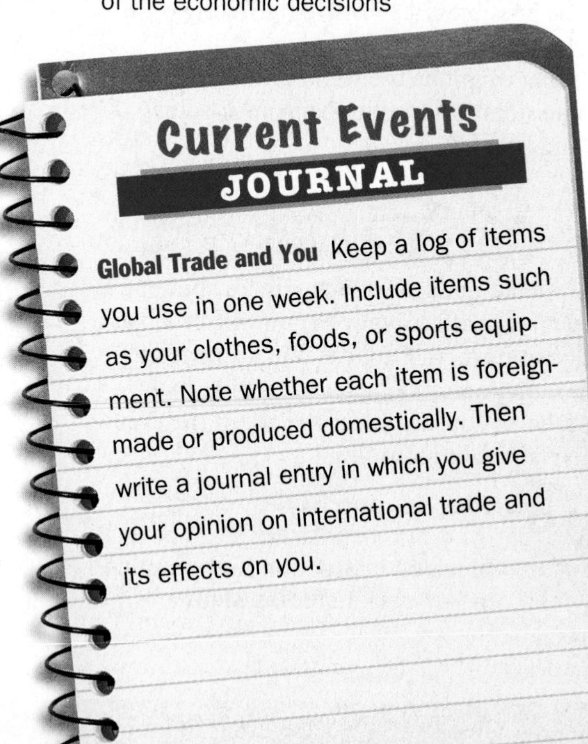

Global Trade and You Keep a log of items you use in one week. Include items such as your clothes, foods, or sports equipment. Note whether each item is foreign-made or produced domestically. Then write a journal entry in which you give your opinion on international trade and its effects on you.

Recalling Facts

1. What are the four factors of production?
2. Which amendment to the Constitution protects citizens' rights to property?
3. What is the role of competition in the free enterprise system?
4. Where are most newly developed nations located?
5. After independence, how did many African leaders try to remedy their nations' economic imbalances?
6. What industrial and agricultural problems were associated with the Soviet Union's economy?
7. What factors threaten the Russian economy today?
8. What are the causes of a lack of national unity in some developing nations?

Understanding Concepts

1. **Free Enterprise** What part of Soviet agricultural reform was similar to free enterprise?
2. **Comparative Government** Why does a communist economic system prevent the development of political parties?
3. **Global Perspectives** What are the differences between the traditional and the new economic goals to promote development in developing nations?

Critical Thinking

1. **Making Comparisons** Use a graphic organizer like the one below to compare ownership of land in a capitalist system with land ownership in a planned economy.

capitalist system	planned economy

2. **Drawing Conclusions** Why might industrialized nations such as the United States exercise influence on developing nations to develop free market economies and democracy?

Interpreting Political Cartoons Activity

1. What comparison is the cartoonist making?
2. Do you think the comparison is a valid one? Why or why not?
3. This cartoon was published in 1993. Are the issues it raises still applicable today? Explain.
4. How do you think the economic situation in a country affects its political climate?

Cooperative Learning Activity

Four Factors of Production
Organize into groups of four. Choose a consumer product, such as an automobile or CD player. Determine each of the four factors of production that went into making the product. Work with group members to create a poster that illustrates the four factors of production involved in making your chosen consumer product.

Technology Activity

Using a Word Processor Find out about the economic conditions in a developing nation. Research the major indicators of the nation's economy, such as the gross national product and major exports and imports. Also find out about the major problems in economic development that the nation faces, and planned solutions. Prepare an illustrated report of your findings. Use the graphic capabilities of your word processor to prepare graphs and charts to include.

Skill Practice Activity

Making Decisions Describe a decision that a student might face today, such as the choice to go to college or to get a job after high school. List the six steps of the decision-making process. Write the questions and information you would consider at each step and what your answers might be. Write what you think would be a wise decision.

Participating in Local Government

Nations of the world are increasingly interdependent. Find out what opportunities your community offers for individual involvement in world issues. For example, are there any organizations or programs that work to end world hunger? Find out how you might contribute to such efforts.

Reference Handbook

Contents

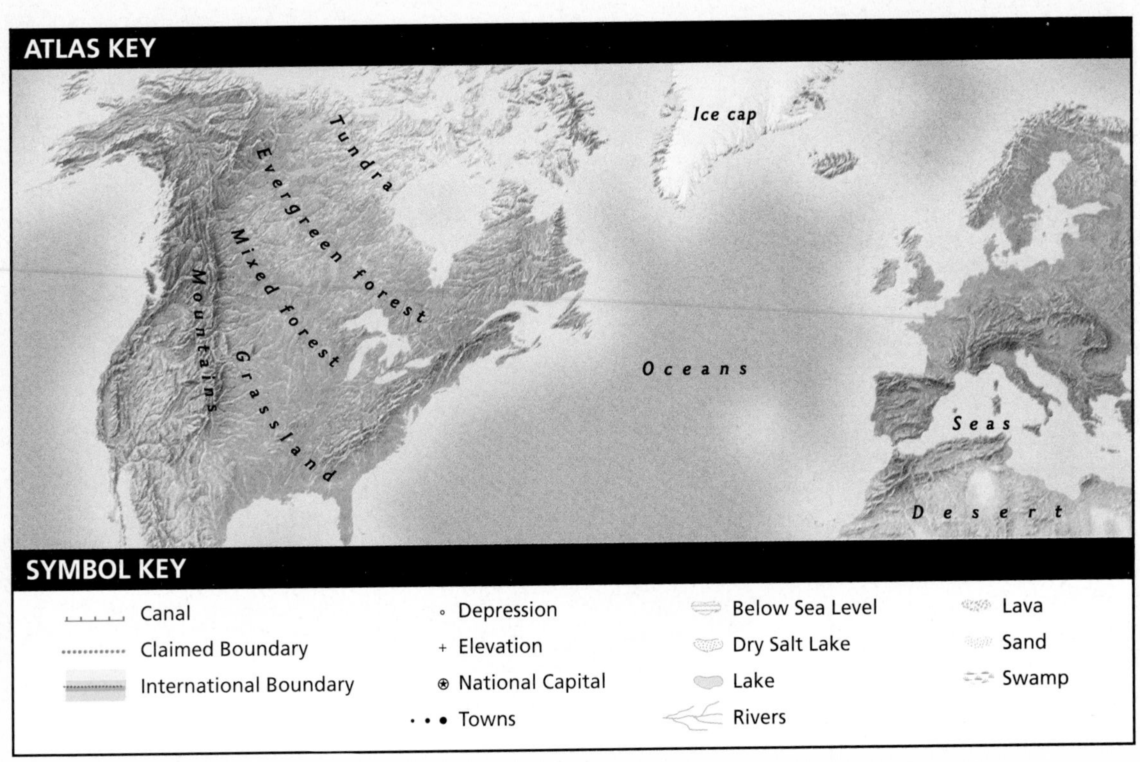

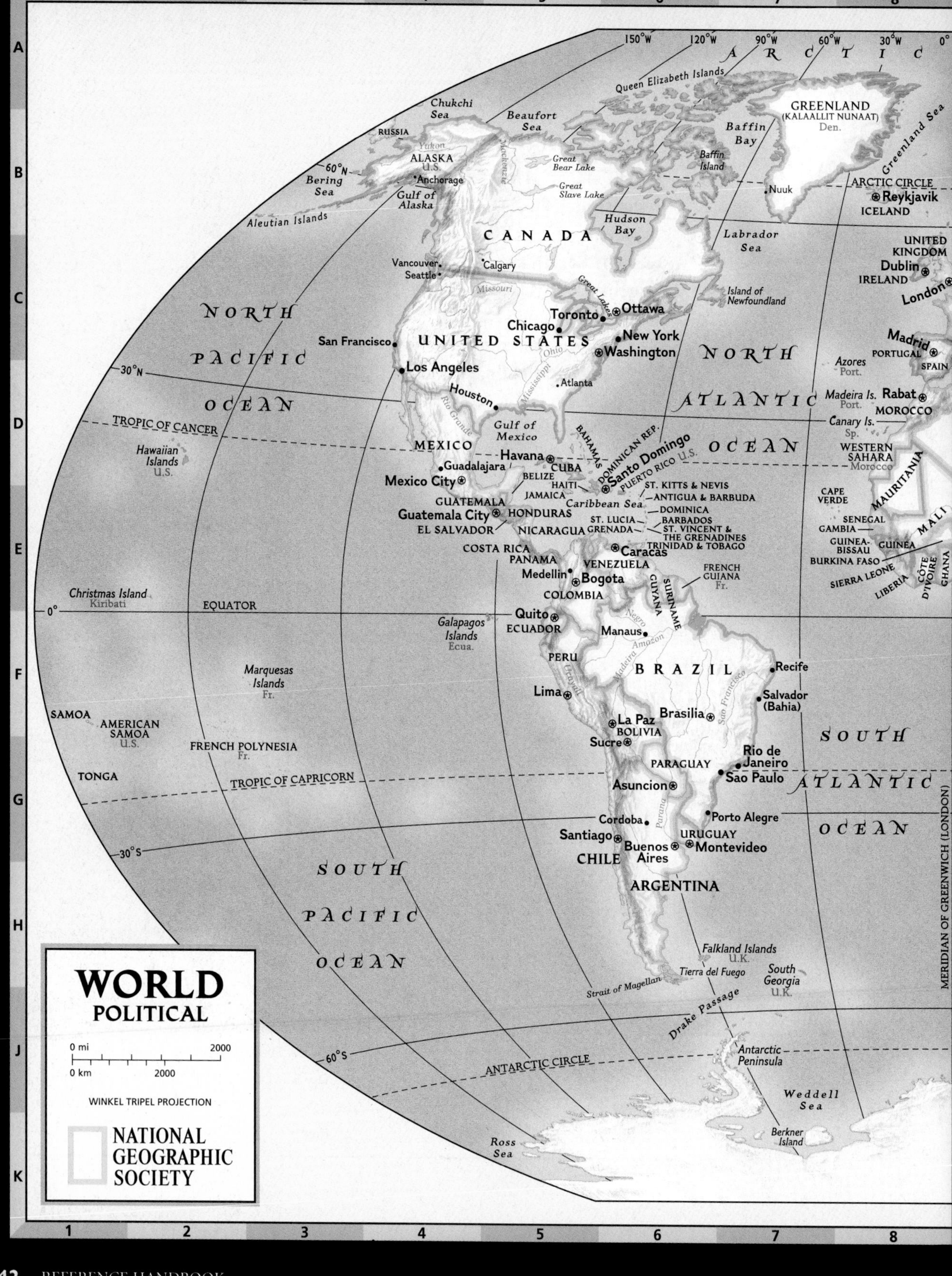

WORLD
POLITICAL
0 mi 2000
0 km 2000
WINKEL TRIPEL PROJECTION
NATIONAL GEOGRAPHIC SOCIETY
NORTH PACIFIC OCEAN
SOUTH PACIFIC OCEAN
NORTH ATLANTIC OCEAN
SOUTH ATLANTIC OCEAN
ARCTIC
CANADA
UNITED STATES
MEXICO
GREENLAND (KALAALLIT NUNAAT) Den.
ALASKA U.S.
RUSSIA
ICELAND
UNITED KINGDOM
IRELAND
PORTUGAL
SPAIN
MOROCCO
WESTERN SAHARA Morocco
MAURITANIA
MALI
CAPE VERDE
SENEGAL
GAMBIA
GUINEA-BISSAU
GUINEA
BURKINA FASO
SIERRA LEONE
LIBERIA
CÔTE D'IVOIRE
GHANA
CUBA
BAHAMAS
DOMINICAN REP.
PUERTO RICO U.S.
HAITI
JAMAICA
BELIZE
GUATEMALA
HONDURAS
EL SALVADOR
NICARAGUA
COSTA RICA
PANAMA
ST. KITTS & NEVIS
ANTIGUA & BARBUDA
DOMINICA
ST. LUCIA
BARBADOS
GRENADA
ST. VINCENT & THE GRENADINES
TRINIDAD & TOBAGO
VENEZUELA
COLOMBIA
GUYANA
SURINAME
FRENCH GUIANA Fr.
ECUADOR
PERU
BRAZIL
BOLIVIA
PARAGUAY
CHILE
ARGENTINA
URUGUAY
Reykjavik
Dublin
London
Madrid
Rabat
Nuuk
Anchorage
Vancouver
Seattle
Calgary
Toronto
Ottawa
Chicago
New York
Washington
San Francisco
Los Angeles
Atlanta
Houston
Havana
Santo Domingo
Guadalajara
Mexico City
Guatemala City
Caracas
Medellín
Bogota
Quito
Manaus
Recife
Salvador (Bahia)
Lima
Brasilia
La Paz
Sucre
Rio de Janeiro
Sao Paulo
Asuncion
Porto Alegre
Cordoba
Santiago
Buenos Aires
Montevideo
Chukchi Sea
Beaufort Sea
Bering Sea
Gulf of Alaska
Aleutian Islands
Queen Elizabeth Islands
Baffin Bay
Baffin Island
Greenland Sea
Great Bear Lake
Great Slave Lake
Hudson Bay
Labrador Sea
Island of Newfoundland
Great Lakes
Yukon
Mackenzie
Missouri
Ohio
Mississippi
Rio Grande
Gulf of Mexico
Caribbean Sea
Azores Port.
Madeira Is. Port.
Canary Is. Sp.
Hawaiian Islands U.S.
Christmas Island Kiribati
Galapagos Islands Ecua.
Marquesas Islands Fr.
SAMOA
AMERICAN SAMOA U.S.
FRENCH POLYNESIA Fr.
TONGA
Negro
Amazon
Madeira
Ucayali
Sao Francisco
Parana
Falkland Islands U.K.
Tierra del Fuego
South Georgia U.K.
Strait of Magellan
Drake Passage
Antarctic Peninsula
Weddell Sea
Berkner Island
Ross Sea
ARCTIC CIRCLE
TROPIC OF CANCER
EQUATOR
TROPIC OF CAPRICORN
ANTARCTIC CIRCLE
MERIDIAN OF GREENWICH (LONDON)
150°W
120°W
90°W
60°W
30°W
0°
60°N
30°N
0°
30°S
60°S
1 2 3 4 5 6 7 8
A B C D E F G H J K

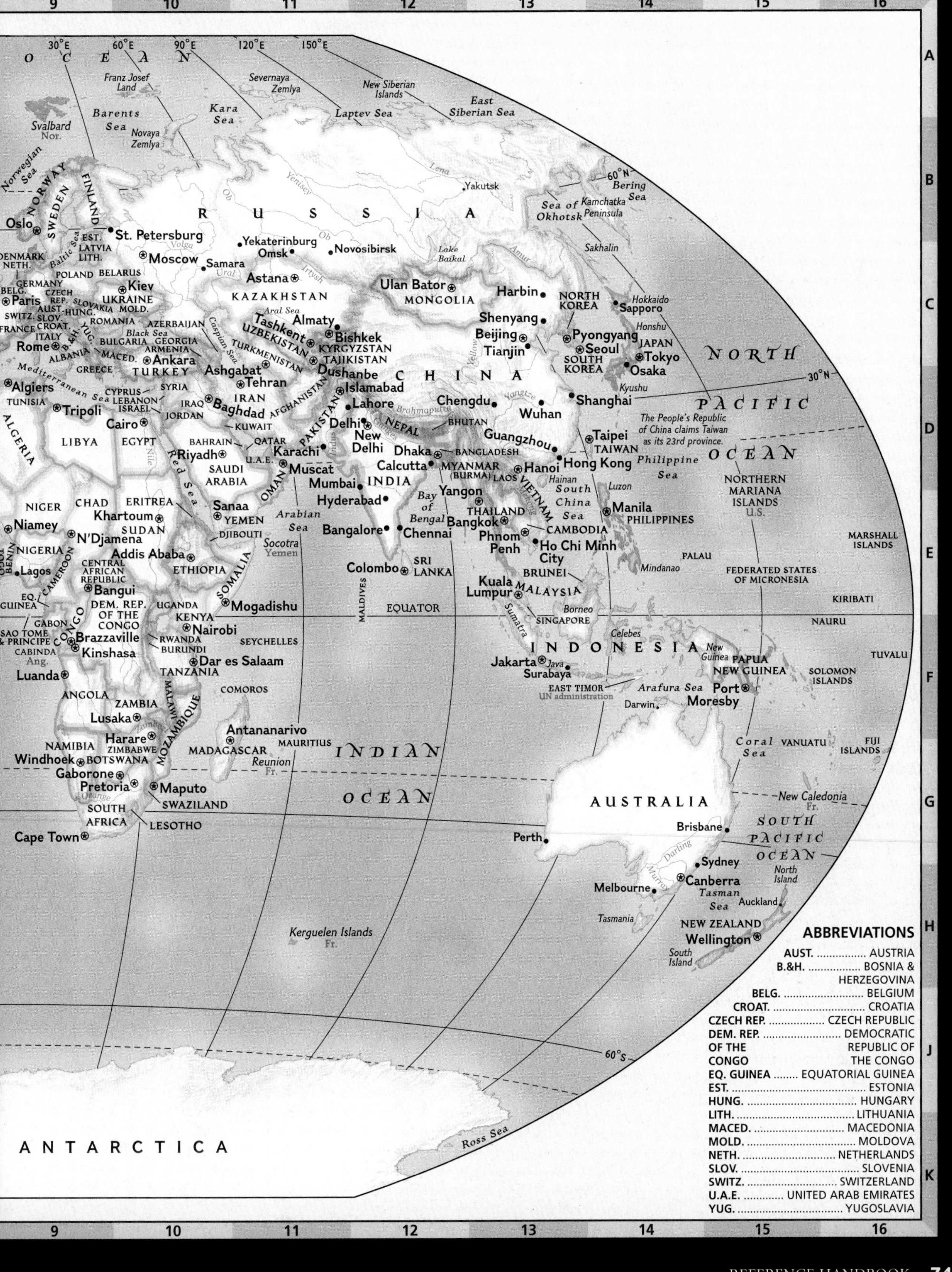
9
10
11
12
13
14
15
16
A
B
C
D
E
F
G
H
J
K
30°E
60°E
90°E
120°E
150°E
60°N
30°N
60°S
O C E A N
Franz Josef Land
Severnaya Zemlya
New Siberian Islands
East Siberian Sea
Laptev Sea
Kara Sea
Barents Sea
Svalbard Nor.
Novaya Zemlya
Norwegian Sea
NORWAY
SWEDEN
FINLAND
Oslo
EST.
LATVIA
LITH.
St. Petersburg
Baltic Sea
DENMARK
NETH.
Moscow
Samara
Volga
Ural
Yekaterinburg
Omsk
Novosibirsk
Ob
Yenisey
Lena
Yakutsk
Irtysh
Lake Baikal
Amur
Sea of Okhotsk
Kamchatka Peninsula
Bering Sea
Sakhalin
R U S S I A
POLAND
BELARUS
GERMANY
BELG.
CZECH REP.
SLOVAKIA
Paris
Kiev
UKRAINE
MOLD.
SWITZ.
AUST.
HUNG.
SLOV.
CROAT.
B.&H.
YUG.
ROMANIA
FRANCE
ITALY
Rome
ALBANIA
MACED.
BULGARIA
Black Sea
GEORGIA
ARMENIA
AZERBAIJAN
Ankara
TURKEY
GREECE
Astana
KAZAKHSTAN
Aral Sea
Caspian Sea
Tashkent
UZBEKISTAN
TURKMENISTAN
Almaty
Bishkek
KYRGYZSTAN
TAJIKISTAN
Ashgabat
Dushanbe
Tehran
IRAN
Ulan Bator
MONGOLIA
Harbin
NORTH KOREA
Hokkaido
Sapporo
Shenyang
Beijing
Tianjin
Yellow
Pyongyang
Seoul
SOUTH KOREA
Honshu
JAPAN
Tokyo
Osaka
Kyushu
C H I N A
Mediterranean Sea
Algiers
TUNISIA
CYPRUS
SYRIA
LEBANON
ISRAEL
IRAQ
Baghdad
JORDAN
AFGHANISTAN
Islamabad
Lahore
PAKISTAN
Brahmaputra
Chengdu
Yangtze
Wuhan
Shanghai
N O R T H
P A C I F I C
O C E A N
The People's Republic of China claims Taiwan as its 23rd province.
Tripoli
ALGERIA
Cairo
LIBYA
EGYPT
Nile
KUWAIT
BAHRAIN
QATAR
U.A.E.
Riyadh
SAUDI ARABIA
Red Sea
Karachi
Indus
Delhi
New Delhi
Ganges
NEPAL
BHUTAN
Guangzhou
Taipei
TAIWAN
Hong Kong
Philippine Sea
Dhaka
BANGLADESH
Calcutta
MYANMAR (BURMA)
LAOS
Hanoi
VIETNAM
Hainan
OMAN
Muscat
Mumbai
INDIA
Hyderabad
Bay of Bengal
Yangon
Mekong
South China Sea
Luzon
NORTHERN MARIANA ISLANDS U.S.
NIGER
CHAD
ERITREA
Khartoum
SUDAN
Sanaa
YEMEN
Arabian Sea
Bangalore
Chennai
THAILAND
Bangkok
CAMBODIA
Phnom Penh
Ho Chi Minh City
Manila
PHILIPPINES
Niamey
N'Djamena
DJIBOUTI
Socotra Yemen
MARSHALL ISLANDS
BENIN
TOGO
NIGERIA
CAMEROON
Addis Ababa
ETHIOPIA
SOMALIA
Colombo
SRI LANKA
PALAU
Mindanao
FEDERATED STATES OF MICRONESIA
BRUNEI
Lagos
CENTRAL AFRICAN REPUBLIC
Bangui
Kuala Lumpur
MALAYSIA
EQ. GUINEA
DEM. REP. OF THE CONGO
UGANDA
Mogadishu
MALDIVES
EQUATOR
Borneo
KIRIBATI
KENYA
Nairobi
Sumatra
SINGAPORE
NAURU
GABON
CONGO
SAO TOME & PRINCIPE
Brazzaville
RWANDA
BURUNDI
SEYCHELLES
Celebes
CABINDA Ang.
Kinshasa
Dar es Salaam
TANZANIA
I N D O N E S I A
New Guinea
PAPUA NEW GUINEA
TUVALU
Jakarta
Java
Surabaya
Luanda
SOLOMON ISLANDS
ANGOLA
COMOROS
EAST TIMOR UN administration
Arafura Sea
Port Moresby
Darwin
ZAMBIA
MALAWI
Lusaka
Zambezi
Antananarivo
MOZAMBIQUE
NAMIBIA
Harare
ZIMBABWE
MAURITIUS
I N D I A N
Coral Sea
VANUATU
FIJI ISLANDS
Windhoek
BOTSWANA
MADAGASCAR
Reunion Fr.
Gaborone
Pretoria
Maputo
Orange
O C E A N
New Caledonia Fr.
SOUTH AFRICA
SWAZILAND
AUSTRALIA
LESOTHO
Brisbane
SOUTH PACIFIC OCEAN
Cape Town
Perth
Darling
Sydney
Murray
Canberra
North Island
Melbourne
Tasman Sea
Auckland
Tasmania
NEW ZEALAND
Kerguelen Islands Fr.
Wellington
South Island
ANTARCTICA
Ross Sea
ABBREVIATIONS
AUST. .... AUSTRIA
B.&H. .... BOSNIA & HERZEGOVINA
BELG. .... BELGIUM
CROAT. .... CROATIA
CZECH REP. .... CZECH REPUBLIC
DEM. REP. OF THE CONGO .... DEMOCRATIC REPUBLIC OF THE CONGO
EQ. GUINEA .... EQUATORIAL GUINEA
EST. .... ESTONIA
HUNG. .... HUNGARY
LITH. .... LITHUANIA
MACED. .... MACEDONIA
MOLD. .... MOLDOVA
NETH. .... NETHERLANDS
SLOV. .... SLOVENIA
SWITZ. .... SWITZERLAND
U.A.E. .... UNITED ARAB EMIRATES
YUG. .... YUGOSLAVIA

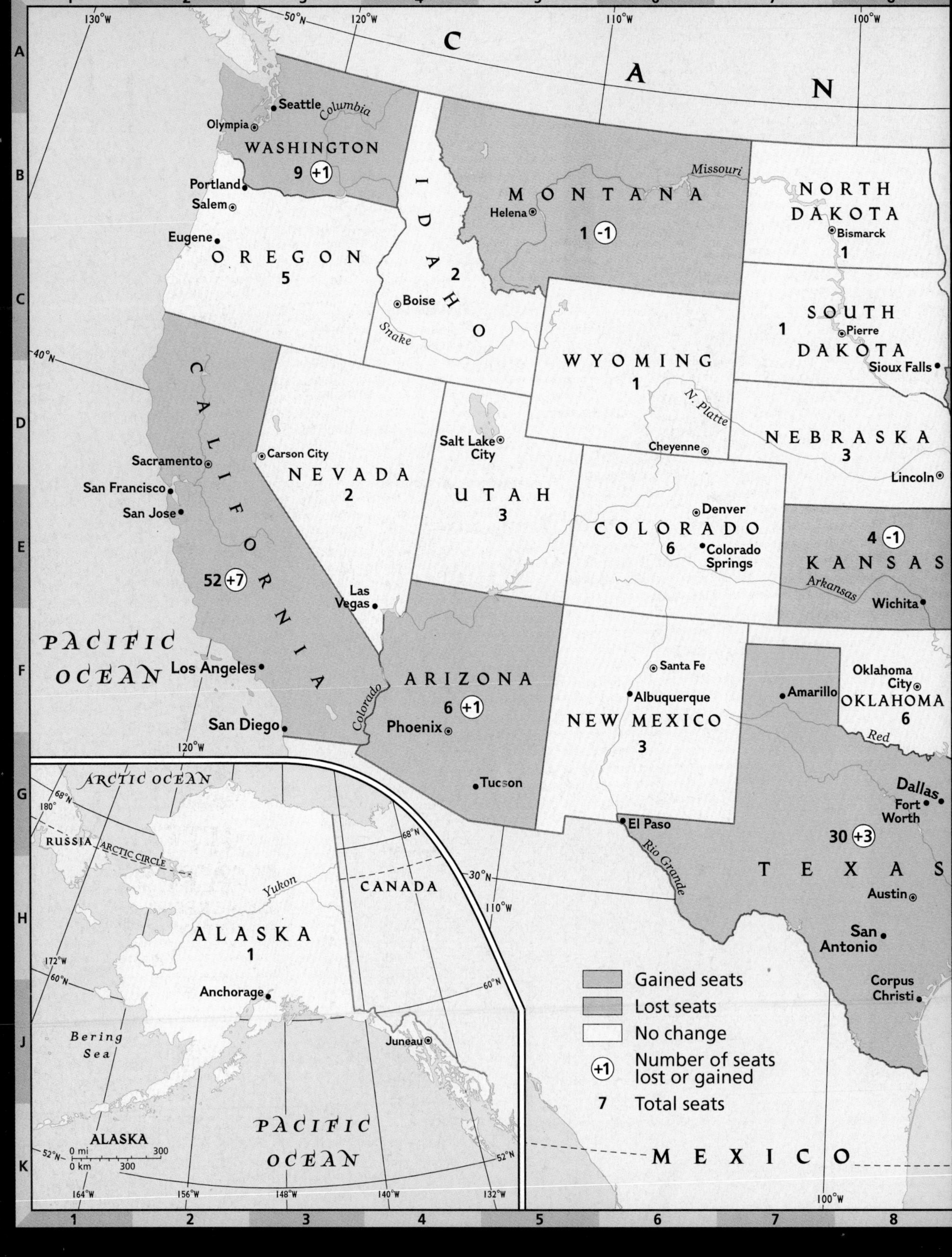

CANADA
PACIFIC OCEAN
WASHINGTON
9 +1
Seattle
Olympia
Columbia
OREGON
5
Portland
Salem
Eugene
IDAHO
2
Boise
Snake
MONTANA
1 -1
Helena
Missouri
NORTH DAKOTA
1
Bismarck
SOUTH DAKOTA
1
Pierre
Sioux Falls
WYOMING
1
Cheyenne
N. Platte
NEBRASKA
3
Lincoln
CALIFORNIA
52 +7
Sacramento
San Francisco
San Jose
Los Angeles
San Diego
NEVADA
2
Carson City
Las Vegas
UTAH
3
Salt Lake City
COLORADO
6
Denver
Colorado Springs
KANSAS
4 -1
Wichita
Arkansas
ARIZONA
6 +1
Phoenix
Tucson
Colorado
NEW MEXICO
3
Santa Fe
Albuquerque
OKLAHOMA
6
Oklahoma City
Red
TEXAS
30 +3
Amarillo
El Paso
Rio Grande
Dallas
Fort Worth
Austin
San Antonio
Corpus Christi
MEXICO
ALASKA
1
Anchorage
Juneau
ARCTIC OCEAN
RUSSIA
ARCTIC CIRCLE
Yukon
Bering Sea
ALASKA
0 mi 300
0 km 300
Gained seats
Lost seats
No change
+1 Number of seats lost or gained
7 Total seats

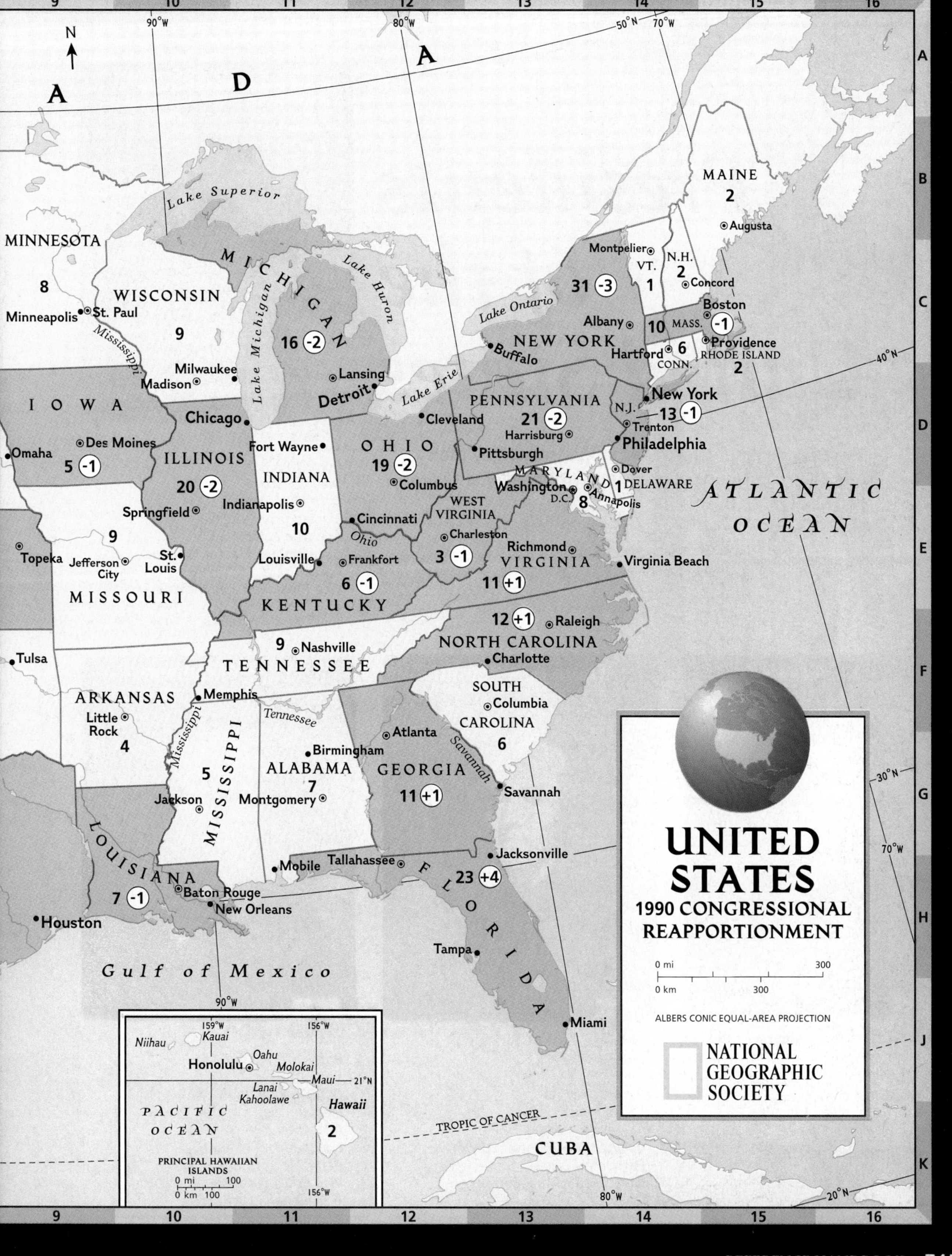
UNITED STATES
1990 CONGRESSIONAL REAPPORTIONMENT
ALBERS CONIC EQUAL-AREA PROJECTION
NATIONAL GEOGRAPHIC SOCIETY
MAINE 2
N.H. 2
VT. 1
31 (-3) NEW YORK
10 MASS. (-1)
6 CONN.
RHODE ISLAND 2
N.J. 13 (-1)
PENNSYLVANIA 21 (-2)
MARYLAND 8
DELAWARE 1
OHIO 19 (-2)
MICHIGAN 16 (-2)
INDIANA 10
ILLINOIS 20 (-2)
WISCONSIN 9
MINNESOTA 8
IOWA 5 (-1)
MISSOURI 9
KENTUCKY 6 (-1)
WEST VIRGINIA 3 (-1)
VIRGINIA 11 (+1)
NORTH CAROLINA 12 (+1)
SOUTH CAROLINA 6
TENNESSEE 9
ARKANSAS 4
MISSISSIPPI 5
ALABAMA 7
GEORGIA 11 (+1)
FLORIDA 23 (+4)
LOUISIANA 7 (-1)
Hawaii 2
ATLANTIC OCEAN
Gulf of Mexico
PACIFIC OCEAN
PRINCIPAL HAWAIIAN ISLANDS
CUBA
TROPIC OF CANCER

Presidents of the United States

The Presidents are portrayed in this section by their official White House portrait (except Presidents Clinton and George W. Bush).

** The Republican Party during this period developed into today's Democratic Party. Today's Republican Party originated in 1854.

George Washington

1 1789–1797

Born: 1732
Died: 1799
Born in: Virginia
Elected from: Virginia
Age when elected: 56
Occupations: Planter, Soldier
Party: None
Vice President: John Adams

John Adams

2 1797–1801

Born: 1735
Died: 1826
Born in: Massachusetts
Elected from: Massachusetts
Age when elected: 61
Occupations: Teacher, Lawyer
Party: Federalist
Vice President: Thomas Jefferson

Thomas Jefferson

3 1801–1809

Born: 1743
Died: 1826
Born in: Virginia
Elected from: Virginia
Age when elected: 57
Occupations: Planter, Lawyer
Party: Republican**
Vice Presidents: Aaron Burr, George Clinton

James Madison

4 1809–1817

Born: 1751
Died: 1836
Born in: Virginia
Elected from: Virginia
Age when elected: 57
Occupation: Planter
Party: Republican**
Vice Presidents: George Clinton, Elbridge Gerry

James Monroe

5

1817–1825

Born: 1758
Died: 1831
Born in: Virginia
Elected from: Virginia
Age when elected: 58
Occupation: Lawyer
Party: Republican**
Vice President: Daniel D. Tompkins

John Quincy Adams

6

1825–1829

Born: 1767
Died: 1848
Born in: Massachusetts
Elected from: Massachusetts
Age when elected: 57
Occupation: Lawyer
Party: Republican**
Vice President: John C. Calhoun

Andrew Jackson

7

1829–1837

Born: 1767
Died: 1845
Born in: South Carolina
Elected from: Tennessee
Age when elected: 61
Occupations: Lawyer, Soldier
Party: Democratic
Vice Presidents: John C. Calhoun, Martin Van Buren

Martin Van Buren

8

1837–1841

Born: 1782
Died: 1862
Born in: New York
Elected from: New York
Age when elected: 54
Occupation: Lawyer
Party: Democratic
Vice President: Richard M. Johnson

William H. Harrison

9

1841

Born: 1773
Died: 1841
Born in: Virginia
Elected from: Ohio
Age when elected: 67
Occupations: Soldier, Planter
Party: Whig
Vice President: John Tyler

John Tyler

10

1841–1845

Born: 1790
Died: 1862
Born in: Virginia
Elected as V.P. from: Virginia
Succeeded Harrison
Age when became President: 51
Occupation: Lawyer
Party: Whig
Vice President: None

James K. Polk

11 1845–1849

Born: 1795
Died: 1849
Born in: North Carolina
Elected from: Tennessee
Age when elected: 49
Occupation: Lawyer
Party: Democratic
Vice President: George M. Dallas

Zachary Taylor

12 1849–1850

Born: 1784
Died: 1850
Born in: Virginia
Elected from: Louisiana
Age when elected: 63
Occupation: Soldier
Party: Whig
Vice President: Millard Fillmore

Millard Fillmore

13 1850–1853

Born: 1800
Died: 1874
Born in: New York
Elected as V.P. from: New York
Succeeded Taylor
Age when became President: 50
Occupation: Lawyer
Party: Whig
Vice President: None

Franklin Pierce

14 1853–1857

Born: 1804
Died: 1869
Born in: New Hampshire
Elected from: New Hampshire
Age when elected: 47
Occupation: Lawyer
Party: Democratic
Vice President: William R. King

James Buchanan

15 1857–1861

Born: 1791
Died: 1868
Born in: Pennsylvania
Elected from: Pennsylvania
Age when elected: 65
Occupation: Lawyer
Party: Democratic
Vice President: John C. Breckinridge

Abraham Lincoln

16 1861–1865

Born: 1809
Died: 1865
Born in: Kentucky
Elected from: Illinois
Age when elected: 51
Occupation: Lawyer
Party: Republican
Vice Presidents: Hannibal Hamlin, Andrew Johnson

Andrew Johnson

17 **1865–1869**

Born: 1808
Died: 1875
Born in: North Carolina
Elected as V.P. from: Tennessee
Age when became President: 55
Succeeded Lincoln
Occupation: Tailor
Party: Republican
Vice President: None

Ulysses S. Grant

18 **1869–1877**

Born: 1822
Died: 1885
Born in: Ohio
Elected from: Illinois
Age when elected: 46
Occupations: Farmer, Soldier
Party: Republican
Vice Presidents: Schuyler Colfax, Henry Wilson

Rutherford B. Hayes

19 **1877–1881**

Born: 1822
Died: 1893
Born in: Ohio
Elected from: Ohio
Age when elected: 54
Occupation: Lawyer
Party: Republican
Vice President: William A. Wheeler

James A. Garfield

20 **1881**

Born: 1831
Died: 1881
Born in: Ohio
Elected from: Ohio
Age when elected: 48
Occupations: Laborer, Professor
Party: Republican
Vice President: Chester A. Arthur

Chester A. Arthur

21 **1881–1885**

Born: 1830
Died: 1886
Born in: Vermont
Elected as V.P. from: New York
Succeeded Garfield
Age when became President: 50
Occupations: Teacher, Lawyer
Party: Republican
Vice President: None

Grover Cleveland

22 24 **1885–89, 1893–97**

Born: 1837 ***Died:*** 1908
Born in: New Jersey
Elected from: New York
Age when elected: 47; 55
Occupation: Lawyer
Party: Democratic
Vice Presidents: Thomas A. Hendricks, Adlai E. Stevenson

Presidents of the United States

Benjamin Harrison

23 **1889–1893**

Born: 1833
Died: 1901
Born in: Ohio
Elected from: Indiana
Age when elected: 55
Occupation: Lawyer
Party: Republican
Vice President: Levi P. Morton

William McKinley

25 **1897–1901**

Born: 1843
Died: 1901
Born in: Ohio
Elected from: Ohio
Age when elected: 53
Occupations: Teacher, Lawyer
Party: Republican
Vice Presidents: Garret Hobart, Theodore Roosevelt

Theodore Roosevelt

26 **1901–1909**

Born: 1858
Died: 1919
Born in: New York
Elected as V.P. from: New York
Succeeded McKinley
Age when became President: 42
Occupations: Historian, Rancher
Party: Republican
Vice President: Charles W. Fairbanks

William H. Taft

27 **1909–1913**

Born: 1857
Died: 1930
Born in: Ohio
Elected from: Ohio
Age when elected: 51
Occupation: Lawyer
Party: Republican
Vice President: James S. Sherman

Woodrow Wilson

28 **1913–1921**

Born: 1856
Died: 1924
Born in: Virginia
Elected from: New Jersey
Age when elected: 55
Occupation: College Professor
Party: Democratic
Vice President: Thomas R. Marshall

Warren G. Harding

29 **1921–1923**

Born: 1865
Died: 1923
Born in: Ohio
Elected from: Ohio
Age when elected: 55
Occupations: Newspaper Editor, Publisher
Party: Republican
Vice President: Calvin Coolidge

Calvin Coolidge

30 **1923–1929**

Born: 1872
Died: 1933
Born in: Vermont
Elected as V.P. from: Massachusetts
Succeeded Harding
Age when became President: 51
Occupation: Lawyer
Party: Republican
Vice President: Charles G. Dawes

Herbert C. Hoover

31 **1929–1933**

Born: 1874
Died: 1964
Born in: Iowa
Elected from: California
Age when elected: 54
Occupation: Engineer
Party: Republican
Vice President: Charles Curtis

Franklin D. Roosevelt

32 **1933–1945**

Born: 1882
Died: 1945
Born in: New York
Elected from: New York
Age when elected: 50
Occupation: Lawyer
Party: Democratic
Vice Presidents: John N. Garner, Henry A. Wallace, Harry S Truman

Harry S. Truman

33 **1945–1953**

Born: 1884
Died: 1972
Born in: Missouri
Elected as V.P. from: Missouri
Succeeded Roosevelt
Age when became President: 60
Occupations: Clerk, Farmer
Party: Democratic
Vice President: Alben W. Barkley

Dwight D. Eisenhower

34 **1953–1961**

Born: 1890
Died: 1969
Born in: Texas
Elected from: New York
Age when elected: 62
Occupation: Soldier
Party: Republican
Vice President: Richard M. Nixon

John F. Kennedy

35 **1961–1963**

Born: 1917
Died: 1963
Born in: Massachusetts
Elected from: Massachusetts
Age when elected: 43
Occupations: Author, Reporter
Party: Democratic
Vice President: Lyndon B. Johnson

Presidents of the United States

Lyndon B. Johnson

36 **1963–1969**

Born: 1908
Died: 1973
Born in: Texas
Elected as V.P. from: Texas
Succeeded Kennedy
Age when became President: 55
Occupation: Teacher
Party: Democratic
Vice President: Hubert H. Humphrey

Richard M. Nixon

37 **1969–1974**

Born: 1913
Died: 1994
Born in: California
Elected from: New York
Age when elected: 55
Occupation: Lawyer
Party: Republican
Vice Presidents: Spiro T. Agnew, Gerald R. Ford

Gerald R. Ford

38 **1974–1977**

Born: 1913
Born in: Nebraska
Appointed by Nixon as V.P. upon Agnew's resignation; assumed presidency upon Nixon's resignation
Age when became President: 61
Occupation: Lawyer
Party: Republican
Vice President: Nelson A. Rockefeller

James E. Carter, Jr.

39 **1977–1981**

Born: 1924
Born in: Georgia
Elected from: Georgia
Age when elected: 52
Occupations: Business, Farmer
Party: Democratic
Vice President: Walter F. Mondale

Ronald W. Reagan

40 **1981–1989**

Born: 1911
Born in: Illinois
Elected from: California
Age when elected: 69
Occupations: Actor, Lecturer
Party: Republican
Vice President: George H.W. Bush

George H.W. Bush

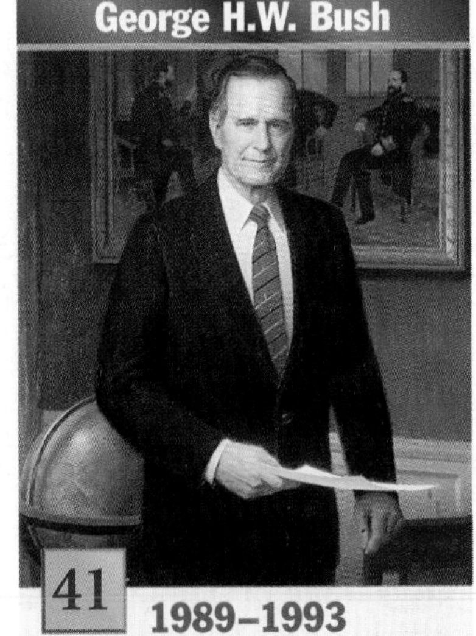

41 **1989–1993**

Born: 1924
Born in: Massachusetts
Elected from: Texas
Age when elected: 64
Occupation: Business
Party: Republican
Vice President: J. Danforth Quayle

William J. Clinton

42

1993–2001

Born: 1946
Born in: Arkansas
Elected from: Arkansas
Age when elected: 46
Occupation: Lawyer
Party: Democratic
Vice President: Albert Gore, Jr.

George W. Bush

43

2001–

Born: 1946
Born in: Connecticut
Elected from: Texas
Age when elected: 54
Occupation: CEO
Party: Republican
Vice President: Richard Cheney

THE WHITE HOUSE . . .
The President's Home

White House Statistics

3 Elevators
5 Major Floors with:
2 Basements
7 Staircases
12 Chimneys
32 Bathrooms
132 Rooms
160 Windows
412 Doors

White House Technology Firsts

1834 Indoor Plumbing
1845 Central Heating
1848 Gas Lighting
1866 Telegraph
1877 Telephone
1891 Electricity
1921 Radio
1926 Electric Refrigerator
1933 Air Conditioning
1942 Bomb Shelter
1947 Television
1979 Computer

Did You Know?

- ***The first baby born in the White House*** was Thomas Jefferson's grandson in 1806.
- ***The first White House wedding held*** was for Dolley Madison's sister in 1812.
- ***General Lafayette visited the White House in 1825*** with his pet alligator, which he kept in the East Room.
- ***Cows grazed on the front lawn of the White House*** up until 1913.
- ***The only president married in the White House*** was Grover Cleveland, in 1886.

Supreme Court Case Summaries

The following case summaries explain the significance of all Supreme Court cases mentioned in the text narrative, except those featured in Supreme Court Cases to Debate.

Abington School District v. Schempp and Murray v. Curlett (1963) struck down a Pennsylvania statute requiring public schools in the state to begin each school day with Bible readings and recitation of the Lord's Prayer. Once again the Supreme Court ruled that the business of government is not to craft and then mandate religious exercises. It held that the establishment clause leaves religious beliefs and religious practices to each individual's choice and expressly commands that government not intrude into this decision-making process.

Adarand Constructors, Inc. v. Pena (1995) announced a major shift in the way the Supreme Court viewed federal affirmative-action programs. Before this case, courts did not give the same level of scrutiny to federal affirmative-actions programs as was given to state and local programs. After this case, all government affirmative-action programs are held to the same standard—they must be justified by a compelling interest.

Adderly v. Florida (1966) again applied the time-place-and-manner rationale. The Supreme Court held that demonstrators could be barred from demonstrating on public grounds near a jail. In so holding, the Court also pointed out that these grounds were not ordinarily open to the public.

Allegheny County v. ACLU (1989) held that a crèche (a Nativity scene) accompanied by a banner reading "Glory to God in the Highest" and centrally displayed in a city/county building violated the establishment clause because it endorsed a particular religious viewpoint.

Arizona v. Fulminante (1991) held that a confession given by one prison inmate, Oreste Fulminante, to another inmate, Anthony Sarivola, in exchange for Sarivola's promise of protection, a confession that Sarivola passed on to police, was involuntary and so could not be used as evidence at Fulminante's later trial for murder.

Arkansas v. Sanders (1979) held that a warrant was required to search luggage taken from a lawfully stopped automobile. The Supreme Court explained that a law enforcement emergency was necessary to dispense with the Fourth Amendment's warrant requirement. Because the search was unlawful, the evidence seized was inadmissible under the exclusionary rule (see *Mapp* v. *Ohio* discussed below).

Baker v. Carr (1962) established that federal courts can hear suits seeking to force state authorities to redraw electoral districts. In this case, the plaintiffs wanted the population of each district to be roughly equal to the population in all other districts. The plaintiffs claimed that the votes of voters in the least populous districts counted as much or more than the votes of voters in the most populous districts and that such an imbalance denied them equal protection of the laws. Before this case, it was thought that federal courts had no authority under the Constitution to decide issues of malapportionment.

Barron v. Baltimore (1833) held that the Fifth Amendment's provision—government must pay if it takes private property for public use—did not apply to the states, but only to the federal government. At the time, the decision supported the view that the Bill of Rights as a whole applied only to the federal government. However, the Supreme Court in subsequent decisions firmly established that most of the rights contained in the Bill of Rights apply to all levels of government—states, counties, cities and towns, as well as to government agencies such as local school boards. In other words, this case has been effectively overruled by cases which apply Fourteenth Amendment protections to the Bill of Rights.

***Bethel School District* v. *Fraser* (1986)** retreated from the expansive view of the First Amendment rights of public school students found in *Tinker* (see below). Here the Supreme Court held that a public high school student did not have a First Amendment right to give a sexually suggestive speech at a school-sponsored assembly, and upheld the three-day suspension of the student who made the speech. In deciding the case, the Court made it clear that students have only a limited right of free speech. According to the Court, a school does not have to tolerate student speech that is inconsistent with its educational mission, even if the same speech would be protected elsewhere.

***Betts* v. *Brady* (1942)** refused to extend the holding of *Powell* v. *Alabama* (see below) to noncapital, i.e., non-death penalty, cases. In this case, the Supreme Court held that poor defendants in noncapital cases are not entitled to an attorney at government expense.

***Bigelow* v. *Virginia* (1975)** established for the first time that commercial speech—speech that proposes a commercial or business transaction—is protected by the First Amendment. The Court held that the Virginia courts had erred because "pure speech" rather than conduct was involved in the advertising.

***Board of Education* v. *Allen* (1968)** upheld a state program that lent state-approved, secular textbooks to religious schools against an establishment clause (U.S. Const. amend. I, cl. 1) challenge. The Supreme Court reasoned that the law had a valid secular purpose—teaching the state's secular curriculum—and that the primary effect of the program neither advanced nor inhibited religion.

***Brandenburg* v. *Ohio* (1969)** overruled *Whitney* v. *California* (see below). In this case, the Supreme Court held that laws that punish people for advocating social change through violence violate the First Amendment. The Court explained that advocacy of an idea, even an idea of violence, is protected by the First Amendment. What is not protected is inciting people to engage in immediate lawless conduct. The Court then reversed the conviction of a member of the Ku Klux Klan for holding a rally and making strong derogatory statements against African Americans and Jews.

***Branzburg* v. *Hayes* (1972)** established that the press may be required to give information in their possession to law enforcement authorities. In this case the Supreme Court upheld findings of contempt against three journalists who refused to testify before grand juries investigating criminal activity. The Court recognized that an effective press must be able to keep the identity of news sources confidential but concluded that news-source confidentiality must yield to the needs of law enforcement.

***Braswell* v. *United States* (1988)** held that the Fifth Amendment's protection against self-incrimination does not extend to an individual who is compelled by court order to surrender a corporation's records. First, the Supreme Court explained that the self-incrimination protection belongs only to an individual. Because a corporation is not an individual, it does not qualify for the protection. Second, the Court pointed out that the self-incrimination protection applies only to testimony, not to books and records.

***Brown* v. *Board of Education* (1954)** overruled *Plessy* v. *Ferguson* (1896) (see below) and abandoned the separate-but-equal doctrine in the context of public schools. In deciding this case, the Supreme Court rejected the idea that truly equivalent but separate schools for African American and white students would be constitutional. The Court explained that the Fourteenth Amendment's command that all persons be accorded the equal protection of the law (U.S. Const. amend. XIV, § 1) is not satisfied simply by ensuring that African American and white schools "have been equalized, or are being equalized, with respect to buildings, curricula, qualifications and salaries, and other tangible factors."

The Court then held that racial segregation in public schools violates the equal protection clause because it is inherently unequal. In other words, nothing can make racially segregated public schools equal under the Constitution because the very fact of separation marks the separated race as inferior. In practical terms, the Court's holding in this case has been extended beyond public education to virtually all public accommodations and activities.

***Buckley* v. *Valeo* (1976)** clarified the meaning of the appointments clause (U.S. Const. art. II, § 2, ¶ 2). The clause specifies how principal and inferior officers are to be appointed. The president names such officers, and the Senate either accepts or rejects the persons named. Also, Congress can allow the president, department heads, or the courts acting alone to appoint inferior officers. In this case the Court ruled that members of the Federal Election Commission were not appointed properly because four of the six commissioners were appointed by an officeholder not mentioned in the appointments clause.

Burstyn v. Wilson (1952) extended the protection of the First Amendment to motion pictures, overruling a 1915 case that held that motion pictures were unprotected. The Supreme Court went on to hold that a state may not ban a film on the ground that it is "sacrilegious," i.e., that it treats one, some, or all religions "with contempt, mockery, scorn and ridicule."

Bush v. Gore (2000) found that a manual recount of disputed presidential ballots in Florida lacked a uniform standard of judging a voter's intent, thus violating the equal protection clause of the Constitution. The court also ruled that there was not enough time to conduct a new manual recount that would pass constitutional standards. The case arose when Republican candidate George W. Bush asked the Court to stop a hand recount. This decision ensured that Bush would receive Florida's electoral votes and win the election.

Bush v. Palm Beach Canvassing Board (2000) was the first time the Supreme Court agreed to hear a case involving a presidential election. The Court reviewed a decision by the Florida Supreme Court to extend the deadline for recounting votes and returned the case to the Florida court for a better explanation of its reasoning.

California v. Acevedo (1991) held that the Fourth Amendment's prohibition of unreasonable searches and seizures does not require a warrant to search inside an automobile as long as police have probable cause to believe that the object to be searched contains contraband.

California v. Greenwood (1988) held that the Fourth Amendment's protection against unreasonable searches and seizures does not extend to the search of a person's garbage after that garbage has been placed for pick up. The Supreme Court explained that an individual does not have a reasonable expectation of privacy in refuse that the owner intends to dispose of.

Chaplinsky v. New Hampshire (1942) announced the "fighting words" doctrine. The defendant, a Jehovah's Witness, was convicted under a state law making it a crime to address any person in public in an "offensive manner"; the offensive manner in this case was using profanity and name-calling in describing the town marshal. In upholding the conviction, the Supreme Court explained that the free speech clause does not protect fighting words—words that have a direct tendency to provoke the person to whom the words are addressed.

Chisholm v. Georgia (1793) stripped the immunity of the states to lawsuits in federal court. The Supreme Court held that a citizen of one state could sue another state in federal court without that state consenting to the suit. The Court's decision created a furor and led to the adoption of the Eleventh Amendment, which protected states from federal court suits by citizens of other states. In 1890 in *Hans* v. *Louisiana*, the Court extended this immunity; unless a state agreed, it could not be sued in federal court by its own citizens.

City of Boerne, Texas v. Flores (1997) struck down the Religious Freedom Restoration Act as an unconstitutional attempt by Congress to expand the Court's reading of the free exercise clause (U.S. Const. amend. I, cl. 1). The Court then held that Congress could not pass legislation that would allow individuals and groups to disobey neutral laws of general application just because the laws might have the indirect effect of making religious practices more difficult.

Clinton v. City of New York (1998) consolidated two challenges to line-item vetoes President Clinton issued in 1997. The Court ruled 6 to 3 in favor of New York City hospitals and Idaho's Snake River Potato Growers, who challenged separate vetoes. Justice Stevens said Congress could not endow the president with power to alter laws without amending the Constitution.

Committee for Public Education v. Regan (1980) held that the establishment clause (U.S. Const. amend. I, cl. 1) is not violated by a program that reimburses religious schools for routine record-keeping and testing services performed by the schools but required by state law.

Cox v. Louisiana (1965) upheld the constitutionality of a statute that prohibited parades near a courthouse. Acknowledging that the First Amendment generally protects marching or picketing, the Supreme Court explained that the special nature of courthouses—specifically, their central role in the administration of justice—justified the statute. The underlying principle justifying the statute is that while government may not be able to prohibit certain speech or speechlike conduct, it can control its time, place, and manner.

Cox v. New Hampshire (1941) upheld the convictions of 68 Jehovah's Witnesses for marching on a public sidewalk without a permit. The Court stressed that the defendants were not being punished for distributing religious leaflets or inviting passersby to a meeting of the religious group. The Court explained that local government officials have the authority to establish time, place, and manner restrictions on the use of public property for expressive purposes and that requiring a permit is a reasonable way for local officials to ensure that marching is not disruptive.

Dartmouth College v. Woodward (1819) held that the state of New Hampshire acted unconstitutionally when it attempted to transfer control of Dartmouth College from the trustees, the governing body of the college, to the state. When the college was created by a charter in 1769, the trustees were given all rights necessary to run the college. The charter, explained the Supreme Court, was a contract protected by the impairments of contracts clause (U.S. Const. art. I, § 10, ¶ 1) from state interference. The Court then held that the trustees' contractual rights were violated when the state removed the trustees and replaced them with the governor and his appointees.

Debs v. United States (1919) followed the decision in *Schenck* v. *United States* (see below). The Supreme Court upheld labor leader Eugene V. Debs's convictions for violating the Federal Espionage Act and obstructing the draft. The basis of the convictions was a speech opposing war in general and World War I in particular. The Court held that Debs's speech was not protected by the free speech clause because it posed a clear and present danger to the nation's war effort.

DeJonge v. Oregon (1937) reinforced earlier Supreme Court holdings that the First Amendment's protection of peaceable assembly and association must be honored by the states. In this case, Dirk DeJonge, a member of the Communist Party, was convicted and sentenced to a seven-year prison term for speaking at a public meeting of the party. In reversing the conviction, the Court held that merely speaking at a meeting of the Communist Party was protected by the First Amendment.

Dennis v. United States (1951) upheld convictions of several Communist Party members for advocating the violent overthrow of the United States government in violation of the federal Smith Act. The Supreme Court applied the clear-and-present-danger test announced in *Schenck* (see below) and once again rejected the claim that the free speech clause protects antigovernment speech and publications.

Dickerson v. United States (2000) overruled a federal law which stated that the admissibility of statements into evidence depended only on whether they were made voluntarily. In doing, the Court upheld the standard set by the *Miranda* decision—statements were admissible only if the suspect had received *Miranda* warnings before being interrogated.

Dred Scott v. Sandford (1857) was decided before the Fourteenth Amendment was added to the Constitution. (The Fourteenth Amendment provides that anyone born or naturalized in the United States is a citizen of the nation and of his or her state of residence.) In this case the Supreme Court held that a slave was property, not a citizen, and thus had no rights under the Constitution. The Court's decision was met with outrage in the North and was a prime factor precipitating the Civil War.

Edwards v. Aguillard (1987) struck down a Louisiana statute requiring public schools to teach "creation science" if they taught evolution. The Supreme Court explained that the effect of the statute was a clear violation of the establishment clause (U.S. Const. amend. I, cl. 1), which is to keep government out of religion and religion out of government.

Engel v. Vitale (1962) held that the establishment clause (U.S. Const. amend. I, cl. 1) was violated by a public school district's practice of starting each school day with a prayer which began: "Almighty God, we acknowledge our dependence upon Thee." The Supreme Court explained that under the establishment clause religion is a personal matter to be guided by individual choice. In short, the Court concluded that the establishment clause was intended to keep government out of religion, thus making it unacceptable for government to compose prayers for anyone to recite.

Scales of justice

Epperson v. Arkansas (1968) held that the state's antievolution law violated the establishment clause (U.S. Const. amend I, cl. 1) because its sole purpose was to remove from the state's public school curriculum a scientific theory found objectionable by fundamentalist Christians. The Supreme Court explained that the law amounts to a clear violation of the establishment clause, which requires that government be neutral with respect to all religious views and practices.

Escobedo v. Illinois (1964) was the forerunner of *Miranda* v. *Arizona* (see below). In this case, the Supreme Court reversed the murder conviction of Danny Escobedo, who gave damaging statements to police during questioning. Throughout the questioning, Escobedo repeatedly but unsuccessfully asked to see his attorney. In holding that Escobedo's Sixth Amendment right to counsel had been violated, the Court explained that an attorney could have assisted Escobedo in invoking his Fifth Amendment privilege against self-incrimination. In other words, an attorney could have told Escobedo when to keep quiet.

Everson v. Board of Education (1947) concluded that a New Jersey township had not violated the establishment clause when it reimbursed parents for the cost of sending their children to school on public transportation. The reimbursement was made to all parents even if their children attended religious schools. The Supreme Court explained that the practice served the public purpose of getting children to school safely; was neutrally administered, neither favoring nor disfavoring anyone on the basis of their religious views; and was not intended to advance religion.

Ex parte Endo (1944) arose out of the detainment of Japanese Americans living on the West Coast during World War II when the nation of Japan was an enemy of the United States. The case began when a citizen of Japanese descent, whose loyalty to the United States was never in doubt, asked to be released from a relocation camp. In this case the Supreme Court held that the federal government has no constitutional basis to detain a loyal citizen.

Ex parte Milligan (1866) established the primacy of the judicial branch in the absence of a bona fide national emergency. The case concerned the military trial of Lambdin Milligan, who was accused by the Army of conspiring to liberate Confederate prisoners from Union prisons during the Civil War. The Supreme Court held that the Constitution prohibits the federal government from trying a civilian in a military court as long as civilian courts are open and available.

Feiner v. New York (1951) upheld the disorderly conduct conviction of Irving Feiner. Feiner was arrested as he was giving a speech on a street corner in a predominantly African American section of a city. Among other things, Feiner said that African Americans "don't have equal rights and they should rise up in arms and fight for them." The Supreme Court said that the First Amendment protected free speech but not the right to use speech to incite a riot.

Fletcher v. Peck (1810) established the principle that a state could not interfere with or impair the value of lawful contract rights. In this case, the Georgia legislature enacted legislation that deprived a purchaser of land of the property. The Supreme Court held that the legislative action violated the impairment of contract clause (U.S. Const. art. I, § 10, ¶ 1) and declared the Georgia statute null and void.

Florida v. J.L. (2000) established that an anonymous tip that a person is carrying a gun fails to justify a stop and frisk of the person by a police officer. Under the Fourth Amendment, such a search is unconstitutional.

Frisby v. Schultz (1988) upheld a so-called focused picketing ordinance that prohibited protesters (anti-abortion protesters, in this case) from picketing a single residence (the house of a physician who performed abortions). However, the ordinance did not prohibit picketing in the general area of the physician's house. The Supreme Court explained that the ordinance was designed to preserve the privacy individuals expect at home. In addition, the ordinance was content-neutral and did not apply more broadly than necessary to protect residential privacy.

Furman v. Georgia (1972) invalidated imposition of the death penalty under state laws then in place. The Supreme Court explained that existing death penalty statutes did not give juries enough guidance in deciding whether or not to impose the death penalty; the result was that the death penalty in many cases was imposed arbitrarily, i.e., without a reasonable basis in the facts and circumstances of the offender or the crime.

Gannett Company, Inc. v. DePasquale (1979) established that neither the press nor the public have a First Amendment right to attend pretrial proceedings, such as a motion to suppress (i.e., keep out) evidence in a criminal case.

Gibbons v. Ogden (1824) made it clear that the authority of Congress to regulate interstate commerce (U.S. Const. art. I, § 8, cl. 3) includes the authority to regulate intrastate commercial activity that bears on, or relates to, interstate commerce. Before this decision, it was thought that the Constitution would permit a state to close its borders to interstate commercial activity—which, in effect, would stop such activity in its tracks. This case says that only Congress can regulate commercial activity that has both intrastate and interstate dimensions.

***Gideon* v. *Wainwright* (1963)** overruled *Betts* v. *Brady* (see above) and held for the first time that poor defendants in criminal cases have the right to a state-paid attorney under the Sixth Amendment. This rule has been refined to apply when the defendant, if convicted, can be sentenced to more than six months in jail.

***Gitlow* v. *New York* (1925)** upheld a conviction for publishing articles that advocated the violent overthrow of democratic governments in general and the government of the United States in particular. In upholding the defendant's conviction under New York's so-called criminal anarchy law, the Court again rejected a free-speech defense while, at the same time, recognizing that the right of free speech is fundamental. According to the Court, a state legislature is entitled to take steps to prevent public disorder.

***Grayned* v. *City of Rockford* (1972)** upheld the convictions of several hundred demonstrators charged with violating a city ordinance that prohibited demonstrations on or near schools while classes were being held. Once again the Court applied the time-place-and-manner doctrine (see *Cox* v. *Louisiana* discussed above): the First Amendment permits persons to demonstrate, but the government can regulate when, where, and how demonstrations are held.

Supreme Court gavel

***Gregg* v. *Georgia* (1976)** specifically held that the death penalty is not necessarily unconstitutional. The Supreme Court went on to uphold, Georgia death penalty statute, explaining that the law provided sufficient safeguards to ensure that the penalty was imposed only as a rational response to the facts of the crime and the circumstances of the offender.

***Gregory* v. *City of Chicago* (1969)** struck down the convictions of several protesters who marched from city hall to the mayor's home to demand that the city's schools be desegregated. The Court held that peaceful protest is protected by the First Amendment.

***Hazelwood School District* v. *Kuhlmeier* (1988)** held that public school officials are in control of the editorial content of a student newspaper published as part of the school's journalism curriculum. Students' First Amendment rights do not include deciding what will and will not be published in a student newspaper that is tied to the school's curriculum.

***Heart of Atlanta Motel, Inc.* v. *United States* (1964)** upheld the Civil Rights Act of 1964, which prohibits racial discrimination by those who provide goods, services, and facilities to the public. The Georgia motel in the case drew its business from other states but refused to rent rooms to African Americans. The Supreme Court explained that Congress had the authority to such discrimination under both the equal protection clause (U.S. Const. amend. XIV, § 1) and the commerce clause (art. I, § 8, cl. 3). With respect to the commerce clause, the Court explained that Congress had ample evidence to conclude that racial discrimination by hotels and motels impedes interstate commerce.

***Hill* v. *Colorado* (2000)** upheld a Colorado law designed to prevent anti-abortion protestors from harrassing people who entered health care facilities. The Court stated that the law made valid restrictions on the time, place, and manner in which protestors could exercise their First Amendment right to free speech.

***Hudson* v. *United States* (1997)** held 5 to 4 that the federal criminal charges in cases of regulatory wrongdoing could follow civil fines, if the fines were not punitive. The Supreme Court had ruled in *United States* v. *Halper* (see below) that civil and criminal penalties could not be imposed for the same act. The Court said *Halper* supported too broad a reading of the double jeopardy clause.

***Hughes* v. *Superior Court* (1950)** upheld the contempt convictions of several individuals for picketing a grocery store in violation of a court order prohibiting the picketing. The picketers wanted the store to hire African Americans in proportion to the percentage of the store's African American customers. While recognizing that labor picketing is protected by the free speech clause (see *Thornhill* v. *Alabama* discussed below), the Supreme Court explained that it does not enjoy the same protection as pure speech. The Court then held that the free speech clause does not bar a state from prohibiting labor picketing aimed at forcing an employer to adopt a hiring quota.

***Hustler Magazine* v. *Falwell* (1988)** held that public officials or public figures subject to parody by the press cannot recover damages (i.e., money) for the emotional distress caused by the parody unless they can prove that the parody was false or was published in reckless disregard of the truth or falsity of its content.

Hutchinson v. Proxmire (1979) articulated the limits of the speech and debate clause (U.S. Const. art. I, § 6), which provides that members of Congress cannot be held criminally or civilly liable for statements made in either house. In this case, however, the Supreme Court held that the clause did not protect Wisconsin senator William Proxmire from being sued for libel. In a press release, at a news conference, and on television news programs, Proxmire claimed that federal funds were wasted in paying for a study of aggressive behavior in animals. Had the senator limited his remarks to a speech on the Senate floor, the speech and debate clause would have protected him from the libel suit; he lost the protection of the clause by making his remarks outside of Congress.

INS v. Chadha (1983) held that legislative action by Congress must comply with the Constitution. In this case, the Supreme Court concluded that the Constitution did not permit one house, acting unilaterally, to override the decision of the attorney general allowing an alien, Chadha, to remain in the United States. The Court said that the attorney general's decision could be set aside only by legislation passed by both houses and signed into law by the president, or passed a second time by a two-thirds vote of both houses in the event of a presidential veto.

International Brotherhood of Teamsters, Local 695 v. Vogt (1950) upheld a state court order prohibiting labor picketing aimed at nonunion employees and seeking to encourage them to join the picketers' union. The Supreme Court explained that a state cannot prohibit any and all labor picketing (see *Thornhill* v. *Alabama*). But, said the Court, a state can prohibit labor picketing in order to preserve the right of each nonunion employee to decide for himself or herself whether or not to join a union.

Jacobson v. Massachusetts (1905) upheld a state law requiring smallpox vaccinations against an individual's claim that submitting to a vaccination would violate his religious beliefs. The law was another example of a neutral law of general application intended to prevent the spread of a communicable disease that could kill. (See *Reynolds* v. *United States* discussed below.) The Supreme Court explained that the state's health and welfare interest took precedence over the individual's free exercise rights.

Jaffee v. Redmond (1996) held for the first time that federal rules of evidence recognize a psychotherapist-patient privilege, which protects confidential communications in that context from compelled disclosure at a criminal trial or in a civil trial. The Supreme Court, however, cautioned that the privilege is not absolute and might be required to yield if, for example, a therapist's disclosure is required to avert serious harm to the patient or another.

Johnson v. Transportation Agency of Santa Clara, California (1987) held that Title VII of the Civil Rights Act of 1964 allows an employer to take gender into account in awarding promotions. The Supreme Court explained that this type of affirmative action is permissible as long as the employer is using the action to remedy the effects of past discrimination against women.

Katz v. United States (1967) overruled *Olmstead* v. *United States* (see below). In this case, the Supreme Court announced that the Fourth Amendment's protection against unreasonable searches and seizures applies to people, not places. In particular, the Court held that the Fourth Amendment applies to telephone wiretaps, and this means, as a general rule, that police must have a court order to place a wiretap.

Kiryas Joel Village School District v. Grumet (1994) struck down as a violation of the establishment clause (U.S. Const. amend. I, cl. 1) a New York statute creating a public school district limited to a single Jewish village and controlled entirely by the leaders of an ultra-Orthodox Jewish sect. The Supreme Court explained that the statute gave the secular authority to educate to a specific religion. Also, because no other religious group had ever received such treatment, the Court said that the establishment clause was violated because the state had singled out the sect for favorable treatment.

Korematsu v. United States (1944) upheld the federal government's authority to exclude Japanese Americans, many of whom were citizens, from designated military areas that included almost the entire West Coast. The government defended the so-called exclusion orders as a necessary response to Japan's attack on Pearl Harbor, which widened World War II from a war against Germany to one against Japan as well. However, in upholding the exclusion orders, the Supreme Court established that courts will subject government actions that discriminate on the basis of race to the most exacting scrutiny, often referred to as strict scrutiny.

Lau v. Nichols (1974) held that the Civil Rights Act of 1964 was violated when San Francisco's public school district refused to instruct children of Chinese ancestry in English. The Supreme Court explained that the Chinese students in the case were not receiving the same education as non-Chinese students as required by the Civil Rights Act, which the school district had agreed to abide by in exchange for receiving federal funds.

Lee* v. *Weisman **(1992)** held that having clergy offer prayers as part of an official public school graduation ceremony is forbidden by the establishment clause of the First Amendment.

Lemon* v. *Kurtzman **(1971)** established a three-part test for determining if a particular government action violates the establishment clause (U.S. Const. amend. I, cl. 1). First, the test asks if the government action has a primary *purpose* of advancing religion; second, if the action has a primary *effect* of advancing religion; and third, if the action risks entangling government in religious affairs or vice versa. The establishment clause is violated if the action fails any one of these tests.

Levitt* v. *Committee for Public Education **(1973)** struck down a New York law under which the state would reimburse religious schools for drafting, grading, and reporting the results of student achievement tests. Because teachers in religious schools prepared the tests, the tests could be used to advance the religious views of the school, a result prohibited by the establishment clause (U.S. Const. amend. I, cl. 1).

Lloyd Corp.* v. *Tanner **(1972)** upheld a shopping center's refusal to allow anti-Vietnam War protesters to distribute flyers on its property. It is elemental that the First Amendment protects only against government action, not private action. The Court concluded that the First Amendment did not apply.

Lynch* v. *Donnelly **(1984)** held that a city-owned crèche (a Nativity scene) included in a Christmas display that also included reindeer, a Santa Claus, and a Christmas tree did not endorse a particular religious viewpoint and thus did not violate the establishment clause (U.S. Const. amend. I, cl. 1). In the Supreme Court's view, the display was a secular holiday display.

Mapp* v. *Ohio **(1961)** extended the exclusionary rule announced in *Weeks* v. *United States* (see below) to state and local law-enforcement officers. After this case, evidence seized in violation of the Fourth Amendment could not be used by the prosecution as evidence of a defendant's guilt in any court—federal, state, or local.

Marbury* v. *Madison **(1803)** established one of the most significant principles of American constitutional law. In this case, the Supreme Court held that it is the Court itself that has the final say on what the Constitution means. It is also the Supreme Court that has the final say in whether or not an act of government—legislative or executive at the federal, state, or local level—violates the Constitution.

Marsh* v. *Chambers **(1983)** held that the establishment clause (U.S. Const. amend. I, cl. 1) was not violated by the practice of the Nebraska legislature to begin its sessions with a prayer. The Supreme Court first noted that the practice had a long history in America, observing that the first Congresses had chaplains. The Court also explained that such a practice when directed to adults is not likely to be perceived as advancing a particular religion or religion in general.

McCollum* v. *Board of Education **(1948)** held that the establishment clause was violated by a public school district's practice of allowing privately paid teachers to hold weekly religion classes in public schools. The Supreme Court explained that the practice used public funds to disseminate religious doctrine, a result flatly at odds with the purpose of the establishment clause.

McCulloch* v. *Maryland **(1819)** established the foundation for the expansive authority of Congress. The Supreme Court held that the necessary and proper clause (U.S. Const. art. I, § 8, cl. 18) allows Congress to do more than the Constitution expressly authorizes it to do. This case says that Congress can enact nearly any law that will help achieve any of the ends set forth in Article I, Section 8. For example, Congress has the express authority to regulate interstate commerce; the necessary and proper clause permits Congress to do so in ways not specified in the Constitution.

Miller* v. *California **(1973)** established the test for determining if a book, movie, television program, etc. is obscene and thus unprotected by the First Amendment. A work is obscene if: 1) the average person would find that the work taken as a whole appeals to prurient interests; 2) the work defines or depicts sexual conduct in a "patently offensive way" as determined by state law; and 3) the work taken as a whole "lacks serious literary, artistic, political, or scientific value."

Minersville School District* v. *Gobitis **(1940)** had held that a state could require public school students to salute the American flag. The Supreme Court explained that a general law (the flag-salute law in this case), not intended to restrict or promote religious views, must be obeyed. This decision didn't last long; it was overruled three years later by *West Virginia State Board of Education* v. *Barnette*, discussed below.

Miranda v. Arizona (1966) held that a person in police custody cannot be questioned unless told that he or she has: 1) the right to remain silent, 2) the right to an attorney (at government expense if the person is unable to pay), and 3) that anything the person says after acknowledging that he or she understands these rights can be used as evidence of guilt at trial. These advisements constitute the well-known *Miranda* warnings and operate to ensure that a person in custody will not give up unknowingly the Fifth Amendment's protection against self-incrimination.

The Supreme Court explained that a person alone in police custody may not understand, even if told, that he or she can remain silent and thus might be misled into believing that questions must be answered. The presence of an attorney is essential.

Mitchell v. Helms (2000) holds that Chapter 2 of the Education Consolidation and Improvement Act of 1981 does not violate the establishment clause of the First Amendment when it provides funds for religiously affiliated schools. The act distributes money to buy equipment and materials for public and private schools.

Mueller v. Allen (1983) upheld a Minnesota law that allowed parents of private school students, whether in sectarian or nonsectarian schools, to deduct educational expenses in computing their state income tax. The Supreme Court explained that the benefit flowed to parents and students and only indirectly, if at all, to religious schools. In addition, the benefit was neutral because it did not depend on the type of private school a student attended. In deciding this case, the Court applied the three-prong *Lemon* test (see above) and concluded that the deduction had a neutral purpose, did not involve government in religious affairs, and, as noted, was neutral and so did not have the effect of advancing religion.

Munn v. Illinois (1876) held that the commerce clause (U.S. Const. art. I, § 8, cl. 3) was not violated by an Illinois law that fixed the maximum prices grain elevators could charge farmers for the short-term storage of grain before it was shipped to processors. The Supreme Court explained that the operation of grain elevators was primarily an intrastate commercial enterprise. In addition, the Court noted that Congress had not acted with respect to interstate commerce in grain and so the Illinois law could not be said to interfere with Congress's authority to regulate interstate commerce.

Near v. Minnesota (1931) established the prior restraint doctrine. The doctrine protects the press (broadly defined to include newspapers, television and radio, filmmakers and distributors, etc.) from government attempts to block publication. Except in extraordinary circumstances, the press must be allowed to publish. If what is published turns out to be unprotected by the First Amendment, the government can take appropriate action. However, to act before publication is to engage in a kind of censorship which the First Amendment does not permit.

Nebraska Press Association v. Stuart (1976) struck down a judge's order that the press covering a mass murder case could not report any facts that "strongly implicated" the defendant. The Supreme Court held that the press cannot be prohibited from reporting what transpires in a courtroom and that, in this case, there were no facts suggesting that press coverage would infringe the defendant's Sixth Amendment right to a fair trial.

New Jersey v. T.L.O. (1985) held that public school officials can search a student's property (a purse) for evidence of wrongdoing (violating the school's no-smoking policy) without having probable cause to believe that the student did anything wrong. It is enough, said the Supreme Court, if school officials have reason to believe that the student violated a rule and that the search will confirm or dispel that suspicion. The Court agreed, however, that the Fourth Amendment protects public school students from unreasonable searches and seizures but not to the degree that adults are protected.

New York Times Co. v. Sullivan (1964) extended the protections afforded to the press by the free press clause (U.S. Const. amend. I). In this case, the Supreme Court held that a public official or public figure suing a publisher for libel (i.e., defamation) must prove that the publisher published a story that he or she knew was false or published the story in "reckless disregard of its truth or falsity," which means that the publisher did not take professionally adequate steps to determine the story's truth or falsity.

New York Times Co. v. United States *(The Pentagon Papers Case)* (1971) reaffirmed the prior restraint doctrine established in *Near* v. *Minnesota* (see above). In this case, the Supreme Court refused to halt publication of the Pentagon Papers, which gave a detailed critical account of the United States's involvement in the Vietnam War. There was, however, considerable disagreement on the Court with four dissenting justices voting to halt publication temporarily to allow the president to show that the documents jeopardized the war effort.

Nix* v. *Williams **(1984)** announced the "inevitable-discovery rule," another example of a situation in which evidence that is otherwise inadmissible becomes admissible. Here the defendant told police where to find the body of a murder victim. The police, however, obtained this information by talking to the defendant without his attorney being present, in violation of the defendant's Sixth Amendment right to counsel. The Supreme Court excused the violation and allowed the information to be used as evidence of the defendant's guilt because the police would have inevitably discovered the body by other lawful means.

Olmstead* v. *United States **(1928)** held that the Fourth Amendment's prohibition against unreasonable searches and seizures applied only to searches and seizures of tangible property like a person's home or a person's briefcase. In this case, the Supreme Court held that the protection did not apply to telephone calls placed from public telephones; these calls could be intercepted by police at will and used as evidence without violating the Fourth Amendment. This case was overruled some 40 years later by *Katz* v. *United States* (see above).

Oregon* v. *Elstad **(1985)** held that a defendant's voluntary but incriminating statement given before being told of his *Miranda* rights does not taint, i.e., ruin and make inadmissible, the same defendant's later confession given after receiving a full recitation of his *Miranda* rights. (The first statement was never used against the defendant.)

Oregon* v. *Smith **(1990)**, officially known as *Employment Division, Department of Human Services of Oregon* v. *Smith*, held that a state may deny unemployment benefits to a person who was fired for the religious use of an illegal drug, peyote. In reaching its decision, the Supreme Court followed the reasoning of an 1879 case, *Reynolds* v. *United States* (see below), and held that a person's free exercise rights are not violated by a neutral law of general application even though the law, as in this case, may penalize a person in the practice of his or her religion.

Payton* v. *New York **(1980)** invalidated a New York statute which authorized police to make warrantless entries into homes to make routine, nonemergency felony arrests. The Supreme Court held that the Fourth Amendment requires a warrant for such routine arrests. The Court's holding means that any evidence seized during the arrest and any statements made by the person arrested could not be used as evidence of guilt at any later criminal trial.

Pierce* v. *Society of Sisters **(1925)** held that parents have a right under the due process clause (U.S. Const. amend. XIV, § 1) to send their children to religious schools as long as the schools meet the secular educational requirements established by state law. The Court also made it clear that while parents have the right to use religious schools, the Constitution forbids states from segregating public school students on the basis of religious affiliation.

Plessy* v. *Ferguson **(1896)** upheld the separate-but-equal doctrine used by Southern states to perpetuate segregation after the Civil War officially ended *de jure*, or law-mandated, segregation. At issue in the case was a Louisiana law requiring passenger trains to have "equal but separated accommodations for the white and colored races." The Supreme Court held that the Fourteenth Amendment's equal protection clause required only equal public facilities for the two races, not equal access to the same facilities. This case was overruled by *Brown* v. *Board of Education* (1954) discussed above.

Police Department of Chicago* v. *Mosley **(1972)** struck down a Chicago, Illinois, ordinance that allowed peaceful labor demonstrations at or near public schools while classes were in session but prohibited all other demonstrations. The Court held that the ordinance was a content-based restriction; it allowed labor demonstrations but not Mosley's single-person demonstration in which he carried a sign alleging that a particular school practiced racial discrimination. Content-based restrictions, the Court explained, almost always violate the First Amendment; while time-place-and-manner restrictions generally are accepted as placing reasonable limits on otherwise protected conduct.

Powell* v. *Alabama **(1932)** established that the due process clause (U.S. Const. amend. XIV, ¶ 1) guarantees the defendant in any death penalty case the right to an attorney. Accordingly, states, not just the federal government, are required, at government expense, to provide an attorney to poor defendants who face the death penalty if convicted.

***Red Lion Broadcasting Co.* v. *FCC* (1969)** is one of a number of Supreme Court cases that make it clear that First Amendment rights of broadcasts are not as broad as the rights of the print media. In this case, the Court upheld two FCC regulations requiring broadcasters to give free reply-time to 1) persons criticized in political editorials and 2) persons who are attacked by others as the latter express their views on a controversial subject.

***Reed* v. *Reed* (1971)** was the first Supreme Court case to hold that discrimination on the basis of sex violates the equal protection clause (U.S. Const. amend. XIV, § 1). At issue in the case was a state law that preferred males to females as the administrators of estates, even though both might be equally qualified to serve as administrators. The Court held that such a mandatory preference serves no purpose but to discriminate—a basic violation of the equal protection clause.

***Regents of the University of California* v. *Bakke* (1978)** was the first Supreme Court decision to suggest that an affirmative action program could be justified on the basis of diversity. The Supreme Court explained that racial quotas were not permissible under the equal protection clause (U.S. Const. amend. XIV, § 1), but that the diversity rationale was a legitimate interest that would allow a state medical school to consider an applicant's race in evaluating his or her application for admission. (Several more recent Supreme Court cases suggest that the diversity rationale is no longer enough to defend an affirmative action program.)

***Reno* v. *American Civil Liberties Union* (1997)** tested the Communications Decency Act that made it a crime to distribute "indecent" material over computer online networks. The Court said that protecting children from pornography did not supersede the right to freedom of expression, adding that the act was unenforceable with the current technology.

***Reno* v. *Condon* (2000)** upheld The Driver's Privacy Protection Act of 1994. The law restricts the ability of a state to disclose a driver's personal information without the driver's consent. According to the Court, the law does not violate states' rights guaranteed in the Tenth Amendment or the Eleventh Amendment provision that suits against a state be tried in a state court.

***Reynolds* v. *Sims* (1964)** extended the one-person, one-vote doctrine announced in *Wesberry* v. *Sanders* to state legislative elections. The Court held that the inequality of representation in the Alabama legislature violated the equal protection clause of the Fourteenth Amendment.

***Reynolds* v. *United States* (1879)** was the first major Supreme Court case to consider the impact of neutral laws of general application on religious practices. (A neutral law of general application is one that is intended to protect the public health and safety and applies to everyone regardless of religious belief or affiliation. Such a law is not intended to affect adversely any religious belief or practice but may have indirect adverse effects.) The case presented a free exercise challenge by a Mormon to a federal law making it unlawful to practice polygamy, i.e., marriage in which a person has more than one spouse. The Mormon religion permitted a male to have more than one wife. The Court upheld the statute, saying that Congress did not have the authority to legislate with respect to religious beliefs but did have the authority to legislate with respect to actions that "subvert good order."

***Rhodes* v. *Chapman* (1981)** held that the Eighth Amendment's prohibition against cruel and unusual punishment is not violated when prison authorities house two inmates in a cell built for only one inmate.

***Richmond Newspapers, Inc.* v. *Virginia* (1980)** established that both the public and the press have a First Amendment right to attend trials. The Supreme Court observed that the importance of a trial is the fundamental fact that the defendant's guilt or innocence is being determined and then explained that the fairness of the guilt/innocence determination is dependent, in part, on the openness of the proceeding.

***Richmond* v. *J.A. Croson Co.* (1989)** held that state and local governments must have a compelling interest, i.e., an exceedingly important interest, in order to implement affirmative-action programs. One such interest is remedying discrimination against racial minorities. However, the Supreme Court struck down a Richmond, Virginia, program that gave at least 30 percent of the city's construction contracts to minority-owned businesses. The Court said there was no proof of racial discrimination, so nothing would be remedied by the program.

***Roe* v. *Wade* (1973)** held that females have a constitutional right under various provisions of the Constitution—most notably, the due process clause (amend. XIV, § 1)—to decide whether or not to terminate a pregnancy. The Supreme Court's decision in this case was the most significant in a long line of decisions over a period of 50 years that recognized a constitutional right of privacy, even though the word *privacy* is not found in the Constitution.

***Santa Fe School District* v. *Doe* (2000)** ruled that the Santa Fe School District violated the establishment clause of the First Amendment when it allowed a student council member to deliver a prayer over the intercom before varsity football games.

***Santobello* v. *New York* (1971)** put the Supreme Court's stamp of approval on plea bargaining. The Supreme Court explained that plea bargaining "is an essential component in the administration of justice." The Court's decision established that a prosecutor must live up to the terms of a plea agreement, although the Court also made it clear that a defendant does not have an absolute right to have the trial judge accept either a guilty plea or a plea agreement.

***Schechter Poultry Corporation* v. *United States* (1935)** overturned the conviction of the employers, who were charged with violating wage and hour limitations of a law adopted under the authority of the National Industrial Recovery Act. The Court held that because the defendants did not sell poultry in interstate commerce, they were not subject to federal regulations on wages and hours.

***Schenck* v. *Pro-Choice Network of Western New York* (1997)** upheld parts of an injunction aimed at anti-abortion protesters and regulating the manner in which they could conduct their protests. The Supreme Court upheld the creation of a fixed 15-foot buffer zone separating protesters from clinic patrons and employees; the Court also upheld a cease-and-desist order under which a protester must move away from any person who indicates that he or she does not want to hear the protester's message. But the Court struck down the "floating buffer zone" that had allowed protesters who maintained a 15-foot distance to move along with patrons and employees.

***Schenck* v. *United States* (1919)** upheld convictions under the Federal Espionage Act. The defendants were charged with distributing leaflets aimed at inciting draft resistance during World War I; their defense was that their antidraft speech was protected by the free speech clause (U.S. Const. amend. I, cl. 2).

The Supreme Court explained that whether or not speech is protected depends on the context in which it occurs. Here, said the Court, the context was the nation's war effort. Because the defendants' antidraft rhetoric created a "clear and present danger" to the success of the war effort, it was not protected speech.

***Sheppard* v. *Maxwell* (1966)** made it clear that a criminal defendant's Sixth Amendment right to a fair trial can justify restrictions on the press's First Amendment rights. The Supreme Court, however, was careful to explain that any restrictions on the press must be no broader than necessary to ensure that the defendant is tried in court and not in the press.

***The Slaughterhouse Cases* (1873)** upheld Louisiana statutes regulating the butcher trade and, specifically, moving butchers out of densely populated sections of New Orleans. The Supreme Court explained that the privileges and immunities clause (U.S. Const. amend. XIV, § 1) only prohibits states from doing something that would impair the general rights of United States citizens, but that there was no right of citizenship that would prohibit a state from regulating businesses in order to protect public health and safety.

This decision was rendered shortly after the Civil War ended and narrowly interpreted the privileges and immunities clause, as well as the due process and equal protection clauses (U.S. Const. amend. XIV, § 1). To the Court, these provisions were meant to secure the rights of the newly freed enslaved persons, not to protect ordinary contract rights of businesspeople.

***Teitel Film Corp.* v. *Cusack* (1968)** struck down a Chicago ordinance under which a police permit was required before any motion picture could be shown. Under the ordinance, it could take between 50 and 57 days to secure a response. Judicial review of a permit denial could take 10 days or more. The Supreme Court explained that the ordinance did not provide for sufficiently prompt action on a permit application and, thus, violated rights of speech and expression protected by the First Amendment.

***Texas* v. *Johnson* (1989)** held that burning an American flag is expressive conduct protected by the First Amendment. Expressive conduct, the Supreme Court explained, is conduct that is intended by the actor to convey a message, and the message that the actor intends to convey is one that observers likely would understand. The Court applied the *O'Brien* test (see *United States* v. *O'Brien*) under which the government can punish a person for conduct that might have an expressive component as long as the punishment advances an important government interest that is unrelated to the content of speech. The Court then reversed the conviction of Gregory Johnson for "desecrating a venerated object"—burning an American flag at the 1984 Republican National Convention to protest the policies of the Reagan administration. The Court explained that Johnson was convicted solely because of the content of his speech.

***Thornhill* v. *Alabama* (1940)** reversed the conviction of the president of a local union for violating an Alabama statute that prohibited only labor picketing. Thornhill was peaceably picketing his employer during an authorized strike when he was arrested and charged. In reaching its decision, the Supreme Court expressly held that the free speech clause protects speech about the facts and circumstances of a labor dispute.

***Tinker* v. *Des Moines School District* (1969)** extended First Amendment protection to public school students in the now-famous statement that "it can hardly be argued that either students or teachers shed their constitutional rights of freedom of speech or expression at the schoolhouse gate." The Supreme Court then held that a public school could not suspend students who wore black armbands to school to symbolize their opposition to the Vietnam War. In so holding, the Court likened the students' conduct to pure speech and decided it on that basis.

***Train* v. *City of New York* (1975)** held that if Congress directs the executive branch to spend funds that Congress has appropriated, the executive branch must do so. In this case, Congress, over a presidential veto, appropriated federal funds for state and local sewer projects. The president directed the head of the Environmental Protection Agency to distribute only some of the appropriated funds. The Supreme Court held that the president must comply with Congress's spending directives.

***Turner Broadcasting System, Inc.* v. *FCC* (1997)** upheld the must-carry provisions of the Cable Television Consumer Protection and Competition Act against a challenge by cable television operators that the provisions violated their free speech rights. The must-carry provisions require a cable operator with 12 or more channels to set aside one-third of its capacity for use by broadcast television stations (e.g., CBS) at no cost. The provisions did not violate the First Amendment because they served several important government interests and did not restrict any more speech than necessary to achieve those interests.

***United States* v. *E.C. Knight Co.* (1895)** gave a very narrow reading to the term *commerce* in deciding if a manufacturing monopoly violated the Sherman Antitrust Act. (Congress used its authority to regulate interstate commerce—U.S. Const. art. I, § 8, cl. 3—to enact the Antitrust Act.) The Supreme Court held that commerce meant only the dollars and cents marketing of goods, not the production of goods that ultimately would be marketed. Note, however, that the Court's decision has been eroded over the years and is no longer valid.

***United States* v. *Eichman* (1990)** struck down the Federal Flag Protection Act because it punishes the content of expressive speech. The Court concluded: "The Government may not prohibit the expression of an idea simply because society finds the idea itself offensive or disagreeable."

***United States* v. *Halper* (1989)** held that the double jeopardy clause (U.S. Const. amend. V, cl. 2), which prohibits multiple punishments for the same offense, can be violated by imposing both a criminal and a civil penalty on an individual for the same conduct. In this case, the conduct was submitting false bills to the federal government. First the defendant received a criminal sanction (imprisonment) after a criminal trial; that penalty was followed by a civil sanction (a large fine) after a civil trial. The Court explained that the fine ($130,000) was punishment under the double jeopardy clause because it was grossly disproportionate to the total amount of the false bills ($585).

***United States* v. *Leon* (1984)** created the good-faith exception to the exclusionary rule. In this case, a magistrate issued an arrest warrant that appeared valid but was later determined to be deficient because the facts on which it was based did not amount to probable cause. However, officers served the warrant and, in the process, uncovered evidence used at Leon's trial. The Supreme Court explained that the neither the officers nor the criminal justice system should be penalized for the magistrate's mistake. The good-faith exception transforms evidence otherwise inadmissible under the Fourth Amendment into admissible evidence.

***United States* v. *Nixon* (1974)** made it clear that the president is not above the law. In the early 1970s, President Nixon was named as an unindicted coconspirator in the criminal investigation that arose in the aftermath of a break-in at the offices of the Democratic Party in Washington, D.C. A federal judge had ordered President Nixon to turn over tapes of conversations he had had with his advisers; Nixon resisted the order, claiming that the conversations were entitled to absolute confidentiality by Article II of the Constitution. The Supreme Court disagreed and held that only those presidential conversations and communications that relate to performing the duties of the office of president are confidential and protected from a judicial order of disclosure.

United States* v. *O'Brien **(1968)** upheld the conviction of David Paul O'Brien for burning his draft card to dramatize his opposition to the Vietnam War, in violation of a regulation requiring a draft registrant to keep his card in his possession at all times. The Court held that symbolic speech was not a defense to a draft-card burning charge because the regulation: 1) served a valid government interest unrelated to the suppression of speech; 2) was narrowly drawn to serve the identified government interest; and 3) left open alternative channels of sending the same message.

United States* v. *Playboy **(2000)** struck down Section 505 of the Telecommunications Act of 1996 because it violated the First Amendment. The act required cable television operators to fully block channels devoted to sexually oriented programs or limit their transmission to hours when children are unlikely to be viewing television. The Court claimed that the way the law addressed the problem was too restrictive.

Vernonia School District 47J* v. *Acton **(1995)** held that the Fourth Amendment's prohibition of unreasonable searches and seizures was not violated by a public school district's policy of conducting random, suspicionless drug tests of all students participating in interscholastic athletics. The Supreme Court explained that the district's interest in combating drug use outweighed the students' privacy interests.

Washington* v. *Davis **(1976)** held that the equal protection clause (U.S. Const. amend. XIV, § 1) is not violated by government actions that have a disproportionate negative impact on members of a particular race or ethnic group. At issue in the case was a test given to police applicants on which white applicants scored higher than African American applicants. The Supreme Court explained that the equal protection clause is violated only by actions taken for the purpose of discriminating against individuals on the basis of race, ethnicity, or other improper factors.

Watkins* v. *United States **(1957)** limited the authority of congressional committees to hold witnesses in contempt for refusing to answer questions. The Supreme Court explained that a witness can be required to answer questions posed by a committee of Congress, but only if the questions are relevant to the committee's purpose. The Court also held that a witness before a congressional committee can invoke the Fifth Amendment's privilege against self-incrimination.

Weeks* v. *United States **(1914)** created the exclusionary rule as the remedy for an unconstitutional search or seizure (U.S. Const. amend. IV). Under the exclusionary rule, evidence seized as a result of an unconstitutional search or seizure cannot be used as evidence of guilt at a later criminal trial. The Supreme Court applied the rule only against federal officers because, at that time, the Bill of Rights was thought to apply only to the federal government.

Wesberry* v. *Sanders **(1964)** established the one-person, one-vote doctrine in elections for the United States House of Representatives. The doctrine ensures that the vote of each voter has the same weight as the vote of every other voter. This decision means that the voting population of each congressional district within a state must be as nearly equal as possible.

West Coast Hotel Co.* v. *Parrish **(1937)** upheld a Washington state statute that authorized a state commission to fix the minimum wages of women and minors. The statute was challenged as a violation of the right to contract. The Supreme Court explained that the right to contract, like most of the rights protected by the due process clause (U.S. Const. amend. XIV, § 1), is not absolute. The Court held that the right to contract was outweighed by the state's interest in protecting the health, safety, and security of vulnerable workers.

West Virginia State Board of Education* v. *Barnette **(1943)** made it clear that the free exercise clause (U.S. Const. amend. I) forbids the government from requiring a person to swear to a belief. The Supreme Court struck down a state law requiring public school students to salute the American flag and recite the Pledge of Allegiance. Parents and students of the Jehovah's Witness faith claimed that the law violated their free exercise rights because their religious precepts prohibited them from pledging allegiance to anything other than God. The Court agreed and held that the state had no interest compelling enough to justify the law.

Westside Community Schools* v. *Mergens **(1990)** upheld the Federal Equal Access Act, which provides that public schools which open their facilities to noncurricular student groups must make their facilities equally available to student religious groups.

Whitney* v. *California **(1927)** upheld the California Criminal Syndicalism Act against a claim that the statute violated First Amendment rights of speech and association. The statute made it a crime for anyone to become a member of any group known to espouse political change, particularly change that would effect the distribution of wealth in the country.

Whren* v. *United States **(1996)** held that the Fourth Amendment's prohibition against unreasonable searches and seizures was not violated when police stopped an automobile for minor traffic violations and discovered illegal drugs in the process. In deciding this case, the Supreme Court rejected the defendant's claim that the real reason the police stopped the vehicle was to search for drugs and that the traffic violations were a pretext. The traffic violations provided probable cause for the stop and that, said the Court, is all the Fourth Amendment requires.

Wisconsin* v. *Mitchell **(1993)** upheld a Wisconsin statute that increased the penalty imposed for certain crimes if the victim was selected on the basis of race. Here the victim of a severe beating was picked because he was African American. The Supreme Court explained that the enhanced penalty did not punish speech; Mitchell remained free to think or say what he pleased on matters of race. The Court also explained that penalties are enhanced in a variety of circumstances (e.g., when a murder victim is a police officer or under or over a certain age), and that the First Amendment is not violated when a murder sentence is enhanced from life imprisonment to death because race was a factor in the killing of the victim.

Wisconsin* v. *Yoder **(1972)** ruled that Wisconsin's compulsory education laws must yield to the concerns of Amish parents that sending their children to public school after the eighth grade exposed the children to influences that undermined their religious faith and religious practices.

Wolman* v. *Walter **(1977)** held that the establishment clause (U.S. Const. amend. I, cl. 1) was not violated by an Ohio law that provided textbooks, testing services, and diagnostic and therapeutic services at state expense to all children, including children attending religious schools. The Supreme Court explained that a general program undertaken to ensure the health and welfare of all children was not unconstitutional simply because the program might provide an indirect benefit to religious schools. However, the Court struck down a provision that reimbursed religious schools for the cost of field trips, because the religious schools determined the purpose and destination of the trips and thus could select such trips based on the support they would lend to the schools' religious precepts.

Woodson* v. *North Carolina **(1976)** held that a state may not make the death penalty mandatory upon conviction for a particular offense. The Supreme Court explained that the death penalty is a particularized punishment; it can be imposed only after a jury (or a judge, in some instances) looks at the offender as an individual and at the facts of the crime and at the offender's character and life history.

Yates* v. *United States **(1957)** reversed the Smith Act convictions of five Communist Party officials. In reaching its decision, the Supreme Court distinguished between teaching and advocating an idea—the violent overthrow of the United States government—and teaching and advocating various concrete violent acts intended to overthrow the government. Speech advocating a violent idea is protected by the free speech clause, while speech advocating violent action is not.

Youngstown Sheet & Tube Co.* v. *Sawyer (the Steel Seizure Case) **(1952)** arose when a nationwide strike of steelworkers threatened to shut down the industry at the height of the Korean War. (Steel production was essential to the war effort.) To avert the strike, President Truman ordered the secretary of commerce to take over the steel mills and keep them running. The Supreme Court held that the president must relinquish control of the mills because he had exceeded his constitutional authority. The Court specifically held that the president's authority as commander in chief did not justify his action. The Court explained that only Congress could "nationalize" an industry; if Congress did so, the president, who is constitutionally required to execute the law, would be authorized to seize and operate the mills.

Zemel* v. *Rusk **(1965)** placed a national-security limitation on a citizen's right to travel abroad. In this case, a citizen tried to get a visa to travel to Cuba, a Communist country with very tense relations with the United States in the early to mid-1960s. The State Department denied the visa request and the Supreme Court affirmed, citing the "weightiest considerations of national security" as illustrated by the Cuban missile crisis of 1962 that had the United States on the brink of war with the Soviet Union.

Zorach* v. *Clauson **(1952)** upheld a New York City program that allowed students to be released early from school to attend religious classes in church buildings, not in public schools as in *McCollum* v. *Board of Education* (see above). The Supreme Court explained that all costs of the program were borne by the participating religions and that no public money, no public facility, and no public employee had any involvement with the program.

Leaders of Government

Chief Justices of the United States

Name and Years of Service	State From Which Appointed	President By Whom Appointed
John Jay (1789–1795)	NY	Washington
John Rutledge (1795)*	SC	Washington
Oliver Ellsworth (1796–1800)	CT	Washington
John Marshall (1801–1835)	VA	John Adams
Roger B. Taney (1836–1864)	MD	Jackson
Salmon P. Chase (1864–1873)	OH	Lincoln
Morrison R. Waite (1874–1888)	OH	Grant
Melville W. Fuller (1888–1910)	IL	Cleveland
Edward D. White (1910–1921)	LA	Taft
William Howard Taft (1921–1930)	CT	Harding
Charles Evans Hughes (1930–1941)	NY	Hoover
Harlan F. Stone (1941–1946)	NY	F.D.Roosevelt
Fred M. Vinson (1946–1953)	KY	Truman
Earl Warren (1953–1969)	CA	Eisenhower
Warren E. Burger (1969–1986)	D.C.	Nixon
William H. Rehnquist (1986–)	AZ	Reagan

** Rutledge was appointed Chief Justice on July 1, 1795, while Congress was not in session. He presided over the August 1795 term of the Supreme Court, but the Senate rejected his appointment on December 15, 1795.*

Senate Majority Leaders

Congress	Years	Leader
62nd	1911–13	Shelby M. Cullom, R–IL
63rd-64th	1913–17	John W. Kern, D–IN
65th	1917–19	Thomas S. Martin, D–VA
66th-67th	1919–24	Henry Cabot Lodge, R–MA
68th-70th	1924–29	Charles Curtis, R–KS
71st-72nd	1929–33	James E. Watson, R–IN
73rd-75th	1933–37	Joseph T. Robinson, D–AR
75th-79th	1937–47	Alben W. Barkley, D–KY
80th	1947–49	Wallace H. White, Jr., R–ME
81st	1949–51	Scott W. Lucas, D–IL
82nd	1951–53	Ernest W. McFarland, D–AZ
83rd	1953–55	Robert A. Taft, R–OH
		William F. Knowland, R–CA
84th-86th	1955–61	Lyndon B. Johnson, D–TX
87th-94th	1961–77	Mike Mansfield, D–MT
95th-96th	1977–81	Robert C. Byrd, D–WV
97th-98th	1981–85	Howard H. Baker, Jr., R–TN
99th	1985–87	Robert Dole, R–KS
100th	1987–89	Robert C. Byrd, D–WV
101st-103rd	1989–95	George J. Mitchell, D–ME
104th	1995–96	Robert Dole, R–KS
104th-106th	1996–	Trent Lott, R–MS

Speakers of the House of Representatives

Congress	Years	Speaker
1st	1789–91	Frederick A.C. Muhlenberg, F–PA
2nd	1791–93	Jonathan Trumbull, F–CT
3rd	1793–95	Frederick A.C. Muhlenberg, F–PA
4th-5th	1795–99	Jonathan Dayton, F–NJ
6th	1799–1801	Theodore Sedgwick, F–MA
7th-9th	1801–07	Nathaniel Macon, D–NC
10th-11th	1807–11	Joseph B. Varnum, D–MA
12th-13th	1811–14	Henry Clay, R–KY
13th	1814–15	Langdon Cheves, D–SC
14th-16th	1815–20	Henry Clay, R–KY
16th	1820–21	John W. Taylor, D–NY
17th	1821–23	Philip P. Barbour, D–VA
18th	1823–25	Henry Clay, R–KY
19th	1825–27	John W. Taylor, D–NY
20th-23rd	1827–34	Andrew Stevenson, D–VA
23rd	1834–35	John Bell, W–TN
24th-25th	1835–39	James K. Polk, D–TN
26th	1839–41	Robert M.T. Hunter, D–VA
27th	1841–43	John White, W–KY
28th	1843–45	John W. Jones, D–VA
29th	1845–47	John W. Davis, D–IN
30th	1847–49	Robert C. Winthrop, W–MA
31st	1849–51	Howell Cobb, D–GA
32nd-33rd	1851–55	Linn Boyd, D–KY
34th	1855–57	Nathaniel P. Banks, R–MA
35th	1857–59	James L. Orr, D–SC
36th	1859–61	William Pennington, R–NJ
37th	1861–63	Galusha A. Grow, R–PA
38th-40th	1863–68	Schuyler Colfax, R–IN
40th	1868–69	Theodore M. Pomeroy, R–NY
41st-43rd	1869–75	James G. Blaine, R–ME
44th	1875–76	Michael C. Kerr, D–IN
44th-46th	1876–81	Samuel J. Randall, D–PA
47th	1881–83	Joseph Warren Keifer, R–OH
48th-50th	1883–89	John G. Carlisle, D–KY
51st	1889–91	Thomas Brackett Reed, R–ME
52nd-53rd	1891–95	Charles F. Crisp, D–GA
54th-55th	1895–99	Thomas Brackett Reed, R–ME
56th-57th	1899–1903	David B. Henderson, R–IA
58th-61st	1903–11	Joseph G. Cannon, R–IL
62nd-65th	1911–19	James B. Clark, D–MO
66th-68th	1919–25	Frederick H. Gillet, R–MA
69th-71st	1925–31	Nicholas Longworth, R–OH
72nd	1931–33	John Nance Garner, D–TX
73rd	1933–34	Henry T. Rainey, D–IL*
74th	1935–36	Joseph W. Byrns, D–TN
74th-76th	1936–40	William B. Bankhead, D–AL
76th-79th	1940–47	Sam Rayburn, D–TX
80th	1947–49	Joseph W. Martin, Jr., R–MA
81st-82nd	1949–53	Sam Rayburn, D–TX
83rd	1953–55	Joseph W. Martin, Jr., R–MA
84th-87th	1955–61	Sam Rayburn, D–TX
87th-91st	1962–71	John W. McCormack, D–MA
92nd-94th	1971–77	Carl B. Albert, D–OK
95th-99th	1977–87	Thomas P. O'Neill, Jr., D–MA
100th-101st	1987–89	Jim C. Wright Jr., D–TX**
101st-103rd	1989–95	Thomas S. Foley, D–WA
104th-105th	1995–99	Newt Gingrich, R–GA
106th	1999–	J. Dennis Hastert, R–IL

* Rainey died in 1934, but was not replaced until the next Congress.
** Wright resigned and was replaced by Foley on June 6, 1989.

Party abbreviations: (D) Democrat, (F) Federalist, (R) Republican, (W) Whig

Declaration of Independence

July 4, 1776

Delegates at the Second Continental Congress faced an enormous task. The war against Great Britain had begun, but to many colonists the purpose for fighting was unclear. As sentiment increased for a complete break with Britain, Congress decided to act. A committee was appointed to prepare a document that declared the thirteen colonies free and independent from Britain. More important, the committee needed to explain why separation was the only fitting solution to long-standing disputes with Parliament and the British Crown. Thomas Jefferson was assigned to write a working draft of this document, which was then revised. It was officially adopted on July 4, 1776. More than any other action of Congress, the Declaration of Independence served to make the American colonists one people.

Liberty Bell

***The Second Continental Congress* by Edward Savage**

In Congress, July 4, 1776. The unanimous Declaration of the thirteen united States of America,

The printed text of the document shows the spelling and punctuation of the parchment original. To aid in comprehension, selected words and their definitions appear in the side margin, along with other explanatory notes.

Preamble

When in the Course of human events, it becomes necessary for one people to dissolve the political bands which have connected them with another, and to assume among the powers of the earth, the separate and equal station to which the Laws of Nature and Nature's God entitle them, a decent respect to the opinions of mankind requires that they should declare the causes which impel them to the separation.—

impel *force*

Declaration of Natural Rights

We hold these truths to be self-evident, that all men are created equal, that they are endowed by their Creator with certain unalienable Rights, that among these are Life, Liberty, and the pursuit of Happiness.—

endowed *provided*

That to secure these rights, Governments are instituted among Men, deriving their just powers from the consent of the governed,—

People create governments to ensure that their natural rights are protected.

That whenever any Form of Government becomes destructive of these ends, it is the Right of the People to alter or to abolish it, and to institute new Government, laying its foundation on such principles and organizing its powers in such form, as to them shall seem most likely to effect their Safety and Happiness. Prudence, indeed, will dictate that Governments long established should not be changed for light and transient causes; and accordingly all experience hath shewn, that mankind are more disposed to suffer, while evils are sufferable, than to right themselves by abolishing the forms to which they are accustomed. But when a long train of abuses and usurpations, pursuing invariably the same Object evinces a design to reduce them under absolute Despotism, it is their right, it is their duty, to throw off such Government, and to provide new Guards for their future security.—

If a government does not serve its purpose, the people have a right to abolish it. Then the people have the right and duty to create a new government that will safeguard their security.

Despotism *unlimited power*

List of Grievances

Such has been the patient sufferance of these Colonies; and such is now the necessity which constrains them to alter their former Systems of Government. The history of the present King of Great Britain is a history of repeated injuries and usurpations, all having in direct object the establishment of an absolute Tyranny over these States. To prove this, let Facts be submitted to a candid world.—

usurpations *unjust uses of power*

Each paragraph lists alleged injustices of George III.

He has refused his Assent to Laws, the most wholesome and necessary for the public good.—

He has forbidden his Governors to pass Laws of immediate and pressing importance, unless suspended in their operation till his Assent should be obtained; and when so suspended, he has utterly neglected to attend to them.—

He has refused to pass other Laws for the accommodation of large districts of people, unless those people would relinquish the right of Representation in the Legislature, a right inestimable to them and formidable to tyrants only.—

relinquish *give up*
inestimable *priceless*

He has called together legislative bodies at places unusual, uncomfortable, and distant from the depository of their public Records, for the sole purpose of fatiguing them into compliance with his measures.—

Annihilation *destruction*

convulsions *violent disturbances*

Naturalization of Foreigners *process by which foreign-born persons become citizens*

tenure *term*

Refers to the British troops sent to the colonies after the French and Indian War.

Refers to the 1766 Declaratory Act.

quartering *lodging*

Refers to the 1774 Quebec Act.

render *make*

abdicated *given up*

perfidy *violation of trust*

He has dissolved Representative Houses repeatedly, for opposing with manly firmness his invasions on the rights of the people.—

He has refused for a long time, after such dissolutions, to cause others to be elected; whereby the Legislative powers, incapable of Annihilation, have returned to the People at large for their exercise; the State remaining in the meantime exposed to all the dangers of invasion from without, and convulsions within.—

He has endeavoured to prevent the population of these States; for that purpose obstructing the Laws for Naturalization of Foreigners; refusing to pass others to encourage their migrations hither, and raising the conditions of new Appropriations of Lands.—

He has obstructed the Administration of Justice, by refusing his Assent to Laws for establishing Judiciary powers.—

He has made Judges dependent on his Will alone, for the tenure of their offices, and the amount and payment of their salaries.—

He has erected a multitude of New Offices, and sent hither swarms of Officers to harass our people, and eat out their substance.—

He has kept among us, in times of peace, Standing Armies without the Consent of our legislatures.—

He has affected to render the Military independent of and superior to the Civil power.—

He has combined with others to subject us to a jurisdiction foreign to our constitution, and unacknowledged by our laws; giving his Assent to their Acts of pretended Legislation:—

For quartering large bodies of troops among us:—

For protecting them, by a mock Trial, from punishment for any Murders which they should commit on the Inhabitants of these States:—

For cutting off our Trade with all parts of the world:—

For imposing Taxes on us without our Consent:—

For depriving us in many cases, of the benefits of Trial by Jury:—

For transporting us beyond Seas to be tried for pretended offences:—

For abolishing the free System of English Laws in a neighbouring Province, establishing therein an Arbitrary government, and enlarging its Boundaries so as to render it at once an example and fit instrument for introducing the same absolute rule into these Colonies:—

For taking away our Charters, abolishing our most valuable Laws, and altering fundamentally the Forms of our Governments:—

For suspending our own Legislatures, and declaring themselves invested with power to legislate for us in all cases whatsoever.—

He has abdicated Government here, by declaring us out of his Protection and waging War against us.—

He has plundered our seas, ravaged our Coasts, burnt our towns, and destroyed the Lives of our people.—

He is at this time transporting large Armies of foreign Mercenaries to compleat the works of death, desolation and tyranny, already begun with circumstances of Cruelty & perfidy scarcely paralleled in the most barbarous ages, and totally unworthy the Head of a civilized nation.—

He has constrained our fellow Citizens taken Captive on the high Seas to bear Arms against their Country, to become the executioners of their friends and Brethren, or to fall themselves by their Hands.—

He has excited domestic insurrections amongst us, and has endeavoured to bring on the inhabitants of our frontiers, the merciless Indian Savages, whose known rule of warfare, is an undistinguished destruction of all ages, sexes and conditions.

In every stage of these Oppressions We have Petitioned for Redress in the most humble terms: Our repeated Petitions have been answered only by repeated injury. A Prince, whose character is thus marked by every act which may define a Tyrant, is unfit to be the ruler of a free people.

Nor have We been wanting in attentions to our British brethren. We have warned them from time to time of attempts by their legislature to extend an unwarrantable jurisdiction over us. We have reminded them of the circumstances of our emigration and settlement here. We have appealed to their native justice and magnanimity, and we have conjured them by the ties of our common kindred to disavow these usurpations, which would inevitably interrupt our connections and correspondence. They too have been deaf to the voice of justice and of consanguinity. We must, therefore, acquiesce in the necessity, which denounces our Separation, and hold them, as we hold the rest of mankind, Enemies in War, in Peace Friends.—

insurrections *rebellions*

Petitioned for Redress *asked formally for a correction of wrongs*

unwarrantable jurisdiction *unjustified authority*

consanguinity *originating from the same ancestor*

Resolution of Independence by the United States

We, therefore, the Representatives of the united States of America, in General Congress, Assembled, appealing to the Supreme Judge of the world for the rectitude of our intentions, do, in the Name, and by Authority of the good People of these Colonies, solemnly publish and declare, That these United Colonies are, and of Right ought to be Free and Independent States; that they are Absolved from all Allegiance to the British Crown, and that all political connection between them and the State of Great Britain, is and ought to be totally dissolved; and that as Free and Independent States, they have full Power to levy War, conclude Peace, contract Alliances, establish Commerce, and to do all other Acts and Things which Independent States may of right do.—

And for the support of this Declaration, with a firm reliance on the protection of divine Providence, we mutually pledge to each other our Lives, our Fortunes and our sacred Honour.

rectitude *rightness*

The signers, as representatives of the American people, declared the colonies independent from Great Britain. Most members signed the document on August 2, 1776.

John Hancock
President from Massachusetts

Georgia
Button Gwinnett
Lyman Hall
George Walton

North Carolina
William Hooper
Joseph Hewes
John Penn

South Carolina
Edward Rutledge
Thomas Heyward, Jr.
Thomas Lynch, Jr.
Arthur Middleton

Maryland
Samuel Chase
William Paca
Thomas Stone
Charles Carroll of Carrollton

Virginia
George Wythe
Richard Henry Lee
Thomas Jefferson
Benjamin Harrison
Thomas Nelson Jr.
Francis Lightfoot Lee
Carter Braxton

Pennsylvania
Robert Morris
Benjamin Rush
Benjamin Franklin
John Morton
George Clymer
James Smith
George Taylor
James Wilson
George Ross

Delaware
Caesar Rodney
George Read
Thomas McKean

New York
William Floyd
Philip Livingston
Francis Lewis
Lewis Morris

New Jersey
Richard Stockton
John Witherspoon
Francis Hopkinson
John Hart
Abraham Clark

New Hampshire
Josiah Bartlett
William Whipple
Matthew Thornton

Massachusetts
Samuel Adams
John Adams
Robert Treat Paine
Elbridge Gerry

Rhode Island
Stephen Hopkins
William Ellery

Connecticut
Samuel Huntington
William Williams
Oliver Wolcott
Roger Sherman

Constitution of the United States

The Constitution of the United States is truly a remarkable document. It was one of the first written constitutions in modern history. The Framers wanted to devise a plan for a strong central government that would unify the country, as well as preserve the ideals of the Declaration of Independence. The document they wrote created a representative legislature, the office of president, a system of courts, and a process for adding amendments. For over 200 years, the flexibility and strength of the Constitution has guided the nation's political leaders. The document has become a symbol of pride and a force for national unity.

The entire text of the Constitution and its amendments follows. For easier study, those passages that have been set aside or changed by the adoption of amendments are printed in blue. Also included are explanatory notes that will help clarify the meaning of each article and section.

The Capitol, Washington, D.C.

Preamble

We, the people of the United States, in Order to form a more perfect Union, establish Justice, insure domestic Tranquility, provide for the common defence, promote the general Welfare, and secure the Blessings of Liberty to ourselves and our Posterity, do ordain and establish this Constitution for the United States of America.

The Preamble introduces the Constitution and sets forth the general purposes for which the government was established. The Preamble also declares that the power of the government comes from the people.

The printed text of the document shows the spelling and punctuation of the parchment original.

Article I

Section 1

All legislative Powers herein granted shall be vested in a Congress of the United States, which shall consist of a Senate and House of Representatives.

Section 2

1. The House of Representatives shall be composed of Members chosen every second Year by the People of the several States, and the Electors in each State shall have the Qualifications requisite for Electors of the most numerous Branch of the State Legislature.
2. No Person shall be a Representative who shall not have attained to the Age of twenty-five Years, and been seven Years a Citizen of the United States, and who shall not, when elected, be an Inhabitant of that State in which he shall be chosen.
3. Representatives and direct Taxes shall be apportioned among the several states which may be included within this Union, according to the respective Numbers, which shall be determined by adding to the whole Number of free Persons, including those bound to Service for a Term of Years, and excluding Indians not taxed, three-fifths of all other Persons. The actual Enumeration shall be made within three Years after the first Meeting of the Congress of the United States, and within every subsequent Term of ten Years, in such Manner as they shall by Law direct. The Number of Representatives shall not exceed one for every thirty Thousand, but each state shall have at Least one Representative; and until such enumeration shall be made, the State of New Hampshire shall be entitled to chuse three; Massachusetts eight, Rhode Island and Providence Plantations one, Connecticut five, New

Article I. The Legislative Branch

Section 1. Congress

The power to make laws is given to a Congress made up of two chambers to represent different interests: the Senate to represent the states; the House to be more responsive to the people's will.

Section 2. House of Representatives

1. **Election and Term of Office** "Electors" means voters. Every two years the voters choose new Congress members to serve in the House of Representatives. The Constitution states that each state may specify who can vote. But the 15th, 19th, 24th, and 26th Amendments have established guidelines that all states must follow regarding the right to vote.
2. **Qualifications** Representatives must be 25 years old, citizens of the United States for 7 years, and residents of the state they represent.
3. **Division of Representatives Among the States** The number of representatives from each state is based on the size of the state's population. Each state is divided into congressional districts, with each district required to be equal in population. Each state is entitled to at least one representative. The number of representatives in the House was set at 435 in 1929. Since then, there has been a reapportionment of seats based on population shifts rather than on addition of seats.

   Only three-fifths of a state's slave population was to be counted in determining the number of representatives elected by the state. Native Americans were not counted at all.

   The "enumeration" referred to is the

census, the population count taken every 10 years since 1790.

4. **Vacancies** Vacancies in the House are filled through special elections called by the state's governor.

5. **Officers** The Speaker is the leader of the majority party in the House and is responsible for choosing the heads of various House committees. "Impeachment" means indictment, or bringing charges against an official.

Section 3. The Senate

1. **Number of Members, Terms of Office, and Voting Procedure** Originally, senators were chosen by the state legislators of their own states. The 17th Amendment changed this, so that senators are now elected directly by the people. There are 100 senators, 2 from each state.

2. **Staggered Elections; Vacancies** One-third of the Senate is elected every two years. The terms of the first Senate's membership was staggered: one group served two years, one four, and one six. All senators now serve a six-year term.

   The 17th Amendment changed the method of filling vacancies in the Senate.

3. **Qualifications** Qualifications for the Senate are more restrictive than those for the House. Senators must be at least 30 years old and they must have been citizens of the United States for at least 9 years. The Framers of the Constitution made the Senate a more elite body in order to produce a further check on the powers of the House of Representatives.

4. **President of the Senate** The vice president's only duty listed in the Constitution is to preside over the Senate. The only real power the vice president has is to cast the deciding vote when there is a tie. However, modern presidents have given their vice presidents new responsibilities.

5. **Other Officers** The Senate selects its other officers, including a presiding officer (president pro tempore) who serves when the vice president is absent or has become president of the United States.

York six, New Jersey four, Pennsylvania eight, Delaware one, Maryland six, Virginia ten; North Carolina five, South Carolina five, and Georgia three.

4. **When vacancies happen in the Representation from any State, the Executive Authority thereof shall issue Writs of Election to fill such Vacancies.**

5. **The House of Representatives shall chuse their Speaker and other Officers; and shall have the sole Power of Impeachment.**

Section 3

1. **The Senate of the United States shall be composed of two Senators from each State, chosen** by the Legislature thereof; **for six Years; and each Senator shall have one Vote.**

2. **Immediately after they shall be assembled in Consequence of the first Election, they shall be divided as equally as may be into three Classes. The Seats of the Senators of the first Class shall be vacated at the Expiration of the second Year, of the second Class at the Expiration of the fourth Year, and of the third Class at the Expiration of the sixth Year, so that one-third may be chosen every second Year; and if Vacancies happen by Resignations, or otherwise,** during the Recess of the Legislature of any State, the Executive thereof may make temporary Appointments until the next Meeting of the Legislature, which shall then fill such Vacancies.

3. **No person shall be a Senator who shall not have attained the Age of thirty Years, and been nine Years a Citizen of the United States, and who shall not, when elected, be an Inhabitant of that State in which he shall be chosen.**

4. **The Vice President of the United States shall be President of the Senate, but shall have no vote, unless they be equally divided.**

5. **The Senate shall chuse their Officers, and also a President pro tempore, in the absence of the Vice-President or when he shall exercise the Office of the President of the United States.**

6. The Senate shall have the sole Power to try all impeachments. When sitting for that purpose they shall be on Oath or Affirmation. When the President of the United States is tried, the Chief Justice shall preside: And no person shall be convicted without the Concurrence of two-thirds of the Members present.

7. Judgment in Cases of Impeachment shall not extend further than to removal from Office, and disqualification to hold and enjoy any Office of Honor, Trust or Profit under the United States: but the Party convicted shall nevertheless be liable and subject to Indictment, Trial, Judgment and Punishment, according to Law.

6. **Trial of Impeachments** When trying a case of impeachment brought by the House, the Senate convenes as a court. The chief justice of the United States acts as the presiding judge, and the Senate acts as the jury. A two-thirds vote of the members present is necessary to convict officials under impeachment charges.

7. **Penalty for Conviction** If the Senate convicts an official, it may only remove the official from office and prevent that person from holding another federal position. However, the convicted official may still be tried for the same offense in a regular court of law.

Section 4

1. The Times, Places, and Manner of holding Elections for Senators and Representatives, shall be prescribed in each state by the Legislature thereof; but the Congress may at any time by Law make or alter such Regulations, except as to the Places of Chusing Senators.

2. The Congress shall assemble at least once in every Year, and such Meeting shall be on the first Monday in December, unless they shall by Law appoint a different Day.

Section 4. Elections and Meetings

1. **Holding Elections** In 1842 Congress required members of the House to be elected from districts in states having more than one representative rather than at large. In 1845 it set the first Tuesday after the first Monday in November as the day for selecting presidential electors.

2. **Meetings** The 20th Amendment, ratified in 1933, has changed the date of the opening of the regular session of Congress to January 3.

Section 5

1. Each House shall be the Judge of the Elections, Returns and Qualifications of its own Members, and a Majority of each shall constitute a Quorum to do Business; but a smaller Number may adjourn from day to day, and may be authorized to compel the Attendance of absent Members, in such Manner, and under such Penalties as each House may provide.

2. Each House may determine the Rules of its Proceedings, punish its Members for disorderly Behaviour, and, with the Concurrence of two-thirds, expel a Member.

Section 5. Organization and Rules of Procedure

1. **Organization** Until 1969 Congress acted as the sole judge of qualifications of its own members. In that year, the Supreme Court ruled that Congress could not legally exclude victorious candidates who met all the requirements listed in Article I, Section 2.

   A "quorum" is the minimum number of members that must be present for the House or Senate to conduct sessions. For a regular House session, a quorum consists of the majority of the House, or 218 of the 435 members.

2. **Rules** Each house sets its own rules, can punish its members for disorderly behavior, and can expel a member by a two-thirds vote.

3. **Journals** In addition to the journals, a complete official record of everything said on the floor, as well as the roll call votes on all bills or issues, is available in the *Congressional Record,* published daily by the Government Printing Office.

4. **Adjournment** Neither house may adjourn for more than three days or move to another location without the approval of the other house.

Section 6. Privileges and Restrictions

1. **Pay and Privileges** To strengthen the federal government, the Founders set congressional salaries to be paid by the United States Treasury rather than by members' respective states. Originally, members were paid $6 per day. Salaries for senators and representatives were $136,700 beginning in 1998.

   The "immunity" privilege means members cannot be sued or be prosecuted for anything they say in Congress. They cannot be arrested while Congress is in session, except for treason, major crimes, or breaking the peace.

2. **Restrictions** "Emoluments" means salaries. The purpose of this clause is to prevent members of Congress from passing laws that would benefit them personally. It also prevents the president from promising them jobs in other branches of the federal government.

Section 7. Passing Laws

1. **Revenue Bills** "Revenue" is income raised by the government. The chief source of government revenue is taxes. All tax laws must originate in the House of Representatives. This ensures that the branch of Congress which is elected by the people every two years has the major role in determining taxes. This clause does not prevent the Senate from amending tax bills.

2. **How Bills Become Laws** A bill may become a law only by passing both houses of Congress and by being signed by the president. If the president disapproves, or vetoes, the bill, it is returned to the house where it originated, along with a written statement of the

3. Each House shall keep a Journal of its Proceedings, and from time to time publish the same, excepting such Parts as may in their Judgment require Secrecy; and the Yeas and Nays of the Members of either House on any question shall, at the desire of one-fifth of those Present, be entered on the Journal.

4. Neither House during the Session of Congress, shall, without the Consent of the other, adjourn for more than three days, nor to any other Place than that in which the two Houses shall be sitting.

Section 6

1. The Senators and Representatives shall receive a Compensation for their Services, to be ascertained by Law, and paid out of the Treasury of the United States. They shall in all Cases, except Treason, Felony and Breach of the Peace be privileged from Arrest during their attendance at the Session of their respective Houses, and in going to and returning from the same; and for any Speech or Debate in either House, they shall not be questioned in any other place.

2. No Senator or Representative shall, during the Time for which he was elected, be appointed to any civil Office under the Authority of the United States, which shall have been created, or the Emoluments whereof shall have been encreased, during such time; and no Person holding any Office under the United States, shall be a Member of either House during his continuance in Office.

Section 7

1. All Bills for raising Revenue shall originate in the House of Representatives; but the Senate may propose or concur with Amendments as on other bills.

2. Every Bill which shall have passed the House of Representatives and the Senate, shall, before it become a Law, be presented to the President of the United States; If he approve he shall sign it, but if not he shall return it, with his Objections, to that House in which it shall have originated, who shall enter the Objections at large on their Journal, and proceed to reconsider it. If after such Reconsideration two-thirds of that House shall agree to pass the bill, it shall be sent, together with the

objections, to the other House, by which it shall likewise be reconsidered, and if approved by two-thirds of that House, it shall become a Law. But in all such Cases the Votes of both Houses shall be determined by Yeas and Nays, and the Names of the Persons voting for and against the Bill shall be entered on the Journal of each House respectively. If any Bill shall not be returned by the President within ten Days (Sundays excepted) after it shall have been presented to him, the Same shall be a Law, in like Manner as if he had signed it, unless the Congress by their Adjournment prevent its Return, in which Case it shall not be a Law.

3. Every Order, Resolution, or Vote to which the Concurrence of the Senate and House of Representatives may be necessary (except on a question of Adjournment) shall be presented to the President of the United States; and before the Same shall take Effect, shall be approved by him, or, being disapproved by him, shall be repassed by two-thirds of the Senate and House of Representatives, according to the Rules and Limitations prescribed in the case of a Bill.

president's objections. If two-thirds of each house approves the bill after the president has vetoed it, it becomes law. In voting to override a president's veto, the votes of all members of Congress must be recorded in the journals or official records. If the president does not sign or veto a bill within 10 days (excluding Sundays), it becomes law. However, if Congress has adjourned during this 10-day period, the bill does not become law. This is known as a "pocket veto."

3. **Presidential Approval or Veto** The Framers included this paragraph to prevent Congress from passing joint resolutions instead of bills to avoid the possibility of a presidential veto. A bill is a draft of a proposed law, whereas a resolution is the legislature's formal expression of opinion or intent on a matter.

Section 8

The Congress shall have the Power

1. To lay and collect Taxes, Duties, Imposts and Excises, to pay the Debts and provide for the common Defence and general Welfare of the United States; but all Duties, Imposts and Excises shall be uniform throughout the United States;
2. To borrow money on the credit of the United States;
3. To regulate Commerce with foreign Nations, and among the several States, and with the Indian Tribes;
4. To establish an uniform Rule of Naturalization, and uniform Laws on the subject of Bankruptcies throughout the United States.
5. To coin Money, regulate the Value thereof, and of foreign Coin, and fix the Standard of Weights and Measures;
6. To provide for the Punishment of counterfeiting the Securities and current Coin of the United States;

Section 8. Powers Granted to Congress

1. **Revenue** This clause gives Congress the power to raise and spend revenue. Taxes must be levied at the same rate throughout the nation.
2. **Borrowing** The federal government borrows money by issuing bonds.
3. **Commerce** The exact meaning of "commerce" has caused controversy. The trend has been to expand its meaning and, consequently, the extent of Congress's powers.
4. **Naturalization and Bankruptcy** "Naturalization" refers to the procedure by which a citizen of a foreign nation becomes a citizen of the United States.
5. **Currency** Control over money is an exclusive federal power; the states are forbidden to issue currency.
6. **Counterfeiting** "Counterfeiting" means illegally imitating or forging.

7. **Post Office** In 1970 the United States Postal Service replaced the Post Office Department.

8. **Copyrights and Patents** Under this provision, Congress has passed copyright and patent laws.

9. **Courts** This provision allows Congress to establish a federal court system.

10. **Piracy** Congress has the power to protect American ships on the high seas.

11. **Declare War** While the Constitution gives Congress the right to declare war, the United States has sent troops into combat without a congressional declaration.

12. **Army** This provision reveals the Framers' fears of a standing army.

13. **Navy** This clause allows Congress to establish a navy.

14. **Rules for Armed Forces** Congress may pass regulations that deal with military discipline.

15. **Militia** The "militia" is now called the National Guard. It is organized by the states.

16. **National Guard** Even though the National Guard is organized by the states, Congress has the authority to pass rules for governing its behavior.

17. **Nation's Capital** This clause grants Congress the right to make laws for Washington, D.C.

18. **Elastic Clause** This is the so-called "elastic clause" of the Constitution and one of its most important provisions. The "necessary and proper" laws must be related to one of the 17 enumerated powers.

7. To establish Post Offices and post Roads;

8. To promote the Progress of Science and useful Arts, by securing for limited Times to Authors and Inventors the exclusive Right to their respective Writings and Discoveries;

9. To constitute Tribunals inferior to the Supreme Court;

10. To define and punish Piracies and Felonies committed on the high Seas, and Offenses against the Law of Nations.

11. To declare War, grant Letters of Marque and Reprisal, and make Rules concerning Captures on Land and Water;

12. To raise and support Armies, but no Appropriation of Money to that Use shall be for a longer Term than two Years;

13. To provide and maintain a Navy;

14. To make Rules for the Government and Regulation of the land and naval forces;

15. To provide for calling forth the Militia to execute the Laws of the Union, suppress Insurrections, and repel Invasions;

16. To provide for organizing, arming, and disciplining, the Militia, and for governing such Part of them as may be employed in the Service of the United States, reserving to the States respectively, the Appointment of the Officers, and the Authority of training the Militia according to the discipline prescribed by Congress;

17. To exercise exclusive Legislation in all Cases whatsoever, over such District (not exceeding ten Miles square) as may, by Cession of particular States, and the acceptance of Congress, become the Seat of Government of the United States, and to exercise like Authority over all Places purchased by the Consent of the Legislature of the State in which the Same shall be, for the Erection of Forts, Magazines, Arsenals, dock-Yards, and other needful Buildings;—And

18. To make all Laws which shall be necessary and proper for carrying into Execution the foregoing Powers, and all other Powers vested by this Constitution in the Government of the United States, or in any Department or Officer thereof.

Section 9

1. The Migration or Importation of such Persons as any of the States now existing shall think proper to admit, shall not be prohibited by the Congress prior to the Year one thousand eight hundred and eight, but a tax or duty may be imposed on such importation, not exceeding ten dollars for each Person.
2. The privilege of the Writ of Habeas Corpus shall not be suspended, unless when in Cases of Rebellion or Invasion the public Safety may require it.
3. No Bill of Attainder or ex post facto Law shall be passed.
4. No capitation, or other direct, Tax shall be laid unless in Proportion to the Census or Enumeration herein before directed to be taken.
5. No Tax or Duty shall be laid on Articles exported from any State.
6. No Preference shall be given by any Regulation of Commerce or Revenue to the Ports of one State over those of another: nor shall Vessels bound to, or from, one State, be obliged to enter, clear, or pay Duties in another.
7. No Money shall be drawn from the Treasury, but in Consequence of Appropriations made by Law; and a regular Statement and Account of the Receipts and Expenditures of all public Money shall be published from time to time.
8. No Title of Nobility shall be granted by the United States:—And no Person holding any Office of Profit or Trust under them, shall, without the Consent of the Congress, accept of any present, Emolument, Office, or Title, of any kind whatever, from any King, Prince, or foreign State.

Section 10

1. No State shall enter into any Treaty, Alliance, or Confederation; grant Letters of Marque and Reprisal; coin Money; emit Bills of Credit; make any Thing but gold and silver Coin a Tender in Payment of Debts; pass any Bill of Attainder; ex post facto Law, or Law impairing the Obligation of Contracts, or grant any Title of Nobility.

Section 9. Powers Denied to the Federal Government

1. **Slave Trade** This paragraph contains the compromise the Framers reached regarding regulation of the slave trade in exchange for Congress's exclusive control over interstate commerce.
2. **Habeas Corpus** *Habeas corpus* is a Latin term meaning "you may have the body." A writ of habeas corpus issued by a judge requires a law official to bring a prisoner to court and show cause for holding the prisoner. The writ may be suspended only during wartime.
3. **Bills of Attainder** A "bill of attainder" is a bill that punishes a person without a jury trial. An "ex post facto" law is one that makes an act a crime after the act has been committed.
4. **Direct Taxes** The 16th Amendment allowed Congress to pass an income tax.
5. **Tax on Exports** Congress may not tax goods that move from one state to another.
6. **Uniformity of Treatment** This prohibition prevents Congress from favoring one state or region over another in the regulation of trade.
7. **Appropriation Law** This clause protects against the misuse of funds. All of the president's expenditures must be made with the permission of Congress.
8. **Titles of Nobility** This clause prevents the development of a nobility in the United States.

Section 10. Powers Denied to the States

1. **Limitations on Power** The states are prohibited from conducting foreign affairs, carrying on a war, or controlling interstate and foreign commerce. States are also not allowed to pass laws that the federal government is prohibited from passing, such as enacting ex post facto laws or bills of attainder. These restrictions on the states were designed, in part, to prevent an overlapping in functions and authority with the federal government that could create conflict and chaos.

2. **Export and Import Taxes** This clause prevents states from levying duties on exports and imports. If states were permitted to tax imports and exports, they could use their taxing power in a way that weakens or destroys Congress's power to control interstate and foreign commerce.

3. **Duties, Armed Forces, War** This clause prohibits states from maintaining an army or navy and from going to war, except in cases where a state is directly attacked. It also forbids states from collecting fees from foreign vessels or from making treaties with other nations. All of these powers are reserved for the federal government.

2. No State shall, without the Consent of the Congress, lay any Imposts or Duties on Imports or Exports, except what may be absolutely necessary for executing its inspection Laws: and the net Produce of all Duties and Imposts, laid by any State on Imports and Exports, shall be for the Use of the Treasury of the United States; and all such Laws shall be subject to the Revision and Controul of the Congress.

3. No State shall, without the Consent of Congress, lay any duty on Tonnage, keep Troops, or Ships of War in time of Peace, enter into any Agreement or Compact with another State, or with a foreign Power, or engage in War, unless actually invaded, or in such imminent Danger as will not admit of delay.

Article II. The Executive Branch

Section 1. President and Vice President

1. **Term of Office** The president is given power to enforce the laws passed by Congress. Both the president and the vice president serve four-year terms. The 22nd Amendment limits the number of terms the president may serve to two.

2. **Election** The Philadelphia Convention had trouble deciding how the president was to be chosen. The system finally agreed upon was indirect election by "electors" chosen for that purpose. The president and vice president are not directly elected. Instead, the president and vice president are elected by presidential electors from each state who form the electoral college. Each state has the number of presidential electors equal to the total number of its senators and representatives. State legislatures determine how the electors are chosen. Originally, the state legislatures chose the electors, but today they are nominated by political parties and elected by the voters. No senator, representative, or any other federal officeholder can serve as an elector.

3. **Former Method of Election** This clause describes the original method of electing the president and vice president. According to this method, each elector voted for two

Article II

Section 1

1. The executive Power shall be vested in a President of the United States of America. He shall hold his Office during the Term of four years, and together with the Vice-President chosen for the same Term, be elected, as follows:

2. Each State shall appoint, in such Manner as the Legislature thereof may direct, a Number of Electors, equal to the whole Number of Senators and Representatives to which the State may be entitled in the Congress: but no Senator or Representative, or Person holding an Office of Trust or Profit under the United States, shall be appointed an Elector.

3. The Electors shall meet in their respective States, and vote by Ballot for two Persons, of whom one at least shall not be an Inhabitant of the same State with themselves. And they shall make a List of all the Persons voted for and of the Number of Votes for each; which List they shall sign and certify, and transmit sealed to the Seat of the Government of the United States, directed to the President of the Senate. The President of the Senate shall, in the Presence of the Senate and House of Representatives, open all the Certificates, and the Votes shall then be counted. The Person having the greatest Number of Votes shall be the President, if such Number be a Majority of the whole Number of Electors appointed; and if

there be more than one who have such Majority, and have an equal Number of Votes, then the House of Representatives shall immediately chuse by Ballot one of them for President; and if no Person have a Majority, then from the five highest on the List the said House shall in like Manner chuse the President. But in chusing the President, the Votes shall be taken by States, the Representation from each State having one Vote; a quorum for this Purpose shall consist of a Member or Members from two-thirds of the States, and a Majority of all the States shall be necessary to a Choice. In every Case, after the Choice of the President, the Person having the greatest Number of Votes of the Electors shall be the Vice-President. But if there should remain two or more who have equal votes, the Senate shall chuse from them by Ballot the Vice President.

4. The Congress may determine the Time of chusing the Electors, and the Day on which they shall give their Votes; which Day shall be the same throughout the United States.

5. No person except a natural born Citizen, or a Citizen of the United States, at the time of the Adoption of this Constitution, shall be eligible to the Office of President; neither shall any Person be eligible to that Office who shall not have attained to the Age of thirty-five years, and been fourteen Years a Resident within the United States.

6. In Case of the Removal of the President from Office, or of his Death, Resignation, or Inability to discharge the Powers and Duties of the said Office, the same shall devolve on the Vice-President, and the Congress may by Law provide for the Case of Removal, Death, Resignation or Inability, both of the President and Vice-President, declaring what Officer shall then act as President, and such Officer shall act accordingly, until the disability be removed, or a President shall be elected.

7. The President shall, at stated Times, receive for his Services a Compensation, which shall neither be encreased nor diminished during the Period for which he shall have been elected, and he shall not receive within that Period any other Emolument from the United States, or any of them.

candidates. The candidate with the most votes (as long as it was a majority) became president. The candidate with the second highest number of votes became vice president. In the election of 1800, the two top candidates received the same number of votes, making it necessary for the House of Representatives to decide the election. To prevent such a situation from recurring, the 12th Amendment was added in 1804.

4. **Date of Elections** Congress selects the date when the presidential electors are chosen and when they vote for president and vice president. All electors must vote on the same day. The first Tuesday after the first Monday in November has been set as the date for presidential elections. Electors cast their votes on the Monday after the second Wednesday in December.

5. **Qualifications** The president must be a citizen of the United States by birth, at least 35 years old, and a resident of the United States for 14 years. See Amendment 22.

6. **Vacancies** If the president dies, resigns, is removed from office by impeachment, or is unable to carry out the duties of the office, the vice president becomes president. (Amendment 25 deals with presidential disability.) If both the president and vice president are unable to serve, Congress has the power to declare by law who acts as president. Congress set the line of succession in the Presidential Succession Act of 1947.

7. **Salary** Originally, the president's salary was $25,000 per year. The president's current salary of $400,000 plus a $50,000 taxable expense account per year was enacted in 1999. The president also receives numerous fringe benefits including a $100,000 nontaxable allowance for travel and entertainment, and living accommodations in two residences—the White House and Camp David. However, the president cannot receive any other income from the United States government or state governments while in office.

8. **Oath of Office** The oath of office is generally administered by the chief justice, but can be administered by any official authorized to administer oaths. All presidents-elect except Washington have been sworn into office by the chief justice. Only Vice Presidents John Tyler, Calvin Coolidge, and Lyndon Johnson in succeeding to the office have been sworn in by someone else.

Section 2. Powers of the President

1. **Military, Cabinet, Pardons** Mention of "the principal officer in each of the executive departments" is the only suggestion of the president's cabinet to be found in the Constitution. The cabinet is a purely advisory body, and its power depends on the president. Each cabinet member is appointed by the president and must be confirmed by the Senate. This clause also makes the president, a civilian, the head of the armed services. This established the principle of civilian control of the military.
2. **Treaties and Appointments** The president is the chief architect of American foreign policy. He or she is responsible for the conduct of foreign relations, or dealings with other countries. All treaties, however, require approval of two-thirds of the senators present. Most federal positions today are filled under the rules and regulations of the civil service system. Most presidential appointees serve at the pleasure of the president. Removal of an official by the president is not subject to congressional approval. But the power can be restricted by conditions set in creating the office.
3. **Vacancies in Offices** The president can temporarily appoint officials to fill vacancies when the Senate is not in session.

Section 3. Duties of the President

Under this provision the president delivers annual State of the Union messages. On occasion, presidents have called Congress into special session to consider particular problems.

The president's duty to receive foreign diplomats also includes the power to ask a foreign country to withdraw its diplomatic officials from

8. Before he enter on the execution of his office, he shall take the following Oath or Affirmation "I do solemnly swear (or affirm) that I will faithfully execute the Office of President of the United States, and will to the best of my Ability, preserve, protect and defend the Constitution of the United States.

Section 2

1. The President shall be Commander in Chief of the Army and Navy of the United States, and of the Militia of the several States, when called into the actual Service of the United States; he may require the Opinion, in writing, of the principal Officer in each of the executive Departments, upon any subject relating to the Duties of their respective Offices, and he shall have Power to Grant Reprieves and Pardons for Offences against the United States, except in Cases of Impeachment.
2. He shall have Power, by and with the Advice and Consent of the Senate, to make Treaties, provided two-thirds of the Senators present concur; and he shall nominate, and by and with the Advice and Consent of the Senate, shall appoint Ambassadors, other public Ministers and Consuls, Judges of the supreme Court, and all other Officers of the United States, whose Appointments are not herein otherwise provided for, and which shall be established by Law. But the Congress may by Law vest the Appointment of such inferior Officers, as they think proper, in the President alone, in the Courts of Law, or in the Heads of Departments.
3. The President shall have Power to fill up all Vacancies that may happen during the Recess of the Senate, by granting Commissions which shall expire at the End of their next Session.

Section 3

He shall from time to time give to Congress Information of the State of the Union, and recommend to their Consideration such Measures as he shall judge necessary and expedient; he may, on extraordinary occasions, convene both Houses, or either of them, and in Case of Disagreement between them, with respect to the Time of Adjournment, he may adjourn them to such Time as he shall think proper; he shall receive

Ambassadors and other public Ministers; he shall take Care that the Laws be faithfully executed, and shall Commission all the Officers of the United States.

Section 4

The President, Vice-President and all civil Officers of the United States, shall be removed from Office on Impeachment for, and Conviction of, Treason, Bribery, or other high Crimes and Misdemeanors.

Article III

Section 1

The Judicial Power of the United States, shall be vested in one supreme Court, and in such inferior Courts as the Congress may from time to time ordain and establish. The judges, both of the supreme and inferior Courts, shall hold their Offices during good Behaviour, and shall, at stated Times, receive for their Services, a Compensation, which shall not be diminished during their Continuance in Office.

Section 2

1. The judicial Power shall extend to all Cases, in Law and Equity, arising under this Constitution, the Laws of the United States, and treaties made, or which shall be made, under their Authority; to all Cases affecting ambassadors, other public ministers and consuls; to all cases of admiralty and maritime Jurisdiction; to Controversies to which the United States shall be a party; to Controversies between two or more states; between a State and Citizens of another State; between Citizens of different States; between Citizens of the same State claiming Lands under Grants of different States, and between a State, or the Citizens thereof, and foreign States, Citizens or Subjects.
2. In all Cases affecting Ambassadors, other public Ministers and Consuls, and those in which a State shall be Party, the supreme Court shall have original Jurisdiction. In all the other Cases before mentioned, the supreme Court shall have appellate Jurisdiction, both as to Law and Fact, with such Exceptions, and under such Regulations as the Congress shall make.

this country. This is called "breaking diplomatic relations" and often carries with it the implied threat of more drastic action, even war. The president likewise has the power of deciding whether or not to recognize foreign governments.

Section 4. Impeachment

This section states the reasons for which the president and vice president may be impeached and removed from office. (See annotations of Article I, Section 3, Clauses 6 and 7.)

Article III. The Judicial Branch

Section 1. Federal Courts

The term *judicial* refers to courts. The Constitution set up only the Supreme Court but provided for the establishment of other federal courts. There are presently nine justices on the Supreme Court. Congress has created a system of federal district courts and courts of appeals, which review certain district court cases. Judges of these courts serve during "good behavior," which means that they usually serve for life or until they choose to retire.

Section 2. Jurisdiction

1. **General Jurisdiction** Use of the words *in law and equity* reflects the fact that American courts took over two kinds of traditional law from Great Britain. The basic law was the "common law," which was based on over five centuries of judicial decisions. "Equity" was a special branch of British law developed to handle cases where common law did not apply.

   Federal courts deal mostly with "statute law," or laws passed by Congress, treaties, and cases involving the Constitution itself. "Admiralty and maritime jurisdiction" covers all sorts of cases involving ships and shipping on the high seas and on rivers, canals, and lakes.
2. **The Supreme Court** When a court has "original jurisdiction" over certain kinds of cases, it means that the court has the authority to be the first court to hear a case. A court with "appellate jurisdiction" hears cases that have been appealed from lower courts. Most Supreme Court cases are heard on appeal from lower courts.

3. **Jury Trials** Except in cases of impeachment, anyone accused of a crime has the right to a trial by jury. The trial must be held in the state where the crime was committed. Jury trial guarantees were strengthened in the 6th, 7th, 8th, and 9th Amendments.

Section 3. Treason

1. **Definition** Knowing that the charge of treason often had been used by monarchs to get rid of people who opposed them, the Framers of the Constitution defined treason carefully, requiring that at least two witnesses be present to testify in court that a treasonable act was committed.

2. **Punishment** Congress is given the power to determine the punishment for treason. The children of a person convicted of treason may not be punished nor may the convicted person's property be taken away from the children. Convictions for treason have been relatively rare in the nation's history.

Article IV. Relations Among the States

Section 1. Official Acts

This provision ensures that each state recognizes the laws, court decisions, and records of all other states. For example, a marriage license or corporation charter issued by one state must be accepted in other states.

Section 2. Mutual Duties of States

1. **Privileges** The "privileges and immunities," or rights of citizens, guarantee each state's citizens equal treatment in all states.

2. **Extradition** "Extradition" means that a person convicted of a crime or a person accused of a crime must be returned to the state where the crime was committed. Thus, a person cannot flee to another state hoping to escape the law.

3. **Fugitive-Slave Clause** Formerly this clause meant that slaves could not become free persons by escaping to free states.

3. The trial of all Crimes, except in Cases of Impeachment, shall be by Jury; and such Trial shall be held in the State where the said Crimes shall have been committed; but when not committed within any State, the Trial shall be at such Place or Places as the Congress may by Law have directed.

Section 3

1. Treason against the United States, shall consist only in levying War against them, or in adhering to their Enemies, giving them Aid and Comfort. No Person shall be convicted of Treason unless on the Testimony of two Witnesses to the same overt Act, or on Confession in open Court.

2. The Congress shall have power to declare the Punishment of Treason, but no Attainder of Treason shall work Corruption of Blood, or Forfeiture except during the Life of the Person attainted.

Article IV

Section 1

Full Faith and Credit shall be given in each State to the public Acts, Records, and judicial Proceedings of every other State. And the Congress may by general Laws prescribe the Manner in which such Acts, Records, and Proceedings shall be proved, and the Effect thereof.

Section 2

1. The Citizens of each State shall be entitled to all Privileges and Immunities of Citizens in the several States.

2. A Person charged in any State with Treason, Felony, or other Crime, who shall flee from Justice, and be found in another State, shall on demand of the executive Authority of the State from which he fled, be delivered up, to be removed to the State having Jurisdiction of the crime.

3. No Person held to Service of Labour in one State, under the Laws thereof, escaping into another, shall, in Consequence of any Law or Regulation therein, be discharged from such Service or Labour, but shall be delivered up on Claim of the Party to whom such Service or Labour may be due.

Section 3

1. New States may be admitted by the Congress into this Union; but no new State shall be formed or erected within the Jurisdiction of any other State; nor any State be formed by the Junction of two or more States, or parts of States, without the Consent of the Legislatures of the States concerned as well as of the Congress.
2. The Congress shall have Power to dispose of and make all needful Rules and Regulations respecting the Territory or other Property belonging to the United States; and nothing in this Constitution shall be so construed as to Prejudice any Claims of the United States, or of any particular State.

Section 3. New States and Territories

1. **New States** Congress has the power to admit new states. It also determines the basic guidelines for applying for statehood. One state, Maine, was created within the original boundaries of another state (Massachusetts) with the consent of Congress and the state.
2. **Territories** Congress has power over federal land. But neither in this clause nor anywhere else in the Constitution is the federal government explicitly empowered to acquire new territory.

Section 4

The United States shall guarantee to every State in this Union a Republican Form of Government, and shall protect each of them against Invasion; and on Application of the Legislature, or of the Executive (when the Legislature cannot be convened) against domestic Violence.

Section 4. Federal Protection for States

This section allows the federal government to send troops into a state to guarantee law and order. The president may send in troops even without the consent of the state government involved.

Article V

The Congress, whenever two-thirds of both Houses shall deem it necessary, shall propose Amendments to this Constitution, or, on the Application of the Legislatures of two-thirds of the several States, shall call a Convention for proposing Amendments, which, in either Case, shall be valid to all Intents and Purposes, as part of this Constitution, when ratified by the Legislatures of three-fourths of the several States, or by Conventions in three-fourths thereof, as the one or the other Mode of Ratification may be proposed by the Congress; Provided that no Amendment which may be made prior to the Year One thousand eight hundred and eight shall in any Manner affect the first and fourth clauses in the Ninth Section of the first Article; and that no State, without its Consent, shall be deprived of its equal Suffrage in the Senate.

Article V. The Amending Process

There are now 27 amendments to the Constitution. The Framers of the Constitution deliberately made it difficult to amend or change the Constitution. Two methods of proposing and ratifying amendments are provided for. A two-thirds majority is needed in Congress to propose an amendment, and at least three-fourths of the states (38 states) must accept the amendment before it can become law. No amendment has yet been proposed by a national convention called by the states, though in the 1980s a convention to propose an amendment requiring a balanced budget had been approved by 32 states.

Article VI

1. All Debts contracted and Engagements entered into, before the Adoption of this Constitution, shall be as valid against the United States under this Constitution as under the Confederation.

Article VI. National Supremacy

1. **Public Debts and Treaties** This section promised that all debts the colonies had incurred during the Revolution and under the Articles of Confederation would be honored by the new United States government.

2. **The Supreme Law** The "supremacy clause" recognized the Constitution and federal laws as supreme when in conflict with those of the states. It was largely based on this clause that Chief Justice John Marshall wrote his historic decision in *McCulloch* v. *Maryland.* The 14th Amendment reinforced the supremacy of federal law over state laws.

3. **Oaths of Office** This clause also declares that no religious test shall be required as a qualification for holding public office. This principle is also asserted in the First Amendment, which forbids Congress to set up an established church or to interfere with the religious freedom of Americans.

2. This Constitution, and the Laws of the United States which shall be made in Pursuance thereof; and all Treaties made, or which shall be made, under the Authority of the United States, shall be the supreme Law of the Land; and the Judges in every State shall be bound thereby, any Thing in the Constitution or Laws of any State to the Contrary notwithstanding.

3. The Senators and Representatives before mentioned, and the Members of the several State Legislatures, and all executive and judicial Officers, both of the United States and of the several States, shall be bound by Oath or Affirmation, to support this Constitution; but no religious Test shall ever be required as a Qualification to any Office or public Trust under the United States.

Article VII. Ratification of the Constitution

Unlike the Articles of Confederation, which required approval of all thirteen states for adoption, the Constitution required approval of only nine of thirteen states. Thirty-nine of the 55 delegates at the Constitutional Convention signed the Constitution. The Constitution went into effect in June 1788.

Article VII

The Ratification of the Conventions of nine States shall be sufficient for the Establishment of this Constitution between the States so ratifying the same.

Done in Convention, by the Unanimous Consent of the States present, the Seventeenth Day of September, in the Year of our Lord one thousand seven hundred and Eighty-seven, and of the Independence of the United States of America the Twelfth. In Witness whereof We have hereunto subscribed our Names.

Signers

George Washington, **President and Deputy from Virginia**

New Hampshire
John Langdon
Nicholas Gilman

Massachusetts
Nathaniel Gorham
Rufus King

Connecticut
William Samuel Johnson
Roger Sherman

New York
Alexander Hamilton

New Jersey
William Livingston
David Brearley
William Paterson
Jonathan Dayton

Pennsylvania
Benjamin Franklin
Thomas Mifflin
Robert Morris
George Clymer
Thomas FitzSimons
Jared Ingersoll
James Wilson
Gouverneur Morris

Delaware
George Read
Gunning Bedford, Jr.
John Dickinson
Richard Bassett
Jacob Broom

Maryland
James McHenry
Daniel of St. Thomas Jenifer
Daniel Carroll

Virginia
John Blair
James Madison, Jr.

North Carolina
William Blount
Richard Dobbs Spaight
Hugh Williamson

South Carolina
John Rutledge
Charles Cotesworth Pinckney
Charles Pinckney
Pierce Butler

Georgia
William Few
Abraham Baldwin

Attest:
William Jackson,
Secretary

Amendment I

Congress shall make no law respecting an establishment of religion, or prohibiting the free exercise thereof; or abridging the freedom of speech, or of the press; or the right of the people peaceably to assemble, and to petition the Government for a redress of grievances.

Amendment II

A well-regulated Militia, being necessary to the security of a free State, the right of the people to keep and bear Arms, shall not be infringed.

Amendment III

No soldier shall, in time of peace be quartered in any house, without the consent of the Owner, nor in time of war, but in a manner to be prescribed by law.

Amendment IV

The right of the people to be secure in their persons, houses, papers, and effects, against unreasonable searches and seizures, shall not be violated, and no Warrants shall issue, but upon probable cause, supported by Oath or affirmation, and particularly describing the place to be searched, and the persons or things to be seized.

Amendment V

No person shall be held to answer for a capital, or otherwise infamous crime, unless on a presentment or indictment of a Grand Jury, except in cases arising in the land or naval forces, or in the Militia, when in actual service in time of War or public danger; nor shall any person be subject for the same offence to be twice put in jeopardy of life or limb; nor shall be compelled in any criminal case to be a witness against himself, nor be deprived of life, liberty, or property, without due process of law; nor shall private property be taken for public use, without just compensation.

Amendment 1.
Freedom of Religion, Speech, Press, and Assembly (1791)

The 1st Amendment protects the civil liberties of individuals in the United States. The 1st Amendment freedoms are not absolute, however. They are limited by the rights of other individuals.

Amendment 2.
Right to Bear Arms (1791)

The purpose of this amendment is to guarantee states the right to keep a militia.

Amendment 3.
Quartering Troops (1791)

This amendment is based on the principle that people have a right to privacy in their own homes. It also reflects the colonists' grievances against the British government before the Revolution. Britain had angered Americans by quartering (housing) troops in private homes.

Amendment 4.
Searches and Seizures (1791)

Like the 3rd Amendment, the 4th Amendment reflects the colonists' desire to protect their privacy. Britain had used writs of assistance (general search warrants) to seek out smuggled goods. Americans wanted to make sure that such searches and seizures would be conducted only when a judge felt that there was "reasonable cause" to conduct them. The Supreme Court has ruled that evidence seized illegally without a search warrant may not be used in court.

Amendment 5.
Rights of Accused Persons (1791)

To bring a "presentment" or "indictment" means to formally charge a person with committing a crime. It is the function of a grand jury to see whether there is enough evidence to bring the accused person to trial. A person may not be tried more than once for the same crime (double jeopardy). Members of the armed services are subject to military law. They may be tried in a court martial. In times of war or a natural disaster, civilians may also be put under martial law. The 5th Amendment also guarantees that persons may not be forced in any criminal case to be a witness against themselves. That is, accused persons may refuse to answer questions on the ground that the answers might tend to incriminate them.

Amendment 6.
Right to Speedy, Fair Trial (1791)

The requirement of a "speedy" trial ensures that an accused person will not be held in jail for a lengthy period as a means of punishing the accused without a trial. A "fair" trial means that the trial must be open to the public and that a jury must hear witnesses and evidence on both sides before deciding the guilt or innocence of a person charged with a crime. This amendment also provides that legal counsel must be provided to a defendant. In 1963, the Supreme Court ruled, in *Gideon* v. *Wainwright,* that if a defendant cannot afford a lawyer, the government must provide one to defend him or her.

Amendment VI

In all criminal prosecutions, the accused shall enjoy the right to a speedy and public trial, by an impartial jury of the State and district wherein the crime shall have been committed, which district shall have been previously ascertained by law, and to be informed of the nature and cause of the accusation; to be confronted with the witnesses against him; to have compulsory process for obtaining witnesses in his favor, and to have the Assistance of Counsel for his defence.

Amendment 7.
Civil Suits (1791)

"Common law" means the law established by previous court decisions. In civil cases where one person sues another for more than $20, a jury trial is provided for. But customarily, federal courts do not hear civil cases unless they involve a good deal more money.

Amendment VII

In suits at common law, where the value in controversy shall exceed twenty dollars, the right of trial by jury shall be preserved, and no fact tried by a jury, shall be otherwise reexamined in any Courts of the United States, than according to the rules of common law.

Amendment 8.
Bail and Punishment (1791)

"Bail" is money that an accused person provides to the court as a guarantee that he or she will be present for a trial. This amendment ensures that neither bail nor punishment for a crime shall be unreasonably severe.

Amendment VIII

Excessive bail shall not be required, nor excessive fines imposed, nor cruel and unusual punishments inflicted.

Amendment 9.
Powers Reserved to the People (1791)

This amendment provides that the people's rights are not limited to those mentioned in the Constitution.

Amendment IX

The enumeration in the Constitution, of certain rights, shall not be construed to deny or disparage others retained by the people.

Amendment 10.
Powers Reserved to the States (1791)

This amendment protects the states and the people from an all-powerful federal government. It provides that the states or the people retain all powers except those denied them or those specifically granted to the federal government. This "reserved powers" provision is a check on the "necessary and proper" power of the federal government provided in the "elastic clause" in Article I, Section 8, Clause 18.

Amendment X

The powers not delegated to the United States by the Constitution, nor prohibited by it to the States, are reserved to the States respectively, or to the people.

Amendment XI

The Judicial power of the United States shall not be construed to extend to any suit in law or equity, commenced or prosecuted against one of the United States by Citizens of another State, or by Citizens or Subjects of any Foreign State.

Amendment XII

The Electors shall meet in their respective States and vote by ballot for President and Vice-President, one of whom, at least, shall not be an inhabitant of the same State with themselves; they shall name in their ballots the person voted for as President, and in distinct ballots the person voted for as Vice-President, and they shall make distinct lists of all persons voted for as President, and of all persons voted for as Vice-President, and of the number of votes for each, which lists they shall sign and certify, and transmit sealed to the seat of the government of the United States, directed to the President of the Senate;—The President of the Senate shall, in the presence of the Senate and House of Representatives, open all the certificates and the votes shall then be counted;—The person having the greatest number of votes for President, shall be the President, if such number be a majority of the whole number of Electors appointed; and if no person have such majority, then from the persons having the highest numbers not exceeding three on the list of those voted for as President, the House of Representatives shall choose immediately, by ballot, the President. But in choosing the President, the votes shall be taken by states, the representation from each state having one vote; a quorum for this purpose shall consist of a member or members from two-thirds of the states, and a majority of all the states shall be necessary to a choice. And if the House of Representatives shall not choose a President whenever the right of choice shall devolve upon them, before the fourth day of March next following, then the Vice-President shall act as President, as in the case of the death or other constitutional disability of the President.—The person having the greatest number of votes as Vice-President, shall be the Vice-President, if such number be a majority of the whole number of Electors appointed, and if no person have a majority, then from the two highest numbers on the list, the Senate shall choose the Vice-President; a quorum for the purpose shall consist of two-thirds of the whole number of Senators, and a majority of the whole number shall be necessary to a choice. But no person constitutionally ineligible to the office of President shall be eligible to that of Vice-President of the United States.

Amendment 11.
Suits Against States (1795)

This amendment provides that a lawsuit brought by a citizen of the United States or a foreign nation against a state must be tried in a state court, not in a federal court. This amendment was passed after the Supreme Court ruled that a federal court could try a lawsuit brought by citizens of South Carolina against a citizen of Georgia. This case, *Chisholm* v. *Georgia,* decided in 1793, was protested by many Americans, who insisted states would lose authority if they could be sued in federal courts.

Amendment 12.
Election of President and Vice President (1804)

This amendment changes the procedure for electing the president and vice president as outlined in Article II, Section 1, Clause 3.

To prevent the recurrence of the election of 1800 whereby a candidate running for vice president (Aaron Burr) could tie a candidate running for president (Thomas Jefferson) and thus force the election into the House of Representatives, the 12th Amendment specifies that the electors are to cast separate ballots for each office. The votes for each office are counted and listed separately. The results are signed, sealed, and sent to the president of the Senate. At a joint session of Congress, the votes are counted. The candidate who receives the most votes, providing it is a majority, is elected president. Other changes include: (1) a reduction from the five to three candidates receiving the most votes among whom the House is to choose if no candidate receives a majority of the electoral votes, and (2) provision for the Senate to choose the vice president from the two highest candidates if neither has received a majority of the electoral votes.

The 12th Amendment does place one restriction on electors. It prohibits electors from voting for two candidates (president and vice president) from their home state.

Amendment 13.
Abolition of Slavery (1865)

This amendment was the final act in ending slavery in the United States. It also prohibits the binding of a person to perform a personal service due to debt. In addition to imprisonment for crime, the Supreme Court has held that the draft is not a violation of the amendment.

This amendment is the first adopted to be divided into sections. It is also the first to contain specifically a provision granting Congress power to enforce it by appropriate legislation.

Amendment 14.
Rights of Citizens (1868)

The clauses of this amendment were intended (1) to penalize Southern states that refused to grant African Americans the vote, (2) to keep former Confederate leaders from serving in government, (3) to forbid payment of the Confederacy's debt by the federal government, and (4) to ensure payment of the war debts owed the federal government.

Section 1. Citizenship Defined By granting citizenship to all persons born in the United States, this amendment granted citizenship to former slaves. The amendment also guaranteed "due process of law." By the 1950s, Supreme Court rulings used the due process clause to protect civil liberties. The last part of Section 1 establishes the doctrine that all citizens are entitled to equal protection of the laws. In 1954 the Supreme Court ruled, in *Brown* v. *Board of Education of Topeka,* that segregation in public schools was unconstitutional because it denied equal protection.

Section 2. Representation in Congress This section reduced the number of members a state had in the House of Representatives if it denied its citizens the right to vote. This section was not implemented, however. Later civil rights laws and the 24th Amendment guaranteed the vote to African Americans.

Section 3. Penalty for Engaging in Insurrection The leaders of the Confederacy were barred from state or federal offices unless Congress agreed to revoke this ban. By the end of Reconstruction all but a few Confederate leaders were allowed to return to public life.

Amendment XIII

Section 1

Neither slavery nor involuntary servitude, except as a punishment for crime whereof the party shall have been duly convicted, shall exist within the United States, or any place subject to their jurisdiction.

Section 2

Congress shall have power to enforce this article by appropriate legislation.

Amendment XIV

Section 1

All persons born or naturalized in the United States, and subject to the jurisdiction thereof, are citizens of the United States and of the State wherein they reside. No State shall make or enforce any law which shall abridge the privileges or immunities of citizens of the United States; nor shall any State deprive any person of life, liberty, or property, without due process of law, nor deny to any person within its jurisdiction the equal protection of the laws.

Section 2

Representatives shall be apportioned among the several States according to their respective numbers, counting the whole number of persons in each State, excluding Indians not taxed. But when the right to vote at any election for the choice of electors for President and Vice-President of the United States, Representatives in Congress, the Executive and Judicial officers of a State, or the members of the Legislature thereof, is denied to any of the male inhabitants of such State, being twenty-one years of age, and citizens of the United States, or in any way abridged, except for participation in rebellion, or other crime, the basis of representation therein shall be reduced in the proportion which the number of such male citizens shall bear to the whole number of male citizens twenty-one years of age in such State.

Section 3

No person shall be a Senator or Representative in Congress, or elector of President and Vice-President, or hold any office, civil or military, under the United States, or under any State, who, having previously taken an oath, as a member of Congress, or as an officer of the United States, or as a member of any State legislature, or as an executive or judicial officer of any State, to support the Constitution of the United States, shall have engaged in insurrection or rebellion against the same, or given aid or comfort to the enemies thereof. But Congress may by a vote of two-thirds of each House, remove such disability.

Section 4

The validity of the public debt of the United States incurred for payment of pensions and bounties for service, authorized by law, including debts in suppressing insurrections or rebellion, shall not be questioned. But neither the United States nor any State shall assume or pay any debt or obligation incurred in aid of insurrection or rebellion against the United States, or any claim for the loss or emancipation of any slave; but all such debts, obligations and claims shall be held illegal and void.

Section 4. Public Debt The public debt incurred by the federal government during the Civil War was valid and could not be questioned by the South. However, the debts of the Confederacy were declared to be illegal. And former slaveholders could not collect compensation for the loss of their slaves.

Section 5

The Congress shall have power to enforce, by appropriate legislation, the provisions of this article.

Section 5. Enforcement Congress was empowered to pass civil rights bills to guarantee the provisions of the amendment.

Amendment XV

Section 1

The right of citizens of the United States to vote shall not be denied or abridged by the United States or by any State on account of race, color, or previous condition of servitude.

Section 2

The Congress shall have power to enforce this article by appropriate legislation.

Amendment 15.
The Right to Vote (1870)

Section 1. Suffrage for African Americans The 15th Amendment replaced Section 2 of the 14th Amendment in guaranteeing African Americans the right to vote; that is, the right of African Americans to vote was not to be left to the states. Yet, despite this prohibition, African Americans were denied the right to vote by many states by such means as poll taxes, literacy tests, and white primaries.

Section 2. Enforcement Congress was given the power to enforce this amendment. During the 1950s and 1960s, it passed successively stronger laws to end racial discrimination in voting rights.

Amendment XVI

The Congress shall have power to lay and collect taxes on incomes, from whatever source derived, without apportionment among several States, and without regard to any census or enumeration.

Amendment 16.
Income Tax (1913)

The origins of this amendment went back to 1895, when the Supreme Court declared a federal income tax unconstitutional. To overcome this Supreme Court decision, this amendment authorized an income tax that was levied on a direct basis.

Amendment 17.
Direct Election of Senators (1913)

Section 1. Method of Election The right to elect senators was given directly to the people of each state. It replaced Article I, Section 3, Clause 1, which empowered state legislatures to elect senators. This amendment was designed not only to make the choice of senators more democratic but also to cut down on corruption and to improve state government.

Section 2. Vacancies A state must order an election to fill a Senate vacancy. A state may empower its governor to appoint a person to fill a Senate seat if a vacancy occurs until an election can be held.

Section 3. Time in Effect This amendment was not to affect any Senate election or temporary appointment until it was in effect.

Amendment XVII

Section 1

The Senate of the United States shall be composed of two Senators from each State, elected by the people thereof, for six years; and each Senator shall have one vote. The electors in each state shall have the qualifications requisite for electors of the most numerous branch of the state legislatures.

Section 2

When vacancies happen in the representation of any State in the Senate, the executive authority of such State shall issue writs of election to fill such vacancies: Provided, that the legislature of any State may empower the executive thereof to make temporary appointments until the people fill the vacancies by election as the legislature may direct.

Section 3

This amendment shall not be so construed as to affect the election or term of any Senator chosen before it becomes valid as part of the Constitution.

Amendment 18.
Prohibition of Alcoholic Beverages (1919)

This amendment prohibited the production, sale, or transportation of alcoholic beverages in the United States. Prohibition proved to be difficult to enforce, especially in states with large urban populations. This amendment was later repealed by the 21st Amendment.

Amendment XVIII

Section 1

After one year from ratification of this article the manufacture, sale, or transportation of intoxicating liquors within, the importation thereof into, or the exportation thereof from the United States and all territory subject to the jurisdiction thereof for beverage purposes is hereby prohibited.

Section 2

The Congress and the several states shall have concurrent power to enforce this article by appropriate legislation.

Section 3

This article shall be inoperative unless it shall have been ratified as an amendment to the Constitution by the legislatures of the several States, as provided in the Constitution, within seven years from the date of the submission hereof to the states of the Congress.

Amendment XIX

Section 1

The right of citizens of the United States to vote shall not be denied or abridged by the United States or by any state on account of sex.

Section 2

Congress shall have power to enforce this article by appropriate legislation.

Amendment XX

Section 1

The terms of the President and Vice President shall end at noon on the 20th day of January, and the terms of the Senators and Representatives at noon on the 3rd day of January, of the years in which such terms would have ended if this article had not been ratified; and the terms of their successors shall then begin.

Section 2

The Congress shall assemble at least once in every year, and such meeting shall begin at noon on the 3rd day of January, unless they shall by law appoint a different day.

Section 3

If, at the time fixed for the beginning of the term of the President, the President elect shall have died, the Vice President elect shall become President. If a President shall not have been chosen before the time fixed for the beginning of his term, or if the President elect shall have failed to qualify, then the Vice President elect shall act as President until a President shall have qualified; and the Congress may by law provide for the case wherein neither a President elect nor a Vice President elect shall have qualified, declaring who shall then act as President, or the manner in which one who is to act shall be selected, and such person shall act accordingly until a President or Vice President shall have qualified.

Section 4

The Congress may by law provide for the case of the death of any of the persons from whom the House of Representatives may choose a President whenever the right of choice shall have devolved upon them, and for the case of the death of any of the persons from whom the Senate may choose a Vice President whenever the right of choice shall have devolved upon them.

Amendment 19. Woman Suffrage (1920)

This amendment, extending the vote to all qualified women in federal and state elections, was a landmark victory for the woman suffrage movement, which had worked to achieve this goal for many years. The women's movement had earlier gained full voting rights for women in four Western states in the late nineteenth century.

Amendment 20. "Lame-Duck" Amendment (1933)

Section 1. New Dates of Terms This amendment had two major purposes: (1) to shorten the time between the president's and vice president's election and inauguration, and (2) to end "lame-duck" sessions of Congress.

When the Constitution first went into effect, transportation and communication were slow and uncertain. It often took many months after the election in November for the president and vice president to travel to Washington, D.C., and prepare for their inauguration on March 4. This amendment ended this long wait for a new administration by fixing January 20 as Inauguration Day.

Section 2. Meeting Time of Congress "Lame-duck" sessions occurred every two years, after the November congressional election. That is, the Congress that held its session in December of an election year was not the newly elected Congress but the old Congress that had been elected two years earlier. This Congress continued to serve for several more months, usually until March of the next year. Often many of its members had failed to be reelected and were called "lame-ducks." The 20th Amendment abolished this lame-duck session, and provided that the new Congress hold its first session soon after the November election, on January 3.

Section 3. Succession of President and Vice President This amendment provides that if the president-elect dies before taking office, the vice president-elect becomes president. In the cases described, Congress will decide on a temporary president.

Section 4. Filling Presidential Vacancy If a presidential candidate dies while an election is being decided in the House, Congress may pass legislation to deal with the situation. Congress has similar power if this occurs when the Senate is deciding a vice-presidential election.

Section 5. Beginning the New Dates Sections 1 and 2 affected the Congress elected in 1934 and President Roosevelt, elected in 1936.

Section 6. Time Limit on Ratification The period for ratification by the states was limited to seven years.

Amendment 21.
Repeal of Prohibition Amendment (1933)

This amendment nullified the 18th Amendment. It is the only amendment ever passed to overturn an earlier amendment. It remained unlawful to transport alcoholic beverages into states that forbade their use. It is the only amendment ratified by special state conventions instead of state legislatures.

Presidential campaign button

Amendment 22.
Limit on Presidential Terms (1951)

This amendment wrote into the Constitution a custom started by Washington, Jefferson, and Madison, whereby presidents limited themselves to two terms in office. Although both Ulysses S. Grant and Theodore Roosevelt sought third terms, the two-term precedent was not broken until Franklin D. Roosevelt was elected to a third term in 1940 and then a fourth term in 1944. The passage of the 22nd Amendment ensures that no president is to be considered indispensable. It also provides that anyone who succeeds to the presidency and serves for more than two years of the term may not be elected more than one more time.

Section 5

Sections 1 and 2 shall take effect on the 15th day of October following the ratification of this article.

Section 6

This article shall be inoperative unless it shall have been ratified as an amendment to the Constitution by the legislatures of three-fourths of the several States within seven years from the date of its submission.

Amendment XXI

Section 1

The eighteenth article of amendment to the Constitution of the United States is hereby repealed.

Section 2

The transportation or importation into any State, Territory, or possession of the United States for delivery or use therein of intoxicating liquors, in violation of the laws thereof, is hereby prohibited.

Section 3

This article shall be inoperative unless it shall have been ratified as an amendment to the Constitution by conventions in the several States, as provided in the Constitution, within seven years from the date of the submission hereof to the States by the Congress.

Amendment XXII

Section 1

No person shall be elected to the office of the President more than twice, and no person who had held the office of President, or acted as President, for more than two years of a term to which some other person was elected President shall be elected to the office of the President more than once.

But this Article shall not apply to any person holding the office of President when this Article was proposed by the Congress, and shall not prevent any person who may be holding the office of President, or acting as President, during the term within which this Article becomes operative from holding the office of President or acting as President during the remainder of such term.

Section 2

This article shall be inoperative unless it shall have been ratified as an amendment to the Constitution by the legislatures of three-fourths of the several States within seven years from the date of its submission to the States by the Congress.

Amendment XXIII

Section 1

The District constituting the seat of Government of the United States shall appoint in such manner as the Congress may direct:

A number of electors of President and Vice President equal to the whole number of Senators and Representatives in Congress to which the District would be entitled if it were a State, but in no event more than the least populous State; they shall be in addition to those appointed by the States, but they shall be considered, for the purposes of the election of President and Vice President, to be electors appointed by a State; and they shall meet in the District and perform such duties as provided by the twelfth article of amendment.

Section 2

The Congress shall have power to enforce this article by appropriate legislation.

Amendment 23.
Presidential Electors for the District of Columbia (1961)

This amendment granted people living in the District of Columbia the right to vote in presidential elections. The District casts three electoral votes. The people of Washington, D.C., still are without representation in Congress.

Amendment XXIV

Section 1

The right of citizens of the United States to vote in any primary or other election for President or Vice President, for electors for President or Vice President, or for Senator or Representative in Congress, shall not be denied or abridged by the United States or any State by reason of failure to pay any poll tax or other tax.

Section 2

The Congress shall have power to enforce this article by appropriate legislation.

Amendment 24.
Abolition of the Poll Tax (1964)

A "poll tax" was a fee that persons were required to pay in order to vote in a number of Southern states. This amendment ended poll taxes as a requirement to vote in any presidential or congressional election. In 1966 the Supreme Court voided poll taxes in state elections as well.

Amendment 25.
Presidential Disability and Succession (1967)

Section 1. Replacing the President The vice president becomes president if the president dies, resigns, or is removed from office.

Section 2. Replacing the Vice President The president is to appoint a new vice president in case of a vacancy in that office, with the approval of the Congress.

The 25th Amendment is unusually precise and explicit because it was intended to solve a serious constitutional problem. Sixteen times in American history, before passage of this amendment, the office of vice president was vacant, but fortunately in none of these cases did the president die or resign.

This amendment was used in 1973, when Vice President Spiro Agnew resigned from office after being charged with accepting bribes. President Richard Nixon then appointed Gerald R. Ford as vice president in accordance with the provisions of the 25th Amendment. A year later, President Nixon resigned during the Watergate scandal, and Ford became president. President Ford then had to fill the vice presidency, which he had left vacant upon assuming the presidency. He named Nelson A. Rockefeller as vice president. Thus both the presidency and vice presidency were held by men who had not been elected to their offices.

Section 3. Replacing the President With Consent If the president informs Congress, in writing, that he or she cannot carry out the duties of the office of president, the vice president becomes acting president.

Section 4. Replacing the President Without Consent If the president is unable to carry out the duties of the office but is unable or unwilling to so notify Congress, the cabinet and the vice president are to inform Congress of this fact. The vice president then becomes acting president. The procedure by which the president may regain the office if he or she recovers is also spelled out in this amendment.

Amendment XXV

Section 1

In case of the removal of the President from office or his death or resignation, the Vice President shall become President.

Section 2

Whenever there is a vacancy in the office of the Vice President, the President shall nominate a Vice President who shall take the office upon confirmation by a majority vote of both houses of Congress.

Section 3

Whenever the President transmits to the President pro tempore of the Senate and the Speaker of the House of Representatives his written declaration that he is unable to discharge the powers and duties of his office, and until he transmits to them a written declaration to the contrary, such powers and duties shall be discharged by the Vice President as Acting President.

Section 4

Whenever the Vice President and a majority of either the principal officers of the executive departments or of such other body as Congress may by law provide, transmit to the President pro tempore of the Senate and the Speaker of the House of Representatives their written declaration that the President is unable to discharge the powers and duties of his office, the Vice President shall immediately assume the power and duties of the office of Acting President.

Thereafter, when the President transmits to the President pro tempore of the Senate and the Speaker of the House of Representatives his written declaration that no inability exists, he shall resume the powers and duties of his office unless the Vice President and a majority of either the principal officers of the executive departments or of such other body as Congress may by law provide, transmit within four days to the President pro tempore of the Senate and the Speaker of the House of Representatives their written declaration that the President is unable to discharge the powers and duties of his office. Thereupon Congress shall decide the issue, assembling within forty-eight hours for that purpose if not in session. If the Congress within twenty-one days after receipt of the latter written declaration, or, if Congress is not in session, within twenty-one days after Congress is required to assemble, determines by two-thirds vote of both houses that the President is unable to discharge the powers and duties of his office, the Vice President shall continue to discharge the same as Acting President; otherwise, the President shall resume the power and duties of his office.

Amendment XXVI

Section 1

The right of citizens of the United States, who are eighteen years of age or older, to vote shall not be denied or abridged by the United States or by any State on account of age.

Section 2

The Congress shall have power to enforce this article by appropriate legislation.

Amendment 26. Eighteen-Year-Old Vote (1971)

This amendment made 18-year-olds eligible to vote in all federal, state, and local elections. Until then, the minimum age had been 21 in most states.

Amendment XXVII

No law, varying the compensation for the services of Senators and Representatives, shall take effect, until an election of Representatives shall have intervened.

Amendment 27. Restraint on Congressional Salaries (1992)

Any increase in the salaries of members of Congress will take effect in the subsequent session of Congress.

Joint session of Congress

Historic Documents

Contents

The Code of Hammurabi

Hammurabi, a Mesopotamian ruler, developed his code of laws around 1700 B.C. This development of written law was a major advance toward justice and order.

Anu and Bel called by name me, Hammurabi, the exalted prince, who feared God, to bring about the rule of righteousness in the land, to destroy the wicked and the evil-doers; so that the strong should not harm the weak; so that I should . . . further the well-being of mankind. . . .

2. If any one bring an accusation against a man, and the accused go to the river and leap into the river, if he sink in the river his accuser shall take possession of his house. But if the river prove that the accused is not guilty, and he escape unhurt, then he who had brought the accusation shall be put to death, while he who leaped into the river shall take possession of the house that had belonged to his accuser. . . .
8. If any one steal cattle or sheep, or an ass, or a pig or a goat, if it belong to a god or to the court, the thief shall pay thirtyfold therefor; if they belonged to a freed man of the king he shall pay tenfold; if the thief has nothing with which to pay he shall be put to death. . . .
21. If any one break a hole into a house (break in to steal), he shall be put to death before that hole and be buried.
22. If any one is committing a robbery and is caught, then he shall be put to death.
23. If the robber is not caught, then shall he who was robbed claim under oath the amount of his loss; then shall the community, and . . . on whose ground and territory and in whose domain it was compensate him for the goods stolen. . . .
53. If any one be too lazy to keep his dam in proper condition, and does not so keep it; if then the dam break and all the fields be flooded, then shall he in whose dam the break occurred be sold for money, and the money shall replace the corn which he has caused to be ruined. . . .

(continued)

Ruins of ancient Babylon

117. If any one fail to meet a claim for debt, and sell himself, his wife, his son, and daughter for money or give them away to forced labor: they shall work for three years in the house of the man who bought them, or the proprietor, and in the fourth year they shall be set free. . . .
136. If any one leave his house, run away, and then his wife go to another house, if then he return, and wishes to take his wife back: because he fled from his home and ran away, the wife of this runaway shall not return to her husband. . . .
142. If a woman quarrel with her husband . . . the reasons for her prejudice must be presented. If she is guiltless, and there is no fault on her part, but he leaves and neglects her, then no guilt attaches to this woman, she shall take her dowry and go back to her father's house.
143. If she is not innocent, but leaves her husband. . . this woman shall be cast into the water. . . .
195. If a son strike his father, his hands shall be hewn off.
196. If a man put out the eye of another man, his eye shall be put out.
197. If he break another man's bone, his bone shall be broken. . . .
199. If he put out the eye of a man's slave, or break the bone of a man's slave, he shall pay one-half of its value.
200. If a man knock out the teeth of his equal, his teeth shall be knocked out. . . .
202. If any one strike the body of a man higher in rank than he, he shall receive sixty blows with an ox-whip in public. . . .
215. If a physician make a large incision with an operating knife and cure it, or if he open a tumor (over an eye) with an operating knife, and saves the eye, he shall receive ten shekels in money. . . .
218. If a physician make a large incision with the operating knife, and kill him, or open a tumor with the operating knife, and cut out the eye, his hands shall be cut off. . . .
229. If a builder build a house for some one, and does not construct it properly, and the house which he built fall in and kill its owner, then that builder shall be put to death. . . .

Laws of justice which Hammurabi, the wise king, established. A righteous law, and pious statute did he teach the land. Hammurabi, the protecting king am I. . . . The king who ruleth among the kings of the cities am I. My words are well considered; there is no wisdom like unto mine. By the command of Shamash, the great judge of heaven and earth, let righteousness go forth in the land. . . .

The Magna Carta

The Magna Carta, signed by King John in 1215, marked a decisive step forward in the development of constitutional government in England. Later it served as a model for colonists who carried its guarantees of legal and political rights to America.

John, by the grace of God, king of England, lord of Ireland, duke of Normandy and Aquitaine, and count of Anjou: to the archbishops, bishops, abbots, earls, barons, justiciaries, foresters, sheriffs, reeves, ministers, and all bailiffs and others his faithful subjects, greeting. . . .

1. We have, in the first place, granted to God, and by this our present charter confirmed for us and our heirs forever that the English church shall be free. . . .

9. Neither we nor our bailiffs shall seize any land or rent for any debt so long as the debtor's chattels are sufficient to discharge the same. . . .

12. No scutage [tax] or aid [subsidy] shall be imposed in our kingdom unless by the common counsel thereof . . . .

14. For obtaining the common counsel of the kingdom concerning the assessment of aids . . . or of scutage, we will cause to be summoned, severally by our letters, the archbishops, bishops, abbots, earls, and great barons; we will also cause to be summoned generally, by our sheriffs and bailiffs, all those who hold lands directly of us, to meet on a fixed day . . . and at a fixed place. . . .

20. A free man shall be amerced [punished] for a small fault only according to the measure thereof, and for a great crime according to its magnitude. . . . None of these amercements shall be imposed except by the oath of honest men of the neighborhood.

21. Earls and barons shall be amerced only by their peers, and only in proportion to the measure of the offense. . . .

38. In the future no bailiff shall upon his own unsupported accusation put any man to trial without producing credible witnesses to the truth of the accusation.

39. No free man shall be taken, imprisoned, disseised [seized], outlawed, banished, or in any way destroyed, nor will we proceed against or prosecute him, except by the lawful judgment of his peers and by the law of the land.

40. To no one will we sell, to none will we deny or delay, right or justice. . . .

42. In the future it shall be lawful . . . for anyone to leave and return to our kingdom safely and securely by land and water, saving his fealty to us. Excepted are those who have been imprisoned or outlawed according to the law of the land. . . .

61. Whereas we, for the honor of God and the amendment of our realm, and in order the better to allay the discord arisen between us and our barons, have granted all these things aforesaid. . . .

63. Wherefore we will, and firmly charge . . . that all men in our kingdom shall have and hold all the aforesaid liberties, rights, and concessions . . . fully, and wholly to them and their heirs. . . in all things and places forever . . . . It is moreover sworn, as well on our part as on the part of the barons, that all these matters aforesaid will be kept in good faith and without deceit. Witness the abovenamed and many others. Given by our hand in the meadow which is called Runnymede. . . .

The English Bill of Rights

In 1689 William of Orange and his wife, Mary, became joint rulers of England after accepting what became known as the Bill of Rights. This document assured the people of certain basic civil rights.

Seal of William and Mary

An act declaring the rights and liberties of the subject and settling the succession of the crown. Whereas the lords spiritual and temporal and commons assembled at Westminster lawfully fully and freely representing all the estates of the people of this realm did upon the thirteenth day of February in the year of our Lord one thousand six hundred eight-eight [-nine] present unto their majesties . . . William and Mary prince and princess of Orange . . . a certain declaration in writing made by the said lords and commons in the words following viz

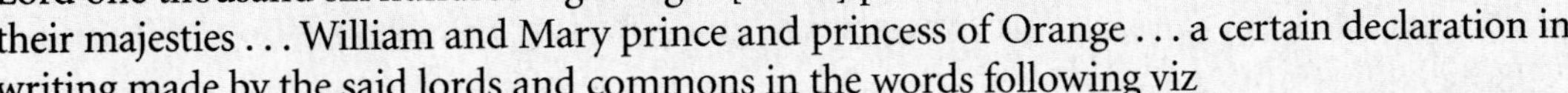

Whereas the late king James the second by the assistance of divers evil counsellors judges and ministers employed by him did endeavor to subvert and extirpate the protestant religion and the laws and liberties of this kingdom.

By assuming and exercising a power of dispensing with and suspending of laws and the execution of laws without consent of parliament. . . .

By levyng money for and to the use of the crown by pretence of prerogative for other time and in other manner than the same was granted by parliament.

By raising and keeping a standing army within this kingdom in time of peace without consent of parliament and quartering soldiers contrary to law. . . .

By violating the freedom of election of members to serve in parliament. . . .

And excessive bail hath been required of persons committed in criminal cases to elude the benefit of the laws made for the liberty of the subjects.

And excessive fines have been imposed.

And illegal and cruel punishments inflicted. . . .

And thereupon the said lords spiritual and temporal and commons . . . do . . . declare

That the pretended power of suspending of laws or the execution of laws by regal authority without consent of parliament is illegal. . . .

That levying money for or to the use of the crown . . . without grant of parliament for longer time or in other manner than the same is or shall be granted is illegal.

That it is the right of the subjects to petition the king and all commitments and prosecutions for such petitioning are illegal.

That the raising or keeping a standing army within the kingdom in time of peace unless it be with consent of parliament is against law. . . .

That election of members of parliament ought to be free. . . .

That excessive bail ought not to be required nor excessive fines imposed nor cruel and unusual punishments inflicted. . . .

The said lords . . . do resolve that William and Mary prince and princess of Orange be and be declared king and queen of England France and Ireland. . . .

The Mayflower Compact

On November 21, 1620, 41 men aboard the Mayflower *drafted this agreement. The Mayflower Compact was the first plan of self-government ever put in force in the English colonies. The original compact has been lost. Mourt's* Relation *(1622) is the earliest source of the text reprinted here.*

This day, before we came to harbor, observing some not well affected to unity and concord, but gave some appearance of faction, it was thought good there should be an association and agreement that we should combine together in one body, and to submit to such government and governors as we should by common consent agree to make and choose, and set our hands to this that follows word for word.

In the name of God, Amen. We whose names are underwritten, the loyal subjects of our dread sovereign lord, King James, by the grace of God, of Great Britain, France, and Ireland, King, Defender of the Faith, etc.

Having undertaken for the glory of God, and advancement of the Christian faith and honor of our king and country, a voyage to plant the first colony in the northern parts of Virginia, do by these present, solemnly and mutually, in the presence of God and one of another, covenant and combine ourselves together into a civil body politic, for our better ordering and preservation and furtherance of the ends aforesaid; and by virtue hereof to enact, constitute, and frame such just and equal laws, ordinances, acts, constitutions, offices from time to time as shall be thought most meet and convenient for the general good of the colony; unto which we promise all due submission and obedience. In witness whereof we have hereunder subscribed our names, Cape Cod, 11th of November, in the year of the reign of our sovereign lord, King James, of England, France, and Ireland 18, and of Scotland 54. Anno Domini 1620.

***Signing of the Compact on the Mayflower* by Edward Percy Moran, c. 1900**

Fundamental Orders of Connecticut

In January 1639, settlers in Connecticut, led by Thomas Hooker, drew up the Fundamental Orders of Connecticut—America's first written constitution. It is essentially a compact among the settlers and a body of laws.

Forasmuch as it has pleased the Almighty God by the wise disposition of His Divine Providence so to order and dispose of things that we, the inhabitants and residents of Windsor, Hartford, and Wethersfield are now cohabiting and dwelling in and upon the river of Conectecotte and the lands thereunto adjoining; and well knowing where a people are gathered together the Word of God requires that, to maintain the peace and union of such a people, there should be an orderly and decent government established according to God, . . . do therefore associate and conjoin ourselves to be as one public state or commonwealth. . . . As also in our civil affairs to be guided and governed according to such laws, rules, orders, and decrees as shall be made, ordered, and decreed, as follows:

1. It is ordered . . . that there shall be yearly two general assemblies or courts; . . . The first shall be called the Court of Election, wherein shall be yearly chosen . . . so many magistrates and other public officers as shall be found requisite. Whereof one to be chosen governor . . . and no other magistrate to be chosen for more than one year; provided aways there be six chosen besides the governor . . . by all that are admitted freemen and have taken the oath of fidelity, and do cohabit within this jurisdiction. . . .
4. It is ordered . . . that no person be chosen governor above once in two years, and that the governor be always a member of some approved congregation, and formerly of the magistracy within this jurisdiction; and all the magistrates freemen of this Commonwealth. . . .
5. It is ordered . . . that to the aforesaid Court of Election the several towns shall send their deputies. . . . Also, the other General Court . . . shall be for making of laws, and any other public occasion which concerns the good of the Commonwealth. . . .
7. It is ordered . . . that . . . the constable or constables of each town shall forthwith give notice distinctly to the inhabitants of the same . . . that . . . they meet and assemble themselves together to elect and choose certain deputies to be at the General Court then following to [manage] the affairs of the Commonwealth; which said deputies shall be chosen by all that are admitted inhabitants in the several towns and have taken the oath of fidelity. . . .
10. It is ordered . . . that every General Court . . . shall consist of the governor, or someone chosen to moderate the Court, and four other magistrates, at least, with the major part of the deputies of the several towns legally chosen. . . . In which said General Courts shall consist the supreme power of the Commonwealth, and they only shall have power to make laws or repeal them, to grant levies, to admit of freemen, dispose of lands undisposed of to several towns or person, and also shall have power to call either Court or magistrate or any other person whatsoever into question for any misdemeanor. . . .

In which Court, the governor or moderator shall have power to order the Court to give liberty of speech, . . . to put all things to vote, and, in case the vote be equal, to have the casting voice. . . .

Two Treatises of Government

John Locke

John Locke's Two Treatises of Government *was published in 1690. The "Second Treatise of Government" states his belief that government is based on an agreement between the people and ruler.*

Of the State of Nature.

To understand Political Power right, and to derive it from its Original, we must consider what State all Men are naturally in, and that is, a State of perfect Freedom to order their Actions, and dispose of their Possessions, and Persons as they think fit, within the bounds of the Law of Nature, without asking leave, or depending upon the Will of any other Man.

A State also of Equality, wherein all the Power and Jurisdiction is reciprocal, no one having more than another. . . .

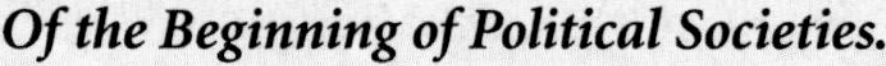

Of the Beginning of Political Societies.

Men being, as has been said, by Nature, all free, equal and independent, no one can be put out of this Estate, and subjected to the Political Power of another, without his own Consent. The only way whereby any one divests himself of his Natural Liberty, and puts on the bonds of Civil Society is by agreeing with other Men to joyn and unite into a Community, for their comfortable, safe, and peaceable living one amongst another, in a secure Enjoyment of their properties, and a greater Security against any that are not of it. This any number of Men may do, because it injures not the Freedom of the rest; they are left as they were in the Liberty of the State of Nature. . . .

For when any number of Men have, by the consent of every individual, made a Community, they have thereby made that Community one Body, with a Power to Act as one Body, which is only by the will and determination of the majority. . . .

Whosoever therefore out of a state of Nature unite into a Community, must be understood to give up all the power, necessary to the ends for which they unite into Society, to the majority of the Community. . . .

Of the Dissolution of Government.

. . . Governments are dissolved from within . . . when the Legislative is altered. . . . First, that when such a single Person or Prince sets up his own Arbitrary Will in place of the Laws, which are the Will of the Society, declared by the Legislative, then the Legislative is changed. . . . Secondly, when the Prince hinders the legislative from . . . acting freely, pursuant to those ends, for which it was Constituted, the Legislative is altered. . . . Thirdly, When by the Arbitrary Power of the Prince, the Electors, or ways of Election are altered, without the Consent, and contrary to the common Interest of the People, there also the Legislative is altered. . . .

In these and the like Cases, when the Government is dissolved, the People are at liberty to provide for themselves, by erecting a new Legislative, differing from the other, by the change of Persons, or Form, or both as they shall find it most for their safety and good. For the Society can never, by the fault of another, lose the Native and Original Right it has to preserve itself. . . .

The Wealth of Nations

Adam Smith, a Scottish economist and philosopher, published An Inquiry into the Nature and Causes of the Wealth of Nations *in 1776. The book offered a detailed description of life and trade in English society. It also scientifically described the basic principles of economics for the first time.*

But it is only for the sake of profit that any man employs a capital in the support of industry; and he will always, therefore, endeavour to employ it in the support of that industry of which the produce is likely to be of the greatest value, or to exchange for the greatest quantity either of money or of other goods. . . .

As every individual, therefore, endeavours as much as he can both to employ his capital in the support of domestic industry, and so to direct that industry that its produce may be of the greatest value; every individual necessarily labours to render the annual revenue of the society as great as he can. He generally, indeed, neither intends to promote the public interest, nor knows how much he is promoting it. . . . By pursuing his own interest he frequently promotes that of the society more effectually than when he really intends to promote it. . . .

What is the species of domestic industry which his capital can employ, and of which the produce is likely to be of the greatest value, every individual, it is evident, can, in his local situation, judge much better than any statesman or lawgiver can do for him. . . .

To give the monopoly of the home-market to the produce of domestic industry, in any particular art or manufacture, is in some measure to direct private people in what manner they ought to employ their capitals, and must, in almost all cases, be either a useless or a hurtful regulation. If the produce of domestic can be brought there as cheap as that of foreign industry, the regulation is evidently useless. If it cannot, it must generally be hurtful. It is the maxim of every prudent master of a family, never to attempt to make at home what it will cost him more to make than to buy. The taylor does not attempt to make his own shoes, but buys them of the shoemaker. The shoemaker does not attempt to make his own clothes, but employs a taylor. The farmer attempts to make neither the one nor the other, but employs those different artificers. All of them find it in their interest to employ their whole industry in a way in which they have some advantage over their neighbours, and to purchase with a part of its produce . . . whatever else they have occasion for.

What is prudence in the conduct of every private family, can scarcely be folly in that of a great kingdom. If a foreign country can supply us with a commodity cheaper than we ourselves can make it, better buy it of them with some part of the produce of our own industry, employed in a way in which we have some advantage. . . . It is certainly not employed to the greatest advantage, when it is thus directed towards an object which it can buy cheaper than it can make.

Adam Smith

Articles of Confederation

In 1776, Richard Henry Lee moved that Congress appoint a committee to draw up articles of confederation among the states. One member of each state was selected. The committee of state delegates revised and adopted John Dickinson's plan of union in 1781.

The Articles of Confederation

Articles of Confederation and Perpetual Union Between the States of New Hampshire, Massachusetts Bay, Rhode Island and Providence Plantations, Connecticut, New York, New Jersey, Pennsylvania, Delaware, Maryland, Virginia, North Carolina, South Carolina, and Georgia.

Article I. The style of this confederacy shall be "The United States of America."

Article II. Each state retains its sovereignty, freedom, and independence, and every power, jurisdiction, and right which is not by this confederation expressly delegated to the United States in Congress assembled.

Article III. The said states hereby severally enter into a firm league of friendship with each other, for their common defense, the security of their liberties, and their mutual and general welfare, binding themselves to assist each other against all force offered to, or attacks made upon them, or any of them, on account of religion, sovereignty, trade, or any other pretense whatever.

Article IV. The better to secure and perpetuate mutual friendship and intercourse among the people of the different states in this union, the free inhabitants of each of these states, paupers, vagabonds, and fugitives from justice excepted, shall be entitled to all privileges and immunities of free citizens in the several states; and the people of each state shall have free ingress and regress to and from any other state and shall enjoy therein all the privileges of trade and commerce, subject to the same duties, impositions, and restrictions as the inhabitants thereof respectively, provided that such restrictions shall not extend so far as to prevent the removal of property imported into any state, to any other state of which the owner is an inhabitant; provided also that no imposition, duties, or restriction shall be laid by any state on the property of the United States, or either of them.

If any person guilty of or charged with treason, felony, or other high misdemeanor in any state shall flee from justice, and be found in any of the United States, he shall, upon demand of the governor or executive power of the state from which he fled, be delivered up and removed to the state having jurisdiction of his offense.

Full faith and credit shall be given in each of these states to the records, acts, and judicial proceedings of the courts and magistrates of every other state.

Article V. For the more convenient management of the general interests of the United

(continued)

States, delegates shall be annually appointed in such manner as the legislature of each state shall direct, to meet in Congress on the first Monday in November, in every year, with a power reserved to each state to recall its delegates, or any of them, at any time within the year and to send others in their stead for the remainder of the year.

No state shall be represented in Congress by less than two nor by more than seven members; and no person shall be capable of being a delegate for more than three years in any term of six years; nor shall any person, being a delegate, be capable of holding any office under the United States for which he, or another for his benefit, receives any salary, fees, or emolument of any kind.

Each state shall maintain its own delegates in a meeting of the states and while they act as members of the Committee of the States.

In determining questions in the United States in Congress assembled, each state shall have one vote.

Freedom of speech and debate in Congress shall not be impeached or questioned in any court or place out of Congress, and the members of Congress shall be protected in their persons from arrests and imprisonments during the time of their going to and from, and attendance on, Congress, except for treason, felony, or breach of the peace.

Article VI. No state, without the consent of the United States in Congress assembled, shall send any embassy to, or receive any embassy from, or enter into any conference, agreement, alliance, or treaty with any king, prince, or state; nor shall any person holding any office of profit or trust under the United States, or any of them, accept of any present, emolument, office, or title of any kind whatever from any king, prince, or foreign state; nor shall the United States in Congress assembled, or any of them, grant any title of nobility.

No two or more states shall enter into any treaty, confederation, or alliance whatever between them without the consent of the United States in Congress assembled, specifying accurately the purposes for which the same is to be entered into and how long it shall continue.

No state shall lay any imposts or duties which may interfere with any stipulations in treaties entered into by the United States in Congress assembled with any king, prince, or state, in pursuance of any treaties already proposed by Congress, to the courts of France and Spain.

No vessels of war shall be kept up in time of peace by any state except such number only as shall be deemed necessary by the United States in Congress assembled for the defense of such state or its trade; nor shall any body of forces be kept up by any state in time of peace except such number only as in the judgment of the United States in Congress assembled shall be deemed requisite to garrison the forts necessary for the defense of such state; but every state shall always keep up a well-regulated and disciplined militia, sufficiently armed and accoutered, and shall provide and constantly have ready for use, in public stores, a due number of field pieces and tents and a proper quantity of arms, ammunition, and camp equipage.

No state shall engage in any war without the consent of the United States in Congress assembled unless such state be actually invaded by enemies, or shall have received certain advice of a resolution being formed by some nation of Indians to invade such state, and the danger is so imminent as not to admit of a delay till the United States in Congress assembled can be consulted; nor shall any state grant commissions to any ships or vessels of war, nor letters of marque or reprisal, except it be after a declaration of war by the United States in

Congress assembled, and then only against the kingdom or state and the subjects thereof against which war has been so declared and under such regulations as shall be established by the United States in Congress assembled, unless such state be infested by pirates, in which case vessels of war may be fitted out for that occasion and kept so long as the danger shall continue or until the United States in Congress assembled shall determine otherwise.

Article VII. When land forces are raised by any state for the common defense, all officers of or under the rank of colonel shall be appointed by the legislature of each state respectively, by whom such forces shall be raised, or in such manner as such state shall direct, and all vacancies shall be filled up by the state which first made the appointment.

Article VIII. All charges of war and all other expenses that shall be incurred for the common defense or general welfare, and allowed by the United States in Congress assembled, shall be defrayed out of a common treasury, which shall be supplied by the several states in proportion to the value of all land within each state, granted to or surveyed for any person, as such land the buildings and improvements thereon shall be estimated according to such mode as the United States in Congress assembled shall from time to time direct and appoint. The taxes for paying that proportion shall be laid and levied by the authority and direction of the legislatures of the several states within the time agreed upon by the United States in Congress assembled.

Article IX. The United States in Congress assembled shall have the sole and exclusive right and power of determining on peace and war, except in the cases mentioned in the sixth article — of sending and receiving ambassadors — entering into treaties and alliances, provided that no treaty of commerce shall be made whereby the legislative power of the respective states shall be restrained from imposing such imposts and duties on foreigners as their own people are subjected to or from prohibiting the exportation or importation of any species of goods or commodities whatsoever — of establishing rules for deciding in all cases what captures on land or water shall be legal, and in what manner prizes taken by land or naval forces in the service of the United States shall be divided or appropriated — of granting letters of marque and reprisal in times of peace — appointing courts for the trial of piracies and felonies committed on the high seas and establishing courts for receiving and determining finally appeals in all cases of captures, provided that no member of Congress shall be appointed a judge in any of the said courts.

The United States in Congress assembled shall also be the last resort on appeal in all disputes and difference now subsisting or that hereafter may arise between two or more states concerning boundary, jurisdiction, or any other cause whatever. . . . Provided, also, that no state shall be deprived of territory for the benefit of the United States.

All controversies concerning the private right of soil claimed under different grants of two or more states, whose jurisdictions as they may respect such lands, and the states which passed such grants are adjusted, the said grants or either of them being at the same time claimed to have originated antecedent to such settlement of jurisdiction shall, on the petition of either party to the Congress of the United States, be finally determined as near as may be in the same manner as is before prescribed for deciding disputes respecting territorial jurisdiction between different states.

The United States in Congress assembled shall also have the sole and exclusive right and power of regulating the alloy and value of coin struck by their own authority or by that of the respective states — fixing the standard of weights and measures throughout the United States — regulating the trade and managing all affairs with the Indians not members of any of the states, provided that the legislative right of any state within its own limits be not infringed or violated — establishing or regulating post offices from one state to another, throughout all the United States, and exacting such postage on the papers passing through the same as may be requisite to defray the expenses of the said office — appointing all officers of the land forces in the service of the United States excepting regimental officers — appointing all the officers of the naval forces, and commissioning all officers whatever in the service of the United States — making rules for the government and regulation of the said land and naval forces, and directing their operations.

The United States in Congress assembled shall have authority to appoint a committee, to sit in the recess of Congress, to be denominated "A Committee of the States," and to consist of one delegate from each state; and to appoint such other committees and civil officers as may be necessary for managing the general affairs of the United States under their direction — to appoint one of their number to preside, provided that no person be allowed to serve in the office of President more than one year in any term of three years; to ascertain the necessary sums of money to be raised for the service of the United States, and to appropriate and apply the same for defraying the public expenses — to borrow money or emit bills on the credit of the United States, transmitting every half-year to the respective states an account of the sums of money so borrowed or emitted — to build and equip a navy — to agree upon the number of land forces, and to make requisitions from each state for its quota, in proportion to the number of white inhabitants in such state, which requisition shall be binding. . . .

Thereupon the legislature of each state shall appoint the regimental officers, raise the men and clothe, arm, and equip them in a soldier-like manner, at the expense of the United States; and the officers and men so clothed, armed, and equipped shall march to the place appointed and within the time agreed on by the United States in Congress assembled. . . .

The United States in Congress assembled shall never engage in a war, nor grant letters of marque and reprisal in time of peace, nor enter into any treaties or alliances, nor coin money, nor regulate the value thereof, nor ascertain the sums and expenses necessary for the defense and welfare of the United States, or any of them, nor emit bills, nor borrow money on the credit of the United States, nor appropriate money, nor agree upon the number of vessels of war to be built or purchased or the number of land or sea forces to be raised, nor appoint a commander in chief of the Army or Navy, unless nine states assent to the same; nor shall a question on any other point, except for adjourning from day to day, be determined unless by the votes of a majority of the United States in Congress assembled. . . .

Article XI. Canada acceding to this Confederation, and joining in the measures of the United States, shall be admitted into and entitled to all the advantages of this union; but no other colony shall be admitted into the same unless such admission be agreed to by nine states.

Article XII. All bills of credit emitted, moneys borrowed, and debts contracted by or under the authority of Congress, before the assembling of the United States, in pursuance of the present Confederation, shall be deemed and considered as a charge against the United States, for payment and satisfaction whereof the said United States and the public faith are hereby solemnly pledged.

The Federalist, No. 10

James Madison wrote several articles supporting ratification of the Constitution for a New York newspaper. In the excerpt below, Madison argues for the idea of a federal republic.

James Madison

Among the numerous advantages promised by a well-constructed Union, none deserves to be more accurately developed than its tendency to break and control the violence of faction. The friend of popular governments never finds himself so much alarmed for their character and fate as when he contemplates their propensity to this dangerous vice. . . . The instability, injustice, and confusion introduced into the public councils have, in truth, been the mortal diseases under which popular governments have everywhere perished. . . . It will be found, indeed, on a candid review of our situation, that some of the distresses under which we labor have been erroneously charged on the operation of our governments; but it will be found, at the same time, that other causes will not alone account for many of our heaviest misfortunes; and, particularly, for that prevailing and increasing distrust of public engagements and alarm for private rights which are echoed from one end of the continent to the other. These must be chiefly, if not wholly, effects of the unsteadiness and injustice with which a factious spirit has tainted our public administration.

By a faction I understand a number of citizens, whether amounting to a majority or minority of the whole, who are united and actuated by some common impulse of passion, or of interest, adverse to the rights of other citizens, or to the permanent and aggregate interests of the community.

There are two methods of curing the mischiefs of faction: the one, by removing its causes; the other, by controlling its effects.

There are again two methods of removing the causes of faction: the one, by destroying the liberty which is essential to its existence; the other, by giving to every citizen the same opinions, the same passions, and the same interests.

It could never be more truly said than of the first remedy that it was worse than the disease. Liberty is to faction what air is to fire, an aliment without which it instantly expires. But it could not be a less folly to abolish liberty, which is essential to political life, because it nourishes faction than it would be to wish the annihilation of air, which is essential to animal life, because it imparts to fire its destructive agency.

The second expedient is as impracticable as the first would be unwise. As long as the reason of man continues fallible, and he is at liberty to exercise it, different opinions will be formed. . . .

The latent causes of faction are thus sown in the nature of man; and we see them everywhere brought into different degrees of activity, according to the different circumstances of civil society. A zeal for different opinions concerning religion, concerning government, and many other points . . . ; an attachment to different leaders ambitiously contending for pre-eminence and power . . . have, in turn, divided mankind into parties, inflamed them with mutual animosity, and rendered them much more disposed to vex and oppress each other than to cooperate for their common good. . . . But the most common and durable source of factions has been the verious and unequal distribution of property. Those who hold and those who are without property have ever formed distinct interests in society. Those who are creditors, and those who are debtors, fall under a like discrimination. A landed interest, a manufacturing interest, a mercantile interest, a moneyed interest, with many lesser interests, grow up of necessity in civilized nations, and divide them into different classes, actuated by different sentiments and views. The regulation of these various and interfering interests forms the principal task of modern legislation and involves the spirit of party and faction in the necessary and ordinary operations of government. . . .

[Y]et what are many of the most important acts of legislation but so many judicial determinations, not indeed concerning the rights of single persons, but concerning the rights of large bodies of citizens? And what are the different classes of legislators but advocates and parties to the causes which they determine? . . .

It is in vain to say that enlightened statesmen will be able to adjust these clashing interests and render them all subservient to the public good. Enlightened statesmen will not always be at the helm. Nor, in many cases, can such an adjustment be made at all without taking into view indirect and remote considerations, which will rarely prevail over the immediate interest which one party may find in disregarding the rights of another or the good of the whole.

The inference to which we are brought is that the *causes* of faction cannot be removed and that relief is only to be sought in the means of controlling its *effects.*

If a faction consists of less than a majority, relief is supplied by the republican principle, which enables the majority to defeat its sinister views by regular vote. It may clog the administration, it may convulse the society; but it will be unable to execute and mask its violence under the forms of the Constitution. When a majority is included in a faction, the form of popular government, on the other hand, enables it to sacrifice to its ruling passion or interest both the public good and the rights of other citizens. To secure the public good and private rights against the danger of such a faction, and at the same time to preserve the spirit and the form of popular government, is then the great object to which our inquiries are directed. . . .

By what means is this object attainable? Evidently by one of two only. Either the existence of the same passion or interest in a majority at the same time must be prevented, or the majority, having such coexistent passion or interest, must be rendered, by their number and local situation, unable to concert and carry into effect schemes of oppression. If the impulse and the opportunity be suffered to coincide, we well know that neither moral nor religious motives can be relied on as an adequate control. They are not found to be such on the injustice and violence of individuals, and lose their efficacy in proportion to the number combined together. . . .

From this view of the subject it may be concluded that a pure democracy, by which I mean a society consisting of a small number of citizens, who assemble and administer the government in person, can admit of no cure for the mischiefs of faction. A common passion or interest will, in almost every case, be felt by a majority of the whole; a communication and concert results from the form of government itself; and there is nothing to check the inducements to sacrifice the weaker party or an obnoxious individual. Hence it is that such democracies have ever been spectacles of turbulence and contention; have ever been found incompatible with personal security or the rights of property; and have in general been as short in their lives as they have been violent in their deaths. . . .

A republic, by which I mean a government in which the scheme of representation takes place, opens a different prospect and promises the cure for which we are seeking. Let us examine the points in which it varies from pure democracy, and we shall comprehend both the nature of the cure and the efficacy which it must derive from the Union.

The two great points of difference between a democracy and a republic are: first, the delegation of the government, in the latter, to a small number of citizens elected by the rest; secondly, the greater number of citizens and greater sphere of country over which the latter may be extended.

The effect of the first difference is, on the one hand, to refine and enlarge the public views by passing them through the medium of a chosen body of citizens, whose wisdom may best discern the true interest of their country and whose patriotism and love of justice will be least likely to sacrifice it to temporary or partial considerations. Under such a regulation it may well happen that the public voice, pronounced by the representatives of the people, will be more consonant to the public good than if pronounced by the people themselves. . . . On the other hand, the effect may be inverted. Men of factious tempers, of local prejudices, or of sinister designs, may, by intrigue, by corruption, or by other means, first obtain the suffrages, and then betray the interests of the people. The question resulting is, whether small or extensive republics are most favorable to the election of proper guardians of the public weal; and it is clearly decided in favor of the latter by two obvious considerations.

In the first place it is to be remarked that however small the republic may be the representatives must be raised to a certain number in order to guard against the cabals of a few; and that however large it may be they must be limited to a certain number in order to guard against the confusion of a multitude. Hence, the number of representatives in the two cases not being in proportion to that of the constituents, and being proportionally greatest in the small republic, it follows that if the proportion of fit characters be not less in the large than in the small republic, the former will present a greater option, and consequently a greater probability of a fit choice.

In the next place, as each representative will be chosen by a greater number of citizens in the large than in the small republic, it will be more difficult for unworthy candidates to practise with success the vicious arts by which elections are too often carried; and the suffrages of the people being more free, will be more likely to center on men who possess the most attractive merit and the most diffusive and established characters.

It must be confessed that in this, as in most other cases, there is a mean, on both sides of which inconveniencies will be found to lie. By enlarging too much the number of electors, you render the representative too little acquainted with all their local circumstances and lesser interests; as by reducing it too much, you render him unduly attached to these, and too little fit to comprehend and pursue great and national objects. The federal Constitution forms a happy combination in this respect; the great and aggregate interests being referred to the national, the local and particular to the State legislatures. . . .

In the extent and proper structure of the Union, therefore, we behold a republican remedy for the diseases most incident to republican government. And according to the degree of pleasure and pride we feel in being republicans ought to be our zeal in cherishing the spirit and supporting the character of federalists.

The Federalist, No. 51

Eagle and crossed flags

To what expedient, then, shall we finally resort, for maintaining in practice the necessary partition of power among the several departments as laid down in the Constitution? . . .

In order to lay a due foundation for that separate and distinct exercise of the different powers of government, which to a certain extent is admitted on all hands to be essential to the preservation of liberty, it is evident that each department should have a will of its own; and consequently should be so constituted that the members of each should have as little agency as possible in the appointment of the members of the others. Were this principle rigorously adhered to, it would require that all the appointments for the supreme executive, legislative, and judiciary magistracies should be drawn from the same fountain of authority, the people. . . .

It is equally evident that the members of each department should be as little dependent as possible on those of the others for the emoluments [finances]annexed to their offices. Were the executive magistrate, or the judges, not independent of the legislature in this particular, their independence in every other would be merely nominal.

But the great security against a gradual concentration of the several powers in the same department consists in giving to those who administer each department the necessary constitutional means and personal motives to resist encroachments of the others. . . . Ambition must be made to counteract ambition. The interest of the man must be connected with the constitutional rights of the place. It may be a reflection on human nature that such devices should be necessary to control the abuses of government. But what is government itself but the greatest of all reflections on human nature? If men were angels, no government would be necessary. If angels were to govern men, neither external nor internal controls on government would be necessary. In framing a government which is to be administered by men over men, the great difficulty lies in this: you must first enable the government to control the governed; and in the next place oblige it to control itself. A dependence on the people is, no doubt, the primary control on the government; but experience has taught mankind the necessity of auxiliary precautions. . . .

But it is not possible to give to each department an equal power of self-defense. In republican government, the legislative authority necessarily predominates. The remedy for this inconveniency is to divide the legislature into different branches; and to render them, by different modes of election and different principles of action, as little connected with each other as the nature of their common functions and their common dependence on the society will admit. It may even be necessary to guard against dangerous encroachments by still further precautions. As the weight of the legislative authority requires that it should be thus divided, the weakness of the executive may require, on the other hand, that it should be fortified. An absolute negative [veto] on the legislature appears, at first view, to be the natural defense with which the executive magistrate should be armed. But perhaps it would be neither altogether safe nor alone sufficient. On ordinary occasions it might not be exerted with

The Federalist, No. 51

(continued)

the requisite firmness, and on extraordinary occasions it might be perfidiously abused. May not this defect of an absolute negative be supplied by some qualified connection between this weaker department and the weaker branch of the stronger department, by which the latter may be led to support the constitutional rights of the former, without being too much detached from the rights of its own department? . . .

There are, moreover, two considerations particularly applicable to the federal system of America, which place that system in a very interesting point of view.

First. In a single republic, all the power surrendered by the people is submitted to the administration of a single government; and the usurpations are guarded against by a division of the government into distinct and separate departments. In the compound republic of America, the power surrendered by the people is first divided between two distinct governments, and then the portion allotted to each subdivided among distinct and separate departments. Hence a double security arises to the rights of the people. The different governments will control each other, at the same time that each will be controlled by itself.

Second. It is of great importance in a republic not only to guard the society against the oppression of its rulers, but to guard one part of the society against the injustice of the other part. Different interests necessarily exist in different classes of citizens. If a majority be united by a common interest, the rights of the minority will be insecure. There are but two methods of providing against this evil: the one by creating a will in the community independent of the majority—that is, of the society itself; the other, by comprehending in the society so many separate descriptions of citizens as will render an unjust combination of a majority of the whole very improbable, if not impracticable. The first method prevails in all governments possessing an hereditary or self-appointed authority. This, at best, is but a precarious security; because a power independent of the society may as well espouse the unjust views of the major as the rightful interests of the minor party, and may possibly be turned against both parties. The second method will be exemplified in the federal republic of the United States. Whilst all authority in it will be derived from and dependent on the society, the society itself will be broken into so many parts, interests and classes of citizens, that the rights of individuals, or of the minority, will be in little danger from interested combinations of the majority. In a free government the security for civil rights must be the same as that for religious rights. It consists in the one case in the multiplicity of interests, and in the other in the multiplicity of sects. The degree of security in both cases will depend on the number of interests and sects; and this may be presumed to depend on the extent of country and number of people comprehended under the same government. This view of the subject must particularly recommend a proper federal system to all the sincere and considerate friends of republican government, since it shows that in exact proportion as the territory of the Union may be formed into more circumscribed Confederacies, or States, oppressive combinations of a majority will be facilitated; the best security, under the republican forms, for the rights of every class of citizen, will be diminished; and consequently the stability and independence of some member of the government, the only other security, must be proportionally increased. Justice is the end of government. It is the end of civil society. It ever has been and ever will be pursued until it be obtained, or until liberty be lost in the pursuit. . . .

Washington's Farewell Address

Washington's Farewell Address was never delivered by him. It was printed in the American Daily Advertiser, *a newspaper in Philadelphia, on September 19, 1796. Designed in part to remove him from consideration for a third presidential term, the address also speaks of the dangers facing the new nation and warns against political parties and sectionalism.*

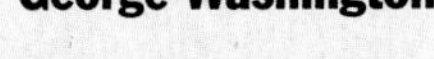

George Washington

Friends and Fellow Citizens:

The period for a new election of a citizen to administer the executive government of the United States being not far distant . . . I should now apprise you of the resolution I have formed to decline being considered among the number of those out of whom a choice is to be made. . . .

The unity of government which constitutes you one people is . . . a main pillar in the edifice of your real independence; the support of your tranquillity at home, your peace abroad; of your safety; of your prosperity in every shape; of that very liberty which you so highly prize. But as it is easy to foresee that, from different causes and from different quarters, much pains will be taken, many artifices employed to weaken in your minds the conviction of this truth. . . .

The name of *American,* which belongs to you, in your national capacity, must always exalt the just pride of patriotism more than any appellation derived from local discriminations. . . .

In contemplating the causes which may disturb our Union, it occurs as matter of serious concern that any ground should have been furnished for characterizing parties by geographical discriminations: Northern and Southern; Atlantic and Western; whence designing men may endeavor to excite a belief that there is a real difference of local interests and views. . . .

Let me now take a more comprehensive view and warn you in the most solemn manner against the baneful effects of the spirit of party generally. . . .

The alternate domination of one faction over another, sharpened by the spirit of revenge natural to party dissension . . . is itself a frightful despotism. . . .

. . . [C]herish the public credit. One method of preserving it is to use it as sparingly as possible, avoiding occasions of expense by cultivating peace, but remembering also that timely disbursements to prepare for danger frequently prevent much greater disbursements to repel it; avoiding likewise the accumulation of debt, not only by shunning occasions of expense but by vigorous exertions in time of peace to discharge the debts which unavoidable wars may have occasioned, not ungenerously throwing upon posterity the burden which we ourselves ought to bear. . . .

The great rule of conduct for us, in regard to foreign nations, is in extending our commercial relations to have with them as little political connection as possible. . . .

In offering you, my countrymen, these counsels of an old and affectionate friend, I dare not hope that they will make the strong and lasting impression I could wish. . . . But if I may even flatter myself that they may be productive of some partial benefit. . . .

The Star-Spangled Banner

During the British bombardment of Fort McHenry during the War of 1812, a young Baltimore lawyer named Francis Scott Key was inspired to write the words to "The Star-Spangled Banner." Congress officially declared it the national anthem in 1931.

Oh, say, can you see, by the dawn's early light,
What so proudly we hailed at the twilight's last gleaming,
Whose broad stripes and bright stars through the perilous fight,
O'er the ramparts we watched were so gallantly streaming?
And the rockets' red glare, the bombs bursting in air,
Gave proof through the night that our flag was still there.
Oh, say, does that star-spangled banner yet wave
O'er the land of the free, and the home of the brave?

On the shore, dimly seen through the mists of the deep,
Where the foe's haughty host in dread silence reposes,
What is that which the breeze, o'er the towering steep,
As it fitfully blows, half conceals, half discloses?
Now it catches the gleam of the morning's first beam,
In full glory reflected, now shines on the stream.
'Tis the star-spangled banner; oh, long may it wave
O'er the land of the free, and the home of the brave!

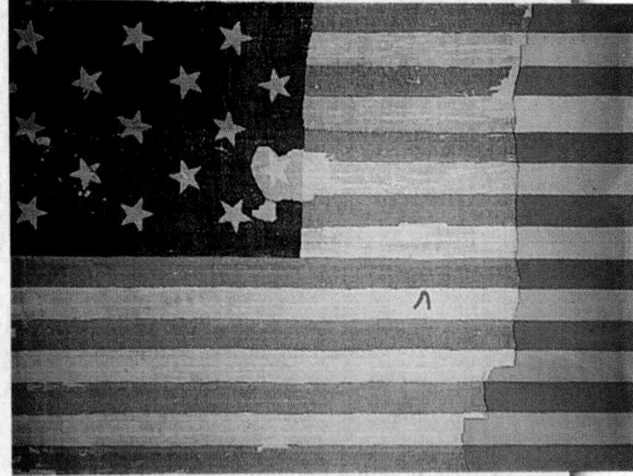

United States flag that flew over Fort McHenry

And where is that band who so vauntingly swore
That the havoc of war and the battle's confusion
A home and a country should leave us no more?
Their blood has washed out their foul footsteps' pollution.
No refuge could save the hireling and slave
From the terror of flight, or the gloom of the grave:
And the star-spangled banner in triumph doth wave
O'er the land of the free, and the home of the brave!

Oh! thus be it ever when freemen shall stand
Between their loved homes and the war's desolation!
Blest with victory and peace, may the heaven-rescued land
Praise the Power that hath made and preserved us a nation!
Then conquer we must, for our cause it is just,
And this be our motto: "In God is our trust!"
And the star-spangled banner in triumph shall wave,
O'er the land of the free, and the home of the brave!

Seneca Falls Declaration

One of the first documents to express the desire for equal rights for women is the Declaration of Sentiments and Resolution, issued in 1848 at the Seneca Falls Convention. Led by Lucretia Mott and Elizabeth Cady Stanton, the delegates adopted a set of resolutions that called for woman suffrage and opportunities for women.

Elizabeth Cady Stanton

When, in the course of human events, it becomes necessary for one portion of the family of man to assume among the people of the earth a position different from that which they have hitherto occupied, but one to which the laws of nature and of nature's God entitle them, a decent respect to the opinions of mankind requires that they should declare the causes that impel them to such a course.

We hold these truths to be self-evident: that all men and women are created equal; that they are endowed by their Creator with certain inalienable rights; that among these are life, liberty, and the pursuit of happiness; that to secure these rights governments are instituted, deriving their just powers from the consent of the governed. Whenever any form of government becomes destructive of these ends, it is the right of those who suffer from it to refuse allegiance to it, and to insist upon the institution of a new government, laying its foundation on such principles, and organizing its powers in such form, as to them shall seem most likely to effect their safety and happiness. . . .

The history of mankind is a history of repeated injuries and usurpations on the part of man toward woman, having in direct object the establishment of an absolute tyranny over her. To prove this, let facts be submitted to a candid world.

He has never permitted her to exercise her inalienable right to the elective franchise.

He has compelled her to submit to laws in the formation of which she had no voice. . . .

He has made her, if married, in the eye of the law, civilly dead.

He has taken from her all right in property, even to the wages she earns. . . .

He has denied her the facilities for obtaining a thorough education, all colleges being closed against her. . . .

He has endeavored, in every way that he could, to destroy her confidence in her own powers, to lessen her self-respect, and to make her willing to lead a dependent and abject life.

Now, in view of this entire disfranchisement . . . we insist that they have immediate admission to all the rights and privileges which belong to them as citizens of the United States. . . .

Resolved, That such laws as conflict, in any way, with the true and substantial happiness of women, are contrary to the great precept of nature and of no validity. . . .

Resolved, that all laws which prevent women from occupying such a station in society as her conscience shall dictate, or which place her in a position inferior to that of man, are . . . of no force or authority. . . .

Resolved, that it is the duty of the women of this country to secure to themselves their sacred right to the elective franchise. . . .

Fourth of July Address

Frederick Douglass

As the city's most distinguished resident, Frederick Douglass was requested to address the citizens of Rochester on the Fourth of July celebration in 1852. The speech he delivered, under the title "What to the Slave is the Fourth of July?", is excerpted below.

Fellow Citizens: Pardon me, and allow me to ask, why am I called upon to speak here today? What have I or those I represent to do with your national independence? Are the great principles of political freedom and of natural justice, embodied in that Declaration of Independence, extended to us? And am I, therefore, called upon to bring our humble offering to the national altar, and to confess the benefits, and express devout gratitude for the blessings resulting from your independence to us? . . .

I say it with a sad sense of disparity between us. I am not included within the pale of this glorious anniversary! Your high independence only reveals the immeasurable distance between us. The blessings in which you this day rejoice are not enjoyed in common. The rich inheritance of justice, liberty, prosperity, and independence bequeathed by your fathers is shared by you, not by me. . . . This Fourth of July is yours, not mine. You may rejoice, I must mourn. . . .

I do not hesitate to declare, with all my soul, that the character and conduct of this nation never looked blacker to me than on this Fourth of July. Whether we turn to the declarations of the past, or to the professions of the present, the conduct of the nation seems equally hideous and revolting. America is false to the past, false to the present, and solemnly binds herself to be false to the future. . . . I will, in the name of humanity, which is outraged, in the name of liberty, which is fettered, in the name of the Constitution and the Bible, which are disregarded and trampled upon, dare to call in question and to denounce, with all the emphasis I can command, everything that serves to perpetuate slavery—the great sin and shame of America! "I will not equivocate; I will not excuse"; I will use the severest language I can command, and yet not one word shall escape me that any man, whose judgment is not blinded by prejudice, or who is not at heart a slave-holder, shall not confess to be right and just. . . .

Would you have me argue that man is entitled to liberty? That he is the rightful owner of his own body? You have already declared it. Must I argue the wrongfulness of slavery? . . . There is not a man beneath the canopy of heaven who does not know that slavery is wrong for him.

What! Am I to argue that it is wrong to make men brutes, to rob them of their liberty, to work them without wages, to keep them ignorant of their relations to their fellow men, to beat them with sticks, to flay their flesh with the lash, to load their limbs with irons, to hunt them with dogs, to sell them at auction, to sunder their families, to knock out their teeth, to burn their flesh, to starve them into obedience and submission to their masters? . . . The feeling of the nation must be quickened; the conscience of the nation must be roused; the propriety of the nation must be startled; the hypocrisy of the nation must be exposed; and its crimes against God and man must be denounced. . . .

The Emancipation Proclamation

On January 1, 1863, President Abraham Lincoln issued the Emancipation Proclamation, which freed all slaves in states under Confederate control. The Proclamation was a significant step toward the Thirteenth Amendment (1865) that ended slavery in the United States.

Abraham Lincoln

Whereas, on the 22nd day of September, in the year of our Lord 1862, a proclamation was issued by the President of the United States, containing, among other things, the following, to wit:

> That on the 1st day of January, in the year of our Lord 1863, all persons held as slaves within any state or designated part of a state, the people whereof shall then be in rebellion against the United States, shall be then, thenceforward, and forever free; and the executive government of the United States, including the military and naval authority thereof, will recognize and maintain the freedom of such persons and will do no act or acts to repress such persons, or any of them, in any efforts they may make for their actual freedom.
>
> That the executive will, on the 1st day January aforesaid, by proclamation, designate the states and parts of states, if any, in which the people thereof, respectively, shall then be in rebellion against the United States; and the fact that any state or the people thereof shall on that day be in good faith represented in the Congress of the United States by members chosen thereto at elections wherein a majority of the qualified voters of such states shall have participated shall, in the absence of strong countervailing testimony, be deemed conclusive evidence that such state and the people thereof are not then in rebellion against the United States.

Now, therefore, I, Abraham Lincoln, President of the United States, by virtue of the power in me vested as commander in chief of the Army and Navy of the United States, in time of actual armed rebellion against the authority and government of the United States, and as a fit and necessary war measure for suppressing said rebellion, do, on this 1st day of January, in the year of our Lord 1863, and in accordance with my purpose so to do, publicly proclaimed for the full period of 100 days from the day first above mentioned, order and designate as the states and parts of states wherein the people thereof, respectively, are this day in rebellion against the United States. . . .

And, by virtue of the power and for the purpose aforesaid, I do order and declare that all persons held as slaves within said designated states and parts of states are, and henceforward shall be, free; and that the executive government of the United States, including the military and naval authorities thereof, will recognize and maintain the freedom of said persons. . .

And upon this act, sincerely believed to be an act of justice, warranted by the Constitution upon military necessity, I invoke the considerate judgment of mankind and the gracious favor of Almighty God.

The Fourteen Points

Leaders (left to right) David Lloyd George of Great Britain, Vittorio Orlando of Italy, Georges Clemenceau of France, and Woodrow Wilson of the United States

On January 8, 1918, President Woodrow Wilson went before Congress to offer a statement of aims called the Fourteen Points.

We entered this war because violations of right had occurred. . . . What we demand in this war, therefore, is . . . that the world be made fit and safe to live in. . . . The only possible programme, as we see it, is this:

I. Open covenants of peace, openly arrived at, after which there shall be no private international understandings of any kind but diplomacy shall proceed always frankly and in the public view.

II. Absolute freedom of navigation upon the seas, outside territorial waters, alike in peace and in war. . . .

III. The removal, so far as possible, of all economic barriers and the establishment of an equality of trade conditions among all the nations. . . .

IV. Adequate guarantees given and taken that national armaments will be reduced to the lowest point consistent with domestic safety.

V. A free, open-minded, and absolutely impartial adjustment of all colonial claims, based upon a strict observance of the principle that in determining all such questions of sovereignty the interests of the populations concerned must have equal weight with the equitable claims of the government whose title is to be determined.

VI. The evacuation of all Russian territory and . . . opportunity for the independent determination of her own political development and national policy. . . .

VII. Belgium . . . must be evacuated and restored. . . .

VIII. All French territory should be freed and the invaded portions restored, and the wrong done to France by Prussia in 1871 in the matter of Alsace-Lorraine should be righted. . . .

IX. A readjustment of the frontiers of Italy should be effected along clearly recognizable lines of nationality.

X. The peoples of Austria-Hungary . . . should be accorded the freest opportunity of autonomous development.

XI. Rumania, Serbia, and Montenegro should be evacuated; occupied territories restored . . . the relations of the several Balkan states to one another determined by friendly counsel along historically established lines of allegiance and nationality. . . .

XII. The Turkish portions of the present Ottoman Empire should be assured a secure sovereignty. . . .

XIII. An independent Polish state should be erected which should include the territories inhabited by indisputably Polish populations. . . .

XIV. A general association of nations must be formed under specific covenants for the purpose of affording mutual guarantees of political independence and territorial integrity. . . .

The Four Freedoms

President Franklin D. Roosevelt delivered this address on January 6, 1941, in his annual message to Congress. Roosevelt called for a world founded on "four essential human freedoms": freedom of speech and expression, freedom of worship, freedom from want, and freedom from fear.

Just as our national policy in internal affairs has been based upon a decent respect for the rights and dignity of all our fellowmen within our gates, so our national policy in foreign affairs has been based on a decent respect for the rights and dignity of all nations, large and small. And the justice of morality must and will win in the end.

Our national policy is this:

First, by an impressive expression of the public will and without regard to partisanship, we are committed to all-inclusive national defense.

Second, by an impressive expression of the public will and without regard to partisanship, we are committed to full support of all those resolute peoples, everywhere, who are resisting aggression and are thereby keeping war away from our Hemisphere. . . .

Roosevelt (left) and British Prime Minister Winston Churchill

Third . . . we are committed to the proposition that principles of morality and considerations for our own security will never permit us to acquiesce in a peace dictated by aggressors. . . .

Let us say to the democracies, "We Americans are vitally concerned in your defense of freedom. We are putting forth our energies, our resources, and our organizing powers to give you the strength to regain and maintain a free world. We shall send you, in ever increasing numbers, ships, planes, tanks, guns. This is our purpose and our pledge."

In fulfillment of this purpose we will not be intimidated by the threats of dictators that they will regard as a breach of international law and as an act of war our aid to the democracies which dare to resist their aggression. . . .

In the future days, which we seek to make secure, we look forward to a world founded upon four essential human freedoms.

The first is freedom of speech and expression everywhere in the world.

The second is freedom of every person to worship God in his own way everywhere in the world.

The third is freedom from want, which, translated into world terms, means economic understandings which will secure to every nation a healthy peacetime life for its inhabitants everywhere in the world.

The fourth is freedom from fear—which, translated into world terms, means a worldwide reduction of armaments to such a point and in such a thorough fashion that no nation will be in a position to commit an act of physical aggression against any neighbor—anywhere in the world. . . .

Charter of the United Nations

United Nations flag

The United Nations Charter was signed on June 26, 1945. It formally established the United Nations, a new international peace organization to succeed the League of Nations. The following excerpt contains Article I of the charter.

We the peoples of the United Nations determined

to save succeeding generations from the scourge of war, which twice in our lifetime has brought untold sorrow to mankind, and

to reaffirm faith in fundamental human rights, in the dignity and worth of the human person, in the equal rights of men and women and of nations large and small, and

to establish conditions under which justice and respect for the obligations arising from treaties and other sources of international law can be maintained, and

to promote social progress and better standards of life in larger freedom,

And for these ends

to practise tolerance and live together in peace with one another as good neighbours, and

to unite our strength to maintain international peace and security, and

to ensure, by the acceptance of principles and the institution of methods, that armed force shall not be used, save in the common interest, and

to employ international machinery for the promotion of the economic and social advancement of all peoples,

Have resolved to combine our efforts to accomplish these aims.

Accordingly, our respective Governments, through representatives assembled in the city of San Francisco, who have exhibited their full powers found to be in good and due form, have agreed to the present Charter of the United Nations and do hereby establish an international organization to be known as the United Nations. . . .

Article 1. The Purposes of the United Nations are:

1. To maintain international peace and security, and to that end: to take effective collective measures for the prevention and removal of threats to the peace, and for the suppression of acts of aggression or other breaches of the peace, and to bring about by peaceful means and in conformity with the principles of justice and international law, adjustment or settlement of international disputes or situations which might lead to a breach of the peace:
2. To develop friendly relations among nations based on respect for the principle of equal rights and self-determination of peoples, and to take other appropriate measures to strengthen universal peace;
3. To achieve international co-operation in solving international problems of an economic, social, cultural, or humanitarian character, and in promoting and encouraging respect for human rights and for fundamental freedoms for all without distinction as to race, sex, language, or religion; and
4. To be a centre for harmonizing the accusations of nations in the attainment of these common ends.

"I Have a Dream"

On August 28, 1963, while Congress debated wide-ranging civil rights legislation, Martin Luther King, Jr., led more than 200,000 people in a march on Washington, D.C. On the steps of the Lincoln Memorial he gave a stirring speech in which he eloquently spoke of his dreams for African Americans and for the United States.

Five score years ago, a great American, in whose symbolic shadow we stand, signed the Emancipation Proclamation. This momentous decree came as a great beacon light of hope to millions of Negro slaves who had been seared in the flames of withering injustice. It came as a joyous daybreak to end the long night of captivity.

But one hundred years later, we must face the tragic fact that the Negro is still not free. One hundred years later, the life of the Negro is still sadly crippled by the manacles of segregation and the chains of discrimination. . . .

There are those who are asking the devotees of civil rights, "When will you be satisfied?"

We can never be satisfied as long as the Negro is the victim of the unspeakable horrors of police brutality.

We can never be satisfied as long as our bodies, heavy with the fatigue of travel, cannot gain lodging in the motels of the highways and the hotels of the cities.

We cannot be satisfied as long as the Negro's basic mobility is from a smaller ghetto to a larger one.

We can never be satisfied as long as a Negro in Mississippi cannot vote and a Negro in New York believes he has nothing for which to vote.

No, no, we are not satisfied, and we will not be satisfied until justice rolls down like waters and righteousness like a mighty stream. . . .

I say to you today, my friends, that in spite of the difficulties and frustrations of the moment I still have a dream. It is a dream deeply rooted in the American dream.

I have a dream that one day this nation will rise up and live out the true meaning of its creed: "We hold these truths to be self-evident; that all men are created equal. "

I have a dream that one day on the red hills of Georgia the sons of former slaves and the sons of former slaveowners will be able to sit down together at the table of brotherhood.

I have a dream that one day even the state of Mississippi, a desert state sweltering with the heat of injustice and oppression, will be transformed into an oasis of freedom and justice.

I have a dream that my four little children will one day live in a nation where they will not be judged by the color of their skin but by the content of their character. . . .

When we let freedom ring, when we let it ring from every village and every hamlet, from every state and every city, we will be able to speed up that day when all of God's children, black men and white men, Jews and Gentiles, Protestants and Catholics, will be able to join hands and sing in the words of the old Negro spiritual, "Free at last! Free at last! Thank God Almighty, we are free at last!"

Election 2000: Albert Gore's Concession Speech

The presidential election of 2000 was one of the closest elections in American history. Although voters cast their ballots on November 7, the winner was not known until December 13 because the Florida race remained too close to call amid a series of legal challenges by both sides. It took the historic intervention of the United States Supreme Court to settle the election by effectively halting the recounting of disputed ballots. On December 13, Vice President Gore formally conceded defeat. Moments later George W. Bush accepted his election as forty-third president of the United States.

Speaker: Albert Gore, Jr., Democratic Party Presidential Candidate

Good evening. Just moments ago, I spoke with George W. Bush and congratulated him on becoming the forty-third president of the United States. . . . I offered to meet with him as soon as possible so that we can start to heal the divisions of the campaign. . . .

Almost a century and a half ago, Senator Stephen Douglas told Abraham Lincoln, who had just defeated him for the presidency, "Partisan feeling must yield to patriotism. I'm with you, Mr. President, and God bless you." Well, in that same spirit, I say to President-elect Bush that what remains of partisan rancor must now be put aside, and may God bless his stewardship of this country. Neither he nor I anticipated this long and difficult road. Certainly neither of us wanted it to happen. Yet it came, and now it has ended, resolved, as it must be resolved, through the honored institutions of our democracy.

Over the library of one of our great law schools is inscribed the motto, "Not under man but under God and law." That's the ruling principle of American freedom, the source of our democratic liberties. I've tried to make it my guide throughout this contest as it has guided America's deliberations of all the complex issues of the past five weeks. Now the U.S. Supreme Court has spoken. Let there be no doubt, while I strongly disagree with the court's decision, I accept it. . . . And tonight, for the sake of the unity of our people and the strength of our democracy, I offer my concession. I also accept my responsibility, which I will discharge unconditionally, to honor the new president-elect and do everything possible to help him bring Americans together in fulfillment of the great vision that our Declaration of Independence defines and that our Constitution affirms and defends. . . .

This has been an extraordinary election. But in one of God's unforeseen paths, this belatedly broken impasse can point us all to a new common ground, for its very closeness can serve to remind us that we are one people with a shared history and a shared destiny. Indeed, that history gives us many examples of contests as hotly debated, as fiercely fought, with their own challenges to the popular will. Other disputes have dragged on for weeks before reaching resolution. And each time, both the victor and the vanquished have accepted the result peacefully and in the spirit of reconciliation. . . .

Now the political struggle is over and we turn again to the unending struggle for the common good of all Americans and for those multitudes around the world who look to us for leadership in the cause of freedom. In the words of our great hymn, "America, America": "Let us crown thy good with brotherhood, from sea to shining to sea." And now, my friends, in a phrase I once addressed to others, it's time for me to go.

Vice President and Mrs. Gore with Senator and Mrs. Lieberman

Election 2000: George W. Bush's Acceptance Speech

Speaker: President-Elect George W. Bush

Tonight I chose to speak from the chamber of the Texas House of Representatives because it has been a home to bipartisan cooperation. Here in a place where Democrats have the majority, Republicans and Democrats have worked together to do what is right for the people we represent. We've had spirited disagreements. And in the end, we found constructive consensus. It is an experience I will always carry with me, an example I will always follow.

The spirit of cooperation I have seen in this hall is what is needed in Washington, D.C. It is the challenge of our moment. After a difficult election, we must put politics behind us and work together to make the promise of America available for every one of our citizens. I am optimistic that we can change the tone in Washington, D.C. I believe things happen for a reason, and I hope the long wait of the last five weeks will heighten a desire to move beyond the bitterness and partisanship of the recent past.

Our nation must rise above a house divided. Americans share hopes and goals and values far more important than any political disagreements. Republicans want the best for our nation, and so do Democrats. Our votes may differ, but not our hopes. I know America wants reconciliation and unity. I know Americans want progress. And we must seize this moment and deliver.

Together, guided by a spirit of common sense, common courtesy, and common goals, we can unite and inspire the American citizens. Together, we will work to make all our public schools excellent. . . . Together we will save Social Security and renew its promise of a secure retirement for generations to come. Together we will strengthen Medicare and offer prescription drug coverage to all of our seniors. Together we will give Americans the broad, fair, and fiscally responsible tax relief they deserve. Together we'll have a bipartisan foreign policy true to our values and true to our friends, and we will address some of society's deepest problems one person at a time, by encouraging and empowering the good hearts and good works of the American people. This is the essence of compassionate conservatism, and it will be a foundation of my administration.

These priorities are not merely Republican concerns or Democratic concerns; they are American responsibilities. During the fall campaign, we differed about the details of these proposals, but there was remarkable consensus about the important issues before us: excellent schools, retirement and health security, tax relief, a strong military, a more civil society. We have discussed our differences. Now it is time to find common ground and build consensus to make America a beacon of opportunity in the twenty-first century. . . .

I have something else to ask you, to ask every American. I ask for you to pray for this great nation. I ask for your prayers for leaders from both parties. I thank you for your prayers for me and my family, and ask you to pray for Vice President Gore and his family. I have faith that with God's help we as a nation will move forward together as one nation, indivisible. And together we will create an America that is open, so every citizen has access to the American dream; an America that is educated, so every child has the keys to realize that dream; and an America that is united in our diversity and our shared American values that are larger than race or party.

President-elect and Mrs. George W. Bush

Congressional Quarterly's United States Data Bank

Contents

Online UPDATE

Visit gov.glencoe.com and click on ***Textbook Updates–United States Data Bank*** for an update of the data.

United States Population Growth, 1980–1998

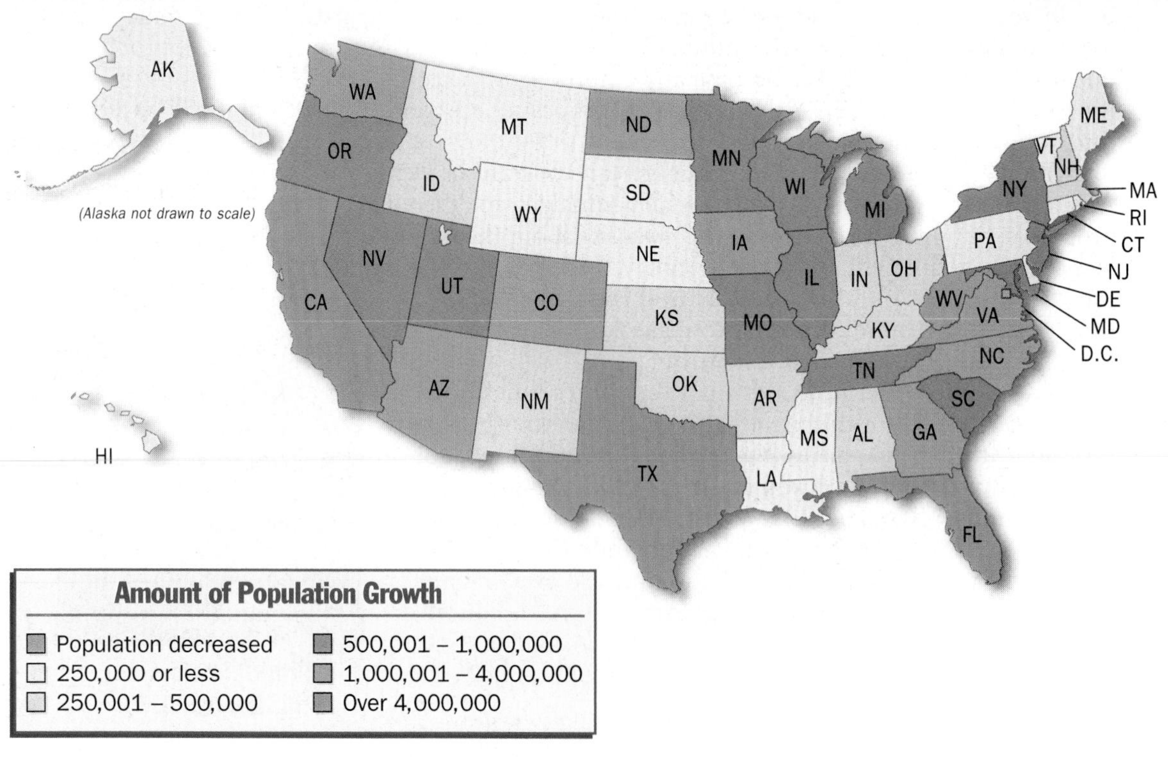

Amount of Population Growth

- Population decreased
- 250,000 or less
- 250,001 – 500,000
- 500,001 – 1,000,000
- 1,000,001 – 4,000,000
- Over 4,000,000

Source: U.S. Bureau of the Census, *Statistical Abstract of the United States: 1999* (Washington, D.C.: 1999).

Crime and the Justice System

Supreme Court Cases

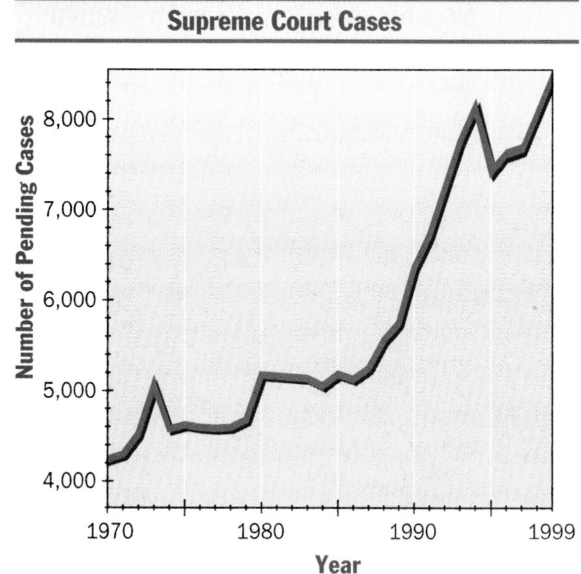

Supreme Court Decisions

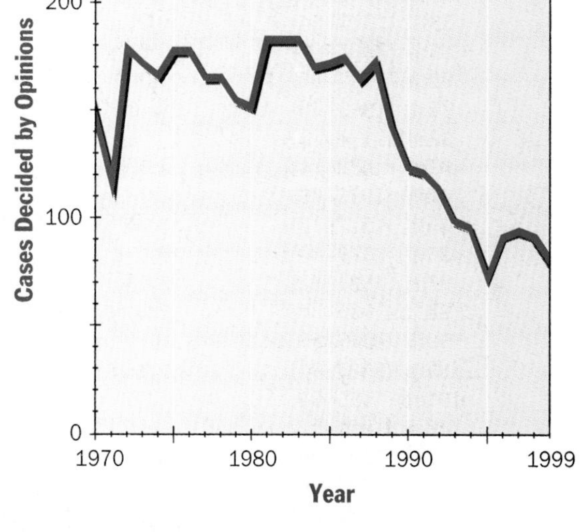

Types of Cases in Federal District Courts, 1997

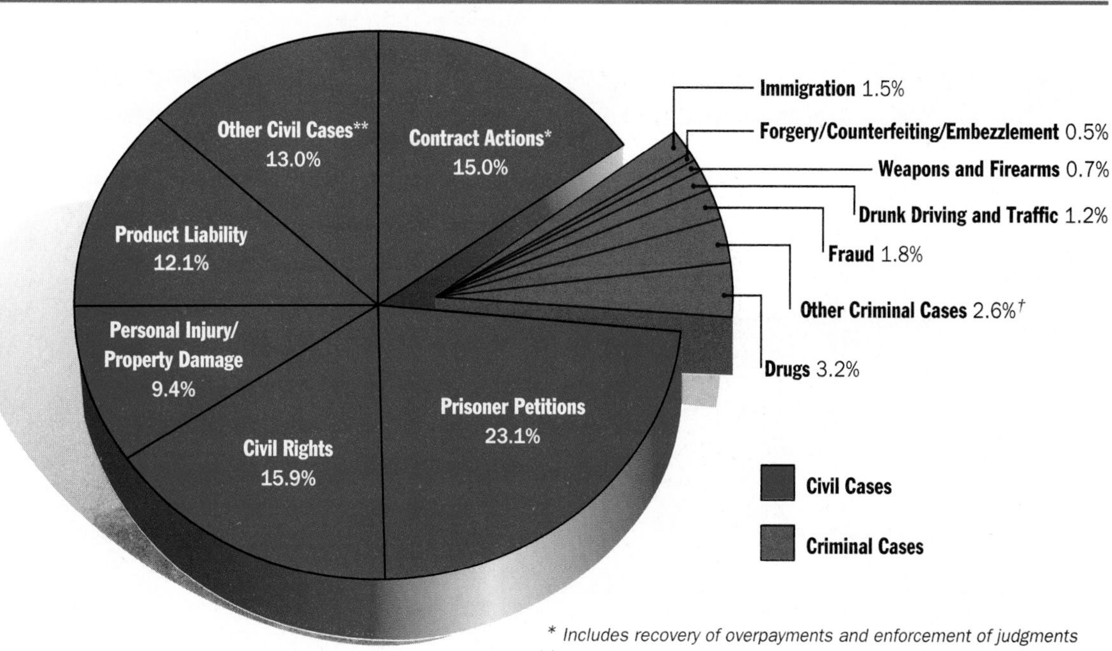

* *Includes recovery of overpayments and enforcement of judgments*
** *Includes bankruptcy, tax suits, labor laws, and social security issues*
† *Includes larceny, theft, homicide, robbery, assault, and burglary*

Sources: Stanley and Niemi, *Vital Statistics on American Politics 1999–2000* (Washington, D.C.: CQ Inc., 2000).
U.S. Bureau of the Census, *Statistical Abstract of the United States: 1999* (Washington, D.C.: 1999).
Supreme Court Public Information Office, *Final Statistical Report, June 29, 2000.*

Congressional Quarterly's United States Data Bank

Bills Introduced, Passed, and Enacted by Congress, 1961–1998

Congress (Years)	BILLS INTRODUCED* House	BILLS INTRODUCED* Senate	BILLS PASSED* House	BILLS PASSED* Senate	BILLS ENACTED
87th (1961–62)	14,328	4,048	1,927	1,953	1,569
88th (1963–64)	14,022	3,457	1,267	1,341	1,026
89th (1965–66)	19,874	4,129	1,565	1,636	1,283
90th (1967–68)	22,060	4,400	1,213	1,376	1,002
91st (1969–70)	21,436	4,867	1,130	1,271	941
92nd (1971–72)	18,561	4,408	970	1,035	768
93rd (1973–74)	18,872	4,524	923	1,115	774
94th (1975–76)	16,982	4,114	968	1,038	729
95th (1977–78)	15,587	3,800	1,027	1,070	803
96th (1979–80)	9,103	3,480	929	977	736
97th (1981–82)	8,094	3,396	704	803	529
98th (1983–84)	7,105	3,454	978	936	677
99th (1985–86)	6,499	3,386	973	940	688
100th (1987–88)	6,263	3,325	1,061	1,002	761
101st (1989–90)	6,683	3,669	968	980	666
102nd (1991–92)	7,771	4,245	932	947	610
103rd (1993–94)	6,647	3,177	749	682	473
104th (1995–96)	4,542	2,266	611	518	337
105th (1997–98)	4,874	2,655	1,174	879	358
106th (1999, 1st session)	4,241	2,352	657	549	173

***Includes House and Senate resolutions, joint resolutions, and concurrent resolutions**

Sources: Stanley and Niemi, *Vital Statistics on American Politics, 1997–1998* (Washington D.C.: CQ Inc., 1997); U.S. Congress, Office of Legislative Information; Ornstein, Mann, and Malbin, *Vital Statistics on Congress 1997–1998* (Washington, D.C.: CQ Inc., 1998), www.thomas.loc.gov.

Federal Revenue by Source, 1999

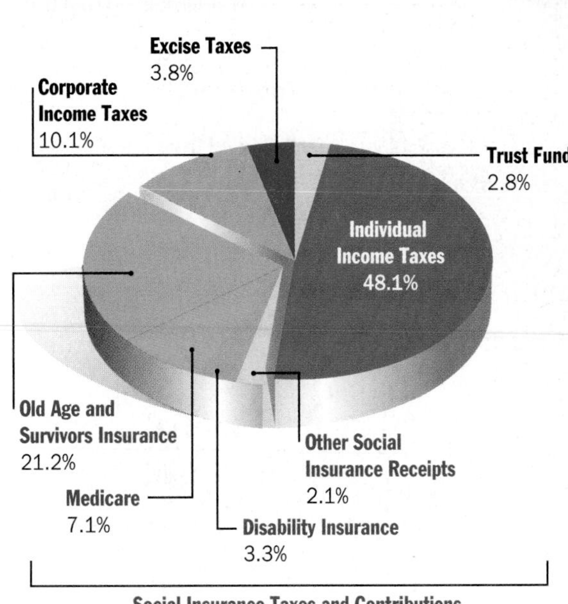

Federal Expenditures by Category, 1999

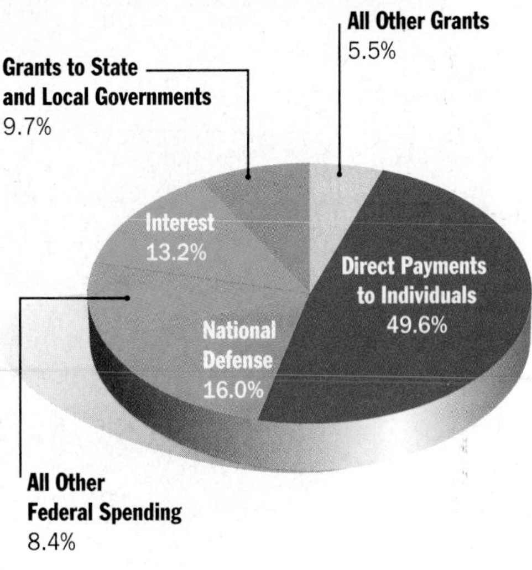

Percentages may not total 100% due to rounding.

Source: U.S. Bureau of the Census, *Statistical Abstract of the United States: 1999* (Washington, D.C.: 1999).

Federal Government Revenues and Expenditures, 1960–1999

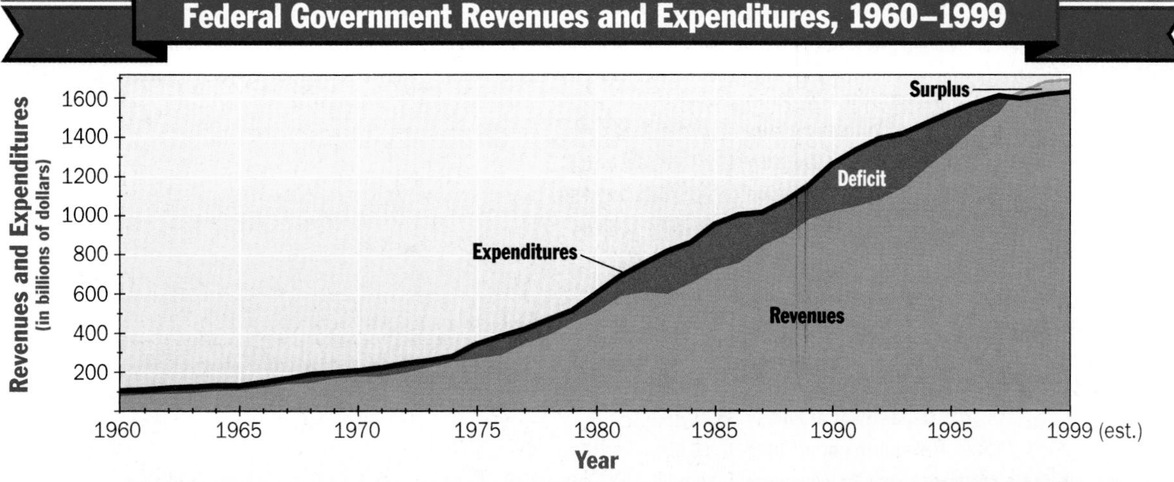

Gross Federal Debt, 1960–1999*

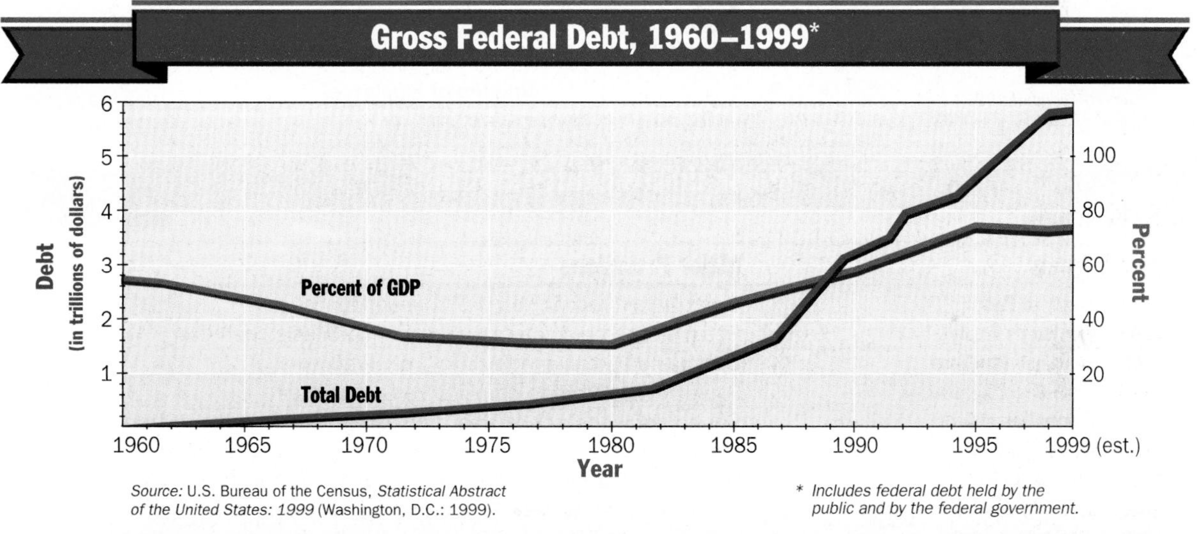

Source: U.S. Bureau of the Census, *Statistical Abstract of the United States: 1999* (Washington, D.C.: 1999).

* *Includes federal debt held by the public and by the federal government.*

National Debt per Capita, 1940–2000*

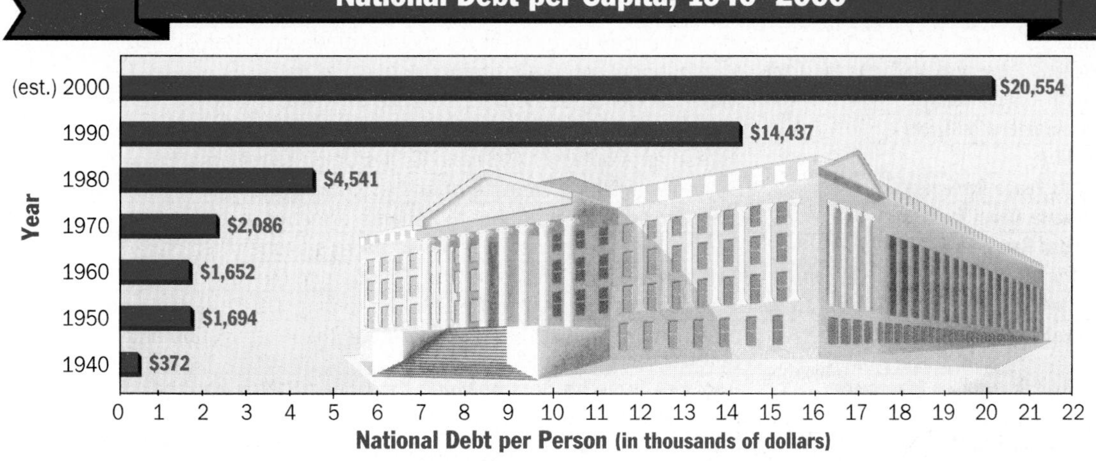

Sources: U.S. Bureau of the Census, U.S. Bureau of Public Debt.

* *Includes federal debt held by the public and by the federal government.*

Executive Department Civilian Employees*

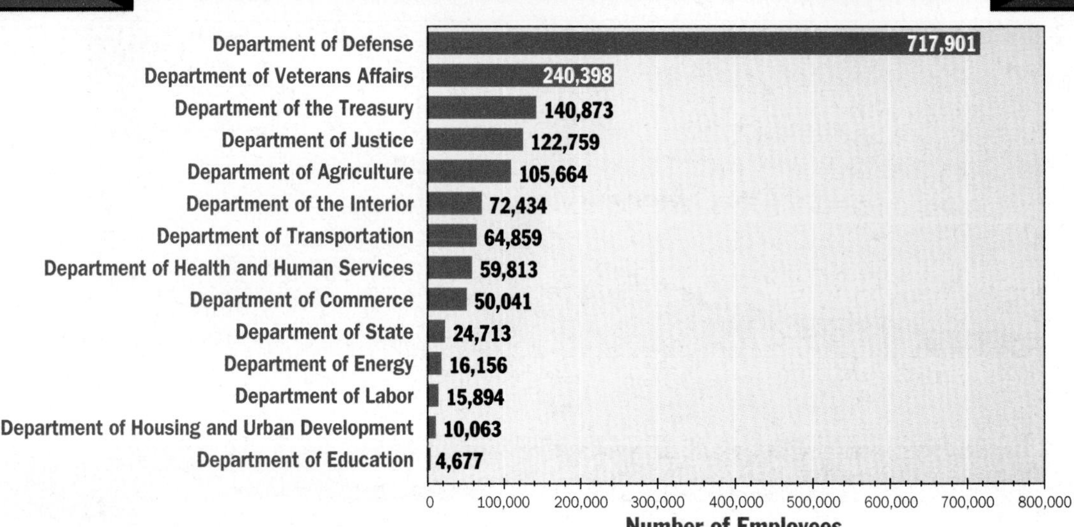

* *as of December 1999*

Source: U.S. Bureau of the Census, *Statistical Abstract of the United States: 1999* (Washington, D.C: 1999).

Major United States Treaties

Year	Treaty	Major Provisions
1783	Treaty of Paris	Great Britain recognized U.S. independence
1795	Pinckney's Treaty	Spain granted U.S. navigation rights on Mississippi River
1803	Louisiana Purchase	U.S. gained Louisiana territory from France
1817	Rush-Bagot Agreement	Signed with Britain to demilitarize Great Lakes
1818	Convention of 1818	Set border with Canada west from Great Lakes as the 49th parallel
1819	Adams-Onís Treaty	Spain ceded Florida; U.S. border set with Spanish territory in West
1846	Oregon Treaty	Signed with Great Britain to settle claims to Oregon country
1848	Treaty of Guadalupe Hidalgo	Ended Mexican War; U.S. gained Southwest and California
1867	Alaska Purchase	U.S. gained Alaska from Russia
1898	Treaty of Paris	Ended Spanish-American War; U.S. gained Puerto Rico and Philippines
1903	Hay-Buneau-Varilla Treaty	Signed with Panama to give U.S. right to build Panama Canal
1947	Rio Pact	Inter-American agreement for security of Western Hemisphere
1947	General Agreement on Tariffs and Trade	Multinational agreement to promote world trade
1949	North Atlantic Treaty	Multinational agreement for defense of Western Europe; created NATO
1968	Nonproliferation Treaty	International agreement to prevent spread of nuclear weapons
1972	SALT I	Agreements between U.S. and Soviet Union to limit nuclear weapons
1973	Paris Peace Agreement	Signed with North Vietnam to end U.S. involvement in Vietnam War
1977	Panama Canal Treaties	Transferred Panama Canal to Panama effective in 1999
1985	Vienna Convention	International agreement to protect Earth's ozone layer
1993	North American Free Trade Agreement	Established duty-free trade with Canada and Mexico
1996	Comprehensive Nuclear Test Ban Treaty	156 countries agreed to halt nuclear testing, US Senate did not ratify.
1996	Counterterrorism Accord	Israel and the US agree to cooperate in the investigation and deterrance of terrorist acts.
1997	Mutual Recognition Agreement	Reduces trade barriers between the United States and the European Community.

Source: U.S. State Department, *Treaties in Force*; Findling, *Dictionary of American Diplomatic History*, 2nd ed. (New York: Greenwood Press, 1989); Axelrod, *American Treaties and Alliances* (Washington, D.C.: CQ, Inc., 2000).

State Facts

State*	Year Admitted	Population 1999 (est.)	Area sq. mile	Capital	Largest City	House Rep. 1990**
1. Delaware	1787	753,538	1,955	Dover	Wilmington	1
2. Pennsylvania	1787	11,994,016	44,820	Harrisburg	Philadelphia	21
3. New Jersey	1787	8,143,412	7,419	Trenton	Newark	13
4. Georgia	1788	7,788,240	57,919	Atlanta	Atlanta	11
5. Connecticut	1788	3,282,031	4,845	Hartford	Bridgeport	6
6. Massachusetts	1788	6,175,169	7,838	Boston	Boston	10
7. Maryland	1788	5,171,634	9,775	Annapolis	Baltimore	8
8. South Carolina	1788	3,885,736	30,111	Columbia	Columbia	6
9. New Hampshire	1788	1,201,134	8,969	Concord	Manchester	2
10. Virginia	1788	6,872,912	39,598	Richmond	Virginia Beach	11
11. New York	1788	18,196,601	47,224	Albany	New York	31
12. North Carolina	1789	7,650,789	48,718	Raleigh	Charlotte	12
13. Rhode Island	1790	990,819	28,164	Providence	Providence	2
14. Vermont	1791	593,740	9,249	Montpelier	Burlington	1
15. Kentucky	1792	3,960,825	39,732	Frankfort	Louisville	6
16. Tennessee	1796	5,483,535	41,220	Nashville	Memphis	9
17. Ohio	1803	11,256,654	40,953	Columbus	Columbus	19
18. Louisiana	1812	4,372,035	43,566	Baton Rouge	New Orleans	7
19. Indiana	1816	5,942,901	35,870	Indianapolis	Indianapolis	10
20. Mississippi	1817	2,768,619	46,914	Jackson	Jackson	5
21. Illinois	1818	12,128,370	55,593	Springfield	Chicago	20
22. Alabama	1819	4,369,862	50,750	Montgomery	Birmingham	7
23. Maine	1820	1,253,040	30,865	Augusta	Portland	2
24. Missouri	1821	5,468,338	68,989	Jefferson City	Kansas City	9
25. Arkansas	1836	2,551,373	52,075	Little Rock	Little Rock	4
26. Michigan	1837	9,863,775	56,809	Lansing	Detroit	16
27. Florida	1845	15,111,244	53,937	Tallahassee	Jacksonville	23
28. Texas	1845	20,044,141	261,914	Austin	Houston	30
29. Iowa	1846	2,869,413	55,875	Des Moines	Des Moines	5
30. Wisconsin	1848	5,250,446	54,314	Madison	Milwaukee	9
31. California	1850	33,145,121	155,973	Sacramento	Los Angeles	52
32. Minnesota	1858	4,775,508	79,617	St. Paul	Minneapolis	8
33. Oregon	1859	3,316,154	96,003	Salem	Portland	5
34. Kansas	1861	2,654,052	81,823	Topeka	Wichita	4
35. West Virginia	1863	1,806,928	24,087	Charleston	Charleston	3
36. Nevada	1864	1,809,253	109,806	Carson City	Las Vegas	2
37. Nebraska	1867	1,666,028	76,878	Lincoln	Omaha	3
38. Colorado	1876	4,056,133	103,729	Denver	Denver	6
39. North Dakota	1889	633,666	68,994	Bismarck	Fargo	1
40. South Dakota	1889	733,133	75,896	Pierre	Sioux Falls	1
41. Montana	1889	882,779	145,556	Helena	Billings	1
42. Washington	1889	5,756,361	66,581	Olympia	Seattle	9
43. Idaho	1890	1,251,700	82,751	Boise	Boise	2
44. Wyoming	1890	479,602	97,105	Cheyenne	Cheyenne	1
45. Utah	1896	2,129,836	82,168	Salt Lake City	Salt Lake City	3
46. Oklahoma	1907	3,358,044	68,679	Oklahoma City	Oklahoma City	6
47. New Mexico	1912	1,739,844	121,365	Santa Fe	Albuquerque	3
48. Arizona	1912	4,778,332	113,642	Phoenix	Phoenix	6
49. Alaska	1959	619,500	570,314	Juneau	Anchorage	1
50. Hawaii	1959	1,185,497	6,423	Honolulu	Honolulu	2
District of Columbia	—	**519,000**	**61**	—	—	
United States	—	**272,690,813**	**3,536,278**	**Washington, D.C.**	**New York**	

*Numbers denote the order in which states were admitted

**Number of members in U.S. House of Representatives

State Revenues and Expenditures

Total State Revenue by Category, 1996

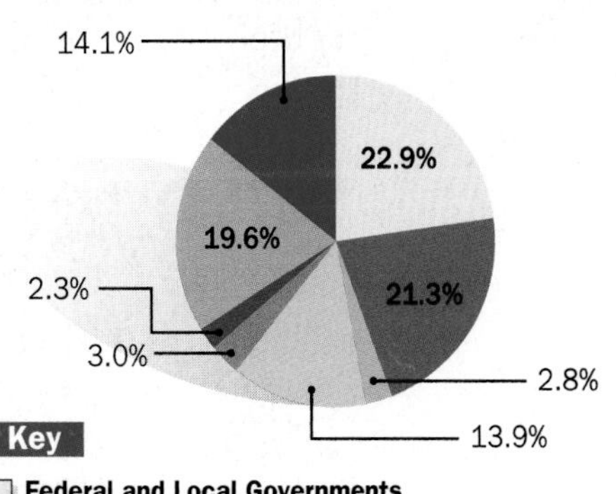

Key

- Federal and Local Governments
- Sales Taxes
- Licenses
- Individual Income Taxes
- Corporate Income Taxes
- Other Taxes
- Public Employees Pension Contributions
- Miscellaneous Revenue

* Percentages do not total 100% due to rounding.
Source: U.S. Bureau of the Census.

Total State Expenditures by Category, 1996

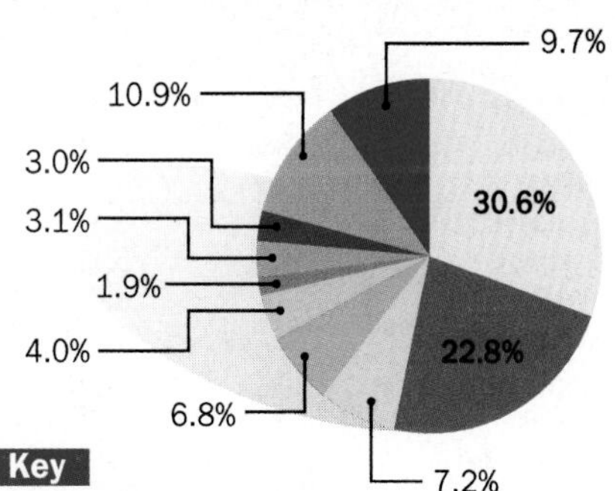

Key

- Education
- Public Welfare
- Hospitals and Health
- Highways
- Police and Corrections
- Natural Resources, Parks and Recreation
- Government Administration
- Interest on Debt
- Public Employees Retirement Benefits
- All Other Expenditures

State Expenditures for Public Education, 1998

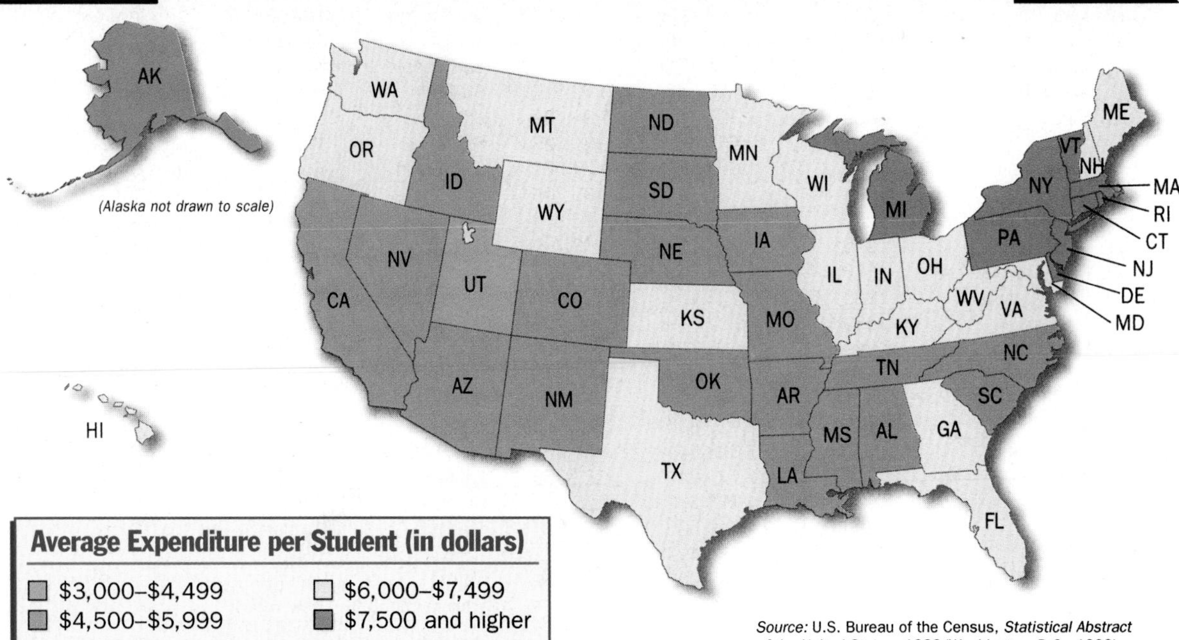

Average Expenditure per Student (in dollars)

- $3,000–$4,499
- $4,500–$5,999
- $6,000–$7,499
- $7,500 and higher

Source: U.S. Bureau of the Census, *Statistical Abstract of the United States: 1999* (Washington, D.C.: 1999).

Size of State Legislatures

State	House Members	Senate Members
Alabama	105	35
Alaska	40	20
Arizona	60	30
Arkansas	100	35
California	80	40
Colorado	65	35
Connecticut	151	36
Delaware	41	21
Florida	120	40
Georgia	180	56
Hawaii	51	25
Idaho	70	35
Illinois	118	59
Indiana	100	50
Iowa	100	50
Kansas	125	40
Kentucky	100	38
Louisiana	105	39
Maine	151	35
Maryland	141	47
Massachusetts	160	40
Michigan	110	38
Minnesota	134	67
Mississippi	122	52
Missouri	163	34
Montana	100	50
Nebraska	N/A	49
Nevada	42	21
New Hampshire	400	24
New Jersey	80	40
New Mexico	70	42
New York	150	61
North Carolina	120	50
North Dakota	98	49
Ohio	99	33
Oklahoma	101	48
Oregon	60	30
Pennsylvania	203	50
Rhode Island	100	50
South Carolina	124	46
South Dakota	70	35
Tennessee	99	33
Texas	150	31
Utah	75	29
Vermont	150	30
Virginia	100	40
Washington	98	49
West Virginia	100	34
Wisconsin	99	33
Wyoming	60	30

Source: Hovey and Hovey, *State Fact Finder, 2000* (Washington D.C.: CQ Inc., 2000).

State Legislators' Compensation

State	Salary (1999)	Expense allowance
Alabama	$1,050	$2,280/month
Alaska	$24,012	$173/day
Arizona	$24,000	$35/day
Arkansas	$12,500	$89/day
California	$99,000	$121/day
Colorado	$30,000	$45/day
Connecticut	$21,788	$0
Delaware	$29,574	$0
Florida	$26,388	$4,093/sess.
Georgia	$11,348	$75/day
Hawaii	$32,000	$80/day
Idaho	$14,760	$75/day
Illinois	$50,803	$85/day
Indiana	$11,600	$112/day
Iowa	$20,758	$86/day
Kansas	$6,485	$80/day
Kentucky	$151/day	$88/day
Louisiana	$16,800	$97/day
Maine	$10,500	$38/day
Maryland	$30,591	$126/day
Massachusetts	$46,410	$9–50/day
Michigan	$55,054	$10,000/year
Minnesota	$31,140	$56/day
Mississippi	$10,000	$99/day
Missouri	$29,080	$68–80/day
Montana	$6,086	$75/day
Nebraska	$12,000	$34–84/day
Nevada	$7,800	federal rate
New Hampshire	$100	$0
New Jersey	$35,000	$0
New Mexico	$0	$124/day
New York	$79,500	$89–130/day
North Carolina	$13,951	$104/day
North Dakota	$12,654	$900/month
Ohio	$42,427	$0
Oklahoma	$38,400	$97/day
Oregon	$14,496	$87/day
Pennsylvania	$59,246	$115/day
Rhode Island	$10,768	$0/day
South Carolina	$10,400	$85/day
South Dakota	$6,000	$95/day
Tennessee	$16,500	$114/day
Texas	$7,200	$118/day
Utah	$4,500	$118/day
Vermont	$9,342	$87/day
Virginia	$18,000	$114/day
Washington	$28,300	$82/day
West Virginia	$15,000	$45–85/day
Wisconsin	$41,809	$75/day
Wyoming	$6,875	$80/day

Source: Hovey and Hovey, *State Fact Finder, 2000* (Washington D.C.: CQ Inc., 2000).

Government Careers Handbook

The United States government is, by far, the nation's largest employer. About two-thirds of federal employees perform white-collar jobs—managers, clerks, engineers, and so on. The remainder are blue-collar workers—painters, heavy equipment operators, mechanics, and electricians, to name just a few. In fact, for nearly every occupation in the private sector, a similar job exists somewhere in the federal government. Fewer than 1 in 10 federal employees works in the Washington, D.C., area. Most blue-collar employees work at naval shipyards, military bases, or on numerous federal construction projects around the country. White-collar federal workers can be found in every city in America.

The Federal Job Market

Every government position falls under one of three job systems. Most white-collar jobs are in the General Schedule, or GS for short. This system assigns each job title to 1 of 15 different levels, based on the experience and expertise needed to do the work. Pay for each position is set according to its classification. The base income for all occupations classified GS-7, for example, is identical no matter how different the jobs are.

The following occupations sample the types of jobs available with the federal government. Although all are entry-level positions, they illustrate a range of duties, job opportunities, and background requirements. Ten are General Schedule positions, because this job category comprises the majority of federal positions. Obviously, however, no list like this one can represent the more than 2,000 occupations at which federal employees currently work.

How to Find Government Jobs and Career Resources on the Net

There are many more careers in the government than the ones listed below. The United States government recruits an average of more than 350,000 new hires each year in hundreds of entry level to professional occupations. Anyone interested in a challenging career with excellent job security and benefits should explore the lucrative government job market.

To locate career resources on the Internet, simply go to a search engine and type in a general topic, such as *government jobs, government careers,* or *federal employment.* You may also wish to look under individual executive departments, such as the Department of State or the Department of Agriculture. To find state or local level government jobs, type in a search topic such as *jobs in California.*

Budget Analyst

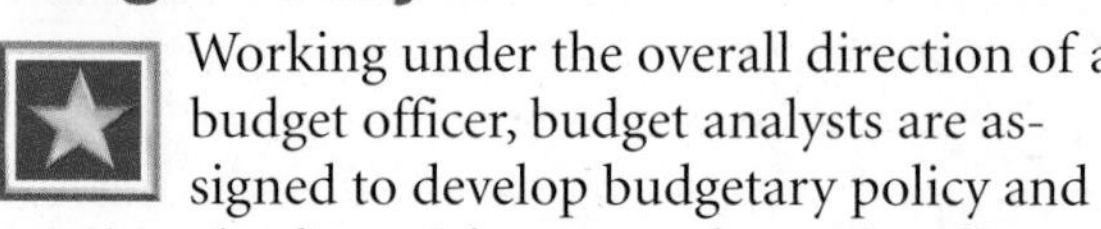

Working under the overall direction of a budget officer, budget analysts are assigned to develop budgetary policy and monitor the financial aspects of specific offices, programs, or activities within the agency that employs them. This responsibility includes making sure that office spending is appropriate and falls within established budgetary guidelines. By analyzing the financial costs and benefits of possible courses of action, budget analysts also help agency managers make policy and operation decisions. In some agencies, budget analysts help determine rates and charges and provide guidance for groups being regulated. Budget analysts work under pressure of tight deadlines and must have highly developed reasoning and communications skills.

Position Requirements: In addition to a written test, applicants are scored on the basis of their experience. Three years of general experience is required. That experience should have provided knowledge of financial and management principles and practices as they apply to organizations. There is no formal education requirement, but most budget analysts have college degrees. A four-year degree substitutes for the experience requirement.

Degrees that include courses in logic, math and statistics, economics, computer science, and other courses that teach techniques used in budget analysis earn high ratings for applicants.

Salary and Outlook: Although more than 12,000 men and women work in the position, there is a high demand for additional budget analysts. Nearly every government department and agency employs at least one. The starting salary is about $22,000 per year, but top pay for this job is more than $100,000.

State and Local Government Opportunities: Many large state and local government agencies also employ budget analysts.

Congressional Aide

Congressional aides perform a variety of roles in the legislative branch. Many staff the special and standing committees of the House and Senate. As attorneys, investigators, researchers, and other specialists, they provide the expertise each committee needs to carry out its work. Other aides serve individual senators and representatives, either in Washington or in their home states and districts. Those on Washington staffs typically work as press aides, administrative assistants, scheduling coordinators, policy specialists, and legislative assistants. Most aides in the home office do "casework," handling constituents' requests for assistance.

Position Requirements: Because civil service laws do not apply to Congress, there are no fixed requirements for congressional aide, nor is there any set path to employment. However, aides tend to be young, well-educated, and have backgrounds in social work, economics, law, political science, and other areas related to the work they perform. A large number have previously served Congress as unpaid student interns or on professional fellowships. Because these are patronage jobs, political connections are important. Many new aides have worked in the campaigns of the legislators who hire them. All committees require a set number of Republicans and Democrats on their staffs.

Salary and Outlook: Here, too, few standards apply. Each legislator receives a fixed amount for salaries and distributes it as he or she sees fit. Top employees can earn over $100,000 annually. Congress employs some 15,000 aides, about two-thirds of whom work for individual senators and representatives. Openings are common, as aides move from staff to staff, to positions in the executive branch, or to jobs in the private sector.

State and Local Government Opportunities: City councils and state legislatures typically employ a small number of aides.

Congressional staff members assist members of Congress with legislative duties.

Air Traffic Controller

Air traffic controllers are responsible for overall safety on commercial flights. Most work in airport control towers, where they make sure that arriving and departing aircraft do not collide by giving pilots taxiing and takeoff instructions and clearances to land. Other air traffic controllers work at en route centers. These controllers use radar to track planes in the air, advising pilots about flight conditions and giving course and altitude instructions when other aircraft are in the area. At flight service centers, a third type of air traffic controller provides pilots with data about terrain, weather conditions, and other information critical to flight safety.

Position Requirements: A college degree, or three years of general work experience, or a combination of college and experience totaling three years is usually required. However, you can also qualify if you have a pilot's license and 350 hours of flight time, an instrument flight rating, or a variety of other experiences with military or civilian aircraft. All candidates must pass a written test, a medical and psychological examination, a drug screen, and a background check. For most positions, your vision must also be corrected to 20/20. Candidates who meet these requirements enter a 16-week training program. Only about half the trainees successfully complete this school.

Salary and Outlook: The Federal Aviation Administration employs about 26,000 air traffic controllers. New positions are often available as the agency increases the size of the air traffic system. Pay begins at about $36,000 a year but controllers who work at the busiest facilities earn higher pay. Average pay for the job is about $50,100 annually.

State and Local Government Opportunities: Few related jobs exist at other levels of government.

Air traffic controller

Correctional Officer

Correctional officers supervise and ensure the custody of criminals in the federal prison system. They are also responsible for guiding prisoner conduct, directing work details, carrying out plans to modify the behavior and attitudes of inmates, and counseling inmates about personal and prison problems. Some correctional officers carry firearms and all are required to complete firearms training. Duties of correctional officers may involve long periods of walking and standing, restraint of prisoners in emergencies, and other physical exertion. The nature of the job may also cause a large amount of mental stress. Successful correctional officers are likely to be flexible, unbiased, understanding, observant, resourceful, stable, and mature.

Position Requirements: Applicants should have at least 3.5 years of general work experience in such areas as rehabilitation counseling, employment counseling, teaching, sales, or in a variety of a community and social services. Any post-high school education may take the place of some work experience, and a college degree with additional course work related to law enforcement can substitute for all of it. While there are no specific height and weight requirements for these positions, applicants must meet a number of other physical standards.

Salary and Outlook: Although there are only about 6,300 correctional officers serving the federal government, the Bureau of Prisons is the fastest growing federal agency. In addition, many current officers move on to other jobs in the prison system. Beginning annual salary is between $21,380 and $23,900, but correctional officers enjoy a faster promotion rate than do other federal employees. The annual average salary for correctional officers is $37,900.

State and Local Government Opportunities: State prison systems also employ correctional officers. So do city and county jails, although their guards may not have that title. The growth of the prison population has increased job opportunities.

Environmental protection specialist

Environmental Protection Specialist

Environmental protection specialists are responsible for monitoring all activities that affect the nation's air, water, and land resources to assure compliance with federal environmental protection laws. Those who are employed by the Environmental Protection Agency primarily evaluate compliance by state and local governments and by private industry. Environmental protection specialists who work for other federal agencies monitor their agency's compliance. Their work involves reviewing agency policies and procedures, helping to develop new agency procedures and techniques when necessary, and making recommendations for further research. Environment protection specialists also provide technical assistance and guidance on environmental laws, regulations, and programs to all private-sector groups that their agency regulates.

Position Requirements: Basic requirements for trainees are a bachelor's degree in any field or three years of relevant work experience, or a combination of education and experience. Nontraining entry-level positions require an additional year's graduate study in an appropriate scientific field, a year of highly specialized experience that is directly related to the job, or a combination that adds up to a year. No written test is required. Applicants are ranked by the quality of their education and experience.

Salary and Outlook: About 2,600 environmental protection specialists work at a number of federal agencies, but most are employed by the Environmental Protection Agency. Environmental protection specialists earn between $26,470 and $85,780.

State and Local Government Opportunities: Largely because of strict and comprehensive federal laws regarding the environment, a need for these positions exists at every level of government.

Food Inspector

Food inspectors assure that the nation's meat supply complies with federal laws governing the wholesomeness and purity of products sold for human consumption. Although they are government employees, food inspectors work in privately owned slaughterhouses and processing plants. Some examine animals before and after slaughter to make sure they are not contaminated and that sanitary procedures are followed. Other food inspectors inspect ingredients that go into processed food, such as canned goods and frozen dinners. Food inspectors often work near machinery in noisy and hazardous environments. Their duties can involve using sharp knives, lifting heavy objects, repeating motions, and working with their hands in water. They must stand for long periods of time, and sometimes must walk on catwalks and slippery floors.

Position Requirements: The qualifications for food inspectors are based on education or experience. To meet the education requirement you should have a college degree in biology, chemistry, zoology, veterinary medicine, food technology, or some appropriate agricultural field. With no degree, you must have three years of relevant experience. This could include work in a stockyard, slaughterhouse or processing plant, on a ranch or farm, or as a veterinary assistant. Applicants must pass a written test and a rigorous physical examination.

Salary and Outlook: The Department of Agriculture employs about 6,200 food inspectors. Most openings are in California, Kansas, Massachusetts, Nebraska, New York, and North Carolina. Starting pay is between $21,370 and $26,470 a year.

State and Local Government Opportunities: State and local health departments and state agriculture departments have similar positions to assure that food products are safe and hygienically prepared.

Foreign Service Officer

Foreign Service Officers work at a variety of jobs at about 250 United States diplomatic posts around the world and in Washington, D.C. Administrative officers coordinate the daily operations of an embassy or consulate. Economics officers analyze economic trends in the host country and promote United States economic interests and policies. Political officers advise, consult, and negotiate with foreign government officials and keep Washington advised of political developments in their host country. Information officers serve as spokespersons, handling all inquiries about the United States and its policies. Consular officers assist Americans who are living or visiting abroad and issue visas to persons wanting to enter the United States. Most new Foreign Service Officers start in this position.

Position Requirements: Although there is no formal education requirement, most Foreign Service Officers have graduate degrees. Applicants must take the difficult Foreign Service Exam. To do well, you should possess excellent writing abilities and a thorough knowledge of government, economics, geography, United States and world history, current events, and world cultures. If you pass the test, you will be invited to a daylong interview that includes two more written tests and an oral exam. New hires spend five years on probation and must master a foreign language.

Salary and Outlook: The Department of State and the United States Information Agency employ Foreign Service Officers. The positions are highly sought. Only a fraction of some 20,000 persons who take the test are hired each year. The beginning salary ranges from $29,900 to $49,100, depending on education, work experience, and foreign language skills. Promotions are competitive.

State and Local Government Opportunities: No similar jobs exist at other levels of government.

National Park Service badge

Postal Clerk/Carrier

Most postal clerks process mail for delivery, using a complicated system that they must memorize. Others sell stamps, weigh packages and perform related customer services. However, senior employees usually hold these "window clerk" positions. Clerks work indoors and may have to stand for long periods of time. Carriers work outdoors collecting and delivering local mail in all kinds of weather. Some carriers drive their assigned route and others walk, carrying mailbags weighing up to 35 pounds. The duties of new clerks and carriers are often interchangeable. Both have to handle sacks of mail that weigh as much as 70 pounds.

Position Requirements: All Americans are eligible to work as postal clerks and carriers. There is no formal education or experience requirement. Applicants must pass a written test and a physical exam, and must meet vision and hearing requirements. (The hearing requirement may be waived for some clerk positions.) Applicants for positions in which driving is required must possess a driver's license from the state where the post office is located. They must have a safe driving record and pass a road test to prove they can operate the type of vehicle they will use on the job.

Salary and Outlook: Postal clerks and carriers are hired by local post offices, according to their needs. Salaries start at about $25,350 per year and can go higher than $39,000. Job opportunities are expected to expand as the volume of mail increases with United States business and population growth. However, the increased use of computerized equipment is gradually changing the sorting clerk job into one of machine operator.

State and Local Government Opportunities: Many large state and local government agencies have mailrooms, which employ mail processing clerks and interoffice delivery personnel.

Park Ranger

Park rangers perform a variety of jobs at national parks, national historical sites, national forests, and on other federal recreational lands. Typical responsibilities include enforcing federal laws and park regulations, providing information, and guiding tours. Firefighting, search and rescue operations, and providing wilderness medical care are also important functions of the position. Park rangers routinely patrol assigned regions in vehicles or on foot to guard against fires and to protect visitors from unsafe conditions. They sometimes must work in extreme temperatures and other harsh weather.

Their duties often require physical exertion in rugged terrain. Rangers may have to be alone on roads or trails for hours, in remote areas and hazardous environments, far from help in event of an emergency.

Position Requirements: The basic qualification for a park ranger is six months of general work experience or one year of college. However, most rangers are hired at an advanced pay grade that requires a bachelor's degree in a field appropriate to the job, or two years of job-related work experience, or a combination of education and experience. There is no written test for any level of ranger position.

Salary and Outlook: Most rangers—more than 12,000—work for the National Park Service and the United States Forest Service. Some part-time jobs are available during the tourist season. The Bureau of Land Management and the Army Corps of Engineers also hire park rangers. Entry-level salaries for rangers are between $21,370 and $32,380. Top pay for a District Ranger is more than $72,500.

State and Local Government Opportunities: State parks and departments of natural resources, local parks and recreation departments, and historical sites operated by state and local governments also hire rangers.

Claim Authorizer / Service Representative

Claims authorizers and service representatives work at the Social Security Administration's 1,300 offices nationwide. Claims authorizers decide who should receive Social Security benefits and how much their benefit should be. Social Security benefits are paid when workers retire or become disabled, on the death of a spouse, or in a number of other circumstances. Regulations for determining eligibility and the amount of the benefit can be complex. Service representatives provide information and help people with benefit-related problems. These can include eligibility questions; lost, late, or incorrect checks; and similar matters. Some service representatives provide help in person at Social Security Administration offices. Others are teleservice representatives, who help people over the phone.

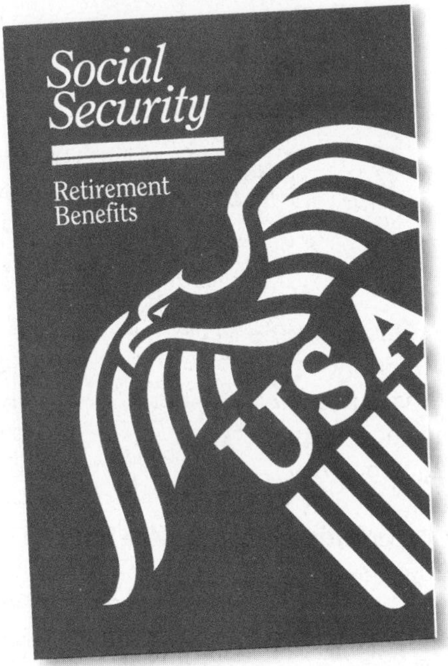

Social insurance administrators distribute information and answer questions.

Position Requirements: Because the duties of these positions are so agency-specific, few outside jobs provide the required related work experience. However, applicants can qualify if they possess a bachelor's degree and pass a written test. The test is waived for graduates whose overall college grade average was at least 3.5 on a 4-point scale.

Salary and Outlook: The government employs nearly 20,000 claims authorizers and 14,000 service representatives. The need for workers in both positions is great. Related claims examining opportunities also exist at the Department of Veterans Affairs and in a few other government agencies. Service representatives initially earn between $19,100 and $21,370 a year and claims authorizers earn between $21,370 and $26,470 to start.

State and Local Government Opportunities: Similar claims examining and service positions exist in state and local human services departments, at state bureaus of workers' compensation, and at state unemployment offices.

Social Worker

Social workers provide helping services as employees of a number of government agencies that work directly with people. Their specific duties may range from carrying out rehabilitation programs for inmates in federal correctional institutions, to counseling patients in government hospitals and clinics or helping families involved in a wide variety of government social welfare programs. Social workers may work with individual clients or with groups. Some help entire communities to develop strategies and resources to prevent or reduce social problems. Others work with adoption programs for children, foster family care, home care services for ill or disabled people, help for mentally disabled or emotionally disturbed clients, and similar professional human service activities.

Position Requirements: While some opportunities exist for those with only undergraduate degrees, the basic requirement for the vast majority of applicants is a master's degree in social work. No written test is required, but many specialized positions require relevant experience in addition to education. Generally, social work performed before earning a master's degree does not meet this requirement. Applicants who have not practiced social work for 10 years or more since earning their degree may be asked to provide evidence that their qualifications meet the standards of current social work practice.

Salary and Outlook: The average pay for social workers is about $52,000 annually. Because of the nature and structure of social work, opportunities exist for supervisors, consultants, and program-development specialists. Generally, additional specialized experience is required to qualify for the upper-level positions.

State and Local Government Opportunities: Most state and local corrections, health, human services, and social welfare agencies also hire social workers.

Treasury Enforcement Agent

Treasury enforcement agents work for the Bureau of Alcohol, Tobacco, and Firearms (BATF), the Internal Revenue Service (IRS), and the United States Customs Service. Although they may conduct noncriminal investigations, the majority of their work involves looking into suspected criminal violations of federal tax laws. Most investigations center on laws related to income tax, money laundering, bootleg tobacco and alcohol products, gambling, and gaming devices. BATF agents investigate violations of federal explosives laws and suspected illegal sales or possession of firearms. Customs agents enforce laws to prevent smuggling of goods across U.S. borders. Agents prepare detailed reports of their investigations, make recommendations about the prosecution of violators, and assist United States Attorneys in preparing cases and during trials. Most Treasury enforcement agents carry firearms and are required to be experts in their use.

Position Requirements: Applicants should have three years of accounting and other related experience, such as in commercial auditing, financial management or business law. However, college courses in accounting and related business or law subjects may be substituted for some or all of this requirement. A year of criminal investigations work, including experience in evidence gathering and in a variety of investigative techniques, is also required. Because of the nature of the job, applicants should be in top physical condition. In addition, they must pass the Treasury Enforcement Agent Exam.

Salary and Outlook: The Department of the Treasury employs about 15,000 enforcement agents—about two-thirds of them as special agents at the IRS. Competition for the positions is intense. Beginning salaries range from $26,880 to $48,250 per year. Experienced special agents can earn up to $72,600.

State and Local Government Opportunities: Some state liquor departments and departments of taxation also hire enforcement agents.

A

abdicate to formally renounce the throne (p. 690)
abridge limit (p. 363)
absentee ballot one that allows a person to vote without going to the polls on Election Day (p. 491)
absolute monarch a monarch that has complete and unlimited power to rule his or her people (p. 19)
acreage allotment the program under which the government pays support prices for farmers' crops grown on an assigned number of acres (p. 586)
administrative assistant member of a lawmaker's personal staff who runs the lawmaker's office, supervises the schedule, and gives advice (p. 147)
administrative law law that spells out the authority, procedures, rules, and regulations to be followed by government agencies (p. 425)
adversary system a judicial system in which opposing lawyers present their strongest cases (p. 428)
advisory opinion a ruling on a law or action that has not been challenged (p. 340)
affidavit a written statement to prove statements of fact signed by a witness under oath (p. 435)
affirmative action government policies that award jobs, government contracts, promotions, admission to schools, and other benefits to minorities and women in order to make up for past discriminations (p. 412)
alien a person who lives in a country where he or she is not a citizen (p. 387)
ambassador an official of the government who represents the nation in diplomatic matters (p. 615)
amendment a change to the Constitution (p. 65)
amicus curiae (uh•mee•kuhs KYUR•ee•EYE) Latin for "friend of the court"; a written brief from an individual or group claiming to have information useful to a court's consideration of a case (p. 333)
amnesty a group pardon to individuals for an offense against the government (pp. 254, 390)
anarchy political disorder (p. 57)
answer a formal response by a defendant to the charges in a complaint (p. 433)
apartheid strict segregation of the races (p. 698)
appellate jurisdiction authority held by a court to hear a case that is appealed from lower court (p. 306)
appropriation approval of government spending (p. 191)
appropriations bill a proposed law to authorize spending money (pp. 160, 191)
arraignment the procedure during which the judge reads the formal charge against the defendant and the defendant pleads guilty or not guilty (p. 441)
arrest warrant an order signed by a judge naming the individual to be arrested for a specific crime (pp. 85, 438)
article one of seven main divisions of the body of the Constitution (p. 64)
assessment the complicated process involved in calculating the value of property to be taxed (p. 674)
at-large as a whole; for example, statewide (p. 128)
audit check more closely (p. 556)
authorization bill a bill that sets up a federal program and specifies how much money may be appropriated for the program (p. 191)
autocracy a system of government in which the power to rule is in the hands of a single individual (p. 18)

B

backgrounders information given by top government officials to reporters who can use it in a story, but cannot reveal their source (p. 535)
balanced budget plan requiring that what the government spends will not exceed its income (p. 77)
bankruptcy the legal proceedings to administer the assets of a person or business that cannot pay its debts (p. 161)
biased sample in polling, a group that does not accurately represent the larger population (p. 520)
bicameral two-house legislative body (p. 641)
bicameral legislature a two-chamber legislature (p. 123)
bilateral treaty agreement between two nations (p. 629)
bill a proposed law (p. 135)
bill of attainder a law that establishes guilt and punishes people without a trial (p. 158)
bipartisan consisting of members of both major political parties (p. 619)
bloc coalition that promotes a common interest (p. 344)
block grant a grant of money to a state or local government for a general purpose (pp. 658, 675)
bond a contractual promise by a borrower to repay a certain sum plus interest by a specified date (p. 657)
borough a political division in Alaska, similar to a county in other states (p. 664)
boss a powerful party leader (p. 465)
bourgeoisie capitalists who own the means of production (p. 29)
brief a written statement setting forth the legal arguments, relevant facts, and precedents supporting one side of a case (p. 333)
broadcast spectrum the range of frequencies over which electronic signals may be sent (p. 547)

bureaucracy government administrators (p. 115)
bureaucrat one who works for a department or agency of the federal government—civil servant (p. 275)

C

cabinet secretaries of the executive departments, the vice president, and other top officials that help the president make decisions and policy (p. 228)
cadre government officials in China (p. 703)
calendar a schedule that lists the order in which bills will be considered in Congress (p. 136)
campaign manager the person responsible for the overall strategy and planning of a campaign (p. 476)
canvass the vote count by the official body that tabulates election returns and certifies the winner (p. 487)
canvassing board the official body that counts votes and certifies the winner (p. 490)
capital the means of production—money, factories, heavy machinery—used to produce other products and goods (p. 718)
capitalism an economic system providing free choice and individual incentive for workers, investors, consumers, and business enterprises (pp. 26, 718)
casework the work that a lawmaker does to help constituents with problems (p. 200)
caseworker a member of a lawmaker's personal staff who handles requests for help from constituents (pp. 148, 201)
caucus a private meeting of party leaders to choose candidates for office (pp. 134, 464)
cede to yield (p. 50)
censure a vote of formal disapproval of a member's actions (p. 129)
census a population count (p. 124)
central clearance Office of Management and Budget's review of all legislative proposals that executive agencies prepare (p. 236)
centralized planning government control of the economy (p. 724)
change of venue new trial location (p. 86)
checks and balances the system where each branch of government exercises some control over the others (p. 65)
civil case one usually involving a dispute between two or more private individuals or organizations (p. 646)
civil law one relating to disputes among two or more individuals or between individuals and the government (pp. 103, 430)
civil rights movement the efforts to end segregation (p. 410)
civil service system practice of government employment based on competitive examinations and merit (p. 286)
civil society a complex network of voluntary associations, economic groups, religious organizations, and many other kinds of groups that exist independent of government (p. 24)
client group individuals and groups who work with a government agency and are most affected by its decisions (p. 295)
closed primary an election in which only members of a political party can vote (p. 465)
closed rule rule that forbids members of Congress to offer amendments to a bill from the floor (p. 190)
closed shop a place of employment where only union members may be hired (p. 583)
cloture a procedure that allows each senator to speak only 1 hour on a bill under debate (p. 140)
cluster sample a polling method that groups people by geographical divisions (p. 521)
coalition government one formed by several parties who combine forces to obtain a majority (p. 454)
collective bargaining the practice of negotiating labor contracts (p. 581)
collective farm farm in which the land is owned by the government but rented to a family (p. 729)
collective naturalization a process by which a group of people become American citizens through an act of Congress (p. 394)
collective security a system by which the participating nations agree to take joint action against a nation that attacks any one of them (p. 629)
command economy an economic system in which the government controls the factors of production (pp. 30, 717)
commission form a form of municipal government that combines executive and legislative powers in an elected commission (p. 667)
committees of correspondence colonial committees urging resistance to the British and keeping in touch with one another as events unfolded (p. 44)
committee staff the people who work for House and Senate committees (p. 147)
common law law made by judges in the process of resolving individual cases (p. 426)
communism an economic system in which the central government directs all major economic decisions (pp. 30, 718)
comparative advantage economic principle that each country should produce those goods it can make more efficiently and trade for other goods (p. 732)

compensation salary (p. 214)
complaint a legal document filed with the court that has jurisdiction over the problem (p. 433)
concurrent jurisdiction authority shared by both federal and state courts (p. 306)
concurrent powers powers that both the national government and the states have (p. 97)
concurrent resolution a resolution that covers matters requiring the action of the House and Senate but on which a law is not needed (p. 182)
concurring opinion the Court's opinion expressing the views of a justice(s) who agree with the majority's conclusions but for different reasons (p. 334)
confederacy a loose union of independent states (p. 12)
conferee member of a conference committee (p. 187)
conference committee a temporary joint committee set up when the House and the Senate have passed different versions of the same bill (p. 144)
conference report compromise bill presented by the conference committee after changes are made (p. 187)
congressional override the power of Congress to pass legislation over a president's veto (p. 249)
conscription compulsory military service; also called a draft (p. 625)
consensus an agreement about basic beliefs (p. 6)
conservation the care and protection of natural resources including the land, lakes, rivers, and forests; oil, natural gas, and other energy sources; and wildlife (p. 651)
conservative one who believes government should be limited, except in supporting traditional values and promoting freedom of opportunity (p. 517)
consolidated democracy a nation that has democratic elections, political parties, constitutional government, an independent judiciary, and usually a market economy (p. 689)
constituent a person a member of Congress has been elected to represent (p. 133)
constitution a plan that provides the rules for government (p. 13)
constitutional commission a group of experts appointed to study a state constitution and recommend changes (p. 639)
constitutional convention a gathering of citizens elected to consider changing or replacing a constitution (p. 639)
constitutional court a court established by Congress under the Constitution (p. 312)
constitutional government a government in which a constitution has authority to place clearly recognized limits on the powers of those who govern (p. 13)
constitutional law law that involves the interpretation and application of the U.S. Constitution and state constitutions (pp. 14, 424)
constitutional monarch a monarch that has shared governmental powers with elected legislatures or serves mainly as a ceremonial leader of a government (p. 19)
consul a government official who heads a consulate in a foreign nation (p. 623)
consulate office that promotes American business and safeguards its travelers in a foreign country (p. 623)
containment the policy designed to keep the Soviet Union from expanding its power (p. 610)
contempt willful obstruction of justice (p. 168)
contract a set of voluntary promises, enforceable by the law, between two or more parties (p. 430)
copyright the exclusive right to publish and sell a literary, musical, or artistic work for a specified period of time (p. 163)
corporate charter a document that gives a corporation legal status (p. 648)
council-manager form a type of municipal government in which legislative and executive powers are separated (p. 668)
counsel an attorney (p. 401)
county the largest political subdivision of a state (p. 663)
county board the governing board of most counties (p. 664)
coup a planned but sudden grab for power (p. 730)
covert secret (p. 265)
criminal case one in which the state brings charges against a citizen for violating the law (p. 646)
criminal justice system system of state and federal courts, police, and prisons that enforce criminal law (p. 437)
criminal law one that defines crimes and provides for their punishment (p. 437)
cross-pressured voter one who is caught between conflicting elements in his or her own life (p. 493)
customs duties taxes levied on goods imported into the United States—tariffs or import duties (p. 557)

D

de facto existing "in fact" rather than legally (p. 265)
defamatory speech false speech that damages a person's good name, character, or reputation (p. 369)
defendant the person against whom a civil or criminal suit is brought in court (p. 433)
delegated powers powers the Constitution grants or delegates to the national government (p. 95)
democracy government in which the people rule (p. 19)

democratic socialism an economic system in which people have control over government through free elections and multiparty systems, but the government owns the basic means of production and makes most economic decisions (p. 28)

denaturalization the loss of citizenship through fraud or deception during the naturalization process (p. 396)

dependent one who depends primarily on another person for basic needs (p. 556)

deregulate to reduce regulations (p. 283)

détente a relaxation of tensions between nations (p. 612)

developing nation a nation only beginning to develop industrially (pp. 16, 722)

direct democracy a form of democracy in which the people govern themselves by voting on issues (p. 20)

direct primary an election in which party members select people to run in the general election (p. 465)

discount rate the interest rate the Federal Reserve System charges member banks for loans (p. 569)

discovery process when both sides prepare for a trial by gathering evidence to support their case (p. 433)

discrimination unfair treatment of individuals based solely on their race, gender, ethnic group, age, physical disability, or religion (p. 407)

dissenting opinion the opinion expressed by a minority of justices in a Court case (p. 334)

divine right belief that certain people are either descended from gods or chosen by gods to rule (p. 8)

double jeopardy retrial of a person who was acquitted in a previous trial for the same crime (p. 404)

due process clause Fourteenth Amendment clause stating that no state may deprive a person of life, liberty, or property without due process of law (p. 308)

due process of law principle in the Fifth Amendment stating that the government must follow proper constitutional procedures in trials and in other actions it takes against individuals (pp. 86, 427)

economics the study of human efforts to satisfy seemingly unlimited wants through the use of limited resources (p. 26)

elastic clause clause in Article I, Section 8 of the Constitution that gives Congress the right to make all laws "necessary and proper" to carry out the powers expressed in the other clauses of Article I (pp. 69, 96, 157)

elector member of a party chosen in each state to formally elect the president and vice president (p. 220)

electoral vote the official vote for president and vice president by electors in each state (p. 220)

embargo an agreement prohibiting trade (p. 44)

embassy an ambassador's official residence and offices in a foreign country (pp. 276, 622)

eminent domain the power of the government to take private property for public use (p. 86)

enabling act the first step in the state admission procedure which enables the people of a territory to prepare a constitution (p. 99)

enemy alien a citizen of a nation with which the United States is at war (p. 387)

entitlement a required government expenditure that continues from one year to the next (pp. 192, 562)

entrepreneur a person who takes a risk to produce goods and services in search of profit (p. 718)

enumerated powers the expressed powers of Congress that are itemized and numbered 1-18 in Article I, Section 8 of the Constitution (pp. 69, 96, 157)

equal time doctrine rule that broadcasters must give equal airtime to candidates for public office (p. 545)

equity a system of rules by which disputes are resolved on the grounds of fairness (p. 426)

establishment clause the First Amendment guarantee that "Congress shall make no law respecting an establishment of religion" (p. 358)

estate tax tax collected on the assets (property and money) of a person who dies (p. 558)

evolutionary theory the theory that the state evolved from the family (p. 8)

excise tax tax on the manufacture, transportation, sale, or consumption of certain items such as gasoline, liquor, or cigarettes (pp. 557, 656)

exclusion the right of Congress to refuse to seat an elected member by a majority vote (p. 129)

exclusionary rule a law stating that any illegally obtained evidence cannot be used in a federal court (p. 399)

executive agreement an agreement made between the president and a head of state (pp. 81, 257, 619)

executive order a rule issued by the president that has the force of law (p. 253)

executive privilege the right of the president and other high-ranking executive officers to refuse to testify before Congress or a court (p. 266)

expatriation giving up one's citizenship by leaving to live in a foreign country (p. 395)

ex post facto law a law that makes a crime of an act that was legal when it was committed (p. 158)

expressed contract a contract in which the terms are specifically stated, usually in writing (p. 430)

expressed powers powers directly stated in the Constitution (pp. 68, 95, 157)
extradite to return a criminal or fugitive who flees across state lines back to the original state (p. 103)
extradition the legal procedure through which a person accused of a crime who has fled to another state is returned to the state where the crime took place (p. 652)
extralegal not sanctioned by law (p. 56)

F

faction a group of people united to promote special interests (p. 503)
factors of production resources that an economy needs to produce goods and services (p. 717)
fairness doctrine rule requiring broadcasters to provide opportunities for the expression of opposing views on issues of public importance (p. 545)
faqih the top religious-political leader in Iran (p. 707)
federal bureaucracy departments and agencies of the federal government—mostly the executive branch (p. 71)
federal grant a sum of money given to a state for a specific purpose (p. 657)
federalism a system in which power is divided between the national and state governments (p. 65)
federal system a government that divides the powers of government between the national government and state or provincial governments (p. 12)
felony a major crime (pp. 399, 438)
filibuster a method of defeating a bill in which a senator talks until a majority either abandons the bill or agrees to modify it (p. 140)
first reading when a bill introduced in Congress is given a title and a number, printed, and distributed (p. 184)
fiscal policy a government's use of spending and taxation to influence the economy (p. 567)
fiscal year a 12-month accounting period (p. 560)
force theory the theory that the state was born of force—when all the people of an area were brought under the authority of one person or group (p. 8)
foreign policy the strategies and goals that guide a nation's relations with other countries (p. 607)
forum medium for discussion (p. 249)
free enterprise the opportunity to control one's own economic decisions (p. 23)
free enterprise system an economic system based on private ownership of the means of production—the capital—and on individual economic freedom (p. 718)
free exercise clause the First Amendment guarantee that prohibits government from unduly interfering with the free exercise of religion (p. 358)
free market economic system in which buyers and sellers make free choices in the marketplace (p. 27)
front-runner the early leader in an election (p. 537)
fundamental right a basic right of the American system or one that is indispensable in a just system (p. 407)

G

gag order an order by a judge barring the press from publishing certain types of information about a pending court case (p. 373)
gentrification the phenomenon of new people moving into a neighborhood, forcing out those who live there, and changing the area's essential character (p. 681)
gerrymander to draw a district's boundaries to gain an advantage in elections (p. 126)
global security the safety of the entire world (p. 708)
government the institution through which the state maintains social order, provides public services, and enforces binding decisions on citizens (p. 8)
government corporation a business that the federal government runs (p. 280)
grandfather clause an exemption in a law for a certain group based on previous conditions (p. 483)
grand jury group that hears charges against a suspect and decides whether there is sufficient evidence to bring the person to trial (pp. 312, 439)
gross national product (GNP) the sum of all goods and services produced in a nation in a year (pp. 568, 728)

H

hearing a session at which a committee listens to testimony from people interested in the bill (p. 184)
heckler's veto public veto of free speech and assembly rights of unpopular groups by claiming demonstrations will result in violence (p. 379)
Holocaust the mass extermination of Jews and other groups by the Nazis during World War II (p. 379)
horse-race coverage media approach of focusing on "winners" and "losers," and "who's ahead," rather than on issues or policy positions (p. 537)
house arrest a sentence which requires an offender to stay at home except for certain functions the court permits (p. 653)
human rights fundamental freedoms (p. 355)
hung jury a jury that is unable to reach a decision (p. 443)

ideological party a political party that focuses on overall change in society rather than on an issue (p. 455)
ideology a set of basic beliefs about life, culture, government, and society (pp. 454, 517)
illegal alien a person without legal permission to be in a country (p. 387)
image mental picture (p. 476)
immunity freedom from prosecution for witnesses whose testimony ties them to illegal acts (p. 169)
impeach to accuse a public official of misconduct in office (p. 79)
impeachment a formal accusation of misconduct in office against a public official (p. 164)
implied contract a contract in which the terms are not expressly stated but can be inferred from the actions of the people involved and the circumstances (p. 430)
implied powers powers that the government requires to carry out the expressed constitutional powers (pp. 96, 157)
impound refuse to spend (p. 337)
impoundment the president's refusal to spend money Congress has voted to fund a program (pp. 175, 253)
income tax the tax levied on individual and corporate earnings (p. 108)
incorporation a process that extended the protections of the Bill of Rights against the actions of state and local governments (p. 356); the process of setting up a legal community under state law (p. 666)
incrementalism the term used to explain that the total budget changes little from year to year (p. 564)
incumbent elected official that is already in office (p. 130)
independent a voter who does not support any particular party (p. 458)
indictment a formal charge by a grand jury (pp. 312, 440)
industrialized nation a nation with large industries and advanced technology that provides a more comfortable way of life than developing nations (p. 16)
information a sworn statement by the prosecution that there is sufficient evidence for a trial (p. 440)
infrastructure the basic facilities of a city, such as paved streets and sidewalks, water pipes, sewers, bridges, and public buildings (p. 680)
inherent powers powers that the national government may exercise simply because it is a government (p. 96)
initiative a method by which citizens propose a constitutional amendment or a law (p. 639)
injunction an order that will stop a particular action or enforce a rule or regulation (pp. 297, 433, 582)
inner cabinet members of the cabinet who wield influence with the president because they head departments that are concerned with national issues (p. 232)
interest group a group of people with common goals who organize to influence government (p. 503)
intergovernmental revenue revenue distributed by one level of government to another (p. 657)
interlocking directorate the same people serving on the boards of directors of competing companies (p. 579)
internationalism involvement in world affairs (p. 609)
international security world stability resulting from the interaction of many nations' policies (p. 708)
interstate commerce trade among the states (pp. 55, 161)
interstate compact a written agreement between two or more states (p. 105)
iron triangle a relationship formed among government agencies, congressional committees, and client groups who work together (p. 298)
isolationism the avoidance of involvement in world affairs (p. 609)
item veto the power to turn down a particular item in a bill without vetoing the entire bill (p. 645)

Jim Crow law law requiring racial segregation in such places as schools, buses, and hotels (p. 408)
joint committee a committee of the House and the Senate that usually acts as a study group and reports its findings back to the House and the Senate (p. 143)
joint resolution a resolution passed by both houses of Congress dealing with unusual or temporary matters, such as correcting an error in an earlier law (p. 182)
judicial activism the philosophy that the Supreme Court should play an active role in shaping national policies by addressing social and political isues (p. 82)
judicial circuit a region containing a United States appellate court (p. 313)
judicial restraint the philosophy that the Supreme Court should avoid taking the initiative on social and political questions (p. 81)
judicial review the power of the Supreme Court to declare laws and actions of local, state, or national governments unconstitutional (pp. 66, 308, 336, 640)
jurisdiction the authority of a court to rule on certain cases (pp. 64, 305)
jury a group of citizens who hear evidence during a trial and give a verdict (pp. 442, 447)

jus sanguinis (YOOS SAHN•gwuh•nuhs) Latin phrase meaning "law of blood"; the principle that grants citizenship on the basis of the citizenship of one's parents (p. 393)

jus soli (YOOS SOH•LEE) Latin phrase meaning "law of the soil"; the principle that grants citizenship to nearly all people born in a country (p. 393)

K

kanyro Japanese term for bureaucratic officials (p. 694)

kibbutzim collective agricultural communes (p. 725)

L

laissez-faire the philosophy that government should keep its hands off the economy (pp. 27, 578)

lame duck an outgoing official serving out the remainder of a term, after retiring or being defeated for reelection (p. 90)

land all natural resources such as soil, water, air, and minerals (p. 717)

law set of rules and standards by which a society governs itself (p. 423)

leak the release of secret information by anonymous government officials to the media (pp. 230, 536)

legislative assistant a member of a lawmaker's personal staff that makes certain that the lawmaker is well informed about proposed legislation (p. 148)

legislative court a court created to help Congress exercise its powers (p. 314)

legislative oversight a continuing review by Congress of how effectively the executive branch carries out the laws Congress passes (p. 169)

legislative veto the provisions Congress wrote into some laws that allowed it to review and cancel actions of executive agencies (p. 171)

liaison officer a cabinet department employee who helps promote good relations with Congress (p. 296)

libel false written or published statements intended to damage a person's reputation (pp. 84, 369, 544)

liberal one who believes the national government should be active in promoting health, education, justice, and equal opportunity (p. 517)

lieutenant governor the presiding officer of the upper house in some state legislatures (p. 642)

life peer a person who has been awarded a title in the House of Lords for outstanding achievement (p. 691)

limited government a system in which the power of the government is limited, not absolute (p. 36)

limited war a war in which the more powerful nation or nations will not go beyond certain limits (p. 709)

line-item veto the power to veto only certain lines or items in a bill (pp. 176, 255)

litigant a person engaged in a lawsuit (p. 307)

lobbying direct contact made by a lobbyist in order to persuade government officials to support the policies their interest group favors (pp. 198, 508)

lobbyist interest group representative (pp. 198, 508)

logrolling an agreement by two or more lawmakers to support each other's bills (p. 202)

M

majority leader the Speaker's top assistant whose job is to help plan the majority party's legislative program and to steer important bills through the House (p. 134)

majority opinion the Court's decision expressing the views of the majority of justices (p. 334)

mandate a formal order given by a higher authority (pp. 245, 658)

mandatory sentencing a system of fixed, required terms of imprisonment for certain types of crimes (p. 651)

market economy an economic system which allows buyers and sellers acting in their individual interests to control the factors of production (p. 717)

marketing quota a limit set among farmers to market only an assigned portion of an overproduced crop (p. 586)

market value the amount of money an owner may expect to receive if property is sold (p. 674)

mass media means of communication, such as television, newspapers, movies, books, and the Internet, that influence large audiences (pp. 515, 527)

mass transit systems such as subways that are used to transport a large number of people (pp. 602, 671)

mayor-council form a form of municipal government in which executive power belongs to an elected mayor, and legislative power to an elected council (p. 666)

media event a visually interesting event designed to reinforce a politician's position on some issue (p. 536)

mediation a process in which each side is given the opportunity to explain its side of the dispute and must listen to the other side (p. 434)

metropolitan area a large city and its surrounding suburbs (p. 671)

metropolitan government a type of government that serves several different communities in the same region (p. 682)

militia armed forces of citizens (p. 85)

misdemeanor a minor crime that is usually punished by a fine or jail sentence of less than one year (p. 438)
mixed economy a system in which the government regulates private enterprise (pp. 575, 721)
moderate one whose beliefs fall somewhere between liberal and conservative views (p. 517)
monarchy autocracy in which a king, queen, or emperor exercises supreme powers of government (p. 19)
monetary policy a government's control of the supply of money and credit to influence the economy (p. 567)
monopoly a business that controls so much of an industry that little or no competition exists (pp. 578, 719)
mortgage a loan taken out to pay for a house (p. 431)
multilateral treaty international agreement signed by several nations (p. 629)
municipality an urban unit of government chartered by a state (p. 665)
mutual defense alliance an agreement between nations to support each other in case of an attack (p. 627)

N

nation group of people united by bonds of race, language, custom, tradition, and, sometimes, religion (p. 6)
national budget the yearly financial plan for the national government (p. 175)
national committee representatives from the 50 state party organizations who run a political party (p. 460)
national convention a gathering of local and state party members chosen to nominate presidential and vice-presidential candidates (p. 460)
national debt the total amount of money the government owes at any given time (pp. 160, 559)
nationalist position a position that favors national action in dealing with problems (p. 106)
nationalization the process by which a government takes control of industry (p. 724)
national security protection of a nation's borders and territories against invasion or control by foreign powers (pp. 608, 708)
national security adviser director of the National Security Council staff (pp. 237, 616)
nation-state a country in which the territory of both the nation and the state coincide (p. 6)
naturalization the legal process by which a person is granted citizenship (p. 392)
necessary and proper clause Article I, Section 8, of the Constitution, which gives Congress the power to make all laws that are necessary and proper for carrying out its duties (pp. 96, 157)
newly developed nation a nation that has had significant or rapid industrial growth in recent years (p. 722)
news briefing a meeting during which a government official makes an announcement or explains a policy, decision, or action (p. 535)
newspaper chain newspaper company that owns many daily and weekly newspapers (p. 528)
news release a ready-made story government officials prepare for members of the press (p. 535)
nominating convention an official public meeting of a party to choose candidates for office (p. 464)
non-resident alien a person from a foreign country who expects to stay in the United States for a short, specified period of time (p. 387)
nuclear proliferation the spread of nuclear weapons (p. 709)

office-group ballot one that lists the candidates together by the office for which they are running (p. 489)
oligarchy a system of government in which a small group holds power (pp. 19, 690)
oligopoly situation when only a few firms dominate a particular industry (pp. 579, 719)
open-market operations the means the Federal Reserve System uses to affect the economy by buying or selling government securities on the open market (p. 570)
open primary an election in which all voters may participate (p. 465)
open shop a place of employment where workers may freely decide whether or not to join a union (p. 583)
opinion a written explanation of a Supreme Court decision; also, in some states, a written interpretation of a state constitution or state laws by the state's attorney general (pp. 322, 331, 645)
ordinance a law (pp. 50, 425)
original jurisdiction the authority of a trial court to be first to hear a case (p. 306)

pardon a release from legal punishment (p. 254)
parish a political division in Louisiana, similar to a county in other states (p. 664)
parliamentary government form of government in which executive and legislative functions both reside in an elected assembly, or parliament (p. 690)
parochial school a school operated by a church or religious group (p. 359)

parole means by which a prisoner is allowed to serve the rest of a sentence in the community under the supervision of a parole officer (p. 653)

party-column ballot one that lists each party's candidates in a column under the party's name (p. 489)

passport a document entitling a traveler to certain protections established by international treaty (p. 623)

patent the exclusive right of an inventor to manufacture, use, and sell his or her invention for a specific period of time (p. 163)

patronage the practice of granting favors to reward party loyalty (pp. 256, 462)

peer group an individual's close friends, religious group, clubs, or work groups (p. 515)

per curiam opinion (puhr KYUR•ee•AHM) a brief unsigned statement of a Supreme Court decision (p. 333)

perjury lying under oath (p. 168)

personal property movable belongings such as clothes and jewelry, as well as intangible items like stocks, bonds, copyrights, and patents (pp. 431, 673)

personal staff the people who work directly for individual senators and representatives (p. 147)

petition an appeal (p. 77)

petit jury a trial jury, usually consisting of 6 or 12 people, that weighs the evidence presented at a trial and renders a verdict (p. 313)

petty offense a minor crime, usually punished by a ticket rather than being arrested (p. 437)

picket to patrol an establishment to convince workers and the public not to enter it (p. 378)

plaintiff person who brings charges in court (p. 433)

plank a section of a political party platform (p. 469)

platform a statement of a political party's principles, beliefs, and positions on vital issues (p. 469)

plea bargaining the process in which a defendant pleads guilty to a lesser crime than the one with which the defendant was originally charged (p. 440)

plurality the largest number of votes in an election (pp. 465, 643)

pocket veto when a president kills a bill passed during the last 10 days Congress is in session by simply refusing to act on it (p. 188)

political action committee (PAC) an organization formed to collect money and provide financial support for political candidates (pp. 130, 475, 477, 511)

political culture a set of shared values and beliefs about a nation and its government (p. 516)

political efficacy an individual's feelings of his or her effectiveness in politics (p. 516)

political party a group of individuals with broad common interests who organize to nominate candidates for office, win elections, conduct government, and determine public policy (pp. 23, 453)

political socialization process by which individuals learn their political beliefs and attitudes through personal background and life experiences (p. 515)

politics the effort to control or influence the conduct and policies of government (p. 14)

polling place the location in a precinct where people vote (p. 488)

poll tax money paid in order to vote (pp. 90, 483)

popular sovereignty rule by the people (p. 65)

pork-barrel legislation laws passed by Congress that appropriate money for local federal projects (p. 202)

preamble a statement in a constitution that sets forth the goals and purposes of government (p. 13)

precedent a model on which to base later decisions or actions (pp. 338, 364, 426)

precinct a voting district (pp. 459, 488)

precinct captain a volunteer who organizes party workers to distribute information about the party and its candidates and to get the voters to the polls (p. 459)

presidential government a form of democratic government in which a president heads the executive branch (p. 692)

presidential succession the order in which officials fill the office of president in case of a vacancy (p. 217)

president pro tempore the Senate member, elected by the Senate, who stands in as president of the Senate in the absence of the vice president (p. 139)

press conference the news media's questioning of a high-level government official (p. 535)

press secretary one of the president's top assistants who is in charge of media relations (p. 239)

presumed innocence the presumption that a person is innocent until proven guilty (p. 428)

price supports the program under which Congress buys farmers' crops if the market price falls below the support price (p. 586)

prime minister the leader of the executive branch of a parliamentary government (p. 691)

prior restraint government censorship of information before it is published or broadcast (pp. 84, 371, 543)

private bill a bill dealing with individual people or places (p. 181)

private law a law that applies to a particular person (p. 390)

probable cause a reasonable basis to believe a person or premises is linked to a crime (p. 85)

procedural due process principle that prohibits arbitrary enforcement of the law, and also provides safeguards to ensure that constitutional and statutory rights are protected by law enforcement (p. 427)
procurement the purchasing of materials (p. 283)
profit the difference between the amount of money used to operate a business and the amount of money the business takes in (p. 720)
progressive tax tax based on a taxpayer's ability to pay (pp. 556, 657)
proletariat workers who produce the goods (p. 29)
propaganda the use of ideas, information, or rumors to influence opinion (p. 495)
proportional representation a system in which several officials are elected to represent the same area in proportion to the votes each party's candidate receives (p. 457); used in presidential primaries to elect delegates in proportion to their popular vote (p. 467)
proportional tax tax that is assessed at the same rate for everyone (p. 657)
public assistance government programs that distribute money to poor people (p. 590)
public bill a bill dealing with general matters and applying to the entire nation (p. 181)
public housing government-subsidized housing for low-income families (p. 600)
public-interest group a group that seeks policy goals that it believes will benefit the nation (p. 506)
public opinion the ideas and attitudes a significant number of Americans hold about issues (p. 514)
public policy the course of action a government takes in response to some issue or problem (p. 112)
public utility an organization that supplies such necessities as electricity, gas, or telephone service (p. 648)
public welfare government efforts to maintain basic health and living conditions for those people who have insufficient resources of their own (p. 654)
public works bill a bill in which Congress appropriates money for local projects (p. 201)
pure speech the verbal expression of thought and opinion before an audience that has chosen to listen (p. 366)

Q

quorum the minimum number of members who must be present to permit a legislative body to take official action (p. 137)
quota a limit on the quantity of a product that may be imported (p. 732)

R

racial discrimination treating members of a race differently simply because of race (p. 408)
random sampling a polling technique in which everyone in the "universe" has an equal chance of being selected (p. 520)
ratify to approve (pp. 48, 76)
ratings a service that provides statistics showing audience size for various media (p. 532)
rational basis test used by a Court to determine whether a state law is reasonably related to an acceptable goal of the government (p. 406)
real property land and whatever is attached to or growing on it (pp. 431, 673)
reapportionment the process of reassigning representation based on population, after every census (p. 124)
redistrict to set up new district lines after reapportionment is complete (p. 125)
referendum a special election (p. 666)
refugee a person fleeing a country to escape persecution or danger (p. 387)
regional security pact a mutual defense treaty among nations of a region (p. 627)
register to enroll one's name with the appropriate local government in order to participate in elections (p. 487)
regressive tax tax in which people with lower incomes pay a larger portion of their income (pp. 557, 657)
representative democracy a form of democracy in which the people elect representatives and give them the responsibility and power to make laws and conduct government (p. 20)
representative government a system of government in which people elect delegates to make laws and conduct government (p. 37)
representative sample a small group of people, typical of the universe, that a pollster questions (p. 520)
reprieve the postponement of legal punishment (p. 254)
republic a government in which voters hold sovereign power; elected representatives, responsible to the people, exercise that power (p. 20)
reserved powers powers that belong strictly to the states (p. 96)
reserve requirement the percentage of money member banks must keep in Federal Reserve Banks as a reserve against their deposits (p. 570)
resident alien a person from a foreign nation who has established permanent residence in the United States (p. 387)

revenue the money a government collects from taxes or other sources (p. 43)
revenue bill a law proposed to raise money (p. 158)
reverse discrimination situation where a qualified individual loses out to an individual chosen because of their race, ethnicity, or gender (p. 414)
revitalization investments in new facilities in an effort to promote economic growth (p. 681)
rider a provision included in a bill on a subject other than the one covered in the bill (p. 182)
riding the circuit traveling to hold court in a justice's assigned region of the country (p. 320)
roll-call vote a voting method used by the Senate in which senators respond "Aye" or "No" as their names are called in alphabetical order (p. 187)
runoff primary a second primary election between the two candidates who received the most votes in the first primary (p. 465)

S

sample group surveyed in an opinion poll (p. 520)
sampling error a measurement of how much the sample results may differ from the sample universe (p. 520)
sanction a measure such as withholding economic aid to influence a foreign government's activities (pp. 630, 698)
scarcity a condition that exists because society does not have all the resources to produce all the goods and services that everyone wants (p. 717)
school board a usually elected local body that governs a school district (p. 673)
search warrant an order signed by a judge describing a specific place to be searched for specific items (p. 85)
secular nonreligious (p. 360)
securities financial instruments, including bonds, notes, and certificates, that are sold as a means of borrowing money with a promise to repay the buyer with interest after a specific time period (pp. 559, 581)
security classification system the provision that information on government activities related to national security and foreign policy may be kept secret (p. 416)
seditious speech speech urging resistance to lawful authority or advocating the overthrow of the government (p. 367)
segregation separation of people from the larger social group (p. 408)
select committee a temporary committee formed to study one specific issue and report its findings to the Senate or the House (p. 142)
self-incrimination testifying against oneself (p. 402)
senatorial courtesy a system in which the president submits the name of a candidate for judicial appointment to the senators from the candidate's state before formally submitting it for full Senate approval (p. 317)
seniority system a system that gives the member of the majority party with the longest uninterrupted service on a particular committee the leadership of that committee (p. 145)
sentence the punishment to be imposed on an offender after a guilty verdict (p. 443)
separate but equal doctrine a policy which held that if facilities for different races were equal, they could be separate (pp. 309, 409)
separation of powers the division of power among the legislative, executive, and judicial branches of government (pp. 40, 65)
sequester to keep isolated (p. 373)
session a period of time during which a legislature meets to conduct business (p. 123)
shah a king (p. 706)
shield law a law that gives reporters some means of protection against being forced to disclose confidential information or sources in state courts (pp. 374, 545)
shock incarceration a prison program involving shorter sentences in a highly structured environment where offenders participate in work, community service, education, and counseling (p. 653)
shock probation program designed to show young offenders how terrible prison life is through brief incarceration followed by supervised release (p. 653)
simple resolution a statement adopted to cover matters affecting only one house of Congress (p. 182)
single-issue party a political party that focuses on one major social, economic, or moral issue (p. 455)
single-member district electoral district in which only one candidate is elected to each office (p. 457)
slander false speech intended to damage a person's reputation (pp. 84, 369)
social consensus when most people in a society accept democratic values and agree about the purpose and limits of government (p. 24)
social contract theory that by contract, people surrender to the state the power needed to maintain order and the state, in turn, agrees to protect its citizens (p. 8)
social insurance government programs designed to help elderly, ill, and unemployed citizens (p. 590)

social insurance tax the money collected by the federal government to pay for major social programs, such as Social Security, Medicare, and unemployment compensation programs (p. 556)
socialism an economic system in which the government owns the basic means of production, distributes the products and wages, and provides social services such as health care and welfare (pp. 28, 718)
soft money money raised by a political party for general purposes, not designated for a candidate (p. 478)
sovereignty the supreme and absolute authority within territorial boundaries (p. 7)
special district a unit of local government that deals with a specific function, such as education, water supply, or transportation (p. 665)
splinter party a political party that splits away from a major party because of some disagreement (p. 455)
spoils system the practice of victorious politicians rewarding their followers with government jobs (p. 285)
spot advertising the brief, frequent, positive descriptions of a candidate or a candidate's major themes broadcast on television or radio (p. 538)
standing committee a permanent committee in Congress that oversees bills that deal with certain kinds of issues (p. 142)
standing vote a voting method used by the House and Senate in which members vote by standing and being counted (p. 187)
stare decisis (STEHR•ee dih•SY•suhs) a Latin term meaning "let the decision stand"; the principle that once the Court rules on a case, its decision serves as a precedent on which to base other decisions (p. 338)
state a political community that occupies a definite territory and has an organized government with the power to make and enforce laws without approval from any higher authority (p. 5)
state central committee committee usually composed largely of representatives from the party's county organizations (p. 460)
state farm farm owned by the government and run like a factory, with farmworkers being paid wages (p. 729)
states' rights position a position that favors state and local action in dealing with problems (p. 106)
statute a law written by a legislative branch (p. 425)
statutory law a law that is written down so that everyone might know and understand it (p. 425)
straight party ticket one where a voter has selected candidates of his or her party only (p. 493)
straw poll an unscientific attempt to measure public opinion (p. 520)
strong-mayor system a type of mayor-council government in which the mayor has strong executive powers (p. 666)
subcommittee a group within a standing committee that specializes in a subcategory of its standing committee's responsibility (p. 142)
subpoena a legal order that a person appear or produce requested documents (p. 168)
substantive due process certain rights of individuals in the application of laws, some that are specified in the Constitution (like free speech) and some that are not specified (like the right of privacy in making personal decisions) (p. 427)
suburb a densely settled territory adjacent to a central city (p. 672)
suffrage the right to vote (p. 481)
summons an official notice of a lawsuit that includes the date, time, and place of the initial court appearance (p. 433)
sunset law a law that requires periodic checks of government agencies to see if they are still needed (p. 112)
sunshine law a law prohibiting public officials from holding meetings not open to the public (p. 113)
supremacy clause statement in Article VI of the Constitution establishing that the Constitution, laws passed by Congress, and treaties of the United States "shall be the supreme Law of the Land" (pp. 64, 97)
suspect classification a classification made on the basis of race or national origin that is subject to strict judicial scrutiny (p. 407)
swing vote the deciding vote (p. 344)
symbolic speech the use of actions and symbols, in addition to or instead of words, to express opinions (p. 366)

T

tariff a tax placed on imports to increase their price in the domestic market (p. 732)
tax the money that people and businesses pay to support the activities of the government (pp. 189, 555)
taxable income the total income of an individual minus certain deductions and personal exemptions (p. 555)
tax credit allows taxpayers to reduce their income tax liability (p. 559)
theocracy a government dominated by religion (p. 453)
third party any political party other than one of the two major parties (p. 455)
ticket the candidates for president and vice president (p. 466)

ticket-splitting voting for candidates from different parties for different offices (p. 489)

tort a wrongful act, other than breach of contract, for which an injured party has the right to sue (p. 432)

totalitarian dictatorship a form of autocratic government where the ideas of leaders are glorified and the government seeks to control all aspects of social and economic life (p. 18)

town meeting a gathering of all the voters of a town to express their opinions and participate in the lawmaking process (p. 665)

township a unit of local government found in some states, usually a subdivision of a county (p. 664)

trading bloc a group of nations that trade without barriers such as tariffs (pp. 710, 733)

traditional economy economic system in which customs dictate the rules for economic activity (p. 717)

transcript a summary record (p. 417)

treaty a formal agreement between the governments of two or more countries (pp. 81, 257, 615)

trial court the court in which a case is originally tried (p. 306)

trust a form of business consolidation in which several corporations combine their stock and allow a board of trustees to operate as a giant enterprise (p. 578)

U

unanimous opinion a Court decision in which all justices vote the same way (p. 334)

uncontrollable government expenditure required by law or resulting from previous budgetary commitments (pp. 192, 562)

unemployment compensation payments to workers who lose their jobs (p. 649)

unemployment insurance programs in which the federal and state governments cooperate to provide help for people who are out of work (p. 592)

unfunded mandates programs ordered but not paid for by federal legislation (p. 588)

unicameral a single-chamber legislature (pp. 48, 641)

union shop a place of employment where workers are required to join a union soon after they have been hired (pp. 583, 649)

unitary system a government that gives all key powers to the national or central government (p. 12)

universe in polling, the group of people that are to be studied (p. 520)

urban renewal programs under which cities apply for federal aid to clear slum areas and rebuild (pp. 599, 678)

verdict decision (p. 443)

veto rejection of a bill (pp. 66, 188)

victim compensation a program in many states whereby the state government provides financial aid to victims of certain crimes (p. 651)

visa a special document, required by certain countries, that is issued by the government of the country that a person wishes to enter (p. 623)

voice vote method in which House or Senate members call out "Aye" or "No" and the Speaker determines which side has the most voice votes (p. 187)

ward a large district comprised of several adjoining precincts (p. 459)

weak-mayor system mayor-council government in which the mayor has limited powers (p. 666)

welfare state a nation that has an economic system, such as socialism, that provides many welfare programs (p. 723)

whip an assistant to the party floor leader in the legislature (p. 135)

wire service an organization that employs reporters throughout the world to collect news stories for subscribers (p. 528)

withholding the money an employer withholds from workers' wages as payment of anticipated income tax (p. 556)

workers' compensation payments people unable to work as a result of job-related injury or ill health receive (p. 649)

writ of certiorari (SUHR•shee•uh•RAR•ee) an order from the Supreme Court to a lower court to send up the records on a case for review (p. 332)

writ of habeas corpus a court order to release a person accused of a crime to court to determine whether he or she has been legally detained (p. 158)

zoning the means a local government uses to regulate the way land and buildings may be used in order to shape community development (p. 669)

Italicized page numbers refer to illustrations. The following abbreviations are used in the index:
m=map, *c*=chart or graph,
p=photograph or picture,
ctn=cartoon, *ptg*=painting, *q*=quote

A

B

C

D

K

M

P

Q

R

S

T

W

abdicate/abdicar renunciar formalmente al trono (pág. 690)
abridge/privar limitar (pág. 363)
absentee ballot/balota ausente la que permite a una persona votar sin ir a la urna electoral en el día de elección (pág. 491)
absolute monarch/monarca absoluto un monarca que tiene poder absoluto e ilimitado para gobernar su gente (pág. 19)
acreage allotment/asignación de acres el programa bajo el cual el gobierno paga precios de apoyo para las cosechas de los agricultores cultivadas en un número de acres asignado (pág. 586)
administrative assistant/auxiliar administrativo miembro del personal propio de un legislador que dirige la oficina del legislador, supervisa el calendario, y da asesoramiento (pág. 147)
administrative law/ley administrativa ley que estipula la autoridad, procedimientos, y reglas para ser seguidos por agencias gubernamentales (pág. 425)
adversary system/sistema adversario sistema judicial en el cual los abogados opositores presentan sus casos más sólidos (pág. 428)
advisory opinion/opinión asesorada una decisión sobre una ley o acción que no ha sido desafiada (pág. 340)
affidavit/declaración jurada una declaración escrita para verificar afirmaciones de hecho firmada bajo juramento (pág. 435)
affirmative action/acción afirmativa política de gobierno que les asigna trabajos, contratos gubernamentales, promociones, admisiones a escuelas, y otros beneficios a minorías y mujeres con el fin de enmendar discriminaciones pasadas (pág. 412)
alien/extranjero una persona que vive en un país donde no es ciudadano (pág. 387)
ambassador/embajador oficial del gobierno que representa la nación en asuntos diplomáticos (pág. 615)
amendment/enmienda un cambio en la Constitución (pág. 65)
amicus curiae término latino que significa "amigo de la corte"; un informe escrito por un individuo o un grupo afirmando tener información útil para la consideración de la corte de un caso (pág. 333)
amnesty/amnistía indulto a un grupo de individuos por una ofensa en contra del gobierno (págs. 254, 390)
anarchy/anarquía desorden político (pág. 57)
answer/respuesta contestación formal por un acusado a los cargos en una demanda (pág. 433)
apartheid segregación estricta de las razas (pág. 698)
appellate jurisdiction/jurisdicción de apelación autoridad tomada por una corte para oír un caso que es apelado de una corte menor (pág. 306)
appropriation/asignación de fondos aprobación de gastos gubernamentales (pág. 191)
appropriations bill/proyecto de ley de asignación de fondos ley propuesta para autorizar el gasto de dinero (págs. 160, 191)
arraignment/acusación procedimiento durante el cual el juez lee el cargo formal contra el acusado y el acusado se declara culpable o no culpable (pág. 441)
arrest warrant/orden de detención orden firmada por un juez nombrando al individuo a ser arrestado por un crimen determinado (págs. 85, 438)
article/artículo una de las siete divisiones principales de la Constitución (pág. 64)
assessment/tasación proceso complicado de calcular el valor de propiedad para el impuesto (pág. 674)
at-large/en general como un todo; por ejemplo, por todo el estado (pág. 128)
audit/intervenir revisar más estrictamente (pág. 556)
authorization bill/proyecto de ley de autorización proyecto de ley que establece un programa federal y especifica cuánto dinero le puede ser asignado (pág. 191)
autocracy/autocracia sistema de gobierno en el cual el poder para dirigir está en manos de un solo individuo (pág. 18)

backgrounders/informes anónimos información dada por altos funcionarios gubernamentales a reporteros que estos pueden usar en una historia pero sin revelar su fuente (pág. 535)
balanced budget/presupuesto balanceado un plan financiero requiriendo que lo que el gobierno federal gasta no excederá su ingreso (pág. 77)
bankruptcy/bancarrota el proceso legal para administrar los bienes de una persona o negocio que no puede pagar sus deudas (pág. 161)
biased sample/muestra sesgada en votación, un grupo que no representa exactamente la mayor población (pág. 520)
bicameral legislatura de dos cámaras (pág. 641)
bicameral legislature/legislatura bicameral legislatura de dos cámaras (pág. 123)
bilateral treaty/tratado bilateral acuerdo firmado por dos naciones (pág. 629)
bill/proyecto de ley ley propuesta (pág. 135)
bill of attainder/orden de culpabilidad una ley que establece la culpabilidad y castiga a una persona sin juicio (pág. 158)
bipartisan/bipartidario que consta de miembros de ambos grandes partidos políticos (pág. 619)
bloc/bloque coalición unida para promocionar un interés común (pág. 344)
block grant/otorgación general grande donación de dinero a un gobierno estatal o local para usar para

un propósito general (págs. 658, 675)

bond/garantía promesa contractual de parte de aquél que pide prestado para volver a pagar cierta cantidad más interés para una fecha específica (pág. 657)

borough/burgo división política en Alaska semejante a un condado en otros estados (pág. 664)

boss/jefe poderoso líder de partido (pág. 465)

bourgeoisie/burguesía capitalistas que poseen los medios de producción (pág. 29)

brief/informe declaración escrita exponiendo los argumentos legales, hechos relevantes, y precedentes apoyando un lado de un caso (pág. 333)

broadcast spectrum/espectro de difusión la variación de frecuencias sobre la cual señales electrónicas pueden ser enviadas (pág. 547)

bureaucracy/burocracia administradores gubernamentales (pág. 115)

bureaucrat/burócrata aquél que trabaja para un departamento o agencia del gobierno federal—servidor civil (pág. 275)

C

cabinet/gabinete los secretarios de los departamentos ejecutivos, el vicepresidente, y otros altos funcionarios que ayudan al presidente a tomar decisiones y hacer políticas (pág. 228)

cadre funcionarios de gobierno en China (pág. 703)

calendar/calendario horario que enumera el orden en el cual los proyectos de ley serán considerados en el Congreso (pág. 136)

campaign manager/director de campaña la persona responsable de la estrategia global y la planeación de una campaña (pág. 476)

canvass/escrutinio el conteo de votos por el cuerpo oficial que tabula las devoluciones electorales y certifica al ganador (pág. 487)

canvassing board/consejo de escrutinio el cuerpo oficial que cuenta los votos y certifica al ganador (pág. 490)

capital los medios de producción—dinero, fábricas, maquinaria pesada—usados para hacer otros productos y bienes (pág. 718)

capitalism/capitalismo un sistema económico proporcionando la libertad de acción e incentivo individual para trabajadores, inversionistas, consumidores, y empresas de negocios (págs. 26, 718)

casework/trabajo particular el trabajo que un legislador hace para ayudar a los constituyentes con sus problemas (pág. 200)

caseworker/asistente social el miembro del personal propio de un legislador quien se encarga de las peticiones de ayuda de los constituyentes (págs. 148, 201)

caucus/junta electoral reunión privada de dirigentes del partido para escoger candidatos a gobierno (págs. 134, 464)

cede/ceder renunciar (pág. 50)

censure/censura voto de desaprobación formal de las acciones de un miembro (pág. 129)

census/censo conteo de población (pág. 124)

central clearance/despacho central revisión por la Oficina de Dirección y Presupuesto de todas las propuestas legislativas que las agencias ejecutivas preparan (pág. 236)

centralized planning/planeación centralizada control de la economía por el gobierno (pág. 724)

change of venue/cambio de jurisdicción nueva localización para un juicio (pág. 86)

checks and balances/control y balances el sistema en que cada ramo del gobierno ejercita algún control sobre los otros (pág. 65)

civil case/caso civil caso generalmente involucrando una disputa entre dos o más individuos privados u organizaciones (pág. 646)

civil law/ley civil una relacionada a disputas entre dos o más individuos o entre individuos y el gobierno (págs. 103, 430)

civil rights movement/movimiento de derechos civiles los esfuerzos para acabar con la segregación (pág. 410)

civil service system/sistema de servicio civil la práctica de empleo gubernamental basado en abiertos exámenes competitivos y mérito (pág. 286)

civil society/sociedad civil una red compleja de asociaciones voluntarias, grupos económicos, organizaciones religiosas, y muchos otros tipos de grupos que existen independientes del gobierno (pág. 24)

client group/grupo de clientes individuos y grupos que trabajan con una agencia gubernamental y que son los más afectados por sus decisiones (pág. 295)

closed primary/elección preliminar cerrada una elección en que sólo los miembros de un partido político pueden votar (pág. 465)

closed rule/norma cerrada una regla que prohibe a miembros del Congreso ofrecer enmiendas a un proyecto de ley pidiendo la palabra (pág. 190)

closed shop/taller cerrado lugar de empleo donde sólo los miembros del sindicato pueden ser contratados (pág. 583)

cloture/clausura procedimiento que permite a cada senador hablar sólo una hora sobre un proyecto de ley bajo debate (pág. 140)

cluster sample/muestra regional método de votación que agrupa a personas por división geográfica (pág. 521)

coalition government/gobierno de coalición uno formado por varios partidos que unen fuerzas para obtener una mayoría (pág. 454)

collective bargaining/negociación colectiva la práctica de negociar contratos laborales (pág. 581)

collective farm/granja colectiva ejido en el cual la tierra es propiedad del gobierno pero arrendada a una familia (pág. 729)

collective naturalization/naturalización colectiva proceso por el cual los miembros de un grupo llegan a ser ciudadanos americanos por medio de un acto del Congreso (pág. 394)

collective security/seguridad colectiva un sistema en el cual las naciones participantes acuerdan tomar acción unida en contra de una nación que ataque a cualquiera de ellas (pág. 629)

command economy/economía de mando un sistema económico en el cual el gobierno controla los elementos de producción (pág. 30, 717)

commission form/forma comisión forma de gobierno municipal que combina los poderes ejecutivo y legislativo en una comisión electa (pág. 667)

committees of correspondence/comités de correspondencia comités de la época colonial que urgían la resistencia a los ingleses y el mantenerse en contacto mientras los eventos se desenvolvían (pág. 44)

committee staff/personal de comité las personas que trabajan para los comités de la Cámara y el Senado (pág. 147)

common law/ley común ley hecha por jueces en el proceso de resolver casos individuales (pág. 426)

communism/comunismo un sistema económico en el cual el gobierno central dirige todas las importantes decisiones económicas (págs. 30, 718)

comparative advantage/ventaja comparativa principio económico de que cada país debe hacer aquellos productos que puede hacer más eficientemente e intercambiar para otros productos (pág. 732)

compensation/compensación salario (pág. 214)

complaint/queja documento legal presentado en la corte que tiene jurisdicción sobre el problema (pág. 433)

concurrent jurisdiction/jurisdicción conjunta autoridad compartida por las cortes federales y estatales (pág. 306)

concurrent powers/poderes comunes poderes tanto del gobierno nacional como de los gobiernos estatales (pág. 97)

concurrent resolution/resolución concurrente resolución que se dirige a asuntos requiriendo la acción de la Cámara y el Senado pero sobre los cuales una ley no es necesaria (pág. 182)

concurring opinion/opinión común la opinión de la Corte expresando la perspectiva de uno o más jueces quienes acuerdan con las conclusiones de la mayoría pero por razones distintas (pág. 334)

confederacy/confederación unión suelta de estados independientes (pág. 12)

conferee miembro de un comité de conferencia (pág. 187)

conference committee/comité de conferencia comité común temporal creado cuando la Cámara y el Senado han aprobado diferentes versiones del mismo proyecto de ley (pág. 144)

conference report/reporte de conferencia el compromiso final del proyecto de ley presentado por el comité de conferencia después de haber hecho cambios (pág. 187)

congressional override/anulación del Congreso el poder del Congreso de aprobar legislación anulando el veto del presidente (pág. 249)

conscription/conscripción servicio militar obligatorio, también llamada la quinta (pág. 625)

consensus/consenso acuerdo sobre creencias básicas (pág. 6)

conservation/conservación cuidado y protección de recursos, incluyendo la tierra, lagos, ríos, y bosques; petróleo, gas natural, y otros recursos de energía; y la vida silvestre (pág. 651)

conservative/conservativo uno que cree que el gobierno debe ser limitado excepto apoyando los valores tradicionales y promoviendo la libertad de oportunidad (pág. 517)

consolidated democracy/democracia consolidada una nación que tiene elecciones democráticas, partidos políticos, gobierno constitucional, judicatura independiente, y generalmente una economía mercadera (pág. 689)

constituent/constituyente una persona a la cual un miembro del Congreso ha sido elegido para representar (pág. 133)

constitution/constitución un plan que provee las normas para el gobierno (pág. 13)

constitutional commission/comisión constitucional un grupo de expertos designados para estudiar la constitución de un estado y recomendar cambios (pág. 639)

constitutional convention/convención constitucional junta de ciudadanos electos para considerar el cambiar o reemplazar una constitución (pág. 639)

constitutional court/corte constitucional una corte establecida por el Congreso bajo la Constitución (pág. 312)

constitutional government/gobierno constitucional un gobierno en el cual una constitución tiene la autoridad de establecer límites claramente reconocidos en los poderes de aquellos que gobiernan (pág. 13)

constitutional law/ley constitucional ley que involucra la interpretación y la aplicación de la Constitución de E.U. y constituciones estatales (págs. 14, 424)

constitutional monarch/monarca constitucional un monarca que tiene poderes gubernamentales compartidos con legislaturas electas o que sirve principalmente como líder ceremonial de un gobierno (pág. 19)

consul/cónsul funcionario gubernamental que encabeza un consulado en una nación extranjera (pág. 623)

consulate/consulado la oficina que promueve los intereses comerciales americanos en un país extranjero y guarda a los viajeros de su nación en ese país (pág. 623)

containment/contención la política diseñada para prohibir que la Unión Soviética expandiera sus poderes (pág. 610)

contempt/rebeldía obstrucción voluntaria de la justicia (pág. 168)

contract/contrato conjunto de promesas voluntarias, que se pueden hacer cumplir a fuerza de ley, entre dos o más partidos (pág. 430)

copyright/derecho de autor derecho exclusivo de publicar y vender un trabajo literario, musical, o artístico por cierto período (pág. 163)

corporate charter/estatuto de corporación documento que da el estatus legal a una sociedad anónima (pág. 648)

council-manager form/forma consejo-director tipo de gobierno municipal en el cual los poderes legislativo y ejecutivo están separados (pág. 668)

counsel/asesor jurídico abogado (pág. 401)

county/condado la mayor subdivisión territorial y política de un estado (pág. 663)

county board/consejo del condado el consejo gobernante de la mayoría de los condados (pág. 664)

coup/golpe una toma del poder planeada pero repentina (pág. 730)

covert/cubierto secreto (pág. 265)

criminal case/caso criminal uno en el cual el estado lleva cargos contra un ciudadano por violar la ley (pág. 646)

criminal justice system/sistema de justicia criminal el sistema de cortes estatales y federales, policías, y prisiones que hacen cumplir la ley criminal (pág. 437)

criminal law/ley criminal aquella que define crímenes y provee por su castigo (pág. 437)

cross-pressured voter/votante bajo presión aquel que se encuentra atrapado entre elementos conflictivos en su propia vida (pág. 493)

customs duties/deberes de aduana los impuestos fijados sobre los productos importados a Estados Unidos—tarifas o deberes de importación (pág. 557)

D

de facto existiendo de hecho en vez de legalmente (pág. 265)

defamatory speech/expresión difamatoria discurso falso que deteriora el buen nombre, carácter, o reputación de una persona (pág. 369)

defendant/acusado la persona contra la cual una demanda civil o criminal es traída (pág. 433)

delegated powers/poderes delegados poderes que la Constitución otorga o delega al gobierno nacional (pág. 95)

democracy/democracia gobierno en el cual la gente manda (pág. 19)

democratic socialism/socialismo democrático un sistema económico en el cual la gente tiene el control sobre el gobierno por medio de la libre elección y el sistema multipartidario, pero el gobierno es dueño de los medios básicos de producción y toma la mayoría de las decisiones económicas (pág. 28)

denaturalization/desnaturalización la pérdida de la ciudadanía por causa de fraude o decepción durante el proceso de la naturalización (pág. 396)

dependent/dependiente aquel que depende principalmente de otra persona por la necesidades básicas (pág. 556)

deregulate/desregular reducir los reglamentos (pág. 283)

détente relajación de la tensión entre países (pág. 612)

developing nation/país en desarrollo una nación apenas comenzando a desarrollarse industrialmente (págs. 16, 722)

direct democracy/democracia directa forma de democracia en la cual la gente se gobierna a sí misma votando en temas (pág. 20)

direct primary/elección preliminar directa elección en la cual miembros del partido seleccionan a personas para postularse en la elección general (pág. 465)

discount rate/tipo de descuento la tasa de interés que el Sistema de Reserva Federal les cobra a los miembros bancos para préstamos (pág. 569)

discovery/descubrimiento el proceso cuando ambos lados preparan para un juicio reuniendo evidencia para apoyar su caso (pág. 433)

discrimination/discriminación tratamiento injusto de individuos basado sólo en su raza, género, grupo étnico, edad, incapacidad física, o religión (pág. 407)

dissenting opinion/opinión disidente la opinión expresada por una minoría de jueces en un caso de la Corte (pág. 334)

divine right/derecho divino la creencia de que ciertas personas son descendientes de dioses o escogidas por dioses para dirigir (pág. 8)

double jeopardy/doble riesgo nuevo juicio de una persona que fue absuelto en un juicio previo por el mismo crimen (pág. 404)

due process clause/cláusula de proceso legal correspondiente cláusula en la Decimocuarta Enmienda estableciendo que ningún estado puede privar a una persona de vida, libertad, o propiedad sin el proceso legal correspondiente (pág. 308)

due process of law/proceso legal correspondiente un principio en la Quinta Enmienda estableciendo que el gobierno debe seguir los procedimientos constitucionales propios en juicios y en otras acciones que toma en contra de individuos (págs. 86, 427)

economics/económica el estudio de los esfuerzos humanos para satisfacer los deseos aparentemente ilimitados por el uso de recursos limitados (pág. 26)

elastic clause/cláusula elástica cláusula en el Artículo I, Sección 8 de la Constitución que otorga al Congreso el derecho de hacer todas las leyes "necesarias y propias" para llevar a cabo los poderes expresados en las otras cláusulas del Artículo I (págs. 69, 96, 157)

elector miembro de un partido político escogido en cada estado para elegir formalmente al presidente y vicepresidente (pág. 220)
electoral vote/voto electoral el voto oficial para presidente y vicepresidente por los electores en cada estado (pág. 220)
embargo acuerdo que prohibe el intercambio (pág. 44)
embassy/embajada la residencia y oficinas oficiales de un embajador en un país extranjero (págs. 276, 622)
eminent domain/dominio eminente el poder del gobierno de quitar propiedades privadas para el uso público (pág. 86)
enabling act/acto capacitador el primer paso en el procedimiento de admisión de un estado el cual permite a la gente de un territorio preparar una constitución (pág. 99)
enemy alien/enemigo extranjero ciudadano de una nación contra la cual Estados Unidos está en guerra (pág. 387)
entitlement/derecho financiero un gasto gubernamental requerido que continúa de un año al otro (págs. 192, 562)
entrepreneur/empresario persona que se arriesga para hacer productos y servicios en busca de ganancias (pág. 718)
enumerated powers/poderes enumerados los poderes expresados del Congreso que son especificados y numerados de 1 a 18 en el Artículo I, Sección 8 de la Constitución (págs. 69, 96, 157)
equal time doctrine/doctrina de tiempo equitativo norma que requiere a las estaciones de difusión dar el tiempo al aire equitativo a candidatos para el cargo público (pág. 545)
equity/equidad sistema de normas por el cual las disputas son resueltas a base de lo justo (pág. 426)
establishment clause/cláusula de establecimiento la garantía de la Primera Enmienda que el Congreso "no hará ninguna ley respecto al establecimiento de religión" (pág. 358)
estate tax/impuesto de herencia impuestos recaudados en los bienes (propiedad y dinero) de una persona que fallece (pág. 558)
evolutionary theory/teoría evolucionaria la teoría de que el estado evolucionó de la familia (pág. 8)
excise tax/impuesto indirecto impuesto en la manufactura, transportación, venta, o consumo de ciertos artículos tales como gasolina, licor, o cigarrillos (págs. 557, 656)
exclusion/exclusión el derecho del Congreso de negarse a sentar a un miembro electo con un voto de mayoría (pág. 129)
exclusionary rule/norma de exclusión una ley estableciendo que cualquier evidencia obtenida ilegalmente no puede ser usada en una corte federal (pág. 399)
executive agreement/acuerdo ejecutivo un acuerdo hecho entre el presidente y un jefe de estado (págs. 81, 257, 619)
executive order/orden ejecutiva una norma emitida por el presidente que tiene la fuerza de ley (pág. 253)
executive privilege/privilegio ejecutivo el derecho del presidente y otros altos funcionarios para rehusarse a atestiguar ante el Congreso o una corte (pág. 266)
expatriation/expatriación renunciar a la ciudadanía por salir para vivir en un país extranjero (pág. 395)
ex post facto law/ley ex post facto una ley que hace crimen de un acto que fue legal cuando fue cometido (pág. 158)
expressed contract/contrato expresado contrato en el cual los términos son específicamente establecidos, generalmente por escrito (pág. 430)
expressed powers/poderes expresados poderes establecidos directamente en la Constitución (págs. 68, 95, 157)
extradite/extraditar regresar al estado original a un criminal o fugitivo que huye cruzando los límites estatales (pág. 103)
extradition/extradición el proceso legal a través del cual una persona acusada de un crimen que ha huido a otro estado es regresado al estado donde el crimen tuvo lugar (pág. 652)
extralegal no permitido por ley (pág. 56)

faction/facción grupo de personas unidas para promover intereses especiales (pág. 503)
factors of production/elementos de producción recursos que una economía necesita para producir bienes y servicios (pág. 717)
fairness doctrine/doctrina justa una norma que requiere que los medios de difusión proporcionan oportunidades para la expresión de ideas opuestas en temas de importancia pública (pág. 545)
faqih el máximo líder político-religioso en Irán (pág. 707)
federal bureaucracy/burocracia federal los departamentos del gobierno federal—en su mayoría del ramo ejecutivo (pág. 71)
federal grant/otorgación federal dinero dado al estado para un propósito específico (pág. 657)
federalism/federalismo un sistema en el cual el poder es dividido entre los gobiernos nacional y estatales (pág. 65)
federal system/sistema federal gobierno que divide los poderes del gobierno entre el gobierno nacional y los gobiernos de los estados o provincias (pág. 12)
felony/crimen un delito grave (págs. 399, 438)
filibuster método de derrotar un proyecto de ley en el cual un senador habla hasta que la mayoría abandona el proyecto o acuerda modificarlo (pág. 140)
first reading/primer informe cuando un proyecto de ley es presentado en el Congreso y es dado un título y número, es impreso y distribuido (pág. 184)

fiscal policy/política fiscal el uso por el gobierno de gastos e impuestos para influenciar la economía (pág. 567)

fiscal year/año fiscal período de contabilidad de 12 meses (pág. 560)

force theory/teoría de fuerza la teoría de que el estado nació a fuerzas—cuando toda la gente de un lugar fue traída bajo la autoridad de una persona o grupo (pág. 8)

foreign policy/política exterior las estrategias y metas que guían las relaciones de una nación con otros países (pág. 607)

forum/foro medio para discusión (pág. 249)

free enterprise/empresa libre la oportunidad de controlar sus propias decisiones económicas (pág. 23)

free enterprise system/sistema de empresa libre un sistema económico basado en la propiedad privada de los medios de producción—el capital—y en la libertad económica individual (pág. 718)

free exercise clause/cláusula de libre ejercicio la garantía en la Primera Enmienda que prohibe al gobierno interferir sin causa con el libre ejercicio de religión (pág. 358)

free market/mercado libre un sistema económico en el cual compradores y vendedores hacen decisiones libres en el mercado (pág. 27)

front-runner/candidato delantero el líder a principios de una elección (pág. 537)

fundamental right/derecho fundamental un derecho básico del sistema americano o uno que es indispensable en un sistema justo (pág. 407)

G

gag order/orden de supresión una orden por un juez prohibiendo a la prensa de publicar ciertos tipos de información sobre un caso judicial pendiente (pág. 373)

gentrification/gentificación el fenómeno de nueva gente mudándose a un vecindario, echando afuera aquellos que viven ahí, y cambiando el carácter esencial del área (pág. 681)

gerrymander trazar los límites de un distrito para ganar ventaja en las elecciones (pág. 126)

global security/seguridad global la seguridad de todo el mundo (pág. 708)

government/gobierno la institución por medio de la cual el estado mantiene el orden social, proporciona servicios públicos, e impone decisiones obligatorias para los ciudadanos (pág. 8)

government corporation/corporación gubernamental una empresa dirigida por el gobierno federal (pág. 280)

grandfather clause/cláusula de abuelo una exención en una ley para cierto grupo basada en condiciones previas (pág. 483)

grand jury/gran jurado el grupo que escucha cargos en contra de una persona sospechosa y decide si hay suficiente evidencia para traer a la persona al juicio (págs. 312, 439)

gross national product (GNP)/producto nacional bruto el total de todos bienes y servicios producidos en una nación en un año (págs. 568, 728)

hearing/audiencia una sesión en la cual un comité escucha el testimonio de gente interesada en el proyecto de ley (pág. 184)

heckler's veto el veto público de la libre expresión y derechos de asamblea de grupos impopulares declarando que las demostraciones resultarán en violencia (pág. 379)

Holocaust/holocausto la exterminación masiva de judíos y otros grupos por los nazis durante la Segunda Guerra Mundial (pág. 379)

horse-race coverage/reportaje de carrera de caballos método de reportaje enfocando en "ganadores" y "perdedores" y en "quién va adelante" mejor que en temas o posiciones políticas (pág. 537)

house arrest/arresto domiciliario una sentencia que requiere a un ofensor quedarse en casa con excepción de ciertas funciones que la corte permite (pág. 653)

human rights/derechos humanos libertades fundamentales (pág. 355)

hung jury/jurado indeciso un jurado que está imposibilitado para llegar a una decisión (pág. 443)

ideological party/partido ideológico partido político que se enfoca en cambios globales en la sociedad más bien que en un tema (pág. 455)

ideology/ideología el conjunto de creencias básicas sobre la vida, cultura, gobierno, y sociedad (págs. 454, 517)

illegal alien/extranjero ilegal persona sin permiso legal para estar en un país (pág. 387)

image/imagen representación mental (pág. 476)

immunity/inmunidad libertad de ser acusado para los testigos cuyo testimonio los ata a actos ilegales (pág. 169)

impeach/acusar acusar a un funcionario de mala conducta en su cargo (pág. 79)

impeachment/acusación acusación formal de mala conducta en el cargo en contra de un oficial público (pág. 164)

implied contract/contrato implícito contrato en el cual los términos no son expresamente citados pero pueden ser deducidos de las acciones de la gente involucrada y las circunstancias (pág. 430)

implied powers/poderes implícitos poderes que el gobierno requiere para llevar a cabo los poderes constitucionales expresados (págs. 96, 157)

impound/confiscar rehusar a gastar (pág. 337)

impoundment/confiscamiento la negativa del presidente de gastar el dinero que el Congreso ha votado para fundar un programa (págs. 175, 253)

income tax/impuesto sobre la renta el impuesto recaudado en ganancias individuales y corporativas (pág. 108)

incorporation/incorporación proceso que extiende la protección de la Declaración de Derechos en contra de las acciones de gobiernos estatales y locales (pág. 356); el proceso de establecer una sociedad legal bajo la ley estatal (pág. 666)

incrementalism/incrementalismo el término usado para explicar que el total del presupuesto cambia poco de un año al otro (pág. 564)

incumbent/titular funcionario gubernamental que ya está en el cargo (pág. 130)

independent/independiente votante que no apoya a un partido político en particular (pág. 458)

indictment/acusación acusación formal por un gran jurado (págs. 312, 440)

industrialized nation/nación industrializada nación con grandes industrias y tecnología avanzada que proporciona una forma de vida más cómoda que la de las naciones en desarrollo (pág. 16)

information/información declaración jurada por la fiscalía afirmando que hay suficiente evidencia para un juicio (pág. 440)

infrastructure/infraestructura las facilidades básicas de una ciudad, tales como calles y banquetas pavimentadas, tubería de agua, puentes, y edificios públicos (pág. 680)

inherent powers/poderes inherentes poderes que el gobierno nacional puede ejercitar simplemente porque es un gobierno (pág. 96)

initiative/iniciativa método por el cual los ciudadanos proponen una enmienda constitucional o una ley (pág. 639)

injunction/mandato judicial orden que detendrá una acción en particular o hará cumplir una norma o reglamentación (págs. 297, 433, 582)

inner cabinet/gabinete interior miembros del gabinete que manejan influencias sobre el presidente porque encabezan departamentos que están interesados con temas nacionales (pág. 232)

interest group/grupo de intereses grupo de personas con objetivos comunes que se organizan para influenciar al gobierno (pág. 503)

intergovernmental revenue/ingresos intergubernamentales ingresos distribuidos de un nivel de gobierno a otro (pág. 657)

interlocking directorate/dirección entrelazada la misma gente sirviendo en las mesas directivas de compañías competentes (pág. 579)

internationalism/internacionalismo involucramiento en asuntos mundiales (pág. 609)

international security/seguridad internacional la estabilidad mundial como resultado de la interacción de la política de muchas naciones (pág. 708)

interstate commerce/comercio interestatal intercambio entre los estados (págs. 55, 161)

interstate compact/compacto interestatal acuerdo escrito entre dos o más estados (pág. 105)

iron triangle/triángulo de hierro relación formada entre agencias gubernamentales, comités congresistas, y grupos de clientes que trabajan juntos (pág. 298)

isolationism/aislacionismo la evasión del involucramiento en asuntos mundiales (pág. 609)

item veto/veto de artículo el poder de rechazar un artículo particular en un proyecto de ley sin vetar el proyecto entero (pág. 645)

J

Jim Crow law/ley Jim Crow ley que requiere la segregación racial en lugares tales como escuelas, autobuses, y hoteles (pág. 408)

joint committee/comité conjunto comité de la Cámara y el Senado que generalmente actúa como grupo de estudio y reporta sus descubrimientos de regreso a la Cámara y el Senado (pág. 143)

joint resolution/resolución conjunta resolución aprobada por las dos cámaras del Congreso que trata de asuntos inusuales o temporales, tal como el corregir un error en una ley previa (pág. 182)

judicial activism/activismo judicial la filosofía que la Suprema Corte debe tomar un papel activo en darle forma a políticas nacionales dirigiéndose a cuestiones sociales y políticas (pág. 82)

judicial circuit/circuito judicial región que contiene una corte de apelación de Estados Unidos (pág. 313)

judicial restraint/represión judicial la filosofía que la Suprema Corte debe evitar tomar la iniciativa en cuestiones sociales y políticas (pág. 81)

judicial review/revisión judicial el poder de la Suprema Corte de declarar inconstitucionales leyes y acciones de gobiernos locales, estatales, o nacional (págs. 66, 308, 336, 640)

jurisdiction/jurisdicción la autoridad de una corte para dictaminar en ciertos casos (págs. 64, 305)

jury/jurado grupo de ciudadanos que escuchan evidencias durante un juicio y dan el veredicto (págs. 442, 447)

jus sanguinis frase latina que quiere decir "ley de sangre"; el principio que otorga la ciudadanía en base de la ciudadanía de los padres (pág. 393)

jus soli frase latina que quiere decir "ley de la tierra"; el principio que otorga la ciudadanía a casi toda persona nacida en un país (pág. 393)

K

kanyro término japonés para funcionarios burocráticos (pág. 694)

kibbutzim comunas agrícolas colectivas (pág. 725)

laissez-faire la filosofía que el gobierno debe mantener sus manos fuera de la economía (págs. 27, 578)

lame duck un funcionario saliente sirviendo el resto de un período después de su retiro o siendo derrotado para reelección (pág. 90)

land/tierra todos los recursos naturales tales como tierra, agua, aire, y minerales (pág. 717)

law/ley conjunto de normas y estándares por los cuales una sociedad se gobierna a sí misma (pág. 423)

leak/divulgación el anuncio de información secreta por funcionarios gubernamentales anónimos a los medios informativos (págs. 230, 536)

legislative assistant/asistente legislativo miembro del personal propio de un legislador que se asegura de que el legislador esté bien informado de legislación propuesta (pág. 148)

legislative court/corte legislativa una corte creada para ayudar al Congreso a ejercitar sus poderes (pág. 314)

legislative oversight/revisión legislativa el repaso continuo del Congreso sobre qué tan efectivamente el ramo ejecutivo ejecuta las leyes que el Congreso aprueba (pág. 169)

legislative veto/veto legislativo provisiones que el Congreso escribió dentro de algunas leyes que le permitieron revisar y cancelar acciones de las agencias ejecutivas (pág. 171)

liaison officer/oficial de enlace empleado de un departamento de gabinete que ayuda a promover las buenas relaciones con el Congreso (pág. 296)

libel/difamación declaración falsa escrita o publicada con intención de dañar la reputación de una persona (págs. 84, 369, 544)

liberal uno que cree que el gobierno nacional debe ser activo promoviendo salud, educación, justicia, y oportunidad equitativa (pág. 517)

lieutenant governor/vicegobernador el oficial presidente en la cámara alta en algunas legislaturas estatales (pág. 642)

life peer/noble de por vida persona a quien le ha sido otorgado un título en la Cámara de Lores por logro sobresaliente (pág. 691)

limited government/gobierno limitado un sistema de gobierno en el cual el poder del gobierno es limitado, no absoluto (pág. 36)

limited war/guerra limitada una guerra en la cual la nación o naciones más poderosas no continuarán más allá de ciertos límites (pág. 709)

line-item veto/veto de línea el poder de vetar sólo ciertas líneas o artículos en un proyecto de ley (págs. 176, 255)

litigant/litigante persona comprometida en una demanda (pág. 307)

lobbying/cabildeo contacto directo hecho por un cabildero con el fin de persuadir a los funcionarios gubernamentales para apoyar la política que su grupo de interés favorece (págs. 198, 508)

lobbyist/cabildero representante de un grupo de interés (págs. 198, 508)

logrolling/intercambio de favores políticos un acuerdo entre dos o más legisladores para apoyarse el uno al otro en sus proyectos de ley (pág. 202)

majority leader/líder mayoritario el asistente máximo del presidente de la Cámara cuyo trabajo es ayudar a planear el programa legislativo del partido mayoritario y dirigir importantes proyectos de ley a través de la Cámara (pág. 134)

majority opinion/opinión mayoritaria decisión de la Corte expresando la perspectiva de la mayoría de los jueces (pág. 334)

mandate/mandato orden formal dada por una autoridad superior (págs. 245, 658)

mandatory sentencing/sentencia mandataria sistema de términos de encarcelamiento fijos y requeridos por ciertos tipos de crímenes (pág. 651)

market economy/economía mercadera un sistema económico que permite a compradores y vendedores actuar en sus propios intereses para controlar los elementos de producción (pág. 717)

marketing quota/cupo mercader límite establecido entre agricultores para vender sólo una porción asignada de una cosecha sobreproducida (pág. 586)

market value/valor de mercado la cantidad de dinero que un propietario espera recibir si su propiedad es vendida (pág. 674)

mass media/medios informativos medios de comunicación, tales como televisión, periódicos, películas, libros, e Internet, que influencian a grandes audiencias (págs. 515, 527)

mass transit/tránsito público sistemas tales como el metro que son usados para transportar a grandes números de personas (págs. 602, 671)

mayor-council form/forma alcalde-consejo forma de gobierno municipal en la cual el poder ejecutivo pertenece a un alcalde electo, y el poder legislativo a un consejo electo (pág. 666)

media event/evento para los medios informativos evento de interés visual diseñado para reforzar la posición de un político en algún tema (pág. 536)

mediation/mediación proceso en el cual cada partido tiene la oportunidad de explicar su lado de la disputa y debe escuchar al otro lado (pág. 434)

metropolitan area/área metropolitana una ciudad grande y sus suburbios alrededores (pág. 671)

metropolitan government/gobierno metropolitano tipo de gobierno que sirve varias comunidades en la misma región (pág. 682)
militia/milicia fuerzas armadas de ciudadanos (pág. 85)
misdemeanor/delito menor un crimen menor que normalmente es castigado por una multa o sentencia de cárcel por menos de un año (pág. 438)
mixed economy/economía mixta un sistema en el cual el gobierno regula empresas privadas (págs. 575, 721)
moderate/moderado aquél cuyas creencias caen entre ideas liberales y conservativas (pág. 517)
monarchy/monarquía autocracia en la cual un rey, reyna, o emperador, ejercita los poderes supremos del gobierno (pág. 19)
monetary policy/política monetaria el control del gobierno del abastecimiento de dinero y crédito para influenciar la economía (pág. 567)
monopoly/monopolio un negocio que controla tanto de una industria que existe poco o nada de competencia (págs. 578, 719)
mortgage/hipoteca préstamo solicitado para pagar una casa (pág. 431)
multilateral treaty/tratado multilateral acuerdo internacional firmado por varias naciones (pág. 629)
municipality/municipalidad unidad urbana de gobierno establecida por carta estatal (pág. 665)
mutual defense alliance/alianza de defensa mutua acuerdo entre naciones para apoyarse la una a la otra en caso de ataque (pág. 627)

N

nation/nación grupo de personas unidas por lazos de raza, lenguaje, costumbre, tradición, y a veces religión (pág. 6)
national budget/presupuesto nacional plan financiero anual para el gobierno nacional (pág. 175)
national committee/comité nacional representantes de las 50 organizaciones estatales de un partido político que lo dirigen (pág. 460)
national convention/convención nacional reunión de miembros locales y estatales de un partido escogidos para nominar a los candidatos para presidente y vicepresidente (pág. 460)
national debt/deuda nacional el total de dinero que el gobierno debe en cualquier momento (págs. 160, 559)
nationalist position/posición nacionalista posición que favorece la acción nacional en tratar problemas (pág. 106)
nationalization/nacionalización el proceso por el cual el gobierno toma control de la industria (pág. 724)
national security/seguridad nacional protección de las fronteras y territorios de una nación en contra de invasiones o el control por poderes extranjeros (págs. 608, 708)
national security adviser/consejero de seguridad nacional director del personal del Consejo de Seguridad Nacional (págs. 237, 616)
nation-state/estado nación un país en el cual el territorio de ambos la nación y el estado coinciden (pág. 6)
naturalization/naturalización el proceso legal por el cual se le otorga a una persona la ciudadanía (pág. 392)
necessary and proper clause/cláusula de necesario y propio Artículo I, Sección 8 de la Constitución, la cual le da al Congreso el poder de aprobar todas las leyes que sean necesarias y propias para hacer cumplir sus deberes (págs. 96, 157)
newly developed nation/nación nuevamente desarrollada nación que ha tenido rápido crecimiento industrial en años recientes (pág. 722)
news briefing/sesión noticiera una junta durante la cual un funcionario gubernamental anuncia o explica una política, decisión, o acción (pág. 535)
newspaper chain/cadena de periódicos compañía de periódicos que posee muchos periódicos diarios y semanales (pág. 528)
news release/comunicado de noticias historia preparada que los funcionarios gubernamentales escriben para los miembros de la prensa (pág. 535)
nominating convention/convención de nominación junta oficial pública de un partido para escoger candidatos para un cargo (pág. 464)
non-resident alien/extranjero no residente persona de un país extranjero que espera quedarse en Estados Unidos por un período corto y específico (pág. 387)
nuclear proliferation/proliferación nuclear la expansión de armas nucleares (pág. 709)

O

office-group ballot/balota de grupo de cargo aquella que enumera los candidatos juntos por el cargo al cual se están postulando (p 489)
oligarchy/oligarquía sistema de gobierno en el cual un pequeño grupo mantiene el poder (págs. 19, 690)
oligopoly/oligopolio situación cuando sólo unas cuantas empresas dominan una industria particular (págs. 579, 719)
open-market operations/operaciones del mercado abierto los medios que el Sistema de Reserva Federal usa para afectar la economía comprando o vendiendo bonos del gobierno u otras seguridades en el mercado abierto (pág. 570)
open primary/elección preliminar abierta una elección en la cual todos los votantes pueden participar (pág. 465)
open shop/taller abierto lugar de empleo donde los trabajadores pueden decidir libremente reunirse o no a una unión (pág. 583)

opinion/opinión explicación escrita de una decisión de la Suprema Corte; también, en algunos estados, una interpretación escrita de la constitución o leyes estatales por el fiscal del estado (págs. 322, 331, 645)
ordinance/ordenanza una ley (págs. 50, 425)
original jurisdiction/jurisdicción original la autoridad de una corte de juicio para ser la primera en escuchar un caso (pág. 306)

pardon/indulto la liberación de castigo legal (pág. 254)
parish/parroquia división política en Luisiana, semejante a un condado en otros estados (pág. 664)
parliamentary government/gobierno parlamentario tipo de gobierno en el cual las funciones ejecutiva y legislativa residen en la asamblea electa, o parlamento (pág. 690)
parochial school/escuela parroquiana escuela operada por una iglesia o grupo religioso (pág. 359)
parole/libertad condicional forma por la cual a un prisionero se le permite servir el resto de una sentencia en la comunidad bajo la supervisión de un oficial (pág. 653)
party-column ballot /balota columnar de partido aquella que enumera a cada candidato de partido en una columna bajo el nombre del partido (pág. 489)
passport/pasaporte documento permitiendo a un viajero cierta protección establecida por tratado internacional (pág. 623)
patent/patente el derecho exclusivo para un inventor de manufacturar, usar, y vender su invención por un período específico (pág. 163)
patronage/patrocinio la práctica de otorgar favores para recompensar la lealtad al partido (págs. 256, 462)
peer group/grupo paritario los amigos cercanos, grupo religioso, clubes, o grupos de trabajo de un individuo (pág. 515)
per curiam opinion/opinión per curiam breve declaración no firmada de una decisión de la Suprema Corte (pág. 333)
perjury/perjurio el mentir bajo juramento (pág. 168)
personal property/propiedad personal pertenencias movibles tales como ropa y joyas, así como artículos intangibles como acciones, bonos, derechos de autor, y patentes (págs. 431, 673)
personal staff/personal propio las personas que trabajan directamente para senadores y representantes individuales, (pág. 147)
petition/petición una solicitud (pág. 77)
petit jury/jurado pequeño jurado de juicio, generalmente de 6 o 12 personas, que considera la evidencia presentada en un juicio y rinde un veredicto (pág. 313)
petty offense/ofensa menor un crimen menor, generalmente castigada con una multa en vez del arresto (pág. 437)
picket/vigilar con piquetes patrullar un establecimiento para convencer a trabajadores y al público de no entrar (pág. 378)
plaintiff/demandante la persona que trae los cargos en una corte (pág. 433)
plank/punto una sección individual del programa político de un partido (pág. 469)
platform/programa político declaración de los principios, creencias, y posiciones en asuntos vitales de un partido político (pág. 469)
plea bargaining/negociación de alegato el proceso en el cual el acusado se declara culpable a un crimen menos grave que él con el cual fue acusado originalmente (pág. 440)
plurality/pluralidad la mayor cantidad de votos en una elección (págs. 465, 643)
pocket veto/veto indirecto cuando un presidente se deshace de un proyecto de ley aprobado durante los últimos 10 días que el Congreso está en sesión simplemente por rehusar a actuar en ello (pág. 188)
political action committee (PAC)/comité de acción política una organización formada para recolectar dinero y proporcionar ayuda financiera a candidatos políticos (págs. 130, 475, 477, 511)
political culture/cultura política el conjunto de valores y creencias compartidos sobre una nación y su gobierno (pág. 516)
political efficacy/eficacia política los sentimientos de un individuo sobre su efectividad en la política (pág. 516)
political party/partido político un grupo de individuos con intereses comunes que se organizan para nominar candidatos para el cargo, ganar elecciones, conducir el gobierno, y determinar la política pública (págs. 23, 453)
political socialization/socialización política el proceso por el cual individuos aprenden sus creencias y actitudes políticas a través de sus antecedentes personales y experiencias de la vida (pág. 515)
politics/política el esfuerzo para controlar o influenciar la conducta y política del gobierno (pág. 14)
polling place/urna electoral el lugar en un recinto donde la gente vota (pág. 488)
poll tax/impuesto al voto dinero pagado para votar (págs. 90, 483)
popular sovereignty/soberanía popular mando por la gente (pág. 65)
pork-barrel legislation leyes aprobadas por el Congreso que asignan dinero para proyectos federales locales (pág. 202)
preamble/preámbulo una declaración en una constitución que estipula los objetivos y propósitos del gobierno (pág. 13)
precedent/precedente modelo en el cual basar decisiones o acciones posteriores (págs. 338, 364, 426)
precinct/recinto distrito electoral (págs. 459, 488)

precinct captain/capitán de recinto un voluntario que organiza los trabajadores del partido para distribuir información acerca del partido y sus candidatos y para urgir a los votantes a las urnas (pág. 459)

presidential government/gobierno presidencial forma de gobierno democrático en la cual el presidente encabeza el ramo ejecutivo (pág. 692)

presidential succession/sucesión presidencial la orden en la cual los funcionarios ocuparán el cargo del presidente en caso de vacante (pág. 217)

president pro tempore/presidente pro tempore el miembro del Senado, electo por el Senado, que suple como presidente del Senado en la ausencia del vicepresidente (pág. 139)

press conference/conferencia de prensa el cuestionamiento por los medios informativos de un alto funcionario gubernamental (pág. 535)

press secretary/secretario de prensa uno de los asistentes máximos del presidente que se encarga de las relaciones con los medios informativos (pág. 239)

presumed innocence/inocencia presunta la presunción de que una persona es inocente hasta comprobarse culpable (pág. 428)

price supports/apoyo de precios el programa bajo el cual el Congreso les compra la cosecha a los agricultores si el precio del mercado cae bajo del precio de apoyo (pág. 586)

prime minister/primer ministro el líder del ramo ejecutivo de un gobierno parlamentario (pág. 691)

prior restraint/restricción anterior la censura por el gobierno de información antes de ser publicada o emitida (págs. 84, 371, 543)

private bill/proyecto de ley privado proyecto de ley que trata de personas o lugares individuales (pág. 181)

private law/ley privada una ley que se aplica a una persona en particular (pág. 390)

probable cause/causa probable base razonable para creer que una persona o un lugar está ligado a un crimen (pág. 85)

procedural due process/proceso de procedimiento correspondiente el principio que prohibe la aplicación arbitraria de la ley, y también provee salvaguardias para asegurar que los derechos constitucionales y estatutarios estén protegidos por la policía (pág. 427)

procurement/adquisición la compra de materiales (pág. 283)

profit/ganancia la diferencia entre la cantidad de dinero usado para operar un negocio y la cantidad de dinero que el negocio recibe (pág. 720)

progressive tax/impuesto progresivo impuesto basado en la habilidad del contribuyente para pagar (págs. 556, 657)

proletariat/proletariado trabajadores que producen los bienes (pág. 29)

propaganda el uso de ideas, información, o rumores para influenciar la opinión (pág. 495)

proportional representation/representación proporcional sistema en el cual varios oficiales son electos para representar la misma área en proporción a los votos que cada candidato de partido recibe (pág. 467); usado en elecciones preliminares presidenciales para elegir delegados en proporción a su voto popular

proportional tax/impuesto proporcional impuesto fijado a la misma tasa para todos (pág. 657)

public assistance/asistencia pública programas gubernamentales que distribuyen dinero a los pobres (pág. 590)

public bill/proyecto de ley público proyecto de ley relacionado con asuntos generales y aplicarse a toda la nación (pág. 181)

public housing/vivienda pública alojamiento subsidiado por el gobierno para familias de bajos ingresos (pág. 600)

public-interest group/grupo de interés público grupo que busca realizar metas políticas que cree que beneficiarán la nación (pág. 506)

public opinion/opinión pública las ideas y actitudes que un número significativo de americanos mantiene sobre temas (pág. 514)

public policy/política pública el curso de acción que un gobierno toma en respuesta a algún tema o problema (pág. 112)

public utility/utilidad pública una organización que administra necesidades tales como electricidad, gas, o servicio telefónico (pág. 648)

public welfare/asistencia social pública esfuerzos del gobierno para mantener la salud y condiciones de vivienda básicas para aquella gente que no tiene suficiente recursos propios (pág. 654)

public works bill/proyecto de ley de trabajos públicos proyecto de ley en el cual el Congreso asigna dinero para los proyectos locales (pág. 201)

pure speech/expresión pura la expresión verbal de pensamiento y opinión ante una audiencia que ha escogido escuchar (pág. 366)

quorum/quórum el número mínimo de miembros que deben estar presentes para permitir a un grupo legislativo de tomar acción oficial (pág. 137)

quota/cuota la limitación de la cantidad de un producto que puede ser importado (pág. 732)

racial discrimination/discriminación racial el tratar diferente a miembros de una raza sólo por su raza (pág. 408)

random sampling/muestreo al azar técnica de votación en la cual cada uno en el universo tiene una oportunidad equitativa de ser escogido (pág. 520)

ratify/ratificar aprobar (págs. 48, 76)

ratings/popularidad servicio que proporciona estadísticas mostrando el tamaño de la audiencia de los medios informativos (pág. 532)

rational basis test/prueba de base racional usada por una corte para determinar si una ley estatal es razonablemente relacionada a una meta aceptable del gobierno (pág. 406)

real property/propiedad real tierra y lo que esté unido o creciendo en ella (págs. 431, 673)

reapportionment/nueva distribución el proceso de asignar de nuevo la representación basada en la población, después de cada censo (pág. 124)

redistrict/delimitar nuevos distritos establecer nuevas líneas de distrito después de que la nueva asignación esté concluida (pág. 125)

referendum/referéndum elección especial (pág. 666)

refugee/refugiado persona huyendo de un país para escapar del peligro y la persecución (pág. 387)

regional security pact/pacto de seguridad regional tratado de defensa mutua entre las naciones de una región (pág. 627)

register/registrarse enlistar su nombre con el gobierno local apropiado con el fin de participar en las elecciones (pág. 487)

regressive tax/impuesto regresivo impuesto en el cual la gente de bajos ingresos paga una mayor porción de sus ingresos (págs. 557, 657)

representative democracy/democracia representativa forma de democracia en la cual la gente elige a representantes y les da la responsabilidad y el poder para hacer leyes y dirigir el gobierno (pág. 20)

representative government/gobierno representativo sistema de gobierno en el cual la gente elige delegados para hacer leyes y dirigir el gobierno (pág. 37)

representative sample/muestra representativa pequeño grupo de gente, típica del universo, al que un encuestador cuestiona (pág. 520)

reprieve/indulto la pospuesta de un castigo legal (pág. 254)

republic/república gobierno en el cual los votantes mantienen el poder soberano; los representantes electos, responsables a la gente, ejercitan ese poder (pág. 20)

reserved powers/poderes reservados poderes que pertenecen estrictamente a los estados (pág. 96)

reserve requirement/requerimiento de reserva el porcentaje de dinero que los bancos miembros deben guardar en Bancos de Reserva Federal como una reserva contra sus depósitos (pág. 570)

resident alien/extranjero residente persona de una nación extranjera que ha establecido la residencia permanente en Estados Unidos (pág. 387)

revenue/ingresos el dinero que un gobierno cobra de impuestos u otras fuentes (pág. 43)

revenue bill/proyecto de ley de ingresos una ley propuesta para juntar dinero (pág. 158)

reverse discrimination/discriminación reversa situación donde un individuo competente pierde a un individuo escogido por su raza, etnicidad, o género (pág. 414)

revitalization/revitalización inversiones en nuevas facilidades en el esfuerzo de promover el crecimiento económico (pág. 681)

rider/cláusula añadida provisión incluida en un proyecto de ley sobre un tema diferente al que es abarcado en el proyecto (pág. 182)

riding the circuit/recorriendo el circuito viajando para presidir el tribunal en la región del país asignada a un juez (pág. 320)

roll-call vote/votación nominal método de votar usado por el Senado en el cual los senadores responden "Sí" o "No" cuando sus nombres son llamados en orden alfabético (pág. 187)

runoff primary/elección preliminar de desempate segunda elección preliminar entre los dos candidatos que recibieron la mayor cantidad de votos en la primera elección preliminar (pág. 465)

S

sample/muestra grupo entrevistado en una encuesta de opinión (pág. 520)

sampling error/error de muestreo la medida de cuánto los resultados de la muestra pueden diferenciarse del universo de la muestra (pág. 520)

sanction/sanción una medida tal como embargar la asistencia económica para influenciar las actividades de un gobierno extranjero (págs. 630, 698)

scarcity/escasez una condición que existe porque la sociedad no tiene todos los recursos para producir todos los bienes y servicios que todos quieren (pág. 717)

school board/mesa directiva escolar un cuerpo local, generalmente electo, que gobierna un distrito escolar (pág. 673)

search warrant/orden de cateo orden firmada por un juez describiendo un lugar específico para ser cateado por artículos específicos (pág. 85)

secular/profano no religioso (pág. 360)

securities/seguridades instrumentos financieros, incluyendo bonos, notas, y certificados, que son vendidos como medios de pedir dinero prestado con la promesa de volver a pagarlo al comprador con intereses después de un período específico (págs. 559, 581)

security classification system/sistema de clasificación de seguridad la provisión de que la información sobre las actividades gubernamentales relacionadas a la seguridad nacional y la política exterior pueden mantenerse en secreto (pág. 416)

seditious speech/expresión sediciosa discurso urgiendo la resistencia a las autoridades legales o el derrocamiento del gobierno (pág. 367)

segregation/segregación separación de personas del grupo social mayor (pág. 408)

select committee/comité selecto un comité temporal formado para estudiar un tema específico y reportar sus descubrimientos al Senado o a la Cámara (pág. 142)

self-incrimination/autoincriminación atestiguando en contra de sí mismo (pág. 402)

senatorial courtesy/cortesía senatorial sistema en el cual el presidente somete el nombre de un candidato para una asignación judicial a los senadores del estado del candidato antes de someterlo formalmente para la aprobación de todo el Senado (pág. 317)

seniority system/sistema de antigüedad sistema que da el liderazgo de un comité al miembro del partido mayoritario con el servicio más largo sin interrumpir en ese comité (pág. 145)

sentence/sentencia el castigo para ser impuesto a un acusado después de un veredicto de culpable (pág. 443)

separate but equal doctrine/doctrina de separadas pero equitativas política que mantuvo que si las facilidades por las diferentes razas fueran iguales podrían ser separadas (págs. 309, 409)

separation of powers/separación de poderes la división de poder entre los ramos de gobierno legislativo, ejecutivo, y judicial (págs. 40, 65)

sequester/secuestrar mantener aislado (pág. 373)

session/sesión un período durante el cual una legislatura se reúne para manejar negocios (pág. 123)

shah un rey (pág. 706)

shield law/ley protectora ley que da a los reporteros alguna forma de protección en contra de ser forzados a revelar información o fuentes de información confidenciales en cortes estatales (págs. 374, 545)

shock incarceration/encarcelamiento a choque programa de prisión involucrando sentencias más cortas en un ambiente altamente estructurado donde los acusados participan en trabajos, servicio a la comunidad, educación, y asesoramiento (pág. 653)

shock probation/libertad condicional a choque programa diseñado para mostrar a los delincuentes juveniles lo terrible de la vida en la prisión a través de un breve encarcelamiento seguido por una libertad supervisada (pág. 653)

simple resolution/resolución simple informe adoptado para cubrir asuntos afectando solamente una cámara del Congreso (pág. 182)

single-issue party/partido de un solo tema partido político que se enfoca en solo un principal tema social, económico, o moral (pág. 455)

single-member district/distrito de un solo miembro distrito electoral en el cual sólo un candidato es electo para cada cargo (pág. 457)

slander/calumnia expresión falsa con la intención de dañar la reputación de una persona (págs. 84, 369)

social consensus/consenso social cuando la mayoría de las personas en una sociedad aceptan valores democráticos y se acuerdan del propósito y límites del gobierno (pág. 24)

social contract/contrato social teoría que, por contrato, la gente entrega al estado el poder necesario para mantener el orden y el estado, a cambio, acuerda proteger a sus ciudadanos (pág. 8)

social insurance/seguro social programas gubernamentales diseñados para ayudar a los ciudadanos ancianos, enfermos, y desempleados (pág. 590)

social insurance tax/impuesto del seguro social dinero cobrado por el gobierno federal para pagar por grandes programas sociales tales como seguro social, cuidado médico, y programas de compensación de desempleo (pág. 556)

socialism/socialismo sistema económico en el cual el gobierno es dueño de los elementos básicos de producción, distribuye los productos y salarios, y proporciona servicios sociales tales como cuidado de salud y asistencia social (págs. 28, 718)

soft money/dinero no asignado dinero juntado por un partido político para propósitos generales que no es asignado a un candidato (pág. 478)

sovereignty/soberanía la absoluta y suprema autoridad dentro de límites territoriales (pág. 7)

special district/distrito especial unidad de gobierno local que trata de una función específica tal como educación, abastecimiento de agua, o transportación (pág. 665)

splinter party/partido disidente partido político que se separa de uno de los grandes partidos a causa de algún desacuerdo (pág. 455)

spoils system/sistema de despojos la práctica de políticos victoriosos compensando a sus seguidores con puestos gubernamentales (pág. 285)

spot advertising/publicidad entre programas las descripciones breves, frecuentes, y positivas de un candidato o de sus importantes temas transmitidas por televisión o radio (pág. 538)

standing committee/comité permanente un comité permanente en el Congreso que supervisa los proyectos de ley que tratan de cierta clase de temas (pág. 142)

standing vote/voto a pie método de votar usado por la Cámara y el Senado en el cual los miembros votan poniéndose a pie y siendo contados (pág. 187)

stare decisis término latino que significa "que permanezca la decisión"; el principio de que alguna vez que la Corte dictamina en un caso, su decisión sirve como precedente en el cual basar otras decisiones (pág. 338)

state/estado comunidad política que ocupa un territorio definido y tiene un gobierno organizado con el poder de hacer leyes y hacerlas cumplir sin la aprobación de cualquier autoridad superior (pág. 5)

state central committee/comité central de estado comité generalmente compuesto en gran parte de representantes de organizaciones del partido de los condados (pág. 460)

state farm/granja estatal ejido propio del gobierno y administrado como una fábrica, con los agricultores siendo asalariados (pág. 729)

states' rights position/posición de derechos estatales posición que favorece acción estatal y local al tratar de problemas (pág. 106)

statute/estatuto ley escrita por un ramo legislativo (pág. 425)

statutory law/ley estatutaria ley que está escrita con el fin de que todo el mundo pueda conocer y entenderla (pág. 425)

straight party ticket/balota partidaria aquella en que el votante selecciona a candidatos de su partido solamente (pág. 493)

straw poll/votación de prueba atento no científico de medir la opinión pública (pág. 520)

strong-mayor system/sistema de alcalde fuerte tipo de gobierno de alcalde-consejo en el cual el alcalde tiene poderes ejecutivos fuertes (pág. 666)

subcommittee/subcomité grupo dentro de un comité permanente que se especializa en una subcategoría de la responsabilidad del comité permanente (pág. 142)

subpoena/citación orden legal para que una persona comparezca o produzca documentos requeridos (pág. 168)

substantive due process/proceso substantivo correspondiente ciertos derechos de individuos en la aplicación de leyes, algunos de los que son especificados en la Constitución (como la libre expresión) y otros de los que no son especificados, (como el derecho de privacidad haciendo decisiones personales) (pág. 427)

suburb/suburbio territorio muy poblada adjunto con una ciudad central (pág. 672)

suffrage/sufragio el derecho al voto (pág. 481)

summons/citación judicial notificación oficial de una demanda que incluye la fecha, tiempo, y lugar de la aparición inicial en la corte (pág. 433)

sunset law/ley de puesta del sol ley que requiere inspecciones periódicas de agencias gubernamentales para ver si todavía son necesarias (pág. 112)

sunshine law/ley del sol ley que prohibe a funcionarios públicos tener reuniones no abiertas al público (pág. 113)

supremacy clause/cláusula de supremacía declaración en el Artículo VI de la Constitución estableciendo que la Constitución, las leyes aprobadas por el Congreso, y los tratados de Estados Unidos "serán la Ley suprema de la Tierra" (págs. 64, 97)

suspect classification/clasificación de sospecho clasificación hecha en la base de raza u origen nacional que es sujeto al severo escrutinio judicial (pág. 407)

swing vote/voto ganador el voto decisivo (pág. 344)

symbolic speech/expresión simbólica el uso de acciones y símbolos, junto con o en lugar de palabras, para expresar opiniones (pág. 366)

T

tariff/tarifa impuesto sobre importaciones para aumentar su precio en el mercado doméstico (pág. 732)

tax/impuesto el dinero que la gente y los negocios pagan para apoyar las actividades del gobierno (págs. 189, 555)

taxable income/renta imponible el total de ingresos de un individuo menos ciertas deducciones y exenciones personales (pág. 555)

tax credit/crédito de impuesto le permite al contribuyente reducir su responsabilidad de impuesto sobre la renta (pág. 559)

theocracy/teocracia gobierno dominado por la religión (pág. 453)

third party/tercer partido cualquier partido político más que los dos partidos mayores (pág. 455)

ticket/candidatura los candidatos para presidente y vicepresidente (pág. 466)

ticket-splitting/balota no partidaria el votar por candidatos de diferentes partidos para los varios cargos (pág. 489)

tort/agravio un acto injusto, más que el incumplimiento de contrato, por el cual el partido dañado tiene derecho de demandar (pág. 432)

totalitarian dictatorship/dictadura totalitaria forma de gobierno autocrático donde las ideas de los líderes son glorificadas y el gobierno busca controlar todo aspecto de la vida social y económica (pág. 18)

town meeting/reunión municipal reunión de todos los votantes de un pueblo para expresar sus opiniones y participar en el proceso de elaboración de las leyes (pág. 665)

township/municipio unidad de gobierno local encontrada en algunos estados, generalmente una subdivisión de un condado (pág. 664)

trading bloc/bloque comerciante un grupo de naciones que intercambian sin barreras tales como tarifas (págs. 710, 733)

traditional economy/economía tradicional sistema económico en el cual el hábito y la costumbre dictan las normas para toda actividad económica (pág. 717)

transcript/transcripción un récord sumario (pág. 417)

treaty/tratado acuerdo formal entre los gobiernos de dos o más países (págs. 81, 257, 615)

trial court/corte de justicia la corte en la cual un caso es originalmente jurado (pág. 306)

trust/cártel forma de consolidación de negocios en la cual varias sociedades anónimas unen sus acciones y permiten que una mesa directiva las dirija como una sola empresa gigante (pág. 578)

unanimous opinion/opinión unánime una decisión de la Corte en la cual todos los jueces votan igual (pág. 334)

uncontrollable/incontrolable gasto gubernamental requerido por ley o resultando de previos compromisos presupuestarios (págs. 192, 562)

unemployment compensation/compensación de desempleo pagos a los trabajadores que pierden su trabajo (pág. 649)

unemployment insurance/seguro de desempleo programas en los cuales los gobiernos federal y estatales cooperan para proporcionar ayuda a personas que no tienen empleo (pág. 592)

unfunded mandates/mandatos sin asignación programas requeridos pero no pagados por la legislación federal (pág. 588)

unicameral legislatura de una cámara (págs. 48, 641)

union shop/taller sindicalizado lugar de empleo donde los trabajadores son requeridos a unirse a la unión al haber sido empleados (págs. 583, 649)

unitary system/sistema unitario gobierno que da todos los poderes clave al gobierno nacional o central (pág. 12)

universe/universo en votación, el grupo de gente que será estudiada (pág. 520)

urban renewal/renovación urbana programas bajo los cuales las ciudades pueden solicitar asistencia federal para limpiar áreas deterioradas y reconstruirlas (págs. 599, 678)

verdict/veredicto decisión (pág. 443)

veto rechazo de un proyecto de ley (págs. 66, 188)

victim compensation/compensación de víctima un programa en varios estados por lo cual el gobierno proporciona ayuda financiera a las víctimas de ciertos crímenes (pág. 651)

visa documento especial, requerido por ciertos países, emitido por el gobierno del país en el que una persona desee entrar (pág. 623)

voice vote/voto a voz método usado por la Cámara y el Senado en el cual los miembros juntos claman "Sí" o "No" y el presidente determina cuál de los lados tiene más votos (pág. 187)

ward/distrito gran distrito que consta de varios recintos adjuntos (pág. 459)

weak-mayor system/sistema de alcalde débil tipo de gobierno alcalde-consejo en el cual el alcalde sólo tiene poderes limitados (pág. 666)

welfare state/estado benefactor nación que tiene un sistema económico, tal como el socialismo, que proporciona varios programas de bienestar social (pág. 723)

whip asistente al jefe de partido en la legislatura (pág. 135)

wire service/servicio difusor una organización que emplea a reporteros por todo el mundo para reunir historias noticieras para suscriptores (pág. 528)

withholding/impuesto retenido el dinero que un empleador retiene del salario de los trabajadores para pagar los impuestos anticipados (pág. 556)

workers' compensation/compensación a trabajadores pagos que reciben las personas imposibilitadas para trabajar como resultado de una herida o mala salud relacionada con el trabajo (pág. 649)

writ of certiorari/orden de certiorari una orden de la Suprema Corte a una corte menor para mandar los registros de un caso para su revisión (pág. 332)

writ of habeas corpus/orden de hábeas corpus una orden de la corte para enviar a una persona acusada de un crimen a la corte para que ésta determine si ha sido legalmente detenida (pág. 158)

zoning/restricciones de edificación medios que un gobierno local utiliza para regular la manera en que la tierra y los edificios pueden ser utilizados para dar forma al desarrollo de una comunidad (pág. 669)

Acknowledgments

Reprinted by arrangement with The Heirs to the Estate of Martin Luther King, Jr., c/o Writers House, Inc. as agent for the proprietor.

Copyright © 1963 by Martin Luther King, Jr., copyright renewed 1991 by Coretta Scott King.

Photo Credits

Picture Research by Pembroke Herbert & Sandi Rygiel, Picture Research Consultants & Archives.

COVER Wes Thompson/The Stock Market.

The following photos appear multiple times. Their first usage is as follows. **ii** (flag) ©PhotoDisc, Inc.; **3** (multimedia tools) Aaron Haupt; **25** (Supreme Court) ©PhotoDisc, Inc.; **32** (notebook) Jerry Davis; **33** clockwise from top right (flag) ©PhotoDisc, Inc., (paper) Jerry Davis, (banner) ©PhotoDisc, Inc., (MA Statehouse) ©PhotoDisc, Inc.; **207** (clipboard) Jerry Davis.

i Wes Thompson/The Stock Market; **iii** Corbis-Bettmann; **iv** (l)UPI/Corbis-Bettmann, (r)US Senate; **v** Supreme Court Historical Society; **vi** Joe Traver/Gamma Liaison; **vii** DPA/Ipol; **viii** Collection of Janice L. & David J. Frent; **ix** (l)Republican National Committee, (r)Mike Derer/Wide World; **x** (t)courtesy Points of Light Foundation, (b)Joseph Sohm/Chromosohm; **xi** William Mercer McLeod; **xiv** Kleponis/Folio; **1** Collection of the Whitney Museum of American Art; **2** "The National Archives of the United States" by Herman Viola, photos Jonathan Wallen, published by Harry N. Abrams, Inc.; **4** Bruce Stoddard/FPG; **5** Bob Daemmrich/Tony Stone Images; **6** (l)Library of Congress, (r)Bob Daemmrich/The ImageWorks; **8** (l)Corbis-Bettmann, (r)courtesy National Portrait Gallery, London; **9** Rhoda Sidney/The Image Works; **10** Michael Anderson/Folio; **11** Cosmo Condina/Tony Stone Images; **12** Mead Art Museum, Amherst College; **13** (l)Independence National Historical Park Collection, (r)Picture Research Consultants & Archives; **14** Collection of Janice L. & David J. Frent; **15** (t)courtesy Laura Epstein, (b)Latent Image; **16** Paul Edmondson/Tony Stone Images; **18** Peter Charlesworth; **19** Erich Lessing/Art Resource, NY; **21** AP/Wide World; **22** Skjold/The Image Works; **23** (l)Chris Corsmeier; (r)Nebraska State Historical Society; **25** UPI/Corbis-Bettmann; **26** Boplop; **27** (l)Corbis-Bettmann, (r)Jeff Greenberg/Folio; **29** Scala/Art Resource, NY; **30** Corbis-Bettmann; **31** Scala/Art Resource, NY; **33** Drawing by Dana Fradon, 1972 The New Yorker Magazine, Inc.; **34** Archive Photos; **35** Picture Research Consultants & Archives; **36** Joe Sohm/Uniphoto; **37** (t)House of Delegates, State Capitol, Richmond VA, (b)Public Record Office; **39** (l)Private Collection, (r)Colonial Williamsburg Foundation; **40** "The National Archives of the United States" by Herman Viola, photos Jonathan Wallen, published by Harry N. Abrams, Inc.; **41** Doug Martin; **42** Lexington Historical Society. Photo by Rob Huntley/Lightstream; **43** (t)Corbis-Bettmann; **44** (l)Crown copyright. Historic Royal Palaces. Photo: David Chalmers (r)Peabody-Essex Museum, Salem MA; **46** (t)Lafayette College Art Collection, Easton PA, (b)Division of Political History, Smithsonian Institution, Washington DC; **48** Painting by Don Troiani, photo courtesy Historical Art Prints, Ltd.; **50** J. Christopher/Uniphoto; **51** (l)Sam Abell/National Geographic Society Image Collection, (r)Picture Research Consultants & Archives; **52** (t)Columbiana Collection, Columbia University, (b)Library of Congress; **53** Deposited by the City of Boston, courtesy Museum of Fine Arts, Boston; **55** (l)H. Armstrong Roberts, (r)Tracy W. McGregor Library, Special Collections Department, University of VA Library; **56** Independence National Historic Park Collection; **58** (l)North Wind Pictures, (r)The Image Bank; **61** Library of Congress; **62** Pete Souza/Folio; **63** Corbis-Bettmann; **67** Tony Auth ©1974 Philadelphia Enquirer. Reprinted with permission of UNIVERSAL PRESS SYNDICATE. All rights reserved.; **68** Collection of Janice L. & David J. Frent; **69** (l)Miriam & Ira D. Wallach Division of Art, Prints and Photographs, New York Public Library. Astor, Lenox & Tilden Foundations, (r)Joseph Sohm/Chromosohm; **70** (l)Steve Liss/Time Magazine, (r)Collection of Janice L. & David J. Frent; **71** (l)White House Historical Association, (r)Chicago Historical Society/Photo Researchers; **72** (l)Geeta Dardick, (r)Sonda Dawes/The Image Works; **73** The Brooklyn Museum. Gift of the Crescent-Hamilton Club; **74** (t)National Archives, (b)Diana Walker/Gamma Liaison; **75** (l)Franklin D. Roosevelt Library, (r)Franklin D. Roosevelt Library; **76** Independence National Historic Park; **78** (l)Martin Levick/Black Star, (r)Schlowsky Photography; **79** Picture Research Consultants & Archives; **80** Diana Walker/Gamma Liaison; **82** UPI/Corbis-Bettmann; **83** Lawrence Ruggeri/Uniphoto; **84** Mark Humphrey/Wide World; **85** © Handelsman from The Cartoon Bank, Inc.; **87** Cheekwood Museum of Art; Museum Purchase through the Bequest of Anita Bevill McMichael; **89** (t)Jeff Bundy/Omaha World-Herald, (b)Gerald Peters Gallery, NY; **93** ©1998 Bob Mankoff from The Cartoon Bank, Inc.; **94** Uniphoto; **95** UPI/Corbis-Bettmann; **96** Joseph Sohm/Chromosohm; **98** Bob Daemmrich Photography; **99** Francis Miller/Life Magazine, ©Time, Inc.; **100** (l)Holt Confer/The ImageWorks, (r)courtesy State of Oklahoma; **101** SuperStock; **104** Chuck Savage/Uniphoto; **106** Bob Daemmrich/Stock Boston; **107** Joseph Sohm/Chromosohm; **108** (l)Library of Congress, (r)Don Uhrbroch/Life Magazine ©Time Inc.; **111** Paul Conklin/Uniphoto; **112** Randy Hampton/Time Life; **113** (l)People Weekly ©1997 Andrew Kaufman, (r)courtesy Points of Light Foundation; **114** (l)Mark Reinstein/Uniphoto, (r)Collection of Janice L. & David J. Frent; **116** (l)Brooks Kraft/Sygma, (r)courtesy Cleveland City Hall; **117** Joe Caputo/Gamma Liaison; **119** ©1998 Bob Mankoff from the Cartoon Bank, Inc.; **120** Kleponis/Folio; **122** Everett Johnson/Folio; **123** Wayne Fisher; **124** (l)courtesy National Portrait Gallery, London, (r)House of Representatives; **131** Wide World; **132** Library of Congress; **133** (l)Diana Walker/Gamma Liaison, (r)Henry Groskinsky; **134** Walter P. Calahan/Folio; **136** Bantam Books; **138** Dennis Brack/Black Star; **139** (l)Scala/Art Resource, NY, (r)Ed Clark, Life Magazine ©Time, Inc.; **141** Dennis Cook/AP/Wide World Photos; **142** John Troha/Black Star; **144** Kamenki Pajic/AP/Wide World photos; **146** Collection of Janice L. & David J. Frent; **147** Mark Cullum/Copley News Service; **148** Dennis Brack/Black Star; **149** (l)"Jefferson" by Rembrandt Peale © White House Historical Association/Photo by National Geographic Society, (r)Robert C. Shafer/Folio; **151** Massachusetts Historical Society; **152** (l)Dennis Brack/Black Star; (c)US Senate; **152-153** UPI/Corbis-Bettmann; **153** (t)George Tames/The New York Times, (b)Najlah Feanny/Saba; **155** Charles Fagan/Associated Features; **156** Mark Groff, Life Magazine ©Time, Inc.; **157** Chet Nunley/Gamma Liaison; **158** (t)Picture Research Consultants & Archives, (b)Numismatic Education Society; **160** David Young Wolff/Tony Stone Images; **161** Collection of the New-York Historical Society; **162** National Museum of American Art, Smithsonian Institution, Washington D.C./Art Resource, NY; **163** (t)West Point Museum, US Military Academy, West Point NY/Photo by Josh Nefsky, (b)Picture Research Consultants & Archives; **164** (l)David Burnett/CONTACT Press Images, (tr)PhotoAssist/courtesy The National Archives, (br)Collection of Janice L. & David J. Frent; **166** Walter Iooss, Jr./Sports Illustrated; **167** UPI/Corbis-Bettmann; **168** (l)JP Laffont/Sygma,(r)Robert Phillips, Life Magazine ©Time, Inc.; **169** Ken Lambert/The Washington Times/Gamma Liaison; **170** (t)courtesy Robin Deykes, (b)Russel Munson/The Stock Market; **172** Tom Horan/Sygma; **173** King Features Syndicate; **175** (l)Picture Research Consultants & Archives, (r)Library of Congress; **177** Aaron Haupt; **179** ©1998 Bob Mankoff from The Cartoon Bank, Inc.; **180** Ashe/Folio; **181** Bob Kelley/Life Magazine ©Time, Inc.; **182** Bob Daemmrich Photography; **186** Dennis Brack/Black Star; **187** US Capitol; **191** (l)John Duricka/Wide World, (r)James Prigoff; **192** Picture Research Consultants & Archives; **193** (l)Collection of The New-York Historical Society, (r)Corbis-Bettmann; **194** Kansas State Historical Society; **195** ©1998 Frank Cotham from The Cartoon Bank, Inc.; **196** (l)Collection of Janice L. & David J. Frent, (r)Collection of Janice L. & David J. Frent; **197** (l)Ed Carreon, (r)Wayne W. Fisher; **199** NASA; **200** Bob Daemmrich Photography; **202** Mark Richards/Contact Press Images; **203** Picture Research Consultants & Archives; **205** (t)courtesy House of Representatives, (b)Joe Marquette/Wide World; **206** (l)Bob Daemmrich/Stock Boston, (r)Rob Huntley/Lightstream; **209** ©1998 Aaron Bacall from The Cartoon Bank, Inc.; **210** SuperStock; **212** Reuters NewMedia Inc./CORBIS; **213** Reagan Library; **214** Charlie Archambault/US News & World Report; **215** "I Have a Dream" Foundation; **216** UPI/Corbis-Bettmann; **218** Ron Edmonds/Wide World; **219** Pool Photo/Newsmakers/Liaison; **220** The Ralph E. Becker Collection/Smithsonian Institution; **221** (l)Collection of Janice L. & David J. Frent, (r)Metropolitan Museum of Art, Gift of Edgar William and Bernice Chrysler Garbisch, 1963. (62.256.7); **223** MTV; **224** Robert King/Newsmakers/Liaison Agency; **226** Collection of Janice L. & David J. Frent; **227** Corbis-Bettmann; **228** The Metropolitan Museum of Art; **229** Itsu Inouye/Wide World; **230** Stock Montage; **231** White House/AP/Wide World Photos; **234** James Colburn/Ipol; **236** Shonna Valeska; **237** Steve Northup, Time Magazine ©Time, Inc.; **238** John Ficara/Sygma; **240** (l)John F. Kennedy Library, (c)National Portrait Gallery, Smithsonian Institution/Art Resource, NY, (r)Library of Congress; **241** (l)Doug Mills/Wide World, (r)John Ficara/Newsweek; **243** ©1998 Bob Mankoff from The Cartoon Bank, Inc.; **244** Owen Franken/CORBIS; **245** Rob Huntley/Lightstream; **247** Library of Congress; **248** (l)UPI/Corbis-Bettmann, (r)Ira Wyman/Sygma; **249** Larry Burrows, Life Magazine ©Time, Inc.; **251** courtesy Central Intelligence Agency; **252** Oliphant ©1973, Denver Post. Distributed by the Los Angeles Times Syndicate. Reprinted with permission; **253** National Archives; **254** Picture Research Consultants & Archives; **255** Karl Rubenthal/LBJ Library; **256** Corporation for National Service; **258** (l)The Metropolitan Museum of Art, Gift of Edgar William and Bernice Chrysler Garbisch, 1963, (r)Dirck Halstead/Gamma Liaison; **259** Smithsonian Institution; **260** (l)Collection of The New-York Historical Society, (r)Ranan R. Lurie; **261** U.S. Coast Guard; **262** (l)Yoichi R. Okamoto/LBJ Library, (r)Porter Gifford/Gamma Liaison; **264** Nixon Presidential Materials Project; **265** The White House; **266** (t)Ed Reinke/Wide World, (b)courtesy Habitat for Humanity; **269** (tl)Collection of Janice L. & David J. Frent, (tc)Collection of Janice L. & David J. Frent, (tr)Collection of Janice L. & David J. Frent, (b)Bill Greenblatt/Newsmakers/Liaison; **270** (t)NBC Photo, (b)Collection of Janice L. & David J. Frent; **273** ©1998 Mike Stevens from The Cartoon Bank, Inc.; **274** Jim Pickerell/Gamma Liaison; **275** courtesy National Transportation Safety Board; **277** Picture Research Consultants & Archives; **279** Uniphoto; **280** NASA; **281** Jeff Greenberg/The Picture Cube; **284** National Postal Museum, Smithsonian Institution; **285** Scott Sachman © National Parks & Conservation Association; **286** Library of Congress; **288** John Emmons/Ipol; **289** Tribune Media Services; **290** Lawrence Migdale/Stock Boston; **291** Doug Martin; **292** Bob Daemmrich/Uniphoto; **293** Larry Downing/Sygma; **294** (l)NASA, (r)Ralph Morse/Life Magazine ©Time, Inc.; **295** Richard Ellis/Sygma; **296** (l)People Weekly ©1997 Neal Preston, (r)Drug Enforcement Administration; **301** Tribune Media Services; **302** Ken Heinen; **304** Bob Daemmrich Photography; **305** "John Marshall" by Febret de Saint Memin, 1801. Duke University Archives; **307** Lisa Biganzoli/National Geographic Society; **309** (l)courtesy The Historic New Orleans Collection, (r)Carl Iwaski, Life Magazine ©Time, Inc.; **310** UPI/Corbis-Bettmann; **311** Nancy Andrews/Wide World; **312** courtesy National Security Archive; **313** (l)Rob Huntley/Lightstream, (r)Susan Farley ©1992 New York Newsday; **315** Bob Daemmrich Photography; **318** (tl)Underwood & Underwood/Corbis-Bettmann, (tr)Emmett Collection, New York Public Library, (b)Joseph J. Scherchel/National Geographic Society Image Collection; **319** Robert Llewellyn; **320** Portrait by John Sydney Hopkinson/Collection of The Supreme Court of The United States; **321** (l)Supreme Court Historical Society, (r)Ken Heinen; **322** (t)Supreme Court Historical Society, (b)Ken Heinen; **324** (t)Jim Brandenburg/Minden Pictures, (b)courtesy Renée Askins;

Acknowledgments and Credits

325 Reuters/Corbis-Bettmann; **326** US Postal Service; **327** Portrait by George Augusta/Collection of The Supreme Court of The United States; **329** ©1981 by Herblock in The Washington Post; **330** Robert Llewellyn; **331** Supreme Court Historical Society; **333** James A. Finley/Wide World; **334** (l)UPI/Corbis-Bettmann, (r)Random House Inc., NY; **335** Erich Solomon; **336** Library of Congress; **337** Bob Daemmrich/Stock Boston; **339** Cartoonists & Writers Syndicate; **340** Nancy Richmond/The Image Works; **341** White House Historical Association; **342** Collection of Janice L. & David J. Frent; **343** Portrait by Bjorn Egeli/Collection of The Supreme Court of The United States; **344** Ken Heinen; **346** (l)Bob Adelman/Magnum, (r)Charles E. Steinheimer, Life Magazine ©Time, Inc.; **347** Tribune Media Services; **348** Franklin D. Roosevelt Library; **349** Ken Heinen; **351** ©1998 Reprinted courtesy Bunny Hoest and Parade Magazine; **352** Barth Falkenberg/Stock Boston; **354** Laina Druskis/Stock Boston; **355** Charles Gupton/Stock Boston; **357** Bob Fitch/Black Star; **358** Picture Research Consultants & Archives; **359** (l)Eric P. Newman Numismatic Education Society, (c)Rob Huntley/Lightstream, (r)Eric Bouvet/Gamma Liaison; **360** Bob Daemmrich Photography; **362** Bob Daemmrich Photography; **364** James Conklin; **365** Audrey Gibson/Washington Stock Photo; **366** courtesy Patrick Griffin/Photo by Wayne W. Fisher; **367** (l)Hiroji Kubota/Magnum, (r)Eddie Adams/Time Magazine; **368** Wide World; **369** Paul S. Conklin; **371** D. Boone/Westlight; **372** (l)UPI/Corbis-Bettmann, (r)Wide World; **373** Glenn Martin/Denver Post/Wide World; **374** Norman Walker/Constitution Magazine; **376** courtesy Simon MOA Management Co., Inc.; **377** Rob Badger/FPG; **378** Rob Huntley/Lightstream; **379** Wide World; **380** Charles Moore/Black Star; **381** (t)Union Summer, (b)Agence France Presse/Corbis-Bettmann; **383** F. Pedrick/The Image Works; **385** ©1985 by Sidney Harris; **386** Joseph Sohm/Chromosohm; **387** Hikaru Iwasaki/National Archives; **388** National Park Service Collection/Gift of Angelo Forgione: **389** Bob Daemmrich Photography; **391** People Weekly © 1993 Ian Cook; **392** (l)Library of Congress, (r)Portrait by George PA Healy/Collection of the Supreme Court of The United States; **393** Bob Daemmrich Photography; **394** Uniphoto; **395** (t)Torsten Kjellstrand, (b)Ranko Chkovic/Sygma; **396, 397** Bob Daemmrich Photography; **398** UPI/Corbis-Bettmann; **399** (t)Therese Frare/Black Star, (b)Bob Daemmrich Photography; **400** Bob Daemmrich Photography; **401** Division of Political History, Smithsonian Institution, Washington DC; **402** (l)Bob Daemmrich Photography, (r)Flip Schulke; **403** UPI/Corbis-Bettmann; **406** Bob Daemmrich Photography; **407** Wide World; **408** (l)Bruce Roberts/Photo Researchers, (r)Collection of Janice L. & David J. Frent; **409** Picture Research Consultants & Archives; **411, 412** Bob Daemmrich Photography; **413** (l)Gary Wagner/Sygma, (r)Walt Zeboski/Wide World; **414** Bob Daemmrich Photography; **415** (l)Collection of Janice L. & David J. Frent, (r)Library of Congress; **416** Topham/The Image Works; **417** Nick Ut/Wide World; **418** Bob Daemmrich Photography; **419** Picture Research Consultants & Archives; **421** Steve Kelley/Copley News Service; **422** David W. Hamilton/The Image Bank; **423** Photri, Inc.; **424** Collection of The New-York Historical Society; **426** Bob Daemmrich Photography; **427** courtesy Tabor Academy; **428** James Wilson/Woodfin Camp & Associates; **429** Greg Smith/Saba; **430** John Biever/Sports Illustrated; **431** (l)courtesy Vernon A. Martin Realtors, (r)Paul Barton/The Stock Market; **432** (l)Corbis-Bettmann, (r)Bob Daemmrich Photography; **433** Bob Daemmrich Photography; **434** (l)Corbis-Bettmann, (r)Bob Daemmrich Photography; **435** John Neubauer; **436** Bob Daemmrich Photography; **437** Ogust/The Image Works; **439** (t)Bob Daemmrich Photography, (b)MADD; **440** courtesy Mary Ellen Beaver; **441** (l)Bob Daemmrich Photography, (r)Bob Daemmrich Photography; **443** Val Mazzenga/Chicago Tribune Magazine; **445** (t)Ilene Perlman/Stock Boston, (b)Bob Daemmrich Photography; **446** (t)Bob Daemmrich Photography, (b)Picture Research Consultants & Archives; **449** Harris/Cartoonists & Writers Syndicate; **450** Shelburne Museum; **452** Najlah Feanny/Saba Press Photos; **453** J.A. Pevlovsky/Sygma; **455** Collection of Janice L. & David J. Frent; **456** (l)Library of Congress, (r)David Woo/Stock Boston; **457** Museum of American Political Life; **458** courtesy Jason Brinton; **459, 460** Collection of Janice L. & David J. Frent; **461** Ted Thai/Time Magazine; **463** Rob Huntley/Lightstream; **464** Collection of Janice L. & David J. Frent; **465** (t)Rick Friedman/Black Star, (b)Larry Hawkins/Eufala Photography; **466** Collection of The New-York Historical Society; **467** (l)Republican National Committee, (r)Mark Burnett; **468** (tl)Collection of Janice L. & David J. Frent, (tr)Collection of Janice L. & David J. Frent, (b)Collection of Janice L. & David J. Frent; **469** Jon Levy/Gamma Liaison; **470** Division of Political History, Smithsonian Institution, Washington DC; **473** ©1978 by Herblock in The Washington Post; **474** Kraft Brooks/Corbis Sygma; **475** TimePix.; **478** Bob Daemmrich/Uniphoto; **479** Toles ©1996 The Buffalo News. Reprinted with permission of UNIVERSAL PRESS SYNDICATE; **481** Charles Gupton/Uniphoto; **482** (t)courtesy Office of the Governor, (b)State of New Jersey; **483** (l)Collection of Janice L. & David J. Frent, (r)Matt Herron; **485** Bob Daemmrich Photography; **486** Matt Meadows; **487** Schlowsky Photography; **490** Allan Tannenbaum/Sygma; **492** Bob Daemmrich Photography; **493** Paul Szep; **498** (t)Collection of Janice L. & David J. Frent, (bl)Collection of Janice L. & David J. Frent, (br)Collection of Janice L. & David J. Frent; **498-499** Collection of Mr. & Mrs. Wilson Pile; **499** Chuck Harrity/US News & World Report; **501** Reprinted by permission of John Trevor, Albuquerque Journal; **502** Bob Daemmrich Photography; **503** MADD; **504** (l)Scott Sachman ©National Parks and Conservation Association, (r)Scott Sachman © National Parks and Conservation Association; **506** Bob Daemmrich Photography; **507** Public Citizen News; **508** (t)Ted Morrison, (b)Mark Burnett; **509** Wide World; **511** Mike Keefe/The Denver Post; **512** courtesy David Laughery; **514** Channel One News; **515** Steve Liss/Time Magazine; **516** Bob Daemmrich Photography; **518** Rick Schmidt/Sygma; **519** Corbis-Bettmann; **525** Mark Cullum/Copley News Service; **526** Doug Mills/Wide World; **527** Picture Research Consultants & Archives; **528** Library of Congress; **530** (t)Picture Research Consultants & Archives, (b)Bob Daemmrich Photography; **531** courtesy CNN; **532** Manuello Paganelli; **533** Donna Cox & Robert Patterson/NCSA; **534** C-SPAN; **535** Wilfredo Lee/Wide World; **536** Charles Phillips/Smithsonian Institution; **537** David McNew/Newsmakers/Liaison Agency; **538** (t)John Zich/Wide World, (b)Scribner's; **540** C-SPAN; **542** Entertainment Weekly; **543** Terrence McCarthy/The New York Times; **544** Les Stone/Corbis Sygma; **545** Federal Communications Commission; **547** Dennis Brack/Black Star; **548** Terry Ashe/Time Magazine; **549** Stephenson/Zuma; **551** Tony Auth. Reprinted with permission of UNIVERSAL PRESS SYNDICATE; **552** Robert Llewellyn/Folio; **554** Terry Ashe/Time Magazine; **555** Culver Pictures; **556** (l)Tribune Media Services, (r)Bob Daemmrich Photography; **558** Bob Daemmrich Photography; **560** Division of Political History, Smithsonian Institution, Washington, DC; **562** Ron Edmunds/Wide World; **563** Steve Warmowski; **565** Internal Revenue Service; **566** Harry Bates/Fortune Magazine; **570** (l)Steven Senne/AP/Wide World Photo, (r)Louis Psihoyos/Matrix; **571** Bob Daemmrich Photgraphy; **573** Raeside/Cartoonists & Writers Syndicate; **574** SuperStock; **575** Bob Daemmrich Photography; **576** International Brotherhood of Teamsters; **577** (t)UPI/Corbis-Bettmann, (b)Bob Daemmrich Photography; **580** Bob Daemmrich Photography; **581** The Oakland Museum; **584** Inga Spence/The Picture Cube; **587** (l)Pete Souza/Gamma Liaison, (r)Environmental Protection Agency; **588** Bill Greene/The Boston Globe; **590** Food and Drug Administration; **593** Nina Berman/Sipa Press; **594** Chuck Harrity/US News & World Report; **596** courtesy Students Against Destructive Decisions; **597** Bob Daemmrich Photography; **598** (l)William Mercer McLeod, (r)Picture Research Consultants & Archives; **600** Jim Lo Scalzo; **601** (l)Lake County (IL)Museum/Curt Teich Postcard Archives, (r)Shelburne Museum, Shelburne VT/Photo by Ken Buris; **603** Jim Lo Scalzo/US News & World Report; **605** Toles ©1996 US News & World Report. Reprinted with permission of UNIVERSAL PRESS SYNDICATE; **606** Wally MacNamee/Sygma; **607** Ron McMillan/Gamma Liaison; **608** Reuters/Corbis-Bettmann; **609** Eric Bouvet/Matrix; **610** (l)The Michael Barson Collection/Past Perfect, (r)Picture Research Consultants & Archives; **611** (t)Jim Storey, (b)Rob Huntley/Lightstream; **612** (l)David Burnett/Contact Press Images, (r)Collection of Janice L. & David J. Frent; **614** Picture Research Consultants & Archives; **615** The White House; **616** US Army; **617** Heidi Levine/Sipa Press; **618** Steve Lehman/Saba; **619** Rothco Cartoons; **621** Jerome Delay/Wide World; **622** Isabel Cutler/Gamma Liaison; **623** Jeffrey Markowitz/Sygma; **626** Bill Gentile/SIPA Press; **627** Larry Lefever from Grant Heilman; **628** Museum of American Political Life/Anderson; **630** Jon Jones/Sygma; **631** Bob Daemmrich Photography; **633** Arcadio/Cartoonists & Writers Syndicate; **634** Frank Siteman/Stock Boston; **636** Jerry Howard/Stock Boston; **637** courtesy The Rhode Island Historical Library; **638** Henry Francis duPont Winterthur Museum; **639** Dan Groshong/Sygma; **641, 643** Bob Daemmrich Photography; **645** courtesy Ron Thornburgh, Secretary of State, State Capitol, Topeka KS; **646** Bob Daemmrich Photography; **648** J. Koontz/The Picture Cube; **649** Bob Daemmrich Photography; **650** (t)L.L. Griffin Photography, (b)Thorney Lieberman; **655** Bob Daemmrich Photography; **656** Camerique/The Picture Cube; **657, 659** Bob Daemmrich Photography; **661** John Klosner; **662** Michael L. Abramson/Life Magazine ©Time, Inc.; **663** Office of the Mayor, Des Moines IA; **665** Bob Daemmrich Photography; **666** M. Fernandes/Washington Stock Photo; **668** Bob Daemmrich Photography; **669** Jeffery Titcomb/Gamma Liaison; **670** (l)Museum of the City of New York, (r)Berle Cherney/Uniphoto; **672** James Blank/Stock Boston; **676** Bill Pugliano/Gamma Liaison; **677** Robert Maass/CORBIS; **678** Rhoda Sidney/Stock Boston; **680** courtesy Gillian Kilberg; **681** Trinity College; **683** Miro Vintoniv/Stock Boston; **685** Signe/Philadelphia Daily News/Cartoonists & Writers Syndicate; **686** Robert Llewellyn; **688** David Turnley/Corbis; **689** Bob Daemmrich Photography; **690** David Cairns/Sipa Press; **695** Rob Huntley/Lightstream; **696** Haviv/Saba; **697** Czarak Sokolowski/Wide World; **699** John Chiasson/Gamma Liaison; **700** (l)Joe Raedle/Newsmakers/Liaison, (r)Wesley Bocxe/newsmakers/Liaison; **702** Joel Simon; **703** Sovfoto/Eastfoto; **704** courtesy Wheels for Humanity; **705** (l)Carl Ho/Reuters/Corbis-Bettmann, (r)Vincent Yu/Wide World; **706** ©1994 Dayton Daily News and Tribune Media Services, Inc. courtesy Grimmy, Inc.; **708** Alexander Tsiaras/Stock Boston; **709** Malcolm Linton/Gamma Liaison; **710** Kindra Clineff/The Picture Cube; **713** Dante Busquets/Gamma Liaison; **715** Henge/Cartoonists & Writers Syndicate; **716** Fritz Hoffman/Network; **717** Bill Gallery/Stock Boston; **718** Tom Wagner/Saba; **720** (t)Jim McHugh/Outline, (b)courtesy Food from the Hood; **721** Wide World; **724** (l)Larry Luxner, (r)Chilean Trade Commission; **725** Picture Research Consultants & Archives; **726** P. Le Segretain/Sygma; **727** Liz Gilbert/Sygma; **728, 729** Sovfoto/Eastfoto; **730** Bob Daemmrich Photography; **731** Sovfoto/Eastfoto; **732** courtesy Pam Ikauniks; **735** Greg Girard/Contact Press Images; **737** Beth A. Keiser/Wide World; **739** Carlson ©1993/Milwaukee Sentinel/Reprinted with permission of UNIVERSAL PRESS SYNDICATE; **740** G. Silverstein/Washington Stock Photo; **746-752** White House Historical Association; **753** (t,c) White House Historical Association, (b) Bush 2000 Campaign; **754** Ken Heinen; **756** Supreme Court Historical Society; **757** Picture Research Consultants & Archives; **759** Rob Huntley/Lightstream; **770** (t)Raza Estakhrian/Tony Stone Images, (b)Historical Society of Pennsylvania; **774** Mark Burnett; **796** Cobalt Productions; **799** Paul Conklin; **801** SuperStock; **803** Corbis-Bettmann; **804** SuperStock; **806, 807** Corbis-Bettmann; **808** Picture Research Consultants & Archives; **812** Corbis-Bettmann; **815** National Gallery of Art, Washington DC; **817** Corbis-Bettmann; **818** Smithsonian Institution; **819** North Wind Picture Archives; **820** National Portrait Gallery/Smithsonian Institution/Art Resource, NY; **821** Smithsonian Institution; **822** UPI/Corbis-Bettmann; **823** Franklin D. Roosevelt Library; **824** Glencoe file photo; **825** Flip Schulke/Black Star; **826** Tim Crosby/Gamma Liaison; **837** Dennis Brack/Black Star; **838** Charlie Westerman/Gamma Liaison; **839** John Chiasson/Gamma Liaison; **841** National Park Service; **842** Social Security Administration.